D1559092

TREASURY *of the* TRUE DHARMA EYE

CONTRIBUTORS

ASSOCIATE EDITOR
Peter Levitt

TRANSLATORS
Robert Aitken
Steve Allen
Reb Anderson
Chozen Jan Bays
Hogen Bays
Edward Brown
Gyokuko Carlson
Kyogen Carlson
Linda Ruth Cutts
Andy Ferguson
Norman Fischer
Gaelyn Godwin
Natalie Goldberg
Joan Halifax
Paul Haller

Blanche Hartman
Arnold Kotler
Taigen Dan Leighton
Peter Levitt
John Daido Loori
Susan Moon
Wendy Egyoku Nakao
Josho Pat Phelan
Lewis Richmond
David Schneider
Jean Selkirk
Alan Senauke
Kazuaki Tanahashi
Katherine Thanas
Mel Weitsman
Dan Welch
Michael Wenger
Philip Whalen

TREASURY *of the* TRUE DHARMA EYE

Zen Master Dogen's *Shobo Genzo*

EDITED BY
Kazuaki Tanahashi

SHAMBHALA
BOULDER • 2012

Shambhala Publications, Inc.
2129 13th Street
Boulder, Colorado 80302
www.shambhala.com

© 2010 by the San Francisco Zen Center

Page 1173 constitutes a continuation of this copyright page.
All rights reserved. No part of this book may be reproduced in
any form or by any means, electronic or mechanical, including
photocopying, recording, or by any information storage and
retrieval system, without permission in writing from the publisher.

9 8 7 6 5

Printed in the United States of America

∞ This edition is printed on acid-free paper that meets the
American National Standards Institute z39.48 Standard.
♻ Shambhala Publications makes every effort to print on recycled
paper. For more information please visit www.shambhala.com.

Shambhala Publications is distributed worldwide
by Penguin Random House, Inc., and its subsidiaries.

Designed by Dede Cummings Designs

The Library of Congress catalogues the previous edition
of this book as follows:
Dogen, 1200–1253.
[Shobo genzo. English]
Treasury of the true dharma eye: Zen master Dogen's
Shobo genzo / edited by Kazuaki Tanahashi.
p. cm.
Includes bibliographical references and index.
ISBN 978-1-59030-474-7 (hardcover—1st ed.)
ISBN 978-1-59030-935-3 (hardcover)
1. Sotoshu—Doctrines—Early works to 1800.
I. Tanahashi, Kazuaki, 1933– II. Title
BQ9449.D654S5313 2010
294.3'85—DC22
2010015405

With deep respect and gratitude to
Zen masters Shunryu Suzuki,
Taizan Maezumi, and Dainin Katagiri,
who pioneered the practice and teaching of
Dogen Zen in North America

ON THE GREAT ROAD OF BUDDHA ancestors there is always unsurpassable practice, continuous and sustained. It forms the circle of the way and is never cut off. Between aspiration, practice, enlightenment, and nirvana, there is not a moment's gap; continuous practice is the circle of the way.

—DOGEN,
"Continuous Practice"

WHEN EVEN FOR A MOMENT you sit upright in samadhi expressing the buddha mudra in the three activities, the whole world of phenomena becomes the buddha's mudra and the entire sky turns into enlightenment.

—DOGEN,
"On the Endeavor of the Way"

CONTENTS

MONASTERY CONSTRUCTION PERIOD, 1243–1245

DAIBUTSU MONASTERY PERIOD, 1245–1246

PREFACE AND
ACKNOWLEDGMENTS

IT IS MY GREAT pleasure to present the lifework of Zen Master Eihei Dogen (1200–1253), an extraordinary meditator, thinker, visionary, teacher, poet, writer, scholar, leader of a spiritual community, and reformer of Buddhism in Japan. We translate the original Japanese title, *Shobo Genzo,* as "Treasury of the True Dharma Eye." The "eye" here indicates the understanding as well as the experience of reality through meditative endeavor.

Dogen offers a practical, profound, and comprehensive teaching on meditation, presented in a series of sections known as fascicles. The word "fascicle," literally a bundle of pages, refers to a section of a written work that is an installment of a larger work. (In the present edition, we refer to the fascicles sometimes as "essays" and sometimes as "texts." Also, for convenience, we refer to the work consistently by its English translation in the introductory comments and notes.)

We present the most comprehensive collection of the *Treasury of the True Dharma Eye* texts. Our basic original text is Kozen's ninety-five-fascicle edition, published in the seventeenth century. In addition, we have included "One Hundred Eight Gates of Realizing Dharma," from Giun's twelve-fascicle version, a thirteenth-century copy not known by Kozen. The inclusion of this fascicle brings our version to ninety-six fascicles.

Dogen's poetic and perplexing essays reveal startling visions and thoughts, often paradoxical and impenetrable. You might call Dogen a thirteenth-century postexistentialist. He sees the world of impermanence, and yet his voice is always active and high-spirited. He challenges us with an urgent question: how do we live each moment fully and meaning-fully? He makes us feel not confined and tiny, but free and enormous.

Since Dogen is one of the greatest writers in Zen Buddhism through-out time and space, this book serves as an overall guide to the history, literature, philosophy, and practice of Zen. As he is also one of the most extensive elucidators of Buddhist scriptures, this book summarizes how he, as an East Asian Buddhist of ancient times, viewed and explained the dharma to his students. Dogen is primarily regarded as the founder of Japan's Soto Zen School where he established forms and procedures for Zen meditation. Today his way of practice is spreading throughout the Western world. You may be surprised how much of the movement in the meditation hall as taught by Dogen in the thirteenth century is practiced in a Zen center in your own city almost seven hundred years later.

I have been extremely fortunate to collaborate in translation with a number of outstanding Zen teachers and writers. I worked with one or two partners in translating each short essay. We examined original sen-tences word by word and came up with the best possible corresponding expressions in English. As associate editor of this work, Peter Levitt has gone over the entire text several times and made valuable suggestions. The strength and consistency of our translations owe much to him. Our intention is to offer a translation that is as accurate as possible, but also one that is inspiring and useful for practitioners of dharma in the West-ern world.

Because Dogen's writing is known for its difficulty, we provide vari-ous kinds of assistance to help readers "decode" the text:

- We present the essays in chronological order (as dated by Dogen) so that readers can trace the development of Dogen's thinking and teaching. In the section "Texts in Relation to Dogen's Life and Translation Credits," we explain the background of each fascicle in relation to other fascicles.
- The Editor's Introduction discusses Dogen's characteristic expres-sions, with examples quoted in the introduction endnotes.
- In the main text, short explanations are enclosed in brackets.
- An extensive glossary at the end of the book provides more detailed explanations of terms and names, as well as linguistic details.

- The words of earlier teachers and other writers that Dogen comments upon are italicized.

Treasury of the True Dharma Eye is the fourth Dogen book project sponsored by the San Francisco Zen Center, following *Moon in a Dewdrop, Enlightenment Unfolds,* and *Beyond Thinking.* I worked for San Francisco Zen Center from 1977 to 1984 as a scholar in residence. Since then the Zen Center has been supporting the Dogen translation projects. Before that, from 1960 to 1968 I worked with Shoichi Nakamura Roshi, my Zen teacher and cotranslator, to produce the first complete modern Japanese translation of Dogen's *Shobo Genzo.* In 1965 Robert Aitken Roshi and I made the first translation of the text "Actualizing the Fundamental Point" included in this book. It has been a half-century journey of conversation with my venerated and beloved master Dogen. I have enjoyed every moment of studying his writing and translating it.

I would like to thank Shunryu Suzuki Roshi for inviting me to speak about Dogen to his students at Soko Temple in 1964, before he founded San Francisco Zen Center. This became a seed for my long-term association with the Zen Center. My gratitude goes to Richard Baker Roshi and the successive abbots of the Zen Center and its officers for supporting the translation project while they were in charge. I am particularly grateful to Michael Wenger Roshi, who has overseen the project as director of publications at the Zen Center and wrote the afterword of this book.

All my cotranslators have been delightful to work with and have taught me tremendously. Mel Weitsman Roshi has been my most frequent translating partner and the one I have worked with longest. Joan Halifax Roshi has invited me to give dharma talks during a number of sesshins and also to lead Dogen seminars.

We benefit a great deal from traditional Soto scholars, including Menzan Zuiho and Bokusan Nishiari. Works by Dr. Doshu Okubo and Dr. Fumio Mastani have always been helpful.

My appreciation goes to Dr. Carl Bielefeldt, Dr. Linda Hess, Dr. William Johnston, Shohaku Okumura Roshi, Christian H. B. Haskett, and Dr. Friederike Boissevain for their expert advice. Thanks to Zen Master Daegak Genthner, Shirley Graham, Roberta Werdinger, Luminous Owl Henkel, Jogen Salzberg, Junna Murakawa, Silvie Senauke,

Mahiru Watanabe, Nathan Wenger, Wolfgang Wilnert, Ann Colburn, Karuna Tanahashi, and Ko Tanahashi for their help in a variety of ways. Our translation project owes much to a grant from the Dragon Mountain Temple.

Norman Fischer Roshi was also the translation editor for *Moon in a Dewdrop* and the author of the introduction to *Beyond Thinking*. Susan Moon, who was translation editor of *Enlightenment Unfolds,* also has helped enliven descriptions of some of the Chinese masters in the glossary. Dan Welch was translation editor for *Beyond Thinking*. Dr. Taigen Dan Leighton, our scholarly editor, checked the glossary and updated our bibliography. Andrew Ferguson provided information on Chinese masters through his book *China's Zen Heritage* and was kind enough to check all the Chinese transliteration as well as the sites on the maps.

It is always wonderful to work with the staff of Shambhala Publications. I am extremely grateful to Peter Turner, Dave O'Neal, Hazel Bercholz, and Ben Gleason for taking on this large project. I thank Kendra Crossen for her excellent copyediting.

KAZUAKI TANAHASHI
Berkeley, California

NOTES TO THE READER

TRANSLITERATION AND PRONUNCIATION

Spellings of Sanskrit words are simplified, and diacritical marks are omitted in the main text. Macrons (to indicate long vowels) and tilde for *ñ* in Sanskrit words are used only in the glossary.

SIMPLIFIED FORM	STANDARD FORM
ch	c, ch
m	m, ṃ, ṇ
ñ	ñ
ri	ri, ṛ
sh	ś, ṣ
t	t, ṭ
th	th, ṭh

Chinese terms are spelled according to the pinyin system. In the following list, the right column gives approximate English pronunciations of unusual letters used in the pinyin system (in the left column):

c	ts
q	ch
x	sh
zh	j

In Japanese words, macrons over long vowels appear for the most part only in the glossary. Macrons are also used in names of texts in the section titled "Texts in Relation to Dogen's Life and Translation Credits." The name Dogen is pronounced with hard *g* as in *gate*.

NAMES

For Japanese names of laypeople, we put the given name first, to conform with English usage; this order is reversed when the names are alphabetized in the glossary and bibliography. The order is not reversed for Buddhist names, such as Eihei Dogen and Chinese laypeople's names. The abbots of Zen monasteries are often referred to by the name of the mountain, monastery, or region where they resided (as in the example of Eihei Dogen of the Eihei Monastery). Similarly, many monasteries are named after the mountains on which they were built.

TIME, DATES, AND THE BUDDHA'S DATES

Years in this book are dated according to the common era (C.E.) and before the common era (B.C.E.), but in referring to months we follow the lunar calendar traditionally used in East Asia. The first to third months correspond to spring, and the other seasons follow in three-month periods. The fifteenth day of each month is the day of the full moon. The lunar calendar occasionally adds an extra month in order to synchronize with the solar year. Even though approximately thirty days of the end of each lunar year run into the next solar year, to avoid confusion, we accord the entire lunar year to its corresponding solar year.

In the traditional East Asian system, a day has twelve hours. The time from sunrise to sunset is divided into six hours. The nighttime is also made up of six hours. In accordance with the movement of the sunrise and sunset, the length of hours in daytime and nighttime change. The diagrams in appendix 8 (p. 945) illustrate the division of the day into portions, according to which monastic practices are performed in an orderly manner.

Traditional East Asian understanding of Shakyamuni Buddha's dates is different from that of contemporary scholars. See *Buddha, Shākyamuni* in the glossary for details.

AGE

People's ages are reckoned according to the traditional East Asian approach, whereby a person is one year old at birth and gains a year on New Year's Day of the East Asian lunar calendar, not on one's birthday.

UNITS OF MEASUREMENT

Please see the glossary at the end of the book for traditional Asian measuring units that appear in the text.

EDITOR'S INTRODUCTION

MEDITATION AS A SELFLESS EXPERIENCE

Meditation (zazen) can be restful and enjoyable, according to Dogen.[1] Its state (samadhi) can be like an ocean that is serene and yet dynamic.[2] Its field can be as vast as spring time, which encompasses all of its flowers, birds, and mountain colors.[3] Being in spring, we hear the sound of a valley stream or become a plum blossom swirling in the wind.[4]

Dogen's poetic descriptions may seem contrary to our usual meditation experience. Often we are troubled with physical pain and sleepiness; our mind may be scattered, and our daily concerns continue to preoccupy us. We may feel that we have had a bad meditation. Dogen, however, seems to show no interest in these specific issues.[5] He simply speaks of the magnificence of meditation and asserts that we can experience luminosity as soon as we start to meditate.[6]

What we think we experience in meditation may be different from what we actually experience. What, then, do we experience? How do we recognize our deep experience and apply it to our daily lives? These are some of the questions Dogen addresses in the essays presented in this volume.

If we were to summarize Dogen's teaching in one word, it might be "nonseparation."[7] In meditation, the body experiences itself as not separate from the mind.[8] The subject becomes not apart from the object.[9]

While our thinking is often limited to the notion of "I," which is occupied by "my" body, "my" mind, and "my" situation, Dogen teaches that we can become selfless in meditation. Then, we are no longer confined by our self-centered worldview and a dominating sense of possessions. Only when we become transparent and let all things speak for themselves can their voices be heard and their true forms appear.[10]

As we calm down and move away from the usual mode of physical and mental activities, we often have a good idea or even, at times, an extraordinary insight during meditation. However, this is only a beginning stage. If we go further, we may experience a dissolving of the notion of the self. Dogen describes such an experience of his own at the climactic moment of his study as "dropping away body and mind."[11]

BEYOND SPACE AND TIME

The distance from here to there is no longer concrete. A meditator walks on the top of a high mountain and swims deep in the ocean, not only becoming an awakened one but also identifying with a fighting spirit.[12] A person who bows becomes one with the person who is bowed to.[13]

Sizes become free of sizes. The depth of a dewdrop is the height of the moon.[14] The entire world is found in a minute particle. Extremely large becomes extremely small, and vice versa.[15] Here is another view of reality distinct from our usual way of seeing.

It is not that duality stops existing or functioning; the small is still small and the large is still large. The body remains the body and the mind remains the mind. Without discerning the differences between things, we could not conduct even the simplest task of our daily lives. And yet, in meditation the distinctions seem to dissolve and lose their usual significance. Dogen calls this kind of nondualistic experience *nirvana*, which exists at each moment of meditation.[16]

Dogen is perhaps the only Zen master in the ancient world who elucidated in detail the paradox of time. For him, time is not separate from existence: time is being.[17]

Certainly, there is the passage of time marked by the movement of the sun or the clock that always manifests in one direction, from the past, to the present, to the future. On the other hand, in some cases we feel that time flies, and in other cases it moves slowly or almost stands still.

In meditation, according to Dogen, time is multidirectional: Yesterday flows into today, and today flows into yesterday; today flows into tomorrow, and tomorrow flows into today. Today also flows into today.[18]

Time flies, yet it does not fly away.[19] This moment, which is inclusive of all times, is timeless.[20]

Further, time is not apart from the one who experiences it: time is the self.[21] Time flows in "I," and "I" makes the time flow. It is selfless "I" that makes time full and complete.[22]

BEYOND LIFE AND DEATH

Time is also life. In the same manner, time is death. Like other Zen teachers, Dogen repeatedly poses an urgent existential question: realizing the brevity of our life, we need to clarify the essential meaning of life and death.[23]

Life and death are often called "birth and death" in Buddhism, based on the understanding that we are born and die innumerable times moment by moment.[24] Meditation is a way to become familiar with life and death. If we realize that we keep on being born and dying all the time, we become intimate with death as well as life. Thus, we may be better prepared for the moment of our departure from this world than we would be otherwise; and this, in turn, reduces our fear of dying.

For Dogen, each moment of our life can be a complete and all-inclusive experience of life.[25] The life of "I" is not separable from the life of the whole—the life of all beings.[26] In the same way, death is a complete and all-inclusive experience.[27]

When we fully live life and fully die death, life is not exclusive of death; death is not exclusive of life. Then life and death are no longer plural but singular as life-and-death or birth-and-death.

It is a dilemma of life: We all die, and yet, avoiding death is no solution. When we thoroughly face death, death becomes "beyond death."[28] Dogen tells us that this is the meaning of "life-and-death" for an awakened person.

ENLIGHTENMENT AND BEYOND

The Zen way of going beyond the barrier of dualism is to meditate in full concentration. This is called "just sitting."[29]

Dogen's invaluable contribution to clarifying the deep meaning of meditation is his introduction of the concept called the "circle of the way." It means that each moment of our meditation encompasses all four elements of meditation: aspiration, practice, enlightenment, and nirvana.[30]

"Aspiration" is determination in pursuit of enlightenment. "Practice" is the effort required for actualizing enlightenment. "Enlightenment" is the awakening of truth, the dharma. "Nirvana," in his case, is the state of profound serenity, in which dualistic thoughts and desires are at rest.[31]

Dogen says that even a moment of meditation by a beginning meditator fully actualizes the unsurpassable realization, whether that is noticed or not.[32] In this way, enlightenment, often regarded as the goal, is itself the path. The path is no other than the goal.[33]

The word "enlightenment," a translation of the Sanskrit word *bodhi* (literally, "awakening"), has layers of meaning:

1. According to Mahayana sutras, Shakyamuni Buddha said, "I have attained the way simultaneously with all sentient beings on the great earth."[34] That is to say that all sentient and insentient beings are illuminated by the Buddha's original enlightenment and thus carry buddha nature—the potential for or the characteristics of enlightenment.[35] In other words, in the Buddha's eye, all are equally enlightened and none are separate from the Buddha.[36] However, this does not mean, from the ordinary, dualistic perspective, that all beings become wise and free of delusion.[37]

2. In Dogen's explanation of the "circle of the way," all those who practice meditation are fully enlightened. Enlightenment is not separate from practice; enlightenment at each moment is no other than the unsurpassable enlightenment.[38] This aspect may be called the unity of practice-enlightenment or practice-realization.[39] Dogen emphasizes practice that is inseparable from enlightenment as the essential practice of the way of awakened ones—the buddha way. The awareness of enlightenment, however, may not necessarily be recognized by everyone all the time, as it is an experience deeper than one grasped by intellect alone.

3. When we practice meditation, we often don't notice that we are already enlightened, and thus we look for enlightenment somewhere other than in practice. Dogen calls this tendency of separation "great delusion."[40] This pursuit, however, provides us with the potential for

"great enlightenment," which is a merging of the unconscious practice-enlightenment and conscious understanding.

This enlightenment can happen unexpectedly and dramatically as a body-and-mind experience of the nonseparation of all things, rather than as a theoretical understanding. Such spiritual breakthroughs, sometimes called "seeing through human nature" (*kensho* in Japanese), may bring forth exuberance. Dogen quotes many such stories of "sudden realization" by ancient Chinese Zen practitioners as cases of study (koans).[41]

However, Dogen discourages his students from striving for breakthroughs, cautioning that this pursuit is based on the notion of a separation between practice and enlightenment.[42] This kind of realization or "attaining the way" takes time and usually follows a series of failed attempts. In regard to this, Dogen says, ". . . even if you are closely engaged in rigorous practices, you may not hit one mark out of one hundred activities. But by following a teacher or a sutra, you may finally hit a mark. This hitting a mark is due to the missing of one hundred marks in the past; it is the maturing of missing one hundred marks in the past."[43]

An awakened person, a buddha, is someone who actualizes enlightenment. If enlightenment is nothing separate from practice, it is clear that all those who practice meditation as recommended in Buddhism are buddhas. And those who have experienced and reached deep understanding of the nonseparation of all things are regarded as ones who have attained the way.

However, for Dogen, attaining the way is not the final goal. He encourages practitioners of the buddha way to go beyond buddhas and leave no trace of enlightenment.[44] That is to say, we are not supposed to remain in the realm of nonduality.

Going beyond the boundary of all things is important. It is wisdom, which is the basis of compassion. Only when we identify ourselves with others can we genuinely act with love toward others. At the same time, however, for practical and ethical reasons in our daily activities, we need to maintain the boundaries of self and other. An enlightened person is someone who embodies the deep understanding of nonduality while acting in accordance with ordinary boundaries, not being bound to either realm but acting freely and harmoniously.[45]

IRONY OF AUTHENTICITY

"Self-realization without a teacher" is seen as a cause of self-righteous-ness and arrogance, and thus is traditionally discouraged in Zen. Dogen, however, is free and radical enough to say that studying dharma with a sutra or a teacher is none other than self-realization without a teacher.[46] As everyone has a different background, character, and situation, one has to arrive at one's own realization. On the other hand, Dogen is ortho-dox enough to say that realization without a teacher *is* to study with the teacher and to study with a scripture.

The single point Dogen repeatedly brings out throughout his teach-ing career is authenticity. He describes himself as one who has authenti-cally received transmission of the true dharma from his teacher, Rujing.[47] All of the effort in his writings is directed toward understanding, enliv-ening, expounding, and transmitting what he sees as the authentic teach-ing of the Buddha.[48] Dogen sometimes uses the words "authentic" and "authentically" several times in one sentence!

The main sources of his inspiration, other than Rujing's words, are Indian Buddhist scriptures and Chinese Zen texts. Dogen draws stories, sayings, verses, and guidelines from these texts to authenticate the prac-tice of the way he is engaged in. Dogen's words "longing for the ancient" well reflect his admiration of and dedication to the teachings of Shakya-muni Buddha and the subsequent dharma descendants up to Rujing.[49]

Some of the earlier Zen practitioners in China were eccentric and wild-spirited, and did not live in monasteries. Dogen draws teachings from their examples, but he himself chooses to follow the tradition of thorough and solemn daily monastic practice. He regards all daily activi-ties, including wearing the robe, cooking, and engaging in administrative work, as sacred. Dogen orchestrates the whole monastic life in ceremo-nial patterns, highly choreographing every movement—when and how to enter the meditation hall, how to bow, how to sit down, how to eat, and even how to use the toilet.[50]

His operating principle is based on guidelines from Chinese Zen monasteries. The seating and movements are organized hierarchically around the abbot as the supreme authority. The status of monastery of-ficers and the dharma ages (years from the time of ordination) of monks are next in line. Geographically, north is regarded as higher than south and the left side as higher than the right side. Perhaps this reflects a combination of ancient Indian custom and the Chinese imperial court system. Everyone in the monastic community is expected to follow the guidelines exactly.[51] By participating in a well-established communal environment, he seems to believe, practitioners can mature their spirituality with little chance to create unwholesome actions.[52]

Being authentic for Dogen means being true not only to the tradition, but to the particularity of each person's experience, which is intuitive and fresh. This may explain why Zen practitioners have produced enormous amounts of literature. The emphasis on spontaneity and individual creativity may explain why Dogen himself produced a unique and extensive body of writing.

It is striking to note that Dogen's obsession with strict monastic guidelines does not confine him in his imaginative and thought-provoking expressions. Rather, his highly patterned daily life becomes the basis for the unprecedented degree of freedom in his use of language. For him, the realm of unbounded imagination derives from reality itself—brought about only by authentic practice.

DOGEN'S STYLE OF WRITING

Dogen was one of the first Buddhist teachers to write in Japanese. (Until then, Japanese students of Buddhism commonly read and wrote in Chinese, which was pronounced in a Japanese approximation of Chinese pronunciation.) He wrote the *Treasury of the True Dharma Eye* in medieval Japanese, although he retained ancient and medieval Chinese forms when quoting from Zen and secular Chinese texts, as well as Buddhist sutras. While some of his poetry was composed in Japanese, Dogen wrote all official statements, most of the monastic guidelines, and many of his poems in Chinese.

The Chinese language has thousands of ideographs and is rich in expressing poetic images and philosophical concepts. Meanwhile, it has no grammatical conjugations and lacks definite parts of speech. The relationship between words is often implicit. Thus, its sentence structure is suggestive and ambiguous.

The Japanese writing system combines Chinese ideographs and Japanese phonetic letters. Its grammar has inflections and parts of speech, so sentence structure is usually explicit. The logical structure of the Japanese language thus allowed Dogen to pioneer a genre of immensely critical essays in his own language.

When Dogen takes up Chinese texts and makes his own translations, he sometimes stretches the original meanings. Part of the poetry and surprise of Dogen's thinking is characterized by this stretching. For example, a line of Rujing's poetry can normally be translated as "Plum blossoms open in early spring." Dogen translates it as "Plum blossoms open early spring." Also, a line from the *Great Pari-nirvana Sutra* is traditionally translated as "All have buddha nature." He translates it as "All beings *are* buddha nature."

At times Dogen also breaks down a Chinese line into individual ideographs and rearranges the sequence. For example: "The mind itself is buddha," "The mind is buddha itself," "Buddha is itself the mind," "The mind itself buddha is," "Buddha is the mind itself."[53]

A fascicle of the *Treasury of the True Dharma Eye* often starts with a summary paragraph in Dogen's own tempered sentences, giving the topic an ultimate value. When he talks about the monastic robe, for example, he describes it as the most essential thing in Buddhist practice. In the same manner, all monastic activities, as well as scriptures, ancestors, and dharma transmission, are given absolute values.

Then, he quotes from Buddhist scriptures, Zen dialogues, or Zen poems and comments on each line, making a detailed examination of the meaning behind the words. He does not hesitate to harshly criticize great masters like Linji and Yunmen, while admiring their teachings in other passages. At the same time, he reveres the accounts of the earliest Chinese masters, such as Bodhidharma and Huineng, the Sixth Ancestor, as well as later ancestors of his lineage.

Dogen focuses on theoretical aspects of the teaching, while constantly reminding students that awakening is beyond thinking. In some of his essays and monastic guidelines, he gives detailed instructions on the practical aspects of zazen and communal activities, often mixed with philosophical interpretations and poetic expressions.

Commenting on earlier Zen masters' words, Dogen develops his own thought and finds a way to expand the meaning of their words to elaborate his understanding of the utmost importance of each moment.

A remarkable example of this is his interpretation of a verse by Yaoshan (ninth-tenth century): "For the time being, stand on a high mountain . . ." From this, Dogen develops his thought that time is no other than being—the concept of "time being," which I alluded to previously.

The Chinese Zen literature contains a number of stories in which teachers of scriptures abandon lecturing in favor of practicing Zen, or in which Zen teachers make comments that appear to question the primacy of the scriptures. Actually, it is not common for Zen teachers to make extensive efforts to examine the meanings of scriptural phrases. It seems that Chinese Zen marked a distinct departure from the Mahayana texts that embody splendorous cosmic mythology and highly systematic theories. Instead, Chinese Zen leaders focused on a practitioner's experience of the very moment in each individual situation. They tended to point to concrete daily objects such as sandals, a whisk, or a walking stick. Parts of the body—top of the head, eyeballs, nostrils, fists, and heels—were their favorite points of reference.

Dogen speaks such Zen language as this. At the same time, however, he conducts a thorough investigation of phrases from a number of sutras, which makes him unique as a Zen teacher. His writings in the *Treasury of the True Dharma Eye* provide a synthesis of these two traditional aspects: studies of scripture that contain vast systematic expressions of the Buddhist teaching, and Zen, which emphasizes direct experience of the essence of Buddhist teaching through meditation.

Most of the texts in the *Treasury of the True Dharma Eye* were delivered to Dogen's practicing community. He may have read the text aloud (as opposed to speaking spontaneously from a rough note) but there is no evidence that he received questions. His main audience consisted of resident monks, and possibly some senior nuns who were his students. Laypeople such as donors and laborers who happened to be working on the monastery construction were at times invited. He also had an invisible audience of heavenly beings, and sometimes describes dharma teachers as "guiding masters of humans and devas."

It is clear that Dogen's thinking and understanding deepened as he wrote his essays. He made a careful revision of his texts with the help of Ejo, his senior student and successor-to-be. Either Dogen or Ejo made final clean copies of the manuscripts.

DECODING THE ZEN PARADOX

Dogen's writings are known for their impenetrability. Zen practitioners who study the *Treasury of the True Dharma Eye* say that it often takes years to understand some passages in the text. The difficulty of his writings comes from the depth of Buddhist thinking in general and the use of Zen stories or words that are enigmatic, plus his own idiosyncratic style of writing.

In exploring the deeper meanings of Zen stories, poetry, teachings, and Buddhist sutras, Dogen expands, twists, and manipulates the meanings of the words from the texts he quotes.[54] By presenting unique and at times outrageous interpretations, he unleashes a great variety of descriptions on the state of meditation.

Dogen makes use of a full range of Zen rhetoric on the paradox of awakening beyond thought. The traditional teaching device includes nonverbal expressions such as silence, shouting, beating, and gestures, which have been recorded in words. Sacrilegious or violent words and absurd images that are intended to crush stereotypical thinking are not uncommon in Zen heritage. Opposite answers to the same question may be given, and different questions may be responded to with the same answer.

Here are examples of other types of Zen rhetoric that Dogen adopts and employs:

1. Startling images: "There is [a mountain] walking, there is [a mountain] flowing, and there is a moment when a mountain gives birth to a mountain child."[55]

2. Upside-down language: "The forest runs around the hunting dog."[56]

3. Tautology: "A fish swims like a fish. . . . A bird flies like a bird."[57]

4. Negative tautology: "An ancient buddha said, 'Mountains are mountains, waters are waters.' These words do not mean mountains are mountains; they mean mountains are mountains."[58]

5. Chopped logic: "At the very moment of asking the meaning of Bodhidharma coming from India, this dharma wheel is *nothing is essential. Nothing is essential* doesn't mean not to utilize or break this dharma wheel. This dharma wheel turns in *nothing is essential.*"[59]

6. Contradiction: "We manifest the voice of insentient beings speaking dharma with the eyes. Investigate the eyes extensively. Because the voice heard by the eyes should be the same as the voice heard by the ears, the voice heard by the eyes is not the same as the voice heard by the ears."[60]

7. The same word with contrasting meanings: "To study the self [selfless universal self] is to forget the self [ego]. To forget the self is to be actualized by myriad things."[61]

8. Opposite uses of the same metaphor: (a) "When Bodhidharma came from India, the root of twining vines [entanglement with letters and theories] was immediately cut off and the pure, single buddha dharma spread. Hope that it will be like this in our country."[62] (b) "'Teacher and disciple practice mutually' is twining vines [intimate interactions] of buddha ancestors."[63]

9. Reversed statement: "An ancient buddha said, 'A painting of a rice cake does not satisfy hunger.' . . . there is no remedy for satisfying hunger other than a painted rice cake."[64]

10. Non sequitur: "Zhaozhou . . . was once asked by a monk, 'I heard that you personally saw Nanquan. Is it true?' Zhaozhou said, 'A giant radish was here in Zhen Region.'"[65]

11. One equals half: "Since intimacy surrounds you, it is fully intimate, half intimate."[66]

12. One equals many: "When even one single thing is serene, myriad things are serene."[67]

13. Seemingly mundane talk: "Zhaozhou, Great Master Zhenji, asked a newly arrived monk, 'Have you been here before?' The monk said, 'Yes, I have been here.' Zhaozhou said, 'Have some tea.'"[68]

These modes of absurdity, contradiction, and double meaning are partly East Asian but mostly Zen, where there is inherent distrust in conventional language and logic. Dogen often makes an effort to crush and penetrate normal intellectual views, going directly to the source of consciousness that is reality itself, before reasoning in duality and nonduality arise. He sometimes calls this mode of communication "intimate language" or "true expression." It is a realm of word beyond word and logic beyond logic.

IMAGE OF TRANSCENDENCE

Awakening starts with the recognition that there are those who are awakened and those who are not. Once awakened, you are free from the distinction between them. This freedom is transcended to the point that there are those who are awakened and those who are not, which appears similar to the beginning stage. On this advanced level of freedom, however, you are totally yourself and act without hindrance.

Thus, there are: affirmation, negation, negation of negation, and negation of "negation of negation." This direction toward the next level of experience can be characterized as: duality, nonduality that is transcendence of duality, transcendence of transcendence, and transcended activities.

This may be seen as a map of freedom, an intellectual analysis. But, in fact, this kind of transcendence is experienced freely and intuitively. Let us examine some of the terms Dogen employs to demonstrate an immediate experience:

"Dropping away body and mind," "casting off limitations," and "hurling away enlightenment" are some of the basic images of release from restricted self-experience. That means you "set aside" usual concerns and are "detached" from both awakening and not awakening.

While you "give up holding back," you are not motionless. Rather, you "break away" and take "the path of letting go." You "leap out," "leap over," and "leap clear." You "jump," "fly beyond," and "leap beyond ancient and present." In Chinese and Japanese, transcending is described as "going beyond" (as in "going beyond buddhas"), which indicates the direction of "going upward," "surpassing" buddhas and ancestors.

The act of "inquiring beyond" and "expressing beyond" is none other than "breaking through the bamboo node [intellect and theories]" and "going beyond discriminatory thoughts" by "breaking open," "penetrating," and "passing through the barrier of dualism." Being "free and transparent" may be possible by "cutting through," "cutting apart," "cutting to the original," "crushing," "smashing," and "vanishing." This is sometimes represented by such graphic expressions as "cracking open particles" and "plucking out eyeballs."

When all preconceived notions of goals and objectives are "lost," you "float free" and "let myriad things advance themselves." That is the "realm of the unconstructed," "beyond knowing," and "beyond think-ing." Here, there is "no effort" and "no creation."

This place of "no doing" is not being lazy or idly thinking about freedom. Instead, it is an experience "beyond obstruction" for the pur-pose of "thorough understanding," "fully actualizing," "realizing through the body," and the "embodiment" of "directly clarifying the source be-yond words." It is not separate from each moment of "sitting through" and "cutting through sitting."

THE TIME WHEN DOGEN LIVED

In Japanese history, the era when Dogen lived is called the Kamakura Period (1185–1333). The preceding periods are the Asuka Period (593–710), the Nara Period (710–794), and the Heian Period (794–1185).

Buddhist doctrine was introduced to Japan through Chinese-language texts from Korea in the mid-sixth century. Since Buddhism was accom-panied by the writing system and advanced technology of a great civili-zation, it quickly received imperial patronage and spread throughout the country. The appointment of Prince Shotoku as the regent, who was to dedicate his life to the practice and propagation of Buddhism, marked the beginning of the Asuka Period.

The grid-shaped city planning of Nara, the new capital of Japan, fol-lowed that of the Chinese capital city Chan'an. The construction of the Todai Temple, which housed an enormous Buddha statue, exemplified a concerted national effort initiated by the monarch to create a society based on the infinite luminosity of the universal buddha light described in the *Avatamsaka Sutra*. The six schools of Buddhism, most of which were based on various philosophical principles, flourished.

A larger-scale planned city of Heian (Kyoto), to the north of Nara, became the imperial capital, where a highly refined court culture devel-oped. Trade with China increased, and a number of monks studied in Tang China, a flourishing world empire. The Shingon (mantra) School, focused on highly ritualized Esoteric Buddhist prayers, became one of the two most influential schools of Buddhism in Japan. The Tendai School—the Japanese form of the Tiantai School in China—was the other powerful school, with a comprehensive Buddhist training center on Mount Hiei in the northeast of Kyoto.

Assimilating with the indigenous Shintoism, Buddhism became an indispensable part of everyday life. Buddhist masters competed with one another to gain imperial patronage, offering a variety of magical prayers. Mount Hiei housed one of the strongest armies of monk-soldiers, who frequently engaged in battles, sometimes burning other monasteries. The Tendai armed forces were known for their frequent demonstrations in Kyoto and for forcing their demands upon the imperial government.

According to Buddhist texts, the period of five hundred years after the time of Shakyamuni Buddha is the Age of True Dharma, which is followed by another five hundred years of the Age of Imitation Dharma. Then the Age of Declining Dharma emerges. Many Japanese Buddhists believed that this last period of no true practice or enlightenment started in 1052. People attributed calamities such as famines, epidemics, social disorder, and wars to the decline of dharma. The wish to attain rebirth in the Pure Land prevailed among those who felt that it was hopeless to attain enlightenment in the present world.

The samurai families—the Taira Clan from the western part of the country and the Minamoto from the east—served as imperial guards and expanded their influence. First, Kiyomori Taira became a powerful military ruler, still serving the emperor. Then, Yoritomo Minamoto defeated the Taira armies in a series of battles and established the Shogun government in Kamakura. This was the beginning of the Kamakura Period. Later, the Hojo Family took over the Kamakura government and called its head "Regent."

Buddhism in this period may be characterized by the emergence of "single practice." Honen and his noted disciple Shinran came into conflict with the Tendai establishment, which forced them into exile, but they succeeded in spreading the wholehearted practice of chanting homage to Amitabha Buddha. Dogen established the Zen practice of "just sitting." Later, Nichiren spread the practice of chanting homage to the *Lotus Sutra—Namu-Myoho-Renge-Kyo*. This "single practice" of Buddhism, in all its variations, appealed to great numbers of farmers, warriors, and court nobles, eventually becoming the mainstream of faith in Japan.

THE EARLY LIFE OF DOGEN

The first biographical account of Dogen was written by Keizan Jokin, who was a dharma successor of Gikai, one of Dogen's senior students. It appears as a chapter of Keizan's book, *Transmission of Light,* completed forty-seven years after Dogen's death. We have included it in appendix 2.

Three other early biographies, all of which were written more than a century after Dogen's death, are also important sources for reconstructing the first part of Dogen's life. They are *Biographies of the First Three Ancestors of the Eihei Monastery (Eihei-ji sanso gyogo-ki),* author unknown, already in existence during the Oei Era (1394–1428); *Biography of the First Ancestor, Zen Master, Priest Dogen (Shoso Dogen zenji osho gyoroku),* author unknown, published in 1673; and *Kenzei's Biography of the Founder Dogen of Eihei (Eihei kaisan gyojo Kenzei-ki)* by Kenzei (1415–1474).[69]

According to the biography by Keizan, Dogen—whose given name is unknown (his name Eihei is taken from the name of his monastery)—was born in 1200 C.E. By Dogen's own words, he was an adopted son of a "minister of the Minamoto family." Keizan identifies Motofusa, Lord of the Pine Palace, as this mysterious person. It seems, however, that a later theory by Soto historians which attributes Michitomo Minatomo (1171–1227) as Dogen's foster father is most convincing. Michitomo was a distinguished poet known as an editor of *Shin Kokin Shu,* a celebrated imperial anthology of waka (a traditional Japanese poem consisting of thirty-one syllables). Dogen presumably received a high tutorial education in Chinese literature and Japanese poetry. He says, "When I was young, I loved studying literature that was not directly connected to Buddhism."[70]

Dogen lost his mother when he was eight (by the Japanese way of reckoning age). Possibly referring to this early misfortune, he himself says, "Realizing the impermanence of life, I began to arouse the way-seeking mind."[71] At thirteen, he visited monk Ryokan, who lived in a hut at the foot of Mount Hiei, northeast of Kyoto, and subsequently entered the monkhood himself. In the following year he was formally ordained by Koen, Head Priest of the Tendai School. Probably Koen was the one who named this novice Buppo Dogen, meaning "Buddha Dharma, Way Source."

Dogen left Mount Hiei after receiving basic training as a monk and studying the scriptures. Later he reflected: "After the aspiration for enlightenment arose, I began to search for dharma, visiting teachers at various places in our country."[72] We don't know whom he visited, except Koin, who was abbot of the Onjo Monastery—a noted Tendai center of esoteric practices—and a dedicated follower of Honen, the main propagator of the Amitabha chanting practice. Dogen recalls: "The late Bishop Koin said, 'The mind of the way is acquired after understanding that one thought embraces all existence in the billion worlds.'"[73] Dogen summarizes the first four years of his pursuit: "I had some understanding of the principle of cause and effect; however, I was not able to clarify the real source of buddha, dharma, and sangha. I only saw the outer forms—the marks and names."[74]

Dogen continues: "Later I entered the chamber of Eisai, Zen Master Senko, and for the first time heard the teaching of the Linji School."[75] Myoan Eisai, who had visited China twice and received dharma transmission from Xuan Huaichang, was among the first to teach Zen in Japan. But because the Tendai establishment was oppressing new movements of Buddhism, he had to teach conventional esoteric practices along with Zen. It was around 1214 when Dogen visited Eisai at the Kennin Monastery in Kyoto, one of the three monasteries Eisai had founded. Eisai was seventy-four years old, and he died the following year.

In 1217, Dogen became a disciple of Butsuju Myozen, Eisai's successor as abbot of the Kennin Monastery. We can assume that Dogen was trained by Myozen in koan studies, which was the principal method of training in the Linji School. Koans are exemplary stories of ancient masters pointing to realization, which are investigated by the students under the personal guidance of their teacher, and may lead to direct experience of the nondual aspect of all things beyond intellect. In 1221, Dogen received a certificate of full accomplishment from Myozen.

Myozen was respected in Kyoto and even gave the bodhisattva precepts to the former emperor Gotakakura, but he was aware of the need to deepen his studies. As China was the only place where he could study authentic Zen, he wanted to follow Eisai's example of traveling to the Middle Kingdom. Dogen, a young but outstanding student at the Kennin Monastery, was allowed to accompany Myozen.

Myozen's party, including Dogen and two other disciples, left Japan from the Port of Hakata on Kyushu Island in the second month of 1223. Two months later, the boat arrived at the then main trading port of Ninbo (in present-day Zhejiang Province). Reflecting on this Dogen writes, "After a voyage of many miles during which I entrusted my phantom body to the billowing waves, I have finally arrived. . . ."[76]

Dogen's first encounter with Chinese Zen happened the following month when he was still on board, waiting for permission to enter a monastery. Myozen, who was acknowledged as Eisai's dharma heir, had already left the boat and been admitted to the monastery. An old monk who was the head cook of a nearby monastery came on board to buy dried mushrooms. After some conversation, Dogen said, "Reverend Head Cook, why don't you concentrate on zazen practice and on the study of the ancient masters' words, rather than troubling yourself by holding the position of head cook and just working?" The old monk laughed and replied, "Good man from a foreign country, you do not yet understand practice or know the meaning of the words of ancient masters." Dogen was surprised and ashamed.[77]

China's highest-ranking Zen monasteries were located in Zhejiang Province, where Dogen arrived. He entered one of them, the Jingde Monastery on Mount Tiantong, also known as Mount Taibai. Soon he noticed monks around him holding up their folded dharma robes, setting them on their heads, and chanting a verse silently with palms together: "How great! The robe of liberation . . ." Seeing this solemn ritual for the first time, he vowed to himself: "However unsuited I might be, I will become an authentic heir of the buddha dharma, receiving authentic transmission of the true dharma, and with compassion show the buddha ancestors' authentically transmitted dharma robes to those in my land."[78]

The abbot of the Jingde Monastery was Wuji Liaopai, in the dharma lineage of Dahui Zonggao who had been the most influential advocate of koan studies in the Linji School. While studying in Liaopai's community for a year and a half, Dogen familiarized himself with formal monastic practices. Then, he started visiting other monasteries in search of a true master.

In early 1225, Dogen went to meet Abbot Yuanzi of the Wannian Monastery at Mount Tiantai, who showed Dogen his document of dharma heritage and offered dharma transmission. Dogen had learned the significance of documents of heritage in the Chinese Buddhist tradition, as the proof of the completion of studies and succession of the dharma lineage. They were often kept strictly confidential, but Dogen had managed to see some and made careful studies of them. Moved by Yuanzi's offer to transmit dharma to him, Dogen bowed and burned incense, but did not accept.

The more closely he saw what was happening in monasteries in the heartland of Chinese Zen, the more he was disappointed. He comments in his journal: "Nowadays elders of different monasteries say that only direct experience without discrimination—to hear the unhearable and to see the unseeable—is the way of buddha ancestors. So they hold up a fist or a whisk, or they shout and beat people with sticks. This kind of teaching doesn't do anything to awaken students. Furthermore, these teachers don't allow students to inquire about the essentials of the Buddha's guidance and they discourage practices that aim to bear fruit in a future birth. Are these teachers really teaching the way of buddha ancestors?"[79]

Dogen also saw corruption in monastic practices. Even documents of dharma heritage that were supposed to be valued with utmost respect were given to those who were not qualified. Monks tended to seek credentials from famous masters who had given dharma heritage to retainers of the king. Some monks, when they grew old, bribed public officials in order to get a temple and hold the abbot's seat.

In 1225, Dogen heard that Rujing, who had been abbot of the Qingliang and Jingci monasteries, had just become abbot of the Jingde Monastery on Mount Tiantong, where Dogen had first stayed. Rujing was a monk from the Caodong School, in which "just sitting," rather than koan studies, was emphasized. He was known as a strict and genuine teacher, not easily admitting monks into his community and often expelling those who did not train seriously. Dogen returned to Mount Tiantong. While he participated in the practice of the monastery as one of hundreds of monks, he wrote to Rujing, explaining why he had come from Japan and requesting the status of a student who could enter the abbot's room for receiving personal guidance. This letter impressed Rujing, who must have heard from officers of the monastery that Dogen was a remarkable student. Rujing wrote back and granted his request, saying, "Yes, you can come informally to ask questions any time, day or night, from now on. Do not worry about formality; we can be like father and son."[80]

On the first day of the fifth month of 1225, Dogen entered the abbot's room and met Rujing for the first time. On this occasion Rujing affirmed his recognition of Dogen and said, "The dharma gate of face-to-face transmission from buddha to buddha, ancestor to ancestor, is actualized now."[81]

This exhilarating time for Dogen was also a time of great loss. Myozen died from illness on the twenty-seventh day of the same month. He had been teacher to Dogen for eight years, as well as a traveling companion and fellow seeker.

Expressing his doubt to Rujing about the current trend of Zen teachers who would emphasize "transmission outside scriptures" and discourage students from studying the Buddha's teaching, Dogen asked for Rujing's comment. Rujing said, "The great road of buddha ancestors is not concerned with inside or outside. . . . We have been followers of the Buddha for a long time. How can we hold views that are outside the way of the Buddha? To teach students the power of the present moment as the only moment is a skillful teaching of buddha ancestors. But this doesn't mean that there is no future result from practice."[82] Thus, Rujing demonstrated that he was an ideal teacher for Dogen, who was seeking Zen that fully embodied the teaching of the Buddha described in scriptures.

While receiving rigorous training from Rujing, Dogen asked him further questions in a respectful but challenging way, showing his sincerity as well as his brilliance. Rujing was confident of himself as an authentic carrier of the Zen tradition, and Dogen sought to experience the heart of his teaching. The culmination of his practice came one day in zazen when he heard Rujing speak in the monks' hall. Reflecting on this experience, Dogen says, "Upon hearing Rujing's words 'dropping off,' I attained the buddha way."[83] In the fall of 1227, after completing his study and receiving a document of heritage from Rujing, Dogen ended his four-year visit to China. He went back to Japan to teach people in his own country.

DOGEN AS A DHARMA TEACHER

In the tenth month of 1227, soon after returning to the Kennin Monastery in Kyoto, Dogen wrote a record of bringing home the relics of Myozen, the former abbot.[84] In the same year he wrote a short manifesto called "Recommending Zazen to All People," in a brief but formal and elaborate Chinese style. This text, a translation of which is included in appendix 1, was his declaration of establishing a new form of Buddhist practice in Japan, based on his understanding of the traditional Zen teaching he had studied in Song-Dynasty China. Dogen was twenty-eight years old in the Japanese way of counting.

The *Treasury of the True Dharma Eye* provides detailed information about the teaching life of Dogen, as he meticulously recorded the dates of creation in the colophons of most of its fascicles. Some other writings of his, including monastic guidelines, were dated. Dogen's students recorded his frequently given formal talks, whose dates either were recorded or can be guessed. We present an outline of his life as a Zen master through textual evidence in the section headed "Texts in Relation to Dogen's Life and Translation Credits."

The first part of Dogen's teaching career was the wandering and preparation period, from age twenty-eight to thirty-four (1227–1233). Then he constructed and taught at a small monastery as abbot: the Kosho Horin Monastery period, from age thirty-four to forty-four (1233–1243). He continued to teach and write during the construction period of a full-scale monastery, from age forty-four to forty-six (1243–1245). Then he taught at the Daibutsu Monastery, later renamed the Eihei Monastery, from age forty-six to fifty-four (1245–1253).

Dogen first intended to spread zazen widely to all people, but he gradually put more and more emphasis on training committed Zen students to the point of saying that attaining the way would only be possible for home leavers (ordained monks and nuns). He gave dharma transmission to a few students, including Ejo—his lifetime teaching assistant and editor, who succeeded him as abbot of Eihei Monastery.

The *Treasury of the True Dharma Eye* is Dogen's lifework, while the *Extensive Record of Priest Eihei Dogen*—edited by his students, Sen'e, Ejo, and Gien—is a huge collection of his texts including formal talks, monastic guidelines, Chinese-style and waka poems, as well as other writings.

Although he rejected calling his community a Zen school or a Buddha Mind school, it was difficult for his dharma descendants to distinguish their group from other schools of Buddhism. Thus, Dogen became regarded as the founder of the Soto School—the Japanese form of the Caodong School, of which Rujing transmitted the lineage to Dogen.

By the efforts of his dharma heirs and descendants, in particular by that of Keizan Jokin (1268–1325), who incorporated Dogen's teaching into that of Esoteric Buddhist practice, the Soto School spread largely in the countryside as its main base. This was in contrast to the Rinzai School, which was supported by the shoguns of the Ashikaga Clan and the emperors during the Muromachi Period (1336–1573), and developed high Zen culture, centering in the city of Kyoto. The Soto School is currently the largest school of Buddhism in Japan.

TRANSMISSION OF THE TEXTS AND LATER SCHOLARSHIP

Originals and hand copies of Dogen's writings were scattered in temples all over Japan. But thanks to traditional and contemporary scholarship, a critical edition that compares variants in all available versions of Dogen's texts has been published and is available for study.[85]

While Dogen's dharma descendants increased, gaining popular support and building temples all over Japan, most of his writings were quickly forgotten. Not one substantial commentary was written on his essays between the fourteenth and seventeenth centuries.

There was a movement in the Soto community after the seventeenth century, however, to restore the founder's spirit. The movement included extensive studies of his writings, resulting in the publication of the *Treasury of the True Dharma Eye* by the Eihei Monastery, along with the emergence of commentaries on Dogen's writings by several monk-scholars.

Studies about Dogen remained in the domain of Soto sectarian scholarship until the 1920s, when Japanese scholars of Western philosophy started to realize the importance of Dogen's thinking. That was when Tetsuro Watsuji's *Shamon Dogen* (Monk Dogen) awakened interest in Dogen's work among intellectuals.

In the 1960s, Dogen began to be recognized as one of the greatest essayists in the history of Japanese literature. His writings were selected for various collections of classical literature. Since the 1960s, six translations of the entire *Treasury of the True Dharma Eye* have been published, making much of Dogen's thought available to Japanese readers.

As Zen meditation began to spread to the Western world in the 1950s, translations of some of Dogen's writings started to appear in Western languages. Over fifty books of Dogen translation and studies have been published in English, which makes Dogen by far the most extensively studied East Asian Buddhist in the Western world. How his influence will extend is yet to be seen.

DOGEN IN OUR TIME

Meditation is increasingly gaining importance in contemporary society. As technology advances and the pace of life becomes faster and faster, participants of the global society feel constantly stressed and driven by anxiety in their efforts to catch up with the speed and complexity of everyday life. In this state of the world, there is a tremendous need for us to slow down, relax, and heal.

Dogen's way, along with meditative arts such as yoga and taichi, can be one of the practices that help us to calm down and remain peaceful while being attentive to body, mind, and outer situations.

Although it is possible for us to meditate for years and still be self-centered, the teaching of the self beyond self—the experience of self-lessness through meditation—is enormously useful. How, then, can we achieve inner freedom? How can we be free from polarizing ourselves from others? How can we be free from dualistic thinking and from language itself? Dogen seems to provide clues to these questions.

Dogen's descriptions of meditation point to a radical expansion of our view of the world. That is, through a meditation-based life, awareness of the interconnection of all things expands our sense of self beyond the conventional confines of a world centered on our personal egos. Thus, the distinction between us and others becomes less significant. More and more we feel the joy and pain of others. This helps us to be compassionate and leads to action that helps others and ourselves by way of loving-kindness.

We may not understand or agree with everything Dogen says: We may not favor his criticism of other Buddhists or non-Buddhists. His teaching may be too austere, too strict, and too monastic for us. His view of history may not accord with contemporary scholarship. However, his unshakable belief in the power of meditation and the immense potential of an individual action can be inspiring.[86]

For Dogen, dreams and illusions have as much reality as actual phenomena. This notion leads us to confirm the power of fantasy and vision, which is often the basis for all types of creative, scientific, and social pursuits. Although Dogen was neither a social reformer nor a peace activist, as a Buddhist he was a pacifist. At the same time, his thoughts on the power of vision can be immensely helpful for those who work for peace and the environment.

Dogen's discourse on karma illuminates the inseparableness of cause and effect. Where there is a cause, whether it is large or small, good or bad, there is and will be an effect. We may not agree with his point, based on Buddhist scriptures, that some of the effects will take place in our future lifetime or lifetimes after death and rebirth. In fact, we may not believe in reincarnation at all. It is possible, however, for us to imagine that our actions will affect others, future generations, and the environment, instead of ourselves alone. We can also see that we, other people, all beings, and the environment are closely interconnected. Thus, it is possible to establish an understanding that all causes have effects, and that there is no cause without effect. Such trust in and identification with causation can be a basis for actions in our time.

Dogen's recommendations on how to brush the teeth and how to use the toilet may no longer be valid, as our lifestyle today is different from that of his time. On the other hand, much of Dogen's instruction on how to sit and move in the meditation hall and how to work in the kitchen still has relevance in Zen monasteries and Zen centers in the Western world. His utmost positivity and trust in the power of action are compelling for those who are discouraged by the enormity of our social problems and who tend to be cynical and inactive. Furthermore, his teaching of sitting up straight helps us to sit, stand, walk and face the world in a forthright way. His ironic statement, "We will thoroughly engage in each activity in order to cultivate fertile conditions to transform the ten directions,"[87] is an excellent reminder that we need to pay full attention to every detail of our work with others in order to prepare ourselves to transform ourselves and, hence, the world.

NOTES

1. Dogen's term for meditation is *zazen*, meaning meditation in a sitting posture. He says, "The zazen I speak of . . . is simply the dharma gate of enjoyment and ease" (Recommending Zazen to All People, p. 908).

2. The state of meditation is called *samadhi*. For Dogen, this samadhi has been passed on by a number of awakened ones from the past. He says, "Buddhas and ancestors continuously maintain ocean mudra [form] samadhi" (Ocean Mudra Samadhi, p. 380).

3. For Dogen, the state of meditation is all-inclusive. It is also in constant movement, which he calls "flowing." He says, "Spring with all its numerous aspects is called flowing. When spring flows there is nothing outside of spring" (The Time Being, p. 108). Dogen encourages meditators to experience this all-inclusive state: "When you paint spring, do not paint willows, plums, peaches, or apricots—just paint spring" (Plum Blossoms, p. 588).

4. Dogen quotes and comments on a poem by Su Dongpo, expressing the poet's understanding which emerged in meditation: "Valley sounds are the long, broad tongue [of the Buddha]. Mountain colors are no other than the unconditioned body [of the Buddha] . . ." (Valley Sounds, Mountain Colors, p. 86).

   Dogen also quotes a poem by his teacher, Rujing, which expresses a state of meditation: "Old plum tree bent and gnarled all at once opens one blossom, two blossoms, three, four, five blossoms, uncountable blossoms, not proud of purity, not proud of fragrance; spreading, becoming spring, blowing over grass and trees . . ." (Plum Blossoms, p. 581).

5. There is no mention of "good meditation" or "bad meditation" in Dogen's extensive writings. Nor does he discuss physical or psychological problems in meditation.

6. "When even for a moment you sit upright in samadhi expressing the buddha mudra [form] in the three activities [body, speech, and thought], the whole world of phenomena becomes the buddha seal [expression] and the entire sky turns into enlightenment" (On the Endeavor of the Way, p. 5).

7. "Nonseparation" may be also described as "undividedness" or "nonduality."

8. The state of meditation Dogen explains is based on general and Zen Buddhist teachings. He says, "In buddha dharma it is always taught that body and mind are not separate, and that essence and characteristics are not two" (On Endeavor of the Way, p. 15). As he uses the words "body" and "mind" not separately from each other, "body-and-mind" can be a suitable translation. For example: "When you see forms or hear sounds, fully engaging body-and-mind, you intuit dharma intimately" (Actualizing the Fundamental Point, p. 30).

9. In continuation of the above line, Dogen says, "Unlike things and their reflections in the mirror, and unlike the moon and its reflection in the water, when one side is illumined, the other side is dark" (ibid., p. 30).

10. "To study the way of enlightenment is to study the self. To study the self is to forget the self. To forget the self is to be actualized by myriad things. When actualized by myriad things, your body and mind as well as the bodies and minds of others drop

away" (ibid., p. 30). Also, "To carry the self forward and illuminate myriad things is delusion. That myriad things come forth and illuminate the self is awakening" (ibid., p. 29).

11. According to Keizan's biography of Dogen: "One day during the late-evening zazen, Rujing said to the assembly, 'Practicing Zen is dropping away body and mind.' Upon hearing this, Dogen suddenly had great realization. Immediately [after zazen], he went up to the abbot's quarters and offered incense to Rujing, who said, 'Why are you offering incense to me?' Dogen said, 'I have dropped away body and mind.' Rujing said, "You have dropped away body and mind. Your body and mind have been dropped away"' (appendix 2, p. 911).

12. Dogen quotes a verse by Yaoshan, a Chinese Zen master: "For the time being, stand on top of the highest peak. For the time being, proceed along the bottom of the deepest ocean. For the time being, three heads and eight arms [of a fighting demon]. For the time being, an eight- or sixteen-foot body [of the Buddha]" (The Time Being, p. 104).

13. A verse by Rujing, Dogen's teacher: "Both the bower and the bowed-to are empty and serene by nature and the way flows freely between them. How wondrous!" (Journal of My Study in China, *Enlightenment Unfolds*, p. 8).

14. "Enlightenment does not divide you, just as the moon does not break the water. You cannot hinder enlightenment, just as a drop of water does not crush the moon in the sky. The depth of the drop is the height of the moon" (Actualizing the Fundamental Point, p. 31).

15. "Understanding these words [about the entire universe] is going beyond buddhas and ancestors by seeing that extremely large is small and extremely small is large" (Awesome Presence of Active Buddhas, p. 264).

16. This is a special usage of the word "nirvana." For Dogen, each moment of practice encompasses this experience. "Between aspiration, practice, enlightenment, and nirvana, there is not a moment's gap; continuous practice is the circle of the way" (Continuous Practice, Part One, p. 332).

17. Dogen elaborates the poem by Yaoshan, quoted in note 12, by saying: "*For the time being* here means time itself is being, and all being is time" (The Time Being, p. 104).

18. "So-called today flows into tomorrow, today flows into yesterday, yesterday flows into today. And today flows into today, tomorrow flows into tomorrow" (ibid., p. 106).

19. "Do not think that time merely flies away. Do not see flying away as the only function of time. If time merely flies away, you would be separated from time" (ibid., p. 106).

20. "'Before the emergence of a single mind, single thought' [immeasurable past] is this very day. Temper your practice without missing this very day" (Old Mirror, p. 215).

21. "In essence, all things in the entire world are linked with one another as moments. Because all moments are the time being, they are your time being" (The Time Being, p. 106).

22. "To fully actualize the [buddha's] golden body with the golden body—to arouse the way-seeking mind, practice, attain enlightenment, and enter nirvana—is nothing but being, nothing but time" (ibid., p. 107).

23. "The real issue here, to clarify birth and to clarify death, is the great matter of causes and effects in the buddha house" (Refrain from Unwholesome Action, p. 103).

24. "... those who clarify the Tathagata's treasury of the true dharma eye, the wondrous heart of nirvana, believe in this principle of birth and death moment by moment" (Arousing the Aspiration for Enlightenment, p. 659).

25. "Birth is just like riding in a boat. You raise the sails and you steer. Although you maneuver the sail and the pole, the boat gives you a ride, and without the boat you couldn't ride. But you ride in the boat, and your riding makes the boat what it is" (Undivided Activity, p. 451).

26. After the line quoted in note 25, Dogen continues: "At just such a moment, there is nothing but the world of the boat. The sky, the water, and the shore are all the boat's world, which is not the same as a world that is not the boat's. Thus, you make birth what it is, you make birth your birth" (ibid., p. 451).

27. "At the moment of death's undivided activity, while it covers the entire earth and the entire sky, it hinders neither death's undivided activity nor birth's undivided activity" (ibid., p. 451).

28. "Death is a phase that is an entire period of itself, with its own past and future. For this reason, death is understood as beyond death" (Birth and Death, p. 885).

29. "Just sitting" is the practice of zazen with no attempt to solve questions or expectation of attainment or enlightenment, and without either repressing or holding on to thoughts and feelings. Dogen emphasized this way of sitting.

30. For the meaning of *nirvana*, see note 16.

31. The essence of what is transmitted in Zen is described as "the treasury of the true dharma eye, the wondrous heart of nirvana." Dogen, however, did not fully explain what he meant by "nirvana" here. So we need to guess from such statements as: "How can you differentiate this into body and mind, and separate birth-and-death from nirvana?" (On Endeavor of the Way, p. 15) and "In awakening there are aspiration, practice, enlightenment, and nirvana. Within the dream there are aspiration, practice, enlightenment, and nirvana. Every awakening within a dream is the genuine form, without regard to large or small, superior or inferior" (Within a Dream Expressing the Dream, p. 437).

32. "Because practice within realization occurs at the moment of practice, the practice of beginner's mind is itself the entire original realization" (On Endeavor of the Way, p. 12).

33. In the "circle of the way" (see n. 16), the way toward enlightenment is not linear, but rather is complete at each moment, encompassing practice and enlightenment.

34. "At age thirty, after practicing continuously, he [the Buddha] attained the way simultaneously with all sentient beings on the great earth" (Continuous Practice, Part One, p. 334).

35. Dogen interprets the statement from the *Maha Pari-nirvana Sutra*, "All sentient beings have buddha nature," as "Living beings all are buddha nature." He reads "all have" (*shitsu u* in Japanese) as "all are" (Buddha Nature, p. 234).

36. "Because earth, grass, trees, walls, tiles, and pebbles in the world of phenomena in the ten directions all engage in buddha activity, those who receive the benefits of the wind and water are inconceivably helped by the buddha's transformation, splendid and unthinkable, and intimately manifest enlightenment" (On Endeavor of the Way, p. 6).

37. The paradox of buddha nature is that although buddha nature *is* all beings, it is only *actualized*. "Buddha nature invariably arises simultaneously with attaining buddhahood" (Buddha Nature, p. 241).

38. "To suppose that practice and realization are not one is a view of those outside the way; in buddha dharma they are inseparable" (On the Endeavor of the Way, p. 12).

39. This concept is called "inseparableness of practice and realization"; or "practice within realization" (ibid., p. 12).

40. "…those who are greatly deluded about realization are sentient beings" (Actualizing the Fundamental Point, p. 29). Here Dogen refers to the term "sentient beings" as those who are not awakened.

41. Early in his teaching career Dogen collected three hundred koans and called them the *Treasury of the True Dharma Eye*, later known as *Shinji* [Chinese] *Shobo Genzo*. He used many of the koans in the essays presented in the present book.

42. In an informal talk Dogen said, "Even if you obtain some ideas by studying koans and words, it may cause you to go further away from the buddha ancestors' path. Instead, dedicate your time to sitting upright, not seeking achievement, and not seeking enlightenment. This is the ancestral way." *Treasury of the True Dharma Eye: Record of Things Heard. Enlightenment Unfolds,* pp. 57–58.

43. Speaking of Mind, Speaking of Essence, p. 493.

44. "When actualized by myriad things, your body and mind as well as the bodies and minds of others drop away. No trace of enlightenment remains, and this no-trace continues endlessly" (Actualizing the Fundamental Point, p. 30).

45. For Dogen's teaching on ethics, see Refrain from Unwholesome Action, pp. 95–103. Also on harmonious practice, "The assembly of students in the hall should blend like milk and water to support the activity of the way" (Regulations for the Auxiliary Cloud Hall at the Kannondori Kosho Gokoku Monastery, p. 39).

46. "When you study buddha dharma with a sutra or with a teacher, you come to realization without a teacher" (Dharma Nature, p. 558).

47. "I, Dogen, first bowed formally to Rujing, my late master, Old Buddha Tiantong, and received transmission face to face on the first day of the fifth month, the first year of Baoqing Era of Great Song, and was thereby allowed to enter the inner chamber" (Face-to-Face Transmission, p. 575).

48. "…I made a vow to myself: However unsuited I may be, I will become an authentic holder of the buddha dharma, receiving authentic transmission of the true dharma,

and with compassion show the buddha ancestors' authentically transmitted dharma robes to those in my land" (Power of the Robe, p. 135; Transmitting the Robe, p. 152).

49. "We come to know the ancient sutras and texts as a result of our longing for the authentic teaching. As we long for the ancient teaching, the sutras of old come forth" (Continuous Practice, Part Two, p. 358).

50. See Practice Period (pp. 724–744) and Guidelines for Practice of the Way (*Beyond Thinking*, pp. 103–117) for procedures in the monks' hall. See Cleansing (pp. 51–56) for instruction on use of the toilet.

51. See Regulations for the Auxiliary Cloud Hall at the Kannondori Kosho Gokoku Monastery, p. 39.

52. See Refrain from Unwholesome Action, p. 95.

53. The Mind Itself Is Buddha, p. 43.

54. For a typical example, see note 35.

55. Mountains and Waters Sutra, p. 156.

56. Spring and Autumn, p. 631.

57. The Point of Zazen, p. 314.

58. Mountains and Waters Sutra, p. 164.

59. The Buddhas' Teaching, p. 280.

60. Insentient Beings Speak Dharma, p. 548.

61. Actualizing the Fundamental Point, p. 30.

62. On the Endeavor of the Way, p. 5.

63. Twining Vines, p. 482.

64. Painting of a Rice Cake, p. 444.

65. Seeing the Buddha, p. 596.

66. Intimate Language, p. 531.

67. Thusness, p. 327.

68. Everyday Activity, p. 621.

69. The four biographies of Dogen mentioned here are included in *Eihei Kaisan Dogen Zenji Gyojo Kenzei-ki,* edited by Kodo Kawamura.

70. Editor's translation of a line from *Treasury of the True Dharma Eye: Record of Things Heard.*

71. Ibid.

72. On the Endeavor of the Way, p. 4.

73. *Treasury of the True Dharma Eye: Record of Things Heard.*

74. Journal of My Study in China, *Enlightenment Unfolds,* p. 3.

75. Ibid.

76. Ibid.

77. Instructions for the Tenzo, *Moon in a Dewdrop,* p. 59.

78. Power of the Robe, p. 135.

79. Journal of My Study in China, *Enlightenment Unfolds,* p. 4.

80. Ibid., p. 3.

81. Face-to-Face Transmission, p. 569.

82. Journal of My Study in China, *Enlightenment Unfolds,* pp. 4–5.
83. Extensive Record of Priest Eihei Dogen, *Beyond Thinking,* p. 145.
84. Record of Bringing Master Myozen's Relics, *Enlightenment Unfolds,* p. 30.
85. Okubo Doshu, ed., *Dogen Zenji Zenshu* (Entire Work of Zen Master Dogen), 3 vols. (Tokyo: Chikuma Shobo, 1970).
86. For example, Dogen says, "The time being of all beings throughout the world in water and on land just actualizes your complete effort right now. All beings of all kinds in the visible and invisible realms are the time being actualized by your complete effort, flowing due to your complete effort" (The Time Being, p. 108).
87. Donation Request for Monks' Hall at the Kannon-dori Monastery, *Enlightenment Unfolds,* p. 47.

TEXTS IN RELATION TO DOGEN'S LIFE AND TRANSLATION CREDITS

IN THIS SECTION we present basic information on all the fascicles, including dates and original titles. We describe them in the context of Dogen's teaching career to provide a timeline of his life as a Zen master.

All the dated fascicles are presented in this book in chronological order. (Undated pieces are placed at the end, in fascicles 85–96.) Dogen's colophons—traditional inscriptions recording such information as date and place of writing—are included in this section as well as in the main text. In addition to the colophons, we drew on *Kenzei's Biography of Dogen* for information about events in Dogen's life. The number of formal talks Dogen gave each year, quoted in this section, is based on *Dogen* by Michio Takeuchi.

The texts in this book are translated from materials published in Doshu Okubo's *Dogen Zenji Zenshu* (Entire Work of Zen Master Dogen). We have also referred to *Dogen Zenji Zenshu,* edited by Tokugen Sakai and colleagues.

"The Editor" in the translator credits refers to Kazuaki Tanahashi. All texts have been closely examined and edited by Peter Levitt and the Editor.

WANDERING PERIOD

1227
RECOMMENDING ZAZEN TO ALL PEOPLE
(FUKAN ZAZEN GI; APPENDIX 1)

Soon after returning from China to Japan, Dogen wrote "Recommending Zazen to All People," which has become one of the most revered texts in the Soto School. This proclamation summarizes his intention to establish a single practice of Zen meditation in Japan. As the colophon states, he wrote this text in Chinese in 1227, the year of his return from China. The original manuscript, edited and handwritten by him in 1233, still exists. We present a translation of the later version.

> Colophon: "Written at the Kannondori Monastery on the fifteenth day, the mid-year [seventh month], the first year of the Tempuku Era [1233]."
> Translated by Edward Brown and the Editor.

1228

On the seventeenth day, the seventh month, of this year, Rujing died. Monk Jiyuan from Mount Tiantong traveled to Japan to inform Dogen of Rujing's death.

1230

When an unusual nationwide famine filled many cities with the dead, Dogen settled in a small temple in Fukakusa, a village to the south of Kyoto.

1231
1. ON THE ENDEAVOR OF THE WAY (BENDŌWA)

"On the Endeavor of the Way" is Dogen's systematic elucidation of his understanding of Zen, based on the principle that practice and enlightenment are inseparable. Using a set of imaginary questions and answers, he responds to doubts and skepticism by those accustomed to conventional Buddhist practices. This essay reflects Dogen's first attempt to express his thinking in the vernacular Japanese language. Until then

Buddhist teachings had been studied and written almost exclusively in the Japanese form of Chinese.

"On the Endeavor of the Way" is highly respected in the Soto School as Dogen's most comprehensive explanation of dharma. However, Dogen did not include the words *Shōbō Genzō*, "Treasury of the True Dharma Eye," at the beginning of its title. When he later edited the *Treasury of the True Dharma Eye*, he did not include this fascicle in either the seventy-five-fascicle or the twelve-fascicle version. The reason why Dogen set aside this text may be that, addressed to an open audience, it reflects his intention to spread dharma broadly, while his teaching evolved toward training a small number of committed students as his community matured.

According to Menzan Zuiho's *Eliminating Wrong Views on the Treasury of the True Dharma Eye (Shōbō Genzō Byakujaku Ketsu*, 1738), this text had been discovered in a courtier's house in Kyoto. Manzan Dohaku included this piece in the appendix of his eighty-four-fascicle version of the *Treasury of the True Dharma Eye* in 1684. Abbot Kozen of the Eihei Monastery included this as the opening piece in his ninety-five-fascicle version of the *Treasury of the True Dharma Eye*, published by the monastery in 1690.

Colophon: "Midautumn day [the fifteenth day of the eighth month], in the third year of the Kanki Era [1231], by Dogen, who has transmitted dharma from Song China."

Translated by Lewis Richmond and the Editor.

KOSHO MONASTERY PERIOD

1233
2. MANIFESTATION OF GREAT PRAJNA
(MAKA HANNYA HARAMITSU)

Dogen's first practice center, Kannondori (Avalokiteshvara's Guiding Power) Monastery, where he was abbot, was established in the spring of 1233 in Fukakusa, south of Kyoto. His first three-month practice period started, as was customary, on the fifteenth day of the fourth month.

(At a summer practice period, traveling monks visit a monastery and join resident practitioners in concentrated meditation, much like the rains retreats established by Shakyamuni Buddha for the monsoon season. Those who complete the period gain one year of dharma age. In the Zen tradition this is the most important time of training. Dogen did not hold a winter practice period.)

Dogen delivered "Manifestation of Great Prajna" as a dharma talk to the Kannondori community, the first text in the series of *Shōbō Genzō*. The official title of the original text is "Shōbō Genzō Maka Hannya Haramitsu." (The following fascicles of *Shōbō Genzō* are similarly titled.)

This is a commentary on the *Prajna Heart Sutra*, one of the most commonly recited scriptures in East Asia. The *Heart Sutra* is regarded as a brief condensation of the entire Mahayana teaching of *shunyata* (emptiness or boundlessness). Its mantra at the end was often believed to have wish-granting magical power in Esoteric Buddhism.

In this fascicle, Dogen challenges the traditional analytical views of phenomena, asserting that all elements are interrelated. Not mentioning the mantra, he hints at his own aversion for highly ritualized and benefit-oriented Esoteric practices. Dogen placed this text second in his seventy-five-fascicle version of the *Treasury of the True Dharma Eye*.

Colophon: "Presented to the assembly of the Kannondori Monastery on a day of the summer practice period in the first year of the Tempuku Era [1233]."
Translated by Edward Brown and the Editor.

3. ACTUALIZING THE FUNDAMENTAL POINT (GENJŌ KŌAN)
Completing his first practice period on the full-moon day (the fifteenth) of the seventh month, Dogen gave this text to his lay student Koshu Yo on the full-moon day of the following month. Koshu must have joined the practice period, and perhaps he was leaving for his home on the southwestern island of Kyushu.

Kōan—the original word for "fundamental point" in the title—usually means an exemplary Zen story given by a teacher to a student for spiritual investigation. But Dogen used the word here to point to the reality of all things that is to be realized.

"Actualizing the Fundamental Point" is probably the best-known and most studied text of all Dogen's writings, both for its summary of his teaching and for its poetic beauty. While other fascicles are focused on the themes indicated by their titles, "Actualizing the Fundamental Point" covers multiple themes, including awakened ones and nonawakened persons, enlightenment and delusion, birth and death, the potential of enlightenment (buddha nature) and actualization of it.

Dogen used this text as the opening fascicle of the seventy-five-fascicle version of the *Treasury of the True Dharma Eye*. He revised this text nineteen years later. Consequently, this text covers a span between the beginning and the end of his monastic teaching. (The earlier manuscript of this fascicle no longer exists.)

> Colophon: *"Written around midautumn, the first year of the Tempuku Era [1233], and given to my lay student Koshu Yo of Kyushu Island. Revised in the fourth year of the Kencho Era [1252]."*
> Translated by Robert Aitken and the Editor. Revised at San Francisco Zen Center and later at Berkeley Zen Center.

1234

Ejo joined Dogen's temporary monastery. Soon he started transcribing Dogen's informal evening talks, creating a text that became known as the *Treasury of the True Dharma Eye: Record of Things Heard (Shōbō Genzō Zuimon-ki)*. Ejo was to be Dogen's lifetime disciple, editor, and dharma successor.

1235

Dogen gave Ejo the bodhisattva precepts. He also wrote a fund-raising letter for construction of a monks' hall at the Kannondori Monastery.

He put together a collection of three hundred Chinese Zen koans, titled the *Treasury of the True Dharma Eye*. Seen as a lifetime notebook for his teaching, this book is known as the *Chinese-Language Treasury of the True Dharma Eye (Shinji Shōbō Genzō)*.

1236

The monks' hall was opened at the monastery. Dogen renamed his practice center the Kosho (Raising Sages) Zen Monastery. (This name was mentioned by Sen'e in the *Extensive Record of Priest Eihei Dogen*.) Ejo was appointed head monk.

1237

Dogen wrote *Instructions for the Tenzo* (*Tenzo Kyōkun*).

Occupied with establishing his monastery, Dogen put aside the writing of the *Treasury of the True Dharma Eye* for nearly five years.

1238

4. ONE BRIGHT PEARL (IKKA MYŌJU)

Dogen presented "One Bright Pearl" to the assembly of the Kannondori Kosho Horin (Avalokiteshvara's Guiding Power, Raising Sages, Treasure Forest) Monastery on the fourth day of the practice period. In this essay he introduces the ancient Chinese Zen master Xuansha, takes up a set of dialogues by him with a student, and offers a thorough examination of the koan. It is the only fascicle Dogen wrote this year.

> Colophon: "Presented to the assembly of Kannondori Kosho Horin Monastery, Uji County, Yamashiro Province, on the eighteenth day, the fourth month, the fourth year of the Katei Era [1238]."
>
> Translated by Edward Brown and the Editor.

1239

5. REGULATIONS FOR THE AUXILIARY CLOUD HALL AT THE KANNONDORI KOSHO GOKOKU MONASTERY (KANNONDŌRI KŌSHŌ GOKOKU-JI JŪ'UN-DŌ SHIKI)

Only three years after the construction of a monks' hall about seventy feet square, it apparently was too small, and an additional monks' hall was built. Unlike most other fascicles of the *Treasury of the True Dharma Eye*, which are short teachings, "Regulations for the Auxiliary Cloud Hall" was intended as a guideline for newcomers who were not yet ready to reside permanently and practice in the main monks' hall.

The monastery name Dogen used here—"Avalokiteshvara's Guiding Power, Raising Sages, Treasure Forest, Protecting the Nation Monastery"—may reflect his wish to gain imperial patronage as a temple for protection of the country. Soon, however, he seemed to have abandoned the idea of seeking such patronage and thus dropped the name Gokoku (Protecting the Nation).

This piece was included in Kozen's ninety-five-fascicle version of the *Treasury of the True Dharma Eye* in 1690. But it had not been included in Dogen's seventy-five or twelve-fascicle version of brief essays.

Colophon: "This was written on the twenty-fifth day, the fourth month, the first year of the En'o Era [1239]."
                                        Translated by Reb Anderson and the Editor.

6. THE MIND ITSELF IS BUDDHA (SOKUSHIN ZEBUTSU)

In the midst of the summer practice period's scorching heat, Dogen delivered the talk "The Mind Itself Is Buddha" to his community. Here he discusses the Buddhist notion of "mind"—which is distinct from a "soul" believed to last after death. Mind is inseparable from body and from all phenomena. In this fascicle he introduces what can be called the "four pillars of buddha dharma"—aspiration, practice, enlightenment, and nirvana.

Colophon: "Presented to the assembly of Kannondori Kosho Horin Monastery, Uji County, Yamashiro Province, on the twenty-fifth day, the fifth month, the first year of the En'o Era [1239]."
                                        Translated by Steve Allen and the Editor.

7. CLEANSING (SENJŌ)

One can assume that Dogen's community members were disciplined in the monks' hall, but relaxed outside the practice place and sloppy in the washroom. In this fascicle, completed in the winter, Dogen explains in detail how to be mindful in using the washroom. For Dogen, body, mind, and the environment cannot be isolated from one another; keeping them clean is an essential practice of dharma.

Colophon: "Presented to the assembly of Kannondori Kosho Horin Monastery, Uji County, Yamashiro Province, on the twenty-third day, the tenth month, the first year of the En'o Era [1239]."
                                        Translated by Peter Levitt and the Editor.

8. WASHING THE FACE (SEMMEN)

"Washing the Face" is a lengthy text presented on the same day as the preceding text, "Cleansing." Dogen offered this piece three times in eleven years, which underscores the importance of the practice of washing the face in his teaching. Kozen's version places this text as the fifty-sixth fascicle, according to the date of its second presentation. Nonetheless, we place it here based on the date of Dogen's first presentation.

Colophons: "Presented to the assembly of the Kannondori Kosho Horin Monastery on the twenty-third day, the tenth month, the first year of the En'o Era [1239]." "Presented again to the assembly of the Yoshimine Temple, Yoshida County, Echizen Province, on the twentieth day, the tenth month, the first year of the Kangen Era [1243]." "Presented once more to the assembly of the Eihei Monastery, Kichijo Mountain, Yoshida County, Echizen Province, on the eleventh day, the first month, the second year of the Kencho Era [1250]."

Translated by Linda Ruth Cutts and the Editor.

1240

9. RECEIVING THE MARROW BY BOWING (RAIHAI TOKUZUI)

Dogen's writing of the *Treasury of the True Dharma Eye* seems to have accelerated around the year 1240. He wrote "Receiving the Marrow by Bowing" before the summer practice period.

Here Dogen focuses with amazing clarity on the equality of accomplished female and male practitioners. Although he had female students, and perhaps allowed them to join the practice, it is likely that, according to custom, they were seated in a low-status position. (In "Continuous Practice, Part Two," Dogen speaks of a Daoist practitioner's being seated lower than nuns in his teacher Rujing's monastery. There is no evidence that Dogen seated nuns differently from his teacher.) So, it is possible to assume that there was prejudice against female practitioners in his community, and outside of it. Among his own students, he may have encountered reluctance to admit nuns to the practice period. On this issue of sexism, we can see that Dogen was radically free of prejudice. At the same time, however, since he was a traditional teacher in a sexist society, his treatment of his female students doesn't seem to have been completely free of discrimination.

Colophon: "Written at the Kannondori Kosho Horin Monastery on the clear-bright day [the fifteenth day from spring solstice], the second year of the En'o Era [1240]."

Translated by Peter Levitt and the Editor.

10. VALLEY SOUNDS, MOUNTAIN COLORS
(KEISEI SANSHOKU)

In every year, the summer practice period started on the full-moon (fifteenth) day of the fourth month. This text was presented on the nineteenth day of the fourth month in the form of *jishu,* which is a semiformal dharma talk. It is likely that Dogen's jishu consisted of reading his draft to the group of practicing students.

In this text, Dogen focuses on stories of three ancient Chinese Zen practitioners who had spiritual breakthroughs in natural settings and expressed their realizations in verses. Dogen repeatedly cautioned his community not to look for such breakthroughs outside their daily practice.

Colophon: "On the fifth day of the practice period, the second year of the En'o Era [1240], this was presented to the assembly of the Kannondori Kosho Horin Monastery."

Translated by Katherine Thanas and the Editor.

11. REFRAIN FROM UNWHOLESOME ACTION
(SHOAKU MAKUSA)

One month after the end of practice period, on the full-moon day—the traditional day of repentance—Dogen delivered this text to those who were still at the monastery. His theme is basic, the "Seven Original Buddhas' precepts." Dogen presents a radically fresh and complete view of the precepts. Refraining from unwholesome or evil action is not a prohibition, but thorough practice, the experience of buddha dharma itself. Dogen had set up a monastic environment so that this would be possible. Of course, those who violated the monastery guidelines were asked to leave.

Colophon: "Presented to the assembly of the Kosho Horin Monastery, Uji County, Yamashiro Province, on the harvest moon day [the fifteenth day], the eighth month, the second year of the En'o Era [1240]."
Translated by Mel Weitsman and the Editor.

12. THE TIME BEING (UJI)

On the first day of the tenth month of 1240, Dogen completed this short but strikingly philosophical text. Deepening one's meditation, one may grasp at once the unity of body and mind, practice and enlightenment, time and being, as well as that of time and self. Time, experienced simultaneously as momentary and timeless, is the essence of Dogen's contemplation.

Colophon: "On the first day of winter [the first day, the tenth month], the first year of the Ninji Era [1240], this was written at the Kosho Horin Monastery."
Translated by Dan Welch and the Editor.

13. POWER OF THE ROBE (KESA KUDOKU)

On the day Dogen completed "The Time Being," he delivered this text, full of practical information about the Buddhist robe. Adorning one's body with an authentic Buddhist robe is essential for actualizing enlightenment. Inverting secular values, he writes that an excrement-cleaning cloth (for cleaning a toilet) is the purest of all materials for making a robe. This is the first text where Dogen quotes extensively from Buddhist scriptures. He made this the third fascicle in his later twelve-fascicle version of the *Treasury of the True Dharma Eye*. Some parts of this fascicle are repeated in "Transmitting the Robe."

Colophon: "This was presented to the assembly of the Kannondori Kosho Horin Monastery on the first day of winter, the first year of the Ninji Era [1240]."
Translated by Blanche Hartman and the Editor.

14. TRANSMITTING THE ROBE (DEN'E)

"Transmitting the Robe" has the same date as "Power of the Robe," and there is much overlap between them. Possibly an original text was divided in two during the process of editing. "Transmitting the Robe" is included in the seventy-five-fascicle version.

Colophon: "This was written at the Kannondori Kosho Horin Monastery on the first day of winter, the first year of the Ninji Era [1240]. Dogen, Shramana who has transmitted dharma from Song [China]."

Translated by Jean Selkirk and the Editor.

15. MOUNTAINS AND WATERS SUTRA (SANSUIKYŌ)

Seventeen days after dating "The Time Being," "Power of the Robe," and "Transmitting the Robe," Dogen presented this highly imaginative and poetic text late at night to his assembly of students.

Colophon: "Presented to the assembly at Kannondori Kosho Horin Monastery at the hour of the Rat [midnight], the eighteenth day, the tenth month, the first year of the Ninji Era [1240]."

Translated by Arnold Kotler and the Editor.

Dogen gave thirty-one formal talks between 1235 and 1240. Formal talks were short ceremonial discourses given in the dharma hall, recorded in Chinese by one of his senior students and later collected in the *Extensive Record of Priest Eihei Dogen.*

1241

16. BUDDHA ANCESTORS (BUSSO)

"Buddha Ancestors" marked Dogen's tenth year of writing and compiling his monumental work. In the New Year, Dogen completed this text, which consists mostly of ancestors' names up to that of his teacher, Rujing. These names have been recited daily by Dogen's countless dharma descendants.

Colophon: "Written and presented at Kannondori Kosho Horin Monastery, Uji County, Yamashiro Province, Japan, on the third day, the first month, the second year of the Ninji Era [1241]."

Translated by Lewis Richmond and the Editor.

17. DOCUMENT OF HERITAGE (SHISHO)

Dogen took three months to prepare the "Document of Heritage." He completed it at the end of spring, but, because of the secret nature of the theme, he did not deliver it to the community. Much of this piece describes his dialogues with monks, including abbots of famous monasteries in China. Demonstrating his extraordinary abilities of memorization and close observation, Dogen speaks of viewing treasured certificates of dharma transmission. He recalls being offered a document of heritage and politely declining the opportunity. He is very critical of the state of Zen in China at that time. He quotes Rujing's words on documents of heritage but, perhaps out of modesty, does not speak of his experience of receiving authentication from Rujing. The second colophon below seems to imply that he continued to edit the text over two years after it was written.

> *Colophons: "On the twenty-seventh day, the third month, the second year of the Ninji Era [1241], this was written at Kannondori Kosho Horin Monastery by monk Dogen, who has transmitted dharma from China." "On the twenty-fourth day, the ninth month, the first year of the Kangan Era [1243], I have hung my traveling stick at the grass-thatched hut in Yoshimine Village, Echizen Province. A written seal."*
>
> Translated by Lewis Richmond and the Editor.

18. DHARMA BLOSSOMS TURN DHARMA BLOSSOMS (HOKKE TEN HOKKE)

In the spring of 1241, Monk Ekan, the main teacher of the Japan Daruma (Bodhidharma) School, joined Dogen's community. This Zen school had been founded by Nonin a half century before. Ekan, who had earlier sent Ejo to study with Dogen, brought along many other students, including Gikai, Giin, and Gien.

Another person who joined the practice period was Etatsu, who seems to have been a newly ordained scholar of the *Lotus Sutra*. Possibly inspired by Etatsu's aspiration for Zen practice, Dogen wrote this fascicle. In the exceptionally long colophon of this fascicle (quoted below), he compares the story of Huineng, the Sixth Chinese Ancestor, guiding a scholar of the sutra, to his own guidance of Etatsu.

"Dharma Blossoms" indicates the *Lotus Sutra,* which is referred to as the Dharma Blossoms Sutra in Chinese. It also means the blossoming of reality. In this fascicle, Dogen plays with the unfolding of this double concept.

Colophon: "*This was written and given to Zen person Etatsu to celebrate his home leaving and entry into the practice of the way, during the summer practice period in the second year of the Ninji Era [1241]. Shaving the head is a good thing. To shave the head over and over again makes a true home leaver. Today's home leaving is the natural fruit of the natural power of the dharma blossoms turning in the past. The dharma blossoms of this moment will certainly bear fruit as dharma blossoms in the future. They are not Shakyamuni's dharma blossoms, nor all buddhas' dharma blossoms, but the dharma blossoms' dharma blossoms. Every day the turning of the dharma blossoms is as it is, beyond perception, beyond knowledge. Dharma blossoms emerge at this moment, beyond knowing, beyond understanding. Past moments are your breathing in and breathing out. Present moments are your breathing in and breathing out. Treasure these moments as dharma blossoms, wondrous and inconceivable. Monk Dogen, who has transmitted dharma from China, founder of the Kannondori Kosho Horin Monastery.*"

Translated by Michael Wenger and the Editor.

19. UNGRASPABLE MIND (SHIN FUKATOKU)

After his story of a *Lotus Sutra* scholar giving up his extensive studies and directly experiencing the meaning of the sutra in the previous fascicle, Dogen here presents the story of a scholar of the *Diamond Sutra*.

Colophon: "*Presented to the assembly of the Kannondori Kosho Horin Monastery, Uji County, Yamashiro Province, in the summer practice period, the second year of the Ninji Era [1241].*"

Translated by Michael Wenger and the Editor.

20. UNGRASPABLE MIND, LATER VERSION
(GO SHIN FUKATOKU)

It seems that after delivering an earlier version of "Ungraspable Mind" to the community, Dogen further edited and expanded the text. This later version was only "written," rather than "presented," during the same practice period.

Dogen included the earlier version in the seventy-five-fascicle version, but not the later version. Kozen included both versions in his Eihei-ji edition.

Colophon: "Written at the Kosho Horin Monastery on a day of summer practice period, the second year of the Ninji Era [1241]."

Translated by Michael Wenger and the Editor.

21. OLD MIRROR (KOKYŌ)

After the end of the practice period, many of the mature Zen students stayed on. This winter Dogen's creative energy burst forth; he wrote six fascicles of the *Treasury of the True Dharma Eye*, beginning with "Old Mirror."

The mirror in ancient China was a disk made of bronze, which needed polishing at times. Reflecting all things, it is a mysterious analogy for awakened mind, like the full moon, an eyeball, or a pearl. Dogen takes up a number of Zen stories, as well as Chinese and Japanese secular stories, on mirror disks, and comments on them with vigor.

Colophon: "Presented to the assembly of the Kannondori Kosho Horin Monastery on the ninth day, the ninth month, the second year of the Ninji Era [1241]."

Translated by Lewis Richmond and the Editor.

22. READING A SUTRA (KANKIN)

Six days after delivering "Old Mirror," Dogen offered this text to the assembly on the first full-moon day of winter. Contrary to the general Chinese Zen adage of "transmission outside the scripture," Dogen emphasizes the invariable value of Buddhist scriptures. He quotes and comments on several Zen stories about scriptures and explains the rites of reading scriptures in a monastery, revealing his extraordinary capacity to observe and describe liturgy in detail.

Colophon: "Presented to the assembly of the Kosho Horin Monastery, Uji County, Yamashiro Province, on the fifteenth day, the ninth month in autumn, the second year of the Ninji Era [1241]."

Translated by John Daido Loori and the Editor.

23. BUDDHA NATURE (BUSSHŌ)

About a month after presenting "Reading a Sutra," Dogen delivered this long and highly theoretical text. He examines and comments on a number of ancient Zen masters' statements on the dilemma of the universality and inconceivability of enlightenment. He exerts himself to uncover the logic in seemingly illogical words on the subject found throughout the Zen tradition.

Dogen later placed this text third in the seventy-five-fascicle version of the *Treasury of the True Dharma Eye*, following "Actualizing the Fundamental Point" and "Manifestation of Great Prajna."

Colophon: "Presented to the assembly of the Kosho Horin Monastery, Uji County, Yamashiro Province, on the fourteenth day, the tenth month, the second year of the Ninji Era [1241]."

Translated by Mel Weitsman and the Editor.

24. AWESOME PRESENCE OF ACTIVE BUDDHAS (GYŌBUTSU IIGI)

Contemplating the expression of buddhahood in "Buddha Nature," Dogen must have been thinking about the aspect of action or practice of buddhas. Practice is what makes a person a buddha. "Awesome Presence of Active Buddhas" was completed about the same time as "Buddha Nature" but was not presented to the community.

Colophon: "Written in the middle of the tenth month, the second year of the Ninji Era [1241], at the Kannondori Horin Monastery by Monk Dogen."

Translated by Taigen Dan Leighton and the Editor.

25. THE BUDDHAS' TEACHING (BUKKYŌ)

Dogen's students who had studied with other Zen masters must have been familiar with the Zen expression "transmission outside the scriptures." Dogen asserts that it is a mistaken notion and explains the Buddhas' expressions by laying out categories of scriptures in the Buddhist canon. The tone of his criticism has sharpened by now.

Colophons: "Presented to the assembly of the Kosho Monastery, Yamashiro Province, on the fourteenth day, the eleventh month, the second year of the Ninji Era [1241]." Presented again "On the seventh day, the eleventh month, the third year of the Ninji Era [1242]."

Translated by Peter Levitt and the Editor.

26. MIRACLES (JINZŪ)

Two days after delivering "The Buddhas' Teaching," Dogen read "Miracles" to the residents of his monastery. For Dogen, the everyday practice of dharma is a series of miracles, while being free from desires is a miracle. Further, going beyond miracles is the ultimate miracle.

> Colophon: "Presented to the assembly of the Kannondori Kosho Horin Monastery on the sixteenth day, the eleventh month, the second year of the Ninji Era [1241]."
>
> Translated by Katherine Thanas and the Editor.

Dogen gave fifty-eight formal talks in 1241.

1242

27. GREAT ENLIGHTENMENT (DAIGO)

"Great Enlightenment" is the first of seventeen fascicles Dogen wrote this year—the most prolific period of his writing career. He revised and presented this text a second time in Echizen Province exactly one year later.

Dogen calls the experience of going beyond the separation of enlightenment and delusion "great enlightenment." In this teaching, enlightenment is not exclusive of delusion. Thus, for him, "great delusion" is not exclusive of enlightenment.

> Colophons: "Abiding at the Kannondori Kosho Horin Monastery, I present this to the assembly on the twenty-eighth day, the first month, the third year of the Ninji Era [1242]." "Staying at the ancient Yoshimine Temple, I revise and present this to the assembly of humans and devas on the twenty-eighth day, the first month, the second year of the Kangen Era [1243]."
>
> Translated by Blanche Hartman and the Editor.

28. THE POINT OF ZAZEN (ZAZEN SHIN)

In "The Point of Zazen," Dogen speaks of the mind of meditation, commenting on two classical stories on the meaning of zazen. He offers sharp criticism of several Chinese writings that were supposed to express the rules and approach of zazen. Then, with great reverence, line by line, he interprets "The Point of Zazen," a verse pointing to the heart of meditation, by Hongzhi Zhengjue. Hongzhi had been a prominent master of the Caodong School in the twelfth century—the lineage Dogen inherited. Hongzhi advocated "silent illumination Zen." Dogen adapted the verse, changing several words and making a stunning improvement. He brought his manuscript to Echizen Province and presented it to his community there a year and a half later.

> *Colophons: "Written at the Kosho Horin Monastery on the eighteenth day, the third month, the third year of the Ninji Era [1242]." "Presented to the assembly at the Yoshimine Temple, Yoshida County, Echizen Province, in the eleventh month of the fourth year of the Ninji Era [1243]."*
> *Translated by Michael Wenger and the Editor; Dogen's poem translated by Philip Whalen and the Editor.*

29. GOING BEYOND BUDDHA (BUKKŌJŌ JI)

Five days after completing "The Point of Zazen," Dogen shared "Going Beyond Buddha" with his monastic community. In this fascicle, he describes the dynamic state of being a buddha by saying, "You reach buddha, and going further, you continue to see buddha."

> *Colophon: "Presented to the assembly at the Kannondori Kosho Horin Monastery on the twenty-third day, the third month, the third year of the Ninji Era [1242]."*
> *Translated by Mel Weitsman and the Editor.*

30. THUSNESS (IMMO)

There was only three days' difference between the delivery of the preceding fascicle, "Going Beyond Buddha," and that of "Thusness." The title, "Immo," is the Japanese translation of the Chinese colloquial word *renmo*. Meaning "in this way," "like this," "like that," "this," or "that," this word is a key term in Zen dialogues. Dogen shows some usages of the word and attempts to decode it with his own style of transcendental language.

Colophon: "Presented to the assembly of Kannondori Kosho Horin Monastery on the twenty-sixth day, the third month, the third year of the Ninji Era (1242)."

Translated by Mel Weitsman and the Editor.

In the spring of 1242, Dogen wrote an afterword to the *Recorded Sayings of Priest Rujing, Sequel.* (Rujing had passed away in 1228, one year after Dogen's departure from the Tiantong Monastery. A two-fascicle book titled the *Recorded Sayings of Priest Rujing* was compiled by Wensu and others, and was published in 1229. This sequel was edited by Yuan, who may have asked Dogen to write this afterword because of the high regard in which Rujing's students held him. The completed book was to be delivered in fall of the same year.)

31A. CONTINUOUS PRACTICE, PART ONE (GYŌJI, JŌ)
31B. CONTINUOUS PRACTICE, PART TWO (GYŌJI, GE)

Seven days after the delivery of "Thusness," Dogen completed an exceptionally long text. It is noteworthy that Dogen first introduces his concept of the "circle of the way" at the beginning of this text.

This text is traditionally divided into two parts and bound into two volumes. In Part One, stories of three Indian ancestors are arranged in chronological order, followed by stories of nineteen Chinese teachers that seem to be thematically arranged. In Part Two, stories of eleven Chinese teachers from Bodhidharma to Rujing are presented, not necessarily in chronological order. Dogen merged these into one fascicle in the seventy-five-fascicle version of the *Treasury of the True Dharma Eye.*

Colophon (31a): "Editing completed on the eighteenth day, the first year of the Ninji Era [1243]. [Dogen]"

Colophon (31b): "Written at the Kannondori Kosho Horin Monastery on the fifth day, the fourth month, the third year of the Ninji Era [1242]."

Translated by Mel Weitsman and the Editor, with David Schneider.

32. OCEAN MUDRA SAMADHI (KAI'IN ZEMMAI)

Dogen had been away from the ocean for some years, residing in a monastery near the Uji River that runs through a flat valley, south of Kyoto.

And yet, the ocean's depth was part of his meditation. In "Ocean Mudra Samadhi" he speaks of samadhi that is as vast and dynamic as an ocean.

Colophon: "Written at the Kannondori Kosho Horin Monastery on the twentieth day, the fourth month, the third year of the Ninji Era [1242]."
                    Translated by Katherine Thanas and the Editor.

33. CONFIRMATION (JUKI)

"Confirmation" is the second fascicle Dogen completed at the beginning of the summer practice period. The monastery had been busy preparing for and entering the practice period. Perhaps Dogen was occupied with daily writing and that is why he did not present "Continuous Practice," "Ocean Mudra Samadhi," and this piece to the community.

The title, "Juki," is a Japanese translation of the Sanskrit word *vyakarana*, meaning "predicting enlightenment"—that is, the Buddha's prediction that a disciple will attain enlightenment in the future. The word suggests a span of time the practitioner will have between receiving a prediction and realizing enlightenment. Dogen presents his view of "prediction" according to the principle of the inseparability of practice and enlightenment.

Colophon: "Written at the Kannondori Kosho Horin Monastery on the twenty-fifth day, the fourth month, in summer, the third year of the Ninji Era [1242]."
                    Translated by Lewis Richmond and the Editor.

34. AVALOKITESHVARA (KANNON)

"Avalokiteshvara" was the fourth fascicle Dogen wrote in the fourth month, and was read to the participants of the practice period. Dogen's first small practice place was called Kannondori (Avalokiteshvara's Guiding Power) Monastery. When it was renamed Kosho Horin Monastery, he still kept the original name, Kannondori, and at times used it for the beginning of the monastery name. It is possible to guess that Avalokiteshvara was his guardian bodhisattva. And yet, Dogen did not speak much about the guiding power of the bodhisattva. Instead, he used the dialogue between two Chinese dharma brothers to unfold the essential Zen understanding of Avalokiteshvara.

Colophon: "Presented to the assembly on the twenty-sixth day, the fourth month, the third year of the Ninji Era [1242]."

Translated by Joan Halifax and the Editor.

35. ARHAT (ARAKAN)

One month after the beginning of the practice period, on the day of the full moon, Dogen offered this teaching, "Arhat," to participants. Arhats are known as sages of early Buddhism, disciples of the Buddha. Mahayana practitioners tended to look down on arhat practice, considering it to be Hinayana, compared with Mahayana bodhisattva practice. Dogen here fully values the arhats' way.

Colophon: "Abiding at the Kannondori Kosho Horin Monastery, Uji County, Yamashiro Province, this was presented to the assembly on the fifteenth day, the fifth month, the third year of the Ninji Era [1242]."

Translated by Peter Levitt and the Editor.

36. CYPRESS TREE (HAKUJUSHI)

Six days after delivering "Arhat," Dogen taught "Cypress Tree." Much of this text reflects on the austere life of the Chinese Zen master Zhaozhou, whose enigmatic words pointing toward a cypress tree's awakened nature are investigated here.

Colophon: "Presented to the assembly of Kannondori Monastery, Uji County, Yamashiro Province, on the twenty-first day, the season of Iris Festival, the fifth month, the third year of the Ninji Era [1242]."

Translated by Katherine Thanas and the Editor.

37. RADIANT LIGHT (KŌMYŌ)

Around the first day of the sixth month, at midpoint of the practice period, Dogen broke the schedule of communal zazen because of the fierce heat and humidity. (He resumed scheduled zazen on the first day of the ninth month, one and a half months after the practice period. Such a three-month break seems to have been common. Dogen mentioned it in his formal talks this year and in 1252.)

On the second day of the sixth month, Dogen delivered this text to the participants in the dark of midnight in the lingering rainy season. He implies that the radiant light of practice-enlightenment was, neverthe-less, right there. As Yunmen said, one can find radiant light in the monks' hall, the buddha hall, the kitchen, and the monastery gate.

Colophon: "Presented to the assembly of the Kannondori Kosho Horin Mon-astery at the fourth segment of the third night period, the second day, the sixth month, the third year of the Ninji Era [1242]. It has been raining for a long time, and raindrops drip from the eaves. Where is the radiant light? The assembly must look and penetrate Yunmen's words."

Translated by Mel Weitsman and the Editor.

38. BODY-AND-MIND STUDY OF THE WAY (SHINJIN GAKUDŌ)

Soon after the practice period ended, on the fifth day of the eighth month, a copy of the newly published *Recorded Sayings of Priest Rujing, Sequel* was delivered from China to Dogen. On the following day he gave a formal talk about it.

According to Dogen, to study buddha dharma is to practice with-out separating body from mind. In this fascicle, however, he temporarily divides the practice into study with mind and study with body, spelling out these two aspects in detail.

Colophon: "This was taught to the assembly of the Horin Monastery on the ninth day, the ninth month, the third year of the Ninji Era [1242]."

Translated by Dan Welch and the Editor.

39. WITHIN A DREAM EXPRESSING THE DREAM (MUCHŪ SETSUMU)

In early winter, twelve days after the presentation of "Body-and-Mind Study of the Way," Dogen delivered "Within a Dream Expressing the Dream" to his monastic community.

Here, Dogen uses the word "dream" to describe the enlightenment of the Buddha, and the meditative experience of all practitioners. Coun-ter to the common notion that dreams are unreal and actual phenomena are real, he asserts that the awakened ones' profound wisdom is concrete, the source of all teaching, while actual phenomena are transient and unreliable.

Colophon: "Presented to the assembly of the Kannondori Kosho Horin Monastery, Uji County, Yamashiro Province, on the twenty-first day, the ninth month, the third year of the Ninji Era [1242]."

Translated by Taigen Dan Leighton and the Editor.

40. EXPRESSIONS (DŌTOKU)

Twelve days after the presentation of "Within a Dream Expressing the Dream," Dogen shared this text, "Expressions," with his assembly. The "expression" here means words, or expressions beyond words, that emerge from one's genuine understanding of reality, unique to the person. In this text, Dogen offers examples of speaking and not speaking.

Colophon: "Written and presented to the assembly of Kannondori Kosho Horin Monastery on the fifth day, the tenth month, the third year of the Ninji Era [1242]."

Translated by Peter Levitt and the Editor.

41. PAINTING OF A RICE CAKE (GABYŌ)

One month after "Expressions" was delivered, Dogen taught this text at his monastery in the middle of winter. Here, Dogen takes up Xiang-yan's famous words "A painting of a rice cake does not satisfy hunger," meaning that descriptive scriptures are not a direct experience of reality. Dogen turns it around in an astounding way. He insists that a painted rice cake alone can satisfy hunger. Although it appears to be an impenetrable paradox, this may be a natural development from his discourse that Buddhist scripture is an entire expression of the Buddha's teaching (as seen in the fascicle "The Buddhas' Teaching").

Colophon: "Presented to the assembly of the Kannondori Kosho Horin Monastery on the fifth day, the eleventh month, the third year of the Ninji Era [1242]."

Translated by Dan Welch and the Editor.

42. UNDIVIDED ACTIVITY (ZENKI)

Two days after presenting his "Painting of a Rice Cake," Dogen taught "The Buddhas' Teaching" to his monastic community for the second time.

In the following month, close to the end of the year, Dogen was invited to give a dharma talk at the Kyoto residence of Lord Yoshishige Hatanao, who was going to be his primary supporter. Yoshishige was a high-ranking officer in the Kyoto office of Minamoto Clan Shogun, then ruler of Japan. This office was close to the Rokuharamitsu (Six Paramita) Monastery, in the Rokuhara area—east of the Kamo River, between Gojo Dori (Fifth Avenue) and Shichijo Dori (Seventh Avenue) in Kyoto.

Addressing an audience of mostly laypeople, in this brief discourse Dogen stresses that each individual should live fully and actively. Possibly this presentation was decisive in Yoshishige's invitation to Dogen to move to Echizen and found a monastery. (Dogen moved most of his community to Echizen seven and a half months later.) Did Yoshishige already have a strong commitment to build a full-scale monastery and support the community? The monastery opened one and a half years later, and Dogen described practice period in a full-scale monastery in "Practice Period" three years later, in 1245.

Colophon: *"Presented to the assembly at the residence of the former governor of Izumo Province, next to the Rokuharamitsu Temple, Kyoto, on the seventeenth day, the twelfth month, the third year of the Ninji Era [1242]."*
Translated by Edward Brown and the Editor.

Dogen gave twenty-six formal dharma talks in 1242.

1243 (IN KYOTO AREA)
43. THE MOON (TSUKI)

Back in Kosho Monastery, Dogen wrote a short piece, "The Moon," soon after New Year's Day, as the first of twenty-two fascicles to be completed this year.

Dogen spells the Japanese title, "Tsuki," meaning "moon," in a very unusual way, using two ideographs, *tsu* (entire) and *ki* (activity). (See "Moon, The" in the glossary for the ideographs.) *Ki* for "activity" also appears in the title of "Undivided Activity," the preceding fascicle. The moon in Buddhism is a metaphor for enlightenment, often represented by a full moon. For Dogen, the moon represents meditation in each moment; the moon waxes and wanes, and yet it is always full. This is the dilemma Dogen explores in this text, which was not presented to the community.

Colophon: "Written at the Kannondori Kosho Horin Monastery on the sixth day, the first month, the fourth year of the Ninji Era [1243]. Monk Dogen."
Translated by Mel Weitsman and the Editor.

44. FLOWERS IN THE SKY (KŪGE)

On the twenty-eighth day of the first month, Dogen delivered "Great Enlightenment" for the second time.

Although his writing was at its peak, he did not complete any other fascicles for two months. What was Dogen doing during this spring? What was more important and pressing than writing his life's work? Was he possibly drawing plans for the construction of his new monastery?

"Flowers in the Sky," meaning "illusion," goes along with such previous fascicles as "Within a Dream Expressing the Dream" and "Painting of a Rice Cake," turning negative images upside down and making them represent the realm of enlightenment.

Colophon: "Presented to the assembly of the Kannondori Kosho Horin Monastery on the tenth day, the third month, the first year of the Kangen Era [1243]."
Translated by Dan Welch and the Editor.

45. OLD BUDDHA MIND (KOBUTSU SHIN)

As was customary, the summer practice period at Dogen's monastery started in the middle of the fourth month. Unusually, he left the community for several days and presented "Old Buddha Mind" at a temple near Yoshishige Hatano's residence, in the city of Kyoto. Perhaps this visit to the city of Kyoto was at the request of Yoshishige. They may well have discussed arrangements to move Dogen's community to Echizen, and the construction of new monastery buildings. Perhaps speaking to his primary supporter, Yoshishige, in this brief presentation Dogen summarizes the mind of ancient buddhas.

Colophon: "Presented to the assembly at the Rokuharamitsu Temple [in Kyoto]
on the twenty-ninth day, the fourth month of the Kangen Era [1243]."
Translated by Joan Halifax and the Editor.

46. BODHISATTVA'S FOUR METHODS OF GUIDANCE (BODAISATTA SHI SHŌHŌ)

Dogen wrote this text five days after his discourse, "Ancient Buddha Mind." The colophon does not say where he wrote it. He may still have been in Kyoto. The fact that Dogen included a description of himself ("Monk Dogen, who transmitted dharma from China"), suggests that he gave the text to Yoshishige. The style is easy and straightforward, explaining the virtues common to lay and ordained practitioners in all Buddhist schools.

Colophon: "Written on the fifth day, the fifth month, the fourth year of Ninji
[1243] by Monk Dogen, who transmitted dharma from China."
Translated by Lewis Richmond and the Editor.

47. TWINING VINES (KATTŌ)

Back in his monastery eight days before the end of the practice period, Dogen gave this talk, "Twining Vines." This was his last known dharma presentation in the vicinity of Kyoto.

Again in this text, Dogen takes up a negative phrase, "twining vines," which normally means "entanglement of words and concepts," and brilliantly turns it around, indicating an intimate and dynamic transmission of dharma.

Colophon: "Presented at the assembly of the Kannondori Kosho Horin Monas-
tery, Uji County, Yamashiro Province, on the seventh day, the seventh month, the
first year of the Kangen Era [1243]."
Translated by Mel Weitsman and the Editor.

As customary, the practice period at the Kosho Monastery ended on the fifteenth day of the seventh month. Several days later, Dogen and most of his community moved to Echizen Province on the Japan Sea.

MONASTERY CONSTRUCTION PERIOD

1243 (IN ECHIZEN)

Leaving Sen'e in charge of the Kosho Monastery, Dogen walked with his students from Fukakusa (south of Kyoto) north, then east to Echizen Province, in early autumn, near the end of the seventh month.

On the seventeenth day of the same month, Yoshishige Hatano and Layman Sakingo, also known as Zen Practitioner Kakunen, found land suitable for Dogen's monastery.

48. THREE REALMS ARE INSEPARABLE FROM MIND (SANGAI YUISHIN)

In the lunar calendar, sometimes an extra day is added to a month, and occasionally an extra month is added to a year. An intercalary seventh month was added in 1243. While Dogen and his community were settling in to a temporary practice place—most probably an ancient temple at the foot of Mount Yoshimine in Echizen—Dogen presented "Three Realms Are Inseparable from Mind" to his faithful students, at the beginning of the month.

The term "three realms" (sangai) is a Buddhist technical term, roughly meaning the entire world of phenomena and beyond. The last part of the original title, "Yuishin," is often translated as "mind only." This phrase refers to the teaching of the *Avatamsaka Sutra* that all things are expression of mind and there is nothing outside of mind. As shown in "Actualizing the Fundamental Point" and "Mind-and-Body Study of the Way," Dogen did not stress "mind only," but spoke of the inseparableness of body and mind, as well as that of mind and all phenomena.

> *Colophon: "Presented to the assembly on Mount Yoshimine on the first day, the intercalary seventh month, the first year of the Kangen Era [1243]."*
> *Translated by Josho Pat Phelan and the Editor.*

49. SPEAKING OF MIND, SPEAKING OF ESSENCE (SESSHIN SESSHŌ)

Dogen inscribed the place and year of presentation but did not put down a date, which was unusual, since he was a meticulous record keeper.

Ejo copied this text on the eleventh day, the first month of the following year. Later, Dogen placed it between "Three Realms Are Inseparable from Mind" and "The Reality of All Things" in his seventy-five-fascicle version, which implies a chronological order. (And yet, no one knows exactly when this fascicle was presented.)

The phrase "speaking of mind, speaking of essence" was at times criticized in the Zen tradition as too theoretical. In fact, Dogen himself had said, "Turning circumstances and turning mind is rejected by the great sage. Speaking of mind and speaking of essence is not agreeable to buddha ancestors" ("Mountains and Waters Sutra"). Here, to the contrary, Dogen emphasizes the importance of expressions of mind and essence. He no longer would merely admire ancient Chinese Zen masters like Linji and Yunmen; he offers harsh criticisms of them. Dogen seems to have developed full confidence as the leader of a monastic community.

> Colophon: "Presented to the assembly of the Yoshimine Temple, Yoshida County, Echizen Province, in the first year of the Kangen Era [1243]."
> Translated by Peter Levitt and the Editor.

50. THE BUDDHA WAY (BUTSUDŌ)

Dogen had some mature Zen students in the Kosho Zen Monastery (as it was called by Sen'e in 1236; see above), who had moved to Echizen with him. Some of them, especially former followers of the Daruma School, such as Ejo and Giun, must have identified themselves as "Zen" practitioners. Dogen needed to say that his teaching did not belong to the "Zen School" or any other sect. He simply taught the "buddha way." He intended to be a genuine disciple of the Buddha, not confined by sectarian limitations. This is a clear departure from his earlier view, presented in "On the Endeavor of the Way," of the Five Schools of Zen as something fixed and authoritative.

> Colophon: "Presented to the assembly of the Yoshimine Temple, Yoshida County, Echizen Province, on the sixteenth day, the ninth month, the first year of the Kangen Era [1243]."
> Translated by Mel Weitsman and the Editor.

51. THE REALITY OF ALL THINGS (SHOHŌ JISSŌ)

On a late autumn day, whose date was forgotten by Dogen or Ejo, Dogen presented "The Reality of All Things" to his community. He criticizes the current state of Chinese Zen and the tendency to view Buddhism, Daoism, and Confucianism as being in accord. Perhaps he listened to the chirping of birds while writing that an ancient master and Rujing equally associated the chirping of birds as expressing the reality of all things.

> Colophon: "Presented to the assembly of the Yoshimine Temple, Echizen Province, Japan, in the ninth month, the first year of the Kangen Era [1243]."
> Translated by Lewis Richmond and the Editor.

52. INTIMATE LANGUAGE (MITSUGO)

"Intimate Language" was also read to Dogen's practicing community in the temporary setting of the Yoshimine Temple in late autumn. For Dogen, "intimate" means direct, close, without gap, and without intermediary words and concepts. Here Dogen writes that the essence of Zen practice is something intimate between the self and the true self, as well as between master and disciple.

> Colophon: "Presented to the assembly of the ancient Yoshimine Temple of Yoshida County, Echizen Province, on the twentieth day, the ninth month, the first year of the Kangen Era [1243]."
> Translated by Michael Wenger and the Editor.

53. BUDDHA SUTRAS (BUKKYŌ)

"Buddha Sutras" is the last piece Dogen wrote and presented during the transitional four-month autumn. In this text, he asserts that no spiritual breakthrough is possible without the aid of Buddhist scriptures, again counter to the common Zen notion of "transmission outside the scriptures."

> Colophon: "Presented to the assembly of the Yoshimine Temple, Yoshida County, Echizen Province, in the ninth month, the first year of the Kangen Era [1243]."
> Translated by Mel Weitsman and the Editor.

54. INSENTIENT BEINGS SPEAK DHARMA (MUJŌ SEPPŌ)

Dogen takes up three ancient Zen dialogues, none of which fully explain what "insentient beings speaking dharma" means. However, Dogen's statement at the beginning, "This speaking dharma is spoken by dharma," seems to offer an important clue. Could it be that dharma is a kind of an insentient being?

> Colophon: "Presented to the assembly of the ancient Yoshimine Temple, Yoshida County, Echizen Province, on the second day, the tenth month, the first year of the Kangen Era [1243]."
> Translated by Alan Senauke and the Editor.

55. DHARMA NATURE (HOSSHŌ)

In the short text "Dharma Nature," Dogen discusses the paradox of enlightenment. Scriptures and teachers cannot bring the self to realization, because all realizations are actualized by the self, and yet without them the self cannot come to realization.

> Colophon: "Presented to the assembly of the Yoshimine Temple, Echizen Province, in early winter [the tenth month], the first year of the Kangen Era [1243]."
> Translated by Peter Levitt and the Editor.

56. DHARANI (DARANI)

Although the day and month of composition were not recorded, the fifty-sixth fascicle offers Dogen's startling explanation of a key Buddhist practice. "Dharani," a Sanskrit word meaning "upholding," "support," or "remembrance," makes a case for chanting magical spells, the heart of Esoteric Buddhist practice. Dogen sees this practice as teacher and disciple bowing to each other.

> Colophon: "Presented to the assembly of the Yoshimine Temple, Echizen Province, in the first year of the Kangen Era [1243]."
> Translated by Joan Halifax and the Editor.

57. FACE-TO-FACE TRANSMISSION (MENJU)

On the twentieth day of the tenth month of 1243, Dogen presented "Washing the Face" to students for the second time, with some additions.

On the same day he presented "Face-to-Face Transmission." Here he emphasizes the authentic transmission of dharma from person to person.

> *Colophon: "Presented to the assembly of the Yoshimine Monastery, Yoshida County, Echizen Province, on the twentieth day, the tenth month, the first year of the Kangen Era [1243]."*
> *Translated by Reb Anderson and the Editor.*

58. RULES FOR ZAZEN (ZAZEN GI)
In the middle of the winter in snow country, Dogen delivered "Rules for Zazen" to his community. This fascicle offers the most basic teaching on zazen. It was probably aimed at monks and lay practitioners assembled to engage in preliminary work for construction scheduled for the following spring. This month he also redelivered "The Point of Zazen," perhaps with his advanced students in mind.

> *Colophon: "Presented to the assembly of the Yoshimine Temple, Yoshida County, Echizen Province, in the eleventh month, the first year of the Kangen Era [1243]."*
> *Translated by Dan Welch and the Editor.*

59. PLUM BLOSSOMS (BAIKA)
In deep winter, anticipating the blooming of plum blossoms, Dogen wrote this fascicle, introducing and commenting on eight poems by Rujing. Earlier this year on the fifth day of the eighth month, the recently compiled *Recorded Sayings of Zen Master Rujing, Sequel* had arrived from China.

> *Colophon: "This was written on the sixth day, the eleventh month, the first year of the Kangen Era [1243], at the Yoshimine Temple, Yoshida County, Echizen Province. Snow is three feet deep all over the land."*
> *Translated by Mel Weitsman and the Editor.*

60. TEN DIRECTIONS (JIPPŌ)
"Ten directions"—the eight compass points plus above and below—includes all the realms of awakening and luminosity. The snow-covered

mountains around him must have inspired Dogen to write this text. But his community was planning to move to a lower altitude, where there was less snow.

> Colophon: *"Presented to the assembly of the Yoshimine Temple, Echizen Province, Japan, on the thirteenth day, the eleventh month, the first year of the Kangen Era [1243]."*
> Translated by Mel Weitsman and the Editor.

61. SEEING THE BUDDHA (KEMBUTSU)

In the mid-eleventh month, Dogen's community was already in the grass-thatched hut at the foot of Yamashi Peak. He addresses in "Seeing the Buddha" the question of physically seeing Shakyamuni Buddha, or experiencing the heart of the Buddha without actually seeing him.

> Colophon: *"Presented to the assembly at Yamashi Peak on the nineteenth day, the eleventh month, the first year of the Kangen Era [1243]."*
> Translated by Gaelyn Godwin and the Editor.

62. ALL-INCLUSIVE STUDY (HENZAN)

Eight days after delivering "Seeing the Buddha," Dogen read "All-Inclusive Study" to his community. The word in the Japanese title (*Henzan*) refers to a Zen student traveling all over to study with various masters. But Dogen uses this word to mean "studying thoroughly with a master (without needing to study with others)." This resonates with Xuansha's words, "Bodhidharma did not come to China. Huike did not go to India."

> Colophon: *"Taught in a grass-thatched hut at the foot of Yamashi Peak, Echizen Province, on the twenty-seventh day, the eleventh month, the first year of the Kangen Era [1243]."*
> Translated by Mel Weitsman and the Editor.

63. EYEBALL (GANZEI)

Eighteen days after "All-Inclusive Study," Dogen delivered "Eyeball" and the following two talks on the same day. In line with "Plum Blossoms,"

Dogen presents six quotations from the *Recorded Sayings of Zen Master Rujing, Sequel* as part of a monthly memorial day for Rujing.

> Colophon: *"Presented to the assembly, at Yamashi Peak, Echizen Province, on the seventeenth day, the twelfth month, the first year of the Kangen Era [1243]."*
> Translated by Peter Levitt and the Editor.

64. EVERYDAY ACTIVITY (KAJŌ)

"Everyday Activity" was delivered on the same day as the preceding text. Again in this fascicle Dogen discusses four quotations from the *Recorded Sayings of Zen Master Rujing, Sequel.*

> Colophon: *"Presented to the assembly at the foot of Yamashi Peak, Echizen Province, on the seventeenth day, the twelfth month, the first year of the Kangen Era [1243]."*
> Translated by Arnold Kotler and the Editor.

65. DRAGON SONG (RYŪGIN)

"Dragon Song" was the last of the nineteen fascicles Dogen wrote in Echizen during the first seven months of 1243, the most prolific time of his life. Strikingly, he does not reference building the monastery, although he must have been very busy preparing for its construction. In this text, he addresses the dynamism and joy of sitting still.

> Colophon: *"Presented to the assembly on the foot of Yamashi Peak on the twenty-fifth day, the twelfth month, the first year of the Kangen Era [1243]."*
> Translated by Mel Weitsman and the Editor.

Dogen gave five formal talks in 1243.

1244

66. SPRING AND AUTUMN (SHUNJŪ)

Although the month and day of "Spring and Autumn" were not recorded, it was possibly delivered in a hut at the foot of Yamashi Peak. It was spring, yet it was too cold to return to the Yoshimine Temple. Dogen's theme is a single koan regarding the Zen way of facing cold and heat. Dogen examines and criticizes six Chinese masters' responses to this koan.

The fact that this fascicle was presented twice hints that some of the residents were away, helping prepare for construction, performing tasks such as cutting wood.

> Colophon: "Presented twice to the assembly in a deep mountain of Echizen in the second year of the Kangen Era [1244]. At the moment of meeting Buddha, the Unicorn Sutra is expounded. An ancestor [Qinquan commenting on Shitou] said, 'Although there are many horns, a single horn is sufficient.'"
> Translated by Katherine Thanas and the Editor.

67. THE MEANING OF BODHIDHARMA'S COMING FROM INDIA (SOSHI SAIRAI I)

As in the preceding fascicle, "Spring and Autumn," the month and day were not recorded in the colophon, but one can assume that Dogen delivered "The Meaning of Bodhidharma's Coming from India," along with five others, in a hut at the foot of Yamashi Peak during the coldest time of the year. In this text, Dogen examines Xiangyan's words on the impossibility of verbally expressing the experience of nonduality.

> Colophon: "Presented to the assembly in a deep mountain of Echizen Province on the fourth day, the second month, the second year of the Kangen Era [1244]."
> Translated by Wendy Egyoku Nakao and the Editor.

68. UDUMBARA BLOSSOM (UDON GE)

In midspring, when the snow began to melt, Dogen and his community returned to the Yoshimine Temple. Presumably, this brief fascicle is directed to a mixture of long-term students and those who had recently arrived for the monastery construction. Dogen speaks of the legend that Shakyamuni Buddha took up a flower and blinked as Mahakashyapa smiled—commonly considered the first Zen transmission. He explains that all awakened ones in the past, present, and future emerge from this exchange.

Colophon: "Presented to the assembly, while residing at the Yoshimine Temple, Echizen Province, on the twelfth day, the second month, the second year of the Kangen Era [1244]."

Translated by Chozen Jan Bays, Hogen Bays, and the Editor.

69. AROUSING THE ASPIRATION FOR THE UNSURPASSABLE (HOTSU MUJŌ SHIN)

Two days after delivering "Udumbara Blossom," Dogen presented this and the following fascicles to his assembly. Some copied versions of these two fascicles have the same title, "Arousing the Aspiration for Enlightenment" (Hotsu Bodai Shin). To avoid confusion, this earlier fascicle was renamed later, possibly by Dogen himself.

Between these brief texts, this fascicle is more directed to lay practitioners of Buddhism, perhaps those who participated in monastery construction, not necessarily limited to Zen practitioners. (Some parts of the text are addressed to monks.) This text mentions virtues, including the construction of buddha images and stupas.

Colophon: "Presented to the assembly of the Yoshimine Temple, Yoshida County, Echizen Province, on the fourteenth day, the second month, the second year of the Kangen Era [1244]."

Translated by Steve Allen and the Editor.

70. AROUSING THE ASPIRATION FOR ENLIGHTENMENT (HOTSU BODAI SHIN)

Delivered on the same day as the preceding fascicle, "Arousing the Aspiration for Enlightenment" is addressed to bodhisattvas and practitioners of "beginner's mind." These two texts deal with a theme common to Buddhism in general.

Colophon: "Presented to the assembly of the Yoshimine Temple, Yoshida County, Echizen Province, on the fourteenth day, the second month, the second year of the Kangen Era [1244]."

Translated by Peter Levitt and the Editor.

71. TATHAGATA'S ENTIRE BODY (NYORAI ZENSHIN)

The day after the preceding fascicles were presented, Dogen delivered "Tathagata's Entire Body" and the following fascicle, "King of Samadhis," on the same day of the full moon. Again, this text runs counter to the common Zen expression "transmission outside the scriptures." Dogen asserts that scriptures are no other than the entire body of the Buddha Shakyamuni.

> Colophon: "Presented to the assembly of the Yoshimine Temple, Yoshida County, Echizen Province, on the fifteenth day, the second month, the second year of the Kangen Era [1244]."
> Translated by John Daido Loori and the Editor.

72. KING OF SAMADHIS (SAMMAI ŌZAMMAI)

Delivered on the same day as "Tathagata's Entire Body," "King of Samadhis" reflects the height of Dogen's creativity and brilliance. It discusses zazen, the heart of Zen practice, in the context of Buddhism in general.

> Colophon: "Presented to the assembly of the Yoshimine Temple on the fifteenth day, the second month, the second year of the Kangen Era [1244]."
> Translated by Norman Fischer and the Editor.

On the nineteenth day of the second month, four days after the delivery of "Tathagata's Entire Body" and "King of Samadhis," ground for the dharma hall of the new monastery was leveled. On the twenty-first day of this month, foundation stones were set and the pillars were erected. On the twenty-second day, the wooden framework of the dharma hall was raised. It was completed four months later.

73. THIRTY-SEVEN WINGS OF ENLIGHTENMENT (SANJŪSHICHI HON BODAI BUMPŌ)

In this long text, "Thirty-seven Wings of Enlightenment," Dogen presents a comprehensive list of Buddhist virtues, not specific to Zen, perhaps addressing home leavers. He emphasizes the necessity of leaving one's household.

Colophon: "Presented to the assembly of the Yoshimine Temple, Echizen Province, on the twenty-fourth day, the second month, the second year of the Kangen Era [1244]."

Translated by Peter Levitt and the Editor.

74. TURNING THE DHARMA WHEEL (TEMBŌRIN)

Still residing temporarily at the Yoshimine Temple, three days after presenting "Thirty-seven Wings of Enlightenment," Dogen read this short text on a general Buddhist theme to his practicing and working community. Here he discusses the authenticity of the *Shurangama Sutra*.

Colophon: "Presented to the assembly of the Yoshimine Monastery, Echizen Province, on the twenty-seventh day, the second month, the second year of the Kangen Era [1244]."

Translated by Taigen Dan Leighton and the Editor.

75. SELF–REALIZATION SAMADHI (JISHŌ ZAMMAI)

Two days after presenting "Turning the Dharma Wheel," Dogen read "Self-Realization Samadhi" to the assembly. In this text he revisits the Buddhist paradox of enlightenment, which he previously discussed in "Speaking of Mind, Speaking of Essence." He explains that scriptures and teachers cannot create self-realization, because all realization is actualized by the self. Yet without them the self cannot be realized.

Colophon: "Presented to the assembly while residing at the Yoshimine Temple on the twenty-ninth day, the second month, the second year of the Kangen Era [1244]."

Translated by Mel Weitsman and the Editor.

76. GREAT PRACTICE (DAI SHUGYŌ)

Nine days later, Dogen read "Great Practice" to his community. This concluded a prolific time at the Yoshimine Temple and the hut on Yamashi Peak. In nine months after arriving in Echizen, Dogen completed twenty-two fascicles of the *Treasury of the True Dharma Eye*.

Here Dogen takes up the Zen parable of an old Zen master who was reborn as a wild fox. Dogen criticizes later Zen masters' comments for not fully expressing the gravity of cause and effect. The subject of karma—one's action and its effect—becomes a critical concern in his teaching from this point on. Some parts of the text in this fascicle overlap those in "Identifying with Cause and Effect."

> *Colophon: "Presented to the assembly of the Yoshimine Temple, Echizen Province, on the ninth day, the third month, the second year of the Kangen Era [1244]."*
> Translated by Dan Welch and the Editor.

There is no record that Dogen held a practice period in 1244. His silence may reflect the intensity of monastery construction and organization. A number of monks arrived in the seventh month.

On the eighteenth day of the seventh month, one day after Rujing's memorial day, Dogen moved from Yoshimine Temple to his new monastery. He opened its dharma hall and named it Daibutsu (Great Buddha) Monastery.

On the fourteenth day of the eighth month, Dogen made a vow to hand carve a Buddha image for the monastery.

On the first day of the ninth month, a ceremony marking completion of the dharma hall was performed.

On the third day of the eleventh month, a framework-raising ceremony for the monks' hall was performed.

Dogen gave six formal talks in 1244.

DAIBUTSU MONASTERY PERIOD

1245
77. SPACE (KOKŪ)
After a year's break, Dogen delivered a short text to his community as his first presentation of the *Treasury of the True Dharma Eye* at the Daibutsu Monastery. In this text, he presents his understanding of space as a boundless and indescribable state of meditation.

Colophon: "This was presented to the assembly of the Daibutsu Monastery, Echizen Province, on the sixth day, the third month, the third year of the Kangen Era [1245]."

Translated by Alan Senauke and the Editor.

78. EATING BOWL (HOU)

Dogen delivered "Eating Bowl" to students at the new monastery six days after "Space." The Buddhist eating bowl is also a begging bowl. Along with the robe, it is a symbol of home leavers and dharma transmission. Here Dogen presents a Zen understanding of the bowl.

Colophon: "Presented to the assembly of the Daibutsu Monastery, Echizen Province, on the twelfth day, the third month, the third year of the Kangen Era [1245]."

Translated by Peter Levitt and the Editor.

79. PRACTICE PERIOD (ANGO)

The first summer practice period at the Daibutsu Monastery started, as was customary, on the full-moon day of the fourth month. It seems that a full-scale monastic compound had been completed by this time. Dogen offers meticulous descriptions of practice period activities in the monastery.

Colophon: "Presented to the assembly of the Daibutsu Monastery, Echizen Province, on the thirteenth day, the sixth month, during the summer practice period, in the third year of the Kangen Era [1245]."

Translated by Norman Fischer and the Editor.

80. SEEING OTHERS' MINDS (TASHIN TSŪ)

In the heat of summer, close to the end of the practice period, Dogen expanded and edited a large section of "Ungraspable Mind" (later version), which had not been presented to the community. Then he delivered this text under a new title to his students. In this fascicle he focuses on the story of a Zen master challenging a miracle worker. He sharply criticizes different Chinese Zen masters' comments on the story.

Colophon: "Presented to the assembly at the Daibutsu Monastery, Echizen Province, on the fourth day, the seventh month, the third year of the Kangen Era [1245]."
Translated by Michael Wenger and the Editor.

81. KING WANTS THE SAINDHAVA (ŌSAKU SENDABA)

In midwinter, three months after the end of the first practice period at the Daibutsu Monastery, Dogen delivered "King Wants the Saindhava." He examines ancient Zen masters' commentaries on the word *saindhava.* Its multiple meanings require mind-to-mind transmission for others to understand its implications.

Colophon: "Presented to the assembly of the Daibutsu Monastery on the twenty-second day, the tenth month, the third year of the Kangen Era [1245]."
Translated by Josho Pat Phelan and the Editor.

Dogen gave fifteen formal talks in 1245.

EIHEI MONASTERY PERIOD

1246

Dogen did not write or deliver any fascicle of the *Treasury of the True Dharma Eye* during the second practice period at the Daibutsu Monastery. It seems that his teaching focus shifted toward creating detailed monastic guidelines, and giving frequent formal talks for his practicing community.

On the full-moon day of the sixth month, Dogen renamed his training center the Eihei (Eternal Peace) Monastery. On this day he completed the *Guidelines for Officers of the Eihei Monastery, Echizen Province, Japan.*

82. INSTRUCTIONS ON KITCHEN WORK (JI KUIN MON)

Soon after the end of the practice period, at the beginning of autumn, Dogen delivered "Instructions on Kitchen Work" to his community.

Similar to his earlier "Guidelines for the Auxiliary Cloud Hall at the Kannondori Kosho Gokoku Monastery," this was initially written as monastic guidelines but was later included in the Eihei-ji edition of the *Treasury of the True Dharma Eye.*

There is a section on duties of the head cook in *Guidelines for Officers of the Eihei Monastery, Echizen Province, Japan,* which he wrote in Chinese two months earlier. But this text, composed in Japanese, seems to be directed to monks and kitchen workers less experienced or educated than the head cook.

> *Introductory note: "Presented to the assembly on the sixth day, the eighth month, the fourth year of the Kangen Era [1246]."*
> *Translated by Peter Levitt and the Editor.*

83. LEAVING THE HOUSEHOLD (SHUKKE)

In midautumn Dogen presented "Leaving the Household" as the only fascicle of the *Treasury of the True Dharma Eye* delivered to his community at the Eihei Monastery.

This is the last-dated piece in the seventy-five-fascicle version (which is identified by Ejo as the "early written version") of the *Treasury of the True Dharma Eye.* The grouping of this version was to be completed sometime after this.

Dogen begins with a Zen reference on receiving precepts and leaving the household, but relies on quotations from the larger body of Buddhist scriptures. He says, "Unsurpassable enlightenment is fulfilled at the moment you leave the household and receive the precepts. It is not fulfilled other than on this day."

> *Colophon: "Presented to the assembly of the Eihei Monastery, Echizen Province, on the fifteenth day, the ninth month, the fourth year of the Kangen Era [1246]."*
> *Translated by Peter Levitt and the Editor.*

Dogen gave seventy-five formal talks in 1246.

In the third month, Tokiyori Hojo became the fifth regent of the Kamakura government. (After the death of the first Shogun, Yoritomo Minamoto, in 1199, successive members of the Hojo Clan became regents of the Kamakura government, gradually taking power. Tokiyori was the one who took full power.) One of the first things he did was to invite Dogen to Kamakura.

1247

Dogen was at the Eihei Monastery during the practice period.

He gave thirty-five formal talks this year. It is possible that he was working on restructuring of the *Treasury of the True Dharma Eye*—the seventy-five- and twelve-fascicle versions.

On the third day of the eighth month, he left for Kamakura to teach laypeople, primarily leaders of the samurai government.

Dogen gave the precepts to a number of people, including Tokiyori. Tokiyori asked Dogen to stay longer and open a monastery in Kamakura, but Dogen declined. Aside from the ten poems he gave Tokiyori's wife, practically none of Dogen's writings remain from this period.

1248

On the thirteenth day of the third month, Dogen returned to the Eihei Monastery, ready to lead the practice period.

He gave fifty-two formal talks this year.

1249

In the first month, Dogen completed the *Guidelines for the Study Hall at the Kissho Mountain, Eihei Monastery.*

He gave fifty-eight formal talks this year.

1250

On the eleventh day of the first month, Dogen delivered "Washing the Face" for the third time.

He gave fifty-one formal talks this year.

1251

Dogen gave sixty-nine formal talks this year.

1252

Dogen revised "Actualizing the Fundamental Point." He may have been
still working on restructuring of the *Treasury of the True Dharma Eye*—
the seventy-five- and twelve-fascicle versions.

He gave fifty-one formal talks this year.

He became sick in the autumn.

1253

84. EIGHT AWAKENINGS OF GREAT BEINGS
(HACHI DAININ GAKU)

At the beginning of the year—the sixth day of the first month—Dogen
wrote "Eight Awakenings of Great Beings." The text consists largely
of quotations from the *Pari-nirvana Admonition Outline Sutra*. He only
added some simple interpretations of Shakyamuni Buddha's last words.
Clearly, as Ejo suggests in his colophon, Dogen intended to mirror the
Buddha's last words in his own final teaching.

> *Colophon: "Written at the Eihei Monastery on the sixth day, the first month, the
> fifth year of the Kencho Era [1253]."*

> *Ejo's colophon: "Now, on the day before the end of the practice period in the
> seventh year of the Kencho Era [1255], I have asked Secretary Gien to copy
> this. I have also proofread it today. This text was written by our late master dur-
> ing his last illness. He rewrote all [seventy-five] fascicles of the* Treasury of the
> True Dharma Eye *he had written in kana [mixture of ideographs and Japanese
> phonetics]. He wanted to add recently written fascicles and altogether create a
> one-hundred-fascicle version. He started writing this text as the twelfth fascicle [of
> the recently written pieces]. Then his sickness advanced, and the compilation of
> the entire text had to stop. Thus, this fascicle is the last teaching left behind by our
> late master. Unfortunately, we are unable to see the one-hundred-fascicle-version
> manuscript. It is indeed most regrettable. Those who long for our late master
> should not fail to copy and maintain this fascicle. It is the last admonition of
> Shakyamuni Buddha, as well as that of our late master."*
>
> *Translated by Reb Anderson and the Editor.*

There is no record of Dogen's formal talks in 1253.

On the eighth day of the seventh month, Dogen became sick again.
Gikai attended to him.

On the fourteenth day of the same month, Dogen appointed Ejo the second abbot of the Eihei Monaster, giving him a robe Dogen himself had sewn.

On the fifth day of the eighth month, at Yoshishige Hatano's request, Dogen left for Kyoto to treat his sickness.

On the fifteenth day of the eighth month, under a harvest moon, he wrote a poem.

> In autumn
> even though I may
> see it again,
> how can I sleep
> with the moon this evening?

On the twenty-eighth day of the eighth month, Dogen passed away at his lay student Kakunen's residence in the city of Kyoto.

FASCICLES NOT DATED BY DOGEN

85. KARMA IN THE THREE PERIODS (SANJI GŌ)

Dogen did not have time to complete and date this manuscript on the general Buddhist theme of karma. It was included, most likely by Ejo, in the twelve-fascicle version of the *Treasury of the True Dharma Eye* as a later manuscript than those in the seventy-five-fascicle version. (The twelve-fascicle version also includes some earlier texts that are strictly for home leavers.)

> *Ejo's colophon: "This was copied at the head monk's office at the Eihei Monastery on the ninth day, the third month, the fifth year of the Kencho Era [1253]."*
> *Translated by Mel Weitsman and the Editor.*

86. FOUR HORSES (SHIME)

A brief text commenting on some selections from pre-Mahayana and Mahayana sutras, "Four Horses" is known as part of the twelve-fascicle version text.

Ejo's colophon: "On a summer practice day of the seventh year of the Kencho Era [1255], I have copied my late master's draft."

Translated by Peter Levitt and the Editor.

87. VIRTUE OF HOME LEAVING (SHUKKE KUDOKU)

Dogen radically expanded his text on a common Buddhist theme that he had brought up in 1246 with "Leaving the Household." "Virtue of Home Leaving" was included in the twelve-fascicle version as the leading piece.

Ejo's colophon: "A day during the summer practice period, the seventh year of the Kencho Era [1255]."

Translated by Paul Haller and the Editor.

88. MAKING OFFERINGS TO BUDDHAS (KUYŌ SHOBUTSU)

Dogen describes various offerings to buddhas, suggesting that such offerings are essential practice for enlightenment. This is one of the fascicles Ejo included in the twelve-fascicle version.

Ejo's colophon: "[Edited during] The summer practice period, the seventh year of the Kencho Era [1265]."

Translated by Natalie Goldberg and the Editor.

89. TAKING REFUGE IN BUDDHA, DHARMA, AND SANGHA (KIE BUPPŌSŌ)

This fascicle is also called "Taking Refuge in the Three Treasures" (Kie Sambō). As Ejo says in his colophon, Dogen did not edit it. After Dogen's death, it was put in the twelve-fascicle version as one of the "recently written pieces."

Ejo's colophon: "Copying of this draft written by our late master was completed on a day of the summer practice period in the seventh year of the Kencho Era [1255]. He could not revise and finalize the manuscript, although he would have made some additions and deletions in the process of editing. Since this is no longer possible, I have preserved his draft as it is."

Translated by Gyokuko Carlson, Kyogen Carlson, and the Editor.

90. IDENTIFYING WITH CAUSE AND EFFECT (SHINJIN INGA)

Examining the same theme as "Great Practice," and possibly written later, "Identifying with Cause and Effect" shows Dogen's mature thinking about cause and effect. Undated and perhaps unedited by Dogen, this fascicle was collected in the twelve-fascicle version.

Ejo's colophon: "During the summer practice period in the seventh year of the Kencho Era [1255], I copied our late master's draft. There may be a second or final version edited by him, but I have used his draft for the time being."
Translated by Katherine Thanas and the Editor.

91. MONK OF THE FOURTH-STAGE MEDITATION (SHIZEN BIKU)

This short piece, interwoven with quotations from pre-Mahayana and Mahayana sutras, is also undated and unedited. It is one of Dogen's later pieces placed in the twelve-fascicle version.

Ejo's colophon: "Copied from a draft [by Dogen] during the practice period of the seventh year of the Kencho Era [1255]."
Translated by Andy Ferguson and the Editor.

92. ONLY A BUDDHA AND A BUDDHA (YUIBUTSU YOBUTSU)

Basing his title on a phrase from the *Lotus Sutra,* Dogen explains in simple language that the full experience of dharma can be passed on only from a buddha to a buddha. This text was not found in either the seventy-five or the twelve-fascicle version. Perhaps Dogen gave it to one of his students in an early time but did not keep a copy of it. It was part of the twenty-eight-fascicle version, transmitted at the Eihei Monastery, and later known as the *Secret Treasury of the True Dharma Eye.* It was included in Kozen's edition.
Translated by Edward Brown and the Editor.

93. BIRTH AND DEATH (SHŌJI)

"Life and death" are often described as "birth and death" in Buddhism, with the understanding that each individual is born and dies in each moment. Like "Only a Buddha and a Buddha," this short fascicle was included in Kozen's edition. It seems to be one of Dogen's earliest pieces, as the writing style and vocabulary are similar to those in "Actualizing the Fundamental Point" and "Undivided Activity."

Translated by Arnold Kotler and the Editor.

94. HEART OF THE WAY (DŌSHIN)

The short text "Heart of the Way" was originally titled "The Buddha Way" (Butsudō), but Kozen renamed it, since there was already another fascicle with that title. Here, Dogen refers to such lay practices as creating a buddha image and printing copies of the *Lotus Sutra.*

Translated by Peter Levitt and the Editor.

95. RECEIVING THE PRECEPTS (JUKAI)

In the twelve-fascicle version, the short undated text "Receiving the Precepts" is second, after "Leaving the Household." Like some other fascicles of this version, it may have been written in the last part of Dogen's life. Drawing examples from ancient Zen masters, Dogen explains the significance of receiving the precepts and describes the procedure for an ordination ceremony.

Translated by Michael Wenger and the Editor.

96. ONE HUNDRED EIGHT GATES OF REALIZING DHARMA (IPPYAKUHACHI HŌMYŌ MON)

Unlike other fascicles of the *Treasury of the True Dharma Eye,* most of "One Hundred Eight Gates of Realizing Dharma" is a long quotation from one sutra. This undated piece lacks a usual introductory section, and Dogen's explanation appears very briefly at the end. It seems to be a rough draft written during the last part of his life. It is placed in the twelve-fascicle version immediately before Dogen's last known text, "Eight Awakenings of Great Beings." This text was not included in Kozen's ninety-five-fascicle version. Because we have included it, our volume has one more fascicle than his seventeenth-century edition.

Translated by Peter Levitt and the Editor.

DOGEN'S LIFE AND TEACHING (APPENDIX 2)

There is a section on Dogen in *Transmission of Light* (*Denkō Roku*) by Keizan Jokin (1268–1325), completed in 1300, nearly half a century after Dogen's death. Keizan's book describes the lives and teachings of Shakyamuni Buddha and fifty-two dharma holders in a lineage through Dogen and Ejo. Keizan, a successor of Gikai and the founder of the Soji Monastery, widely disseminated Dogen's teaching among priests and laity, and is regarded as the second founder of the Soto School.

Translated by Susan Moon and the Editor.

WANDERING PERIOD

1227–1233

I

ON THE ENDEAVOR OF THE WAY

ALL BUDDHA TATHAGATAS who individually transmit inconceivable dharma, actualizing unsurpassable, complete enlightenment, have a wondrous art, supreme and unconditioned. Receptive samadhi is its mark; only buddhas transmit it to buddhas without veering off. Sitting upright, practicing Zen, is the authentic gate to free yourself in the unconfined realm of this samadhi.

Although this inconceivable dharma is abundant in each person, it is not actualized without practice, and it is not experienced without realization. When you release it, it fills your hand—how could it be limited to one or many? When you speak it, it fills your mouth—it is not bounded by length or width.

All buddhas continuously abide in this dharma, and do not leave traces of consciousness about where they are. Sentient beings continuously move about in this dharma, but where they are is not clear in their consciousness.

The concentrated endeavor of the way I am speaking of allows all things to come forth in realization so they may practice going beyond in the path of letting go. Passing through the barrier [of dualism] and dropping off limitations in this way, how could you be hindered by nodes in bamboo or knots in wood [concepts and theories]?

After the aspiration for enlightenment arose, I began to search for dharma, visiting teachers at various places in our country. Then I met priest Myozen, of the Kennin Monastery, with whom I trained for nine years, and thus I learned a little about the teaching of the Rinzai School. Priest Myozen alone, as a senior disciple, authentically received transmission of the unsurpassable buddha dharma from Eisai; no one can be compared with Myozen.

Later I went to Great Song China, visited masters on both sides of the Zhe River, and heard the teachings of the Five Schools. Finally, I became a student of Zen Master Rujing of Taibai Peak and completed my life's quest of the great matter.

Then, around the beginning of the Shaoding Era [1228–1233 C.E.] of Great Song, I came back to Japan with the vision of spreading the teaching and saving sentient beings—a heavy burden on my shoulders. And yet I have put aside the hope of having the teaching prevail everywhere until the time of surging opportunity. For the time being I wander about like a cloud or a waterweed, and let the wind of the ancient sages be heard.

There may be true students who are not concerned with fame and gain who allow their aspiration for enlightenment to guide them and earnestly desire to practice the buddha way. They may be misguided by incapable teachers and obstructed from the correct understanding; intoxicated in confusion, they may sink into the realm of delusion for a long time. How can they nourish the correct seed of prajna and encounter the time of attaining the way? Since I am wandering about, which mountain or river can they call on? Because of my concern for them, I would like to record the standards of Zen monasteries that I personally saw and heard in Great Song, as well as the profound principle that has been transmitted by my master. I wish to leave for students of the way the authentic teaching of the buddha house. This is indeed the essence:

The great master Shakyamuni entrusted dharma to Mahakashyapa at the assembly on Vulture Peak; it was then authentically transmitted from ancestor to ancestor down to Venerable Bodhidharma. Bodhidharma went to China and entrusted dharma to the great master Huike; this was the beginning of dharma transmission in the eastern country. In this way, by direct transmission, it reached Huineng, the Sixth Ancestor, Zen Master Dajian. Then the authentic buddha dharma spread in China, and the teaching that is not concerned with concepts and theories took form.

At that time there were two outstanding disciples of Huineng: Nanyue Huairang and Qingyuan Xingsi. They both equally received the buddha seal, as guiding masters of humans and devas. Their two lineages spread, and later the Five Gates opened: the Fayan School, the Guiyang School, the Caodong School, the Yunmen School, and the Linji School. At present in Great Song China only the Linji School prospers throughout the country. But in spite of their different styles, each of the Five Schools holds the one seal of the buddha mind.

In China after the Later Han Dynasty [25–220 C.E.], the teachings of Buddhist scriptures were introduced and spread all over the land, but there was no conclusive teaching as yet. When Bodhidharma came from India [527 C.E.], the root of twining vines was immediately cut off and the pure, single buddha dharma spread. Hope that it will be like this in our country.

Now, all ancestors and all buddhas who uphold buddha dharma have made it the true path of unfolding enlightenment to sit upright, practicing in the midst of receptive samadhi. Those who attained enlightenment in India and China followed this way. Thus, teachers and disciples intimately transmitted this excellent art as the essence of the teaching.

In the authentic tradition of our heritage, it is said that this directly transmitted, straightforward buddha dharma is the unsurpassable of the unsurpassable. From the first time you meet a master, without depending on incense offering, bowing, chanting buddha names, repentance, or reading scriptures, just wholeheartedly sit, and thus drop away body and mind.

When even for a moment you sit upright in samadhi expressing the buddha mudra [form] in the three activities [body, speech, and thought], the whole world of phenomena becomes the buddha mudra and the entire sky turns into enlightenment. Accordingly, all buddha tathagatas increase dharma bliss, the original source, and renew their magnificence in the awakening of the way. Furthermore, all beings in the world of phenomena in the ten directions and the six paths, including the three lower paths, at once obtain pure body and mind, realize the state of great emancipation, and manifest the original face. At this moment, all things actualize true awakening; myriad objects partake of the buddha body; and sitting upright, a glorious one under the bodhi tree, you immediately leap beyond the boundary of awakening. Then, you turn the unsurpassably great dharma wheel and expound the profound wisdom, ultimate and unconditioned.

This broad awakening comes back to you, and a path opens up to help you invisibly. Thus, in zazen you invariably drop away body and mind, cut through fragmented concepts and thoughts from the past, and realize essential buddha dharma. You cultivate buddha activity at innumerable practice places of buddha tathagatas everywhere, provide the opportunity for everyone to engage in ongoing buddhahood, and vigorously uplift the dharma of going beyond buddha.

Because earth, grass, trees, walls, tiles, and pebbles in the world of phenomena in the ten directions all engage in buddha activity, those who receive the benefits of the wind and water are inconceivably helped by the buddha's transformation, splendid and unthinkable, and intimately manifest enlightenment. Those who receive these benefits of water and fire widely engage in circulating the buddha's transformation based on original realization. Because of this, all those who live with you and speak with you also receive immeasurable buddha virtue, practice continuously, and extensively unfold the endless, unremitting, unthinkable, unnameable buddha dharma throughout the entire world of phenomena.

All this, however, does not appear within perception. Because it is unconstructedness in stillness, it is immediate realization. If practice and realization were two things, as it appears to an ordinary person, each could be recognized separately. But what can be met with recognition is not realization itself, because realization is not reached with a discriminating mind.

In stillness, mind and object merge in realization and go beyond enlightenment. Thus, in the state of receptive samadhi, without disturbing its quality or moving a single particle, you engage the vast buddha activity, the extremely profound and subtle buddha transformation.

Grasses, trees, and lands that are embraced by this way of transformation together radiate a great light and endlessly expound the inconceivable, profound dharma. Grass, trees, and walls bring forth the teaching to all beings, including common people and sages; all beings in response extend this dharma to grass, trees, and walls. Thus, the realm of self-awakening and awakening others invariably holds the mark of realization with nothing lacking, and realization itself is manifested without ceasing for a moment.

This being so, the zazen of even one person at one moment imperceptibly accords with all things and fully resonates through all time. Thus, in the past, future, and present of the limitless universe, this zazen carries on the buddha's transformation endlessly and timelessly. Each moment of zazen is equally the wholeness of practice, equally the wholeness of realization.

This is so not only while sitting; like a hammer striking emptiness, before and after its exquisite sound permeates everywhere. How can it be limited to this time and space? Myriad beings all manifest original practice, original face; it is impossible to measure. Even if all buddhas of the ten directions, as innumerable as the sands of the Ganges, exert their strength and with the buddha wisdom try to measure the merit of one person's zazen, they will not be able to fully comprehend it.

Question 1: We have now heard that the merit of zazen is lofty and great. But an ignorant person may be doubtful and say, "There are many gates for buddha dharma. Why do you recommend zazen exclusively?"
Answer: Because this is the front gate for buddha dharma.

Question 2: Why do you regard zazen alone as the front gate?
Answer: The great master Shakyamuni authentically transmitted this splendid method of attaining the way, and all buddha tathagatas of the past, future, and present attain the way by practicing zazen. For this reason it has been transmitted as the front gate. Furthermore, all ancestors in India and China attained the way by practicing zazen. Thus, I now teach this front gate to human beings and devas.

Question 3: We understand that you have studied the path of the buddha ancestors and authentically transmit the tathagatas' excellent art. This is beyond the reach of ordinary thought. However, reading sutras or chanting buddha's name must be causes and conditions of enlightenment. How can zazen, just sitting uselessly doing nothing, be depended upon for attaining enlightenment?

Answer: If you think that the samadhi of all buddhas, their unsurpassable great art, is just sitting uselessly doing nothing, you malign the Great Vehicle. Such misunderstanding is like saying there is no water when you are in the middle of the ocean. Just now, all buddhas sit serenely at ease in receptive samadhi. Is this not the actualization of vast merit? What a pity that your eye is not yet open, that your mind is still intoxicated!

The realm of all buddhas is inconceivable. It cannot be reached by intellect—much less can those who have no trust or who lack wisdom know it. Only those who have the great capacity of genuine trust can enter this realm. Those who have no trust are unable to accept it, however much they hear it. Even at the assembly on Vulture Peak, there were those who were told by Shakyamuni Buddha, "You may leave if you wish."

When genuine trust arises, practice and study with a teacher. If it does not, wait for a while. It is regrettable if you have not received the beneficence of the buddha dharma.

Also, what do you understand of the merit attained by reading sutras, chanting buddha's name, and so on? It is futile to think that just moving the tongue and making a sound is meritorious Buddhist activity. If you regard these as the buddha dharma, it will be farther and farther away.

Actually, the meaning of studying sutras is that if you understand and follow the rules of practice for sudden or gradual realization taught by the Buddha, you will unmistakably attain enlightenment. In studying sutras you should not expend thoughts in the vain hope that they will be helpful for attaining realization.

To attempt to reach the buddha way by chanting buddha's name thousands of times is like foolishly trying to go south while heading north, or to fit a square peg into a round hole. To be consumed with words and letters while ignorant of the way of practice is like a physician forgetting how to prescribe medicine; what use can it be? People who chant all the time are just like frogs croaking day and night in spring fields; their effort will be of no use whatsoever. Even worse off are those deluded by fame and gain who cannot give up such practices, because their acquisitiveness is so deep. Such people existed in the past; are there not even more today? What a pity, indeed!

Just understand that when a master who has attained the way with a clear mind authentically transmits to a student who has merged with realization, then the wondrous dharma of the Seven Original Buddhas, in its essence, is actualized and maintained. This cannot be known by those who study words. Therefore, set aside your doubt, practice zazen under an authentic teacher, and actualize buddhas' receptive samadhi.

Question 4: The Lotus School and the Avatamsaka School, which have been transmitted to Japan, both expound the ultimate of Mahayana teaching. Furthermore, the teaching of the Mantra School was directly transmitted by Vairochana Tathagata to Vajrasattva, and its lineage from teacher to disciple since then has not been interupted. This teaching expounds "Mind itself is buddha," and "Everyone's mind becomes buddha." They also advocate the authentic enlightenment of the Five Buddhas within one sitting, instead of practice through many eons. It is regarded as the supreme buddha dharma. What extraordinary aspect of the practice you mention makes you recommend it, disregarding the practice of other schools?
Answer: You should know that in the buddha house we do not discuss superiority or inferiority of the teaching; nor do we concern ourselves with the depth or shallowness of the dharma, but only with the genuineness of practice.

There are those who, attracted by grass, flowers, mountains, and waters, flow into the buddha way; and there are those who, grasping soil, rocks, sand, and pebbles, uphold the buddha seal. Although the boundless words of the Buddha permeate myriad things, the turning of the great dharma wheel is contained inside a single particle of dust. In this sense, the line "Mind itself is buddha" is the moon reflected on water, and the teaching "Sitting itself is becoming buddha" is a reflection in the mirror. Do not be concerned with the splendor of the words. By showing the buddha ancestors' excellent way of direct transmission, I am just recommending the practice of the immediate realization of enlightenment, hoping that you will become a true practitioner of the way.

For the transmission of buddha dharma, the teacher should be a person who has merged with realization. Scholars concerned with words and letters cannot do it; this would be like the blind leading the blind.

Those within the gate of the buddha ancestors' authentic transmission venerate an accomplished adept who has attained the way and merged with realization, and entrust this master with the upholding of buddha dharma. Accordingly, when spirit beings of the visible and invisible realms come to pay homage, or when arhats who have attained the fruits of realization come to inquire about the dharma, this master will not fail to clarify the means to illumine their mind-ground. This is not known in other teachings. Buddha's disciples should study the buddha dharma alone.

Know that fundamentally you do not lack unsurpassed enlightenment, and you are replete with it continuously. But you may not realize it, and may be in the habit of arousing discriminatory views, and regard them as real. Without noticing, you miss the great way, and your efforts will be fruitless. Such discriminatory views create flowers of emptiness.

You may imagine the twelvefold causation of rebirth, or the twenty-five existences, and have such views as the Three or Five Vehicles, and whether the Buddha exists or not. But do not take up these views and regard them as the correct way of practicing buddha dharma.

Instead, sit zazen wholeheartedly, conform to the buddha form, and let go of all things. Then, leaping beyond the boundary of delusion and enlightenment, free from the paths of ordinary and sacred, unconstrained by ordinary thinking, immediately wander at ease, enriched with great enlightenment. When you practice in this way, how can those who are concerned about the traps and snares of words and letters be compared to you?

Question 5: Among the three learnings there is the practice of samadhi, and among the six practices there is the practice of dhyana. Both of these have been studied by all bodhisattvas from the moment of arousing the aspiration for enlightenment, and both are practiced by the clever and dull. The zazen you speak of seems to be something like this. Why do you say that the true teaching of the Tathagata is contained in it?

Answer: Your question arises because the treasury of the true dharma eye, the single great matter of the Tathagata, the unsurpassable great dharma, has been named the Zen [Dhyana] School. You should know that the name "Zen [Chan] School" appeared in China and spread eastward. It was not heard of in India. When the great master Bodhidharma sat facing the wall at the Shaolin Temple on Mount Song for nine years, neither monks nor laypeople knew the Buddha's true teaching, so they called him the Brahman who concentrated on zazen. Subsequently, all buddha ancestors of every generation always devoted themselves to zazen. Heedless laypeople who saw them, without knowing the truth, informally called them the Zazen School. Later the word *za*—sitting—was dropped, and nowadays it is called the Zen School.

The meaning of this teaching has been made clear through the discourses of our ancestors. Do not identify zazen with the dhyana or samadhi of the six practices or the three learnings.

The authenticity of the transmission of this buddha dharma is unhidden through all time. Long ago at the assembly on Vulture Peak the Tathagata entrusted Venerable Mahakashyapa alone with the unsurpassable, great teaching—the treasury of the true dharma eye, the wondrous heart of nirvana. This event was witnessed by devas in the heavenly world; do not doubt it. The buddha dharma is protected by these devas and its merit does not decrease.

Know that the practice of zazen is the complete path of buddha dharma, and nothing can be compared to it.

Question 6: Why, among the four bodily presences taught in the buddha house, do you emphasize sitting alone, recommend Zen samadhi, and expound entry into realization?

Answer: It is impossible to know completely the methods by which all buddhas from the past practiced and entered realization, one after another. It is hard to know, but if you look into it, all buddhas are engaged in zazen as the source of realization. Don't look for anything else.

Extolling it, an ancestor said [in the *Guidelines for Zen Monasteries*], "Zazen is the dharma gate of enjoyment and ease." Thus, we know that sitting practice, among the four bodily presences, is the way of enjoyment and ease. Furthermore, it is not merely the practice of one or two buddhas, but all buddha ancestors practiced in this way.

Question 7: While it is clear that those who have not yet realized buddha dharma should practice zazen and attain realization, for those who have already understood the buddha's correct teaching, what should they expect from zazen?

Answer: Although we should not talk about dreams with careless people, nor give a boat pole to a woodcutter, nevertheless I will give instruction about this.

To suppose that practice and realization are not one is a view of those outside the way; in buddha dharma they are inseparable. Because practice within realization occurs at the moment of practice, the practice of beginner's mind is itself the entire original realization.

When giving instruction for zazen practice, we say that you should not have any expectation for realization outside of practice, since this is the immediate original realization. Because this is the realization of practice, there is no boundary in realization. Because this is the practice of realization, there is no beginning in practice.

In this way, Shakyamuni Tathagata and Venerable Mahakashyapa were both fulfilled by practice within realization; great master Bodhidharma and Huineng—high ancestor Dajian—were drawn in and turned by practice within realization. The ancient way of abiding in buddha dharma has always been like this.

Practice just here is not apart from realization. Fortunately, each one of us has individually inherited this wondrous practice; each beginner's endeavor of the way brings forth original realization in the realm of the unconstructed. Know that in order not to divide this realization, which is inseparable from practice, buddha ancestors always caution you not to be lax in your practice. Release this wondrous practice and original realization fills your hands. Liberate original realization and wondrous practice is upheld throughout your body.

As I personally saw in Great Song, the Zen monasteries in various places all had meditation halls where five to six hundred, or even up to two thousand monks, practiced zazen day and night. When I asked the abbots of these monasteries, masters who had inherited the seal [authentic experience] of buddha mind, about the essential meaning of buddha dharma, I was told that practice and realization are not two different things.

Therefore, I recommend to students who are already studying with a teacher, as well as all those outstanding people who seek the truth of buddha dharma, to practice zazen and endeavor in the way under the guidance of an authentic teacher, and investigate the teaching of the buddha ancestors without distinguishing between beginning or advanced, and without being concerned about ordinary or sacred.

An ancient ancestor once said, "It is not that there is no practice and no realization; it is just that they cannot be divided." It has also been said that "Someone who sees the way practices the way." Understand that practice is endeavor in the midst of attaining the way.

Question 8: In the past, various teachers went to Tang China, became transmitters of the dharma, and spread the scriptural teaching widely throughout Japan. Why did they ignore a practice such as you have described and introduce only scriptural teaching?
Answer: The reason these ancient teachers did not introduce this dharma is that the time was not yet ripe.

Question 9: Did those masters in ancient times understand this dharma?
Answer: If they had understood it, it would have spread.

Question 10: One master said:

Do not grieve over birth [life] and death. There is an immediate way to be free from birth and death, namely, to know the principle that the nature of mind is permanent.

It [the principle] means that because this body is already alive, it will eventually die, but the mind-nature will not perish. You should recognize that mind-nature exists within your body and is not affected by birth and death. This is its inherent nature. The body is a temporary form; it dies here and is born there, and is not fixed. Mind is permanent; it does not change through the past, future, or present.

To understand this is to be free from birth and death. If you understand this principle, you become free from ordinary birth and death and enter the ocean of mind-nature when your body perishes. When you flow into the ocean of nature, you attain the wondrous virtue of all buddha tathagatas. Even though you realize this now, because your body is formed as a result of deluded actions from past lives, you are not the same as all sages. If you do not recognize this principle, you will go around in birth and death forever. Therefore, you should hasten to understand that mind-nature is permanent. If you just spend your whole life leisurely sitting, what can you expect?

Does such a statement as this accord with the path of all buddhas and ancestors?

Answer: The view you have mentioned is not at all the buddha dharma, but rather the view of Shrenika, an outsider, who said:

> There is a soul in one's body, and this soul, on encountering conditions, recognizes good and bad, right and wrong. To discern aching and itching, or to know pain and pleasure, is also this soul's capacity. However, when the body is destroyed, the soul comes out and is born in another world. So it appears to be dead here, but since there is birth in another place, it is permanent without dying.

To follow this view and regard it as the Buddha's teaching is more foolish than grasping a piece of stone and regarding it as gold. Such shameful ignorance cannot be compared to anything. National Teacher Huizhong of Great Tang criticized this deeply. To take up the mistaken view that mind is permanent and forms perish, while regarding this as equal to the wondrous teaching of all buddhas, or to create the causes of birth and death while wishing to be apart from birth and death—is this not foolish? It is most pitiable. Just understand it as the mistaken view of someone outside the way and do not listen to it.

As I cannot refrain from being sympathetic, let me disabuse you of your mistaken view. In buddha dharma it is always taught that body and mind are not separate, and that essence and characteristics are not two. This has been known throughout India and China, so there is no room for mistake.

In fact, from the perspective of permanence, all things are permanent; body and mind are not separate. From the perspective of cessation, all things cease; essence and characteristics cannot be divided. How can you say body perishes but mind is permanent? Is it not against the authentic principle? Furthermore, you should understand that birth-and-death is itself nirvana. Nirvana is not realized outside of birth-and-death. Even if you think that mind is permanent apart from the body, and mistakenly assume that buddha wisdom is separate from birth-and-death, the mind of this assumption still arises and perishes momentarily and is not permanent. Is it not truly ephemeral?

Reflect that the teaching of the oneness of body and mind is always being expounded in the buddha dharma. How, then, can mind alone leave the body and not cease when the body ceases? If body and mind are inseparable sometimes and not inseparable at other times, the Buddha's teaching would be false. To think that birth-and-death must be rejected is the mistake of ignoring buddha dharma. You must refrain from this.

The so-called "dharma gate of the whole reality of mind-nature" in buddha dharma includes the entire world of phenomena without separating essence from characteristics or birth from death. Nothing, not even enlightenment or nirvana, is outside of mind-nature. All things and all phenomena are just one mind; nothing is excluded or unrelated. It is taught that all dharma gates are equally one mind, and there is no differentiation. This is the understanding of mind-nature in the buddha house. How can you differentiate this into body and mind, and separate birth-and-death from nirvana? Already, you are a buddha child. Do not listen to the tongues of mad people, quoting an outsider's view.

Question 11: Should those who are entirely engaged in zazen strictly follow the precepts?

Answer: Holding to the precepts and engaging in pure actions is the rule of the Zen Gate (School) and the teaching of buddha ancestors. Even those who have not yet received the precepts or have broken the precepts can still receive the benefit of zazen.

Question 12: Is it all right for those who practice zazen also to engage in chanting mantras or in the practice of shamatha [calming the mind] and vipashyana [analytical introspection]?
Answer: When I was in China and asked masters about the essence of the teaching, I was told that none of the ancestors who authentically transmitted the buddha seal in India and China in the past or present had ever engaged in such a combination of practices. Indeed, without devoting yourself to one thing, you cannot penetrate the one wisdom.

Question 13: Should zazen be practiced by lay men and women, or should it be practiced solely by home leavers?
Answer: The ancestors say, "In understanding buddha dharma, men and women, nobles and commoners, are not distinguished."

Question 14: Home leavers are free from various involvements and do not have hindrances in zazen in pursuit of the way. How can the laity, who are variously occupied, practice single-mindedly and accord with the buddha way, which is unconditioned?
Answer: Buddha ancestors, out of their kindness, have opened the wide gate of compassion in order to let all sentient beings enter realization. Who among humans and heavenly beings cannot enter?

If you look back to ancient times, the examples are many. To begin with, Emperors Dai and Shun had many obligations on the throne; nevertheless, they practiced zazen in pursuit of the way, and penetrated the great way of buddha ancestors. Ministers Li and Fang [Pei Xiu] both closely served their emperors but they practiced zazen, pursued the way, and entered realization in the great way of buddha ancestors.

This just depends on whether or not you have the willingness. It does not matter whether you are a layperson or a home leaver. Those who can discern excellence invariably come to trust in this practice. Those who regard worldly affairs as a hindrance to buddha dharma think only that there is no buddha dharma in the secular world; they do not understand that there is no secular world in buddha dharma.

Recently, there was a high official of Great Song, Minister Feng, who was an adept in the ancestral way. He once wrote a poem concerning his view of practice:

> I enjoy zazen between my official duties
> and seldom sleep lying on a bed.
> Although I appear to be a minister,
> I'm known as a Buddhist elder
>   throughout the country.

Although he was busy in his official duties, he attained the way because he had a deep intention toward the buddha way. When considering someone like him, reflect on yourself and illuminate the present with the past.

In Song China, kings and ministers, officials and common people, men and women, grounded their intention on the ancestral way. Both warriors and literary people aroused the intention to practice Zen and study the way. Among those who pursued this intention, many of them illuminated their mind-ground. From this we understand that worldly duties do not hinder the buddha dharma.

When the true buddha dharma is spread widely in the nation, the rule of the monarch is peaceful because all buddhas and devas protect it unceasingly. If the rule is peaceful, the buddha dharma gains eminence.

When Shakyamuni Buddha was alive, even those who previously had committed serious crimes or had mistaken views attained the way. In the assemblies of the ancestors, hunters and woodcutters attained enlightenment. As it was so for them at that time, it is so for anyone now. Just seek the teaching of an authentic master.

Question 15: Can we attain realization if we practice, even in this last age of decline?

Answer: In the scriptural schools they explain various categories, but in the true Mahayana teachings dharma is not divided into periods of truth, imitation, and decline. Instead, it is taught that everyone attains the way by practice. Particularly in this authentically transmitted teaching of zazen, you are filled with the treasure you already have, entering dharma and leaving bondage behind. Those who practice know whether realization is attained or not, just as those who drink water know whether it is hot or cold.

Question 16: Someone once said:

> In buddha dharma, if you comprehend the meaning of "Mind itself is buddha," that will be sufficient without any chanting of sutras or practicing the buddha way. To know that "buddha dharma originally lies in the self" is the completion of attaining the way. Other than this, you need not seek from anyone else.

Why should you be troubled with practicing zazen and pursuing the way?
Answer: This statement is entirely groundless. If what you say is true, then whoever has a mind would immediately understand the meaning of buddha dharma. You should know that buddha dharma is studied by giving up the view of self and other.

If the understanding of "Self itself is buddha" were the attaining of the way, Shakyamuni Buddha would not have taken the trouble to elucidate the way. Let me illuminate this with an excellent case of an ancient master:

Once a monk called Director Xuanze was in the assembly of Zen Master Fayan. Fayan asked him, "Director Xuanze, how long have you been in my community?"

Xuanze said, "I have been studying with you for three years."

Fayan said, "You are a recent member of the community. Why don't you ask me about buddha dharma?"

Xuanze said, "I cannot deceive you, sir. When I was studying with Zen Master Qingfeng [Baizhao Zhiyuan], I mastered the state of ease and joy in buddha dharma."

Fayan said, "With what words did you enter this understanding?"

Xuanze said, "When I asked Qingfeng, 'What is the self of a Zen student?' he said, 'The fire spirits are here to look for fire.'"

Fayan said, "That is a good statement. But I'm afraid you did not understand it."

Xuanze said, "The fire spirits belong to fire. So I understood that fire looks for fire and self looks for self."

The master said, "Indeed, you did not understand. If buddha dharma were like that, it would not have been transmitted until now."

Then Xuanze was distressed and left the monastery. But on his way he said to himself, "The master is a renowned teacher in this country, a great leader of five hundred monks. His criticism of my fault ought to have some point."

He went back to Fayan, apologized, and said, "What is the self of a Zen student?"

Fayan said, "The fire spirits are here to look for fire."

Upon hearing this statement, Xuanze had a great realization of buddha dharma.

In this way, we know that mere recognition of "Self itself is buddha" is not penetrating buddha dharma. If the understanding of "Self itself is buddha" were buddha dharma, Fayan would not have given such criticism or guidance. Just inquire about the rules of practice as soon as you meet a master, single-mindedly practice zazen, and pursue the way, without leaving a half-understanding in your mind. Then the excellent art of buddha dharma will not be in vain.

Question 17: We have heard that in India and China there have been people in the past and present who realized the way on hearing the sound of bamboo being struck, or who understood the mind when seeing the color of blossoms. Great Master Shakyamuni was awakened to the way when he saw the morning star, and Venerable Ananda understood the dharma when a banner pole fell down. Furthermore, among the Five Houses after the six early ancestors in China, there were many who realized the mind-ground with one word or half a phrase. Not all of them necessarily practiced zazen in pursuit of the way; is this not so?

Answer: Of those who clarified the mind upon seeing a form, or who realized the way upon hearing a sound, not one had any intellectual thinking regarding the endeavor of the way and not one was concerned about their self other than their original self.

Question 18: People in India and China are straightforward by nature. As they are in the center of civilization, when buddha dharma is taught to them, they can immediately enter it. People in our country since ancient times have been bereft of compassionate wisdom, and it is difficult for the right seed of prajna to be nourished. This is because we are uncivilized. Is it not regrettable? Thus, the monks in our country are inferior to even the laity in those great countries. Our entire nation is foolish and narrow-minded, and we are deeply attached to visible merit and fond of worldly values. If such people do zazen, can they immediately realize buddha dharma?

Answer: What you say is correct. Among people in our own country, compassionate wisdom does not yet prevail, and their nature is rather coarse. Even if the true dharma is explained to them, its nectar becomes poisonous. They easily pursue fame and gain, and it is difficult for them to be free from delusion.

However, to enter the realization of buddha dharma, one does not need the worldly wisdom of humans and devas as a boat for fleeing the world. When the Buddha was alive, one person realized the four fruits of attainment when he was hit by a ball; another understood the great way by wearing a robe in jest. They were both ignorant people, like beasts, but with the aid of genuine trust they were able to be free from delusion. A laywoman serving food to an ignorant old monk sitting in silence was enlightened. This did not depend upon wisdom, scripture, words, or speech; it was only brought about by genuine trust.

Now, Shakyamuni Buddha's teaching has been spread in the billion worlds for about two thousand years. Those countries are not necessarily the countries of compassionate wisdom, and the people are not necessarily sharp and intelligent. However, the Tathagata's true dharma in essence has a great inconceivable meritorious power, and spreads in those countries when the time is ripe.

If you practice with genuine trust, you will attain the way, regardless of being sharp or dull. Do not think that buddha dharma cannot be understood in this country because this is not a country of compassionate wisdom and people are foolish. In fact, everyone has the seed of prajna in abundance; it is only that they have rarely realized it and have not yet fully received buddha dharma.

This exchange of questions and answers may have been rather confusing; a number of times flowers of emptiness were made to bloom. However, since the meaning of zazen in pursuit of the way has not been transmitted in this country, those who wish to know about it may be regretful. Therefore, for the sake of those who wish to practice, I have recorded some of the essential teachings of the clear-eyed teachers, which I learned in China. Beyond this, guidelines for practice places and the regulations for monasteries are more than I can mention now. They should not be presented casually.

Our country lies to the east of the dragon ocean, far from China, but the Buddha's teaching was transmitted eastward to Japan, about the time of Emperors Kimmei and Yomei. This is the good fortune of our people, yet the philosophy and rituals have been entangled, and authentic practice was not established. Now, if you make patched robes and mended bowls your whole life, build a thatched-roofed hut near a mossy cliff or white rock, and practice sitting upright, you immediately go beyond buddha and directly master the great matter of your life's study. This is the admonition of Dragon Fang [Longya], the transmitted way of practice of Mount Rooster-Foot [where Mahakashyapa practiced]. Concerning the method of zazen, I would refer you to "Recommending Zazen to All People," which I wrote during the Karoku Era [1225–1227].

Although a king's edict is needed for spreading dharma in the country, if we think of the Buddha entrusting the dharma to kings and ministers on Vulture Peak, all the kings and ministers who have appeared in the billion worlds are born because of their wish from a previous birth to protect and guard buddha dharma. Where this teaching prevails, is there any place that is not a buddha land? Thus, spreading the way of buddha ancestors does not depend upon place or circumstance. Just consider that today is the beginning.

I have written this to leave for people of excellence who aspire to practice buddha dharma and for true students who wander like water-weeds, seeking the way.

Midautumn day [the fifteenth day of the eighth month], in the third year of the Kanki Era [1231], by Dogen, who has transmitted dharma from Song China.

Kosho Monastery Period

─────

1233–1243

2

MANIFESTATION OF GREAT PRAJNA

AVALOKITESHVARA BODHISATTVA, WHILE experiencing deeply the manifestation of prajna [wisdom beyond wisdom], clearly saw with the entire body that all five skandhas are empty. These five skandhas [streams of body and mind]—form, feeling, perception, inclination, and discernment—are fivefold prajna. Clear seeing is prajna. To expound this teaching, it is said [in the *Maha Prajna Paramita Heart Sutra*] that form is emptiness and emptiness is form. Form is form. Emptiness is emptiness [boundlessness]. One hundred grasses are thus. Myriad forms are thus.

The manifestation of the twelvefold prajna [the prajna of the six senses and their objects] means twelve types of entering [into buddha dharma].

There is the eighteenfold prajna: the prajna of eyes, ears, nose, tongue, body, and mind; the prajna of sight, sound, smell, taste, touch, and objects of mind; also the prajna of the corresponding consciousness of eyes, ears, nose, tongue, body, and mind.

There is the fourfold [noble truth] prajna: suffering, craving, freedom from suffering, and the path. There is the sixfold [manifestation] prajna: generosity, precepts, patience, vigor, contemplation, and prajna.

There is the singlefold prajna: unsurpassable, complete enlightenment, actualized at this very moment. There is the manifestation of the threefold prajna: the past, present, and future. There is the sixfold [great element] prajna: earth, water, fire, air, space, and consciousness. The fourfold [bodily posture] prajna: walking, standing, sitting, and lying down, common in daily activities.

In the assembly of Shakyamuni Buddha there was a monk who said to himself:

> I will take refuge in this very profound manifestation of prajna. Although nothing arises or perishes in the midst of this manifestation of prajna, the precept skandha, the samadhi skandha, the wisdom skandha, the emancipation skandha, and the emancipation of views skandha are established. The fruits of entering the stream, of once-returning, of no-longer-returning, and of the arhat are established. The pratyeka-buddha's enlightenment is established. The unsurpassable, complete enlightenment is established. Buddha, dharma, and sangha treasures are established. The turning of the wondrous dharma wheel and awakening sentient beings are established.

The Buddha read the monk's mind and said to him, "That's right, that's right. The very profound manifestation of prajna is subtle and fathomless."

This monk's understanding was that taking refuge in all things is taking refuge in prajna that does not arise or perish. At the very moment of taking refuge, the prajna that establishes precepts, samadhi, wisdom, and awakening sentient beings is actualized. This prajna is called emptiness. So the actualization of emptiness is established. This is the manifestation of prajna that is extremely subtle and fathomless.

Indra asked Elder Subhuti, "Great reverend, if bodhisattvas, great beings, want to experience the profound manifestation of prajna, how should they study?"

Subhuti said, "Lord Indra of Kausika, if bodhisattvas, great beings, want to experience the profound manifestation of prajna, they should study as they would study empty space."

Thus, studying prajna is empty space, empty space is studying prajna.

Then, Indra asked the Buddha, "World-Honored One, if good men and women receive, recite, reflect upon, and explain to others the profound manifestation of the prajna you have explained, how should I protect them? Please teach me."

Subhuti answered for the Buddha, "Lord Indra of Kausika, do you think there is anything you need to protect?"

Indra said, "No, great reverend, I don't see anything I need to protect."

Subhuti said, "Lord Indra of Kausika, if good men and women practice the profound manifestation of the prajna, which the Buddha has explained, that itself is protection. If they do so, they will not stray from it. So you should know that in case humans or nonhumans want to find a way to harm good men and women, it will not be possible. Lord Indra of Kausika, protecting the profound manifestation of prajna, which the Buddha has explained, and protecting the bodhisattvas who practice it, are not different from protecting empty space."

Thus, know that receiving, reciting, or reflecting upon the profound manifestation of prajna is no other than protecting prajna. Intending to protect is receiving, reciting, and so forth.

Rujing, my late master, Old Buddha, said:

The entire body is a mouth [wind-bell] hanging in empty space,
regardless of the wind from the east, west, south, or north,
joining the whole universe in chiming out prajna.
Ting-ting, ting-ting, ting-ting.

This is an authentic heir of buddha ancestors speaking prajna. The entire body is prajna. The entire other is prajna. The entire self is prajna. The entire east, west, south, and north is prajna.

Shakyamuni Buddha said:

Shariputra, sentient beings should dedicate themselves and pay respect to this prajna just as to the living Buddha. They should reflect upon the manifestation of prajna just as they dedicate themselves and pay respect to the Buddha, the World-Honored One. Why so? Because the manifestation of prajna is no other than the Buddha, the World-Honored One. The Buddha, the World-Honored One, is no other than the manifestation of prajna. The manifestation of prajna is itself the Buddha, the World-Honored One. The Buddha, the World-Honored One, is the manifestation of prajna. Why so? Shariputra, unsurpassable, complete enlightenment of all tathagatas has emerged from the manifestation of prajna. Shariputra, bodhisattvas, great beings, pratyeka-buddhas, arhats, never-returners, once-returners, stream enterers have all emerged from the manifestation of prajna. Shariputra, the ten ways of wholesome actions in the world, the four stages of meditation, the four samadhis in formlessness, and the five miraculous powers have all emerged from the manifestation of prajna.

Thus, the Buddha, the World-Honored One, is the manifestation of prajna. The manifestation of prajna is all things. All things are aspects of emptiness—not arising [beyond arising], not perishing, not defiled, not pure, not increasing, and not decreasing. To actualize the manifestation of prajna is to actualize the Buddha, the World-Honored One.

———————

Look into this. Study this. To dedicate yourself and take refuge in the manifestation of prajna is to see and uphold the Buddha, the World-Honored One. It is to be the Buddha, the World-Honored One, seeing and accepting.

Presented to the assembly of the Kannondori Monastery on a day of the summer practice period in the first year of the Tempuku Era [1233].

3

ACTUALIZING THE
FUNDAMENTAL POINT

As all things are buddha dharma, there is delusion, realization, practice, birth [life] and death, buddhas and sentient beings. As myriad things are without an abiding self, there is no delusion, no realization, no buddha, no sentient being, no birth and death. The buddha way, in essence, is leaping clear of abundance and lack; thus there is birth and death, delusion and realization, sentient beings and buddhas. Yet in attachment blossoms fall, and in aversion weeds spread.

———

To carry the self forward and illuminate myriad things is delusion. That myriad things come forth and illuminate the self is awakening.

Those who have great realization of delusion are buddhas; those who are greatly deluded about realization are sentient beings. Further, there are those who continue realizing beyond realization and those who are in delusion throughout delusion.

When buddhas are truly buddhas, they do not necessarily notice that they are buddhas. However, they are actualized buddhas, who go on actualizing buddha.

When you see forms or hear sounds, fully engaging body-and-mind, you intuit dharma intimately. Unlike things and their reflections in the mirror, and unlike the moon and its reflection in the water, when one side is illumined, the other side is dark.

To study the way of enlightenment is to study the self. To study the self is to forget the self. To forget the self is to be actualized by myriad things. When actualized by myriad things, your body and mind as well as the bodies and minds of others drop away. No trace of enlightenment remains, and this no-trace continues endlessly.

When you first seek dharma, you imagine you are far away from its environs. At the moment when dharma is authentically transmitted, you are immediately your original self.

When you ride in a boat and watch the shore, you might assume that the shore is moving. But when you keep your eyes closely on the boat, you can see that the boat moves. Similarly, if you examine myriad things with a confused body and mind, you might suppose that your mind and essence are permanent. When you practice intimately and return to where you are, it will be clear that nothing at all has unchanging self.

Firewood becomes ash, and does not become firewood again. Yet, do not suppose that the ash is after and the firewood before. Understand that firewood abides in its condition as firewood, which fully includes before and after, while it is independent of before and after. Ash abides in its condition as ash, which fully includes before and after. Just as firewood does not become firewood again after it is ash, you do not return to birth after death.

This being so, it is an established way in buddha dharma to deny that birth turns into death. Accordingly, birth is understood as beyond birth. It is an unshakable teaching in the Buddha's discourse that death does not turn into birth. Accordingly, death is understood as beyond death.

Birth is a condition complete in this moment. Death is a condition complete in this moment. They are like winter and spring. You do not call winter the beginning of spring, nor summer the end of spring.

Enlightenment is like the moon reflected on the water. The moon does not get wet, nor is the water broken. Although its light is wide and great, the moon is reflected even in a puddle an inch wide. The whole moon and the entire sky are reflected in dewdrops on the grass, or even in one drop of water.

Enlightenment does not divide you, just as the moon does not break the water. You cannot hinder enlightenment, just as a drop of water does not crush the moon in the sky. The depth of the drop is the height of the moon. Each reflection, however long or short its duration, manifests the vastness of the dewdrop, and realizes the limitlessness of the moonlight in the sky.

When dharma does not fill your whole body and mind, you may assume it is already sufficient. When dharma fills your body and mind, you understand that something is missing. For example, when you sail out in a boat to the middle of the ocean where no land is in sight, and view the four directions, the ocean looks circular, and does not look any other way. But the ocean is neither round nor square; its features are infinite in variety. It is like a palace. It is like a jewel. It only looks circular as far as you can see at that time. All things are like this.

Although there are many features in the dusty world and the world beyond conditions, you see and understand only what your eye of practice can reach. In order to learn the nature of the myriad things, you must know that although they may look round or square, the other features of oceans and mountains are infinite in variety; whole worlds are there. It is so not only around you, but also directly beneath your feet, or in a drop of water.

A fish swims in the ocean, and no matter how far it swims, there is no end to the water. A bird flies in the sky, and no matter how far it flies, there is no end to the air. However, the fish and the bird have never left their elements. When their activity is large, their field is large. When their need is small, their field is small. Thus, each of them totally covers its full range, and each of them totally experiences its realm. If the bird leaves the air, it will die at once. If the fish leaves the water, it will die at once.

Know that water is life and air is life. The bird is life and the fish is life. Life must be the bird and life must be the fish. You can go further. There is practice-enlightenment, which encompasses limited and un-limited life.

Now, if a bird or a fish tries to reach the end of its element before moving in it, this bird or this fish will not find its way or its place. When you find your place where you are, practice occurs, actualizing the fundamental point. When you find your way at this moment, practice oc-curs, actualizing the fundamental point; for the place, the way, is neither large nor small, neither yours nor others'. The place, the way, has not car-ried over from the past, and it is not merely arising now. Accordingly, in the practice-enlightenment of the buddha way, to attain one thing is to penetrate one thing; to meet one practice is to sustain one practice.

Here is the place; here the way unfolds. The boundary of realization is not distinct, for the realization comes forth simultaneously with the full experience of buddha dharma. Do not suppose that what you at-tain becomes your knowledge and is grasped by your intellect. Although actualized immediately, what is inconceivable may not be apparent. Its emergence is beyond your knowledge.

Mayu, Zen Master Baoche, was fanning himself. A monk approached and said, "Master, the nature of wind is permanent and there is no place it does not reach. Why, then, do you fan yourself?"

"Although you understand that the nature of wind is permanent," Mayu replied, "you do not understand the meaning of its reaching everywhere."

"What is the meaning of its reaching everywhere?" asked the monk.

Mayu just kept fanning himself.

The monk bowed deeply.

The actualization of the buddha dharma, the vital path of its authentic transmission, is like this. If you say that you do not need to fan yourself because the nature of wind is permanent and you can have wind without fanning, you understand neither permanence nor the nature of wind. The nature of wind is permanent; because of that, the wind of the buddha house brings forth the gold of the earth and ripens the cream of the long river.

Written around midautumn, the first year of the Tempuku Era [1233], and given to my lay student Koshu Yo of Kyushu Island. Revised in the fourth year of the Kencho Era [1252].

4

ONE BRIGHT PEARL

Xuansha, Great Master Zongyi, of Mount Xuansha, Fu Region, China, of the Saha World, used to be called Shibei. His family name was Xie. When he was a householder, he loved fishing and boating on the Nantai River, doing as fishermen do.

At the beginning of the Xiantong Era [860–873] a golden-scaled fish came to him without his seeking it, and he suddenly had the urge to leave the dusty world. So he gave up his boat and went off into the mountains. He was thirty years old when he realized the precariousness of the floating world and the preciousness of the buddha way. Then he went to Mount Xuefeng and studied with Xuefeng, Great Master Zhenjiao, endeavoring in the way day and night.

One day, as he was leaving the mountain with his traveling bag to visit other monasteries to further his study, his toe hit a rock and began to bleed. In sharp pain he suddenly had a realization and said to himself, "If my body doesn't exist, where does this pain come from?" So he went back to see Xuefeng.

Xuefeng said, "What's happening, Ascetic Bei [Shibei]?"

Xuansha said, "No one can be fooled."

Xuefeng loved his words and said, "Who doesn't know these words, yet who else could say them?" Then he said, "Why doesn't Ascetic Bei with the traveling bag go and study all over?"

Xuansha said, "Bodhidharma didn't come to China. Huike didn't go to India."

Xuefeng praised him.

Although Xuansha was a fisherman who had never read sutras even in dreams, he focused on his intention to practice and was strongly determined. Xuefeng saw his practice excel in the community and regarded him as an outstanding student. The coarse cotton robe Xuansha had on all the time was worn out and tattered, so he put on a paper robe beneath it. He sometimes added dried mugwort grass to cover himself. He did not study with anyone other than Xuefeng. In this way, he acquired the capacity to inherit Xuefeng's dharma.

———————

Some years after attaining the way, Xuansha instructed his students, saying, "The entire world of the ten directions is one bright pearl."

Once a monk asked him, "I heard that you said, 'The entire world of the ten directions is one bright pearl.' How should I understand this?"

Xuansha said, "The entire world of the ten directions is one bright pearl. What do you do with your understanding?"

The next day Xuansha asked the monk, "The entire world of the ten directions is one bright pearl. How do you understand this?"

The monk said, "The entire world of the ten directions is one bright pearl. What do you do with your understanding?"

Xuansha said, "I see that you have worked out a way to get through the demon's cave on the black mountain."

———————

Xuansha is the first one to say, *The entire world of the ten directions is one bright pearl*. It means the entire world of the ten directions is neither vast nor minute, neither square nor round. It is not neutral, not active, and not obvious. Because it is beyond the coming or going of birth and death, it is the coming and going of birth and death. Thus, past days have already left here and the present moment starts from here. When we investigate the entire world of the ten directions, who can see it as bits and pieces, who can talk about it as something solid?

The entire world of the ten directions means that you ceaselessly chase things and make them into the self, and you chase the self and make it into things. When emotions arise, wisdom is pushed aside. By seeing this as separation, teacher and student turn their heads and exchange their faces, unroll the great matter and harmonize their understanding. Because you chase the self and make it into things, the entire world of the ten directions is ceaseless. Because you take initiative, you do more than distantly see the essential matter.

One bright pearl is not merely the name [of an object] but an expression of understanding. Although there have been people who thought that it was only a name, *one bright pearl* directly experiences ten thousand years. While the entire past has not yet departed, the entire present is just now arriving. Here is the now of the body, the now of the mind. This is the bright pearl; it is not limited to grass and trees here and there, or even to mountains and rivers in the universe.

How should I understand this? These words appear to be the monk's expression of ignorance, but the great function emerges right here, actualizing the great principle [that enlightenment encompasses time and space]. Step forward and penetrate one foot of water, one foot of wave, ten feet of pearl, ten feet of illumination.

In expressing his understanding, Xuansha said, *The entire world of the ten directions is one bright pearl. What do you do with your understanding?* These words are an expression that buddhas inherit from buddhas, ancestors inherit from ancestors, and Xuansha inherits from Xuansha. If you do not want to inherit this expression, there may be a way not to do so. But even if you totally avoid it for a while, this expression arises all-inclusively right now.

The next day Xuansha asked the monk, *The entire world of the ten directions is one bright pearl. How do you understand this?* This is an expression that takes up yesterday's statement and, adding another layer, blows it back today. His question today pushes down yesterday's nodding laugh.

The monk said, *The entire world of the ten directions is one bright pearl. What do you do with your understanding?* Speak! This is riding the robber's horse to chase the robber [the self looking for the self]. An authentic buddha speaking to you walks in the midst of various beings. Now turn the light inward and illuminate yourself. How many ways do you understand this? You may say, "seven pieces of milk cake" or "five pieces of herb cake." Yet, there is teaching and practice south of Xian and north of Tan [anywhere].

Xuansha said, *I see that you have worked out a way to get through the demon's cave on the black mountain.* Know that the sun face and moon face have not switched over since ancient times. The sun face emerges with the sun face, and the moon face emerges with the moon face. So, even in the sixth month [height of summer], do not say your nature is hot. The timeless thusness of this one bright pearl is boundless. It is just that the entire world of the ten directions is one bright pearl, not two or three. The entire body is one true dharma eye, the true body, a single phrase. The entire body is illumination; the entire body is the entire mind. When the entire body is the entire body, there is no hindrance. It is gently curved and turns round and round.

With the power of the bright pearl manifesting in this way, Avalokiteshvara and Maitreya see form and hear sound; old buddhas and new buddhas reveal their bodies and expound dharma. At this very moment the bright pearl hangs in space or is sewn inside the robe; it is hidden under the gill [of a dragon] or in the hair. This is one bright pearl, the entire world of the ten directions. Although it is sewn inside the robe, do not try to hang it outside the robe. Although it is hidden under the gill or in the hair, do not try to take it out.

A man sewed a valuable pearl inside the clothes of a dear friend who was drunk [as told in the *Lotus Sutra*]. A dear friend always gives a valuable pearl. When a pearl is sewn inside one's clothes, one is always drunk. This is one bright pearl, the entire world of the ten directions. All things, turning or not turning [seen when one is drunk or sober], are one bright pearl. Knowing the bright pearl is one bright pearl. This is how it is with one bright pearl.

This being so, although you may say, "I am not a bright pearl," you should not doubt. Whether you doubt it or not, such doubt comes from a limited view. Limited views are merely limited.

How lovely is one bright pearl's infinite colors and shades! Bits and pieces of its colors and shades express the entire world of the ten directions. No one can take it away, or throw a tile at it in the marketplace. Do not be concerned about falling or not falling into cause and effect in the six paths. Not ignoring cause and effect, from beginning to end, is the face of the bright pearl, is the eye of the bright pearl.

To think or not to think one hundred times about what the bright pearl is or is not is like gathering and binding weeds [to trap yourself]. But when you clarify the body and mind as the bright pearl through the dharma words of Xuansha, you understand that mind is not the self.

Who is concerned whether or not appearing and disappearing are the bright pearl? Even if you are concerned, that does not mean you are not the bright pearl. It is not something outside of the bright pearl that causes practice and thought. Therefore, forward or back, your every step in the demon's cave on the black mountain is one bright pearl.

Presented to the assembly of the Kannondori Kosho Horin Monastery, Uji County, Yamashiro Province, on the eighteenth day, the fourth month, the fourth year of the Katei Era [1238].

5

REGULATIONS FOR THE AUXILIARY CLOUD HALL AT THE KANNONDORI KOSHO GOKOKU MONASTERY

THOSE WHO HAVE way-seeking mind and wish to abandon fame and gain should enter. Those who are half-hearted and lack sincerity should not enter. If the entry is a mistake, after some consideration one may be asked to leave.

Know that when the way-seeking mind is aroused within, there is immediate freedom from fame and gain. In the vastness of the billion worlds, true heirs of dharma are rare. In spite of the long history of our country you should make the present moment the true source, having compassion for later generations by giving emphasis to the present.

The assembly of students in the hall should blend like milk and water to support the activity of the way. Although now for some period you are either guest or host, later you will be buddha ancestors equally throughout time. Therefore, you should not forget the feeling of gratitude. It is rare to meet one another and practice what is rare to practice.

This is called the body and mind of buddha dharma; you will certainly become a buddha ancestor.

Having left your home and birthplace, now you depend on clouds and you depend on water. The support to you and your practice given by this assembly of students surpasses that which was given by your father and mother. Your father and mother are temporarily close to you in birth and death, but this assembly of students is your companion in the buddha way of enlightenment for all time.

Do not look for a chance to go out. But, if necessary, going out is permitted once a month. People in the past lived in the remote mountains and practiced far away in the forests. Not only were they free from nearly all worldly affairs, but they also relinquished all relationships. You should learn the heart of their hiding brilliance and obscuring traces. Now is the time for the fire on your head to be brushed off. Is it not sad if you waste this time, concerning yourself with secular affairs? Life is impermanent and unreliable. No one knows where and when this dew-like existence will drop from the grass. Not recognizing impermanence is truly regrettable.

Do not read books in the hall, even Zen texts, and do not bring in personal correspondence. In the hall you should endeavor in the way of realizing the great matter. When facing the bright window, you should illuminate the mind with the authentic teaching. Do not waste a moment. Concentrate your effort.

Day or night, always inform the director of the hall where you are going to be. Do not play around according to your own impulses; your actions affect the discipline of the entire assembly. Who knows? This may be the last day of your life. It would be truly regrettable to die while indulging in pleasures.

Do not be concerned with the faults of others. Do not see others' faults with a hateful mind. There is an old saying that if you stop seeing others' faults, then naturally seniors are venerated and juniors are revered. Do not imitate others' faults; just cultivate virtue. The Buddha prohibited unwholesome actions but did not tell us to despise those who practice unwholesome actions.

Whether carrying out either important matters or trifles, always consult with the director of the hall. Those who do things without consulting with the director of the hall should leave. If you neglect the formality of guest and host, you can understand neither the true nor the conditional.

Inside or near the hall, do not put your heads together and talk loudly. The director should prohibit this.

Do not do chanting circumambulation in the hall.

Do not hold or carry beads in the hall. Do not enter or leave with your hands hanging down.

Do not chant the names of buddhas or sutras in the hall. However, this is permitted when supporters request sutra chanting on a particular occasion. Do not spit, blow your nose, or laugh loudly. Be sobered by the fact that the work of the way is not yet mastered. Regret the subtle passage of time, which is eating away this opportunity for practice of the way. Then you may have the sense of being a fish in a small puddle.

Those assembled in the hall should not wear brocade but rather things like paper robes. Those who understood the way in the past were all like this.

Do not enter the hall intoxicated with wine. If you do so by accident, you should make a formal repentance. Do not have wine brought into the hall. Do not enter the hall smelling of onions.

Quarreling persons should go out of the hall, because their quarreling not only hinders their own work in the way but also that of others. Those who see such quarreling and do not stop it are equally at fault.

Those who do not follow the guidelines of the hall should be removed. Those who are amused by or in sympathy with such students are also at fault.

Do not show the inside of the hall to visiting monks or laypeople, as this may disturb the students. Do not speak loudly with guests near the hall, and do not talk about practice in a self-praising way, in order to get offerings. However, those who have a long-standing intention to practice or those who are on pilgrimage may be allowed inside. In such cases, always consult the director of the hall beforehand.

Practice zazen in this hall just as in the monks' hall. Never neglect early morning zazen or the evening practice instruction period.

At mealtime, those who drop monks' bowls or utensils on the floor should be fined according to the regulations of the monastery.

The admonitions of buddha ancestors should always be followed. The pure guidelines of the monastery are to be inscribed in your bones and mind.

Wish to be serenely composed for your entire life and to practice the way free of expectations.

These regulations are the body and mind of the ancient buddhas. Respect and follow them.

This was written on the twenty-fifth day, the fourth month, the first year of the En'o Era [1239].

6

THE MIND ITSELF IS BUDDHA

WHAT BUDDHAS AND ancestors have maintained without exception is "The mind itself is buddha." However, this particular expression was not known in India; it was first heard in China.

Many students misunderstand this teaching, as they do not file a file about it [examine it thoroughly]. Because they do not file a file, they fall into a group of those outside the way. Upon hearing the phrase *The mind itself is buddha*, ignorant people think that the thoughts and awareness of ordinary beings, who have not aroused the aspiration for enlightenment, are already buddhas. They think in this way because they have not yet met an authentic teacher.

———————

Shrenika, who lived in India, was one of those outside the way. This was his theory:

The great road lies within this body right now. How it works is easy to know: The soul [everlasting consciousness] discerns pain and pleasure, cold and heat, aching and itching. It is not obstructed by things and is not concerned with objects. While things come and go and objects are born and perish, the soul exists without changing. It pervades all sentient beings both ordinary and sacred.

Although there are flowers of emptiness, which are false reality, as soon as an embracing wisdom appears even for a moment, things disappear and objects perish. The soul, the original nature, alone is clearly permanent. When the body is broken, the soul comes out of it unbroken. It is just like the owner of a house on fire who comes out of it safely.

What is luminous is called the nature of an awakened or wise person, a buddha. This is awakening. Self and other equally possess this nature. Both enlightenment and delusion are connected with it.

Whatever things or objects may be, the soul is different from them and is unchanged for eons. The objects that exist right now are real only if the soul abides in them. As these objects arise from the soul, the original nature, they are true reality. But they are not permanent; they exist and then disappear.

As the soul intuitively knows bright and dark, it is called a knowing spirit. It is also called the true self, the source of awakening, true nature, or true body. To realize such a true nature is described as returning to permanence. This soul is called a great being that returns to reality.

After such realization, the soul does not transmigrate in birth and death; it enters the ocean of the true nature of no birth and death. There is no reality other than this. When this true nature is not revealed, the three realms and the six paths emerge one after another.

This was Shrenika's theory.

————

Huizhong, National Teacher Dazheng, of Tang China, asked a monk, "Where have you come from?"

The monk said, "I have come from the south."

Huizhong asked, "What kind of teachers are there in the south?"

The monk replied, "There are many."

Huizhong asked, "How do they teach?"

The monk said, "Teachers there directly help students to realize that the mind itself is buddha. They say, 'Buddha means awakening. All of you already possess the nature of seeing, hearing, understanding, and knowing. This nature can cause you to raise your eyebrows and blink. It functions in the past and future. It fills your body. If you touch your head, the head knows it. If you touch your leg, the leg knows it. Thus, it is called correct, pervasive knowing. There is no buddha other than this. Your body is within birth and death, but mind nature has neither been born nor died since beginningless time. The body is born and dies just like the skin a snake leaves behind, the bones a dragon replaces with new ones, or a house the owner walks away from. Your body is impermanent, but your nature is permanent.' This is roughly what they teach in the south."

Huizhong said, "If it is so, their teaching is no different from that of Shrenika, an outsider of the way. He says, 'Inside your body there is a spirit. It knows aching and itching. When your body is destroyed, the spirit leaves, just like the owner of a house that is on fire who escapes from it. The house is impermanent, but the owner is permanent.'

"If we examine these theories, neither of them is closer to the truth than the other. When I traveled to various places, I heard many accounts of this kind of teaching. It has been particularly popular in recent times. They gather together three or five hundred monks and tell them that this is the essential teaching of the south. By taking up the *Platform Sutra*, altering the text, mixing in coarse stories, and leaving out sacred teachings, they confuse later generations. How can we call their statements teachings? How painful it is that our school is in such decline! If seeing, hearing, understanding, and knowing were buddha nature, Vimalakirti would not have said, 'Dharma is different from seeing, hearing, understanding, and knowing. To practice seeing, hearing, understanding, and knowing is only to practice seeing, hearing, understanding, and knowing. It is not seeking dharma.'"

Huizhong, a senior disciple of Huineng, Old Buddha Caoxi [the Sixth Ancestor], was a great teacher of humans and devas. Clarify his essential teaching and make it a standard for study.

The mind itself is buddha, which has been maintained by buddha ancestors, is not something those outside of the way or practitioners of the Two Lesser Vehicles can even dream of. Only buddha ancestors together with buddha ancestors have been actualizing and penetrating *The mind itself is buddha*. Thus, it has been heard, practiced, and realized. Buddha's one hundred grasses have been taken up; they have been made to disappear. However, this cannot be explained as the sixteen-foot golden body [of the Buddha].

This is the fundamental point, which does not wait for actualization. It does not avoid being decomposed. In itself, there are three realms—there is no walking away. *Itself* is not merely inseparable from mind. The mind is a wall. It is not stained by muddy water; it is not created.

Study thoroughly: "The mind itself is buddha," "The mind is buddha itself," "Buddha is itself the mind," "The mind itself Buddha is," "Buddha is the mind itself." By studying thoroughly in this way and taking up *The mind itself is buddha*, you authentically transmit it to *The mind itself is buddha*. It has been authentically transmitted until today.

The mind that has been authentically transmitted is: one mind is all things, all things are one mind.

Thus, an ancient teacher said, "If you realize this mind, there is not an inch of land left on earth."

Know that when you realize this mind, the entire sky collapses and the whole earth explodes. Or, if you realize this mind, the earth raises its surface by three inches.

————————

Ancient masters [Yangshan and Guishan] said to each other, "What is the wondrous clear mind?" "I say it is mountains, rivers, and the earth; it is the sun, the moon, and stars."

Thus, we know that the mind is mountains, rivers, and the earth; the mind is the sun, the moon, and stars. What is said here is not more, not less.

Mountains, rivers, and earth mind are just mountains, rivers, and the earth. There are no extra waves or sprays [in this mind]. The sun, the moon, and stars mind is just the sun, the moon, and stars. There is no extra fog or mist. The coming and going of birth and death mind is just the coming and going of birth and death. There is no extra delusion or enlightenment. The walls, tiles, and pebbles mind is just the walls, tiles, and pebbles. There is no extra mud or water. Four great elements and five skandhas mind are just four great elements and five skandhas. There is no extra horse or monkey. The chair and whisk mind is just the chair and whisk. There is no extra bamboo or wood.

This being so, *The mind itself is buddha* does not divide *The mind itself is buddha*. Buddhas do not divide buddhas. Thus, *The mind itself is buddha* indicates buddhas of aspiration, practice, enlightenment, and nirvana. Those who have not actualized aspiration, practice, enlightenment, and nirvana do not experience *The mind itself is buddha*.

Even if you arouse the aspiration for enlightenment and actualize practice-realization for a moment, that is *The mind itself is buddha*. Even if you arouse the aspiration for enlightenment and actualize practice-realization within the most minute particle, that is *The mind itself is buddha*. Even if you arouse the aspiration for enlightenment and actualize practice-realization for innumerable kalpas, that is *The mind itself is buddha*. Even if you arouse the aspiration for enlightenment and actualize practice-realization in a flash of thought, that is *The mind itself is buddha*. Even if you arouse the aspiration for enlightenment and actualize practice-realization within half a fist, that is *The mind itself is buddha*.

Those who say that practicing for an eon to become buddha is not *The mind itself is buddha* have not seen, known, and studied *The mind itself is buddha*. They have not met an authentic teacher who expounds *The mind itself is buddha*.

The buddhas spoken of here are none other than Shakyamuni Buddha. Shakyamuni Buddha is *The mind itself is buddha*. When all buddhas in the past, present, and future are buddhas, they unfailingly become Shakyamuni Buddha. This is "The mind itself is buddha."

Presented to the assembly of the Kannondori Kosho Horin Monastery, Uji County, Yamashiro Province, on the twenty-fifth day, the fifth month, the first year of the En'o Era [1239].

7

CLEANSING

THE PRACTICE-REALIZATION THAT buddha ancestors have guarded and maintained is called nondefilement.

Nanyue Huairang, who would later become Great Master Dahui of the Guanyin Monastery, Mount Nanyue, was once asked by Huineng, the Sixth Ancestor, "Do you depend on practice-realization?"

Nanyue said, "It is not that there is no practice-realization. It is just that it should not be defiled."

Huineng said, "This nondefilement is what all buddhas have mindfully guarded. You are like this. I am like this. All ancestors in India were also like this."

––––––––––

The *Sutra of the Three Thousand Guidelines for Pure Conduct* says, "To cleanse your body means to wash away the excrement and urine and to cut your ten fingernails."

Thus, even if the body and mind are undefiled, there are methods of cleansing the body, cleansing the mind. It is not only cleansing the body and mind, but also cleansing the entire land, cleansing the places [of sitting] under trees.

Even if the land is not polluted, cleansing it is the intention of all buddhas. They do not turn their backs on it or give it up even after they reach the buddha fruit.

The essential meaning of cleansing is difficult to fathom. The method [of cleansing] is itself the essential meaning. Attaining the way is the method.

The "Pure Conduct" Chapter of the *Avatamsaka Sutra* says:

When you defecate and urinate, vow to remove defilement and become free from sexual desire, anger, and ignorance together with all sentient beings. When you arrive at the water, vow to go toward the unsurpassable way and attain the dharma beyond worldly affairs together with all sentient beings. When you cleanse with the water, vow to embody pure patience and become fully undefiled together with all sentient beings.

Water is not necessarily pure or impure by origin. The body is not necessarily pure or impure by origin. All things are like this. Water is not sentient or insentient. The body is not sentient or insentient. All things are like this.

The teaching of the Buddha, the World-Honored One, is like this. It is not that you purify the body with water; there is a method to maintain buddha dharma with buddha dharma. This is called cleansing.

You authentically receive this cleansing in person with the single body-mind of buddha ancestors. This is to see and hear a single phrase of buddha ancestors. It is to abide clearly in a sole radiant light of buddha ancestors. This is to actualize immeasurable, boundless merit.

At the very moment of embodying the awesome presence of this practice in body-mind, the timeless original practice is fully accomplished. Thus, the body-mind of this practice is originally actualized.

Cut your ten fingernails. The ten fingernails mean all your nails. Cut your toenails in the same way. According to one sutra, if the tips of your nails are longer than a grain of barley, you are found faulty. So, do not grow your nails long. Keeping long nails is following the example of outsiders of the way. Frequently cut your nails.

Among monks in Great Song, however, many who are not equipped with the eye of study keep long nails. The tips of the nails of some of them are one or two *sun* long, or even three or four. This is against dharma; they do not have a body-mind of buddha dharma. They are like this because they do not follow the ancient custom of the buddha house. Masters who maintain the way are not like that.

In addition, there are those who keep their hair long. This is also against dharma. Do not mistake such behavior by some monks in Great Song for true dharma.

———————

Rujing, my late master, Old Buddha, deeply cautioned against those monks who keep their hair and nails long, by saying, "Those who do not shave their heads are neither laity nor monks. They are animals. Among ancient buddha ancestors, who did not shave their heads? Those who do not understand cleansing hair are truly animals."

As he taught the assembly in this way, many of those who hadn't shaved for years shaved their heads.

When he ascended to the teaching seat [for a formal talk] or when he gave an informal talk, he would snap his fingers loudly and scold:

Those who keep long hair and nails meaninglessly without knowing the reason should be pitied for violating dharma, even if they have the body-mind of the Southern Continent, Jambudvipa.

As the ancestral way has been in decline for the last two or three hundred years, there are a number of such people. They become the heads of monasteries, being authorized to receive the titles of masters, and pretend to guide others. This does not benefit humans and devas.

In the monasteries all over China there is not a single person who has the aspiration for the way, and for a long time there has not been one who has attained the way. There are only groups of those who are decadent.

When Rujing taught the assembly in this way, none of those who were mistakenly called elders of monasteries in various directions were resentful or spoke back.

Know that keeping long hair has been cautioned against by buddha ancestors, and keeping long nails is a conduct of those outside the way.

A descendant of buddha ancestors should not indulge in behavior that is against dharma. Cleanse your body-mind. Cut your nails and shave your head. Do not be negligent in washing off excrement and urine.

––––––––––

Shariputra once converted a person outside the way with his awesome presence [in the practice of cleansing]. This is not what the person wanted or what Shariputra tried to achieve, but where the awesome presence of a buddha ancestor was actualized, the practitioner of the crooked teaching surrendered.

When you practice under a tree or in an open field, there is no toilet, so cleanse yourself with some dirt and water from a nearby river or valley brook. You may not find ash, so use two rows of seven pellets of dirt.

The way to use two rows of seven pellets of dirt is first to take off the dharma robe, fold it, and set it to the side. Then take up brown dirt, not so dark, and make pellets as large as soybeans. Set them on a rock or something nearby in two rows, seven in each row. Also set up a stone for rubbing [for washing hands]. Then defecate, and afterward use a piece of wood or paper. When you are done, go to the water and cleanse yourself. First use three pellets of dirt. Put one on your palm, mix it with water to make it liquid, and wash off the urine. With another pellet, wash yourself of the excrement in the same way. [Repeat this a few times.] Take up another pellet and clean the place where the excrement has dropped. Finally, use another pellet to wash your hands in the same way.

Since monks started living in monasteries, a toilet house has been used. It is called the "east building." It used to be called the "brook house." It is sometimes called the "wash house." This is a building essential to an abode of monks.

––––––––––

For going to the east building, always carry a hand towel. To do so, fold the towel in two [the long way] and hang it [folded in half again] over the left sleeve of the outer robe near the elbow.

At the east building hang the hand towel on the bamboo hanger, just as you hang it over your sleeve. If you are wearing a kashaya of nine or five strips, hang it beside the towel. Hang them carefully so that they don't fall down. Don't throw them. Remember the ideograph on the bamboo hanger. Ideographs are written on white sheets of paper, cut in circles like a full moon, and arrayed in a row on the bamboo hangers. By remembering the ideograph, you know where you have put your outer robe. As a number of monks use this building, do not confuse your hanging position with someone else's.

Meanwhile, if other monks come and stand in line, greet them with your hands in shashu. You don't necessarily stand face to face and bow to each other, but just bring your hands in shashu up to your chest and show a sign of greeting. In the east building, even if you don't wear an outer robe, make a gesture of greeting in this way.

If you have not yet used your hands for cleansing, and if you are not holding anything in your hands, hold them in shashu for greeting. If you have already used a hand or are holding something in one hand, use the other hand for greeting. To do so, hold your palm up, slightly cup your fingers just as if you were scooping water, and lower your head. If someone else greets you in this way, return the greeting in the same way. If you greet someone else in this way, the person should do so as well.

Before using the toilet, take off and hang your upper robe and outer robe on the bamboo hanger, next to the hand towel. Put the backs of the sleeves of the outer robe together, hold the armpit part of the sleeves [with the right hand], and pull up to keep the sleeves overlapped. At that time, hold the rear neck part of the outer robe with the left hand so that the ends of the sleeves, as well as both lapels, overlap each other. Then fold the outer robe vertically to make sure that the ends of the sleeves are aligned with the lapels. Fold the outer robe again vertically and bring the top part of the outer robe over the bamboo hanger. The lower part of the outer robe and the sleeves hang on your side of the bamboo hanger, while the waist part of the outer robe touches the bamboo hanger.

Then, cross both sides of the towel, which is already hanging, pull them around the outer robe, and tie a knot two or three times to keep the outer robe from slipping down. After this, bow to the outer robe. Next, take a strap and tie the sleeves of your underclothes across your armpits over your shoulders [in the undergarment].

Then, walk to the toilet area, get water in the wooden bucket, carry it with the right hand, and step into the toilet room. When pouring water into the bucket, do not fill it—make it nine out of ten. Change your sandals in front of the toilet door. Put on the cattail sandals [provided at the toilet] and leave your own straw sandals in front of the toilet. This is called "changing sandals."

The *Guidelines for Zen Monasteries* says, "When you want to go to the wash house, go early enough. Do not hurry and create accidents. Fold your kashaya and put it on the shelf, or hang it on a bamboo hanger in the wash house."

Step inside and slide the door shut with the left hand. Pour a bit of water into the wooden barrel. Then, place the bucket in front of you where it is supposed to be. While standing, snap the fingers [of the right hand] three times [for removing impurity], while keeping the left hand in a fist on the left side of the waist.

Pull the bottom and corners of your undergarment, face the door, put your feet on both sides of the top of the barrel, squat, and defecate. Do not stain the sides. Do not soil the front and back [of the barrel top].

Be silent the entire time. Do not converse through the wall or chant aloud. Do not spit in a disturbing manner. Do not groan. Do not write on the wall. Do not draw on the earthen floor with the toilet stick.

After defecating, use the stick for wiping. Another way is to use paper. In this case, do not use paper that has been already used or has been written on.

Be aware of whether the stick is clean or dirty. The stick is triangular [made of bamboo or wood], about eight *sun* long, and as thick as a thumb. Some sticks are lacquered, while others are not. Dirty sticks are put into the dirty stick container. Clean sticks are found on the table close to the edge of the wooden barrel.

After the stick or paper is used, take up the bucket with the right hand, wet the left hand well, cup it, pour water into it, and first wash urine from yourself three times. Then wash off the excrement. Wash properly and make your body clean. During this process, do not tilt the bucket roughly, pour too much water, or quickly lose water by overfilling the cupped hand.

After washing your body, put the bucket back in its position. Use the stick or paper to dry both areas of your body thoroughly. Then, pull and straighten up the bottom and corners of the underclothes with your right hand. When you carry the bucket with the right hand and leave the toilet, take off the cattail sandals and put on your straw sandals. Then, go to the washing area and return the bucket to its original position.

Next, wash your hands. Pick up an ash ladle with the right hand, scoop up some ash, and place it on a tile. Add some drops of water to it with your right hand and wash the soiled [left] hand. You wash it by rubbing it on the tile, just like sharpening a rusty knife. Wash it with ash three times. Then, place dirt on the tile, add drops of water, and wash the hand three more times. After that, get some honey locust powder with the right hand, dip both hands into water in a small wooden bucket, and wash them well. Wash your hands thoroughly up to the wrist. Wash them with complete attention and sincerity. Thus, wash three times with ash, three times with dirt, and once with honey locust powder. In this way, washing seven times at each use of the toilet is the right amount. Finally, wash your hands in a large wooden bucket. At this time, don't use herb or ash but rinse your hands with cold or warm water. After washing, put the used water into a small bucket. Get fresh water in the large bucket and rinse your hands again.

The *Avatamsaka Sutra* says:

> Washing my hands with water,
> may all sentient beings
> attain excellent hands
> for maintaining buddha dharma.

When you hold a dipper, always use the right hand. Do not make noise. Do not carelessly splatter water, sprinkle honey locust powder, or wet the wash area.

Dry your hands with a towel for common use or with your own towel. Then, walk to the bamboo hanger where your outer robe is hanging, untie your strap, and hang it on the hanger. Put your palms together, untie the towel, and put on the outer robe.

Then, hang the towel over the left elbow and perfume your hands. In the common area, there is a stick of aloeswood carved in the shape of a treasure jar. It is as thick as a thumb and four times as long as four finger-widths. A string about one *shaku* [one foot] long is threaded through the holes on both ends of this aloeswood, which is hung on a bamboo hanger. If you rub this stick with both hands, they become fragrant.

When you hang your strap on the bamboo hanger, do not put it on top of another; keep the straps from being entangled with each other.

This procedure [for using the toilet] is to cleanse the buddha land, to beautify the buddha land. Follow this procedure thoroughly.

Do not act hastily. Do not think of getting it over with and going back quickly. Quietly think of the teaching: "In the wash house, dharma is not expounded." Do not make observations on the monks who are on their way to the toilet.

For cleansing in the toilet room, cold water is suitable. It is said that hot water may cause stomach upset. For washing hands, it is all right to use warm water. The wash house is equipped with a kettle for this purpose.

The *Guidelines for Zen Monasteries* says, "Even late at night, keep water heated and oil [for the lamp] burning. Make hot water available at all times so the monks are not interrupted." In this way we know that both hot and cold water are used in the wash room.

If the toilet gets dirty, shut the door and put up a "Dirty" sign. If the bucket is dropped by mistake, also shut the door and put up a "Wet" sign. Do not use the toilets when you see such signs. If you are entering a dirty or wet toilet and someone else signals to you by snapping their fingers, stay outside for a moment [to let the person clean the toilet].

The *Guidelines for Zen Monasteries* says, "Those who fail to cleanse are not allowed to sit on the meditation platform, venerate the three treasures, and receive reverence from others."

The *Sutra of the Three Thousand Guidelines for Pure Conduct* says, "Those who do not cleanse themselves of urine or excrement are accountable for a dushkrita [light wrongdoing] conduct. They are not allowed to sit on the monks' pure sitting cushions and venerate the three treasures. Even if they do so, there will be no benefit."

Thus, in the practice place of endeavor of the way, make this cleansing procedure a priority. How can you not venerate the three treasures?

How can you not receive reverence from others? How can you not revere others?

In the practice places of buddha ancestors, there is always the awesome practice of this cleansing. Among those who practice in the practice places of buddha ancestors, there is always the awesome practice of this cleansing. Cleansing is not forced by the self, but is the conduct of awesome practice itself. Cleansing is the continuous procedure of all buddhas. Cleansing is the everyday activity of all ancestors. It is the buddha procedure not only of all buddhas in this realm, but of buddhas in the ten directions. It is the buddha procedure of the pure land and impure land.

Those who hear little think that buddhas don't have a procedure in the wash house or that the procedure for buddhas in the Saha World is different from that of buddhas in the pure land. This is not the study of the way.

Know that the matter of being clean or dirty is like drips of blood for those who have left the household. Sometimes it is gentle, and other times it is severe. Thus, be aware that all buddhas use a wash house.

Chapter 14 of the *Compiled Precepts in Ten Sections for Chanting* says:

Novice Rahula stayed at the Buddha's wash house and the Buddha noticed it. Stroking Rahula's head with the right hand, the Buddha told him in a verse:

> You stay here not because of poverty,
> nor because of having lost wealth,
> but for the sake of seeking the way.
> A home leaver should thus bear hardship.

As you see, there is a wash house in the practice place of the Buddha. The awesome practice inside the Buddha's wash house is cleansing, which has been transmitted from ancestor to ancestor. That the buddha procedure is still being practiced is an auspicious joy for those who long for the ancient way. This is encountering what is rare to encounter.

Above all, the Tathagata graciously expounded dharma to Rahula inside the wash house. The wash house is a place of assembly for the Buddha turning the dharma wheel. The procedure in this practice place has been authentically transmitted by buddha ancestors.

Chapter 34 of the *Great Sangha Precepts [Scripture]* says: "The wash house should not be placed in the east or north side [of the monastery], but in the south or west side. A place for urination should be also like this."

Follow this format, this is a plan for monasteries in India—the buildings where the Tathagata is still present. Know that this format is not only the buddha procedure of a single buddha, but of the practice places—monasteries—of the Seven Original Buddhas. This was not initiated [by Shakyamuni Buddha], but it has been the awesome practice of all buddhas.

If you build a monastery and practice buddha dharma before clarifying this matter, there may be a number of mistakes, the awesome practice may not be complete, and buddha enlightenment may not be actualized. When you construct a practice place and found a monastery, follow the dharma procedure authentically transmitted by buddha ancestors. Since this dharma procedure is of authentic heirs and of authentic transmission, its merit has been accumulated.

Without being authentically transmitted heirs of buddha ancestors, you have not yet known the body-mind of buddha dharma. Without knowing the body-mind of buddha dharma, you have not yet clarified the buddha work. That the buddha dharma of Shakyamuni Buddha has spread throughout the ten directions means that the body-mind of the Buddha is actualized. The very moment of the body-mind of the Buddha being actualized is just this.

Presented to the assembly of the Kannondori Kosho Horin Monastery, Uji County, Yamashiro Province, on the twenty-third day, the tenth month, the first year of the En'o Era [1239].

8

WASHING THE FACE

THE *LOTUS SUTRA* says, "If you spread oil on your body after removing dirt, and wear fresh robes, you are clean inside and outside."

This dharma was expounded by the Tathagata at the lotus assembly when he taught those who were engaged in the four practices of enjoyment and ease. It is not equal to other teachings and not the same as accounts in other sutras.

Thus, cleansing body and mind, spreading scented oil on the body after removing dirt, is a primary buddha dharma. To wear fresh clothes is a dharma of purification. By washing away dirt and spreading scented oil on the body, you are clean inside and outside. When you are clean inside and outside, your body, mind, and environs are all clean.

But those who are ignorant and do not hear and practice buddha dharma say, "Although you can wash your skin, you have five main organs and six sub-organs in your body. If you don't wash all your organs, you are not purified." Those who make such a statement have not yet heard and known buddha dharma. They have not encountered an authentic teacher, a descendant of buddha ancestors.

Now, study the true dharma of buddha ancestors, discarding the words of those with outrageously crooked views. The boundary of all phenomena cannot be determined, and the inside and outside of various elements are ungraspable. Thus, the inside and outside of body and mind are ungraspable. However, a bodhisattva of the final body washes the kashaya and cleanses the body and mind before sitting in the place of enlightenment and attaining the way. This is the awesome ritual of buddhas of the past, present, and future in the ten directions. A bodhisattva of the final body has the most venerable and supreme merit, wisdom, body, mind, and splendor, different from others in all aspects. Our way of washing and cleansing should be like that.

A person's body and mind change according to situations and time. A billion worlds can be sat through within a single sitting. Even so, at that very moment the body and mind cannot be measured by self or other. It is the power of buddha dharma. The scale of the body and mind is not five or six feet, because the five or six feet is not unchangeable.

Where the body is neither bounded nor boundless, it is not limited to this world or that world, to the entire world or the immeasurable entire world. As in an old saying, "What is it here? Describe it roughly or in detail."

The scale of mind cannot be known by thinking and discernment, either. It cannot be known by beyond thinking and beyond discernment. The scale of body and mind is like this; so is the scale of cleansing. To take up this scale of cleansing, practicing and realizing it, is what buddhas and ancestors have cared for.

Do not make your scheming self a priority. Do not make your calculating self real. By washing and cleansing, you thoroughly take up the scale of body and mind and purify them. Even the four great elements and five skandhas, and what is indestructible [in the body and mind], can be purified by cleansing.

Do not merely think that rinsing with water makes things clean. How can water be originally pure or impure? Even if water is originally pure or impure, we do not say that water makes the places it reaches pure or impure. Only when you maintain the practice and realization of buddha ancestors, the buddha dharma of washing with water and cleansing with water, is water transmitted. By practicing and realizing in this way, you leap over purity, penetrate impurity, and drop away beyond purity and beyond impurity. In this way, the teaching of washing what is not yet defiled and washing what is greatly pure is maintained in the way of buddha ancestors alone. It is not known by those outside the way.

If the statement by those who are ignorant were true, even if you grind the five organs and six sub-organs into powder, make them into emptiness, and wash them with the entire ocean, how could the body and mind be pure if you don't wash inside the particles? How could you attain purity without washing inside the emptiness? But those who are ignorant don't know the way to cleanse emptiness.

You take up emptiness and wash emptiness, take up emptiness and wash body and mind. If you accept washing with trust in this way, you maintain the practice and realization of buddha ancestors.

When you wash in the true dharma authentically transmitted by buddhas and ancestors, the inside and outside of body and mind, as well as the inside, the outside, and the in-between of the five organs, six sub-organs, body, mind, environs, the world of phenomena, and empty space are immediately cleansed. When you cleanse with incense and flowers, the past, present, future, causes and conditions, actions and effects are immediately purified.

The Buddha said, "After three bathings and three scentings, your body and mind are cleansed."

Thus, the way to purify the body and purify the mind is always scenting yourself at each bath. You continue in this way, make three bathings and three scentings, bow to the Buddha, turn [chant] the sutra, do zazen, and do walking meditation. If you are going to go back to zazen after walking meditation, always wash your feet. Even when your feet are not dirty, it is customary for buddha ancestors to do so.

In the *three bathings and three scentings,* one bathing means to take a bath. The entire body bathes. After that, you put on the robe as usual, burn fine incense, and scent inside the upper part of the robe, the kashaya, and the place of sitting. Then, take another bath and make another scenting. This is practiced three times. This is the way customary in the dharma. It is not that the six sense roots and the six dusts are renewed, but the power of cleansing is actualized. Do not doubt it. In buddha dharma, the virtue of purity is actualized even when the three poisons and four confusions have not been removed.

When you wash yourself with aloeswood, do not break it into pieces or grind it into powder, but use a whole piece to rub your body. In buddha dharma there is a formal way of cleansing the body. Accordingly, cleanse the body, the mind, the feet, the face, the eyes, the mouth, the hands, the head, the eating bowls, and the kashaya, and wash away urine and excrement. This is an authentic way of all buddhas and ancestors in the past, present, and future.

For making offerings to buddha, dharma, and sangha, use various sticks of incense. First, wash the hands, rinse the mouth, and put on clean robes. Pour pure water into a clean basin, wash and purify the incense, and then make offerings to the realm of buddha, dharma, and sangha. May we wash the sandalwood incense from Mount Malaya [in India] with the water of eight virtues from Anavatapta Lake and make offerings to the three treasures!

The way of washing the face was transmitted from India and spread in China. Although it is described as a guideline in the precept scriptures, the transmission of the teaching by buddhas and ancestors [in the Zen tradition] is an authentic way. It has not only been practiced by buddhas and ancestors for hundreds of years, but it has also been widely practiced for billions of eons before and after. Washing the face is not merely removing filth; it is the life vein of buddha ancestors.

According to the guideline, if someone doesn't wash the face, one who bows and one who is bowed to are both at fault. One who bows and one who is bowed to are originally empty, and originally dropped away [free]. Thus, always wash your face.

The time for washing the face is either at the fifth night period or at dawn. When Rujing, my late master, was abbot of the Tiantong Monastery, he designated the last part of the third night period for washing the face.

Wear a one- or two-piece robe, carry a hand towel, and go to the sink for washing the face. The hand towel is a regular-width cloth twelve *shaku* [feet] long. It should not be white. A white cloth is prohibited.

———————

The *Sutra of Three Thousand Guidelines for Pure Conduct* says:

For using a hand towel, there are five guidelines: Dry yourself with the top and bottom ends of it; dry the hands with one end and the face with the other; don't wipe the nose with it; rinse it as if you wipe off filth; don't wipe the entire body with it. Also, take it with you when you bathe.

Guard and maintain your towel in this way. Fold it in two and hang it over your left elbow. Dry the face with one half of it and the hands with the other half. *Don't wipe the nose* means not to wipe inside the nose or wipe off the snivel. You should not wipe the armpits, back, stomach, navel, thighs, or legs with the hand towel.

When it becomes filthy, wash it and dry it over a fire or in the sun. Do not use it for washing your body while bathing.

The sink for washing the face for the cloud hall [monks' hall] is at an added area behind the hall. It is to the west of the illumination hall [study hall]. There is a building plan [that includes this area] transmitted until now. In residential huts and individual quarters, sinks for washing the face are situated in convenient places. The abbot's place for washing the face is situated in the abbot's quarters. Sinks for elder monks and senior teachers are also provided in convenient places. If the abbot sleeps in the cloud hall, he should wash his face at the sink behind the hall.

When you get to the sink, hang the towel around your neck. Pull both ends forward from both sides of the neck, push the ends to the back under your armpits, cross the towel at your back, bring its ends to the front, and tie it on your chest. In this way the lapel of your day robe is covered by the towel and the sleeves are tied up higher than your elbows. The forearms and hands are exposed, just as when you tie a sash [for holding up tucked sleeves].

In case you wash your face at the sink behind the monks' hall, pick up a face-washing basin, get some warm water in the cauldron, and set it in the sink. If you are somewhere else, pour some warm water from the warm wooden tub.

Then, use a willow twig. The way of chewing a willow twig has long been lost and there is no place for using it at monasteries in Great Song China. But we do have a place for using a willow twig at the Kichijo Mountain Eihei Monastery. So this is a current practice.

First, chew a willow twig: Pick one with the right hand and chant a vow.

The "Pure Practice" chapter of the *Avatamsaka Sutra* says:

> Holding a willow twig I vow:
> May all beings attain
> the true dharma and
> experience original purity.

Before chewing the willow twig, chant:

> Chewing a willow twig I vow:
> May all beings attain
> a fang that subdues and
> crushes all delusions.

Then chew the willow twig.

The length of a willow twig can be four, eight, twelve, or sixteen times the thickness of a finger.

Chapter 34 of the *Great Sangha Precepts [Scripture]* says, "Use the tooth sticks according to their length. The longest ones are the length of sixteen fingers thick, and the shortest ones are the length of four fingers thick."

Know that a tooth stick should not be shorter than four fingers thick. Ones that are longer than sixteen fingers thick do not fit. The thickness of a finger means that of the little finger. However, there are no restrictions on how thin the fingers can be [as a measuring standard]. The tooth stick is in the shape of the little finger; one end is thick and the other thin. You chew its thick end thoroughly into fiber.

———

The *Sutra of Three Thousand Guidelines for Pure Conduct* says, "Do not chew more than three *bu* [three tenths of one *sun* (inch)] of it."

You chew the tooth stick repeatedly and brush the surface of the teeth as if you were polishing them. Brush and rinse several times. Mindfully brush the gums also. Brush and clean in between the teeth. With frequent rinsing, your mouth is cleansed. Then scrape the tongue.

The *Sutra of Three Thousand Guidelines for Pure Conduct* says, "There are five guidelines for scraping the tongue: Do not practice excessively; stop when bleeding; do not make a large hand motion that may stain your robe; do not throw away the willow twig and hit someone else; always practice it in a sheltered place."

What is called "three tongue scrapings" means to scrape the tongue while holding water in your mouth three times. It does not mean scraping in three strokes. Remember to stop if you start bleeding. Scrape the tongue thoroughly in this way.

The *Sutra of Three Thousand Guidelines for Pure Conduct* says, "Cleansing the mouth means to chew the willow twig, rinse the mouth, and scrape the tongue."

Thus, buddha ancestors and their descendants have protected and maintained the use of a willow twig.

[The *Wise and Fools Sutra* says:]

Once, the Buddha was with one thousand two hundred fifty monks in the Bamboo Grove of Rajagriha. It was the first day of the twelfth month. King Prasenajit prepared a meal for them. In the early morning he handed a willow twig to the Buddha, who received it, chewed it, and threw the rest onto the ground. It started growing into a tree; its roots and stems emerged thickly. It became five hundred *yojna* high. Its branches and leaves spread like clouds and covered all over. It opened blossoms as large as wheels. It bore fruit as large as jars. Its roots, stems, branches, and leaves were all made of seven treasures, which were extremely beautiful, reflecting and illuminating various colors, overshadowing the sun and the moon. Its fruits were as sweet as nectar and its fragrance permeated everywhere and pleased everyone. When the wind blew, the rustling of its branches and leaves created sublime music and expounded dharma, which no one tired of. Seeing this transformation, all people deepened their faith. The Buddha spoke of dharma in response to the understanding of all those who heard and opened their hearts. A great number of seekers received the buddha fruits and ascended to heaven.

Thus, a way to make an offering to the Buddha is to offer a willow twig in the early morning. Then you offer various things. Although there are many stories about offering a willow twig to the Buddha and letting the Buddha use a willow twig, since you need to know it, I have now presented this story of King Prasenajit's offering, which became a tall tree.

On the same day, six teachers outside the way were defeated by the Buddha and ran away in fright. They all jumped into water and were drowned.

[According to the *Wise and Fools Sutra:*] "Nine hundred million followers of the six teachers outside the way went to see the Buddha and asked him to make them his disciples. The Buddha said, 'Come, monks.' Then, they all became monks with their hair and beards dropped away and their bodies wrapped in dharma robes. The Buddha expounded essential dharma. Their desires being dissolved, they all became arhats."

In this way, because the Tathagata used a willow twig, humans and devas made offering of it to the Tathagata. We clearly know that chewing a willow twig is maintained by buddhas, bodhisattvas, and their disciples. Without using it, the way of using it will be neglected. It would be deplorable not to use it.

––––––––––

The *Indra's Net Bodhisattva Sutra* says:

You, children of the Buddha, should practice asceticism day and night, doing zazen in winter and summer, and participate in a practice period in summer. Always use a willow twig, washing powder, three robes, a jar, bowls, a sitting mat, a walking stick, an incense bowl, a water bag, a towel, a knife, a flint stone, tweezers, a straw mat, sutras, a precept book, a Buddha image, and a bodhisattva image. When you bodhisattvas practice asceticism or wander one or two hundred *li*, you should always carry these eighteen items. Practice asceticism from the fifteenth day of the first month to the fifteenth day of the third month, and from the fifteenth day of the eighth month to the fifteenth day of the tenth month. During these periods carry these eighteen items just like the two wings of a bird.

Do not leave out even one of these eighteen items. If you do not follow this teaching, it would be like a bird missing one of its wings. Even if it has the other wing, it would not be able to fly. Then, it would not be able to follow the path of birds. A bodhisattva is like this. Without being equipped with these eighteen types of wings, the practice of the bodhisattva way would not be possible.

Among the eighteen items, a willow twig is listed first. It is the first thing to carry. Those who clarify the use of a willow twig are bodhisattvas who clarify buddha dharma. Those who do not yet clarify this have not yet dreamed of buddha dharma. This being so, seeing a willow twig is seeing a buddha ancestor.

If someone asks you, "What is the essential matter?" say, "I have fortunately met Old Man Eihei chewing a willow twig."

This bodhisattva precept of the *Indra's Net Bodhisattva Sutra* has been maintained in the past, present, and future by bodhisattvas of the past, present, and future. Thus, a willow twig has been maintained in the past, present, and future.

———

The *Guidelines for Zen Monasteries* says:

The *Indra's Net Bodhisattva Sutra* expounds the ten grave and forty-eight minor precepts. Be familiar with the precepts by reading and chanting them. Know how to maintain them, how not to violate them, how to be open to them, and how to control yourself. Depend on these sacred words uttered by the [Buddha's] golden mouth and do not mistakenly follow mediocre fellows.

Know that the teaching authentically transmitted by buddhas and ancestors is like this. To contradict it is not the buddha way, not buddha dharma, not the ancestral way.

However, willow twigs are not seen in Great Song China nowadays. When I first saw various mountains and monasteries there in the fourth month of the sixteenth year of the Katei Era [1224], monks and people of high and low status in or out of government did not know about willow twigs. As none of the monks knew about them, they would be embarrassed and confused when I asked them about willow twigs. What a pity that the pure dharma has diminished!

Those who cleanse their mouths use a brush. It is made of horse hair cut about one *sun* long and planted like a horse mane in about a two-*sun*-long rectangle on one end of a cow horn, six or seven *sun* long, and three-tenths of a *sun* thick. They wash their teeth with such a brush. It is not suited as a tool for monks. As it is an impure tool, it is not a tool for buddha dharma. Even laypeople who worship devas should avoid such a brush.

Such brushes are also used by monks and laypeople for removing dust from their shoes or brushing their hair. They vary in size but are the same type of tool. Yet, they are only used by one person out of ten thousand.

So, monks and laypeople in Great Song China have bad breath. When they speak, their breath can be smelled two or three *shaku* away, which is hard to bear. Those who call themselves reverend teachers who have attained the way, or guiding masters of humans and devas, are not aware of the way to rinse the mouth, scrape the tongue, and chew a willow twig. The decline of the great way of buddha ancestors is beyond measure.

Risking our dewdroplike life in crossing the ocean of ten thousand *li* and crossing mountains and rivers of a foreign land, we seek the way. However, it is our lamentable fortune to see such a decline of dharma. How much of the pure dharma has perished before us? It is regrettable, truly regrettable.

On the other hand, both monks and laypeople in and out of the imperial court in Japan see and hear about a willow twig. To do so is to hear and see the buddha light. But their way of chewing a willow twig is not in accordance with the way, and the practice of brushing the tongue has not been transmitted; their practice is coarse. Compared with those in Song who don't know about a willow twig, people here are aware of the excellent practice. Sorcerers also use willow twigs. Know that a willow twig is a tool for being away from the dusty world. It is a means for cleansing.

The *Sutra of Three Thousand Guidelines for Pure Conduct* says:

There are five ways for using a willow twig: Cut wood according to the guidelines; crush the willow twig according to guidelines; do not chew more than one-third of the willow twig; for the gum where a tooth is missing, put the willow twig inside the gap and chew it three times; wash your eyes with the rinsing water.

We now cup the water we used for chewing the willow twig in the right hand and rinse the mouth; this comes from the teaching of the *Three Thousand Guidelines for Monks*. This has been taught in Japanese households since olden times.

The way of scraping the tongue was transmitted [from China] by Eisai. Before you discard the willow twig after use, you tear it from its chewed end into two pieces. Place the sharp side of one of the torn pieces onto the tongue and scrape it. Then, put water in your cupped right hand, rinse the mouth, and scrape the tongue several times. You keep scraping with the blade of the torn willow twig almost until the tongue starts to bleed.

When you rinse the mouth, chant this mantra from the *Avatamsaka Sutra* to yourself:

> By my rinsing the mouth and teeth,
> may all beings
> face the gate of pure dharma
> and attain ultimate emancipation.

Rinse a number of times while washing inside the mouth, including the back of the lips, the bottom of the tongue, and the bottom of the upper jaw, with the front tips of the index finger, middle finger, and ring finger, as if you were licking them. If you have just eaten oily food, use acacia powder.

After using the willow twig, discard it behind the screen. Snap your fingers three times after discarding it. There is a bucket for discarded willow twigs at the sink in the back of the monks' hall. Discard it somewhere else in other places. Spit out the water for rinsing the mouth outside the bucket.

———————

Next, wash your face: Scoop up some warm water in the face basin with your hands and wash all over from the forehead, eyebrows, eyes, nostrils, inside the ears, and jaws, to the cheeks. First, take some warm water [with a dipper], and wet and rub all parts. Do not leak saliva or snivel into the water. While washing in this way, do not waste the warm water by overflowing the basin or splattering. Wash your face until it is filthless and the grease is removed. Wash the back of the earlobes so that there is no liquid there. Wash inside the eyelids so that there is no sand in the eyes. Wash the hair and top of the head also. This is a sacred procedure. After washing the face and draining the water, snap your fingers three times.

Then, dry your face with the towel. Wipe it well and dry it completely. After that, untie the towel, fold it in half, and hang it over the left elbow.

At the sink behind the monks' hall, face-washing towels for common use are provided. They are pieces of white cloth. There is also a wooden box with charcoal fire in it [to dry hands]. There is no lack of towels for everyone. Dry your face and head with one. You can also use your own towel.

At the time of washing the face, do not make noise by allowing a dipper to drip, or in any other way. Do not splatter the warm water and wet a nearby place.

Reflect quietly and rejoice that although we live in the last five hundred years [of the three periods of five hundred years after the time of Shakyamuni Buddha] in a faraway island of a remote country, as our wholesome karma from the past has not decayed, we have authentically received the awesome procedure of ancient buddhas, practice it, and realize it without staining it. Walk with light steps and speak quietly while returning to the cloud hall.

The huts for elder practitioners need to have sinks for washing the face. Not to wash the face goes against the guidelines. At the time of washing the face, skin medicine may be used.

————————

Chewing a willow twig and washing the face is the true dharma of ancient buddhas. It should be practiced and realized by those who practice the way with way-seeking heart. If warm water is not available, use cold water, which also is an old way, ancient dharma. When warm or cold water is not available in the early morning, wipe your face thoroughly, spread fragrant herbs or incense powder, then bow to the Buddha, burn incense, chant sutras, and do zazen.

Without washing the face, all the practices would lack authenticity.

Presented to the assembly of the Kannondori Kosho Horin Monastery on the twenty-third day, the tenth month, the first year of En'o Era [1239].

POSTSCRIPT

In India and China, all people, including kings, princes, ministers, officials, laity, monks, noble and ordinary men and women, and farmers, wash their faces. They have face-washing basins in their homes, made of silver or hard tin. They offer washing their faces to the shrines of devas and gods. They offer washing their faces to the stupas of buddha ancestors. Both laypeople and monks, after washing their faces, dress up and bow to devas, gods, ancestors, and parents. They bow to their teachers, the three treasures, myriad spirits in the three realms, and the lords of the ten directions. Nowadays, farmers, rural workers, fishermen, and woodcutters don't forget to wash their faces. Yet, they do not chew willow sticks.

In Japan, the king, ministers, the young and old, the noble and ordinary, laity and monks, don't forget to chew a willow twig and rinse their mouths. But they don't wash their faces. One gain, one loss.

To maintain both washing the face and chewing the willow twig is to fulfill what is lacking. It is the illuminated presence of buddha ancestors.

Presented again to the assembly of the Yoshimine Temple, Yoshida County, Echizen Province, on the twentieth day, the tenth month, the first year of the Kangen Era [1243].

Presented once more to the assembly of the Eihei Monastery, Kichijo Mountain, Yoshida County, Echizen Province, on the eleventh day, the first month, the second year of the Kencho Era [1250].

9

RECEIVING THE MARROW BY BOWING

I N THE PRACTICE of unsurpassable, complete enlightenment, what is most difficult is to find a guiding teacher. The guiding teacher should be a strong person, regardless of being a male or female. The teacher should be a person of thusness, with excellent knowledge and wild fox [transformative] spirit, whether living in the past or present. This is the face [essence] of attaining the marrow, the guiding virtue. This is "not ignoring cause and effect," and "You and I are just this."

After you encounter your guiding teacher, practice diligently in the endeavor of the way, casting off myriad conditions, without sparing a moment. Practice with heart, practice with beyond heart, practice even with half a heart. In this way, brush off the fire on your head [practice with urgency], or stand on your toes [practice intensely].

If you practice in this way, you will not be destroyed by jealous demons; the ancestor [Huike] who cut off his arm and attained the [Bodhidharma's] marrow becomes not other [than you]. The master who drops away body and mind is you yourself.

You attain the marrow and are invariably transmitted dharma through your utmost sincerity and trusting heart. There is no path that comes from anything other than sincere trust; there is no direction that emerges from itself.

Thus, you regard dharma as weighty and your own body as lightly weighted. You retreat from the world and make the way your abode. If you consider your own body weightier than dharma, dharma is not transmitted to you and you will not be able to attain the way.

Although the aspiration for making dharma weighty is not limited to a single path, and does not depend on instructions from others, let me make one or two points.

Regarding dharma as weighty means this: If you encounter someone who maintains the great dharma, having received the acknowledgment—"You have attained my marrow"—whether the person is a pillar or a lantern, a buddha, wild fox, demon, man or woman, you should keep your body and mind on the zazen seat and attend to the person even for immeasurable eons. It is common to attain body and mind, which are just like widely spread rice plants, flax, bamboo, or reed. But it is rare to encounter dharma.

———————

Shakyamuni Buddha said:

In encountering teachers who expound unsurpassable enlightenment, do not consider their caste or facial appearance; do not dislike their shortcomings or judge their activities. Just value their prajna and feed them daily with one hundred or one thousand ounces of gold. Offer them celestial meals. Sprinkle celestial flowers for them. Bow and pay respect to them three times a day, and do not arouse the mind of confusion.

If you act in this way, the path of enlightenment will certainly have a place. This is how I have practiced since I aroused the aspiration for enlightenment, and now I have attained unsurpassable, complete enlightenment.

Thus, look to trees and rocks, fields and villages, to expound dharma. Ask pillars about dharma and investigate with walls.

In the past, Indra bowed to a wild fox to inquire about dharma. This fox was known as a great bodhisattva. This action by Indra was not based on the fox's high or low status of being.

However, foolish people who have not heard buddha dharma call themselves great monks and would not bow to younger ones who have attained dharma. Those who have matured practice over a long period of time would not bow to latecomers who have attained dharma. Those who have certificates as masters would not bow to others who have not been certified. Those who are in charge of dharma matters would not bow to other monks who have attained dharma. Those who are bishops would not bow to laymen and laywomen who have attained dharma. Bodhisattvas of three classes and ten stages would not bow to nuns who have attained dharma. Those who are imperial descendants would not bow to retainers who have attained dharma. Such foolish people have neither seen nor heard the buddha way, just like the one who groundlessly left parents and wandered in another land.

When Zhaozhou, who would later become Great Master Zhenji, of the Tang Dynasty aroused the aspiration for enlightenment and was about to begin a journey, he said to himself, "I will ask about dharma of anyone who surpasses me, even a seven-year-old. I will teach anyone who is behind me, even a one-hundred-year-old."

When asking a seven-year-old about dharma, an old man like Zhaozhou bows. It is an extraordinary aspiration, the mind art of an old buddha.

It is an excellent custom of study that when a nun has attained the way, attained dharma, and started to teach, monks who seek dharma and study join her assembly, bow to her, and ask about the way. It is just like finding water at the time of thirst.

Zhixian [Guanxi] of China was a revered teacher in the lineage of Linji.

Once Linji saw Zhixian approaching and grabbed him. Zhixian said, "I understand it."

Linji let him loose and said, "You are free to have a meal here."

Thus, Zhixian became a student of Linji.

After leaving Linji, he went to see Moshan. She said, "Where are you from?"

Zhixian said, "From the entrance."

Moshan said, "Why don't you close it off?"

Zhixian was silent. He made a bow and expressed himself as a student of Moshan's. Then he asked: "How is Moshan [Mount Mo]?"

Moshan said, "It does not show its peak."

Zhixian said, "Who is the person inside the mountain?"

Moshan said, "It is beyond man and woman."

Zhixian said, "How come you don't change?"

Moshan said, "I am not a wild fox spirit. Why should I change?"

Zhixian bowed. Then he aroused the aspiration for enlightenment and worked as head of the garden for three years.

Later he became the abbot of a monastery and said to the assembly, "I received half a ladle [of gruel] at Old Man Linji's and another half at Old Woman Moshan's. So I had a full ladle and have been satisfied up to this moment."

Now, when we hear this story we long for such an ancient encounter. Moshan was an outstanding student of Gaoan Dayu. Her life vein had the power to become Zhixian's Old Woman. Linji was an heir of Huangbo, Zen Master Xiyun. His endeavor of the way had the power to become Zhixian's Old Man. Old Woman means mother, and Old Man means father.

The fact that Zhixian bowed to Nun Liaoran of Moshan and asked for dharma was an excellent example of aspiration, a model for latecomers. It should be called hammering open the gate bar or breaking through a bamboo node.

Nun Miaoxin was a student of Yangshan. When Yangshan was looking for someone to fill the position of the director of the guesthouse at the foot of Mount Yangshan, he asked his senior students, who had served as officers, to make a recommendation. After some discussion, Yangshan said, "Although Miaoxin is a woman, she has heroic aspiration. She should be suited to serve as the director of the guesthouse."

Everyone agreed, and Miaoxin was appointed to the position. None of Yangshan's other students resented the decision. As it was not a minor position, those who recommended Miaoxin were careful about this selection.

While Miaoxin filled this position, there was a group of seventeen monks from Shu, in the west, who were on the road in search of a master. On their way to climb up to Yangshan's monastery, they stopped and stayed at the guesthouse. While they rested in the evening, they discussed the story about the wind and the banner of Huineng, High Ancestor of Caoxi. The seventeen monks' interpretations were all wrong.

Miaoxin, who overheard the discussion outside the room, said, "How wasteful! How many pairs of straw sandals have these seventeen blind donkeys worn out? They haven't even dreamed of buddha dharma."

Her assistant worker told them that Miaoxin had not approved their understanding. Instead of being upset with her disapproval, the monks were ashamed of their lack of understanding. They got formally dressed, offered incense, bowed, and asked her to teach.

Miaoxin said, "Come closer."

When the seventeen monks were still getting closer, Miaoxin said, "It is not that wind flaps. It is not that the banner flaps. It is not that your mind flaps."

Hearing her words, all seventeen monks had realization. They thanked her and formally became her students. Soon after, they went back to Shu without climbing up to Yangshan's monastery. Indeed, this is nothing the bodhisattvas of three classes or ten stages can come up with. It is work transmitted by buddha ancestors from heir to heir.

Thus, even nowadays when the position of abbot or head monk is not filled, you should request a nun who has attained dharma to assume the position. However aged or senior a monk may be, what's the use of someone who has not attained the way? The master of an assembly should be a person of a clear eye.

Those who are drowned in the body and mind of villagers are often so stubborn that even laypeople may ridicule them. It is not worth mentioning in buddha dharma. Some refuse to bow to female teachers who have received dharma transmission. Because these people lack knowledge and study, they are close to animals and far from buddha ancestors.

If such people are deeply determined to throw their body and mind wholeheartedly into buddha dharma, buddha dharma takes pity on them without fail. Foolish humans and devas still have the capacity to feel the

truth. How should the authentic dharma of all buddhas not have compassion to respond to sincere hearts? Even mud, rocks, sand, and pebbles
have hearts to be affected by sincerity.

Today, nuns stay in monasteries of Great Song. When the attainment
of dharma by one of them is acknowledged and she is appointed abbess
of a nunnery by the government, she ascends the teaching seat in the
monastery where she is staying. All monks, including the abbot, assemble, stand, and listen to her dharma discourse. Some monks ask questions.
This has been the custom since ancient times.

One who has attained dharma is a true authentic buddha and should
not be regarded as the same as before. When we see the person, someone
who is new and extraordinary sees us. When we see the person, today
sees today.

When arhats, pratyeka-buddhas, or bodhisattvas of the three stages
and ten classes come to a nun who maintains the treasury of the true
dharma eye, they should bow and ask about dharma, and she should
receive their bow.

Why are men special? Emptiness is emptiness. Four great elements
are four great elements. Five skandhas are five skandhas. Women are just
like that. Both men and women attain the way. You should honor attainment of the way. Do not discriminate between men and women. This is
the most wondrous principle of the buddha way.

Also, those who are called laity in Song China are people who have
not left their households. Some of them are married and have their
abodes. Others are celibate but may still have much wordly concern.
However, monks with cloud robes and mist sleeves visit laypeople who
have clarified dharma, bow to them, and inquire about the way, just as
they do to masters who have left their households. They should also do
so to accomplished women and even to animals.

On the other hand, even a one-hundred-year-old monk who has not
dreamed of the essentials of buddha dharma cannot be closed to men
and women who have attained dharma. Such a person should not be
respected more than as a host or a guest.

Even seven-year-old girls who practice buddha dharma and express buddha dharma are guiding teachers of the four types of disciples

[monks, nuns, laymen, and laywomen]; they are compassionate parents of sentient beings. They are like dragon princesses who have attained buddhahood. You should make an offering and respect them just as you respect buddha tathagatas. This is an authentic custom of the buddha way. Those who do not know this custom and do not receive it should be pitied.

Written at the Kannondori Kosho Horin Monastery on the clear-bright day [the fifteenth day from spring solstice], the second year of the En'o Era [1240].

POSTSCRIPT

There have been women on the throne in Japan and China. The entire land is ruled by the monarch, and all people become her subjects. This is not done to respect the human form but to respect the position. Since of old, nuns have been respected solely for their attainment of dharma, and not for their human form.

Again, if there is a nun who has become an arhat, all the merits that follow the four fruits come and assemble around her. Who among humans and devas comes close to the merits of the four fruits? No devas in the three realms can equal the merits; none of them are worth as much. So, they all revere the merits.

Furthermore, who would not revere someone who has aroused the great heart of the bodhisattva and received transmission of the Tathagata's authentic dharma? Not to revere such a person is naturally ridiculous. Not to revere your own unsurpassable enlightenment is to foolishly slander dharma.

In Japan, some daughters of the emperor or ministers have positions similar to that of the empress. Some empresses hold Buddhist titles. Some of these women have shaven heads and others don't. Monks who are greedy for fame and love to receive benefits rush to their houses and keep hitting their foreheads on these women's footwear. This is even lower than being their retainers. There are many of those who become their servants and simply grow old. What a pity that they were born in this remote small nation and are not aware that this is a corrupt custom! This does not happen in India or China, but only in our country. It is lamentable.

They shave their faces and heads in vain and break the Tathagata's authentic dharma. It is a serious wrongdoing. It is sad that they forget that the worldly path is made of dreams, phantoms, and empty blossoms, and are bound as servants of these women. They act like this for the sake of a worldly path. Why don't they revere those who should be revered for the sake of unsurpassable enlightenment? They act like this because they have little aspiration to regard dharma as weighty and they are not filled with the aspiration to seek dharma.

When they greedily receive treasures, they think it is justifiable to receive donations, particularly from women. When you seek dharma you should have an aspiration that goes beyond this kind of thinking. If you do so, grass, trees, and walls will give out true dharma; all things in heaven and earth will offer true dharma. This is a principle you should know without fail. Even if you meet a true teacher, if you don't arouse this aspiration to seek dharma, you won't receive the benefit of dharma water. Endeavor thoroughly.

———

Those who are extremely stupid think that women are merely the objects of sexual desire and treat women in this way. The Buddha's children should not be like this. If we discriminate against women because we see them merely as objects of sexual desire, do we also discriminate against all men for the same reason?

For the cause of defilement, men can be the object, women can be the object, those who are neither men nor women can be the object, phantoms and flowers of emptiness can be the object. There were those who were trapped by impure conduct while looking at images on water or gazing at the sun. Gods can be the objects, demons can be the objects. We cannot finish counting all the causes of impure conduct. It is said that there are eighty-four thousand objects. Do we not look at them or discard them all?

The *Precept Scripture* says, "The [sexual] use of one of the two parts of a male body or the three parts of a female body is a grave crime. Those who have committed this crime should be expelled from the sangha."

Thus, if we exclude those who become the objects of sexual desire, we have to exclude all men and women so that they have no chance to be ordained. Thoroughly investigate this.

There are men outside the way who have no wives. Although they don't have wives, if they do not enter buddha dharma, they are those outside the way who hold wrong views.

Among the Buddha's disciples, there are laymen and laywomen who are married. Although they are married, they are the Buddha's disciples; no others among humans and devas can stand shoulder to shoulder with them.

There was a foolish monk who made a vow never to look at a woman, birth after birth, world after world. What was this vow based on—the worldly method, buddha dharma, the outsider's method, or the celestial demon's method?

What is the fault of women? What is the virtue of men? There are unwholesome men, and there are wholesome women. Hoping to hear dharma and leave the household does not depend on being female or male.

Before becoming free from delusion, men and women are equally not free from delusion. At the time of becoming free from delusion and realizing the truth, there is no difference between men and women.

If you vow for a long time not to look at women, do you leave out women when you vow to save numberless sentient beings? If you do so, you are not a bodhisattva. How can you call it the Buddha's compassion? This is merely nonsense spoken by a soaking-drunk shravaka. Humans and devas should not believe in such a practice.

If you exclude those who have broken precepts, you may exclude all bodhisattvas. If you exclude those who may break precepts in the future, you may exclude all bodhisattvas who arouse the aspiration for enlightenment. If you exclude them in such a way, you need to exclude everyone. Then, how can buddha dharma be actualized? To make such vows is the mad intention of fools who don't know buddha dharma. It should be lamented.

If you make such a vow [as not looking at women], is it that Shakyamuni Buddha and all bodhisattvas in his lifetime had broken precepts? Was their aspiration for enlightenment shallower than yours? Quietly ponder this.

Was it not possible for the ancestor who was entrusted with dharma [Mahakashyapa] and all bodhisattvas during the Buddha's lifetime to practice unless they made such a vow? With such a vow, not only are you unable to awaken women, you are also unable to go and hear women who have attained dharma and expound dharma for humans and devas. If you don't go and hear them teach, you are not bodhisattvas but those outside the way.

When we look at Great Song China, there are monks who seem to have trained for a long time merely counting the sands in the ocean [studying letters] and wandering around in the ocean of birth and death. On the other hand, there are women who have studied with teachers, endeavored in the way, and become guiding teachers of humans and devas.

There was an old woman who refused to sell a rice cake [to Deshan] and discarded it. What a pity, there are male monks who count the sands in the ocean of teaching and have never dreamed of buddha dharma!

When you see an object, learn to clarify it. Being scared of it and only trying to avoid it is the teaching and practice of shravakas in the Lesser Vehicle. If you give up the east and hide in the west, it is not that there is no object in the west. Even if you keep escaping, there are objects afar and objects nearby. This is not the way of emancipation. The farther away you push objects, the deeper you may be attached to them.

———————

There is one ridiculous custom in Japan. This is called a "secluded area" or "a Mahayana practice place," where nuns and laywomen are not allowed to enter. This crooked custom has been going on for a long time, and people do not think about it. Those who study ancient teachings do not try to change it. Those who study extensively do not question it.

This custom is sometimes advocated as the avatar's establishment or the ancient sage's style, without being challenged. If we laughed about it, our stomachs would be exhausted.

Who is the avatar—a wise person, a sage, a god, or a demon? Is it a bodhisattva of the ten stages or three classes? Is it a bodhisattva of enlightenment equal to buddhas, or one of wondrous enlightenment? Or, do people believe that they cannot be free from the transmigration of birth and death unless they change authentic customs?

In fact, Great Master Shakyamuni attained unsurpassable, complete enlightenment and clarified all that needed to be clarified. He practiced all that needed to be practiced. He was emancipated from all that needed emancipation. Who nowadays can even come close to him?

In the assembly of the Buddha since his lifetime, there are four types of disciples—monks, nuns, laymen, and laywomen. There are also eight types of guardian deities, thirty-seven wings of enlightenment, and eighty-four thousand dharma gates. They all form buddha realms, creating buddha assemblies. Which of these assemblies lacks nuns, laywomen, laymen, or the eight types of guardian deities?

Do not look for a secluded area that is purer than the buddha assemblies that existed while the Buddha was alive. Such a secluded area is a place of heavenly demons. The rules for a buddha assembly do not vary between this world and that, or one thousand buddhas in the past, present, and future. Know that to have different rules is not a buddha assembly.

The so-called four fruits are the ultimate ranks. Both in Mahayana and Hinayana the merits of the four fruits are not differentiated. When a number of nuns realize the four fruits, there is no place in the three realms or in the buddha land of the ten directions that they cannot reach. Who can block their practice?

Having wondrous enlightenment is an unsurpassable stage. When women become buddhas of this stage, what in all directions cannot be thoroughly experienced? Who can try to block them and keep them from arriving at this stage? They attain the power of broadly illuminating all the ten directions. What is the point of creating a secluded area?

Or, do you want to block heavenly women and keep them from getting to this secluded area? Do you also want to block goddesses and keep them from getting to this secluded area? Heavenly women and goddesses are those who have not yet become free from delusions. They are still sentient beings who transmigrate. Sometimes they break precepts and sometimes they don't. Human females and animal females also at times break precepts, and at times don't. Who is going to block the way of heavenly women and goddesses? They join the buddha assemblies of the past, present, and future and practice at the buddha places. If there are places different from the buddha places and buddha assemblies, who can trust them as places of buddha dharma? Such secluded areas are of utmost stupidity and only confuse worldly people. It is more foolish than foxes who try to protect their holes from humans.

The ranks of the Buddha's disciples, either bodhisattvas or shravakas, are: first, monks; second, nuns; third, laymen; and fourth, laywomen. This status has long been known among devas and humans. The second-ranking disciples of the Buddha are higher than a wheel-turning king or Indra. There is no place these disciples cannot go. Their high status cannot be compared to that of kings or ministers of a small country in a remote land.

When I look at practice places that do not allow nuns, I see that men who are country people, farmers, and woodcutters still go in freely. None of the kings, ministers, government officers, and prime ministers are prohibited from entering.

Who, including farmers and these others, can compare to nuns in terms of the practice of the way and attainment of ranks [of the disciples of the Buddha]? Whether it is debated on the basis of worldly law or the buddha dharma, country people should not enter where nuns enter.

The basis for a "secluded area" is an extreme confusion. This custom was initiated in our small country. What a pity that children of the compassionate father [the Buddha] of the three realms are blocked from entering some places in this country!

Some of those who live in the so-called secluded areas do not avoid the ten unwholesome actions and commit the ten grave offenses. Is it that these areas are criminal places and those who do not commit crimes are excluded? Furthermore, the five grave crimes are regarded as the most serious of unwholesome actions. Those who live in the secluded areas may also commit such crimes. Such demon realms should be opened up. If they study the Buddha's teaching and enter the Buddha's world, it will certainly be an act to return the kindness of the Buddha.

Were the ancient teachers who built the secluded areas aware of the meaning of creating it? From whom did they receive such a teaching? Whose seal of approval did they have?

Buddhas, sentient beings, the great earth, vast space, who enter the great area established by all buddhas, are liberated from bondage and return to the source that is buddhas' wondrous dharma. This being so, sentient beings who step into this area even once receive the buddha merit. It is the merit of not veering off and attaining purity.

When one place of practice is established, all the worlds of phenomena are established. When it is once established, all the worlds of phenomena are established. There is an area of practice established with water. There is an area established with mind. There is also an area established with emptiness. This is something to be transmitted from person to person.

To establish an area of practice, after sprinkling nectar water, taking refuge [in the three treasures], and purifying the ground, we chant a verse: "This area and all worlds of phenomena have been purely established." Do senior monks who talk about the secluded areas know the meaning of this phrase?

I suppose they don't understand that in establishing an area of practice, all worlds of phenomena are established. Perhaps they are intoxicated with the wine of shravakas and regard a small area as a great area. I hope they will quickly come out of their everyday intoxication and merge with the worlds of phenomena that are a great area of all buddhas.

All sentient beings should bow to and revere the merit of receiving the [Buddha's] broad offering of awakening. Who would not call it the marrow of attaining the way?

IO

VALLEY SOUNDS, MOUNTAIN COLORS

IN THE TRANSMISSION of unsurpassable, complete enlightenment by numberless buddha ancestors, various practices have arisen. Study such examples as ancient practitioners crushing their bones and Huike chopping off his arm. Embody in yourself the dedication of a boy spreading his hair on muddy ground for the Buddha to walk on.

Slipping out of your old skin, not constrained by past views, you manifest immediately what has been dormant for boundless eons. As this very moment manifests, "I" don't know, "who" doesn't know, "you" have no expectations, and "the buddha eye" sees beyond seeing. This experience is beyond the realm of human thinking.

In Song China there was a man who called himself Layman Dongpo. He was originally named Shi of the Su family, and his initiatory name was Zidan. A literary genius, he studied the way of dragons and elephants in the ocean of awakening. He descended deep chasms and soared freely through clouds.

One night when Dongpo visited Mount Lu, he was enlightened upon hearing the sound of the valley stream. He composed the following verse, which he presented to Changzong:

> Valley sounds are the long, broad tongue.
> Mountain colors are no other than the
> unconditioned body.
> Eighty-four thousand verses are heard through
> the night.
> What can I say about this in the future?

Seeing this verse, Changzong approved his understanding.

Changzong, also called Zen Master Zhaojiao, was a dharma heir of Huanglong, Zen Master Huinan, who was a dharma heir of Chuyuan, Zen Master Ciming.

Another time when Dongpo met with Liaoyuan, Zen Master Foyin, Liaoyuan transmitted the buddha precepts to him with a dharma robe, which Dongpo later wore when practicing. Dongpo presented Liaoyuan with a jeweled belt. People talked about this exchange as something extraordinary.

The valley sounds of Dongpo would refresh practitioners of later generations. How sad for those who miss the dharma of the manifested buddha body! How are mountain colors seen and valley sounds heard otherwise? Are mountain colors and valley sounds one phrase or half a phrase? Are they eighty-four thousand verses of scripture? You may regret that mountains and waters conceal sounds and colors, but you may also rejoice that the moment of enlightenment emerges through mountains and waters.

The tongue [of the Buddha] does not take a break. The colors are beyond coming and going. Are the sounds and colors intimate when they are apparent, or are they intimate when they are obscured? Are they one whole expression or half an expression? During past springs and autumns, Dongpo had not seen or heard the mountains and waters. He saw and heard them for the first time that night. Bodhisattvas who study the way, open your minds to mountains flowing and to water not flowing.

Dongpo had this awakening soon after he heard Changzong talk about insentient beings speaking dharma. Although Dongpo did not leap when he heard Changzong's words, towering billows flew into the sky upon his hearing the sounds of the valley. Was it the valley sounds or the tide of awakening that jolted Dongpo?

I suspect that Changzong's voices of insentient beings speaking dharma are resounding even now, still blended with the sounds of the night's stream. Who can fathom this water? Is it a bucketful or does it fill whole oceans?

In the end let me ask you: Was it Dongpo who was awakened or the mountains and waters that were awakened? Who today sees right away with a clear eye the long, broad tongue and the unconditioned body [of the Buddha]?

————————

Xiangyan Zhixian studied at the assembly of Guishan Lingyou, Zen Master Dayuan, on Mount Gui.

Guishan said, "You are bright and knowledgeable. Say something about yourself before your parents were born, but don't use words learned from commentaries."

Xiangyan tried and tried but could not say anything. He pored through many books he had collected over the years but could not come up with anything. Deeply ashamed, he burned the books and said, "A painting of a rice cake does not satisfy hunger. I will be just a cooking monk, not expecting to understand buddha dharma in this lifetime."

A cooking monk means one who supports the assembly by cooking rice, an equivalent of a kitchen assistant in our country. He followed this vow for years.

One day Xiangyan said to Guishan, "My mind is undifferentiated; I cannot speak. Can you speak for me, Master?"

Guishan said, "I wouldn't mind explaining it to you, but if I did, you would resent me in the future."

Sometime later, Xiangyan went to the memorial site of Nanyang Huizhong, National Teacher Dazheng, at Mount Wudang, and built himself a hut. For company, he planted some bamboo.

One day, while he was sweeping the path, a pebble flew up and struck a bamboo. At the unexpected sound, Xiangyan had thorough awakening. After bathing and cleansing himself, he faced Mount Gui, offered incense, prostrated himself, and said, "Master, if you had spoken for me at that time, this could not have happened. Your kindness is deeper than my parents'." Then he wrote a poem:

> One stroke dissolves knowledge.
> Struggle no longer needed.
> I will follow the ancient path
> not lapsing into quietude.
> Noble conduct beyond sound and form—
> no trace anywhere.
> Those who have mastered the way
> may call this an unsurpassable activity.

He presented this poem to Guishan, who said, "This fellow has gone through."

One spring day, after practicing for thirty years, Lingyun, who would later become Zen Master Zhiqin, walked into the mountains. While resting he saw peach blossoms in full bloom in a distant village and was suddenly awakened. He wrote this poem, which he presented to Guishan:

> For thirty years I have looked for a sword
>   master.
> Many times leaves fell, new ones sprouted.
> One glimpse of peach blossoms—
> now no more doubts, just this.

Guishan said, "One who enters with ripened conditions will never leave." He approved Lingyun in this way.

Who does not enter with ripened causes? Who enters and then goes away? This awakening is not limited to Lingyun. If mountain colors were not the unconditioned body, how could this awakening have occurred? This is how he inherited dharma from Guishan.

Once a monk asked Changsha, Zen Master Jingcen, "How do you turn mountains, rivers, and the great earth into the self?"

Changsha said, "How do you turn the self into mountains, rivers, and the great earth?"

Saying that the self returns to the self is not contradicted by saying that the self is mountains, rivers, and the great earth.

Langye Huijue, Great Master Guangzhao, was a dharma descendant of Nanyue. Once Zhixuan, a lecturer on scriptures, asked Langye, "If originally unconditioned, how do mountains, rivers, and the great earth suddenly emerge?"

Langye responded, "If originally unconditioned, how do mountains, rivers, and the great earth suddenly emerge?"

Now we know. Mountains, rivers, and the great earth, which are originally unconditioned, should not be mistaken for mountains, rivers, and the great earth. The sutra master had never heard this, so he did not understand mountains, rivers, and the great earth as just mountains, rivers, and the great earth.

Know that without mountain colors and valley sounds, [Shakyamuni Buddha's] taking up the flower and [Huike's] attaining the marrow would not have taken place. Because of the power of valley sounds and mountain colors, the Buddha with the great earth and sentient beings simultaneously attains the way, and countless buddhas become enlightened upon seeing the morning star. Such skin bags are earlier sages whose aspiration for seeking dharma is profound. People today should be inspired by predecessors like these. Authentic study, free of concern for fame and gain, should be based on such aspiration.

In this remote nation in recent days those who genuinely seek buddha dharma are rare—it is not that there are none. Many people leave their households, appearing free from worldly matters, but in fact they use the buddha way to seek fame and gain. What a pity! How sad that they waste their time in unilluminated trades! When will they break away and attain the way? If they meet a true teacher, how will they recognize the true dragon?

Rujing, my late master, Old Buddha, called such people "pitiful fel-lows." Because of unwholesome causes in previous lives, they do not seek dharma for the sake of dharma. In this life, they are suspicious of the true dragon when they see it, and are put off by genuine dharma when they encounter it. As their body, mind, flesh, and bones are not ready to follow dharma, they are unable to receive it. Because the lineage of the ancestral school started long ago, the aspiration for enlightenment has become a distant dream. How pitiful that people do not know about or see treasure even though they were born on a mountain of treasure! Where can they find dharma treasure?

———

As soon as you arouse the aspiration for enlightenment, even if you transmigrate in the six realms and four forms of birth, transmigration itself will be your vow for enlightenment. Although you may have wasted time so far, you should vow immediately, before this present life ends:

Together with all sentient beings, may I hear the true
    dharma from this birth throughout future births.
When I hear the true dharma, I will not doubt or distrust it.
When I encounter the true dharma, I will relinquish
    ordinary affairs and uphold the buddha dharma.
Thus, may I realize the way together with the great earth
    and all sentient beings.

This vow is the ground for genuine aspiration. Do not slacken in this determination.

———

Japan is a remote land where people are extremely ignorant. Neither sages nor geniuses have been known to arise here, and genuine students of the way are rare. When we talk about way-seeking mind, those with-out it become resentful instead of reflecting on themselves.

When you arouse the aspiration for enlightenment, try to keep your practice private. Praising your own practice is out of the question. Peo-ple nowadays rarely seek the truth. Deficient in practice and realization, they seek recognition for their effort and want others to acknowledge that their practice and understanding are in accord. This is delusion on top of delusion. Abandon such confused thinking.

Among those who study the way, it is rare to find determination for true dharma. Such determination is the buddha radiance, the buddha mind, which has been transmitted from buddha to buddha.

From the time of the Tathagata to this day, there have been many concerned with fame and gain in the study of the way. But if they meet a true master and turn toward true dharma, they will readily attain the way. Know that there is a disease for fame and gain among practitioners of the way. Among beginners as well as longtime practitioners, some have the opportunity to receive the teaching, while others don't. Some long for the ancient way, but there are also demons who slander the teaching. Do not be attached or upset in either case. When you remember how few realize the three poisons as the three poisons, you no longer have resentment.

Do not forget the joyful aspiration that arises when you first seek the way. When you arouse the aspiration for enlightenment, you do not seek dharma in order to be respected by others. You abandon fame and gain, and without veering off you aspire to attain the way. You do not look for respect or gifts from kings or ministers. Even though these may come to you, it should not be your primary intention to become entangled with humans and devas. But foolish people, even those with way-seeking mind, quickly forget their original aspiration and hope for offerings from humans and devas. Receiving such offerings, they rejoice that the merit of buddha dharma has arrived. When kings and ministers come to take refuge in the buddha, foolish teachers may feel rewarded. This is a hazard of practice. Remember to have compassion for them, but do not rejoice.

Do you recall that the Buddha said these golden words? "Even now, at the time of the Tathagata, there are many who are antagonistic." Thus, foolish people do not understand the wise; small-minded ones regard great sages as enemies.

Also, the ancestors in India were sometimes overpowered by kings, those outside the way, or practitioners of the Two Lesser Vehicles. It was not that the ancestors lacked deep understanding or that those others excelled.

When Bodhidharma came from India and stayed at Mount Song, neither the Emperor of Liang nor the Emperor of Wei understood him. At that time there were two critics, Scripture Master Bodhiruchi and Precept Master Guangtong. They were afraid they would lose their fame and gain to a true teacher, so they tried to block him. It was as if they were trying to cover the sun. They were worse than Devadatta, who lived at the time of the Buddha. What a pity! The fame and gain they were attached to would have been discarded like excrement by Bodhidharma. This behavior was the result of their lack of understanding buddha dharma. They were like dogs barking at a well-intentioned person.

Do not resent such dogs, but vow to guide them with this blessing: "Dogs, arouse the aspiration for enlightenment." An old sage said, "There are animals who have human faces." On the other hand, there are demons who take refuge in the Buddha and make offerings to him.

———————

An earlier buddha said, "Do not get close to kings, princes, ministers, administrators, Brahmans, and laypeople."

Practitioners should remember this admonition so that, as their practice advances, the merit of their bodhisattva effort with beginner's mind will accumulate.

———————

There are stories of Indra, who came down to test the aspiration of a practitioner, or of the demon Papiyas, who obstructed people's practice. Such things happen when practitioners cannot free themselves from desire for fame and gain. But such things do not happen to those who have great compassion and whose vow to guide sentient beings is vast and mature.

Through the merit of practice you may be given the gift of an entire nation, and this may appear to be a great achievement in the world. But do not be blinded; look deeply on such an occasion. Foolish people may rejoice, but they are like dogs licking a dry bone. Wise people and sages reject this just as worldly people are disgusted by excrement.

———————

In general, when you are a beginner you cannot fathom the buddha way. Your assumptions do not hit the mark. The fact that you cannot fathom the buddha way as a beginner does not mean that you lack ultimate understanding, but it does mean that you do not recognize the deepest point.

Endeavor wholeheartedly to follow the path of earlier sages. You may have to climb mountains and cross oceans when you look for a teacher to inquire about the way. Look for a teacher and search for understanding with all-encompassing effort, as if you were coming down from heaven or emerging from the ground. When you encounter a true teacher, you invoke sentient beings as well as insentient beings. You hear with the body, you hear with the mind.

To hear with the ear is an everyday matter, but to hear with the eye is not always so. When you see buddha, you see self-buddha, other-buddha, a large buddha, a small buddha. Do not be frightened by a large buddha. Do not be put off by a small buddha. Just see large and small buddhas as valley sounds and mountain colors, as a broad, long tongue, and as eighty-four thousand verses. This is liberation, this is outstanding seeing.

There is a common saying that expresses this: "Totally superb, totally solid." An earlier buddha said: "It covers heaven, it encompasses the earth." This is the purity of a spring pine, the magnificence of an autumn chrysanthemum. Just this.

When you reach this realm, you are a master of humans and devas. If you teach others before arriving in this realm, you will do great harm to them. Without knowing the spring pine or the autumn chrysanthemum, how can you nourish others and how can you cut through their roots of confusion?

When you are lazy or doubtful, repent before the buddhas with a sincere mind. If you do so, the power of repentance will purify and help you. This power will nurture trust and effort free from hindrance. Once pure trust emerges, self and others are simultaneously turned. This benefit reaches both sentient and insentient beings.

Repentance is: "Although my past unwholesome actions have accumulated, causing hindrance in the study of the way, may buddhas and ancestors release me from these actions and liberate me. May the merit of practicing dharma fill inexhaustible worlds of phenomena. May compassion be extended to me."

Before awakening, buddha ancestors were like you. Upon awakening, you will become buddha ancestors. When you look at buddha ancestors, you are a buddha ancestor. When you look at their aspiration for enlightenment, you have the aspiration. Working with compassion this way and that, you achieve facility and you let facility drop away.

Thus, Longya said:

> If you did not attain enlightenment in the past, do so now.
> Liberate this body that is the culmination of many lifetimes.
> Before enlightenment, ancient buddhas were like us.
> When enlightened, we will be like those of old.

This is the understanding of a realized buddha. We should reflect on it. This is the exact point of a realized buddha.

With repentance you will certainly receive invisible help from buddha ancestors. Repent to the buddhas with mind and body. The power of repentance melts the roots of unwholesomeness. This is the single color of true practice, the true heart of trust, the true body of trust.

———

When you have true practice, then valley sounds and colors, mountain colors and sounds, all reveal the eighty-four thousand verses. When you are free from fame, profit, body, and mind, the valleys and mountains are also free. Through the night the valley sounds and mountain colors do and do not actualize the eighty-four thousand verses. When your capacity to talk about valleys and mountains as valleys and mountains is not yet mature, who can see and hear you as valley sounds and mountain colors?

On the fifth day of the practice period, the second year of the En'o Era [1240], this was presented to the assembly of the Kannondori Kosho Horin Monastery.

11

REFRAIN FROM UNWHOLESOME ACTION

ANCIENT BUDDHAS SAY:

> Refrain from unwholesome action.
> Do wholesome action.
> Purify your own mind.
> This is the teaching of all buddhas.

This teaching has been authentically transmitted from earlier buddhas to later buddhas of the future as the Seven Original Buddhas' general precepts in the ancestral school. Later buddhas received these precepts from earlier buddhas. This teaching is not limited to the Seven Original Buddhas; it is the teaching of all buddhas. Thoroughly investigate this point.

This dharma way of the Seven Original Buddhas is always the dharma way of the Seven Original Buddhas. Transmitting and receiving these precepts is a mutual activity. This is the teaching of all buddhas—the teaching, practice, and enlightenment of hundreds, thousands, and myriads of buddhas.

Unwholesome action is [the manifestation of] one of the three natures: the wholesome action nature, the unwholesome action nature, and the neutral nature. The unwholesome action nature is unborn, just as the wholesome action nature and neutral nature are unborn. These three natures are also nondefiled and are reality. However, these three natures are manifested in various ways.

As for unwholesome action, unwholesome action in this world and unwholesome action in other worlds are sometimes the same and sometimes different. Unwholesome action in former times and unwholesome action in the present time are sometimes the same and sometimes different. Unwholesome action in the deva world and unwholesome action in the human world are sometimes the same and sometimes different. Furthermore, there is a great difference between the buddha way and the worldly realm in what is called unwholesome action, wholesome action, or neutral action. Wholesome action and unwholesome action are time, although time is neither wholesome action nor unwholesome action. Wholesome action and unwholesome action are dharma, although dharma is neither wholesome action nor unwholesome action. As dharma is all-inclusive, unwholesome action is all-inclusive. As dharma is all-inclusive, wholesome action is all-inclusive.

When you listen, study, practice, and realize unsurpassable, complete enlightenment, it is deep, vast, and wondrous. You learn this unsurpassable enlightenment either by following a teacher or by following a sutra. First you understand it as *refrain from unwholesome action*. If you do not understand it as *refrain from unwholesome action*, it is not true buddha dharma, but the speech of demons. Know that to understand unsurpassable enlightenment as *refrain from unwholesome action* is the true buddha dharma.

Refrain from unwholesome action. This is not what ordinary people first interpret it to mean, although it may sound like it when we hear enlightenment expounded as a teaching of enlightenment. We understand in this way because it is an expression of unsurpassable enlightenment. It is words of enlightenment, therefore it is spoken enlightenment. Moved by what is spoken and heard—unsurpassable enlightenment—you vow to refrain from unwholesome action and practice refraining from unwholesome action.

When you refrain from unwholesome action, the power of practice is immediately actualized. This is actualized on the scale of the entire earth, the entire universe, all time, and all dharmas. This is the scale of *refrain from*.

This very person at this very moment abides in the place, comes from it, and goes to it, where no unwholesome action is created. No unwholesome action is created, although the person appears to be faced with the conditions of creating unwholesome action or of associating with those who create unwholesome action.

When the power of *refrain from* is actualized, unwholesome action does not manifest as unwholesome action. Unwholesome action has no fixed form. You can pick it up or let it go. At the moment we understand this, we know that unwholesome action does not overcome a person and a person does not destroy unwholesome action.

————————

When you arouse your entire mind and let it practice, and when you arouse your entire body and let it practice, eight or nine out of ten are accomplished before questioning, and *refrain from unwholesome action* is actualized after knowing. When you bring forth your body-mind and practice, and when you bring forth the body-mind and practice of others, the power of practice with the four elements and the five skandhas is immediately actualized. Without defiling the self of the four elements and the five skandhas, the four elements and the five skandhas of today are practiced. The power of the four elements and the five skandhas practiced at this moment actualizes the practice of the four elements and the five skandhas in the past.

When you move mountains, rivers, and earth, as well as the sun, the moon, and stars to practice, they in return move you to practice. This is not the open eye of just one time, but the vital eye of all times. Because it is all the open eye, the vital eye of all times, you move all buddhas and all ancestors to practice, to listen to the teaching, and to realize the fruit.

Since all buddhas and ancestors have not allowed the teaching, practice, and enlightenment to be divided, the teaching, practice, and enlightenment have not hindered all buddhas and ancestors. For this reason, when you move buddhas and ancestors to practice, none of them are separated from before or after your realization, either in the past, present, or future. At the time when sentient beings become buddhas and ancestors, they become buddhas and ancestors without hindering the buddhas and ancestors who already exist. Ponder this point closely while walking, abiding, sitting, and lying down throughout the twelve hours of the day. It is not that a sentient being is destroyed, taken away, or lost by becoming a buddha ancestor, but a sentient being is dropped away.

You allow the cause and effect of wholesome and unwholesome actions to practice. It is not that you put cause and effect into action or that you create cause and effect, but cause and effect at times allow you to practice.

The original face of cause and effect is already clear. Because this is dropping away, it is *refrain from*, unborn, impermanent, not ignoring, and not dropping.

When you study in this way, you realize that unwholesome action is none other than *refrained from*. Assisted by this realization, you see through, and by sitting you cut through refraining from unwholesome action.

At the beginning, middle, and end, as refraining from unwholesome action is actualized, then unwholesome action does not arise through causes and conditions. It is just *refrain from*. Unwholesome action does not cease through causes and conditions. It is just *refrain from*. As unwholesome action is all-inclusive, all dharmas are all-inclusive.

Those who only know that unwholesome action arises through causes and conditions and do not see that causes and conditions themselves are *refrain from* should be pitied. Because buddha seeds come forth through conditions, conditions come forth through buddha seeds.

It is not that unwholesome action does not exist, but it is just *refrain from*. It is not that unwholesome action does exist, it is just *refrain from*. Unwholesome action is not emptiness, but it is just *refrain from*. Unwholesome action is not form, but it is just *refrain from*.

Unwholesome action is not *refrain from*, it is just *refrain from*. For example, a spring pine is neither nonexistent nor existent. It is *refrain from*. Autumn chrysanthemum is neither nonexistent nor existent. It is *refrain from*. All buddhas are neither nonexistent nor existent. They are *refrain from*. Pillars, lanterns, whisk, and staff are neither existent nor nonexistent. They are *refrain from*. Self is neither existent nor nonexistent. It is *refrain from*.

Studying in this way actualizes the fundamental point. The fundamental point is actualized. Investigate this through host [self] and investigate this through guest [other].

Since this is so, regretting that you have created what should not be created is also inevitably the practice of *refrain from*. Nevertheless, intending to create unwholesome action just because you hear that unwholesome action is *refrain from* is just like walking north to try to get to the southern county of Yue.

Refrain from and *unwholesome action* are not only "the well seeing the donkey," but also the well seeing the well [inseparable from each other], the donkey seeing the donkey, the person seeing the person, the mountain seeing the mountain. Just as we speak in this way, *unwholesome action* is *refrain from*.

It is said, "Buddha's true dharma body is like the empty sky. It manifests forms responding to conditions just like the moon reflected in the water." Because it is *refrain from* that responds to things, it is *refrain from* that manifests forms. It is just like emptiness that claps toward the left and toward the right [without hindrance], like the moon reflected in water. The moon is fully immersed in the water. In this way *refrain from* is actualized without doubt.

Do wholesome action. This wholesome action is [manifestation of] one of the three natures. Although there are many varieties of wholesome action, there is no wholesome action that is already actualized and waiting for someone to practice it. At the very moment of doing wholesome action, there is no wholesome action that does not come forth.

Although myriads of wholesome actions are formless, they arrive at the place where wholesome action is done faster than a magnet drawing iron. Its power is stronger than a vairambhaka storm. The great earth, mountains, rivers, the lands of the world, or the increasing effect of action cannot hinder the intentional encounter of wholesome action.

However, there is a principle that views of wholesome action vary in the world. The views define what is wholesome action. It is just the same as all buddhas in the past, present, and future expounding dharma. Buddhas expounding dharma while they are in the world is just time. They expound nondiscriminating dharma according to their life spans and the dimensions of their bodies.

This being so, wholesome action by a person who practices trust is far different from wholesome action by a person who practices dharma. Nevertheless, they are not two separate dharmas. It is like a shramana's keeping the precepts and a bodhisattva's breaking the precepts.

Wholesome action does not arise due to causes and conditions, nor does it cease due to causes and conditions. Although wholesome action is all phenomena, all phenomena are not wholesome action. Causes and conditions, as well as wholesome actions, equally begin in completeness and end in completeness.

Although wholesome action is *do*, it is not self, and not known by the self. It is not other, and not known by other. In knowing, there is self and other. In seeing, there is self and other. Thus, the vital eye of each is within the sun and within the moon.

This is *do*. At the very moment of *do*, the fundamental point is actualized. Yet, it is not the beginning or the end of the fundamental point. It is not the eternal abiding of the fundamental point. Should this not be called *do*?

Although practicing wholesome action is *do*, it cannot be discerned. Although this *do* is a vital eye, it cannot be discerned. *Do* is not actualized for the sake of discernment. Discernment by the vital eye is not the same as discernment by something else.

Wholesome action is neither existent nor nonexistent, neither form nor emptiness. It is just *do*. Actualizing at any place or actualizing at any moment is inevitably *do*. This *do* always actualizes all that is wholesome action. Although actualizing *do* is the fundamental point, it is neither arising nor ceasing, neither causes nor conditions. The entering, abiding, and departing of *do* is also like this. When one wholesome action among all wholesome actions is *do*, all things, the whole body, and the true ground altogether are moved to *do*.

Both cause and effect of wholesome action actualize the fundamental point through *do*. Cause is not before and effect is not after. Cause is complete and effect is complete. Cause is all-inclusive just as dharma is all-inclusive. Effect is all-inclusive just as dharma is all-inclusive. Although effect is experienced, induced by cause, one is not before and the other is not after. We say that both before and after are all-inclusive.

———

Purify your own mind. This means that you *refrain from*. Purify through *refrain from*. You that is *your own*. You that is *mind*. *Your own* that refrains from. Mind that refrains from. Mind that does. Purify through *do*. Your own *do*. You *do*. This is the teaching of all buddhas.

Buddhas are like Shiva [creator of the world]. While the spirits of Shiva are sometimes the same and sometimes different, they are not necessarily buddhas. Buddhas are also like wheel-turning kings. However, not all the wheel-turning kings are necessarily buddhas. Investigate and study this point. Those who do not examine what buddhas are may appear to strive with great effort, but they are sentient beings who only suffer and are not practitioners of the buddha way. Refraining from [unwholesome action] and doing [wholesome action] are like "The donkey has not left, yet the horse has arrived."

Bai Zhuyi of the Tang Dynasty was the lay student of Ruman, Zen Master Fuguang, and a dharma descendant of Mazu, Zen Master Daji of Jiangxi.

When he was governor of Hang province, he studied with Zen Master Daolin of Niaoke.

One day Zhuyi said, "What is the essential meaning of buddha dharma?"

Daolin said, "Refrain from unwholesome action, do wholesome action."

Zhuyi said, "If that is so, a three-year-old child could say it."

Daolin said, "A three-year-old child may say this, but even an eighty-year-old person cannot practice it."

Zhuyi bowed in gratitude and left.

Zhuyi, a descendant of General Bai, was an extraordinary poet. He was regarded as a man of letters who had lived twenty-four lifetimes as a poet. He was sometimes called Manjushri or Maitreya. There was no place he was not known and no place his writing did not circulate.

However, he was a beginner and a latecomer in the buddha way. It seems that he had never dreamed of the true meaning of *refrain from unwholesome action* and *do wholesome action*. He thought that Daolin presented this phrase in a merely intellectual way. Zhuyi had not heard and did not know that *refrain from unwholesome action* and *do wholesome action* are teachings of the buddha way, which are thousands and myriads of years old and apply to now and then. He responded in the way he did because he was not standing in the buddha dharma and did not understand the buddha dharma.

Even if you caution against doing unwholesome action by intention, and encourage doing wholesome action by intention, you actualize *refrain from*. On the whole, in the buddha dharma, what you first hear from a teacher and what you finally achieve are the same. This is called genuine from head to tail. It is also called "inconceivable cause, inconceivable effect," or "buddha cause, buddha effect." Cause and effect in the buddha way is neither a heterogeneous maturing nor a homogenous stream. Since this is so, without buddha cause, buddha effect cannot be experienced. Because Daolin expressed this essential teaching, it was buddha dharma.

Even if unwholesome action fills worlds upon worlds, and swallows up all things upon all things, *refrain from* is emancipation. Wholesome action is wholesome action in the beginning, middle, and end. It is the true essence, marks, substance, and activity of *do*, as it is. Because Zhuyi did not follow this track, he said, "Even a three-year-old can say this." Lacking the capacity for true expression, he uttered these words.

What a pity, Zhuyi! Why did you say this? Because you have not touched upon buddha wind [the buddha teaching]. Do you know about a three-year-old child? Do you understand the principle of a child's inherent capacity? Those who understand know that a three-year-old child also understands all buddhas in the three worlds. How can those who cannot understand all buddhas in the three worlds understand a three-year-old child? Do not think that to face a person is to understand a person. Do not think that not to face a person is not to understand a person.

Those who understand a speck of dust understand the entire world. Those who master one thing master myriad things. Those who do not master myriad things do not master one thing. Because those who study mastering see myriad things as well as one thing through penetration, those who study a speck of dust simultaneously study the entire world.

It is extremely foolish to assume that a three-year-old child cannot express buddha dharma and that what a three-year-old child says is easy.

The real issue here, to clarify birth and to clarify death, is the great matter of causes and effects in the buddha house.

An old master said, "When you are born, you have the capacity to roar like a lion." The capacity to roar like a lion is a virtue of the Tathagata turning the dharma wheel. It is turning the dharma wheel.

Another old master said, "The coming and going of birth and death is the true human body."

In this way, to clarify the true human body and to have the virtue of roaring like a lion are indeed the great matter, and are not to be taken lightly. For this reason, to understand the words and practice of a three-year-old child is a great matter of causes and conditions. This is sometimes the same and sometimes not the same as the words and the practice of all buddhas in the three worlds.

Because Zhuyi was ignorant and had never heard the expression of the three-year-old child, without even questioning it he responded as he did. He did not even hear Daolin's voice of the way, which was louder than thunder. He wanted to point out that Daolin failed to hit the mark and said, "*a three-year-old child could say it.*" In this way he failed to hear the lion's roar of the child and missed the turning dharma wheel of the Zen master.

Daolin pitied him and responded further: *Even if a three-year-old child can say this, even an eighty-year-old person cannot practice it.* This means that the words of the three-year-old child hit the mark. Thoroughly study these words. *Even an eighty-year-old person cannot practice it.* Thoroughly investigate these words.

The child's expression is entrusted to you; it is not entrusted to the child. The old person's practice of the unattainable is entrusted to you; it is not entrusted to the old person. To understand, speak, and live in this way is the point of the buddha dharma.

Presented to the assembly of the Kosho Horin Monastery, Uji County, Yamashiro Province, on the harvest moon day [the fifteenth day], the eighth month, the second year of the En'o Era [1240].

12

THE TIME BEING

A<small>N ANCIENT BUDDHA</small> [Yaoshan] said:

> For the time being, stand on top of the highest peak.
> For the time being, proceed along the bottom of the
> deepest ocean.
> For the time being, three heads and eight arms [of a
> fighting demon].
> For the time being, an eight- or sixteen-foot body
> [of the Buddha].
> For the time being, a staff or whisk.
> For the time being, a pillar or lantern.
> For the time being, the children of [common
> families] Zhang and Li.
> For the time being, the earth and sky.

For the time being here means time itself is being, and all being is time. A golden sixteen-foot body is time; because it is time, there is the radiant illumination of time. Study it as the twelve hours of the present. *Three heads and eight arms* is time; because it is time, it is not separate from the twelve hours of the present.

Even though you do not measure the hours of the day as long or short, far or near, you still call it twelve hours. Because the signs of time's coming and going are obvious, people do not doubt it. Although they do not doubt it, they do not understand it. Or, when sentient beings doubt what they do not understand, their doubt is not firmly fixed. Because of that, their past doubts do not necessarily coincide with the present doubt. Yet, doubt itself is nothing but time.

The way the self arrays itself is the form of the entire world. See each thing in this entire world as a moment of time.

Things do not hinder one another, just as moments do not hinder one another. The way-seeking mind arises in this moment. A way-seeking moment arises in this mind. It is the same with practice and with attaining the way.

Thus, the self setting itself out in array sees itself. This is the understanding that the self is time.

Know that in this way there are myriads of forms and hundreds of grasses [all things] throughout the entire earth, and yet each grass and each form itself is the entire earth. The study of this is the beginning of practice.

When you are at this place, there is just one grass, there is just one form; there is understanding of form and beyond understanding of form; there is understanding of grass and beyond understanding of grass. Since there is nothing but just this moment, the time being is all the time there is. Grass being, form being, are both time.

Each moment is all being, each moment is the entire world. Reflect now whether any being or any world is left out of the present moment.

Yet, an ordinary person who does not understand buddha dharma may hear the words *time being* this way: "For a while I was three heads and eight arms. For a while I was an eight- or sixteen-foot body. This is like having crossed over rivers and climbed mountains. Even though the mountains and rivers still exist, I have already passed them and now reside in the jeweled palace and vermilion tower. Those mountains and rivers are as distant from me as heaven is from earth."

It is not that simple. At the time the mountains were climbed and the rivers were crossed, you were present. Time is not separate from you, and as you are present, time does not go away.

As time is not marked by coming and going, the moment you climbed the mountains is the time being right now. If time keeps coming and going, you are the time being right now. This is the meaning of the time being.

Does this time being not swallow up the moment when you climbed the mountains and the moment when you resided in the jeweled palace and vermilion tower? Does it not spit them out?

Three heads and eight arms may be yesterday's time. An eight- or sixteen-foot body may be today's time. Yet, yesterday and today are both in the moment when you directly enter the mountains and see myriad peaks. Yesterday's time and today's time do not go away.

Three heads and eight arms move forward as your time being. It looks as if they are far away, but they are here and now. The eight- or sixteen-foot body moves forward as your time being. It looks as if it is nearby, but it is exactly here. Thus, a pine tree is time, bamboo is time.

———————

Do not think that time merely flies away. Do not see flying away as the only function of time. If time merely flies away, you would be separated from time. The reason you do not clearly understand the time being is that you think of time only as passing.

In essence, all things in the entire world are linked with one another as moments. Because all moments are the time being, they are your time being.

———————

The time being has a characteristic of flowing. So-called today flows into tomorrow, today flows into yesterday, yesterday flows into today. And today flows into today, tomorrow flows into tomorrow.

Because flowing is a characteristic of time, moments of past and present do not overlap or line up side by side. [Zen master] Qingyuan is time, Huangbo is time, Mazu is time, Shitou is time, because self and other are already time. Practice-enlightenment is time. Being splattered with mud and getting wet with water [to awaken others] is also time.

Although the views of an ordinary person and the causes and conditions of those views are what the ordinary person sees, they are not necessarily the ordinary person's reality. The reality merely manifests itself for the time being as an ordinary person. Because you think your time or your being is not reality, you believe that the sixteen-foot golden body is not you.

However, your attempts to escape from being the sixteen-foot golden body are nothing but bits and pieces of the time being. Those who have not yet confirmed this should look into it deeply. The hours of Horse and Sheep, which are arrayed in the world now, are actualized by ascendings and descendings of the time being at each moment. The rat is time, the tiger is time, sentient beings are time, buddhas are time.

At this moment, you enlighten the entire world with three heads and eight arms; you enlighten the entire world with the sixteen-foot golden body. To fully actualize the entire world with the entire world is called thorough practice.

To fully actualize the golden body with the golden body—to arouse the way-seeking mind, practice, attain enlightenment, and enter nirvana—is nothing but being, nothing but time.

Just actualize all time as all being; there is nothing extra. An "extra being" is thoroughly an extra being. Thus, the time being half-actualized is half of the time being completely actualized, and a moment that seems to be missed is also completely being. In the same way, even the moment before or after the moment that appears to be missed is also the time being complete in itself. Vigorously abiding in each moment is the time

being. Do not mistakenly confuse it as nonbeing. Do not forcefully assert it as being.

   You may suppose that time is only passing away, and not understand
that time never arrives. Although understanding itself is time, understanding does not depend on its own arrival.
   People only see time's coming and going, and do not thoroughly
understand that the time being abides in each moment. Then, when can
they penetrate the barrier? Even if people recognized the time being in
each moment, who could give expression to this recognition? Even if
they could give expression to this recognition for a long time, who could
stop looking for the realization of the original face? According to an ordinary person's view of the time being, even enlightenment and nirvana
as the time being would be merely aspects of coming and going.

   The time being is entirely actualized without being caught up in
nets or cages. Deva kings and heavenly beings appearing right and left
are the time being of your complete effort right now. The time being
of all beings throughout the world in water and on land just actualizes
your complete effort right now. All beings of all kinds in the visible and
invisible realms are the time being actualized by your complete effort,
flowing due to your complete effort.
   Closely examine this flowing; without your complete effort right
now, nothing would be actualized, nothing would flow.

   Do not think flowing is like wind and rain moving from east to west.
The entire world is not unchangeable, not immovable. It flows. Flowing
is like spring. Spring with all its numerous aspects is called flowing. When
spring flows, there is nothing outside of spring. Study this in detail.
   Spring always flows through spring. Although flowing itself is not
spring, flowing occurs throughout spring. Thus, flowing is complete at
just this moment of spring. Examine this thoroughly, coming and going.
   In your study of flowing, if you imagine the objective to be outside
yourself and that you flow and move through hundreds and thousands

of worlds, for hundreds, thousands, and myriad of eons, you have not
devotedly studied the buddha way.

———————

Yaoshan, who would later become Great Master Hongdao, instructed
by Shitou, Great Master Wuji, once went to study with Mazu, Zen Master Daji of Jiangxi.

Yaoshan asked, "I am familiar with the teaching of the Three Vehicles and Twelve Divisions of scripture. But what is the meaning of
Bodhidharma coming from India?"

Mazu replied:

> For the time being, have him raise his eyebrows
>   and blink.
> For the time being, do not have him raise his
>   eyebrows and blink.
> For the time being, to have him raise his
>   eyebrows and blink is right.
> For the time being, to have him raise his
>   eyebrows and blink is not right.

Hearing these words, Yaoshan experienced great enlightenment and
said to Mazu, "When I was studying with Shitou, it was like a mosquito
trying to bite an iron bull."

What Mazu said is not the same as other people's words. The *eyebrows*
and *eyes* are mountains and oceans, because mountains and oceans are
eyebrows and eyes. *Have him raise his eyebrows* is to see the mountains.
Have him blink is to understand the oceans. The *right* answer belongs to
him, and he is activated by your having him raise his eyebrows and blink.
Not right does not mean not having him raise his eyebrows and blink.
Not to have him raise his eyebrows and blink does not mean not right.
These are all equally the time being.

Mountains are time. Oceans are time. If they were not time, there
would be no mountains or oceans. Do not think that mountains and
oceans here and now are not time. If time is annihilated, mountains and

oceans are annihilated. As time is not annihilated, mountains and oceans are not annihilated.

This being so, the morning star appears, the Tathagata appears, the eye appears, and holding up a flower appears. Each is time. If it were not time, it could not be thus.

———————

Shexian, Zen Master Guixing, is an heir of Shoushan and a dharma descendant of Linji. One day he taught the assembly:

> For the time being, mind arrives, but words do not.
> For the time being, words arrive, but mind does not.
> For the time being, both mind and words arrive.
> For the time being, neither mind nor words arrive.

Both mind and words are the time being. Both arriving and not-arriving are the time being. When the moment of arriving has not appeared, the moment of not-arriving is here. Mind is a donkey [that has not yet left], words are a horse [that has already arrived]. Having-already-arrived is words and not-having-left is mind. Arriving is not "coming," not-arriving is not "not yet."

———————

The time being is like this. Arriving is fulfilled by arriving, but not by not-arriving. Not-arriving is fulfilled by not-arriving, but not by arriving. Mind fulfills mind and sees mind; words fulfill words and see words. Fulfilling fulfills fulfilling and sees fulfilling. Fulfilling is nothing but fulfilling. This is time.

As fulfilling is caused by you, there is no fulfilling that is separate from you. Thus, you go out and meet someone. Someone meets someone. You meet yourself. Going out meets going out. If these do not actualize time, they cannot be thus.

———————

Mind is the moment of actualizing the fundamental point; words are the moment of going beyond, unlocking the barrier. Arriving is the moment of casting off the body; not-arriving is the moment of being one with just this, while being free from just this. In this way you must endeavor to actualize the time being.

————————

The old masters have thus uttered these words, but is there nothing further to say? You should say:

> Mind and words arriving partially are the time being.
> Mind and words not arriving partially are the time being.

Further, you should examine the time being:

> To have him raise the eyebrows and blink is half the time being.
> To have him raise the eyebrows and blink is the time being missed.
> Not to have him raise the eyebrows and blink is half the time being.
> Not to have him raise the eyebrows and blink is the time being missed.

Thus, to study thoroughly, coming and going, and to study thoroughly, arriving and beyond arriving, are the time being of this moment.

On the first day of winter [the first day, the tenth month], the first year of the Ninji Era [1240], this was written at the Kosho Horin Monastery.

13

POWER OF THE ROBE

BODHIDHARMA, THE HIGH Ancestor of Mount Song, alone transmitted the authentic teaching of the robe to China. He is the twenty-eighth-generation ancestor from Shakyamuni Buddha. In India twenty-eight generations of ancestors transmitted this teaching from heir to heir. The Twenty-eighth Ancestor entered China and became the First Ancestor there. After transmission of the teaching through five generations in China, Huineng of Caoxi became the thirty-third-generation ancestor. He is called the Sixth Chinese Ancestor.

Huineng, who would later become Zen Master Dajian, received a robe from Hongren at Mount Huangmei and maintained it for the rest of his life. This robe is still enshrined at the Baolin Monastery in Mount Caoxi, where he taught.

Over the generations, one emperor after another requested that the robe be brought to the palace. When it was, people made offerings and bowed to it. Thus, the robe has been worshipped as a sacred object. Emperors Zong, Su, and Dai of the Tang Dynasty occasionally invited the robe to be brought to the palace. Each time it was brought and each time it was returned, an imperial messenger accompanied it.

Once, when Emperor Dai sent this buddha robe back to Mount Caoxi, he proclaimed: "We order Liu Chongjing, the Nation's Chief

General, to transport the robe with great respect. We regard this robe as a national treasure. You should place it in the main temple with appropriate procedures. Make sure that the monks are notified of our command and protect the robe without fail."

There is more merit in seeing the buddha robe, hearing the teaching of it, and making offerings to it than in presiding over the billion worlds. To be the king of a nation where the robe exists is an outstanding birth among innumerable births and deaths; it is indeed the most supreme birth.

In the billion worlds where the Buddha's teaching reaches, is there any place that has no kashaya robe? Yet, Bodhidharma alone authentically transmitted the buddha kashaya face to face, heir to heir. Teachers who were not in this lineage were not given the buddha kashaya.

A transmission in the lineage of Bodhisattva Bhadrapala, a descendant of Prajnatara, the Twenty-seventh Ancestor, reached Dharma Teacher Sengzhao, but no buddha kashaya was transmitted to him.

Daoxin, the Fourth Ancestor in China, guided Niutou, who would later become Zen Master Farong, but did not give him a buddha kashaya.

Although the power of the Tathagata's dharma is not lacking and its benefit is broad for thousands of years, even for those who did not receive heir-to-heir transmission of kashaya, those who received authentic heir-to-heir transmission of kashaya are not the same as those who didn't. Therefore, when humans or devas receive a robe, they should receive one authentically transmitted by the buddha ancestors.

In India and China, even laypeople received kashaya in the Ages of True Dharma and Imitation Dharma. Nowadays, in the lands remote from India when the buddha dharma is thin and declining, those who shave their heads and faces, calling themselves the Buddha's disciples, do not maintain the kashaya. They do not believe, know, or understand that the kashaya is to be maintained. What a pity! How can they know its form, color, and measurement? How can they know the proper way to wear it?

A kashaya has been called the garment of emancipation. The hindrances of actions and defilements, and the effects of unwholesome action are all removed by it. If a dragon obtains a small piece of kashaya, it can be cured of febrile diseases. If an ox touches a kashaya with one of its horns, its past wrongdoings disappear. When buddhas attain the way, they always wear a kashaya. Know that its power is unsurpassable and most venerable.

It is regrettable that we have been born in a remote land in the Age of Declining Dharma. However, we have the joy of meeting the teaching of the robe transmitted from buddha to buddha, heir to heir. In what lineage has Shakyamuni's teaching of the robe been transmitted as authentically as it has been in ours? Who would not show reverence and make offerings upon meeting the teaching of the robe? You should make such offerings just for one day, even if you need to give up immeasurable lives to do so. You should vow to meet, uphold, revere, and make offerings to the robe, birth after birth, generation after generation.

We are thousands of miles away from the land where the Buddha was born, on the other side of mountains and oceans. We are unable to go there, but due to the influence of our past good actions, we are no longer blocked by mountains and oceans nor excluded by our ignorance in this remote place. We have met the true teaching and are determined to practice it day and night. We maintain, uphold, and guard the kashaya continuously.

Thus, the power of the kashaya is actualized through our practice, not merely with one or two buddhas but with as many buddhas as the sands of the Ganges. Even if it is your own practice, you should revere it, rejoice in it, and wholeheartedly express gratitude for the profound gift transmitted by the ancestral teachers. Even animals repay kindness; how should humans not recognize the kind help by others? If you do not understand kindness, you are more foolish than animals.

The power of the buddha robe, the buddha dharma, cannot be known and understood except by ancestors who transmit the Buddha's true dharma. When you follow the path of buddhas, you should joyfully appreciate the buddha robe, the buddha dharma. You should continue this authentic transmission even for hundreds and thousands of future generations. This is buddha dharma freshly actualized.

Authentic transmission is not like mixing water with milk, but rather like the crown prince being installed as king. You can use milk mixed with water if there is not enough milk. But don't mix milk with oil, lacquer, or wine. If there is authentic transmission, even an ordinary teacher of a mediocre lineage can be regarded as milk. How much more so with the authentic transmission of buddhas and ancestors? It is like the installation of the crown prince. Even worldly people say that a king only wears the former king's robe. How could a buddha's child wear a robe other than the buddha robe?

Since the tenth year of the Yongping Era [67 C.E.] of Emperor Xiaoming of the Later Han Dynasty, monks and laypeople often went back and forth between India and China. But none of them said that they had met an ancestor in India who had authentic transmission from buddha ancestors. Thus, there was no lineage of face-to-face transmission from the Tathagata. These seekers only studied with masters of sutras and treatises and brought back Sanskrit scriptures. They did not say they had met ancestors who had authentically inherited buddha dharma. They did not say there were ancestors who had transmitted the buddha kashaya. Thus, we know that those people did not enter deeply into the chamber of buddha dharma and clarify the meaning of the correct transmission of the buddha ancestors.

The Tathagata Shakyamuni entrusted the treasury of the true dharma eye, the unsurpassable enlightenment, to Mahakashyapa along with the kashaya which had been transmitted by his teacher, Kashyapa Buddha. The robe was transmitted heir to heir for thirty-three generations, to Huineng. The shape, color, and measurements were intimately transmitted. After that, dharma descendants of Qingyuan and Nanyue, transmitting the dharma, sewed and wore the ancestral dharma. The teaching of washing and maintaining the robe was not known except by those who studied in the chamber of a master who had transmitted this teaching face to face.

———————

There are three types of kashaya: a five-panel robe, a seven-panel robe, and a great robe [sanghati robe] such as a nine-panel robe. One who is engaged in authentic practice receives only such robes as these, which are enough to offer to the body, and does not keep other types of robes. For work and traveling far or near, a five-panel robe is worn.

For conducting formal activities or joining the assembly, a seven-panel robe is worn. For guiding humans and devas and arousing their respect and trust, you should wear a great robe such as a nine-panel robe. A five-panel robe is worn indoors, and a seven-panel robe is worn while with other monks. A great robe is worn when entering the palace or in town.

Also, a five-panel robe is worn when it is mild; a seven-panel robe is added on top of it when it is cold. A great robe is further added when it is severely cold. Long ago in midwinter, when it was so cold that the bamboo was cracking, the Tathagata wore a five-panel robe in the early evening. Later at night it got colder, so he added a seven-panel robe. At the end of the night when it became even colder, he further added a great robe. The Buddha then thought, "In the future when the cold is severe, good monks can use these three robes to warm the body."

———

These are ways to wear the kashaya: The most common way is to leave the right shoulder uncovered. There is also a way to cover both shoulders, which is customary for tathagatas and elders. When both shoulders are covered, the chest is either covered or revealed. Both shoulders are covered when a great kashaya of more than sixty panels is worn.

When you put on a kashaya, you start by placing both ends on your left shoulder and upper arm, hanging the ends over your left elbow. If you put on a great kashaya, you start by bringing the ends over the left shoulder and letting them hang down in back. There are many other ways to put on a kashaya. You should study deeply and make inquiries of your teacher.

For hundreds of years during the Liang, Chen, Sui, Tang, and Song dynasties, a number of scholars of Mahayana and Hinayana gave up lecturing on scripture, having learned that it was not the ultimate teaching. Intending to study the authentically transmitted dharma of buddha ancestors, they would invariably drop off their old robes and receive an authentically transmitted kashaya. This is departing from the limited and turning to the genuine.

The Tathagata's dharma is rooted in India, where teachers in the past and present have gone beyond the limited views of ordinary people. As the realms of buddhas and the realms of sentient beings are neither limited nor unlimited, the teaching, practice, practitioner, and essence of Mahayana and Hinayana cannot be contained by ordinary people's views. However, in China, practitioners often ignore teachings from India and regard recent interpretations with limited views as buddha dharma, which is a mistake.

Those who arouse an aspiration and wish to receive a kashaya should receive an authentically transmitted one. Do not receive a kashaya with a new design. What is called an authentically transmitted kashaya is what has been transmitted from Bodhidharma and Huineng, heir to heir directly from the Tathagata, without a generation's gap. This is the authentically transmitted kashaya worn by dharma heirs and dharma descendants. Newly designed kashayas in China are not appropriate. The kashayas worn by monks from India in the past and present are all like the buddha ancestors' authentically transmitted kashayas. None of them wore kashayas like those newly made by monks of the Precept School in China. Those who are ignorant believe in the kashayas of the Precept School, but those who have clear understanding do not.

The power of the kashaya transmitted by buddha ancestors is clear and easy to accept. The authentic transmission has been handed down from person to person. The true form has been shown to us directly. It still exists, as this dharma has been inherited up to the present. The ancestors who received a kashaya are all teachers and students who merged their minds and received dharma. Therefore, you should make a kashaya in the manner authentically transmitted by buddha ancestors.

As this is the authentic transmission, ordinary people and sages, humans and devas, as well as dragon kings, all know it. To be born to the abundance of this dharma and to wear a kashaya even once and maintain it for a moment is no other than wearing an amulet that assures the attainment of unsurpassable enlightenment.

When one phrase or one verse permeates your body and mind, it becomes a seed of illumination for limitless kalpas, and this brings you to unsurpassable enlightenment. When one dharma or one wholesome action permeates your body and mind, it is also like this.

Moment by moment a thought appears and disappears without abiding. Moment by moment a body appears and disappears without abiding. Yet, the power of practice always matures. A kashaya is neither made nor not made, neither abiding nor not abiding. It is the ultimate realm of buddha and buddha. A practitioner who receives it unfailingly attains and experiences its power.

Those who have no wholesome past actions cannot see, wear, receive, and understand a kashaya even if they live for one, two, or innumerable lifetimes. When I look at practitioners in China and Japan, I see that there are those who are able to wear a kashaya and those who are not. Their ability to wear one does not depend on how noble or lowly they are, how wise or ignorant they are, but on their wholesome past actions. Therefore, those who have received a kashaya should rejoice in their wholesome past actions, without doubting their accumulated merit. Those who have not received a kashaya should wish for one. Try to sow a seed of a kashaya immediately in this lifetime. Those who cannot receive one because of their hindrances should repent to buddha tathagatas and the three treasures.

How strongly people in other countries wish to have the Tathagata's authentic transmission of the dharma of the robe in their countries, just as in China! How deep their regret is and how sorrowful they are that they do not have it! With what fortune have we encountered the authentic transmission of the World-Honored One's robe dharma! This is due to the great power of our having nurtured prajna in the past.

Now, in this unwholesome time—the Age of Declining Dharma— people have no regret that they do not have authentic transmission, but they are jealous that others do. They seem like a gang of demons. What they believe and what they practice are not genuine, but only bound by their past actions. They should take refuge in the authentically transmitted buddha dharma as the true place of return in studying the buddha way.

You should know that a kashaya is what all buddhas respect and take refuge in. It is the buddha body, the buddha mind. It is called the clothing of emancipation, the robe of the field of benefaction, the robe beyond form, the unsurpassable robe, the robe of patience, the Tathagata's robe, the robe of great love and great compassion, the robe as a victorious banner, and the robe of unsurpassable, complete enlightenment. Receive it indeed with utmost respect. This is why you should not alter it.

———————

Either silk or common cloth is used as the material for a robe, according to the situation. It is not necessarily true that common cloth is pure and silk is impure. On the other hand, it would be unreasonable and laughable to exclude common cloth and only choose silk. According to the usual practice of buddhas, the robe of discarded cloth is regarded as excellent.

There are ten types of discarded cloth, including burned cloth, cloth chewed by oxen, cloth chewed by rats, and cloth from corpses. People throughout India throw away such cloth on streets or fields, just as we do with excrement-cleaning cloth. So, a robe of discarded cloth is actually called a robe of excrement-cleaning cloth. Practitioners pick up such cloths, wash them, and repair them for use. There can be pieces of silk and common cloth among them. Give up discrimination between silk and common cloth, and study the meaning of discarded cloth. Long ago a monk washed such a robe of discarded cloth in Anavatapta Lake, when the dragon king rained down flowers in admiration and respect.

There are teachers in the Lesser Vehicles who groundlessly say that threads are incarnated bodies of the tree god. Practitioners of the Great Vehicle should laugh about it. Which thread is not an incarnated body? Those who have ears to hear about incarnated bodies may not have the eyes to see them. Know that among the cloths you pick up, there can be common cloth and silk. Because cloth is made differently in different regions, it is difficult to identify the materials. Eyes cannot see the difference. Do not discuss whether the material you pick up is silk or common cloth. Just call it discarded cloth.

Even if a human or a deva turns into discarded cloth, it is not sentient but just discarded cloth. Even if a pine or chrysanthemum turns into discarded cloth, it is not insentient but just discarded cloth. Discarded cloth is actualized only when you accept that discarded cloth is beyond silk or common cloth, not gold, silver, or a pearl. Discarded cloth is not yet dreamed of by those who have not yet given up discrimination between silk and common cloth.

Once a monk asked Old Buddha [Huineng], "Is the robe you received at midnight at Mount Huangmei common cloth or silk? What is it?"

Huineng said, "Not common cloth, not silk."

Know that a kashaya is neither silk nor common cloth. This is a profound teaching of the buddha way.

———

Venerable Shanavasin is the third entrusted ancestor of the dharma treasury. He was born wearing a layperson's robe. The robe turned into a kashaya when he became a monk.

Nun Shuklayah was born with a kashaya, birth after birth, and in between, as a result of offering a carpet to the Buddha.

When we meet Shakyamuni Buddha and leave the household, the lay clothing we acquire at birth immediately turns into a kashaya, just as Shanavasin's did. Thus, a kashaya is neither silk nor common cloth. The power of buddha dharma transforms body, mind, and all things in this way.

It is clear that our body, mind, and environs are immediately transformed when we leave the household and receive the precepts. But we often do not notice this because of our ignorance. This effect of buddha dharma is applied not only to Shanavasin and Nun Shuklayah but to us all. Do not doubt this great benefit. Endeavor to clarify this point. The kashaya that covers the body of one who has received the precepts is not limited to common cloth or silk. The Buddha's transformation is beyond our comprehension. The pearl hidden inside the robe is beyond the understanding of those who count letters.

———

Study the shape, color, and measurement of buddhas' kashayas. See whether they have size or are sizeless, whether they have form or are formless. This is what the ancestors in India and China in the past and at present have studied and authentically transmitted. Those who see and hear this original inheritance that has come from ancestor to ancestor and yet do not accept it cannot be excused. This is due to their ignorance and distrust. It is throwing away the true and seeking the false, giving up the essential and wishing for the trivial, making light of the Tathagata.

Those who arouse the aspiration for enlightenment should without fail receive the authentic transmission of the ancestors. As dharma descendants we have not only encountered the rarely encountered buddha dharma, but we have seen, studied, and received the authentically transmitted buddha kashaya. In this way we see the Tathagata, we hear the Buddha expound the dharma, we are illuminated by the Buddha, we enjoy the Buddha's enjoyment, we receive the one-to-one transmission of the Buddha's mind, and we attain the Buddha's marrow. Thus, we are intimately wrapped in the kashaya of Shakyamuni Buddha. We personally accompany the Buddha and receive this kashaya from the Buddha.

This is how to wash a kashaya: You put it unfolded into a clean wooden tub, cover it with thoroughly boiled water that has been purified by incense, and leave it for one hour [roughly two hours by the modern way of counting]. Another way is to boil water mixed with pure ash and cover the kashaya until the water cools. Nowadays it is common to use ash water. It is called *aku no yu* in Japan.

When the ash water cools, rinse the kashaya many times with clear, hot water. Do not scrub it with your hands or stomp on it. After thus removing sweat and oil stains, mix fragrant powder of sandalwood or aloeswood with cold water and rinse the kashaya in it.

Then, hang it on a clean rod to dry. When it is completely dry, fold it and put it high on the altar. Burn incense, spread flower petals on the altar, circumambulate the kashaya clockwise a few times, and bow to it. After three, six, or nine full bows, kneel and put your palms together, then hold up the kashaya with both hands, chant the kashaya verse, and put it on properly.

The World-Honored One, Shakyamuni Buddha, said to the great assembly:

Good assembly, long ago in my previous life when I was with Ratnakosha Buddha, I was called Mahakaruna Bodhisattva. Once, in front of the Ratnakosha Buddha, I made these vows:

Ratnakosha Buddha, after I attain buddhahood, there may be those who, following my teaching, leave the household and wear a kashaya, and still break important precepts, hold wrong views, or ignore the three treasures. And there may be monks, nuns, laymen, or laywomen who arouse respectful minds and honor the great robe, revering the buddha, dharma, and sangha. I vow that there will not be even one such person in the Three Vehicles who misses receiving a prediction of enlightenment or turns away from my teaching. Otherwise, this would contradict the vows of all buddhas who have been present for limitless eons in the worlds of the ten directions, and thus I would not attain unsurpassable, complete enlightenment.

Ratnakosha Buddha, after I attain buddhahood, if any devas, dragons, humans, or nonhumans revere, make offering to, or admire one who wears the kashaya, I vow that such beings, who see even a small piece of kashaya, will practice in the Three Vehicles without regressing.

If there are sentient beings overcome by hunger or thirst, poverty-stricken, or in most humble positions, as well as hungry ghosts, who obtain a piece of a kashaya no bigger than a hand, I vow that such beings will be satisfied with food and drink, and that their wishes will be immediately actualized.

If there are sentient beings who are in conflict, harbor grudges, and fight one another, or if there are devas, dragons, gandharvas, asuras, garudas, kinnaras, mahoragas, kumbhandas, pisachas, humans, or nonhumans who fight one another, I vow that if such beings think of a kashaya, then compassionate mind, gentle mind, generous mind, serene mind, wholesome mind will rise and they will attain purity.

If people who battle, quarrel, or are in legal conflicts bring a patch of kashaya for self-protection and pay respect to it, they will always be victorious and overcome difficulties, because others will not harm, confuse, or belittle them.

Ratnakosha Buddha, if my kashaya did not possess the above five sacred powers, I would be deceiving all buddhas who have been present for limitless eons in the world of the ten directions, and I would not achieve unsurpassable, complete enlightenment for conducting buddha activities in the future; thus I would be without wholesome dharma and unable to overcome those who are outside the way.

Good assembly, Ratnakosha Buddha then extended his golden right arm, stroked Mahakaruna Bodhisattva on the head, and said in admiration, "Splendid, splendid, courageous bodhisattva. Your vow is a rare treasure that expresses great wisdom. You will actualize unsurpassable, complete enlightenment and your kashaya robe will possess those five sacred powers and cause immeasurable benefit."

Good assembly, upon hearing Ratnakosha Buddha's admiration, Mahakaruna Bodhisattva rejoiced and became exuberant. Then Ratnakosha Buddha extended his golden right arm, with long and slender fingers and palm as soft as a feathery celestial robe. Ratnakosha Buddha stroked the bodhisattva on the head and turned him into a youth of twenty.

Good assembly, all the devas, dragons, gandharvas, humans, and nonhumans placed their hands together and dedicated flowers and music to Mahakaruna Bodhisattva. They continued to admire the bodhisattva while they sat still.

From the time when Shakyamuni Buddha was alive in this world up to the present, these five sacred powers of the kashaya have been described in sutras and precept texts for bodhisattvas and shravakas. Indeed, the kashaya is a buddha robe of all buddhas of the past, present, and future. Although the power of all kashayas is unlimited, receiving a kashaya from the heritage of Shakyamuni Buddha excels receiving a kashaya from the heritage of other buddhas.

The reason for this is that Shakyamuni Buddha made these vows to initiate the power of the kashaya in his former life as Mahakaruna Bodhisattva when he made five hundred vast vows to Ratnakosha Buddha. The power of the kashaya is unlimited and beyond thought. Thus, what transmits the skin, flesh, bones, and marrow of the World-Honored One is the kashaya robe. Ancestors who have transmitted the treasury of the true dharma eye have always authentically transmitted a kashaya.

Sentient beings who maintain and pay respect to a kashaya have always attained the way within two or three lifetimes. Even wearing the kashaya as a joke or for profit can lead to attainment of the way.

Ancestor Nagarjuna said, "Home leavers in buddha dharma, you can resolve your crimes and attain liberation even if you break precepts and commit crimes, as mentioned in the *Sutra on the Former Birth of Nun Utpalavarna:*"

> At the time when the Buddha was in this world, Nun Utpalavarna attained six miraculous powers and became an arhat. She visited noble householders and talked about the life of home leavers. She encouraged noble women to become nuns.
>
> They said, "We are young and beautiful. It would be hard to keep the precepts."
>
> Utpalavarna said, "It's all right to break the precepts. Leave the household first."
>
> The women said, "If we break the precepts, we will fall into hell. How can we do that?"
>
> Utpalavarna said, "Then go ahead and fall into hell."
>
> They laughed and said, "We would be punished in hell. How can we fall into hell?"
>
> Utpalavarna said, "Reflecting on my former life, I was an entertainer, putting on various costumes and speaking memorized lines. Once, I put on a nun's clothes for a joke. As a result of this action, I was reborn as a nun at the time of Kashyapa Buddha. Because of my high status and proper conduct, I grew arrogant and broke a precept. I fell into hell and experienced various punishments. In my next birth I met Shakyamuni Buddha, left the household, attained six miraculous powers, and became an arhat. From this I know that if you leave the household and receive precepts, even if you break a precept, you can become an arhat because of the merit of the precepts you have received. But you cannot attain the way if you only create unwholesome deeds without receiving the precepts. I was once a criminal falling in and out of hell. If a mere criminal dies and enters hell, there is nothing to attain. So, you should know that even if you break a precept, you can attain the fruit of the way."

The cause of Nun Utpalavarna's becoming an arhat in this story is none other than putting on a kashaya for a joke. In her second birth, she became a nun at the time of Kashyapa Buddha, and in her third birth she became a great arhat at the time of Shakyamuni Buddha and accomplished the three types of knowledge and six miraculous powers.

The three types of knowledge are the celestial eye, knowing the past, and knowing how to remove desires. The six miraculous powers are the power of celestial activity, insight into others' minds, the celestial eye, the celestial ear, knowing the past, and removing desires.

Indeed, a mere criminal dies in vain and enters hell. The criminal comes out of hell and becomes a criminal. As Utpalavarna had a causal connection with the precepts, even though she broke a precept, she was able to attain the way. As a result of putting on a kashaya for a joke, she could attain the way even in her third birth. How much more likely you are to attain the way if you arouse a pure heart of trust and put on a kashaya for the sake of unsurpassable enlightenment! Can the merit not be complete? Even further, the merit of maintaining a kashaya with utmost respect throughout a lifetime is vast and boundless.

Those who arouse the aspiration for enlightenment should immediately receive a kashaya. To encounter this fortunate life but not to plant buddha seeds is regrettable. Having received a human body in this world, Jambudvipa, you have a chance to meet Shakyamuni Buddha's dharma, to share life with ancestors who are heirs of buddha dharma, and to receive a kashaya that has been directly transmitted from person to person. It would be a pity not to do this and to spend your life in vain.

In the authentic transmission of the kashaya, only transmission through the ancestors is authentic heritage. Transmission through other teachers cannot compare to this. However, even if you receive a kashaya from a teacher without transmission, the merit is profound. How much more merit there is in receiving a kashaya from an authentic teacher of heir-to-heir, face-to-face transmission! Indeed, in this way you become a dharma child and a dharma grandchild of the Tathagata. This is truly to inherit the Tathagata's skin, flesh, bones, and marrow.

The kashaya is transmitted through buddhas of the ten directions in the past, present, and future without a break. Buddhas, bodhisattvas, shravakas, and pratyeka-buddhas of the ten directions in the past, present, and future maintain it.

For making a kashaya, coarse cloth is basic. When coarse cloth is not available, more finely woven cloth may be used. In case there is neither coarse cloth nor finely woven cloth, plain silk may be used. When none of these are available, patterned or open-weave silk may be used. This is permitted by the Tathagata. When no cloth is available, the Tathagata permits making a leather kashaya.

Kashaya materials should be dyed blue, yellow, red, black, or purple. The color should be subdued and indistinct. The Tathagata always wore a kashaya of skin color. This is the original kashaya color.

The kashaya transmitted by Bodhidharma was bluish black. It was made of cotton from India, which is still kept at Mount Caoxi. This kashaya was transmitted for twenty-eight generations in India and five generations in China to Huineng of Mount Caoxi. Now, disciples of Huineng maintain the tradition of this buddha robe. Monks of other lineages have nothing close to it.

There are three types of kashaya material: excrement-cleaning cloths, animal hair or bird feathers, and patched cloths. I have already mentioned that a robe usually consists of excrement-cleaning cloth. A robe made of animal hair or bird feathers is called a down robe. A robe made of patched cloths is made of old, worn-out cloths. Cloths desirable by worldly standards are not used.

[The *One Hundred One Practices of the Sarvastivada School* says:]

Senior Monk Upali said to the World-Honored One, "Great virtuous World-Honored One, how many panels does a great robe have?"

The Buddha said, "There are nine kinds of robes. The number of panels may be nine, eleven, thirteen, fifteen, seventeen, nineteen, twenty-one, twenty-three, or twenty-five. The first three kinds of great robes consist of panels of one short and two long pieces of cloth. The second three kinds of great robes consist of panels of one short and three long pieces of cloth. The last three kinds of great robes consist of panels of one short and four long pieces of cloth. A robe with more panels is not standard."

Upali said, "Great virtuous World-Honored One, how many sizes of great robes are there?"

The Buddha said, "There are three sizes: large, medium, and small. A large robe measures three *hasta* [the length from elbow to middle fingertip] vertically and five *hasta* horizontally. A small robe measures two and a half *hasta* vertically and four and a half *hasta* horizontally. A medium robe measures between these two."

Upali said, "Great virtuous World-Honored One, how many panels does an uttarasangha [outer] robe have?"

The Buddha said, "It has seven panels. Each panel consists of one short and two long pieces of cloth."

Upali said, "Great virtuous World-Honored One, what are the sizes of an uttarasangha robe?"

The Buddha said, "There are three sizes. A large robe measures three *hasta* vertically and five *hasta* horizontally. A small robe measures half a *hasta* less each way. A medium robe measures between these two."

Upali said, "Great virtuous World-Honored One, how many panels does an antarvasa [inner] robe have?"

The Buddha said, "It has five panels. Each panel consists of one short and one long piece of cloth."

Upali said, "Great virtuous World-Honored One, what are the sizes of an antarvasa robe?"

The Buddha said, "There are three sizes: large, medium, and small. A large antarvasa robe measures three *hasta* vertically and five *hasta* horizontally. A small and a medium antarvasa robe measure the same as the uttarasangha robe."

The Buddha also said, "There are two other types of antarvasa robe. One measures two *hasta* vertically and five *hasta* horizontally. The other measures two *hasta* vertically and four *hasta* horizontally."

The sanghati robe is the double robe. The uttarasangha robe is the outer robe. The antarvasa robe is the inner or under robe. The sanghati robe is also called the great robe, the visiting palace robe, or the expounding dharma robe. The uttarasangha robe is a seven-panel robe. It is a less formal robe for joining the assembly. The antarvasa is a five-panel robe, which is an informal or a work robe.

Always maintain these three types of robes. Also, there is a sixty-panel sanghati robe. Maintain this.

Some sources say that the height of human bodies varies corresponding to the maximum life span, which ranges between 80,000 years and 100 years. Other sources say that the height of human bodies does not vary. It is a correct teaching to say it does not vary. But the heights of a buddha's body and a human body are different. Human bodies can be measured, but the buddha's body cannot. Thus, when Shakyamuni Buddha wore the past Kashyapa Buddha's robe, it was neither too long nor too wide. When the future Maitreya Tathagata wears Shakyamuni Buddha's robe, it will be neither too short nor too narrow. Be aware that a buddha's body is beyond long and short. Brahma, the king of gods who resides high in the form realm, could not see the top of the Buddha's head. Maudgalyayana, a disciple of the Buddha, traveled all the way to the Heaven of Shining Banner and still heard the Buddha's voice. Thus, the Buddha was seen and heard near and far. How marvelous it is! All the merits of the Tathagata are like this. Keep this in mind.

———————

A kashaya varies according to how it is sewn. It may be made of rectangular pieces sewn together, of narrow strips sewn in the same pattern onto one large piece, of one piece tucked and hemmed, or of one piece plain and flat. These are all authentic ways of sewing. You should choose the way of sewing to suit the cloth you have received. The Buddha said, "The kashayas of the buddhas of the past, present, and future are always stitched."

In acquiring materials, purity is of primary concern. What is called excrement-cleaning cloth is regarded as being of utmost purity. Buddhas of the past, present, and future all recognize its purity. Cloth that is donated by faithful laypeople is pure. Cloth that is purchased in a marketplace with donated money is also pure. Although there are guidelines for the length of time to spend on sewing, we live in a remote land in a time of declining dharma, so the most important thing for you is to sew a kashaya when the trusting heart arises, and then receive it.

———————

It is an essential characteristic of Mahayana that even a layperson, whether human or celestial, receives a kashaya. King Brahma and Shakyamuni both wore a kashaya. These are outstanding examples in the desire realm and in the form realm, and cannot be comprehended by ordinary human beings.

Lay bodhisattvas also wear kashayas. In China, Emperor Wu of the Liang Dynasty and Emperor Yang of the Sui Dynasty both wore a kashaya. Emperors Dai and Su [of the Tang Dyanasty] also wore a kashaya, studied with monks, and received the bodhisattva precepts. Other lay men and women of the past and present also have received a kashaya together with the Buddhist precepts.

In Japan, Prince Shotoku wore a kashaya and expounded such sutras as the *Lotus Sutra* and the *Shrimala Devi Sutra*, when he perceived the marvel of celestial flowers raining down. Since then the buddha dharma has spread widely in our country. Prince Shotoku was not only the Regent of the Nation, but also a guiding master of humans and devas. A messenger of the Buddha, he was both father and mother of sentient beings. Although the form, color, and measurements of a kashaya were not transmitted accurately in Japan, still, because of Prince Shotoku's influence, we are able to see and hear about kashayas. If he had not introduced the Buddha's teaching, it would have been a great loss to us.

Later, Emperor Shomu also received a kashaya and the bodhisattva precepts. In this way, even those who are on a throne or those who are retainers can receive a kashaya and the bodhisattva precepts. There is no wholesome fortune for humans that excels this.

Some sources say that the kashaya worn by laypeople is called "a single-stitch robe" or "a lay robe" and that double stitching is not used for that. Other sources say that when laypeople go to the practice place, they wear three types of dharma robes and use tooth-cleaning twigs, rinsing water, eating utensils, and sitting mats to engage in pure practice just as monks do. These are words of ancient masters. However, in the direct transmission of buddha ancestors, the kashaya given to kings, ministers, lay practitioners, and warriors is invariably double-stitched. Laborer Lu [Huineng] did receive the buddha kashaya when he was a layman, which is an excellent precedent.

The kashaya is a banner of the Buddha's disciple. When you have received a kashaya, wear it respectfully every day.

First, put it on top of your head, place your palms together, and recite this verse:

Great is the robe of liberation,
the robe beyond form, the field of benefaction!
I wear the Tathagata's teaching
to awaken countless beings.

Then put it on. Visualize your teacher, or visualize a stupa in the kashaya. Also recite this verse when you put on the kashaya after washing it.

The Buddha said, "When you shave your head and wear a kashaya, you are protected by all buddhas. Having left the household, you are given offerings by celestial beings."

From this, know without doubt that as soon as you shave your head and wear a kashaya, you are guarded by all buddhas. With this protection, you fully realize unsurpassable enlightenment. Thus, you are given offerings by humans and devas.

The World-Honored One said to Monk Junanaprabha:

The dharma robe brings forth the ten excellent merits: It covers your body, providing modesty and the practice of wholesome conduct. It protects you from cold, heat, insects, beasts, and snakes, and provides comfort in the practice of the way. It manifests the form of a mendicant home leaver and arouses joy in those who see it, relieving them of ill intentions. It is a sacred banner of humans and devas. It causes those who revere it and bow to it to be born in the heaven of purity. By wearing it, you arouse the thought of a sacred banner, avert wrongdoing, and bring forth benefaction. It has been dyed with subdued color to help you become free from the five-sense desires, undefiled by greed and attachment. It is the Buddha's pure robe that transforms delusion forever and creates a wholesome field of benefaction. When you wear it your unwholesome actions will disappear and the path of the ten wholesome actions will increase moment by moment. It is like an excellent rice field that nurtures the bodhisattva mind. It is like armor that protects you from the poison arrows of delusion.

Thus, Monk Junanaprabha understood that, thanks to these ten excellent merits, all buddhas in the past, present, and future, all pratyeka-buddhas, shramanas, and pure home leavers, wear the kashaya while they sit on the sacred platform of emancipation, holding the sword of wisdom to subdue the demon of delusion, and together enter nirvana.

Then the World-Honored One said in a verse:

> Listen carefully, Monk Junanaprabha.
> The robe of the field of great benefaction has ten
> > excellent merits:
> While worldly clothes increase defilement,
> the dharma robe of the Tathagata does not.
> The dharma robe provides modesty, completes
> > repentance,
> and creates the field of benefaction.
> It protects you from cold, heat, and poisonous creatures
> and strengthens your way-seeking mind
> for attaining the ultimate understanding.
> Manifesting the form of a mendicant home leaver,
> it frees people from greed and desire, removes five wrong
> > views,
> and helps you to hold authentic practice.
> By revering and bowing to the sacred-banner kashaya,
> you will have the benefaction of King Brahma.
> When you wear the kashaya, visualize a stupa
> creating benefaction, eliminating unwholesomeness,
> and joining humans and devas.
> The noble form of the kashaya arouses respect
> in a true seeker who becomes free from worldly dust.
> All buddhas praise it as an excellent field
> most beneficial to sentient beings.
> The inconceivable miraculous power of the kashaya
> nurtures practice for enlightenment.
> The sprout of practice grows in the spring field;
> the splendid fruit of enlightenment is like a harvest in
> > autumn.

The kashaya is true armor, impenetrable as diamond,
the deadly arrows of delusion cannot pierce it.

I have now recited the ten excellent merits of kashaya.
For eons, more comments could be made, but I'll say this:
A dragon who wears even a shred of kashaya
can't be devoured by a gold-winged garuda.
A person who holds a kashaya while crossing the ocean
will not fear dragons, fish, or harmful beings.
Lightning and thunder, heaven's wrath,
will not frighten a monk who wears a kashaya.
When a layperson carries a kashaya with respect,
no evil spirits draw near.
When you arouse the beginner's mind,
leave home and worldly affairs to practice the way,
demon palaces in the ten directions will tremble
and you will immediately realize the dharma king's body.

These ten excellent merits encompass the wide-ranging merit of the buddha way. Understand clearly the merits expounded in these prose and verse lines. Do not put them aside after reading, but continue to study them phrase by phrase. These excellent merits come from the power of the kashaya, not from the power of a practitioner's vigor or long practice.

The Buddha said, "The miraculous power of the kashaya is beyond thought." It is not something ordinary people or wise sages can comprehend. When the dharma king's body is immediately actualized, the kashaya is always worn. Those who do not wear a kashaya have never actualized the dharma king's body.

––––––

The robe of utmost purity is one made of excrement-cleaning cloth. Its merits are clearly and extensively stated in sutras and commentaries of the Great and Lesser Vehicles, which you should inquire into and study broadly. You should also study about other materials for robes. Buddha ancestors who have always understood and transmitted the robe of excrement-cleaning cloth cannot be compared to those who have not.

The *Agama Midiaka Sutra* says:

Venerable assembly, suppose there is someone whose practice is pure in body, but not pure in speech and mind. If you see this person and feel disgust, the disgust needs to be removed.

Venerable assembly, suppose there is someone whose practice is not pure in body, but pure in speech and mind. If you see this person and feel disgust, the disgust needs to be removed. How is this removed?

Venerable assembly, it's like a monk who practices outdoors and finds stained cloth. When he sees cloth discarded in the toilet which is stained with excrement, urine, mucus, or other impurities, he picks it up with his left hand, opens it with his right hand, tears it up, and saves the parts that are not stained or damaged.

Venerable assembly, suppose there is someone whose practice is not pure in body, but pure in speech and mind. Do not think of this practice as impure in body, but just think of this practice as pure in speech and mind. If you see the impurity and feel disgust, the disgust needs to be removed.

This is the way for a monk who practices outdoors and collects discarded cloths. There are four types as well as ten types of discarded cloths. When you collect cloths, you should save pieces without holes. Also, the parts heavily stained with urine and excrement are not taken. Save the pieces that can be washed clean.

The ten types of discarded cloths are those that have been chewed by cows, gnawed by rats, burned, stained by menstrual blood, stained during childbirth, used as a shrine robe, found in a cemetery, used as an offering with a prayer, given by royalty, and used as a shroud. These cloths are abandoned by people and not ordinarily used anymore. You pick them up and turn them into pure material for the kashaya.

This is what buddhas in the past, present, and future admire and use. Thus, discarded cloths have been respected and guarded by humans, devas, and dragons. You should pick up such discarded cloths, the material of utmost purity, to create a kashaya. There is no robe like this in Japan now. Even if you look for one, you don't encounter it. How sorrowful! Even if you search, you won't find one in this small, remote country.

To make a kashaya, you should use pure material given by donors, offered by humans or devas, or purchased with the earnings from pure livelihood. Discarded cloth, as well as cloth obtained by pure livelihood, is neither silk, cotton, gold, silver, jade, nor brocade, but is nothing other than discarded cloth. It is used not for making tattered or elegant clothes, but just for the sake of buddha dharma. To wear this cloth is to transmit the skin, flesh, bones, and marrow of buddhas of the past, present, and future, to transmit the treasury of the true dharma eye. Do not ask humans and devas about the power of the robe. Just study it with buddha ancestors.

POSTSCRIPT

Once, when I was in Song China, practicing on a long sitting platform, I observed the monks around me. At the beginning of zazen in the morning, they would hold up their kashayas, place them on their heads, and chant a verse quietly with palms together:

> Great is the robe of liberation,
> the robe beyond form, the field of benefaction!
> I wear the Tathagata's teaching
> to awaken countless beings.

This was the first time I had seen the kashaya held up in this way, and I rejoiced, tears wetting the collar of my robe. Although I had read this verse of veneration for the kashaya in the *Agama Sutra,* I had not known the procedure. Now, I saw it with my own eyes. In my joy I also felt sorry that there had been no master to teach this to me and no good friend to recommend it in Japan. How sad that so much time had been wasted! But I also rejoiced in my wholesome past actions [that caused me to experience this]. If I had stayed in my land, how could I have sat side by side with the monks who had received and were wearing the buddha robe? My sadness and joy brought endless tears.

Then, I made a vow to myself: However unsuited I may be, I will become an authentic holder of the buddha dharma, receiving authentic transmission of the true dharma, and with compassion show the buddha ancestors' authentically transmitted dharma robes to those in my land. I rejoice that the vow I made at that time has not been in vain, and that there have been many bodhisattvas, lay and ordained, who have received the kashaya in Japan. Those who maintain the kashaya should always venerate it day and night. This brings forth most excellent merit. To see or hear one line of the kashaya verse is not limited to seeing and hearing it as if we were trees and rocks, but pervades the nine realms of sentient beings.

———————

In the tenth month of the seventeenth year of the Jiading Era of Song China [1224], two Korean monks visited Qingyuan Prefecture. One was named Zixuan, and the other Jingyun. They were men of letters who often discussed the meaning of sutras, but just like laypeople they did not have kashayas or bowls. What a pity! They had shaven heads but not the manners of monks. This was perhaps because they had come from a small country in a remote land. When some monks from Japan visit other countries, they might be like Zixuan and his company.

———————

During the twelve years of his practice before attaining the way, Shakyamuni Buddha venerated the kashaya without putting it aside. As a remote descendant, you should keep this in mind. Turn your head away from worshipping heaven, gods, kings, and retainers for the sake of name and gain, and joyfully dedicate yourself to venerating the buddha robe.

This was presented to the assembly of the Kannondori Kosho Horin Monastery on the first day of winter, the first year of the Ninji Era [1240].

14

TRANSMITTING THE ROBE

BODHIDHARMA, THE HIGH Ancestor of Mount Song, alone transmitted the authentic teaching of the robe to China. He is the twenty-eighth-generation ancestor from Shakyamuni Buddha. In India twenty-eight generations of ancestors transmitted this teaching from heir to heir. Then six generations of ancestors clearly transmitted it in China. Altogether, thirty-three generations of ancestors transmitted it in India and China.

Huineng, Zen Master Dajian, the Thirty-third Ancestor, received a robe from Hongren at midnight on Mount Huangmei and maintained it for the rest of his life. This robe is still enshrined at the Baolin Monastery in Mount Caoxi [where he taught].

Over the generations, one emperor after another requested that this robe be brought to the palace. When it was, people made offerings and bowed to it. Thus, the robe has been worshipped as a sacred object. Emperors Zong, Su, and Dai of the Tang Dynasty occasionally invited the robe to be brought to the palace for worship. Each time it was brought and each time it was returned, the emperor issued an edict and ordered an imperial messenger to accompany it. This is how they paid reverence to the robe.

Once, when Emperor Dai sent this buddha robe back to Mount Caoxi, he proclaimed: "We order Liu Chongjing, the Nation's Chief General, to transport the robe with great respect. We regard this robe as a national treasure. You should place it in the main temple with appropriate procedures. Make sure that the monks are notified of our command and unfailingly protect the robe."

In this way, some emperors in particular regarded the robe as a national treasure. Indeed, holding the buddha robe in their country is a greater fortune than presiding over the billion worlds. It cannot be compared to the Bian's giant jewel, which became the national emblem from generation to generation but would not come close to the rare treasure transmitted from buddha to buddha.

Since the time of the Great Tang Dynasty, those in black robes and white robes [home leavers and laypeople] who have bowed to this robe all have great capacity to have trust in the dharma. Without being helped by wholesome actions in the past, how can they personally bow to the buddha robe authentically transmitted from buddha to buddha? Those with skin, flesh, bones, and marrow [of the Buddha] should rejoice. Those who are unable to receive it with trust should deplore that they are not seeds of buddhas, although that is the result of their past actions.

Even laypeople say that to see an action of a person is to see the person. Similarly, to bow to a buddha's robe now is to see the buddha. You should construct hundreds and thousands of stupas and make offerings to the buddha robe. Those even in the deva realm and in the ocean who have hearts should revere the robe. Those in the human realm who know the sincerity and excellence of the wheel-turning kings should revere this robe.

What a pity that some heads of state didn't know that there was such a valuable treasure in their country [China]! Some of them, confused by the teaching of Daoist practitioners, abolished buddha dharma. They wore cloth headwear instead of putting on the kashaya, and spoke about attaining longevity. There were such heads of state in the Tang and Song Dynasties. Although they were emperors, they were lowlier than their subjects. Quietly observe this.

Buddha robes are present in our country [Japan]. Ponder if this is a land of wearing a buddha robe.

A buddha robe excels relics. Wheel-turning kings, lions, and humans have relics. Even pratyeka-buddhas have relics. But wheel-turning kings, lions, and humans do not necessarily have kashayas. Only buddhas have kashayas. So, deeply revere the kashaya.

Many foolish people nowadays revere relics but don't know about a kashaya. They rarely know that a kashaya should be maintained and protected. This is so because they have hardly heard about the value of a kashaya from their predecessors and have not yet learned about the authentic transmission of buddha dharma.

If we ponder the time when Shakyamuni Buddha was alive, this was only two thousand and some years ago. Many national treasures and divine objects that have been transmitted until now are older than that. Buddha dharma and the buddha robe are recent and new. They have unfolded in fields and villages for merely fifty generations. Yet, their benefits are wondrous. Although those national treasures and divine objects still have merit, the buddha robe is beyond comparison. While those national treasures and divine objects have not been authentically transmitted from heir to heir, the buddha robe has been authentically transmitted from heir to heir.

Know that one attains the way upon hearing the four-line verse or upon hearing one phrase. Why does the four-line verse or the one phrase have such miraculous power? Because they are both buddha dharma. Now, the supreme [excrement-cleaning] robe, [often in the form of] the nine-panel robe, has been authentically transmitted with buddha dharma. They should not be inferior to the four-line verse. They should not have less miraculous effect than the one phrase.

This being so, for these two thousand and some years, all those who have trust in and practice dharma, who are student followers of the Buddha, have maintained and protected kashayas as their own bodies and minds. Those who are ignorant of the true dharma of all buddhas do not venerate kashayas. Although Indra and the Dragon King of Anavatapta Lake are both lay kings of deva worlds, they maintain and protect kashayas.

But those who have shaved their heads and call themselves children of the Buddha don't know that a kashaya is to be received and maintained. How should they know its shape, color, and measurements? Do they know how to put it on? Further, they have not even dreamed of the awesome manner of wearing it.

From ancient times, a kashaya is known as a robe for removing fever or a robe of emancipation. Its merit is immeasurable. The three types of fever a dragon suffers from are removed with the merit of a kashaya. When buddhas attain the way, they always wear the kashaya.

Even if you were born in this remote land and have encountered the decline of dharma, if you compare the difference between having and not having transmission [of a robe], you should receive with trust, maintain, and protect an authentically transmitted robe.

In what other houses have both the robe and dharma of Shakyamuni Buddha been truly transmitted as in our house? They exist only in the buddha way. Encountering the robe and dharma, who can be lax on revering and dedicating to them? Dedicate yourself even if you need to give up lives as many as the sands of the Ganges for one day of revering the robe. Vow to encounter and revere it birth after birth, world after world.

We were born beyond mountains and oceans more than one hundred thousand *li* away from the land where the Buddha was born. We are uncivilized and foolish. However, if you receive and maintain a kashaya even for a day and night, and study one phrase or one verse of it, you will have the merit of making an offering not only to one or two buddhas but also to countless, one hundred, thousand, billion buddhas. Even if this is done by you, revere, love, and appreciate your action.

Thoroughly express your gratitude for the great kindness of the ancestors who have transmitted the robe and dharma. Even animals repay others' kindness. How can a human not know others' kindness? If you didn't appreciate others' kindness, you would be worse and more foolish than animals.

The merit of a kashaya is not even dreamed of by those who are not ancestors and do not transmit the Buddha's true dharma. How then can they clarify the shape, color, and measurements of a kashaya? Those who long for the traces of buddhas should long for their kashayas. If this authentic transmission is authentically transmitted, this is indeed buddha dharma even one hundred, one thousand, and myriad generations later. The proof of this realization is evident.

Even a layperson [Lord Qing] said, "If it were not the late king's robe, I would not wear it. If it were not the late king's law, I would not follow it." The buddha way is just like that. Other than the late buddha's dharma robe, what would you wear in the practice of the buddha way and serving all buddhas? Those who do not wear this cannot enter the buddhas' assembly.

Since the tenth year of the Yongping Era [67 C.E.] of the Emperor Xiaoming of the Later Han Dynasty, monks and laypeople often went back and forth between India and China. But none of them said that they had met an ancestor in India who had authentic transmission from buddha ancestors. Thus, there was no lineage of face-to-face transmission from the Tathagata. These seekers only studied with masters of sutras and treatises and brought back only names and aspects of buddha dharma. They did not say they had met ancestors who had authentically inherited buddha dharma. They did not say there were ancestors who had transmitted the buddha kashaya. Therefore, those people did not enter deeply into the chamber of buddha dharma and clarify the meaning of the authentic transmission of the buddha ancestors.

They only think that the kashaya is a robe and don't know that it is valued in buddha dharma. It is a pity, indeed. A buddha robe is transmitted to and received by an authentic heir of the treasury of the true dharma eye. It is a commonly known fact among humans and devas that there are no ancestors authentically transmitting the dharma treasury who have not seen and heard of the buddha robe. Thus, the authentic transmission and learning of the shape, color, and measurements, and the great merit, as well as the body, mind, bones, and marrow of a buddha kashaya, lie only in the authentically transmitted work of the buddha house. This is not known in the teaching of various Agama schools. What has been independently created by practitioners nowadays is not authentic transmission by authentic heirs.

The Tathagata Shakyamuni, our great teacher, entrusted the treasury of the true dharma eye, the unsurpassable enlightenment, to Mahakashyapa along with the kashaya. The robe was transmitted heir to heir for thirty-three generations to Huineng. The shape, color, and measurements have been intimately transmitted, freshly received, and maintained until now. This is an authentic transmission that each of the high ancestors of the Five Schools received and maintained. For forty or fifty generations, teacher and disciple without exception have sewn and worn the kashaya. This has been transmitted afresh from buddha to buddha in merged realization generation after generation.

———————

According to the authentically transmitted instruction of the Buddha, a kashaya can be made of:

Nine panels, each panel consisting of three long pieces and one short piece of cloth

Nine panels, each panel consisting of four long pieces and one short piece of cloth

Eleven panels, each panel consisting of three long pieces and one short piece of cloth, or of four long pieces and one short piece of cloth

Thirteen panels, each panel consisting of three long pieces and one short piece of cloth, or of four long pieces and one short piece of cloth

Fifteen panels, each panel consisting of four long pieces and one short piece of cloth

Seventeen panels, each panel consisting of four long pieces and one short piece of cloth

Nineteen panels, each panel consisting of four long pieces and one short piece of cloth

Twenty-one panels, each panel consisting of four long pieces and one short piece of cloth

Twenty-three panels, each panel consisting of four long pieces and one short piece of cloth

Twenty-five panels, each panel consisting of four long pieces and one short piece of cloth

Two hundred fifty panels, each panel consisting of four long pieces and one short piece of cloth

> Eighty-four thousand panels, each panel consisting of eight long
> pieces and one short piece of cloth

This is a summary. There are other types of kashayas. All these are
outer robes. Both laypeople and monks receive and maintain them. To
receive and maintain them means to wear them and not to keep them
folded without use.

Those who shave their heads and faces but hate and fear kashayas
without receiving and maintaining them are demons or people outside
the way.

Baizhang, Zen Master Dazhi, said, "Those who lack wholesome seeds
planted in the past avoid and dislike a kashaya. They fear and avoid true
dharma."

———————

The Buddha said:

> If a sentient being, after entering my dharma, commits a heavy crime
> or falls into crooked views, but reveres the outer robe with mindfulness,
> receiving and maintaining it, other buddhas and I will certainly give a
> prediction of enlightenment in the Three Vehicles to such a person, who
> will become a buddha. If a deva, a dragon, a human being, or a demon
> reveres the merit of even a small piece of kashaya, they will practice
> unremittingly in the Three Vehicles. If a spirit being or a sentient being
> acquires even a four-*sun* piece of a kashaya, the being will have sufficient
> food and drink. If sentient beings have a fight and are about to fall into a
> crooked view, but think of the power of a kashaya, they can arouse com-
> passion and return to purity with the power of a kashaya. If someone in
> a battlefield carries a small piece of a kashaya and reveres it, the person
> will certainly attain emancipation.

Thus, we know that the power of a kashaya is unsurpassable and
wondrous. Where it is accepted and maintained with trust, there is always the receiving of a prediction of enlightenment and attaining of no-
remittance. Not only Shakyamuni Buddha but all other buddhas teach in
this way. Know that the essence and form of all buddhas is the kashaya.

Thus, the Buddha said, "Those who fall into unwholesome paths avoid a monk's great robe." So, if you feel like avoiding a kashaya upon hearing and seeing it, you should lament that you are about to fall into an unwholesome path. Repent for this.

When Shakyamuni Buddha was about to leave his palace and enter the mountains for the first time, a tree god held up an outer robe and said, "If you wear this robe with reverence, you will be protected from harm by demons." It is said that the Buddha revered it and wore it for twelve years without ceasing. This is a story told by scriptures, including the *Agama Sutra*.

It is also said that a kashaya is an auspicious robe. Those who wear it invariably attain an excellent place. There has never been a time in the world when this robe has not emerged. Its emergence at any moment is a matter of timeless kalpas. A matter of timeless kalpas is its arrival at any moment. To attain a kashaya is to attain the emblem of the Buddha. This being so, among all buddha tathagatas there is no one who has not received and maintained it. There is no one who has received and maintained a kashaya and has not become a buddha.

———————

There are various ways to wear the kashaya. The most common way is to leave the right shoulder uncovered.

There is also a way to cover both shoulders. In this case, you align both edges of the robe to your left shoulder and elbow, with the front edge in front and the back edge underneath it. At times the Buddha wore the kashaya in this way. This is not, however, seen or heard by shravakas or taught by scriptures, including the *Agama Sutra*.

The method of wearing a kashaya in the buddha way has been invariably received and maintained by ancestors who have received the true dharma that is present. When receiving a kashaya, you should always receive it from such an ancestor. A kashaya transmitted by buddha ancestors is authentically transmitted from buddha to buddha without fail. It is a kashaya of earlier buddhas and later buddhas, old buddhas and new buddhas. It transforms the way and transforms buddhas. In authentically transforming the past, present, and future, a kashaya is transmitted from past to present, from present to future, from present to past, from past to past, from present to present, from future to future, from future to present, from future to past. It is authentic transmission only between buddha and buddha.

This being so, for hundreds of years since Bodhidharma came to China, and from the Tang to Song Dynasties, a number of scholars experienced realization and those in the scriptural and precepts schools entered buddha dharma. They gave up their worn-out robes that had come from the old nests [teachings] and received kashayas authentically transmitted in the buddha way. Such incidents are recorded in books including the *[Jingde Record of] Transmission of the Lamp*, the *Extensive Transmission of the Lamp*, the *Continuous Transmission of the Lamp*, and the *Universal Transmission of the Lamp*. This marked a departure from the limited views of the scriptural and precepts schools to revering the great way that had been authentically transmitted by buddha ancestors. Such people all became buddha ancestors.

Those who are in the present should also study with ancient ancestors. If you are to receive a kashaya, authentically receive an authentically transmitted kashaya. Receive it with trust. Do not receive a forged kashaya.

Speaking of an authentically transmitted kashaya, the one authentically transmitted from Shaolin [Bodhidharma] through Caoxi [Huineng] has been passed on from heir to heir without missing even one generation. In this way, the work of the way has been exactly passed on, and the buddha robe has been intimately handed down. The buddha way is authentically transmitted to the buddha way. It does not depend on the hearsay of an idle person.

There is a common saying: "One thousand hearings do not match one seeing. One thousand seeings do not match one attainment." If we reflect on this, even one thousand seeings and ten thousand hearings cannot match one attainment, an authentic receiving of the buddha robe.

Those who doubt authentic transmission have not dreamed of it, but authentic transmission of the buddha robe is more intimate than hearing about a buddha sutra. Even one thousand sutras and ten thousand attainments cannot match one realization. Buddha ancestors are the merging of realization. Do not follow the mediocre schools of scripture and precepts.

The power of the robe in the ancestral gate [school] has actually been transmitted in its original form. It has been received and inherited up until now without a break. Those who authentically receive it are all dharma-transmitted ancestors who have merged with realization. They excel bodhisattvas of the ten stages and three classes. See it, revere it, bow to it, and place it on your head.

That you accept the teaching of authentic transmission of this buddha robe in your body and mind with trust is a sign of encountering the Buddha. Not to be able to receive this dharma is a life to be lamented. Deeply affirm that covering your body with this kashaya even once is an amulet of protection for ensuring enlightenment.

It is said that if you dye your mind with one phrase or one verse of teaching, it will become timelessly radiant without lack. To dye your body and mind with a single dharma is just like this.

Although the mind has no abode and is not possessed by the self, its power is concrete. Although the body has no abode, its power is concrete. A kashaya also neither comes nor goes. It is not possessed by the self or other; it abides where it is maintained and assists the one who maintains it. The power of what is attained by the kashaya must also be like this.

Making a kashaya is not limited to the ordinary or sages. Its meaning cannot be thoroughly understood by bodhisattvas of the ten stages and three classes. Those who don't have seeds of enlightenment planted in the past do not see, hear about, and know a kashaya even for one lifetime, two lifetimes, or innumerable lifetimes. How then can they receive and maintain it?

There are those who comprehend the merit of a kashaya touching their bodies even once, and there are those who don't. Those who understand this merit should rejoice, and those who don't should hope for it. Those who cannot should lament.

Within and outside the billion worlds, both humans and devas widely see, hear, and know that the buddha robe has only been transmitted inside the gate of buddha ancestors. Also, the facts about the buddha robe are known inside the ancestral gate alone, and not inside other gates.

Those who resent themselves for not knowing about the buddha robe are foolish. Even if they are well versed in eighty-four thousand samadhis and dharanis, if they have not authentically received the buddha ancestors' dharma of the robe and have not clarified the authentic transmission of the kashaya, they are not authentic heirs of buddhas.

How many sentient beings in other realms would wish that the buddha robe had been authentically transmitted in their own lands just as it has been transmitted to China? They may be ashamed or have deep sorrow.

Indeed, we encounter the dharma of the Tathagatha, the World-Honored One's authentically transmitted way of the robe. It is due to the seeds of great merit planted in the past. Nowadays, in this unwholesome time in the world of declining dharma, there are a number of groups of demons who are not ashamed of not having authentic transmission but are jealous of it. Where they abide and what they possess are not their true self. To authentically receive the true dharma alone is the straight path of studying the Buddha.

———————

Know that a kashaya is the buddha body, buddha mind. It is called a robe of emancipation, a field of benefaction. It is called a robe of patience, a robe beyond form. It is called a robe of compassion, a robe of the Tathagata, a robe of unsurpassable, complete enlightenment. Receive and maintain it accordingly.

Nowadays in Great Song China, those who call themselves students of precepts [practitioners of the Precept School] are not ashamed, resentful, or even aware of receiving incomprehensible teachings in their house, because they are intoxicated with the wine of shravakas. Following their own minor thinking, such people have altered the kashaya that was transmitted from India and used for a long time through Han and Tang China. This is based on their limited views, of which they should be ashamed. If a robe that comes from such minor thinking is worn, much of the buddha form will be missing. Because they did not extensively study the buddha guidelines, they have created such a robe. It is clear that the body-mind of the Tathagata has been authentically transmitted in the ancestral gate alone, and has not flown into the work of their houses. If they had known the buddha guidelines even one out of ten thousand, they would not have destroyed the buddha robe in this way. They do not even clarify scriptural text and the essence of it.

———————

Being confined to coarse cloth as the material for a kashaya grossly contradicts buddha dharma and in particular violates the buddha robe. A disciple of the Buddha should not wear such a violated robe. How so? Those who insist on coarse cloth only emphasize material and forget the spirit of the buddha robe. What a pity! The view of shravakas in the Lesser Vehicles misses the point. Let me say this: when their view on the cloth is crushed, the buddha robe emerges.

More than one or two buddhas have worn a kashaya made of silk that they denounce. According to the buddha guidelines, excrement-cleaning cloth is regarded as excellent pure material for making a kashaya.

Silk, cotton, and other kinds of cloth are listed among the ten types of excrement-cleaning cloth. Then, is it that silk cannot be used as excrement-cleaning cloth? Those who do not accept this go against the buddha way. If they exclude silk, they should exclude common cloth.

Why do they exclude silk? Because they say silk is produced by killing silkworms. This should be greatly ridiculed. Isn't common cloth related to living beings? Without being liberated from the ordinary view of sentient and insentient, how can they know the buddha kashaya?

Also, there are those who explain silk as the product of incarnated bodies [of a tree god] and confuse others. This should also be ridiculed. What is not a product of transformative birth? Such people may trust their ears to hear about transformation but doubt their eyes that see transformation. It seems they have eyes but don't have ears, or they have ears but don't have eyes. Where are their ears and eyes?

Know that among the cloths you pick up, there can be silklike cloths and common cloths among them. When you use them for making a kashaya, you should not call it silk or common cloth, but just call it excrement-cleaning cloth. As it is excrement-cleaning cloth, it is neither silk nor common cloth. Even if a human or a deva turns into discarded cloth, it is not sentient but just discarded cloth. Even if a pine or chrysanthemum turns into discarded cloth, it is not insentient but just discarded cloth.

When you know that excrement-cleaning cloth is beyond silk and common cloth and beyond a jewel, excrement-cleaning cloth emerges and you encounter excrement-cleaning cloth. Those who haven't given up discrimination between silk and common cloth have never dreamed of excrement-cleaning cloth. If those who make a kashaya of coarse cloth and maintain it for lifetimes are not aware of this way of seeing the material for a kashaya, this is not authentically receiving the buddha robe.

Among various types of kashaya, there are a common-cloth kashaya, a silk kashaya, and a leather kashaya. They are all worn by buddhas—buddha robes with buddha merit.

While there is authentically transmitted teaching on kashaya, those who have not been freed from ordinary views make light of buddha dharma, do not believe in the buddha words, and try to follow ordinary thinking. They must be called people outside the way who have been entrusted with buddha dharma. They are among the group of those who destroy the true dharma.

Some also say that they have altered the buddha robe by following the teaching of devas. Perhaps they want to be a heavenly buddha or have become a type of deva. However, the Buddha's disciples should expound buddha dharma to devas, instead of inquiring into the way of devas. How pitiful! Those who have not authentically received buddha dharma speak in this way.

Devas and the Buddha's descendants hold varied views, and devas come down [to the human realm] to inquire of the Buddha's descendants about dharma. It is because the deva views and the Buddha views are far different from each other.

Discard the minor views of shravakas in the Precept School, and do not accept their views. Know that they are views of the Lesser School.

The Buddha said, "Those who kill their parents repent, but those who slander the dharma do not." Thus, the path of minor views and doubts is not the original intention of the Buddha. The great road of buddha dharma cannot be reached by the Lesser Vehicles. No one other than those in the ancestral way with the entrusted dharma treasure knows of the authentic transmission of the Buddha's great precepts.

Long ago, at midnight on Mount Huangmei, the robe dharma of the Buddha was authentically transmitted to the top of Huineng's head. This is indeed an authentic transmission of transmitting the dharma and the robe. This took place because Hongren knew who the true person was. Had Hongren been one of those of four fruits [arhats], bodhisattvas of three classes or ten stages, or of masters of treatises and scriptures, he would have transmitted the dharma and robe to Shenxiu and not to Huineng. However, because the buddha ancestor selected a buddha ancestor beyond the path of the ordinary or sacred, Huineng became the Sixth Ancestor. Know that the heir-to-heir practice of buddha ancestors knowing a person and knowing the self does not lie in a fathomable place.

Later, a monk asked Huineng, "Is the robe transmitted to you at midnight on Mount Huangmei made of common cloth, silk, or fine cotton? What is it, after all?"

Huineng said, "It is not made of common cloth, silk, or fine cotton."

Remember these words of the High Ancestor of Caoxi. The buddha robe is beyond silk, common cloth, and cotton. Those who ignore this and groundlessly call it silk, common cloth, or cotton are slandering the buddha dharma. How can they know the buddha robe?

Furthermore, there are those who are told [by the Buddha] to come and receive the precepts. The kashayas they receive go beyond the distinction of silk or common cloth. This is the Buddha's admonition.

The lay clothes Shanavasin was wearing were transformed into a kashaya when he became a monk. Reflect quietly on this story. Do not ignore it as if you had not heard of it.

There is further teaching on the kashaya authentically transmitted from buddha to buddha, from ancestor to ancestor. Those who count letters are not aware of it and cannot fathom it. Indeed, how can the one thousand varieties and ten thousand transformations of the buddha way be limited to the realm of mediocre schools? There is samadhi and there is dharani. Those who count the sands of the Ganges do not see the pearl sewn inside the robe.

Regard the shape, color, and measurements of the kashaya authentically transmitted by buddha ancestors as the true base of all buddhas' kashaya. This model has existed for a long time in India and China, from ancient times up to the present day. Those who discern right and wrong have realized it.

Even if there are those outside the ancestral way who call some robes kashayas, there are no true ancestors who allow them to be their branches and leaves [descendants]. How can they nurture the seeds of wholesome roots? How, then, can they attain the fruit?

Now, we do not only see and hear the buddha dharma that has not been encountered for vast kalpas, but we also see, hear, study, and maintain the buddha robe. This is no other than seeing the Buddha. This is to hear the buddha voice, radiate the buddha light, and experience the buddha experience. This is to receive the buddha mind from person to person, attaining the buddha marrow.

———————

The material for making a kashaya should always be pure. Pure material is something that is donated by a donor with pure trust, bought in a marketplace, sent by devas, or given by dragon kings or demon kings. Pure donations or pure leather offered by the king or ministers can also be used.

Also, ten types of excrement-cleaning cloth are regarded as pure. They are: cloth chewed by oxen, cloth chewed by rats, burned cloth, cloth that is stained with menstrual blood, cloth stained in childbirth, cloth picked up at a shrine, cloth picked up at a cemetery, cloth for prayers, cloth given by the king and ministers, and shrouds.

These types of cloth are regarded as pure material for making a kashaya. They are discarded in the lay world but utilized in the buddha way. The values in the lay world and in the buddha way can be measured in this manner.

Thus, if you look for pure material, look for these ten types of cloth. Know what is pure and understand what is impure when acquiring them. Know the mind and understand the body. Acquire the ten types of cloth and think over the purity of silk and common cloth.

It is extremely foolish to assume that a robe made of excrement-cleaning cloth is used merely for shabby appearance. This type of robe has been used in the buddha dharma to dress cleanly and magnificently. In the buddha dharma, to wear a poor-looking robe means to wear an impure robe made of brocade, gold, silver, and rare jewels.

In the buddha way of this and other worlds, to use a clean and magnificent robe means to use a robe made of one of the ten types of cloth. This is not only going beyond purity and impurity but also becoming free from the realm of delusion and no-delusion, going beyond form and consciousness, while not being concerned with gain and loss.

Those who wholeheartedly receive and maintain the authentic transmission are buddha ancestors because when they are buddha ancestors they receive authentic transmission. They receive and maintain this, authentically transmitted, as buddha ancestors not depending on the emergence and no-emergence of body or mind.

It is lamentable that monks and nuns have not worn a kashaya for a long time in Japan. Rejoice that you receive and maintain it now. Lay men and women who receive and maintain the precepts should wear a kashaya of five, seven, or nine panels. How should home leavers not wear it?

It is said that those who are Indra and the Six Deva Kings of the desire realm, up to male prostitutes, female prostitutes, and servants, should receive the buddha precepts and wear a kashaya. How, then, should the Buddha's descendants not wear the buddha robe? Even animals should receive the buddha precepts and wear a kashaya. Why should buddha children not wear the buddha robe?

In this way, those who are the Buddha's descendants, regardless of being devas or humans, the king and officials, beyond the boundaries of laity, home leavers, servants, and animals, should receive the buddha precepts and a kashaya. This is indeed a straight way to the buddha place.

When you wash a kashaya, sprinkle powdered incense and flower petals into water. When the kashaya is washed, rinsed, and dried, you should fold it, set it on a high place, and venerate it with incense and flowers: After making three bows, kneel down and place it on your head, put your palms together, and chant this verse:

> Great is the robe of liberation,
> the robe beyond form, the field of benefaction!
> I wear the Tathagata's teaching
> to awaken countless beings.

Chant this three times. Then, stand up and put it on.

Once, when I was in Song China, practicing on a long sitting plat-form, I observed the monks around me. At the beginning of zazen in the morning, they would hold up their kashayas, place them on their heads, and chant the robe verse quietly with palms together. This was the first time I had seen the putting on of the kashaya in this way and I rejoiced, tears wetting the collar of my robe. Although I had read this verse of venerating the kashaya in the *Agama Sutra,* I had not known the proce-dure. At that moment, I saw it with my own eyes. In my joy I also felt sorrow that there had been no master to teach this to me and no good friend to recommend it in Japan. How sad that so much time had been wasted!

But I also rejoiced in my wholesome past actions. If I had stayed in my land, how could I have sat side by side with the monks who had re-ceived and were wearing the buddha robe? My sadness and joy brought endless tears.

Then, I made a vow to myself: However unsuited I may be, I will become an authentic holder of the buddha dharma, receiving authentic transmission of the true dharma, and I will compassionately show people in my land the buddha ancestors' authentically transmitted dharma robe.

The vow I made at that time must not have been in vain, thanks to the invisible assistance of true trust. The buddha children who receive and maintain the kashaya now should endeavor in the practice of rever-ing it day and night. This brings forth genuine merit. The effect of seeing and hearing one line of the kashaya verse may extend to trees and rocks. The power of the authentically transmitted kashaya is rare to encounter in the ten directions.

In the tenth month of the seventeenth year of the Jiading Era of Song China [1224], two Korean monks visited Qingyuan Prefecture. One was named Zixuan, and the other Jingyun. They were men of let-ters who often discussed the meaning of sutras, but they did not have kashayas or bowls as if they had been laypeople. What a pity! They had shaven heads but did not have the manners of monks. This was perhaps because they had come from a small country in a remote land. When monks from Japan visit other countries, they might be like these monks.

During the twelve years of his practice before attaining the way, Shakyamuni Buddha venerated the kashaya without putting it aside. As his remote descendant, you should keep this in mind. Turn your head away from worshipping heaven, gods, kings, and retainers for the sake of name and gain, and joyfully dedicate yourself to venerating the buddha robe.

This was written at the Kannondori Kosho Horin Monastery on the first day of winter, the first year of the Ninji Era [1240]. Dogen, Shramana who has transmitted dharma from Song China.

15

MOUNTAINS AND WATERS SUTRA

MOUNTAINS AND WATERS right now actualize the ancient buddha expression. Each, abiding in its condition, unfolds its full potential. Because mountains and waters have been active since before the
Empty Eon, they are alive at this moment. Because they have been the
self since before form arose, they are emancipation actualized.

Because mountains are high and broad, their way of riding the clouds
always extends from the mountains; their wondrous power of soaring in
the wind comes freely from the mountains.

Priest Daokai of Mount Furong said to the assembly, "The green mountains are always walking; a stone woman gives birth to a child at night."

Mountains do not lack the characteristics of mountains. Therefore,
they always abide in ease and always walk. Examine in detail the characteristic of the mountains' walking.

Mountains' walking is just like human walking. Accordingly, do not
doubt mountains' walking even though it does not look the same as
human walking. The buddha ancestor's words point to walking. This is
fundamental understanding. Penetrate these words.

Because green mountains walk, they are permanent. Although they walk more swiftly than the wind, someone in the mountains does not notice or understand it. "In the mountains" means the blossoming of the entire world. People outside the mountains do not notice or understand the mountains' walking. Those without eyes to see mountains cannot notice, understand, see, or hear this reality.

If you doubt mountains' walking, you do not know your own walking; it is not that you do not walk, but that you do not know or understand your own walking. Since you do know your own walking, you should fully know the green mountains' walking.

Green mountains are neither sentient nor insentient. You are neither sentient nor insentient. At this moment, you cannot doubt the green mountains' walking.

———

You may not notice that you study the green mountains, using numerous worlds of phenomena as your standards. Clearly examine the green mountains' walking and your own walking. Examine walking backward and backward walking, and investigate the fact that walking forward and backward has never stopped since the very moment before form arose, since the time of the King of the Empty Eon.

If walking had stopped, buddha ancestors would not have appeared. If walking ends, the buddha dharma cannot reach the present. Walking forward does not cease; walking backward does not cease. Walking forward does not obstruct walking backward. Walking backward does not obstruct walking forward. This is called the mountains' flow and the flowing mountains.

———

Green mountains thoroughly practice walking and eastern mountains thoroughly practice traveling on water. Accordingly, these activities are a mountain's practice. Keeping its own form, without changing body and mind, a mountain always practices in every place.

Don't slander by saying that a green mountain cannot walk and an eastern mountain cannot travel on water. When your understanding is shallow, you doubt the phrase *Green mountains are always walking.* When your learning is immature, you are shocked by the words "flowing mountains." Without fully understanding even the words "flowing water," you drown in small views and narrow understanding.

Yet, the characteristics of mountains manifest their form and life force. There is walking, there is flowing, and there is a moment when a mountain gives birth to a mountain child. Because mountains are buddha ancestors, buddha ancestors appear in this way.

Even if you have an eye to see mountains as grass, trees, earth, rocks, or walls, do not be confused or swayed by it; this is not complete realization. Even if there is a moment when you view mountains as the seven treasures' splendor, this is not returning to the source. Even if you understand mountains as the realm where all buddhas practice, this understanding is not something to be attached to. Even if you have the highest understanding of mountains as all buddhas' wondrous characteristics, the truth is not only this. These are conditioned views. This is not the understanding of buddha ancestors, but merely looking through a bamboo pipe at a corner of the sky.

Turning circumstances and turning mind is rejected by the great sage. Speaking of mind and speaking of essence is not agreeable to buddha ancestors. Seeing into mind and seeing into essence is the activity of people outside the way. Confined words and phrases do not lead to liberation. There is something free from all of these views. That is: *Green mountains are always walking,* and *Eastern mountains travel on water.* Study this in detail.

———

A stone woman gives birth to a child at night means that the moment when a barren woman gives birth to a child is called night.

There are male stones, female stones, and nonmale, nonfemale stones. Placed in the sky and in the earth, they are called heavenly stones and earthly stones. These are explained in the ordinary world, but not many people know about it.

Understand the meaning of *gives birth to a child.* At the moment of giving birth to a child, is the mother separate from the child? Study not only that you become a mother when your child is born, but also that you become a child. This is to actualize giving birth in practice-realization. Study and investigate this thoroughly.

Yunmen, Great Master Kuangzhen, said, "Eastern mountains travel on water."

The meaning of these words brought forth that all mountains are eastern mountains, and all eastern mountains travel on water. Because of this, Nine Mountains, Mount Sumeru, and other mountains appear and have practice-realization. These are called *eastern mountains*. However, could Yunmen penetrate the skin, flesh, bones, and marrow of the eastern mountains and their vital practice-realization?

Now, in Great Song China there are careless fellows who form groups; they cannot be set straight by the few true masters. They say that the statement "Eastern mountains travel on water," or Nanquan's story of a sickle, is illogical; what they mean is that any words having to do with logical thought are not buddha ancestors' Zen words, and that only illogical stories are buddha ancestors' expressions. In this way they consider Huangbo's striking with a staff and Linji's shout as beyond logic and unconcerned with thought; they regard these as words of great enlightenment that precede the arising of form.

They say, "Ancient masters used expedient phrases, which are beyond understanding, to slash entangled vines." Those who say this have never seen a true master, and they have no eye of understanding. They are immature, foolish fellows not even worth discussing. In China these two or three hundred years, there have been many groups of demons and six types of heretical thinkers. What a pity! The great road of buddha ancestors is crumbling. People who hold this view are not even as good as shravakas of the Lesser Vehicles and are more foolish than those outside the way. They are neither laypeople nor monks, neither human nor heavenly beings. They are more stupid than animals that learn the buddha way.

The illogical stories mentioned by those bald-headed fellows are only illogical for them, not for buddha ancestors. Even though they do not understand, they should not neglect studying the buddha ancestors' path of understanding. Even if it is beyond understanding in the end, their present understanding is off the mark.

I have personally seen and heard many people like this in Song China. How sad that they do not know about the phrases of logical thought, or penetrating logical thought in phrases! When I laughed at them in China, they had no response and remained silent. Their idea about illogical words is only a distorted view. Even if there is no teacher to show them the original truth, their belief in spontaneous enlightenment is a view of those outside the way.

Know that *eastern mountains travel on water* is the bones and marrow of the buddha ancestors. All waters appear at the foot of the eastern mountains. Accordingly, all mountains ride on clouds and walk in the sky. All mountains are the tops of the heads of all waters. Walking beyond and walking within are both done on water. All mountains walk with their toes on waters and make them splash. Thus, in walking there are seven vertical paths and eight horizontal paths. This is practice-realization.

Water is neither strong nor weak, neither wet nor dry, neither moving nor still, neither cold nor hot, neither existent nor nonexistent, neither deluded nor enlightened. When water solidifies, it is harder than a diamond. Who can crack it? When water melts, it is softer than milk. Who can destroy it? Do not doubt that these are the characteristics water manifests. Reflect on the moment when you see water of the ten directions as water of the ten directions.

This is not merely studying the moment when human and heavenly beings see water; this is studying the moment when water sees water. Because water practices and realizes water, water expresses water. Actualize the path where self encounters self. Go forward and backward, leaping beyond the vital path where other fathoms other.

Not all beings see mountains and waters in the same way. Some beings see water as a jeweled ornament, but they do not regard jeweled ornaments as water. What in the human realm corresponds to their water? We only see their jeweled ornaments as water.

Some beings see water as wondrous blossoms, but they do not use blossoms as water. Hungry ghosts see water as raging fire or pus and blood. Dragons and fish see water as a palace or a pavilion. Some beings see water as the seven treasures or a wish-granting jewel. Some beings see water as a forest or a wall. Some see it as the dharma nature of pure liberation, the true human body, or the form of the body and the essence of mind. Human beings see water as water. Water is seen as dead or alive depending on [the seer's] causes and conditions.

Thus, the views of all beings are not the same. Question this matter now. Are there many ways to see one thing, or is it a mistake to see many forms as one thing? Pursue this beyond the limit of pursuit. Accordingly, endeavors in practice-realization of the way are not limited to one or two kinds. The thoroughly actualized realm has one thousand kinds and ten thousand ways.

When we think about the meaning of this, it seems that there is water for various beings but there is no original water—there is no water common to all types of beings. But water for these various kinds of beings does not depend on mind or body, does not arise from actions, does not depend on self or other. Water's freedom depends only on water.

In this way, water is not just earth, water, fire, wind, space, or consciousness. Water is not blue, yellow, red, white, or black. Water is not form, sound, smell, taste, touch, or mind. But water as earth, water, fire, wind, and space actualizes itself.

This being so, it is difficult to say who has created this land and palace right now or how such things have been created. To say that the world is resting on the wheel of space or on the wheel of wind is not the truth of the self or the truth of others. Such a statement is based only on a small view of assumptions. People speak this way because they think that it is impossible for things to exist without having a place to rest.

———————

The Buddha said, "All things are ultimately unbound. There is nowhere that they permanently abide."

Know that even though all things are unbound and not tied to anything, they abide in their own condition. However, when most human beings see water, they only see that it flows unceasingly. This is a limited human view; there are actually many kinds of flowing. Water flows on the earth, in the sky, upward, and downward. It flows around a single curve or into many bottomless abysses. When it rises it becomes clouds. When it descends it forms abysses.

————————

Wenzi said, "The path of water is such that when it rises to the sky, it becomes raindrops; when it falls to the ground, it becomes rivers."

Even a secular person can speak this way. You who call yourselves descendants of buddha ancestors should feel ashamed of being more ignorant than an ordinary person. The path of water is not noticed by water, but is actualized by water. It is not unnoticed by water, but is actualized by water.

When it rises to the sky, it becomes raindrops means that water rises to the heavens and skies and forms raindrops. Raindrops vary according to the different worlds. To say that there are places water does not reach is the teaching of the shravakas in the Lesser Vehicles or the mistaken teaching of people outside the way. Water exists inside fire and inside mind, thought, and discernment. Water also reaches inside realization of buddha nature.

When it falls to the ground, it becomes rivers means that when water reaches the ground it turns into rivers. The essence of the rivers becomes a wise person.

Ordinary fools and mediocre people nowadays think that water is always in rivers or oceans, but this is not so. There are rivers and oceans within water. Thus, even where there is not a river or an ocean, there is water. It is just that when water falls down to the ground, it manifests the characteristics of rivers and oceans.

Also, do not think that where water forms rivers or oceans there is no world and there is no buddha land. Even in a drop of water innumerable buddha lands appear. Accordingly, it is not that there is only water in the buddha land or a buddha land in water.

Where water abides is not concerned with the past, future, present, or the worlds of phenomena. Yet, water is the fundamental point actualized. Where buddha ancestors reach, water never fails to reach. Where water reaches, buddha ancestors never fail to be present. Thus, buddha ancestors always take up water and make it their body and mind, make it their thought.

In this way, the words "Water does not rise" are not found in scriptures inside or outside [of buddha dharma]. The path of water runs upward, downward, and in all directions.

However, one buddha sutra does say, "Fire and air go upward, earth and water go downward." This *upward* and *downward* require examination. Examine this from the point of view of the buddha way. Although you use the word *downward* to describe the direction earth and water go, earth and water do not actually go downward. In the same way, the direction fire and air go is called *upward*.

The world of phenomena is not limited by up, down, or the cardinal directions. They are tentatively designated according to the directions in which four great elements, five great elements, or six great elements go. The Heaven of No Thought should not be regarded as *upward* nor should Avichi Hell be regarded as *downward*. The Avichi Hell is the entire world of phenomena; the Heaven of No Thought is the entire world of phenomena.

———

Now, when dragons and fish see water as a palace, it may be like human beings seeing a palace. They may not think it flows. If an outsider tells them, "What you see as a palace is running water," the dragons and fish may be astonished, just as we are when we hear the words *Mountains flow*. Nevertheless, there may be some dragons and fish who understand that the railings and pillars of palaces and pavilions are flowing water.

Quietly reflect and ponder the meaning of this. If you do not learn to penetrate your superficial views, you will not be free from the body and mind of an ordinary person. Then you will not thoroughly experience the land of buddha ancestors, or even the land or the palace of ordinary people.

At this time, human beings deeply know that what is in the ocean and the river is water, but do not know what dragons and fish see and use as water. Do not foolishly suppose that what we see as water is used as water by all other beings. You who study with buddhas should not be limited to human views when you see water. Go further and study water in the buddha way. Study how you view the water used by buddha ancestors. Study whether there is water or no water in the house of buddha ancestors.

———————

Mountains have been the abode of great sages from the limitless past to the limitless present. Wise people and sages all have mountains as their inner chamber, as their body and mind. Because of wise people and sages, mountains are actualized.

You may think that in mountains many wise people and great sages are assembled. But after entering the mountains, not a single person meets another. There is just the vital activity of the mountains. There is no trace of anyone having entered the mountains.

When you see mountains from the ordinary world, and when you meet mountains while in mountains, the mountains' head and eye are viewed quite differently. Your idea or view of mountains not flowing is not the same as the view of dragons and fish. Human and heavenly beings have attained a position concerning their own worlds that other beings may doubt or may not have the capacity to doubt.

Do not remain bewildered and skeptical when you hear the words *Mountains flow;* but study these words with buddha ancestors. When you take up one view, you see mountains flowing, and when you take up another view, mountains are not flowing. One time mountains are flowing, another time they are not flowing. If you do not fully understand this, you do not understand the true dharma wheel of the Tathagata.

An ancient buddha said, "If you do not wish to incur the cause for Unceasing Hell, do not slander the true dharma wheel of the Tathagata." Carve these words on your skin, flesh, bones, and marrow; on your body, mind, and environs; on emptiness and on form. They are already carved on trees and rocks, on fields and villages.

———————

Although mountains belong to the nation, mountains belong to people who love them. When mountains love their master, such a virtuous sage or wise person enters the mountains. Since mountains belong to the sages and wise people living there, trees and rocks become abundant and birds and animals are inspired. This is so because the sages and wise people extend their virtue.

Know for a fact that mountains are fond of wise people and sages. Rulers have visited mountains to pay homage to wise people or to ask for instructions from great sages. These have been excellent precedences in the past and present. At such times these rulers treat the sages as teachers, disregarding the protocol of the usual world. The imperial power has no authority over the wise people in the mountains. Mountains are apart from the human world. At the time the Yellow Emperor visited Mount Kongdong to pay homage to Guangcheng, he walked on his knees, touched his forehead to the ground, and asked for instruction.

When Shakyamuni Buddha left his father's palace and entered the mountains, his father, the king, did not resent the mountains, nor was he suspicious of those who taught the prince in the mountains. The twelve years of Shakyamuni Buddha's practice of the way were mostly spent in the mountains, and his opening of the way occurred in the mountains. Thus, even his father, a wheel-turning king, did not wield authority in the mountains.

Know that mountains are not the realm of human beings or the realm of heavenly beings. Do not view mountains from the standard of human thought. If you do not judge mountains' flowing by the human understanding of flowing, you will not doubt mountains' flowing and not flowing.

On the other hand, from ancient times wise people and sages have often lived on water. When they live on water, they catch fish, catch human beings, and catch the way. These were all ancient ways of being on water, following wind and streams. Furthermore, there is catching the self, catching catching, being caught by catching, and being caught by the way.

Priest Decheng abruptly left Mount Yao and lived on the river. There he produced a successor, the wise sage of the Huating River [Jiashan Shanhui]. Is this not catching a fish, catching a person, catching water, or catching the self? The disciple seeing Decheng is Decheng. Decheng guiding his disciple is meeting a [true] person.

It is not only that there is water in the world, but there is a world in water. It is not merely in water. There is a world of sentient beings in clouds. There is a world of sentient beings in the air. There is a world of sentient beings in fire. There is a world of sentient beings on earth. There is a world of sentient beings in the world of phenomena. There is a world of sentient beings in a blade of grass. There is a world of sentient beings in one staff.

Wherever there is a world of sentient beings, there is a world of buddha ancestors. Thoroughly examine the meaning of this.

In this way, water is the true dragon's palace. It is not flowing downward. To regard water as only flowing is to slander water with the word *flowing*. This would be the same as insisting that water does not flow.

Water is just the true thusness of water. Water is water's complete characteristics; it is not flowing. When you investigate the flowing and not-flowing of a handful of water, thorough experience of all things is immediately actualized.

There are mountains hidden in treasures. There are mountains hidden in swamps. There are mountains hidden in the sky. There are mountains hidden in mountains. There are mountains hidden in hiddenness. This is how we study.

An ancient buddha said, "Mountains are mountains, waters are waters." These words do not mean mountains are mountains; they mean mountains are mountains.

In this way, investigate mountains thoroughly. When you investigate mountains thoroughly, this becomes the endeavor within the mountains.

Such mountains and waters of themselves become wise persons and sages.

Presented to the assembly at Kannondori Kosho Horin Monastery at the hour of the Rat [midnight], the eighteenth day, the tenth month, the first year of the Ninji Era [1240].

16

BUDDHA ANCESTORS

ACTUALIZING BUDDHA ANCESTORS means to uphold and see them in veneration. It is not limited to buddhas of the past, present, and future, but it is going beyond buddhas who are going beyond themselves. It is taking up those who have maintained the face and eye of buddha ancestors, formally bowing and encountering them. They have manifested the power of the buddha ancestors, dwelt in it, and actualized it in the body.

The buddha ancestors are:

Vipashin (Boundless Discourse) Buddha, Honored One
Shikhin (Fire) Buddha, Honored One
Vishvabhu (Universal Compassion) Buddha, Honored One
Krakucchanda (Gold Wizard) Buddha, Honored One
Kanakamuni (Golden Sage) Buddha, Honored One
Kashyapa (Drinking Light) Buddha, Honored One
Shakyamuni (Patient Silence) Buddha, Honored One

Mahakashyapa, Honored One
Ananda, Honored One
Shanavasin, Honored One
Upagupta, Honored One
Dhritaka, Honored One
Micchaka, Honored One
Vasumitra, Honored One
Buddhanandi, Honored One
Buddhamitra, Honored One
Parshva, Honored One
Punyayashas, Honored One
Ashvaghosha, Honored One
Kapimala, Honored One
Nagarjuna, Honored One
Kanadeva, Honored One
Rahulata, Honored One
Sanghanandi, Honored One
Gayashata, Honored One
Kumarata, Honored One
Jayata, Honored One
Vasubandhu, Honored One
Manorhita, Honored One
Haklenayashas, Honored One
Simhabhikshu, Honored One
Basiasita, Honored One
Punyamitra, Honored One
Prajnatara, Honored One

Bodhidharma, Honored One
Huike, Honored One
Sengcan, Honored One
Daoxin, Honored One
Hongren, Honored One
Huineng, Honored One
Xingsi, Honored One
Xiqian, Honored One
Weiyan, Honored One

Tansheng, Honored One
Liangjie, Honored One
Daoying, Honored One
Daopi, Honored One
Guanzhi, Honored One
Yuanguan, Honored One
Jingxuan, Honored One
Yiqing, Honored One
Daokai, Honored One
Zichun, Honored One
Qingliao, Honored One
Zhongque, Honored One
Zhijian, Honored One
Rujing, Honored One.

———————

I saw Rujing, my late master, Old Buddha Tiantong, at the time of summer practice period in the first year of the Baoqing Era [1227] of Great Song, and with a formal bow completed receiving these buddha ancestors.

This can only occur between a buddha and a buddha.

Written and presented at Kannondori Kosho Horin Monastery, Uji County, Yamashiro Province, Japan, on the third day, the first month, the second year of the Ninji Era [1241].

17

DOCUMENT OF HERITAGE

A BUDDHA IS TRANSMITTED dharma only from a buddha, an ancestor only from an ancestor, through merging realization in direct transmission. In this way, it is the unsurpassable enlightenment. It is impossible to give the seal of realization without being a buddha, and it is impossible to become a buddha without receiving the seal of realization from a buddha. Who else, other than a buddha, can certify this realization as the most venerable, the most unsurpassable?

When you have the seal of realization from a buddha, you have realization without a teacher, realization without self. This being so, it is said, "A buddha receives realization from a buddha; an ancestor merges realization with an ancestor." The meaning of this teaching cannot be understood by those who are not buddhas. How then can it be measured by bodhisattvas of the ten stages or even those in the stage of enlightenment equal to buddhas'?

Furthermore, how can it be discerned by masters of sutras or treatises? Even if they explain it, they still do not understand it.

———

Since a buddha receives dharma from a buddha, the buddha way is thoroughly experienced by a buddha and a buddha; there is no moment of the way without a buddha and a buddha. For example, rocks inherit from rocks, jewels inherit from jewels. When a chrysanthemum inherits from a chrysanthemum and a pine gives the seal of realization to a pine, the preceding chrysanthemum is one with the following chrysanthemum and the preceding pine is one with the following pine. Those who do not understand this, even when they hear the words "authentic transmission from buddha to buddha," have no idea what it means; they do not know heritage from buddha to buddha in merged realization of ancestor and ancestor. What a pity! They appear to be a buddha family but they are not buddha heirs, nor are they heir-buddhas.

———————

Huineng, the Sixth Ancestor of Caoxi, once gave a discourse to the assembly: "There are forty ancestors from the Seven Original Buddhas to myself, and there are forty ancestors from myself to the Seven Original Buddhas."

This is clearly the meaning of the authentic heritage of buddha ancestors. The Seven Original Buddhas include those who appeared in the last eon and those who appeared in the present eon. Nevertheless, the continuation of face-to-face transmission of the forty ancestors is the buddha way and the buddha heritage.

Thus, proceeding from Huineng to the Seven Original Buddhas is the buddha heritage of forty ancestors. And going beyond from the Seven Original Buddhas to Huineng is the buddha heritage of forty buddhas.

The buddha way, the ancestor way, is like this. Without merging realization and without buddha ancestors, there is no buddha wisdom and there is no thorough ancestral experience. Without buddha wisdom, there is no accepting buddha; without thorough experience, there is no merging of realization between ancestors.

———————

The forty ancestors here represent only recent buddhas. Furthermore, the mutual heritage between buddhas and buddhas is deep and vast, neither backing up nor turning away, neither cut off nor stopped.

This means that although Shakyamuni Buddha had realized the way before the Seven Original Buddhas, he finally received dharma from Kashyapa Buddha. Again, although he realized the way on the eighth day of the twelfth month in the thirtieth year since his birth, it is realization of the way before the Seven Original Buddhas. It is realization of the way simultaneously with all buddhas shoulder to shoulder, realization of the way before all buddhas, realization of the way after all buddhas.

Furthermore, there is an understanding that Kashyapa Buddha, in turn, received dharma from Shakyamuni Buddha. If you do not clarify this, you do not understand the buddha way. If you do not clarify the buddha way, you are not an heir of the buddha. The buddha's heir means the buddha's child.

Shakyamuni Buddha once caused Ananda to ask, "Whose disciples were all buddhas of the past?"

Shakyamuni Buddha answered, "All buddhas of the past are disciples of myself, Shakyamuni Buddha."

The presence of all buddhas is like this. To see all buddhas, to succeed in all buddhas, to fulfill the way, is the buddha way of all buddhas. In this buddha way, the document of heritage is always given at the time of transmitting dharma. Those without dharma heritage are people outside the way who believe in spontaneous enlightenment. If the buddha way had not clearly established dharma heritage, how could it have come down to the present?

For this reason, when a buddha becomes a buddha, a document of heritage is given to a buddha's heir buddha, and this document of heritage is given by a buddha's heir buddha.

The meaning of the document of heritage is this: you understand the sun, the moon, and stars, and inherit dharma; you attain skin, flesh, bones, and marrow, and inherit dharma; you inherit a robe or staff, a pine branch or whisk, an udumbara blossom or a brocade robe; you receive straw sandals or an arched bamboo staff.

At the time of dharma heritage, the document is handwritten with the blood of the finger or the tongue. Or, it is handwritten with oil or milk. Every one of these is a document of heritage.

Those who entrust and those who receive this heritage are both the buddha's heirs. Indeed, whenever buddha ancestors are actualized, dharma heritage is actualized. At the time of actualization, innumerable buddha ancestors arrive without expectation and receive dharma without seeking. Those who inherit dharma are all buddha ancestors.

In China, since the time Bodhidharma, the Twenty-eighth Ancestor, came from India, the principle that there is dharma heritage in the buddha way has been authentically understood. Before that time, it had never been spoken of. This is something that had never been known in India by teachers of scriptures or treatises. This is something that has never been reached by bodhisattvas or even by teachers of dharani who study the meaning of the Tripitaka. What a pity! Although they have received a human body as a vessel of the way, they are uselessly entangled by the net of scriptures; they do not understand the method of breaking through, and cannot realize the moment of leaping out. This being so, you must study the way in detail and wholeheartedly determine to thoroughly experience it.

When I was in China, I had the opportunity to bow to some documents of heritage. There were various kinds.

One of those who showed me documents of heritage was Visiting Abbot Weiyi at Mount Tiantong, a former abbot of the Guangfu Monastery. He was a man from Yue, like Rujing, my late master. So Rujing would say, "Ask Abbot Weiyi about the customs of my region."

One day Weiyi said, "Old writings worth seeing are treasures of humankind. How many of them have you seen?"

I said, "I have seen a few."

Then he said, "I have a scroll of old writing. I will show it to you at your convenience." He brought it to me. It was a document of heritage of the Fayan lineage that he had obtained from the articles left behind by an old master. So it was not what Weiyi himself had received.

The document said, "The First Ancestor, Mahakashyapa, was awakened by Shakyamuni Buddha. Shakyamuni Buddha was awakened by Kashyapa Buddha."

Upon seeing this, I was firmly convinced that there is dharma heritage between an authentic heir and an authentic heir. This was a teaching

I had never seen before. At that moment the buddha ancestors had invisibly responded to my wish and helped me, a descendant of theirs. I had never been moved so much.

When elder Zongyue was filling the position of head monk at Mount Tiantong, he showed me a document of heritage of the Yunmen lineage. The name of the teacher giving the document of heritage and the names of some Indian and all Chinese ancestors were written side by side, and below that was the name of the person receiving the document. The name of this new ancestor was directly connected to those of the buddha ancestors. Therefore, all the names of the more than forty ancestors from the Tathagata are joined together with the name of the new heir. It was as though each of them had given heritage to the heir. Mahakashyapa, Ananda, and others were lined up just as in other lineages.

I asked Zongyue, the head monk, "Reverend, there is some difference among the Five Schools in the arrangement of names on the documents of heritage. Why is that so? If it came directly from India, why is there such a difference?"

Zongyue said, "Even if there is a vast difference, just understand that buddhas of Mount Yunmen are like this. For what reason is Venerable Shakyamuni revered? He is revered for his awakening of the way. For what reason is great master Yunmen revered? He is revered for his awakening of the way."

Upon hearing these words, I had some understanding.

Those who are heads of the large monasteries in Jiangsu and Zhenjiang provinces now are mostly heirs of the Linji, Yunmen, and Dongshan lineages.

But among students, particularly among those who call themselves descendants of Linji, some intend wrongdoing. Usually those studying in the community of a master request a scroll of the master's portrait and a scroll of his dharma words in order to prepare to meet the standard requirement of dharma heritage. But these fellows ask the attendants of masters for dharma words and portraits, and collect and hide many of them. When they are old they bribe public officials to get a temple and hold the abbot's seat without having received dharma from the masters whose dharma words and portraits they obtained. Instead, they receive dharma from the famous masters of the time or from the masters who have given dharma heritage to retainers of the king. They covet fame without regard to attaining dharma.

What a pity that there are such crooked habits at this wicked time of decayed teaching! Not even one of those fellows has ever dreamed of the way of buddha ancestors.

————————

Now, the masters' dharma words or portraits are also given to lecturers of scripture schools as well as lay men and women. They are even given to workers in the monasteries or to merchants. This is evident by the records of various masters.

In many cases, monks who are not qualified eagerly desire proof of dharma heritage and ask for a scroll of calligraphy. Although their teachers are distressed by this, they reluctantly take up the brush. In such cases the teacher does not follow the traditional format, but writes only that the person has studied with him.

The recent way is that when students gain accomplishment under a master, they receive dharma from that master as their dharma teacher. Some monks sitting on a long platform, who have not received a seal from a master but have only received guidance in the abbot's room or listened to the formal lectures, constantly refer to what was given by their master after they become abbots of temples. On the other hand, many students only accept those with whom they have broken open the great matter as their dharma teachers.

————————

Also, there was a priest named Chuan, a descendant of Priest Qing-yuan, Zen Master Fuyan of Longmen. This Chuan, a librarian, also had a document of heritage. At the beginning of the Jiading Era [1208–1224], when librarian Chuan was sick, senior monk Ryuzen, a Japanese, took good care of him. Because Ryuzen worked hard, librarian Chuan, grateful for help during his illness, took out his document of heritage and let Ryuzen see it, saying, "This is a thing not commonly shown, but I will let you pay homage to it."

About eight years after that, in the autumn of the sixteenth year of the Jiading Era [1223], when I was first staying at Mount Tiantong, Ryuzen cordially requested that librarian Chuan show this document of heritage to me. In this document of heritage, the names of the forty-five ancestors from the Seven Original Buddhas through Linji were lined up, and the names and monograms of masters after Linji were written inside a drawn circle. The name of the new heir was written at the end under the date. In this way a difference was made between the masters before and after Linji.

———

Rujing, my late master, abbot of Mount Tiantong, strictly prohibited students from unjustifiably claiming to have received dharma heritage. His assembly was an ancient buddha's assembly, restoring the monastic tradition. He himself did not wear a brocade robe. Although he had received the brocade robe of Zen Master Daokai of Mount Furong, he did not use it during formal or informal lectures. In fact, he never wore a brocade robe in his entire lifetime as an abbot. Those who were knowledgeable, as well as those who were not, admired him and respected him as a true master.

———

In his lectures, Rujing often admonished all practitioners of the way:

Recently, there are a number of monks who borrow the name of the ancestor way, wear robes unsuitably, grow their hair, and get by in the world by having their titles as Zen masters registered. What a pity! Who can help them? I only regret that so few elders in this world have way-seeking mind and practice the way. Those who have seen or heard of the significance of the document of heritage or dharma heritage are even rarer—not one person out of a hundred or a thousand. Thus, the ancestor way has declined.

When he said this, other elders in China did not contradict him.

Thus, when you make sincere effort in the way, you will know about the document of heritage. To know about this is the study of the way.

———————

On the document of heritage of the Linji lineage, the student's name is written, followed by the words "This person has studied with me," "This person has joined my assembly," "This person has entered my chamber," or "This person has inherited dharma from me." Then the names of the ancestors of the past are written in the traditional sequence.

Also, in the Linji School there is an oral instruction that the dharma succession is given not necessarily by the first teacher or the last teacher, but by the right teacher; this is the principle of direct heritage.

One of the Linji lineage's documents of heritage, which I actually saw, is written as follows:

> Librarian Liaopai, a courageous man, is my disciple. I have studied with Priest Zonggao of Mount Jing. Zonggao succeeded Keqin of Mount Jia. Keqin succeeded Fayan of Yangqi. Fayan succeeded Shouduan of Haihui. Shouduan succeeded Fanghui of Yangqi. Fanghui succeeded Chuyuan of Ciming. Chuyuan succeeded Shanzhao of Fenyang. Shanzhao succeeded Xingnian of Shoushan. Xingnian succeeded Yanzhao of Fengxue. Yanzhao succeeded Huiyong of Nanyuan. Huiyong succeeded Cunjiang of Xinghua. Cunjiang is senior heir of the High Ancestor Linji.

This document was given by Deguang, Zen Master Fuzhao of Mount Ayuwang, to Wuji Liaopai. When Wuji was the abbot of Mount Tiantong, Chiyu, a junior priest, privately brought it to Liaoran Hall and showed it to me. It was the twenty-first day of the first month, the seventeenth year of the Jiading Era [1224] of Great Song. What a joy it was! It was only possible by the invisible help of buddha ancestors. I saw it after offering incense and formally bowing to it.

The reason I requested to see this document of heritage was that Director Shiguang personally told me about it in Serene Light Hall around the seventh month of the previous year.

So I asked Shiguang, "Who keeps it?"

He said, "It is in the master abbot's quarters. If you request cordially, you may be able to see it." After I heard this, day and night I wanted to see it. Then later I rendered my wholehearted request to Junior Priest Chiyu.

The document was written on a mounted piece of white silk. The outside of the scroll was made of red brocade; the axis ends were of jade. It was about nine *sun* in height and over seven *shaku* long. Most people were not allowed to see it.

I thanked Chiyu. Also, I went to see Abbot Wuji immediately, offered incense, and thanked him. Then he said, "Few people know about this, and now you do, elder. This is a fulfillment of your practice of the way." I was very pleased.

———

When I visited Mount Tiantai and Mount Yadang later in the Baoqing Era [1225–1228], I went to the Wannian Monastery of Pingtian [on Mount Tiantai]. The abbot there was priest Yuanzi of Fu Region, under whom the monastery had prospered. He had succeeded Abbot Zhongjian after his retirement.

Upon my first greeting him, Abbot Yuanzi talked about the teaching of the buddha ancestors. When he mentioned Yangshan's dharma succession from Great Guishan, he said, "You haven't seen the document of heritage here in my quarters, have you?"

I replied, "No, unfortunately I haven't."

Abbot Yuanzi got up, took out the document of heritage, and, holding it up, said:

Following the dharma admonition of buddha ancestors, I have not shown this even to a close disciple or an old attendant monk. But when I went to the city to see the governor and stayed there, as I do occasionally, I had a dream. In this dream a distinguished priest who seemed to be Zen Master Fachang of Mount Damei appeared, holding up a branch of plum blossoms. He said, "If a true person comes who has disembarked from a boat, do not withhold these flowers." And he gave me the plum blossoms. Still in the dream, I exclaimed, "Why shouldn't I give him thirty blows before he leaves the boat?" Then before five days had passed, you came to meet me, elder. Of course you have disembarked from a boat, and this document of heritage is written on brocade that has a design of plum blossoms. Since you must be the one Damei was referring to, in accordance with the dream I have taken this document out. Do you wish to inherit dharma from me? I would not withhold it if so.

I could not help being moved. Although I should have requested to receive a document of heritage from him, I only offered incense, bowed, and paid homage to him with deep respect. At that time there was present an incense attendant named Faning. He said that it was the first time he had ever seen the document of heritage.

I said to myself, "This event indeed could not have happened without the invisible help of buddha ancestors. As a foolish man from a remote country, by what fortune have I been able to see a document of heritage once again?" Tears wet my sleeves. At that time the Vimalakirti Hall and the Great Hall of Mount Tiantai were quiet, without anyone around.

This document of heritage was written on white brocade with a pattern of fallen plum blossoms. Its height was over nine *sun* and its length over one *hiro* [sixty *sun*]. Its axis ends were made of yellow jade. The outside of the scroll was brocade.

On my way back to Tiantong from Mount Tiantai, I stayed at the entry hall of the Husheng Monastery on Mount Damei. At that time I had an auspicious dream that the ancestor Damei came up to me and gave me a branch of plum blossoms in full bloom. This image of the ancestor was worthy of great respect. The branch was one *shaku* tall and one *shaku* wide. Aren't these plum blossoms as rare as an udumbara blossom? This dream was just as real as being awake. I have never before told this story to anyone in China or Japan.

———————

The document of heritage written in our lineage from Dongshan is different from that written in the Linji and other lineages.

Our document of heritage was originally written inside the robe [body and mind] of buddha ancestors. Qingyuan, High Ancestor, wrote it with the pure blood taken from his own finger in front of [his teacher] Huineng, the Sixth Ancestor of Caoxi, and then authentically received it. It has been said that his blood was mixed with Huineng's blood when it was written. It has also been said that the ceremony of harmonizing blood was done by Bodhidharma, the First Ancestor, and Huike, the Second Ancestor. Such statements as "This is my heir" or "He has studied with me" are not written on our documents of heritage, but only the names of ancestors, including the Seven Original Buddhas, are written.

Thus, Huineng's blood spirit is graciously harmonized with Qingyuan's pure blood, and Qingyuan's pure blood is intimately harmonized with Huineng's own blood. Only great ancestor Qingyuan directly received the seal of realization in this way, and no other ancestors can be compared to him. Those who know this agree that buddha dharma has been transmitted only through Qingyuan.

POSTSCRIPT

Rujing said, "All buddhas have dharma heritage without fail. That is to say, Shakyamuni Buddha received dharma from Kashyapa Buddha. Kashyapa Buddha received it from Kanakamuni Buddha. Kanakamuni Buddha received it from Krakucchanda Buddha. Accept it with trust that buddhas have received dharma from buddhas in this way until now. This is the way of studying buddhas."

Then I said, "Shakyamuni Buddha came out into the world and attained the way after the pari-nirvana of Kashyapa Buddha. Furthermore, how could the buddha of the present eon inherit from the buddha of the previous eon? What is the meaning of this?"

Rujing said:

What you mentioned is the view of scriptural schools or the way of bodhisattvas of the ten stages and three classes, which is different from the way of direct heritage of buddha ancestors. Our way of transmission between buddhas and buddhas is not like that.

We understand that Shakyamuni Buddha did inherit dharma from Kashyapa Buddha. And we learn that Kashyapa Buddha entered pari-nirvana after giving dharma heritage to Shakyamuni Buddha. If Shakyamuni Buddha had not received dharma from Kashyapa Buddha, it would be the same as the group of six bald-headed rascals [during the Buddha's time] who believe in spontaneous enlightenment. Who, then, could believe in Shakyamuni Buddha?

Because of this heritage from buddha to buddha until now, each buddha is an heir. Buddhas are not lined up, nor are they gathered to-gether, but they just inherit from each other. Thus, we understand.

It has nothing to do with measurements that are taught in various Agama Schools, such as eons or long lifetimes. If you say that dharma heritage started from Shakyamuni Buddha, it would be only about two thousand years old, which is not so old. And the heritage would range only over forty generations, which is rather new. But buddha heritage should not be understood in this way. We understand that Shakyamuni Buddha received dharma from Kashyapa Buddha, and Kashyapa Buddha received dharma from Shakyamuni Buddha. When you understand in this way, it is the true dharma heritage of all buddhas and all ancestors.

Then, for the first time, I not only accepted that there is dharma heritage of buddha ancestors, but I also was able to get out of the old pit I had been in up to that time.

On the twenty-seventh day, the third month, the second year of the Ninji Era [1241], this was written at the Kannondori Kosho Horin Monastery by monk Dogen, who has transmitted dharma from China.

On the twenty-fourth day, the ninth month, the first year of the Kangan Era [1243], I have hung my traveling stick at the grass-thatched hut in Yoshimine Village, Echizen Province. A written seal.

18

Dharma Blossoms Turn
Dharma Blossoms

T HE BUDDHA LANDS of the ten directions are just dharma blossoms. Here, all buddhas of the ten directions in the past and present who abide in unsurpassed, complete enlightenment turn dharma blossoms and are turned by dharma blossoms. In this way there is the original practice of bodhisattvas, not turning back or veering away; there is the most profound, immeasurable wisdom of buddhas; there is the serene, subtle samadhi difficult to comprehend and difficult to enter.

Manjushri, the awakened one, speaks of dharma blossoms [in the *Lotus Sutra*] as the ocean of buddha lands where only buddhas are together with buddhas. Shakyamuni Buddha speaks of dharma blossoms thus: "I know form as suchness. So do the buddhas in the ten directions." He then says, "The buddhas in the ten directions and I know it well," and "I want sentient beings to open themselves and enter this realization."

Samantabhadra activates the turning of dharma blossoms of unthinkable power and spreads unsurpassed, complete enlightenment, profound and timeless, in the Jambudvipa world, where grass and trees large and small are equally nourished by moistening rain. The turning of dharma blossoms extends to places where it is not known. As Samantabhadra's turning of dharma blossoms occurs, a great assembly gathers on Vulture Peak. Seeing the coming of Samantabhadra, Shakyamuni Buddha acknowledges his arrival with illuminating light from the white tuft on his forehead.

During the assembly, Manjushri contemplates and speaks to Maitreya, turning dharma blossoms and immediately predicting his future enlightenment. Samantabhadra, buddhas, Manjushri, and the great assembly, all thoroughly understand the turning of dharma blossoms, which is wholesome at the beginning, middle, and end.

In this way dharma blossoms emerge as: "The One Vehicle alone is the essential teaching." Because this emergence is the essential teaching, the Buddha says, "Only a buddha together with a buddha can fully experience the reality of all things."

The dharma is always One Buddha Vehicle. Only buddhas can help buddhas to fully experience this reality. All buddhas, including the Seven Original Buddhas, help other buddhas to fully experience this reality and make it possible for Shakyamuni Buddha to attain the way. This occurs in the buddha lands in the ten directions, encompassing India and China. This is the dharma that reached Huineng, the Thirty-third Ancestor, Zen Master Dajian. It is the One Vehicle dharma of buddhas alone fully experiencing reality. This alone is the one essential matter, One Buddha Vehicle.

At this very moment, buddhas emerge in the world; they emerge right here. The transmission of Qingyuan's buddha wind until now, the spreading of Nanyue's dharma gate into the world, is the emergence of the Tathagata's knowledge of thusness. Truly, the dharma blossoms fully experience *only a buddha together with a buddha*, unfold, and enter the realization of a buddha heir, an heir buddha.

This is called the *Wondrous Lotus Flowers Dharma Sutra*. It teaches the dharma to bodhisattvas. As these dharmas are all dharmas, Vulture Peak, empty sky, ocean, and earth are all lotus flowers. This is reality; this is thusness. It is things abiding in their condition. It is the great essential matter. It is buddha knowledge, the continuous abiding in worldly aspects, thusness, the timeless lifespan of tathagatas, immeasurable profundity. It is the impermanence of all things. It is the lotus flower samadhi. It is Shakyamuni Buddha. It is turning dharma blossoms and dharma turning blossoms. It is the treasury of the true dharma eye, the wondrous heart of nirvana. It is manifesting the body and awakening beings. It is giving a prediction of enlightenment and bringing forth a buddha, maintaining and abiding in dharma.

———————

A monk called Fada visited the assembly of Huineng, Zen Master Dajian of the Baolin Monastery, Mount Caoxi, Shao Region, Guangdong, Tang China. He boasted that he had chanted the *Lotus Sutra* three thousand times.

Huineng said to him, "Even if you have chanted the sutra ten thousand times, if you don't understand the meaning of it, you won't even know your own errors."

Fada said, "Because I am stupid, I have only been able to follow the words and chant. How can I understand the meaning of it?"

Huineng said, "Chant it for me. I will elucidate its meaning for you."

Fada chanted the sutra.

At chapter 2, "Skillful Means," Huineng said, "Stop. The essential meaning of this sutra is the cause of the Buddha's emergence into the world. Many parables are expounded, but there is nothing more than this. This cause is the single essential matter. What is the single essential matter? It is the buddha unfolding knowledge and entering realization. You are originally buddha knowledge. You who have this knowledge are a buddha. You should trust right now that the buddha knowledge is your own mind."

Then he taught with a verse:

> When your mind is deluded, you are turned by the
> dharma blossoms.
> When your mind is enlightened, you turn the dharma
> blossoms.
> If you cannot clarify the meaning after chanting the
> sutra at great length, you become its enemy.
> Thinking beyond thinking is right.
> Thinking about thinking is wrong.
> If thinking and beyond thinking do not divide the mind
> you can steer the white-ox cart endlessly.

Hearing this verse, Fada further asked Huineng, "The sutra says, 'Great shramanas and bodhisattvas all exhaust their thinking and analyzing, but they cannot fathom the Buddha's wisdom.' Leading ordinary people to understand their own mind is called the Buddha's knowledge. Only those who are of excellent capacity avoid doubting and slandering the Buddha's teaching. The sutra also talks about three types of carts. How different is the great-ox cart from the white-ox cart? Please, master, would you teach me?"

Huineng said:

The meaning of the sutra is clear. It is you who are deluded. Those in the Three Vehicles cannot fathom the Buddha's wisdom because they think and analyze. However hard you think and project, you remain far away. The Buddha only expounds for ordinary people, not for buddhas. Those who walk away from the Buddha's sermons look for the three carts elsewhere. Yet they are already seated on the white-ox cart outside the gate.

The sutra clearly tells you "not two, not three." Why don't you understand this? The three carts are expedient means; they were taught in the past. The One Vehicle is reality; it is here now. I want you to leave the expedient means of the past to the past and return to reality. When you return to reality, it is not merely a name. Know that all things are rare treasures that belong to you. Receive and make use of them. Do not regard these treasures as belonging to your parents or your child. Do not feel that you have to use them. This is the meaning of the *Lotus Sutra*. Chant it every moment from kalpa to kalpa, day and night, without opening a scroll of the sutra.

Rejoicing in these instructions, Fada presented this verse of admiration:

After chanting the sutra three thousand times
I was annihilated by Caoxi's single verse.
Without clarifying the meaning of birth in life,
how can one end madness throughout lifetimes?
Although there are expedient carts pulled by sheep, deer,
    or oxen,

wholesomeness is manifest in the beginning, middle, and end.
Who is aware that the King of Dharma
abides in the burning house?

Upon receiving this poem, Huineng said, "From now on, you will be
called the Sutra-Chanting Monk."

This is how Fada studied with Huineng. Since then, the dharma blossoms of the dharma blossoms turning and turning the dharma blossoms
have been expounded. This had not been heard of before their dialogue.
Indeed, to clarify buddha's knowledge is itself the treasury of the true
dharma eye, it is itself the buddha ancestor. You can see from Fada's case
that those who vainly count letters, as numerous as pebbles and sands [of
the Ganges], cannot understand.

In order to fathom the true meaning of the dharma, thoroughly
study the ancestor's teaching as a single great matter. Do not try to learn
it through other vehicles. The thusness of reality and the true characteristics, true form, true function, true cause and effect of the dharma blossoms turning, had not existed or been spoken of before Huineng.

What is spoken of as *turned by dharma blossoms* is *your mind is deluded.*
Your mind is deluded is no other than *turned by dharma blossoms.* Thus, the
deluded mind is turned by dharma blossoms. The meaning is that while
the deluded mind is no other than all phenomena, reality is turned by
dharma blossoms. To be turned in this way is neither to be rejoiced in
nor sought after, neither to attain nor to arrive.

This being so, dharma blossom turning is not two, not three. As there
is only One Buddha Vehicle, and the dharma blossoms turning and being turned are, in reality, One Buddha Vehicle, one great matter, these
are bits and pieces [of One Vehicle] alone. Thus, do not resent delusion.
What you practice is the bodhisattva way, seeing buddhas through the
original practice of the bodhisattva. Each unfolding of the teaching, each
entering into enlightenment, is dharma blossoms turning.

There is delusion in the burning house, delusion at the gate, delusion away from the gate, delusion in front of the gate, delusion inside
the gate. Inside-the-gate, away-from-the-gate, as well as at-the-gate, and

the burning house are actualized in delusion. This is the unfolding of the teaching and entering enlightenment on the white-ox cart.

When you enter majestically, riding the white-ox cart, do you regard the ground as the place of entering, or do you see the burning house as the place of departing? Do you fully regard being at the gate as passing the gate?

Know that the cart wheel turns the burning house, unfolds the teaching and enters enlightenment. The ground turns the burning house, unfolds the teaching, and enters enlightenment. At-the-gate turns the entire gate, unfolds the teaching, and enters enlightenment. Innumerable gates turn the one gate, unfold the teaching, and enter enlightenment. Each unfolding of the teaching and each entrance into enlightenment turns the innumerable gates, unfolds the teaching, and enters enlightenment. Turning unfolds the teaching and enters enlightenment inside the gate. Turning unfolds the teaching and enters enlightenment away from the gate. Turning of the ground inside the burning house unfolds the teaching and enters enlightenment.

Thus, the burning house is beyond understanding, and the ground is beyond knowing. Who regards the turning of the three realms as the wheel of the One Vehicle? Who regards unfolding the teaching and entering enlightenment as going in and out of the gate? If you seek the cart wheel instead of the burning house, how many turnings will there be? If you desire the burning house and not the ground, how profound will it be? Do you fully understand the ground as the equanimity of Vulture Peak? Do you practice the evenness of the ground on Vulture Peak? Thoroughly engage in the practice to make "the place where sentient beings rejoice" into "my [the Buddha's] indestructible Pure Land."

[The *Lotus Sutra* says,] "I wholeheartedly wish to see the Buddha."

Study thoroughly whether this *I* is you or other. There is attaining the way by sharing the [buddha] body, and there is attaining the way with the entire body.

"Appearing together on Vulture Peak" took place because the Buddha's body-and-mind was not held back. There is unfolding the teaching and entering enlightenment by "always being present and expounding dharma." There is unfolding the teaching and entering enlightenment through "manifesting nirvana by skillful means."

Who has trust in understanding and trust in beyond understanding, when the Buddha says, "They do not see me, although I am close to them."

"The place filled with celestial beings" is the land of Shakyamuni Buddha and Vairochana Buddha—the land of eternal, serene light. Encompassing the four lands within ourselves, we abide in the buddha land of one thusness.

When you see a speck of dust, it is not that you do not see the world of phenomena. When you realize the world of phenomena, it is not that you do not realize a speck of dust. When buddhas realize the world of phenomena, they do not keep you from realization. Wholesomeness is manifest in the beginning, middle, and end.

Thus, realization is reality right now. Even shocks, doubts, fears, and frights are none other than reality right now. However, with buddha knowledge it is different; seeing a speck of dust is different from sitting within a speck of dust. Even when you sit in the world of phenomena, it is not broad. Even when you sit in a speck of dust, it is not narrow. If you are not fully present, you do not fully sit. If you are fully present, you are free of how large or narrow it is where you are. Thus, you have thoroughly experienced the essential unfolding of dharma blossoms.

Is it that the manifestation and essence of your practice now originates in the world of phenomena or in a speck of dust? Have no shocks and doubts, no fears or frights. Just this turning of dharma blossoms is the original practice, deep and wide. In seeing the speck of dust and seeing the world of phenomena, there is no attempt to create or measure. Even those who attempt to create or measure do so in accordance with dharma blossoms.

When you hear the words "unfold the teaching and enter enlightenment," understand that the buddhas want sentient beings to do so. "Opening the buddha wisdom" is the dharma blossoms turning; this is "manifesting buddha wisdom." "Realizing buddha wisdom" is the dharma blossoms turning; this is entering buddha wisdom. "Manifesting buddha wisdom" is the dharma blossoms turning; this is realizing buddha wisdom.

This is the dharma blossoms turning, opening the teaching and entering enlightenment; each is a way of thorough practice. Truly the buddha tathagatas' realization of wisdom is turning broad and profound dharma blossoms. Giving a prediction of enlightenment is the unfolding of the buddha wisdom by the self. It is not the dharma blossoms turning to be given to others. This is what is meant by the words *When your mind is deluded, it is turned by the dharma blossoms.*

When your mind is enlightened, you turn the dharma blossoms means that you turn the dharma blossoms. That is to say, when the dharma blossoms fully turn you, you are empowered to turn the dharma blossoms. While the original turning never stops, you return to turn the dharma blossoms. While the donkey [delusion] has not left, the horse [enlightenment] has arrived. This is the single great matter manifesting here and now.

Although bodhisattvas who emerge from the earth into myriad worlds are the great sages of timeless dharma blossoms, still they emerge now turned by themselves and turned by others. Do not regard emerging from the earth alone as turning the dharma blossoms. Regard emerging from the sky also as turning the dharma blossoms. Know with buddha wisdom that bodhisattvas emerge not only from the earth or the sky, but also from the dharma blossoms.

At the moment of dharma blossoming, invariably the parent is young and the child is old. It is not that the child is not a child and the parent is not a parent. Yet, you need to learn that the child [you] is indeed old and the parent [dharma] is truly young. Do not be like those who lack trust and are startled by this statement. What is usually distrusted is that now is a moment of dharma blossoming. Nevertheless, trust and turn the dharma blossoms as "in the time of the Buddha." Turned by the unfolding of the teaching and by entering enlightenment, bodhisattvas emerge from the earth. Turned by buddha wisdom, bodhisattvas emerge from the earth.

At the moment of turning the dharma blossoms there is the enlightened mind of the dharma blossoms, there are the dharma blossoms of enlightened mind. They are below and above in the air. What is below or above in the air is none other than the turning of the dharma blossoms. This is the Buddha's timeless life span.

Turn the dharma blossoms [of understanding] that the Buddha's life span, the dharma blossoms, the world of phenomena, and the mind are actualized below and above in the air. Thus, below and above are nothing but the manifestation of the turning of the dharma blossoms.

Sometimes the dharma blossoms are turned into three types of herbs, and sometimes they are turned into two types of trees. Do not wait to possess enlightenment. Do not wonder about not possessing enlightenment. To turn the self and aspire to enlightenment is to be in the southern buddha land. To attain the way is to join the Vulture Peak assembly of the southern buddha land. To be on Vulture Peak is itself to turn the dharma blossoms. There are assemblies in the air of buddha lands in the ten directions. They are embodiments of the turning of the dharma blossoms. Thus, the dharma blossoms of the buddha lands in the ten directions are turned. There is not a gap for even a speck of dust.

"Form is emptiness" is the turning of dharma blossoms, beyond coming and beyond going. "Emptiness is form" is the turning of dharma blossoms, beyond birth and beyond death. This is not only when the Buddha was in the world and when he has passed away.

That another person is intimate with you is that you are intimate with the person. To express respect is to give a gift like a pearl hidden in the hair or sewn into the robe [as told in the *Lotus Sutra*]. Thoroughly examine such moments [as dharma blossoms turning].

There is the turning of the dharma blossoms actualizing a jeweled tower five hundred *yojana* high in front of the Buddha [Shakyamuni]. There is the turning of the dharma blossoms actualizing the Buddha [Prabhutaratna] sitting in a tower two hundred *yojana* wide. There is the turning of the dharma blossoms actualizing bodhisattvas emerging from the ground and abiding in the air, when mind is without hindrance and form is without hindrance. There is the turning of the dharma blossoms actualizing bodhisattvas emerging from the sky and abiding in the ground, while immersed in the eye and immersed in the body. There is Vulture Peak in the tower, and a jeweled tower in Vulture Peak. The jeweled tower stands in the air. The air is air as the jeweled tower. The ancient buddha [Prabhutaratna] sits side by side with the Vulture Peak Buddha [Shakyamuni] in the tower, and the Vulture Peak Buddha enters realization for the Buddha in the tower.

The Vulture Peak Buddha turns the dharma blossoms with body, mind, and the whole environs. Emerging on Vulture Peak means the buddha in the tower manifests, remaining in the ancient buddha land

and timelessly passing away. When you investigate emerging and entering, do not follow commonplace ideas or the interpretations of those in the Two Lesser Vehicles. Just study the turning of the dharma blossoms. Timelessly passing away is magnificient realization embodied by the Buddha. It is not limited to inside the tower, in front of the buddha, the treasure stupa, empty space, the world of phenomena, or Vulture Peak. It is not limited to half a realm or the entire realm. It is not limited to the condition of phenomena. It is just beyond thinking.

There is the turning of dharma blossoms, manifesting a buddha body and expounding dharma, manifesting this body and expounding dharma. There is the turning of dharma blossoms manifesting as Devadatta, and there is the turning of dharma blossoms by saying, "You may leave this assembly if you wish." Do not assume the time you wait [for the Buddha] with joined hands gazing upward to be sixty short eons. You may call the time of wholehearted waiting innumerable eons, yet you cannot measure buddha wisdom. You cannot equate the duration of wholehearted waiting to the size of buddha wisdom.

Do not assume that this turning of dharma blossoms is limited to the path of a bodhisattva's original practice. At the assembly of the lotus blossoms, there is the act of turning dharma blossoms—"Today the Tathagata expounds the Great Vehicle." Dharma blossoms are dharma blossoms right now, beyond perception and knowledge, beyond knowing and understanding. Thus, innumerable eons are one hairbreadth moment of the turning of dharma blossoms. It is a straightforward expression of the Buddha's incalculable life span.

It has been several hundred years since the *Lotus Sutra* was transmitted and started turning the dharma blossoms in China. Many people have written commentaries. Some of them have been outstanding teachers. But no one has attained and activated the essence of turning the lotus blossoms like Huineng, Old Buddha, High Ancestor of Caoxi. To hear it now and encounter it now is an ancient buddha meeting an ancient buddha. Are we not in the land of an ancient buddha?

Rejoice! From eon to eon there have been dharma blossoms. From day to night there have been dharma blossoms. As dharma blossoms have been active from eon to eon, from day to night, whether your body and mind are strong or weak, they are dharma blossoms. Such blossoms are a rare treasure, radiant light, a practice place, broad and vast, great and timeless. When your mind is deluded, you are turned by the dharma blossoms. When your mind is enlightened, you turn the dharma blossoms. Indeed, this is dharma blossoms turning dharma blossoms.

[Let me repeat:] When your mind is deluded, you are turned by the dharma blossoms. When your mind is enlightened, you turn the dharma blossoms. When you thoroughly experience this, it is dharma blossoms turning dharma blossoms.

To honor and dedicate yourself to this teaching is no other than dharma blossoms turning dharma blossoms.

This was written and given to Zen person Etatsu to celebrate his home leaving and entry into the practice of the way, during the summer practice period in the second year of the Ninji Era [1241]. Shaving the head is a good thing. To shave the head over and over again makes a true home leaver. Today's home leaving is the natural fruit of the natural power of dharma blossoms turning in the past. The dharma blossoms of this moment will certainly bear fruit as dharma blossoms in the future. They are not Shakyamuni's dharma blossoms, nor all buddhas' dharma blossoms, but the dharma blossoms' dharma blossoms. Every day the turning of the dharma blossoms is as it is, beyond perception, beyond knowledge. Dharma blossoms emerge at this moment, beyond knowing, beyond understanding. Past moments are your breathing in and breathing out. Present moments are your breathing in and breathing out. Treasure these moments as dharma blossoms, wondrous and inconceivable. Monk Dogen, who has transmitted dharma from China, founder of the Kannondori Kosho Horin Monastery.

19

UNGRASPABLE MIND

SHAKYAMUNI BUDDHA SAYS, "The past mind is ungraspable. The present mind is ungraspable. The future mind is ungraspable."

This has been a point of study by buddha ancestors who have gouged out the caves and baskets [limited dualistic views] from what is ungraspable in the past, present, and future. They have used the caves and baskets of the self to do so.

This self is ungraspable mind. Thinking and discerning at this very moment is ungraspable mind. The entire body that utilizes the twelve hours of a day is ungraspable mind.

Buddha ancestors understood mind that is ungraspable from the time they entered the inner chambers [of their masters]. Without entering the inner chambers, there would not have been questioning, answering, seeing, and hearing about ungraspable mind. This is not even dreamed of by those who are masters of sutras and treatises, or by shravakas and pratyeka-buddhas.

Here is a familiar example:

Deshan Xuanjian was proclaiming that he had mastered the *Diamond Sutra*, calling himself Diamond King Chou. He claimed that he was particularly familiar with Xinlong's commentary. He had collected twelve bundles of commentaries. It appeared that he was incomparable. However, he was merely a descendant of dharma teachers of letters

Once, hearing about the unsurpassable dharma transmitted heir to heir in the south, Deshan felt very competitive. He learned about the assembly of Longtan, Zen Master Chongxin, so he crossed mountains and rivers carrying his books to meet him. On his way he stopped to catch his breath and saw an old woman.

Deshan said to her, "What do you do?"

The old woman said, "I sell rice cakes."

Deshan said, "Please sell me some."

The old woman said, "What will you do with them, reverend?"

Deshan said, "I will eat them to refresh myself."

The old woman said, "What are you carrying?"

Deshan said, "Haven't you heard of me? I am Diamond King Chou. I specialize in the *Diamond Sutra*. There is no part of it I haven't mastered. These are important commentaries on the sutra."

The old woman said, "May I ask you a question?"

Deshan said, "Of course, ask me anything."

The old woman said, "I was told that the *Diamond Sutra* says, 'The past mind is ungraspable. The present mind is ungraspable. The future mind is ungraspable.' With which mind will you satisfy your hunger with these cakes? If you can answer, I will give you some cakes. Otherwise, I will not."

Dumbfounded, Deshan was unable to answer. The old woman flapped her sleeves and went away without giving Deshan any rice cakes.

How regrettable! The king of commentators, who wrote commentaries on hundreds of scrolls, a lecturer for decades, was so easily defeated by a humble old woman with a single question. There is great difference between those who have entered an authentic teacher's chamber and received transmission, and those who have not.

Deshan said to himself, "A painted rice cake does not satisfy hunger." He is now known as a dharma heir of Longtan.

Reflecting on this story, it is clear that Deshan had not clarified the matter. Even after meeting Longtan, he must have feared the old woman. He was an immature student and not an old buddha going beyond realization.

Although the old woman shut him up, we cannot say whether she was a person of true understanding. It is possible that she had heard of ungraspable mind and asked this question, thinking that mind is ineffable.

If Deshan had been fully awakened, he would have been able to respond and discern whether or not the old woman was a person of true understanding. But since Deshan was not yet Deshan, we do not know or see through the old woman's understanding.

Those who nowadays wear cloud robes and mist sleeves [monks], who laugh at Deshan for being unable to respond and praise the old woman for her brilliance, are foolish. We may doubt the old woman's understanding because, when Deshan could not answer, she could have said, "Reverend, you cannot answer my question. Ask me the same question and I will give you an answer." If she could have answered Deshan, it would have been clear that she was truly a person of realization.

Asking a question is not yet making a statement. There has never been a case since olden times where someone who said nothing was regarded as a person of realization.

Groundless self-proclamations are useless just as in the case of Deshan. Those who have not made a right statement should not be accepted, just as in the case of the old woman.

Try to speak for Deshan. When asked by the old woman, he should have said, "If so, don't sell me rice cakes." If he had done so, it would have been a sharp investigation of the way.

Deshan may ask the old woman, "The past mind is ungraspable. The present mind is ungraspable. The future mind is ungraspable. With which mind will you satisfy your hunger with these cakes?"

Then, the old woman should say, "Reverend, you only know that rice cakes satisfy your hunger. You don't know that mind satisfies the rice cakes' hunger, or that mind satisfies the mind's hunger."

If she says so, Deshan will try to find an answer.

At that moment, she should pick up three pieces of rice cake and offer them to Deshan. When Deshan moves to receive them, the old woman should say, "The past mind is ungraspable. The present mind is ungraspable. The future mind is ungraspable."

Again, Deshan may open his hand to receive the rice cakes. The old woman should pick one up, hit Deshan with it, and say, "A corpse with no spirit. Don't be dumbfounded."

If Deshan speaks upon hearing these words, it will be good. If not, the old woman should continue to say more. Merely flapping her sleeves and going away are not like holding a stinging bee inside the sleeves [is not sharp enough].

Deshan did not say to the old woman, "I cannot answer. Please speak for me." Thus, he did not say what he was supposed to say, and did not ask what he was supposed to ask.

What a pity! Deshan and the old woman's discussion on past mind and future mind has not been grasped by the future mind.

Deshan does not seem to have acquired clarity even after that. His actions were only coarse. As he studied with Longtan for a long time, he must have had occasion to break Longtan's head horn [surpass the teacher] and to receive the pearl from the gill [of the dragon]. But he only blew at a candle and was short of transmission of the lamp.

Accordingly, monks who study the way should always make a diligent effort. Those who take an easy path are not adequate. Those who make a diligent effort are buddha ancestors.

The inexhaustibility of mind is to buy a piece of painted rice cake and chew it up in a single bite.

Presented to the assembly of the Kannondori Kosho Horin Monastery, Uji County, Yamashiro Province, in the summer practice period, the second year of the Ninji Era [1241].

20

UNGRASPABLE MIND, LATER VERSION

THE UNGRASPABLE MIND is all buddhas. Buddhas have maintained this as unsurpassable enlightenment.

The *Diamond Sutra* says, "The past mind is ungraspable. The present mind is ungraspable. The future mind is ungraspable."

This is the ungraspable mind of the three realms [desire, form, and no-form realms], the ungraspable mind of all things, which is maintained and actualized by the ungraspable mind as all buddhas.

This understanding cannot be realized without studying with buddhas, and cannot be authentically transmitted without studying with ancestors. To study means to practice with the sixteen-foot golden body and to practice with a blade of grass. To study with all buddhas means to practice with skin, flesh, bones, and marrow, and to practice with [Mahakashyapa's] smile.

That is, it means to practice with a buddha who has authentically transmitted the treasury of the true dharma eye heir to heir; to practice directly pointing to the mind seal of buddhas and ancestors; and to receive the bones, marrow, and face, as well as the body, hair, and skin. Those who have not studied the buddha way, who have not entered the ancestors' chambers, have not experienced this. Those who have not asked or spoken about dharma have not even dreamed of it.

———————

When Deshan was well versed in the *Diamond Sutra* but not yet fully realized, he was called Diamond King Chou. He was foremost among eight hundred scholars. He not only was familiar with Xinlong's commentary, but had collected twelve bundles of commentaries. There was no one like him.

Hearing about a teacher in the south who had received heir-to-heir transmission of the unsurpassable way, Deshan crossed mountains and rivers carrying his books to meet him. Approaching Longtan, he stopped to catch his breath and saw an old woman.

Deshan said to her, "What do you do?"

The old woman said, "I sell rice cakes."

Deshan said, "Please sell me some."

The old woman said, "What will you do with them, reverend?"

Deshan said, "I will eat them to refresh myself."

The old woman said, "What are you carrying?"

Deshan said, "Haven't you heard of me? I am Diamond King Chou. I specialize in the *Diamond Sutra*. There is no part of it I haven't mastered. These are important commentaries on the sutra."

The old woman said, "May I ask you a question?"

Deshan said, "Of course, ask me anything."

The old woman said, "I was told that the *Diamond Sutra* says, 'The past mind is ungraspable. The present mind is ungraspable. The future mind is ungraspable.' With which mind will you satisfy your hunger with these cakes? If you can answer, I will give you some cakes. Otherwise, I will not."

Dumbfounded, Deshan was unable to answer. The old woman abruptly flapped her sleeves and went away without giving Deshan any rice cakes.

How regrettable! The king of commentators, who wrote commentaries on hundreds of scrolls, a lecturer for decades, was easily defeated by a humble old woman with a single question. There is a great difference between those who have entered an authentic teacher's chamber and received transmission, and those who have not.

Those who hear the word *ungraspable* and think that everyone's mind is equally ungraspable have no vitality. Those who think that mind is *ungraspable* because everyone has mind miss the point.

Deshan at that moment realized for the first time that a painted rice cake does not satisfy hunger and that one needs to meet a true teacher in order to practice the way. Hence he met Longtan, actualized the vital way of teacher and disciple, and became a true person. He became not only a high ancestor to Yunmen and Fayan but also a guiding teacher for humans and devas.

As I reflect on this story, it is clear that Deshan at that time had not clarified the matter. Although the old woman shut him up, we cannot say whether she was a person of true understanding. It is possible that she had heard of ungraspable mind and asked this question, thinking that mind is ineffable.

If Deshan had been fully awakened, he would have been able to respond and discern whether the old woman was a person of true understanding. But as Deshan was not yet Deshan, we do not know or see through the old woman's understanding. Doubt about the old woman remains. Seeing Deshan unable to say a word, she should have said, "Reverend, if you cannot answer, why don't you ask me? I will answer it for you."

If Deshan had asked and the old woman had expressed herself, her true understanding would have been revealed. The bones, marrow, and faces of the ancient buddhas, as well as their light and auspiciousness, would have revealed the virtue of studying together. Thus, Deshan, the old woman, ungraspableness, exhaustibleness, the rice cake, and the mind would have become free from grasping and from letting go.

The buddha mind encompasses the past, present, and future. Although this mind and the past, present, and future are not apart by even a hairbreadth, if we separate them they would be as distant as eighteen thousand miles.

When asked about the past mind, say, "Ungraspable." When asked about the present mind, say, "Ungraspable." When asked about the future mind, say, "Ungraspable."

It means that there is no mind that is called ungraspable. But it is described as ungraspable for the time being. Do not say the mind cannot be exhausted; just say it is ungraspable. Do not say the mind can be exhausted; just say it is ungraspable.

When asked about the past mind that is ungraspable, say, "Birth and death come and go." When asked about the present mind that is ungraspable, say, "Birth and death come and go." When asked about the future mind that is ungraspable, say "Birth and death come and go."

There is buddha mind that is walls, tiles, and pebbles. Buddhas in the past, present, and future realize it as ungraspable. Walls, tiles, and pebbles are just buddha mind. Buddhas in the past, present, and future realize them as ungraspable.

Furthermore, the ungraspableness of mountains, rivers, and the great earth is within the self; the ungraspableness is the mind. There is also the ungraspableness of "With no place to abide, the mind emerges." All buddhas in the ten directions expound eighty thousand dharma gates in each lifetime. The mind that is ungraspable is like this.

At the time of Nanyang Huizhong, National Teacher Dazheng, Tripitaka Master Daer came from India to the capital city [of Chang'yan in China]. He claimed that he had mastered the power of seeing others' minds. Emperor Su of the Tang Dynasty asked Huizhong to test him. Daer saw Huizhong, bowed to him, and stood on the right side of him.

Huizhong said, "Have you mastered the power of seeing others' minds?"

Daer said, "Not really."

Huizhong said, "Tell me where this old monk is."

Daer said, "You are the teacher of the nation, reverend. Why are you in the West River enjoying the racing boats?"

Huizhong paused for a while and said, "Tell me where am I now."

Daer said, "You are the teacher of the nation, reverend. Why are you on the Tianjin Bridge watching monkeys play?"

Huizhong again said, "Tell me where I am."

Daer tried to see for some time but could not see where Huizhong was.

Huizhong shouted: "You are possessed by the spirit of a wild fox. You don't have the power of seeing others' minds."

Daer remained silent.

It is not good not to understand this. A buddha ancestor and a Tripitaka master are not the same. They are as far apart from each other as heaven and earth. A buddha ancestor clarifies buddha dharma and a Tripitaka master does not. Indeed, a layperson can be a Tripitaka master who specializes in literature. So, even if Daer not only was well versed in the languages of India but also had mastery in seeing others' minds, he had never dreamed of the body and mind of the buddha way. Upon his encounter with Huizhong, he was defeated.

In studying the mind in the buddha way, all things are mind, the three realms are inseparable from mind, inseparable from mind is inseparable from mind, buddha is mind. Do not mistake the mind of the self or of other in the buddha way. Do not vainly float down the West River. Do not imagine the Tianjin Bridge. In order to maintain the body and mind of the buddha way, study the mastery of wisdom in the buddha way. In this buddha way, the entire earth is all mind; it does not change by appearing and disappearing. The entire dharma is all mind. Understand the entire mind as mastery of wisdom.

Daer did not see this. He was merely a wild fox spirit. Therefore, he did not see Huizhong's mind and understand his mind from his first two questions. He was a wild fox spirit wastefully fooling with racing boats and playing monkeys. How could he have seen Huizhong? It is clear that he did not know where Huizhong was.

Daer did not hear the words in Huizhong's third question, *Tell me where this old monk is.* If he had heard them, he would have asked the meaning of the question. But he didn't, so he missed the question.

If Daer had studied buddha dharma, he would have heard Huizhong's words and seen Huizhong's mind. Because he had not studied buddha dharma, he wasted the opportunity of meeting the guiding master of humans and devas. How pitiful! How sad!

How can a scholar of the Tripitaka come close to the practice of buddha ancestors? Furthermore, treatise masters and Tripitaka masters in India may never understand Huizhong's practice. What a Tripitaka master knows should be known by Indra or a treatise master. What Indra or a treatise master knows may be reached by a bodhisattva in the ten stages or three classes, or a bodhisattva who is a candidate to be a buddha. But the body and mind of Huizhong cannot be known by a bodhisattva in the ten stages or three classes, or a bodhisattva who is a candidate to be a buddha. To speak of body and mind in the buddha house is like this. Know this and trust that this is so.

———

The dharma of our great master Shakyamuni Buddha is not the same as that of a wild fox spirit in the Two Lesser Vehicles or those outside the way. Thus, venerable masters since ancient times have investigated this story. Here are some examples.

A monk asked Zhaozhou, "Why didn't Daer see where Huizhong was?"

Zhaozhou said, "Huizhong was on top of Daer's nostrils, so he could not see Huizhong."

A monk asked Xuansha, "Why did Daer not see Huizhong, who was on top of his nostrils?"

Xuansha said, "Because he was too close."

Haihui Shouduan said, "If Huizhong was on top of Daer's nostrils, why was it difficult to see? Because Daer did not know that Huizhong was inside his eyeball."

Also, Xuansha criticized Daer by saying, "Say! Did you actually see Huizhong the first two times?"

Xuedou [Zhongxian] said, "You lost. You lost."

A monk asked Yangshan, "Why could Daer not answer the third time even after taking a long time?"

Yangshan said, "The first two times he was merged with an object of mind. But later he entered receptive samadhi. That's why he could not see Huizhong."

These five masters strike the point but still miss Huizhong's practice. It's like saying Daer did not get it for the third time but did for the first two times. This is how they miss it. Those who study later should be aware of it.

I have two doubts about these five masters. One: They did not know why Huizhong had tested Daer. Two: They did not know the body and mind of Huizhong.

Now, the reason I say that they did not know why Huizhong had tested Daer is this: Huizhong said, *Tell me where this old monk is.* This is how he asked Daer if he knew buddha dharma. If Daer had known buddha dharma, he should have investigated Huizhong's question in buddha dharma. To investigate it in buddha dharma is to ask where Huizhong was in here, there, unsurpassable enlightenment, realization of prajna, emptiness, the earth, a grass-roof hut, or a place of treasure.

Daer did not understand Huizhong's mind and wastefully presented a view of an ordinary person or the Two Lesser Vehicles.

Huizhong asked again, *Tell me where this old monk is.* For this Daer presented another fruitless statement.

Huizhong finally asked, *Tell me where this old monk is.* Daer thought about it for some time but did not say anything. He was dumbfounded. Then Huizhong scolded him and said, *You are possessed by the spirit of a wild fox. You don't have the power of seeing others' minds.* But Daer could not say anything.

When I reflect on this story, all five masters thought that Huizhong's criticism indicated that Daer knew where he was the first two times but did not know the third time. It is not so. Huizhong scolded that Daer was a mere fox spirit and had not even dreamed of buddha dharma. It is not that Daer knew where he was for the first two times but did not for the third time. Huizhong's scolding Daer scolded him all the way.

Huizhong's point was: Is there seeing others' minds in buddha dharma? If so, investigate "others" in buddha dharma, investigate "mind" in buddha dharma, and investigate "understanding" in buddha dharma. However, Huizhong thought Daer's statements had nothing to do with buddha dharma and could not be called buddha dharma. The reason he tested him three times was that even if Daer had a right answer for the third time, what he said the first two times were not the teaching of buddha dharma and it was not what Huizhong was asking for; so Daer should be criticized. Huizhong asked him three times to see whether Daer had understood the true meaning of the question.

Secondly, I say these five masters did not understand Huizhong's mind. The reason is: The body and mind of Huizhong were not known and understood by Daer. They cannot be reached by bodhisattvas of the ten stages or three classes. They cannot be clarified by candidates for buddhas or those who have understanding equal to enlightenment. How could they be understood by an ordinary person like Daer? Clearly understand this.

Those who suppose that Daer can know and reach the body and mind of Huizhong do so because they themselves do not know the body and mind of Huizhong. If you say that those who understand others' minds can know Huizhong, then would practitioners of the Lesser Vehicles understand him? No. They cannot even get close to Huizhong. Nowadays there are many practitioners of the Lesser Vehicles who read Mahayana scriptures. They do not know the body and mind of Huizhong either. And they do not even dream of the body and mind of buddha dharma. You should know that even if they read Mahayana scriptures, they are practitioners of Hinayana. The body and mind of Huizhong are not to be understood by those who practice miraculous powers.

The body and mind of Huizhong cannot be measured by Huizhong himself. The reason is that practice is never about the intention to become a buddha. Therefore, even a buddha eye cannot see them. The activity is dropped away from a birdcage or a fishing net. It is not bound by a birdcage or a fishing net.

The five masters' views should be altogether seen through. Zhaozhou said, *Huizhong was on top of Daer's nostrils, so he could not see Huizhong.* What does this mean? He was mistaken, as he discussed branches without clarifying the root. How could Huizhong be on top of Daer's nostrils? Daer did not have nostrils. Also, Zhaozhou gives the impression that Huizhong and Daer had seen each other. But they were not close to each other. A person with clear eyes should understand this.

Xuansha said, *Because he was too close.* Daer was not even close. He was not in Huizhong's neighborhood. How could Xuansha say *too close?* He did not know *too close,* he did not study *too close.* This is far, far away from buddha dharma.

Yangshan said, *The first two times he was merged with the object of mind. But later he entered receptive samadhi. That's why he could not see Huizhong.* Although his fame as Small Shakyamuni prevailed even in India, it's not that he was faultless. If he says that true encountering is always merged with the object of mind, it is just like saying there is no true encountering of buddha ancestors, or just like saying there is no act of making a prediction and creating a buddha. Yangshan indicated that Daer knew where Huizhong was the first two times. I should say Yangshan did not know even a hairbreadth of Huizhong's teaching.

Also, Xuansha criticized Daer by saying, *Did you actually see Huizhong the first two times?* This statement appears to express what needs to be expressed. But Xuansha seems to indicate that Daer's seeing Huizhong was like not seeing him. This is not correct.

Hearing Xuansha, Xuedou said, *You lost. You lost.* Xuedou said so since he had approved Xuansha. He should not have said so if he had not.

Haihui Shouduan said, *If Huizhong was on top of Daer's nostrils, why was it difficult to see? Because Daer did not know that Huizhong was inside his eyeball.* He also discusses the third time. He should have denied Daer's seeing of Huizhong the first two times, but he didn't. How could he know that Huizhong was on top of Daer's nose or inside his eyeball?

These five old masters were not clear about Huizhong's teaching. It looks as if they did not pursue buddha dharma enough.

Know that Huizhong is a buddha who excelled in his time. He had authentically received transmission of the treasury of true dharma eye. That is why scholars of the Lesser Vehicles who study scriptures and treatises did not come close to him.

"Seeing others' mind" can be seen as seeing others' thought from the Lesser Vehicles' viewpoint. It is wrong to think that such scholars of the Lesser Vehicles who study scriptures and treatises understood one half or even the tip of one hair of Huizhong. You should just know that they had no idea about Huizhong's teaching.

You might think that Daer knew where Huizhong was the first two times but not the third time; that he should not be criticized because he was right two out of three times, and that he was not completely wrong. Then who would criticize Daer, and who would trust Huizhong?

Huizhong's intention was to criticize Daer for not experiencing the body and mind of buddha dharma. The five masters made such mistakes. None of them grasped Huizhong's teaching.

Huizhong expressed the ungraspable mind of the buddha way. It is hard to believe that those who did not understand this one teaching do understand other teachings. Know that ancient teachers sometimes made mistake after mistake.

———

Once a monk asked Huizhong, "What is the mind of an ancient buddha?"

Huizhong said, "Walls, tiles, and pebbles."

This is ungraspable mind.

Another time a monk asked Huizhong, "What is the permanent mind of all buddhas?"

Huizhong said, "It was good to see the emperor."

This is again investigating ungraspable mind.

Indra once asked Huizhong, "How do we get liberated from everyday activities?"

Huizhong said, "You get liberated by practicing the way."

Indra asked further, "What is the way?"

Huizhong said, "Momentary mind is the way."

Indra said, "What is the momentary mind?"

Huizhong raised a finger and said, "This is the base of prajna. That is the net of pearls."

Indra made a deep bow.

There are many discussions on body and mind from the viewpoint of the buddha way in the assemblies of buddhas and ancestors. To study them is beyond the intellectual reach of the ordinary and sacred. Study mind that is ungraspable.

Written at the Kosho Horin Monastery on a day of summer practice period, the second year of the Ninji Era [1241].

21

OLD MIRROR

WHAT ALL BUDDHAS and ancestors have maintained and transmitted, person to person, is an old mirror. This is one seeing, one
face; one image, one casting [of the bronze mirror]; one practice and
one realization. When a barbarian comes, a barbarian appears in eighteen
thousand forms. When a Chinese person comes, a Chinese person appears in myriad years in one moment. When the old comes, the old appears. When the new comes, the new appears. When a buddha comes, a
buddha appears. When an ancestor comes, an ancestor appears.

––––––––––

Venerable Gayashata, the Eighteenth Ancestor, was a man from Madhya,
India. His family name was Uddaka-Ramaputta. His father's name was
Heavenly Canopy, and his mother's name was Sacred Direction. She had
a dream of a great deity looking into a large mirror. Soon she became
pregnant, and in seven days she gave birth to Gayashata. At birth Gayashata's skin was like polished lapis lazuli. Before he was first bathed, he
was naturally clean and fragrant. He always liked to be quiet and spoke
differently from ordinary children.

He was born together with a clear round mirror. This was extraordinary. "Born together" does not mean that the round mirror came from

his mother's womb. Gayashata was born from his mother's womb, but at the time of his birth this mirror appeared spontaneously close to Gayashata and became his everyday companion.

This mirror was not ordinary. When the boy approached, the mirror would stand up, as if it were being held by his hands, and reflect his face. When he went away, the mirror would follow him, reflecting his body. When he slept, the mirror would cover him just like a flower canopy. When he sat up, the mirror would be in front of him. Thus, the mirror accompanied the boy in all his activities.

All the buddha teachings from the past, present, and future could be seen in the mirror. Every aspect of heavenly and human affairs was clearly reflected in the mirror. This mirror could reveal any teaching, ancient or current, more clearly than the scriptures. However, when the boy left home and received the precepts, the mirror disappeared. People near and far admired these extraordinary occurrences.

Although this cannot be compared with anything in this Saha World, we should consider whether anything similar can be found in any world. Know that scriptures carved on trees and stones, teachers active in farmlands and villages, yellow paper and red scrolls—these are all round mirrors. How can we regard Gayashata as exceptional?

Once, when Gayashata was traveling, he saw Venerable Sanghanandi and approached him.

Sanghanandi asked him, "What expression do you have at hand?"

Understand that this is not merely a question.

Gayashata said in verse:

> All buddhas are a great round mirror.
> There is no obscuration inside or out.
> Two people have one understanding.
> Minds and eyes are alike.

How was the great round mirror of all buddhas born together with Gayashata? From his birth, he brought forward the clarity of the great round mirror. All buddhas equally study and see this mirror. All buddhas are cast images of this mirror.

The great round mirror is beyond wisdom and truth, beyond essence and characteristics. Although there is something called a great round mirror in the teaching of the ten sages and three classes [of bodhisattvas], it is not the same as this great round mirror of all buddhas. Not all buddhas are limited to wisdom. Buddhas have wisdom, but we do not regard wisdom as buddhas. Know that speaking of wisdom is not the ultimate expression of the buddha way.

Even if you see or hear that the great round mirror of all buddhas is born together with you, there is a further teaching. This great round mirror does not belong to this life or another life. It is not a jade mirror, a bronze mirror, a flesh mirror, or a marrow mirror.

Is this verse spoken by the round mirror or by the boy? Even though the boy expounded this four-line verse, he had never studied it in scriptures or with a teacher. He said this by holding up the round mirror. From the time he was an infant he was always looking at this mirror. It seemed that he had this understanding from birth. Was the great round mirror born together with the boy, or was the boy born together with the great round mirror? They must have been born together before and after.

The great round mirror is the power of all buddhas. *There is no obscuration inside or out* means that there is no inside other than outside, and no outside that has any obscuration inside. This mirror has no front or back.

As for *two people have one understanding* and *their minds and eyes are alike*, being *alike* means one person meets another. The image inside has mind, eye, and one understanding. The reflection outside has mind, eye, and one understanding. The bodies, minds, and environs [of the two people] that emerge are alike inside and outside. There is neither self nor other. Two people encounter, two people are alike. Other is called self, self becomes other.

Minds and eyes are alike means the minds are like the minds, the eyes are like the eyes. Being alike is minds and eyes. It is just like saying that both minds and eyes are alike. Minds are alike just as the Third Ancestor [Jianzhi—Mirror Wisdom] or the Sixth Ancestor [Dajian—Great Mirror]. Eye and eye are alike just as the eye of the way is immersed in the eye.

This is the meaning of Gayashata's words. This is what he presented to Sanghanandi upon meeting him. Take up these words and study the buddha face, ancestor face, of the great round mirror as a family member of the old mirror.

———————

When Huineng, who would later become Zen Master Dajian, [the Sixth Chinese Ancestor, that is] the Thirty-third Ancestor [after Mahakashyapa], was practicing in the dharma assembly of Hongren, the Fifth Ancestor, on Mount Huangmei, he wrote a verse on a wall and presented it to Hongren:

> Bodhi is not a tree,
> the clear mirror has no stand,
> from the beginning there is not a single thing:
> In what place can there be dust?

Study these words. People in later times have called Huineng an old buddha. For example, Keqin, Zen Master Yuanwu, said, "Homage to the true Old Buddha of Caoxi."

Thus, know that the clear mirror Huineng spoke of is *from the beginning there is not a single thing: In what place can there be dust?* The clear mirror with no stand is the life vein. Investigate it. Everything that is clear is the clear mirror. So it is said, "When brightness comes, meet it with brightness."

How can there be dust anywhere? So, it is nowhere. Furthermore, in the entire world of the ten directions, is there any dust that is not the mirror? How can dust that is not the mirror stay on the mirror? Know that the whole world is not the dusty world, but is the face of the old mirror.

———————

A monk in the assembly of Nanyue, Great Master Dahui, asked, "When the mirror casts a reflection, where does the light go?"

Nanyue said, "Where has the face before you became a monk gone?"

The monk said, "How come the mirror does not shine after casting a reflection?"

Nanyue said, "Even if it does not shine, there is not a single point of deception at all."

Nanyue's words express the realization that whatever is reflected in the mirror forms images. Although the mirror is neither gold nor jade, beyond illumination or reflection, still, it casts reflections—this is the ultimate study of the mirror.

Where does the light go is when the mirror casts a reflection. That means images go to where there are images, and reflections reflect the mirror.

Where has the face before you became a monk gone? illuminates the face by holding up the mirror. At this moment, which face is the face of the self?

Even if it does not shine, there is not a single point of deception means the mirror does not shine and does not deceive. Understand it as "The ocean dries up and yet does not reveal the bottom." Do not disturb it, do not rattle it.

Still, investigate further: Take up images and cast [create] a mirror. At this very moment, with a hundred thousand myriad illuminations, every point is deception.

———————

Xuefeng, Great Master Zhenjiao, once taught the assembly, "If you want to understand the essential matter, it is like an old mirror I have in myself. When a barbarian comes, a barbarian appears. When a Chinese person comes, a Chinese person appears."

Xuansha came out and said, "What about the moment when you encounter the emergence of a bright mirror all of a sudden?"

Xuefeng said, "Both the barbarian and the Chinese person disappear."

Xuansha said, "I have a different understanding."

Xuefeng said, "How do you understand?"

Xuansha said, "Please ask me a question."

Xuefeng said, "What about the moment when you encounter the emergence of a bright mirror all of a sudden?"

Xuansha said, "One hundred broken pieces."

For the moment, investigate the essential matter spoken of by Xuefeng—what is it? For the moment, take a look at Xuefeng's old mirror. The words *like an old mirror I have in myself* mean that the mirror is completely boundless and not limited to outside or inside. It is a pearl rolling on a board.

When a barbarian comes, a barbarian appears is [a thorough experience of] one red beard. *When a Chinese person comes, a Chinese person appears* means that this person has lived [in a civilized land] altogether with the three or five elements since the beginning of time. Xuefeng manifested the Chinese person with the power of the old mirror. Because this Chinese person is not merely a Chinese person, *a Chinese person appears.* Regarding Xuefeng's words, *Both the barbarian and the Chinese person disappear,* I say further that the mirror also disappears.

Regarding Xuansha's words *broken into one hundred pieces,* let me say: Now I am demanding of you: Give me back the broken pieces. How can you give me the bright mirror?

———————

The Yellow Emperor had a set of twelve mirrors. According to legend, they were given by the God of Heaven. In another account they were given to the emperor by Guangcheng at Mount Kongdong.

Each mirror was used at each hour of the day, each month of the year, and each year of the twelve-year cycle.

It is said that these mirrors were the scriptures of Guangcheng, who taught the emperor that these mirrors represented the twelve hours of the day and so on, and that the emperor should use these mirrors to reflect on past and present.

If the twelve hours are not mirrors, how can one reflect on past and present? If the twelve hours are not mirrors, how can reflection be possible?

What we call twelve hours are twelve faces. Twelve faces are twelve mirrors. Past and present are the making of twelve mirrors.

Guangcheng taught this understanding to the emperor. Although these words were by someone outside the way, they represent a mirror where *a Chinese person appears.*

The Yellow Emperor, who arrived in a carriage, walked on his knees into the Kong Cave and asked Guangcheng about the way.

Guangcheng said, "Mirrors are the basis of yin and yang that govern you. There are three mirrors within you: heaven, earth, and humanity. These mirrors neither see nor hear. If you hold them in your mind and remain serene, your body will be just right—always serene, always pure. Your body will not disturb your mind, and you will be able to live long."

In olden times emperors governed the world and the great way with these three mirrors. Those who clarified the great way were regarded as lords of heaven and earth.

A worldly person said, "Emperor Tai [of the Tang Dynasty] regarded others as his mirrors. He reflected on the security and insecurity of the nation in this way." This emperor used one of the three mirrors.

In terms of regarding others as mirrors, you might think that if one asks those who have studied extensively about past and present, one will be advised which person of ability to use. You might think of how emperors obtained wise courtiers like Weizheng or Fang Xuanling. But this is not what is meant by the words *Emperor Tai regarded others as his mirrors*.

To regard others as mirrors means to regard mirrors as mirrors, oneself as mirrors, the five elements as mirrors, and the five virtues as mirrors. When we observe the coming and going of others, there is no trace in coming and there is no direction in going. This is the meaning of human mirrors.

From wise to foolish, people are as varied and complex as the change of weather. There are human faces, mirror faces, sun faces, moon faces. The spirit of the Five Mountains and the Four Rivers purifies the Four Seas for generations. This is an influence of the mirrors.

The remarks about Emperor Tai mean that he saw through others and assessed their complexity. It is not that he asked those who had studied extensively for their advice.

Japan has had three sacred mirrors since the time of the gods. They have been transmitted until this day along with the sacred jade and sword. The mirrors are kept separately in the Grand Shrine in Ise Province, in the Hinokuma Shrine in Kii Province, and in the household office of the Imperial Palace.

From this we know that nations have transmitted mirrors. To maintain the mirrors is to maintain the nation. Legend says that these three mirrors have been transmitted as divine seats, given by the God of Heaven. Thus, the well-tempered bronze of the mirrors is a manifestation of yin and yang.

It seems that when the new comes, the new appears; when the old comes, the old appears. What reflects the old and the new is an old mirror.

————

Xuefeng's words may be interpreted thus: When a Korean person comes, a Korean person appears; when a Japanese person comes, a Japanese person appears. When a deva comes, a deva appears. When a human comes, a human appears.

Even when we study coming and appearing in this way, we don't necessarily know the roots and branches of appearing. It is just that we encounter appearing. We should not assume that coming and appearing are knowing and understanding.

Xuefeng said, *When a barbarian comes, a barbarian appears.* Does it mean that a barbarian's coming is a barbarian's appearing? The coming of a barbarian is the straightforward coming of a barbarian, and the appearing of a barbarian is the straightforward appearing of a barbarian. It is not that coming is for the purpose of appearing. Although an old mirror is an old mirror, you should study in this way.

Xuansha came out and said, "What about the moment when you encounter the emergence of a bright mirror all of a sudden?" Clarify these words. What is the meaning of *bright*?

He meant that the coming is not necessarily a barbarian. He meant that this bright mirror should not be regarded as a barbarian appearing.

Although the coming of a bright mirror is the coming of a bright mirror, it is not the coming of two mirrors. Although it is not two mirrors, an old mirror is an old mirror; a bright mirror is a bright mirror. The realization of an old mirror and a bright mirror has been expressed by Xuefeng and Xuansha. Their words are the essence and form of the buddha way.

Know that Xuansha's words *the coming of a bright mirror* are seven penetrations and eight masteries, the crystal clarity of the eight-faceted jewel among enlightened statements. It is like [Sansheng's words,] "I will go out immediately to meet a person," and "As soon as I come out, I will guide the person."

Then, is the brightness of *a bright mirror* the same as or different from the oldness of *an old mirror*? Is the bright mirror old? Is the old mirror bright? Do not simply assume that the words *an old mirror* mean that it is bright.

The essence of the words [by Xuansha] is "I am like this. You are like this. All ancestors in India are like this." Quickly polish your understanding.

An ancestor said, "An old mirror is polished." Is it so with a bright mirror? How is it? Extensively study the words of the buddha ancestor.

Xuefeng's reply, *Both the barbarian and the Chinese person disappear,* means the barbarian and the Chinese person disappear together at the moment of a bright mirror. What is the meaning of both disappearing? While the coming and appearing of the barbarian and the Chinese person do not hinder the old mirror, why do they both disappear?

Even if Xuefeng said, *When a barbarian comes, a barbarian appears,* and *when a Chinese person comes, a Chinese person appears,* the coming of a bright mirror is the coming of a bright mirror. Thus, the barbarian and the Chinese person who appear in an old mirror together disappear together. This being so, in these words by Xuefeng, there is an old mirror, a bright mirror. Be clear about the teaching that the moment when a bright mirror truly comes does not hinder the barbarian that appears in an old mirror.

Xuefeng's words *When a barbarian comes, a barbarian appears, when a Chinese person comes, a Chinese person appears* do not indicate that the barbarian or the Chinese person come and appear on the face of an old mirror, on the back of an old mirror, or outside of an old mirror. His words do not indicate that the barbarian and the Chinese person come and appear together with an old mirror.

Listen to Xuefeng's words. The moment of the barbarian and the Chinese person coming and appearing actualizes the coming and appearing of a barbarian and the Chinese person in an old mirror. To say that the mirror still exists when both the barbarian and the Chinese person disappear is to be ignorant about appearing and to be negligent about coming. It is more than confusion.

Then, Xuansha said, *I have a different understanding.* Xuefeng said, *How do you understand?* Xuansha said, *Please ask me a question.* Do not miss this request by Xuansha. It is not hurling insight between parent and child [master and student]. When Xuansha requested his master to ask him a question, he must have known what was going to be asked. When the thunder of questioning arises, there is no way to escape.

Xuefeng said, *What about the moment when you encounter the emergence of a bright mirror all of a sudden?* This question is one piece of old mirror the parent and child investigate together.

Xuansha said, *One hundred broken pieces.* These words mean one hundred, one thousand, or ten thousand pieces. The moment of encountering the emergence of a bright mirror all of a sudden is *one hundred broken pieces.* To study and realize *one hundred broken pieces* is a bright mirror, because letting the bright mirror express itself must be in the form of *one hundred broken pieces.* Where miscellaneous pieces are hanging, there is the bright mirror. Do not try to peek into a moment when a bright mirror is not miscellaneous pieces or when there are no miscellaneous pieces. A bright mirror is just one hundred broken pieces. To face the one hundred broken pieces is to face a solitary sheer peak.

Then, is the *one hundred broken pieces* spoken of by Xuansha an expression of an old mirror or a bright mirror? This is when you should ask for a turning word. This is no longer a talk about an old mirror or a bright mirror. You could still keep asking about an old mirror or a bright mirror. But, do sand, pebbles, and walls get to the tip of your tongue and not turn into one hundred broken pieces when you question Xuansha's words?

In what form are the broken pieces manifested? [I say:] The moon in an ancient blue sky.

———————

When Xuefeng, Great Master Zhenjiao, was walking with Sansheng, who would later become Zen Master Huiran, they saw a troop of monkeys.

Xuefeng said, "Each of these apes carries an old mirror on its back."

Sansheng said, "Why do you call what is nameless for eons an old mirror?"

Xuefeng said, "A scratch is made."

Sansheng said, "What's the urgency? I don't know the words."
Xuefeng said, "It is this old monk's fault."

Investigate these words thoroughly. *Apes* means monkeys. But what are the apes Xuefeng saw? Ask in this way and endeavor further without minding the passage of time.

Each carries an old mirror means that even if an old mirror is buddhas and ancestors, an old mirror can be beyond going beyond buddhas and ancestors. *Each of these apes carries an old mirror on its back* means that a mirror is neither large nor small, but just an old mirror. *Carries on its back* is like mounting a painting of the Buddha by gluing a piece of paper to its back. An ape has an old mirror mounted on it. But what kind of glue is used?

Let me ask you: If an ape is backed by an old mirror, is an old mirror backed by an ape? An old mirror is backed by an old mirror. An ape is backed by an ape.

Each . . . carries on its back must not be a groundless statement. It is an expression that is just right. Is the right expression an ape or an old mirror? What is the right expression? Are we or are we not already apes? Whom should we ask? To have an ape within the self is not known by self or other. The self is in the self; there is no need to look for it.

Sansheng said, *Why do you call what is nameless for eons an old mirror?*

This is an expression by Sansheng to authenticate an old mirror. *Eons* means before the emergence of a single mind, single thought. No name comes out for eons. *Nameless* is sun face, moon face, an old mirror face, a bright mirror face of these eons. When nameless is truly nameless, eons are not eons. When eons are not eons, Sansheng's expression is beyond an expression.

"Before the emergence of a single mind, single thought" is this very day. Temper your practice without missing this very day. Indeed, the statement *nameless for eons* is renowned. How can you call it an old mirror? A dragon head, a snake tail?

Responding to Sansheng's statement, Xuefeng should have said, "An old mirror. An old mirror." But instead, Xuefeng said, *A scratch is made.*

It means that a scratch has emerged. How can there be a scratch on an old mirror? *A scratch is made* must mean *nameless for eons.*

A scratch means an old mirror is nameless for eons. A scratch on an old mirror is an entire old mirror. As Sansheng had not come out of the cave—a scratch on an old mirror—the question he asked is completely a scratch on an old mirror.

Thus, study that a scratch can be made on an old mirror, and that what is scratched is also an old mirror. This is the study of an old mirror.

Sansheng continued: *What's the urgency? I don't know the words.*

He was asking what the urgency was. Was the urgency about today or tomorrow, self or other, the entire world of the ten directions or in the country of Great Tang? Investigate this thoroughly.

Regarding *I don't know the words,* there are expressed words, unexpressed words, and completed words. The teaching of words is actualized now.

For example, how about the words, "I have attained the way simultaneously with sentient beings on the great earth"? In this way, words should not be like an elaborately woven brocade [decorative endeavor] or facing each other. It is like, "I don't know who faces me" [as Emperor Wu said to Bodhidharma]; it is facing but not-knowing each other. It is not that there are no words, but just not-knowing. Not-knowing is a straightforward bare heart. It is bright and clear not-seeing.

Xuefeng said, *It is this old monk's fault.* This statement may be interpreted to mean that Xuefeng admitted his mistake in the earlier expression. But it is not the case. *This old monk* is an accomplished master in the house [of the Buddha], who wholeheartedly practices being an old monk and nothing else. In one thousand changes and ten thousand transformations, into a god's head and a demon's face, the practice of the way is just being one old monk. Buddhas come and ancestors come, while myriad years arise in a single moment, yet the practice of the way is just being one old monk. The *fault* is the abbot's being busy.

Reflecting on this dialogue, Xuefeng is a horn of Deshan's lineage, and Sansheng is an outstanding disciple of Linji. Both masters, being descendants of Qingyuan and Nanyue, equally hold respectable lineages. They maintained an old mirror in this way. This is a model for those who practice later.

Xuefeng taught the assembly: "When the world is ten feet wide, an old mirror is ten feet wide. When the world is one foot wide, an old mirror is one foot wide."

Then Xuansha said, pointing to the furnace, "Tell us. How wide is that furnace?"

Xuefeng said, "It is as wide as an old mirror."

Xuansha said, "Reverend master, your heels have not yet touched the ground."

Ten feet wide is called the world. The world is ten feet wide. *One foot wide* is called the world. The world is one foot wide. It is the *ten feet wide* of the present moment. It is the *one foot wide* of the present moment. There is no other *one foot wide* or *ten feet wide* than this.

Reflecting on this dialogue, people in the secular world say that the size of the billion worlds, the inexhaustible world of phenomena, is immeasurable and boundless. But it is a limited view of themselves, similar to pointing to a nearby village. On the other hand [in buddha dharma], we take up the world and understand it as ten feet wide. Thus, Xuefeng said, *When the world is ten feet wide, an old mirror is ten feet wide.* When we study this *ten feet wide,* we get a glimpse of the breadth of the world.

Hearing the phrase *an old mirror,* you may think it is like a thin sheet of ice. But it is not so. Although the breadth of *ten feet* is no other than the breadth of the world, you should investigate whether or not the outlook of an old mirror conforms to the boundlessness of the world.

An old mirror is not like a pearl. Do not view it as bright or dark, square or round. Even if the world of the ten directions is one bright pearl, it is not exactly the same as an old mirror.

This being so, an old mirror is not affected by the coming and appearing of a barbarian or a Chinese person. It is crystal clear vertically and horizontally all the way. An old mirror is neither multiple nor large. *Wide* indicates the measure of it. It does not mean breadth. *Wide* is like measuring two or three inches, or counting seven or eight pieces. In the arithmetic of the buddha way, great enlightenment and beyond enlightenment are counted as two or three ounces, and buddha ancestors are counted as fivefold or tenfold. Ten feet is the breadth of an old mirror. The breadth of an old mirror is singlefold.

Xuansha said, *How wide is that furnace?* There is nothing hidden in this statement. Study it as a one-thousand-year-old and ten-thousand-year-old statement.

When you see a furnace, who is the one that sees? When you see a furnace, it is not seven feet or eight feet. Xuansha's question was not a confused statement. It actualizes something remarkable. It is like saying, "What has thus come?"

How wide is not asking about the size in an ordinary way. It is an understanding of being emancipated right where you are. This should not be doubted. Listen to Xuansha's words for a teaching that the characteristics of a furnace are beyond measurement. Do not drop the ball you are holding on the ground; just smash it. This is endeavor.

Xuefeng said, *It is as wide as an old mirror.* Reflect quietly on these words. He did not say that the furnace is one foot wide. It is not that to say *one foot* is right and to say *as wide as an old mirror* is wrong. Just reflect on the practice of saying, *It is as wide as an old mirror.*

Many people think that Xuefeng was wrong in not saying, "one foot wide." Investigate, however, the completeness of being *wide*. Reflect on one whole piece of *an old mirror*. Do not miss the practice of *like*. It is like [Xiangyan's] saying, "Hold up a vital posture on the old path. Do not fall into stagnancy."

Xuansha said, *Reverend master, your heels have not yet touched the ground.* What he meant by *reverend master,* or reverend priest, is not necessarily Xuefeng. Xuefeng is a reverend master.

Ask where the heels are. Investigate what the heels are. Investigate whether the heels are the treasury of the true dharma eye, the empty sky, the entire earth, or the life vein. Are they many, one, half, or one hundred thousand [heels]? Study in this way.

What is the ground in *your heels have not yet touched the ground*? The great earth is called the ground according to the views of one kind of being. Among other beings, some see it as the inconceivable dharma gate of emancipation, while others see it as the place where all buddhas practice the way.

So, what is the ground the heels are supposed to touch? Is the ground real existence or real nonexistence? Or, does *the ground* mean that there is not even an inch of it in the great way? Ask in this way and that way. Say it to self and others.

Is it right or wrong that the heels touch the ground? Why did Xuansha say that Xuefeng's heels *have not yet touched the ground*? At the very moment when there is not an inch of land on the great earth, touching the ground is *not yet,* and not touching the ground is *not yet.*

Thus, *your heels have not yet touched the ground* is the activity of the reverend master. It is work of the heels.

————————

Guotai, Zen Master Hongtao of the Guotai Monastery, Mount Jinhua, Wu Region, was asked by a monk, "What is an old mirror that is not yet polished?"

Guotai said, "An old mirror."

The monk asked, "What is an old mirror that is already polished?"

Guotai said, "An old mirror."

Know that the old mirror spoken of now is an old mirror throughout the time when it is polished, before it is polished, and after it is polished. Thus, when you polish it, you polish the entire old mirror. It is not that you apply mercury or something else to an old mirror and polish it. Although it is not the self polishing or polishing the self, it is polishing an old mirror.

It is not that an old mirror is dull when it is not yet polished. It is stained but not dull. It is an old mirror that has life.

You polish a mirror and make it a mirror. You polish a tile and make it a mirror. You polish a tile and make it a tile. You polish a mirror and make it a tile. Also, you polish but do not accomplish, or you accomplish but do not polish. These are all works in the house of buddha ancestors.

————————

Mazu of Jiangxi practiced with Nanyue, who intimately transmitted the mind seal to him. This was the beginning of polishing a tile.

Living in the Chuanfa Temple, Mazu was engaged in continuous practice of zazen for over a decade. Ponder his sitting on a rainy night in a thatched-roof hut. There is no account that he skipped sitting on a cold platform when stranded by snow.

When Nanyue visited his hut, Mazu stood up.
Nanyue said, "What have you been doing these days?"
Mazu said, "I have been just sitting."
Nanyue said, "What is your intention in just sitting?"
Mazu said, "I intend to become a buddha."
Then Nanyue picked up a tile and started polishing it on a stone near Mazu's hut.
Mazu said, "Master, what are you doing?"
Nanyue said, "Polishing a tile."
Mazu said, "Why are you polishing the tile?"
Nanyue said, "I am trying to make a mirror."
Mazu said, "How can you polish a tile and make a mirror?"
Nanyue said, "How can you do zazen and become a buddha?"

People have been interpreting this great story for hundreds of years as Nanyue's encouragement to Mazu. It is not necessarily so. The activity of a great sage is far beyond ordinary understanding.

Without polishing a tile, how can a great sage have the skillful means to make a true person? The capacity of making a true person is the bones and marrow of buddha ancestors. Although it is fabricated, it is a furnishing [essential] of the house. Without being furniture or equipment, Nanyue's teaching could not have been transmitted in the buddha house. In particular, this immediately guided Mazu. From this we know that the work authentically transmitted by buddha ancestors is no other than directly pointing.

Indeed, at the moment a polished tile becomes a mirror, Mazu becomes a buddha. At the moment Mazu becomes a buddha, Mazu immediately becomes Mazu. At the moment Mazu becomes Mazu, zazen immediately becomes zazen.

Thus, polishing a tile and turning it into a mirror has been maintained as the bones and marrow of the ancient buddha. This being so, there is an old mirror made of a tile. Although this mirror is polished, it has never been defiled. It is not that the tile is dirty. It is just that a tile that is a tile is polished. To actualize the work of making a mirror in this way is the endeavor of buddha ancestors.

If polishing a tile did not make a mirror, polishing a mirror would not make a mirror either. Who can doubt this? This making is making a buddha, making a mirror.

There may be those who question whether polishing a mirror becomes polishing a tile by mistake. The time of polishing cannot be fathomed by the measure of other times.

Nanyue's expression, however, is an expression of expressions. Thus, polishing a tile is making a mirror. Those of you nowadays should also try to polish a tile to make a mirror. It will certainly be a mirror.

If a tile does not become a mirror, a human being does not become a buddha. If you look down at a tile as a lump of mud, you look down at a human being as a lump of mud. If a human has mind, a tile should have mind. Who knows that there is a mirror that is brought forth as a tile and is actualized as a tile? Who knows that there is a mirror that is brought forth as a mirror and is actualized as a mirror?

Presented to the assembly of the Kannondori Kosho Horin Monastery on the ninth day, the ninth month, the second year of the Ninji Era [1241].

22

READING A SUTRA

THE PRACTICE AND realization of unsurpassable, complete enlightenment is brought forth sometimes by a teacher and sometimes by a sutra. A teacher is a buddha ancestor of the entire self. A sutra is a sutra of the entire self. We say this because you yourself are the self of all buddha ancestors, and the self of all sutras.

Although it is called the self, it is not bound by "you" and "I." It is a vital eyeball, a vital fist. Thus, there is remembering, reading, chanting, copying, receiving, and maintaining a sutra. All of these are the practice-realization of buddha ancestors.

To encounter a sutra, however, is not easy. Among the innumerable lands, it is difficult to hear the name of a sutra. Even in the assembly of buddha ancestors, it is difficult to hear the name of a sutra. Even among receivers of the life veins [of buddha dharma], there are those who have not even heard the name of a sutra.

Without being buddha ancestors, it is impossible to see, hear, read, chant, and understand the meaning of a sutra. Upon studying with a buddha ancestor, you also study a sutra. Then the hearing, maintaining, receiving, and expounding of a sutra is actualized in arriving, hearing, and speaking through ears, eyes, nose, tongue, body, and mind.

Those who expound discourses of teaching outside the way for the sake of seeking fame cannot practice the buddha sutras that have been transmitted by carvings on trees and rocks, being spread in fields and villages, being demonstrated in a great number of lands, and expounded in empty space.

————————

Yaoshan, Great Master Hongdao, had not given a dharma talk for some time. The director of the monastery said to him, "The assembly has been wishing to have your compassionate admonition for a long time."

Yaoshan said, "Hit the bell."

The director hit the bell and assembled the monks.

Yaoshan ascended the teaching seat. After a while he got down and went back to the abbot's quarters.

The director followed him and said, "You promised to expound dharma to the assembly. How come you did not say a word?"

Yaoshan said, "Sutras have sutra scholars. Treatises have treatise scholars. What do you expect from this old monk?"

What Yaoshan taught is that a fist has a fist teacher and an eyeball has an eyeball teacher.

However, ask Yaoshan, "It is not that I expect something from you. But, master, what kind of teacher are you?"

————————

A monk called Fada, a chanter of the *Lotus Sutra*, visited the assembly of Huineng, Zen Master Dajian of the Baolin Monastery, Mount Caoxi, Shao Region.

Huineng taught him with a verse:

> When your mind is deluded, you are turned by the
>   dharma blossoms.
> When your mind is enlightened, you turn the
>   dharma blossoms.
> If you cannot clarify the meaning after chanting the
>   sutra at great length, you become its enemy.
> Thinking beyond thinking is right.
> Thinking about thinking is wrong.

> If thinking and beyond thinking do not divide the
> mind,
> you can steer the white-ox vehicle endlessly.

In this way, when you are deluded, you are turned by dharma blossoms. Further, when you leap beyond delusion and enlightenment, dharma blossoms turn dharma blossoms.

Rejoicing in these instructions, Fada presented this verse of admiration:

> After chanting the sutra three thousand times
> I was annihilated by Caoxi's single verse.
> Without clarifying the meaning of birth in life,
> how can one end madness throughout lifetimes?
> Although there are expedient carts pulled by
> sheep, deer, or oxen,
> wholesomeness is manifest in the beginning,
> middle, and end.
> Who is aware that the King of Dharma
> abides in the burning house?

Upon receiving this poem, Huineng said, "From now on, you will be called the Sutra-Chanting Monk."

Know that there was a sutra-chanting monk in the buddha way who was personally named by Huineng. The chanting of Sutra-Chanting Monk is neither chanting nor beyond chanting. It cannot be measured by being or beyond being. Indeed, this is not putting down the scrolls [of the *Lotus Sutra*] for eons and not lacking a moment of chanting the sutra. From the sutra to the sutra there is nothing other than the sutra.

———

Prajnatara, the Twenty-seventh Ancestor, was once offered a midday meal by the King of East India.

The King asked him, "Everyone turns [reads] a sutra except you, venerable. Why is this so?"

Prajnatara said, "While exhaling I do not follow conditions. While inhaling I do not abide in the realm of skandhas. I turn hundreds, thousands, myriads, and billions of scrolls of sutras, not merely one or two."

Venerable Prajnatara is a seed from East India, the twenty-seventh-generation authentic dharma heir after Mahakashyapa. He had authentically received all furnishings [essentials] of the buddha house. He had maintained the top of the head, eyeball, fist, and nostril, as well as the staff, bowl, robe, bones, and marrow. He is our early ancestor and we are his cloud [monk] descendants.

What Prajnatara emphasized is that not only was he free from following conditions while exhaling, but also conditions were free from following him while he exhaled. Even if conditions are the top of the head or eyeball, the entire body or entire mind brings them here, takes them away, brings them here again; just be free from following conditions. Being free from following is thoroughly following. You hit a stone and you sound the stone [There is no separation between you and conditions].

Although exhaling is no other than conditions, do not follow conditions. Although you may not have known the activity of inhaling and exhaling for uncountable kalpas, the time when you know it has just arrived right now. This being so, you hear about being free from abiding in the realm of skandhas and not following conditions.

This is the moment when conditions thoroughly investigate inhaling, and so on. This moment has never happened before, nor will it happen in the future. This moment is just right now.

The realm of skandhas means the realm of five skandhas: form, perception, feeling, inclination, and discernment. To be free from abiding in five skandhas is to live in the world where five skandhas have not been divided.

As Prajnatara took up this key [of nonduality], the sutras he turned were not limited to one or two, but were hundreds, thousands, myriads, and billions of scrolls. He spoke of so many, but it is immeasurable.

Prajnatara regarded not abiding in the realm of skandhas while exhaling as hundreds, thousands, myriads, and billions of scrolls of sutras. But this cannot be counted by ordinary people or sages. It is not in the realm of ordinary people or sages. Thus, it can neither be measured by the intellect of those who are wise, nor be guessed by the wisdom of those who have knowledge. Neither can it be discussed by the intellect of those who are beyond wise, nor can it be arrived at by the wisdom of those who have knowledge beyond knowledge. Rather, it is buddha ancestors' practice-realization, skin, flesh, bones, marrow, eyeball, fist, top of the head, nostril, staff, whisk, leaping away from making.

———

Zhaozhou, Great Master Zhenji of the Guanyin Monastery, Zhao Region, was once given a donation and asked to rotate [chant] the canon by an old woman.

He got off the meditation platform, walked around it, and said to the messenger, "The canon has been rotated."

The messenger went back to the old woman and reported this.

The old woman said, "I asked the master to rotate the entire canon. Why did he only rotate half of the canon?"

It is clear that rotating the entire canon or half of the canon is rotating three scrolls of sutra for the old woman. *The canon has been rotated* is Zhaozhou's entire canon.

How the canon is rotated is Zhaozhou walking around the meditation platform, the meditation platform walking around Zhaozhou, Zhaozhou walking around Zhaozhou, the meditation platform walking around the meditation platform. And yet, not all rotating of the canon is walking around the meditation platform, or the walking of the meditation platform.

———

Dasui, Great Master Shenzhoa of Mount Dasui, Yi Region, whose priest name was Fazhen, inherited dharma from Changqing, Zen Master Da'an. He was once given a donation and asked to rotate the canon by an old woman.

Dasui walked around the meditation platform and said to the messenger, "The canon has been rotated."

The messenger went back to the old woman and reported this.

The old woman said, "I asked the master to rotate the entire canon. Why did he only rotate half of the canon?"

Now, do not interpret this as Dasui walking around the meditation platform or as the meditation platform walking around Dasui. This is not only a circle of a fist or an eyeball, but drawing a circle, creating a circle.

However, did the old woman have an eye or not? She said, *Why did he only rotate half of the canon?* Although these words may have been authentically transmitted by a fist, she should have spoken further, "I asked the master to rotate the entire canon. Why did he merely fool with his spirit?" Even if she said this by mistake, she would have been someone with an eye.

———

Dongshan, Great Master Wuben, High Ancestor, was once given a meal offering and a donation, and asked to rotate the canon by a government official. Dongshan got off the meditation platform and bowed to the official.

The official bowed back.

Dongshan led him and walked around the meditation platform. Then he bowed to him. After a while Dongshan asked him, "Do you understand it?"

The official said, "No, I don't."

Dongshan said, "You and I have chanted the canon together. How come you don't understand it?"

You and I have chanted the canon together—this is clear. It is not that walking around the meditation platform is chanting the canon, nor is it that chanting the canon is walking around the meditation platform. And yet, listen to the compassionate admonition of Dongshan.

This story was presented by Rujing, my late master, Old Buddha, as abbot of the Tiantong Monastery, when a donor from Korea visited and asked him to have the assembly chant a sutra and to give a dharma talk.

After his talk, Rujing drew a large circle with a whisk [in the air] and said, "Today I have rotated the canon for you."

Then he threw down the whisk and descended the teaching seat.

You should rotate Rujing's words, which cannot be compared with the words of others.

Now, do you use a single eye or half an eye to rotate the canon? For

Dongshan's words and Rujing's words—how much of the eye or the tongue is used? See it thoroughly.

———

Yaoshan, Great Master Hongdao, never allowed his students to read a sutra. But one day he himself was reading a sutra.

A monk asked, "Master, you never allow us to read a sutra. How come you are reading one now?"

Yaoshan said, "I need to shelter my eyes [be one with the sutra]."

The monk said, "Can I imitate you?"

Yaoshan said, "If you read a sutra, even a calf skin would be pierced."

The words *I need to shelter my eyes* are expressed by the sheltering eyes themselves. Sheltering eyes is crushing the eyeballs, crushing the sutra, totally eyes sheltering, and totally sheltering eyes. Sheltering the eyes is opening the eyes within sheltering, vital eyes within sheltering, vital sheltering within the eyes. It is adding eyelids on top of eyelids. It is taking up the eyes within sheltering, eyes taking up sheltering. Thus, if the eyeball is not a sutra, the power of sheltering the eyes will not be manifested.

Even a calf skin would be pierced means [you become] the entire calf skin, the entire skin of a calf, taking up a calf and making leather. Thus, skin, flesh, bones, and marrow, as well as horns and nostrils, become activities of a calf. At the time of *imitating you,* a calf becoming an eyeball is called sheltering the eyes. An eyeball becomes a calf.

———

Yefu, Zen Master Daochuan, said:

> Billions of offerings to buddhas create boundless
>   benefaction.
> How can it compare to reading an ancient teaching?
> Yet, letters are merely inked on white paper.
> Please open your eyes and see through immediately.

Know that the virtues of making offerings to ancient buddhas and reading an ancient teaching stand shoulder to shoulder, going beyond measure. Still, an ancient teaching is inked on white paper. Who knows if this is an ancient teaching? Thoroughly study the meaning of this.

———

Yunju, Great Master Hongjue of Mount Yunju, once saw a monk silently reading a sutra in his room. He asked the monk through the window, "Reverend, what sutra are you reading?"

The monk said, "The *Vimalakirti Sutra.*"

Yunju said, "I am not asking you about the *Vimalakirti Sutra.* What sutra are you reading?"

At this the monk entered realization.

Yunju's question—*What sutra are you reading?*—addressed a single path of silently reading throughout a vast time span. Without speaking about what the monk was reading, this question put a dead snake on the road [woke him up]. Thus, this question—*What sutra*—emerged. The monk unmistakably encountered a person [himself]. So he said, *The Vimalakirti Sutra.*

To read a sutra is to take up and assemble all buddha ancestors, turn them into an eyeball, and read it. At this very moment buddha ancestors become buddhas, expound dharma, expound buddha, and become. Without this moment of reading a sutra, the top of the head and the face of buddha ancestors had not actualized.

———

Currently in the assemblies of buddha ancestors, there are a variety of occasions for reciting a sutra. For example: a donor comes to the monastery and asks the assembly of monks to recite a sutra regularly or on a particular occasion; the assembly aspires to do so on their own; or the assembly recites a sutra for a deceased monk.

When a donor requests the assembly of monks to recite a sutra, the director of the monks' hall hangs a plaque announcing a sutra recitation in front of the monks' hall and other quarters at the morning meal time on the scheduled day. After the meal, the director spreads the bowing mat in front of the image of the Sacred Monk, and, when the time comes, strikes the bell in front of the monks' hall three times. Or the bell can be struck just once, according to the direction of the abbot.

Following the sound of the bell, the head monk and the assembly of monks, in kashaya, enter the monks' hall and sit on their assigned seats facing out. Then, the abbot enters the hall, makes a standing bow to the Sacred Monk, offers incense, and sits on the abbot's chair. After this, young helpers bring the sutra books.

The sutra books have been assembled in the kitchen to be transported in due time. The books are placed either in a box or on a tray. Monks receive sutra books, open them, and start reciting.

At this time the monastery host brings the donor into the hall. The donor receives a portable incense burner in front of the hall, holds it up, and enters the hall. The portable incense burner has been kept in a communal area of the monastery. A worker puts incense into a box beforehand, sets it in front of the hall, and hands the incense to the donor at the host's signal. The host and the donor go into the hall from the southern side of its front entrance.

The donor goes to the Sacred Monk, burns incense, and makes three bows, while holding the incense burner. In the meantime, the monastery host slightly faces the donor while standing with hands in shashu at the northern side.

After bowing, the donor turns around in a rightward direction and makes a standing bow to the abbot while holding up the incense burner. The abbot, remaining seated on the chair, holds up the sutra book [between the thumbs and index fingers] with hands in gassho, and receives the donor's greeting.

Then, the donor turns to the north, performs a standing bow, and makes a circumambulation in the hall, starting in front of the head monk's seat. This is led by the monastery host. When the greeting circuit is over, the donor returns to the Sacred Monk and makes a standing bow while holding up the incense burner. At this time, the monastery host stands with hands in shashu facing north in the south side of the entrance. After bowing to the Sacred Monk, the donor follows the host out of the hall, walks around in front of the hall, enters the hall again, and makes three bows to the Sacred Monk.

Then, the donor sits on a crossed-legged chair for the conclusion of the recitation. This chair is placed facing south near the pole to the north of the Sacred Monk. Or it is placed facing north near the pole in the opposite side. After the donor is seated, the monastery host makes a standing bow to the donor and takes a seat.

It is possible to have the recitation of a gatha while the donor makes a greeting circuit. The gatha chanters' seats can be either to the right or left of the Sacred Monk, according to circumstances. Fine incense, such as aloeswood, or incense sticks are inserted into the portable incense burner and burned. This incense is prepared by the donor. When the donor makes a circumambulation, the assembly of monks hold their hands in gassho.

Next, the recitation honorarium is presented. The amount of the honorarium is decided by the donor. Sometimes materials such as cotton or fans are presented. This offering is delivered by the donor, a monastery officer, or an assistant worker. It is placed in front of each monk, not in the monk's hand. Each monk receives it with a gassho.

The honorarium can be presented at the midday meal on the day of recitation. In this case, after the donated meal, the head monk hits the umpan with a mallet once and distributes the honorarium.

A sheet of paper on which the intention of the donation is written is posted on the pole north of the Sacred Monk.

When you read a sutra in the monks' hall, recite it in a soft voice rather than a spirited one. Or, open the sutra book and just look at the letters. It is not actually reading, but looking at the sutra.

For such a ritual, hundreds and thousands of copies of sutras—such as the *Diamond Sutra*, the "Universal Gate" and "Blissful Practice" chapters of the *Lotus Sutra,* and the *Suvarna Prabhasottama King Sutra*—are kept in monasteries. Each monk reads a copy.

After the recitation, the novices walk with the box or tray of sutra books in front of everyone's seat. The monks return the books to it. When you take and return the book, you do gassho. That is: after gassho, you take the book, and after you return it, do gassho. Then everyone in gassho recites the dedication in a soft voice.

For the recitation of a sutra in the communal area [the recitation hall] of the monastery, all the procedures—including the work of the director [of the monastery in this case], burning incense, bowing, the greeting circuit, and offering an honorarium—are the same as those for the recitation for a donor.

If one of the monks becomes a donor and requests the assembly to recite a sutra, it will be the same as in the case for a lay donor. The procedures include burning incense, bowing, the greeting circuit, and offering an honorarium. The monastery host leads the donor just like a lay donor.

———————

A sutra is also recited for the time of celebration for the Emperor. If the Emperor's birthday is the fifteenth day of the first month, the recitation begins on the fifteenth day of the twelfth month of the previous year, when no formal talk is offered.

Two long sitting platforms are set up before the image of Shakyamuni Buddha in the buddha hall. The platforms are placed in parallel on the east and west sides. Between the platforms, tables are set up, on which sutra books are placed. The sutra can be the *Diamond Sutra*, the *Virtuous King Sutra,* the *Lotus Sutra*, the *Most Excellent King Sutra*, or the *Suvarna Prabhasottama Sutra.*

A certain number of monks per day are assigned to conduct recitation in the buddha hall. Snacks are offered to these monks before the midday meal. Snacks can be a bowl of noodles and a bowl of warm food, or six or seven steamed cakes and a bowl of warm food. The steamed cakes are also served in a bowl, without chopsticks or a spoon. Monks take the snacks while they remain seated for recitation.

The snacks are set on the tables for the sutra books, without using additional small tables. While snacks are eaten, the sutra books remain on the tables. After the snack is over, monks leave the seats one by one, rinse their mouths, and return to continue recitation.

This recitation is done daily from the time of the morning meal to that of the midday meal. A drum is hit three times during the midday meal, signaling the end of recitation; those who have been chanting leave their seats.

From the first day of recitation, a plaque reading "The practice place in celebration of the Emperor's birthday" is hung under the east eave in front of the buddha hall. The plaque is yellow. Also, an intent of celebration is written on yellow paper mounted on a lattice panel. This plaque is posted on the eastern pole in the front area inside the buddha hall. The abbot's name in two ideographs is written on a small red or white sheet of paper, which is pasted underneath the date on the plaque.

Recitation is done in this way: On the day of the Emperor's birthday the abbot ascends the teaching seat and offers words of celebration. This is an ancient custom that has not become outdated.

Sometimes a monk aspires to recite a sutra. A monastery has a recitation hall in the communal area where recitation is practiced. It follows the guidelines presented above.

———————

Yaoshan, Great Master Hongdao, asked novice Gao, "Did you get it by reading a sutra or from personal guidance?"

Gao said, "I didn't get it by reading a sutra or from personal guidance."

Yaoshan said, "There are many who don't read a sutra or receive personal guidance. How come they don't get it?"

Gao said, "I can't say they don't get it. Perhaps they don't want to hit the mark."

While there are those who do or do not hit the mark in the house of buddha ancestors, reading a sutra and receiving personal instructions are essentials for everyday use.

Presented to the assembly of the Kosho Horin Monastery, Uji County, Yamashiro Province, on the fifteenth day, the ninth month in autumn, the second year of the Ninji Era [1241].

23

BUDDHA NATURE

SHAKYAMUNI BUDDHA SAID, "Living beings all are buddha nature. The Tathagata is continuously abiding and not subject to change."

As this is the lion roar of our great teacher Shakyamuni turning the wheel of dharma, it is the top of the head and the eyeball of all buddhas and ancestors. It has been practiced for two thousand one hundred nineteen years (up to this day, the second year of the Ninji Era of Japan). It has been maintained by more than fifty generations of authentic heirs (up to Rujing, my late master, Priest Tiantong)—twenty-eight generations in India and twenty-three generations in China. Buddha ancestors of the ten directions have also maintained it.

What is the meaning of the World-Honored One's teaching? It is the turning dharma wheel of "What has thus come?"

Living beings are also called "sentient beings," "various beings," or "various kinds." The *all are* is none other than sentient beings and living beings.

Thus, all are buddha nature. One form of all beings is sentient beings. At this very moment, the inside and outside of sentient beings are the *all are* of buddha nature. This understanding is not only the skin, flesh, bones, and marrow of a person-to-person transmission, but "You have attained my skin, flesh, bones, and marrow."

Know that the *are* of *all are buddha nature* is beyond are and are not. *All are* are the buddha words, the buddha tongue. They are the eyeball of buddha ancestors and the nostrils of patched-robed monks. The words *all are* are not limited to embryonic beings, original beings, inconceivable beings, or any other kind of beings. Furthermore, they do not mean causal beings or imaginary beings. *All are* are free from mind, object, essence, or aspects. This being so, the body, mind, and environs of *Living beings all are* [buddha nature] are not limited to the increasing power of action, imaginary causation, things as they are, or the practice realization of miraculous powers.

If *Living beings all have* were so, actualizing the way by all sages, the enlightenment of all buddhas, and the eye of buddha ancestors would be [caused by] the increasing power of action, imaginary causation, and so forth. But it is not so. In the entire world, there is no extra speck of dust. Buddha nature is immediate, and there is no second person [nothing outside], just as it is said, "Cut through the original person beyond knowing; action consciousness continues without ceasing." Buddha nature is not the being of imaginary causation, because "Nothing is hidden in the entire world."

"Nothing is hidden in the entire world" does not necessarily mean "The entire world is full of beings." To say, "The entire world is self-existence" is a crooked view held by those outside the way. What is not hidden is not original beings, as it encompasses past and present. It is not an embryonic being, as it is not affected by even one speck of dust from outside. It is not a suddenly emerged being, as it is shared by all beings. It is not a beginningless being, as it is "What has thus come?" It is not an embryonic being, as "Everyday mind is the way."

Know that in the midst of *all are*, sentient beings are hard to find. If you thoroughly understand *all are*, *all are* will be penetrated and dropped off.

———

Hearing the term "buddha nature," many students mistakenly regard it as the self explained by Shrenika, a teacher outside the way. They think this because they have not met a true person, the true self, a true teacher. They mistakenly regard the conscious mind, which is caused by the movement of air and fire, as the awareness and understanding of buddha nature. But who says that buddha nature has awareness or understanding? Even though those who are aware or understand are buddhas, buddha nature is neither awareness nor understanding.

Furthermore, the buddhas' awareness, of which they speak, is not the same awareness they mistakenly regard as awareness. The movement of air and fire is not the cause of buddhas' awareness. It is just that the awareness is one or two buddha faces, ancestor faces.

A number of ancient masters and early sages went to India and returned to China to guide humans and devas. They have been as common as rice, flax, bamboo, and reeds from the time of the Han and Tang dynasties until the time of the present Song Dynasty. Many of them regard the movement of air and fire as the awareness of buddha nature. What a pity! They make this kind of mistake because their study of the way is coarse. Those who are mature, as well as beginners in studying the buddha way, should not fall into this.

When you observe awareness, you know that awareness is not movement. When you observe movement, you know that movement is not thus. When you truly understand movement, you truly understand awareness. Studying "buddha" and "nature," when you get one, you get the other.

Buddha nature is no other than *all are*, because *all are* is buddha nature. *All are* is not a hundred broken pieces. *All are* is not a single rail of iron. As it is a held-up fist [something dynamic], it is not limited to large or small. When it is called buddha nature, it cannot be put shoulder to shoulder with all sages, it cannot be put shoulder to shoulder with buddha nature.

Some people think that buddha nature is like seeds of grass and trees: when dharma rain is abundant, sprouts and stems grow; branches, leaves, flowers, and fruit mature; and their fruit contains seeds. Such a view is an assumption of ordinary people. If you come up with such an assumption, investigate thoroughly that each and every seed, flower, and fruit is itself pure mind.

A fruit has seeds that are not visible but develop roots, stems, and so forth. The elements of the plants are not assembled from outside, but branches and twigs grow. Not limited to inside or outside, the growth of plants is not in vain, past and present. Thus, even if you take up the view of ordinary people, the roots, stems, branches, and leaves are the *all are* of buddha nature that rises and perishes simultaneously with all things.

———————

The Buddha said, "If you want to understand buddha nature, you should intimately observe cause and effect over time. When the time is ripe, buddha nature manifests."

The words *to understand buddha nature* do not only mean to know but also to practice it, to realize it, to expound it, and to let go of it. Expounding it, practicing it, realizing it, letting go of it, missing it, and not missing it are all *cause and effect over time.*

You observe cause and effect over time through observation of cause and effect over time. You observe it with a whisk, a staff, and so forth. However, you may observe it through the wisdom of desire, the wisdom of beyond desire, original enlightenment, embryonic enlightenment, no-enlightenment, or true enlightenment.

Intimately observe is not limited to observing, being observed, correct observation, or wrong observation; it is *intimately observe*. As it is intimate observing, it is not self-observation or other's observation. Intimate observing is cause and effect as they are over time, and it is beyond cause and effect. It is buddha nature as it is. It is becoming free of the body of buddha nature. It is buddha and buddha as they are, [buddha] nature and nature as they are.

Hearing the words *when the time is ripe*, many people both in the past and present have thought that it means we should wait until buddha nature manifests in the future; that as a result of practice we will eventually encounter the time when buddha nature manifests; and that when the time is not ripe, buddha nature will not manifest even if we inquire about dharma from a teacher and endeavor in the practice of the way. They think in this way and stay in the [secular] world of red dust fruitlessly while keeping a monk's appearance. Such people appear to be those outside of the way who believe in spontaneous enlightenment.

The words *If you want to understand buddha nature* mean "if you want to understand buddha nature immediately." *Observe cause and effect over time* means "You should know cause and effect over time." *You should intimately observe cause and effect over time* means that if you want to know buddha nature, it is no other than knowing cause and effect over time. *When the time is ripe* means that the time has already arrived. How can we doubt it? A time of doubting also is a time when buddha nature is present to the self.

Know that *when the time is ripe* means that the twelve hours of the day are not passed in vain. *When the time is* is like saying "when the time has arrived." "When the time has arrived" is not the arrival of buddha nature. Thus, when the time has arrived, buddha nature is already actualized. This principle is self-evident. Generally, there is no time when the time has not yet arrived; there is no buddha nature that is not actualized.

Venerable Ashvaghosha, the Twelfth Ancestor, explained the ocean of buddha nature to Kapimala, the Thirteenth Ancestor, to be: "Mountains, rivers, and the great earth—all depend on it. Various samadhis and the six miraculous powers emerge from it."

Thus, mountains, rivers, and the great earth are all the ocean of buddha nature. *All depend on it* means that at the very moment when they depend on it, they are mountains, rivers, and the great earth. Know that the form of the ocean of buddha nature is like this. It is not concerned with inside, outside, or in between. This being so, to see mountains and rivers is to see buddha nature; to see buddha nature is to see the fins of a donkey and the beak of a horse. *All depend on* means to totally depend on. Thus, you understand and go beyond understanding.

Ashvaghosha said, *Various samadhis and the six miraculous powers emerge from it*. Know that the "emerging" and "not yet emerging" of various samadhis equally depend on buddha nature; the emerging of the six miraculous powers from here and not here all depend on buddha nature.

The *six miraculous powers* are not those taught in the Agama School. The *six* is the realization of the six miraculous powers of three three before and three three after [countless]. So, do not think that the six miraculous powers are limited to the one hundred grasses bright and clear and the mind of buddha ancestors bright and clear. Even though you may be limited by the thought of the six miraculous powers, you are immersed in the vastness of the ocean of buddha nature.

———————

Hongren, the Fifth Chinese Ancestor, Zen Master Daman, was from Huangmei, Qi Region. He was born without a father. He acquired the way when he was young. In his earlier life he had been growing pine trees on West Mountain in Qi Region when he met Daoxin, the Fourth Ancestor, who was traveling through the region. Daoxin said to him, "I want to transmit dharma to you. But you are too old. I will wait for you until you return."

Hongren agreed. He entered the body of a daughter of the Zhou family and was reborn through her. After he was born, he was cast away into the brackish water of the harbor. But a spirit guarded him from harm for seven days. He was rescued by someone and was brought up until he was seven years old, when he saw Daoxin on the street in Huangmei.

Daoxin said to himself, "This is a little child, but his appearance is extraordinary, not like any other." So he said to Hongren, "What is your name?"

Hongren said, "I have a name, but it is not an ordinary name."

"What is it?"

Hongren said, "It is buddha nature."

Daoxin said, "You have no buddha nature."

Hongren said, "As buddha nature is empty, you say I have no buddha nature."

Realizing that Hongren was a dharma vessel, Daoxin asked him to be his attendant and later entrusted him with the treasury of the true dharma eye. Hongren lived on the East Mountain of Huangmei and circulated the profound wind [teaching].

Thus, when we study the dialogue of these ancestors, Daoxin's words *What is your name?* have significance. In ancient times people would ask others what country and which family they were from. It means "You must have come from a certain family." It is just like saying, "You are like this. I am like this."

Hongren's words *I have a name, but it is not an ordinary name* mean that to have this name is to have no ordinary name. An ordinary name is not it.

Daoxing's words *What is it?* mean what is *it*? *It* is called *what*. That is the *name*. *It* makes *what*. *What* makes *it*. The name is *it*. The name is *what*. *It* is presented as mugwort tea or green tea. *It* is daily tea and rice.

Hongren's words *It is buddha nature* mean that *it* is buddha nature. Because *it* is *what*, it is buddha. Is *it* merely understood as *what name*? Even when *it* is not *it*, it is buddha nature. This being so, although *it* is *what* and *it* is buddha, when Hongren drops off and slips through, the name is always present. His is Zhou. However, he did not receive the name from his father or his ancestors, and he did not resemble his mother. Who can stand shoulder to shoulder with him?

By saying *You have no buddha nature*, Daoxin was saying that although Hongren is not "who he is" and it's up to him to determine who he is, he has *no buddha nature* [he is beyond buddha nature]. Learn and study what kind of moment it is when there is *no buddha nature*. Is it *no buddha nature* on the top of the buddha's head, or is it *no buddha nature* that is going beyond? Do not be stuck with seven penetrations or search for eight masteries.

No buddha nature is sometimes understood as the samadhi of this one moment. Ask whether there is *no buddha nature* when buddha nature attains buddhahood. Ask whether there is *no buddha nature* that arouses the aspiration [for enlightenment]. Have a pillar ask this question, or ask a pillar this question. Have buddha nature ask this question.

In this way, the words *no buddha nature* are heard all the way from the ancestral chamber of Daoxin. These words are seen and heard on Mount Huangmei, in Zhou Province, and Mount Guishan. Be sure to endeavor with the words *no buddha nature* without being put off by the words. In tracing *no buddha nature*, there, straight on, is the standard of *what*, the moment of *you*, the response of *it*, and the name *Zhou*.

Hongren's words *As buddha nature is empty, you say I have no buddha nature* express clearly that *empty* is not *no*. In speaking of the emptiness of buddha nature, he did not say half a pound or eight ounces; he just said *no [buddha nature]*. As it is *empty*, he did not call it empty. As it is *no [buddha nature]*, he did not call it *no*. As buddha nature is empty, he called it *no*. Thus, bits and pieces of *no* are a standard for speaking about emptiness. Emptiness is the measure of speaking *no [buddha nature]*.

Empty mentioned here is not that of "Form is emptiness." "Form is emptiness" does not mean to force form to be emptiness or to break up emptiness to establish form.

Rather, it is the emptiness of "Emptiness is emptiness." *Emptiness is emptiness* means there is a piece of rock hanging in emptiness. Thus, Daoxin and Hongren talked about *no buddha nature*, buddha nature that is empty, and buddha nature that is existence.

———

Huineng, who would later become Zen Master Dajian of Mount Caoxi, the Sixth Ancestor, went to Huangmei to meet Hongren, the Fifth Ancestor. Hongren said, "Where are you from?"

Huineng said, "From Lingnan."

Hongren said, "What do you seek?"

Huineng said, "I seek to become a buddha."

Hongren said, "People from Lingnan have no buddha nature. How can you become a buddha?"

Hongren's words *People from Lingnan have no buddha nature* do not mean that people from Lingnan do not have buddha nature, or that they do have buddha nature. Rather, he was saying that people from Lingnan *have no-buddha* [beyond-buddha] *nature*.

His words, *How can you become a buddha?* is asking what kind of becoming a buddha Huineng intended.

There are few earlier teachers who clarified the essentials of buddha nature. It's not what teachers of the *Agama Sutras*, other sutras, and treatises understand. It has only been transmitted person to person to the descendants of buddha ancestors.

The essential of buddha nature is that buddha nature is embodied not before but after you attain buddhahood. Buddha nature invariably arises simultaneously with attaining buddhahood. You should thoroughly investigate this principle, studying and endeavoring for twenty or thirty years. This is not something bodhisattvas of the ten stages or the three classes can clarify.

The words "Sentient beings have buddha nature" or "Sentient beings have no buddha nature" point to this principle. To understand that buddha nature is embodied after attaining buddhahood is hitting a mark right on. To study otherwise is not buddha dharma. Without this understanding, buddha dharma would not have reached to this day. Not understanding this principle is not clarifying, seeing, or hearing the attainment of buddhahood.

This is why Hongren said, *People from Lingnan have no buddha nature,* when he was offering guidance to Huineng. What is rare to encounter and hear when first seeing a buddha and hearing dharma is the teaching that sentient beings have no buddha nature. What to rejoice upon in following a teacher and studying sutras is to hear the teaching that sentient beings have no buddha nature. Those who are not immersed in seeing, hearing, and knowing that sentient beings without exception have no buddha nature have not yet seen, heard, or known buddha nature.

When Huineng wholeheartedly sought to become a buddha and Hongren helped him to become a buddha, he had no other words or skillful means than saying *People from Lingnan have no buddha nature.* Know that to say and hear no-buddha nature is a direct way to become a buddha. Thus, at the very moment of no-buddha nature you become a buddha. Those who have not seen, heard, or spoken no-buddha nature have not yet become a buddha.

Huineng said, "There are people from the south and people from the north, but in buddha nature there is no south or north."

Take up these words and investigate the meaning behind them. Reflect with a bare heart upon the words *south* and *north.* His words have a point—a view that people become buddhas but buddha nature doesn't become people. Was Huineng aware of it or not?

Buddhas, including Kashyapa Buddha and Shakyamuni Buddha, are empowered to say *Living beings all are buddha nature* when they are buddhas and turning the dharma wheel, by receiving a portion of the all-inclusive power of the words *no buddha nature* spoken by Hongren and Huineng. How could the words *Living beings all are buddha nature* not inherit dharma from the *no* of *no buddha nature*?

In this way, the words *no buddha nature* are heard far away from the chamber of Hongren and Huineng. Since Huineng was already a true person at that time, he should have further investigated the words *no buddha nature*. He should have asked, "Aside from whether one has buddha nature or not, how is buddha nature?" He should also have asked, "What is buddha nature?" Upon hearing the words buddha nature, people nowadays also discuss whether one has buddha nature or no buddha nature without asking what buddha nature is. This is hasty and careless.

Thus, study the "no" of all "nos" through the *no* of *no buddha nature*. Dive over and over again into the statement of Huineng, *There are people from the south and people from the north, but in buddha nature there is no south or north*. Work on it and quietly let go of it.

Some foolish people assume that Huineng's statement means that people from the south differ from those from the north because of their qualities, but that buddha nature goes beyond south or north, as it is empty and fluid. This is ignorant beyond measure. Disregard such a crooked view and study straightforwardly.

Later, Huineng taught his disciple Xinchang by saying, "Impermanence is itself buddha nature. Permanence is the mind that discriminates the wholesomeness and unwholesomeness of all things."

The *impermanence* Huineng speaks of is beyond the grasp of outsiders or practitioners of the Lesser Vehicles. Teachers and descendants of these people talk about impermanence, but they have not yet fully understood it.

Impermanence expounds, practices, and realizes impermanence; all this is impermanence. Manifesting a [buddha] body and expounding dharma with the buddha body—this is buddha nature. Further, it is to manifest a tall dharma body and to manifest a short dharma body. Constantly being a sage is impermanence. Constantly being an ordinary person is impermanence.

This is the meaning of Huineng's words *Impermanence is itself buddha nature*. To say that those who are constantly sages or ordinary people cannot be buddha nature is a limited view, the narrow thinking of foolish people. Their understanding of buddha falls short. Their understanding of buddha nature falls short.

Permanence means no turning. "No turning" is not affected by the passage of coming and going, although there are such changes as becoming free from desire or allowing desire itself to become free. This is permanence. Grass, trees, and forests are impermanent; they are buddha nature. Humans, things, body, and mind are impermanent; they are buddha nature. Land, mountains, and rivers are impermanent, as they are buddha nature. Unsurpassable, complete enlightenment is impermanent, as it is buddha nature. Great pari-nirvana is buddha nature, as it is impermanence. Practitioners of the Lesser Vehicles who hold limited views, and teachers and commentators of the Tripitaka, should be startled at this statement of Huineng. If they aren't, they must be a group of outsider demons.

———————

Venerable Nagarjuna, the Fourteenth Ancestor, is called Dragon Tree, Dragon Excellence, or Dragon Ferocity in China. He was a man from western India who went to southern India. People there believed in practices that bring good fortune. When Nagarjuna expounded dharma to people, one of them said, "The best things in the world are practices that bring good fortune. Even if you talk about buddha nature, no one can see it."

Nagarjuna replied, "If you want to see buddha nature, first let go of your pride."

The man said, "Is buddha nature large or small?"

Nagarjuna said, "Buddha nature is neither large nor small, neither broad nor narrow. It has neither goodness nor rewards. It has neither death nor birth."

Realizing that Nagarjuna's teaching was extraordinary, the man's aspiration was turned around. Then, while sitting, Nagarjuna manifested a body of complete freedom in the shape of a full moon. The assembly could hear his dharma talk, but they could not see him.

In the assembly there was someone called Kanadeva, the son of a wealthy man, who said to the assembly, "Do you understand this?"

People said, "We cannot see the master but we can hear him. Our minds do not understand what's happening, and our bodies have not experienced such a thing."

Kanadeva said, "This is how the master manifests the form of buddha nature and shows it to us. The reason is that the samadhi of no-form has taken the shape of a full moon. Buddha nature is vast, empty, and clear."

Just as Kanadeva said this, Nagarjuna appeared on his seat and taught in verse:

> This body manifests a full moon
> expressing the bodies of all buddhas,
> teaching that it has no particular shape,
> expressing that revealing it is neither sound nor form.

Thus, know that a true expression is not done by sound or form, and a true teaching has no particular shape. Nagarjuna expounded on buddha nature countless times. What is shown here is just an example.

You should reflect without fail on Nagarjuna's words *If you want to see buddha nature, first let go of your pride.* It's not that you cannot see buddha nature, but to see it, you first need to let go of your pride. Because you are complex, there are many types of pride. There are myriad ways to let go of pride, and when you do, you see buddha nature. This is to see buddha nature with your eyes.

Do not regard Nagarjuna's words *Buddha nature is neither large nor small* as ordinary people or those in the Lesser Vehicle do. Stubborn people believe that buddha nature is enormous. This is the piling up of crooked thoughts. To be immersed in Nagarjuna's words *neither large nor small* is to discern them as spoken just now. This discernment is a cause for listening. Listen to his verse now. He says, *This body manifests a full moon expressing the bodies of all buddhas.* As he manifested the body expressing all buddhas' bodies, the body took the shape of a full moon. Thus, you should study that everything both long and short, square and round, is manifested in the shape of a full moon. If you are ignorant about the body or the manifestation, you are ignorant not only about the shape of the full moon but about the bodies of the buddhas.

Foolish people may think that Nagarjuna manifested the shape of a full moon tentatively. This is a crooked thought of rascals who have not inherited the buddha way. When and where could he have manifested a form that was not his own body? Know that Nagarjuna was sitting on the teaching seat, just as everyone is sitting right now. This body manifests the shape of a full moon. Manifestation of the body is not limited to square or round, existent or nonexistent, revealed or hidden. Manifestation of this body is not limited to eighty-four thousand skandhas; it is just manifestation of this body. You speak of a full moon, but what about a crescent moon or sliver moon?

As this manifestation of the body is to *first let go of your pride*, it is not Nagarjuna but the bodies of all buddhas. As this manifestation expresses all buddhas, it becomes free from all buddhas. Thus, it is not limited to the realm of buddhas.

Even if there may be a void similar to the full moon of buddha nature, it cannot be compared with that full moon. Furthermore, expression [of buddha nature] is neither sound nor form. The manifestation of this body is neither form nor mind, nor is it in the realm of the skandhas. Although the manifestation of this body may look like the realm of the skandhas, it is expressing the bodies of the buddhas. This is expounding dharma; it is having no form. When having no form is the samadhi of no-form, the body is manifested.

Although the assembly saw the shape of a full moon, what they did not see was a turning point of expounding dharma, the manifestation of a free body beyond form and sound. This hiding and revealing is the going back and forth of the full moon.

At the very moment when Nagarjuna sat on his seat and manifested the body of freedom, the whole assembly only heard dharma without seeing him. His heir, Kanadeva, clearly understood the meaning of the full-moon shape, of the manifestation of the body, of the nature of all buddhas, and of the bodies of all buddhas. Although there were many who entered Nagarjuna's room and received water, vessel to vessel, there was no one who could compare with Kanadeva, who was a venerable student sharing the seat with Nagarjuna, and was a guiding master of the assembly on the half seat. He authentically received the treasury of the true dharma eye, the unsurpassable great dharma, just like Venerable Mahakashyapa did on Vulture Peak.

Previously, Nagarjuna was a Brahman master outside the buddha dharma. When his mind was turned, he sent away the students who had been studying with him. After he became a buddha ancestor, Kanadeva alone received the treasury of the great dharma as an authentic heir. This is a person-to-person transmission of the unsurpassable buddha way.

However, a crooked group of people who hid their falsehood and groundlessly called themselves dharma heirs of Nagarjuna Bodhisattva compiled treatises and interpretations. Many of them were attributed to Nagarjuna although they were not by him. Those who had been driven away by him were confusing both humans and devas with these texts. Disciples of the Buddha should know that the teachings that were not passed on by Kanadeva are not the words of Nagarjuna. You can genuinely trust the teaching through Kanadeva. But many people knowingly accept the false teaching. We should deplore the foolishness of those who slander great prajna.

Kanadeva pointed to Nagarjuna's manifested body and said to the assembly, *This is how the master manifests the form of buddha nature and shows it to us. The reason is that the samadhi of no-form has taken the shape of a full moon. Buddha nature is vast, empty, and clear.* Who, among those skin bags here and there, seeing and hearing the buddha dharma spread in the billion worlds of phenomena of humans and devas, can say that the body of Nagarjuna was manifesting as buddha nature? In the billion worlds Kanadeva alone could say this. Others merely said that buddha nature is neither seen with the eyes, nor heard with the ears, nor known through consciousness. As they didn't know that Nagarjuna's manifestation of the body was buddha nature, they could not say so. Even though Ancestor Nagarjuna did not withhold his teaching, they could not see or hear it, as their eyes and ears were covered. They were unable to realize it, as their body consciousness had not arisen. When they saw and bowed to the samadhi of no-form that had taken the shape of a full moon, they could not see it.

As Kanadeva says, *Buddha nature is vast, empty, and clear.* Thus, manifesting the body is itself expounding buddha nature, vast, empty, and clear. Expounding buddha nature is that body manifested [in a full-moon shape], expressing the bodies of all buddhas. Are there one or two buddhas who embody this expression? The buddha bodies are a manifestation of that body. Also, buddha nature is manifested as that body.

The buddha ancestors' perception that discerns the four great elements and the five skandhas is also a working of this manifested body. The skandhas, places, and realms are like this in all buddhas' bodies. All merits are this merit. All buddhas' merits are fully expressed and encompassed by this manifested body. The coming and going of all the innumerable, boundless merits are part of the working of this manifested body.

However, those in early and later generations in the three countries [India, China, and Japan] who studied dharma later than Nagarjuna and Kanadeva have not spoken as these masters did. How many scholars of sutras and treatises have missed Nagarjuna and Kanadeva's words? From the early times in China, people tried to paint this story, but they have not been able to paint it on body, mind, emptiness, or the wall. They have only painted the story with the tips of their brush. They have merely painted a mirrorlike circle on the dharma seat and claimed it as Nagarjuna's manifestation of the full-moon body. For hundreds of years such paintings have been specks of gold [hindrances] in human eyes, but no one has pointed out that these paintings are false. What a pity! Myriad interpretations are off the mark.

If people think that Nagarjuna's manifestation of the full-moon shape is merely a single circle, they truly see a piece of a painted rice cake. It is fooling others; such laughing kills people.

How sad, none of those in China, laity or home leavers, have taken Nagarjuna's words seriously or understood Kanadeva's statement! How, then, can they become intimate with Nagarjuna's manifestation of the body? This is to be ignorant about the circular moon while missing the full moon. This is because they have neither studied the past nor longed for the past. Old buddhas and new buddhas, you should meet the true manifestation of the body instead of admiring a painted rice cake.

Know that when you paint the manifestation of a full moon, do it on a dharma seat. Raising an eyebrow and blinking are just this. The treasury of the true dharma eye—skin, flesh, bones. and marrow—is just sitting solidly. Breaking into a smile is transmitted, making a buddha and making an ancestor.

Without a moon shape, your painting will have no shape of thusness, no expounding of dharma, no sound or form, and no use. When you express the manifestation of the [buddha] body, paint a circular moon shape. When you paint a circular moon shape, paint a circular moon shape, actualize a circular moon shape, because the manifestation of body is a circular moon shape. When you paint a circular moon shape, paint a full moon, actualize a full moon. Thus, unless you paint the manifestation of the body, a circular moon shape, a full moon, and buddha bodies, you are not embodying the expression and painting the expounding of dharma, but merely creating a piece of painted rice cake. What's the use of it? Look quickly. Who will be satisfied or not satisfied right at this moment? The moon is circular. The circle is the manifestation of the body. When you study the circle, don't regard it as a coin or a piece of cake. The manifested body is a circular moon. It has the shape of a full moon. See the circle in a coin or in a rice cake.

When I was wandering, I arrived at Great Song China. In the autumn of the sixteenth year of the Jiading Era [1224], I visited the Ayuwang Mountain Guanli Monastery for the first time. There on the walls of the western hallway, I saw paintings of the thirty-three ancestors of India. I did not have understanding at that time. Later, during the summer practice period of the first year of the Baoqing Era [1225], I visited the monastery again. I walked along the hallway with Guest Coordinator Chenggui from the western district of Shu. I asked him, "What is this painting?"

Chenggui said, "Nagarjuna manifesting his body in the shape of a full moon." He had no nostrils on his face and no wisdom in his explanation.

I said, "Truly it looks like a piece of painted rice cake."

Although Chenggui burst into laughter, he had no sword in his laughter and no ability to tear off the painted rice cake. We exchanged a few words on our way to the relic hall and the six excellent places, but he did not even come up with any doubts. Other monks who spoke to us had no idea.

So I said to Chenggui, "I will ask the abbot." The abbot of the monastery at that time was Priest Daguang.

Then, Chenggui said, "He doesn't have nostrils. He cannot answer. How can he know?" So, I decided not to speak with Daguang.

Although Chenggui spoke in this way, he did not seem to have realization. Those who joined the conversation did not have any remarkable expressions. The abbots of this monastery in the past and present did not question them and correct their views.

Never paint what cannot be painted. Paint straightforwardly what needs to be painted. Yet, [Nagarjuna's] manifestation of the body in the shape of a full moon had never been painted.

In fact, as people are not awakened from the assumption that buddha nature is thought and consciousness, they seem to miss the expressions of "have buddha nature" and "have no buddha nature." Those who learn that the point needs to be expressed are rare. Know that this negligence is due to giving up the subject. Among the abbots of various monasteries there are those who never mention buddha nature throughout their lifetimes.

Some of these abbots say, "Those who listen to the [Buddha's] teachings discuss buddha nature. Monks who practice Zen should not talk about it." Those who say such things are truly beasts. What kind of demons attempt to mix with and defile the way of our Buddha Tathagata? Is there listening to the teaching in the buddha way? Is there practicing Zen in the buddha way? Know that there is nothing like listening to the teaching or practicing Zen in the buddha way.

Yanguan, National Teacher Qi'an of Hang Region, who was a dharma heir of Mazu, once said to his assembly, "Living beings all have buddha nature."

Immediately investigate these words. All living beings have their own karma, practice, body-mind, and environs; their views vary. Ordinary people, those outside the way, those in the Three Vehicles and the Five Vehicles, are all different.

What are called *living beings* in the buddha way encompasses all those who have heart. All those who have heart are living beings. Those who have no heart are also living beings. All living beings are heart. Thus, heart is all living beings.

All living beings have buddha nature. Grass, trees, land, and earth are heart. As they are heart, they are living beings. As they are living beings they have buddha nature. Sun, moon, stars are all heart. As they are heart, they are living beings. As they are living beings, they have buddha nature. The statement of Yanguan *have buddha nature* means this. If not, it is not *have buddha nature* taught in the buddha way.

The meaning of Yanguan's words is that living beings alone have buddha nature. Those who are not living beings do not have buddha nature.

Now, ask him, "Do all living beings have or not have buddha nature?" In this way, question and examine his understanding.

Study that Yanguan did not say, "Living beings all are buddha nature," but rather: "Living beings all have buddha nature." Drop off the *have* of *have buddha nature*. Dropping off is one solid rail of iron. One solid rail of iron is the bird's path.

Thus, living beings all have buddha nature. These words not only penetrate living beings but penetrate buddha nature. Although Yanguan could not find a thorough expression, he did not miss the mark. It is not that his expression has no valuable teaching. But he may not have understood the deep meaning of his own words that embody the four great elements and the five skandhas, as well as skin, flesh, bones, and marrow. Thus, an expression is sometimes the result of a lifetime. Also, birth after birth can depend on an expression.

Guishan, Zen Master Dayuan of Mount Gui, once told his assembly, "Entire living beings have no buddha nature."

Among the humans and devas who have heard his words, some have had a great capacity to rejoice. But it is not that there has been no one who was shocked or suspicious.

Shakyamuni Buddha's expounding of the way was *Living beings all are buddha nature.* What Guishan said was *Entire living beings have no buddha nature.* These two statements—*all are* and *have no*—are far apart. Whether Guishan's statement is right or wrong can be questioned. However, *Entire living beings have no buddha nature* stands high in the buddha way.

Yanguan's statement *have buddha nature* can be likened to joining hands with an ancient buddha, or two people holding one walking stick. But Guishan's statement is not like that; it is a single stick swallowing both people.

Yanguan is an heir of Mazu, and Guishan is a descendant of Mazu. However, the descendant is advanced in Mazu's way and the heir is not yet mature. Guishan makes an essential statement by saying, *Entire living beings have no buddha nature,* which does not fall off the straight line. This is how he maintained the sutra in his own house.

Inquire further about how it is that living beings all are buddha nature or all have buddha nature. If living beings all *have* buddha nature, they must be a group of demons. It is covering all living beings with demons.

As buddha nature is buddha nature, living beings are living beings. It is not that living beings originally possess buddha nature. Even if they beckon to buddha nature, it will not come. Do not say that Zhang drinks wine and Li gets drunk [that the two are not separate]. Those who originally *have* buddha nature are not living beings. If they are living beings [who have buddha nature], they are not [separately] buddha nature.

Thus, Baizhang said, "To say 'Entire living beings all have buddha nature' is to slander buddha, dharma, and sangha. To say 'Living beings have no buddha nature' is also to slander buddha, dharma, and sangha."

In this way, *have buddha nature* and *have no buddha nature* are both slandering. Although it is slandering, you can still inquire about it. Ask Guishan and Baizhang, and hear their responses: "Slandering is not out of the question. But does buddha nature expound dharma?" If buddha nature expounds dharma, it must be immersed in expounding dharma. If it expounds dharma, it must go together with hearing it.

Also, ask Guishan: "Even if you say, 'Entire living beings have no buddha nature,' you are not saying, 'Entire buddha nature has no living beings' or 'Entire buddha nature has no buddha nature.' Furthermore, you have not yet dreamed of 'Entire buddhas have no buddha nature.'" Look into this.

————————

Baizhang, Great Master Dazhi, said to his assembly:

The Buddha is the supreme vehicle. He is established in the buddha way as the one who has wisdom that is the highest of the highest. The Buddha has buddha nature. He is the guiding master who has attained unobstructed wind, unobstructed wisdom. Thus, he is the master of cause and effect, and freely uses happiness that comes with wisdom, transporting cause and effect on this cart. Abiding in birth, he is not held up by birth. Abiding in death, he is not obstructed by death. Abiding in the five skandhas, he is not obstructed by the five skandhas. He comes and goes freely with no difficulty, just like passing through an open gate. Thus, he brings every being, regardless of position or capacity, even an ant, into the inconceivable pure and wondrous land.

This is Baizhang's point. The so-called five skandhas are the indestructible [buddha] body. The [Buddha's] work is like going through an open gate unobstructed by the five skandhas. Engaged in birth, do not be held up by birth. Engaged in death, do not be held up by death. Do not be attached to birth. Do not groundlessly fear death. Already there is buddha nature.

Those who are shaken by death and try to avoid it are outside the way. Those who realize pressing conditions and utilize them as unobstructed wind are buddhas of the supreme vehicle. Where these buddhas abide is the pure and wondrous land.

Huangbo was sitting in the tea room while visiting Nanquan's monastery.

Nanquan asked, "What is the meaning of clearly seeing buddha nature by practicing samadhi and wisdom equally?"

Huangbo said, "It can be done by not depending upon a single thing for twelve hours."

Nanquan said, "Isn't that another elder's view?"

Huangbo said, "Not really."

Nanquan said, "Putting aside for the moment the money for the gruel you have eaten, whom should I reimburse for the straw sandals?"

Huangbo stopped.

The words *practicing samadhi and wisdom equally* do not mean that clearly seeing buddha nature is possible by equally practicing samadhi and wisdom. Instead, where there is the cultivation of wisdom, there is *practicing samadhi and wisdom equally*. What they mean is that samadhi and wisdom are practiced equally when buddha nature is clearly seen. Nanquan was asking the meaning of this principle. It is just like asking, "Who clearly sees buddha nature?" It is also like asking the meaning of "buddha nature is clearly seen by equally cultivating buddha nature."

Huangbo's words *It can be done by not depending upon a single thing for twelve hours* mean that even though the twelve hours abide in the twelve hours, they are *not depending*. *Not depending upon a single thing* is clearly seeing buddha nature because *not depending* is *twelve hours*.

At what moment and to which land do these twelve hours arrive? Are the twelve hours spoken of here twelve hours of humans? Are there twelve hours somewhere else? Is it that the twelve hours in the silver world have arrived temporarily? Whether the twelve hours are in this land or in another realm, they are *not depending*. They are just twelve hours, they are *not depending*.

Nanquan's words to Huangbo, *Isn't that a view of another elder?* are like asking, "Is this really your own view?" Even if *you* are asked whether this is your own view, don't turn around and say it is. Even if this view fits *you* exactly, it may not fit Huangbo. Huangbo is not limited by *you*. The view of another elder is vastly revealed all the way through.

Huangbo's words *Not really* are based on a custom in Song China of not saying so even if one has a clear view. Therefore, *not really* does not mean "not really." Do not assume that these words mean what they seem to mean. Even if the view of another is that of the elder, even if the view of another elder is that of Huangbo, what you should say is *not really*. A water buffalo comes out and bellows; to say it like this is to say it completely. Say the meaning of saying, the saying of saying it completely.

Nanquan said, *Putting aside for the moment the money for the gruel you have eaten, whom should I reimburse for the straw sandals?* It means that although he wasn't concerned about what Huangbo had contributed to the monastery for gruel, he wanted to return Huangbo's money for the sandals.

Study the meaning of this, life after life. Investigate why Nanquan wanted the matter of the money for gruel to be set aside for the moment. How do you understand the money for straw sandals? It means wearing out countless pairs of sandals in way-seeking travels.

Speak! "If you don't return the money, I won't be wearing sandals." Or say, "A couple of pairs of sandals." This is a complete expression. This is an essential response.

Huangbo stopped. He was silent. It does not mean that he stopped

because he was not approved by Nanquan, or that he did not understand. A monk of true color is not like that. Know that speaking by not
speaking is like a sword hidden within laughter. This is sufficient gruel
and sufficient rice for clearly seeing buddha nature.

———————

Regarding this dialogue, Guishan asked Yangshan, "Is it that Huangbo
did not harmonize with Nanquan?"

Yangshan said, "That's not the case. Huangbo had the power to trap
a tiger."

Guishan said, "Your way of seeing has grown."

In this way Guishan questioned whether Huangbo understood Nanquan or not. Yangshan's reply *Huangbo had the power to trap a tiger* means
that trapping a tiger is grabbing the head of the tiger. To trap and grab a
tiger is to walk in the midst of a variety of beings. Clearly seeing buddha
nature is opening a single eye. Clearly seeing buddha nature is letting go
of the single eye.

Say it quickly! Clearly seeing buddha nature is seeing how large it is.
Neither half a thing nor an entire thing is to be depended upon. One
hundred things, one thousand things, are *not depending*. One hundred
times, one thousand times, are *not depending*.

So it is said: "Baskets and cages are one. Within time there are twelve
hours to depend upon or not to depend upon. It is like the way twining
vines depend upon a tree. Within heaven and throughout heaven, latecomers have no words."

———————

A monk asked Zhaozhou, Great Master Zhenji, "Does a dog have
buddha nature?"

Clarify the meaning of this question. A dog is a dog. It is not that this
monk was asking whether a dog has buddha nature or not. He was asking whether an iron person still practices the way. To happen to encounter Zhaozhou's poisonous hand may look unfortunate for this monk, but
it is like the lingering trace of seeing half a sage after thirty years.

Zhaozhou said, "No."

When you hear this word, a direction for study emerges. The *no* that
buddha nature itself calls forth must be like this. The *no* that the dog

itself calls forth must be like this. The *no* that bystanders call forth must be like this. This *no* holds the moment that dissolves a rock.

The monk said, "All sentient beings have buddha nature. How come a dog has no buddha nature?"

He meant that if sentient beings have no buddha nature, buddha nature must be *no* and a dog must be *no*. The monk asked the meaning of that. How is it that a dog's buddha nature depends upon *no*?

Zhaozhou said, "Because it has total ignorance."

He meant that *it has* is total ignorance. In the light of total ignorance and of *it has*, the dog is *no*, buddha nature is *no*. If total ignorance has not yet merged with a dog, how should a dog meet buddha nature? Even if both dog and buddha nature are let go of and taken in, still it is nothing but total ignorance all the way through.

Later another monk asked Zhaozhou, "Does a dog have buddha nature?"

This question indicates that the monk knew Zhaozhou's teaching. To speak of or inquire about buddha nature in this way was an everyday matter for buddha ancestors.

Zhaozhou said, "Yes."

This *yes* is not that of the commentators in the scriptural schools or the theorists of the Sarvastivada School. Go beyond and study the buddha *yes*. Buddha yes is Zhaozhou yes. Zhaozhou yes is dog yes. Dog yes is buddha nature yes.

The monk said, "If it [buddha nature] already is, how does it get into the dog's skin bag [body]?"

What he meant was: When we ask whether it is being now, being past, or *already is*, the *already is*, although it looks like all beings, is all-inclusive and clear. Does "already is" *get into* or not? The practice of *get into the dog's skin bag* should not be ignored.

Zhaozhou said, "It intentionally obstructs."

Although it has spread widely as words in the common world, this is Zhaozhou's statement. What he meant was knowingly committing. There are few who question these words. Aside from being difficult to clarify the words *get into*, they are not relevant.

In fact, "If you want to know the person of no death in the hut, how can you leave this skin bag right now?" Whoever the person of no death might be, when does that person not leave the skin bag?

Intentionally obstructing does not necessarily get it into the skin bag. Getting it into the skin bag is not necessarily *intentionally obstructing. Intentionally* means *obstructing.*

Know that this *obstructing* encompasses the practice of becoming free from the body. This is spoken of as *get into.* When the practice of becoming free from the body is fully encompassed, it is encompassed in self and others. This being so, do not easily say that a donkey comes before and a horse comes after [one follows after the other].

––––––––––

Thus, Yunju, High Ancestor, said, "When you study matters of buddha dharma, stop having your mind stuck on it." In this way, you may have studied a portion of buddha dharma mistakenly for days and months, as a dog that gets buddha nature into the skin bag. Although it is intentionally obstructing, it is being buddha nature.

––––––––––

At the assembly of Changsha Jingcen, Government Secretary Zhu asked, "When an earthworm is cut in half, both heads [pieces] move. In which head is buddha nature?"

Changsha said, "No illusion."

Zhu said, "What about moving?"

Changsha said, "Air and fire are not yet scattered."

In regard to Zhu's words, *When an earthworm is cut in half,* is it definite that the earthworm is in one piece before it is cut? It is not so in the everyday activities of buddha ancestors. An earthworm is not of one piece in origin, nor is it of two pieces after being cut. Thoroughly study the expressions "one" and "two."

Both heads move. Were they one head before being cut? Is buddha going beyond buddha of one head? The words *both heads* have nothing to do with whether Zhu had understanding or not. Do not ignore this question. Is it that the separated pieces are actually of one head and there is another head somewhere else? In regard to *move,* "Move delusions in samadhi and pull them out with wisdom" are both *move.*

In which head is buddha nature? Ask, "When buddha nature is cut in half, where is the earthworm's head?" Express this thoroughly.

Both heads move. In which head is buddha nature? Does it mean that buddha nature cannot abide if both heads move? Or, is Zhu asking in which motion buddha dharma abides while both heads move?

Changsha said, *No illusion.* What is the point? He cautions not to have illusion. Then, is he saying that there is no illusion when both heads move and that moving is not illusion? Does he simply mean that buddha nature has no illusion? Or, does he mean that there is no need to talk about buddha nature or both heads; there is just no illusion? Investigate his words thoroughly.

Zhu said, *What about moving?* Does he mean that moving adds another layer of buddha nature, or that what is moving is not buddha nature?

Changsha's words *Air and fire are not yet scattered* must cause buddha nature to manifest. Is it buddha nature, air, or fire [that is manifested]? Do not say buddha nature emerges together with air and fire. Do not say that when one emerges, the others do not. Do not say that air and fire are no other than buddha nature.

Thus, Changsha did not say that an earthworm has buddha nature, nor did he say that an earthworm has no buddha nature. He just said *No illusion,* then *Air and fire are not yet scattered.* Fathom the vital activities of buddha dharma through his words. Quietly ponder his statement *Air and fire are not yet scattered.* What is the point of *not yet scattered?* Does he mean that air and fire are assembled, but the moment of their being scattered has not arrived? It is not so. *Air and fire are not yet scattered* means the Buddha expounds dharma. *Not yet scattered air and fire* means dharma expounds the Buddha.

This is the arrival of the moment when dharma is expounded [by the Buddha] in one sound. It is the arrival of the moment when expounding dharma is one sound. Dharma is one sound, because it is the dharma of one sound.

Also, to assume that buddha nature exists only at the time of birth [life] and not at the time of death is [a result of] the least learning and shallow understanding. At the moment of birth, there is buddha nature and there is beyond buddha nature. At the moment of death, there is buddha nature and there is beyond buddha nature.

If *scattered* and *not yet scattered* of air and fire is discussed, buddha nature is scattered and not yet scattered. At the time of *scattered,* there is buddha nature and there is beyond buddha nature. At the time of *not yet scattered,* there is buddha nature and there is beyond buddha nature. This being so, it is those outside the way who mistakenly believe that buddha nature does or does not exist according to whether something does or does not move, that the spirit does or does not exist according to whether one does or does not have consciousness, and that essential nature does or does not exist according to whether one does or does not know.

From beginningless time, many ignorant people mistook consciousness for buddha nature, the original person. It is totally laughable.

If we discuss buddha nature further, it should not be splattered with mud or wet with water [overexplained]—it is walls, tiles, and pebbles. In expressing beyond, what is buddha nature? Can you say in detail? [I say it is like a demon with] Three heads and eight arms.

Presented to the assembly of the Kosho Horin Monastery, Uji County, Yamashiro Province, on the fourteenth day, the tenth month, the second year of the Ninji Era [1241].

24

Awesome Presence
of Active Buddhas

Buddhas at all times practice complete awesome presence; thus they are active buddhas. Active buddhas are neither reward-body buddhas nor incarnate-body buddhas, neither self-manifested buddhas nor buddhas manifested from others. Active buddhas are neither originally enlightened nor enlightened at some particular time, neither naturally enlightened nor without enlightenment. Such buddhas can never compare to active buddhas.

Know that buddhas in the buddha way do not wait for awakening. Active buddhas alone fully experience the vital process on the path of going beyond buddha. This is something that self-manifested buddhas have never dreamed of.

Because active buddhas manifest awesome presence in every situation, they bring forth awesome presence with their body. Thus, their transformative function flows out in their speech, reaching throughout time, space, buddhas, and activities. Without being an active buddha, you cannot be liberated from bondage to buddha and bondage to dharma, and you will be pulled into the cult of buddha-demons and dharma-demons.

"Bondage to buddha" means being bound by the view that our perception and cognition of enlightenment is actually enlightenment. Experiencing such views even for a moment, you cannot expect to meet liberation, and you will remain mistaken.

Seeing enlightenment as nothing but enlightenment may appear as a view that corresponds to enlightenment. Who would imagine calling it a crooked view? But this is like tying yourself up without a rope. Becoming further and further bound up, the tree you are tied to will not topple, and the wisteria vine binding you will not wither. In vain you struggle inside a pit in the vicinity of buddha, without seeing this as a sickness of the dharma body or as a trap of the reward body.

Teachers of buddha dharma, such as scholars of the sutras and treatises who listen to the buddha way from afar, say that "to arouse a view of dharma nature within dharma nature is no other than ignorance." These teachers talk about arousing a view of dharma nature without clarifying the bondage to dharma nature; they only accumulate the bondage of ignorance. They do not know about the bondage to dharma nature. Although this is regrettable, their awareness of the accumulation of the bondage of ignorance can be the seed for arousing the aspiration for enlightenment.

Now, active buddhas are never bound by such ties. This being so [it is said in the *Lotus Sutra*], "In the past I practiced the bodhisattva way and have attained this long life span, still now unexhausted, covering vast numbers of years."

Know that it is not that the life span of the bodhisattva has continued without end only until now, or not that the life span of the Buddha has prevailed only in the past, but what is called *vast numbers* is a total, inclusive attainment. What is called *still now* is the total life span. Even if *in the past I practiced* is one solid piece of iron ten thousand miles long, it casts away hundreds of years vertically and horizontally.

This being so, practice-realization is neither existence nor beyond existence. Practice-realization is not defiled [divided]. Although there are hundreds, thousands, and myriads [of practice-realizations] in a place where there is no buddha and no person, practice-realization does not defile active buddhas. Thus, there is no division in the practice-realization of active buddhas. It is not that there is no separation of practice-realization, but that this nondefilement is not nonexistent.

———————

Huineng of Caoxi [the Sixth Ancestor] said [to Nanyue], "This very nondefilement is what is attentively maintained by all buddhas. You are also like this. I am like this. All the ancestors in India are also like this."

Because *You are also like this*, there are all buddhas. Because *I am like this*, there are all buddhas. Indeed, it is beyond me and beyond you. In this nondefilement, *I* as I am, *attentively maintained by all buddhas*, is the awesome presence of an active buddha. *You* as you are, *attentively maintained by all buddhas*, is the awesome presence of an active buddha.

Because *I am like this*, the teacher is excellent. Because *you are also like this*, the disciple is strong. The teacher's excellence and disciple's strength are the complete wisdom and practice of active buddhas. Penetrate *What is attentively maintained by all buddhas*, as well as *I am like this* and *You are also like this*.

Even if this statement by Huineng were not about "me," how could it not be about "you"? What is attentively maintained by active buddhas, and what is thoroughly mastered by active buddhas, is like this. Thus, we know practice and realization are not concerned with essence or forms, roots or branches. While the everyday activities of active buddhas unfailingly allow buddhas to practice, active buddhas allow everyday activities to practice. This is to abandon your body for dharma, to abandon dharma for your body. This is to give up holding back your life, to hold on fully to your life. The awesome presence not only lets go of dharma for the sake of the dharma, it also lets go of dharma for the sake of mind. Do not forget that this letting go is unlimited.

Do not take up the buddha measure to measure and analyze the great way. The buddha measure is one step, just like an open blossom. Do not hold out the mind measure to grope for and deliberate about the awesome presence. The mind measure is a single face, like the world. The measure of a single blade of grass is clearly the measure of the buddha ancestor mind—one blade that recognizes the whereabouts of active buddhas.

Even if you recognize that one mind measure encompasses innumerable buddha measures, when you try to measure the active buddhas' appearance by the motion and stillness of their visage, it is undoubtedly beyond measure. Since their conduct is beyond measure, measuring does not hit the mark, is not useful, and cannot be gauged.

———————

Now, there is another point for investigating the awesome presence of active buddhas. When "Buddha is none other than the self" comes thus, the awesome presence of *I am like this* and *You are also like this* indicates "I alone know this." Yet, the dropping away of "The buddhas in the ten directions are also like this" is not only the single avenue.

Accordingly, an old buddha [Hongzhi Zhengjiao] said, "Reach over to grasp what's there, and bring its workings right here."

When you take on sustaining this, all things, bodies, actions, and buddhas become intimate with you. These actions, things, bodies, and buddhas are simply covered [immersed] in acceptance. Because they are simply covered in acceptance, through acceptance they are just dropped off.

The covered eye is the radiance of one hundred grass tips; do not be swayed [into thinking] that it does not see one thing, does not see a single matter. The covered eye reaches this thing and that thing. Throughout journeys, while taking on coming and going, or while leaving and entering by the same gate, nothing is hidden in the entire world, and so the World-Honored One's intimate language, intimate realization, intimate practice, and intimate entrustment are present.

Leaving the gate there is grass, entering the gate there is grass, though there is not a bit of grass for myriad miles. Such "entering" and "leaving" are not essential. Grasping by entering does not wait for the letting go of leaving; these are mere apparitions of blossoms in the sky.

Who would regard this apparition of blossoms in the sky as taking up a mistake and settling in with the mistake? Stepping forward misses, stepping backward misses, taking one step misses, taking two steps misses, and so there are mistakes upon mistakes.

Heaven and earth are far distant [due to our mistakes], and yet the ultimate way is not difficult. Thoroughly understand that in the awesome presence, and the presence of awe, the great way is wide open.

Know that upon emerging in birth, all emerge together on the way, and that upon entering death, all enter together on the way. From the head down to the tail, the awesome presence of rolling the pearl and of turning the jewel is manifested.

———————

That which allows one part of a buddha's awesome presence is the entire universe, the entire earth, as well as the entirety of birth and death, coming and going, of innumerable lands and lotus blossoms. Each of these innumerable lands and lotus blossoms is one part.

Students may think that "the entire universe" refers to this Southern Continent of Jambudvipa, or all the Four Continents. Some may think of it as China or Japan. Regarding "the entire earth," they think it is one billion worlds, or simply one province or prefecture. When you examine "the entire earth" or "the entire universe," investigate them three or five times without stopping, even though you already see them as vast.

Understanding these words [about the entire universe] is going beyond buddhas and ancestors by seeing that extremely large is small and extremely small is large. Although this seems like denying that there is any such thing as large or small, this [understanding] is the awesome presence of active buddhas.

Understand that the awesome presence of the entire universe and the awesome presence of the entire earth as revealed by buddhas and ancestors are the unhidden inclusive world. This is not only the unhidden inclusive world, but the awesome presence within a single active buddha.

———————

In expounding the buddha way, womb birth and transformation birth are usually mentioned, but not moisture birth and egg birth. Furthermore, it has not even been dreamed that there could be births other than these four types. Even further, has it been seen, heard, or realized that there are these four types of birth beyond the four types of birth? In the great way of buddhas and ancestors, it has been intimately and explicitly transmitted that there are four types of birth beyond [the usual understanding of] these four types of birth. What groups of people have not heard, known, or clarified this understanding?

As these four types of birth are already known, how many types of death are there? Are there four types of death for the four types of birth, or are there two or three types of death? Are there five or six, one thousand, or ten thousand deaths? To have even a little doubt about this point is part of the inquiry.

Now, consider whether there are beings among these four types who only have birth without death. Are there any beings who only transmit death and do not transmit birth? Study whether or not there are beings who have birth alone or death without birth.

There are people who hear the phrase "beyond birth" but do not clarify it, ignoring their body-and-mind endeavor. This is extreme foolishness. They should be called beasts who cannot even reach the four categories of beings with the capacity for faith, for understanding dharma, or for sudden or gradual awakening. How is this so? Even though they hear the words "beyond birth," they need to question the meaning. And they do not ask further about beyond buddha, beyond the way, beyond mind, beyond extinction, beyond "beyond birth," beyond world of phenomena, beyond dharma nature, or beyond death. They are like oxen and horses who vainly think only of water and grass.

Know that birth-and-death is the activity of the buddha way; birth-and-death is the furnishings [essentials] of the buddha house. It is utilized when it needs to be utilized; it is fully clarified when it is clarified. Accordingly, all buddhas are clear about the implements of birth-and-death, and fully achieve their utilization. How can those who are ignorant of this realm of birth and death be called a person, or someone who has completed birth, or accomplished death? Do not believe that you are sunk in birth and death, or even think that you exist in birth and death. Do not blindly believe, or misunderstand, or disregard birth and death as merely birth and death.

Some people say that buddhas only appear in the human realm, and think that they do not appear in other realms or worlds. If that were true, all realms would have been human realms when the Buddha was alive. This is like saying that human buddhas alone are venerable ones. However, there must be buddhas in the deva realm as well as buddhas in the buddha realm. Those who think that buddhas appear only in the human realm have not yet entered the inner chamber of buddha ancestors.

———

An ancestor said, "Shakyamuni Buddha received transmission of the true dharma from Kashyapa Buddha, went to Tushita Heaven to teach, and still abides there."

Indeed, know that Shakyamuni of the human realm spread the teaching through his manifestation of pari-nirvana, but Shakyamuni in the heavenly realm still abides there, teaching devas. Students should know that Shakyamuni of the human realm reveals infinitely varied expressions, actions, and teachings, auspiciously illuminating a portion of the human realm. It is foolish not to notice that Shakyamuni in the heavenly realm teaches in far more varied ways, in one thousand styles, in ten thousand gates.

Do not ignore that the essential meaning of the great way, transmitted authentically from buddha to buddha alone, goes beyond cutting off, and drops away what is beginningless and endless. It has been authentically transmitted only in the buddha way. This activity has never been known or heard of by other beings.

Where active buddhas teach, there are beings that are not limited to the four types of birth. There are realms not limited to heavenly beings, humans, or the world of phenomena. When you look into the awesome presence of active buddhas, do not use the eyes of heavenly beings or humans. Do not use the deluded thinking of heavenly beings or humans. Do not try to analyze it using human or heavenly faculties. Even bodhisattvas of the ten stages and three classes have not clarified this, so how could the analytical thinking of humans and devas reach it? When human calculation is small, knowledge is small. When a life span is fleeting, thinking is fleeting. Then, how is it possible to make calculations about the awesome presence of active buddhas?

This being so, do not accept as children of the Buddha any groups who regard mere human views as the buddha dharma, or who limit buddha dharma to human dharmas. They are merely sentient beings conditioned by karma who have not yet heard the dharma or practiced the way with body and mind. Neither their life, death, views, and learning, nor their walking, standing, sitting, and lying down, are in accord with dharma. Such kinds of beings have not been nurtured or benefited by dharma.

Active buddhas love neither original enlightenment nor acquired enlightenment, and neither possess nor do not possess enlightenment—this is true indeed.

Worldly people carry on deliberations about thinking and not thinking, having enlightenment or not having enlightenment, and fundamental or acquired enlightenment. These are merely worldly people's categories, which have not been transmitted from buddha to buddha. The thinking of worldly people and the thinking of buddhas are completely different and cannot be compared. The original enlightenment discussed by worldly people and the original enlightenment actualized by buddhas are as far apart from each other as heaven and earth; they are beyond comparison. Even the deliberations of bodhisattvas of the ten stages or three classes do not match the expressions of buddhas. How can worldly people, vainly counting grains of sand, make accurate assessments?

Nevertheless, there are many people who merely agree to the crooked, inverted views of worldly people or of those outside the way, and then mistakenly regard such views as the realm of buddhas. Buddhas say that the unwholesome roots of such people are deep and heavy, and they are to be pitied. However endless the unwholesome roots of such people may be, this tendency is their burden. For now, look into this and release it. Grasping such obstructions and involving yourself with them are not a good direction to pursue.

———————

The awesome presence of active buddhas right now is beyond obstruction. Totally encompassed by buddhas, active buddhas are free from obstruction as they penetrate the vital path of being splattered by mud and soaked in water. Active buddhas transform devas in the heavenly realm and transform humans in the human realm. This is the power of opening blossoms and the power of the world arising. There has never been a gap in active buddhas' transformative work. This being so, there is complete dropping of self and other, outstanding in coming and going.

Immediately going to and coming from Tushita Heaven, this is immediately Tushita Heaven. Immediately going to and coming from blissful ease, this is immediately blissful ease. This is immediate and complete

dropping of Tushita Heaven, and this is immediate and complete dropping of blissful ease. This is the immediate crushing of blissful ease in
Tushita Heaven into a hundred pieces. This is no other than the immediate grasping and letting go of blissful ease in Tushita Heaven. This is
swallowing up everything in one gulp.

Know that this blissful ease in Tushita Heaven is no other than transmigration, coming and going, within heavenly halls and the Pure Land.
Because this blissful ease is the practice of coming and going, one practices equally in heavenly halls and the Pure Land.

Because this is great enlightenment, it is equally great enlightenment
[within heavenly halls and the Pure Land]. In great delusion, it is equally
great delusion. This is simply the toes wiggling in the sandals [noth-
ing special] for active buddhas. Sometimes it is the sound of a fart or
the smell of shit throughout the single path [of active buddhas]. This is
smelled with the nostrils, and heard with the ears, body, and practice.
Further, there is a moment of attaining "my skin, flesh, bones, and marrow." Beyond this, there is no practice attained from others.

In regard to freely penetrating the great way that completes birth
and masters death, there is an ancient statement, "A great sage surrenders
birth and death to the mind, surrenders birth and death to the body, surrenders birth and death to the way, surrenders birth and death to birth
and death." As this teaching is actualized without limitation in the past
and present, the awesome presence of active buddhas is thoroughly practiced immediately.

The teaching of birth and death, body and mind, as the circle of the
way is actualized at once. Thoroughly practicing, thoroughly clarifying,
is not forced. It is just like recognizing the shadow of deluded thought
and turning the light to shine within. The clarity of clarity beyond clarity prevails in the activity of buddhas. This is totally surrendering to
practice.

To understand the meaning of totally surrendering, you should thoroughly investigate mind. In the steadfastness of thorough investigation,
all phenomena are the unadorned clarity of mind. You know and understand that the three realms of desire, form, and formlessness are merely
elaborate divisions of mind. Although your knowing and understanding

are part of all phenomena, you actualize the home village of the self. This is no other than your everyday activity.

This being so, the continuous effort to grasp the point in phrases and to seek eloquence beyond words is to take hold beyond taking hold and to let go beyond letting go.

In this endeavor, what is birth? What is death? What are body and mind? What are giving and taking? What are surrendering and rejecting? Is there no encounter while entering and exiting the same gate? Is there hiding the body but exposing the horns within a single move? Do we understand from great deliberation, or know with considerate intention? Is this endeavor one bright pearl or the entire treasury of the sutras? Is it a single monk's staff or a single layer of the face? Does this occur thirty years later or in myriad years within one moment? Examine this in detail, and make a detailed study of this examination. In this detailed examination, you hear sounds with your entire eye and see colors with your entire ear.

Further, opening the single eye of a monk is going beyond phenomena before one's eyes, going beyond objects before one's eyes. There is the composure of smiling and blinking. This is the moment of the awesome presence of an active buddha. Not pulled by things or pulling things, not creating or producing causal conditions, not original nature or dharma nature, not abiding in one's conditions, not original being, and not merely accepting any of these as suchness—this is simply the awesome presence of an active buddha.

This being so, the fluctuating circumstances of the body and phenomena are left to the mind and phenomena. For now, the awesome presence of dropping off birth and dropping off death is solely surrendered to buddha. Thus, there is an understanding: "All things are inseparable from mind, and the three realms are inseparable from mind." Further, in an expression that goes beyond, there is a statement that "inseparable from mind" is called "walls and pebbles." Where there is nothing inseparable from mind, there are no walls and pebbles.

The point is that the awesome presence of active buddhas is entrusted to the mind, phenomena, and the body. This awesome presence cannot be reached through the understandings of acquired enlightenment or original enlightenment. Furthermore, how can it be reached by those outside the way, those in the Two Vehicles, or bodhisattvas of the three classes or ten stages?

This awesome presence is not comprehended by any person, and is beyond comprehension on any level. However lively it may be, each branch is just as it is. Is it one long piece of iron? Is it both ends of a worm moving? One long piece of iron is neither long nor short; both ends moving are neither self nor other.

When the power of unrolling the matter and hurling insightful flashes is put into practice, the awesomeness encompasses all things, and the eye becomes lofty through the entire world. There is illumination that is not hindered by taking in or letting go. It is the monks' hall, the buddha hall, the kitchen, or the monastery gate. Further, there is illumination that does not take in or let go. It is also the monks' hall, the buddha hall, the kitchen, or the monastery gate.

Moreover, there is an eye that penetrates the ten directions and receives the entire earth. This eye is in front of the mind and behind the mind. Such an eye, ear, nose, tongue, body, and mind have the dazzling power of illumination. Thus, there are buddhas in the past, present, and future who maintain what is beyond knowing, and there are cats and white oxen who launch the insightful response of already knowing. This is grabbing the ox's nose and having an eye. This expresses the dharma of active buddhas and allows the dharma of active buddhas.

Xuefeng, Great Master Zhenjiao, said to the assembly, "The buddhas in the past, present, and future abide in flames and turn the great dharma wheel."

Xuansha, who would later become Great Master Zongyi, said in response, "As flames expound dharma to all the buddhas in the past, present, and future, all the buddhas remain standing and listen."

Keqin, Zen Master Yuanwu, later commented on their words: "One says the monkey is white; the other says it is black. They hurl insightful flashes at each other; spirits emerge and demons vanish. Blazing flames in the spreading sky are buddhas expounding dharma; the spreading sky in blazing flames is dharma expounding buddhas. Amid the winds, these two masters cut apart the tangle of twining vines and with a single statement crush Vimalakirti in his silence."

Now, *buddhas in the past, present, and future* means all buddhas. Active buddhas are all buddhas in the past, present, and future. All buddhas in the ten directions are none other than these buddhas in the three times. Expounding fully, buddhas speak like this throughout the past, present, and future. If you want to inquire about the active buddhas, they are exactly the buddhas in the past, present, and future. With or without knowing, they are none other than active buddhas as all buddhas in the three times.

This being so, the three ancient buddhas—Xuefeng, Xuansha, and Keqin—spoke like this to express their understanding of buddhas in the three times.

Study the meaning of Xuefeng's statement *The buddhas in the past, present, and future abide in flames and turn the great dharma wheel.* The practice place of the buddhas in the three times turning the dharma wheel is invariably inside flames. Inside flames is always buddhas' place of practice. Teachers of sutras and commentaries have never heard this, and those outside the way, or in the Two Lesser Vehicles, cannot know it. Know that the flames around all buddhas are not the same as the flames of other beings. Shed light on whether or not other beings are within flames.

Study how the buddhas in the three times transform beings within flames. When they abide within flames, are the flames and buddhas intimate or are they separate? Are the buddhas and their surroundings integrated or are they independent? Are they of one piece or divided?

In turning the great dharma wheel there is turning the self, turning insightful flashes. This is unrolling the matter and hurling insightful flashes, turning dharma and dharma turning. This is called turning the dharma wheel.

Even if the entire great earth is entirely in flames, there must be the dharma wheel turning the flame wheel, the dharma wheel turning all buddhas, the dharma wheel turning the dharma wheel, and the dharma wheel turning past, present, and future.

This being so, flames are the great practice place of all buddhas turning the dharma wheel. If you try to assess this with the measurements of realms, time, human capacity, or ordinary or sacred, you cannot hit the mark. Because it cannot be assessed by these calculations, all buddhas in the three times abide in flames and turn the great dharma wheel. As they are called all buddhas in the three times, they go beyond these measurements. Because it is the practice place of buddhas in the three times turning the dharma wheel, there are flames. Because there are flames, it is the practice place of all buddhas.

Xuansha said, *As flames expound dharma to all the buddhas in the past, present, and future, all the buddhas remain standing and listen.* You may hear this statement and say that Xuansha's words are a more complete utterance than Xuefeng's words, but it is not necessarily so. Know that Xuefeng's statement is different from Xuansha's. That is, Xuefeng speaks about the place where all buddhas in the three times turn the great dharma wheel, while Xuansha speaks about all buddhas in the three times listening to the dharma.

Xuefeng's statement is indeed about turning the dharma, but he does not actually discuss listening or not listening to dharma at the place of turning dharma. Thus, it does not sound as if turning the dharma is always listening to the dharma. Moreover, Xuefeng in his teaching did not say that buddhas in the three times expound dharma for the sake of flames. Nor did he say that buddhas in the three times turn the great dharma wheel for the sake of the buddhas in the three times, nor that flames turn the great dharma wheel for the sake of the flames. Is there any difference between the words *turning the dharma wheel* and *turning the great dharma wheel*? Turning the dharma wheel is not limited to expounding the dharma. Isn't expounding the dharma necessarily for the sake of others? Thus, it is not that the words of Xuefeng have not exhausted the meaning of the words that he should have said.

Definitely study in detail Xuefeng's words *abiding in flames and turning the great dharma wheel.* Don't be confused by Xuansha's words.

Penetrating Xuefeng's statement awesomely presents the awesome presence of buddhas. The flames that contain the buddhas in the three times prevail not only in one or two limitless worlds of phenomena, and do not merely fill one or two particles of dust. In an attempt to discern the great dharma wheel's turning, do not measure it as large or small, wide or narrow. Turning the great dharma wheel is neither for the self nor for others, neither for expounding nor for listening.

Xuansha said, *As flames expound dharma to all the buddhas in the past, present, and future, all the buddhas remain standing and listen.* Although he said flames expound dharma to the buddhas in the three times, he did not say that flames turn the dharma wheel. Furthermore, he did not say that buddhas in the three times turn the dharma wheel. Although all buddhas in the three times remain standing and listening, how can the flames turn the dharma wheel of the buddhas in the three times? Do the flames that expound dharma for the buddhas in the three times also turn the great dharma wheel or not? Xuansha did not say that turning the dharma wheel occurs at this moment. He did not say that the dharma wheel does not turn. However, it might be supposed that Xuansha carelessly interpreted the turning of the dharma wheel as expounding the dharma wheel. If so, he did not yet comprehend the statement of Xuefeng.

Xuansha knew that when flames expound dharma for the buddhas in the three times, the buddhas all remain standing and listen to the dharma. However, he did not realize that where the flames turn the dharma wheel, the flames remain standing and listen to the dharma. He did not say that where the flames turn the dharma wheel, the flames altogether turn the dharma wheel. All buddhas of the three times listening to the dharma are the dharma of all buddhas, which is not dependent on others. Do not consider the flames as dharma, as buddha, or even as flames. Indeed, do not ignore the statements of this master and his disciple. This is to say that they are not only red-bearded barbarians, but that they are barbarians with red beards.

Although Xuansha's words are like this, there is something you should study with great effort. Without regard to the limited views of the Great Vehicle or Lesser Vehicles held by teachers of sutras and treatises, just study the true characteristics that have been authentically transmitted from buddha to buddha, ancestor to ancestor.

All the buddhas remain standing and listen. This is not limited to the views of the Great Vehicle or Lesser Vehicle. Teachers of sutras and treatises only know that buddhas expound dharma in response to the readiness of those who hear it. But they do not say that buddhas listen to the dharma, that buddhas practice, and that buddhas accomplish buddhahood.

Regarding Xuansha's words, *All the buddhas remain standing and listen,* this is the essence and experience of buddhas' listening. Do not regard the capacity to expound the dharma as superior, and the capacity to listen to the dharma as inferior. If those who speak are venerable, those who listen are venerable as well.

————————

Shakyamuni Buddha said, "To expound this *Lotus Sutra* is to see me. To expound it for the sake of even one person is difficult."

Thus, being able to expound the dharma is to see Shakyamuni Buddha, because *to see me* is itself Shakyamuni Buddha.

The Buddha also said, "After I pass away, to listen to and to accept this sutra, and to inquire into its meaning, will be quite difficult."

Know that it is equally difficult to listen to and accept this sutra. Expounding and listening are not a matter of superior or inferior. Even if those who remain standing and listening are the most venerable buddhas, nevertheless they remain and listen to dharma, because all buddhas of the three times remain and listen to dharma. As the fruit of buddhahood is already present, they do not listen to dharma to achieve buddhahood; as [Xuansha] indicated, they are already buddhas of the three times.

Know that the buddhas in the three times are buddhas who remain and listen to the dharma expounded by flames. The transformative function of this single phrase cannot be traced in a linear manner. If you try to trace it, the arrowhead and the shaft will crush each other. Flames definitely expound dharma for the buddhas of the three times. With bits and pieces of red heart, an iron tree blossoms and the world becomes fragrant. Let me ask: When buddhas remain standing and listen to the flames expound dharma, ultimately what is it that is actualized? This is wisdom surpassing the master, wisdom equaling the master. Further, there are buddhas in the three times investigating the inner sanctum of master and disciple.

Keqin's words *The monkey is white* do not conflict with the other monkey's being black. Thus, [Keqin comments that] Xuefeng and Xuansha hurl insightful flashes at each other as spirits emerge and demons vanish. Although there is a path that Xuefeng travels together with Xuansha, yet does not enter together with Xuansha, is it the case that the flames are all buddhas, or that all buddhas are the flames? Xuansha's mind interchanges black and white, emerging and vanishing like spirits and demons, while Xuefeng's voice and form do not remain in the realm of black and white. Further, see that Xuansha's statement is just right, beyond just right; and Xuefeng's statement takes it up and releases it.

Keqin has a statement that is not the same as Xuansha's and not the same as Xuefeng's: *Blazing flames in the spreading sky are buddhas expounding dharma; the spreading sky in blazing flames is dharma expounding buddhas.* This statement has been truly an illumination for those who have studied ever since. Even if you do not notice the blazing flames, if you are covered by the spreading sky, you have your share and others have theirs. Wherever the entire sky covers, there are always blazing flames. Even though you dislike these blazing flames and look somewhere else, how could it be otherwise?

Rejoice! Although your skin bag was born far from the sages, and although this moment is distant from the sages, you have encountered the transforming guidance of the spreading sky that can still be heard. Although *buddhas expounding dharma* has been heard, how many layers of ignorance we have suffered from because of not having heard the statement *dharma expounding buddhas*! Accordingly, it is simply that all buddhas in the three times are expounded by dharma throughout the three times, and all dharmas in the three times are expounded by buddhas throughout the three times.

It is the spreading sky alone that cuts apart the tangle of twining vines amid the winds. A single statement crushes both Vimalakirti and those who are not Vimalakirti, and nothing remains.

———

Thus, dharma expounds buddha, dharma practices buddha, dharma verifies buddha. Buddha expounds dharma, buddha practices buddha, buddha makes buddha. This is all the awesome presence of active buddhas. Throughout heaven and earth, throughout past and present, what they have attained is not insignificant, what they have clarified is not to be utilized casually.

Written in the middle of the tenth month, the second year of the Ninji Era [1241], at the Kannondori Horin Monastery by Monk Dogen.

25

THE BUDDHAS' TEACHING

THE ACTUALIZED EXPRESSION of all buddhas is the buddhas'
teaching. Because buddha ancestors express this teaching for all
buddha ancestors, it is authentically transmitted for the sake of teaching.
This is turning the dharma wheel. Within the eyeball of this dharma
wheel, you actualize all buddha ancestors and have all buddhas enter
pari-nirvana.

These buddha ancestors invariably emerge in a single particle and
enter nirvana in a single particle. They emerge in the entire world and
enter nirvana in the entire world. They emerge in a single moment
and emerge in the ocean of multiple eons. And yet, their emergence
in a single particle in a single moment lacks no merit. This cannot be
replaced by their emergence in the entire world, in the ocean of multiple eons.

This being so, do not say that buddhas who attain the way in the
morning and enter nirvana that evening lack merit. If you say that one
day contains little merit, then eighty years of human life is not long
enough. When you compare the eighty years of human life with ten or
twenty eons, it would be like one day and eighty years, and the merits of
this buddha and that buddha could not be discerned. If you compare the

merit of a long eon and timeless life with the merit of eighty years, there would be no room for doubt.

In this way, the buddhas' teaching is the buddha who teaches. It is the merit thoroughly experienced by buddha ancestors. It is not that buddhas are high and broad and their teaching of dharma is low and narrow.

Know that if buddhas are large, their teaching is large; if buddhas are small, their teaching is small. Thus, know that buddhas and their teaching cannot be measured as large or small. It is beyond the aspects of wholesome, unwholesome, or neutral. It is not a teaching for oneself or others.

––––––––––

A teacher says:

Old Man Shakya expounded the teaching of the sutras throughout his lifetime. In addition, he authentically transmitted the dharma of one mind, the supreme vehicle, to Mahakashyapa. This has been passed down from person to person. Due to this, his teaching is a groundless theory presented in accordance with the capacity of listeners. Meanwhile, the dharma of one mind is the true nature of reality. This authentically transmitted single mind is called transmission outside of scriptures. It does not equal words in the Three Vehicles and the Twelve Divisions of the teaching. Because this mind is the supreme vehicle, it is called directly pointing to the human mind, seeing original nature, and becoming a buddha.

This statement is not at all a work of buddha dharma. It has no vital path of leaping beyond and no awesome presence wherever the body reaches.

Even if those who make such a statement were to call themselves pioneering teachers hundreds and thousands of years in the future, regard them as neither clarifying nor mastering buddha dharma or the buddha way. Why? Because they don't know the Buddha, the teaching, the mind, inside, or outside. The reason is that they have never heard buddha dharma.

When we speak of buddhas, those who don't know the origin and effect of buddhas and their boundaries of coming and going cannot be called disciples of the Buddha. To talk only about *this authentically trans-*

mitted single mind, while excluding authentic transmission of the buddhas' teaching, is not to know buddha dharma. They do not know the single mind of the buddhas' teaching. They have not heard of the single mind of the buddhas' teaching.

They speak of the buddhas' teaching outside of the single mind. Their single mind is not the single mind. They speak of the single mind outside of the buddhas' teaching. The buddhas' teaching they speak of is not the buddhas' teaching. Even if they have inherited the mistaken view of transmission outside the teaching, their words and truth do not fit each other because they do not yet know inside from outside.

How can buddha ancestors who have transmitted the treasury of the true dharma eye person to person not transmit the buddhas' teaching person to person? Furthermore, how would Old Man Shakya set up a teaching that is not a work of the buddha house? If Old Man Shakya lets the teaching be transmitted from person to person, which buddha ancestors can deny the teaching? Thus, what is called the *supreme vehicle* is the Three Vehicles and the Twelve Divisions of teaching, the great treasury and small treasury [Mahayana and Hinayana canons].

Know that what is called buddha mind is the Buddha's eyeball, a broken wooden dipper. Since it is all things and the three realms, it is mountains, oceans, lands, the sun, the moon, and stars. The buddhas' teaching is myriad things in all places. What is called outside is right here, arriving right here.

Since authentic transmission is conducted from self to self, the self is within authentic transmission. You authentically inherit one mind from one mind. Thus, there is one mind in authentic transmission. *The dharma of one mind, the supreme vehicle*, is mud, stone, sand, and pebbles. Since mud, stone, sand, and pebbles are one mind, the mud, stone, sand, and pebbles are mud, stone, sand, and pebbles. If you speak of *the dharma of one mind, the supreme vehicle*, you should understand it like this.

However, those who talk about transmission outside the teaching do not understand this meaning. So, do not believe the wrong view of transmission outside the teaching and thereby misunderstand buddhas' teaching.

If these people were right, the buddhas' teaching should be called transmission outside the mind. If we were to say so, neither one phrase nor half a verse of the buddhas' teaching would have been transmitted to us. If we do not say transmission outside the mind, we should not say transmission outside the teaching.

Mahakashyapa is already the head of the dharma treasury as the heir of Shakyamuni Buddha. He authentically inherited the treasury of the true dharma eye and upholds the buddha way. It is biased to say that he should not have authentically inherited the buddhas' teaching.

Know that if you authentically inherit one phrase, you authentically inherit one dharma. If you inherit one phrase, you inherit mountains and you inherit waters. You cannot be separated from this very place.

Shakyamuni Buddha authentically transmitted his treasury of the true dharma eye, unsurpassable enlightenment, to Mahakashyapa alone and to no one else. Authentic transmission was unquestionably to Mahakashyapa. Thus, all those who study truth in buddha dharma in the past and present always investigate thoroughly with buddha ancestors to determine the authenticity of teaching from the past. They do not ask others for this. Those who are not authenticated by buddha ancestors are not buddha ancestors. Those who want to be authenticated should be authenticated by buddha ancestors. The reason is that the original teachers of mastering the dharma wheel are buddha ancestors.

Buddha ancestors alone, being past and present buddhas, clarify and authentically transmit the expression of existence and nonexistence as well as the expression of emptiness and form.

————————

Baling was once asked by a monk, "Is the heart of an ancestor the same as the heart of the teaching?"

Baling said, "When it is cold, a rooster climbs the tree and a duck gets into water."

Study this expression, encounter the ancestral meaning of the buddha way, see, and hear the teaching of the buddha way. This monk was in fact asking whether or not the heart of an ancestor is truly the heart of an ancestor. Baling's answer addresses a distinction, but it is not the same as the distinction discussed by those who are bound by distinction. In this way, because the heart of an ancestor and the heart of the teaching are beyond distinction, distinction is addressed. Baling's answer is just like saying, "Don't ask about distinction."

Xuansha was once asked by a monk, "If the Three Vehicles and the Twelve Divisions of the teaching are not essential, what is the meaning of Bodhidharma's coming from India?"

Xuansha replied, "The Three Vehicles and the Twelve Divisions of the teaching are not essential; nothing is essential."

The monk asked this question with the assumption, as is commonly understood, that *the Three Vehicles and the Twelve Divisions of the teaching* are mere details in buddha dharma. He wanted to know the meaning of Bodhidharma's coming from India [the heart of buddha dharma], which he assumed should be other than these details. The monk did not understand that the Three Vehicles and the Twelve Divisions of the teaching are the meaning of Bodhidharma's coming from India. Further, how could he have understood that the complete assemblage of eighty-four thousand dharma gates is the meaning of Bodhidharma's coming from India?

Investigate this thoroughly now. How can the Three Vehicles and the Twelve Divisions of the teaching not be essential? And, if they are essential, what are the guidelines? Is it possible that the study of the meaning of Bodhidharma's coming from India is actualized even when the Three Vehicles and the Twelve Divisions of the teaching are disregarded? The monk's question was not without significance.

Xuansha said, *The Three Vehicles and the Twelve Divisions of the teaching are not essential; nothing is essential.* This statement is a dharma wheel. Study thoroughly that when this dharma wheel is turned, the buddhas' teaching abides in the buddhas' teaching.

The meaning of Xuansha's reply is that the Three Vehicles and the Twelve Divisions of the teaching are the buddha ancestors' dharma wheel, which turns in the place where there are buddha ancestors and in the place where there are no buddha ancestors. It turns equally before and after the time of ancestors.

Further, the Three Vehicles and the Twelve Divisions of the teaching have the function of turning buddha ancestors. At the very moment of asking the meaning of Bodhidharma's coming from India, this dharma wheel is *nothing is essential*. *Nothing is essential* doesn't mean not to utilize or break this dharma wheel. This dharma wheel turns in *nothing is essential*.

See that Xuansha did not say that the Three Vehicles and the Twelve Divisions of the teaching did not exist; he said that they were not essential. Because they are not essential, they are the Three Vehicles and the Twelve Divisions of the teaching. Because they are the Three Vehicles and the Twelve Divisions of the teaching, they are beyond the Three Vehicles and the Twelve Divisions of the teaching. Thus, Xuansha said, the Three Vehicles and the Twelve Divisions of the teaching are not essential.

Let me offer an outline of the Three Vehicles and the Twelve Divisions of the teaching.

The Three Vehicles:
The first of the Three Vehicles is the Shravaka Vehicle. This vehicle is attained through the four noble truths. They are: The truth of suffering; the truth of the causes of suffering; the truth of the cessation of suffering; and the truth of the [eightfold] path. By learning and practicing these truths, you become free from birth, aging, sickness, and death, and fully experience pari-nirvana.

To say that the truths of suffering and the causes of suffering are ordinary and the truths of ceasing suffering and the path are primary in practicing the four noble truths is a view of scriptural commentators. In the practice of buddha dharma, all four noble truths are understood only by buddha and buddha; all four noble truths are things in their own conditions; all four noble truths are reality; all four noble truths are buddha nature. This being so, they do not require a discussion about not being born or not being created, because in the four noble truths *nothing is essential*.

The second vehicle is the Pratyeka-buddha Vehicle. This is a path to reach pari-nirvana by observing the twelvefold causation. It consists of: ignorance, inclination, discernment, name and form, six objects of perception, contact, feeling, craving, grasping, becoming, birth, decay and death.

When you observe these twelve causes, you examine them from the viewpoint of subject and object, cause and effect, in the past, present, and future. In this examination, the turning of the wheel is not essential at all; cause and effect are not essential at all.

Know that if ignorance is one mind, inclination and discernment, and so on, are one mind. If ignorance perishes, inclination and discernment, and so on, perish. If ignorance is nirvana, inclination and discernment, and so on, are nirvana. We say so because birth is itself perishing. Ignorance is a phrase of expression. Discernment, name and form, and so on, are also like this.

Know that ignorance, inclination, and so on, are no other than [Qingyuan's statement]: "I have a hatchet. I live with it in this mountain." [I am intimate with what I have.] Ignorance, inclination, and so on, are no other than "When I left the monastery, I asked the abbot to give me the hatchet."

The third vehicle is the Bodhisattva Vehicle. It is to achieve unsurpassable, complete enlightenment through the teaching, practice, and realization of the six paramitas. Achieving them is not creating, not not-creating, not initiating, not newly making, not achieving for a long time, not original practice, and not not-making. It is just achieving unsurpassable, complete enlightenment.

The six paramitas [realizations] are: the paramita of giving, the paramita of precepts, the paramita of patience, the paramita of effort, the paramita of meditation, and the paramita of prajna [wisdom beyond wisdom]. These are all unsurpassable enlightenment, beyond any discussion of not-born and not-created.

It is not necessarily that the paramita of giving comes first and the paramita of prajna comes last. A sutra says, "A bodhisattva of sharp capacity makes prajna first and giving last. A bodhisattva of dull capacity makes giving first and prajna last." However, the paramita of patience can come first, and the paramita of meditation can come first. Thirty-six [six times six] paramitas can be actualized. From one basket [container], another basket is reached.

Paramita means "arriving at the other shore" [of enlightenment]. Although the other shore does not have the appearance or trace from olden times, arriving is actualized. Arriving is the fundamental point. Do not think that practice leads to the other shore. Because there is practice on the other shore, when you practice, the other shore arrives. It is because this practice embodies the capacity to actualize all realms.

The Twelve Divisions of the teaching:

Sutra—a scripture in prose
Geya—a teaching reiterated in verse
Vyakarana—a prediction of enlightenment
Gatha—a verse for chanting
Udana—a teaching expounded not in response to a question
Nidana—an explanation of causes [of unwholesome things]
Avadana—a parable
Itivrittaka—a past life [of a disciple of the Buddha]
Jataka—a past life [of the Buddha]
Vaipulya—a broad teaching
Adbhuta-dharma—an unprecedented [magical] story
Upadesha—a philosophical discussion

The Tathagata personally expounded conditional and real matters of the world of skandhas, surroundings, and perceptions for sentient beings. This is called a sutra.

He also reiterated his explanation of these matters in verses of four, five, six, seven, or eight syllables. This is called a geya.

Or he personally predicted a future event of a sentient being, such as a dove or a sparrow becoming a buddha. This is called a vyakarana.

The Tathagata explained matters of the world in a solitary verse. This is called a gatha.

He explained matters of the world without someone asking him a question. This is called an udana.

He summarized unwholesome matters of the world and provided precepts. This is called a nidana.

He explained matters of the world with a parable. This is called an avadana.

He explained past lives of the Buddha's disciples. This is called an itivrittaka.

He explained matters of a past life. This is called a jataka.

He explained broad matters of the world. This is called a vaipulya.

He explained matters unprecedented in the world. This is called an adbhuta-dharma.

And he discussed matters of the world. This is called an upadesha.

These Twelve Divisions of scriptures have been created to give joy to sentient beings. They are the established explanations of the world.

It is rare to hear the names of the Twelve Divisions of the teaching. These names are heard when buddha dharma is spread in the world, and they are not heard when buddha dharma perishes. They are also not heard when buddha dharma is not yet spread. Those who cultivate wholesome roots for a long time and see the Buddha hear these names. Those who hear them are bound to receive unsurpassable, complete enlightenment before long.

Each of these Twelve Divisions is called a sutra. They are called the Twelve Divisions of the teaching or the Twelve Divisions of sutras.

Each of the Twelve Divisions of the teaching contains the Twelve Divisions of the teaching; they are one hundred forty-four divisions of the teaching. As each of the Twelve Divisions of the teaching embodies the Twelve Divisions of the teaching, they are one division of the teaching.

However, the number twelve is not the amount before or after a billion. The Twelve Divisions of the teaching are the eyeball of buddha ancestors, the bones and marrow of buddha ancestors, the work of the house of buddha ancestors, the radiant light of buddha ancestors, the splendor of buddha ancestors, the land of buddha ancestors. To see the Twelve Divisions of the teaching is to see buddha ancestors. To express buddha ancestors is to express the Twelve Divisions of the teaching.

This being so, Qingyuan's lowering his one leg [as a sign of approving Shitou] is the Three Vehicles and the Twelve Divisions of the teaching. Nanyue's statement "Your words were close but did not hit the mark" is no other than the Three Vehicles and the Twelve Divisions of the teaching.

Xuansha's statement, *The Three Vehicles and the Twelve Divisions of the teaching are not essential* is also like this. When you take up this expression, there are only buddha ancestors. There is not half a person, not one thing other than buddha ancestors. Not even one thing has risen.

How is it? Say, "Nothing is essential!"

———————

Also, there are Nine Divisions, or nine divisions of the teaching. They are:

Sutra
Gatha
Itivrittaka
Jataka
Adbhuta-dharma
Nidana
Avadana
Geya
Upadesha

As each of these nine divisions includes nine divisions, there are eighty-one divisions. As each of these nine divisions embodies one division, there are nine divisions.

Without the capacity to return to one division, there cannot be nine divisions. As there is the capacity to return to one division, one division returns to one division. For this reason, there are eighty-one divisions. This is the division of just this, the division of the self, the division of a whisk, the division of a walking stick, the division of the treasury of the true dharma eye.

———————

Shakykamuni Buddha said, "I expound these nine divisions of dharma to suit all beings. This is the basis for entering the Great Vehicle. Thus, I expound these scriptures."

Know that *I* is the Tathagata. His face, eyes, body, and mind are expressed. This *I* is already the nine divisions of dharma. The nine divisions of dharma are the *I*. Each phrase, each verse, expounded now is the nine divisions of dharma. Because of *I,* the nine divisions of dharma are expounded *to suit all beings.*

This being so, all birth of sentient beings is born inside this. That is why *I expound these scriptures.* All death dies inside this. That is why *I expound these scriptures.* All thoughts and actions are the reason why *I expound these scriptures.* The Tathagata guides all beings and helps them to enter the buddha way. That is why *I expound these scriptures.*

All beings follow *I expound these nine divisions of dharma. To follow* is to follow others, the self, all beings, birth, I, and this. As all beings are invariably *I,* they are every line of the nine divisions of dharma.

The basis for entering the Great Vehicle means the basis for realizing the Great Vehicle, practicing the Great Vehicle, listening to the Great Vehicle, and expounding the Great Vehicle.

This does not mean that all beings attain the way spontaneously. They are a part of attaining the way. *Entering* is *the basis. The basis* is from beginning to end.

The Buddha expounds dharma. Dharma expounds the Buddha. Dharma is expounded by the Buddha. The Buddha is expounded by dharma. The flame [of discourse] expounds the Buddha, expounds dharma. The Buddha expounds the flame. Dharma expounds the flame.

These scriptures have a reason for the Tathagata to expound, to expound *thus.* Even if we try to expound these scriptures, it is impossible. This being so, the Tathagata says, *Thus, I expound these scriptures.*

Expounding *thus* is the entire world. The entire world is expounding *thus.* This buddha and that buddha equally call them *these scriptures.* The realm of self and the realm of others equally expound *these scriptures.* Thus, *I expound these scriptures.*

These scriptures are the buddhas' teachings. Know that the teachings of the buddhas are as many as the sands of the Ganges, a bamboo stick, and a whisk. The sands of the Ganges of the buddhas' teachings are a staff and a fist.

Know that the Three Vehicles, the Twelve Divisions of the teaching, and so on, are the eyeball of buddha ancestors. How can those who do not open this eyeball be descendants of buddha ancestors? How can those who do not take them up inherit the authentic eye of buddha ancestors? Those who have not mastered the treasury of the true dharma eye are not dharma descendants of the Seven Original Buddhas.

Presented to the assembly of the Kosho Monastery, Yamashiro Province, on the fourteenth day, the eleventh month, the second year of the Ninji Era [1241].

[Presented again] On the seventh day, the eleventh month, the third year of the Ninji Era [1242].

26

MIRACLES

THE MIRACLES I am speaking of are the daily activities of buddhas, which they do not neglect to practice. There are six miracles
[freedom from the six-sense desires], one miracle, going beyond miracles,
and unsurpassable miracles. Miracles are practiced three thousand times
in the morning and eight hundred times in the evening. Miracles arise
simultaneously with buddhas but are not known by buddhas. Miracles
disappear with buddhas but do not overwhelm buddhas.

Miracles occur equally in heaven and on earth. Miracles occur
throughout practice and enlightenment whenever buddhas search in the
Himalayas or practice like a tree or a rock. When the buddhas before
Shakyamuni Buddha appeared as his disciples, bringing a robe and a
stupa to him, he said, "This is a miracle caused by the inconceivable
power of all buddhas." Thus, we know that this miracle can also happen
to buddhas now and buddhas in the future.

Guishan is the thirty-seventh ancestor, a direct descendant of
Shakyamuni Buddha. He was a dharma heir of Baizhang, Zen Master
Dazhi. Today, buddha ancestors in the ten directions, even those who

do not call themselves descendants of Guishan, are all in fact his remote descendants.

One day, while Guishan was lying down, Yangshan Huiji came to see him. Guishan turned to face the wall.

Yangshan said, "I am your student. Please don't be formal."

Guishan started to get up.

Yangshan rose to leave.

Guishan said, "Huiji."

Yangshan returned.

Guishan said, "Let me tell you about my dream."

Yangshan leaned forward to listen.

Guishan said simply, "Would you interpret my dream for me? I want to see how you do it."

In response Yangshan brought a basin of water and a towel. Guishan washed his face and sat up. Then Xiangyan came in.

Guishan said, "Huiji and I have been sharing miracles. This is no small matter."

Xiangyan said, "I was next door and heard you."

Guishan said to him, "Why don't you try now?"

Xiangyan made a bowl of tea and brought it to him.

Guishan praised them, saying, "You two students surpass even Shari-putra and Maudgalyayana with your miraculous activity!"

If you want to understand buddhas' miracles, you should study Gui-shan's words. As *this is no small matter,* practicing miracles is studying the buddha way. Not practicing miracles is not studying the buddha way. This miraculous activity is transmitted heir to heir. Do not study miracles from those outside the way, those in the Two Lesser Vehicles, or interpreters of sutras.

When we study Guishan's miracles, we see that they were unsurpass-able; each action was extraordinary. Beginning with Guishan lying down, there are: turning to face the wall, getting up, calling *Huiji,* talking about the dream, washing his face, and sitting up. Yangshan leaned forward to listen, and brought a basin of water and a towel. Guishan then described this as: *Huiji and I have been sharing miracles.* Study these miracles.

These ancestors who authentically transmitted buddha dharma talked in this way. Do not merely interpret it as Guishan expressing his dream by washing his face. Regard their interaction as a series of miracles.

Guishan said, *This is no small matter.* His understanding of miracles is different from that of practitioners who follow the Lesser Vehicles, have limited understanding, or hold small views. It is not the same as that of bodhisattvas of the ten stages and three classes. People of limited views study minor miracles and attain limited understanding. They do not experience the great miracles of buddha ancestors.

These are miracles of buddhas, and miracles going beyond buddha. Those who study such miracles are beyond the reach of demons or those outside the way. Teachers and interpreters of sutras have never heard of this teaching, nor would they have accepted it even if they had heard. Rather than studying great miracles, teachers and interpreters of sutras, those outside the way, and practitioners of the Two Lesser Vehicles study minor miracles.

Buddhas abide in and transmit great miracles, buddha miracles. Had it not been for buddha miracles, Yangshan would not have brought water and a towel, and Guishan would not have turned to the wall as he was lying down, nor sat up after washing his face.

Encompassed by the power of great miracles, minor miracles occur. Great miracles include minor miracles but minor miracles do not know great miracles. Minor miracles are a tuft of hair breathing in the vast ocean, a mustard seed storing Mount Sumeru, the top of the head spouting water, or feet spreading fire. Miracles like these are minor miracles. The five or six miraculous powers are minor miracles. Those who practice them never dream of buddha miracles. The reason I call them minor miracles is that they are limited by circumstances and depend upon special practices and realizations. They may occur in this lifetime but not in another lifetime. They may be available to some people but not to others. They may appear in this land but not elsewhere. They may appear at times other than the present moment but not at the present moment.

Great miracles are not like that. The teaching, practice, and enlightenment of buddhas are all actualized through miracles. They are actualized not only in the realm of buddhas but also in the realm of going beyond buddhas. The transformative power of miracle buddhas is indeed beyond thinking. This power appears before the buddha bodies appear, and is

290 · TREASURY OF THE TRUE DHARMA EYE

not concerned with the past, present, or future. The aspiration, practice, enlightenment, and nirvana of all buddhas would not have appeared without buddha miracles.

In the inexhaustible ocean of the world of phenomena, the power of buddha miracles is unchanging. A tuft of hair not only breathes in the great ocean but it maintains, realizes, utilizes, and breathes out the great ocean. When this activity arises, it encompasses all worlds of phenomena. However, do not assume that there are no other activities that encompass all worlds of phenomena.

A mustard seed containing Mount Sumeru is also like this. A mustard seed breathes out Mount Sumeru and actualizes the inexhaustible ocean of the world of phenomena. When a tuft of hair or a mustard seed breathes out a great ocean, breathing out happens in one moment, and it happens in myriad eons. Breathing out myriad eons and breathing out one moment happen simultaneously. How are a tuft of hair and a mustard seed brought forth? They are brought forth by miracles. This bringing forth is miracles. What enables a tuft of hair and a mustard seed to do things like that? Miracles enable them to do so. Miracles bring forth miracles. Do not think that miracles sometimes do and sometimes do not happen in the past, present, or future. Buddhas alone abide in miracles.

———————

Layman Pangyun was an outstanding person in the ancestral seat. He not only trained with Mazu and Shitou, but met and studied with many enlightened teachers. One day he said, "Miracles are nothing other than fetching water and carrying firewood."

Thoroughly investigate the meaning of these words. *Fetching water* means drawing and carrying water. Sometimes you do it yourself and sometimes you have others do it. Those who practice this are all miracle buddhas. Although miracles are noticed once in a while, miracles are miracles. It is not that things perish or are eliminated when they are unnoticed. Things are just as they are even when unnoticed. Even when people do not know that fetching water is a miracle, fetching water is undeniably a miracle.

Carrying firewood means doing the labor of hauling, as in the time of Huineng, the Sixth Ancestor. Even if you do not know that miracles happen three thousand times in the morning and eight hundred times in the evening, miracles are actualized. Those who see and hear the wondrous activities of miracles by buddha tathagatas do not fail to attain the way. Attaining the way of all buddhas is always completed by the power of miracles.

Causing water to spout out of the head is a practice of the Lesser Vehicles. It is merely a minor miracle. On the other hand, fetching water is a great miracle. The custom of fetching water and carrying firewood has not declined, as people have not ignored it. It has come down from ancient times to today, and it has been transmitted from there to here. Thus, miracles have not declined even for a moment. Such are great miracles, which are *no small matter.*

––––––––––––

Dongshan Liangjie, who would later become Great Master Wuben, was once attendant to Yunyan, who said, "Liangjie, what are miracles?"

Dongshan politely brought his hands together at his chest and stood near him.

Yunyan asked again, "What are miracles?"

Dongshan bade farewell and walked away.

In this story, words are heard and the meaning of miracles is understood. There is merging, like a box and its cover joining. Know that it is a miracle to have a disciple like Dongshan who does not veer off, or to have a high ancestor like Yunyan who does not come forward. Do not think that the miracles they are speaking of are the same as those outside the way or in the Two Lesser Vehicles.

On the road of buddhas there are also great miracles that happen at the top or bottom of the body. The entire world of ten directions is the true body of a single monk. Thus, the Nine Mountains and the Eight Seas around Mount Sumeru, as well as the ocean of thusness and the ocean of all wisdom, are no other than water spouting from the top, bottom, and center of the body. It is also water spouting from the top, bottom, and center of the formless body. The spouting out of fire is also like this.

Not only is there the spouting out of water, fire, and air, but also there is the spouting out of buddhas from the top and bottom of the body. There is the spouting of ancestors from the top and bottom of the body. There is the spouting of immeasurable eons from the top and bottom of the body. There is also the spouting out of the ocean of the world of phenomena and the swallowing of the ocean of the world of phenomena from the top of the body. To spit out the lands of the world seven or eight times and to swallow them two or three times is also like this. The four, five, or six great elements, all elements, and immeasurable elements, are also great miracles that appear and disappear, are spit out, and swallowed. The great earth and empty space are miracles that are swallowed and spit out.

Miracles have the power of being activated by a mustard seed and responding to a tuft of hair. Miracles arise, abide, and return to the source beyond the reach of consciousness. The various aspects of buddha miracles are beyond long or short—how can this be measured by discriminatory thinking?

———

Long ago, when a sorcerer who had the five miraculous powers was attending the Buddha, he asked, "You have six miraculous powers and I have five. What is the one I am missing?"

The Buddha called to him, "Sorcerer."

"Yes," he responded.

The Buddha said, "What miraculous power are you asking about?"

Thoroughly study the meaning of this dialogue. How did the sorcerer know that the Buddha had six miraculous powers? The Buddha has immeasurable miraculous wisdom, which is not limited to six miraculous powers. Even if you see six miraculous powers, you cannot master them. How can those who have lesser miraculous powers dream of the Buddha's six miraculous powers?

You should say, "When the sorcerer saw Old Man Shakyamuni, did he actually see the Buddha? When he saw the Buddha, did he actually see Old Man Shakyamuni? If the sorcerer saw Old Man Shakyamuni and recognized the Buddha, did he also see himself, the sorcerer of the five miraculous powers?"

Study the sorcerer's questions and study going beyond this dialogue. Isn't this question about the Buddha's six miraculous powers like counting the treasure of a neighbor? What is the meaning of Old Man Sha-kyamuni's words, *What miraculous power are you asking about?* He did not say whether the sorcerer has this miraculous power or not. Even if Old Man Shakyamuni had spoken about it, how would the sorcerer have understood the single miraculous power? Although the sorcerer had five miraculous powers, they are not the same as the five miraculous powers of the Buddha.

Although the sorcerer's powers may look like those of the Buddha, how can his powers compare to those of the Buddha? If the sorcerer attained even one of the Buddha's powers, he could meet the Buddha by this power.

When we see the sorcerer, he had powers similar to the Buddha's, and when we see the Buddha, he had powers similar to the sorcerer's. But the sorcerer did not have the Buddha's miraculous powers. If one of the sorcerer's powers could not reach one of the Buddha's powers, none of his five powers could be equal to those of the Buddha.

So what is the use of asking the Buddha, *What miraculous power am I missing?* Old Man Shakyamuni meant that the sorcerer should have asked about the powers the sorcerer already had. The sorcerer had not even mastered one of those powers. In this way the Buddha's miraculous powers and other people's miraculous powers look alike but in fact are completely different.

———

About the Buddha's six types of miracles, Linji, Great Master Hui-zhao, said:

> According to an old teacher, the excellent marks of the Buddha Tatha-gata's body are listed to accommodate the needs of people's minds. To counter the common tendency toward nihilistic views, such provisional names as the thirty-two marks or the eighty appearances of the Bud-dha are used as expedient means. But they are imaginary concepts. Such a body is itself not awakening. Having no form is the Buddha's true form.
>
> You say that the Buddha's six types of miracles are wondrous. Devas, sorcerers, fighting spirits, and demons also have miraculous powers. Are they buddhas? Followers of the way, do not be mistaken. A fighting spirit

defeated by Indra took his eighty-four thousand retainers and hid inside a hole of a lotus root. Do you call this a miracle?

The miracles I have described [of these devas, sorcerers, fighting spirits, and demons] are the result of past actions or present situations. But the six types of miracles of a buddha are different. A buddha enters forms, sounds, smells, tastes, touchables, and objects of mind and is not confused by them. Thus, a buddha masters the six-sense objects, which are all marked with emptiness. A buddha is free of conditions. Even having a body of five skandhas accompanied by desire, a buddha does not depend on anything. A buddha practices miracles that are grounded on the earth.

Followers of the way, a true buddha has no form, and the true dharma has no marks. From your mind's illusions, marks and appearances are created. What you get is a wild fox's spirit, which is the view of those outside the way, and not of a true buddha.

Thus, the six types of miracles of the buddhas cannot be reached by devas, demons, or those of the Two Lesser Vehicles. The six types of miracles of the buddha way cannot be measured. They are only transmitted to disciples of the buddha way, person to person, but not to others. Those who have not inherited such miracles do not know them. Know that those who have not inherited such miracles are not persons of the buddha way.

————————

Baizhang, Zen Master Dazhi, said:

The eyes, ears, nose, and tongue are not defiled by form or formlessness. This nondefilement is called receiving the four-line verse of vows and receiving the four fruits of the arhats. Leaving no trace in the six sense organs is called the six types of miracles. Not to be hindered by either form or formlessness, and not to depend on intellectual understanding, are miracles. Not abiding in these miracles is called "going beyond miracles." A bodhisattva who goes beyond miracles does not leave traces. This is a person going beyond buddha. It is a most wondrous person, a heavenly self.

The miracles transmitted by buddha ancestors are as Baizhang described. A miracle buddha is one who goes beyond buddha, a most wondrous person, an uncreated self, a bodhisattva of going beyond miracles. Miracles do not depend upon intellectual understanding, do not abide in themselves, and are not hindered by things. There are the six types of miracles in the buddha way, which have been maintained by buddhas ceaselessly. There has not been a single buddha who has not maintained them. Those who do not maintain them are not buddhas. These six types of miracles leave no trace in the six sense organs.

———————

An old teacher [Yongjia] said, "The six types of miracles are neither empty nor not empty. A circle of light is neither inside nor outside."

Neither inside nor outside means leaving no trace. When you practice, study, and realize no-trace, you are not disturbed by the six sense organs. Those who are disturbed should receive thirty blows.

The six types of miracles should be studied like this. How can those who are not authentic heirs of the buddha house learn about this? They mistakenly regard running around inside and outside as the practice of returning home.

The four fruits of the arhats are the essentials of the buddha way. But no teachers of the Tripitaka have authentically transmitted them. How can those who study letters or wander in remote lands receive these fruits? Those who are satisfied with minor achievements cannot master them. The four fruits are transmitted only by buddha and buddha. The so-called four fruits are to receive the four lines of verse, and this means that eyes, ears, nose, and tongue are undefiled by all things. Undefiled means unstained. Unstained means undivided mind—"I am always intimate with this."

The six types of miracles and the four fruits of the buddha way have been authentically transmitted in this manner. Know that anything different from this is not buddha dharma. Thus, the buddha dharma is always actualized through miracles. When actualized, a drop of water swallows the great ocean and a speck of dust hurls out a high mountain. Who can doubt that these are miracles?

Presented to the assembly of the Kannondori Kosho Horin Monastery on the sixteenth day, the eleventh month, the second year of the Ninji Era [1241].

27

GREAT ENLIGHTENMENT

THE GREAT WAY of the buddhas has been transmitted with intimate attention; the work of the ancestors has been unfolded evenly and broadly. Thus, great enlightenment is actualized, and beyond enlightenment is the decisive way. In this way, enlightenment is realized and played with; enlightenment disappears in the practice of letting go. This is the everyday activity of buddha ancestors. Enlightenment taken up activates the twelve hours of the day. Enlightenment hurled away is activated by the twelve hours of the day. Furthermore, leaping beyond the mechanism of time there is twiddling with a mud ball and twiddling with spirit.

Although it should be thoroughly understood that buddha ancestors are invariably actualized from great enlightenment, it is not that the entire experience of great enlightenment should be regarded as buddha ancestors, and it is not that the entire experience of buddha ancestors should be regarded as entire great enlightenment. Buddha ancestors leap beyond the boundary of great enlightenment, and great enlightenment has a face that leaps beyond buddha ancestors.

Now, human capacity is greatly varied. For example, there are those who already have understanding at birth. At birth they are free from birth. That means they understand with the body at the beginning, middle, and end of birth. There are those who understand through study, ultimately understanding the self through practice. That means they practice with the body—the skin, flesh, bones, and marrow of study.

Besides those who have understanding at birth or through study, there are those who have understanding as buddhas. They go beyond the boundary of self and other, having no limit in this very place, and are not concerned with the notion of self and other. There are also those who understand without teachers. Although they do not rely upon teachers, sutras, essence, or form, and they do not turn the self around nor merge with others, nevertheless all things are revealed.

Among these types of people, don't regard one as sharp and another as dull. Various types of people, as they are, actualize various types of accomplishments. Examine what sentient or insentient being is without understanding at birth. If one has understanding at birth, one has enlightenment at birth, realization at birth, and practice at birth. Thus, the buddha ancestors who are already excellent tamers of beings are regarded as those who have enlightenment at birth. This is so because their birth has brought forth enlightenment. Indeed, this is enlightenment at birth that is filled with great enlightenment. This is the study of taking up enlightenment. Thus, one is greatly enlightened by taking up the three realms, by taking up one hundred grasses, by taking up the four great elements, by taking up buddha ancestors, and by taking up the fundamental point. All these are further attaining great enlightenment by taking up great enlightenment. The very moment for this is just now.

Linji, Great Master Huizhao, said, "In the great nation of Tang China, if you look for a single person who is not enlightened, it is hard to find one."

This statement by Linji is the skin, flesh, bones, and marrow of the authentic stream, which is not mistaken. *In the great nation of Tang China* means within the eyeball of self, which is not limited to the entire world or the dusty world.

If you look for a single person who is not enlightened in just this, you cannot find one. The self of yesterday's self is not unenlightened.

The self of today's other is not unenlightened. Among the past and present of mountain-beings and water-beings, no one is unenlightened. Students of the way should study Linji's statement in this way without wasting time.

However, you should further study the heart of the work in the ancestral school. Now, ask Linji, "If you only know that it is hard to find an unenlightened person and do not know that it is hard to find an enlightened one, it is not yet sufficient. It is impossible to say that you have thoroughly understood the fact that it is hard to find an unenlightened one. Even if it is hard to find an unenlightened one, have you not seen half a person who is not yet enlightened but has a serene face and magnificent composure?"

Thus, do not admit that the statement *In the great nation of Tang China, if you look for a single person who is not enlightened, it is hard to find one* expresses an ultimate understanding. Try to find two or three Tang Chinas within one person or half a person. Is it or is it not hard to find one? When you have the eye to see this, you can be regarded as a mature buddha ancestor.

Jingzhao Xiujing, Great Master Baozhi, of the Huayan Monastery in Jingzhao, was a dharma heir of Dongshan. Once a monk asked him, "What happens when a greatly enlightened person becomes deluded?"

Jingzhao said, "A broken mirror no longer reflects images. Fallen flowers hardly ever climb up the tree."

The monk's question was like a mere question, but it was a dharma talk to the assembly. Outside the assembly of the Huayan Monastery this would not have been spoken. And one who was not a dharma heir of Dongshan could not have responded like this. Indeed, he was someone mature enough to sit on the seat of a buddha ancestor.

The so-called *greatly enlightened person* has neither been enlightened from the beginning nor received enlightenment from somewhere else. Great enlightenment is not something one encounters when one is old, after having worked for a long time as an ordinary monk in a communal place of the monastery. It does not emerge by pulling it out from oneself; nevertheless, one is greatly enlightened.

Don't regard not being deluded as great enlightenment. Don't try to become deluded to obtain the seeds for great enlightenment. A greatly enlightened person is further greatly enlightened. A greatly deluded person is further greatly enlightened. Just as there is one who is greatly enlightened, there is a greatly enlightened buddha, greatly enlightened earth, water, fire, air, and emptiness; a greatly enlightened pillar and lantern. This is the meaning of *a greatly enlightened person* in the monk's question.

What happens when a greatly enlightened person becomes deluded? This is indeed a question to be asked. Jingzhao did not avoid it. This question has been admired in Zen monasteries as a meritorious work of a buddha ancestor. Investigate it.

Is a greatly enlightened person who becomes deluded the same as an unenlightened person? When a greatly enlightened person becomes deluded, does the person use great enlightenment to create delusion? Does the person bring delusion from somewhere else and become deluded by covering the great enlightenment with delusion? Is it that a greatly enlightened person does not destroy great enlightenment but practices delusion? Or, is it that *a greatly enlightened person becomes deluded* means delusion brings forth another great enlightenment? Study thoroughly in this way.

Is it that great enlightenment is a single hand, or is it that becoming deluded is a single hand? To inquire how a greatly enlightened person can become deluded should be the ultimate point of study. Know that there is great enlightenment that makes becoming deluded intimate.

Accordingly, it is not that recognizing the thief as one's own child is delusion, nor is it that recognizing one's own child as the thief is delusion. It is just that great enlightenment is to recognize the thief as the thief. Delusion is to recognize one's own child as one's own child. Adding a little to a lot is great enlightenment. Taking out a little from a little is delusion. Accordingly, look for a deluded person and encounter a greatly enlightened one just as you grasp the deluded one. Is the self right now delusion or not delusion? Examine this and bring it to yourself. This is called encountering a buddha ancestor.

Jingzhao said, *A broken mirror no longer reflects images. Fallen flowers hardly ever climb up the tree.* This teaching speaks of the moment when the mirror is broken. It is wrong to study the moment of *broken mirror* and compare it to the time when the mirror is not broken. It is a mistake to interpret Jingzhao's words to mean that a greatly enlightened person is no longer deluded, because the person neither reflects images nor climbs up the tree. This is not a study of the way as it is.

If what ordinary people think were right, you should ask, "What is the everyday activity of a greatly enlightened person?" They might say, "Can such a person still become deluded?" That is not how we should understand the dialogue between Jingzhao and the monk.

When the monk said, *What happens when a greatly enlightened person becomes deluded?* he was asking about the very moment a greatly enlightened person becomes deluded. The very moment when these words are uttered, a broken mirror no longer reflects images and fallen flowers hardly ever climb up the tree. When fallen flowers are just fallen flowers, even if they get up to the top of a one-hundred-foot pole, they are still fallen flowers. When a broken mirror is just a broken mirror, whatever activities occur, they are merely broken pieces that no longer reflect images. Take up the teaching of the words *a broken mirror* and *fallen flowers,* and study the moment when a greatly enlightened person becomes deluded.

Do not regard great enlightenment as becoming a buddha, returning to the source, and manifesting a buddha body. Do not regard becoming deluded as returning to be a sentient being. People with mistaken views talk about breaking great enlightenment and returning to be a sentient being. But Jingzhao was implying neither that great enlightenment gets broken or lost, nor that delusion appears. Do not think like those who have mistaken views.

Indeed, great enlightenment is limitless, delusion is limitless, and delusion does not hinder great enlightenment; take up threefold great enlightenment and turn it into a half-fold minor delusion. Thus, the Himalayas are greatly enlightened to benefit the Himalayas. Wood and stone are greatly enlightened taking the forms of wood and stone.

Buddhas' great enlightenment is greatly enlightened for the sake of sentient beings. Sentient beings' great enlightenment is greatly enlightened by buddhas' great enlightenment. This goes beyond before and after. Great enlightenment right at this moment is not self, not other. Great enlightenment does not come from somewhere else—the ditch is filled in and the stream is stopped up. Great enlightenment does not go away—stop following others. How? Follow all the way through.

Mihu of Jingzhao sent a monk to ask Yangshan, "Do people nowadays depend upon enlightenment?"

Yangshan said, "It's not that they are not enlightened, but how can they avoid falling into the secondary?"

The monk returned and reported this to Mihu, who then approved Yangshan.

The *nowadays* spoken of here is the right now of each of you. Even if you think of the past, present, and future millions of times, all time is this very moment, right now. Where you are is nothing but this very moment. Furthermore, an eyeball is this moment, a nostril is this moment.

Quietly investigate this question: *Do people nowadays depend upon enlightenment?* Renew this question in your heart; renew this question in the top of your head.

These days shaven-headed monks in Song China look in vain for enlightenment, saying that enlightenment is the true goal, though they don't seem to be illuminated by the light of buddha ancestors. Because of laziness they miss the opportunity of studying with true teachers. They might not be able to attain liberation even if they were to encounter the emergence of authentic buddhas.

Mihu's question does not mean that there is no enlightenment, that there is enlightenment, or that enlightenment comes from somewhere else. This question asks whether or not people depend upon enlightenment. It is like saying, "How are people nowadays enlightened?"

If you speak of "achieving enlightenment," you may think that you don't usually have enlightenment. If you say, "Enlightenment comes," you may wonder where it comes from. If you say, "I have become enlightened," you may suppose that enlightenment has a beginning. Mihu did not speak that way. When he spoke of enlightenment, he simply asked about *depend upon enlightenment.*

Yangshan's words *how can they help but fall into the secondary* mean that the secondary is also enlightenment. *The secondary* is like saying "to become enlightened," "to get enlightenment," or "enlightenment has come." It means that "becoming" and "coming" are enlightenment.

It may look as if Yangshan was cautious about falling into the secondary and was denying a secondary enlightenment. But the secondary that becomes enlightenment is no other than the secondary that is true enlightenment. This being so, even the secondary, the hundredth, or the thousandth is enlightenment. It is not that the secondary is capped by the primary.

Don't say that yesterday's self was the true self but today's self is the secondary self. Don't say that enlightenment just now was not there yesterday. It is not that enlightenment has begun this moment. Study in this way. Thus, great enlightenment is black, great enlightenment is white.

Abiding at the Kannondori Kosho Horin Monastery, I present this to the assembly on the twenty-eighth day, the first month, the third year of the Ninji Era [1242].

Staying at the ancient Yoshimine Temple, I revise and present this to the assembly of humans and devas on the twenty-eighth day, the first month, the second year of the Kangen Era [1243].

28

THE POINT OF ZAZEN

Yaoshan, Great Master Hongdao, was sitting. A monk asked him, "In steadfast sitting, what do you think?"

Yaoshan said, "Think not-thinking."

"How do you think not-thinking?"

Yaoshan replied, "Beyond thinking."

Realizing these words of Yaoshan, you should investigate and receive the authentic transmission of steadfast sitting. This is the thorough study of steadfast sitting transmitted in the buddha way.

Yaoshan is not the only one who spoke of thinking in steadfast sitting. His words, however, were extraordinary. *Think not-thinking* is the skin, flesh, bones, and marrow of thinking and the skin, flesh, bones, and marrow of not-thinking.

The monk said, *How do you think not-thinking?* However ancient not-thinking is, still we are asked how to think it. Is there not-thinking in steadfast sitting? How can going beyond steadfast sitting not be understood? One who is not shallow and foolish can ask and think about steadfast sitting.

Yaoshan said, *Beyond thinking.* The activity of beyond thinking is crystal clear. In order to think not-thinking, beyond thinking is always used.

In beyond thinking, there is somebody that sustains you. Even if it is you who are sitting steadfastly, you not only are thinking but are upholding steadfast sitting. When sitting steadfastly, how can steadfast sitting think steadfast sitting? Thus, sitting steadfastly is not buddha thought, dharma thought, enlightenment thought, or realization thought.

This teaching was directly transmitted person to person from Shakyamuni Buddha to Yaoshan through thirty-six generations of ancestors. That means if you go beyond thirty-six generations from Yaoshan, you go back to Shakyamuni Buddha. What was authentically transmitted thus was *think not-thinking*.

However, careless students in recent times say, "The endeavor of zazen is completed when your heart is quiescent, as zazen is a place of calmness." Such a view does not even reach that of students of the Lesser Vehicles, and is inferior to the teachings of human and deva vehicles. How can we call them students of buddha dharma? In present-day Song China, there are many practitioners who hold such views. The decline of the ancestral path is truly lamentable.

There are also people who say, "Practicing zazen is essential for those who are beginners or those who have started studying recently, but it is not necessarily the activity of buddha ancestors. Activity in daily life is Zen, and sitting is Zen. In speaking and in silence, in motion and stillness, your body should be tranquil. Do not be concerned only with the practice of zazen." Many of those who call themselves descendants of Linji hold such a view. They say so because they have not received the transmission of the right livelihood of buddha dharma.

Who are beginners? Are there any who are not beginners? When do you leave the beginner's mind? Know that in the definitive study of the buddha dharma, you engage in zazen and endeavor in the way. At the heart of the teaching is a practicing buddha who does not seek to become a buddha. As a practicing buddha does not become a buddha, the fundamental point is realized.

The embodiment of buddha is not becoming a buddha. When you break through the snares and cages [of words and concepts], a sitting buddha does not hinder becoming a buddha. Right now, you have the ability to enter the realm of buddha and enter the realms of demons throughout the ages. Going forward and going backward, you personally have the freedom of overflowing ditches, overflowing valleys.

Mazu, Zen Master Daji of Jiangxi, studied with Nanyue, Zen Master Dahui. After intimately receiving Nanyue's mind seal, Mazu was continuously engaged in zazen.

One day Nanyue went up to him and said, "Virtuous one, what's your intention in doing zazen?"

Quietly ponder this question. Was Nanyue asking if Mazu had the intention of going beyond zazen, if he had an intention outside of zazen, or if he had no intention at all? Was Nanyue asking what kind of intention emerges while doing zazen? Investigate this thoroughly.

Love a true dragon instead of loving a carved one. However, know that both carved and true dragons have the ability to produce clouds and rain. Do not treasure or belittle what is far away, but be intimate with it. Do not treasure or belittle what is near, but be intimate with it. Do not make light or a big deal of what you see with your eyes. Do not make light or a big deal of what you hear with your ears. Rather, illuminate your eyes and ears.

Mazu said, "My intention is to become a buddha."

Clarify these words. What is the meaning of *become a buddha*? Does *become a buddha* mean being made buddha by another buddha, or buddha making oneself buddha? Is this the emergence of one or two buddhas? Is the intention to become buddha dropping off, or is dropping off the intention to become buddha? Does this mean that however many ways there are to become buddha, to be immersed in this intention to become a buddha is the intention to become buddha?

Know that Mazu meant that zazen is inevitably the intention to become buddha, and that zazen is inevitably becoming buddha with intention. Intention is prior to becoming a buddha and after becoming a buddha. Intention is the very moment of becoming buddha.

I ask you: How much of becoming buddha is being immersed in intention? This immersion is immersed in immersion. Immersion is always a direct expression of totally becoming buddha, every bit of completely intending to become buddha. Do not avoid even a bit of intention. If you avoid it, you lose your body and miss your life. When you lose your body and miss your life, this too is immersion in intention.

Nanyue picked up a tile and started to polish it on a rock.

Mazu said, "What are you doing?"

Indeed, who does not see this as polishing a tile? Who can see this as polishing a tile? So Mazu asked, *What are you doing?*

What are you doing? is no other than polishing a tile. Whether in this world or in another world, polishing a tile has never ceased. Do not regard your view as the only view. In any activity, there is always this question.

Those who see buddha without knowing and understanding buddha see water without understanding water, and see mountains without knowing mountains. To hastily conclude that what's happening in front of you is a dead end is not a study of buddha.

Nanyue said, "I am polishing this tile to make a mirror."

Clarify these words. Polishing a tile to make a mirror has a deep meaning; it is not a false statement, but actualizes the fundamental point. Although a tile is a tile and a mirror is a mirror, there are many ways to investigate the meaning of polishing. An ancient bright mirror, a bright mirror, comes from polishing a tile. Without knowing that all mirrors come from polishing tiles, you will not see or hear the words, mouth, or breath of buddha ancestors.

Mazu said, "How can you make a mirror by polishing a tile?"

Indeed, by polishing a tile and doing nothing else, an iron-willed practitioner does not make a mirror. Even if making a mirror is not polishing a tile, a mirror is immediately there.

Nanyue said, "How can you become a buddha by doing zazen?"

Be clear that zazen is not working toward becoming a buddha. The teaching that becoming a buddha has nothing to do with zazen is evident.

Mazu said, "Then, how so?"

These words may seem to be asking one thing but in fact are asking another. It is like close friends meeting; each is intimate with the other. *How so?* addresses both zazen and becoming a buddha at the same time.

Nanyue said, "When driving a cart, if it stops moving, do you whip the cart or the ox?"

In regard to *driving a cart*, what is moving and what is stopping? Does it mean that water flowing is the cart moving or water not flowing is the cart moving? You can also say that flowing is water not moving. There is a time when water's moving is not-flowing. Thus, when you investigate the cart not moving, there is stopping and not stopping; it depends on time. The word *stopping* does not merely mean not moving.

In regards to Nanyue's words *Do you whip the cart or the ox?* is it that you sometimes hit the cart and sometimes hit the ox? Is hitting the cart the same or not the same as hitting the ox? In the secular world, there is no custom of hitting the cart. Although there is no custom of common people hitting the cart, in the buddha way there is the practice of hitting the cart; this is the eye of study. Even if you realize the practice of hitting the cart, it is not the same as hitting the ox. Study this thoroughly.

Although hitting the ox is commonly practiced, you should investigate hitting the ox in the buddha way. Is it hitting a living buffalo, an iron ox, or a clay ox? Is it hitting with a whip, with the entire world, or with the whole mind? Is it hitting the marrow, hitting with the fist? How about fist hitting fist, and ox hitting ox?

Mazu was silent.

Do not ignore this silence. This is hurling a tile to attract a jewel, turning the head and turning the face. This silence cannot be taken away.

Nanyue then instructed: "If you practice sitting Zen, you practice sitting buddha."

Investigate this statement and understand the pivotal point of the ancestral school. Those who miss the essential meaning of the practice of sitting Zen may say that it is the practice of sitting buddha. But how can those who are not authentic descendants be sure that the practice of sitting Zen is the practice of sitting buddha? Know that the zazen of beginner's mind is the beginning of zazen. The beginning of zazen is the beginning of sitting buddha.

Nanyue continued: "If you practice sitting Zen, [you will know that] Zen is not about sitting or lying down."

What Nanyue meant is that zazen is zazen, and it is not limited to sitting or lying down. This teaching has been transmitted person to person; thus boundless sitting and lying down are the self [beyond self]. When you reflect on your life activities, are they intimate with zazen or remote from it? Is there enlightenment in zazen, or is there delusion? Is there one whose wisdom penetrates zazen?

Nanyue said further: "In the practice of sitting buddha, the buddha has no fixed form."

Nanyue spoke the words in this way. The reason why sitting buddha is neither singular nor plural is that sitting buddha is adorned with no fixed form. To speak of no fixed form is to speak of buddha's form. As buddha has no fixed form, there is no escape from sitting buddha. Adorned with buddha's no-fixed form, the practice of zazen is itself sitting buddha. In the dharma beyond condition, who can discriminate buddha from not-buddha? Falling away before discrimination, sitting buddha is sitting buddha.

Nanyue said, "If you sit buddha, you kill [go beyond] buddha."

When you study sitting buddha further in this way, it has an aspect of *kill buddha*. At the very moment of sitting buddha there is killing buddha. If you want to find the extraordinary luminosity of killing buddha, always sit buddha. *Kill* may be an ordinary word that people commonly use, but its meaning here is totally different. Study how it is that sitting buddha is killing buddha. Investigate the fact that the buddha is itself *killing buddha*. Study killing and not killing a true person.

Nanyue said, "If you are identified with [confined by] the sitting form, you have not reached the heart of the matter."

Identified with the sitting form, spoken of here, is to defile and abandon the sitting form. The reason is that when one is sitting buddha, it is impossible not to be identified with the sitting form. However clear the sitting form is, the heart of the matter cannot be reached, because it is impossible not to be one with the sitting form. To penetrate this is called "letting go of body and mind."

Those who have not practiced sitting do not reach the heart of the matter. The heart of the matter is sitting time, sitting person, sitting buddha, and the practice of sitting buddha.

The sitting of mere sitting and mere lying down is not sitting buddha. Although usual sitting looks like sitting buddha or buddha sitting, it is not so. A person becomes buddha, becoming a buddha person. However, all people do not become buddhas. Buddhas are not all people, because buddhas are not limited to people. An ordinary person is not necessarily buddha, buddha is not necessarily an ordinary person. Sitting buddha is like this.

In this way Nanyue was a profound teacher and Mazu was a thorough student. Mazu realized sitting buddha as becoming buddha, and Nanyue taught becoming buddha as sitting buddha. At Nanyue's assembly there was this kind of investigation, and at Yaoshan's assembly there was that dialogue. Know that what buddhas and ancestors have regarded as the pivotal point is sitting buddha. Those who are buddha ancestors employ this pivotal point. Those who aren't have never dreamed of it.

Transmission of buddha dharma in the west and east [India and China] is no other than transmission of sitting buddha. This is the pivotal point. Where buddha dharma is not transmitted, zazen is not transmitted. What has been passed on person to person is the essential teaching of zazen alone. Those who have not intimately received this teaching are not buddha ancestors.

Without clarifying this single matter, you cannot clarify myriad matters and practices. Without clarifying them, you cannot be regarded as one who has attained the way with clear eye and cannot join buddha ancestors of the past and present. Thus, buddha ancestors unfailingly receive and transmit zazen person to person.

To be illuminated by buddha ancestors is to endeavor in the thorough practice of zazen. Those who are ignorant mistakenly think that buddha light is like sunlight, moonlight, or the glowing of a jewel. But sunlight, moonlight, or the glowing of a jewel is merely a physical manifestation in the transmigration through the six paths, and cannot be compared to buddha light. Buddha light is to receive and listen to one phrase of teaching, to maintain and guard one dharma, and to transmit zazen person to person. Without being illuminated by such light, accepting and maintaining zazen is not possible.

Since ancient times few have understood zazen as it is. Even the heads of high-ranking monasteries in China nowadays do not know and study the meaning of zazen. There are only a few who clearly understand it. Monasteries have schedules for zazen; the abbots and resident monks keep the practice of zazen as essential and encourage students to practice zazen. But few of them seem to understand the meaning of what they are doing.

Some masters have written texts titled "Essentials of Zazen." A few others have written "Rules for Zazen," and a few more have written "The Point of Zazen." Among these texts, none of those titled "Essentials of Zazen" are worthwhile. No version of "Rules for Zazen" clarifies the practice. They were written by those who did not know zazen, as they had not received the transmission of zazen person to person. "The Point of Zazen" included in the *Jingde Record of Transmission of the Lamp* and "Essentials of Zazen" included in the *Jiatai Record of the Universal Lamp* are also like this.

What a pity! They visited and abided in monasteries of the ten directions and practiced all their lives, but they did not make a thorough effort even for one sitting. Sitting had not immersed in them and endeavor had not encountered them. It is not that zazen avoided them, but that they were carelessly intoxicated. They did not aspire to a genuine effort.

Their texts merely aim to return to the source and origin, trying to cease thinking and to be still. That does not even come up to taking the steps of visualization, purification, nurturing, and attainment, or the view of the bodhisattvas of the last ten stages approaching buddha's enlightenment. How could they have received and transmitted the buddha ancestors' zazen? The Song Dynasty compilers of Zen texts included these writings by mistake. Those who study now should not pay attention to such writings.

"The Point of Zazen," written by Zhengjiao, Zen Master Hongzhi of the Tiantong Jingde Monastery, Mount Taibai, Qingyuan Prefecture, China, is a work of a buddha ancestor. It is a true point of zazen, with penetrating words. It is the only light that illuminates the inside and outside of the world of phenomena. It is buddha ancestor among buddha ancestors of past and present. Earlier buddhas and later buddhas have been led to zazen by this teaching. Present buddhas and past buddhas are actualized by this "Point of Zazen." The text is as follows:

> The hub of buddhas' activity,
> the turning of the ancestors' hub,

is known free of forms,
illuminated beyond conditions.

As it is known free of forms,
the knowledge is subtle.
As it is illuminated beyond conditions,
the illumination is wondrous.

When the knowledge is subtle,
there is no thought of discrimination.
When the illumination is wondrous,
there is not the slightest hint.

Where there is no thought of discrimination,
the knowledge is extraordinary with no comparison.
Where there is not the slightest hint,
the illumination has nothing to grasp.

The water is clear to the bottom
where the fish swims without moving.
The sky is vast and boundless
where the bird flies away and disappears.

The *point* presented here is the manifestation of great function, the awesome presence beyond sound and form, bamboo knots and wood grains [standards] before the parents were born. It is joyously not slandering buddha ancestors, not avoiding the death of body and mind. It is as extraordinary as having a head that is three feet tall and a neck that is two inches short.

The hub of buddhas' activity: Buddhas do not fail to make buddhas the hub. This hub is manifested. That is zazen.

The turning of the ancestors' hub: One's late master spoke beyond words. This understanding is the basis of ancestors, of transmitting dharma, and of transmitting the robe. Turning heads and exchanging faces is the hub of buddhas' activity. Turning faces and exchanging heads is the turning of the ancestors' hub.

Is known free of forms: This knowing is not, of course, conscious knowing. Conscious knowing is small. This knowing is not comprehension. Comprehension is created. Thus, this knowing is free of forms. Being free of forms is this knowing. Don't regard it as all-inclusive knowledge. Don't limit it to self-knowledge. Being free of forms is "When brightness [duality] comes, meet it with brightness. When darkness [nonduality] comes, meet it with darkness," "Sit through the skin you were born with."

Illuminated beyond conditions: This illumination is not illuminating everything or illuminating with brilliance. Being beyond condition is this illumination. Illumination does not turn to conditions, as conditions are already illumination. *Beyond* means the entire world is not hidden, a broken world does not appear. It is subtle and wondrous. It is interchangeable and not interchangeable.

When the knowledge is subtle, there is no thought of discrimination: Thought as knowledge does not depend on other-power. Knowledge is a shape, and a shape is mountains and rivers. The mountains and rivers are subtle. Subtle is wondrous. When you utilize it, it is lively. When you create a dragon, it is not limited inside or outside of the dragon gate. To utilize a bit of this knowledge is to know by bringing forth mountains and rivers of the entire world with all their force. If you don't have knowledge by being intimate with mountains and rivers, there is not a shred or scrap of knowledge. Do not grieve that discernment and discrimination come slowly. Buddhas who have already discerned are already being actualized. *There is no thought of discrimination* means there is already merging. There is already merging is actualization. Thus, *there is no thought of discrimination* is not meeting even one person.

When the illumination is wondrous, there is not the slightest hint: The slightest is the entire world. The illumination is naturally wondrous and luminous. Thus, it looks as if it hadn't arrived. Do not doubt your eyes. Do not believe your ears. To directly clarify the source beyond words and not to grasp cases [koans] through words is illumination. This being so, illumination is not comparing, not grasping. To maintain illumination is extraordinary and to accept it as complete is no other than doubting it thoroughly.

The water is clear to the bottom where the fish swims without moving. Water hanging in the sky does not get to the bottom. Furthermore, water that fills a vessel is not as clear as the water mentioned here. Water that is boundless is described as *clear to the bottom.* When the fish swims in this water, it is not motionless. It goes for myriad miles. There is no way to measure it and there is no shore to limit it. There is no sky for the fish to fly in and no bottom to get to, and there is no shore where someone sees the fish. In fact, there is no one who sees the fish. If you speak of recognizing the fish, there is merely water clear to the bottom. The activity of zazen is just like the fish swimming. Who can measure how many thousands and myriads of miles there are in zazen? Its journey is the entire body going on the path where no bird flies.

The sky is vast and boundless where the bird flies away and disappears: The vast sky does not hang above. What hangs above is not called the vast sky. Furthermore, what encompasses all space is not called vast sky. What is neither revealed nor hidden, neither inside nor outside, is called vast sky. If the bird flies in this sky, it just flies in the sky. The activity of flying in the sky is immeasurable. Flying in the sky is the entire world; it is the entire world flying in the sky. Although we don't know how far the flying goes, we say it beyond saying—we say *flies away*. It is "Go away with no string on your straw sandals." When the sky flies away, the bird flies away. When the bird flies away, the sky flies away. When you speak about the investigation of flying, it is right here. This is the point of steadfast sitting. Even if you go myriad miles, it is right here.

This is "The Point of Zazen" by Zhengjiao. Among the old masters throughout time, no one has written "The Point of Zazen" like this. If the stinky skin bags here and there would try to say something like this, they might not be able to do so in one or more lifetimes. There is no text like Zhengjiao's. Rujing, my late master, would refer to him on his teaching seat as Old Buddha Hongzhi and would not refer to other teachers as Old Buddha. One who has the eye to see a true person recognizes the voice of buddha ancestors. Thus, we know that there is a buddha ancestor in the lineage of Dongshan.

More than eighty years have passed since the time of Zhengjiao. After his text, I have written my version of "The Point of Zazen." It is the eighteenth day, the third month, the third year of the Ninji Era [1242]. It has been eighty-five years since Zhengjiao passed away on the eighth day, the tenth month, the twenty-seventh year of the Shaoxing Era [1157]. This is my text:

THE POINT OF ZAZEN

The hub of buddhas' activity,
the turning of the ancestors' hub,
moves along with beyond thinking
and is completed in the realm of beyond merging.

As it moves along with beyond thinking,
its appearing is immediate.
As it is completed in the realm of beyond merging,
completeness itself is realization.

When its appearing is intimate,
you have no illusion.
When completeness reveals itself,
it is neither real nor apparent.

When you have immediacy without illusion,
immediacy is "dropping away" with no obstacles.
Realization, beyond real or apparent,
is effort without expectation.

Clear water all the way to the bottom;
a fish swims like a fish.
Vast sky transparent throughout;
a bird flies like a bird.

Although Zhengjiao's text is not incomplete, zazen may be spoken of in this way. All descendants of buddha ancestors should practice zazen as the single great matter. It is the authentic seal transmitted from person to person.

Written at the Kosho Horin Monastery on the eighteenth day, the third month, the third year of the Ninji Era [1242].

Presented to the assembly at the Yoshimine Temple, Yoshida County, Echizen Province, in the eleventh month, the fourth year of the Ninji Era [1243].

29

GOING BEYOND BUDDHA

DONGSHAN, HIGH ANCESTOR, Great Master Wuben of Mount Dong, Yun Region, is the direct heir of Yunyan, Great Master Wuzhu of Mount Yunyan, Tan Region. He is the thirty-eighth going-beyond ancestor from the Tathagata. He is the thirty-eighth ancestor going beyond himself.

Dongshan once taught the assembly, "Concerning realization-through-the-body of going beyond buddha, I would like to talk a little."
A monk said, "What is this talk?"
Dongshan said, "When I talk, you don't hear it."
The monk said, "Do you hear it?"
Dongshan said, "Wait till I don't talk, then you hear it."

The words spoken here, *going beyond buddha,* originally came from Dongshan. Other buddha ancestors have studied his words and realized through-the-body going beyond buddha. Know that going beyond buddha is neither causality nor fruition. However, there is realization-through-the-body and complete attainment of *you don't hear it* at the moment *when I talk.*

Without going beyond buddha, you do not realize through-the-body going beyond buddha. Without talking, you do not realize through-the-body going beyond buddha. Going beyond buddha and talking neither reveal each other nor hide each other, neither give to nor take from each other. This being so, talking brings forth going beyond buddha.

When going beyond buddha is actualized, *you do not hear it. You do not hear it* means buddha-going-beyond-buddha is not heard by the self. At the time of talking, you do not hear it. Know that talking is not stained by either hearing or not-hearing. It is not concerned with hearing or not-hearing.

You are concealed within not-hearing. You are concealed within talking. It is like meeting a person and not meeting a person; being thus and not thus. When you talk, you don't hear it. The meaning of *you don't hear it* is that you are not hindered by the tongue or ears, you are not seen through by the eyes, you are not shielded by body and mind. This is not-hearing. Do not try to take this up and regard it as talking. Not-hearing is not talking. It is just that at the time of talking you do not hear it. Dongshan's words *When I talk, you don't hear it* mean that talking, from beginning to end, is just like wisteria vines entangled with each other. Talking is entangled with talking, it is permeated by talking.

The monk said, *Do you hear it?* This does not mean that he is asking if the master hears the talking; he is not asking about the master or his talking. Instead, the monk is asking whether he should study direct hearing as the master talks. That is to say, he is asking whether talking is talking and hearing is hearing. Even if you can say something about it, it is beyond your speech.

Examine thoroughly the words of Dongshan, *Wait till I don't talk, then you hear it.* At the very moment of talking, there is no direct hearing. Direct hearing comes forth at the moment of not-talking.

It is not that you unfortunately miss the moment of not-talking and must wait for not-talking. Direct hearing is not merely observing. It is true observation. It is not at the moment of direct hearing that talking goes away and is confined somewhere. It is not at the time of talking that direct hearing hides its body in the eye of talking and resounds like thunder. It is just that you do not hear at the time of talking; you directly hear at the time of not-talking.

This is the meaning of *I would like to talk a little* and *realization-through-the-body of going beyond buddha*. That is to realize through-the-body direct hearing at the time of talking. This being so, Dongshan said, *Wait till I don't talk, then you hear it*. However, going beyond buddha is not before the Seven Original Buddhas. It is the Seven Original Buddhas going beyond.

Dongshan, High Ancestor, Great Master Wuben, taught the assembly, "You should know someone going beyond buddha."
A monk asked, "Who is someone going beyond buddha?"
The master said, "Not-buddha."

Later Yunmen interpreted this: "The name is unattainable, the form is unattainable, therefore the person is 'not.'"
Baofu said, "Buddha-not."
Fayan also said, "Provisionally, the person is called buddha."

The buddha ancestor going beyond a buddha ancestor is Dongshan. The reason is that though there are many other buddhas and ancestors, they have never dreamed of the words "going beyond buddha." If this were spoken to Deshan or Linji, they would not get it right. Neither Yantou nor Xuefeng would be awakened even if their bodies were crushed and shattered with the blow of a fist.

Dongshan's words *realization-through-the-body of going beyond buddha, I would like to talk a little,* and *You should know someone going beyond buddha* cannot be fully realized merely by practice and enlightenment through one, two, three, four, five eons, or one hundred great eons. Only those who study the inconceivable road can realize it.

Know that there is someone going beyond buddha. This is the full activity of playing with the spirit. So, understand going beyond buddha by taking up an ancient buddha and raising a fist. To see through this is to know someone who goes beyond buddha and someone who goes beyond *not-buddha.*

The words of Dongshan do not mean that you should be someone who goes beyond buddha, or that you should meet someone who goes beyond buddha. He just means that you should know that there is someone who goes beyond buddha. The key to this barrier is not-knowing someone who goes beyond buddha, and not-knowing someone who goes beyond not-buddha.

Someone who goes beyond buddha in this way is not-buddha. When you are asked "What is not-buddha?" consider: You do not call the person not-buddha because the person precedes buddha. You do not call the person not-buddha because the person follows buddha. You do not call the person not-buddha because the person surpasses buddha.

The person is not-buddha merely because of going beyond buddha. "Not-buddha" is so called because buddha's face is dropped away, buddha's body and mind are dropped away.

———————

Jingyin, Zen Master Kumu, in Dongjing, whose priest name is Facheng, an heir of Furong, taught the assembly: "As I know about going beyond buddha, I have something to say. Answer now, good students! What is going beyond buddha? Someone has a child who does not have six sense organs and lacks seven consciousnesses. He is a great icchantika, a kind of not-buddha. When he meets a buddha he kills the buddha, and when he meets an ancestor he kills the ancestor. The heavens cannot contain this person. Hell does not have a gate to let him in. All of you! Do you know this person?"

After waiting for a while he said, "If you don't see saindhava, it's like talking a lot in deep sleep."

Not have six sense organs can be described as "The eyeballs have become tallow beads, the nostrils have become bamboo pipes, and the skull has turned into a shit dipper. What is the meaning of all this?"

In this way, the *six sense* organs are not there. Because there are no six sense organs, this person has gone through the forge and bellows and has become a metal buddha. He has gone through a great ocean and has become a clay buddha. He has gone through the fire and has become a wooden buddha.

Lacks seven consciousnesses means this person is a broken wooden dipper. Although he kills a buddha, he meets the buddha. Because he meets a buddha, he kills the buddha. If he tries to enter the heavens, the heavens are annihilated. If he goes toward hell, hell will burst immediately.

If he meets face to face, his face breaks into a smile and there is no saindhava. Although he is in deep sleep, he talks a lot.

Understand that this means all the mountains and the entire land
know the self. Jewels and stones are all crushed into pieces. Quietly study
and pursue this teaching of Jingyin. Do not neglect it.

———————

Yunju Daoying, who would later become Zen Master Hongjue of
Mount Yunju, went to study with High Ancestor Dongshan.

Dongshan said, "What is your name?"

Yunju said, "Daoying."

Dongshan said, "Say something beyond that."

Yunju said, "When I say something beyond, I am not called
Daoying."

Dongshan said, "When I was with Yunyan, we spoke just like this."

Examine in detail the words between this master and disciple. *When
I say something beyond, I am not called Daoying* is Yunju's going beyond.
Know that in addition to the usual Yunju, there is someone beyond, who
is not called Daoying. From the moment *When I say something beyond, I
am not called Daoying* is actualized, he is truly Yunju.

However, do not say that he is Daoying when he is going beyond.
When he was asked by Dongshan, *Say something beyond that*, even if he
had replied, *When I say something beyond, I am called Daoying*, it would still
be the words of going beyond. Why is it so? Yunju immediately leaps
into the top of the head and hides his own body. Since he hides his own
body, his form is revealed.

———————

Caoshan Benji studied with Dongshan, High Ancestor. Dongshan
said, "What is your name?"

Caoshan said, "Benji."

Dongshan said, "Say something beyond that."

Caoshan said, "I will not say."

Dongshan asked again, "Why will you not say?"

Caoshan said, "No-name Benji."

Dongshan approved it.

It is not that there is nothing to say in going beyond, but there is no saying. *Why will you not say?* Because of *no-name Benji.* Therefore, saying in going beyond is no-saying. No-saying in going beyond is no-name. Benji of no-name is saying going beyond. Thus, he is Benji no-name.

Thus, there is no-Benji. No-name drops away. Benji drops away.

————————

Panshan, Zen Master Baoji, said, "The single path of going beyond—a thousand sages, no transmission."

The single path of going beyond is the utterance of Panshan alone. He did not say "buddha going beyond" or "someone going beyond," but he said *the single path of going beyond.*

It means that even if thousands of sages appear all together, the single path of going beyond is not transmitted. *No transmission* means a thousand sages protect that which is not transmitted. You may be able to understand in this way. But there is something further to say about this. It is not that a thousand sages or a thousand wise people do not exist, but that a single path of going beyond is not merely the realm of the sages or of the wise.

————————

Zhimen, Zen Master Guangzuo, was once asked by a monk, "What is going beyond buddha?"

He said, "To hold up the sun and the moon on top of a staff."

This means that you are completely covered by the sun and the moon on top of a staff. This is buddha going beyond. When you penetrate the staff that holds up the sun and the moon, the entire universe is dark. This is buddha going beyond. It is not that the sun and the moon are the staff. *On top of a staff* means the entire staff.

————————

Daowu, who would later become Zen master of the Tianhuang Monastery, visited the assembly of Shitou, Great Master Wuji, and asked, "What is the fundamental meaning of buddha dharma?"

Shitou said, "Not to attain, not to know."

Daowu said, "Is there a further turning point in going beyond?"
Shitou said, "The vast sky does not keep white clouds from flying."

Now, Shitou is the second generation from Caoxi [Huineng]. Daowu of the Tianhuang Monastery is a younger dharma brother of Yaoshan. When Daowu asked Shitou about *the fundamental meaning of buddha dharma*, it is not a question asked by a beginner or someone who had recently started. Daowu asked this question when he was ready to understand the fundamental meaning if he heard it.

Shitou said, *Not to attain, not to know.* Understand that in buddha dharma the fundamental meaning is in the initial aspiration, as well as in the ultimate level. This fundamental meaning is not to attain. It is not that there is no aspiration, no practice, or no enlightenment. But simply, not-attaining. The fundamental meaning is not to know. Practice-enlightenment is not nonexistent or existent, but is not to know, not to attain.

Again, the fundamental meaning is not to attain, not to know. It is not that there is no sacred truth, no practice-enlightenment, but simply not to attain, not to know. It is not that there is a sacred truth and practice-enlightenment, but simply not to attain, not to know.

Daowu said, *Is there a further turning point in going beyond?* It means that when the turning point is actualized, going beyond is actualized. *Turning point* is a provisional expression. The provisional expression is all buddhas, all ancestors. In speaking of it, there is *further*. Even if there is *further*, do not neglect *going beyond*. Speak accordingly.

The vast sky does not hinder the white clouds from flying. These are Shitou's words. The vast sky does not hinder the vast sky. Just as the vast sky does not hinder the vast sky from flying, white clouds do not hinder white clouds. White clouds fly with no hindrance. White clouds' flying does not hinder the vast sky's flying. Not hindering others is not hindering self.

It is not that self and others need or have no hindrance. None of these requires no-hindrance or remains in no-hindrance. This is the no-hindrance brought out in the phrase *The vast sky does not hinder the white clouds from flying.*

Right now, raise the eyebrow of the eye of study and see through the emergence of buddhas, ancestors, self, and others. This is a case of asking one question and answering ten. In asking one question and answering ten, the person who asks one question is the true person; the person who answers ten is the true person.

———————

Huangbo said, "Those who have left the household should understand things that have come from the past. Niutou, Great Master Farong, a disciple of Fourth Ancestor Daoxin, explained vertically and horizontally but did not know the key to the barrier of going beyond. With your own eye and brain you should discern the correct school from the incorrect."

Huangbo's words *things that have come from the past* mean that which has been authentically transmitted from buddha ancestors. This is called the treasury of the true dharma eye, the wondrous heart of nirvana. Although it is in yourself, you should understand it. Although it is in yourself, it is beyond your understanding. Those who have not received authentic buddha-to-buddha transmission have never dreamed of it.

Huangbo, as the dharma heir of Baizhang, exceeds Baizhang and, as a dharma descendant of Mazu, exceeds Mazu. In three or four generations of the ancestral school, there was no one who could stand shoulder to shoulder with Huangbo. Huangbo alone made it clear that Niutou [Ox Head] did not have two horns. Other buddha ancestors had not noticed it.

Niutou, Zen Master Farong of Mount Niutou, was a respected teacher, a disciple of Dayi Daoxin, the Fourth Ancestor. When compared to that of Indian or Chinese sutra masters and treatise masters, his discourse was not inadequate. But regrettably he had not realized the key to the barrier of going beyond.

If you do not have the key to the barrier of things that have come from the past, how can you discern correct from incorrect in buddha dharma? You are merely someone who studies words and phrases. Thus, knowing, practicing, and realizing the key to the barrier of going beyond is not something ordinary people can accomplish. However, where there is true endeavor, the key is realized.

Going beyond buddha means that you reach buddha, and going further, you continue to see buddha. It is not the same as sentient beings' seeing buddha. Therefore, if your seeing buddha is merely the same as sentient beings' seeing buddha, it is not seeing buddha. If your seeing buddha is merely the same as sentient beings' seeing buddha, it is seeing buddha mistakenly; how can you experience going beyond buddha?

Know that Huangbo's words *going beyond* cannot be understood by careless people of these times. Their dharma discourses cannot reach that of Niutou. Even if their dharma discourses equaled that of Niutou, they would be merely Niutou's dharma brothers. How can they have the key to the barrier of going beyond? Other bodhisattvas of the ten stages or three classes can never have the key to the barrier of going beyond. How can they open and close the barrier of going beyond? This is the eye of study. One who has the key to the barrier of going beyond goes beyond buddha, realizing through-the-body going beyond buddha.

Presented to the assembly at the Kannondori Kosho Horin Monastery on the twenty-third day, the third month, the third year of the Ninji Era [1242].

30

THUSNESS

Yunju, Great Master Hongjue of Mount Yunju, an heir of Dongshan, is a thirty-ninth-generation dharma descendant of Shakyamuni Buddha. He is an authentic ancestor of the Dongshan School. One day he said to the assembly, "You are trying to attain thusness, yet you are already a person of thusness. As you are already a person of thusness, why be worried about thusness?"

It means that one who aspires to experience thusness is immediately a person of thusness. If so, why be worried about thusness?

For the time being, we will regard the teaching by Yunju, "immediately getting to unsurpassable enlightenment," as thusness. Within this unsurpassable manifestation of enlightenment, the entire world of the ten directions is but a small portion; enlightenment exceeds the boundary of the entire world.

You are an accoutrement that exists in the entire world of the ten directions. How do you know it to be thus? You know it because your body and mind are not you; they appear in the entire world of the ten directions.

Your body is not you; your life is transported, moving in time without stopping even for a moment. Where has your youthful face gone? When you search for it, there is no trace. When you ponder deeply, there are many from the past whom you cannot encounter again. The pure mind does not stay; it comes and goes in fragments. Even if there is truth, it does not stay within the boundary of yourself.

Because of thusness, you arouse a boundless aspiration for enlightenment. Once this aspiration arises, you let go of what you have been playing with. You come forward to hear what you have never heard and realize what is not yet realized. This is not at all self-doing. Know that it is so because you are a person of thusness.

How do you know that you are a person of thusness? You know it because you want to attain thusness. As you already have the face and eye of a person of thusness, do not worry about thusness now. Even if you worry, it is thusness not to be worried about.

Also, do not be startled at the thusness of thusness. Even if there is thusness that you are startled at or wonder about, it is thusness. It is thusness not to be startled at.

Do not measure this with the yardstick of buddha or mind. Do not measure it with the yardstick of the world of phenomena or the entire world. It is just *If you are already a person of thusness, why be worried about thusness?*

This being so, thusness of sound and form is thus; thusness of body and mind is thus; thusness of all buddhas is thus.

For example, when you understand the moment of falling to the ground as thusness, you will not doubt the moment of falling to the ground at the moment of getting up.

Since ancient times, these words have been spoken in both India and the deva world: "One who falls to the ground uses the ground to stand up. One who ignores the ground and tries to stand cannot." The meaning is that those who fall down on the earth stand up on the earth; it is impossible to get up without using the earth.

Some people interpret this as great enlightenment, which is the desirable way to become free from body and mind. Thus, when being asked how buddhas attain the way, they say that it is like those who fall to the ground and use the ground to stand up.

Thoroughly investigate this and penetrate the views from the past, the future, and this very moment. Great enlightenment, beyond enlightenment, further delusion, and loss of delusion are immersed in enlightenment, immersed in delusion. They all fall to the ground and get up using the ground.

This is an expression above the heavens and below the heavens. It is an expression from India and China, from the past and present. It is an expression of old and new buddhas. It leaves nothing uncovered and lacks nothing.

This being so, those who only understand thus but miss beyond understanding thus have not thoroughly studied this expression. Even though the expression of an old buddha has been passed down as thus, when you hear the expression of an old buddha as an old buddha, you should inquire beyond.

Even if it had not been spoken in India or in the deva world, you should say something further in this way: "If one who falls to the ground uses the ground to stand up, it is not possible even for immeasurable eons."

Here is one vital path for getting up: "One who falls to the ground uses the sky to stand up. One who falls to the sky uses the ground to stand up." Without being thus, you can never get up. This has always been the way with all buddhas and ancestors.

Someone may ask, "How far apart are the sky and the ground from each other?" In response to such a question, you might reply, "The sky and the ground are eighteen thousand miles apart. One who falls to the ground uses the sky to stand up. One who ignores the sky and tries to stand cannot. One who falls to the sky uses the ground to stand up. One who ignores the ground and tries to stand cannot."

Those who are unable to express this have not yet known and seen the measure of the ground and the sky in the buddha way.

Sanghanandi, the Seventeenth Ancestor, acquired his dharma heir, Gayashata, in the following way:

Hearing a wind bell ringing outside the hall, he asked Gayashata, "Is it the wind or the bell that is ringing?"

Gayashata said, "Neither the wind nor the bell. It is the mind ringing."

Sanghanandi asked, "What is the mind?"

Gayashata said, "Altogether serene."

Sanghanandi said, "Splendid, splendid. Who other than you will succeed in my path?"

Thus, the treasury of the true dharma eye was transmitted to Gayashata.

This is to study that the mind is ringing while the wind is not ringing. This is to study that the mind is ringing while the bell is not ringing. Even if the mind ringing is thus, it is altogether serene.

This story was transmitted from India to China and has been regarded as a standard for study of the way, but many have misunderstood it as follows: Gayashata's statement—*Neither the wind nor the bell. It is the mind ringing*—means that at the very moment of listening, a thought arises. This arising of a thought is called mind. Without this mind-thought, how can one relate to the sound of the bell ringing? Because listening manifests with this thought, it should be regarded as the root of listening. Therefore, Gayashata said, *It is the mind ringing.*

This is a wrong view. They say this because they have not acquired the power of authentic teachers. This is like an interpretation by commentators in linguistics, but it is not the deep study of the buddha way.

On the other hand, those who have studied with authentic heirs of the buddha way take up unsurpassable enlightenment, the treasury of the true dharma eye, and call it serene, nondoing, samadhi, or dharani. The meaning of this is that when even one single thing is serene, myriad things are serene. If the blowing of the wind is serene, the ringing of the bell is serene. This is why Gayashata said, "Altogether serene."

You may say the mind that is ringing is not the wind ringing; the mind that is ringing is not the bell ringing; the mind that is ringing is not the mind that is ringing. Investigate thusness intimately and just

328 · TREASURY OF THE TRUE DHARMA EYE

say, "The wind rings. The bell rings. The blowing rings. The ringing rings." You realize thusness not because *why be worried about thusness?* but because "why pursue thusness?"

———————

Huineng, who would later become the Thirty-third Ancestor, Zen Master Dajian, was staying at the Faxing Monastery, in Guang Province, before his head was shaved.

There were two monks from India debating. One of them said, "The banner is flapping."

The other said, "The wind is flapping."

They went back and forth and could not settle the question. Then Huineng said, "It is not the banner that is flapping. It is not the wind that is flapping. It is your mind that is flapping."

Hearing this, the monks immediately agreed with him.

In this way, Huineng expressed that the wind, the banner, and the flapping are altogether the mind. Even if you hear Huineng's words now, you may not understand them. How, then, do you experience his words? How does this expression of thusness emerge?

Hearing his words, *It is your mind that is flapping*, you may think that he meant "It is your mind that is flapping." If so, not seeing Huineng or not knowing Huineng, you are not a dharma descendant of Huineng.

As a descendant, in order to experience Huineng's words and experience them by receiving his body, hair, and skin, you should thus say: "Let go of the words *It is your mind that is flapping*, and say, 'It is you that is flapping.'"

How does this expression of thusness emerge? It is because what flaps is what flaps, and you are you. As he was already a person of thusness, this expression of thusness emerges.

In his early life, Huineng was a woodcutter in Xin Province. He thoroughly understood mountains and rivers. Even as he endeavored and cut to the original source, how could he have contemplated inside a luminous window and studied in stillness the ancient teaching to illuminate the mind? With whom could he have studied to cleanse himself with snow?

One day in a marketplace he heard someone chanting a sutra. It was neither what he was waiting for nor what others had recommended to him. Having lost his father when quite young, he had been the sole support of his mother. He did not know that one bright pearl hidden in the robe could illuminate and break open the entire universe.

As soon as he attained clarity, he left his old mother and looked for a teacher. It is a rare case for people. No one takes the obligation and love toward parents lightly. But since he regarded dharma as weightier than his obligation and love, he left his mother. This is the meaning of the words [in the *Lotus Sutra*] "If you hear with wisdom, you trust and understand what you hear immediately."

This kind of wisdom can neither be acquired from someone else nor be aroused by oneself. Wisdom is transmitted to wisdom; wisdom searches for wisdom. Once, wisdom formed the bodies of five hundred bats [who listened to the dharma]; they had no other bodies and minds. At another time, wisdom was intimate within the bodies of ten thousand fish; even without conditions or causes, they could immediately attain understanding upon hearing the dharma.

Wisdom neither comes nor enters. It is just like when the god of spring encounters spring. Wisdom is neither with thought nor without thought. Wisdom is neither with mind nor without mind. How can it be concerned with large or small? How can it be discussed as delusion or enlightenment?

It means that without knowing what buddha dharma is and without having heard it, one does not look for and wish for it. But upon hearing dharma, one regards obligations as less weighty and forgets about oneself. It is because the body-and-mind that has wisdom is no longer the self. This is called *you trust and understand what you hear immediately.*

We do not know how many rounds of birth and death we go through wastefully in the dusty world, in spite of having this wisdom. It is just like a stone containing jade; the jade does not know that it is inside the stone, and the stone does not know that it contains the jade. A person discovers and removes the jade. This is not what the jade expected or what the stone was waiting for. It does not depend on the stone's view or the jade's thought. Likewise, although a person and wisdom are not acquainted with each other, without exception the way is heard by wisdom.

It is said [in the *Lotus Sutra*] that one with no wisdom who doubts will be lost forever. Although wisdom is neither being nor nonbeing, there is the being of a timeless spring pine and the nonbeing of fallen chrysanthemum blossoms. At the moment of no-wisdom, unsurpassable enlightenment becomes doubt; all things are altogether doubted. At that moment, one is lost forever; the words one hears and the things to realize become no other than doubt.

There is no self—no place to hide in the all-inclusive world. There is no other—just one straight rod of iron for myriad miles. Even as branches grow thus, there is only one vehicle of dharma in the entire world. Even as leaves fall thus, things abide in their conditions, and there is the aspect of the world as permanent. Thus, being wisdom and being no wisdom are like sun face and moon face [day and night of the same day].

As he was a person of thusness, Huineng attained clarity. Later he went to Mount Huangmei and met Hongren, Zen Master Daman. Hongren then assigned him to work as a laborer. Huineng pounded rice day and night for eight months.

Once, in the middle of the night, Hongren slipped into the pounding hut and asked Huineng, "Is the rice hulled now?"

Huineng said, "Hulled but not yet sifted."

Hongren tapped the mortar with his cane three times. Huineng shuffled the rice three times. This is regarded as the moment when teacher and student merged. Although neither known by the self nor understood by others, the transmission of dharma and the transmission of the robe took place at this very moment of thusness.

Once Shitou, Great Master Wuji of Mount Nanyue, was asked by Yaoshan, "I have a rough idea about the Three Vehicles and the Twelve Divisions of the scriptures. I have heard of the teaching from the south about directly pointing to the human mind, seeing through one's nature, and becoming a buddha. I beg you, reverend, please give me your compassionate instruction."

This is a question by Yaoshan, who had previously been a lecturer. He was well versed in the Three Vehicles and the Twelve Divisions of the scriptures. Thus, he was not ignorant of buddha dharma. Long ago, there was no particular school of Buddhism, so studying the Three Vehicles and the Twelve Divisions of the scriptures was the only way. Nowadays, most people are dull and try to analyze buddha dharma by establishing various doctrines. This is not the buddha way of awakening with dharma.

Shitou replied, "Thusness is ungraspable. Beyond thusness is ungraspable. Both thusness and beyond thusness are ungraspable. How about you?"

This is Shitou's statement for the benefit of Yaoshan. Indeed, as both thusness and beyond thusness are ungraspable, thusness is ungraspable, beyond thusness is ungraspable. Thusness is as it is. The function of this word is neither limited nor not limited.

Study thusness as ungraspable. Inquire about ungraspability in thusness. This thusness, this ungraspability, is not merely concerned with buddha thoughts. Understanding is ungraspable. Enlightenment is ungraspable.

––––––––––

Huineng, Zen Master Dajian of Mount Caoxi, once instructed Nanyue, who would later become Zen Master Dahui: "What is it that thus comes?"

Study thoroughly his statement that all things are invariably *what*, as *what* is beyond doubt, beyond understanding, but, just *what*. Study thoroughly that the one thing is no other than *what*. *What* is not to be doubted. *What* thus comes.

Presented to the assembly of the Kannondori Kosho Horin Monastery on the twenty-sixth day, the third month, the third year of the Ninji Era [1242].

31A

CONTINUOUS PRACTICE,
PART ONE

O N THE GREAT road of buddha ancestors there is always unsurpassable practice, continuous and sustained. It forms the circle of
the way and is never cut off. Between aspiration, practice, enlightenment, and nirvana, there is not a moment's gap; continuous practice is
the circle of the way. This being so, continuous practice is undivided, not
forced by you or others. The power of this continuous practice confirms
you as well as others. It means your practice affects the entire earth and
the entire sky in the ten directions. Although not noticed by others or
by yourself, it is so.

Accordingly, by the continuous practice of all buddhas and ancestors,
your practice is actualized and your great road opens up. By your continuous practice, the continuous practice of all buddhas is actualized and
the great road of all buddhas opens up. Your continuous practice creates
the circle of the way. By this practice, buddha ancestors abide as buddha, not-abide as buddha, have buddha mind, and attain buddha without
cutting off.

Because of this practice, there are the sun, the moon, and stars. Because
of this practice, there are the great earth and the open sky. Because of

this practice, there are body, mind, and their environs. Because of this practice, there are the four great elements and the five skandhas. Continuous practice is not necessarily something people in the world love, but it should be the true place of return for everyone. Because of the continuous practice of all buddhas of the past, present, and future, all buddhas of the past, present, and future are actualized.

The effect of such sustained practice is sometimes not hidden. Therefore, you aspire to practice. The effect is sometimes not apparent. Therefore, you may not see, hear, or know it. Understand that although it is not revealed, it is not hidden.

As it is not divided by what is hidden, apparent, existent, or not existent, you may not notice the causal conditions that led you to be engaged in the practice that actualizes you at this very moment of unknowing. The reason you don't see it is that becoming conscious of it is not anything remarkable. Investigate in detail that it is so because the causal condition [the aspiration] is no other than continuous practice, though continuous practice is not limited by the causal condition.

Continuous practice that actualizes itself is no other than your continuous practice right now. The now of this practice is not originally possessed by the self. The now of this practice does not come and go, enter and depart. The word "now" does not exist before continuous practice. The moment when it is actualized is called now. This being so, your continuous practice of this day is a seed of all buddhas and the practice of all buddhas. All buddhas are actualized and sustained by your continuous practice.

By not sustaining your continuous practice, you would be excluding buddhas, not nurturing buddhas, excluding continuous practice, not being born and dying simultaneously with all buddhas, and not studying and practicing with all buddhas. Blossoms opening and leaves falling now are the actualization of continuous practice. Polishing a mirror or breaking a mirror is no other than this practice.

Even if you might try to ignore it in order to hide a crooked intention and escape from it, this ignoring would also be continuous practice. To go off here and there looking for continuous practice appears similar to the aspiration for it. But it is like leaving behind the treasure at the home of your true parent and wandering poor in another land. Wandering through wind and water at the risk of your life, you should not discard the treasure of your own parent. While you were searching in this way, the dharma treasure would be missed. This being so, continuous practice should not slacken even for a moment.

Compassionate Father, Great Teacher Shakyamuni Buddha, was engaged in continuous practice in the deep mountains from the time he was nineteen years old. At age thirty, after practicing continuously, he attained the way simultaneously with all sentient beings on the great earth. Until he was eighty years old, his practice was sustained in mountains, forests, and monasteries. He did not return to the palace nor did he claim any property. He wore the same robes and held the same bowls throughout his lifetime. From the time he began teaching he was not alone even for a day or for an hour. He did not reject offerings from humans and devas. He was patient with the criticism of people outside the way. Wearing the pure robes and begging for food, the Buddha's lifetime of teaching was nothing but continuous practice.

Mahakashyapa, the Eighth Ancestor [after the Seven Original Buddhas], is Shakyamuni Buddha's heir. Throughout his lifetime he was engaged without negligence in the twelve ascetic practices: (1) Not to accept invitations from people, to practice begging daily, and not to receive money as an alternative for food. (2) To stay on mountains and not in villages or towns. (3) Not to ask for or accept clothing, but to take clothing from the dead in cemeteries, and dye and sew the cloth for robes. (4) To take shelter under a tree in the field. (5) To have one meal a day, which is called sangha asanika. (6) Not to lie down day or night, but to practice walking meditation and sleep sitting up, which is called "sangha naishadika." (7) To own three robes and nothing more and not to lie down with a robe on. (8) To live in cemeteries rather than in monasteries or houses; to sit zazen and seek the way while gazing at skeletons. (9) To seek out a solitary place, with no desire to lie down with or to be close to others. (10) To eat fruit before the meal and not after. (11) To sit in an open space and not to desire to sleep under a tree or in a house. (12) Not to eat meat or cream and not to rub the body with flax oil.

These are called the twelve ascetic practices. Venerable Mahakashyapa did not turn back or deviate from them throughout his lifetime. Even after authentically receiving the Tathagata's treasury of the true dharma eye, he did not retire from these practices.

Once the Buddha said, "You are old now. You should eat like the rest of the monks."

Mahakashyapa said, "If I had not encountered the Tathagata, I would have remained a self-enlightened buddha, living in mountains and forests. Fortunately, I have met the Tathagata. This is a beneficent gift of dharma. So, I cannot forgo my ascetic practice and eat like the rest of the monks."

The Tathagata admired his determination. At another time Mahakashyapa looked exhausted because of his ascetic practices, and the monks looked down on him. Then the Tathagata graciously called Mahakashyapa up to him and offered him half of his seat. Thus, Mahakashyapa sat on the Tathagata's seat. Know that Mahakashyapa was the most senior monk in the assembly of the Buddha. It is impossible to list all the practices he did in his lifetime.

––––––––

Venerable Parshva, who would later become the Tenth Ancestor, did not lay himself down on his side to sleep throughout his lifetime. Although he started his practice in his eighties, he soon received the great dharma, one to one. As he did not waste a moment, within three years he received the true eye of complete enlightenment.

Parshva was in his mother's womb for sixty years and was born with long, gray hair. As he had a vow not to lay himself down on his side to sleep, he was called Venerable Undefiled Sides. In order to pick up a sutra in the dark, he would radiate his inner light, an ability he had from birth.

When Parshva was about to give up his household and wear a monk's robe at the age of eighty, a young boy in the town criticized him, saying, "You are ignorant. What you are going to do doesn't make sense. Monks maintain two types of practice: learning samadhi and chanting. You are too old and frail to learn these things. You will only confuse the pure stream and eat monks' food in vain."

Hearing this criticism, he thanked the boy and reaffirmed his vow: "Until I master the Tripitaka, become free of desires in the three realms, achieve the six miraculous powers, and attain the eight types of emancipation, I will not lie down on my side."

After that he did not skip even one day of contemplation while walking, sitting, and standing. During the day he studied the teachings and at night he practiced tranquil concentration. After three years he mastered the Tripitaka. He became free of desires in the three realms and attained proficiency in the three types of knowledge.

Parshva was in his mother's womb for sixty years before his birth. Did he seek the way in the womb? Eighty years after his birth, he left his household to study the way. It was one hundred and forty years after he was conceived. Although outstanding, he was older and more frail than anyone else. In the womb he was old and after birth he was old. However, he did not mind people's criticism and had unrelenting determination. That is why after only three years his endeavor to attain the way was fulfilled. Upon seeing him and being inspired by him, how could we be slack in our endeavor? Do not be hindered by old age and frailty.

Birth is hard to fathom. Is this birth or not? Is this old age or not? The views of water by four types of beings vary. We should just focus our aspiration and endeavor on the practice of the way. We should understand that the practice of the way is no other than seeing into birth and death, yet our practice is not bound by birth and death.

It is extremely foolish of people nowadays to put aside the endeavor of the way when they become fifty or sixty years old, even seventy or eighty. If we are concerned about how many months and years we have lived, this is merely a limited human view, which has nothing to do with the study of the way. Do not consider whether you are in your prime or old and frail. Single-mindedly aspire to study and master the way, standing shoulder to shoulder with Parshva. Do not look back or cling to a heap of dust in the graveyard. If you do not have single-minded aspiration and are not awakened, who would pity you? Practice to see directly just as you would add eyeballs to a skeleton lying in the wilderness.

Huineng, who would later become the Sixth Chinese Ancestor, was a woodcutter from Xin Region, who could hardly be called learned. He lost his father when very young and was brought up by his old mother. He worked as a woodcutter to support her. Upon hearing a phrase from a sutra at the crossroads in town, he left his mother and set out in search of dharma. He was a great vessel, rare for any time, an outstanding practitioner of the way. Separating from his loving mother must have been more difficult than cutting off his own arm; setting aside his filial obligation was not lightly done.

Throwing himself into Hongren's assembly on Mount Huangmei, Huineng pounded rice day and night for eight months without sleep or rest. He received the authentic transmission of the robe and bowl at midnight. After being entrusted with the dharma he continued to pound rice for eight years, traveling with a grinding stone on his back. Even after he emerged in the world and expounded dharma to awaken people, he did not neglect this grinding stone. His continuous practice was rare in the world.

———————

Mazu of Jianxi did zazen for twenty years and received the intimate seal from Nanyue. Thus, Mazu, when expounding dharma and saving people, did not say anything that might discourage anyone from practicing zazen. Whenever new students arrived, he would allow them to intimately receive the mind seal. He was always the first one to engage in communal work and was not lax even when he was old. The current school of Linji is descended from Mazu.

———————

Yunyan and Daowu both studied with Yaoshan. Together they made a vow to study single-mindedly without laying their sides on the platform for forty years.

Yunyan transmitted dharma to Dongshan, who would later become Great Master Wuben. Dongshan said, "Twenty years ago I wanted to be just one piece, and I have been engaged in zazen ever since."

Nowadays this statement is widely acclaimed.

———————

Yunju, who would later become Great Master Hongjiao, was always served food by a heavenly being when he was living in his hermitage called Sanfeng [Three Peak] Hut. During that time, Yunju went to study with Dongshan, under whose teaching he settled the great matter of the way and returned to his hut. When the heavenly being brought food again, he looked for Yunju for three days but could not see him. Without depending on heavenly offerings, Yunju was fully dedicating himself to the great way. Ponder his aspiration for practice.

———————

From the time he was the attendant to Mazu until he died, Baizhang, who would later become Zen Master Dazhi, did not let a single day pass without working for the assembly or for others. He graciously gave us the model of "A day of no work is a day of no eating." When Baizhang was old, he labored just like those in their prime. The assembly was concerned about him, but he did not stop working. At last some students hid the tools from him during the work period. He refused to eat that day, expressing his regret that he could not join the assembly's communal work. This is Baizhang's exemplification of "A day of no work is a day of no eating." The wind of the Linji School, which is now widely spread in Song China, as well as the wind of other schools, represents the continuous practice of Baizhang's profound teaching.

———————

When Priest Jingqing was abbot of his monastery, he was so inconspicuous that the deities of the region never saw his face, nor did they even hear about him.

———————

Sanping, who would later become Zen Master Yizhong, used to receive meals that were delivered by devas. After encountering his teacher Dadian, Sanping could no longer be found by the devas.

———————

Changqing Da'an was called the Second Guishan. He said, "I lived on Mount Gui for twenty years. I ate Mount Gui's rice and shit Mount Gui's shit. I was not studying the words of Ancestor Guishan [Lingyou] but was just taming a water buffalo, wandering around all day long."

Know that raising a single water buffalo is the sustained practice of living on Mount Gui for twenty years. Ancestor Guishan had studied in the assembly of Baizhang. Quietly think about and remember Changqing's activities of those twenty years. There are many who study Guishan's words, but the continuous practice of *not studying the words of Ancestor Guishan* is rare.

———————

Zhaozhou, Priest Congsen, who would later become Great Master Zhenji of the Guanyin Monastery, first aroused the way-seeking mind at the age of sixty-one. He traveled around, carrying a water gourd and a staff with metal rings on top. He kept telling himself, "I will inquire about dharma of anyone who excels me, even a seven-year-old child. I will teach dharma to anyone who has less understanding, even a hundred-year-old."

Thus, he studied and understood Nanquan's way. It was an endeavor of twenty years. Finally, when he was eighty years old, he became abbot of the Guanyin Monastery, east of the city of Zhao Province [Zhaozhou]. After that, he guided humans and devas for forty years.

Zhaozhou did not write a single letter of request to donors. The monks' hall was small and without front or back platforms. Once, a leg of a sitting platform broke. He replaced it with a charred stick from the fireplace, tying it on with a rope, and used it for many years. When an officer asked for permission to get a new leg, he did not allow it. Follow the spirit of this old buddha.

Zhaozhou became abbot after receiving dharma transmission in his eighties. This was authentic transmission of the true dharma. People called him Old Buddha. Those who have not yet received true transmission of the dharma are lightweights compared with Zhaozhou. Those of you who are younger than eighty may be more active than Zhaozhou. But how can you younger lightweights be equal to him even in his old age? Keeping this in mind, strive in the path of continuous practice.

During the forty years Zhaozhou taught, he did not store worldly property. There was not a grain of rice in the monastery. So, the monks would pick up chestnuts and acorns for food, and they would adjust the mealtime to fit the situation. Indeed this was the spirit of the dragons and elephants of the past. You should long for such practice.

———

Zhaozhou once said to the assembly, "If you do not leave the monastery in your lifetime and do not speak for five or ten years, no one can call you speechless. Even buddhas would not know what to make of you."

Zhaozhou expresses sustained practice in this way. You should know that *not speak for five or ten years* may have the appearance of being speechless, but because of the merit of *do not leave the monastery* and *do not speak,* it is not the same as being speechless. The buddha way is like this. One who is capable of speaking but doesn't speak is not like an ordinary person who has not heard the voice of the way. Thus, unsurpassable continuous practice is *not leave the monastery. Not leave the monastery* is total speech that is dropping off. Most people do not know, nor speak of, going beyond speechless. No one keeps them from speaking of it, but nevertheless they don't speak of it. They do not discover or understand that to go beyond speechless is to express thusness. How regrettable!

Quietly engage in the sustained practice of *not leave the monastery.* Do not be swayed east or west by the winds of east and west. The spring breeze and the autumn moon of five or ten years, unbeknownst to us, have the ring of emancipation beyond sound and form. This voice is not known to the self, not understood by the self. Learn to treasure each moment of sustained practice. Do not assume that not to speak is useless. It is entering the monastery, leaving the monastery. The bird's path is the forest. The entire world is the forest, the monastery.

Mount Damei is in Qingyuan Prefecture. Fachang from Xiangyang founded the Husheng Monastery on this mountain. When studying in the assembly of Mazu, Fachang asked him, "What is buddha?"

Mazu said, "Mind itself is buddha."

Upon hearing these words, Fachang had realization.

Fachang climbed to the top of Mount Damei and dwelt there in a hut. He ate pinecones and wore lotus leaves, as there were many lotus plants in a small pond on that mountain. He practiced zazen for over thirty years, and was completely detached from human affairs. Without paying attention to which day it was, he only saw the green and yellow of the surrounding mountains. These were rugged years.

During zazen he set an iron stupa of eight *cun* in height on his head. It was like wearing a jeweled crown. As his intention was not to let the stupa fall down, he would not sleep. This stupa is still listed as a stored treasure at the Husheng Monastery. He practiced in this way continuously, without slackening.

After many years, a monk from the assembly of Yanguan went to the mountain looking for wood to make a staff. He lost his way and after a while found himself in front of Fachang's hut. Seeing Fachang, he asked, "How long have you been on this mountain?"

Fachang said, "I have seen nothing but the green and yellow of the surrounding mountains."

The monk said, "How do I get off this mountain?"

Fachang said, "Follow the stream."

Mystified by Fachang, the monk went back and told Yanguan about him.

Yanguan said, "When I was in Jiangxi, I saw a monk like that, but I haven't heard of him since. This might be him."

Yanguan sent the monk to Fachang and invited him to come to the monastery. Fachang would not leave the mountain but responded with a poem:

> A decayed tree remains in the cold forest.
> Meeting springs, there is no change of mind.
> Woodcutters see me, but I ignore them.
> How come the wood master seeks me out?

Fachang stayed on the mountain. Later, when he was about to move deeper into the mountain, he wrote this poem:

> Wearing lotus leaves from this pond—inexhaustible.
> Eating pine nuts from several trees—still more left.

> Having been spotted by people from the world,
> I am moving my hut further away.

So he moved his abode.

Later his teacher Mazu sent a monk to Fachang to ask him, "Reverend, when you studied with Mazu, what did you understand that led you to live on this mountain?"

Fachang said, "Mazu said to me, 'Mind itself is buddha.' That's why I am living here."

The monk said, "Nowadays buddha dharma is different."

Fachang said, "How is it different?"

The monk said, "Mazu says, 'Beyond mind, beyond buddha.'"

Fachang said, "That old man always confuses people. Let it be 'beyond mind, beyond buddha.' As for me, mind itself is none other than buddha."

The monk brought Fachang's response to Mazu.

Mazu said, "The plum is ripe."

This story is widely known among humans and devas. Tianlong is Fachang's excellent student. Tianlong's heir, Juzhi, is Fachang's dharma grandchild. Jiazhi of Korea transmitted Fachang's dharma and became the first ancestor of his country. All masters in Korea are dharma descendants of Fachang.

While Fachang was alive, a tiger and an elephant attended him without contending with each other. After he died, the tiger and elephant carried rocks and mud to help erect a tower for him. This tower still exists in the Husheng Monastery.

Fachang's sustained practice has been admired by teachers both past and present. Those who do not appreciate him lack wisdom. To suppose that buddha dharma is present in the pursuit of fame and gain is a limited and foolish view.

———

Fayan, Zen Master Wuzu, said:

When our founder [Yangqi Fanghui] became abbot of Yangqi, the monastery buildings were old and dilapidated, barely able to provide shelter from wind and rain. It was deep winter and all the buildings were badly in need of repair. The monks' hall in particular was damaged to the point where snow and hail would pile up on the sitting platforms and there was hardly any place to settle down. It was very hard to do zazen there. The elders of the monastery were so concerned that they made a request to Yangqi to have the buildings repaired.

Yangqi said, "According to the Buddha's teaching, this is the time when the human life span is decreasing, and the high lands and the deep valleys are always changing. How can we achieve complete satisfaction in all things? Sages in the past sat under trees and did walking meditation on bare ground. These are excellent examples, the profound teaching of practicing emptiness. You have left the household to study the way and are not yet accustomed to the daily activities with hands and legs. You are only forty or fifty years old. How can you have the leisure to enjoy a comfortable building?" Thus, Yangqi did not approve their request. On the following day, he sat on the teaching seat and presented this poem to the assembly:

> When I began living here in this building with crumbling walls,
> all the platforms were covered by jewels of snow.
> Scrunching up my shoulders to my neck, I sigh into darkness,
> reflecting on ancient ones abiding under a tree.

Even though the monks' hall was still in disrepair, monks in cloud robes and mist sleeves from the Four Seas and Five Lakes of China wanted to practice in Yangqi's assembly. We should be joyous that there were so many who were immersed in the way. You should dye your mind with his words and inscribe them in your ears.

Later, Fayan gave an instruction, saying, "Practice does not go beyond thinking. Thinking does not go beyond practice."

Take this teaching seriously, thinking of it day and night and putting it into practice morning and evening. Do not be like those who are blown about by winds from the east, west, south, and north.

———————

In Japan even the Imperial Palace is not a magnificent edifice but is built of coarse, plain wood. How can monks who study the way live in a luxurious building? Such a building can only be acquired by devious means; cases of acquisition through pure means are rare. I am not talking about something you may already possess. But do not try to acquire something luxurious. A grass hut and a plain wooden hermitage were abodes loved by ancient sages. Those who study nowadays should long for and study this simplicity.

Although the Yellow Emperor, Emperor Yao, and Emperor Shun were worldly monarchs in China, they lived in grass huts. They set excellent examples for the world.

The *Shizi* says, "If you want to know the deeds of the Yellow Emperor, you should see his abode called the Thatched Palace. If you want to see the deeds of emperors Yao and Shun, you should see their Zongzhang Palace. The Yellow Emperor's abode was roofed with grass. That is why it was called the Thatched Palace. Yao and Shun's residence was also roofed with grass. And it was called the Headquarters."

Keep in mind that these palaces were thatched with grass. If we compare ourselves to the Yellow Emperor, Emperor Yao, or Emperor Shun, the gap is wider than that between heaven and earth. Those emperors made thatched-roof buildings their quarters. If laypeople could live in grass huts, how should monks make tall buildings with breathtaking views their abode? It would be shameful. People of old lived under trees in the forest. Both laypeople and home leavers love such places.

The Yellow Emperor was a disciple of a Daoist named Guangcheng, who lived in a grotto called Kongdong. Many kings and ministers of Great Song China still follow the Yellow Emperor's example. Knowing that people in the dusty realms lived humbly, how can home leavers be more worldly or more murky than they?

――――――――

Among the buddha ancestors of the past, many received offerings from devas. However, after they attained the way, the devas' celestial eyes could not see them and demonic spirits could no longer communicate with them. Be aware of this.

When devas and gods follow the practice of buddha ancestors, they have a way to approach them. But when buddha ancestors actualize going beyond, devas and gods have no way to find and come close to them. So Nanquan said, "As I lack the power of practice, a spirit is able to find me."

Know from this that to be seen by spirits means that your power of practice is lacking.

———————

The guardian spirit of the monastery buildings at Tiantong on Mount Taibai said to Hongzhi, Abbot Zhengjiao, "I know that you have been abbot of this monastery for over ten years. But whenever I go to see you in your sleeping quarters, I cannot quite reach you."

This is indeed an example of someone who was engaged in the way. The monastery on Mount Tiantong was originally a small practice place. When Hongzhi was abbot, he abolished the Daoist temple, the nunnery, and the scriptural seminary and turned the compound into the current Jingde Monastery.

After Hongzhi died, Wang Boxiang, the imperial historian, was writing a biography of Hongzhi. Someone said, "You should record that Hongzhi plundered the Daoist temple, the nunnery, and the scriptural seminary and turned the compound into the current Jingde Monastery." Boxiang said, "It should not be recorded, because it is not a meritorious thing for a monk to do." People of his time agreed with Boxiang.

Know that such a thing is what a worldly person might tend to do and should not be seen as the achievement of a monk. Upon entering the buddha way, you go beyond the humans and devas of the three realms, and you are no longer measured by the standards of those in the three realms. Examine this closely. Study it thoroughly involving body, speech, mind, and your surroundings. The continuous practice of buddha ancestors has the great power to awaken both humans and devas, who, however, may not notice that they are helped by it.

———————

In the continuous practice of the way of buddha ancestors, do not be concerned about whether you are a great or a modest hermit, whether you are brilliant or dull. Just forsake name and gain forever and don't be bound by myriad conditions. Do not waste the passing time. Brush off the fire on top of your head. Do not wait for great enlightenment, as great enlightenment is the tea and rice of daily activity. Do not wish for beyond enlightenment, as beyond enlightenment is a jewel concealed in your hair.

If you have a home, leave your home. If you have beloved ones, leave them. If you have fame, abandon it. If you have gain, escape from it. If you have fields, get rid of them. If you have relatives, separate from them. If you don't have name and gain, stay away from them. Why should you not remain free from them, while those who already have name and gain need to give them up? This is the single track of continuous practice.

To forsake name and gain in this lifetime and practice one thing thoroughly is the vast continuous practice of the Buddha's timeless life. This continuous practice is bound to be sustained by continuous practice. Love and respect your body, mind, and self that are engaged in this continuous practice.

———————

Daci, Zen Master Huanzhong, said, "Speaking ten feet does not compare to practicing one foot. Speaking one foot does not compare to practicing one inch."

It may appear that Daci was warning the people of his day not to ignore continuous practice and not to forget about mastering the buddha way. However, he was not saying that speaking ten feet is of no value, but rather that the practice of one foot has greater power. The comparison between speech and practice is not limited to one foot or ten feet. It is also like Mount Sumeru and a poppy seed. Sumeru reveals its entire size. A poppy seed reveals its entire size. The great moment of continuous practice is like this. This is not speaking to himself but speaking to Huanzhong [Boundless World].

———————

Dongshan, Great Master Wuben, said, "Speak what cannot be practiced. Practice what cannot be spoken."

These are words spoken by the high ancestor. It means that practice clarifies the way to speech and there is a way that speech approaches practice. This being so, you practice all day while speaking all day. You practice what cannot be practiced and you speak what cannot be spoken.

———————

Yunju, Great Master Hongjue, investigating Dongshan's words seven or eight ways, said, "At the time of speaking, there is no road of practice. At the time of practice, there is no path of speaking."

His words show that it is not that there is neither practicing nor speaking. At the time of speaking, you do not leave the monastery for your lifetime. At the time of practicing, you wash the head and request Xuefeng to shave it. You should not waste the time of speaking or the time of practicing.

———————

Buddha ancestors have said since ancient times, "Living for one hundred years without encountering a buddha does not compare to living for one day and arousing the determination for the way."

These are not merely the words of one or two buddhas; they have been spoken and practiced by all buddhas. Within the cycles of birth and death for myriad kalpas, one day of continuous practice is a bright jewel in the banded hair, the ancient mirror of all-inclusive birth and all-inclusive death. It is a day of rejoicing. The power of continuous practice is itself rejoicing.

When the power of your continuous practice is not sufficient and you have not received the bones and marrow of buddha ancestors, you are not valuing the body-mind of buddha ancestors, nor are you taking joy in the face of buddha ancestors. Although the face, bones, and marrow of buddha ancestors are beyond going and not going, beyond coming and not coming, they are always transmitted through one day's continuous practice. Therefore, each day is valuable. A hundred years lived in vain is a regrettable passage of time, a remorseful life as a living corpse. But even if you run around as a servant of sound and form for a hundred years, if you attain one day of continuous practice, you not only attain the practice of one hundred years, but you awaken others for a hundred years. The living body of this one day is a living body to revere, a form to revere. If you live for one day merged with the activity of the buddhas, this one day is considered as excellent as many kalpas of lifetimes.

Even when you are uncertain, do not use this one day wastefully. It is a rare treasure to value. Do not compare it to an enormous jewel. Do not compare it to a dragon's bright pearl. Old sages valued this one day more than their own living bodies. Reflect on this quietly. A dragon's pearl may be found. An enormous jewel may be acquired. But this one day out of a hundred years cannot be retrieved once it is lost. What skillful means can retrieve a day that has passed? No historical documents have recorded any such means. Not to waste time is to contain the passage of days and months within your skin bag without leaking. Thus, sages and wise ones in olden times valued each moment, each day, and each month more than their own eyeballs or the nation's land. To waste the passage of time is to be confused and stained in the floating world of name and gain. Not to miss the passage of time is to be in the way for the sake of the way.

Once you have clarity, do not neglect a single day. Wholeheartedly practice for the sake of the way and speak for the sake of the way. We know that buddha ancestors of old did not neglect each day's endeavor. Reflect on this every day. Sit near a bright window and reflect on this, on mellow and flower-filled days. Sit in a plain building and remember it on a solitary rainy evening. Why do the moments of time steal your endeavor? They not only steal one day but steal the merit of many kalpas. What kind of enemy is the passage of time? How regrettable! Your loss of time would all be because of your negligence of practice. If you were not intimate with yourself, you would resent yourself.

It is not that buddha ancestors lacked family obligations and attachments, but they abandoned them. It is not that buddha ancestors were not bound by relationships, but they let them go. Even if you are bound by relationships, you cannot keep them. If you do not throw away family obligations and attachments, the family obligations and attachments will throw you away. If you want to cherish the family obligations and attachments, then cherish them. To cherish the family obligations and attachments means to be free from them.

Nanyue, Priest Huairang, who would later become Zen Master Dahui, went to study with Huineng, the Sixth Ancestor, and was his attendant for fifteen years. He received the way and the craft, just like someone receiving a vessel of water from another. Such an example from olden times should be longed for.

There must have been a lot of hardship during the wind and frost of those fifteen years. In spite of it, Nanyue single-heartedly pursued his investigation. This is a mirror for later generations. Without charcoal in the cold stove, he slept alone in an empty hall. Without lamplight on summer evenings, he sat at a window by himself. Not having one piece of knowledge or a half of understanding, he reached the place of no effort, going beyond study. This is no other than continuous practice. As Nanyue had subtly abandoned greed for name and love for gain, he simply accumulated the power of continuous practice day by day. Do not forget the meaning of this. His statement to Huineng, "Speaking about it won't hit the mark," expresses his continuous practice of eight years. Such continuous practice is rare throughout the past and present, aspired to by those who are wise and those who are not.

———————

Xiangyan, who would later become Zen Master Zhixian, cultivated the way with Guishan. When Xiangyan tried to come up with one phrase of understanding, he could not utter it even after trying several times. In anguish, he burned his sutras and books of commentary, and took up the practice of serving meals for many years. Then, he climbed up Mount Wudang, to visit the remains of Huizhong, National Teacher Dazheng of Nanyang, and built a retreat hut there. One day when he was sweeping the path, a pebble flew up and struck a bamboo. At the crack he suddenly had realization.

Later he became abbot of the Xiangyan Monastery and maintained the practice of one bowl and one robe. He lived his life discreetly in this monastery of extraordinary rocks and clear springs, and rarely left the mountain. Many spots where he practiced are still there.

———————

Linji, who would later become Great Master Huizhao, an heir of Huangbo, was in Huangbo's assembly for three years. After concentrated endeavor of the way, following the encouragement of his senior dharma brother, Venerable Chen of Mu Region, he asked Huangbo three times about the essential meaning of buddha dharma. He received sixty blows of the stick, but still he did not slacken his determination. He was sent to see Dayu and had great realization. This was the result of his study with these two reverend masters, Huangbo and Chen.

Linji and Deshan are called heroes of the ancestral seats. But how can Deshan compare to Linji? Indeed, Linji was extraordinary. Those who were ordinary in his time excel those who are outstanding in our time. It is said that Linji strove whole-heartedly and his continuous practice was extraordinary. None of us can guess how it was.

When Linji was at the assembly of Huangbo, he planted cedar and pine trees with Huangbo. Huangbo asked him, "Why are we planting so many trees deep in this mountain?"

Linji said, "First, for the landscape around the monastery. Second, as a landmark for later generations." Then he hit the ground twice with his hoe.

Huangbo held up his staff and said, "That's why I have just given you thirty blows."

Linji heaved a deep sigh.

Huangbo said, "When you receive my teaching, it will flourish in the world."

In this way, know that when they planted cedar and pine trees after attaining the way, they were carrying hoes in their hands. *When you receive my teaching, it will flourish in the world* is a result of this. Transmit person to person and directly point to this ancient example of planting trees. Both Huangbo and Linji planted trees.

In the past Huangbo had the continuous practice of joining the workers in the Da'an Monastery and cleaning the halls. He swept the buddha hall and the dharma hall. He did not wait for the continuous practice of cleaning the mind and cleaning the lamp. It was at this time that he encountered Minister Pei.

————————

Emperor Xuan of the Tang Dynasty was the second son of Emperor Xian. He was bright from the time he was young. He loved to sit in the lotus position and would do zazen in the palace.

Emperor Mu was Xuan's elder brother. When Mu was reigning, Xuan went to the throne room, sat on the throne early in the morning, and pretended to greet his retainers. The ministers saw this and, thinking he was out of his mind, reported it to the Emperor. Seeing this, Mu stroked

Xuan's head and said, "Brother, you have inherited the excellent qualities of our family lineage." At that time Xuan was thirteen years old.

Mu passed away in the fourth year of the Changqing Era [825].
He had three sons: Jing, Wen, and Wu. Jing inherited the throne but
passed away three years later. One year after Wen was installed, the ministers rebelled and replaced him with Wu. Xuan, not yet having been
enthroned, lived in the country of his nephew. Wu called Xuan "my
dull uncle."

Wu was on the throne during the Huichang Era [841–846], when
he prohibited Buddhist teaching. One day he summoned Xuan and had
him beaten into unconsciousness and soaked with urine as punishment
for having climbed up onto Mu's throne a long time before. Xuan was
left in the imperial garden. When he regained consciousness, he left his
homeland. Disguising himself, Xuan joined the assembly of Xiangyan,
Zen Master Zhixian, had his head shaved, and became a novice. However, he did not receive the full precepts.

As a novice, Xuan traveled to various places with his teacher, Xiangyan. When they arrived at Mount Lu, Xiangyan wrote a verse beside the
waterfall there:

> The water gouges the cliff and pounds the
>   rocks unceasingly.
> Even from a distance we know how high it is.

Xiangyan was trying to engage Xuan, to see how mature he was.
Xuan added a verse:

> How can the valley stream be blocked?
> It will end up in the ocean as billows.

Seeing these lines, Xiangyan realized that Xuan was no ordinary person. Later, Xuan went to the assembly of Yanguan, National Teacher
Qi'an of Hang Region, and served as secretary of the monastery. At that
time Huangbo was head monk. Thus, Xuan was sharing the meditation
platform with Huangbo.

When Huangbo went to the buddha hall and made prostrations to
the Buddha, the secretary joined him and said, "Seek without being

attached to the buddha. Seek without being attached to the dharma. Seek without being attached to the sangha. Elder, why are you making prostrations?"

In response, Huangbo slapped the novice secretary and said, "'Seek without being attached to the buddha. Seek without being attached to the dharma. Seek without being attached to the sangha. Therefore, we make prostrations like this."

Then Huangbo slapped him again.

Xuan said, "That's pretty rough."

Huangbo said, "What is right here? How can you say it's rough?" and gave him another slap.

Xuan was silent.

After Wu's reign ended, Xuan returned to the laity and ascended the throne. He stopped Wu's persecution of Buddhism and reinstituted the Buddhist teaching.

Before he was installed as emperor, he left his father's kingdom and traveled widely, practicing the way wholeheartedly. It is said that while emperor, he enjoyed practicing zazen day and night. Indeed, Xuan had been a pitiable wanderer after his father passed away and again after his brother passed away. He was punished and beaten, as ordered by his nephew Wu. But his aspiration did not waver and he continued his practice. His genuine continuous practice was an excellent example, rare in history.

Xuefeng, Priest Yicun, who would later become Great Master Zhen-jiao, never slackened in zazen day and night from the time he aroused the way-seeking mind. During the long course of traveling and visiting various monasteries, he did not discriminate among them, but hung up his traveling staff and joined their practice. He did not relax his effort and completely perished in zazen. After that, he founded an unadorned monastery on Mount Xuefeng,

When Xuefeng began to study with masters, he traveled to Dong-shan nine times and to Touzi three times. His effort was so outstanding that when teachers nowadays encourage continuous practice, pure and solemn, they use "Xuefeng's lofty aspiration" as an example.

Although Xuefeng's dullness is not different from others', his brilliance is beyond comparison. This is due to his continuous practice. Those of you who follow the way these days should wash yourselves with the snow of Xuefeng [Snow Peak]. If you quietly reflect on the muscle power of Xuefeng to study at various monasteries, you will see that it is no other than the spiritual bone power he carried over from former lives.

———————

Nowadays, when you join the assemblies of various masters who maintain the way, and you want to receive instructions, it is hard to find an opportunity. Not merely twenty or thirty skin bags, but one hundred or one thousand faces all desire to return to the true source. The day of the masters' guiding hand ends at sunset. The evening of pounding rice goes quickly. At the time when the masters expound dharma, you may lack eyes and ears; your seeing and hearing may be blocked. When you are ready, your teacher's time may come to an end. While senior reverend masters clap their hands in laughter, those of you who are newly ordained and low in seniority may have difficulty even joining the assembly at the end of the mat.

There are those who do and those who do not enter the inner chambers. There are those who do and those who do not hear the essential words of the teachers. The passage of time is faster than an arrow. Life is more fragile than a dewdrop. Even when you have teachers, you may not be able to study with them. When you want to study with teachers, you may not have them. I have personally seen and heard of such cases.

Although great teachers all have the power to know people, it is rare to have a good relationship with a teacher and become intimate while cultivating the way. When Xuefeng visited Dongshan and Touzi, he must have had a hard time. We can all sympathize with the dharma aspiration of his continuous practice. Those who don't study or practice will be filled with regret.

Editing completed on the eighteenth day, the first year of the Ninji Era [1243].
[Dogen]

31B

CONTINUOUS PRACTICE,
PART TWO

BODHIDHARMA CAME FROM India to China at the request of his teacher, Venerable Prajnatara. How severe the wind and snow was throughout his three-year journey! How innumerable the waves of the ocean, under clouds and mist, as he sailed toward an unknown country! This journey is beyond the imagination of those attached to body and life.

This continuous practice is due solely to his great compassionate determination to transmit dharma and to save deluded beings. It is continuous practice because of his dedication to transmitting dharma, because of the all-inclusive world where dharma is to be transmitted, because the entire world of the ten directions is the true path, and because the entire world of the ten directions is the entire world of the ten directions. What place is not Bodhidharma's palace? What palace could hinder his practice of the way?

Thus, Bodhidharma left India. As his vow was to save deluded beings, he had no doubt or fear. As what he embodied was the all-inclusive practice for saving deluded beings, he had no doubt or fear. Bidding farewell to the country of his father, the king, he sailed on a large ship through the South Sea and entered the Province of Guang. Although there were many people on board, including his attendant monks, no record of the voyage has remained. No one knows what happened to his entourage.

On the twenty-first day, the ninth month, the eighth year of the Putong Era [527 C.E.] of the Kingdom of Liang, Xiaoang, Governor of Guang Province, officially welcomed Bodhidharma. Carrying out his duty, he reported Bodhidharma's arrival to Emperor Wu. It was the first day of the tenth month. Reviewing the report with delight, Emperor Wu sent a messenger to Bodhidharma to invite him to the palace.

Bodhidharma went to the capital city of Jinling and met with Wu, who said, "Ever since I became Emperor, I have built temples, copied sutras, and approved the ordination of more monks than I can count. What is the merit of having done all this?"

Bodhidharma said, "There is no merit."

The Emperor said, "Why is that so?"

Bodhidharma said, "These are minor achievements of humans and devas, which become the causes of desire. They are like shadows of forms and not real."

The Emperor said, "What is real merit?"

Bodhidharma said, "When pure wisdom is complete, the essence is empty and serene. Such merit cannot be attained through worldly actions."

The Emperor said, "What is the foremost sacred truth?"

Bodhidharma said, "Vast emptiness, nothing sacred."

The Emperor said, "Who is it that faces me?"

Bodhidharma said, "I don't know."

The Emperor did not understand. Bodhidharma knew that there was no merging [between the two] and the time was not ripe. Thus, without a word he left on the nineteenth day of the tenth month and traveled north of the River Yangzi.

He arrived in Luoyang in the Kingdom of Wei on the twenty-third day of the eleventh month of the same year. He stayed at the Shaolin Temple of Mount Song, where he sat facing the wall in silence day after day. But the Emperor [Xiaoming] of Wei was unaware of his presence and was not ashamed of being unaware of it.

Bodhidharma was from the warrior class in southern India, a prince of a major kingdom, where sophisticated customs had been developed. In contrast, the customs of the minor kingdom of Wei must have looked uncivilized in the eyes of Bodhidharma, but it did not affect him. He did not abandon the country or people. Although he was attacked by the monk Bodhiruchi, he did not defend himself, nor did he hate him. He was not resentful of Precept Master Guangtong's bad intention, but simply ignored him.

Although Bodhidharma did many outstanding things, he was often regarded as an ordinary Tripitaka master or a scholar of sutras and commentaries because of the lack of understanding and small-mindedness of some monks in China. People thought Bodhidharma expounded the dharma gate of the Zen School. They saw no difference between his true teaching and the teachings of scholarly commentators.

Bodhidharma is the twenty-eighth authentic heir of Shakyamuni Buddha. He left the large kingdom of his father to save sentient beings of the eastern country. Who can be compared to him? If he had not come from India, how could sentient beings of China see and hear the Buddha's true dharma? They would have been stuck with countless names and forms. Now, some barbarians like us, who have hair and horns, are able to hear the true dharma. Today even farmers and village people can see and hear it because of the continuous practice of Bodhidharma who voyaged to China.

China was much less civilized than India. Their customs were not as wholesome as those of India. An outstanding sage like Bodhidharma, who had received and maintained the treasury of dharma, would not have bothered to go, had he not had great patience and vast compassion. There was no established place for practice, and few people in China who would be able to appreciate a true teacher.

Bodhidharma stayed on Mount Song for nine years. People called him a wall-gazing Brahman. Later historians listed him as a practitioner of learning meditation. But that is not the whole truth. The ancestor alone transmitted the treasury of the true dharma eye, buddha to buddha, heir to heir.

The *Record within the Forest* by Shimen [Rock Gate] says:

Bodhidharma at first visited the Kingdom of Liang and then the Kingdom of Wei. He then went to Mount Song and rested his traveling staff at the Shaolin Temple, where he simply sat at ease facing the wall. It was not a step-by-step practice of learning meditation. For a long time people could not guess why he was doing it, so they regarded Bodhidharma as a practitioner of learning meditation.

Now, meditation is only one of the many activities of Zen. It does not cover the entire practice of the sage. But those who recorded the history of that time classified him among practitioners of learning meditation and lumped him together with those who engaged in the static practice of a decayed tree and dead ash. The sage is not limited to meditation, yet does not contradict meditation. It is like the practice of *Ijing* [I-ching] not being limited to yin and yang, yet not contradicting yin and yang.

When Emperor Wu of Liang met Bodhidharma, the Emperor asked, "What is the primary meaning of the sacred truth?" Bodhidharma said, "Vast emptiness, nothing sacred." The Emperor asked further, "Who is facing me?" Bodhidharma said, "I don't know." Had he not been so familiar with the local language, he would not have communicated so well.

Thus, it is clear that Bodhidharma moved from Liang to Wei. He walked to Mount Song and stayed at the Shaolin Temple. Although he sat in stillness facing the wall, he was not engaged in so-called learning meditation. Although he had not brought even one volume of sutra, he was a genuine master who transmitted true dharma. However, historians without understanding classified him in the section on teachers of learning meditation. This was the utmost stupidity, which is lamentable.

When Bodhidharma arrived on Mount Song, a doglike monk barked at him. What a pity! How foolish! With what mind could one ignore Bodhidharma's compassionate gift? How could one fail to repay his kindness? In the worldly realm, there are those who do not forget the kindness of others. People call them worthy beings. The great kindness of Bodhidharma surpasses that of one's parents. His compassion is beyond filial love.

The lowly birth of Japanese people is amazing, if we think about it. Not having been born in the center of the world, we haven't seen the flourishing land. We haven't known sages nor seen the wise. There has been no one who has ascended to heaven from our land, Japan. We are all equally immature. From the time our nation was founded, no one has guided laypeople. We have never heard of anyone purifying the nation, as no one has known what is pure and what is murky. We are not familiar with yin and yang, or with heaven, earth, and humans. How, then, could we understand the undulation of the five types of matter? This ignorance comes from not knowing the sound and form before our very eyes. It is the result of not knowing the sutras, nor having true teachers with whom to study them.

Having no true teachers, we do not know how many scores of volumes, how many hundreds of verses, and how many thousands of words the sutras have. We just read the remote aspects of the writing, instead of understanding the essential meaning of the thousands of verses and myriad words. We come to know the ancient sutras and texts as a result of our longing for the authentic teaching. As we long for the ancient teaching, the sutras of old come forth.

The founders of the Han and Wei dynasties in China—Emperors Gao and Tai—understood the verses of heaven and transmitted the expression of the terrestrial forms. When we clarify their words, the fundamentals of heaven, earth, and humans are understood. People who have not encountered the guidance of such virtuous leaders do not know what it is to truly serve the emperor or to truly serve their parents. They are unfortunate subjects of the Emperor and unfortunate children of their parents. As subjects or children, they miss a precious jewel and waste the passage of time. Born into such a family, they have no authority to govern, and cling to petty positions. Thus, the nation is murky, rarely known for its purity. Since we have a lowly life in such a remote land as Japan where the Tathagata's true dharma is not heard, what is the use of clinging to this bodily life? Why do we cling to this bodily life, and to what do we devote ourselves?

Those who have a worthy and noble life should not cling to it for anything, even for the sake of dharma. This is also true for those with a lowly life. On the other hand, if those with a lowly life dedicate themselves to following the way for the sake of dharma, their life is worthier than the life of the heavenly devas, a wheel-turning king, the gods of heaven and earth, or sentient beings in the three realms.

Now, Bodhidharma, the First Chinese Ancestor, was the third son of the King of Xiangzhi in southern India. As a prince from a royal family, of noble background, he was to be respected. But in the remote land of China, people did not know how to respect him. They had no incense, flowers, royal cushions, or palace for him. Japan is an even more distant steep cliff away, where no one knows how to honor a prince from a great nation. Even if we learn the manners, we may have difficulty in mastering them. The way to honor a lord is different from the way to honor royalty; one way is less formal than the other. But here we can't tell the difference, as we are unaware of the degrees of nobility even among ourselves. As we don't understand the difference, we don't know the degrees of our own nobility.

Bodhidharma was a dharma heir, twenty-eight generations from Shakyamuni Buddha. After he attained the way, his importance increased. A great sage, the most venerable one, he followed his teacher's request to transmit dharma for saving beings and did not cling to his bodily life. In China they had not seen a buddha child, an authentic heir, nor had anyone received person-to-person transmission of the ancestral face. No one had met a buddha before Bodhidharma appeared. No buddhas other than his descendants emerged in China after that.

It is possible to meet the Buddha when the udumbara blossom is in bloom. People count the years looking forward to this. But the coming of the First Ancestor from India will never happen again. And yet those who call themselves descendants of the ancestors are like the one in the Kingdom of Chu who treasured an ordinary green stone, thinking it was jade. Unable to tell jade from stone, they think that teachers of sutras and treatises are equal to Bodhidharma. It is so because of their limited learning and shallow understanding. Those who do not recognize the authentic seed of prajna do not become descendants of the ancestral path. They wander around in the crooked paths of name and concept. How sad!

Even after the Putong Era of the Kingdom of Liang, there were monks who went to India. For what reason? It is quite stupid. Because of their unwholesome past actions, they wander around in a foreign land. Step by step they go on the crooked paths of slandering dharma. Step by step they go farther away from their parental land. What do they gain by arriving in India? They merely bear hardships traveling through mountains and waters. As they do not know the true meaning of teachings brought from India and buddha dharma transmitted eastward to China, they get lost in India.

Although they are supposed to seek for buddha dharma, they lack the right aspiration for buddha dharma, and so even in India they do not meet a true teacher, but only teachers of treatises and sutras. The reason for this is that although there are true teachers in India, seekers who lack the right mind to search for true dharma cannot find them. We have never heard of people who went to India and met true teachers. If they had done so, they would have spoken about it. But because they didn't go, they did not speak about it.

Also, in China there have been many monks who have depended upon sutras and treatises without seeking true dharma, even after Bodhidharma came from India. Although they read sutras and treatises, they are ignorant about the meaning of them. This dark activity comes not only from today's action but also from unwholesome actions of the past. In this lifetime they do not learn the true teaching of the Tathagata, are not illuminated by the face-to-face transmission of the Tathagata, do not actualize the buddha mind of the Tathagata, and do not listen to the wind of the house of all buddhas. It is regrettable.

There were many people like that in the Sui, Tang, and Song dynasties. But even if those who have once nurtured the seeds of prajna enter the gate unintentionally, they are freed from counting sands and become descendants of Bodhidharma. They are persons of excellent roots, the highest of the high, persons of good seeds, while those who are ignorant merely lodge forever in the huts of sutras and treatises.

Therefore, we should look up at the profound teaching that Bodhidharma brought from India without avoiding or abhorring the steep path. For what other purpose should we save our stinky skin bags?

Xiangyan said:

> Hundreds of plans, thousands of means,
> your body is dust in the tomb.
> Don't say white hair has no words.
> It is a message from the yellow springs [realm of death].

Thus, even if you make hundreds of plans and create thousands of means to save yourselves, in the end you will turn to dust in the tomb. Furthermore, driven by a king of a small nation and his retainers, you run around east and west, with thousands of hardships and myriad sufferings of body and mind. You give your life over to loyalty, even to the extent of following your king to the grave. A future driven by worldly obligations is clouds and mists of darkness. Many people since olden times have been occupied by minor pursuits and have given up their lives. Those human lives might have been saved, as they could have become vessels of the way.

Now that you have met the true dharma, study it even if you have to give up the lives of hundreds and thousands of kalpas. Why would you give up your life for worthless petty people instead of devoting yourself to the broad and profound buddha dharma? Neither those who are wise nor those who are not should hesitate in making this decision. Think quietly. When the true dharma is not spread, you cannot meet it even if you want to give up your life for it. Wish right now for the self that meets the true dharma. Be ashamed of the self that would not offer your life for the sake of the true dharma. If there is anything to be ashamed of, it is this.

This being so, to appreciate the great gift of Bodhidharma is the continuous practice of this day. Do not look back on your bodily life. Do not cling to worldly obligations and love that put you lower than birds and beasts. Even if you cling to that love, you cannot maintain it forever. Do not hold on to the house of the family that is like trash. Even if you retreat to that place, it cannot be your ultimate abode.

The wise buddha ancestors in olden times let go of the seven types of treasure and a thousand servants, leaving behind jeweled palaces and vermilion towers. They saw these luxuries as drool and manure. These actions by the ancient buddha ancestors exemplify their kindness.

Even a sick sparrow remembered the beneficence of someone who had cared for it, and presented a jade ring that carried a prediction of an auspicious future. A captured tortoise did not forget the beneficence of someone who helped release it, and exhibited its tortoise figure in all the seals the person commissioned. How sad that some with human faces lack the virtue of these creatures!

Your ability to see buddhas and hear dharma right now is the result of the compassionate continuous practice of each buddha ancestor. Without the one-to-one transmission of buddha ancestors, how could the dharma have reached us today? You should gratefully repay the beneficence of having received one phrase, one dharma. How much more beneficent is the unsurpassed great dharma, the treasury of the true dharma eye? How could you not repay it with gratitude? You should vow to surrender to this day your lifetimes, which could be as immeasurable as the sands of the Ganges.

Your corpse of a body, which is dedicated to dharma, should be revered with bows and offerings, generation after generation. Such a corpse is what devas and dragon kings respect, guard, and admire for the obvious reason. There has been a Brahman custom for a long time in India to sell and buy skulls, because people there revere the merit of the skulls of those who have practiced dharma. If you don't dedicate your bodily life to the way right now, the power of practicing dharma will not arrive. To fully engage without sparing your bodily life is to mature your practice of dharma. Then your skull will be revered. But who would bow to your skull if you do not dedicate yourself to the way? Who would want to sell or buy such a skull found in a field? You will be regretful when your spirit looks back to this day, if you do not dedicate yourself to the way.

A demon beat the bones of his own corpse for his unwholesome past actions, and a deva bowed to his own skeleton for his wholesome past actions. Thinking upon the time when your body will turn to dust or mud, you should care about the future generations without self-concern. Then, those who see your remains will be moved to tears. Even if you turn to dust or mud, leaving a skull that people might want to avoid, you will be very fortunate if you engage in continuous practice of the true buddha dharma.

Thus, do not fear the suffering from cold. Suffering from cold has never crushed the way. Only be concerned about not practicing. Lack of practice leaves a person divided and hinders the way. Do not be put off by the suffering from heat. Suffering from heat has never crushed the way. Only be concerned about not practicing. Lack of practice leaves a person divided and hinders the way.

The Buddha accepted an offering of barley for horses as food for himself. Sages of olden times lived on bracken in the mountains. These are excellent examples for both buddhas and laity. Do not be like a demon looking for blood or milk. A day of fully engaged activity is the continuous practice of all buddhas.

———————

Huike, who would later become Great Master Zhengzong Pujue, the Second Ancestor of China, was admired even by gods and demons. He was a teacher of high virtue, a broad-minded person, respected equally by monks and laypeople.

He lived long in the capital city of Luoyang and read widely. Such a person is rarely encountered. His understanding was high and his virtue weighty.

One day a spirit appeared in his dream and said to Huike, "This is not a place to stay if you want to harvest the fruit. The great road is not far away. You should go south."

The next day he had a piercing headache and asked his teacher, Zen Master Baojing of Mount Xiang near Luoyang, to help relieve it. Then a voice from the sky was heard, "This is not a usual headache. Your bones are being replaced."

Huike told Baojing about his dream. Taking a look at his head, which had the appearance of five peaks sticking out, Baojing said, "You have an auspicious appearance, which shows that you are destined to have realization. The spirit's message for you to go south must mean that Bodhidharma, the great practitioner of the Shaolin Temple, is your teacher."

The spirit who had spoken to Huike was the guardian deity for his endless practice of the way.

Following Baojing's instruction, Huike went to see Bodhidharma at Shaoshi Peak. It was a severely cold winter night, said to be the ninth day of the twelfth month. Even without heavy rain or snow, on such a winter night in the deep mountains it would be impossible for a person to stand outdoors. It was a horrendous season when bamboo cracked. A great snow covered the entire mountain. Huike searched in the snow for a trail. Who knows the extent of his hardship?

Finally Huike reached Bodhidharma's dwelling, but was not allowed to enter. Bodhidharma did not turn around. Throughout the night Huike did not sleep, sit, or rest. He stood firmly until dawn. The night snow seemed to have no mercy, piling higher and burying him up to his waist. Every drop of his tears froze. Seeing his frozen tears, he shed even more tears. Looking at his own body, he thought to himself, "A seeker in the past crushed his bones, extracted his marrow, and squeezed his blood to feed the starving people. Another seeker laid down his hair on the muddy road to let the Buddha pass. Another threw his body off the cliff to feed a tiger. They were like that. Then who am I?" Thus, his aspiration became stronger.

Those who study nowadays should not forget Huike's words *They were like that. Then who am I?* If we forget, we will drown for numberless kalpas. Thus, Huike addressed himself in this way, strengthening his aspiration for dharma. He did not mind being covered by snow. When we imagine the hair-raising ordeal of that long night, we are struck with terror.

At dawn Bodhidharma took notice and asked, "What do you seek? Why have you stood in the snow for so long?"

Shedding more tears, Huike said, "All I wish is that you compassionately open the gate of sweet dew in order to awaken many beings."

Bodhidharma said, "The unsurpassed, inconceivable way of all buddhas must be practiced hard and consistently for vast kalpas. You must bear what is unbearable. But if you wish with small virtue, small wisdom, and casual, arrogant mind for the true vehicle, you will toil in vain."

Then Huike was encouraged. Unnoticed by Bodhidharma, he took a sharp knife, cut off his left arm, and offered it to him.

Bodhidharma knew then that Huike was a dharma vessel, and said, "When buddhas first seek the way, they give up bodily form for the sake of dharma. Now that I see your determination, you are invited to pursue the way here."

Thus, Huike entered Bodhidharma's inner chamber, attending to him with great diligence for eight years. Huike was indeed an example and a great guide for humans and devas to follow. Such great diligence had not been heard of either in India or China. When it comes to "smiling," you should study Mahakashyapa. And when it comes to attaining the marrow, you should study Huike.

Reflecting quietly, we know that even if Bodhidharma had come from India thousands of times, without the continuous practice of Huike there would not be a great number of students and practitioners today. Now, as we see and hear the true dharma, we should express our gratitude to Huike. Most ways of expressing gratitude may miss the mark. Giving up the life of your body is not enough. A castle is not solid enough, as it can be taken by others or given away to a family. The life of the body can be given to impermanence, a lord, or a crooked way. Therefore, none of these are suitable offerings. Continuous practice, day after day, is the most appropriate way of expressing gratitude.

This means that you practice continuously, without wasting a single day of your life, without using it for your own sake. Why is it so? Your life is a fortunate outcome of continuous practice from the past. You should express your gratitude immediately. How sad and shameful to waste this body, which has benefited from the continuous practice of buddha ancestors, by becoming a slave of family, and surrendering to their vanities, without noticing the fall! Or, the body may be mistakenly given to that horrendous robber, the demon of fame and gain.

If ever you value fame and gain, then be compassionate to fame and gain. If you are compassionate to fame and gain, you will not allow them to break the body that can become a buddha ancestor. Being compassionate to family and relatives is also like this. Do not think that fame and gain are phantoms and illusions, but regard them as sentient beings. If you are not compassionate to fame and gain, you will accumulate unwholesome actions. The true eye of study should be like this.

Thoughtful people in the world express gratitude for receiving gold, silver, or rare treasures. They also express gratitude for receiving kind words. Who can forget the great gift of seeing and hearing the Tathagata's unsurpassable true dharma, being aware that this is itself a rare treasure of a lifetime? The bones and skulls of those who did not turn back from this continuous practice are enshrined in seven-treasure pagodas, receiving respect and offerings by humans and devas. When you become aware of such a great gift, you should attentively repay the mountain of benevolence, without allowing your life to disappear like a dewdrop on the grass. This is continuous practice. The power of this practice is that you yourself practice as an ancestral buddha.

The First and Second Chinese Ancestors did not found monasteries, so they were not occupied by grass cutting. Nor did the Third and Fourth Ancestors. Thus they remained free of administrative duties. The Fifth and Sixth Ancestors did not build their own monasteries. Neither did Qingyuan nor Nanyue.

———————

Shitou did zazen on a large rock where he had a thatched hut. He sat continuously without sleeping day and night. Although he did not ignore work, he did not fail to do zazen throughout the day. Nowadays the descendants of his teacher Qingyuan are spread throughout China, benefiting humans and devas. This is due to the great determination and solid, continuous practice of Shitou. The current Yunmen and Fayan lines are also descended from Shitou.

———————

When Daoxin, who would later become Zen Master Dayi, the Fourth Chinese Ancestor, was fourteen, he met Sengcan, the Third Chinese Ancestor, and then labored for nine years. After inheriting the authentic teaching of buddha ancestors, Daoxin kept his mind gathered and did not sleep with his side on the mat for almost sixty years. In his guidance he did not discriminate between enemies and friends, so his virtue prevailed among humans and devas.

In the sixteenth year of the Zhenguan Era [642], Emperor Tai, in admiration of Daoxin's flavor of the way, invited him to the capital, wishing to test the hue of his dharma. Daoxin respectfully declined three times, claiming ill health. At the fourth summons, the Emperor ordered the messenger to cut off Daoxin's head if he declined again. The messenger saw Daoxin and relayed the imperial order to him. With complete composure Daoxin stretched out his neck and made ready for the sword. Extremely impressed, the messenger went back to the capital and wrote a report to the Emperor, who admired Daoxin even more. He expressed his appreciation by sending Daoxin a gift of rare silk.

Thus, the continuous practice of Daoxin, who was not attached to his bodily life as bodily life and tried to avoid becoming intimate with kings and ministers, is something rarely encountered in a thousand years. Because Emperor Tai was a just king, Daoxin had nothing against him. The Emperor admired Daoxin because he did not spare his own bodily life and was willing to die. Daoxin focused on his continuous practice, not without reason but with respect for the passage of time. Compared with the current tendency in this declining age when many people try to find favor with the emperors, Daoxin's refusal of the three imperial requests is remarkable.

On the fourth day, the intercalary ninth month, the second year of the Yonghui Era [651] during the reign of Emperor Gao, Daoxin gave instruction to his students, saying, "All things are liberated. You should guard your mind and teach future generations."

After saying this, he sat at ease and passed away. He was seventy-two years old. A stupa was built for him on the mountain. On the eighth day of the fourth month of the following year, the door to the stupa opened of itself, and inside it, his body looked as if he were alive. After that his students kept the door open.

Know Daoxin's words: *All things are liberated.* It is not merely that all things are empty or all things are all things, but that all things are liberated. Daoxin had continuous practice before and after entering the stupa. To assume that all living beings die is a narrow view. To assume that the dead do not perceive is a limited idea. Do not follow these views when you study the way. There may be those who go beyond death. There may be dead people who perceive.

Xuansha, who would later become Great Master Zongyi, was from Min Prefecture, Fu Region. His family name was Xie and his dharma name was Shibei. He was fond of dropping a fishing line ever since he was little. Later he supported himself by fishing from a tiny boat on the River Nantai. At the beginning of the Xiantong Era [860–874] of the Tang Dynasty, when he was thirty, he had an urge to leave the dusty world. So he gave up his boat, went to see Furong, Zen Master Lingxun, and dropped his hair. He received the monk precepts from Precept Master Daoxuan of the Kaiyuan Monastery in Jiangnan. He wore a simple cotton robe and straw sandals, ate barely enough to sustain life, and sat zazen all day long. People thought him extraordinary.

Xuansha was originally a dharma brother of Xuefeng Yicun, but studied with him closely as a student. Xuefeng called him Ascetic Bei [Shibei] because of his rigorous practice.

One day Xuefeng asked, "Where is Ascetic Bei heading?"

Xuansha said, "He is not misleading anyone."

Later, Xuefeng called Xuansha and asked, "Why doesn't Ascetic Bei travel all around to study?"

Xuansha said, "Bodhidharma didn't come to China. The Second Ancestor didn't go to India."

Xuefeng approved his words.

When Xuefeng became abbot on Mount Xianggu, later called Mount Xuefeng, Xuansha accompanied him as his assistant. Because of their collaboration, many excellent students assembled in the monastery. Xuansha continued to enter the abbot's room to receive guidance from before dawn till late at night. Students who lacked decisive understanding would ask Xuansha to go with them to see Xuefeng. Sometimes Xuefeng would say to them, "Why don't you ask Ascetic Bei?" As caring as Xuefeng, Xuansha would not hesitate to respond to Xuefeng's request.

Without Xuansha's outstanding continuous practice, such dedication would not have been possible. The continuous practice of sitting zazen all day long is rare. While there are many who run around after sound and form, there are few who sit zazen all day long. Those of you who come later should fear wasting your remaining time and endeavor to sit zazen the whole day.

Changqing, Priest Huileng, was a revered teacher under Xuefeng. He visited and practiced with Xuefeng and Xuansha for almost twenty-nine years. During this time he wore out twenty sitting mats. Those who love zazen nowadays regard Changqing as an excellent ancient example.

There are many who long for him but few who measure up to him. His three-decade endeavor was not without results; he suddenly had great awakening when he was rolling up a bamboo shade.

He did not go back to his hometown to see his relations or chat with his fellow students for thirty years. He practiced single-mindedly and continuously, questioning over and over without negligence. What a sharp capacity! What a great root! We learn from sutras about those who have solid determination. But those of you who seek what should be sought and are ashamed of what should be ashamed of need to encounter Changqing. Unfortunately, there are many who do not have way-seeking mind, are poor in conduct, and are bound by fame and gain.

Guishan, who would later become Zen Master Dayuan, went to the steep and rocky Mount Gui immediately after receiving a confirmation of enlightenment from Baizhang. He mingled with birds and beasts, assembled a thatched hut, and tempered his practice. While living on acorns and chestnuts, he was not intimidated by storms or snow. Without temple or property, he actualized continuous practice for forty years. Later this place became a monastery renowned throughout China, where excellent practitioners like dragons and elephants came to follow in his footsteps.

If you vow to establish a temple, do not be swayed by human concerns, but maintain the strict continuous practice of buddha dharma. Where the practice is tempered, even without a [monks'] hall, is a place of enlightenment of old buddhas. The teaching given outdoors under a tree may be heard afar. Such a place can be a sacred domain for a long time. Indeed, the continuous practice of one person will merge with the place of the way of all buddhas.

Foolish people in this declining age are consumed with erecting magnificent temple buildings. Buddha ancestors have never wished for such temple buildings. You uselessly decorate the halls before you clarify your own eye. Rather than making offerings to buddhas, you are turning the house of all buddhas into a pitfall of fame and gain. Quietly ponder the continuous practice of the ancient Guishan. In order to do this, identify yourself with Guishan.

The sobbing rain of deep night pierces moss and pierces rock. On a snowy night of winter when even animals are rarely seen, how could the aromas from people's houses reach you? This kind of search is impossible without the continuous practice of taking your own life lightly and regarding dharma as precious. Without cutting grass or moving earth and lumber, Guishan was fully engaged in tempering practice of the way.

What a deep feeling we have for him! With what great determination the hardship was endured by the authentic heir transmitting the true dharma on the steep mountain! It is said about Mount Gui that there is a pond and a brook where ice accumulates and fog becomes dense. It is not an inviting place for retreat, but it is where Guishan's practice of the buddha way and the depth of the mountains were merged and renewed.

Continuous practice is not something we should take casually. If we do not repay the gift of the hardship of Guishan's continuous practice, how can we, who aspire to study, identify with him as if he were sitting in front of us? Due to the power and the guiding merit of his continuous practice, the wheel of air [a layer upon which the world is settled] is not upset, the world is not broken, the palace of devas is calm, and human lands are maintained.

Although we are not direct descendants of Guishan, he is an ancestor of the teaching. Later, Yangshan went to study and attend him. Yangshan, who had studied with Baizhang, was like Shariputra, who gave one hundred answers to ten questions. Attending Guishan, he spent three years watching over a buffalo. This kind of continuous practice has been cut off and not seen in recent years. Such a statement by Yangshan as "spending three years watching over a buffalo" cannot otherwise be heard.

———

Ancestor Daokai of Mount Furong is a true source of actualizing continuous practice. Offered a purple robe and the title of Zen Master Dingzhao by the Emperor, he did not accept them. His letter declining them upset the Emperor, but Daokai persisted in refusing these honors. When he had a hut on Mount Furong, hundreds of monks and laypeople gathered there. The flavor of his one daily bowl of watery gruel, which drove most of them away, is still talked about.

Once, Daokai vowed never to go to a feast and said to the assembly:

Home leavers should not avoid hardship. Seeking freedom from birth and death, rest your mind, stop worrying, and cut off dependence on relations. That's why you are called home leavers. How can you receive luxurious offerings and be immersed in ordinary life? You should cast off this, that, and everything in between. Regard whatever you see and hear as a flower planted on a rock. When you encounter fame and gain, regard them as a dust mote in your eye.

It is not that fame and gain haven't been experienced or known from beginningless time; rather they are like the head that cannot help seeing the tail. Why should you struggle and long for them? If you don't stop longing now, when will you? Thus, the ancient sages teach you to let go right at this very moment. If you do so, what will remain? If you attain calmness of mind, buddha ancestors will be like something extra and all the things in the world will be inevitably flameless and plain. Only then can you merge with the place of suchness.

Don't you see? Yinshan [Longshan] did not see anyone throughout his life. Zhaozhou did not speak one phrase throughout his life. Biandan picked acorns for his meals. Fachang made a robe of lotus leaves. Ascetic Zhiyi only wore paper. Senior Monk Xuantai only wore cotton. Shishuang Qingzhu built a hall and practiced with the assembly of those who sat like dead trees [without lying down]. What you need to do is let your mind perish.

Touzi Datong asked his students to wash the rice that he cooked together with them. Thus, what you need to do is to minimize your concerns. This is how the ancient sages encouraged themselves. Had they not thought their practices worthwhile, they would not have simplified their daily activities. Practitioners, if you have realization with your whole body, you will be a person of no lack. If you don't hit the mark, you will waste your effort.

Daokai continued:

I have become head of this monastery in spite of having achieved nothing worth mentioning. How can I sit on this seat and neglect the trust of the ancient sages? I want to follow the example of the teachers of old who were abbots of monasteries. After consulting with all of you, I have decided not to go out of the monastery, attend feasts, or ask for donations. We will divide one year's harvest from our fields into three-hundred-sixty-day portions and use them accordingly. But we will not reduce the number of monks in the assembly. When there is enough rice, we will cook rice. When there is not enough, we will make gruel by adding water. When there is less rice, we will make watery gruel. When we accept new monks, we will serve tea that is nothing special. Tea will be made ready in the tea room for all to serve themselves. We will do only what is essential, eliminating all the rest, in order to concentrate on the endeavor of the way.

Here, the livelihood is complete and the landscape is not dull. Flowers smile and birds sing. Wooden horses whine and stone oxen run. Green mountains far away are faint and spring water nearby is soundless. Monkeys on the mountain ridges chatter and dewdrops wet the midnight moon. Cranes caw in the forests and the winds swirl around the dawn pines. When spring wind rises, a dead tree roars like a dragon. At the time of falling leaves, the shivering forest scatters blossoms. The jewel steps delineate moss patterns. Human faces take on shades of mist. Sounds are serene. Remote from worldly affairs, this one taste is subtle—nothing in particular.

Today I am supposed to present the gate of the house to all of you. This is already off the track. Even so, I go on lecturing and giving instructions in the abbot's room. I take up a mallet and swing a whisk. I shout to the east and strike the west. My face grimaces as if I were having a seizure. I feel as if I were belittling you students and betraying the ancient sages.

Don't you see? Bodhidharma came from India, got to the foot of Shaoshi Peak, and faced the wall for nine years. Huike stood in the snow and cut off his arm. What hardship! Bodhidharma did not say a word and Huike did not ask a question. But can you call Bodhidharma a person of not doing? Can you regard Huike as not seeking a master? Whenever I speak about examples of ancient sages, I feel there is no place to hide. I am ashamed that we who come later are so soft and weak.

These days, people make offerings of a hundred flavors to others and say, "As I have fulfilled the four types of offerings to monks, I feel ready to arouse the aspiration for enlightenment." But I fear that such people do not know how to move their hands and legs, and will be separated from the reality of birth and death of the world. Time flies like an arrow and their regret may be deep.

There are times when others have awakened me with their merit. But I am not forcing you to follow my advice. Have you seen this verse by a teacher of old?

Rice without millet from fields in the mountains,
yellow pickled vegetables—
eat as you like.
Otherwise, leave it to east and west.
Please, fellow travelers, each of you make an effort.
Take care.

These words of Daokai are the bones and marrow of the ancestral school, transmitted person to person. Although there are many examples of Daokai's continuous practice, I am only presenting this talk. Those of us who come after Daokai should long for and study the continuous practice he tempered on Mount Furong. It was the genuine form and spirit of Shakyamuni Buddha at Jeta Grove.

———————

Mazu, who would later become Zen Master Daji of the Kaiyuan Monastery, Hong Region, Jiangxi, was from Shifang Prefecture, Han Region. His priest name is Daoyi. He studied with Nanyue and was his attendant for over ten years. Once he was about to visit his hometown and got halfway there but turned around and went back to the monastery. When he returned, he offered incense and bowed to Nanyue, who wrote a verse for him:

> Let me advise you not to go home.
> At home the way is not practiced.
> Old women in the neighborhood
> would call you by your childhood name.

Respectfully receiving these dharma words, Mazu made a vow not to go in the direction of Han Region in this or any other lifetime. Not taking one step closer to his old home, Mazu stayed in Jiangxi and traveled all over the region. Other than speaking of "Mind itself is buddha," he did not give any words of guidance. However, he was an authentic heir of Nanyue, a life vein for humans and devas.

What is the meaning of *not to go home*? How does one not go home? Returning to east, west, south, or north is no more than the falling and rising of the self. Indeed, the way is not practiced by going home. Practice continuously, examining whether the way is practiced or not, either by going home or not going home. Why is the way not practiced by going home? Is the way hindered by not practicing? Is it hindered by the self?

Nanyue did not say, "Old women in the neighborhood might call you by your childhood name." But he did say, *Old women in the neighborhood would call you by your childhood name.* Why did he say so? Why did Mazu accept these dharma words? Because when you go south, the earth goes south. Other directions are also like this. It is a narrow view to deny this point by seeing Mount Sumeru or the great ocean as merely large and separate from you, or to miss this point by using the sun, the moon, and stars as a measure for comparison.

———

Hongren, who would later become the Fifth Chinese Ancestor, Zen Master Daman, was a man from Huangmei. His lay name was Zhou, after his mother's family. Like Laozi [Lao-tzu], he was born without a father. From age seven, when he received transmission of dharma, until age seventy-four, he maintained the treasury of the true dharma eye of buddha ancestors. During this time he discreetly entrusted the robe of dharma to Laborer Huineng [the Sixth Ancestor]. Hongren's was an incomparable continuous practice. Because he did not bring forth the robe of dharma for [his most learned student] Senior Monk Shenxiu but entrusted it to Laborer Huineng, the life of the true dharma has not been cut off.

———

Rujing, my late master, Priest Tiantong, was from Yue. At age nineteen he abandoned scriptural studies and engaged in practice, and he did not turn around even at age seventy. When offered a purple robe with the title of master from the Emperor Ning in the Jiading Era [1208–1224], he sent a letter politely declining it. Monks in the ten directions respected him for his action and those, both near and far, who were knowledgeable rejoiced over it. The Emperor was extremely impressed and sent him an offering of tea. Those who heard of this admired it as something rare at the time. Rujing's action is indeed a genuine continuous practice.

I say this because loving fame is worse than breaking a precept.

Breaking a precept is a transgression at a particular time. Loving fame is like an ailment of a lifetime. Do not foolishly hold on to fame, or do not ignorantly accept it. Not to accept fame is continuous practice. To abandon it is continuous practice.

The titles of master for the first six ancestors were all given posthumously by emperors. These ancestors did not receive their titles out of love of fame. Likewise, you should give up love of fame within birth and death, and simply wish for the continuous practice of buddha ancestors. Do not be like devouring creatures. To greedily love the self, which is of slight significance, doesn't take you above the level of creatures and beasts. To abandon fame and gain is rare for humans and devas, but all buddha ancestors have done so.

Some say, "I seek fame and love gain for the benefit of sentient beings." This is a greatly mistaken view held by heretics within the buddha dharma, as well as by a troop of demons who slander the true dharma. Does this view mean that the buddha ancestors who do not seek fame and gain are unable to benefit sentient beings? What a laugh! What a laugh! Not-seeking can benefit beings. How is it so? Those who, without understanding this, promote what is not beneficial as beneficial are a troop of demons. Sentient beings helped by such demons are bound for hell. Such demons should deplore that their lives are in darkness. Do not regard such ignorant ones as beneficent beings.

Thus, declining the offer of a title of master has been an excellent custom since olden times. This is something that those of us in later generations should fully understand. To see Rujing in person was to meet that person.

Leaving home at nineteen, looking for a teacher, Rujing engaged in the endeavor of the way, without retreating or turning around. Until the age of sixty-five he still had not become close to or even seen an emperor, nor become intimate with ministers or government officials. Not only did he not accept a purple robe, he did not wear any brocade throughout his life. He only wore a black kashaya and a combined robe for formal talks and for giving instruction in the abbot's room.

Instructing the monks, Rujing said:

For the practice of Zen in pursuit of the way, maintaining the mind of the way is primary. It is deplorable that the ancestral way has declined in the last two hundred years. There have been few skin bags who have expressed a phrase of understanding.

At the time when I hung my walking staff at Mount Jing, Fuzhao Deguang was abbot. He said in his dharma talk, "Studying buddha dharma, the path of Zen, you should not look for phrases by others. Each of you should have your own understanding." Thus, he did not oversee the monks' hall and did not guide the many monks who were studying there. Instead, he spent his time entertaining visiting dignitaries. Not understanding the working of buddha dharma, he was simply greedy for name and loved gain.

If it were enough to merely have our own understanding of buddha dharma, why have there always been determined old gimlets who traveled around looking for teachers? Indeed, Deguang had not yet mastered Zen. Nowadays, the elders of monasteries in various places are just like Deguang with their lack of way-seeking mind. How can they hold buddha dharma in their hands? It is regrettable, indeed!

Although Rujing said this to the assembly that included many of Deguang's students, none of them were resentful.

Rujing also said, "To practice Zen is to drop away body and mind. You can actualize it by just sitting, without relying on burning incense, bowing, chanting Buddha's name, repentance, or reading sutras."

In Song China, there are a great many skin bags, not merely hundreds, who regard themselves as Zen practitioners, calling themselves descendants of the ancestral school. But those who encourage just sitting as just sitting are rarely heard of. Within the country of Four Seas and Five Lakes [China], Rujing was the only one. Elders all over admired him, even though he did not admire them. But there are also leaders of large temples who do not know of him. Although born in China, they are like a herd of beasts. They have not studied what they should have studied, while merely wasting the passage of time. What a pity! Those who do not know about Rujing mistakenly regard idle chatter and confused talk as the teaching style of buddha ancestors.

Rujing sometimes said in his talk in the dharma hall:

Since I was nineteen, I have visited monasteries all over but have not met teachers to guide humans. Since then, I have not spent even one day or night without covering a zazen cushion. Since I became abbot,

I have not chatted with people from my hometown. This is because I feel urgent about the passing of time. I have always stayed in the building where I hung my walking stick, without going to visit other huts or dormitories of the monastery. How could I spend time enjoying the mountainside or admiring waterscapes?

I have been doing zazen not only in the monks' hall and other communal places, but also alone in quiet towers and screened-in places. I always carry a cushion so I can sit at the foot of a rock. My hope has been to thoroughly penetrate the diamond seat. Sometimes my buttocks get raw, but still I sit harder.

I am now sixty-five. Although my bones are aged and my head is dull, I don't yet understand zazen. But, because I care about my fellow practitioners in the ten directions, I live in this monastery and transmit the way to the assembly, beginning with dawn instruction. I do this because I wonder, where is the buddha dharma among the elders of other places?

He spoke in this way on a teaching seat. Also, Rujing would not accept gifts from monks who arrived from other places.

Superintendent Zhao, a grandson of Emperor Ning, who was a commanding military officer and agricultural administrator of Ming Region, invited Rujing to the capital to give a dharma talk. At that time Zhao presented ten thousand silver coins to him. Rujing thanked him and said, "I have come to give a customary lecture on the treasury of the true dharma eye, wondrous heart of nirvana. I am dedicating the merit to the well-being of your late father. But I will not accept the silver coins. Monks have no need of these things. I greatly appreciate your kindness, but as usual I must decline your offer."

Zhao said, "Master, as a relative of His Imperial Majesty, I am respected everywhere and I have wealth. On this memorial day of my late father I would like to give him support in another world. Why can't you accept my offering? I feel greatly fortunate to have you here today. With your great compassion and great kindness, please accept my humble gift."

Rujing said, "Your Excellency, your request cannot be refused. But I have a question. When I expounded dharma, did you understand it?"

Zhao said, "I was simply delighted to hear it."

Rujing said, "You are brilliantly illuminating my words. I am honored. I just wish for the happiness of your late father, who was invoked today. Please explain to me what I said in my discourse. If you can, I will accept the silver. If you cannot, then please keep it for yourself."

Zhao said, "When I think about it, your composure and movement were excellent."

Rujing said, "That's what I did. How about what you heard?"

Zhao hesitated.

Rujing said, "Your late father's happiness is already fulfilled. Your gift should be left to his decision." Thus he bade farewell.

Zhao said, "I regret that you did not accept my offering. But I rejoice in seeing you." So saying, Zhao saw Rujing off.

Monks and laity on both sides of the Zhe River [Zhejiang Province] admired Rujing. This was recorded in the journal of Attendant Monk Ping, who said, "An old master like this is hard to meet. Where else could we possibly find someone so accomplished?"

Who in any direction would decline the offering of ten thousand blocks of silver? A teacher of old said, "Gold, silver, and jewels should be regarded as excrement. Even if you see them as gold and silver, it is customary for monks not to accept them." Rujing followed this teaching; others did not. He would often say, "In the past three hundred years there have been few teachers like myself. Therefore, it is imperative that you practice diligently with me in the endeavor of the way."

In his assembly there was someone called Daosheng from Mian Region in Shu, who was a Daoist. A party of five practitioners including him made a vow: "We will master the great way of buddha ancestors in our lifetime. We will not go back to our hometowns until we do."

Rujing was delighted with their vow and allowed them to join walking and sitting meditation with the assembly. In the order of seating, he placed them right after the nuns [presumably a low-status position]. It was rare for Daoists to practice in a Zen monastery like this.

Also, a monk called Shanru from Fu Region made a vow: "I will not take a step toward my home in the south, but will single-mindedly study the great way of buddha ancestors." I personally witnessed many students like this in Rujing's assembly. There are few like them in the assemblies of other masters. The continuous practice at Rujing's assembly was outstanding amongst monks of Great Song China. Those who do not aspire to practice as they did should be sorrowful. Even when we meet the buddha dharma, we don't necessarily respond to it. How much less fortunate is our body and mind if we don't meet the buddha dharma at all!

Think quietly. Life does not last long. To realize even a few lines of the buddha ancestors' words is to realize the buddha ancestors. How is this so? Since buddha ancestors are body and mind as one, one phrase or two are the buddha ancestors' warm body-mind. Their body-mind comes forth and realizes your body-mind. At the very moment of realization, this realization comes forth and realizes your body-mind. This life realizes the life of many lifetimes. By becoming a buddha and becoming an ancestor, you go beyond buddha and go beyond ancestor.

———————

Accounts of continuous practice are like this. Do not run around after fame and gain in the realm of sound and form. Not to run around is the continuous practice that has been transmitted person to person by buddha ancestors. Mature hermits, beginning hermits, one person, or half a person, I ask you to throw away myriad matters and conditions, and to continuously practice the continuous practice of buddha ancestors.

Written at the Kannondori Kosho Horin Monastery, on the fifth day, the fourth month, the third year of the Ninji Era [1243].

32

OCEAN MUDRA SAMADHI

B<small>UDDHAS AND ANCESTORS</small> continuously maintain ocean mudra [form] samadhi. While swimming in this samadhi, they expound, realize, and practice. Traveling through water includes journeying along the ocean bottom. This is called "coursing along the bottom of the deepest ocean."

This ocean differs from the sea of birth and death where buddhas vow to guide beings drifting in birth and death to the shore of liberation. Each buddha ancestor breaks through the bamboo node [intellectual thinking] and passes the barrier individually; this is done only through the power of the ocean mudra samadhi.

———

The Buddha said:

Elements come together and form this body. At the time of appearing, elements appear. At the time of disappearing, elements disappear. When elements appear, I do not say "I" appear. When elements disappear, I do not say "I" disappear. Past moments and future moments do not arise sequentially. Past elements and future elements do not arise in alignment. This is the meaning of ocean mudra samadhi.

Closely investigate these words by the Buddha. Attaining the way and entering realization do not necessarily require extensive learning or explanation. Anyone can attain the way through a simple verse of four lines. Even scholars with extensive knowledge can enter realization through a one-line verse. But these words by the Buddha are not about searching for original enlightenment or gaining initial enlightenment. Although buddhas and ancestors manifest original or initial enlightenment, original or initial enlightenment is not buddha ancestors.

At the very moment of ocean mudra samadhi, elements come together and the Buddha's words *elements come together* are manifested. This is the moment of *form this body*.

This body is a coming together of elements. It is not merely a coming together; it is elements coming together. A body formed in this way is described as *this body*.

The Buddha said, *At the time of appearing, elements appear.* This appearing does not leave any mark of appearing; therefore, appearing does not enter one's perception or knowledge. Thus, the Buddha said, *I do not say "I" appear.* It is not that there is someone else who perceives or thinks that the person appears; it is just that you see beyond, and you drop away your initial understanding.

As the time [of ocean mudra samadhi] is not other than appearing, appearing is the arrival of time. What is it that appears? Appearing appears. Because appearing is time, appearing does not fail to fully manifest skin, flesh, bones, and marrow. As appearing is a coming together, appearing is this body, appearing is *"I" appear,* appearing is all elements coming together. What appears is not merely sound and form. All elements appear as *"I" appear* and as *I do not say "I" appear.*

Not say is not "not expressing," because expressing is not saying. The time of appearing [in ocean mudra samadhi] is when elements appear, which is not the same as the twelve hours of the day [ordinary time]. All elements are the time of appearing, not the time when the three realms appear.

An ancient buddha said, "Fire appears all of a sudden."

Fire here means elements appear together but are not sequential.

An ancient buddha said, "What about the moment when appearing and disappearing continue endlessly?"

Appearing and disappearing continue endlessly while self appears and disappears. Reflect on the words *continue endlessly* and let them continue endlessly. Allow the moments of appearing and disappearing to continue and discontinue as the life stream of buddha ancestors.

The moment when appearing and disappearing continue endlessly is "What appears and disappears?" This means "With this body I awaken beings," "Now I manifest this body," "I expound dharma," "Past mind is unattainable," "You have attained my marrow," "You have attained my bones." This is "What appears and disappears?"

———————

[The Buddha said,] *When elements disappear, I do not say "I" disappear.* The moment when *I do not say "I" disappear* is the moment when elements disappear. What disappears are elements disappearing. Although disappearing, they are elements. Because they are elements, they are not affected by delusion. Because they are not affected by delusion, they are not divided. This undividedness is all buddhas and ancestors. In the words [spoken by Huineng], "You are like this," what is not *you*? All past moments and all future moments are *you*. When he said, "I am like this," what is not *I*? Past moments and future moments are all *I*.

Disappearing has been magnificently expressed as countless hands and eyes [of Avalokiteshvara Bodhisattva]. It is unsurpassable nirvana. It is called death. It is called freedom from attachment. It is called the abiding place.

Hands and eyes are expressions of disappearing. Not saying *I* at the moment of appearing and not saying *I* at the moment of disappearing appear together, but do not disappear at the same time. There are past elements that disappear and future elements that disappear. There are elements that are moments in the past and elements that are moments in the future. Being is past and future elements. Being is past and future moments. Things that are not sequential are being. Things that are not aligned are being.

Talking about things that are not sequential and not aligned explains eight or nine out of ten. To regard the four great elements and five skandhas as the hands and eyes of disappearing is to take them up and pursue understanding. To see four great elements and five skandhas as the path of disappearing is going beyond, encountering reality. The entire body is hands and eyes, not lacking anything. The full range of the body is hands and eyes, not lacking anything. Disappearing is the activity of buddha ancestors.

While the Buddha says *not sequential* and *not aligned,* nevertheless appearing arises in the beginning, middle, and end. This may be seen as officially not allowing a needle, but unofficially permitting carriages and horses to pass.

In the beginning, middle, and end, disappearing is neither sequential nor aligned. Although elements appear *all of a sudden* where past elements disappeared, it is not that disappearing turns into appearing, but that elements appear. Because elements appear completely, they are neither sequential nor aligned. It does not mean that disappearings succeed disappearings or are aligned with disappearings. Disappearing is complete disappearing in the beginning, middle, and end. Disappearing meets disappearing, with nothing taken away; the entire mind knows there is disappearing.

Although elements disappear *all of a sudden* where past elements appeared, it is not that appearing turns into disappearing, but that elements disappear. Because elements disappear completely, they are neither sequential nor aligned.

Whether it is just appearing or just disappearing, in ocean mudra samadhi, all elements are as they are. It is not that there is no practice and realization, it is just that they are not divided. This is called ocean mudra samadhi.

Samadhi is actualization; it is expression. It is the time of night when a hand is reaching back, groping for a pillow. When the hand reaches back for a pillow at night, this groping is not limited to thousands and millions of eons, but is [as the Buddha says in the *Lotus Sutra*] "I am always in the ocean expounding the wondrous *Lotus Sutra*."

The Buddha said, *I do not say "I" appear.* This means, *I am always in the ocean.* From his front side the Buddha always teaches, "When one wave moves, thousands of waves follow." From his back he teaches the *Lotus Sutra,* expounding "When thousands of waves move, one wave follows."

Even if you cast a one-thousand-foot or a ten-thousand-foot fishing line, regrettably it only goes straight down. Both front and back spoken of here are *I am in the ocean*. They are just like the front and back of the head. The front and back of the head means placing one head on top of another.

It is not that there is a person *in the ocean*. The ocean of "I am in the ocean" is not an abode of people in the world. It is not where sages love to be. It is just "I am alone in the ocean." Thus, the Buddha said, *I am always in the ocean expounding*.

This ocean does not belong to inside, outside, or in-between. It is just *I am always expounding the Lotus Sutra*. The Buddha does not abide in the east, west, south, or north. The whole boat is empty; it returns full of moonlight. This return is a true place of settling. Who could call it stagnant water? It is actualized in the ultimate dimensions of the buddha dharma. This is called the mudra of water mudra.

Let me speak further. It is the mudra of emptiness. It is the mudra of mud. The water mudra of water is not necessarily the mudra of ocean. Going beyond is the mudra of ocean mudra. This is called ocean mudra, water mudra, mud mudra, and mind mudra. By transmitting the mind mudra, you mudra [form] water, you mudra mud, you mudra emptiness.

———————

Caoshan, Great Master Yuanzheng, was asked by a monk, "From the scriptures we learn that an ocean does not retain corpses. What is the ocean?"

Caoshan said, "That which contains myriad things."

The monk said, "The ocean does not keep corpses. Why?"

Caoshan said, "Those who have stopped breathing do not remain as they are."

The monk said, "The ocean contains myriad things, but those who have stopped breathing do not remain as they are. Why?"

Caoshan said, "Myriad things stop breathing when they don't function anymore."

Caoshan, a dharma brother of Yunju, was right on the mark of Dongshan's teaching. *From the scriptures we learn* refers to the correct teaching of buddha ancestors. It is not the teaching of ordinary sages, nor is it a lesser teaching of the buddha dharma.

The ocean that *does not retain corpses* is not the open water, an enclosed sea, or even one of the Eight Seas. This is not what the monk asked Caoshan. The monk understands what is not the ocean as the ocean, but also understands the ocean as the ocean.

A sea is not the ocean. The ocean is not necessarily an abyss of water with eight powers or nine trenches of salt water; the ocean is where all elements come together. It is not limited to deep water. This being so, the monk's question *What is the ocean?* refers to an ocean that is not known by humans and devas. The one who asked this question wanted to shake up fixed views.

Not retaining corpses is [as Puhua said], "When brightness arises, meet it with brightness; when darkness arises, meet it with darkness." A corpse is as indestructible as ash, meaning [as Fachang said], "through countless springs, there is no change of mind." A corpse such as this has not been seen before; therefore it is unknown.

Caoshan's words *That which contains myriad things* indicates the deep ocean. The point of his words is not about one thing that contains myriad things but about just containing myriad things. He did not merely mean that the deep ocean contains myriad things, but that what contains myriad things is nothing other than the deep ocean.

Recognized or not, myriad things are just myriad things. Encountering the buddha face and the ancestor face is nothing other than fully recognizing myriad things as myriad things. Because myriad things are all-inclusive, you do not merely stand atop the highest peak or travel along the bottom of the deepest ocean. Being all-inclusive is just like this; letting go is just like that. What is called the ocean of buddha nature or Vairochana's ocean storehouse is just myriad things. Although the ocean surface is invisible, there is no doubt about the practice of swimming in it.

Duofu described a grove of bamboo as "one or two stalks are bent and three or four stalks are leaning." Although he referred to myriad things, why did he not say, "One thousand or ten thousand stalks are bent"? Why did he not say, "one thousand or ten thousand groves"? Do not forget that a grove of bamboo is like that. This is what is meant by Caoshan's words *That which contains myriad things.*

The monk's statement, *Those who have stopped breathing do not remain as they are. Why?* appears to be a question, but it is actually an understanding of what it is. When doubt arises, just encounter doubt. In investigating thusness, the monk said, *Those who have stopped breathing do not remain as they are. Why?* and *The ocean does not retain corpses. Why?* This is the meaning of his words: *The ocean contains myriad things, but those who have stopped breathing do not remain as they are. Why?* Know that containing does not allow things to remain as they are. Containing is not-retaining. Even if myriad things were nothing but corpses, for ten thousand years the ocean would never retain them unchanged. The old monk, who does not remain the same, makes his move.

Caoshan's words, *Myriad things stop breathing when they don't function anymore* mean that even if myriad things do or do not stop breathing, they do not remain as they are. Even if corpses are corpses, the practice of being one with myriad things should be able to contain them; the practice should be all-containing. In the past and future of myriad things, there is a function that goes beyond not-breathing.

This is the blind leading the blind. The meaning of the blind leading the blind is that a blind one leads a blind one [teacher and student merge]; blind ones lead blind ones. When blind ones lead blind ones, all things are contained. Containing contains all things.

In the great way of going beyond, no endeavor is complete without being one with myriad things. This is ocean mudra samadhi.

Written at the Kannondori Kosho Horin Monastery on the twentieth day, the fourth month, the third year of the Ninji Era [1242].

33

CONFIRMATION

THE GREAT WAY uniquely transmitted by buddhas and ancestors is confirmation. Those who have not studied buddhas and ancestors have never dreamed of it.

At the time of confirmation, even those who have not aroused the aspiration for enlightenment are confirmed. Those with no buddha nature are confirmed; those with buddha nature are confirmed. Body is confirmed, no-body is confirmed. All buddhas are confirmed. All buddhas maintain the confirmation of all buddhas.

Do not assume that you become a buddha after attaining confirmation; do not suppose that you attain confirmation after becoming a buddha. At the time of confirmation there is becoming a buddha; at the time of confirmation there is practice.

Accordingly, all buddhas have confirmation; buddhas going beyond buddhas have confirmation. The self is confirmed. Body and mind are confirmed. When you complete study and fully understand confirmation, you fulfill your study and fully understand the buddha way.

Before having the body, there is confirmation. After having the body, there is confirmation. There is confirmation that is recognized by the self, and there is confirmation that is not recognized by the self. There is confirmation recognized by others, and there is confirmation not recognized by others.

Know that confirmation actualizes the self. Confirmation is the self of actualization. Thus, what has been directly transmitted between buddha and buddha, between ancestor and ancestor, is none other than confirmation. There is not a single thing that is not confirmation. How can it be otherwise for mountains, rivers, earth, Mount Sumeru, or great oceans? There is not one, or a half of the third child of Zhang, or the fourth child of Li [an ordinary person] who is without confirmation.

Confirmation studied thoroughly in this way is speaking one phrase, hearing one phrase; beyond understanding of one phrase, understanding of one phrase; practicing and discoursing. Confirmation causes walking backward, walking forward. Sitting and wearing a robe at this moment could not be actualized without authentic confirmation. Because actualizing is putting the robe on your head and joining your palms together, actualizing is confirmation.

The Buddha said:

There are many kinds of confirmation. Briefly speaking, there are eight kinds: confirmation known to oneself but not to others; confirmation known to everyone but not to oneself; confirmation known to oneself and everyone; confirmation not known to oneself or to anyone else; confirmation recognized by those who are nearby but not by those who are distant; confirmation recognized by those distant but not by those nearby; confirmation recognized by both those nearby and those distant; and confirmation recognized by neither those nearby nor those distant.

Thus, do not think that confirmation is only known to the spirit of this present skin-bag body. Do not say that a person who is not enlightened should not be easily confirmed. It is usually thought in the world that a person is confirmed when the merit of the practice is complete and becoming a buddha is determined; but it is not so in the buddha way. Following a master and hearing one phrase, or following a sutra and learning one phrase, is itself attaining confirmation, because it is the original practice of all buddhas and because it is a wholesome root of a hundred grasses.

When confirmation is expressed, those who attain confirmation are all people in the ultimate realm. Know that even one particle of dust is unsurpassable; even one particle of dust is going beyond itself. How could confirmation not be one particle of dust? How could confirmation not be one thing? How could confirmation not be myriad things? How could confirmation not be practice and enlightenment? How could confirmation not be buddhas and ancestors? How could confirmation not be pursuit and endeavor of the way? How could confirmation not be great enlightenment and great delusion?

Confirmation is "When my essential teaching reaches you, it will vigorously rise in the world." Confirmation is "You are like this; I am like this." Confirmation is a guidepost. Confirmation is beyond your knowledge. Confirmation is the face breaking into a smile. Confirmation is the coming and going of birth and death.

Confirmation is the entire world of the ten directions. Confirmation is "The whole world is not hidden."

Xuansha, who would later be Great Master Zongyi, once accompanied Xuefeng. Xuefeng pointed to the ground in front of him and said, "This piece of rice field would be a good spot for a seamless tower."

Xuansha said, "How high would it be?"

Xuefeng just looked up and down.

Xuansha said, "You do not lack the meritorious reward of human and heavenly beings. However, master, you have not dreamed of the confirmation on Vulture Peak."

Xuefeng said, "How about you?"

Xuansha said, "Seven or eight feet."

Xuansha's words *However, master, you have not dreamed of the confirmation on Vulture Peak* do not mean that Xuefeng was not confirmed on Vulture Peak, nor do they mean that Xuefeng was confirmed on Vulture Peak. It means that Xuefeng has not dreamed of the confirmation on Vulture Peak.

The confirmation on Vulture Peak is said from a lofty perspective. It is "I have the treasury of the true dharma eye, the wondrous heart of nirvana. I now entrust it to Mahakashyapa."

———————

Know that in the simultaneous practice of the moment when Qing-yuan confirms Shitou, Mahakashyapa is also comfirmed by Qingyuan. Qingyuan also gives Shakyamuni confirmation. So, it is clear that for each buddha and ancestor there is entrustment of the treasury of the true dharma eye.

In this way Huineng confirmed Qingyuan. When Qingyuan is confirmed by Huineng, Qingyuan becomes Qingyuan by this confirmation. At this moment, the practice of Huineng and other ancestors is directly actualized and realized by Qingyuan's confirmation. This is called "One hundred grasses are bright and clear, buddha ancestors' minds are bright and clear." This being so, how can buddha ancestors not be one hundred grasses? How can one hundred grasses not be you or myself?

Do not stupidly assume that what you have is always known to you, or seen by you. It is not so. Things you know are not necessarily your possessions. Your possessions are not necessarily what you see or what you know. Therefore, do not consider that whatever diverges from your knowledge or thought is not your possession. In particular, *confirmation on Vulture Peak* means Shakyamuni Buddha's confirmation. This confirmation has been confirmed to Shakyamuni Buddha by Shakyamuni Buddha. Someone who is not in accord with this way is not confirmed.

There is no hindrance in confirming someone who is already confirmed, and nothing extra is added in confirming someone who has not been confirmed. Having nothing lacking or extra is the way all buddha ancestors are confirmed by all buddha ancestors.

———————

In this regard, an ancient buddha said:

> From olden times to now, raising the whisk
>   clarifies east and west.
> The great meaning is subtle and not easy to grasp.
> Without a teacher transmitting it,
>   what profound words can you see?

In studying Xuansha's asking the height of the seamless tower, there needs to be an answer to, *How high would it be*? It was not five hundred or eighty thousand *yojana*. Nor did it exclude looking up and down.

Xuansha said, *You do not lack the meritorious reward of human and heavenly beings*. But showing the height of the seamless tower by looking up and down is not Shakyamuni Buddha's confirmation. To attain Shakyamuni Buddha's confirmation is to say, *Seven or eight feet*. To examine Shakyamuni Buddha's true confirmation is accomplished by the words *Seven or eight feet*.

Whether the words *Seven or eight feet* are right or not, confirmation was accomplished by Xuefeng, and confirmation was accomplished by Xuansha. Still further, you should bring up the confirmation and speak of the height of the seamless tower. To speak about buddha dharma by bringing up what is not confirmation is not true expression.

When the self understands, hears, and speaks the true self, invariably the fundamental point is actualized by confirmation. Confirmation itself brings forth the effort that is manifested simultaneously with confirmation. In order to fully actualize confirmation, countless buddhas and ancestors have realized authentic awakening. The power realized by confirmation brings forth all buddhas. For this reason it is said, "Only because of one great matter [all buddhas] appear." The meaning is that, while going beyond, no-self never fails to attain confirmation of no-self. In this way, all buddhas attain confirmation of all buddhas.

Now, confirmation is given and accepted by raising one hand, raising two hands, raising one thousand hands and eyes. Confirmation is actualized by taking up an udumbara blossom or a brocade robe. These are not forced but are natural activities of confirmation. There is confirmation attained from inside, confirmation attained from outside. For thoroughly studying the meaning of inside and outside, study about confirmation. Study of the way of confirmation is one rod of iron ten thousand miles long. Sitting like a rock in confirmation is one moment that is myriad years.

An ancient buddha said, "Successively attaining buddhahood, [buddhas] continuing to confirm."

Attaining buddhahood spoken of here is always *successively*. As part of *successively* you attain buddhahood. Confirmation turns this *attaining buddhahood*. This turning keeps on continuously, moving on to the next turning. It continues happening. This happening is making. This making is not the making of a limited body, a limited situation, a limited thought, or a limited mind.

Thoroughly investigate making or not making a situation in terms of turning. Thoroughly investigate making or not making in terms of turning.

All buddhas and ancestors who appear now are turned by making. The coming of the five buddhas and six ancestors from India has been turned by making.

Furthermore, drawing water and carrying firewood have been turned. The appearance of "mind itself is buddha" has been turned. The pari-nirvana of "mind itself is buddha" is not just one or two rare pari-nirvanas. Make countless pari-nirvanas countless pari-nirvanas. Make countless attainings of the way countless attainings of the way. Make countless forms of the Buddha countless forms of the Buddha. This is successively attaining buddhahood and successively attaining pari-nirvana. It is successively attaining confirmation, successively attaining turning.

Turning is not originally existent, but just seven penetrations and eight masteries. To see and meet each face of the buddhas and ancestors is *successively*. Even if you try to escape, there is no gap in the turning of buddhas and ancestors' confirmation.

————————

An ancient buddha said, "I now hear from the Buddha about the magnificent confirmation and about receiving it continuously; my body and mind fully rejoice."

Magnificent confirmation is always *I now hear from the Buddha*. *Receiving it continuously* is *my body and mind fully rejoice*. *Continuously* means *I now*. It is not concerned with self and other in the past, present, and future. It is just *hearing from the Buddha* and not hearing from others. It is not delusion or enlightenment, not sentient beings, not grass, trees, or countries, but it is hearing from the Buddha. It is magnificent confirmation. It is continuously receiving.

Continuously means not to stay in one spot even for a moment, but to have body and mind fully rejoicing. *Receiving it continuously* and *rejoice* are no other than studying simultaneously and all-inclusively with the body, studying simultaneously and all-inclusively with the mind. Furthermore, body is inclusive of mind, and mind is inclusive of body. Therefore, it is called inclusive body and mind. This is all-inclusive world, all-inclusive direction, all-inclusive body, all-inclusive mind. This is extraordinary oneness of rejoicing. When this rejoicing lets people clearly rejoice in sleeping and waking, or in delusion and enlightenment, this rejoicing is intimate with each of them but not separate from any of them. For this reason, this is the magnificent confirmation that is received continuously.

———————

Shakyamuni Buddha said to eighty-thousand mahasattvas through Bhaishajyaraja Bodhisattva:

> Bhaishajyaraja, if you look at countless devas, dragon kings, yakshas, gandharvas, asuras, garudas, kinnaras, mahoragas, humans, nonhumans, monks, nuns, laymen, and laywomen in this great assembly, there are those who seek to be shravakas, pratyeka-buddhas, or buddhas. Among such beings, if there are those who come in front of the Buddha who hear one verse or phrase of the *Sutra of Wondrous Dharma Blossoms,* and are delighted even for a moment, I will confirm them all equally, and they will attain unsurpassable, complete enlightenment.

Thus, even though those who are assembled—deva kings, dragon kings, four or eight types of beings—have different pursuits and understanding, who hears a line of verse that is not the inconceivable dharma? How can your thought, *even for a moment* delight in other teachings? *Such beings* means dharma-blossom beings. *Those who come in front of the Buddha* means all of those who abide in the Buddha. Even if there are those who appear in myriad forms as humans or nonhumans, and even if they are scattered like hundreds of grasses, they are *such beings. Such beings* are *I will confirm them all equally. I will confirm them all equally* is, from beginning to end, *They will attain unsurpassable, complete enlightenment.*

Shakyamuni Buddha said to Bhaishajyaraja Bodhisattva, *if there are those who come in front of the Buddha who hear one verse or phrase of the Sutra of Wondrous Dharma Blossoms, and are delighted even for a moment . . . they will attain unsurpassable, complete enlightenment.*

When is *after the pari-nirvana of the Tathagata?* Is it after forty-nine years, after eighty years? For now let us say eighty years. *If there are those who hear one verse or phrase of the Sutra of Wondrous Dharma Blossoms, and are delighted even for a moment*—is this to hear it with wisdom or without wisdom? Is it to hear it by mistake or not by mistake?

If you explain to others, it is heard by *if there are those . . .* Do not be concerned whether they are those with wisdom or without wisdom. Say that when they hear the *Sutra of Wondrous Dharma Blossoms*, even with the immeasurably profound wisdom of all buddhas, to hear is one phrase, to hear is one verse, to hear is to be delighted for one moment.

At this moment, *they will attain unsurpassable, complete enlightenment.* There is confirmation—*I will confirm them all equally.* Do not leave it to the ignorant third son of Zhang [ordinary person]. Devote yourself to a detailed study of this matter.

Being *delighted even for a moment* is those who hear. At this moment, there is no room to set skin, flesh, bones, or marrow on your head. Being given this confirmation of unsurpassable, complete enlightenment means, "My wish is already fulfilled." Be a skin bag like this. Thus, all wishes are fulfilled. In this way, there are people who are called *those who hear.*

There is confirmation by taking up a pine branch; there is confirmation by taking up an udumbara blossom. There is confirmation by blinking. There is confirmation by breaking into a smile. There is an example of transmitting straw sandals. This is not what can be easily thought about or understood.

There is confirmation of, "My body is thus." There is confirmation of, "Your body is thus." It means that the past, present, and future are confirmation. Because it is the past, present, and future within confirmation, it is actualized by confirming the self and by confirming others.

———

Vimalakirti said to Maitreya:

Maitreya, the World-Honored One has confirmed that you attain unsur-passable, complete enlightenment in your lifetime. In which life—past, present, or future birth—do you receive it?

If you say past birth, past birth has already perished. If you say future birth, future birth has not come yet. If you say present birth, present birth does not abide. The Buddha says, "Bhikshus, the present moment is birth, old age, and death."

If you say that you receive confirmation in beyond birth, beyond birth is the true stage. In the true stage, there is no receiving confirma-tion; there is no attaining unsurpassable, complete enlightenment.

Maitreya, how do you receive confirmation in your lifetime? Do you say you receive it in thusness-birth, or do you say you receive it in thusness-death? If you say you receive it in thusness-birth, thusness does not have birth. If you say you receive it in thusness-death, thusness does not have death.

All sentient beings are like this. All things are like this. All sages and wise ones are like this. You are also like this. If you receive confirmation, all sentient beings receive confirmation. The reason is that thusness is not two, not many. If you attain unsurpassable, complete enlightenment, all sentient beings also attain it. The reason is that all sentient beings are aspects of enlightenment.

The Tathagata did not deny Vimalakirti's statement. Accordingly, Maitreya's attaining confirmation is already determined. In this way, all sentient beings' attaining confirmation is also determined. Without sen-tient beings receiving confirmation, there is no confirmation of Mai-treya. *All sentient beings are aspects of enlightenment.* Enlightenment receives confirmation from enlightenment.

Receiving confirmation is the life of today. Since all sentient beings arouse the aspiration for enlightenment simultaneously with Maitreya, this is receiving confirmation together, and attaining the way together.

However, Vimalakirti's words, *In the true stage there is no receiving confir-mation,* show that he did not know that the true stage is itself confirma-tion, and he did not say that the true stage is itself enlightenment.

Vimalakirti also says, "Past birth has already perished . . . future birth has not come yet . . . present birth does not abide." But past has not necessarily already perished, future has not necessarily not come yet, and present does not necessarily not abide. Even when you regard having-already-perished, not-yet-come, and not-abiding, as the past, future, and present, you should clarify that not-yet-come is itself the past, present, and future. Accordingly, confirmation is attained in both birth and death. Enlightenment is attained in both birth and death.

When all sentient beings receive confirmation, Maitreya also receives confirmation. Now I ask you, Vimalakirti: Is Maitreya the same as sentient beings or different from them? Answer! You said, "If Maitreya received confirmation, all sentient beings receive confirmation." If you say Maitreya is not a sentient being, sentient beings are not sentient beings, and Maitreya is not Maitreya. How is it so? Then, Vimalakirti is not Vimalakirti. If you are not Vimalakirti, you cannot make this statement.

Therefore, you should say: When confirmation causes all sentient beings to exist, all sentient beings and Maitreya exist. Confirmation causes all things to be as they are.

Written at the Kannondori Kosho Horin Monastery on the twenty-fifth day, the fourth month in summer, the third year of the Ninji Era [1242].

34

AVALOKITESHVARA

YUNYAN, WHO WOULD later become Great Master Wuzhu, asked
[his senior dharma brother] Daowu, who would later become
Great Master Xiuyi, "What does the bodhisattva of great compassion do
with so many hands and eyes?"

Daowu said, "Like someone reaching back for the pillow at night."

Yunyan said, "I got it. I got it."

Daowu said, "What did you get?"

Yunyan said, "All over the body are hands and eyes."

Daowu said, "You have said it well. But it's eight or nine out of ten."

Yunyan said, "I am just this. How about yourself, brother?"

Daowu said, "Wherever the body reaches, it is hands and eyes."

Although there have been a number of statements about Avalokiteshvara before and after Yunyan and Daowu, they are not as good as
the statements made by these two. If you want to study Avalokiteshvara,
you should thoroughly investigate their words.

The *bodhisattva of great compassion* is Avalokiteshvara—"One who
perceives the cries of the world," also called "One who has complete
freedom in perceiving." This bodhisattva is regarded as the parent of all
buddhas. Do not assume that this bodhisattva has not mastered the way

as much as buddhas. In fact, Avalokiteshvara was True Dharma Illumination Tathagata in a previous life.

Study and focus on Yunyan's words: *What does the bodhisattva of great compassion do with so many hands and eyes?* There are schools [of Buddhism] that cherish Avalokiteshvara, and schools that have no relationship with this bodhisattva.

Yunyan had a connection with Avalokiteshvara and pondered the bodhisattva together with Daowu. Not only one or two, but hundreds and thousands of Avalokiteshvaras are with Yunyan.

Yunyan and his dharma descendants alone make Avalokiteshvara truly Avalokiteshvara. How is this so? The Avalokiteshvara expressed by Yunyan is thoroughly expressed, while the Avalokiteshvara expressed by others is not. The Avalokiteshvara expressed by others merely has twelve faces. Yunyan's Avalokiteshvara is not like that. The Avalokiteshvara expressed by others merely has one thousand hands and eyes. Yunyan's Avalokiteshvara is not like that. The Avalokiteshvara expressed by others merely has eighty-four thousand hands and eyes. Yunyan's Avalokiteshvara is not like that. How do we know this?

The *so many hands and eyes* of the bodhisattva of great compassion expressed by Yunyan is not limited to eighty-four thousand hands and eyes, not to speak of such numbers as twelve or thirty-two or -three. *So many* means a great many. It is as many as possible, not limited to any number. As it is not limited to any number, it is not limited to beyond boundary and measure [not limited to the infinite]. Study the scale of *so many* in this way. It even goes beyond the boundary of beyond boundary and measure.

When Yunyan asked this question, Daowu did not disapprove of it. He saw deep meaning in the question.

Yunyan and Daowu studied shoulder to shoulder in Yaoshan's community and journeyed together for forty years. Investigating ancient and new cases, they rejected incorrect views and confirmed each other's understanding. Having been together like this, Yunyan presented his understanding on that day, and Daowu confirmed it.

Know that the words *many hands and eyes* were equally expressed by these two ancient buddhas. The words *many hands and eyes* were studied simultaneously by Yunyan and Daowu.

What does the bodhisattva of great compassion do? This is a question directed to Daowu. This question is not the same as that of the bodhi-sattvas of ten stages or three classes. This question brings forth an expression of understanding. It brings forth hands and eyes.

As the question was presented—*What does the bodhisattva of great compassion do with so many hands and eyes?*—there are old buddhas and new buddhas who have become buddhas through the power of working on this question. The question can be "How does the bodhisattva use so many hands and eyes?" "How is it?" "How does the bodhisattva manage [so many hands and eyes]?" or "What do you say?"

Daowu said, *Like someone reaching back for the pillow at night.* He meant that it is just like searching for the pillow at night. *Reaching back* means groping for it. *At night* means in utter darkness. It is as clear as "looking at a mountain in the daytime."

Using the hands and eyes is *like someone reaching back for the pillow at night.* Study the use of the hands and eyes in this way. Investigate a nighttime that is thought of in the daytime, and a nighttime experienced in the nighttime. Investigate a nighttime that is neither daytime nor nighttime. *Someone reaching back for the pillow* may not be understood as Avalokiteshvara using the hands and eyes, but there is no way to escape it.

Is the so-called *someone* merely someone? Or is it an ordinary person, yet not ordinary? If you understand *someone* as an ordinary person in the buddha way, and do not take it as "merely someone," then there is something to study about *reaching back for the pillow.*

The pillow has a point that must be investigated. *Night* is not merely the night of the day and the night of humans and devas. Know that what is expressed here is not grabbing, pulling, or pushing the pillow.

When you investigate Daowu's words, *reaching back for the pillow at night,* see and don't miss that there are eyes that can see the night. There is no limit to the hand reaching out for the pillow. If the hand reaches backward, is there an eye that can see what is behind? Clarify the meaning of an eye at night.

Is this a world of eyes on hands? Is this someone who has eyes on hands? Do eyes and hands fly like a roar of thunder? Have the eyes and hands been working in one or many ways, from beginning to end?

If you investigate the use of so many hands and eyes, the bodhisattva of great compassion may only appear to be a bodhisattva of hands and eyes. If someone questions this, say, "How does the bodhisattva of hands and eyes use so many bodhisattvas of great compassion?"

Know that even though the hands and eyes do not hinder each other, how you use them is how you let them be used, and how you use them as they are.

In understanding things as they are, *the hands and eyes all over* are never hidden, nor are they waiting for the moment of understanding *the hands and eyes all over*. Even though there are these or those hands and eyes that are not hidden, they are not the self, mountains or rivers, sun face or moon face, and not "Mind itself is buddha."

Yunyen said, *I got it, I got it*. He did not mean he understood Daowu's words. The *I got it, I got it* makes his experience of the bodhisattva using the hands and eyes a true experience. Daowu used his words boundlessly just like this. He entered that very day boundlessly just like this.

Daowu said, *What did you get?* This means that although Yunyan's *I got it* does not hinder *I got it,* Daowu's response was *What did you get?*

Already there was *I got it,* and you got it. Is it not that the eyes got it, and the hands got it? Is *I got it* actualized or not actualized?

While it is [true that it was] I who *got it,* it is [true that it was] you who were asked: *What did you get?* This requires investigation.

Regarding Yunyan's words *All over the body are hands and eyes,* when people lecture on *reaching back for the pillow,* many of them explain that there are hands and eyes all over Avalokiteshvara's body. To describe Avalokiteshvara that way may be explaining Avalokiteshvara, but this is not thoroughly expressing the bodhisattva.

Yunyan's words *All over the body are hands and eyes* do not mean that there are hands and eyes all over Avalokiteshvara's body. Even if *all over* means all over the world, the very body, hands, and eyes [of Avalokiteshvara] are not covered by this *all over*. Even if the body, hands, and eyes have the power to cover everything, they are not the hands and eyes that would confiscate goods from the marketplace. No views, practice, or words can exactly express the power of the hands and eyes.

So many hands and eyes means more than one thousand, ten thousand, eighty-four thousand; more than beyond boundary and measure. This is not only so for *All over the body are hands and eyes,* but also for expounding dharma to awaken sentient beings, and for causing the land to radiate light.

In this way, Yunyan's words mean that all over the body are no other than hands and eyes. It is not that there are hands and eyes all over Avalokiteshvara's body. Investigate this. Do not be surprised that Avalokiteshvara uses and manages the hands and eyes that are no other than all over the body.

Daowu said: *You have said it well. But it's eight or nine out of ten.* This means that Yunyan's expression was well presented. *You have said it well* means Yunyan is right, and there is nothing unexpressed. If Daowu had meant that Yunyan did not express right understanding, he would only have said, *It's eight or nine out of ten.*

Study the true meaning of Daowu's words. Even when someone expresses ten out of ten, if it is without mastery of the way, it is not complete. On the other hand, when what should be presented is presented, someone expressing eight or nine out of ten should be regarded as someone who has expressed ten out of ten.

The moment of hitting the mark, which can be expressed in one hundred, one thousand, or ten thousand ways, Yunyan expressed in merely eight or nine out of ten with little effort. Truly, his capacity is wondrous. Bringing forth the entire world of the ten directions with one hundred, one thousand, or ten thousand efforts is better than bringing forth nothing. And yet, bringing it forth with a single effort is extraordinary. This is the meaning of *You got eight or nine out of ten.*

However, hearing the buddha ancestor's words—*You got eight or nine out of ten*—people assume that Yunyan expressed only eight or nine while he should have expressed ten out of ten. If buddha dharma were like that, it would not have reached today. The *eight or nine* is like one hundred or one thousand. It means so many. From one point of view, it means beyond eight or nine. You should study the dharma talks of buddha ancestors in this way.

Yunyan said, *I am just this. How about yourself?* He said *just this* in response to Daowu's *You got eight or nine out of ten.* It is like "I leave no trace" or "The arms are long but the sleeves are short" [the way as it is]. It is not that he said *I am just this* because he had not expressed his understanding well enough.

Daowu said, *Wherever the body reaches, it is hands and eyes.* He did not mean that the hands and eyes reach as hands and eyes. The hands and eyes that reach wherever the body reaches is expressed as *Wherever the body reaches, it is hands and eyes.*

Thus, Daowu did not say that the [Avalokiteshvara's] body is hands and eyes. While using so many hands and eyes so many times, the hands and eyes are invariably *Wherever the body reaches, it is hands and eyes.*

You might be asked, "How does the bodhisattva use so many bodies and minds?" Then you might say, "Wherever the body reaches, it is just this."

Between Yunyan's *all over the body* and Daowu's *wherever the body reaches,* it is not that one has expressed thoroughly and the other has not. Yunyan's *all over the body* and Daowu's *wherever the body reaches* cannot be compared to each other. Each one has expressed it thoroughly in regard to *so many hands and eyes.*

In this way, the Avalokiteshvara expressed by Old Man Shakyamuni has only one thousand eyes, twelve faces, thirty-three bodies, or eighty-four thousand manifestations. Yunyan and Daowu's Avalokiteshvara has numberless hands and eyes. However, it is not a question of more or less. When you practice the numberless hands and eyes of Avalokiteshvara, expressed by Yunyan and Daowu, all buddhas experience Avalokiteshvara's samadhi eight or nine out of ten.

Presented to the assembly on the twenty-sixth day, the fourth month, the third year of the Ninji Era [1242].

POSTSCRIPT

Since buddha dharma was brought from India [to China], many buddha ancestors have talked about Avalokiteshvara, but none of them match Yunyan and Daowu. That is why I am presenting only this case now.

Yongjia, Great Master Zhenjiao, said, "Not to see even one dharma is called a tathagata. This is the one who perceives with freedom [Avalokiteshvara]."

This confirms that the Tathagata and Avalokiteshvara both reveal their own bodies, but they are not separate bodies.

Mayu and Linji had understanding of the true hands and eyes. It is one of the many dialogues on Avalokiteshvara.

Yunmen spoke of Avalokiteshvara who "sees form and clarifies the mind, hears sound and realizes the way."

Which form or sound does Avalokiteshvara not see or hear?

Baizhang spoke of Avalokiteshvara "entering reality."

In the assembly described by the *Shurangama Sutra*, there is Avalokiteshvara of complete mastery.

In the assembly described by the *Lotus Sutra*, there is Avalokiteshvara who manifests the universal gate.

Avalokiteshvaras described by these ancients all work together with buddhas, mountains, rivers, and earth. Although working together with buddhas, mountains, rivers, and earth, these Avalokiteshvaras are still one or two manifestations of countless hands and eyes.

Presented to the assembly on the twenty-sixth day, the fourth month, the third year of the Ninji Era [1242].

35

ARHAT

[IT IS SAID IN the *Lotus Sutra:*] "An arhat is one who has transformed all afflictions, has no more delusion, has driven away self-interest, has removed all forms of bondage, and has achieved freedom of mind."

This is a great arhat, who has obtained the fourth and final fruit in practicing with the Buddha. This is a buddha arhat.

Afflictions are a broken dipper with a missing handle, used a great many times. *Has transformed all afflictions* means that the entire body of the dipper has made a leap. *Has driven away self-interest* means coming in and out of the top of the head. *Has removed all forms of bondage* means nothing is hidden in the world of the ten directions. *Freedom of mind* can be understood as "flat in a high place and flat in a low place." In this way, there are walls, tiles, and pebbles. *Freedom* means the undivided activity of mind that is actualized. *Has no more delusion* is not giving rise to delusions—delusion is obstructed by delusion.

The miraculous powers, wisdom, meditation, dharma expounding, guidance, and radiating light of an arhat are not the same as those of people outside the way or heavenly demons. An arhat's vision of one hundred buddha worlds is not similar to that of an ordinary person's.

One says that barbarians' hair is red, while the other says that there are barbarians with red hair.

Entering nirvana is an arhat's practice of entering a fist. Thus, it is the wondrous heart of nirvana—there is no place to avoid. One who enters a nostril is a true arhat. One who has not entered a nostril is not an arhat.

———————

It is said [in the *Lotus Sutra*], "Today we are true arhats. We will let the Buddha's enlightened voice be heard by all."

We will let the Buddha's enlightened voice be heard by all means to let all beings hear the Buddha's teaching. Why should this be limited to buddhas and disciples? To let all those who have knowledge, wisdom, skin, flesh, bones, and marrow hear it is to let it be heard by all beings. Those who have knowledge and wisdom are the land, grass, trees, walls, tiles, and pebbles. Those who sway, fall, prosper, and decline, and those who come and go in birth and death, all hear it. *We will let the Buddha's enlightened voice be heard by all* should not be understood to mean merely that the entire world has ears.

———————

Shakyamuni Buddha said [in the *Lotus Sutra*], "If some of my disciples call themselves arhats or pratyeka-buddhas and do not understand that all tathagatas only teach bodhisattva works, they are not the Buddha's disciples. Neither are they arhats nor pratyeka-buddhas."

The Buddha's statement *only teach bodhisattva works* means that "I and buddhas in the ten directions know this very well." It means, "Only buddha and buddha thoroughly understand the reality of all things." It is unsurpassable, complete enlightenment.

Thus, the way bodhisattvas and buddhas call themselves, and the way arhats and pratyeka-buddhas call themselves, should be the same. Why so? Because they both understand that all tathagatas only teach bodhisattva works.

———————

A teacher of old said, "In the shravaka [Hinayana] sutras, an arhat is regarded as the buddha ground."

This statement is a clarification of the buddha way. It is not only a theory memorized by teachers of treatises, but also a common understanding in the buddha way. Study the teaching that regards an arhat as the buddha ground. Study the teaching that regards the buddha ground as an arhat.

There is not a single extra particle or thing other than the arhat fruit. How can there be extra complete enlightenment other than this? There is not a single extra particle or thing other than unsurpassable, complete enlightenment. How can there be four extra paths and fruits other than this?

At this very moment, when an arhat brings up all things, there is no eight *lian* or half a *jin* in all things. What an arhat brings up is mind beyond this, buddha beyond this, and thing beyond this. It is buddha eye beyond seeing. It cannot be discussed as before or after eighty thousand kalpas. Study an arhat's power of plucking the eyeball. Extra things are entirely extra things.

———————

Shakyamuni Buddha said [in the *Lotus Sutra*], "These monks and nuns think they have become arhats, attained their final bodies, and thoroughly experienced nirvana, so they do not seek unsurpassable, complete enlightenment. Such people are arrogant. It is groundless to be truly an arhat and not believe in unsurpassable, complete enlightenment."

To believe in unsurpassable, complete enlightenment is proof of being an arhat. To believe in unsurpassable, complete enlightenment is to be entrusted with it, to receive transmission of it person to person, and to practice and realize it.

To be truly an arhat is not to attain the final body, or thoroughly experience nirvana, for an arhat does seek unsurpassable, complete enlightenment. To seek unsurpassable, complete enlightenment is to fool with an eyeball, to sit facing the wall, and to open the eye facing the wall. Although abiding in the all-inclusive realm, an arhat appears like a spirit and disappears like a demon. Although abiding in all time, there is a constant tossing back and forth of an insightful flash.

This is called seeking unsurpassable, complete enlightenment. Thus, it is seeking to be an arhat. Seeking to be an arhat is to be satisfied with gruel, to be satisfied with cooked rice.

———————

Keqin, Zen Master Yuanwu of Mount Jia, said:

After realization, people of old would go deeply into a mountain, a weed grove, or a stone cave, and cook meals in a broken pot for ten or twenty years. They would forget all about the human world and reject its dusty treasures. But today you may not want to do that.

Just hide your name, obscure your traces, and remain an old gimlet. Merge with realization and experience receptive samadhi according to your capacity. Remove the effects of your past actions and become free from old habits. If your capacity is greater, help others, create wisdom relationships, polish the tips of your feet, and mature. Just as if you were picking one or even half a blade of grass from a thick patch of weeds, join those who have wisdom and help them to get away from the chain of birth and death. In this way, you can benefit future generations and repay the deep kindness of buddha ancestors.

Or, if it so happens that the fruit that has lived through frost and dew ripens, take this fruit into the world to transform humans and devas, responding to situations and following circumstances, but without ever having a seeking mind.

Why depend on influential people and follow worldly trends while confusing common people and ignoring sages, grasping for benefit and looking for fame? This would only cause you to fall into an unceasing hell.

Even if you do not have an opportunity to be active in the world, if you simply do not create causes that lead you to hell, you will be an arhat truly free from the dusty world.

Thus, a patch-robed monk of genuine form is a true arhat free from the dusty world. If you want to know the characteristics of an arhat, it is just this. Do not be confused by words of treatises in India. Jiashan of China is a buddha ancestor who has received authentic transmission person to person.

———————

Baizhang, Zen Master Dazhi of Mount Baizhang, Hong Region, said, "Eyes, ears, nose, tongue, body, and mind are not stained by greed for things that do or do not exist. This is called receiving and maintaining the four-line verse. It is called the four fruits."

These eyes, ears, nose, tongue, body, and mind, that are not confined by self or other, cannot be measured or thoroughly experienced from beginning to end. Thus, the entire body is unstained by greed. It is unstained by things that do or do not exist. The entirety of receiving and maintaining the four-line verse is called *not stained*. It is also called the four fruits. One who has attained the four fruits is an arhat.

This being so, the eyes, ears, nose, tongue, body, and mind that are actualized right now are an arhat, free and transparent from root to twig. To arrive at a barrier is receiving and maintaining the four-line verse. This is the four fruits. Transparent top, transparent bottom, the whole body is actualized. Not a hairbreadth slips away.

In the end, how should we say what it is? It is thus:

Within the ordinary, the arhat is immersed in all things.
Within the sacred, the arhat is liberated.
The arhat and all things practice together.
Realizing arhat is being immersed in arhat—
an old fist before the King of the Empty Eon.

Abiding at the Kannondori Kosho Horin Monastery, Uji County, Yamashiro Province, this is presented to the assembly on the fifteenth day, the fifth month, the third year of the Ninji Era [1242].

36

CYPRESS TREE

ZHAOZHOU, WHO WOULD later become Great Master Zhenji, the thirty-seventh ancestor from Shakyamuni Tathagata, first aroused the aspiration for enlightenment at age sixty-one, and left home to study the way.

At this time he vowed, "I will teach even a hundred-year-old person who has less understanding than I. I will inquire about the way even from a seven-year-old child who surpasses my understanding."

Having made this vow, he journeyed south. While asking about the way, he got to Mount Nanquan and bowed to Nanquan, Priest Puyuan.

Nanquan was lying down in the abbot's room. When he saw Zhaozhou, he asked, "Where are you from?"

Zhaozhou said, "The Ruixiang [Auspicious Image] Monastery."

Nanquan asked, "Is there an auspicious image over there?"

Zhaozhou replied, "There is no auspicious image, but there is a reclining Tathagata."

Hearing this, Nanquan sat up and said, "Are you a novice with a teacher?"

Zhaozhou said, "Yes, I am a novice with a teacher."

Nanquan asked, "Who is your teacher?"

Zhaozhou said, "It is still cold in early spring. I respectfully bow to you and wish you an auspicious life."

Nanquan called the practice coordinator and said, "Take care of this novice."

From that time, Zhaozhou stayed at Nanquan's monastery without ever leaving. He endeavored in the way for thirty years, avoiding inessential activities, not wasting time.

After receiving transmission of the way, he resided as abbot at the Guanyin Monastery in Zhao Region for thirty years. His abbacy was unique. One day he said:

> With an empty stomach I look at smoke rising from
>   nearby kitchens.
> Having bidden farewell to dumplings and steamed bread
>   last year,
> my mouth still waters thinking of them.
> There is little room for mindfulness but much for
>   despair.
> From a hundred neighboring houses, no one gives to the
>   monastery.
> Visitors come for tea,
> but not finding a treat, they leave unhappy.

How pathetic! Zhaozhou's monastery rarely even fired up its stove to boil plain rice. They hadn't tasted various flavors for more than a year. One hundred neighbors came for tea; those who didn't want tea stayed away. Visitors bringing gifts of tea come from outside the village. Even though monks were searching for a master, they might not be dragons and elephants remembering to bring food offerings.

At another time Zhaozhou said:

> Reflecting on home leavers in the world,
> I wonder how many abbots like myself
> have only broken bamboo strips on a dirt bed.
> My pillow of woven willow twigs lacks a cover.
> There is no incense to offer to the sacred image.
> Only the smell of cow dung rises from the incense bowl.

From these words you can feel the purity of Zhaozhou's monastery. Learn from this excellent example. However, he did not have many monks, fewer than twenty, because it was difficult to follow such a practice. The monks' hall was small, without front and back sitting platforms. No lanterns were lit at night and no charcoal burned in winter. You could call it a pitiable life for his old age. The pure practice of the old buddha was like this.

Once, a leg of one of the sitting platforms broke. Zhaozhou replaced it with a burned stick that had rope tied around it. It was like that for some years. When a monastery officer wanted to repair it, Zhaozhou would not allow it. This is an unparalleled example throughout time.

Usually there was no grain visible in the gruel, and hungry monks sat next to drafty windows. He and the assembly often picked nuts for their meals.

Nowadays, we who follow his teaching admire his pure practice. Although we cannot come up to Zhaozhou's standard, we keep it in mind, longing for the ancient way.

Once, he said to the assembly, "I was in the south for thirty years engaged wholeheartedly in zazen. Students, if you want to realize the single great matter, clarify what is essential through zazen. If you practice three years, five years, twenty or thirty years, and still have not attained the way, you can cut off this old monk's head and make a urine dipper from it."

This was his commitment. Indeed, endeavor in zazen is the straight path of the buddha way. Clarify the principle through sitting and seeing.

Later someone commented: "Zhaozhou is an ancient buddha."

———————

Zhaozhou was asked by a monk, "What is the meaning of Bodhidharma's coming from India?"

Zhaozhou said, "The cypress tree in the garden."

The monk said, "Reverend, please do not use an object to guide me."

Zhaozhou said, "I am not using an object."

The monk said, "What is the meaning of Bodhidharma's coming from India?"

Zhaozhou said, "The cypress tree in the garden."

Although this koan originated with Zhaozhou, all buddhas have in fact created it with their whole bodies. Who could own it?

What we should learn from this is that the cypress tree in the garden is not an object, Bodhidharma's coming from India is not an object, and the cypress tree is not the self.

Thus, there is just *Reverend, please do not use an object to guide me,* and just *I am not using an object.*

Which *reverend* is hindered by *reverend*? If not hindered, the *reverend* is *I*. Which *I* is hindered by *I*? Even if the *I* is hindered, it is a true person. What object is hindered by *Bodhidharma's coming from India*? An object is always *Bodhidharma's coming from India.* However, *Bodhidharma's coming from India* and the object are not sequential.

Bodhidharma's coming from India is not necessarily the treasury of the true dharma eye, the wondrous heart of nirvana. It is beyond this mind, beyond this buddha, beyond this object.

The question *What is the meaning of Bodhidharma's coming from India?* is not only a question, or the teacher and student sharing the same view. At the very moment of asking, has not one of them seen through? How much has the other attained? In further give and take, neither one is wrong.

Thus, there is missing the mark on top of missing the mark. Because it is missing on top of missing, it is continuous missing. Is it not receiving voidness and sending back an echo? Because vast spirit has no contradiction, *The cypress tree in the garden.*

Without being an object, it cannot be a cypress tree. Even if it is an object, *I am not using an object,* and *Reverend, please do not use an object to guide me.*

The cypress tree is not in an old shrine. As it is not in an old shrine, it is totally immersed. As it is totally immersed, "I have endeavored." Because "I have endeavored," *I am not using an object.* Then, with what does Zhaozhou teach? "I am like this."

———————

Zhaozhou was asked by a monk, "Does the cypress tree have buddha nature?"

Zhaozhou answered, "It does."

The monk said, "When does it become buddha?"

Zhaozhou said, "When the sky falls to the ground."

The monk said, "When does that happen?"

Zhaozhou said, "When the cypress tree becomes buddha."

Now, listen to these words of Zhaozhou, while not abandoning the questions of the monk. The times of Zhaozhou's words, *When the sky falls to the ground* and *When the cypress tree becomes buddha*, are not separate.

The monk questioned the cypress tree, buddha nature, becoming a buddha, and when. He also questioned the sky and falling.

In response to the monk's question, Zhaozhou said, *It does,* meaning the cypress tree has buddha nature. Fully explore this statement and freely let flow the life stream of buddha ancestors.

That the cypress tree has buddha nature could not ordinarily be spoken of; it had not yet been spoken about. The cypress tree does have buddha nature. Clarify how: Is the status of the cypress tree that has buddha nature high or low? Inquire about its life span and physical dimensions. Ask about its social class and clan. Are hundreds and thousands of cypress trees in one class or in different families?

Does the cypress tree become buddha, practice, and arouse the aspiration for enlightenment? Or does it become buddha but does not practice or arouse the aspiration for enlightenment? What kind of relationship exists between the cypress tree and the sky? Does the cypress tree become buddha when the sky falls because the treeness of the cypress tree is always the sky? Is the status of the cypress tree in the sky its beginning or ultimate stage? Investigate this thoroughly in detail.

Let me ask Old Man Zhaozhou: "If you are one of the withered cypress trees sprouting from one root, what do you do?"

That the cypress tree has buddha nature is not the understanding of those outside the way or those in the Two Lesser Vehicles. Nor has it been seen or heard of by teachers of sutras or treatises. Even further, can it be expounded by the flowery words of withered trees and dead ash? The followers of Zhaozhou alone study and investigate this.

Zhaozhou's indication "The cypress tree has buddha nature" raises such questions as: Is the cypress tree totally immersed in the cypress tree? Is buddha nature totally immersed in buddha nature? More than a few buddhas have explored these words, but not all those that have buddha faces investigate such words. Even among buddhas, there are some who can say them and some who cannot.

The words *When the sky falls to the ground* do not refer to something impossible. Every time the cypress tree becomes buddha, the sky falls. Sounds of falling are not hidden, but are louder than hundreds and thousands of thunder strikes. The time when the cypress tree becomes buddha is provisionally within the twelve hours and yet is beyond the twelve hours. The sky that falls is not the same sky seen by ordinary people and sages, but an entirety of sky beyond that. Others do not see it. Zhaozhou alone sees it.

The ground the sky falls to is not possessed by ordinary people or sages, but there is an entirety of ground beyond that. Light and shadow do not reach it. Zhaozhou alone reaches it. At the moment the sky falls, even the sun, moon, mountains, and rivers will face it.

Who says that buddha nature unfailingly becomes buddha? Buddha nature is magnificence actualized after becoming buddha. Further, there is buddha nature that is born together and practiced together upon becoming buddha.

Thus, the cypress tree and buddha nature are neither different sounds nor the same tune. That is to say, not necessarily either. What is this? Investigate thoroughly.

Presented to the assembly of Kannondori Monastery, Uji County, Yamashiro Province, on the twenty-first day, the season of Iris Festival, the fifth month, the third year of the Ninji Era [1242].

37

RADIANT LIGHT

I N A FORMAL talk, Changsha, Great Master Zhaoxian, of Hunan,
Great Song China, said, "The entire world of the ten directions is a
shramana's [monk's] single eye. The entire world of the ten directions is
a shramana's everyday speech. The entire world of the ten directions is a
shramana's entire body. The entire world of the ten directions is the radiant light of the self. The entire world of the ten directions is within the
radiant light of the self. In the entire world of the ten directions, there is
not a single person that is not the self."

Make sure to endeavor in the practice of the buddha way. Those who
practice should not be coarse or distant. Even so, there have been few
practitioners of the way who have mastered this radiant light.

Emperor Xiaoming of the Later Han Dynasty, China, was the fourth
son of Emperor Guangwu. His given name was Zhuang, and his posthumous name was Emperor Xian. During his reign, in the tenth year of
the Yongping Era [67 C.E.], Matanga and Dharmaratna introduced the
Buddha's teaching to China for the first time. At the scripture-burning

platform they defeated the Daoists who had mistaken views, by demonstrating the miraculous power of the buddhas.

Later on, in the Putong Era [520–527] during the reign of Emperor Wu of the Kingdom of Liang, Bodhidharma traveled from India to the south sea province of Guang. He was an authentic heir of the treasury of the true dharma eye. He was the twenty-eighth-generation dharma descendant from Shakyamuni Buddha. He hung his traveling staff at the Shaolin Temple, Shaoshi Peak, Mount Song. As the First Zen Ancestor in China, Bodhidharma transmitted dharma to Huike, the Second Ancestor, Zen Master Dazu. This is intimacy within the radiant light of buddha ancestors.

Until that time no one in China had seen or heard of the radiant light of buddha ancestors. Who, then, was even aware of the radiant light of the self? Even though people had been carrying the radiant light within their heads and encountering it all the time, they still did not practice it as their own eyeballs. Thus, they do not clarify the shape and function of radiant light. Because they avoided encountering the radiant light, their radiant light was missing radiant light. Although missing is itself radiant light, they were immersed in missing.

Those stinky skin bags who miss the point think that both buddha light and human light are red, white, blue, or yellow, like fire light or water light, pearl light or jewel light, the dragon king's light, or sun or moon light. However hard they study with teachers and sutras, if they hear about the radiant light and think it must be like the way of a firefly, it is not the study with ultimate insight. There have been many like that from the Han, Sui, Tang, and Song dynasties until now. Do not study with such dharma teachers of letters. Do not listen to such confused views of meditation teachers.

The radiant light of buddha ancestors spoken of here is the entire world of the ten directions, as well as all buddhas and all ancestors, only buddha and buddha, buddha light, and light buddha. Buddha ancestors maintain buddha ancestors as radiant light. They practice and realize this radiant light and become buddhas, sit as buddhas, and realize buddhas.

This being so, it is said [in the *Lotus Sutra*], "This light illuminates the eighteen thousand eastern buddha lands." These words are radiant light. This light is buddha light. Illuminating the east is the east illuminating. This east is not the east of the common world; it is the center of the world of phenomena, in the middle of the fist. Although it covers the east, the radiant light is eight *ryo* [ounces]. Study that there is east in this land and in other lands, and that there is east in the east.

In regard to the *eighteen thousand*, ten thousand is half a fist, half this mind. It is not necessarily thousands. It is not tens of thousands or one million. The buddha land is within an eyeball. To see and hear the words *illuminates the eighteen thousand eastern buddha lands*, and to assume it is like extending a piece of white silk toward the east, is not the study of the way. The entire world of the ten directions is just the east. The east is called the entire world of the ten directions. This being so, there is the entire world of the ten directions. The words that express *the entire world of the ten directions* are heard by the *eighteen thousand* buddha lands.

Emperor Xiang of the Tang Dynasty was the father of Emperors Mu and Xuan, and the grandfather of Emperors Jing, Wen, and Wu. On the night when he held a ceremony revering the Buddha's relics in the palace, a radiant light appeared. Xiang was delighted. Most of his courtiers congratulated him the following morning.

But there was a courtier called Han Yu, whose given name was Tuizhi, with the posthumous name Lord Wen. He had been studying as a lay student of buddha ancestors. He did not express congratulations.

Emperor Xian said, "All other courtiers are congratulating me. My lord, why do you alone not do so?"

Han Yu said, "I have read in Buddhist literature that buddha light is not blue, yellow, red, or white. It must have been the light of a guardian dragon god."

The Emperor said, "What is buddha light?"

Han Yu was silent.

Han Yu was a layperson who had a courageous spirit. He was a person turning the heavens and turning the earth. To study as he did is the beginning study of the way. Not to study in this way is to go against the way. Even if one expounds a sutra and causes heavenly flowers to rain down, if one does not get to this point, it is a vain endeavor. Even if bodhisattvas of the ten stages and three classes speak with the same voice as Han Yu, that is the aspiration for enlightenment, and that is practice-realization.

Yet, there is something Han Yu did not understand about Buddhist literature. How did he study the words that buddha light is not blue, yellow, red, or white? If he had the ability to see that what is blue, yellow, red, or white is not buddha light, he should not see buddha light as blue, yellow, red, or white. If Emperor Xiang had been a buddha ancestor, he would have challenged him in this way.

Thus, bright radiant light is one hundred grasses. The radiant light of one hundred grasses cannot give or take roots, stems, branches, and leaves as well as flowers, fruits, light, and colors.

There is radiant light of the five paths, there is radiant light of the six paths. Where there is, how would you talk about the light and the radiance? How do the mountains and rivers appear all of a sudden?

Study closely Changsha's words, *The entire world of the ten directions is the radiant light of the self.* Study that radiant light is the self of the entire world of the ten directions.

The coming and going of birth and death are the coming and going of radiant light. Going beyond ordinary and sacred is the blue and red of radiant light. Becoming a buddha and becoming an ancestor are the black and yellow of radiant light. It is not that there is no practice-realization; it is just defilement [expression] of radiant light. Grass, trees, tiles, and walls, as well as skin, flesh, bones, and marrow are the red and white of radiant light. Haze, mist, water, and rocks, as well as the path of a bird and the profound way, are rotating circles of radiant light.

To see and hear the radiant light of the self are the actual realization of encountering buddha, the actual realization of seeing the Buddha.

The entire world of the ten directions is the self. This self is the entire world of the ten directions. There is no way to avoid it. Even if there is a way to avoid it, it is the vital path of going beyond the self. The skull right now is seven feet tall. That is the shape, the form of the entire world of the ten directions. The entire world of the ten directions practiced and realized in the buddha way is the skull and skeleton, as well as skin, flesh, bones, and marrow.

———————

Yunmen, Great Master Daciyun Kuangzhen, is a thirty-ninth-generation descendant of the Tathagata, the World-Honored One. He transmitted dharma to Xuefeng, Great Master Zhenjiao. Although he was a latecomer in the buddha's assembly, he was a hero on an ancestral seat. Who can say that a radiant light buddha has not appeared on Mount Yunmen?

Once, he ascended the teaching seat and said to the assembly, "Each and every person embodies the radiant light. If you try to see it, it is totally invisible. Then, what is each and every person's radiant light?"

No one in the assembly answered.

Yunmen answered for them, "The monks' hall, the buddha hall, the kitchen, and the monastery gate."

Yunmen did not say that each and every person's radiant light will appear later, has appeared in the past, or is appearing nearby. Clearly hear the words, *Each and every person embodies the radiant light.* Assemble one hundred or one thousand Yunmens and make them investigate together and speak in one voice. *Each and every person embodies the radiant light* is not Yunmen's personal statement; everyone's light takes itself up and makes this statement. *Each and every person embodies the radiant light* means all humanity embodies the radiant light.

Radiant light means each and every person. Each and every person takes up the radiant light and sees its body, mind, and environs. There is a person where each and every radiant light embodies a person. There is a person where radiant light is the self. There is a person where each and every person embodies a person. There is radiant light where each and every radiant light embodies radiant light. There is embodiment where each and every embodiment embodies. There is each and every where each and every [self] embodies each and every.

Thus, know that the radiant light that each and every person embodies is each and every person that is actualized. It is each and every person that each and every light embodies.

Let me ask you, Yunmen, "What do you call each and every person? What do you call radiant light?"

Yunmen said, *Then, what is each and every person's radiant light?* This question is radiant light; it is a statement that kills doubt. Thus, each and every person who responds to it is a person of radiant light.

No one in the assembly answered. Even if they had had hundreds and thousands of statements to make, they chose to express themselves by not responding. This is the treasury of the true dharma eye, the wondrous heart of nirvana, authentically transmitted by buddha ancestors.

Yunmen spoke for them: *The monks' hall, the buddha hall, the kitchen, and the monastery gate. Spoke for them* means Yunmen spoke for himself, he spoke for the assembly, he spoke for the radiant light, he spoke for the monks' hall, the buddha hall, the kitchen, and the monastery gate.

However, what did he call the buddha hall, the kitchen, and the monastery gate? He may not have called the whole assembly of monks, as well as everyone else, the buddha hall, the kitchen, and the monastery gate. How many buddha halls, kitchens, and monastery gates did he mean? Which is Yunmen, the Seven Original Buddhas, the four times seven [twenty-eight Indian ancestors], the two times three [the first six Chinese ancestors], the fist, or the nostril?

Even if the buddha hall, the kitchen, and the monastery gate are buddha ancestors, they cannot avoid being each and every person. Thus, there is no *each and every person* [that does not embody radiant light]. In this way, there is no buddha in the hall of being buddha, no buddha in the hall of being no buddha. There is buddha of being light, buddha of no light, no buddha light, and being buddha light.

Xuefeng, Great Master Zhenjiao, said to the assembly, "I have met each and every person in front of the monks' hall."

This is the moment when Xuefeng's entire body is an eyeball. This is the moment when Xuefeng meets Xuefeng and the monks' hall meets the monks' hall.

Regarding the statement by Xuefeng, Baofu asked Ehu, "Setting aside being in front of the monks' hall for the moment, at which Land

View Pavilion or Crow Stone Peak did Xuefeng meet each and every person?"

Ehu quickly walked back to the abbot's quarters.

Baofu entered the monks' hall.

This is the emergence of an outstanding statement. This is the meaning of meeting. This is meeting the monks' hall.

Dizang, Great Master Zheying of the Dizang Monastery, said, "The tenzo [head cook] enters the kitchen."

This statement reaches a time long before the Seven Original Buddhas.

Presented to the assembly of the Kannondori Kosho Horin Monastery at the fourth segment of the third night period, the second day, the sixth month, the third year of the Ninji Era [1242]. It has been raining for a long time, and raindrops keep dripping from the eaves. Where is the radiant light? The assembly must look and break through Yunmen's words.

38

BODY-AND-MIND
STUDY OF THE WAY

WITHOUT PRACTICE, THE buddha way cannot be attained. Without study, it remains remote.

Nanyue, Zen Master Dahui, said, "It is not that there is no practice and no realization; it is just that they cannot be divided."

Not to study the buddha way is to fall into the realm of outsiders and those without enlightenment. All preceding and succeeding buddhas without exception practice the buddha way.

———————

For the time being let us say there are two approaches to studying the buddha way: to study with mind and to study with body.

To study with mind means to study with various aspects of mind, such as consciousness, emotion, and intellect. After resonating with the way and arousing the aspiration for enlightenment, take refuge in the great way of buddha ancestors and devote yourself to the practice of way-seeking mind. Even if you have not yet aroused the way-seeking mind, follow the examples of buddha ancestors who did arouse the way-seeking mind in former times.

There is the aspiration for enlightenment, bits and pieces of straightforward mind, the mind of ancient buddhas, everyday mind, and the inseparable-from-the-three-realms mind. Sometimes you study the way by casting off the mind. Sometimes you study the way by taking up the mind. Either way, study the way with thinking and study the way not-thinking.

To authentically inherit and transmit the brocade robe, to say, "You have attained my marrow," to make three bows and return to the original place, or to pound rice and receive the robe—this is studying mind with mind.

Shaving the head and wearing the robe is itself turning the mind and illuminating the mind. Leaving the castle and entering the mountains is leaving one mind and entering one mind. To directly enter the mountains is to think not-thinking. To leave the world behind is beyond thinking.

Those who have rolled up this matter into wide-open eyeballs are two or three bushels. Those who have tampered with it by karma-consciousness are thousands and millions of pieces.

When you study the way in this manner, having merit, the result may come of itself; having the result, merit may not arrive. You will secretly borrow the nostrils of buddha ancestors and have them exhale; taking up the hoof of a donkey, you will have it imprint the seal of enlightenment. These are authentic examples of the ancient tradition.

———————

Now, mountains, rivers, earth, the sun, the moon, and stars are mind. At just this moment, what is it that appears directly in front of you? "Mountains, rivers, and earth" do not merely mean the mountains, rivers, and earth where you are standing. There are various kinds of mountains, such as Great Sumeru and Small Sumeru; some mountains extend widely, some rise up steeply. A billion worlds and innumerable lands can be found in a mountain. There are mountains suspended in form; there are mountains suspended in emptiness.

There are also many kinds of waters: heavenly rivers, earthly rivers, and the four great rivers. There are lakes without heat; in the Great Northern Continent there are four Anavatapta Lakes, there are oceans and rivers. There are oceans and pools.

Earth is not necessarily ground, and ground is not necessarily earth. There is earth-ground, there is mind-ground, there is treasure-ground. Although the varieties are innumerable, it is not that there is no earth, but without doubt there is a world where emptiness is earth.

The sun, the moon, and stars as seen by humans and by devas are not the same, and the views of them by various beings differ widely. Views about one mind differ as well. Yet these views are nothing but mind. Is it inside or outside? Does it come or go? Is there more of it at birth or not? Is there less of it at death or not? How do we understand this birth and death, and views of birth and death?

All this is merely a moment or two of mind. A moment or two of mind is a moment of mountains, rivers, and earth, or two moments of mountains, rivers, and earth. Because mountains, rivers, earth, and so forth neither exist nor do not exist, they are not large or small, not attainable or unattainable, not knowable or unknowable, not penetrable or impenetrable. They neither change with realization, nor change without realization. Just wholeheartedly accept with trust that to study the way with mind is this mountains-rivers-and-earth mind itself thoroughly engaged in studying the way.

This trust and acceptance is neither large nor small, neither existent nor nonexistent. To study in this manner—understanding that home is no home, abandoning home, and entering the homeless life—is not measurable as large or small, near or far. It is beyond beginning or end, beyond ascending or descending. Unrolling the matter, it is seven or eight feet. Responding immediately, it benefits the self and others. All this is nothing but the study of the way.

———

Because the study of the way is like this, walls, tiles, and pebbles are mind. Other than this there are no three realms inseparable from mind, and no universe inseparable from mind. Mind is walls, tiles, and pebbles, put together before the Xiantong Era [860–873] and taken apart after the Xiantong Era, splattered with mud and soaking wet. Binding the self with no rope, mind has the power to attract a pearl, and the ability to be a pearl in water. Some days the pearl is melted. Sometimes it is crushed. There are times when this pearl is reduced to extremely fine powder.

Mind does not converse with bare pillars or rub shoulders with hanging lanterns. In this manner the mind studies the way running barefoot—who can get a glimpse of it? The mind studies the way turning somersaults—all things tumble over with it. At this time a wall crumbling away allows you to study the ten directions, and the gateless gate allows you to study the four quarters.

———

The aspiration for enlightenment can occur within birth-and-death, within nirvana. It can also occur without concern for birth-and-death and nirvana. It does not depend upon the place where it occurs, nor is it hindered by the place where it occurs.

Conditions do not arouse it, and knowledge does not arouse it. The aspiration for enlightenment arouses itself. This arousing is the aspiration for enlightenment. The aspiration for enlightenment is neither existent nor nonexistent, neither wholesome nor unwholesome nor neutral. It is not the result of past actions. Even beings in the blissful realms can arouse it. The aspiration for enlightenment arises just at the time of arising; it is not limited by conditions.

At the very moment when the aspiration for enlightenment is aroused, the entire world of phenomena arouses the aspiration for enlightenment. Although the aspiration for enlightenment seems to create conditions, it actually does not encounter conditions. The aspiration for enlightenment and conditions together hold out a single hand—a single hand held out freely, a single hand held out in the midst of all being. Thus, the aspiration for enlightenment is aroused even in the realms of hell, hungry ghosts, animals, and fighting spirits.

"Bits and pieces of straightforward mind" means all the bits and pieces moment after moment are straightforward mind. Not only one or two pieces, but all bits and pieces. The lotus leaf is completely round, round as a mirror. The tip of the water chestnut is extremely sharp, sharp as a gimlet.

Although straightforward mind resembles a mirror, it is bits and pieces. Even if it resembles a gimlet, it is bits and pieces.

———

As for the mind of ancient buddhas, a monk once asked Huizhong, National Teacher Dazheng, "What is the mind of ancient buddhas?"

Huizhong said, "Walls, tiles, and pebbles."

Thus, know that the mind of the ancient buddhas is not merely walls, tiles, and pebbles; and that walls, tiles, and pebbles are not merely called the mind of the ancient buddhas. The mind of the ancient buddhas is studied in this way.

"Everyday mind" means to maintain everyday mind in this world or in any world. Yesterday goes forth from this moment, and today comes forth from this place. While going the boundless sky goes, and while coming the entire earth comes. This is everyday mind.

Everyday mind opens the gate of the inner chamber. Because thousands of gates and myriads of doors open and close all at once, it is everyday mind. Now, this boundless sky and entire earth are like unrecognized words, a voice from the deep. Words are all-inclusive, mind is all-inclusive, things are all-inclusive.

Although there is birth and death in each moment of this life of birth and death, the body after the final body is never known. Even though you do not know it, if you arouse the aspiration for enlightenment, you will move forward on the way of enlightenment. The moment is already here. Do not doubt it in the least. Even if you should doubt it, this is nothing but everyday mind.

To study the way with body means to study the way with your own body. It is the study of the way using this lump of red flesh. The body comes forth from the study of the way. Everything that comes forth from the study of the way is the true human body.

The entire world of the ten directions is nothing but the true human body. The coming and going of birth and death is the true human body.

To turn this body around, abandoning the ten unwholesome actions, keeping the eight precepts, taking refuge in the three treasures, and leaving home and entering the homeless life, is the true study of the way. For this reason it is called the true human body. Those who follow this must not be like outsiders who hold the view of spontaneous enlightenment.

Baizhang, Zen Master Dazhi, said, "If you are attached to the view that original purity and original emancipation are buddha, or to Zen practice, you are a follower of the outsiders' way of spontaneous enlightenment."

This teaching is not the broken furniture of an abandoned house, but the collected efforts and accumulated virtue of studying the way. The body suddenly leaps up, transparently clear in eight facets. It drops away, while entwined around a tree like wisteria.

Baizhang's words are nothing but manifesting this body, awakening beings, and expounding the dharma; manifesting another's body, awakening beings, and expounding the dharma; beyond manifesting this body, awakening beings, and expounding the dharma; beyond manifesting another's body, awakening beings, and expounding the dharma. Then again, his words are beyond expounding the dharma.

Thus, at the moment of dropping away the body, there is a voice that stops all sound. At the moment of renouncing worldly life, the arm is cut off and the marrow is attained. Even if you begin to study the way before the eon of the King of Emptiness, still your practice as a descendant of yourself is endless.

"The entire world of the ten directions" means that all ten directions are the entire world. East, west, south, north, the four midpoints, up, and down are the ten directions. Consider the moment when front and back, vertical and horizontal, are thoroughly reached. To consider means to understand and to resolve that this human body, undivided by self and others, is the entire world of the ten directions. This is to hear what has never been heard, because directions are all-inclusive and all worlds are alike.

"The human body" means the four great elements and the five skandhas. However, none of these elements or objects are fully understood by ordinary people; only sages thoroughly master them.

Now, penetrate the ten directions within one particle of dust, but do not confine them to one particle of dust. Construct a monks' hall and a buddha hall within a single particle of dust, and construct the entire world in the monks' hall and the buddha hall. In this way the human body is constructed, and such construction comes from the human body. This is the meaning of "The entire world of the ten directions is the true human body." Do not follow the mistaken views of spontaneous or natural enlightenment.

Because it is not in the realm of the measurable, the true human body is not broad or narrow. The entire world of the ten directions is eighty-four thousand dharma-expounding skandhas, eighty-four thousand samadhis, and eighty-four thousand dharanis.

Because the eighty-four thousand dharma-expounding skandhas are turning the dharma wheel, the moment the dharma wheel is turned, the true human body covers the whole universe and extends throughout all time. It is not that the true human body is unlimited; the true human body is just the true human body. At this moment it is you, at this moment it is I, that is the true human body, the entire world of the ten directions. Study the way without missing these points.

Even if you were to renounce the body or accept the body for three great eons, for thirteen great eons, or for innumerable eons, by all means this is the moment to study the way, to study the way backward and forward.

To bow all the way to the floor and to bow standing is awesome presence in motion and stillness. Painting a decayed tree and polishing a brick of dead ash continue without stopping. Even though calendar days are short and urgent, study of the way in this manner is profound and deep.

Although the life of those who have abandoned home and entered the homeless realm may appear bleak and lonely, it should not be confused with that of worldly woodcutters. Even if home leavers are continually active, their life is not the same as that of farmers. In the study of the true human body, do not get caught up in discussions of delusion or enlightenment, good or bad. Do not stay in the realm of wrong or right, true or false.

"Coming and going of birth and death is the true human body" means that even though birth-and-death is where ordinary people drift about, it is where great sages are liberated. Merely going beyond the ordinary and surpassing the sage is not the true human body. Although there are two or seven kinds of birth and death, when they are thoroughly mastered they are not to be feared, as each one of them is nothing but birth and death. How is this so? Not abandoning birth, you see death. Not abandoning death, you see birth. Birth does not hinder death. Death does not hinder birth.

Neither birth nor death is known by ordinary people. Birth is like a cypress tree. Death is like an iron person. Even if a cypress tree were to hinder a cypress tree, birth is never hindered by death. Accordingly, birth and death are the study of the way. Birth is not like one sheet of cloth; death is not like two rolls of cloth. Death is not the opposite of birth; birth does not precede death.

––––––––––

Keqin, Zen Master Yuanwu, said:

> Birth is the emergence of undivided activity.
> Death is the emergence of undivided activity.
> Filling up the great empty sky,
> straightforward mind is always bits and pieces.

Quietly pursue and examine these words. Although Keqin said this, he did not understand that birth-and-death further overflows undivided activity.

When you study coming and going, in coming there is birth-and-death, in going there is birth-and-death. In birth there is coming and going, in death there is coming and going. Coming and going are to fly in and fly out with the entire world of the ten directions as two or three wings, and to walk forward and backward with the entire world of the ten directions as three or five feet.

With birth and death as its head and tail, the entire world of the ten directions, the true human body, freely turns the body and flaps the brain. When turning the body and flapping the brain, it is the size of a penny, it is inside a particle of dust. It is the vast, flat earth, it is a sheer eight-thousand-foot cliff. Where there is a sheer eight-thousand-foot cliff, there is the vast, flat earth. In this way, the true human body is manifested as the Southern and Northern Continents. To examine this is the study of the way.

The true human body is the bones and marrow of the realm beyond consciousness and unconsciousness. Just raising this up is the study of the way.

This was taught to the assembly of the Horin Monastery on the ninth day, the ninth month, the third year of the Ninji Era [1242].

39

WITHIN A DREAM
EXPRESSING THE DREAM

THE PATH OF all buddhas and ancestors arises before the first forms emerge; it cannot be spoken of using conventional views. This being so, in the realm of buddha ancestors there is the active power of buddhas going beyond buddhas. Since this realm is not a matter of the passage of time, their lives are neither long nor short, neither quick nor slow. This cannot be judged in an ordinary manner. Thus, the dharma wheel has been set to turn since before the first sign of forms emerged. The great merit needs no reward, and becomes the guidepost for all ages. Within a dream this is the dream you express. Because awakening is seen within awakening, the dream is expressed within a dream.

The place where the dream is expressed within a dream is the land and the assembly of buddha ancestors. The buddhas' lands and their assemblies, the ancestors' way and their seats, are awakening throughout awakening, and express the dream within a dream. When you meet such speech and expressions, do not regard them as other than the buddhas' assembly; it is buddha turning the dharma wheel. This dharma wheel encompasses all the ten directions and the eight facets of a clear crystal, and so the great oceans, Mount Sumeru, the lands, and all buddhas are actualized. This is the dream expressed within a dream, prior to all dreams.

Every dewdrop manifested in every realm is a dream. This dream is the glowing clarity of the hundred grasses. What requires questioning is this very point. What is confusing is this very point. At this time, there are dream grasses, grasses within, expressive grasses, and so on. When we study this, then roots, stems, branches, leaves, flowers, and fruits, as well as radiance and color, are all the great dream. Do not mistake them as merely dreamy.

However, those who do not wish to study buddha dharma believe that expressing the dream within a dream means speaking of unreal dream grass as real, like piling delusion upon delusion. But this is not true. When you say, "Within confusion is just confusion," still you should follow the path in the vast sky known as "delusion throughout delusion." You should endeavor to investigate just this thoroughly.

———————

The expressing of the dream within a dream is all buddhas. All buddhas are wind and rain, water and fire. We respectfully maintain these names of buddhas, and also pay homage to those names of other buddhas. To express the dream within a dream is the ancient buddhas; it is to ride in this treasure boat and directly arrive in the practice place. Directly arriving in the practice place is riding in this treasure boat. Meandering dreams and direct dreams, holding and letting go, all freely flow like gusting breezes.

The dharma wheel is just like this; turning the great dharma-wheel-world is immeasurable and boundless. It turns even within a single particle, ebbing and flowing ceaselessly within the particle. Accordingly, whenever such a dharma is turned, even an antagonist nods and smiles. Wherever such a dharma is turned, it freely circulates like the flowing breezes.

Thus, the endless turning of dharma traverses the entire land. In the all-embracing world, cause and effect are not ignored, and all buddhas are unsurpassable. Know that being present in all situations, the guiding way of all buddhas in the amassing of expressions of dharma is boundlessly transforming. Do not search for the limits of dharma in the past and future.

All things leave and all things arrive right here. This being so, one plants twining vines and gets entangled in twining vines. This is the characteristic of unsurpassable enlightenment. Just as enlightenment is limitless, sentient beings are limitless and unsurpassable. Just as cages and snares are limitless, emancipation from them is limitless. The actualization of the fundamental point is: "I grant you thirty blows." This is the actualization of expressing the dream within a dream.

Thus, a tree with no roots, the ground where no light or shade falls, and a valley where no shouts echo are no other than the actualized expressions of the dream within a dream. This is neither the realm of humans nor of heavenly beings, and cannot be judged by ordinary people. Who could doubt that a dream is enlightenment, since it is not within the purview of doubt? Who could recognize this dream, since it is not related to recognition? Since unsurpassable enlightenment is unsurpassable enlightenment, so the dream is called a dream.

———————

There are inner dreams, dream expressions, expressions of dreams, and dreams inside. Without being within a dream, there is no expression of dreams. Without expressing dreams, there is no being within a dream. Without expressing dreams, there are no buddhas. Without being within a dream, buddhas do not emerge and turn the wondrous dharma wheel. This dharma wheel is no other than a buddha together with a buddha, and a dream expressed within a dream. Simply expressing the dream within a dream is itself buddhas and ancestors, the assembly of unsurpassable enlightenment. Furthermore, going beyond the dharma body is itself expressing the dream within a dream.

Here is the encounter of a buddha with a buddha. No attachments are needed to the head, eyes, marrow, and brain, or body, flesh, hands, and feet. Without attachment, one who buys gold sells gold. This is called the mystery of mysteries, the wonder of wonders, the awakening of awakenings, the head top above the head. This is the daily activity of buddha ancestors. When you study this head top, you may think that the head only means a human skull, without understanding that it is the crown of Vairochana Buddha. How can you realize it as the tips of the bright, clear hundred grasses? Who knows that this is the head as it is?

Since ancient times the phrase "the head top placed above the head" has been spoken. Hearing this phrase, foolish people think that it cautions against adding something extra. Usually they refer to something that should not occur when they say, "How can you add a head on top of a head?" Actually, isn't this a mistake?

The expression of the dream within a dream can be aroused by both ordinary people and sages. Moreover, the expression of the dream within a dream by both ordinary people and sages arose yesterday and develops today. Know that yesterday's expression of the dream within a dream was the recognition of this expression as expressing the dream within a dream. The present expression of the dream within a dream is to experience right now this expression as expressing the dream within a dream. Indeed, this is the marvelous joy of meeting a buddha.

We should regret that, although the dream of the buddha ancestors' bright hundred grass tops is apparent, clearer than a hundred thousand suns and moons, the ignorant do not see it. What a pity! The head that is "the head placed above the head" is exactly the head tops of a hundred grasses, thousands of types of heads, the ten thousand kinds of heads, the heads throughout the body, the heads of the entire world unconcealed, the heads of the entire world of the ten directions, the heads of teacher and student that join in a single phrase, the head top of a one-hundred-foot pole. "Placing" and "above" in "placing the head top above the head" are both heads. Study and investigate this.

Thus, the passage "All buddhas and their unsurpassable, complete enlightenment emerge from this [Diamond] sutra" is exactly expressing the dream within a dream, which has always been the head placed atop the head. This sutra, while expressing the dream within a dream, brings forth buddhas with their unsurpassed enlightenment. These buddhas, with their enlightenment, in turn speak this sutra, which is the established expression of the dream within a dream.

As the cause of a dream is not obscure, the effect of the dream is not ignored. This is indeed one mallet striking one thousand or ten thousand blows, one thousand or ten thousand mallets striking one or half a blow. As it is so, a thing of suchness expresses the dream within a dream; a person of suchness expresses the dream within a dream. A thing beyond suchness expresses the dream within a dream; a person beyond suchness expresses the dream within a dream. This understanding has been acknowledged as crystal clear. What is called "talking all day long about a dream within a dream" is no other than the actual expression of the dream within a dream.

An ancient buddha said, "Now I express the dream within a dream for you. All buddhas in the past, present, and future express the dream within a dream. The six early generations of Chinese ancestors express the dream within a dream."

Study and clarify these words. Shakyamuni Buddha holding up the flower and blinking is exactly the expression of the dream within a dream. Huike doing prostrations and attaining the marrow is also the expression of the dream within a dream.

Making one brief utterance, beyond understanding and beyond knowing, is the expression of the dream within a dream. As the expression of the dream within a dream is the thousand hands and eyes of Avalokiteshvara that function by many means, the power of seeing colors and sounds, and hearing colors and sounds, is fully maintained. The manifesting body is the expression of the dream within a dream. The expressions of dreams and of myriad aspects of dharma are the expression of the dream within a dream. Taking hold and letting go are the expressions of the dream within a dream. Directly pointing is expressing the dream; hitting the mark is expressing the dream.

When you take hold or when you let go, you need to study the common balancing scale. As soon as you understand it, the measuring of ounces and pounds will become clear and will express the dream within a dream. Without knowing ounces and pounds, and without reaching the level balance, there is no actualization of the balance point. When you attain balanced equilibrium, you will see the balance point. Achieving balance does not depend on the objects being weighed, on the balancing scale, or on the activity of weighing, but just hangs on emptiness. Thus, deeply consider that without attaining balance you do not experience solidity. Just hanging on its own in emptiness, the expression of the dream within a dream allows objects to float free in emptiness. Within emptiness, stable balance is manifested. Stable balance is the great way of the balance scale. While suspending emptiness and suspending objects, whether as emptiness or as forms, expression of the dream within a dream brings level balance.

There is no liberation other than expression of the dream within a dream. The dream is the entire great earth; the entire great earth is stable. Thus, the inexhaustibility of turning the head and pivoting the brain [actualizing freedom] is just your awakening of the dream within a dream—identifying with and actualizing the dream within a dream.

———————

Shakyamuni Buddha said in a verse [in the *Lotus Sutra*]:

> All buddhas, with bodies of golden hue,
> splendidly adorned with a hundred auspicious marks,
> hear the dharma and expound it for others.
> Such is the fine dream that ever occurs.
> In the dream you are made king,
> then forsake palace and household entourage,
> along with utmost satisfaction of the five-sense
>   desires,
> and travel to the site of practice
> under the bodhi tree.
> On the lion's seat
> in search of the way, after seven days
> you attain the wisdom of the buddhas,
> completing the unsurpassable way.
> Arising and turning the dharma wheel,
> you expound the dharma for the four groups of
>   practitioners
> throughout thousands of millions of kalpas,
> expressing the wondrous dharma free of flaws,
> and liberating innumerable sentient beings.
> Finally you enter pari-nirvana,
> like the smoke dispersing as the lamp is extinguished.
> If later in the unwholesome world
> one expounds this foremost dharma,
> one will produce great benefit,
> like the merit just described.

Study this discourse of the Buddha, and thoroughly investigate this buddha assembly of the buddhas [in the *Lotus Sutra*]. This dream of buddhas is not an analogy. As the wondrous dharma of all buddhas is mastered only by a buddha together with a buddha, all dharmas awakened in the dream are genuine forms. In awakening there is aspiration, practice, enlightenment, and nirvana. Within the dream there is aspiration, practice, enlightenment, and nirvana. Every awakening within a dream is the genuine form, without regard to large or small, superior or inferior.

However, on hearing the words in the passage, *In the dream you are made king,* people in the past and present mistakenly think that, due to the power of expounding *this foremost dharma,* mere night dreams may become like this dream of buddhas. Those who think like this have not yet clarified the Buddha's discourse.

Awakening and dreaming are from the beginning one suchness, the genuine reality. The buddha dharma, even if it were an analogy, is the genuine reality. As it is not an analogy, *made king in the dream* is the reality of the buddha dharma.

Shakyamuni Buddha and all buddhas and ancestors each arouse the mind, cultivate practice, and attain universal true awakening within a dream. This being so, the Buddha's path of transforming the Saha World throughout his lifetime is indeed created in a dream.

In search of the way, after seven days is the measure of attained buddha wisdom. As for what is described, *Turning the dharma wheel . . . throughout thousands of millions of kalpas . . . liberating innumerable sentient beings*—these fluctuations within a dream cannot be traced.

All buddhas, with bodies of golden hue, splendidly adorned with a hundred auspicious marks, hear the dharma and expound it for others. Such is the fine dream that ever occurs. These words clearly show that this *fine dream* is illuminated as *all buddhas.*

There is the *ever occurring* of the Tathagata's words; it is not only hundreds of years of dreaming. *Expounding it for others* is manifesting the body. *Hearing the dharma* is hearing sounds with the eye, and with the mind. It is hearing sounds in the old nest, and before the empty kalpa.

Since it is said that *All buddhas, with bodies of golden hue, splendidly adorned with a hundred auspicious marks,* we can directly realize beyond any doubt that this *fine dream* is itself *all buddhas with bodies.* Although within awakening the buddhas' transformations never cease, the buddha ancestors' emergence is itself the creation of a dream within a dream. Be mindful of not slandering the buddha dharma. When you practice not slandering the buddha dharma, this path of the tathagatas is immediately actualized.

Presented to the assembly of the Kannondori Kosho Horin Monastery, Uji County, Yamashiro Province, on the twenty-first day, the ninth month, the third year of the Ninji Era [1242].

40

EXPRESSIONS

ALL BUDDHAS AND ancestors are expressions. Thus, when buddha ancestors intend to select buddha ancestors, they always ask, "Do you have your expression?"

This question is asked with the mind and with the body. It is asked with a walking stick or a whisk. It is asked with a pillar or a lantern. Those who are not buddha ancestors do not ask this and do not answer this, since they are not in the position to do so.

Such an expression is not obtained by following others or by the power of oneself. Where there is a thorough inquiry of a buddha ancestor, there is an expression of a buddha ancestor.

Within the expression, those in the past practiced and became thoroughly realized; you in the present pursue and endeavor in the way. When you pursue a buddha ancestor as a buddha ancestor, and understand the buddha ancestor's expression, this expression spontaneously becomes the practice of three years, eight, thirty, or forty years. It makes an utmost effort, and creates an expression.

———————

[Dogen's note on the back of the following text says: "The thirty years or twenty years (of practice) are the years and months created by expressions. These years and months bring their efforts together to help create expressions."]

Then, even for decades, there is not a single gap in expression. Thus, the understanding at the moment of thorough realization should be authentic. As this understanding is recognized as authentic, what is expressed now is beyond doubt. This being so, there is an expression right now, an understanding right now. An expression right now and an understanding in the past are a single track, myriad miles. The practice right now is practiced by the expression and by the understanding.

The grip of this practice accumulates in months and years and lets go of the practice from the months and years in the past. When it is about to drop away, the skin, flesh, bones, and marrow also affirm the dropping away; the nation, land, mountains, and rivers together affirm the dropping away. When you intend to get to the dropping away as an ultimate treasure place, this intention is a manifestation [of the expression]. So, at this very moment, an expression is actualized without being waited for. Although this is not an effort of the mind or the body, a spontaneous expression arises. When it is expressed, you won't feel unfamiliar or suspicious.

And yet, when you express such an expression, you beyond-express a beyond-expression. Even if you recognize that you express within an expression, if you do not thoroughly realize beyond-expression as beyond-expression, it is not yet the face of a buddha ancestor, nor is it a buddha ancestor's bones and marrow.

In this way, how can the expression of bowing three times and standing in the original position [by Huike] be the same as an expression of those who view the skin, flesh, bones, and marrow [as separate from one another]? The expression of those who view the skin, flesh, bones, and marrow cannot touch or include the expression of bowing three times and standing in the original position. An encounter of you with other as an encounter of separate beings remains an encounter of other with you as an encounter of separate beings.

You have expression and beyond-expression. Other has expression and beyond-expression. Expression has you and other. Beyond-expression has you and other.

———

Zhaozhou, Great Master Zhenji, said, "If you sit steadfastly without leaving the monastery for a lifetime, and do not speak for five or ten years, no one will call you speechless. After that, even buddhas will not equal you."

In this way, when you think of the practice and endeavor of not leaving the monastery for a lifetime, staying in the monastery for five or ten years, going through frost and flowers, the steadfast sitting that has been sat through is a certain expression. Walking, sitting, and lying down *without leaving the monastery* is the practice of *no one will call you speechless*. Although how the lifetime comes about is beyond our knowledge, if you activate *without leaving the monastery*, you do not leave the monastery.

What kind of invisible path is there between the lifetime and the monastery? Just investigate steadfast sitting. Do not avoid no-expression. No-expression is expression from beginning to end.

Steadfast sitting is one lifetime, two lifetimes, not merely one time, two times. If you sit steadfastly without speaking for five or ten years, even buddhas will not ignore you. Indeed, such steadfast sitting without speaking is something buddha eyes cannot see, buddha power cannot pull away, and buddhas cannot question.

What Zhaozhou meant is that the expression of beyond-expression in steadfast sitting is why buddhas cannot call the person speechless or beyond speechless. Thus, not leaving the monastery for a lifetime is not leaving expression for a lifetime. Sitting steadfastly without speaking for five or six years is expression for five or six years.

It is not leaving beyond-expression for a lifetime, or expression beyond attainment for five or six years. It is cutting through one hundred, one thousand buddhas, by sitting. It is one hundred, one thousand buddhas cutting through you by sitting.

This being so, what is expressed by buddha ancestors is not leaving the monastery for a lifetime. Even if you are speechless, you have expression. Do not assume that a speechless person cannot express.

It is not that one who can express is not speechless. A speechless person can also express. The speechless voice is heard. Listen to the speechless voice.

Without being a speechless person, how can you encounter a speechless person, how can you speak with someone who is speechless?

When you are already a speechless person, how do you encounter one, how do you speak with one? Investigate in this way and thoroughly study someone who is speechless.

———

In the assembly of Xuefeng, Great Master Zhenjiao, there was a monk who built a thatched-roof hermitage at the foot of a mountain. He did not shave for years. No one knew what was happening in the hermitage, and his life in the mountain was solitary. He would go to the nearby valley brook, fetch water with the wooden dipper he himself had made, and drink it. Indeed, he was a valley drinker.

As he spent days and months in this way, his practice was noticed by another monk, who went to see him and asked, "What is the meaning of Bodhidharma's coming from India?"

The hermit said, "The valley is deep, the dipper handle is long."

The monk was so shocked that he did not bow, nor did he ask for teaching. He went up to the mountain and told Xuefeng the story.

Hearing this, Xuefeng said, "It is quite amazing. If he is like that, I should go over and check him out."

What Xuefeng meant was that the hermit seemed amazingly accomplished, but he wanted to examine how he was doing.

So, one day, Xuefeng had his attendant monk carry a razor and rushed to the hermitage. As soon as Xuefeng saw the hermit, he said, "If you have expression, I will not shave your head."

Be aware of this statement. Xuefeng's words sound like he would not shave the hermit's head if the hermit had expression. How is it? Is it that if the expression was truly expression, Xuefeng would not shave the hermit's head? You should listen to this expression with the power of listening. Speak about it to those who have the power of listening.

Hearing Xuefeng's words, the hermit washed his head and came back to Xuefeng. Is this bringing expression or beyond-expression?

Xuefeng shaved the hermit's head.

This story is indeed like the emergence of an udumbara blossom— rare to encounter and rare to hear. It is beyond the realm of seven or ten sages. It is beyond the understanding of three or seven wisdom beings. Teachers of sutras and treatises or practitioners of supernormal powers cannot measure it. To encounter the emergence of a buddha is to hear a story such as this.

Now, what is the meaning of Xuefeng's words, *If you have expression, I will not shave your head*? When people who have not yet attained expression hear this, those with capacity may be astonished and those without may be confused.

Xuefeng did not ask the hermit about a buddha, and the hermit did not speak of the way. Xuefeng did not ask him about samadhi, and the hermit did not speak of dharani. Although Xuefeng's words may have sounded like a question, they were expression. Examine this thoroughly.

In this situation, when the hermit was challenged by Xuefeng's expression, he was not confused, because he had genuine understanding. Without hiding his style of practice, he washed his head and came back to Xuefeng. This is a dharma realization that even a buddha with buddha wisdom cannot get near. It is emergence of a [buddha] body, expounding of dharma, awakening of sentient beings, and coming with a washed head.

If Xuefeng had not been a true person, he would have thrown down the razor and burst into laughter. However, he was a true person with great capacity, so he shaved the hermit's head.

Indeed, if Xuefeng and the hermit had not been "only a buddha and a buddha," it would not have happened this way. If they had not been one buddha in two buddhas, it would not have happened this way. If they had not been a dragon and a dragon, it would not have happened this way. Although a dragon's pearl is tirelessly spared by the dragon, it naturally falls into the hand of a person of understanding.

Know that Xuefeng checked out the hermit and the hermit encountered Xuefeng. With expression and beyond-expression, one got his head shaved and the other shaved his head.

Thus, good friends of expression have a way to visit unexpectedly. Friends beyond-expression have a place to be acquainted without expectation. Where there is the practice of getting acquainted, expression is actualized.

Written and presented to the assembly of the Kannondori Kosho Horin Monastery on the fifth day, the tenth month, the third year of the Ninji Era [1242].

41

PAINTING OF A RICE CAKE

A<small>LL BUDDHAS ARE</small> realization; thus all things are realization. Yet, no buddhas or things have the same characteristics; none have the same mind. Although there are no identical characteristics or minds, at the moment of your actualization, numerous actualizations manifest without hindrance. At the moment of your manifestation, numerous manifestations come forth without touching one another. This is the straightforward teaching of the ancestors.

Do not use the measure of oneness or difference as the criterion of your study. Thus, it is said, "To reach one thing is to reach myriad things."

To reach one thing does not take away its inherent characteristics. Just as reaching does not make one thing separate, it does not make one thing not separate. To try to make it not different is a hindrance. When you allow reaching to be unhindered by reaching, one reaching is myriad reachings. One reaching is one thing. Reaching one thing is reaching myriad things.

———————

An ancient buddha [Xiangyan Zhixian] said, "A painting of a rice cake does not satisfy hunger."

Those in cloud robes and mist sleeves who study this statement, as well as bodhisattvas and shravakas who come from the ten directions, differ in name and position; the skin and flesh of divine heads or of demon faces in the ten directions differ, sometimes thick, sometimes thin.

This statement has been studied by ancient buddhas and present buddhas; it has become a theme to ponder by seekers in grass-roofed huts and under trees. When they transmit their teaching, they say, "This statement means that studying the sutras and commentaries does not nourish true wisdom." Or they suppose it means that to study the sutras of the Three Vehicles or the One Vehicle is not the way of complete enlightenment.

However, to think this statement means that expedient teachings are useless is a great mistake. This is not the authentic transmission of the ancestors' teaching; it obscures the words of the buddha ancestors. If you do not understand this one buddha's phrase, who could acknowledge that you have thoroughly understood the words of other buddhas?

To say *A painting of a rice cake does not satisfy hunger* is like saying, "to refrain from unwholesome action and do wholesome action." It is like saying, "What is it that thus comes?" It is like saying, "I am always intimate with this." Investigate it in this way.

There are few who have even seen through this *painting of a rice cake,* and none of them has thoroughly understood it. How is this so? When I inquired of a few skin bags in the past, they had never questioned or investigated this matter. They were unconcerned with it, as if it were someone else's gossip.

Know that a painted rice cake is your face after your parents were born, your face before your parents were born. Thus, although it is neither born nor unborn, the moment when a painted rice cake is made of rice flour is the moment of actualizing of the way. Do not see this moment as affected by the limited view that a painted rice cake comes and goes.

The paints for painting rice cakes are the same as those used for painting mountains and waters. For painting mountains and waters, blue and red paints are used; for painting rice cakes, rice flour is used. Thus, they are painted in the same way, and they are examined in the same way.

Accordingly, *painted rice cake* spoken of here means that sesame rice cakes, herb rice cakes, milk rice cakes, toasted rice cakes, millet rice cakes, and the like are all actualized in the painting. Thus, understand that a painting is all-inclusive, a rice cake is all-inclusive, things are all-inclusive. In this way, all rice cakes actualized right now are nothing but a painted rice cake.

If you look for some other kind of painted rice cake, you will never find it, you will never grasp it. A painted rice cake at once appears and does not appear. This being so, it has no mark of old or young, and has no trace of coming or going. Just here, the land of painted rice cakes is revealed and confirmed.

The phrase *does not satisfy hunger* means this hunger, not the ordinary matter of the twelve hours, never encounters a painted rice cake. Even if you were to eat a painted rice cake, it would never put an end to this hunger. Rice cakes are not separate from hunger. Rice cakes are not separate from rice cakes. Thus, these activities and teachings cannot be given away. Hunger is a single staff maneuvered horizontally and vertically through a thousand changes and myriad forms. A rice cake is the wholeness of body and mind actualized. A rice cake is blue, yellow, red, and white as well as long, short, square, and round.

When mountains and waters are painted, blue, green, and red paints are used, strange rocks and wondrous stones are used, the four jewels and the seven treasures are used. Rice cakes are painted in the same manner. When a person is painted, the four great elements and the five skandhas are used. When a buddha is painted, not only a clay altar or lump of earth is used, but the thirty-two marks, a blade of grass, and the cultivation of wisdom for incalculable eons are used. As a buddha has been painted on a single scroll in this way, all buddhas are painted buddhas, and all painted buddhas are actual buddhas.

Examine a painted buddha, and examine a painted rice cake. Which is the black stone tortoise and which is the iron staff? Which is form and which is mind? Pursue and investigate this in detail. When you penetrate this matter, the coming and going of birth and death is a painting. Unsurpassed enlightenment is a painting. The entire universe and the open sky are nothing but a painting.

An ancient buddha said:

> Attaining the way—a thousand snowflakes disappear.
> Painting green mountains—several scrolls appear.

This is an utterance of great enlightenment, actualized practice in the endeavor of the way. Accordingly, at the moment of attaining the way, green mountains and white snow are painted on countless scrolls. Motion and stillness are nothing but a painting. Our endeavor at this moment is brought forth entirely from a painting.

The ten names and the three miraculous powers are a painting on a scroll. The roots, capacities, awakenings, and noble path are also a painting on a scroll. If you say a painting is not real, then the myriad things are not real. If the myriad things are not real, then buddha dharma is not real. As buddha dharma is real, a painted rice cake is real.

Yunmen, Great Master Kuangzhen, was once asked by a monk, "What is your statement about going beyond buddhas and surpassing ancestors?"

Yunmen said, "A sesame rice cake."

Quietly examine these words. When this sesame rice cake is actualized, an ancient teacher gives expression to going beyond buddhas and surpassing the ancestors. An iron person asks this question and students understand it. Thus, this expression is complete. Unrolling the matter and hurling insightful flashes as a sesame rice cake is itself two or three painted rice cakes. Yunmen's is a statement that goes beyond buddhas and surpasses ancestors—an activity that enters buddhas and enters demons.

Rujing, my late master, said, "A tall bamboo and a plantain enter a painting."

This phrase means that things beyond measure are actualized together in a painting. A tall bamboo is long. Although it is moved by yin and yang, the months and years of the tall bamboo move yin and yang. The months and years of yin and yang are beyond measure. Although the great sages understand yin and yang, they cannot measure it. Yin and yang are all-inclusive phenomena, all-inclusive scale, and the all-inclusive way.

Yin and yang spoken of here have nothing to do with views held by those outside the way or those in the Two Vehicles. Yin and yang belong to the tall bamboo. They are the passage of time of the tall bamboo and the world of the tall bamboo. All buddhas of the ten directions are the family of the tall bamboo.

Know that the entire heaven and earth are the roots, stem, branches, and leaves of the tall bamboo. This makes heaven and earth timeless; this makes the great oceans, Mount Sumeru, and the worlds of the ten directions indestructible. A walking stick and an arched bamboo stick are old and beyond old.

A plantain has earth, water, fire, air, and emptiness, as well as mind, consciousness, and wisdom as its roots, stems, branches, leaves, flowers, fruits, colors, and forms. Accordingly, the plantain wears the autumn wind and is torn in the autumn wind. We know that it is pure and clear, and that not a single particle is excluded.

There is no muscle in the eye. There is no pigment in the paints. This is emancipation right here. As emancipation is not a matter of time, it is not concerned with a discussion of a certain moment or instant. Taking up this understanding, make earth, water, fire, and air your vital activity; make mind, consciousness, and wisdom your great death. In this manner, the activities of the [buddha] house have been passed on with spring, autumn, winter, and summer as furnishings [essentials].

Now, the fluctuations of the tall bamboo and the plantain are a painting. Those who experience great awakening upon hearing the sound of bamboo, whether they are snakes or dragons [ordinary or extraordinary practitioners], are all paintings. Do not doubt it with the limited view that separates ordinary from sacred.

That bamboo pole is just long. This pole is just short. This pole is just long. That pole is just short. As these are all paintings, the painted forms of long and short always accord with each other. When you paint something long, you cannot help painting something short. Thoroughly investigate the meaning of this. As the entire world and all phenomena are a painting, human existence appears from a painting, and buddha ancestors are actualized from a painting.

―――――――

Since this is so, there is no remedy for satisfying hunger other than a painted rice cake. Without painted hunger, you never become a true person. There is no understanding other than painted satisfaction. In fact, satisfying hunger, satisfying beyond hunger, not satisfying hunger, and not satisfying beyond hunger cannot be attained or spoken of without painted hunger. For now, study all of these as a painted rice cake.

When you understand this teaching with your body and mind, you will thoroughly experience the ability to turn things and be turned by things. If this is not done, the power of the study of the way is not yet realized. To enact this ability is to actualize the painting of enlightenment.

Presented to the assembly of the Kannondori Kosho Horin Monastery on the fifth day, the eleventh month, the third year of the Ninji Era [1242].

42

UNDIVIDED ACTIVITY

THE GREAT WAY of all buddhas, thoroughly practiced, is emancipation and realization.

"Emancipation" means that in birth [life] you are emancipated from birth [life], and in death you are emancipated from death. Thus, there is detachment from birth-and-death and penetration of birth-and-death. Such is the complete practice of the great way. There is letting go of birth-and-death and vitalizing birth-and-death. Such is the thorough practice of the great way.

"Realization" is birth; birth is realization. At the time of realization there is nothing but birth totally actualized, nothing but death totally actualized.

Such activity makes birth wholly birth and death wholly death. Actualized just so at this moment, this activity is neither large nor small, neither immeasurable nor measurable, neither remote nor near. Birth right now is undivided activity. Undivided activity is birth right now.

Birth neither comes nor goes. Birth neither appears nor is already existing. Thus, birth is totally manifested and death is totally manifested.

Know that there are innumerable beings in yourself, where there is birth and there is death.

Quietly think over whether birth and all things that arise together with birth are inseparable or not. There is neither a moment nor a thing that is apart from birth. There is neither an object nor a mind that is apart from birth.

Birth is just like riding in a boat. You raise the sails and you steer. Although you maneuver the sail and the pole, the boat gives you a ride, and without the boat you couldn't ride. But you ride in the boat, and your riding makes the boat what it is. Investigate a moment such as this. At just such a moment, there is nothing but the world of the boat. The sky, the water, and the shore are all the boat's world, which is not the same as a world that is not the boat's. Thus, you make birth what it is, you make birth your birth.

When you ride in a boat, your body, mind, and environs together are the undivided activity of the boat. The entire earth and the entire sky are both the undivided activity of the boat. Thus, birth is nothing but you; you are nothing but birth.

———————

Keqin, Zen Master Yuanwu of Mount Jia, said, "Birth is undivided activity. Death is undivided activity."

Clarify and investigate these words. What you should investigate is: While the undivided activity of birth has no beginning or end, and covers the entire earth and the entire sky, it hinders neither birth's undivided activity nor death's undivided activity. At the moment of death's undivided activity, while it covers the entire earth and the entire sky, it hinders neither death's undivided activity nor birth's undivided activity. This being so, birth does not hinder death; death does not hinder birth.

———————

Both the entire earth and the entire sky appear in birth as well as in death. However, it is not that one and the same entire earth and sky are fully manifested in birth and in death: although not one, not different; although not different, not the same; although not the same, not many.

Similarly, in birth there is the undivided activity of all things, and in death there is the undivided activity of all things. There is undivided activity in what is not birth and not death. There is birth and there is death in undivided activity.

This being so, the undivided activity of birth and death is like a young person bending and stretching, or it is like someone asleep at night searching for the pillow. This is realization in vast, wondrous light.

At just such a moment you may suppose that because realization is manifested in undivided activity, there was no realization prior to this. However, prior to this realization, undivided activity was manifested. The undivided activity manifested previously does not hinder the present realization of undivided activity. Thus, your understanding can be manifested moment after moment.

Presented to the assembly at the residence of the former governor of Izumo Province, next to the Rokuharamitsu Temple, Kyoto, on the seventeenth day, the twelfth month, the third year of the Ninji Era [1242].

43

THE MOON

FULLY ACTUALIZING MOONS is not limited to "three three before" [moons on the first nine days of a lunar-calendar month] or "three three after" [moons on the last days of a month]. Moons fully actualized are not limited to "three three before" or "three three after."

Since this is so, Shakyamuni Buddha said, "Buddha's true dharma body as it is, is open sky. In response to things, forms appear. Thus is the moon in water."

The thusness of *Thus is the moon in water* is the moon in water. It is water thusness, moon thusness, thusness within, within thusness. *Thus* does not mean "like something." *Thus* means exactly.

Buddha's true dharma body is the *as it is* of open sky. This open sky is the *as it is* of buddha's true dharma body. Because it is buddha's true dharma body, the entire earth, the entire universe, all phenomena, and all appearances are open sky. Hundreds of grasses and myriad forms—each appearing *as it is*—are nothing but buddha's true dharma body, thusness of the moon in water.

The time when the moon appears is not necessarily night. Night is not necessarily dark. Do not be limited to the narrow views held by human beings. Even where there is no sun or moon, there is day and night. Sun and moon are not day and night; each is *as it is*.

The moon is not one moon or two moons, not thousands of moons or myriads of moons. Even if the moon itself holds the view of one moon or two moons, that is merely the moon's view. It is not necessarily the words or understanding of the buddha way.

Even if you say, "There was a moon last night," the moon you see tonight is not last night's moon. Thoroughly study that tonight's moon, from beginning to end, is tonight's moon. Although there is a moon, it is neither new nor old, because a moon succeeds in a moon.

———

Panshan, Zen Master Baoji, said, "The mind moon is alone and full. Its light swallows myriad forms. Moonlight does not illuminate objects. Objects do not exist. Light and objects both disappear. What is this?"

What is said here is that buddha ancestors and buddha heirs always have the mind moon, because they make moon their mind. There is no mind that is not moon, and there is no moon that is not mind.

Alone and full means nothing lacking. Beyond two or three is called *myriad forms*. Myriad forms are moonlight, not merely forms. Accordingly, *Its light swallows myriad forms.* Myriad forms completely swallow moonlight. Here moonlight swallowing moonlight is called *Its light swallows myriad forms.* That is to say, the moon swallows the moon, the moonlight swallows the moon. Therefore, it is said, *Moonlight does not illuminate objects. Objects do not exist.*

Since this is so, at the moment of awakening others with a buddha body, a buddha body comes forth and expounds dharma; at the moment of awakening others with the boundless body, the boundless body manifests and expounds dharma. This is nothing but turning the dharma wheel within the moon. No matter whether the yin spirit or the yang spirit illuminates, no matter whether the moon is a fire jewel or a water jewel, a buddha body is immediately actualized.

This mind is the moon. This moon of itself is mind. This is penetrating and comprehending the mind of buddha ancestors and buddha heirs.

———

An ancient buddha said, "A single mind is all things. All things are a single mind."

Thus, mind is all things, all things are mind. Since mind is the moon, the moon is the moon. Since mind, which is all things, is completely moon, the all-inclusive world is the all-inclusive moon; the entire body is the entire moon. Amid the "three three before and three three after" in the myriad years of this moment, what is not the moon?

Sun-Face Buddha, Moon-Face Buddha—our body, mind, and environs—are also within the moon. The coming and going of birth and death is also the moon. The entire world of the ten directions is the up and down, the left and right of the moon. Everyday activity at this moment is hundreds of grasses brilliant in the moon, the mind of ancestors brilliant in the moon.

Touzi, Great Master Ciji of Shu Region, was once asked by a monk, "When the moon is not yet full, what then?"

The master said, "Swallow three or four."

The monk said, "After it is full, what then?"

The master said, "Spit out seven or eight."

What is examined here is *not yet full* and *after it is full*. Both are the moon's activity. Each of the three or four moons is a complete moon that is *not yet full*. Each of the seven or eight moons is a complete moon that is *after it is full*.

To swallow is three or four. At this moment, the moon that is *not yet full* is actualized. To spit out is seven or eight. At this moment, *after it is full* is actualized.

When the moon swallows the moon, that is three or four. In swallowing, the moon is brought forth. The moon is swallowing actualized. When the moon spits out the moon, that is seven or eight. In spitting out, the moon is brought forth. The moon is spitting out actualized.

Thus, there is total swallowing, total spitting out. The whole earth and the whole sky are spit out. The whole sky and the whole earth are swallowed. Swallow yourself and swallow others. Spit out yourself and spit out others.

Shakyamuni Buddha said to Vajragarbha Bodhisattva, "When you look at deep water and shift your eyes, the water sways. Your fixed eyes can turn fire around. When the clouds fly, the moon travels; when a boat goes, the shore moves. It is just like this."

Thoroughly study and understand, *When the clouds fly, the moon travels; when a boat goes, the shore moves.* Do not study in haste. Do not follow ordinary thinking. But those who see and hear the Buddha's discourse as the Buddha's discourse are rare. If you study it as the Buddha's discourse, the round, full enlightenment is not limited to body and mind, or to enlightenment and nirvana. Enlightenment and nirvana are not necessarily the round, full enlightenment, nor are they body and mind.

The Tathagata says, *When the clouds fly, the moon travels,* and *when a boat goes, the shore moves.* In this way the moon travels when the clouds move, and the shore moves when the boat goes. The meaning of these words is that clouds and moon travel at the same time; they walk together with no beginning or end, no before or after. The boat and the shore travel at the same time; they walk together without starting or stopping, without floating or turning.

When you study someone's movement, the movement is not merely starting or stopping. The movement that starts or stops is not that person's. Do not take up starting or stopping and regard it as the person's movement. The clouds' flying, the moon's traveling, the boat's going, and the shore's moving are all like this. Do not foolishly be limited by a narrow view.

The clouds' flying is not concerned with east, west, south, or north. The moon's traveling has not ceased day or night from ancient times to the present. Do not forget this. The boat's going and the shore's moving are not bound by the past, present, or future, but actualize the past, present, and future. This being so, "full and not hungry just now" is possible.

Foolish people think that because clouds run we see the immovable moon as moving, and because a boat goes we see the immovable shore as moving. But if they are right, why did the Tathagata speak as he did? The meaning of buddha dharma cannot be measured by the narrow views of human or heavenly beings. Although it is immeasurable, buddha dharma is practiced in accordance with the listeners' capacities. Who is unable to take up the boat or shore over and over? Who is unable to see through the clouds or moon immediately?

Know that the Tathagata's words do not make a metaphor of clouds for dharma suchness, of the moon for dharma suchness, of the boat for dharma suchness, or of the shore for dharma suchness. Quietly examine and penetrate this. One step of the moon is the Tathagata's round, full enlightenment. The Tathagata's round, full enlightenment is the motion of the moon. The moon is beyond moving or not moving, beyond going forward or backward. The moon's motion is not an analogy. It is the essence of *alone and full*.

Know that even though the moon passes quickly it is beyond beginning, middle, or end. Thus, there is the first-month moon and the second-month moon. The first and the second are both the moon. Right practice is the moon. Right offering is the moon. Snapping the sleeves and walking away is the moon.

Round and pointed are not concerned with the cycle of coming and going. The moon is beyond coming and going; it goes freely and grasps firmly coming and going, beyond coming and going. Manifesting wind and streams, the moons are as they are.

Written at the Kannondori Kosho Horin Monastery on the sixth day, the first month, the fourth year of the Ninji Era [1243]. Monk Dogen.

44

FLOWERS IN THE SKY

BODHIDHARMA, HIGH ANCESTOR, said, "One blossom opens five petals. Fruit forms naturally."

Study the moment of the blossom's blooming and of its light and color. The blossom consists of five petals. The blossoming of the five petals is one blossom. The true meaning of this blossom leads to [his words]: "I am originally in this land to transmit dharma and save deluded sentient beings." This is a point of study of its light and color. It means: "The forming of the fruit is up to you." This is the meaning of *Fruit forms naturally*.

Forms naturally means to practice causes and experience the effects. There are causes in the common world. There are effects in the common world. You practice causes and effects in the common world and experience causes and effects in the common world.

Naturally [self thusness] means of itself. *Self* is invariably *you*. It is four great elements and five skandhas. Because it is [as Linji said] "let it be a true person of no rank," it is beyond self and other. This being so, what is indefinite is called self. *Thusness* is to accept what is as it is.

Forms naturally is the moment of the blossoming and forming of fruit. It is the moment to transmit dharma and save deluded sentient beings. It is like the time and place of the unfolding of an utpala [blue lotus] blossom that are the time and place of a blazing fire. Sparks of a gimlet and flames are all the place of unfolding and the time of aligning of an utpala blossom. Without being the time and place of an utpala blossom, not even a blink of fire is born, not even a blink of fire is activated.

Know that within a blink of fire, one hundred, one thousand utpala blossoms unfold on earth and in the sky. They unfold in the past and at present. To see and hear the present moment and present place of fire is to hear and see utpala blossoms. Without fail, see and hear the time and place of utpala blossoms.

An ancient master [Tong'an Changcha] said, "Utpala blossoms open inside fire."

In this way, utpala blossoms definitely unfold in fire. If you want to know what is inside fire, it is the place where utpala blossoms unfold. You need to exclude human views and deva views, and learn what is inside fire. If you would doubt this, you would doubt lotus blossoms born in water, or you would doubt the variety of blossoms on branches and twigs. If you doubt this, you would also doubt the stable ground of material worlds. However, you don't doubt these. Those who are not buddha ancestors do not know that the opening of blossoms raises the world.

The opening of blossoms is three three before, three three after [countless]. To fulfill these numbers, all phenomena are gathered and make the blossoms colorful. Let this understanding manifest and fathom spring and autumn. It is not only that spring and autumn have blossoms and fruit, but the time being always has blossoms and fruit.

Both blossoms and fruit maintain moments. All moments maintain blossoms and fruit. This being so, one hundred grasses all have blossoms and fruit. All trees have blossoms and fruit. Trees of gold, silver, copper, iron, coral, and crystal all have blossoms and fruit. Trees of earth, water, fire, air, space all have blossoms and fruit. Human trees have blossoms. Decayed trees have blossoms.

In the midst of these blossoms, the World-Honored One spoke of flowers in the open sky [illusory flowers]. But those who hear little and see little do not know what kind of color, light, leaves, and blossoms the flowers in the sky carry. They only hear the words *flowers in the sky*.

Know that there are teachings about flowers in the sky in the buddha way. People outside the way do not know the teachings about flowers in the sky. How can they understand them?

Only buddhas and ancestors know the opening and falling of flowers in the sky [sky blossoms] and earth blossoms, and the opening and falling of world blossoms. They alone know that flowers in the sky, earth blossoms, and world blossoms are sutras. This is a standard of studying buddhas.

Because what buddha ancestors ride on are flowers in the sky, the buddha world and all buddha dharmas are flowers in the sky. But mediocre and foolish people think that the *obscured eyes* in the Tathagata's statement "What is seen by obscured eyes are flowers in the sky" means the confused eyes of sentient beings. Because their sick eyes are already confused, they think that flowers in the sky are seen in pure space. Being attached to this view, they mistakenly see that none of the three realms and the six paths, existent buddhas and nonexistent buddhas, exist. If such deluded seeing stops, they may stop seeing such flowers in the sky and think the Tathagata said that in original emptiness there are no flowers.

What a pity! They do not know from beginning to end the moment of flowers in the sky spoken by the Tathagata. The meanings of "obscured eyes" and "flowers in the sky" have not been grasped by ordinary people and those outside the way.

Buddha tathagatas practice these flowers in the sky and attain the robe, the way of sitting, and entering the room. They attain the way and the fruit of buddhahood.

Taking up a flower and blinking are both the fundamental point actualized by obscured eyes and flowers in the sky. That the treasury of the true dharma eye, the wondrous heart of nirvana, has been authentically transmitted without cutting off is called obscured eyes and flowers in the sky. Enlightenment, nirvana, dharma body, self nature, and so on are two or three petals of the five petals of flowers unfolding in the sky.

Shakyamuni Buddha said, "Someone who has obscured eyes sees flowers in the sky. When this disease is removed, flowers in the sky disappear."

There have been no scholars who clarify this teaching. Because they don't know *the sky,* they don't know the *flowers in the sky.* Because they don't know *flowers in the sky,* they don't know, see, encounter, and become *a person with obscured eyes.*

Encounter a person with obscured eyes, and know and see the flowers in the sky. After seeing the flowers in the sky, also see that the flowers disappear in the sky. To think that the flowers in the sky stop existing once they disappear is a view in the Lesser Vehicle.

When the flowers in the sky are invisible, in what way do they exist? Mediocre scholars today only see that the flowers in the sky should be discarded. They don't know the great matter after the flowers in the sky, or the seeding, blooming, and falling of the flowers in the sky. These scholars merely regard where the atmosphere is as the sky, and where the sun, the moon, and stars hang as the sky. So, they assume that the so-called flowers in the sky change colors, float in the air like clouds, move toward east and west, up and down, blown by the wind. To regard the four great elements that create and are created, all things in the material world, the original enlightenment, and basic nature as flowers in the sky is ignorant. Such scholars don't know that there are the four great elements and the others due to all things. They don't know that the material worlds rest in their conditions due to all things. They only think that all things exist due to material worlds.

They only think that flowers in the sky exist due to obscured eyes. And they do not realize that flowers in the sky cause obscured eyes.

Know that a person with obscured eyes in the buddha way is a person of the original enlightenment, of wondrous enlightenment, of all buddhas, of the three realms, of buddha going beyond buddha. Do not misunderstand that obscuring is illusion. Do not think that there is reality other than that. Such a point is a lesser view. If obscurity and flowers [in the sky] are illusion, a view such as to create and be created is also illusion. If everything is illusion, truth cannot be established. If there is no truth to be established, the point that obscurity and flowers [in the sky] are illusion cannot be established.

When enlightenment is obscurity, all things around enlightenment are things that adorn obscurity. When delusion is obscurity, all things around delusion are things that adorn obscurity.

Say for the time being that as obscurity and the eyes are equal, the sky and flowers are equal. As obscurity and the eyes are beyond birth, the sky and flowers are beyond birth. As all things are reality, obscurity and flowers are reality.

Do not discuss the past, present, and future. As flowers in the sky are not conditioned by beginning, middle, and end, and as they are not obstructed by birth and death, flowers in the sky cause birth and death to be birth and death.

Flowers in the sky are born in the sky and perish in the sky. They are born in obscurity and perish in obscurity. They are born in flowers and perish in flowers. Further, flowers in the sky are like this in other places and times.

In studying flowers in the sky, there should be a number of ways. There are views by obscured eyes, by clear eyes, by buddha eyes, and by ancestor eyes. There are views by way-seeking eyes, by blind eyes, by three thousand years, by eight hundred years, by one hundred eons, by innumerable eons. As all of these see flowers in the sky, the sky looks different, flowers appear varied.

Know that the sky is just one blade of grass. In this sky, flowers always bloom. It is like flowers blooming on one hundred blades of grass. In order to express this teaching, the Tathagata says that in the sky there are originally no flowers.

Although there are originally no flowers, there are flowers such as peach, apricot, plum, and willow. So we say that a plum tree did not blossom yesterday, but blossoms in spring.

Thus, when the time comes, flowers open. This is the moment of flowers, the arrival of flowers. At this very moment of flowers arriving, there is no other way. Plum and willow flowers unfailingly bloom on plum and willow trees. You see the flowers and know plum and willow trees. You understand flowers by looking at plum and willow trees. Peach and apricot flowers have never bloomed on plum and willow trees. Plum and willow flowers bloom on plum and willow trees. Peach and apricot flowers bloom on peach and apricot trees. Flowers in the sky bloom in the sky in just this way. They do not bloom on other grasses or trees.

Seeing the colors of flowers in the sky, you fathom the limitlessness of fruit in the sky. Seeing the opening and falling of flowers in the sky, study the spring and autumn of flowers in the sky. The spring of flowers in the sky and the spring of other flowers should be the same. Just as there are a variety of flowers in the sky, there should be a variety of springtimes. This being so, there are springs and autumns in the past and present.

Those who assume that flowers in the sky are not real and other flowers are real have not seen or heard the Buddha's teaching. To hear the words that the sky originally had no flowers and assume that the flowers in the sky that did not exist do exist now is a lesser view based on shallow thinking. Step forward and think deeply.

An ancestor [Huike] said, "Flowers are beyond birth."

When this teaching is realized, flowers are beyond birth, beyond death; flowers are beyond flowers, the sky is beyond the sky. Do not be confused about the before and after of flowers. Do not get into a theoretical discussion of whether flowers exist or not.

Flowers always appear to be dyed by colors, but colors are not necessarily flowers. Times [seasons] also have colors, such as blue, yellow, red, white, and so on. Spring draws flowers, and flowers draw spring.

Zhang Zhuo, who had an outstanding literary capacity, was a lay student of Shishuang. He wrote a poem on his realization:

> Radiant light serenely illuminates the sands of the Ganges.
> The ordinary and sages, beings with spirits, are equally my
>   home.
> A single moment is beyond birth, actualizing the
>   undivided.
> A subtle movement of the six sense roots shelters the
>   clouds.

Removing delusions increases sickness.
Going toward true thusness is also wrong.
Follow the worldly conditions with no hindrance.
Nirvana and birth-and-death are both flowers in the sky.

Radiant light serenely illuminates the sands of the Ganges. This radiant light renews actualizing the monks' hall, buddha hall, kitchen, and monastery gate. *The sands of the Ganges* are radiant light actualized, actualizing radiant light.

The ordinary and sages, beings with spirits, are equally my home. It is not that the difference among the ordinary and sages, as well as beings with spirits, does not exist. Just do not slander them because of their differences.

A single moment is beyond birth, actualizing the undivided. Moment after moment is a single moment. It is beyond birth. It completely actualizes all things. Thus, it is expressed as *a single moment is beyond birth.*

A subtle movement of the six sense roots shelters the clouds. The six sense roots—eyes, ears, nose, tongue, body, and mind—are not merely two or three, but three and three [in a great variety] before and after. Their movement is like that of Mount Sumeru, the earth, the six sense roots, and like a subtle movement. As their movement is like that of Mount Sumeru, their no-movement is also that of Mount Sumeru. It forms clouds, it forms water.

Removing delusions increases sickness. It is not that there has been no sickness. There is buddha sickness, ancestor sickness [desire to be a buddha and ancestor]. Removing such sickness with wisdom adds sickness, increases sickness. At the very moment of removing sickness, there is delusion. Removing sickness and having delusion are simultaneous and beyond simultaneous. Delusion always comes with a way to remove it.

Going toward true thusness is also wrong. To go against true thusness is a mistake. To go toward true thusness is a mistake. True thusness is going against and going toward. There is true thusness in going against it and in going toward it. Who knows that such a mistake is also true thusness?

Follow the worldly conditions with no hindrance. The worldly conditions follow the worldly conditions. Following and further following are worldly conditions. This is called no hindrance. Hindrance and no hindrance are covered by the eye that sees through.

Nirvana and birth-and-death are both flowers in the sky. What is called nirvana is unsurpassable, complete enlightenment. It is the abode of buddha ancestors and their followers. Birth-and-death is a true human body. Although both nirvana and birth-and-death are the way of buddha ancestors and their followers, they are flowers in the sky. The root, stem, branches, leaves, blossoms, fruit, light, and colors of flowers in the sky are all open blossoms of flowers in the sky. Flowers in the sky are bound to bear fruit in the sky, dropping seeds in the sky.

Because the three realms we see and hear now are the opening of five-petal flowers in the sky, it is not like the three realms seeing the three realms. This is the reality of all things, the flower of all things. Furthermore, study that all things that cannot be measured are equally flowers in the sky, fruit in the sky, which are not different from plum, willow, peach, and apricot.

———————

Lingxun, who would later become the abbot at Mount Furong, Fu Region of Song China, asked Guizong, Zen Master Zhizhen of the Guizong Monastery, upon first studying with him, "What is the buddha?"

Guizong said, "If I answer you, would you believe it?"

Lingxun said, "How should I not believe your truthful words?"

Guizong said, "You are it."

Lingxun said, "How should I maintain it?"

Guizong replied, "If you have a spot of obscurity, flowers in the sky will scatter."

This statement by Guizong, *If you have a spot of obscurity, flowers in the sky will scatter* is an expression by a buddha who maintains [buddhahood]. Thus, know that the scattering of obscurity and flowers [in the sky] actualizes all buddhas. The flowers and fruit of the eyes in the sky are maintained by all buddhas. Guizong actualizes the eyes by obscurity. He actualizes flowers in the sky in the eyes. He actualizes the eyes in flowers in the sky.

Flowers in the sky are in the eye, while a bit of obscurity scatters. One eye is in the sky, while all obscurity scatters. Thus, obscurity is totally actualized. The eye is totally actualized. The sky is totally actualized.

The flowers are totally actualized. Scattering is one thousand eyes. There are eyes wherever the body reaches.

When and where there is one eye, there are flowers in the sky, there are flowers in the eye. The flowers in one eye are called flowers in the sky. The expression of the flowers in the eye needs to be clarified.

This being so, Langya, Great Master Guangzhao of Mount Langya said:

> How splendid! Buddhas in the ten directions are originally flowers in the eye. If you want to know the flowers in the eye, they are originally buddhas in the ten directions. If you want to know buddhas in the ten directions, they are not flowers in the eye. If you want to know flowers in the eye, they are not buddhas in the ten directions.
>
> If you clarify this, the faults belong to the buddhas in the ten directions. If you have not clarified this, shravakas dance and pratyeka-buddhas dress up.

Know that it is not that the buddhas in the ten directions are not real, but that they are originally flowers in the eye. The buddhas in the ten directions abide in the eye. Other than being in the eye, there is no abode for the buddhas.

Flowers in the eye are neither nonexistent nor existent, neither illusory nor real; they are just buddhas in the ten directions.

If you want to know the buddhas in the ten directions, they are not flowers in the eye. If you want to know flowers in the eye, they don't seem to be the buddhas in the ten directions.

This being so, both grasping clearly and not grasping clearly are flowers in the eye, the buddhas in the ten directions. *Want to know* and *they are not* both actualize *How splendid!*

The teaching of flowers in the sky and flowers on the earth expressed by buddhas and ancestors is as wondrous as this.

Commentators on sutras and treatises may have heard of flowers in the sky, but the life vein [tradition] of flowers on the earth is not seen or heard by those who are not buddha ancestors. There is an expression by a buddha ancestor who was familiar with the life vein of flowers on the earth:

Shimen, Zen Master Huiche of Mount Shimen, Great Song, was a venerated heir of Liangshan. Once a monk asked him, "What is the treasure inside the mountain?" The point of this question is just like asking, "What is the buddha?" or "What is the way?"

Shimen replied, "Flowers in the sky emerge from the earth. The whole nation has no way to buy them."

This statement cannot be seen as secondary to other statements. People everywhere usually discuss flowers in the sky as illusory flowers and speak of flowers in the sky as being born in the sky and perishing in the sky. There have not been people who understand flowers that *emerge from the sky*. How can they know flowers that *emerge from the earth*? Shimen alone understood it.

Emerge from the earth means from the earth in the beginning, middle, and end. *Emerge* means to open. Flowers in the sky emerge from the entire earth, open blossoms, emerging from the entire earth.

The whole nation has no way to buy them means that it is not that the whole nation does not buy them; it is just that there is no way to buy them.

There are flowers in the sky that emerge from the earth. There is the entire earth that emerges from the flowers and opens. Thus, know that flowers in the sky emerge and open both the earth and the sky.

Presented to the assembly of the Kannondori Kosho Horin Monastery on the tenth day, the third month, the first year of the Kangen Era [1243].

45

OLD BUDDHA MIND

THE ANCESTRAL TEACHING was transmitted by forty ancestors from the Seven Original Buddhas to Huineng of Caoxi. There were forty ancestors from Huineng to the Seven Original Buddhas.

Because the Seven Original Buddhas had the power of going upward and going downward, the dharma reached Huineng and it reached the Seven Original Buddhas. Because Huineng had the power of going upward and going downward, the dharma has been authentically transmitted from the Seven Original Buddhas and from Huineng to buddhas of later times.

Buddhas are not only before and after. At the time of Shakyamuni Buddha, there were buddhas in the ten directions. At the time of Qingyuan, there was Nanyue. At the time of Nanyue, there was Qingyuan. Or, at the time of Shitou, there was Mazu of Jianxi. They did not obstruct each other, although it is not that they did not interact with each other. Study thoroughly that there has been such manifestations as these.

As these forty buddha ancestors are old buddhas, they have bodies and minds. They have illumination and land with a timeless past and something that never existed in the past. Having something that never existed in the past and having a timeless past are equally the manifestation of old buddhas.

To study the way of old buddhas is to realize the way of old buddhas—generations and generations of old buddhas. What we call old buddhas are old of new and old, but they leap beyond old and new. They are directly old and new.

Rujing, my late master, said, "I have encountered Old Buddha Hongzhi."

From this I guess that there is an old buddha in the house of Tiantong, and there is Tiantong in the house of an old buddha.

Keqin, Zen Master Yuanwu, said, "I bow to Caoxi [Huineng], true Old Buddha."

Know that we should bow to the thirty-third-generation ancestor from Shakyamuni Buddha [Huineng], as Old Buddha. Because Keqin had an old buddha's splendid illumination, he made such a bow upon encountering the old buddha. Thus, chew on the head and tail of Huineng and grab hold of the nose of an old buddha. One who grabs hold of this is an old buddha.

Sushan said, "On top of Dayu Peak there is an old buddha shining light that reaches here."

Know that Sushan had already encountered the old buddha. Do not look anywhere else. Where the old buddha can be found is on top of Dayu Peak. One who is not an old buddha does not know where the old buddha is. One who knows where the old buddha can be found is an old buddha.

Xuefeng said, "Zhaozhou, Old Buddha."

Know that although Zhaozhou was an old buddha, if Xuefeng had not been given the ability to be an old buddha, he would not have mastered the craft of meeting the old buddha. The practice right now is to study with an old buddha, which is benefited by the old buddha who practices silence responding to questions.

Old Man Xuefeng is still well. The teaching style of an old buddha and the awesome presence of an old buddha cannot be imitated and equaled by one who is not an old buddha. This being so, study the wholesomeness of the beginning, middle, and end of Zhaozhou and experience the timelessness of the old buddha.

———

Huizhong, National Teacher Dazheng of the Guangzhai Monastery in Xijing, was a dharma heir of Huineng. He was equally revered by emperors of humans and devas. It was rare to see or hear of a master like him in China. Not only was he the dharma teacher to four emperors, but one of them pulled his cart into the imperial court. Further, he was invited to Indra's palace and went up to heaven to expound the dharma to Indra in the assembly of devas.

Huizhong was once asked by a monk, "What is the mind of an old buddha?"

He replied, "Walls, tiles, and pebbles."

The monk's question was no different from asking, "What is this?" or "What is that?" This was expressed by the question, which became an expression of realization throughout the past and present.

Thus, myriad trees and a hundred grasses with blooming flowers are an expression of an old buddha. This is an old buddha's expression, an old buddha's question. The Nine Mountains and Eight Seas that emerge in the world are the moon face and sun face of an old buddha—the skin, flesh, bones, and marrow of an old buddha.

Further, there must be an active buddha with old mind, a realizing buddha with old mind, becoming buddha of old mind, becoming mind of buddha oldness, as old mind is the mind of oldness. Because mind buddha is always old, old mind is a chair, bamboo, and wood.

[It is as Xuansha said,] "Even if we look in the entire world for a single person who understands buddha dharma, it is impossible to find one." "Reverend, what do you call it?"

At this very moment of causation and in the empty space of the dusty world there is nothing other than old mind. To maintain old mind and to maintain an old buddha are like maintaining two heads on one face or painting two heads on one body.

Huizhong said, *Walls, tiles, and pebbles.* This statement shows that there is an expression stepping toward walls, tiles, and pebbles. This is walls, tiles, and pebbles. It is a straight way of expression. There is also an expression by walls, tiles, and pebbles that steps backward within walls, tiles, and pebbles. Where these expressions emerge and complete, a cliff of one thousand rocks and myriad rocks stands; walls all over the earth and all over heaven stand; there is one or half a piece of tile; or there is a large or small tip of a pebble. This is not only mind, but a body, as well as their environs.

This being so, ask, "What are walls, tiles, and pebbles?"

In response, say, "Old buddha mind."

Then, investigate further: What are so-called walls? What are called walls? What shape are they? Study thoroughly in this way.

Does making cause walls to appear? Do walls cause making to appear? Are walls made or not? Are they sentient or insentient? Do they or do they not emerge right here?

Even if they appear in the deva realm or human realm, in this or another world, while you investigate thoroughly, old buddha mind is walls, tiles, and pebbles. Old buddha mind and walls, tiles, and pebbles have not been separated even by a particle.

———————

Jianyuan, Zen Master Zhongxing, was asked by a monk, "What is the mind of old buddha?"

Jianyuan said, "The entire world falls apart."

The monk asked further, "What happens when the entire world falls apart?"

Jianyuan said, "I would rather not have my body."

The so-called worlds are all buddha worlds of the ten directions. There is not a world that is not a buddha world. Study the entire world and how it falls apart. Do not study it in the self. Because you don't study it in the self, the very moment of falling apart is one path, two, three, four, or five paths—thus, inexhaustible paths.

Each path is *I would rather not have my body. My body* is *I would rather not have.* Value the now, and don't let yourself fail to be old buddha mind.

Indeed, old buddha mind stands like a wall before the Seven Original Buddhas. It sprouted after the Seven Original Buddhas. Old buddha mind blossoms before all buddhas. It bears fruit after all buddhas. Old buddha mind drops away before old buddha mind.

Presented to the assembly at the Rokuharamitsu Temple [in Kyoto] on the twenty-ninth day, the fourth month of the Kangen Era [1243].

46

THE BODHISATTVA'S FOUR
METHODS OF GUIDANCE

T HE BODHISATTVA'S FOUR methods of guidance are giving, kind
speech, beneficial action, and identity action.

"Giving" means nongreed. Nongreed means not to covet. Not to
covet means not to curry favor. Even if you govern the Four Continents,
you should always convey the authentic path with nongreed. It is like
giving away unneeded belongings to someone you don't know, offering
flowers blooming on a distant mountain to the Tathagata, or, again, offering treasures you had in your former life to sentient beings. Whether it
is of teaching or of material, each gift has its value and is worth giving.
Even if the gift is not your own, there is no reason to abstain from giving. The question is not whether the gift is valuable but whether there is
genuine merit.

When you leave the way to the way, you attain the way. At the time
of attaining the way, the way is always left to the way. When treasure is
left just as treasure, treasure becomes giving. You give yourself to yourself and others to others. The power of the causal relations of giving

reaches to devas, human beings, and even enlightened sages. When giving becomes actual, such causal relations are immediately formed.

The Buddha said, "When a person who practices giving goes to an assembly, people take notice." Know that the mind of such a person communicates subtly with others. This being so, give even a phrase or verse of the truth; it will be a wholesome seed for this and other lifetimes. Give your valuables, even a penny or a blade of grass; it will be a wholesome root for this and other lifetimes. The truth can turn into valuables; valuables can turn into the truth. This is all because the giver is willing.

A king [Emperor Tai of the Tang Dynasty] gave his beard as medicine to cure his retainer's disease. A child offered sand to Buddha and became King [Ashoka] in a later birth. They were not greedy for reward but only shared what they could. To launch a boat or build a bridge is an act of giving. If you study giving closely, you see that to accept a body and to give up the body are both giving. Making a living and producing things can be nothing other than giving. To leave flowers to the wind, to leave birds to the seasons, are also acts of giving.

Great King Ashoka was able to offer enough food for hundreds of monks with half a myrobalan fruit. People who practice giving should understand that King Ashoka thus proved the greatness of giving. Not only should you make an effort to give, but also be mindful of every opportunity to give. You are born into this present life because you originally embodied the merit of giving [in the past].

The Buddha said, "If you are to practice giving to yourself, how much more so to your parents, wife, and children."

Thus, know that to give to yourself is a part of giving. To give to your family is also giving. Even when you give a particle of dust, you should rejoice in your own act, because you authentically transmit the merit of all buddhas, and begin to practice an act of a bodhisattva. The mind of a sentient being is difficult to change. Keep on changing the minds of sentient beings, from the moment that you offer one valuable, to the moment that they attain the way. This should be initiated by giving. Thus, giving is the first of the six paramitas [realizations].

Mind is beyond measure. Things given are beyond measure. And yet, in giving, mind transforms the gift and the gift transforms mind.

"Kind speech" means that when you see sentient beings, you arouse the heart of compassion and offer words of loving care. It is contrary to cruel or violent speech.

In the secular world, there is the custom of asking after someone's health. In the buddha way there is the phrase, "Please treasure yourself" and the respectful address to seniors, "May I ask how you are?" It is kind speech to speak to sentient beings as you would to a baby.

Praise those with virtue; pity those without it. If kind speech is offered, little by little kind speech expands. Thus, even kind speech that is not ordinarily known or seen comes into being. Be willing to practice it for this entire present life; do not give up, world after world, life after life. Kind speech is the basis for reconciling rulers and subduing enemies. Those who hear kind speech from you have a delighted expression and a joyful mind. Those who hear of your kind speech will be deeply touched; they will always remember it.

Know that kind speech arises from kind heart, and kind heart from the seed of compassionate heart. Ponder the fact that kind speech is not just praising the merit of others; it has the power to turn the destiny of the nation.

"Beneficial action" is skillfully to benefit all classes of sentient beings; that is, to care about their distant and near future, and to help them by using skillful means. In ancient times, someone helped a caged tortoise; another took care of a sick sparrow. They did not expect a reward; they were moved to do so only for the sake of beneficial action.

Foolish people think that if they help others first, their own benefit will be lost, but this is not so. Beneficial action is an act of oneness, benefiting self and others together.

To greet petitioners, a lord of old stopped three times in the middle of his bath to arrange his hair, and three times left his dinner table. He did this solely with the intention of benefiting others. He did not mind instructing even subjects of other lords. Thus, benefit friend and enemy equally. Benefit self and others alike. If you have this heart, even beneficial action for the sake of grass, trees, wind, and water is spontaneous

476 · TREASURY OF THE TRUE DHARMA EYE

and unremitting. This being so, make a wholehearted effort to help the ignorant.

————————

"Identity action" means nondifference. It is nondifference from self, nondifference from others. For example, in the human world the Tathagata took the form of a human being. From this we know that he did the same in other realms. When we know identity action, self and others are one.

Lute, song, and wine are one with human beings, devas, and spirit beings. Human beings are one with lute, song, and wine. Lute, song, and wine are one with lute, song, and wine. Human beings are one with human beings; devas are one with devas; spirit beings are one with spirit beings. To understand this is to understand identity action.

"Action" means right form, dignity, correct manner. This means that you cause yourself to be in identity with others after causing others to be in identity with you. However, the relationship of self and others varies limitlessly according to circumstances.

The *Guanzi* says, "The ocean does not exclude water; that is why it is large. The mountain does not exclude soil; that is why it is high. A wise lord does not exclude people; that is why he has many subjects."

That the ocean does not exclude water is identity action. Water does not exclude the ocean either. This being so, water comes together to form the ocean. Soil piles up to form mountains.

My understanding is that because the ocean itself does not exclude the ocean, it is the ocean and it is large. Because mountains do not exclude mountains, they are mountains and they are high. Because a wise lord does not weary of people, his people assemble. "People" means the nation. "A wise lord" means ruler of the nation. A ruler is not supposed to weary of people. "Not to weary of people" does not mean to give no reward or punishment. Although a ruler gives reward and punishment, he does not weary of people. In ancient times, when people were less complicated, there was neither legal reward nor punishment in the country. The concept of reward and punishment was different. Even at present, there should be some people who seek the way without expecting a reward. This is beyond the understanding of ignorant people. Because a wise lord understands this, he does not weary of people.

People form a nation and seek a wise lord, but as they do not completely know the reason why a wise lord is wise, they only hope to be supported by the wise lord. They do not notice that they are the ones who support the wise lord. In this way, the principle of identity action is applied to both a wise lord and all people. This being so, identity action is a vow of bodhisattvas.

With a gentle expression, practice identity action for all people.

———————

Each of these four methods of guidance includes all four. Thus, there are sixteen methods of guiding sentient beings.

Written on the fifth day, the fifth month, the fourth year of the Ninji Era [1243] by Monk Dogen, who transmitted dharma from China.

47

TWINING VINES

A T THE ASSEMBLY on Vulture Peak, only Mahakashyapa, through realization, received Shakyamuni Buddha's treasury of the true dharma eye, unsurpassable enlightenment. By a direct transmission of authentic realization through twenty-eight generations, it reached venerable Bodhidharma.

Bodhidharma went to China and entrusted the treasury of the true dharma eye, unsurpassable enlightenment, to Dazu Huike, who would later become Great Master Zhengzong Pujue, and confirmed him as the Second Ancestor. Because the Twenty-eighth Ancestor in India went to China as the first teacher there, he is also called the First Chinese Ancestor. The Twenty-ninth Ancestor is called the Second Chinese Ancestor. This is the custom in China.

Bodhidharma once studied with Venerable Prajnatara and through realization directly received the admonitions of the buddha, the bones of the way. In realization he attained the source through the source and made it the root of branches and leaves.

Although there are a number of sages who try to study by cutting off the root of twining vines [expressions], they do not regard the cutting of twining vines with twining vines as "cutting through" [fully comprehending]. Also, they do not know entangling twining vines by further entangling them. Furthermore, how can they understand inheriting twining vines through twining vines? Those who notice that inheriting dharma is twining vines are rare. There is no one who has learned it, and there is no one who has spoken about it. How is it possible for many to have realized it?

Rujing, my late master, Old Buddha, said, "Gourd vines entangle with gourd vines."

This teaching has never been seen or heard in the various directions of the past and present. Rujing alone spoke it. *Gourd vines entangle with gourd vines* means that buddha ancestors thoroughly experience buddha ancestors; buddha ancestors merge with buddha ancestors in realization. This is transmitting mind by mind.

Bodhidharma once said to his students, "The time has come. Can you express your understanding?"

Then one of the students, Daofu, said, "My present view is that we should neither be attached to letters nor be apart from letters, and allow the way to function freely."

Bodhidharma said, "You have attained my skin."

The nun Zongchi said, "My view is that it is like the joy of seeing Akshobhya Buddha's land just once and not again."

Bodhidharma said, "You have attained my flesh."

Daoyu said, "The four great elements are originally empty, and the five skandhas do not exist. Therefore, I see nothing to be attained."

Bodhidharma said, "You have attained my bones."

Finally, Huike bowed three times, stood up, and returned to where he was.

Bodhidharma said, "You have attained my marrow." Thus, he confirmed Huike as the Second Ancestor and transmitted dharma and the robe to him.

Investigate these words of Bodhidharma: *You have attained my skin . . . flesh . . . bones . . . marrow.* These are the ancestor's words. All four students had attainment and understanding. Each one's attainment and understanding is skin, flesh, bones, and marrow leaping out of body and mind; skin, flesh, bones, and marrow dropping away body and mind. Do not see or hear the ancestor with a limited understanding of these statements. Otherwise what was spoken and heard will not be fully grasped.

However, those who have not received authentic transmission think that Bodhidharma's words *skin . . . flesh . . . bones . . . marrow* are not equal in depth, and because the views of the four students vary, one may seem to be closer than the others. They think that skin and flesh are not as close as bones and marrow. They think that Huike was acknowledged as attaining the marrow because his view was better than those of the others. People who speak in this way have not yet studied with buddha ancestors and do not have transmission of the ancestor way.

Know that *skin . . . flesh . . . bones . . . marrow* do not mean that one understanding is deeper than another. Even if there are superior or inferior views, in Bodhidharma's words there is only attaining *my*. It means that neither the phrase *You have attained my marrow* nor the phrase *You have attained my bones* is more essential than the other for guiding a person in holding up grass [endeavor] or dropping grass [beyond endeavor]. It is like holding up a flower or transmitting a robe. From the beginning, Bodhidharma's confirmation of each one was equal. Although his confirmation was equal, the four views were not necessarily equal. However varied the four views are, Bodhidharma's words are just Bodhidharma's words. In fact, words and understanding do not necessarily match.

For example, Bodhidharma said to the four students, *You have attained my skin,* and so forth. Had he hundreds or thousands of students after Huike, he would have spoken hundreds or thousands of words. There should be no limit. Because he had only four students he spoke of *skin . . . flesh . . . bones . . . marrow.* But the words not spoken, and yet to be spoken, should be many.

Know that even to Huike, Bodhidharma could have said, *You have attained my skin.* Even saying, *You have attained my skin,* he could have transmitted the treasury of the true dharma eye to Huike as the Second Ancestor. It does not go by the superiority or inferiority of attaining the flesh or attaining the marrow.

Even to Daofu, Daoyu, or Zongchi, Bodhidharma could have said,

You have attained my marrow. Even though they attained the skin, he could have transmitted dharma to them. Bodhidharma's body-and-mind is Bodhidharma's skin, flesh, bones, and marrow. It is not that the marrow is close and the skin is far.

Now, to receive the seal of *You have attained my skin* by having the eye of studying is to fully attain the ancestor. There is an ancestor whose full body is skin, an ancestor whose full body is flesh, an ancestor whose full body is bones, and an ancestor whose full body is marrow. There is an ancestor whose full body is mind, an ancestor whose full body is body, an ancestor whose full mind is mind. There is an ancestor whose full ancestor is ancestor. And there is an ancestor whose full body is "attaining myself," "attaining yourself."

In this way, when these ancestors appear together and speak to hundreds and thousands of students, they say, *You have attained my skin*. Even if the ancestors in hundreds and thousands of words indicate skin, flesh, bones, and marrow in this way, people outside will think superficially about skin, flesh, bones, and marrow.

If there had been six or seven students in Bodhidharma's community, he would have said, "You have attained my mind," "You have attained my body," "You have attained my buddhahood," "You have attained my eye," or "You have attained my realization." This is the moment when *you* are now an ancestor, and this is the time when *you* are now Huike.

Examine thoroughly the meaning of *have attained*. Know that there is "You have attained me," "I have attained you," "[This is] attaining me and you," and "[This is] attaining you and me." Upon studying an ancestor's body-and-mind, if you say that inside and outside are not one or that the entire body is not the full body, you are not in the land where the buddha ancestors appear.

To attain skin is to attain bones, flesh, and marrow. To attain bones, flesh, and marrow is to attain skin, flesh, and face. It is to understand not only that all the worlds of the ten directions are the true body, but that they are skin, flesh, bones, and marrow. In this way, "You attain my robe," and "You attain the dharma."

Thus, words are bits and pieces leaping out; teacher and disciple practice mutually. What is heard is bits and pieces leaping out; teacher and disciple practice mutually.

"Teacher and disciple practice mutually" is twining vines of buddha ancestors. "Twining vines of buddha ancestors" is the life stream of skin, flesh, bones, and marrow. Taking up a flower and blinking are twining vines. Breaking into a smile is skin, flesh, bones, and marrow.

Study further; the seeds of twining vines have the power of dropping away body. Branches, leaves, flowers, and fruit of twining vines do and do not interpenetrate one another. Thus, buddha ancestors appear, and the fundamental point is actualized.

───────

Zhaozhou, Great Master Zhenji, said to his assembly, "Mahakashyapa transmitted to Ananda. Now say! To whom did Bodhidharma transmit?"

A monk said, "The Second Ancestor attained his marrow. How about it?"

Zhaozhou said, "Do not slander the Second Ancestor." He also said, "If Bodhidharma means 'Someone who has reached the outside attains the skin, someone who has reached the inside attains the bones,' then tell me: What does someone who has reached even deeper inside get?"

The monk said, "What does attaining the marrow mean?"

Zhaozhou said, "Just know about skin. There is no marrow to depend upon in my body."

The monk said, "What is marrow?"

Zhaozhou said, "At that place you don't feel the skin."

Thus, know: When you don't even feel the skin, how can you feel the marrow? When you feel the skin, you can attain the marrow. Thus, study the meaning of *At that place you don't feel the skin*.

A monk asked, *What does attaining the marrow mean?* Then, Zhaozhou said, *Just know the skin. There is no marrow to depend upon in my body.* When you know the skin, there is no need to search for the marrow. This is truly attaining the marrow. Being so, the question *The Second Ancestor attained his marrow. How about it?* appeared.

When you penetrate the moment of Mahakashyapa transmitting to Ananda, Ananda hides his body in Mahakashyapa, and Mahakashyapa hides his body in Ananda. Thus, at the moment of [teacher and student] meeting for transmission, the practice of exchanging face, skin, flesh, bones, and marrow cannot be avoided. Because of this, Zhaozhou said, *Now say! To whom did Bodhidharma transmit?*

When Bodhidharma gives transmission, he is Bodhidharma. When the Second Ancestor attains the marrow, he is Bodhidharma. By studying the meaning of this, buddha dharma has continued to be buddha dharma to this day. If not, buddha dharma would not have reached to this day. Quietly pursue and investigate the meaning of this point for yourself and others.

Zhaozhou said, *If Bodhidharma means, "Someone who has reached the outside attains the skin, someone who has reached the inside attains the bones," then tell me: What does someone who has reached even deeper inside get?* Directly understand the meaning of *outside* [essential] and *inside* [essential]. When you discuss *outside*, skin, flesh, bones, and marrow are all outside. When you discuss *inside*, skin, flesh, bones, and marrow are all inside.

This being so, these four Bodhidharmas altogether mastered hundreds and thousands of myriad bits and pieces beyond skin, flesh, bones, and marrow. Do not suppose that you cannot go beyond the marrow. You can go threefold, fivefold beyond.

This teaching of Zhaozhou, an ancient buddha, is a buddha's words. It is not what other masters like Linji, Deshan, Guishan, and Yunmen either reached or dreamed of. How could they talk about it? Some careless elders of recent times do not even know that it exists. If you were to tell them about it, they would be shocked.

Xuedou, Zen Master Mingjue, said, "Zhaozhou and Muzhou—both Zhous—are ancient buddhas."

The words of Zhaozhou, an ancient buddha, are realization of buddha dharma, understanding of expressions in the past.

Xuefeng, Great Master Zhenjiao, said, "Zhaozhou is an ancient buddha."

The former buddha ancestor admired Zhaozhou as an ancient buddha, and the latter buddha ancestor admired Zhaozhou as an ancient buddha. Thus, we know that he was an ancient buddha who went beyond buddhas of the past and present. In this way, the entanglement of skin, flesh, bones, and marrow is an essential expression by an ancient

484 · TREASURY OF THE TRUE DHARMA EYE

buddha of "You have attained me." Thoroughly study and examine this expression.

It is said that Bodhidharma returned to India. I have learned that this is wrong. What Songyun saw on the road as Bodhidharma [heading west] could not have been actual. How could Songyun have discovered Bodhidharma's destination? It is correct to learn and understand that his ashes were laid to rest in Mount Xionger after he passed away.

Presented at the assembly of the Kannondori Kosho Horin Monastery, Uji County, Yamashiro Province, on the seventh day, the seventh month, the first year of the Kangen Era [1243].

MONASTERY
CONSTRUCTION PERIOD

———

1243–1245

48

THREE REALMS ARE
INSEPARABLE FROM MIND

GREAT MASTER SHAKYAMUNI said [in the *Avatamsaka Sutra*], "The three realms are inseparable from single mind. There is nothing outside of mind. Mind, the Buddha, and sentient beings are not divided."

This passage expresses a complete actualization of the Buddha's lifetime. A complete actualization of the Buddha's lifetime is an utmost actualization of complete wholeness. Whatever effort it may embody, it is an effortless effort. Thus, the Tathagata's words, *The three realms are inseparable from single mind,* are an entire actualization of the entire Tathagata. His whole lifetime is this single passage.

The three realms are the entire world. This does not mean that the three realms are merely mind, because, however many crystal-clear facets they may have, the three realms are still the three realms. Even if you mistakenly see something outside the three realms, that is not correct at all.

Inside, outside, and in between are all in the three realms. Beginning, later, and in between are all in the three realms.

The three realms are seen just as the three realms. What is not seen as the three realms is the three realms seen incorrectly. In the three realms what is seen as the three realms are old nests [views] as well as new buds [views]. Old nests see the three realms and new buds see the three realms.

Thus, Great Master Shakya said, "Nothing sees the three realms better than the three realms."

What is seen is no other than the three realms. The three realms are just seen as the three realms.

The three realms are neither originally present nor arising at this moment. They neither appear spontaneously nor are they produced by causation. The three realms are not a matter of the beginning, middle, or end.

You leave the three realms or you are present in the three realms. This is dynamic work encountering dynamic work, twining vines growing twining vines. Being present in the three realms, you are seen by the three realms. What is seen by the three realms is what is seen within the three realms. What is seen within the three realms is actualizing the three realms, is the three realms being actualized, and is actualizing the fundamental point.

In this way, you cause the three realms to become actualized as aspiration, practice, enlightenment, and nirvana. This means [as the Buddha said,] *these three realms are all my beings.*

Thus, Great Master Shakyamuni said, "Now these three realms are all my beings. All sentient beings in these realms are my children."

As these three realms are the Tathagata's beings, the entire world is the three realms. These three realms are the entire world.

Now these means the past, present, and future. The past, present, and future actualized do not hinder *now these*. *Now these* actualized affect the past, present, and future.

My beings are the true human body of the entire world of the ten directions; a shramana's single eye of the entire world of the ten directions. Sentient beings are the true human body of the entire world of the ten directions. Because each sentient being is a living being, they are beings.

My children is the total actualization of the children. Thus, the children who receive body, hair, and skin from compassionate parents do not harm the body or ignore it and are regarded as the children actualized. Right now, it is neither that the parent is before and the children are after, nor that the children are before and the parent is after, nor that the parent and children stand shoulder to shoulder. This is the meaning of *my children*.

Without inheriting it, you are [inherently] the Tathagata's child. Without earning it, you are already the Tathagata's child. It is beyond the aspect of coming and going. It is beyond the measure of large and small. It is beyond the discussion of old and young.

Maintain old and young just as old and young of buddha ancestors. In this way, the parent is young while the child is old; the parent is old while the child is young; the parent is old while the child is old; and the parent is young while the child is young.

One who studies the oldness of the parent is not the child. One who has not passed the youth of a child is not the parent. Thoroughly investigate the oldness and youth of the child and the oldness and youth of the parent. Don't be negligent. There are a parent and a child who are born at the same time. There are a parent and a child who die at the same time. There are a parent and a child who are born beyond time. There are a parent and a child who die beyond time.

Without hindering the compassionate parent, a child can be born. Without hindering the child, a compassionate parent is actualized.

There are sentient beings with mind. There are sentient beings with no mind. There is a child with mind. There is a child with no mind. These children—*my children*—are all Shakyamuni Buddha's heirs.

All sentient beings of the past, present, and future in the entire ten directions are buddhas of the past, present, and future in the entire ten directions. *My children* of all buddhas are sentient beings. The compassionate parents of sentient beings are all buddhas.

Thus, the flowers and fruit of one hundred grasses are *my beings* of all buddhas. Rocks and stones, large and small, are *my beings* of all buddhas. Their places of serene abiding are forests and fields. The forests and fields are their places of seclusion.

However, the Tathagata only talked about *my children.* He did not speak about himself as the parent. Study this thoroughly.

Great Master Shakyamuni said, "The responding, transformed, and dharma bodies of all buddhas do not go beyond the three realms. There are no sentient beings outside the three realms. Where else would the Buddha teach? Thus, I say that an outsider's theory, in the *Great Existence Sutra,* that there is a storehouse of sentient beings outside the three realms is not a teaching of the Seven Original Buddhas."

Investigate and clarify that the responding, transformed, and dharma bodies of all buddhas are always in the three realms. The three realms have no outside. The Tathagata is not outside. Walls are not outside.

Because the three realms have no outside, sentient beings are not outside. Where else would the Buddha teach without sentient beings? What the Buddha teaches are always sentient beings.

Know that the *storehouse of sentient beings* is a theory in the *Great Existence Sutra* outside the way. It is not in a sutra by the Seven Original Buddhas.

What is inseparable from mind is not limited to one, two, or three realms. It is not outside the three realms. What is inseparable from mind cannot be mistaken. It is conceived by consciousness, and yet it is not conceived by consciousness. It is walls, tiles, and pebbles. It is mountains, rivers, and the great earth.

Mind is skin, flesh, bones, and marrow. Mind is taking up a flower and smiling. There is having mind, and having no mind. There is mind with a body, and mind with no body. There is mind before the body, and mind after the body. For the birth of a body, there is womb birth, egg birth, moisture birth, and transformation birth. For the birth of a mind, there is womb birth, egg birth, moisture birth, and transformation birth.

Blue, yellow, red, and white are mind. Long, short, square, and round are mind. The coming and going of birth and death are mind. Year, month, day, and hour are mind. Dream, phantom, and empty flower are mind. Water, foam, splash, and flame are mind. Spring flowers and autumn moon are mind. All things that arise and fall are mind.

However, they cannot be destroyed. Thus, there is mind where there are all things that are real. There is mind that is experienced only between a buddha and a buddha.

————————

Xuansha, Great Master Zongyi, asked Luohan Guichen, who would later become Great Master Zheying, "How do you understand the three realms inseparable from mind?"

Luohan pointed to a chair and said, "Master, what do you call it?"

Xuansha said, "A chair."

Luohan said, "Master, you don't understand the three realms inseparable from mind."

Xuansha said, "I call it something made of bamboo and wood. How do you call it?"

Luohan said, "I also call it something made of bamboo and wood."

Xuansha said, "Looking throughout the entire earth, I cannot find a single person who understands buddha dharma."

Xuansha asked, *How do you understand the three realms inseparable from mind?* What is understood and what is not understood are equally the three realms inseparable from mind. The three realms are not yet understood. So, Luohan pointed to a chair and said, *Master, what do you call it?* Know that *how do you understand?* is no other than *what do you call it?*

Speak about Xuansha's words, *A chair*. Are these words of understanding the three realms or not understanding the three realms? Are they or are they not words of the three realms? Are they an expression of a chair or of Xuansha? Try to express it thoroughly. Try to understand it thoroughly. Try to practice it thoroughly.

Luohan said, *Master, you don't understand the three realms inseparable from mind*. These words are like asking Zhaozhou, "Master, where do you live?" Zhaozhou may say, "East Gate," or "South Gate." He may say, "West Gate," or "North Gate." Furthermore, he may say, "East of Zhao Region [Zhaozhou]," or "South of Zhao Region."

Even if you understand the three realms inseparable from mind, you should still thoroughly investigate not understanding the three realms inseparable from mind. Furthermore, there are the three realms inseparable from mind beyond understanding and not understanding.

Xuansha said, *I call it something made of bamboo and wood.* Penetrate the nodes and grains [phrase] of this statement unprecedented and never to be matched. Before he responded in this way, what had it been called? Had it been regarded as *something made of bamboo and wood,* crystal clear from beginning, middle, and end? Are Xuansha's words an expression of the three realms inseparable from mind or beyond an expression of the three realms inseparable from mind?

Know that even if Xuansha first spoke of the three realms as *a chair,* as inseparable from mind, or as the three realms, he now speaks of the three realms as *something made of bamboo and wood.*

Luohan said, *I also call it something made of bamboo and wood.* This response is expressed between teacher and student, face to face, who studied together from head to tail. Investigate thoroughly if Xuansha's words *something made of bamboo and wood* and Luohan's words *I also call it something made of bamboo and wood* are the same or not, right to the point or not.

Xuansha said, *Looking throughout the entire earth, I cannot find a single person who understands buddha dharma.* Also study these words carefully.

Know that Xuansha simply called the three realms *something made of bamboo and wood,* and Luohan also called the three realms *something made of bamboo and wood.* They did not yet understand the three realms inseparable from mind. They did not go beyond understanding the three realms inseparable from mind. They did not express the three realms. They did not go beyond expressing the three realms inseparable from mind.

Thus, ask Xuansha, "Even if you say, *Looking throughout the entire earth, I cannot find a single person who understands buddha dharma,* tell me: What do you call the entire earth?"

Thoroughly investigate in this way.

Presented to the assembly on Mount Yoshimine on the first day, the intercalary seventh month, the first year of the Kangen Era [1243].

49

SPEAKING OF MIND, SPEAKING OF ESSENCE

SHENSHAN, WHO WOULD later become Zen Master Sengmi, was traveling with Dongshan, who would later become Zen Master Wuben.

Dongshan pointed to a temple near the road and said, "Inside that temple someone is speaking of mind, speaking of essence."

Shenshan said, "Who is that?"

Dongshan said, "My dharma uncle, your question has completely killed that person."

Shenshan said, "Who is speaking of mind, speaking of essence?"

Dongshan said, "In death, find life."

Speaking of mind, speaking of essence is the great foundation of the buddha way. It actualizes buddhas and ancestors from there. Without speaking of mind, speaking of essence, there is no turning of the wondrous dharma wheel, no aspiration and practice, no attaining the way together with all beings on earth, no sentient beings beyond buddha nature.

To take up a flower and blink is speaking of mind, speaking of essence. To bow and return to the original position is speaking of mind, speaking of essence. Bodhidharma going to the kingdom of Liang is speaking of mind, speaking of essence. To transmit the robe at midnight is speaking of mind, speaking of essence. To take up a staff is speaking of mind, speaking of essence. To lay down a whisk is speaking of mind, speaking of essence. All the merits of buddhas and ancestors are speaking of mind, speaking of essence.

There is ordinary speaking of mind, speaking of essence. There is speaking of mind, speaking of essence by walls, tiles, and pebbles.

It is said that when mind arises, various things arise, and when mind perishes, various things perish. Yet, there is a time when mind is no other than speaking, and there is a time when essence is no other than speaking.

However, mediocre people who have not penetrated mind and have not mastered essence do not know speaking of mind, speaking of essence. They do not know talks on profundity or wonder. So, they say and teach that speaking of mind, speaking of essence are not words of buddha ancestors. Because they do not know speaking of mind, speaking of essence as speaking of mind, speaking of essence, they regard speaking of mind, speaking of essence as speaking of mind, speaking of essence. This happens because they do not examine openings and blockages in the buddha way.

———————

In a later time there was someone called Zonggao, Zen Master Dahui of Mount Jia, who said, "Because people nowadays are fond of speaking of mind, speaking of essence, and talks on profundity and wonder, they are delayed in attaining the way. When you throw away both mind and essence, forget both profundity and wonder, and become free from the manifestation of these two aspects, you merge with realization."

This statement does not follow the teachings of buddha ancestors in sutras or reflect the gems of buddha ancestors. Because of this, Zonggao assumed that mind is merely intellect and awareness. He was not aware that intellect and awareness are [only a part of] mind. He mistakenly thought that essence is [limited to being] still and serene, and did not know about the existence or nonexistence of buddha nature, dharma nature. He had never seen thusness nature. Because of this, he had a mistaken view of buddha dharma.

Instead, the mind that buddha ancestors speak of is skin, flesh, bones, and marrow. The essence that buddha ancestors maintain is a bamboo stick and a wooden staff. The profundity that buddha ancestors merge with in realization is pillars and lanterns. The wonder that buddha ancestors take up is knowing, seeing, understanding, and merging.

From the beginning, buddha ancestors who are truly buddha ancestors listen to, expound, practice, and realize this mind essence. They maintain and practice the profound wonder. Those who do so are called descendants who study buddha ancestors. Otherwise, it is not studying the way.

In this way Zonggao did not attain the way at the time for *attaining the way*, and did not go beyond attaining the way at the time for going beyond attaining the way. He missed both the time for attaining and beyond attaining.

When Zonggao said *throw away both mind and essence,* he meant that a small portion of mind makes speaking [of it] possible. It is one out of one hundred, one thousand, ten thousand, or one hundred million minds. When he said *forget both profundity and wonder,* only a small portion of *talks on profundity* is speaking.

Without studying this key point and simply speaking of *throw away,* he may think of being released from the hands, or escaping from the body. This is not yet freedom from the limited view of the Lesser Vehicles. How could he have reached the utmost profundity of the Great Vehicle? Further, how could he know the key for going beyond? It is impossible to say that Zonggao had consumed the tea and rice of buddha ancestors.

To study with a master and endeavor is no other than thoroughly experiencing speaking of mind, speaking of essence at this very moment in your body and mind, and studying through before and after life. There are not two or three things [other than this single matter].

————————

Once Bodhidharma said to Huike, "If you put all the outside conditions to rest, your mind will not be agitated. With your mind like a wall, you will enter enlightenment."

Huike spoke of mind, spoke of essence in various ways but could not merge with realization for a long time. But one day he got it all of a sudden. So, he said to Bodhidharma, "Now I have put all the conditions to rest for the first time."

Knowing that Huike had realization, Bodhidharma did not push him further. He only said, "Have you attained annihilation?"

Huike said, "No, I haven't."

Bodhidharma said, "What is your experience?"

Huike said, "It is always so clear that I cannot explain it."

Bodhidharma said, "This is the essential mind transmitted by all buddhas and ancestors from the past. You have now attained it. Maintain it well."

Some people doubt this story and others expound it. Nevertheless, it is one of the stories about Huike studying with Bodhidharma. At first, when Huike examined speaking of mind, speaking of essence, he did not have realization. After accumulating effort and developing virtue, he finally understood Bodhidharma's words.

Foolish people say that when Huike first examined speaking of mind, speaking of essence, he did not understand it, because speaking of mind, speaking of essence was at fault. They say that Huike later had realization by throwing away speaking of mind, speaking of essence. They say so because they do not thoroughly understand the words *with your mind like a wall, you will enter enlightenment.* They lack discernment in study of the way.

The reason for this is that soon after you arouse the aspiration for enlightenment and begin the practice of the buddha way, even if you are closely engaged in rigorous practices, you may not hit one mark out of one hundred activities. But by following a teacher or by following a sutra, you may finally hit a mark. This hitting a mark is due to the missing of one hundred marks in the past; it is the maturing of missing one hundred marks in the past.

Listening to the teaching, practicing the way, and attaining realization are all like this. Although yesterday's speaking of mind, speaking of essence missed one hundred marks, this missing directly hits the mark today.

Even if you are immature and cannot attain mastery at the beginning of practicing the buddha way, you should not give up the buddha way and try to attain it by going through other ways. It is difficult for those who are not familiar with the process of practicing the buddha way to clarify the openings and blockages of the buddha way.

The buddha way is the buddha way even when you first arouse the aspiration for enlightenment. It is the buddha way when you attain authentic enlightenment. It is the buddha way altogether at the beginning, in the middle, and at the end. It is like journeying a long distance; one step is within one thousand *li*, one thousand steps are within one thousand *li*. The first step and the one-thousandth step are different, but are equally within the one thousand *li*.

But extreme fools think that you haven't reached the buddha way while studying it, and that you experience the buddha way only at the time of having the fruit [of enlightenment]. They think so because they don't know taking up and expounding the way, taking up and practicing the way, taking up and realizing the way. People learn that only those who are deluded practice the buddha way and have great enlightenment. They do not know or hear that even those who are not deluded practice the buddha way and have great enlightenment. So, they think such a thing.

As speaking of mind, speaking of essence before merging with realization is the buddha way, you speak of mind, speak of essence, and merge with realization. Do not assume that merging with realization only means that a deluded person becomes greatly enlightened for the first time. A deluded person becomes greatly enlightened. An enlightened person becomes greatly enlightened. A person who is beyond enlightened becomes greatly enlightened. A person who is beyond deluded becomes greatly enlightened. A person who has merged with realization merges with realization.

This being so, speaking of mind, speaking of essence is straightforward buddha dharma. Zonggao did not understand this point and advised not to speak of mind, speak of essence. This is not a teaching of buddha dharma. Still, there is no one in Great Song China nowadays to even come close to Zonggao.

———————

Dongshan, venerable alone among all ancestors, had penetrated speaking of mind, speaking of essence, as speaking of mind, speaking of essence. Ancestors in various places who had not penetrated this did not speak of it as in the story of Dongshan and Shenshan [mentioned earlier].

Dongshan said to Shenshan, *Inside that temple there is someone speaking of mind, speaking of essence.* The ancestral teaching expressed in this statement has been authentically transmitted by Dongshan's dharma descendants since he emerged in the world. Those in other gates have not seen or heard it, even in a dream. Then how should they know the way to receive and study it, even in a dream? This has only been handed down heir to heir. How can those who don't receive it master the foundation of the buddha way?

The meaning of Dongshan's statement is that, inside and outside, there is someone speaking of mind, speaking of essence; that outside and inside, mind is speaking; and outside and inside, essence is speaking. Endeavor to study this thoroughly. There has been no speaking that is not essence. There has been no mind that is not speaking.

What is called buddha nature is all speaking. What is called beyond buddha nature is all speaking. When you study the nature of buddha nature, not to study having buddha nature is not the study of the way; not to study having beyond buddha nature is not the study of the way.

Those who study that speaking is essence are authentic descendants of buddha ancestors. Those who accept with trust that essence is no other than speaking are buddha ancestors who are authentic descendants.

To say that mind shakes while nature remains still is an outsider's view. To say that essence is still and serene while forms change is an outsider's view. The study of mind, the study of essence in the buddha way is not like that. The practice of mind, the practice of essence in the buddha way is not the same as that of outsiders. The clarification of mind, the clarification of essence, in the buddha way is not shared by those outside the way.

In the buddha way there is speaking of mind, speaking of essence by someone; there is speaking of mind, speaking of essence by a person beyond; there is beyond speaking of mind, speaking of essence by someone; there is beyond speaking of mind, speaking of essence by a person beyond. There is speaking of mind as well as not yet speaking of mind. There is speaking of essence as well as not yet speaking of essence.

If you do not study speaking of mind by a person beyond, you have not yet reached the field [of realization]. If you do not study speaking of mind by someone, you have not yet reached the field. Speaking of mind studies a person beyond. A person beyond studies speaking of mind. Speaking of mind studies the person. The person studies speaking of mind.

The total expression by Linji is "a person with no rank," but he has not expressed "a person with rank." The rest of the study and the expression have not been realized. We should say that he did not yet arrive on the ground of thorough study.

Because speaking of mind, speaking of essence is no other than speaking of buddha, speaking of ancestor, you should see with your ears and see with your eyes.

In this story, Shenshan said, *Who is that?* For actualizing this statement, Shenshan could have ridden on this statement before and after. *Who is that?* is a speaking of mind, speaking of essence *inside*. Thus, when *Who is that?* is said, or when *Who is that?* is thought, there is speaking of mind, speaking of essence.

Such speaking of mind, speaking of essence has not been known by others. Not recognizing their own son as the thief, they regard the thief as their son.

Dongshan said, *My dharma uncle, your question has completely killed* [fully illuminated] *that person.* Hearing this statement, mediocre people who study the way think that someone who speaks of mind, speaks of essence is immediately killed by the question, *Who is that?* They think that this question indicates that Shenshan did not even realize whether or not he was right in front of the person. They think that Shenshan had no view at all, so this was a dead phrase. But it is not necessarily so.

Those who have penetrated this speaking of mind, speaking of essence are rare. *Completely killed* is not being killed one or two out of ten. Rather, it is being killed ten out of ten.

At this very moment when Shenshan asked the question, who can say that it did not shelter the sky and cover the earth? This question— *Who is that?*—is illuminating the past, cutting through; illuminating the present, cutting through; illuminating the future, cutting through; illuminating this very moment, cutting through.

Shenshan asked again, *Who is speaking of mind, speaking of essence?* Although the *who* he said before and this *who* are like three Zhangs [with the same family name], they are like four Lis [with different personalities].

Dongshan said, *In death, find life.* Do not assume that *in death* means being completely killed. It is not that Dongshan pointed to speaking of mind, speaking of essence and said that this is the *who.*

This *who* is *someone* who speaks of mind, speaks of essence. Do not assume that this *someone* cannot expect to be *completely killed* [fully illuminated].

Dongshan's statement *In death, find life,* actualizes the form and sound of *someone is speaking of mind, speaking of essence.* The *completely killed* includes death that is one or two out of ten [incomplete death]. Although life is fully life, it is not that death turns into life. It is life that drops away from beginning to end.

——————

In the buddha way, ancestor way, there has been the teaching of speaking of mind, speaking of essence. This has been thoroughly examined. When you study this further, you are *completely killed,* and actualize the experience of *find life.*

Know that from the Tang Dynasty until today there have been many who do not understand that speaking of mind, speaking of essence is the buddha way. They are not familiar with speaking of mind, speaking of essence in teaching, practice, and realization. As a result, they make confused statements. What a pity! They should be saved from the moment before this lifetime and after this lifetime.

Let me say that speaking of mind, speaking of essence is an essential point of the Seven Original Buddhas.

Presented to the assembly of the Yoshimine Temple, Yoshida County, Echizen Province, in the first year of the Kangen Era [1243].

50

THE BUDDHA WAY

Huineng, Old Buddha Caoxi, once instructed the assembly, "From myself to the Seven Original Buddhas of the Past, we count forty ancestors."

When we investigate this statement, there are forty buddhas from the Seven Original Buddhas to Huineng. When you count buddhas and ancestors, you count in this way. If you count in this way, the Seven Original Buddhas are seven ancestors. The thirty-three ancestors are thirty-three buddhas. What Huineng says is so. This is the buddha's authentically transmitted instruction. The direct heirs alone authentically transmitted this way of counting.

From Shakyamuni Buddha through Huineng there are thirty-four ancestors. The succession of buddhas and ancestors is handed down in the same way that Mahakashyapa met the Tathagata and the Tathagata attained Mahakashyapa.

In the same way that Shakyamuni Buddha studied with Kashyapa Buddha, masters and disciples exist to this day. In this way the treasury of the true dharma eye has been handed down from person to person. The essential life of buddha dharma is just this authentic transmission.

Because buddha dharma is authentically transmitted in this way, it is the direct succession of entrusting.

This being so, the function, the essence, of the buddha way, is present with nothing lacking. This has been transmitted from India to China for eighteen thousand *li*. It has been transmitted from Buddha's lifetime to the present day for over two thousand years.

Those who do not study this, do not correctly see the treasury of the true dharma eye, the wondrous heart of nirvana, which has been authentically transmitted by buddhas and ancestors. They groundlessly call it the "Zen School." They call ancestors Zen ancestors, and then title the teachers Zen masters. Or, some people call themselves Zen students or the House of Zen. These are branches and leaves [forms] rooted in mistaken views.

In India and China from ancient times to the present, there has not been such a name as "Zen School." Those who groundlessly refer to themselves in this way are demons who violate the buddha way, enemies who are not welcomed by buddhas and ancestors.

The *Record within the Forests* by Shimen says:

Bodhidharma first went from Liang to Wei. Walking to the foot of Mount Song, he leaned his walking stick at Shaolin. He just sat quietly facing the wall. It was not learning meditation, but because people could not understand his intention, they regarded Bodhidharma's sitting as learning meditation.

Now, Zen meditation is part of all activities. How can it completely cover this sage? But when writing history, people of his time put him in the lineage of learning meditation, together with practitioners of decayed trees and dead ash.

This sage, however, never was limited to Zen meditation, and yet he was not apart from Zen meditation. It is just like in the *Ijing* [I-ching] that comes out from yin and yang, yet is not apart from yin and yang.

To call Bodhidharma the Twenty-eighth Ancestor is based on calling Mahakashyapa the First Ancestor. Bodhidharma is the Thirty-fifth Ancestor from Vipashyin Buddha [the First Original Buddha]. The Zen meditation of these Seven Original Buddhas and twenty-eight generations does not necessarily exhaust the way of enlightenment. For this reason, Shimen said, *Zen meditation is part of all activities. How can it completely cover this sage?*

Shimen had seen a [true] person to some extent. He had entered the inner chamber of the ancestors' teaching, so he could say this. This is a rare and hard thing to meet with in the land of Great Song China these days. Even if it is Zen meditation, you should not call yourselves the "Zen School." Realize that Zen meditation is not the entire practice in buddha dharma.

Therefore, those who intentionally call the great road of authentic transmission from buddha to buddha the "Zen School" have not seen, heard, or succeeded in the buddha way even in a dream. Do not think that there is buddha dharma in those who call themselves the "Zen School." Who started calling themselves the "Zen School"? None of the buddhas and ancestors called themselves the "Zen School." Only Papiyas, the king of demons, called his group the "Zen School." Those who use the name of Papiyas belong to the "Demon School" and are not descendants of buddha ancestors.

In front of innumerable beings on Vulture Peak, the World-Honored One held up an udumbara blossom and blinked. The entire assembly was silent. Mahakashyapa alone broke into a smile. The World-Honored One said, "I have the treasury of the true dharma eye, the wondrous heart of nirvana. This, along with the robe, is entrusted to Mahakashyapa."

What the World-Honored One entrusted to Mahakashyapa was *I have the treasury of the true dharma eye, the wondrous heart of nirvana.* There is no record of his saying, "I have the Zen School. This is entrusted to Mahakashyapa." He said, *along with the robe*, but did not say, "along with the Zen School." Thus, while the World-Honored One was alive, the name "Zen School" was not heard.

Bodhidharma, the First Chinese Ancestor, once instructed Huike, the Second Ancestor: "The unsurpassable, wondrous way of all buddhas is to make effort in difficult and painful practices for vast eons, bearing what is hard to bear. Do not seek the true vehicle with little virtue, shallow wisdom, or a careless or proud mind."

Bodhidharma also said, "The dharma seal of all buddhas is not obtained from a person." Again, he said, "The Tathagata entrusted the treasury of the true dharma eye to Mahakashyapa."

What is spoken here is the unsurpassable wondrous way of all buddhas, the treasury of the true dharma eye, and the dharma seal of all buddhas. At that time there was no name the "Zen School," and there were no stories referring to the "Zen School."

This treasury of the true dharma eye has been transmitted face to face by raising eyebrows and blinking. It has been transmitted and received with body, mind, bones, and marrow. It has been transmitted and received before the body and after the body. It has been transmitted and received within mind and outside of mind.

The name "Zen School" was not heard at the assembly of the World-Honored One and Mahakashyapa. The name "Zen School" was not heard at the assemblies of the First and Second Chinese Ancestors. The name "Zen School" was not heard at the assemblies of the Fifth and Sixth Chinese Ancestors. The name "Zen School" was not heard at the assemblies of Qingyuan and Nanyue. When did this name begin to be used and who started it? Possibly some students who were not actually students, and surreptitiously destroyed or stole the teaching, may have begun using this name.

For later students to mistakenly use the name "Zen School" is to damage the gate of buddhas and ancestors, and is not permitted by buddhas and ancestors. It makes you think that there is a teaching called the "Zen School" besides the teaching of buddhas and ancestors. This is the erroneous way outside the teaching of buddhas and ancestors.

You who are descendants of buddhas and ancestors should study the bones, marrow, and face of buddhas and ancestors. Throw yourself into the way of buddhas and ancestors. Do not deviate from this and study outside the way. That you have a human body and mind is a rare thing, which is the result of endeavor in the way from olden times. Receiving this gracious result, do not mistakenly become a student outside the way; it is not returning gratitude to buddhas and ancestors.

Recently, in the entire land of Great Song China, people in mediocre schools have heard this false name, "Zen School." Many ordinary people hear the false name "Zen School," "Bodhidharma School," or "Buddha Mind School," and are confused. These are groundless statements of those who have not yet known the great way of buddhas and ancestors, and have not seen, heard, or accepted that there is the treasury of the true dharma eye. How can those who know the treasury of the true dharma eye mistakenly call the buddha way by these false names?

Thus, Shitou, Great Master Wuji of Mount Nanyue, ascended the teaching seat and said to the assembly, "Our dharma gate has been transmitted from past buddhas. It is not concerned with Zen meditation or effort, but it just reaches the buddha knowledge."

Know that the buddha ancestor who has authentically received transmission from the Seven Original Buddhas speaks this way. The words *Our dharma gate has been transmitted from past buddhas* are actualized. But the words "Our Zen School has been transmitted from past buddhas" are not actualized. Without singling out Zen meditation or effort, buddha knowledge is reached. Without excluding effort or Zen meditation, what is reached is buddha knowledge.

This is the entrusting of *I have the treasury of the true dharma eye. Our* means *I have. Dharma gate* means *the true dharma. Our, I have*, and *my marrow* are the entrusting of "You have attained" [as Bodhidharma said].

Shitou was the heir of Qingyuan, High Ancestor. He alone entered Qingyuan's inner chamber. His head was shaved by Huineng, Old Buddha Caoxi. Therefore, Huineng was his ancestor and father. Qingyuan was his elder brother and teacher. Shitou alone was a person of excellence in the buddha way and occupied the ancestor seat. The authentic transmission of the buddha way reached Shitou alone. Fruit and branches of the word *actualized* are completely beyond the *old* of an old buddha, the eternal now of an old buddha. Make his teaching the eyeball of the treasury of the true dharma eye. Do not compare Shitou to other teachers. Those who do not understand compare him to Mazu of Jiangxi, but it is a mistake to do so.

In this way, know that the buddha way that has been transmitted from past buddhas is not called Zen meditation, so how could there be the name "Zen School"? Clearly understand that it is an extreme mistake to use the name "Zen School." Those who are ignorant assume that there is an "existence school" and an "emptiness school." They feel bad not having a special name as a school, as if there is nothing to study. But the buddha way is not like that. It should be determined that in the past there was no such name as "Zen School."

However, those of mediocre streams in recent times are foolish and do not know the authentic teaching. They have not received transmission from past buddhas and mistakenly say, "In buddha dharma, there are five schools that have various flavors." This is a characteristic of the declining teaching. There is not yet one person or one-half a person to crush this view. Rujing, my late master, Old Buddha Tiantong, for the first time, took pity on them. This is the way things go with human beings and teaching.

Rujing, my late master, ascended the teaching seat and taught the assembly: "Nowadays, this person and that person constantly say that Yunmen, Fayan, Guiyang, Linji, and Caodong have separate teachings. This is not buddha dharma. This is not the ancestral way."

The emergence of such a statement is difficult to meet with even in a thousand years. Rujing alone spoke in this way. It is difficult for such to be heard in the ten directions. Only in his assembly of wholeness was it heard. And yet, among the one thousand monks [who practiced with him], there was no one who had the ear to hear, or the eye to see. Given this, is there anyone capable of hearing with the entire mind, or hearing through the body? Even if they hear it with their entire bodies and minds for billions of eons, they cannot take up the entire body and mind of Rujing to hear it, realize it, believe it, and drop it away.

What a pity! People in the ten directions of the land of Great Song think that Rujing can be compared shoulder to shoulder with the elders of their own monasteries. Do those who think like this have eyes, or not? Some of them think that Rujing can be compared shoulder to shoulder with Linji or Deshan. I should say that these people also have not yet met either Rujing or Linji.

Before I formally bowed to Rujing, Old Buddha, I was trying to thoroughly study the profound teaching of the "Five Schools." But after I formally bowed to Rujing, I understood clearly that the "Five Schools" are groundlessly named.

In this way, when the buddha dharma was flourishing in China, there was no such designation as "Five Schools," and there were no teachers of old to expound the teaching using the name of the "Five Schools." After the buddha dharma became shallow and declined, the name "Five Schools" groundlessly appeared. This is because people have been negligent in study and not intimate in the endeavor of the way.

Those who look for genuine practice in the way of clouds and water should neither give it any thought nor bother to remember the differences in style of teaching. It is the same with the Three Mysteries, the Three Essentials, the Four Positions of Subject and Object, the Four Positions of Illumination and Function, and the Nine Ties of Teaching. The same can be said of the Three Phrases, the Five Ranks, and the Ten Equal Wisdoms.

The words of Old Man Shakyamuni are not confined to such narrow definitions as these, which are not regarded as great. Such theories were not spoken or heard at Shaolin or Caoxi. How sad! The bald-headed ones who have not heard dharma in this age of decline have ignorant eyes in body and mind and consequently talk about such things. Those who are descendants of buddha ancestors should not speak in such a way. Such confused theories as these have never been heard in the abode of buddha ancestors.

Flatterers in later times did not hear the entire words in buddha dharma and did not have complete trust in the ancestors' words. They were ignorant of the original self, became proud of what little they had learned, and established names such as the "Five Schools." Since these names were established, childish students have stopped studying the way in pursuit of the root and mistakenly follow the branches. They have no spirit of longing for the ancient, and their practice is mixed with worldly ways. To pay attention to worldly ways is admonished even by secular teachers.

———————

King Wen asked Minister Tai, "You made an effort to recommend wise people, but as yet there is no result. The world is even more disturbed. What is the cause of this crisis?"

The minister answered, "If you hire wise ones and do not use them, it is hiring in name only and the fruit is not attained."

King Wen said, "Where is the fault?"

The minister said, "The fault lies in adopting what worldly people admire and not adopting truth."

King Wen said, "What is the meaning of adopting what is admired by worldly people?"

The minister said, "If you listen to what ordinary people admire, you regard wisdom as not wisdom, knowledge as not knowledge, loyalty as not loyalty, trust as not trust. If you regard those who are considered wise by the worldly as wise, and regard those who are criticized by the worldly as incapable, then those who are popular advance and those who are not popular withdraw. Consequently, wicked people form groups and overwhelm the wise ones; loyal and innocent retainers are killed, and wicked retainers fill the ranks with false honor. This is how the world has become even more confused and why the country cannot avoid a crisis."

Thus, a secular person grieves over the crisis in society. The Buddha's children should grieve over the crisis in buddha dharma and the buddha way. The cause of the crisis lies in mistakenly paying attention to the words of worldly people. If you listen to what worldly people admire, you cannot attain true wisdom. If you wish to attain true wisdom, you should have resources to reflect on the past and see to the future.

Those who are admired by worldly people are not necessarily wise ones or sages. Those who are criticized by worldly people are not necessarily wise ones or sages. However, consider, and do not confuse those who are wise and criticized with those who are false and honored. Not to use the wise ones is the loss of the nation. To promote incapable ones is the regret of the nation.

To maintain the names of the "Five Schools" nowadays is the confusion of worldly people. There are many who follow this worldly custom, but there are few who know this worldly custom as just a worldly custom. You can regard those who guide worldly people as sages, but those who follow the ways of worldly people are extremely foolish. How can they know the Buddha's true teaching? How can they become buddhas and ancestors?

The teaching has been directly transmitted from the Seven Original Buddhas. How can it be like the Five Divisions of the Precept School established in India by those who depend upon letters and interpret their meaning? In this way, know that ancestors who regard the true life of the buddha dharma as the true life have never said that there are various gates such as the "Five Schools." Those who think that there are "Five Schools" in the buddha way are not authentic heirs of the Seven Original Buddhas.

———————

Rujing taught the assembly, "In recent years the ancestors' way has been discarded and there are many groups of demons and beasts. They frequently discuss the different flavors of the Five Houses. How shameful! How shameful!"

Thus we know that the twenty-eight ancestors in India and the twenty-two ancestors in China have never expounded the differences of the "Five Schools." All the ancestors have this in common. Those who discuss the "Five Schools" and say that each has its own teaching confuse people of the world, through their limited learning and shallow understanding. If buddhas had established their own ways within the buddha way, how could the buddha way have reached this day? Mahakashyapa might have become independent. Ananda might have become independent. If becoming independent were the correct way, buddha dharma would have perished in India.

Who would long for the ancient teaching if everyone became independent? Who could discern authentic from inauthentic in the teaching if everyone became independent? If authentic and inauthentic are not distinguished, who could tell buddha dharma from what it is not? If you do not understand the meaning of this, it cannot be called the buddha way.

The names of the "Five Schools" were not established when the ancestor of each school was still alive. After the ancestors who were regarded as the founders of the "Five Schools" passed away, the mediocre streams of their students whose eyes were not yet clear and whose feet were not able to walk began using these names without asking their teachers, contrary to their ancestors. This is clear and it is known by everyone.

Guishan, Zen Master Dayuan of Mount Gui, was an heir of Baizhang, Zen Master Dazhi. He lived on Mount Gui when Baizhang was alive. Guishan never said that buddha dharma should be called the "Guiyang [Guishan and Yangshan] School." Nor did Baizhang say that he should abide on Mount Gui and call his teaching the "Guiyang School." Neither Guishan nor his master spoke of it in this way. Thus, know that this is a groundless name.

Do not look to Yangshan as the perpetrator, although the "Guiyang School" partly bears his name. If he had the need to call it after his name, he would have done that. But since there was no need to, he did not name it after himself in the past, nor would he do so in the present.

There is no such name as the "Caoxi School," the "Nanyue School," the "Xijiang School," or the "Baizhang School." Guishan should not be different from Huineng of Caoxi. He should not excel Huineng. In fact, he should not even reach to Huineng.

One word or half a phrase spoken by Guishan is not necessarily carried equally on one staff with Yangshan. If you establish the name of the school, you should call it the "Guishan School" or the "Dagui [Great Guishan] School." But there is no reason and no ground for calling it the "Guiyang School."

Had it been appropriate to call it the "Guiyang School," they would have done so when the two masters were alive. But they did not name it while they were alive. Why did they not do so? Those who go against their fathers and ancestors and call their teaching the "Guiyang School," although there was no such name while the two masters were alive, are unfilial descendants. This is not the original wish of Guishan or the straightforward will of Yangshan. There is no such authentic transmission from the true masters. It is clear that these names were groundlessly created by those who were mistaken. Do not spread it in the ten directions.

Linji, Great Master Huizhao, abandoned the house gate of lecturing sutras and became a student of Huangbo. He was struck by Huangbo's staff on three occasions; all together sixty blows. He went to study with Dayu and experienced realization. Later, he was abbot of the Linji Monastery in Zhen Province.

As he did not fully master Huangbo's mind, he did not speak one phrase or half a phrase to the effect that the buddha dharma he had inherited should be called the "Linji School." Nor did he indicate it by raising a fist or holding up a whisk. However, the mediocre stream of his students, without protecting their teacher's accomplishment in buddha dharma, initiated the name "Linji School" by mistake. Rather, they should have done what was in accord with the daily life of Linji. Since this would go against the way of Huangbo, they should have refrained from initiating such a name.

In fact, when Linji was about to pass away, he entrusted Sansheng, who would later become Zen Master Huiran, and said, "After I pass away, do not let my treasury of the true dharma eye be extinguished."

Sansheng said, "How would I let your treasury of the true dharma eye be extinguished?"

Linji said, "If someone asks you about it, how would you respond?"

Sansheng shouted.

Linji said, "Who would have guessed that my treasury of the true dharma eye has reached as far as this blind donkey and perished?"

The master and disciple spoke to each other in this way. Linji did not say, "Do not let my Zen School be extinguished," "Do not let my Linji School be extinguished," or "Do not let my school be extinguished." Rather, he just said, *Do not let my treasury of the true dharma eye be extin-*

guished. Clearly know that the great road authentically transmitted by buddhas and ancestors should not be called the "Zen School" or the "Linji School."

———————

This being so, never call it the "Zen School." Even if *extinguished* is the essence of the treasury of the true dharma eye, it is entrusted in this way. *Reached as far as this blind donkey and perished* is a true entrustment. Who would guess? Inside the gate of Linji, there was only Sansheng. Neither his older nor younger fellow practitioners were in the same rank—this is how they are arrayed under the bright window.

The story of Linji and Sansheng is that of buddha ancestors. Linji's entrustment now is the entrustment on Vulture Peak long ago. Thus, it is clear that you should not use the name "Linji School."

———————

Yunmen, Great Master Kuangzhen, once studied with Venerable Master Chen. Thus, he is a descendant of Huangbo. Later he succeeded Xuefeng, who did not tell him to call the treasury of the true dharma eye "Yunmen School." But without knowing that "Guiyang School" and "Linji School" were groundless names, his students initiated the name "Yunmen School." If the effort of Yunmen had been to establish a new school, it could not be admitted as the body and mind of the buddha dharma. To associate him with the name of the school is just like regarding the emperor as a person of humble rank.

———————

Zen Master Great Fayan of the Qingliang Monastery is an heir of Dizang and a dharma descendant of Xuansha. His teaching was free from mistakes. "Great Fayan" was his official title. He did not say even one word among one thousand words, or one phrase among ten thousand phrases, to indicate that the treasury of the true dharma eye should be named after him, nor did he initiate a "Fayan School." However, his students did initiate the name "Fayan School." If Fayan were teaching at present, he would cut off the groundless name "Fayan School." Fayan has already passed away, and there is no one who can correct this disastrous error. Even one thousand or ten thousand years later, those who want to be filial to Zen Master Fayan should not use this name. To refrain from doing so is the best way to be filial.

In fact, Yunmen and Fayan are descendants of Qingyuan, High Ancestor, from whom the bones of the way and the marrow of the dharma have been transmitted.

———

Dongshan, High Ancestor, Great Master Wuben, succeeded in dharma from Yunyan. Yunyan is an authentic heir of Yaoshan. Yaoshan is an authentic heir of Shitou. Shitou is the single heir of High Ancestor Qingyuan. Without having two or three to compare shoulder to shoulder, Shitou alone authentically transmitted the accomplishment of the way. The true life of the buddha way has remained in China thanks to Shitou, who authentically transmitted dharma completely.

Qingyuan spread the teaching of Huineng at Mount Qingyuan when Huineng himself was teaching. Huineng let Qingyuan appear in the world and let the world see and hear him while he himself was still alive. Qingyuan was the authentic heir of authentic heirs, high ancestor of high ancestors. Concerning his study and emergence in the world, no one could be compared to him. Yet, even those who could not be compared to him at that time would excel at present. Those who study the way should make a special point of knowing this.

———

Huineng, Old Buddha Caoxi, taught human beings and devas at the time of his pari-nirvana. On this occasion, Shitou advanced and asked Huineng which teacher he should study with. Huineng said, "Go and see Xingsi [Qingyuan]." He did not say, "Go and see Huairang [Nanyue]." Thus, the ancient buddha's treasury of the true dharma eye was authentically transmitted by Qingyuan alone. Even if Qingyuan and Nanyue are acknowledged as excellent students who both attained the way, Qingyuan is the only authentic disciple. Huineng confirmed his disciple Qingyuan as his heir. Thus, Huineng became the father of Qingyuan when Qingyuan became his heir. In this way, Qingyuan's attaining the marrow is clear. The authentic heritage of the ancestral teaching is clear.

As an heir, the fourth generation from Qingyuan, Dongshan authentically succeeded in the treasury of the true dharma eye and opened the eye to the wondrous heart of nirvana. Other than this, there is no transmission or school. He never taught the assembly, either with a fist or by blinking, that they should call themselves the "Caodong School." Furthermore, since he had no mediocre stream among his students, no student called it the "Dongshan School," let alone the "Caodong School."

The name "Caodong School" seems to be a combination of Dongshan and Caoshan. If so, Yunju and Tong'an should also be added. Yunju is a guiding master of humans and devas, more venerable than Caoshan. I suppose that the "Caodong School" is so called because skin bags outside presumed that Dongshan was someone who could be compared shoulder to shoulder with them. It is like floating clouds covering the world beneath the bright sun.

———————

Rujing, my late master, said: "Although there are a number of those in all directions who ascend the lion seat and are regarded as masters of humans and devas, there are none who understand buddha dharma."

Thus, they [such false teachers] established the teaching of the "Five Schools" and are stagnant with phrases on top of phrases. They are truly enemies of buddha ancestors.

Sometimes the sect of Huanglong, Zen Master Huinan, is called the "Huanglong School," but people will soon know about the mistake.

In fact, when the World-Honored One was alive, he did not call his teaching the "Buddha School," "Vulture Peak School," or "Jeta Grove School." He did not call it "My Mind School" or the "Buddha Mind School." In which discourses did he call it the "Buddha Mind School"? Why, then, do people nowadays call it the "Buddha Mind School"? For what reason would the World-Honored One name the teaching after his mind? How would the teaching be the "mind"?

If there is to be a "Buddha Mind School," there should be a "Buddha Body School," "Buddha Eye School," "Buddha Ear School," or "Buddha Nose-and-Tongue School." There should be a "Buddha Marrow School," "Buddha Bones School," "Buddha Leg School," or "Buddha Land School." But there are none of these. Therefore, know that the "Buddha Mind School" is a false name.

When Shakyamuni Buddha broadly took up the reality of all things in the buddha land of the ten directions, and taught in the buddha land of the ten directions, he did not say that he had established a school in the buddha land of the ten directions. If the name "school" is within the teaching of buddha ancestors, it should exist in the buddha land. If it were in the buddha land, the name would form a part of the Buddha's discourses. But it does not, so we know that the name "school" is not an accoutrement of the buddha land. The ancestors did not speak of the name "school," so we know that it is not one of the furnishings of the ancestors' abode. This not only is ridiculed by other people and prohibited by all buddhas, but is also ridiculed by the self. Refrain from using these names. Do not say there are Five Houses in the Buddha's teaching.

———————

Later on, there was a childish fellow called Zhicong [meaning Wisdom Brilliance]. He collected one or two phrases of the ancestors. He spoke about the teachings of the Five Houses and called them the *Human and Deva Eyes*. People do not understand this, and some of those who are beginners or immature students think that it is authentic and hide the book in their robes. It is not "human and deva eyes," but it blinds human and deva eyes. How could it have the power of completely covering the treasury of the true dharma eye?

This text, the *Human and Deva Eyes*, was edited by Senior Monk Zhicong in the Wannian Monastery of Mount Tiantai about the twelfth month, the fifteenth year of the Chunzhi Era (1188). This was done recently, but it could possibly be accepted if the statements were correct. However, his work is confusion as well as ignorance. There is no eye of studies or eye of practice, not to mention the eye of seeing buddha ancestors. This text should not be used. The editor is not as wise and brilliant as his name implies; rather he is foolish and blind. He collected the words of those who had not known or met themselves, and he did not collect the words of those who are true persons. So we know that he did not recognize true persons.

People who study scriptures in China tend to talk about schools, because they like to make comparisons among them. But the treasury of the true dharma eye of buddha ancestors has been entrusted from heir to heir. There is no way to compare it, and there is nothing it can be confused with.

However, careless elders of the present day groundlessly use the names of the schools in an attempt to establish themselves without being concerned with the buddha way. The buddha way is not their buddha way. It is the buddha way of all buddhas and ancestors. It is the buddha way of the buddha way.

———————

Minister Tai said to King Wen, "The world is not one person's world; it is the world's world."

Even a secular person has such wisdom and such words. You, children inside the house of buddhas and ancestors, should not groundlessly let your ignorance obscure the great way by naming yourselves after a school. It is ridiculous. If you do so, you are not people of the buddha way.

If there were to be the name of a school, the World-Honored One would have used it himself. But he did not. How can you as his descendant do that after his pari-nirvana? Who is more skillful than the World-Honored One? No one is. Creating such a name has no merit. If you go against the authentic way of buddha ancestors, and establish a school yourself, how can there be Buddha's descendants who regard your school as their school? Reflect on the past and think of the present, and do not make a mistake.

The only wishes of the World-Honored One's disciples who were left behind were not to vary one hairbreadth from how he was when he was alive in the world, to be concerned about not reaching one millionth part of him, to rejoice upon arriving, and not to go against his will. In this way, vow to see and meet the World-Honored One birth after birth and hear his teaching.

To oppose the teaching of the World-Honored One, which was given while he was alive, and to establish the name of a school is not to be a disciple of the Tathagata or a descendant of ancestors. It is worse than committing a serious crime. Practitioners of dharma who neglect the Tathagatha's unsurpassed enlightenment and call themselves by the name of their own school take lightly, oppose, and ignore the teachers of the past. It is a lack of faith in the merit of the World-Honored One in the days when he was alive in the world. There is no buddha dharma in the house of such people.

For this reason, upon authentically succeeding in the work of studying buddhas, do not attempt to learn the names of the schools. What buddhas and ancestors entrust and authentically transmit is the treasury of the true dharma eye, unsurpassed enlightenment. All the dharma that belongs to buddha ancestors has been entrusted by the buddhas. There is no new extra dharma. This is the bones of the dharma and marrow of the way.

Presented to the assembly of the Yoshimine Temple, Yoshida County, Echizen Province, on the sixteenth day, the ninth month, the first year of the Kangen Era [1243].

51

THE REALITY OF ALL THINGS

ACTUALIZING BUDDHA ANCESTORS is reality thoroughly experienced. Reality is all things. All things are reality thusness; original nature thusness; body thusness; mind thusness; world thusness; cloud and rain thusness; walking, standing, sitting, and lying down thusness; sadness, joy, motion, and stillness thusness; staff and whisk thusness; taking up the flower and smiling thusness; inheriting dharma and giving predictions thusness; studying and endeavor of the way thusness; pine purity and bamboo joints thusness.

Shakyamuni Buddha said [in the *Lotus Sutra*]:

Only a buddha and a buddha can thoroughly experience the reality of all things. What is called *all things* is reality thusness, original nature thusness, body thusness, capacity thusness, activity thusness, cause thusness, condition thusness, effect thusness, reward thusness, root-branch-and-beyond thusness.

The Tathagata's words *root-branch-and-beyond thusness* is the self-expression of the reality of all things, the self-expression of all teachers.

It is studying together as one, because studying is no other than studying together as one.

Only a buddha and a buddha is the reality of all things. The Reality of all things is only a buddha and a buddha. Only a buddha is all things. And a buddha is all things. When you hear the words *all things,* do not assume it is one or many. When you hear the word *reality,* do not study it as void or original nature. *Reality* is *only a buddha; reality* is *and a buddha.*

Can experience is *only a buddha; thoroughly* is *and a buddha. All things* are all things that are *only a buddha. Reality* is *and a buddha.* When all things are truly all things, they are called *only a buddha.* When all things are *reality,* they are called *and a buddha.*

Thus, when all things are all things, there is reality thusness, original nature thusness. When reality is reality, there is reality thusness, original nature thusness. That *only a buddha and a buddha* appear in the world is speaking, practice, and realization of the reality of all things. Speaking is *can thoroughly experience.* Although *thoroughly,* it is *can experience,* because it is beyond beginning, middle, and end; it is reality thusness, original nature thusness. Thus, it is described as "wholesome in the beginning, middle, and end."

Can thoroughly experience is *the reality of all things. The Reality of all things* is reality thusness. Reality thusness is *can thoroughly experience* original nature thusness. *Original nature thusness* is *can thoroughly experience* body thusness. *Body thusness* is *can thoroughly experience* capacity thusness. *Capacity thusness* is *can thoroughly experience* activity thusness. *Activity thusness* is *can thoroughly experience* cause thusness. *Cause thusness* is *can thoroughly experience* condition thusness. *Condition thusness* is *can thoroughly experience* effect thusness. *Effect thusness* is *can thoroughly experience* reward thusness. *Reward thusness* is *can thoroughly experience* root-branch-and-beyond thusness.

The words *root-branch-and-beyond thusness* are indeed thusness actualized. This being so, the effect in the buddha stage is beyond an effect in cause and effect. Thus, the effect in cause and effect is no other than the effect in the buddha stage. Because this effect is immersed in form, original nature, body, and capacity, then form, original nature, body, and capacity of all things are immeasurably and boundlessly reality. Because this effect is beyond form, original nature, body, and capacity, then form, original nature, body, and capacity of all things are all together reality.

When you become one with reality, then such words as *original nature,* *body,* and *capacity*—immersed in effect, reward, cause, and condition—hit the mark eight or nine out of ten. When you become one with reality, then original nature, body, and capacity—immersed in effect, reward, cause, and condition—hit the mark ten out of ten.

Reality thusness is not one reality, nor is it one thusness. It is thusness immeasurable, boundless, unspeakable, and unfathomable. Do not make one hundred or one thousand as a measure. Make all things a measure. Make the measure of reality the measure.

It means that *only a buddha and a buddha* can thoroughly experience the reality of all things; *only a buddha and a buddha* can thoroughly experience the true nature of all things; *only a buddha and a buddha* can thoroughly experience the true body of all things; *only a buddha and a buddha* can thoroughly experience the true capacity of all things; *only a buddha and a buddha* can thoroughly experience the true activity of all things; *only a buddha and a buddha* can thoroughly experience the true cause of all things; *only a buddha and a buddha* can thoroughly experience the true condition of all things; *only a buddha and a buddha* can thoroughly experience the true effect of all things; *only a buddha and a buddha* can thoroughly experience the true reward of all things; *only a buddha and a buddha* can thoroughly experience the true root-branch-and-beyond of all things.

———————

In this way, the buddha land in the ten directions is just *only a buddha and a buddha.* There is no one or half *only a buddha and a buddha* other than this. *Only* and *and* are to possess *body* in *body* and to realize *reality* in *reality.* It is like having original nature as body and letting it be original nature.

In this way, Shakyamuni Buddha said [in the *Lotus Sutra*], "I and buddhas in the ten directions can understand this."

Thus, the very moment of *can understand* and the very moment of *can understand this* are equally each and every [experience of] time being. If *I* were different from *buddhas in the ten directions,* how could the Buddha have actualized the words *I and buddhas in the ten directions*? Because this place is beyond the ten directions, the ten directions are in this place.

This being so, to encounter all things that are reality means that spring enters blossoms and a person encounters spring. The moon illuminates the moon and a person meets the self. Or, a person sees fire. These are equally the true meaning of encountering.

In this way, reality studying reality is called a buddha ancestor receiving transmission of dharma from a buddha ancestor. This is all things confirming the enlightenment of all things. It is *only a buddha* transmits dharma to *only a buddha; and a buddha* receives transmission of dharma from *and a buddha.*

Thus, there is the coming and going of birth and death. Thus, there is aspiration, practice, enlightenment, and nirvana. In taking up aspiration, practice, enlightenment, and nirvana, you thoroughly study and guide the coming and going of birth and death and the true human body; you grab hold of them and you let go of them. Making this the life vein, blossoms open and fruit is born. Making this bones and marrow, there is Mahakashyapa and there is Ananda.

The reality thusness of wind, rain, water, and fire *can thoroughly experience*. The original nature thusness of blue, yellow, red, and white *can thoroughly experience*. With this body and capacity, you transform the ordinary and enter the sacred. With this effect and reward, you go beyond buddha and beyond ancestor. Through this cause and condition, you pick up dirt and turn it into gold. Through this effect and reward, there is transmission of dharma and entrustment of the robe.

The Tathagata said [in the *Lotus Sutra*], "Thus, I expound the mudra of reality."

It means: *Thus, I* practice *the mudra* [definite expression] *of reality. Thus, I* listen to *the mudra of reality. Thus, I* realize *the mudra of reality.* Study thoroughly and experience thoroughly in this way. The meaning of this is like "A pearl rolls on a board and a board rolls on a pearl" [the dynamic interaction of subject and object, practice and enlightenment].

The Chandra Surya Pradipa Buddha said [in the *Lotus Sutra*], "I have expounded the meaning of the reality of all things to you."

Study this statement and know that buddha ancestors unfailingly make expounding the meaning of reality a single great matter. Buddha ancestors, together with the eighteen realms, unfold the meaning of reality. Before body and mind, after body and mind, at the very moment of body and mind [in the past, present, and future], they expound reality, original nature, body, capacity, and so on. Those who do not thoroughly experience, expound, understand, and beyond-understand reality are not buddha ancestors; they are demons and animals.

––––––––––

Shakyamuni Buddha said [in the *Lotus Sutra*], "The entire unsurpassable, complete enlightenment of all bodhisattvas belongs to this sutra. This sutra opens the gate of skillful means and demonstrates reality."

What are called *all bodhisattvas* are all buddhas. Buddhas and bodhisattvas are not different types of beings. It is not that one is older and the other is younger, or that one is superior and the other is inferior. This bodhisattva and that bodhisattva are not two beings, not self and other. They are not limited to the past, future, and present, but there is a dharma procedure of practicing the bodhisattva path for becoming a buddha.

Bodhisattvas become buddhas at the first moment of arousing the aspiration for enlightenment, and they become buddhas at the place of wondrous enlightenment. There are bodhisattvas who have become buddhas uncountable times—one hundred, one thousand, ten thousand billion times. Those who speak of abolishing practice and doing nothing after becoming buddhas are ordinary people who do not know the path of buddha ancestors.

What are called *all bodhisattvas* are the original ancestors of all buddhas. All buddhas are the original teachers of all bodhisattvas. Even if unsurpassable enlightenment is practiced and realized in the past, present, or future, before the body and after the mind, it is altogether *this sutra* in the beginning, middle, and end. *Belongs* and being made to belong are altogether *this sutra*. At this very moment, you realize *all bodhisattvas* mentioned in this sutra.

The sutra is neither sentient nor insentient, neither created nor uncreated. Yet, upon realizing a bodhisattva, realizing a person, realizing reality, and realizing the sutra, the gate of skillful means opens. The gate of skillful means is an unsurpassable merit of the buddha fruit, things abiding in the world of phenomena, and the everlasting reality of the world.

The gate of skillful means is not a temporary art. It is the study of the entire world of the ten directions. It is taking up the reality of all things and studying it. Even if this gate of skillful means covers the world of the ten directions in the entire world of the ten directions, without being *all bodhisattvas,* this cannot be experienced.

––––––––––

Xuefeng said, "The entire great earth is a gate of emancipation. Even if I invite people, they would not get through it."

Thus, know that although the entire great earth is a gate of emancipation, going in and out of it is not easy; there are not many who go in and out. Even if they are invited, they would not go in and out. Even if they are not invited, they would not go in and out. Those who step forward may miss it. Those who step backward may stand still. How so? If you try to have others go in and out of the gate, it moves farther away. If you have a gate that accepts others, it is possible for them to go in and out.

––––––––––

Shakyamuni Buddha's words *opens the gate of skillful means* demonstrate reality. *Demonstrates reality* is all through time in the beginning, middle, and end, independent from one another. When the gate of skillful means truly opens, it opens in the entire world of the ten directions. If you see the entire world of the ten directions at this very moment, you see a sight that has never been seen. That brings forth the entire world of the ten directions onefold, twofold, in three pieces, or in four pieces, and lets the gate of skillful means open. Thus, although the gate of skillful means is seen as opening equally, a number of entire worlds of the ten directions are seen as being actualized as a small part of opening the gate of skillful means. Such activities are due to the power of the sutra.

Demonstrating reality is having the entire world hear the phrase *the reality of all things* and having the entire world attain the way. It is to let the entire person understand the meaning of *the reality of all things* and let the entire dharma emerge.

This being so, the unsurpassable enlightenment of the Forty Buddhas, Forty Ancestors [from the Seven Original Buddhas to Huineng, the Sixth Chinese Ancestor], all belongs to *this sutra.* Enlightenment belongs to *this sutra,* and *this sutra* belongs to enlightenment. Both the sitting mat and the sounding board that are no other than unsurpassable enlightenment belong to *this sutra*. Taking up a flower and smiling, as well as bowing and attaining the marrow, belong to *this sutra*. *This sutra* belongs to these activities. This is opening the gate of skillful means and demonstrating reality.

———

However, coarse people in recent Song China expound reality falsely without knowing the settling place and without seeing the treasure place. They further study the words of Laozi [Lao-tzu] and Zhuangzi [Chuang-tzu]. They say that these teachings are identical to the great road of buddha ancestors. They also insist that the Three Teachings are in accord, explaining that they are like the tripod of a worshipping bowl, which would tip over if it were without one of the legs. It is extreme stupidity, not worth examining.

Do not accept that those who say such things have learned buddha dharma. The reasons for not doing so are as follows: We regard buddha dharma as having originated in India. The Buddha lived for eighty years and expounded dharma for fifty years, when he taught humans and devas. He transformed all sentient beings who entered the buddha way. After that, the twenty-eight ancestors authentically transmitted his teaching. This is the peak, the most wondrous and venerable. Various people outside the way and heavenly demons were all subdued by the Buddha. Humans and devas who have become buddhas and ancestors are countless.

Although Confucianism and Daoism have not entered India, no one speaks of the buddha way as incomplete. If the Three Teachings had been one, when buddha dharma appeared in India, Confucianism and Daoism would have appeared. However, buddha dharma is "I alone am venerable above and under heaven." Reflect on that time. Do not forget it.

The phrase "accord of the Three Teachings" does not even come close to a child's mumbling. Those who insist on this are those who destroy buddha dharma. There are so many of them. They take the appearance of guiding masters of humans and devas. Some of them have even become emperors' teachers. Great Song China has been in the time of the decline of buddha dharma. Rujing, my late master, warned of this.

Such people [who advocate the accord of the Three Teachings] are seeds of those in the Lesser Vehicles or those outside the way. For a couple of hundred years there have been such people who don't know even the existence of reality. When they study authentic buddha dharma, they only speak of becoming free from birth and death. Also, there have been those who don't know how to study the authentic dharma of buddha ancestors. They only understand imitating the ancients while living in a monastery. What a pity that the ancestral way is in decline! This is what venerable masters who have mastered the way deplore. Do not pay attention to the theories of such people. Just pity them.

———————

Keqin, Zen Master Yuanwu, said, "The coming and going of birth and death are the true human body."

Take up this statement, know yourself, and investigate buddha dharma.

———————

Changsha said, "The entire world of the ten directions is the true human body. The entire world of the ten directions is within the radiant light of the self."

This statement is not known by the elders of many monasteries in Great Song China today as something to study, not to speak of being studied by them. If you take this up and ask about it, they may blush and remain silent.

Rujing, my late master Old Buddha, said, "The elders of many monasteries lack illuminating the past and illuminating the present. They haven't mastered the meaning of buddha dharma. Being asked about the entire world of the ten directions and so forth, they don't know the answer. It looks as though some of them had never heard of such a question."

After hearing this, I asked elders of monasteries such a question; few of them had heard about it. What a pity that they occupy their positions while uttering vain speeches!

———————

Once, Ying'an Tanhua said to monk Dehui:

> If you want to make understanding easy, get to the place of arousing the mind and moving thoughts during the twelve hours [all day]. If you have contact with these moving thoughts, you immediately understand what is ungraspable. It is like a great void that has no trace of void. Front and back are one. Both the knower and the known are invisible. Both implicit and explicit perish. Past, present, and future are equal. Upon arriving at this state, you are called a leisurely person of no more studying and no more doing.

This is a phrase of Old Man Ying'an's fully concerted expression. It appears that he chased a shadow and did not know the real meaning of ceasing.

Is there not buddha dharma when the front and back are not one? What are the front and back? Also, he regards the void with no form as a statement of buddha ancestors. What does he regard as the void? In my opinion, he did not know or see the void. He did not take up or strike the void.

Ying'an spoke of *arousing the mind and moving thoughts.* However, it is possible to say that the mind does not move. Then, how can you arouse the mind during the twelve hours of the day? Mind does not move and enter into the twelve hours of the day. The twelve hours do not move in twelve [separate] minds. If they did, how could you arouse the mind?

What are moving thoughts? Do thoughts move or not-move? Do thoughts not-move or not not-move? What is movement? And what is not-movement? What do you call thoughts? Are thoughts in twelve hours? Is twelve hours in thoughts? Is there a moment when neither of them exists?

Ying'an said, *Get to the place . . . during the twelve hours,* and you can *make understanding easy.* What do you call easy understanding? Do you say that it is easy to understand the way of buddha ancestors? However, as buddha dharma is beyond easy or difficult to understand, Nanyue and Mazu both practiced thoroughly with their teacher [Huineng].

Ying'an said, *you immediately understand what is ungraspable.* This reveals that he had not even dreamed of the buddha ancestors' way. With his ability, how can he speak of understanding easily or not? It is clear that he had not yet thoroughly studied the great way of buddha ancestors. If buddha dharma were like this, how could it have reached this day?

Even Ying'an was like this. Yet, if we look for someone like him among the elders of monasteries nowadays, it is impossible to meet one even for long eons. Even if we look piercingly hard, we cannot find anyone like Ying'an. Therefore, many people in recent times approve of him. However, it is hard to acknowledge that buddha dharma had reached him. He was still a latecomer on the monastic seats—an ordinary person. At least he had a spirit for knowing a true person. But, as they do not know a true person, elders nowadays do not know themselves,

Although Ying'an had not mastered buddha dharma, he had studied the way. On the other hand, the elders of monasteries nowadays have not studied the way. While Ying'an heard good words, the words did not enter his ears and were not seen by his ears; they did not enter his eyes and were not heard by his eyes.

Ying'an was like this in the past, but he must be self-enlightened by now. The seniors of monasteries in Great Song China today don't look into the inside and outside of Ying'an, thus, sounds and forms are all outside of their realm. Such people do not know whether the reality of buddha dharma expressed by buddha ancestors is the words of buddha ancestors or not. This being so, none of the elders or other clumsy fellows in these two or three hundred years have seen and explained reality.

––––––––––

Rujing gave a dharma talk in the abbot's room one evening:

> I, Tiantong, have a calf tonight.
> The golden-faced Gautama takes up reality.
> Even if you want to buy it, it has no price.
> The chirp of a cuckoo is heard from above a solitary cloud.

In this way, a venerable master who excels in the buddha way speaks of reality. Those who do not know and have not studied the buddha way do not speak of reality.

This verse was presented around the third month, the second year of the Baoqing Era [1226] of Great Song China. It was close to the fourth time period late at night; I heard a drum hit three times in the north.

I took up my [folded] bowing cloth, wore a kashaya, and went out of the cloud [monks'] hall. A plaque signaling permission to enter the abbot's room was hanging.

I followed other monks and went in the direction of the dharma hall. Passing the west wall of the dharma hall, I climbed up the west stairway of the Serene Light Hall [abbot's quarters west]. I climbed up the west stairway of the Great Light Treasury Hall [abbot's quarters east]. From the southern part of the standing screen, I approached the table with an incense burner, burned incense, and bowed. I thought that those who wished to enter the abbot's room must be standing in line, but no other monk was there.

A reed screen was hanging at the entrance of the Wondrous Plateau [abbot's main quarters]. I heard the faint dharma voice of the great abbot priest. At that time Zukun, the practice coordinator from Xichuan, arrived and burned incense after me. When we quietly looked up at the Wondrous Plateau, we saw a crowd of monks standing from the east end to the west end of the hall. Then the dharma talk started, which I listened to while standing in the back of the crowd.

Rujing told a story about Zen Master Fachang of Damei, living in the monastery. Many monks shed tears when they heard about Fachang's assembly wearing lotus leaves and eating pine nuts. Rujing also told a detailed story about Shakyamuni Buddha's practice period. Many listeners shed tears.

Rujing then said, "A practice period here at Mount Tiantong is approaching. It is spring now, not cold and not hot. This is the time favorable for zazen. Fellow practitioners, why not do zazen?"

Thus, he spoke and presented the above verse. After reading this verse, he struck the right side of his Zen chair with his right hand and said, "Now enter the room."

When some of the monks were inside the abbot's room, Rujing said, "A nightingale chirps. Bamboo on the mountain cracks." He spoke in this way but did not say anything more. Although many monks entered the room, they remained in silent awe.

This way of inviting monks to enter the abbot's room is not practiced in other monasteries. Rujing alone practiced in this way. At the time of his giving a dharma talk, the assembly of monks would stand around chairs and screens. As they kept standing, monks near the entrance would enter the room, and those who had finished visiting would go out of the gate of the abbot's quarters as usual. The rest of the monks would keep standing, so they could see and hear the formal movement of those who entered the room as well as the dignified bearing of the abbot priest as he spoke. This format has not been found in other monasteries, where the seniors do not practice in this way.

In the usual manner of entering the abbot's room, monks try to get ahead of others, but in this way of entering the room, monks want to follow. Be aware of the difference in people's minds.

It is the first year of the Kangen Era [1243] now. The passage of time is swift, and it has been eighteen years since then. I don't remember how many mountains and rivers I have crossed from Mount Tiantong to here, but I have been engraving in my body, mind, bones, and marrow his magnificent words and stunning phrases as reality. I believe Rujing's dharma talk and the monks entering his room at that time have been memorable for many monks. It was a serene night while the faint light of the moon was leaking through the pavilion and nightingales were chirping continuously.

Xuansha, Great Master Zongyi, was on his way to the dharma hall when he heard the swallow's voice.

He said [in his dharma talk], "The swallow's voice deeply speaks of reality and well expounds the heart of the dharma."

Then, he descended from the teaching seat.

Later, a monk asked him for teaching by saying, "I don't understand it."

Xuansha said, "Go away. No one believes you."

You may think that Xuansha's statement, *The swallow's voice deeply speaks of reality* means that swallows alone deeply speak of reality. But it is not so. He did hear the chirping of swallows on his way. It is not that swallows were speaking of reality. It is not that Xuansha was speaking of reality. They were not divided into two, but at that very moment there was speaking of reality.

Study this story thoroughly for now. There was Xuansha's walking on his way there. There was hearing the chirping of swallows. There was a statement, *The swallow's voice deeply speaks of reality and well expounds the heart of the dharma.* There was descending from his teaching seat. There was a monk asking him by saying, *I don't understand it.* There was Xuansha saying, *Go away. No one believes you.* The monk's statement, *I don't understand it,* was not necessarily asking about reality, but was a life vein of buddha ancestors—bones and marrow of the treasury of the true dharma eye.

Know that whether this monk had asked for instruction by saying, "I understand it," or by saying, "I speak it," Xuansha would invariably have said, *Go away. No one believes you.* It is not that Xuansha said, *Go away. No one believes you* because the monk understood it but said he did not understand it.

Indeed, even if you are an ordinary person and not like this monk, you experience the reality of all things. When reality is actualized in this way at this time and place, you are directly connected to the life vein of buddha ancestors. In the lineage of Qingyuan, this was actualized [by Xuansha].

Know that reality is an authentic vein that has been transmitted from heir to heir. All things are only a buddha and a buddha thoroughly investigated. Only a buddha and a buddha are splendid just as they are.

Presented to the assembly of the Yoshimine Temple, Echizen Province, Japan, in the ninth month, the first year of the Kangen Era [1243].

52

INTIMATE LANGUAGE

ACTUALIZING THE FUNDAMENTAL point, you realize the great road maintained by all buddhas. "You are like this. I am like this. Keep it well," is revealed.

Yunju, Great Master Hongjiao, was asked by an imperial minister who brought an offering, "The World-Honored One had intimate language, and Mahakashyapa did not conceal it. What was the World-Honored One's language?"

Yunju said, "Your Excellency."

"Yes," he responded.

Yunju asked, "Do you understand it?"

The minister said, "No, I don't."

Yunju said, "If you don't understand it, the World-Honored One had intimate language. If you understand it, Mahakashyapa did not conceal it."

Yunju, a teacher of humans and devas, is the fifth-generation direct heir of Qingyuan. A great sage of the ten directions, he guides sentient beings and insentient beings. The forty-sixth-generation heir of the buddhas [including the Seven Original Buddhas], Yunju spoke dharma for buddha ancestors. Celestial beings sent offerings to his Three Peak Hut, but after he received dharma transmission upon attaining the way, he went beyond the realm of devas and no longer received offerings from them.

The World-Honored One had intimate language, and Mahakashyapa did not conceal it had been transmitted by the forty-six buddhas through Yunju. Still, these words were the original face of Yunju. This understanding cannot be grasped by ordinary humans. It does not come from outside. It has not existed from the beginning. It is not newly acquired.

The intimate language spoken of here was not only put forth by Shakyamuni Buddha, the World-Honored One, but also by all buddha ancestors. When there is the World-Honored One, there is intimate language. When there is intimate language, Mahakashyapa does not conceal it. Since there are hundreds and thousands of World-Honored Ones, there are hundreds and thousands of Mahakashyapas. Study this point without fail, as if cutting through what is impossible to cut through. Investigate it in detail little by little, hundreds and thousands of times, instead of trying to understand it all at once. Do not assume that you understand it right away. Yunju was already a world-honored one, so he had intimate language and Mahakashyapa did not conceal it. But do not regard the minister's response to Yunju as intimate language.

Yunju said to the minister, *If you don't understand it, the World-Honored One had intimate language. If you understand it, Mahakashyapa did not conceal it.*

Aspire to investigate these words for many eons. Yunju's words *If you don't understand it,* are a world-honored one's intimate language. Not understanding is not the same as going blank. Not understanding does not mean that you don't know.

By saying, *If you don't understand it,* Yunju is encouraging practice without words. Investigate this. Then, Yunju said, *If you understand it . . .* He did not mean that the minister should rest on his understanding.

Among the gates to the study of buddha dharma, there is a key to understanding buddha dharma and to going beyond understanding buddha dharma. Without meeting a true teacher, you wouldn't even know there is a key. You might mistakenly think that what cannot be seen or heard is intimate language.

Yunju did not mean that Mahakashyapa had not concealed it just because the minister understood it. Not concealing can happen with not understanding. Do not think that anyone can see and hear not-concealing. Not-concealing is already present. Investigate the very moment when nothing is concealed.

Do not think that the realm you don't know is intimate language. At the very moment when you go beyond understanding buddha dharma, there is intimate language. This is when the World-Honored One has intimate language. This is when the World-Honored One is present.

However, those who have not heard the teachings of true masters, although they sit in the teaching seat, have not even dreamed of intimate language. They mistakenly say:

> The passage, *The World-Honored One had intimate language* means that he held up a flower and blinked to the assembly of innumerable beings on Vulture Peak. The reason for this is that the teaching by words is shallow and limited to forms, so the Buddha used no words, took up a flower and blinked. This was the very moment of presenting intimate language. But the assembly of innumerable beings did not understand. That is why this is secret language for the assembly of innumerable beings. *Mahakashyapa did not conceal it* means that he smiled when he saw the flower and the blinking, as if he had already known them; nothing was concealed from him. This is a true understanding, which has been transmitted from person to person.

There are an enormous number of people who believe in such a theory. They comprise communities all over China. What a pity! The degeneration of the buddha way has resulted from this. Those who have clear eyes should turn these people around one by one.

If the World-Honored One's words were shallow, his holding up a flower and blinking would also be shallow. Those who say that the World-Honored One's words are limited to forms are not students of buddha dharma. Although they know that words have form, they do not yet know that the World-Honored One does not have form. They are not yet free from ordinary ways of thinking. Buddha ancestors drop away all experience of body and mind. They use words to turn the dharma wheel. Hearing their words many people are benefited. Those who have trust in dharma and practice dharma are guided in the realm of buddha ancestors and in the realm of going beyond buddha ancestors.

Didn't the innumerable beings in the assembly understand the intimate language of holding up the flower and blinking? Understand that they stand shoulder to shoulder with Mahakashyapa, they are born simultaneously with the World-Honored One. The innumerable beings are none other than the innumerable beings. Arousing the aspiration for enlightenment at the very same moment, they take the same path and abide on the same earth.

The innumerable beings see the Buddha and hear the dharma with wisdom that knows and with wisdom that goes beyond knowing. Seeing one buddha, they see as many buddhas as the sands of the Ganges. At the assembly of each buddha, there are millions and billions of beings. Understand that each buddha demonstrates the moment when holding up the flower and blinking emerge. What is seen is not obscure; what is heard is clear. This is mind eye, body eye, mind ear, and body ear.

————————

How do you understand Mahakashyapa's breaking into a smile? Speak! Those with mistaken views call it secret language and regard his smile as not concealing the secrecy. That is stupidity piled upon stupidity.

Upon seeing Mahakashyapa smile, the World-Honored One said, *I have the treasury of the true dharma eye, the wondrous heart of nirvana. I entrust this to Mahakashyapa.* Is this statement words or no words? If the World-Honored One avoided words and preferred holding up a flower, he would have held up the flower again and again. How could Mahakashyapa have understood him, and how could the assembly of beings have heard him? Do not pay attention to people's mistaken explanations.

The World-Honored One has intimate language, intimate practice, and intimate realization. But ignorant people think *intimate* means that which is known by the self and not by others. Those east and west, past and present, who think and speak this way are not following the buddha way. If what they think were true, those who do not study would have much intimacy, while those who study would have little intimacy. Would those who study extensively have no intimacy? What about those who have the celestial eye, celestial ear, dharma eye, dharma ear, buddha eye, or buddha ear? Would they have no intimate language or intimate heart?

Intimate language, intimate heart, and intimate action in buddha dharma are not like that. When you encounter a person, you invariably hear intimate language and speak intimate language. When you know yourself, you know intimate action. Thus, buddha ancestors can thoroughly actualize this intimate heart and intimate language. Know that where there are buddha ancestors, intimate language and intimate action are immediately manifest. *Intimate* means close and inseparable. There is no gap. Intimacy embraces buddha ancestors. It embraces you. It embraces the self. It embraces action. It embraces generations. It embraces merit. It embraces intimacy.

When intimate language encounters an intimate person, the buddha eye sees the unseen. Intimate action is not known by self or other, but the intimate self alone knows it. Each intimate other goes beyond understanding. Since intimacy surrounds you, it is fully intimate, half intimate.

Clearly study this. Indeed, intimacy comes forth at the place where the person becomes [a buddha], at the moment when understanding takes place. Such a person is an authentic heir of buddha ancestors. Right now is the very moment when you are intimate with yourself, intimate with other. You are intimate with buddha ancestors, intimate with other beings. This being so, intimacy renews intimacy. Because the teaching of practice-enlightenment is the way of buddha ancestors, it is intimacy that penetrates buddha ancestors. Thus, intimacy penetrates intimacy.

––––––––––

Xuedou, Old Master, said to his assembly:

> The World-Honored One has intimate language.
> Mahakashyapa does not conceal it.
> Night rain causes the blossoms to fall.
> The fragrant water reaches everywhere.

Night rain causes the blossoms to fall and *The fragrant water reaches every- where,* spoken here by Xuedou, are intimate. Study this and examine the eyeballs and nostrils of buddha ancestors. This is not somewhere Linji or Deshan can arrive. Open the nostrils within the eyeballs, and sharpen the nose tip within the ears. With the entire body and mind, study the realm where the ear, nose, and eye are neither old nor new. This is how blossoms and rain open up the world.

The fragrant water reaches everywhere, spoken by Xuedou, conceals the body and reveals the form. This being so, in the daily practice of the buddha ancestors' school, the passage *The World-Honored One had intimate language, and Mahakashyapa does not conceal it,* is studied and penetrated. Each of the Seven Original Buddhas has studied intimate language like this. Thus, Mahakashyapa and Shakyamuni Buddha have completely manifested intimate language.

Presented to the assembly of the ancient Yoshimine Temple of Yoshida County, Echizen Province, on the twentieth day, the ninth month, the first year of the Kangen Era [1243].

53

BUDDHA SUTRAS

I N THE BUDDHA sutras, there is teaching for bodhisattvas and there
is teaching for buddhas. Both are instruments of the great way. The
instruments accompany the master and the master uses the instruments.

Because of this, buddhas and ancestors of India and China followed
the teachers and followed the sutras; there has never been a gap between
arousing the aspiration for enlightenment, practice, and the fruit thereof.
Arousing the aspiration for enlightenment depends on sutras and teachers. Practice depends on sutras and teachers. The fruit of enlightenment
is one and intimate with sutras and teachers.

Before a movement [asking a question] and after the words are simultaneous study with sutras and teachers. Within a movement and inside
the words are also simultaneous study with sutras and teachers.

A teacher always penetrates the sutras. To penetrate means to make
the sutras the land, the body, and the mind. A teacher makes the sutras a
structure for guiding others. A teacher makes the sitting, lying down, and
walking; father and mother; and descendants. Using the sutras as practice
and understanding, a teacher fully masters the sutras. A teacher's washing
the face and having tea are the ancient sutras.

The sutras give birth to a teacher. The sixty blows of Huangbo's staff nourished his descendants. The three taps of the stick by [Fifth Ancestor Daman Hongren of] Huangmei caused the transmission of the robe and the entrustment of the dharma.

Realizing the way upon seeing peach blossoms, hearing a stone striking bamboo, and seeing the morning star are nothing but sutras nourishing teachers. Sometimes there is a skin bag or a fist that attains the eye and attains a sutra. Sometimes there is a wooden dipper or a lacquer bucket that attains a sutra and attains the eye.

The sutras are the entire world of the ten directions. There is no moment or place that is not sutras. The sutras are written in letters of the supreme principle and of the secular principles. The sutras are written in letters of heavenly beings, human beings, animals, fighting spirits, one hundred grasses, or ten thousand trees. This being so, what is long, short, square, and round, as well as what is blue, yellow, red, and white, arrayed densely in the entire world of the ten directions, are no other than letters of the sutras and the surface of the sutras. Regard them as the instruments of the great way, and as the sutras of the buddha house.

These sutras spread throughout all time and circulate in all lands. These sutras open the gate of teaching for people without neglecting anyone on the entire earth. These sutras open the gate of teaching for the insentient, saving all beings on the entire earth. They teach all buddhas and bodhisattvas in all lands throughout the entire world. They open the gate of skillful means, and they open the gate of abiding in their conditions without abandoning one thing, or even half a thing, demonstrating reality.

Thus, buddhas and bodhisattvas make no contrivance of their own by way of thought or no-thought. Each makes a great vow to attain the sutras.

The moment when you determine to attain the sutras is not past or present, because past and present are the time when you already attain the sutras. What emerges in the face of the entire world of the ten directions is the attaining of the sutras.

When you read, recite, and penetrate the sutras, buddha wisdom, spontaneous wisdom, or no-teacher wisdom are manifested prior to the mind and prior to the body. At this time there is nothing new or extra-ordinary that makes you wonder. That the sutras are held, read, and recited by you means that the sutras guide you. Their function before the words and outside the phrases, beneath the surface and above the knots, is nothing but scattering blossoms and penetrating blossoms.

———————

These sutras are called dharma. There are eighty-four thousand streams of expounding dharma. In these sutras, there are letters such as "All buddhas attain authentic enlightenment," "All buddhas who abide in the world," and "All buddhas enter pari-nirvana." "Thus come" and "thus go" are both letters in the sutras, dharma letters within dharma.

Holding up a flower and blinking, and breaking into a smile, are ancient sutras authentically transmitted from the Seven Original Bud-dhas. Snow up to the waist and [Huike] cutting off an arm, or bowing formally and attaining the marrow, are ancient sutras transmitted from master to disciple. [Hongren] Transmitting dharma and finally entrusting the robe [to Huineng] is to arrive at the moment of entrusting the entire scroll of extensive letters. [Hongren] Tapping the mortar three times and [Huineng] sifting the rice three times is to cause the sutra to extend its hands, and to cause the sutra to directly transmit the sutra.

Not only that, but, "What has thus come?" is one thousand sutras for teaching all buddhas, ten thousand sutras for teaching all bodhisat-tvas. "Speaking about it won't hit the mark" expounds the eighty thou-sand skandhas and the Twelve Divisions [of sutras]. Furthermore, a fist, a heel, a staff, or a whisk, is itself an old sutra, a new sutra, an existent sutra, an empty sutra. Endeavor of the way in the practicing commu-nity, and the practice of sitting zazen, is unquestionably a buddha sutra from beginning to end and from end to beginning. In this way, you inscribe sutras on bodhi leaves, and you inscribe sutras on the surface of the void.

———————

In fact, one motion and two stillnesses of buddhas and ancestors in grasping firmly and letting go are the opening and closing of the sutras. As you study what is limitless as the measure of limits, you receive sutras and extend sutras from nostrils, from toe tips. You receive and extend sutras before your parents were born, and before the time of the King of the Empty Eon.

You receive sutras and expound sutras by means of mountains, rivers, and earth, or by means of the sun, the moon, and stars. Likewise, you hold sutras and transmit sutras with the self before the Empty Eon, or with body and mind before the original face. You actualize such sutras by cracking open particles. You bring forth such sutras by cracking open the world of phenomena.

Venerable Prajnatara, the Twenty-seventh Ancestor, said, "While exhaling I do not follow conditions, and while inhaling I do not abide in the world of skandhas. I turn [read] the sutras in this way, not one or two sutras but hundreds, thousands, millions, and billions."

Listen to these words of the ancestor and study that sutras are turned at the place of exhaling and inhaling. To know the place of turning sutras is to know the place of the existence of sutras. As turning is being turned, and turning the sutras is sutras turning, knowing all is seeing all.

———————

Rujing, my late master, would say, "In our place, burning incense, bowing, chanting the Buddha's name, repentance, and reading sutras are not essential. Just sit, endeavor in the way, and drop away body and mind."

There are few who clarify the meaning of these words. How is it so? If you call reading sutras reading sutras, you get divided. If you don't call reading sutras reading sutras, you are against it. You cannot get it with words. You cannot get it without words. Say it quickly. Say it quickly.

Study this point. Because of this essential meaning, a teacher of old said, "Reading sutras carries the eye of reading sutras." Know that without sutras in the past and present, such a statement as this would not be possible. Study that there is reading sutras while dropping away and there is reading sutras for beyond use.

This being so, one or half a person who studies [dharma] unfailingly receives and maintains buddha sutras in order to be a buddha child; do not wastefully study the crooked views outside the way. As the treasury of the true dharma eye actualized right now is no other than buddha sutras, all buddha sutras are the treasury of the true dharma eye. They are neither the same nor different, neither the self nor other.

Know that as there are many aspects within the treasury of the true dharma eye, you cannot fully clarify it. Yet, the treasury of the true dharma eye is expounded. There is no way you cannot have trust in it. Buddha sutras are like this. There are a number of them, but what you receive with trust is your one verse or your one phrase. Do not try to understand eighty thousand verses or phrases.

Thus, even if you don't have the mastery of buddha sutras, do not mistakenly say that buddha sutras are not buddha dharma. If you see through with a true eye what you regard as the bones and marrow of buddha ancestors, they may be merely later studies depending on letters. It may be the same as receiving and maintaining one verse or one phrase, or it may not be as close as receiving and maintaining one verse or one phrase. Do not slander the Buddha's true dharma with your shallow understanding.

There are no voices or forms that are more beneficial than buddha sutras. Voices and forms delude you, and yet you tend to seek them and be greedy for them. On the other hand, buddha sutras do not delude you. Do not slander them with a lack of trust in them.

———————

Nevertheless, all types of coarse, stinky skin bags have said for a couple of hundred years, "Don't keep the phrases of ancestral teachers in mind. Furthermore, don't take a long look at or use the teachings of sutras. Instead, just keep your body and mind like a decayed tree or dead ash. Be like a broken wooden dipper or a barrel with no bottom."

Those who speak in this way are a band of those outside the way, of heavenly demons. They take up theories that should not be taken up. Because of such people, the buddha ancestors' dharma has vainly become a dharma of crazy confusion. What a pity! How sad!

Even a broken wooden dipper and a barrel with no bottom are ancient sutras of buddha ancestors. There are few buddha ancestors who understand the number of scrolls and the contents of such sutras. To say that buddha sutras are not buddha dharma is not to observe the occasions when buddha ancestors used sutras, not to study the occasions when buddha ancestors emerged from sutras, and not to know the degree of intimacy between buddha ancestors and buddha sutras.

Hasty people who say such things are as many as stalks of straw, flax, bamboo, and reed. They ascend the lion seats and lead monasteries all over as teachers of humans and devas. Those who are hasty have studied with teachers who were hasty and do not know what is hasty. As they do not know it, they do not wish to be otherwise. How sad that they follow the ignorant and remain ignorant!

As they lack the body and mind of buddha dharma, they do not know how the manner of the body should be and how the state of the mind should be. As they have not clarified existence and beyond existence, when they are asked questions they merely raise a fist without knowing its meaning. As they have not understood the paths of right and wrong, when they are asked questions they raise a whisk without knowing meaning. Or, upon guiding students, they take up Linji's "Four Understandings" and "Four Illuminations," Yunmen's "Three Phrases," Dongshan's "Three Roads" and "Five Ranks," and so on, as the standards of studying the way.

Rujing, my late master, Priest Tiantong, often laughed about it and said, "How can buddha study be like that? The great road of buddha ancestors often speaks of the body and speaks of the mind. When we study it, there is no sufficient time to experience it thoroughly. With what leisure could we accept the latecomer's phrases? Know that elders in many places lack way-seeking mind and clearly have not studied the body and mind of buddha dharma."

This is how Rujing taught the assembly.

———————

Indeed, Linji is a latecomer in the assembly of Huangbo. After receiving sixty blows of a staff, he went to study with Dayu. Upon hearing the story about an old woman's heart, he reflected on his practice up until then, and went back to Huangbo. Hearing about this, people think that Linji alone succeeded in Huangbo's buddha dharma. They even think Linji excelled Huangbo. This is not true at all.

Although Linji studied in the assembly of Huangbo, when Venerable Chen encouraged him to ask questions, it is said that he did not know what to ask. When he had not yet clarified the great matter and listened to a dharma discourse as a student of the way, how could he be dumbfounded like this? Thus, we know he did not have an outstanding capacity to learn.

Also, Linji never had the aspiration to exceed his teacher. None of his statements exceeded his teacher's. On the other hand, Huangbo had statements that exceeded his teacher's; he had the wisdom that exceeded his teacher's. He spoke words that no other buddhas had spoken. He understood the dharma that no other ancestors had understood. Huangbo is an old buddha who went beyond past and present. He was more venerable than Baizhang, and more brilliant than Mazu.

Linji did not have such excellent spirit. Why not? He did not make a statement even in a dream that had never been spoken since olden times. It looks as if he understood many while forgetting one, and he mastered one while troubled with many. How could we regard his "Four Understandings" as having a flavor of the way and use them as pointers for studying dharma?

Yunmen was a student of Xuefeng. He was regarded as a great master of humans and devas, but he still had room to study. To regard Yunmen as attaining the most essential is sorrowful.

What did buddha ancestors make the standard of studying the way before Linji came and before Yunmen emerged? Know that the work of the way was not transmitted to their houses.

Because people do not have anything to depend upon, they say such things [as regarding buddha sutras as not being buddha dharma]. These people make out buddha sutras to be desolate. Do not follow them.

If you throw away buddha sutras, you might as well throw away Linji and Yunmen as well. If buddha sutras were not meant to be used, there would be no water to drink and no dipper with which to scoop water.

The teaching of the "Three Roads" and the "Five Ranks" of Dongshan, High Ancestor, are knots and wood grains [theories] and are not in the realm to be known by hasty people. His teaching has been authentically transmitted, and the buddha work is directly pointing. It cannot be compared with the teachings of other schools.

———————

Hasty people also say that the teachings of Daoism, Confucianism, and Buddhism ultimately accord, while there are only differences in their gates of entry. Sometimes they compare these teachings to the tripod of a worshiping vessel. This is what monks in the country of Great Song frequently discuss.

Buddha dharma has already left the ground and perished for those who speak in this way. Or, we can say that buddha dharma hasn't reached them even in the shape of a minute particle. Such people try to explain the similarities of buddha dharma to other teachings and mistakenly say that buddha sutras are not necessary because there is a separate teaching within the gate of the ancestors. They say so because they haven't glimpsed the boundary of buddha dharma with their minor capacity.

They say buddha sutras should not be used. Then, would they use ancestor sutras? There are many teachings in the ancestral ways that resemble teachings of buddha sutras. How should they make selections for their use? If they say there is an ancestral way outside of the buddha way, who would believe in the ancestral way?

Ancestors are ancestors because they authentically transmit the buddha way. How could those who have not transmitted the buddha way be called ancestors? We venerate Bodhidharma, the First Chinese Ancestor, because he is the Twenty-eighth Indian Ancestor. If you speak of the ancestral way outside of the buddha way, it should be difficult to acknowledge the Tenth Ancestor or the Twentieth Ancestor in India. We venerate ancestors who have succeeded in the person-to-person transmission because of the weightiness of the buddha way. With what face could those who have not authentically transmitted the buddha way encounter humans and devas? Furthermore, it is impossible to turn around the aspiration for longing for the Buddha and follow those who are not in the buddha way.

Now, the reason why these insane, hasty people take the buddha way lightly is that they are unable to take up with determination the dharma that is inherent in the buddha way. The ignorance in comparing the Daoist and Confucian teachings with the Buddha's teaching, even for the time being, is not only deplorable but creates conditions for wrongdoing, representing a decline of the nation. It shows the desolation of the three treasures.

The ways of Confucius and Laozi cannot be compared with the way of the arhats. Further, how can they come close to bodhisattvas whose enlightenment is equal to buddhas or bodhisattvas of wondrous enlightenment? The teachings of Confucius and Laozi regard the insight of sages as great manifestation of the universe. But even in one lifetime or many lifetimes they can never clarify the cause and effect of great sages. Although they see the motion and stillness of body and mind as the doing of not-doing, they are unable to cut through and clarify the reality of the entire world of the ten directions. In fact, the teachings of Confucius and Laozi are inferior to buddha dharma by far more than the distance between heaven and earth. To discuss these teachings on the same level groundlessly slanders buddha dharma, and slanders Confucius and Laozi.

Even if the teachings of Confucius and Laozi are fine and subtle, how can elders of recent times get a glimpse of them, even in countless years, let alone understand their outlines? They have instructions and trainings, which are not easily mastered by mediocre people nowadays. Yet, there is no one who tries to practice their teachings. The particle of one is not the same as that of the other. Furthermore, who among later practitioners would grasp the depth of buddha sutras? While clarifying none of the teachings, they groundlessly speak of the accord of the Three Teachings.

Such people in Great Song China are awarded the title of Master and hold positions as teachers, being shameless in the past and present, and confusingly interpret the buddha way. It is hard to admit that they have buddha dharma. These elders insist that buddha sutras are not the true intention of the buddha way, but that the ancestral transmission is the true intention in which extraordinary subtlety has been transmitted. These statements represent extreme stupidity expressed by mad and confused people.

In contrast, not one line or half a phrase in the authentic transmission of ancestors has anything extraordinary that differs from buddha sutras. It is just that buddha sutras and the ancestral way have been equally transmitted and spread from Shakyamuni Buddha. However, the ancestral transmission has been carried on from heir to heir. How else should we know, clarify, and chant buddha sutras?

A teacher of old said, "You are deluded about the sutras. The sutras don't delude you."

There are a number of stories about ancient teachers reading buddha sutras.

Say to those who are hasty, "If buddha sutras were to be cast away as you suggest, you might as well cast away buddha mind and buddha body. If you were to cast away buddha body and buddha mind, you might as well cast away buddha children. If you were to cast away buddha children, you might as well cast away the buddha way. If you were to cast away the buddha way, how should you not cast away the ancestral way? If you were to cast away the buddha way and the ancestral way altogether, you would be like a mere bald-headed farmer; who could say that you are not qualified to be beaten with a stick? You would not only be driven by kings and ministers, but tortured by Old Man Yama [King of Hell].

Because elders in recent times merely carry certificates issued by kings and ministers, and call themselves the heads of monasteries, they speak of such insane things [as ignoring buddha sutras]. But no one is able to discern their statements. Rujing, my late master, alone laughed at them, while elders in other monasteries were not aware of the problem.

In general, do not assume that monks in other countries must have words they have clarified, and that masters of emperors in large nations must have something they have mastered. Sentient beings in other countries do not necessarily carry the seeds of monkhood. Wholesome beings are wholesome, and unwholesome beings are unwholesome. In all three realms of the world of phenomena, types of sentient beings are similar.

To be the master of the emperor, a person of the way is not necessarily selected. The emperor doesn't know who is a person of the way. He only hears his courtiers' recommendations and makes an appointment. In the past and present, there have been persons of the way who have become teachers of the emperor, while there also have been persons not of the way who have become teachers of the emperor. Those who are appointed in a murky age are not people of the way. Those who are not appointed in a murky age are people of the way. The reason for this is that there are ages when people of the way are recognized and there are ages when people of the way are not recognized.

Do not forget that there was Shenxiu at the time of Huangmei. Shenxiu was a teacher of the emperor who expounded dharma facing the imperial screen. He was a senior monk among seven hundred high monks. Remember also that there was Worker Lu [Huineng] in the same assembly. After being a woodcutter, he became a monastery worker. He stopped carrying wood and worked at the task of pounding rice. Although he was regrettably low in status, he was distinguished in laity and excelled in monkhood, attaining dharma and receiving the robe. Such a thing had never been heard of even in India—a rare outstanding precedent that only occurred in China. The seven hundred high monks could not stand shoulder to shoulder with Worker Lu; dragons and elephants [excellent practitioners] in the nation had no way to find his trace. Truly, Worker Lu succeeded to the thirty-third ancestral position as a buddha heir. Had his teacher Hongren, the Fifth Chinese Ancestor, not been someone who could recognize a true person, it would not have been possible.

Quietly ponder this point. Do not take it carelessly. Hope to attain the power of recognizing true persons. Not to be able to recognize true persons is a great sickness of self and other, a great sickness of the world. To have broad and great knowledge is not essential. Hurry and look for the eye and power to recognize true persons. Without this power, you would sink in vast eons.

This being so, know that there are always buddha sutras in the buddha way, study the broad expressions and deep meanings with mountains and oceans, and make them the standard for the endeavor of the way.

Presented to the assembly of the Yoshimine Temple, Yoshida County, Echizen Province, in the ninth month, the first year of the Kangen Era [1243].

54

INSENTIENT BEINGS
SPEAK DHARMA

SPEAKING DHARMA BY means of speaking dharma actualizes the fundamental point that buddha ancestors entrust to buddha ancestors. This speaking dharma is spoken by dharma.

Speaking dharma is neither sentient nor insentient. It is neither creating nor not creating. It is not caused by creating or not creating. It doesn't depend on conditions. This being so, just as birds fly in the air, speaking dharma leaves no trace. It is just given to Buddhist practitioners.

When the great road is complete, speaking dharma is complete. When the dharma treasury is entrusted, speaking dharma is entrusted. When a flower is held up, speaking dharma is held up. When a robe is transmitted, speaking dharma is transmitted. In this way, all buddhas, all ancestors, have maintained speaking dharma since before the King of the Empty Eon. Expounding dharma has been their fundamental practice since the time before all buddhas.

Do not think that buddha ancestors alone have brought forth speaking dharma. Speaking dharma has brought forth buddha ancestors. This speaking dharma is not limited to the teachings of eighty-four thousand dharma gates, but opens up the teachings of immeasurable, boundless gates.

Do not think that dharma spoken by earlier buddhas was spoken by later buddhas. Just as earlier buddhas don't become later buddhas, earlier speaking dharma does not become later speaking dharma. Thus, Shakyamuni Buddha said, "Just as all buddhas in the three worlds spoke dharma, I now speak indiscernible dharma."

In this way, just as each buddha employs speaking dharma, all buddhas employ speaking dharma. Just as each buddha transmits speaking dharma, all buddhas transmit speaking dharma.

Insentient beings' speaking dharma was transmitted from the ancient buddhas to the Seven Original Buddhas, and it has been transmitted from the Seven Original Buddhas to the present day. In this speaking dharma by insentient beings there are all buddhas, all ancestors. Do not think that the dharma I am speaking now is something new that has not been transmitted. Do not think that what has been transmitted since ancient times is an old pit of demons.

———————

Huizhong, National Teacher Dazheng of the Guangzhai Monastery in the city of Xijing, in Great Tang, was asked by a monk, "Do insentient beings understand dharma when it's spoken?"

Huizhong replied, "Obviously, insentient beings always speak dharma. The speaking never stops."

The monk asked, "Why don't I hear it?"

Huizhong said, "You don't hear it, but that doesn't mean others don't hear it."

The monk said, "Tell me, who hears it?"

Huizhong responded, "All the sages do."

The monk asked, "Do you hear it, sir?"

"No, I don't hear it."

The monk persisted, "If you don't hear it, how do you know that insentient beings understand this dharma?"

Huizhong responded, "This fortunate person doesn't hear it. If I did, I would be equal to all sages. Then you could not hear me expound dharma."

The monk said, "If so, human beings would be left out."

Huizhong said, "But I speak to humans, not to sages."

The monk asked, "What happens to sentient beings after they hear you?"

Huizhong responded, "They are no longer sentient beings."

Beginners and latecomers who look into insentient beings speaking dharma should directly study this story of Huizhong.

Huizhong said, *Obviously, insentient beings always speak dharma. The speaking never stops. Always* is a part of all time. *The speaking never stops* means there is no break in speaking dharma. Just because insentient beings do not use the voice or the manner of sentient beings in speaking dharma, you should not suppose that the way insentient beings speak dharma is different from the way sentient beings speak dharma.

The buddha way does not appropriate the voice of sentient beings and apply it to the voice of insentient beings. Insentient beings do not necessarily speak dharma with a voice heard by the ears. Similarly, sentient beings do not speak dharma with the voice heard by the ears. Now ask yourself, ask others, and inquire, "What are sentient beings? What are insentient beings?"

In this way, concentrate and study closely what *insentient beings always speak dharma* is. Foolish people may think that the sound of trees, or the opening and falling of leaves and flowers, is insentient beings speaking dharma. Such people are not studying buddha dharma. If it were so, who would know and hear insentient beings speaking dharma? Reflect now: are there grass, trees, and forests in the world of insentient beings? Is the world of insentient beings mixed with the world of sentient beings? Furthermore, to regard grass and trees as insentient beings is not thoroughgoing. To regard insentient beings as grass, trees, tiles, and pebbles is not enough.

Even if you hold a human view that regards grass, trees, and so on as insentient, you cannot grasp them by ordinary thinking. The reason is that there is a distinct difference between trees in heaven and trees in the human world. Those that grow in China and those that grow elsewhere are not the same. Plants in the ocean and those on mountains are completely different. Furthermore, there are trees that spread in space and trees that spread in clouds. Among hundreds of grasses and myriad trees that grow in air or in fire, there are those that should be understood as sentient, and those that should not be seen as insentient. There are grasses and trees that are like humans and beasts. They cannot be classified as either sentient or insentient. In sorcery, the trees, stones, flowers, fruits, and water are difficult to speak of even if you believe what you see. It is impossible to generalize about things in all corners of the world only by seeing and knowing about grass and trees in Japan.

Huizhong said, *All the sages do.* It means that in the assembly where insentient beings speak dharma, all sages stand and listen. All sages and insentient beings actualize listening and actualize speaking. Insentient beings speak dharma for all sages. Is this sacred or ordinary? If you experience with your body the way insentient beings speak dharma, you will grasp with your body how all sages hear. As soon as you grasp this with your body, you can comprehend the realm of sages. In this way, you should practice the celestial path of going beyond ordinary and going beyond sacred.

Huizhong said, *I don't hear it.* Do not suppose that these words are easy to understand. Does he "not hear" as he goes beyond ordinary and sacred? Or does he "not hear" because he tears apart the old convention of ordinary and sacred? Investigate this and let the words come through.

Huizhong said, *This fortunate person doesn't hear it. If I did, I would be equal to all sages.* This presentation is not one or two phrases. The fortunate person is neither ordinary nor sacred. Is this a buddha ancestor? Because buddha ancestors go beyond ordinary and sacred, what all sages hear is not the same.

Huizhong said, *Then you could not hear me expound dharma.* Work on these words and prepare the enlightenment of all buddhas and sages. The essence is that insentient beings speak dharma, and all sages hear it; Huizhong speaks dharma, and this monk hears it. Day by day and month by month, make this matter the focus of your study. Now, ask Huizhong, "I am not asking you what happens when sentient beings hear it. But what happens at the precise moment when sentient beings hear the dharma expounded?"

Dongshan, who would later become High Ancestor Great Master Wuben, studied with his teacher Yunyan, Great Priest, Early Ancestor.

Dongshan asked Yunyan, "Who can hear insentient beings speak dharma?"

Yunyan said, "Insentient beings hear insentient beings speak dharma."

Dongshan asked, "Do you hear it, sir?"

Yunyan said, "If I heard it, you could not hear me speak dharma."

Dongshan responded: "Being so, I don't hear you speak dharma."

Yunyan replied, "You haven't been hearing me speak dharma. How could you hear insentient beings speak dharma?"

Dongshan responded by presenting this poem:

> How splendid! How wondrous!
> Inconceivable! Insentient beings speak dharma.
> The ears never hear it.
> Only the eyes do.

Dongshan asked, *Who can hear insentient beings speak dharma?* Investigate this question in detail throughout your life, throughout many lives. The question also can work as a statement. This statement is the skin, flesh, bones, and marrow. It is not merely transmitting mind with mind. This "transmitting mind with mind" is a common notion of beginning and advanced students. However, the key to practice is taking up the robe and transmitting it, taking up dharma and transmitting it. How can people nowadays master this matter in three or four months?

Dongshan had heard about the words of Huizhong, *Insentient beings speak dharma. . . . All sages can hear it.* But he inquired further: *Who can hear insentient beings speak dharma?* Is Dongshan agreeing or not agreeing with Huizhong? Is this a question or a statement? If Dongshan was not agreeing with Huizhong, why did he speak this way? If he was agreeing with Huizhong, why did he speak this way?

Yunyan said, *Insentient beings hear insentient beings speak dharma.* Transmit this blood vein and experience body and mind dropping away. Insentient beings hearing insentient beings speak dharma is essentially all buddhas hearing all buddhas speak dharma. In the assembly of beings, those who hear insentient beings speak dharma are insentient, whether they are sentient beings or insentient beings, ordinary or sacred.

With these essentials you should determine if past or present teachings are true or false. Even if a teaching was brought from India, if it has not been authentically transmitted by genuine masters, do not adopt it. Even if the lineage of teaching has lasted for thousands of years, if there is not an authentic succession from heir to heir, it's not worth inheriting. Today, authentically transmitted teaching has already spread across the eastern lands. You can easily distinguish what is genuine or false.

When you hear, *Sentient beings hear sentient beings speak dharma,* accept this as the bones and marrow of all buddhas and ancestors. When you hear the words of Yunyan and Huizhong and wrestle with them, the sages who speak what all sages hear are insentient. Insentient beings who speak what insentient beings hear are sages. Since insentient beings speaking dharma are insentient, what they speak is insentient. This is how insentient beings speak dharma. This is how speaking dharma is insentient.

Dongshan responded: *Being so, I don't hear you speak dharma. Being so* here refers to Yunyan's words, *Insentient beings hear insentient beings speak dharma.* Because insentient beings hear insentient beings speak dharma, Dongshan said, *I don't hear you speak dharma.* At this moment, Dongshan not only became part of the audience, but also revealed his towering determination to speak dharma for insentient beings. He not only experienced insentient beings speaking dharma, but he thoroughly took hold of hearing and not hearing insentient beings speak dharma. From there he experienced sentient beings speaking, not speaking, already having spoken, now speaking, and just speaking dharma. Furthermore, he clarified the hearing and the not-hearing of the dharma spoken by sentient beings and insentient beings.

Actually, hearing dharma is not limited to ear sense and ear consciousness. You hear dharma with complete power, complete mind, complete body, and complete way from before your parents were born, before the Empty Eon, through the entire future, the unlimited future. You can hear dharma with body first and mind last.

Such ways of hearing the dharma are all effective. Don't think that you are not benefited by hearing the dharma if it does not reach your mind consciousness. Effacing mind, dropping body, you hear the dharma and see the result. With no mind and no body, you should hear dharma and benefit from it. Experiencing such moments is how all buddha ancestors become buddhas and attain ancestorhood.

Ordinary people cannot understand that dharma power transforms body and mind. The boundary of body and mind cannot be encompassed. When the effect of hearing dharma is planted in the field of body and mind, it never decays. It is bound to grow and bear fruit.

Foolish people may think that when we hear dharma, if we do not advance in understanding and cannot remember the teaching, there will be no benefit from it. They say it is essential to learn broadly and memorize extensively with our entire body and mind. They think that forgetting the teaching, absentmindedly leaving the place of instruction, creates no benefit and no accomplishment. They think in this way because they have not met a genuine teacher and encountered themselves. One who has not received authentic transmission face to face cannot be a genuine teacher. A genuine teacher is one who has received transmission authentically from buddha to buddha.

Indeed, to memorize in mind consciousness and not to forget is exactly how the power of hearing the dharma encompasses the mind and encompasses consciousness. At the very moment when this is done, you realize the power of encompassing body; encompassing past body, encompassing mind; encompassing past mind, encompassing future mind; encompassing cause and condition, action and result; encompassing form, essence, body, and activity; encompassing buddha; encompassing ancestor; encompassing self and other; and encompassing skin, flesh, bones, and marrow. The power of encompassing speech and encompassing sitting and lying down is manifest throughout the entire earth and sky.

The power of hearing dharma is not easy to know. But when we join the great assembly of buddha ancestors, and study their skin, flesh, bones, and marrow, there is no instant when the power of speaking dharma does not work, and there is no place where the power of hearing dharma does not extend. The tides of timelessness bring forth sudden or gradual effects. Thus, learning broadly and memorizing extensively are not to be abandoned. However, they are not the only key. Students should know about this. Dongshan understood it.

Yunyan replied: *You haven't been hearing me speak dharma. How could you hear insentient beings speak dharma?* This is how Yunyan pulled open the lapels of his own robe and with the bones and marrow of the ancestors certified that Dongshan had actualized enlightenment on top of enlightenment. *You haven't been hearing me speak dharma.* Ordinary people can't say this. He was assuring Dongshan that however variously insentient beings speak dharma, Dongshan should not be lost in thought about it. The transmission at this moment was truly subtle and pivotal. Ordinary sages cannot easily understand it.

Dongshan responded by presenting this poem: *How splendid! How wondrous! Inconceivable! Insentient beings speak dharma.* Thus, insentient beings and their speaking dharma are both difficult to think about. What are the so-called insentient beings? Study that they are neither ordinary nor sacred, neither sentient nor insentient. Ordinary and sacred, sentient and insentient [in a usual sense], may be reached by thinking whether they are speaking or not speaking. Now it is inconceivable, splendid, and wondrous. What is splendid and wondrous cannot be reached by the wisdom and consciousness of the ordinary or the sacred. Heavenly beings and ordinary humans cannot assess it.

The ears never hear it. Even with heavenly ears or with dharma ears of all realms and all times, it cannot be understood through what is heard. Even with an ear on the wall or an ear on a stick, insentient beings speaking dharma cannot be heard, because it is not a sound that is the object of the ear. It is not that hearing with ears does not happen, but that it is impossible to hear even if we try for hundreds and thousands of eons. Insentient beings speaking dharma is the awesome manifestation of the single way beyond sound and form. Insentient beings speaking dharma is beyond the pit that ordinary beings and sages fall into.

Only the eyes do. Some people may think that this statement means that the coming and going of grass, trees, flowers, and birds viewed by humans are what eyes hear. This view is mistaken. It is not at all buddha dharma. There is no such understanding in the buddha dharma.

When we study Dongshan's words *Only the eyes do,* it means we hear the voice of insentient beings speaking dharma with the eyes. We manifest the voice of insentient beings speaking dharma with the eyes. Investigate the eyes extensively. Because the voice heard by the eyes should be the same as the voice heard by the ears, the voice heard by the eyes is not the same as the voice heard by the ears. Do not think that eyes have ear organs. Do not think that eyes are ears. Do not think that voice appears in the eyes.

———————

An ancient teacher [Xuansha] said, "The entire world of the ten directions is no other than a monk's single eye."

Don't suppose that you can understand Dongshan's words, *Only the eyes do,* by hearing it with a monk's single eye. When you study the ancient teacher's words, *The entire world of the ten directions is no other than a monk's single eye,* the entire world of the ten directions is no other than a monk's single eye. Furthermore, there are eyes on one thousand hands, one thousand true dharma eyes, one thousand ear eyes, one thousand tongue eyes, one thousand mind eyes, one thousand eyes throughout the mind, one thousand eyes throughout the body, one thousand eyes on top of a stick, one thousand eyes on the extremities of the body, one thousand eyes on the extremities of the mind, one thousand dead eyes in the midst of death, one thousand living eyes in the midst of life, one thousand eyes of self, one thousand eyes of other, one thousand eyes on top of eyes, one thousand eyes of study, one thousand vertical eyes, and one thousand horizontal eyes.

This being so, even if you study these entire eyes as the entire world, still it is not the embodiment of eyes. Urgently investigate hearing with the eyes insentient beings speaking dharma.

The meaning of Dongshan's words is that insentient beings speaking dharma cannot be understood by ears. The eyes can hear the voice. Furthermore, there is hearing voice throughout the body and there is hearing voice wherever the body can reach. Even if you do not embody hearing the voice with the eyes, you should master with your body *insentient beings hear insentient beings speaking dharma,* and let go of *insentient beings hear insentient beings speaking dharma.*

———————

As this teaching has been transmitted, Rujing, my late teacher, Old Buddha Tiantong, said, "Gourd with its tendrils is entwined with gourd."

This is the speaking dharma of insentient beings, which transmits Yunyan's true eye, his bones and marrow. Because all speaking dharma is insentient, insentient beings speak dharma. This is a venerable example. Insentient beings are those who speak dharma for insentient beings.

What do you call insentient beings? Know, those who hear insentient beings speak dharma are thus. What do you call speaking dharma? Know, those who do not know insentient beings are thus.

———————

Touzi, Great Master Ciji of Shu Province, whose priest name was Datong, was an heir of Cuiwei, Zen Master Wuxue. Touzi was called Old Buddha Touzi by Mingjiao [Xuedou Zhongxian]. He was once asked by a monk, "What is insentient beings speaking dharma?"

Touzi replied, "Don't bad-mouth them."

What Touzi says here is indeed the dharma standard of the old buddha, a settling point of the ancestral teaching. Insentient beings speaking dharma and the speaking dharma of insentient beings are equally beyond bad-mouthing. Know that insentient beings speaking dharma is the totality of buddha ancestors. It is not known by followers of Linji or Deshan. Only buddha ancestors penetrate this.

Presented to the assembly of the ancient Yoshimine Temple, Yoshida County, Echizen Province, on the second day, the tenth month, the first year of the Kangen Era [1243].

55

DHARMA NATURE

WHEN YOU STUDY buddha dharma with a sutra or with a teacher, you come to realization without a teacher. Coming to realization without a teacher occurs due to dharma nature.

Even if you have knowledge by birth, you should always look for a teacher and inquire about the way. Even if you have beyond-knowledge by birth, you should always practice in the endeavor of the way. Who does not have knowledge by birth? And yet, study a sutra and follow a teacher.

Know that to encounter a sutra or a teacher and experience dharma-nature samadhi is called the knowledge by birth of dharma-nature samadhi through encountering dharma-nature samadhi. This is acquiring knowledge of a past life, acquiring the three miraculous powers, and realizing unsurpassable, complete enlightenment.

You encounter knowledge by birth and study knowledge by birth. You encounter knowledge without a teacher and spontaneous knowledge, and authentically transmit knowledge without a teacher and spontaneous knowledge.

Without having knowledge by birth, you cannot hear dharma nature and you cannot realize dharma nature even if you encounter a sutra or a teacher. The great way is not like someone who drinks water and therefore knows whether it is cold or warm.

All buddhas, all bodhisattvas, and all sentient beings clarify the great road of all dharma nature with the power of knowledge by birth. That you clarify the great road of dharma nature with a sutra and a teacher is no other than clarifying dharma nature by yourself.

Sutras are dharma nature that is you yourself. A teacher is dharma nature that is you yourself. Dharma nature is a teacher. Dharma nature is you yourself. Because dharma nature is you yourself, it is not you tempted by those outside the way or a group of demons. Dharma nature has no outside-the-way and no demons. It is just that you have a morning meal, you have a midday meal, and you have tea.

However, those who call themselves students for two or three decades keep being dumbfounded upon hearing a discussion on dharma nature; they pass their lives in this way. Those who call themselves longtimers in monasteries, who are seated in a bent-wood teaching chair, can only climb in and out of a pit of confusion with their bodies, minds, and environs when they hear the voice of dharma nature and see its form. Their reaction proves that they mistakenly think that dharma nature emerges even after the three realms and the ten directions we live in collapse. They also mistakenly think that such dharma nature is separate from all phenomena in this moment.

The meaning of dharma nature is not like that. All phenomena and dharma nature go beyond arguments about whether they are the same or different, about whether they are identical or separate. What is not past, present, and future, not permanent or impermanent, not form, perception, feeling, inclination, and discernment, is dharma nature.

———————

Mazu, Zen Master Daji of Jiangxi, said, "No sentient beings have the need to come out of dharma-nature samadhi for innumerable eons. They stay in dharma nature forever, wearing a robe, eating a meal, and exchanging words. These activities of the six sense organs and all other activities are no other than dharma nature."

The dharma nature spoken of by Mazu is dharma nature speaking of dharma nature. It practices together with Mazu. It practices together with dharma nature.

I hear this. So how should I not speak of it? Dharma nature rides on Mazu [meaning Horse Ancestor]. A person takes a meal, and a meal takes a person.

Once being dharma nature, you don't leave dharma-nature samadhi. You don't leave dharma nature before being dharma nature. You don't leave dharma nature after being dharma nature. Dharma nature, together with immeasurable eons, is dharma-nature samadhi. Dharma nature is called immeasurable eons.

Thus, just this right now is dharma nature. Dharma nature is just this right now. Wearing a robe and eating a meal is dharma-nature samadhi wearing a robe and having a meal. Dharma nature that is a robe is actualized. Dharma nature that is a meal is actualized. Dharma nature no other than eating is actualized. Dharma nature no other than wearing is actualized.

Without wearing a robe and eating a meal, without exchanging words, and without the activities of the six sense organs and all other activities, there is no dharma-nature samadhi and there is no entering dharma nature.

The actualized expression of just now was handed down from buddha to buddha through Shakyamuni Buddha. It was authentically transmitted from ancestor to ancestor through Mazu. It has been authentically handed down from buddha to buddha, from ancestor to ancestor, by means of dharma-nature samadhi. Budddhas and ancestors enliven dharma nature without the need to enter it.

Even though dharma teachers of letters speak of dharma nature, it is not the dharma nature spoken of by Mazu. The statement that sentient beings who have not come out of dharma nature can never be dharma nature may happen to have a point. Yet, such a statement is three or four more pieces of dharma nature. Talks and activities to deny dharma nature are also dharma nature.

Days and months in immeasurable eons are the passage of dharma nature. Present and future are also like this. Thinking that one is far from dharma nature, making the scale of one's body the scale of body and mind is dharma nature. Both thinking and not-thinking are dharma nature. Those who think that water does not flow or trees do not grow and decay in what is called dharma nature are people outside the way.

————————

Shakyamuni Buddha said, "Aspects of thusness are no other than the nature of thusness."

Thus, flowers blossoming and leaves falling are *the nature of thusness*.

But foolish people think that there cannot be flowers blossoming and leaves falling in the realm of dharma nature. If you think in this way, don't ask others, but just pretend that your doubt is your expression. Repeat it a few times as if quoting from others. Then you will be able to be released from your doubt.

Such a doubt is not wrong; it merely lacks clarity. Even after you have clarity, do not let your earlier thinking disappear.

Flowers blossoming and leaves falling are no other than flowers blossoming and leaves falling. The thought that there cannot be flowers blossoming and leaves falling in dharma nature is itself dharma nature. It is thought that doubts and is released from doubt. Thus, it is thought that, as it is, is dharma nature. The entire thought of the thought of dharma nature has such a face [characteristic].

No other than dharma nature, mentioned by Mazu, expresses eight or nine out of ten; but there is much he did not express. He did not say: "All dharma nature is without the need to leave dharma nature," "All dharma nature is entirely dharma nature," "All sentient beings are without the need to leave sentient beings," "All sentient beings are a small part of dharma nature," "All sentient beings are a small part of sentient beings," "All dharma nature is half of sentient beings," "Half of sentient beings are half of dharma nature," "Beyond sentient beings is dharma nature," "Dharma nature is beyond sentient beings," "Dharma nature is released from dharma nature," or "Sentient beings are released from sentient beings."

What we hear from Mazu is merely, *No sentient beings have the need to come out of dharma-nature samadhi*. But he did not say, "Dharma nature has no need to come out of sentient-being samadhi," or "Dharma-nature samadhi goes in and out of sentient-being samadhi."

Furthermore, what is not heard from Mazu are: "Dharma nature becomes buddha," "Sentient beings realize dharma nature," or "Insentient beings do not have the need to come out of dharma nature."

Now, ask Mazu: "What do you call sentient beings? If you call dharma nature sentient beings, it is no other than 'What has thus come?' If you call sentient beings sentient beings, it is no other than 'Your words are close but have not hit the mark.'"

Tell me what it is. Tell me quickly.

Presented to the assembly of the Yoshimine Temple, Echizen Province, in early winter [the tenth month], the first year of the Kangen Era [1243].

56

DHARANI

IF YOUR EYE of study is clear, your true dharma eye is clear. As your true dharma eye is clear, you have a clear eye of study. What authentically transmits this essential matter is no other than the power to see a great teacher. This is a great matter. This is a great dharani [total sustenance]. What is called a great teacher is a buddha ancestor. Always serve the buddha ancestor by bringing a towel and a water jar [as Yangshan did for Guishan].

Thus, the disciple bringing tea and the teacher drinking it actualizes the essential heart. It actualizes miracles. The disciple bringing a basin of water and the teacher taking a wash is unaffected by the surroundings. It is being aware in the adjacent room of what is happening [as in the Guishan story].

This is not only studying the essential heart of buddha ancestors, but encountering one or two buddha ancestors who are immersed in the essential heart. It is not only receiving miracles of buddha ancestors, but experiencing seven or eight buddha ancestors who are immersed in miracles.

The miracles of all buddha ancestors are thoroughly experienced by this bundle of activities [of serving the teacher]. The essential heart of all buddha ancestors is thoroughly experienced by this single act. This being so, it is not inappropriate to greet your teacher by offering celestial flowers and celestial incense. Yet, you are a true descendant of buddha ancestors by greeting your teacher and offering the wholehearted dharani.

————————

The great dharani is a formal greeting. Because a formal greeting is a great dharani, you encounter the actualization of a formal greeting. The phrase "formal greeting" originated in China and has been widely used for a long time. It has not been transmitted by Indra or from India, but from buddha ancestors. It is not in the realm of sound or form. Do not wonder if it came from before or after the King of the Empty Eon.

A formal greeting means burning incense and bowing. A root teacher is someone who has ordained you or has transmitted dharma to you. These two may be the same person. You stay with and see your root teacher. This is the dharani of making greetings. Be close to your teacher without long absences.

At the beginning and the end of a practice period, on winter solstice as well as at the beginning and in the middle of a month, make a point to offer incense and bow to your teacher. A good time for this is before or after the morning meal.

Dress formally and go to the teacher's hall. To dress formally means to wear the kashaya, carry the folded bowing cloth, wear clean sandals and socks, and carry a stick of incense or a block of aloeswood. In this way you meet your teacher and make a greeting statement. Then your teacher's attending monk readies an incense burner and lights a candle. If the teacher is seated on a chair, light the incense and offer it by setting it in the incense burner. If the teacher is behind the screen, set the incense in the burner outside the screen. If the teacher is lying down or having a meal, burn and offer the incense in the same manner.

If the teacher is standing, say, "Master, please sit down." Or say, "Master, please make yourself comfortable." There are many other ways to ask your teacher to sit down. After your teacher is seated, you make a greeting statement while you bend forward in a formal manner. Then, you go to the incense burner in front of you and set upright the incense you have brought.

This is the way for carrying and burning the incense: You carry it under the lapel of your robe, inside the robe above the belt, or inside a sleeve; this is up to you. After the greeting, you take the incense out. If the incense is wrapped in paper, you turn your upper body toward the left, take off the paper, hold up the incense with both hands [turn back, light it], and set it in the incense burner. Set it upright without leaning. After setting it, you turn around to the right in shashu, walk in front of your teacher, bow, and make a greeting statement. Then, you spread the bowing cloth, and bow.

You bow nine or twelve times. After the bowing is over, fold up the bowing cloth and continue your greeting statement.

Or, spread the bowing cloth once, make three formal bows, and offer seasonal greetings.

The nine bows I have mentioned means spreading the bowing cloth and making three most formal bows; repeat this three times without being interrupted by a seasonal greeting. This form has been handed down from the Seven Original Buddhas. This essential teaching has been authentically transmitted. That is why we follow this form. Such greetings have not been abandoned since ancient times.

Besides these greetings, you bow to the teacher upon receiving dharma teachings or asking for materials to study. For example, when Huike expressed his understanding to Bodhidharma, he made three bows. Upon expressing the essence of the treasury of the true dharma eye, Huike made these bows. Know that bowing is the treasury of the true dharma eye. The treasury of the true dharma eye is a great dharani.

When asking for instruction, one "hitting bow" has recently been practiced. An ancient way is bowing three times: to express gratitude for a teaching, three bows or nine bows are not necessarily practiced. It can be semiformal bows [bowing down with the face touching the fourfold bowing cloth] or six bows. These are both bowing down with the head touching the floor. They are called the utmost bowing in India. For this you hit the floor with your forehead. You repeat it until you start bleeding. The bowing cloth is spread in this case also. For one bow, three or six bows, you hit the floor with your forehead. This is called hitting bows.

In the secular world also there are bows, such as nine types of bows.

When you receive a dharma instruction, you can do indefinite bows. That is to bow ceaselessly, one hundred or one thousand times.

These bows have been practiced in the assemblies of buddha ancestors. Follow the instructions of your teacher and practice it according
to the guidelines. When bowing remains in the world, buddha dharma
remains. When bowing disappears, buddha dharma disappears.

In bowing to the root teacher who has transmitted dharma to you,
you do so regardless of time and place. You bow while you lie down or
while you have your meal. You bow while you use the toilet. You bow
beyond the wall or beyond mountains and rivers. You bow beyond eons.
You bow beyond the coming and going of birth and death. You bow
beyond enlightenment and nirvana.

Although you bow in various ways, your root teacher does not bow
back but merely keeps the palms together. The teacher may move to
make a slight bow, but this seldom takes place.

You face north for such bowing. Your root teacher sits upright, facing south. You stand in front of the teacher, facing north, and bow to the
teacher. This is an essential procedure. It has been taught that when your
true faith of taking refuge arises, your bowing toward the north will
always happen.

Thus, when the World-Honored One was alive, all humans, devas,
and dragons who took refuge in the Buddha, faced north and respectfully bowed to the World-Honored One.

The five monks—Ajnatakaundinya, Assaji, Mahanaman, Bhadrika,
and Vappa—were the first ones, after the Tathagata attained the way, to
spontaneously stand up, face toward the north, and offer him bows. When
those outside the way and demons give up wrong views and take refuge
in the Buddha, they always face north and make an offering of bows.

Since then, all those who have joined the assemblies of ancestors
of the twenty-eight generations in India, and all generations in China,
and all those taking refuge in the true dharma, without exception have
bowed toward the north. This has been affirmed by the true dharma and
not planned by teachers and disciples. This is a great dharani.

[A sutra says,] "A great dharani is called complete enlightenment. A
great dharani is called a formal greeting. A great dharani is to actualize

bowing. A great dharani is called a kashaya. A great dharani is called the treasury of the true dharma eye."

By chanting this dharani, you calm and protect the entire great earth. By chanting this dharani, you calm and manifest the worlds of the entire directions. By chanting this dharani, you calm and actualize the realm of all time, you calm and create entire buddha realms, you calm and penetrate inside and outside the hut. Investigate thoroughly that a great dharani is just like this.

All dharanis make this dharani their consonants and vowels. All dharanis are actualized as relations of this dharani. All buddha ancestors arouse aspiration, endeavor in the way, attain the way, and turn the dharma wheel from the gate of this dharani.

This being so, you who are a descendant of buddha ancestors, should thoroughly investigate this dharani.

To be wrapped in the robe of Shakyamuni Buddha is to be wrapped in the robes of all buddhas in the ten directions. To be wrapped in the robe of Shakyamuni Buddha is to be wrapped in a kashaya. A kashaya is an emblem of buddha assemblies. It is rare to encounter, rare to practice.

We happen to have received human bodies, although we were born in a remote land. However ignorant we might be, the wholesome root of the dharani we nurtured in the past is manifested, and now we have encountered the dharma of Shakyamuni Buddha.

When you bow to buddha ancestors who are nurtured by themselves or by others at places of one hundred grasses [in the midst of all phenomena], you experience Shakyamuni Buddha's attainment of the way, effort in the way, and dharani—miraculous transformation. When you bow to ancient buddhas and present buddhas in countless billions of eons, it is the moment of being wrapped in Shakyamuni Buddha's robe.

Once your body is wrapped in a kashaya, you attain Shakyamuni Buddha's flesh, hands and feet, head and eyes, marrow and brains, radiant light, and turning of the wheel of dharma. You wear a kashaya in this way. This actualizes the power of the robe. You vow and make offerings to Shakyamuni Buddha by maintaining, enjoying, protecting, and wearing the kashaya. By doing so, the practice of countless eons is thoroughly experienced.

To bow to and make offerings to Shakyamuni Buddha is to bow to and make offerings to the root teacher who has transmitted dharma to you, and to bow to and make offerings to the root teacher who has shaved your head. This is no other than seeing Shakyamuni Buddha, offering dharma to Shakyamuni Buddha, offering dharani to Shakyamuni Buddha.

Rujing, my late master, Old Buddha Tiantong, said, "To bow in deep snow [as Huike did], or to bow in rice bran [as Huineng did]—these are excellent examples, ancient precedents, great dharanis."

Presented to the assembly of the Yoshimine Temple, Echizen Province, in the first year of the Kangen Era [1243].

57

FACE-TO-FACE TRANSMISSION

ONCE, ON VULTURE Peak in India, in the midst of a vast assembly of beings, Shakyamuni Buddha held up an udumbara blossom and blinked. Mahakashyapa smiled. Then Shakyamuni Buddha said, "I have the treasury of the true dharma eye, the wondrous heart of nirvana. I entrust it to Mahakashyapa."

This is the meaning of transmitting the treasury of the true dharma eye, face to face, from buddha to buddha, from ancestor to ancestor. It was authentically transmitted through the Seven Original Buddhas to Mahakashyapa. From Mahakashyapa there were twenty-eight transmissions up to and including Bodhidharma. Venerable Bodhidharma himself went to China and gave face-to-face transmission to Huike, Great Master Zhengzong Pujue. There were five transmissions through to Huineng, Great Master Dajian of Mount Caoxi. Then there were seventeen transmissions through Rujing, my late master, Old Buddha Tiantong of the renowned Mount Taibai, Qingyuan Prefecture, Great Song.

————————

I first offered incense and bowed formally to Rujing in the abbot's room—Wondrous Light Terrace—on the first day, the fifth month, of the

first year of the Baoqing Era of Great Song [1225]. He also saw me for
the first time. Upon this occasion he transmitted dharma to me, finger to
finger, face to face, and said, "The dharma gate of face-to-face transmission from buddha to buddha, ancestor to ancestor, is actualized now."

This itself is holding up a flower on Vulture Peak, or attaining the
marrow at Mount Song. It is transmitting the robe at Mount Huangmei,
or the face-to-face transmission at Mount Dong. This is buddha ancestors transmitting the treasury of the eye face to face. It occurs only in
our teaching. Other people have not even dreamed of it.

Face-to-face means between buddha ancestors' faces; when Shakyamuni Buddha was in the assembly of Kashyapa Buddha, he received
this transmission from Kashyapa Buddha and has passed it on. There are
no buddhas without receiving face-to-face transmission from the buddha face.

Shakyamuni Buddha, by seeing Mahakashyapa, intimately entrusted
him with the dharma. Ananda or Rahula were not equal to Mahakashyapa, who received the intimate entrustment. Nor were all the great
bodhisattvas, who were unable to sit in Mahakashyapa's seat.

The World-Honored One and Mahakashyapa sat together on the
same seat and wore the same robe. This occurred only once in the Buddha's life. Thus, Mahakashyapa received the World-Honored One's transmission directly face to face, mind to mind, body to body, and eye to
eye. Mahakashyapa respectfully greeted Shakyamuni Buddha while making offerings and bowing formally. Thousands of times Mahakashyapa
had pounded his bones and crushed his body. His face was no longer
his own. Thus, he received the Tathagata's face through face-to-face
transmission.

———

Shakyamuni Buddha saw Mahakashyapa in person. Mahakashyapa
saw Venerable Ananda in person, and Ananda bowed formally to
Mahakashyapa's buddha face. This is face-to-face transmission. Ananda
maintained this face-to-face transmission, closely guided Shanavasin,
and transmitted face to face. When Shanavasin respectfully saw Venerable Ananda, he received face-to-face transmission, just face to face.

Thus, the authentic ancestors of all generations have continued face-to-face transmission, disciple seeing teacher, and teacher seeing disciple. An ancestor, a teacher, or a disciple cannot be a buddha or an ancestor without having face-to-face transmission.

It is like pouring water into the ocean and spreading it endlessly, or like transmitting the lamp and allowing it to shine ceaselessly. In thousands of millions of transmissions, the trunk and branches are one, breaking an eggshell by pecking from the inside and outside at once.

Day and night Mahakashyapa closely attended Shakyamuni Buddha, and spent his whole life intimately illuminated by the buddha face. How long this has been happening is beyond comprehension. Quietly and joyously reflect on this.

Thus, Mahakashyapa bowed formally to Shakyamuni Buddha's face. Shakyamuni Buddha's eyes were reflected in his eyes, and his eyes were reflected in Shakyamuni Buddha's eyes. This is the buddha eye; this is the buddha face. It has been transmitted face to face without a generation's gap until now. This is face-to-face transmission.

All these authentic heirs are the buddha face; each of them has received face-to-face transmission from the original buddha face. Bowing formally to this authentic face-to-face transmission is bowing to the Seven Original Buddhas, including Shakyamuni Buddha, and bowing and making offerings to Mahakashyapa and the rest of the twenty-eight Indian buddha ancestors.

The face and eyeball of buddha ancestors are like this. To see these buddha ancestors is to see the Seven Original Buddhas, including Shakyamuni Buddha. Exactly at this moment, buddha ancestors are intimately transmitting themselves.

A face-to-face-transmitting buddha transmits to a face-to-face-transmitting buddha. A face-to-face-transmitting buddha is transmitted from vine to vine, without being cut off. Such transmission is transmitted from eye to eye, with the eye open. It is transmitted from face to face, with the face revealed.

Face-to-face transmission is given and received in the presence of the buddha face. Mind is taken up, transmitted to mind, and received by mind. Body is manifested and transmitted to body. In other regions or countries, this is regarded as the original heritage. In China and eastward, there is face-to-face transmission only within the house of authentically transmitted buddha ancestors. Thus, the true eye that always sees the Tathagata anew has been transmitted.

———

At the time of bowing formally to Shakyamuni Buddha's face, the fifty-one buddha ancestors and the Seven Original Buddhas are not present side by side or in one line. But it is face-to-face transmission among all the buddha ancestors at the same time. If you do not see in just one generation all the masters, you are not a disciple. If you do not see in just one generation all the disciples, you are not a master. Masters and disciples always see one another when transmitting and receiving dharma. This is the realization of the way, face-to-face transmission of the ancestral source. Thus, masters and disciples bring forth the luminous face of the Tathagata.

Accordingly, this face-to-face transmission is actualizing the face and continuing the transmission of Shakyamuni Buddha through thousands and thousands of years, or hundreds and billions of eons. When the World-Honored One, Mahakashyapa, and other members of the fifty-one buddha ancestors, and the Seven Original Buddhas appear, their shadows appear, their light appears, their bodies appear, and their minds appear. An invisible leg or a sharpened nose appears. Even without knowing one word or understanding half a phrase, the teacher sees the student from within, and the student lowers the top of the head; this is authentic face-to-face transmission.

Venerate this face-to-face transmission. If the traces of mind were only projected in the field of mind, they would not be of great value. However, if you receive face-to-face transmission by exchanging your face, and if you give face-to-face transmission by turning your head, the face skin is three inches thick and ten feet thin.

This face skin is the great round mirror of all buddhas. Because they have the great round mirror as their face skin, they are unmarred inside and outside. A great round mirror transmits to a great round mirror.

You who rightly transmit the true eye that directly sees Shakyamuni Buddha are more intimate with Shakyamuni Buddha than Shakyamuni Buddha is with himself. With this eye you see and bring forth numerous past and future Shakyamuni Buddhas. Therefore, in order to express adoration to Shakyamuni Buddha, you should profoundly venerate this authentic face-to-face transmission and with formal bows acknowledge the extreme rarity of meeting with it. This is to bow formally to the Tathagata and to be given face-to-face transmission by the Tathagata. You may wonder if it is the self that now sees the unchanging practice of authentic transmission of the face-to-face-transmitting tathagatas. Whether it is the self or other that sees this transmission, you should treasure and protect it.

It is taught in the buddha's house that those who bow formally to the Eight Pagodas are liberated from the hindrances of unwholesome actions and experience the fruit of the way. These pagodas are the actualization of Shakyamuni Buddha's way. They were built where he was born, where he turned the dharma wheel, attained the way, entered parinirvana, at the city of Kanyakubja, and at Amrapali Grove, thus completing the earth and the sky. They were built by way of sounds, smells, tastes, touchables, mental phenomena, and forms. The fruit of the way is realized by formally bowing to the Eight Pagodas. This is a common practice in India performed by laypeople and monks, by devas and human beings who devotedly make offerings and prostrations. These pagodas are equal to one volume of the scripture.

A buddha scripture is like this. Even beyond that, the practice of the thirty-seven wings of enlightenment and attaining the fruit of the way in each and every birth is actualized by allowing the trace of Shakyamuni Buddha's practice throughout time. This is to prevail as the authentic way everywhere and to be clearly expressed in past and present.

Know that, although wind and rain wear them down, the Eight Pagodas, standing layer upon layer through numerous frosts and flowers, are not diminished in their merit, remaining in emptiness and form. Because of this, even if you have delusion and hindrance, when you practice the [fivefold] root, the [fivefold] power, the limbs of enlightenment, and the noble path, the power of the Eight Pagodas is still vital in your practice and realization.

The benefaction of Shakyamuni Buddha is like this. Even so, face-to-face transmission is incomparably greater than the Eight Pagodas. The thirty-seven wings of enlightenment are rooted in the buddha face, the buddha mind, the buddha body, the buddha way, the buddha nose, and the buddha tongue. The benefaction of the Eight Pagodas is also based on the buddha face and so forth. While practicing the vital path of penetration, you who study dharma should think deeply day and night about this and quietly rejoice.

———

Now, our country surpasses other countries and our way alone is unsurpassable. In other places there are not many people who are like us. The reason I say so is this: Although the teaching of the assembly on Vulture Peak has spread in the ten directions, still the Chinese masters are the only authentic heirs of the great master [Bodhidharma] of Shaolin, and only the descendants of the great master [Huineng] of Mount Caoxi have transmitted this dharma face to face up to the present.

This is a splendid opportunity for buddha dharma to freshly enter into mud and water. If you do not realize the fruit at this moment, when will you realize it? If you do not cut off delusion at this moment, when will you cut off delusion? If you do not become a buddha at this moment, when will you? If you do not sit as a buddha at this moment, when will you practice as an active buddha? Diligently examine this in detail.

———

Shakyamuni Buddha graciously entrusted and transmitted dharma face to face to Mahakashyapa, saying, *I have the treasury of the true dharma eye. I entrust it to Mahakashyapa.*

At the assembly of Mount Song, Bodhidharma said to Huike, who would later become the Second Ancestor, "You have attained my marrow."

From this we know that entrusting the treasury of the true dharma eye and saying, "You have attained my marrow" is this very face-to-face transmission. At the exact moment of jumping beyond your ordinary bones and marrow, there is the buddha ancestor's transmission face to face. The face-to-face transmission of great enlightenment, the face-to-face transmission of the mind seal, is extraordinary. Transmission is never exhausted; there is never a lack of enlightenment.

Now, the great way of buddha ancestors is only giving and receiving face to face, receiving and giving face to face; there is nothing excessive and there is nothing lacking. Faithfully and joyously realize when your own face meets someone who has received this transmission face to face.

I, Dogen, first bowed formally to Rujing, my late master, Old Buddha Tiantong, and received transmission face to face on the first day of the fifth month, the first year of Baoqing Era of Great Song [1225], and was thereby allowed to enter the inner chamber. I was able to enact this face-to-face transmission by dropping away body and mind, and I have established this transmission in Japan.

Presented to the assembly of the Yoshimine Temple, Yoshida County, Echizen Province on the twentieth day, the tenth month, the first year of the Kangen Era [1243].

POSTSCRIPT

Among those who had not heard or learned about the meaning of such face-to-face transmission in the buddha way, there was someone called Zen Master Chenggu, of the Jianfu Monastery in the Jingyou Era [1034–1038] during the reign of Emperor Ren of Great Song. He ascended the teaching seat and said:

> Yunmen, Great Master Kuangzhen, is now present. Do you see him? If you do, you are the same as I. Do you see him? Do you see him? If you understand this immediately, you have got it; but do not boast.
>
> This is like Huangbo, who, when he heard Baizhang present the story of great master Mazu's shout, experienced great understanding. Then Baizhang asked him, "Are you great master Mazu's heir or not?" Huangbo said, "I know the great master, but in a word, I haven't seen him. If I inherit from him, I fear I will lose my descendants."
>
> Attention, everyone! Since it was already five years after the death of great master Mazu, Huangbo said that he had not seen him. Thus, we know that Huangbo's view was incomplete. That is to say, he had only one eye. But I am not like that. I know great master Yunmen, and I have seen great master Yunmen. Therefore, I am great master Yunmen's heir.

But more than one hundred years have passed since the death of Yunmen. Then, how can we say that I have personally seen him? Do you understand this? Those who have reached this state, I will approve. But those who have dim eyes will produce doubt and slander in their mind, so they cannot see and explain it. Those of you who have not seen, can you get it now? Please take care of yourselves.

Chenggu, admitting that you know great master Yunmen and have seen him, has great master Yunmen seen you or not? If great master Yunmen has not seen you, you cannot be great master Yunmen's heir. Because great master Yunmen has not seen you, you cannot say that great master Yunmen has seen you. Thus, we know that you and great master Yunmen have not yet seen each other.

In the past, present, and future of the Seven Original Buddhas and all buddhas, which of the buddha ancestors have received dharma without the teacher and disciple seeing each other? Chenggu, you should not say that Huangbo's view was incomplete. How can you evaluate Huangbo's practice, and how can you evaluate Huangbo's words? Huangbo was an authentic buddha; he thoroughly knew about dharma transmission. But you have never dreamed of the meaning of dharma transmission. Huangbo received dharma transmission from his teacher and he maintained the dharma of this ancestor. Huangbo met and saw his teacher. But you have neither seen a teacher nor known an ancestor. You neither know the self nor see the self. No teacher has seen you, and your eye as a teacher has not yet opened. The truth is that your view is incomplete, your succession of dharma is incomplete.

Chenggu, do you understand that great master Yunmen is a dharma descendant of Huangbo? How can you evaluate the words of Baizhang and Huangbo? You cannot even evaluate the words of Yunmen. The words of Baizhang and Huangbo are presented by those who are able to study and are evaluated by those who have directly experienced dropping away. But you do not study and you do not experience dropping away; you do not understand and you cannot evaluate it.

You say that Huangbo did not receive dharma from great master Ma [Mazu] although it was less than five years since great master Ma's death. Your understanding is not worth a laugh. If you are to receive dharma, you will receive it only after innumerable eons. If not, you will not receive it after half a day or even after a moment. You are a totally ignorant fool who has not yet seen the sun-face moon-face [various aspects] of the buddha way.

You say that you are great master Yunmen's heir although more than one hundred years have passed since the death of Yunmen. Have you received dharma from Yunmen because you have monumental power? You are as ignorant as a three-year-old child. Does this mean that someone who receives dharma from Yunmen one thousand years later will have a power ten times as great as yours?

Let me rescue you now. Study these words: Baizhang said, *Are you great master Mazu's heir?* This does not mean that Huangbo was asked to inherit dharma from great master Mazu. You should now study these words of the combating lion. By studying the story of a black tortoise climbing up a tree backward, you should investigate the vital way of moving forward and moving backward. Upon inheriting dharma there is this kind of study. Huangbo's words *I fear I will lose my descendants* cannot be evaluated by you. Do you understand what he meant by *my* and *descendants*? You must examine this in detail; the meaning is already manifested, and nothing is hidden.

However, someone called Weibai, Zen Master Fuguo, ignorant of the dharma heritage of buddha ancestors, listed Chenggu as a dharma heir of Yunmen. It is a mistake. Those who study the way later should not naively think that Chenggu had mastered the way.

Chenggu, if dharma heritage can be attained through literature as you imply, do all those who reach understanding by reading sutras receive dharma from Shakyamuni Buddha? It is never so. Understanding by sutras always requires an authentic master's seal of approval.

Your words show that you have not yet read the recorded sayings of Yunmen. Only those who have seen Yunmen's words have received dharma from Yunmen. But you have not yet seen Yunmen with your own eyes; you have not yet seen the self with your own eyes. You have not seen Yunmen with Yunmen's eyes; you have not seen the self with Yunmen's eyes.

There are many people like you who have not thoroughly studied. Continually buy straw sandals and seek an authentic master from whom to receive dharma. You should not say that you have received dharma from great master Yunmen. If you do so, you will enter the stream of those outside the way. Even Baizhang would be mistaken if he talked like you.

58

Rules for Zazen

Practicing Zen is zazen. For zazen, a quiet place is suitable. Lay out a thick mat. Do not let in drafts or smoke, rain or dew. Protect and maintain the place that contains your body. There are examples from the past of sitting on a diamond seat and sitting on a flat stone covered with a thick layer of grass. Day or night, the place of sitting should not be dark; it should be kept warm in winter and cool in summer.

Set aside all involvements and let the myriad things rest. Zazen is not thinking of good, not thinking of bad. It is not conscious endeavor. It is not introspection. Do not desire to become a buddha. Let sitting or lying down drop away. Be moderate in eating and drinking. Mindful of the passing of time, engage yourself in zazen as though saving your head from fire. On Mount Huangmei, Hongren, the Fifth Ancestor, practiced zazen to the exclusion of all other activities.

When sitting zazen, wear the kashaya and use a round cushion. The cushion should not be placed all the way under the legs, but only under the buttocks. In this way the crossed legs rest on the [soft] mat and the backbone is supported with the round cushion. This is the method used by all buddha ancestors for zazen.

Sit either in the half-lotus position or in the full-lotus position. For the full-lotus put the right foot on the left thigh and the left foot on the right thigh. The toes should lie along the thighs, not extending beyond. For the half-lotus position, simply put the left foot on the right thigh.

Loosen your robes and arrange them in an orderly way. Place the right hand on the left foot and the left hand on the right hand, with the ends of the thumbs lightly touching each other. With the hands in this position, place them close to the body so that the joined thumb-tips are at the navel.

Straighten your body and sit upright. Do not lean to the left or right; do not bend forward or backward. Your ears should be in line with your shoulders, and your nose in line with your navel.

Rest your tongue against the roof of your mouth, and breathe through your nose. Lips and teeth should be closed. Eyes should be open, neither too wide, nor too narrow. Having adjusted body and mind in this manner, take a breath and exhale fully.

Sit solidly in samadhi and think not-thinking. How do you think not-thinking? Beyond thinking. This is the art of zazen.

Zazen is not learning to do concentration. It is the dharma gate of great ease and joy. It is undivided practice-realization.

Presented to the assembly of the Yoshimine Temple, Yoshida County, Echizen Province, in the eleventh month, the first year of the Kangen Era [1243].

59

PLUM BLOSSOMS

RUJING, MY LATE master, Old Buddha Tiantong, was the thirtieth abbot of the Tiantong Jingde Monastery, renowned Mount Taibai, Qingyuan Prefecture, Great Song. He ascended the teaching seat and said to the assembly:

> Tiantong's first phrase of midwinter:
> Old plum tree bent and gnarled
> all at once opens one blossom, two blossoms,
> three, four, five blossoms, uncountable blossoms,
> not proud of purity,
> not proud of fragrance;
> spreading, becoming spring,
> blowing over grass and trees,
> balding the head of a patch-robed monk.
> Whirling, quickly changing into wild wind, stormy rain,
> falling, snow all over the earth.
> The old plum tree is boundless.
> A hard cold rubs the nostrils.

The old plum tree spoken of here is boundless. *All at once* its blossoms open, and of itself the fruit is born.

It forms spring; it forms winter. It arouses wild wind and stormy rain. It is the head of a patch-robed monk; it is the eyeball of an ancient buddha. It becomes grass and trees; it becomes pure fragrance. Its whirling, miraculous quick transformation has no limit. Furthermore, the treeness of the great earth, high sky, bright sun, and clear moon derives from the treeness of the old plum tree. They have always been entangled, vine with vine.

When the old plum tree suddenly opens, the world of blossoming flowers arises. At the moment when the world of blossoming flowers arises, spring arrives. There is a single blossom that opens five petals. At this moment of a single blossom, there are three, four, and five blossoms, hundreds, thousands, myriads, billions of blossoms—countless blossoms. These blossomings are not-being-proud-of one, two, or countless branches of the old plum tree. An udumbara blossom and blue lotus blossoms are also one or two branches of the old plum tree's blossoms. Blossoming is the old plum tree's offering.

The old plum tree is within the human world and the heavenly world. The old plum tree manifests both human and heavenly worlds in its treeness. Thus, hundreds and thousands of blossoms are called both human and heavenly blossoms. Myriads and billions of blossoms are buddha ancestor blossoms. In such a moment, "All buddhas have appeared in the world!" is shouted; "The ancestor was originally in this land!" is shouted.

———————

Rujing ascended the teaching seat and said to the assembly:

> When Gautama's eyeball vanishes,
> plum blossoms in snow, just one branch,
> become thorn branches, here, everywhere, right now.
> Laughing, spring wind blows madly.

This is the time for all human and heavenly beings to turn toward attaining the way, as the old buddha's dharma wheel is turned to the extreme limit of the entire world. Even clouds, rain, wind, and water, as well as grass, trees, and insects, do not fail to receive the benefit of this teaching. Heaven, earth, and land are vigorously turned by this dharma wheel. To hear words never heard before is to hear these words. To attain what has never existed is to attain this teaching. This is the dharma wheel that cannot be seen or heard without having some inconceivable good fortune.

Now in Great Song China, both inside and outside of its one hundred and eighty regions, there are uncountable mountain temples and town temples. Many monks abide there, but those who have not seen Rujing are many, and those who have seen him are few. Further, fewer have heard his words, not to mention those who have personally met with him face to face. Even fewer have been allowed to enter his chamber. Among these few, how many have been allowed to take refuge in his skin, flesh, bones, and marrow, eyeball and face?

Rujing did not easily allow monks to join his monastery. He would say, "Those who are accustomed to a lax way-seeking mind cannot stay in this place." He would chase them out and say, "What can we do with those who have not realized original self? Such dogs stir people up. They should not be permitted to join the monastery."

I have personally seen and heard this. I think to myself, "Which roots of unwholesome actions made it impossible for them to abide with the master even though they were from the same country? With what fortune was I allowed not only to join the monastery, but to enter the chamber whenever I wished, to take refuge in his venerable form, and to listen to the dharma words, even though I was someone from a remote country? Although I was foolish and ignorant, it is an excellent causal relationship that is not at all hollow."

When Rujing was giving guidance in Song China, there were those who could receive personal guidance from him and those who could not. Now that he has left Song China, it is darker than dark night. Why? Because there is no old buddha like Rujing—before or after him. Therefore, you who study later should think about this upon hearing these words. Do not think that human and heavenly beings everywhere see and hear this dharma wheel.

The *plum blossoms in snow* is the emergence of an udumbara blossom. How often do we see the eyeball of the true dharma of our Buddha

Tathagata but do not smile, missing his blink? Now we authentically receive and accept that plum blossoms in snow are truly the Tathagata's eyeball. We take them up and hold them as the eye at the top of the head, as the pupil of the eye.

When we enter into plum blossoms and fully study them, there is no room for doubt to arise. They are already the eyeball of "Alone above and below the heavens, I am the honored one," and again, "most honored in the world of phenomena."

Thus, heavenly blossoms in heaven, heavenly blossoms in the human world, mandara blossoms raining from heaven, great mandara blossoms, manjushaka blossoms, great manjushaka blossoms, and all blossoms of inexhaustible lands in the ten directions are one family of plum blossoms in snow. Because they bloom as offerings of plum blossoms, billions of blossoms are one family of plum blossoms. They should be called young plum blossoms. Furthermore, flowers in the sky, flowers on the earth, and flowers of samadhi are all the large and small members of plum blossoms' family.

To form billions of lands within blossoms and to bloom in the land is the gift of plum blossoms. Without the offering of plum blossoms there is no offering of rain or dew. The life vein consists of plum blossoms. Do not regard plum blossoms merely as snow all over the Shaolin Temple of Mount Song. They are the Tathagata's eyeball illuminating overhead and underfoot. Do not regard plum blossoms merely as snow of the Snow Mountains or the Snow Palace. They are the Old Gautama's eyeball of true dharma. The eyeballs of the five eyes are fully manifested in this place. The eyeballs of one thousand eyes are completed in this eyeball.

Indeed, Old Gautama's radiant light of body-mind contains not one unillumined particle of the reality of all things. Even if there is a difference of views between human and heavenly beings, and the minds of ordinary and sacred are separate from one another, snow-all-over is earth, earth is snow-all-over. Without snow-all-over there is no earth in the entire world. The intimate outside-inside of this snow-all-over is Old Gautama's eyeball.

Know that blossoms and ground are entirely beyond birth. Because blossoms are beyond birth, ground is beyond birth. Because blossoms and ground are entirely beyond birth, eyeball is beyond birth. "Beyond birth" means unsurpassed enlightenment. To see it just this moment is *plum blossoms in snow just one branch*. Ground and blossoms, birth permeating birth. This *snow, all over* means snow completely covers outside and inside.

The entire world is mind ground; the entire world is blossom heart. Because the entire world is blossom heart, the entire world is plum blossoms. Because the entire world is plum blossoms, the entire world is Gautama's eyeball.

Here, everywhere, right now is mountains, rivers, and earth. Everything, every moment, is realization everywhere of "I am originally in this land, transmit dharma, and save deluded minds. One blossom opens five petals. The fruit matures of itself [as expressed by Bodhidharma]." Although there is the coming [of buddha dharma] from India and proceeding eastward, this is the everywhere of plum blossoms right now.

Realization of this *right now* is nothing other than *become thorn branches everywhere right now*. A great branch is the right now of old branches and new branches. A small twig is the everywhere of old twigs and new twigs. Study this place as everywhere and study everywhere as now.

Within three, four, five, or six blossoms is within countless blossoms. Blossoms embody deep, vast characteristics of inside, and reveal high and vast characteristics of outside. This outside-inside is the blooming of one blossom. Because there is *just one branch*, there are no other branches, no other trees. Every place reached by one branch is right now. This is Old Man Gautama. Because it is just one branch, it is entrusting, heir to heir.

This being so, "I have the treasury of the true dharma eye. This is entrusted to Mahakashyapa" and "You have attained my marrow." This realization everywhere leaves nothing that is not deeply revered. Thus, five petals open; the five petals are plum blossoms.

Accordingly, there are Seven Original Buddha ancestors, twenty-eight Indian ancestors, six early Chinese ancestors, and nineteen later Chinese ancestors. They are all just one stem opening five petals, five petals in just one stem. Practicing thoroughly one branch and practicing thoroughly five petals is plum-blossoms-in-snow authentically receiving, entrusting, and encountering. Turning body and mind inside the ceaseless murmuring of just one branch, clouds and moon are one, valleys and mountains are separate.

However, those who have no penetrating eye say, "'One blossom opens five petals' means that Bodhidharma brings forth the five early Chinese ancestors. Because this line of five ancestors cannot be equaled by those coming either before or after, they are called five petals." This statement is not worth criticizing. Those who say so do not study with buddhas and ancestors. What a pity! How can the road of five petals in one blossom be limited to the five ancestors? Are those who came after Huineng, the Sixth Ancestor, not to be mentioned? This does not even attain the level of childish talk! Never pay attention to such statements.

Rujing ascended the teaching seat at the beginning of a year and said:

> The first day of the year is auspicious.
> Myriad things are all new.
> In prostration, the great assembly reflects:
> Plum blossoms open early spring.

I reflect quietly: Even if all the old gimlets in the past, present, and future drop away the body in the entire ten directions, unless they can say, "Plum blossoms open early spring," who can acknowledge them as those who have mastered the way? Rujing alone is the old buddha of old buddhas.

He means that, accompanied by the opening of plum blossoms, the entire spring comes forth early. Myriad springs are one or two characteristics of plum blossoms. One spring causes myriad things to be all new, and causes all things to be on the first day of the year. *Auspicious* means the true eyeball. Myriad things are not merely the past, present, and future, but both before and after the King of the Empty Eon. Because immeasurable, inexhaustible past, present, and future are entirely new, this newness drops away newness. Therefore, in prostration the great assembly reflects, because the great assembly that reflects in prostration is just this.

Rujing ascended the teaching seat and said to the assembly:

> One word—precisely!
> The long ages do not move.
> Willow eyes arouse new twigs.
> Plum blossoms fill old branches.

This means that the endeavor of the way throughout a hundred great eons is, from beginning to end, *One word—precisely!* Practice in the moment of a thought is both before and after *The long ages do not move.*

This causes the new twigs to grow thickly and makes the eyeballs clear and bright. Although they are new twigs, they are eyes. Although they are nothing but eyes, they are seen as new twigs. Penetrate this newness as *Myriad things are all new.*

Plum blossoms fill old branches means that plum blossoms are totally old branches and pervade old branches: old branches are nothing but plum blossoms. In this way blossoms and branches merge. Blossoms and branches are born of the same moment. At once blossoms and branches are filled. Because blossoms and branches are filled as one, "I have the true dharma. This is entrusted to Mahakashyapa." Each face is filled with taking up the flower; each blossom is filled with breaking into a smile.

Rujing ascended the teaching seat and said to the assembly:

> Willows flourish a sash.
> Plum blossoms wear an armband.

This armband is not a brocade or a jewel. It is plum blossoms blooming. Plum blossoms blooming is "My marrow has attained you."

When King Prasenajit invited Venerable Pindola and offered a noon meal, the king said, "I have heard that you saw the Buddha in person. Is that so?"

Pindola answered by raising his eyebrow with his hand.

Rujing said in his poem:

> Raising an eyebrow, he answers the question.
> He saw the Buddha in person and does not deceive.
> Still he is worthy of offerings from the world.
> Spring lies in plum twigs accompanied by snow—cold.

The story is that King Prasenajit once asked Pindola whether he had seen the Buddha or not. To see the Buddha is to become a buddha. To become a buddha is to raise the eyebrow. Even if Pindola had realized the fruit of an arhat, unless he was a true arhat he could not have seen the Buddha. Unless he saw the Buddha, he could not have become a buddha. Unless he became a buddha, he could not have raised the eyebrow.

Know that Venerable Pindola was a face-to-face transmission disciple of Shakyamuni Buddha and, having realized the four fruits of the way, was awaiting the emergence of another buddha—how could he not have seen Shakyamuni Buddha? *Saw the Buddha* is not just seeing a buddha but seeing Shakyamuni Buddha as Shakyamuni Buddha seeing himself. It has been studied in this way. When King Prasenajit opened this eye of study, he met a skilled hand that raised the eyebrow.

Have a penetrating buddha eye that calmly looks into the meaning of *saw the Buddha in person*. This spring lies neither in the human world nor in a buddha land, but in plum twigs. How do we know this? It is snow and cold, raising eyebrows.

———————

Rujing said:

> The original face is beyond birth and death.
> Spring in plum blossoms enters into a painting.

When you paint spring, do not paint willows, plums, peaches, or apricots—just paint spring. To paint willows, plums, peaches, or apricots is to paint willows, plums, peaches, or apricots. It is not yet painting spring.

It is not that spring cannot be painted, but aside from Rujing, there is no one in India or China who has painted spring. He alone was a sharp-pointed brush that painted spring.

This *spring* is spring in the painting as it *enters into a painting*. He does not use other means, but lets plum blossoms initiate spring. He lets spring enter into a painting and into a tree. This is skillful means.

Because Rujing clarifies the treasury of the true dharma eye, he authentically transmits it to buddha ancestors who assemble in the ten directions of the past, present, and future. In this way he thoroughly masters the eyeball and opens up plum blossoms.

This was written on the sixth day, the eleventh month, the first year of the Kangen Era [1243], at the Yoshimine Temple, Yoshida County, Echizen Province. Snow is three feet deep, all over the land.

POSTSCRIPT

If a doubt arises and you think that plum blossoms are not Gautama's eyeball, consider whether anything other than plum blossoms may be seen as his eyeball. If you seek the eyeball elsewhere, you will not recognize it even though you are facing it, because meeting is not consummated. This day is not this day of an individual; it is this day of the great house. Realize plum blossoms as the eyeball right now. Stop seeking any further!

———————

Rujing said:

Bright, bright! Clear, clear!
Stop seeking in the images of plum blossoms.
Throughout past and present they bring rain and form clouds.
Past and present, solitary and silent—where are the boundaries?

Thus, to form clouds and to bring rain is the activity of plum blossoms. The movement of clouds and rain is a thousand forms and myriad colors, a thousand merits and myriad characteristics of plum blossoms.

Throughout past and present is plum blossoms; plum blossoms are called past and present.

———

Once, Wuzu, Zen Master Fayan, said:

> North wind harmonized with snow shakes the valley forest.
> Myriad things are hidden, but regret is not deep.
> Mountain plums alone are high-spirited,
> spitting out winter's cold heart, just before the end of the year.

In this way, without penetrating the activities of plum blossoms it is hard to know winter's cold heart. Some aspects of plum blossoms harmonize with north wind and form snow. Thus, I know that to spread wind, to form snow, to make the year sequential, and to cause the valley forest and myriad things to be, are all due to the power of plum blossoms.

———

Senior Fu of Taiyuan said, in praise of the way of enlightenment:

> In olden days when I was not yet awakened,
> the sound of a painted horn was the sound of sorrow.
> Now, on my pillow there is no idle dream.
> Letting go, plum blossoms blow vast and small.

Senior Fu had been a lecturer before. He was opened up by the head cook of Mount Jia and experienced great realization, allowing plum blossoms, the spring wind, to blow vast and small.

60

TEN DIRECTIONS

A SINGLE FIST, JUST this, is the ten directions. A sincere heart, just one, is simply the ten directions crystal clear. The ten directions squeeze out the marrow from the bone.

––––––––––

Shakyamuni Buddha said to the assembly, "In the buddha land of the ten directions, there is only the dharma of the One Vehicle."

The ten directions spoken of here have taken up the buddha land and made it what it is. Thus, without taking it up, there can be no buddha land. Because it is the buddha land, the Buddha is its host.

This Saha World can be called Shakyamuni Buddha's land. Take up this Saha World, clarify whether it is eight *liang* or half a *jin*, and examine whether the buddha land of the ten directions is seven or eight feet.

The ten directions enter one direction and enter one buddha. This being so, the ten directions appear in the ten directions. Because the ten directions are one direction, this direction, self direction, present direction, and the ten directions are the eyeball direction, fist direction, bare pillar direction, and lantern direction. The ten direction buddhas in the ten direction land are neither large nor small, neither pure nor stained.

Thus, "only a buddha and a buddha" in the ten directions admire one another. To slander one another and talk about merits and shortcomings, good and bad, cannot be regarded as turning the dharma wheel or expounding dharma. But rather, all buddhas and buddha children support and greet one another. In receiving the buddha ancestors' dharma, you study in this way without criticizing and insulting one another as do those demons outside the way.

When we open the Buddha sutras transmitted to China, and look at the details of Shakyamuni Buddha's lifetime of teaching, we see that he never regarded some buddhas as inferior and other buddhas as superior, nor did he call some buddhas not buddhas. What is not found in the Buddha's teaching are judgments on other buddhas. Words of other buddhas criticizing Shakyamuni Buddha are not known, either.

Regarding this, Shakyamuni Buddha said to the assembly, "I just know the essence. So do the buddhas in the ten directions."

Know that *I just know the essence* is to draw a circle. The drawn circle means "That pole is that long. This pole is this long."

The Buddha's words, *in the ten directions* means: "I just know the essence. So does Shakyamuni Buddha." It is no other than "I just realize the essence. So do the buddhas in this direction." It is *I* form, *know* form, *this* form, *all* form, *ten directions* form, Saha Land form, Shakyamuni Buddha form.

All these forms are buddha sutras. All buddhas and buddha lands are not two. They are neither sentient nor insentient, neither delusion nor enlightenment, neither wholesome nor unwholesome, nor neutral, neither pure nor defiled, neither forming nor maintaining, neither disintegrating nor empty. They are neither permanent nor impermanent, neither existent nor nonexistent, neither self nor other. They are free from the four views [on existence and nonexistence]; they go beyond the one hundred negations. They are just the ten directions, just the buddha lands. Thus, the ten directions have a head but no tail.

———————

Changsha Jingcen, said to the assembly, "The entire world of the ten directions is a single eye of a monk."

It means the single eye of monk Gautama. The single eye of monk Gautama is "I have the treasury of the true dharma eye." Even if he had entrusted it to Ananda, it would be the single eye of monk Gautama. Corners and spots in the world of the ten directions are the objects of Gautama's eye. This entire world of the ten directions is one within the monk's eye. There are eyes that go beyond this.

[Changsha continued,] "The entire world of the ten directions is the everyday words of a monk."

Everyday means ordinary. As a colloquial expression in Japan, we say "common." Thus, a monk's common words are the entire world of the ten directions. The words and speech are straightforward, as everyday words are the entire world of the ten directions. Investigate clearly that the entire world of the ten directions is everyday words.

As the ten directions are inexhaustible, they are the entire ten directions. Words are used in an everyday manner. It is like searching for a horse, salt, water, and a chalice [all called *saindhava*]. It is like offering water, a chalice, salt, and a horse. Who knows that a great person beyond measure turns body and turns brain within this phrase? It is turning words within a phrase. It is the everyday activity of an ocean mouth and a mountain tongue [of the Buddha]. Thus, one covers the mouth and covers the ears. This is the true thusness of the ten directions.

[Changsha continued further,] "The entire world of the ten directions is the whole body of a monk."

One hand points to heaven. This is heaven. One hand points to the earth. This is the earth. Thus, "In heaven above and earth below, I alone am the honored one." This is the entire world of the ten directions that is the whole body of a monk. The head top, eyes, nostrils, skin, flesh, bones, and marrow—each is the monk's body that penetrates the entire ten directions. It does so without disturbing the entire ten directions. It takes up the monk's body of the entire ten directions, and sees the monk's body of the entire ten directions without measuring.

[Changsha continued,] "The entire world of the ten directions is the radiant light of the self."

The self means nostrils before the birth of your parents. The nostrils, being by accident in the hand of the self, are called the entire world of the ten directions. Yet, the self is right here, actualizing the fundamental point, opening the hall, and seeing the Buddha.

Although the eyeball has been switched to a black bead by someone else, going straight ahead you meet the assembly of a great house.
Although calling is easy and responding is difficult, when you are called,
you turn your head. When you turn your head, what use can it be? Still,
you turn your head toward the person who called.

A meal waits for you to eat it. A robe waits for you to wear it. What
a pity you don't take it while it wants you to. I have already given you
thirty blows.

[Changsha continued,] "The entire world of the ten directions is
within the radiant light of the self."

The eyelid, just one piece, is called *the radiant light of the self*. When it
opens all of a sudden, it is called *within*. What you see in the eye is called
the entire ten directions. This being so, sleeping on the same bed, you
both know there is an opening in the cover.

[Changsha continues,] "In the entire world of the ten directions,
there is no single person that is not the self."

Thus, each practitioner, each fist, in the ten directions, cannot help
but be the self. There are no ten directions that are not the self. Each and
every self is the ten directions. The ten directions of each and every self
are intimately immersed in the ten directions. Because the life vein of
each and every self is altogether in the hand of the self, the self passes on
the original nourishment to the self.

How now are Bodhidharma's eye and Gautama's nostrils in the
womb of a bare pillar? Let me say: "They come and go. The ten directions leave everything to all ten directions."

———

Xuansha, Great Master Zongyi, said, "The entire world of the ten
directions is one bright pearl."

From this we clearly know that one bright pearl is the entire world
of the ten directions. Those with divine heads and demon faces abide
in this bright pearl as their grotto hut. Descendants of buddha ancestors
make it their eye. Male and female householders regard it as the head top
and fist. Beginners and latecomers regard it as putting on the robe and
eating a meal. My late master Rujing called it a mud ball and threw it at
my fellow practitioners.

As it is a move transmitted person to person, the eyeball of the ancestral school has been plucked out. When it is plucked out, the entire ancestral school makes a move. This bright pearl shines within the eyeball.

Priest [Yuezhou] Qianfeng was asked by a monk, "The World-Honored Ones in the ten directions are all on the one path to nirvana. Let me ask you: Where is the path?"

Qianfeng drew a line with his staff in the air and said, "It's here."

Qianfeng's words *It's here* mean the ten directions. The World-Honored Ones is the staff. The staff is *It's here*. The one path is no other than the ten directions.

However, do not hide the staff inside Gautama's nostrils. Do not stick the staff in the staff's nostrils.

Yet, do not accept that Old Man Qianfeng has already dealt with the World-Honored Ones in the ten directions, all on the one path. Just say, *It's here*. It is not that *It's here* does not exist. Is it not that Old Man Qianfeng has been confused by a staff after all?

Know that vitalizing the nostrils is no other than the ten directions.

Presented to the assembly of the Yoshimine Temple, Echizen Province, Japan, on the thirteenth day, the eleventh month, the first year of the Kangen Era [1243].

61

SEEING THE BUDDHA

SHAKYAMUNI BUDDHA SAID [in the *Diamond Sutra*] to the assembly, "When you see forms and beyond forms, you see the Tathagata."

You see forms and beyond forms is seeing through [forms and beyond] with the body. Thus, *you see the Tathagata*. When the practice of opening the eye to see the Tathagata is actualized, you see the Buddha. The vital path of seeing the Buddha is the practice of seeing the Buddha.

When you see buddha-as-self elsewhere and buddha-as-self outside of buddha, they may be seen [as indistinguishable] as branches and vines. However, when you study seeing the Buddha, understand seeing the Buddha, drop away seeing the Buddha, vitally grasp seeing the Buddha, and utilize seeing the Buddha, it is [varied] like seeing the Sun-Face Buddha and seeing the Moon-Face Buddha.

These ways of seeing the Buddha are equally seeing the Buddha with inexhaustible faces, with inexhaustible bodies, with inexhaustible minds, and with inexhaustible hands and eyes.

From the moment of arousing the aspiration for enlightenment, you take steps on the journey in the endeavor of the way. Merging with realization and thorough understanding are all the vital eye, bones, and marrow that run into seeing the Buddha. This being so, the total world of self, the total direction of other, this and that, are all the practice of seeing the Buddha.

In investigating the Tathagata's statement, *When you see forms and beyond forms*, those who lack the eye of study assume that to see forms as beyond forms is itself seeing the Tathagata. They think that since forms are beyond forms, they are the Tathagata. Although a part of their small view is like this, the meaning of the Buddha's statement is not so.

Know that to see through forms and to see through beyond forms is actually seeing the Tathagata. There is Tathagata, and there is beyond Tathagata.

———————

Fayan, Great Zen Master of the Qingliang Monastery, said, "If you see that all forms are beyond forms, you don't see the Tathagata."

These words by Fayan are words of seeing the Buddha. When we examine these words, they stand out and extend their hands. Listen to his words with your ears. Listen to his words of seeing the Buddha with your eyes.

Those who studied the meaning of his words in the past say:

All forms are Tathagata forms. There is never a single form that merges with what is not the Tathagata forms. Never regard forms as beyond forms. To do so is to escape from your own parents. Because these forms are nothing but the Tathagata forms, Fayan said that all forms are all forms.

However, these words by Fayan are the utmost statement of the Mahayana, confirmed by masters in various places. Accept his words with trust and practice, and do not take them lightly like feathers flying in the east or west wind. See thoroughly that all forms are Tathagata forms and not beyond forms. See the Buddha in this way, make up your mind, realize trust, and maintain these words. Chant these words and become familiar with them.

Thus, keep seeing and hearing these words with your ears and eyes. Have the words drop away in your body, mind, bones, and marrow. Have the words seen through your mountains, rivers, and entire world. This is the practice of studying with buddha ancestors.

Do not think that your own words and actions cannot awaken your own eye. Turned by your own turning words, you see and drop away your own turning of buddha ancestors. This is the everyday activity of buddha ancestors.

In this way, there is a single path to study. No forms are beyond forms, beyond forms are all forms. Because beyond forms are all forms, beyond forms are indeed beyond forms. Study that forms that are called beyond forms, and forms that are called all forms, are both Tathagata forms.

Inside the house of study, there are two types of commentaries— those made by seeing the scriptures and those made without seeing the scriptures. This is what a vital eye studies. If you have not penetrated the scriptures by seeing with the eye, it is not studying thoroughly with the eye. Without studying thoroughly with the eye, you do not see the Buddha.

In seeing the Buddha, there is seeing where forms are and seeing where beyond forms are. It is [as Huineng said] "I don't understand buddha dharma."

In not seeing the Buddha, there is seeing where forms are and seeing where beyond forms are. It is [as Huineng said] "There is someone who understands buddha dharma." This is understanding Fayan's words eight or nine out of ten.

This being so, say further on this matter of grave importance: "If you see the reality of all things, that is to see the Tathagata."

All of these words have been caused by the teaching of Shakyamuni Buddha, and are not the skin, flesh, bones, and marrow of any others.

When Shakyamuni Buddha taught at Vulture Peak, Bhaishajyaraja Bodhisattva said to the assembly, "If you get close to a dharma teacher, you will directly attain the bodhisattva way. If you follow the teacher and practice, you will see buddhas as many as the sands of the Ganges."

To *get close to a dharma teacher* is like Huike attending Bodhidharma for eight years. Consequently, he grasped Bodhidharma's marrow with his whole arms. It is also like Nanyue practicing for fifteen years. To attain the teacher's marrow is called to *get close to*.

The bodhisattva way is [as Huineng said]: "I am like this. You are like this." It is to *directly attain* activities of a twining vine on a branch [intimate practice with the teacher]. To *directly attain* is not drawing something from the past or initiating something new for the future. It is not grasping what is prevailing at present. But it is to drop away from getting close to the teacher. Thus, all attaining is directly attaining.

To *follow the teacher and practice* is to enliven the ancient precedent of being an attendant monk to the teacher. Study this thoroughly. At the very moment of practicing this, there is hitting the mark of seeing. That is where you see buddhas as the sands of the Ganges. Buddhas as many as the sands of the Ganges are vital and active—each and every one of them. However, do not get busy trying to see buddhas as many as the sands of the Ganges. First of all, endeavor to follow the teacher and practice. *If you follow the teacher and practice, you will see buddhas.*

Shakyamuni Buddha said to all the realized beings, "Enter deep into samadhi and see buddhas in the ten directions."

The entire world is *deep*, because it is in the buddha land of the ten directions. It is neither broad nor narrow, neither large nor small. When you take up one side, the other side comes with it. This is called total inclusion.

The entire world is not seven feet, eight feet, or ten feet. It is total inclusion without outside. It is just *enter*.

To *enter deep* is samadhi. To *enter deep* is to *see buddhas in the ten directions*. Because of "entering so deep inside that no one can guide the person," to *enter deep* is to *see buddhas in the ten directions*. Because "Even if you brought it, the person would not accept it" [as Dongshan said], buddhas are in the ten directions.

To *enter deep* is for a long, long time not to leave. To *see buddhas in the ten directions* is just to see the Tathagata lying down.

Samadhi is to enter but not to come out. If you are not suspicious and fearful of a true dragon, you have no doubts to let go of at the very moment of seeing the Buddha.

Because you see the Buddha by seeing the Buddha, you enter deep in samadhi from samadhi. It is not that the experience of samadhi, seeing the Buddha, and entering deep was created by a person of leisurely practice in the past and has been transmitted to another person in the present. Although it is not a newly sprouted bud, it is as it is. All transmission of the way, succeeding in the work, is like this. Practicing cause and receiving effect is like this.

———

Shakyamuni Buddha said to Samantabhadra Bodhisattva, "Know that those who receive, chant, memorize, study, and copy this *Lotus Sutra* immediately see Shakyamuni Buddha, just like hearing the sutra from the Buddha's own mouth."

That all buddhas *see Shakyamuni Buddha* and become Shakyamuni Buddha is called attaining the way and becoming buddhas. Such buddha activity is unfailingly attained through all seven types of practice. Those who engage in these know the very person as the very person. Because they are in the place of seeing Shakyamuni Buddha, they *see Shakyamuni Buddha, just like hearing the sutra from the Buddha's own mouth.*

Shakyamuni Buddha has been Shakyamuni Buddha since he saw Shakyamuni Buddha. This being so, the voices from his tongue cover the billion worlds. What place in mountains and oceans is not buddha scripture? Thus, only those who copy the sutra *see Shakyamuni Buddha.*

The buddha mouth is always open throughout myriad years. What moments are not sutras? Thus, only those who accept the sutra *see Shakyamuni Buddha.*

The function of the eyes, ears, nose, and so on [in seeing the Buddha], must also be like this. The everyday activity of taking and discarding, before and after, right and left, is also like this.

How could we not rejoice to be born in the presence of the sutra and see Shakyamuni Buddha? You have been born to encounter Shakyamuni Buddha. When you encourage your body and mind, and receive, chant, memorize, practice, and copy the *Lotus Sutra*, you *immediately see Shakyamuni Buddha.*

Just like hearing the sutra from the Buddha's own mouth—who would not rush to hear it? Those who do not immediately practice it are sentient beings who lack benefaction and wisdom. *Know that* those who study and practice it *immediately see Shakyamuni Buddha.*

———————

Shakyamuni Buddha said to the assembly, "Good men and women, listen to my teaching that the life span of the Buddha is timeless, and understand it with trust in your deep heart. Then, you will immediately see the Buddha, who always abides and teaches on Vulture Peak surrounded by great bodhisattvas and shravakas. You will also see that the surface of this Saha World is vast and flat, made of lapis lazuli."

Deep heart means the Saha World. *Understand it with trust* means not avoiding. Who would not understand with trust the forthright and truthful words of the Buddha?

To encounter this sutra is a condition that ought to be understood with trust. The Buddha vowed to be born in this Saha World in order to understand the *Lotus Sutra* and his timeless life with trust in his *deep heart*.

The Tathagata's extraordinary power, compassionate power, timeless life power takes up your heart to lead you to understand with trust [his teaching that the life span of the Buddha is timeless]. The Tathagata's power takes up your body, the entire world, buddha ancestors, all things, reality, skin, flesh, bones, and marrow, and the coming and going of birth and death, to lead you to understand with trust. This understanding with trust is to see the Buddha.

Thus, know that you have the eye on top of the mind and see the Buddha; you attain the eye of understanding with trust and see the Buddha.

Not only do you see the Buddha, but you *see the Buddha, who always abides and teaches on Vulture Peak*. Always abiding on Vulture Peak is no other than the Tathagata's life span. *Thus, see the Buddha, who always abides on Vulture Peak* means that the Tathagata and Vulture Peak from the past always abide; the Tathagata and Vulture Peak from now on always abide. It is that the bodhisattvas and shravakas [who surround the Tathagata] also always abide. It is that his teaching always abides.

You see that the Saha World with its lapis lazuli ground is vast and flat. Don't sway in seeing the Saha World. A high place is vast and flat in the high place, and a low place is vast and flat in the low place. Where we are is a lapis lazuli ground. Do not look down on it as merely vast and flat.

The surface of this Saha World is vast and flat, made of lapis lazuli is like this. If you don't see where we are as a lapis lazuli ground, Vulture Peak would not be Vulture Peak, Shakyamuni Buddha would not be Shakyamuni Buddha. Understanding that where we are is a lapis lazuli ground is no other than understanding it with trust in your deep heart. It is to see the Buddha.

———————

Shakyamuni Buddha said to the assembly, "When you single-mindedly want to see the Buddha and do not spare your life, I appear on Vulture Peak together with the assembly of monks."

The single-mindedness spoken of now is not that of ordinary people or those in the Two Vehicles. It is the single-minded pursuit to see the Buddha. The single-minded pursuit to see the Buddha is *Vulture Peak*. It is *together with the assembly of monks*. When each of you at this very moment aspires to see the Buddha, you do so with Vulture Peak mind.

Thus, a single mind is no other than Vulture Peak. How can a single body not come forth together with the single mind? How can a single body and mind come forth together?

The body and mind are like this. Those who live timeless life, as well as those who live transient life, are also like this. In this way, you leave your self-sparing mind to the mind of only sparing the unsurpassable way. Thus, *I appear on Vulture Peak together with the assembly of monks* is the single mind aspiring to see the Buddha.

———————

Shakyamuni Buddha said to the assembly, "If you expound this sutra, you see me as Prabhutaratna [Many Jewels] Tathagata, and all other incarnated buddhas."

Expound this sutra means "Although I abide here permanently, with my miraculous power I keep confused sentient beings from seeing me, however near they may be."
On the front and back of the Tathagata of miraculous power, there is the power of *you see me*.

Shakyamuni Buddha said to the assembly, "Those who maintain this sutra see me. They also see Prabhutaratna Buddha and all buddhas who share the same body."

Because the Tathagata is determined to maintain this sutra, he always recommends this sutra to you. When there are those who maintain this sutra, they invariably see Shakyamuni Buddha. Thus, we know that if you see the Buddha, you maintain the sutra. Those who maintain the sutra see the Buddha.

Thus, those of you who maintain one verse or one phrase [of this sutra] see Shakyamuni Buddha, Prabhutaratna Buddha, and the incarnated buddhas. You receive the transmission of the treasury of the dharma, the true eye of the Buddha, and you see the life of the Buddha. You receive the eye going beyond, the eye on top of the head, and the nostril of the Buddha.

———

[According to the *Lotus Sutra:*]
Jaradhara Garjita Ghosha Susvara Nakshatra Raja Sankusumitabhijna Buddha said to King Subhavyuha, "Great King, know that a good teacher is a great cause and condition. Guided by a good teacher, you get to see the Buddha by arousing the aspiration for unsurpassable, complete enlightenment."

The great dharma assembly [of Jaradhara Garjita Ghosha Susvara Nakshatra Raja Sankusumitabhijna Buddha] is not yet over. Although we say buddhas of the past, present, and future, their past, present, and future are not the same as those of ordinary people's view. Past is the top of your mind; present is your fist; future is the back of your brain.

Thus, Jaradhara Garjita Ghosha Susvara Nakshatra Raja Sankusumitabhijna Buddha actualizes the top of his mind, sees the Buddha. The words *see the Buddha* mean this. *Guided by a good teacher* is to *see the Buddha*. To *see the Buddha* is to arouse the aspiration for unsurpassable, complete enlightenment. Arousing the aspiration for unsurpassable, complete enlightenment is, from head to tail, seeing the Buddha.

Shakyamuni Buddha said, "Those who practice virtue with gentleness and openness see me expounding dharma here."

Virtue means splattering mud and getting wet in water, or following waves to chase waves. To practice this is called the *gentleness and openness* of "You are like this. I am like this." This is to see the Buddha in the mud, to see the Buddha with the heart of the waves. This is to encounter the Buddha who is *expounding dharma here.*

Recently in Great Song China there are a great number of fellows with little seeing and hearing who call themselves Zen masters but don't know the vertical and horizontal of buddha dharma. They merely memorize two or three phrases by Linji or Yunmen, regard these words as the entire path of buddha dharma.

If buddha dharma were encompassed by a couple of phrases by Linji or Yunmen, it would not have reached this day. It is not possible to call Linji or Yunmen the most venerable in buddha dharma. Furthermore, those fellows nowadays who are short of phrases have not come close to Linji or Yunmen.

Because they are dull, they slander buddha scriptures without studying and clarifying the meaning of them. They are not descendants of buddha ancestors and should be regarded as part of the flock outside the way. How can they reach the realm of seeing the Buddha? They cannot even reach the teachings of Confucius and Laozi. Those of you who are inside the house of buddha ancestors should not pay attention to those fellows who call themselves Zen masters. Instead, practice thoroughly and penetrate with your body the eye of seeing the Buddha.

Rujing, my late master, Old Buddha Tiantong, said, "King Prasenajit asked Pindola, 'Venerable Master, I hear that you personally have seen the Buddha. Is it true?' Pindola responded by brushing up his eyebrows with his hand."

Then, Rujing taught in a verse:

> Pindola raised his eyebrows and answered the king's question.
> No doubt he had personally seen the Buddha.
> Until now he has been worthy of offerings from the four
>   quarters of the world.
> Spring is within a plum twig, bearing the snow—cold.

Seeing the Buddha here does not mean seeing the Buddha as self or seeing the Buddha as other, but it means seeing the Buddha [Shakyamuni]. Because one branch of plum blossoms sees one branch of plum blossoms, blossoms are open, bright and clear.

The king's question was whether Pindola had seen the Buddha and become a buddha. Pindola clearly raised his eyebrows. This was the proof that he had seen the Buddha. This should not be confused. This fact has not ceased *until now*, revealing that Pindola is *worthy of offerings*. Thus, the fact that Pindola had personally seen the Buddha cannot be doubted.

The question *Have you personally seen the Buddha?* asked by the king of three hundred million people [Prasenajit] meant whether Pindola had seen the Buddha in this way. It is not seeing the thirty-two marks of the Buddha. Seeing the thirty-two marks of the Buddha can be done by anybody.

There are a number of humans, devas, shravakas, and pratyekabuddhas who do not know the meaning of truly seeing the Buddha [and say that they haven't seen the Buddha]. It is just like saying that they have hardly seen a whisk being raised [teaching being given], although they see a whisk being raised quite often.

To see the Buddha is to be seen by the Buddha. However hard you may try to hide it, your seeing the Buddha comes forth and lets itself leak out [be revealed]. This is how seeing the Buddha works. Endeavor with your bodies and minds as numerous as the sands of the Ganges and investigate thoroughly the meaning of Pindola raising his eyebrows.

Even if you lived together with Shakyamuni Buddha day and night for one hundred, one thousand, or ten thousand eons, if you did not have the ability to raise your eyebrows, this would not be seeing the Buddha. On the other hand, even if you are far away from the Buddha by hundreds of thousands of *li* and by over two thousand years, if you personally actualize the ability of raising your eyebrows, you have seen Shakyamuni Buddha since the time before the King of the Empty Eon. It is seeing one branch of plum blossoms, seeing spring in a branch of plum blossoms.

Thus, personally seeing the Buddha is formally bowing three times, greeting with hands joined together, smiling, a fist striking thunder, sitting on the cushion in meditation posture.

———

Venerable Pindola went to King Ashoka's palace to receive a meal offering. After the king distributed incense to the monks, he bowed to Pindola and asked, "I heard that you have personally seen the Buddha. Is it true?"

Pindola brushed up his eyebrows with his hand and asked, "Do you understand it?"

The king said, "No, I don't."

Pindola said, "When the Dragon King of Anavatapta Lake invited all buddhas and offered a feast, I was one of those who were present."

When King Ashoka asked Pindola if he had *personally seen the Buddha,* he was trying to see if the venerable teacher was actually venerable. Responding to this question, Pindola immediately brushed up his eyebrows. This is to actualize seeing the Buddha in this world. This is to personally show having become a buddha.

Pindola said, *When the Dragon King of Anavatapta Lake invited all buddhas and offered a feast, I was one of those who were present.* Know that in the assembly of invited buddhas, the attendees of "only a buddha and a buddha" are as numerous as stalks of straw, flax, bamboo, and reeds. This is beyond the reach of arhats who have attained the four fruits, or pratyeka-buddhas. Even if such practitioners come, don't regard them as members of *invited* buddhas.

However, Pindola proclaimed that he was *one of those who were present* when all buddhas were invited. This is a boundless self-expression. It is clear that he did see the Buddha. When the Dragon King *invited all buddhas,* not only Shakyamuni Buddha but also countless and endless buddhas of the ten directions in the past, present, and future were invited. The buddhas who were invited personally saw Shakyamuni Buddha without separation. The point of *seeing the Buddha*, seeing the teacher, seeing the self, seeing yourself, is also like this.

Anavatapta Lake is also called Annoktapta Lake, the lake of no suffering from heat.

———

Baoning, Zen Master Renyong, said in a verse:

> Our Buddha personally sees Pindola,
> whose eyebrows are long, whose hair is short, and whose
> eyes look vulgar.
> King Ashoka was still suspicious.
> OM MANI SHRI SURYA [Homage to the jewel that shines like
> the sun].

This verse does not present a complete expression, but I am quoting it for your further study.

———

Zhaozhou, Great Master Zhenji, was once asked by a monk, "I heard that you personally saw Nanquan. Is it true?"

Zhaozhou said, "A giant radish was here in Zhen Region."

The manifestation of this expression is proof that Zhaozhou had personally seen Nanquan. It is not having words or having no-words, not having teaching words or having conversational words. It is not raising the eyebrows or brushing up the eyebrows, but it is directly seeing the eyebrows. Even if Zhaozhou was a genius standing alone, he could not have said this without personally seeing Nanquan.

Zhaozhou said, *A giant radish was here in Zhen Region,* when he was abbot of the Zhenji Monastery in Doujia Garden, Zhen Region. He was later given the title Great Master Zhenji. In this way, from the time when he practiced opening the eye of seeing the Buddha, he held the authentic transmission of the buddha ancestors' treasury of the true dharma eye. When the treasury of the true dharma eye is authentically transmitted, the gentle and awesome presence of seeing the Buddha is actualized. Right here, see the Buddha enormously and magnificently.

Presented to the assembly at Yamashi Peak on the nineteenth day, the eleventh month, the first year of the Kangen Era [1243].

62

ALL-INCLUSIVE STUDY

THE GREAT WAY of buddha ancestors is to penetrate the ultimate realm, soaring with no strings attached or like clouds arising below your feet.

This being so, "The world of blossoming flowers arises," and "I am always intimate with this." Accordingly, sweet melon has a sweet stem, bitter gourd has a bitter root. Sweet melon and its stem are sweet through and through. Thus, the way has been studied thoroughly.

Xuansha, who would later become Zen Master Zongyi, was called upon by his master Xuefeng, who said, "Ascetic Bei, why don't you go toward all-inclusive study?"

Xuansha said, "Bodhidharma did not come to China. Huike did not go to India."

Xuefeng was deeply impressed with this.

All-inclusive study here means to study by doing cartwheels, where "Sacred truth doesn't do anything. What degrees can there be?"

Nanyue, who would later become Zen Master Dahui, first went to meet Huineng, the Old Buddha of Caoxi. Huineng said, "What is it that thus comes?"

Nanyue studied this lump of mud all-inclusively for eight years and finally presented a move to Huineng: "I understand now. When I first came here, you instructed me: 'What is it that thus comes?'"

Then, Huineng said, "How do you understand it?"

Nanyue said, "Speaking about it won't hit the mark."

This is the actualization of all-inclusive study, the realization of eight years [seven years and some months].

Huineng said, "Does it depend on practice and realization?"

Dahui said, "It is not that there is no practice and no realization, it is just that they cannot be divided."

Then Huineng said, "I am like this, you are like this, and all the buddha ancestors in India are also like this."

After this, Nanyue praticed all-inclusively for eight more years; counting from beginning to end, it was an all-inclusive study of fifteen years.

To *thus come* is all-inclusive study. To open up the hall and see all buddhas and all ancestors where *Speaking about it won't hit the mark* is all-inclusive study.

Since entering into and seeing the picture, there have been sixty-five hundred thousand myriad billions of turning bodies of all-inclusive study. Leisurely entering the monastery and leisurely leaving the monastery are not all-inclusive study. Seeing with the entire eyeball is all-inclusive study. Getting all the way through is all-inclusive study. To understand whether the face skin is thick or not is all-inclusive study.

The meaning of *all-inclusive study* as asserted by Xuefeng does not mean that he encouraged Xuansha to leave the monastery, or go north or come south. His expression provoked the all-inclusive study of Xuansha's words *Bodhidharma did not come to China. Huike did not go to India.*

Xuansha's words *Bodhidharma did not come to China* do not confusedly state that Bodhidharma did not come although he actually did come. They mean that there is not an inch of land on earth. This *Bodhidharma* is the tip of the life vein. Even if the entire eastern land appears to accompany him, his body is not turned, nor is it moved by the words. Because Bodhidharma did not come to China, he faces China. Even if China sees the buddha face, the ancestor face, it is not that Bodhidharma came to China. To grasp the buddha ancestor is to lose his nostrils.

The lands do not lie to east or west. East-and-west has nothing to do with lands. *Huike did not go to India* means that to study India all-inclusively, you need not go to India. Should Huike go to India, he would miss his arm.

What then is the meaning of Huike, the Second Ancestor, not going to India? He leaped into the eyeball of the blue-eyed one [Bodhidharma]; there was no need to go to India. Had he not leaped into the blue eyes, he should have gone to India. Plucking out Bodhidharma's eyeball is all-inclusive study. To go to India or to go to China is not all-inclusive study. To visit Tiantai or Nanyue or to reach Wutai or heaven is not all-inclusive study. If the Four Seas and Five Lakes are not penetrated, it is not all-inclusive study. To go back and forth on the Four Seas and Five Lakes is not to allow the Four Seas and Five Lakes to study all-inclusively. By treading back and forth, you will make the road smooth, the ground beneath your feet will become smooth, but all-inclusive study will be lost.

Because Xuansha studied all-inclusively the understanding of "The entire universe of the ten directions is the true human body," he reached the understanding of *Bodhidharma did not come to China. Huike did not go to India.*

All-inclusive study means "If the top of a stone is large, the bottom is large. If the top of the stone is small, the bottom is small." Without changing the top of a stone, you allow the stone to be large or to be small. To study a hundred thousand myriad things only as a hundred thousand myriad things is not yet all-inclusive study. To turn a hundred thousand myriad bodies even in half a statement is all-inclusive study.

For example, "Just hit the earth when you hit the earth" is all-inclusive study. Merely hitting the earth once, hitting the sky once, or hitting the four directions and eight directions once is not all-inclusive study. But Juzhi's studying with Tianlong and attaining one finger is all-inclusive study. Juzhi's just raising one finger is all-inclusive study.

Xuansha taught the assembly, "Old Man Shakyamuni and I studied together."

A monk came up and asked, "I wonder, whom did you two study with?"

Xuansha said, "We studied with the third son of Xie [Xuansha] on a fishing boat."

Old Man Shakyamuni's study from beginning to end is itself studying together with Old Man Xuansha. Xuansha's study from beginning to end is studying closely together with Old Man Shakyamuni. Between Old Man Shakyamuni and Old Man Xuansha, there is no one study that is more complete or incomplete than another. This is the meaning of all-inclusive study. Old Man Shakyamuni is an ancient buddha because he studied together with Old Man Xuansha. Old Man Xuansha is a descendant because he studied together with Old Man Shakyamuni. Study the meaning of this all-inclusively.

Clarify the words, *We studied with the third son of Xie on a fishing boat.* This is to study all-inclusively in pursuit of the moment when Old Man Shakyamuni and Old Man Xuansha studied together at the same time. When Xuansha saw the third son of Xie on the fishing boat, they were sharing study. When the third son of Xie saw the bald-headed fellow [himself] on Mount Xuansha, they were sharing study.

Studying together or not studying together—you should allow yourself and others to reflect on this. Old Man Xuansha and Old Man Shakyamuni studied together, studied all-inclusively. Together study all-inclusively: "With whom did the third son of Xie and Xuansha study?"

If the meaning of all-inclusive study does not appear, then studying the self is not attained, studying the self is not complete; studying others is not attained, studying others is not complete; studying a true person is not attained, studying yourself is not attained; studying the fist is not attained, studying the eyeball is not attained; self hooking self is not attained, catching the fish without a hook is not attained.

If you thoroughly experience all-inclusive study, all-inclusive study is dropped away. When the ocean is dry, no bottom is visible. When a person is dead, no mind remains. "The ocean is dry" means the entire ocean is completely dry. The ocean is dry and you cannot see the bottom. Not remaining and completely remaining—both are the person's mind. When a person is dead, the mind does not remain. When death is taken up, the mind does not remain. This being so, know that the entire person is mind, the entire mind is the person. In this way, investigate thoroughly from top to bottom.

Rujing, my late master, Old Buddha Tiantong, was once asked to give a discourse when accomplished priests, who were elders from various places, assembled. He ascended the teaching seat and said:

> The great road has no gate. It leaps out from the heads of all of you. The open sky has no road. It enters into my nostrils. In this way we meet as Gautama's bandits, or Linji's troublemakers. Ha! The great house tumbles down and spring wind swirls. Astonished, apricot blossoms fly and scatter—red.

This discourse was given when Rujing was abbot of the Qingliang Monastery in Jiankang Prefecture, when he was visited by temple elders from various places. These accomplished priests and Rujing had known one another as teacher and disciples or had been students together. He had friends like this in all directions. They got together and asked him for a discourse. Elders who did not have a teaching phrase were not his associates and were not included. Only the most venerable priests were requested to attend.

Rujing's all-inclusive study cannot be fully accomplished by everyone. There has not been an ancient buddha like him for two or three hundred years in Great Song. As *The great road has no gate*, it is four or five thousand avenues of pleasure quarters, two or three myriads of wind-and-string pavilions.

But when the whole body of the great road leaps out, it leaps out from the head, not from anywhere else. In the same way, it enters the nostrils. Both leaping out and entering are studies of the way. Those who have not leaped out of the head or inhaled the body through the nostrils are not students of the way or persons of all-inclusive study. Study the meaning of all-inclusive study just with Xuansha.

Long ago Daoxin, who would later become the Fourth Ancestor, studied with Sengcan, the Third Ancestor, for nine years. This is all-inclusive study.

Later Nanquan, Zen Master Puyuan, lived in Chiyang for almost thirty years. This is all-inclusive study without leaving the mountain.

Yunyan, Daowu, and others engaged in practice when they were at Mount Yao for forty years. This is all-inclusive study.

Long ago Huike, who would later become the Second Ancestor, practiced at Mount Song for eight years. He studied all-inclusively the skin, flesh, bones, and marrow.

All-inclusive study is just single-minded sitting, dropping away body and mind. At the moment of going there, you go there; at the moment of coming here, you come here. There is no gap. Just in this way, the entire body all-inclusively studies the great road's entire body.

Stepping over the head of Vairochana is samadhi without conflict. To attain this firmly is to step over the head of Vairochana.

The complete practice of all-inclusive study by leaping out is gourd leaping out from gourd. For a long time the gourd's head has been the practice place. Its vital force is vines. Gourd studies gourd all-inclusively. In this way a blade of grass is actualized. This is all-inclusive study.

Taught in a grass-thatched hut at the foot of Yamashi Peak, Echizen Province, on the twenty-seventh day, the eleventh month, the first year of the Kangen Era [1243].

63

EYEBALL

UPHOLDING STUDY THROUGH a billion eons and turning it into a ball is eighty-four thousand eyeballs.

––––––––––

When Rujing, my late master, Old Buddha Tiantong, was abbot of the Ruiyan Monastery, he ascended the teaching seat and said to the assembly:

> Autumn wind clear, autumn moon bright.
> Earth, mountains, and rivers reveal an eyeball.
> I, Ruiyan, glance with this one eye and encounter you.
> Alternating the stick and shout, I test the patch-robed
>   monks.

Test the patch-robed monks means to examine whether they are authentic buddhas or not. The essential method is *alternating the stick and shout.* This is *glance with this one eye.* Actualizing this activity is an eyeball.

Mountains, rivers, and earth are the eyeball revealed before the emergence of the Empty Eon. It is *autumn wind clear;* it grows old. It is *autumn moon bright;* it does not grow old. Even the Four Great Oceans cannot be

616   ·   TREASURY OF THE TRUE DHARMA EYE

compared with *autumn wind clear. Autumn moon bright* is brighter than a thousand suns and moons. Clear and bright are mountains, rivers, and earth—an eyeball. Patch-robed monks are buddha ancestors. Regardless of great enlightenment, regardless of beyond enlightenment, regardless of before or after the first sign of the Empty Eon, being eyeballs is being buddha ancestors. Testing is an eyeball revealed, glancing actualized, vitalizing the eyeball.

Encountering is meeting. Encountering, meeting, is the tip of the eye. The eyeball is roaring thunder.

Do not think that the entire body is large and the entire eye is small. Often in the past, even those who were regarded as old and great assumed that the body is large and the eye is small. This is because they were not equipped with an eyeball.

———————

When Dongshan, who would later become Great Master Wuben, was at the assembly of Yunyan, he saw Yunyan making straw sandals. Dongshan asked him, "Please, may I have an eyeball?"

Yunyan said, "To whom did you give away yours?"

Dongshan said, "I did not have one."

Yunyan said, "Yes, you did. Where did you put it?"

Dongshan was silent.

Yunyan said, "You are asking for an eyeball. Isn't your asking an eyeball?"

Dogshan said, "It's not an eyeball."

Yunyan clicked his tongue.

In this way, all-illuminating study is to ask for an eyeball. To engage in the endeavor of the way in the cloud hall, to get to the dharma hall, to enter the hall for sleeping, are all asking for an eyeball. To join the assembly as it arrives and to join the assembly as it leaves is no other than asking for an eyeball. It is clear that the eyeball is not self, and not other.

Thus, Dongshan said, *Please, may I have an eyeball?* From this we know that we should not ask someone else for what is self or what is other.

Yunyan instructed: *To whom did you give away yours?* This is the moment of *you.* This is the point of *to whom.*

Dongshan said, *I did not have one.* This is an eyeball expressing itself.

Quietly investigate and pursue the meaning of such an actualized expression.

Yunyan said, *Where did you put it?* The eyeball of this expression is that the *not* of *I did not have one* is no other than *Where did you put it?* And *Where did you put it?* means *Yes, you did.* Understand that this is an expression of thusness.

Dongshan was silent. This does not mean that his mind was clouded. His statement shows that he had retreated to the edge of consciousness.

Yunyan said, *You are asking for an eyeball. Isn't your asking an eyeball?* This is the knot and grain [signs] of glancing with an eyeball. It is a vital crushing of an eyeball. What Yunyan showed is that an eyeball asks for an eyeball, water draws water, and mountains flow to mountains. His statement is an expression [of compassion] for us to journey among other types of beings and to be born among the same type of beings.

Dogshan said, *It's not an eyeball.* This is an eyeball expounding itself. See that a vital eyeball is expressing itself where there are body, mind, and thinking beyond an eyeball, as well as words beyond an eyeball.

Buddhas in the past, present, and future stand and listen to the eyeball turn and expound the great dharma wheel. Inside the chamber of investigating thoroughly, buddhas leap into the eyeball and arouse aspiration, engage in practice, and realize great enlightenment. This eyeball is neither self nor other. As it has no hindrance, these great actions are without hindrance.

In this regard, a teacher of old said, "How splendid buddhas in the ten directions are! From the beginning, they are blossoms in an eye."

Buddhas in the ten directions spoken of here are an eyeball. *Blossoms in an eye* are *buddhas in the ten directions.* It is, therefore, an eyeball inheriting the entirety of an eyeball while stepping forward and backward, while sitting and sleeping. This is grasping and letting go within an eyeball.

Rujing, my late master, Old Buddha, said, "Pluck out Bodhidharma's eyeball, turn it into a mud ball, and strike a person."

Then, raising his voice, he said, "Look. The ocean is dry below its bottom. The high waves strike the sky."

This is an instruction given to the ocean of monks at the abbot's quarters of the Qingliang Monastery. *Turn it into a mud ball, and strike a person* means to make a person. Because of turning, each person reveals the original face. With Bodhidharma's eyeball, true persons are made, and we make true persons. This is what he meant by saying *turn it into a mud ball, and strike a person.*

Because true persons are made of the eyeball, the fist that strikes a person in the cloud hall, the stick that makes a person in the dharma hall, the bamboo stick and whisk that strike a person in the abbot's quarters, are all Bodhidharma's eyeball.

Pluck out Bodhidharma's eyeball, turn it into a mud ball, and strike means what people nowadays call a meeting with the master, asking questions, engaging in early morning practice, or endeavor in sitting. What kind of person is struck? That is: *The ocean is dry below its bottom. The high waves strike the sky.*

———

Rujing ascended the teaching seat and said in admiration of the Tathagata's attaining enlightenment:

> A wild fox spirit hides in grass for six years,
> leaps—its entire body is twining vines.
> Smashing the eyeball, there is nothing to
>   seek.
> Deceived, people call it enlightenment at
>   the morning star.

That the Tathagata was enlightened upon seeing the morning star is how outsiders talk about the moment of smashing the eyeball right now. This is, however, its *entire body is twining vines.* Thus, it leaps effortlessly.

There is nothing to seek means that there is nothing to seek in actualizing and not yet actualizing.

———

Rujing ascended the teaching seat and said:

> When Gautama's eyeball is smashed,
> plum blossoms in snow, just one branch,
> become thorn twigs, here, right now.
> Laughing, spring wind blows madly.

Let me say: Gautama's eyeball is not merely one, two, or three. Which eyeball is smashed now? Is there an eyeball that is called *smashed*? In this very thusness, there is an eyeball that is *plum blossoms in snow, just one branch*. This eyeball comes before spring and overflows the heart of spring.

Rujing ascended the teaching seat and said:

> Great rain keeps pouring.
> The great clear sky is wide open.
> A toad sings and an earthworm murmurs.
> An ancient buddha has not left,
> raising a diamond eyeball.
> Damn! Twining vines, twining vines.

A diamond eyeball is *Great rain keeps pouring, the great clear sky is wide open*. It is *A toad sings and an earthworm murmurs*. Because of not having left, it is *an ancient buddha*. Even if *an ancient buddha* has left, it is not the same as the "having left" of one who is not *an ancient buddha*.

Rujing ascended the teaching seat and said:

> The sun is in the south, the day is longest.
> Within the eyeball there is illumination.
> Within the nostrils there is exhalation.

Being continuous right now, from winter solstice to the New Year, daytime becomes longer, yet continuity drops away. This is *Within the eyeball there is illumination*. It is to see a mountain inside the sun. The awesome activity of practice is thus.

————————

Rujing ascended the teaching seat at the Jingci Monastery, Linan Prefecture, and said:

> This morning marks the first day of the second month.
> The whisk pulls out the eyeball.
> This is as clear as a mirror,
> as black as lacquer.
> It rushes to leap and
> swallows the universe—one color.
> Yet my disciples hit the fence and hit the wall.
> What is it?
> Exhaust your thinking and burst out laughing.
> Ha, ha! Leave everything to the spring wind till
>   nothing is left.

Hit the fence and hit the wall is hitting the entire fence and hitting the entire wall. Here is an eyeball. This is an eyeball that is this morning, the first day, and the second month. It is a whisk that is an eyeball. Because it rushes to leap, it is this morning. Because it swallows the universe one thousand or ten thousand times, it is the second month. At the time when your thinking is exhausted, it is the first day.

Actualizing an eyeball's vital activity is just like this.

Presented to the assembly at Yamashi Peak, Echizen Province, on the seventeenth day, the twelfth month, the first year of the Kangen Era [1243].

64

EVERYDAY ACTIVITY

I N THE DOMAIN of buddha ancestors, drinking tea and eating rice are everyday activity. Drinking tea and eating rice have been transmitted for a long time and are present right now. Thus, the buddha ancestors' vital activity of drinking tea and eating rice comes to us.

Priest Daokai, who would later become abbot of Mount Dayang, asked Touzi [Yiqing], "It is said that the thoughts and words of buddha ancestors are everyday tea and rice. Besides this, are there any words or phrases for teaching?"

Touzi said, "Tell me, when the emperor issues a decree in his territory, does he depend upon [ancient] Emperors Yu, Tang, Yao, or Shun?"

As Daokai was about to open his mouth, Touzi covered it with his whisk. "While you were thinking, you've already received thirty blows."

Daokai was then awakened. He bowed deeply and began to leave.

Touzi said, "Wait, reverend."

Daokai did not turn around, and Touzi said, "Have you reached the ground of no-doubt?"

Daokai covered his ears with his hands and left.

From this, clearly understand that the thoughts and words of buddha ancestors are their everyday tea and rice. Ordinary coarse tea and plain rice are buddhas' thoughts, ancestors' phrases. Because buddha ancestors prepare tea and rice, tea and rice maintain buddha ancestors. Accordingly, they need no powers other than this tea and rice, and they have no need to use powers as buddha ancestors.

Investigate and study the expression *Does he depend upon Emperors Yu, Tang, Yao, or Shun?* Leap over the summit of the question *Besides this, are there any words or phrases for teaching?* Try to see whether leaping is possible or not.

Shitou, Great Master Wuji, at the Shitou Hut on Mount Nanyue, said:

> I have built a grass hut where no coins are kept.
> Having had rice, I am ready for a leisurely nap.

Having had rice—words come, words go, words come and go, filled with buddha ancestors' thoughts and phrases. Not yet having rice means not yet being satisfied. However, the point of *having had rice* and *a leisurely nap* is actualized before having rice, while having rice, and after having rice. To assume that the experience of having rice lies only after *having had rice* is the mere study of four or five *sho* [small amount] of rice.

Rujing taught the assembly:

> I heard that a monk asked Baizhang, "What is an extraordinary thing?" Baizhang said, "Sitting alone on Daxiong Peak. The assembly cannot move the person. For now, let the person totally sit." Today if someone were to ask me, "What is an extraordinary thing?" I would say, "Is anything extraordinary? How was it? The bowl of Jingci has moved; I'm eating rice in Tiantong."

In the domain of buddha ancestors there is always something extraordinary. This is *sitting alone on Daxiong Peak.* Being allowed to totally sit is itself an extraordinary thing. Even more extraordinary is *The bowl of Jingci has moved; I'm eating rice in Tiantong.*

Each and every extraordinary activity is simply eating rice. Thus, sitting alone on Daxiong Peak is just eating rice. The monk's bowl is used for having rice, and what is used for having rice is the monk's bowl. It is *the bowl of Jingci* and it is *having rice in Tiantong.* Being satisfied is to know rice. Eating rice is to be satisfied. To know is to be satisfied with rice. To be satisfied is to continue eating.

Now, what is the monk's bowl? I say it is not wood and it is not black lacquer. Is it an immovable rock? Is it an iron person? It is bottomless. It has no nostrils. One mouthful swallows the open sky. The open sky is received with palms together.

Rujing once taught the assembly at the buddha hall of the Ruiyan Jingtu Monastery of Tai Region:

> When hunger comes, have rice.
> When fatigue comes, sleep.
> Furnace and bellows, each covers the entire sky.

When hunger comes is the vital activity of a person who has had rice. A person who has not had rice has not had hunger. Since this is so, a person who gets hungry every day is someone who has had rice. Understand this completely. *When fatigue comes* means that there is fatigue in the midst of fatigue; it springs forth completely from the summit of fatigue. Accordingly, the entire body is completely turned right now by the activity of the entire body.

Sleep is to sleep using the buddha eye, dharma eye, wisdom eye, ancestor eye, and pillar-and-lantern eye.

Rujing once accepted an invitation and moved to the Jingci Monastery of Linan Prefecture from the Ruiyan Monastery of Tai Region, ascended the seat, and said:

Half a year, just having rice and sitting on Wan Peak.
This sitting cuts through thousands of layers of misty clouds.
One sudden clap of roaring thunder.
Spring in the mystic village—apricot blossoms are red.

The teaching of buddha ancestors who transmit the Buddha's life-long practice is entirely *having rice and sitting on Wan Peak*. To study and practice the inheritance of the Buddha's ancestral wisdom is to bring forth the vital activity of having rice. *Half a year, . . . sitting on Wan Peak* is called having rice. You cannot tell how many layers of misty clouds this sitting cuts through. However sudden the roar of thunder may be, spring apricot blossoms are just red. *Mystic village* means red through and through right now. This is having rice. Wan Peak is the name of a peak that represents the Ruiyan Monastery.

———————

Rujing once taught the assembly at the buddha hall of the Ruiyan Monastery, Qingyuan Prefecture, Ming Region:

Wondrous golden form
wears a robe and eats rice.
So I bow to you;
go to sleep early and wake up late. Ha!
Discuss the profound, expound the inconceivable—endless.
I avoid the self-deception of holding up a flower.

Immediately penetrate this. *Wondrous golden form* means wearing a robe and eating rice. Wearing a robe and eating rice is wondrous golden form. Do not wonder who is wearing a robe and eating rice. Do not say whose wondrous golden form it is.

Speaking in this way is complete expression. This is the meaning of *So I bow to you*. Thus "I have already had rice. You have just bowed to the rice." This is because "I completely avoid holding up a flower."

———————

Changqing, Priest Da'an, Zen Master Yuanzhi, of the Changqing Monastery, Fu Region, ascended the seat and taught the assembly:

I have been at Mount Gui for thirty years and have been eating Mount Gui's rice and shitting Mount Gui's shit. I have not studied Guishan's Zen but just see a single water buffalo. When it wanders off the road and begins grazing, I yank it back. When it trespasses onto other people's rice fields, I whip it. In this way, I have been taming it for a long time. Such an adorable one! It understands human speech and now has transformed into a white ox. All day long it walks round and round in front of us. Even if we try to drive it away, it does not leave.

Clearly accept this teaching. Thirty years of pursuit in the assembly of buddha ancestors is eating rice. There are no other pursuits. If you actualize this endeavor of eating rice, invariably you will see the buffalo.

———————

Zhaozhou, Great Master Zhenji, asked a newly arrived monk, "Have you been here before?"
The monk said, "Yes, I have been here."
Zhaozhou said, "Have some tea."

Later, he asked another monk, "Have you been here before?"
The monk said, "No, I have not been here."
Zhaozhou said, "Have some tea."

The temple director then asked Zhaozhou, "Why do you say, 'Have some tea' to someone who has been here, and 'Have some tea' to someone who has not?"
Zhaozhou said, "Director."
"Yes."
Zhaozhou said, "Have some tea."

Zhaozhou's word *here* does not mean the top of the head, the nostrils, or Zhaozhou. Since *here* leaps off here, a monk said, *I have been here*, and another said, *I have not been here*. It means: What is now? Whatever is here, just say, "I have been here" or "I have not been here."

———————

Regarding this, Rujing said:

> Who in the picture of a wineshop
> faces you and drinks Zhaozhou's tea?

Thus, the everyday activity of buddha ancestors is nothing but having tea and eating rice.

Presented to the assembly at the foot of Yamashi Peak, Echizen Province, on the seventeenth day, the twelfth month, the first year of the Kangen Era [1243].

65

DRAGON SONG

Touzi, Great Master Ciji of Shu Region, was once asked by a monk, "Is there a dragon singing in a withered tree?"

Touzi replied, "I say there is a lion roaring in a skull."

Discussions about a withered tree and dead ash [composure in stillness] are originally teachings outside the way. But the withered tree spoken of by those outside the way and that spoken of by buddha ancestors are far apart. Those outside the way talk about a withered tree, but they don't authentically know it; how can they hear the dragon singing? They think that a withered tree is a dead tree which does not grow leaves in spring.

The withered tree spoken of by buddha ancestors is the understanding of the ocean drying up. The ocean drying up is the tree withering. The tree withering encounters spring. The immovability of the tree is its witheredness. The mountain trees, ocean trees, and sky trees right now are all withered trees. That which sprouts buds is a dragon singing in a withered tree. Those who embrace it one hundredfold, one thousandfold, and one myriadfold are descendants of the withered tree.

The form, essence, body, and power of this witheredness are a withered stake spoken of by a buddha ancestor [Sushan Guangren]. It is beyond a withered stake. There are mountain valley trees, and fields-of-village trees. The mountain valley trees are called pines and cypresses in the common world. The fields-of-village trees are called humans and devas in the common world. Those that depend on roots and spread leaves are called buddha ancestors. They all go back to the essence. This is to be studied. This is the tall dharma body of a withered tree and the short dharma body of a withered tree.

Without a withered tree there wouldn't be the dragon singing. Without a withered tree the dragon's singing wouldn't be smashed. "I have encountered spring many times, but the mind has not changed" [a line by Damei Fachang] is the dragon singing with complete witheredness. Although the dragon's singing does not conform with gong, shang, jue, zhi, yu [do, re, mi, fa, so], gong, shang, jue, zhi, yu are the before and after, two or three elements of the dragon's singing.

In this way, the monk's words, *Is there a dragon singing in a withered tree?* emerge for the first time as a question and a statement for immeasurable eons. As for Touzi's response, *I say there is a lion roaring in a skull*—what could hinder it? It keeps bending self and pushing other without ceasing. The skull covers the entire field.

Xiangyan, Great Master Xideng of Xiangyan Monastery, was once asked by a monk, "What is the way?"

Xiangyan said, "A dragon is singing in a withered tree."

The monk said, "I don't understand."

Xiangyan said, "An eyeball in the skull."

Later a monk asked Shishuang, "What is a dragon singing in a withered tree?"

Shishuang said, "It still holds joy."

The monk asked, "What is the eyeball in the skull?"

Shishuang said, "It still holds consciousness."

Later a monk asked Caoshan, "What is a dragon singing in a withered tree?"

Caoshan said, "The blood vein does not get cut off."

The monk asked, "What is the eyeball in the skull?"

Caoshan said, "It does not dry up."

The monk said, "I wonder if anyone has heard it?"

Caoshan said, "In the entire world there is no one who has not heard it."

The monk said, "I wonder what kind of song the dragon sings?"

Caoshan said, "No one knows what kind of song the dragon sings. All who hear it lose it."

The one who questions hearing and singing is not the one who sings the dragon's tune. The dragon's tune has its own melody. *In a withered tree* or *in a skull* are neither inside nor outside, neither self nor other. It is right now and a long time ago.

It still holds joy is growing a horn on the head. *It still holds consciousness,* is the skin dropping away completely.

Caoshan's words *The blood vein does not get cut off* are not avoided, turning the body in the word vein. *It does not dry up* means that the ocean's dryness never reaches to the bottom. Since the never-reaching is itself dryness, it is dryness beyond dryness.

To ask *if anyone has heard it* is like asking if there is anyone who has not gotten it. In regard to Caoshan's statement, *In the entire world there is no one who has not heard it,* ask further: "Never mind the fact that there is no one who has not heard it; where is the dragon's song at the time when no one in the entire world has heard it? Say it quickly, quickly!"

I wonder if anyone has heard it. Regarding this question, say: "The dragon song is howling and humming in muddy water, exhaling through the nostrils."

No one knows what kind of song the dragon sings is to have a dragon in the song. *All who hear it lose it* [become completely selfless] is something we should treasure.

Now, the dragon songs of Xiangyan, Shishuang, and Caoshan come forth, forming clouds and forming water. They go beyond words, beyond saying eyeballs in the skull. This is thousands and myriad pieces of the dragon song. *It still holds joy* is the croaking of frogs. *It still holds consciousness* is the singing of earthworms. Thus, the blood vein does not get cut off, a gourd succeeds a gourd. As *it does not dry up*, a pillar conceives a child; a lantern faces a lantern.

> *Presented to the assembly on the foot of Yamashi Peak on the twenty-fifth day, the twelfth month, the first year of the Kangen Era [1243].*

66

SPRING AND AUTUMN

DONGSHAN, GREAT MASTER Wuben, was once asked by a monk, "When cold or heat comes, how can we avoid it?"

Dongshan said, "Why don't you go where there is no cold or heat?"

The monk said, "What do you mean by 'where there is no cold or heat'?"

Dongshan said, "When it is cold, cold finishes the monk. When it is hot, heat demolishes the monk."

This story has often been examined in the past. Many of you should also pursue it now. Buddha ancestors have never failed to master this matter, and those who have mastered it are buddha ancestors. Buddha ancestors in India and China, both past and present, often made this issue the face and eye of their realization. To bring forth this face and eye is the fundamental point of buddha ancestors.

This being so, examine in detail the monk's question *When cold or heat comes, how can we avoid it?* This is to study the very moment when cold comes or the moment when heat comes. This cold or heat—complete cold or complete heat—is itself cold or heat. Accordingly, when either comes, it comes from the summit of cold or the summit of heat, and manifests from the eyeball of cold itself or heat itself. This summit is where there is no cold or heat. This eyeball is where there is no cold or heat.

Dongshan's words *When it is cold, cold finishes the monk. When it is hot, heat demolishes the monk* show how it is when the moment arrives. Even if there is the expression *When it is cold, cold finishes,* it is not necessary that when it is hot, heat demolishes the expression. Cold penetrates the root of cold, heat penetrates the root of heat. Even if you try millions of times to avoid cold or heat, it is like trying to put a tail where the head is. Cold is the vital eyeball of the ancestral school. Heat is the warm skin and flesh of my late master.

Jingyin Kumu, is an heir of Furong. His priest name is Facheng. He said:

> Many of you examine this dialogue and say, "This monk's question already falls into differentiation. Dongshan's answer brings the matter to oneness. The monk understood the meaning of Dongshan's words and entered oneness. Dongshan then entered differentiation."
>
> To analyze in such a way is to denigrate the ancient sage and lower yourself. Can't you understand these words? When I hear your interpretations, the meaning is decorated and seems beautiful, but if your interpretations accumulate over time, they become a disease. If you, advanced wanderers, want to master this matter, you should understand the treasury of the true dharma eye of this ancient ancestor Dongshan. Other buddha ancestors' words are just the play of hot water in a bowl. Now, let me ask you: in the end, what is the place of no cold or heat? Do you understand?

> In the jade pavilion, a kingfisher builds a nest.
> In the gold palace, ducks are enclosed.

Kumu is a descendant of Dongshan and a distinguished person in the ancestral seat. Here he warns many of those who pay homage to Dongshan, High Ancestor, Great Master, in the caved house of differentiation and oneness. If buddha dharma had been transmitted merely through the investigation of differentiation and oneness, how could it have reached this day?

Peasants or stray cats who have never understood the inner chamber of Dongshan, and who have not passed the threshold of the buddha dharma, mistakenly say that Dongshan guided students with his theory of Five Ranks of differentiation and oneness. This is a confused view. Do not pay attention to it, but just study thoroughly that the ancient ancestor has the treasury of the true dharma eye.

Hongzhi, Zen Master of Mount Tiantong, Qingyuan Prefecture, is an heir of Danxia. (His priest name is Zhenjiao.) He said:

> When you take up this dialogue, it is like you and me playing a game of go. If you do not respond to my move, I'll swallow you up. Only when you penetrate this, will you understand the meaning of Dongshan's words. I, Tiantong, cannot help adding this note:
>
>> I see no cold or heat whatsoever.
>> The great ocean has just dried up.
>> Let me tell you, a giant tortoise is lying in front of you.
>> It's funny you are setting up a fishing pole on the sand.

Suppose there is a game of go; who are the two players? If you say that you and I are playing go, it means you have a handicap of eight stones. If you have a handicap of eight stones, it is no longer a game.

What is the meaning of this? When you answer, answer this way: You play go with yourself; the opponents become one. Thus, steadying your mind and turning your body, examine Hongzhi's words, *If you do not respond to my move.* That means *you* are not yet you. Do not neglect the words, *I'll swallow you up.* Mud is within mud. Wash your feet, wash the tassel on your hat. A jewel is within a jewel, illuminating other, illuminating the self.

Keqin, Zen Master Yuanwu of Mount Jia, is an heir of Fayan, of Mount Wuzu. About this case he said:

A board rolls on a pearl and a pearl rolls on a board.
Differentiation within oneness; oneness within
    differentiation.
A mountain goat hangs by its horns on a branch,
    leaving no trace.
A hunting dog runs in the forest, taking empty steps.

The words *A board rolls on a pearl* appear before the light and cut off the future—rarely heard in the past and present. Until now it has only been said that things do not abide, like pearls rolling on a board. However, now a mountain goat hangs by its horns in emptiness. The forest runs around the hunting dog.

Xuedou, Zen Master Mingjiao of the Zisheng Monastery on Mount Xuedou, Qingyuan Prefecture, is an heir of Beita Guangzuo. (His priest name is Zhongxian.) Once, he said:

Reaching out your arms is climbing the ten-
    thousand-foot cliff.
Oneness and differentiation are not necessarily fixed.
The old lapis lazuli hall brightly illuminates the
    moon.
A fierce dog tiptoes up the stairs of emptiness.

Xuedou is a third-generation dharma descendant of Yunmen. He should be called a mature skin bag. By saying *Reaching out your arms is climbing the ten-thousand-foot cliff,* he seems to show an extraordinary mark, but it is not necessarily so. The matter discussed between the monk and Dongshan is not necessarily limited to extending the arms, not extending the arms, going into the world, or not going into the world. Furthermore, why did he emphasize the words *differentiation* and *oneness*? It seems that Xuedou could not deal with this matter without the view of differentiation and oneness. The reason he does not grasp this study by the nose is that he has not reached the neighborhood of Dongshan and does not see the great house of buddha dharma. He should take up his sandals and inquire further. Do not mistakenly say that Dongshan's buddha dharma is the Five Ranks of oneness and differentiation.

———————

Tianning, Zen Master Changling, Shouzhuo of the Tianning Monastery in Dongjing, wrote a poem on this case:

> Within differentiation there is oneness.
> Within oneness there is differentiation.
> Drifting in the human world hundreds and
>   thousands of years,
> again and again we want to depart but cannot.
> In front of the gate just as before, weeds abound.

Although he talks about differentiation and oneness, somehow he has touched it. Indeed there is something he has touched. What is within differentiation?

———————

Fuxing of Mount Gui, Tan Region, is an heir of Yuanwu. (His priest name is Fatai.) He said:

> The place where there is no cold or heat leads to you.
> A decayed tree brings forth blossoms once again.
> It's like looking at the mark on the boat for the sword
>   dropped into the water.
> Even now you are in the midst of cold ash.

These words have some power of crushing the fundamental point underfoot while raising it overhead.

———————

Letan Zhantang, Zen Master Wenzhun, said:

> When it is hot, heat prevails; in cold, cold prevails.
> From the beginning, cold and heat do not interfere
>   with each other.

Moving through the heavens, you become well
versed in worldly affairs.
On your honorable head you wear a wild boar hat.

Now, I [Dogen] ask you, "What is not-interfering?" Answer quick, quick!

———————

Heshan, Zen Master Fudeng of Mount He, Hu Region (whose priest name is priest Shouxun), is an heir of Taiping Huiqin, Zen Master Fujian. He said:

"Where there is no cold or heat" is Dongshan's phrase.
This place is where a number of Zen persons get lost.
Go for fire when it is cold, and cool yourself when it is hot.
All your life you can avoid cold and heat.

Although Heshan is a dharma descendant of Wuzu Fayan, his words appear to be child's talk. However, *All your life you can avoid cold and heat* hints at his later maturity as a great old master. *All your life* is your entire life; *avoid cold and heat* is nothing other than dropping away body and mind.

———————

Various masters of different generations smacked their lips in presenting their capping verses, but they did not even come close to Dongshan. The reason is that they mistakenly talked about cooling off and warming up without understanding cold or heat in the everyday activities of buddha ancestors. This is most pitiful. What did they learn about cold or heat from their old masters? How sad that the ancestral way has declined!

Only after you understand the meaning of cold and heat, permeate the moment of cold and heat, and activate cold and heat, should you add a capping verse to explain the words of Dongshan. Otherwise, you are not as good as those who know nothing. Even in the secular world the understanding of sun and moon, and how to abide with all things, varies according to sages, learned people, virtuous people, and ignorant people.

Don't think that cold and heat in the buddha way are the same as the cold and heat that ignorant people talk about. Investigate this directly.

Presented twice to the assembly in a deep mountain of Echizen in the second year of the Kangen Era [1244]. At the moment of meeting Buddha, the Unicorn Sutra is expounded. An ancestor [Qingyuan commenting on Shitou] said, "Although there are many horns, a single horn is sufficient."

67

THE MEANING OF BODHIDHARMA COMING FROM INDIA

XIANGYAN, GREAT MASTER Xideng of the Xiangyan Monastery, whose priest name was Zhixian, was a dharma heir of Guishan.

He once said to the assembly, "What if you are hanging by your teeth from a tree branch on a one-thousand-foot cliff, with no place for your hands or feet to reach. All of a sudden someone under the tree asks you, 'What is the meaning of Bodhidharma coming from India?' If you open your mouth to respond, you will lose your life. If you don't respond, you don't attend to the question. Tell me, what would you do?"

Then, senior monk Zhao from Hutou came out and said, "Master, I will not ask you about being in a tree. But tell me, what happens before climbing the tree?"

Xiangyan burst into laughter.

Many people have investigated and discussed this case, but few have spoken penetrating words about it. Most have been dumbfounded.

However, if we think about this case by taking up not-thinking and beyond thinking, we can have the experience of sharing a cushion with

Old Man Xiangyan. If you sit steadfastly together with Xiangyan on the same cushion, you must understand this case thoroughly before he opens his mouth. Seeing it thoroughly, you will not only steal Xiangyan's eyeball, but also take up Shakyamuni Buddha's treasury of the true dharma eye.

Now, quietly examine the words *What if you are hanging by your teeth from a tree branch on a one-thousand-foot cliff?* What is *you*?

Do not see a pillar as separate from a stake. Do not miss encountering self and other in the smile of a buddha face, an ancestor face. The tree from which you are hanging is neither the entire great earth nor the top of a one-hundred-foot pole. It is a one-thousand-foot cliff. You drop away within the one-thousand-foot cliff.

There is time to fall from the tree as well as to climb it. *What if you are hanging by your teeth from a tree branch on a one-thousand-foot cliff?* Know that there was the time you climbed it.

Thus, going up is one thousand feet, going down is one thousand feet. Going toward the left is one thousand feet, going toward the right is one thousand feet. Here is one thousand feet, there is one thousand feet. You are one thousand feet, climbing is one thousand feet. The one thousand feet spoken of is just like this.

Let me ask you: what is the size of one thousand feet? Let me say it is just like the size of an old mirror, a furnace, or a seamless tower.

By your teeth from a tree branch. What are the teeth? Even if you don't know the entire mouth opening, you should first look for the branch, check its leaves, and know where your mouth is. What grasps the branch are the teeth. Thus, the entire teeth are the branch, the entire branch is the teeth. The whole body is the mouth. The whole mouth is the whole body.

The tree steps on the tree. Thus, it is said that the feet don't step on the tree; the feet step on themselves. The branch climbs on itself. Thus, it is said that the hands do not climb on the branch; the hands climb on themselves. This being so, the heels step forward and backward; the hand makes a fist and opens.

People here and there think that this case is about hanging in emptiness. But is hanging in emptiness the same as hanging from a tree by your teeth?

All of a sudden someone under the tree asks you, "What is the meaning of Bodhidharma coming from India?" This line may suggest that there is someone under the tree. It may be a person tree. There is a person under a person. Thus, the tree questions the tree. The person questions the person. The entire tree is the entire question. This is taking up the meaning of Bodhidharma coming from India by inquiring, *What is the meaning of Bodhidharma coming from India?*

The one who is inquiring also hangs from the tree by the teeth and questions. Without hanging from the tree by the teeth, the questioning is not possible, the voice does not fill the mouth, and the mouth is not filled with words. When you ask the meaning of Bodhidharma coming from India, you ask, while hanging by your teeth, the meaning of Bodhidharma coming from India.

If you open your mouth to respond, you will lose your life. Now, examine intimately the words *if you open your mouth to respond.* It is said that there is a way to respond by not opening your mouth. Then you will not lose your life.

Opening or not opening your mouth does not hinder *hanging by your teeth from a tree branch.* Opening and closing are not necessarily the activity of the entire mouth. But the entire mouth opens or closes. Thus, hanging by your teeth is the entire mouth's everyday activity. Opening or closing does not hinder the entire mouth.

Does *open your mouth to respond* mean to respond by opening the branch or by opening the meaning of Bodhidharma coming from India? If the response does not open the meaning of Bodhidharma coming from India, it does not respond to the question. The entire body maintains life, and we cannot say you will lose your life. If you have already lost your life, you cannot respond.

However, what Xiangyan meant was that you should dare to respond and just lose your life.

Know that when you don't respond, you maintain life; when you respond, you twirl your body and vitalize life. From this we see that each person filling the mouth is expression. Respond to another, respond to yourself. Ask another, ask yourself. This is hanging on expression by the teeth. Hanging on expression *by your teeth* is *hanging by your teeth from a tree branch.* Responding to another is opening the mouth in the mouth.

Not responding to another does not attend to the other's question, but it does attend to your own question.

Thus, know that buddhas and ancestors who respond to the question, *What is the meaning of Bodhidharma coming from India?* all respond at the very moment of hanging by their teeth from a tree branch. Buddhas and ancestors who ask, *What is the meaning of Bodhidharma coming from India?* all ask the question at the very moment of hanging by their teeth from a tree branch .

———————

Xuedou, Priest Zhongxian, also called Zen Master Mingjiao, said, "Speaking in a tree is easy, but speaking under the tree is difficult. I am already in a tree. Bring me your question."

Regarding *bring me your question*, however hard one tries, it is regrettable that the question comes slowly and that it comes after the answer.

Let me ask the old gimlets throughout past and present: Xiangyan's bursting into laughter—is it speaking in the tree or speaking under the tree? Is it or is it not responding to the question, *What is the meaning of Bodhidharma coming from India?* Tell me, how do you see it?

Presented to the assembly in a deep mountain of Echizen Province on the fourth day, the second month, the second year of the Kangen Era [1244].

68

UDUMBARA BLOSSOM

AT THE ASSEMBLY of a million beings on Vulture Peak, the World-Honored One held up an udumbara blossom and blinked. Then, Mahakashyapa smiled. The World-Honored One said, "I have the treasury of the true dharma eye, the wondrous heart of nirvana. I entrust it to Mahakashyapa."

The Seven Original Buddhas and all buddhas equally hold up this flower. They realize and manifest holding up the flower of going beyond. They break open and clarify holding up the flower right at this moment. This being so, going beyond and going within, self and other, and the going forward and going back of holding up the flower are altogether holding up the entire flower. This is flower dimension, buddha dimension, mind dimension, and body dimension.

No matter how many times a flower is held up, it is transmission and entrusting [of the dharma] face to face, heir to heir. The World-Honored One's holding up the flower has not been abandoned. Your holding up the flower that the World-Honored One held up is your inheriting the World-Honored One. As the moment of holding up the flower is throughout time, you are with the World-Honored One, holding up the flower.

Holding up a flower means a flower holding up a flower. The flower can be a plum blossom, spring blossom, snow blossom, or lotus. The five petals of a plum blossom are three hundred sixty or more assemblies, five thousand forty-eight fascicles [of sutras], Three Vehicles and Twelve Divisions [of the Buddha's teaching], as well as three types and ten stages of bodhisattvas. And yet, it is beyond the understanding of three types and ten stages of bodhisattvas.

In this flower, there is a great basket [of scriptures], there is something extraordinary. This is called "the world of blossoming flowers arises."

"One flower opens five petals. The fruit matures of itself" [from a verse by Bodhidharma] means the entire body upholds the entire body. Seeing peach blossoms and smashing the eyeball, or hearing the sound of green bamboo and obscuring the ear consciousness, is the right now of holding up the flower. Cutting the arm in deep snow, or bowing and attaining the marrow, is the unfolding of the blossom of itself. Husking rice in the stone mortar and having a robe transmitted deep in the night is the flower holding up itself. All these are the life root in the hand of the World-Honored One.

Now, holding up a flower existed before the World-Honored One attained enlightenment. It took place at the same time that the World-Honored One attained enlightenment. It has taken place after he attained enlightenment. In this way the flower attains enlightenment. Holding up the flower goes beyond these times. Arousing the aspiration for enlightenment and receiving initiation, as well as practice, realization, and continuation, all stir up the spring wind of holding up the flower.

Thus, Gautama, the World-Honored One, entered the flower and hid in emptiness. He must have held up the nostrils. He did hold up the void and called it holding up the flower. Holding up the flower is holding it up with the eyeball, with mind consciousness, with the nostrils, and with holding up the flower.

Mountains, rivers, sun, moon, wind, and rain, as well as humans, animals, grass, and trees—each and all has been held up. This is holding up the flower. The coming and going of birth and death is a variety of blossoms and their colors. For us to study in this way is holding up the blossom.

The Buddha said [in the *Lotus Sutra*], "It is like an udumbara blossom. All beings love and enjoy it."

All beings here means buddha ancestors who manifest or hide their bodies. Grass, trees, and insects all have radiant light. *Love and enjoy it* means that the skin, flesh, bones, and marrow of each one of them is vital now. Thus, all are the udumbara blossom. That is why it is so extraordinary.

———————

Blinking takes place when the Tathagata sits through under the tree and replaces his eyeball with the morning star. At that moment Mahakashyapa smiles. His face immediately changes and is replaced with the face of taking up the flower.

When the Tathagata blinks, our eyeball is immediately smashed. This blinking of the Tathagata is itself taking up the flower. It is the udumbara flower opening of itself.

At the very moment of taking up the flower, all Gautamas, all Mahakashyapas, all sentient beings, all of us hold up a single hand and together take up the flower. This has never ceased till now. Within this hand is the samadhi of hiding the body, which is called the four great elements and the five skandhas.

I have is entrusting. Entrusting is *I have*. Entrusting is always immersed in *I have*. *I have* is the head top. You study *I have* by grasping the measurement of the head top. When you take up *I have* and replace it with entrusting, you uphold the treasury of the true dharma eye.

———————

Bodhidharma coming from India is holding up a flower. Holding up a flower is called playing with the spirit. Playing with the spirit is just sitting, dropping away body and mind. To become a buddha and to become an ancestor is called playing with the spirit. To put on a robe and to eat a meal is called playing with the spirit. Buddhas and ancestors mastering cases [of study] is no other than playing with the spirit. You are encountered by the buddha hall and you encounter the monks' hall. That is for the flower to deepen its color and for the color to add the brightness.

Further, you take up the han in the monks' hall and strike it in the cloud, or you hold the flute in the buddha hall and play it at the bottom of water. This is when you happen to make a tune of plum blossoms.

———————

Thus, Rujing, my late master, Old Buddha, said:

> When Gautama's eyeball is smashed,
> plum blossoms in snow, just one branch,
> become thorn bushes, here, everywhere, right now.
> Laughing, spring wind blows madly.

Now, the Tathagata's eyeball happened to be a plum blossom. The plum blossom forms thorns that spread all over. The Tathagata hides his body inside this eyeball, inside the plum blossom. The plum blossom hides itself in the thorns, then it blows spring wind. Thus it rejoices in plum blossom music.

Rujing said:

> What Lingyun saw are open peach blossoms.
> What I see is fallen peach blossoms.

Know that Lingyun had realization upon seeing the open peach blossoms. His direct experience should not be doubted. The fallen peach blossoms are what Rujing saw. The opening of peach blossoms is stimulated by the spring wind. The falling of peach blossoms is regretted by the spring wind. However deeply regretted by the spring wind, the peach blossoms fall and drop away one's body and mind.

Presented to the assembly, while residing at the Yoshimine Temple, Echizen Province, on the twelfth day, the second month, the second year of the Kangen Era [1244].

69

AROUSING THE ASPIRATION FOR THE UNSURPASSABLE

THE HIGH ANCESTOR of India [Shakyamuni Buddha] said, "The Snow Mountains [the Himalayas] are like great nirvana."

Know that this is a precise analogy, intimate and direct. To take up *the Snow Mountains* is to speak of the Snow Mountains. To take up *great nirvana* is to speak of great nirvana.

———

Bodhidharma, the First Ancestor of China, said, "Mind is like wood and stone."

What is called *mind* here is the mind that is thusness, the mind of the entire earth, the mind of self and other. The mind of buddha ancestors in the ten directions, the mind of heavenly dragons, and the mind of other beings are like wood and stone. There is no mind other than this.

The mind of wood and stone is not bound to the realms of existence, nonexistence, emptiness, or form. With the mind of wood and the mind of stone, you arouse the aspiration for enlightenment, practice, and actualize realization because your mind is wood and your mind is stone.

With the dynamic capacity of the mind of wood and the mind of stone, "thinking not-thinking" is actualized right now. As soon as you see and hear the wind [teaching] in the mind of wood and the mind of stone, you surpass the realms outside the way. There is no buddha way other than this.

———————

Huizhong, Great Master Dazheng, said, "Walls, tiles, and pebbles are the ancient buddha mind."

Study and see through the whereabouts of these walls, tiles, and pebbles. Ask, "What has manifested in this way?" The ancient buddha mind is not bound to the realm of the King of the Empty Eon. It is being satisfied with each meal. It is being satisfied with grass and water. Investigating in this way and sitting as a buddha, being a buddha, is called arousing the aspiration for enlightenment.

Now, the cause for the aspiration for enlightenment does not lie anywhere else. The aspiration for enlightenment is aroused by the aspiration for enlightenment itself. To arouse the aspiration for enlightenment is to pick up a blade of grass and manifest a buddha image, to take up a rootless tree and create a sutra.

To arouse the aspiration for enlightenment is to make an offering of sand or rice water to the Buddha. It is to make an offering of a handful of food to sentient beings. It is to make an offering of a bouquet of flowers to the Buddha. To practice a small virtuous act with the encouragement of someone else, or to bow to the Buddha following a demon's deceptive advice, is also arousing the aspiration for enlightenment.

Further, you abandon the household by realizing that your house is not a true house. You enter the mountain and practice dharma. You create a buddha image and build a stupa. You chant a sutra and recite the Buddha's name. You look for a teacher and inquire about the way. You sit in meditation posture. You bow to the three treasures. You recite homage to the Buddha.

Thus, eighty thousand skandhas [all phenomena] become the causes and conditions for arousing the aspiration for enlightenment. There are those who arouse the aspiration for enlightenment in a dream and attain the way. There are those who arouse the aspiration for enlightenment and attain the way while intoxicated. There are those who attain the way when they see flowers flying or leaves falling. Others attain the way among peach blossoms or green bamboo. Some attain the way in a deva realm or in the ocean. They all attain the way.

All these cases arouse the aspiration for enlightenment within arousing the aspiration for enlightenment, in body and mind, in the bodies and minds of all buddhas, in the skin, flesh, bones, and marrow of all buddhas.

This being so, building stupas, creating buddha images, and other practices right now are exactly arousing the aspiration for enlightenment, the aspiration for directly becoming a buddha. This should not be abandoned along the way. Such practices are called merit beyond purpose, merit beyond making. This is visualizing true thusness, visualizing dharma nature. This is integrating the samadhis of all buddhas. This is attaining the dharani of all buddhas. This is the heart of unsurpassable, complete enlightenment. This is the fruit of an arhat. This is the actualizing of a buddha. Other than this, there is no dharma beyond purpose and beyond doing.

———————

However, foolish people in the Lesser Vehicles say, "Creating images of the Buddha or building stupas is work of purposeful doing; this should be avoided. To give rest to thinking and focus the mind is free of doing. Not producing anything and not making anything is genuine practice. Visualizing dharma nature and its reality is a practice beyond doing."

To speak in this way has been a custom in India and China from ancient times to the present. Consequently, while people commit grave and serious crimes, they do not create buddha images or build stupas. While they are lost in a forest of delusion, they do not recite the Buddha's name or read sutras. They not only destroy the seeds of [rebirth as] humans or devas but also deny their own buddha nature, their own tathagata nature. How sad!

Although they have encountered the time of the buddha, dharma, and sangha, they have turned into the enemies of the buddha, dharma, and sangha. Although they have climbed the mountain of the three treasures, they return empty-handed. Although they have entered the ocean of the three treasures, they return empty-handed. That means they have encountered the emergence of a thousand buddhas and ten thousand ancestors, but they do not have the opportunity to cross over [to the shore of enlightenment], and miss the direction to arouse the aspiration for enlightenment. This occurs because they follow those outside the way and do not follow the sutras and true teachers.

Quickly abandon the view that building stupas and other practices do not arouse the aspiration for enlightenment. Cleanse your mind, body, ears, and eyes, and disregard such views. Just follow the buddha sutras, follow true teachers, take refuge in true dharma, and study buddha dharma.

In the great way of buddha dharma, there are thousands of sutras in one particle, there are countless buddhas in one particle. Both a blade of grass and a tree are the body and mind. Because myriad things are beyond birth, the one mind is beyond birth. Because all things are reality, one particle is reality. Thus, the one mind is all things. All things are the one mind, the entire body.

If building stupas and other practices were purposeful activity, then enlightenment, the fruit of awakening, and the buddha nature of true thusness would also be purposeful activity. Because the buddha nature of true thusness is not purposeful activity, building stupas and other practices are not purposeful activity. These activities are beyond purpose, beyond desire.

Know and trust that building stupas and related practices are no other than the aspiration for enlightenment. From this the vow of practice grows and does not decay for a billion eons. This is called seeing the Buddha and hearing the dharma.

Know that creating buddha images and building stupas by assembling wood and stone, piling up dirt, collecting gold, silver, and the seven treasures, is no other than creating buddha images and building stupas by assembling the one mind. This is creating buddha images by collecting emptiness on top of emptiness. This is creating buddha images by taking up mind on top of mind. This is building stupas by laying stupas on top of stupas. This is creating buddha images by actualizing buddhas on top of buddhas.

This being so, a sutra [the *Lotus Sutra*] says, "When this is contemplated, all buddhas in the ten directions emerge."

Know that when one contemplating buddha emerges, all contemplating buddhas in the ten directions emerge. When one thing becomes a buddha, all things become buddhas.

———————

Shakyamuni Buddha said, "When the morning star appeared, I attained the way simultaneously with all sentient beings and the great earth."

Thus, aspiration, practice, enlightenment, and nirvana must be *simultaneously* aspiration, practice, enlightenment, and nirvana [with all sentient beings]. The body and mind of the buddha way is grass, trees, tiles, and pebbles, as well as wind, rain, water, and fire. To turn them around and make them the buddha way—this is the aspiration for enlightenment.

Hold up empty space to build a stupa and create a buddha image. Scoop up valley water to build a stupa and create a buddha image. This is arousing the aspiration for unsurpassable, complete enlightenment. This is arousing for enlightenment one aspiration one hundred times, one thousand times, myriad times. This is practice and realization.

This being so, those who think that arousing the aspiration only happens once, although practice for attaining one realization happens innumerable times, have not heard, known, or encountered buddha dharma.

Arousing the aspiration for enlightenment one thousand times, one billion times, is not other than arousing the aspiration for enlightenment one time. Arousing the aspiration for enlightenment by one thousand billion people is not other than arousing one aspiration. Arousing the aspiration for enlightenment one time is arousing the aspiration for enlightenment one thousand times, one billion times. Practice, realization, and the turning of the dharma are also like this.

If you are not grass and trees, how can you have body and mind? If you are not body and mind, how can you be grass and trees? It is so because you cannot be grass and trees without being grass and trees.

Zazen, the endeavor of the way, is arousing the aspiration for enlightenment. Arousing the aspiration is neither one nor many. Zazen is neither one nor many, neither two nor three. It cannot be divided, either. Thoroughly investigate each and every zazen in this way.

If the process of assembling grass, trees, and the seven treasures to build a stupa and create a buddha image were a purposeful activity and not attaining the way, then the thirty-seven wings of enlightenment would also be a purposeful activity; endeavoring in the practice with the bodies and minds of humans and devas of the three realms would also be a purposeful activity and would not enable you to arrive at the ultimate ground of enlightenment.

Grass, trees, tiles, and pebbles, as well as the four great elements and the five skandhas, are all equally inseparable mind, equally marks of reality. The entire world of the ten directions, the buddha nature of thusness, is equally things abiding in their conditions.

How can there be grass, trees, and so on within the buddha nature of thusness? How can grass, trees, and so on not be buddha nature? All things are neither created nor not created, but are reality. Reality is reality as it is.

Thusness is the body and mind right now. Arouse the aspiration with this body and mind. Do not avoid stepping on water and stepping on stones. To take up just one blade of grass and create a sixteen-foot golden body, or to take up a particle of dust and build a stupa shrine of an ancient buddha, arouses the aspiration for enlightenment. It is to see buddha and hear buddha. It is to see dharma and hear dharma. It is to become buddha and practice buddha.

———————

Shakyamuni Buddha said, "Laymen, laywomen, good men, and good women make an offering of their spouses and children to the three treasures. They make an offering of themselves to the three treasures. All monks receive such faithful offerings. How can you, monks, not practice diligently?"

Know that [laypeople] offering food and drink, clothes, bedding, medicine, monk's huts, fields, and forests to the three treasures is no other than offering the flesh, skin, bones, and marrow of themselves, their spouses, or their children. By doing so, they are already in the meritorious ocean of the three treasures. They are in one community. As they are in one community, they are with the three treasures. The virtue of the three treasures is actualized in the skin, flesh, bones, and marrow of their spouses and children. This is diligent endeavor of the way.

Right now, take up the essence and form of the World-Honored One and grasp the skin, flesh, bones, and marrow of the buddha way. This faithful offering arouses the aspiration. How can monks who receive such an offering not diligently practice from beginning to end?

Thus, when a particle arouses the aspiration, one mind follows and arouses the aspiration. When one mind follows and arouses the aspiration, one emptiness follows and arouses the aspiration. When you, whether learned or not learned, arouse the aspiration, you acquire the seed of one buddha nature.

When you turn the four great elements and the five skandhas and practice sincerely, you attain the way. When you turn grass, trees, tiles, and walls, and practice sincerely, you attain the way. It is so because the four great elements and the five skandhas, as well as grass, trees, tiles, and walls, practice together with you. They have the same nature, the same mind and life, the same body and capacity as you.

This being so, many of those who come from the assembly of buddha ancestors endeavor in the way of taking up grass and having the heart of trees. This is how it is with arousing the aspiration for enlightenment.

———————

Hongren, who would later become the Fifth Chinese Ancestor, was once a practitioner who planted pine trees. Linji practiced planting pine and cedar trees on Mount Huangbo. Old Man Liu planted pine trees on Mount Dong. These practitioners took up the purity of pine and cypress and plucked out an eyeball of buddha ancestors. This is actualizing the power of playing with and opening the vital eyeball. Building a stupa and creating a buddha image are playing with an eyeball, tasting the aspiration, and letting the aspiration be aroused.

Without attaining the eyeball of building a stupa and so on, buddha ancestors would not attain the way. Only after attaining the eyeball of creating a buddha image do you become a buddha and become an ancestor.

To say, "Building a stupa and so on, which will turn into dust, is not true merit. On the other hand, to train to be beyond birth is a solid practice, which cannot be defiled by dust," is not the Buddha's words. If you say that a stupa will turn to dust, then what is beyond birth will also turn to dust. If what is beyond birth does not turn to dust, a stupa will not turn to dust. What is this place of dust? Do you call it purposefully made or not?

———

A sutra [the *Avatamsaka Sutra*] says:

> Upon first arousing the aspiration in birth and
>   death,
> the bodhisattva wholeheartedly seeks enlightenment
> solidly without being swayed.
> The merit of this single intention is so deep and
>   boundless
> that even in countless eons the Tathagata cannot
>   fully explain it.

Clearly know that taking up birth and death to arouse the aspiration is *wholeheartedly seeks enlightenment*. This single intention should be the same as one blade of grass and one tree; they are one birth and one death.

The merit of this single intention is deep without boundary, vast without boundary. Even if the Tathagata tries to comprehend it using countless eons as words, it cannot be fully exhausted. It is inexhaustible just as the bottom remains when the ocean dries up, or the heart remains after a person dies.

Just as the single intention is deep and boundless, one blade of grass, one tree, one stone, or one tile is deep and boundless. If a blade of grass or a stone is seven or eight feet, the single intention is seven or eight feet. Arousing the aspiration is also seven or eight feet.

Thus, going deeply into a mountain and contemplating the buddha way are easy. Building a stupa and creating a buddha image are very difficult. Both types of practice require endeavor without slack. But the practice of taking up mind [contemplation] and the practice taken up by the mind [building a stupa and so on] are far apart from each other. In this way, arousing the aspiration for enlightenment accumulates, actualizing buddha ancestors.

> *Presented to the assembly of the Yoshimine Temple, Yoshida County, Echizen Province on the fourteenth day, the second month, the second year of the Kangen Era [1244].*

70

AROUSING THE ASPIRATION
FOR ENLIGHTENMENT

THERE ARE THREE types of consciousness: One is chitta, which is called "discerning mind." Another is hridaya [heart], which is translated as "grass and tree consciousness." The last is vriddha [center, essence], which is translated as "essential assembling consciousness."

Among these types of consciousness, discerning mind is used for arousing the aspiration for bodhi [bodhichitta]. *Bodhi* [enlightenment] is an Indian word, translated into Chinese as *dao* [way or enlightenment]. *Chitta* is also an Indian word, meaning in this case "discerning mind." Without discerning mind, the aspiration for enlightenment cannot be aroused. It is not that discerning mind is the aspiration for enlightenment, but that the aspiration for enlightenment is aroused with discerning mind.

Arousing the aspiration for enlightenment is making a vow to bring all sentient beings [to the shore of enlightenment] before you bring yourself, and actualizing the vow. Even a humble person who arouses this aspiration is already a guiding teacher of all sentient beings.

This aspiration is neither originally existent nor does it emerge all of a sudden. It is neither one nor many. It is neither spontaneous nor formed gradually. This aspiration is not in yourself, nor are you in it.

This aspiration is not pervasive in this world of phenomena. It is neither before nor after. It is neither existent nor nonexistent. It is neither self nature nor other nature. It is neither common nature nor causeless nature.

Yet, in response to affinity [between the teacher and the student], the aspiration for enlightenment arises. It is not given by buddhas or bodhisattvas, and it is not created by yourself. The aspiration arises in response to affinity, thus it is not spontaneous.

This aspiration for enlightenment has been aroused mostly by humans who live in the Southern Continent, Jambudvipa. It has also been aroused by those who abide in the eight difficult situations [to attain enlightenment], but not by most of them.

After arousing the aspiration for enlightenment, bodhisattvas practice for many eons, for one hundred great eons. They practice for countless eons, become buddhas, awaken, and benefit sentient beings through this bodhisattva determination. Or, they practice for countless eons for the benefit of sentient beings, enjoying their bodhisattva determination to help sentient beings cross over before they themselves cross over and become buddhas.

The meaning of the aspiration for enlightenment is to endeavor without ceasing—in body, speech, and thought—to help all sentient beings to arouse the aspiration for enlightenment. This leads them into the buddha way. To provide sentient beings merely with worldly pleasure is not beneficial to them.

Arousing such aspiration, and the practice-realization of it, goes far beyond the boundary of practice and realization, delusion and enlightenment. It excels in the three realms and is outstanding among all things. It is not anything that shravakas and pratyeka-buddhas can reach.

———————

Kashyapa Bodhisattva [Mahakashyapa] extolled Shakyamuni Buddha with a verse:

Although beginner's mind and ultimate mind are
    indistinguishable,
the beginner's mind is more difficult.
I bow to the beginner's mind
that lets others awaken first.
Already a teacher of humans and devas,
the beginner's mind excels the mind of
a shravaka or of a pratyeka-buddha.
Such aspiration is outstanding in the three realms,
so it is called unsurpassable.

Arousing the aspiration means to intend to awaken others before yourself. This is called the beginner's aspiration for enlightenment. After arousing this aspiration, you encounter and make offerings to see buddhas. You see buddhas, hear dharma, and arouse further aspiration for enlightenment. It is just like adding frost on top of snow.

The *ultimate mind* means attaining enlightenment, the buddha fruit. If you compare unsurpassable, complete enlightenment with the beginner's aspiration for enlightenment, it is like comparing a blaze that destroys the world with the blinking of a firefly. Yet, if you arouse the intention of awakening others first, these two are *indistinguishable*.

———

[The *Lotus Sutra* says:] "I [the Tathagata] always hold in mind how to help sentient beings enter the unsurpassable way and immediately attain buddha bodies."

This is exactly the timeless activity of the Tathagata in his aspiration, practice, and fruit of realization.

To benefit sentient beings is to help them arouse the aspiration to awaken other sentient beings before awakening themselves. Do not think of yourself as becoming a buddha by helping people to arouse the aspiration to awaken others before awakening themselves. Even when your merit for becoming a buddha has matured, you turn it around and dedicate it to others so that they may become buddhas, attaining the way.

This aspiration is not self, not other, and does not come from somewhere else. However, after arousing this aspiration, when taking up the great earth, all of it turns into gold; when stirring the great ocean, it immediately turns into nectar. After arousing this aspiration, if you hold mud, stones, or pebbles, they also take up the aspiration for enlightenment; if you practice splashes of water, bubbles, or flames, they intimately bring forth the aspiration for enlightenment. Thus, the offering of land, castles, spouses, children, men and women, the seven treasures, heads, eyes, marrow, brains, bodies, flesh, and limbs, is crowded with arousing the aspiration for enlightenment, the vital activity of the aspiration for enlightenment.

Although chitta is neither near nor far, neither self nor other, if you are unremitting in the aspiration for awakening others first with this chitta, this is arousing the aspiration for enlightenment. Thus, the offering of grass, trees, tiles, pebbles, gold, silver, and the rare treasures that sentient beings cling to as their own possessions, to the aspiration for enlightenment—is this not also arousing the aspiration for enlightenment?

It is not without cause that minds and all things, self and other, come together; therefore, at the moment you arouse the aspiration for enlightenment, myriad things become conditions that increase this aspiration. At each moment, all aspirations for enlightenment and attainments of the way are born and perish. If they were not born and did not perish at each moment, the unwholesome actions of the past moments would not go away. If the unwholesome actions in the past moments did not go away, wholesome actions in their future moments would not manifest at this moment.

The scale of this moment can only be known by the Tathagata. "The mind of this moment manifests one word. The word of this moment expounds one letter" [as in the *Abhidharma Mahavibhasha Shastra*].

This can only be done by the Tathagata, and not by other sages.

There are sixty-five moments when a strong person snaps the fingers and the five skandhas are born and perish. Ordinary people are not aware of it.

Ordinary people know about the moments as uncountable as the sands of the Ganges. But they are not aware that there are six billion four hundred million ninety-nine thousand nine hundred eighty moments within one day and night when the five skandhas are born and perish.

Because they are not aware of this, they do not arouse the aspiration for enlightenment. Those who do not know and do not believe in buddha dharma do not believe in birth and death at each moment. On the other hand, those who clarify the Tathagata's treasury of the true dharma eye, the wondrous heart of nirvana, believe in this principle of birth and death moment by moment.

You now encounter the Tathagata's teaching and appear to clarify matters, but you may only know moments for being as uncountable as the sands of the Ganges and may believe that time works in this way. You may not understand the entire teaching of the World-Honored One, just as you may not know the scale of a moment. Those of you who study should not be proud of yourselves. You may not know what is extremely small or extremely large.

If sentient beings rely on the Tathagata's ability of the way, they see one billion worlds. From the present existence you reach an intermediary existence, and from an intermediary existence you reach a future existence, passing through moment by moment. In this way, beyond your intention, you pass through birth and death driven by your karma, without stopping even for a moment.

With the body and mind that migrate through birth and death, you should arouse the aspiration for enlightenment to awaken others first. Even if you spare your body and mind from the way of arousing the aspiration for enlightenment in the course of birth, aging, sickness, and death, you cannot in the end keep them as your own possessions.

———————

The life of a sentient being changes swiftly through birth and death without ceasing.

During the lifetime of the World-Honored One, a monk visited him, bowed to the ground, touching his feet, looked at him, and said, "How fast does the life of a sentient being change through birth and death?"

The Buddha said, "I can explain it, but you won't understand it."

The monk said, "Would you show it to me by an analogy?"

The Buddha said, "Let me explain it to you. It is like four excellent archers who take their bows and arrows and stand together back to back. When they are about to shoot, a fast runner comes up to them and says, 'Shoot your arrows all at once. I will catch all of them without dropping a single one to the ground.' What do you think of this man? Is he not fast?"

The monk said, "Yes, World-Honored One, he is very fast."

The Buddha said, "This man is not as fast as a demon who runs on the ground. This demon is not as fast as a flying demon. This flying demon is not as fast as the Four Deva Kings. These deva kings are not as fast as the sun and the moon. The sun and the moon are not as fast as the devas who pull the cart of the sun and the moon. These devas fly around very fast. However, the change of life through birth and death is faster than these devas. It flows moment by moment without stopping."

How our life changes moment by moment, flowing through birth and death, is like this. You practitioners should not forget it for even an instant of thought. If you arouse the thought of bringing others across first while in this swift change through birth and death, a timeless life span is immediately actualized.

All buddhas of the ten directions in the past, present, and future, including the Seven Original Buddhas, the World-Honored Ones; the twenty-eight ancestors of India; the six early ancestors of China; as well as other ancestors who transmit the Buddha's treasury of the true dharma eye, the wondrous heart of nirvana, have all maintained the aspiration for enlightenment. Those who have not aroused the aspiration for enlightenment are not ancestors.

The one hundred twentieth question in the *Guidelines for Zen Monasteries* says, "Have you realized the aspiration for enlightenment?"

Know that the study of the way of buddha ancestors invariably makes realizing the aspiration for enlightenment a priority. This is customary for buddha ancestors.

Realized the aspiration means to become clear about it. It is not great enlightenment. Even if you suddenly realize the ten stages [of bodhisattvas], still you are a bodhisattva. The twenty-eight ancestors of India, the six early ancestors of China, and all other great ancestors are in fact bodhisattvas, and not buddhas, shravakas, or pratyeka-buddhas.

Those who study the way nowadays are bodhisattvas and not shra-vakas. Not one of them has clarified it. They groundlessly call themselves monks or robe wearers but don't know who they are. What a pity that the ancient ancestral way has declined!

However, whether you are a layperson, a home leaver, a deva, or a human, whether you are suffering or in bliss, you should quickly arouse the aspiration for bringing others across before yourself. Although the realm of sentient beings is neither bounded nor boundless, you should arouse the aspiration for bringing others across before yourself. This is the aspiration for enlightenment.

Before descending to the Jambudvipa Continent, a bodhisattva who is a candidate to be a buddha gives the final discourse in Tushita Heaven and says, "The aspiration for enlightenment is a gate of clarifying dharma; it does not cut off the three treasures."

We clearly know in this way that *not cut off the three treasures* is the power of the aspiration for enlightenment. After arousing the aspiration for enlightenment, guard it tightly without relenting.

———————

The Buddha said:

What is the one thing that bodhisattvas guard? It is the aspiration for enlightenment. Bodhisattvas, great beings, always endeavor to guard this aspiration for enlightenment just as people in the world protect their only child. It is like a one-eyed person protecting the working eye, or people traveling in a vast wilderness protecting their guide. Bodhisattvas guard the aspiration for enlightenment in this way.

Because bodhisattvas guard the aspiration for enlightenment, they attain unsurpassable, complete enlightenment. Because bodhisattvas attain unsurpassable, complete enlightenment, they embody consistency, enjoyment, freedom, and purity. This is unsurpassable great pari-nirvana. Thus, bodhisattvas guard this one thing.

The Buddha's words about guarding the aspiration for enlighten-ment are like this. The reason for guarding it without relenting is that, as is commonly known, there are three things that can be born but that are hard to ripen. They are fish eggs, myrobalan fruit, and the aspiration of bodhisattvas. As there are many who turn away and lose their aspiration, you should always be careful not to lose your aspiration. For this reason, you guard your aspiration for enlightenment.

Often, the reason beginning bodhisattvas lose their aspiration for enlightenment is that they haven't met authentic teachers. If they don't meet authentic teachers, they don't listen to true dharma. If they don't listen to true dharma, they deny cause and effect, emancipation, the three treasures, and all things in the present and future. Then, they are wastefully attached to the five desires of the present moment and lose the possibility of enlightenment in the future.

In order to distract a practicing bodhisattva, Demon Papiyas or someone like him disguises himself as the Buddha or a parent, teacher, relative, or deva, approaches the bodhisattva, and makes up a statement like: "The buddha way is long, far away, and painful, which is most worrisome. It's best to become free from birth and death first, then bring across sentient beings." Hearing these words, practitioners turn away from their aspiration for enlightenment and their bodhisattva practice.

Know that such words are a demon's statement. Bodhisattvas should be aware of this and not follow such words. Never give up the vow of practice to awaken other sentient beings first. Know that any words that are against this vow are a statement of demons, those outside the way, or unwholesome friends. Do not pay attention to such words.

———

[The *Treatise on Realization of Great Wisdom* by Nagarjuna says:]

There are four types of demons: demons of delusions, demons of the five skandhas, demons of death, and the celestial king of demons.

"Demons of delusions" include those of one hundred eight delusions. They can be classified as eighty-four thousand delusions.

"Demons of the five skandhas" are causes and conditions of delusions interacting with one another. They come from the four great elements, as well as from things consisting of the four elements in the body and the root of the eyes. They are called the "form skandha."

The perception of all things, including one hundred eight delusions, is called the "perception skandha." Innumerable large and small feelings interacting, including a sense of possession, are called the "feeling skandha."

The suitable and unsuitable mental activity that arouses greed and anger, based on the mind of liking and disliking, is called the "inclination skandha."

The six sense organs and their objects interact with one another and cause six types of consciousness. These six types of consciousness interact with one another and form immeasurable, boundless mind. This is called the "discernment skandha."

"Demons of death" means that, because of the impermanence of all things, the life span of the five skandhas, as well as the three matters—consciousness, warmth, and life that has lasted thus far—are destroyed. This is why they are called "demons of death."

The "celestial king of demons" is the lord of the desire realm. As he is deeply attached to worldly pleasures and the love of possessing things, he arouses crooked views and is jealous of the practice of all sages' path of nirvana. This is called the "celestial king of demons."

Mara (demon) is an Indian word. In China it is translated as "Taker of Life." Although demons of death can take people's lives, other demons can also take life, as well as the life of wisdom. This is why they are called "Killers."

Question: The demons of the five skandhas include three other types of demons. Why are they classified as four types of demons?

Answer: They are indeed one type of demon. But in order to show [their] various aspects, they are explained as four types.

These are Ancestor Nagarjuna's explanations. You practitioners should be aware of them and study them diligently. Do not be tempted by demons and lose your guard, turning away from the aspiration for enlightenment. This is called guarding the aspiration for enlightenment.

Presented to the assembly of the Yoshimine Temple, Yoshida County, Echizen Province, on the fourteenth day, the second month, the second year of the Kangen Era [1244].

71

TATHAGATA'S ENTIRE BODY

ONCE, ON VULTURE PEAK in Rajagraha, Shakyamuni Buddha said to Bhaishajyaraja Bodhisattva Mahasattva:

> Bhaishajyaraja, wherever a sutra is expounded, read, chanted, copied, or kept, a seven-treasure stupa, tall, wide, and solemn, is erected, but do not enshrine the Buddha's relics in it. The reason is that a stupa embodies the Tathagata's entire body. Make offerings of all sorts of flowers, incense, jewels, canopies, banners, music, and chanting verses to respect, revere, and admire the stupa. When people see this stupa, bow, and make offerings to it, they know that they are closer to unsurpassable, complete enlightenment.

In this way, a sutra is expounded, read, chanted, and copied. A sutra is reality. To build *a seven-treasure stupa* is to build reality. The stupa's height and breadth are the scale of reality. *A stupa embodies the Tathagata's entire body* means a stupa is the Tathagata's entire body.

Thus, expounding, reading, chanting, copying, and so on, are the Tathagata's entire body. *Make offerings of all sorts of flowers, incense, jewels, canopies, banners, music, and chanting verses to respect, revere, and admire the stupa.* Or, offer heavenly flowers, heavenly incense, and heavenly canopies, and so on. These are all marks of reality. Or, offer excellent flowers, excellent incense, renowned robes, and renowned garments of the human realm. These are all marks of reality.

A stupa *is erected, but do not enshrine the Buddha's relics in it:* from this we know that a sutra is the relics of the Tathagata, the entire body of the Tathagata.

There is no greater merit than seeing and hearing golden words uttered by the Buddha. Hurry up and accumulate effort and virtue. When you see people bow and make offerings to the stupa, know that *they are closer to unsurpassable, complete enlightenment.* When you see the tower, sincerely bow and make offerings to it. Thus, all come *closer to* unsurpassable, complete enlightenment. *Closer to* is not come close to or go close to. Unsurpassable, complete enlightenment is all *closer to.*

Right now, when you see those who receive, chant, elucidate, and copy a sutra, you are seeing this stupa. Rejoice that all are close to unsurpassable, complete enlightenment.

This being so, a sutra is the Tathagata's entire body. To bow to a sutra is to bow to the Tathagata's entire body. To encounter a sutra is to encounter the Tathagata's entire body.

A sutra is the relics of the Tathagata. So, the relics of the Tathagata are a sutra. Even if you know that a sutra is the relics of the Tathagata, if you don't know that the relics of the Tathagata are a sutra, it is not the buddha way.

The reality of all things right now is a sutra. Human realms, deva realms, ocean, empty space, this land, and other lands are the reality of all things, a sutra, relics. Hold, chant, elucidate, and copy the relics and unfold enlightenment. This is to follow a sutra.

There are relics of ancient buddhas, present buddhas, pratyeka-buddhas, wheel-turning kings, and lions [kings of dharma], and there are relics of wooden buddhas and painted buddhas. There are also relics of humans. Nowadays, among buddha ancestors in China, there are those who manifest relics while they are alive, and there are many who manifest relics after being cremated. Such relics are all sutras.

Shakyamuni Buddha said to the assembly, "I practiced the bodhisattva path in my past life. The long life I have achieved by this has not been exhausted. My life span will be doubled in my future life."

The relics of eighty-four *to* [approximately twenty-five bushels] are no other than the Tathagata's timeless life. How much is the life span of one who practiced the bodhisattva path in the past life beyond the boundary of the billion worlds? This is the Tathagata's entire body, a sutra.

Prajna Kuta Bodhisattva said [in the *Lotus Sutra*], "I see that Shakyamuni Buddha was engaged in difficult and painful practice through innumerable eons, piling up effort, accumulating virtue, and ceaselessly pursuing the bodhisattva path. When I observe the billion worlds, there is not even a poppy seed that is not a place where this bodhisattva gave up his life for the sake of other beings. Thus, he achieved the path of enlightenment."

From this I know that the billion worlds are a piece of his compassionate heart, a bit of his boundless realm, the Tathagata's entire body. It is beyond whether he did or did not give up his life.

Relics are neither before nor after the Buddha, nor do they stand shoulder to shoulder with the Buddha. Being engaged in difficult and rigorous practice through innumerable eons is the Buddha's womb and abdomen activities, the Buddha's skin, flesh, bones, and marrow. This is spoken of as *ceaselessly*. He makes further effort after attaining buddhahood. He goes further and further, giving guidance to the billion worlds. This is the activity of the Tathagata's entire body.

Presented to the assembly of the Yoshimine Temple, Yoshida County, Echizen Province, on the fifteenth day, the second month, the second year of the Kangen Era [1244].

72

KING OF SAMADHIS

To transcend the world directly, to manifest the magnificence of the buddha ancestors' house—this is sitting in the meditation posture. To leap over the heads of outsiders and demons, and become a true person inside the buddha ancestors' room—this is sitting in the meditation posture. To sit in the meditation posture is to transcend the deepest and most intimate teaching of buddha ancestors. Thus, buddha ancestors practice this way without needing to do anything else.

Know that the world of sitting practice is far different from other worlds. Clarify this for yourself, then activate the aspiration, practice, enlightenment, and nirvana of the buddha ancestors. Study the world at the very moment of sitting. Is it vertical or horizontal? At the very moment of sitting, what is sitting? Is it an acrobat's graceful somersault or the rapid darting of a fish? Is it thinking or not thinking? Is it doing or not doing? Is it sitting within sitting? Is it sitting within body-mind? Is it sitting letting go of sitting within sitting, or letting go of sitting within body-mind? Investigate this in every possible way. Sit in the body's meditation posture. Sit in the mind's meditation posture. Sit in the meditation posture of letting go of body-mind.

Rujing, my late master, Old Buddha, said, "Practicing Zen is letting go of body and mind. It can only be done by wholehearted sitting; incense offering, bowing, chanting Buddha's name, repentance, and sutra reading are not pivotal."

Rujing is the only one in four or five hundred years who has plucked out the eye of the buddha ancestors, and sat down inside that eye. There are few in China who can stand shoulder to shoulder with him. Perhaps there are some who have understood that sitting is buddha dharma and buddha dharma is sitting. And perhaps there are some who have personally experienced that sitting is buddha dharma. But there is no one else who has personally experienced that sitting is sitting, and so there is no one else who upholds buddha dharma as buddha dharma.

Thus, there is sitting with the mind, which is not the same as sitting with the body. There is sitting with the body, which is not the same as sitting with the mind. There is sitting letting go of body-mind, which is not the same as sitting letting go of body-mind. To experience this is to merge the practice and understanding of the buddha ancestors. Maintain this insight. Investigate this awareness.

———————

Shakyamuni Buddha said to the assembly, "When you sit in the meditation posture, you realize samadhi in body and mind, and give rise to an awesome virtue that people respect. Like the sun illuminating and refreshing the world, this sitting removes obscurities from the mind and lightens the body so that exhaustion is set aside. Enlightenment becomes as natural as a dragon curled up at rest. A demon is frightened even by a picture of someone sitting in the meditation posture; how much more so by a living person who realizes the way sitting motionless and at ease."

As the Buddha said, a demon is startled and frightened by even a picture of someone sitting in the meditation posture and even more frightened by a living person sitting that way. So we know that the merit of such sitting is immeasurable. This ordinary everyday sitting is itself boundless joy.

Shakyamuni Buddha continued speaking to the assembly: "Therefore, you should sit in the meditation posture."

Then the Tathagata, the World-Honored One, taught his disciples how to sit and said to them:

> Some outsiders try to practice by standing on tiptoes, others by standing continuously, and still others by adopting the yoga posture of hooking their feet over their shoulders. These people develop unbalanced minds that flounder in an ocean of delusion because their postures are unnatural. Why do I teach my disciples to sit up straight in the meditation posture? Because it is easy to regulate the mind when the body is upright. If the body is straight, the mind is not dull. Instead, the mind is forthright, the intention is true, and mindfulness is present. If the mind scatters or the body leans, gather together your body-mind and resume the upright posture. If you want to manifest samadhi and enter it, you should gather together all distracted thought and scattered mind within this posture. Practice in this way and you will manifest and intimately enter the king of samadhis.

Thus, we clearly know that sitting in the meditation posture is itself the king of samadhis. It is itself entering realization. All other samadhis serve the king of samadhis.

———————

Sitting in the meditation posture is a forthright body, a forthright mind, a forthright body-mind, a forthright buddha ancestor, a forthright practice-realization, a forthright top of the head, and a forthright life stream.

When you sit in the meditation posture, the skin, flesh, bones, and marrow of a human being are immediately vivid in the king of samadhis. The World-Honored One always sat in this meditation posture, and all his disciples authentically transmitted it. The World-Honored One taught humans and devas how to sit in this meditation posture. It is the mind seal authentically transmitted by the Seven Original Buddhas.

Shakyamuni Buddha sat in this meditation posture under the bodhi tree for fifty small eons, sixty great eons, and innumerable unclassifiable eons. Perhaps he sat for three weeks, or maybe only for a few hours. In any case, the Buddha's zazen is the turning of the wondrous wheel of dharma; his lifetime guidance is contained within it. Nothing is lacking.

The yellow scrolls and red rolls of the sutras are all here. In this moment of sitting, buddha sees buddha and all beings attain buddhahood.

Soon after Bodhidharma, the First Chinese Ancestor, arrived from India, he sat zazen facing the wall in the meditation posture for nine years at the Shaolin Temple, Shaoshi Peak of Mount Song. Since then the head and eyeball of his practice have prevailed all over China. Bodhidharma's life stream is just this sitting in the meditation posture. Before he came from India, people in China had not truly known sitting in the meditation posture. But after he arrived, they came to know it. Thus, for one lifetime, for myriad lifetimes, from head to toe, without leaving the monastery and without concern for other activities, wholeheartedly sit in the meditation posture day and night—this is the king of samadhis.

Presented to the assembly of the Yoshimine Temple on the fifteenth day, the second month, the second year of the Kangen Era [1244].

73

THIRTY-SEVEN WINGS
OF ENLIGHTENMENT

THE FUNDAMENTAL POINT set by ancient buddhas is the teaching, practice, and realization of the thirty-seven wings of enlightenment. Climbing and descending its classifications like twining vines is further twining vines [dynamic interaction] of the fundamental point. This is calling and actualizing buddhas, calling and actualizing ancestors.

————————

First, the four abodes of mindfulness are also called the four places of mindfulness. They are: visualizing the body as impure, visualizing perception as suffering, visualizing mind as impermanent, and visualizing that things are without a permanent and independent self.

"Visualizing the body as impure" means that the single skin bag [body] visualizing the body is the entire world of the ten directions. Because it is a true body, it visualizes the body as impure, leaping along a vital path. Not leaping must be not visualizing, not having the body, not practicing, not speaking, not having visualized. Know that visualizing is actualized, leaping along is actualized.

"Visualizing" is everyday walking, sweeping the ground, cleaning the meditation platform. You sweep the ground with the question: "Which month is it?" You sweep the ground and clean the meditation platform with the answer, "It is the second month." Thus, you do so with the entire great earth.

"Visualizing the body" is body visualizing. It is the body visualizing and not anything else visualizing. This very visualizing is outstanding. When body visualizing is actualized, mind visualizing does not search and is not actualized. This being so, body visualizing is diamond samadhi, shurangama [solid] samadhi. These are both visualizing the body as impure.

Now, the meaning of seeing the morning star at dawn is called "visualizing the body as impure." It is not discriminating pure from impure. Rather, [it is inevitable that] having the body is impure, manifesting the body is impure.

Study in this way: When a demon becomes a buddha, you take up a demon and turn the demon into a buddha. When a buddha becomes a buddha, you take up a buddha, paint a buddha, and turn the buddha into a buddha. When a person becomes a buddha, you take up a person, prepare the person, and turn the person into a buddha. Study thoroughly that at the place of taking up, the path unfolds right where you are.

This is like washing the robe. The water is defiled by the robe and the robe is soaked by the water. While you wash with water and with some more water, you use the water. This is washing the robe. If you don't see cleanness at the first or second washing, you keep washing. After the water goes, you get some more water. Even when the robe is clean, you keep on washing. You use the water of all beings, which is suitable for washing the robe. When the water is soiled, you know there are fish.

You wash the robe together with the robes of various beings. Endeavoring in this way, the fundamental point of washing the robe is actualized. Thus, you understand purity. It means that dipping the robe in water is not necessarily the original intention; to defile the water with the robe is not necessarily the original intention. However, washing the robe with defiled water is the original intention of washing the robe.

Furthermore, there is a way to wash the robe with fire, air, earth, water, and space. There is a way to wash earth, water, fire, air, and space with earth, water, fire, air, and space.

The meaning of visualizing the body as impure is also like this. Thus, to cover the body, to cover visualizing, to cover impurity, is no other than the kashaya wrapped around the body born from the mother. If the kashaya were not wrapped around the body born from the mother, buddha ancestors would not have used it. How can this understanding be limited to Shanavasin [whose lay clothes turned into a buddha robe]? Keep this principle in mind and study thoroughly.

"Visualizing perception as suffering" means suffering is perception. Perception is not perception of self, other, existence, or nonexistence. It is perception of the living body, suffering [bitterness] of the living body.

"Visualizing perception as suffering" means seeing that the living body turns from a sweet melon into a bitter gourd. Thus, skin, flesh, bones, and marrow are bitter. Those with mind and those without mind are both bitter. To realize this is a part of the practice-realization of miracles—the miracle of leaping out of the calyx [of a sweet melon] and leaping out of the roots [of a bitter gourd].

"It is said that sentient beings are suffering. Furthermore, suffering is sentient beings." [Words spoken by Jingqing Daofu.] Sentient beings are not self, not other. This statement—*Furthermore, suffering is sentient beings*—cannot fool others.

Although a sweet melon is sweet all the way to the calyx, and a bitter gourd is bitter all the way to the root, bitterness [suffering] cannot be easily grasped. So, ask yourself: what is suffering?

In regard to "visualizing mind as impermanent," Huineng, Old Buddha of Caoxi, said, "Impermanence is no other than buddha nature."

In this way, all types of impermanence understood by various beings are buddha nature.

Yongjia, Great Master Zhenjiao, said, "All phenomena are impermanent and everything is empty. This is the great, complete enlightenment of the Tathagata."

In this way, "visualizing mind as impermanent" is no other than the great, complete enlightenment of the Tathagata—the Tathagata of the great, complete enlightenment. Even if the mind tries not to visualize this, as mind changes with all things, where there is mind, there is visualization. Arriving at unsurpassable, complete enlightenment, actualizing unsurpassable, complete enlightenment, is impermanence, visualizing mind.

Mind, which is not necessarily permanent, is free of the four basic modes of discernment and beyond the one hundred types of negation. This being so, walls, tiles, and pebbles, large and small stones, are mind. They are impermanence. This is visualizing.

"Visualizing that things are without a permanent and independent self" is "A tall person has a tall dharma body, a short person has a short dharma body."

As the self is activities actualized, it is not a permanent and independent self. A dog has no buddha nature; a dog has buddha nature. No beings have buddha nature; no buddha nature has beings. No buddhas have beings; no buddhas have buddhas. No buddha nature has buddha nature. No beings have beings.

Thus, study "no beings have things" as visualizing that things are without a permanent and independent self. Know that the entire body leaps out of twining vines [entanglement] of the self.

———————

Shakyamuni Buddha said, "All buddhas and bodhisattvas always abide in the practice and make it their sacred womb."

In this way, all buddhas and bodhisattvas make these four abodes of mindfulness their sacred womb. Know that it is the sacred womb of bodhisattvas of enlightenment equal to that of buddhas, and it is the sacred womb of bodhisattvas of wondrous enlightenment.

Buddhas who are beyond the stage of bodhisattvas of wondrous enlightenment also make the four abodes their sacred womb. Bodhisattvas who leap beyond the bodhisattvas whose enlightenment equals that of buddhas, and those of inconceivable enlightenment, also make these four abodes of mindfulness their sacred womb. Indeed, the skin, flesh, bones, and marrow of all buddhas and all ancestors are just these four abodes of mindfulness.

The four right stoppings are also called the four right efforts. They are: Not arousing an unwholesome action that has not arisen, stopping an unwholesome action that has arisen, arousing a wholesome action that has not arisen, and allowing a wholesome action that has arisen to increase.

In regard to "not arousing an unwholesome action that has not arisen," there is no clear definition of an *unwholesome action*. It has been called this merely in accordance with the lands and realms. And yet, "not arousing what has not arisen" has been called buddha dharma and has been authentically transmitted.

According to the theory of those outside the way, an unwholesome action that has not arisen is rooted in the permanent self that has not sprouted. However, it is not so in buddha dharma.

For now, ask yourself: where does the unwholesome action lie before it arises? If you say that it lies in the future [apart from the self], you will remain an outsider of the way who holds a nihilistic view. If you say that the future comes and becomes the present, it is not a statement of buddha dharma; the past, present, and future would be confused. If the past, present, and future are confused, all things would be confused. If all things are confused, the reality of all things would be confused. If the reality of all things is confused, [transmission between] "only a buddha and a buddha" would be confused. This being so, we don't say that the future will later become the present.

Ask yourself further: What do you regard as *an unwholesome action that has not arisen?* Who knows this and sees this? If you can know and see this, there must already be a moment that has not arisen and a moment that has not not-arisen. If so, you cannot call it something that has not yet arisen, but rather you should call it something that has already arisen.

You should study *not arousing an unwholesome action that has not arisen* without following the views of those outside the way. An accumulated unwholesome action that fills the sky [whole world] is called an unwholesome action that has not arisen. That is *not arousing an unwholesome action. Not arousing* is "speaking of the permanence of all things yesterday and speaking of the impermanence of all things today" [beyond the discussion of permanence and impermanence].

In regard to "stopping an unwholesome action that has arisen," *has arisen* means entirely arisen. Entirely arisen means half arisen. Half arisen is rising right now. Rising right now is fully immersed in rising, leaping beyond the top of rising.

Stopping an unwholesome action that has arisen is Devadatta falling into hell while being alive, and Devadatta receiving a prediction of enlightenment while being alive. It is entering into a donkey womb while being alive, becoming a buddha while being alive.

Take up the meaning of this teaching and study about *stopping*. Stopping is stopping by leaping beyond and going through stopping.

"Arousing a wholesome action that has not arisen" means being filled with your face before your parents are born, clearly taking up the matter before things emerge, understanding what is before the King of the Empty Eon.

In regard to "allowing a wholesome action that has arisen to increase," it is not that you increase a wholesome action that has arisen, but that you allow a wholesome action that has arisen to increase. It is seeing the morning star and letting others see the morning star. It is the eye becoming the morning star.

It is like [Mazu] saying, "For thirty years after the barbarians' invasion, the monastery has not been short of salt and vinegar." Because you let a wholesome action increase, it has already arisen. Thus, the valley is deep and the dipper handle is long. Because he [Bodhidharma] was, he came [to China].

———————

The four elements of supernormal power are: the supernormal power of desire, the supernormal power of mind, the supernormal power of effort, and the supernormal power of contemplation.

The supernormal power of desire is the intention of body-mind to become a buddha, to sleep well, to be the self, and to bow to you.

The supernormal power of desire is not limited to the causes and conditions of body-mind. Rather, it is like a bird flying in the boundless sky, or a fish swimming at the bottom of deep water.

The supernormal power of mind is walls, tiles, pebbles, mountains, rivers, and the great earth. It is every part of the three realms. It is a brilliant red bamboo or wooden chair.

Because we cannot exhaust using the supernormal power of mind, there is buddha ancestor mind, mind of the ordinary and sages, mind of grass and trees, and the mind that changes. Fully exhausting mind is the supernormal power of mind.

The supernormal power of effort is walking straight ahead on top of a one-hundred-foot bamboo pole. Where is the top of a one-hundred-foot bamboo pole? It is beyond straight ahead and beyond grasping.

It is not that there is no one walking straight ahead. Where is right here? You speak of stepping forward and stepping backward. At the very moment of the supernormal power of effort, the entire world of the ten directions arrives, following the supernormal power of effort; the entire world of the ten directions reaches, following the supernormal power of effort.

In regard to the supernormal power of contemplation, all buddha ancestors have vast karma consciousness and are not based in any particular place. There is body contemplation, mind contemplation, perception contemplation, straw sandal contemplation, the self before the Empty Eon contemplation.

The supernormal power of contemplation is also called the four aspects of the fulfillment of wishes. It means no hesitation.

Shakyamuni Buddha said, "Arriving without moving forward is called the fulfillment of wishes."

Thus, the supernormal power of contemplation is as pointed as the tip of a gimlet, and as sharp as the blade of a chisel.

The fivefold root is the root of trust, the root of effort, the root of mindfulness, the root of samadhi, and the root of wisdom.

Know that the root of trust is not self, not others. It is not forced by the self, nor is it created by the self or led by others. Because it is not established by the self, it has been intimately entrusted throughout east and west.

The entire body embodying trust is called trust. Trust invariably follows and is followed by the stage of the buddha fruit. Without being at the stage of the buddha fruit, trust is not actualized.

So, it is said [in the *Treatise on Realization of Great Wisdom*], "Trust makes it possible to enter the great ocean of buddha dharma." Where trust is actualized, buddha ancestors are actualized.

The root of effort is to reflect on just sitting. Ceasing is unable to cease, being greatly occupied and yet not being occupied. Occupied and not occupied are the first month, the second month.

Shakyamuni Buddha said, "I always make an effort. That is why I have attained unsurpassable, complete enlightenment."

Always make an effort is the entire past, present, and future, from head to tail. *I always make an effort* is *I have attained unsurpassable, complete enlightenment. I have attained unsurpassable, complete enlightenment,* therefore *I always make an effort.*

If not so, how would it be *always make an effort*? If not so, how would it be *I have attained*? Teachers of treatises and scriptures do not see or hear the meaning of this. How could they have studied it?

The root of mindfulness is the red flesh ball of a decayed tree. A red flesh ball is called a decayed tree. A decayed tree is the root of mindfulness.

What the self has searched for is mindfulness. There is mindfulness at the time of having a body. There is mindfulness at the time of having no mind. There is mindfulness with mind. There is mindfulness with no body.

The life root of the entire earth person is the root of mindfulness. The life root of the entire ten directions buddha is the root of mindfulness.

There are multiple persons in a single mindfulness. There are multiple mindfulnesses in a single person. However, there is a person with mindfulness, and there is a person without mindfulness.

It is not that a person always has mindfulness. It is not that mindfulness is always hanging on a person. May it be so, there is virtue in maintaining the root of mindfulness and thoroughly experiencing the root of mindfulness.

The root of samadhi is refraining from touching the eyebrows and brushing up the eyebrows. Thus, it is beyond obscuring cause and effect, and beyond falling into cause and effect.

From this root of samadhi, you enter the donkey's womb, the horse's womb.

It is like a stone wrapped around a jade. Do not say the entire stone is a jade. It is also like the earth topped with the mountain. Do not say the entire earth is the mountain. Even so, you leap out and leap in from the top of the mountain.

The root of wisdom is not known beyond the knowledge of buddhas in the past, present, and future. But it is known by badgers and white cows. Do not say why this is so. This cannot be explained. It is just like breath going through nostrils or a fist having fingertips.

A donkey remains a donkey. A well sees a well. Thus, a root succeeds in a root.

———————

The fivefold power is the power of trust, the power of effort, the power of mindfulness, the power of samadhi, and the power of wisdom.

The power of trust is to be fooled by the self and have nowhere to escape. It is to be called by someone else and turn your head around. It is to be just here from birth to old age. It is letting go of falling down seven times and falling down eight times. Trust is like a crystal that purifies the water [it is put into]. Transmitting dharma and transmitting the robe are trust. It is transmitting buddhas and transmitting ancestors.

The power of effort is to speak of what action cannot express, to act what speaking cannot express. Thus, when speaking one *sun*, there is nothing like speaking one *sun*. When acting one *sun,* there is nothing like acting one *sun*. Effort within effort is the power of effort.

The power of mindfulness is to be a coarse person by grabbing another's nostrils. Thus, nostrils grab the person. It is to hurl a pearl and attract a pearl, to hurl a tile and attract a tile. Not yet hurling is worth receiving thirty blows. Even if people in the world use it, it will not wear out.

The power of samadhi is like a child having a mother or a mother having a child. It is like a child having a child or a mother having a mother.

However, it is not like exchanging the head with the face or buying gold with gold. It is just that singing becomes louder and louder.

The power of wisdom is deep in time. It is like a boat meeting the river crossing.

Thus, it was said in ancient times [in the *Lotus Sutra*], "It is like the river crossing meeting a boat."

The meaning of this phrase is that the river crossing cannot be separated from a boat. That the river crossing does not hinder the river crossing is called a boat. Spring is long and ice melts.

———

The seven limbs of enlightenment are: the selection limb of enlightenment, the effort limb of enlightenment, the joy limb of enlightenment, the retreat limb of enlightenment, the letting-go limb of enlightenment, the samadhi limb of enlightenment, and the mindfulness limb of enlightenment.

In regard to the selection limb of enlightenment [as in the poem "Engraving Trust in the Heart"], "Even if there is a hairbreadth of difference, you are as far away as heaven from earth. This being so, the ultimate way is not difficult, it is just that selection is necessary.

The effort limb of enlightenment is not to take advantage in the marketplace. Prices are set and values are known for buying and selling. It appears to be bending your body and pushing others, but even the entire body is not crushed when it is beaten. Before you have sold a turning word, you encounter a customer who buys a turning mind. Before a donkey matter is done, a horse matter arrives.

The joy limb of enlightenment is an old woman's mind intimate with drops of blood. The great compassionate one with one thousand arms and eyes [Avalokiteshvara] is quite busy. In the snow of the twelfth month, plum blossoms begin to leak out their fragrance, predicting the cold assembly [of monks] in the following spring.

And yet, the joy limb of enlightenment is vibrant and full of laughter.

In regard to the retreat limb of enlightenment, when you are with yourself, don't form a group with yourself; when you are with others, don't form a group with others. It is in the spirit of "You have not attained what I have attained." It is like speaking with blazing clarity, traveling through other types of beings.

In regard to the letting-go limb of enlightenment, it is like saying, "Even if I bring it forth, you may not accept it." It is also like saying, "A Chinese person learns a Chinese way of walking. A Persian person looks for ivory."

In regard to the samadhi limb of enlightenment, by concentrating on things that are about to arise, you have the eye of seeing things that are about to arise. The self pokes the self's nostrils. The self grabs the rope [through the nostrils], and the self pulls the rope. Thus, you get to tame a single water buffalo.

In regard to the mindfulness limb of enlightenment, a pillar walks in the sky. The mouth looks like an oak leaf and the eyes are like eyebrows. In the candana [incense] tree forest, candana is burned. In the lion's cave, a lion roars.

———

The eightfold noble path limb [of enlightenment] is also called the eightfold noble path. It consists of: the right view path limb, the right thought path limb, the right speech path limb, the right action path limb, the right livelihood path limb, the right effort path limb, the right mindfulness path limb, and the right samadhi path limb.

The right view path limb is hiding the body within an eyeball. This being so, the body before [this life] must embody the eye of the body before. Because it magnificently sees the self in the past, it actualizes the fundamental point. It is what has been intimately seen in the past. Those who do not hide the body within an eyeball are not buddha ancestors.

In regard to the right thought path limb, when you hold a right thought, all buddhas in the ten directions emerge. Thus, the emergence of the ten directions, the emergence of all buddhas, takes place at the moment of holding a right thought.

Although the moment of holding a right thought is not the self and is beyond others, at this very moment when a thought is held, you get to Varanasi [where the Buddha first taught]. Varanasi is where this thought is.

An ancient buddha [Yaoshan] said, "Think not-thinking. How do you think not-thinking? Beyond thinking."

This is right thinking, right contemplation. Sitting and breaking through the cushion is right thinking.

In regard to the right speech path limb, a mute is not a mute to the mute. A mute does not make an expression among people, but people in the mute world are not mutes. They do not look for sages [outside of themselves]. They do not add anything to their own spirits.

This is to study hanging the mouth on the wall, hanging all mouths on all walls.

The right action path limb is leaving the household and practicing the way, entering a mountain and attaining realization.

Shakyamuni Buddha said, "The thirty-seven wings of enlightenment are a monk's action."

A monk's action is neither the Great Vehicle nor the Lesser Vehicles. Among monks, there are buddha monks, bodhisattva monks, shravaka monks, and so on.

Those who have not left the household do not succeed in the right action of buddha ancestors, nor do they authentically transmit the great way of buddha dharma. Although laypeople study the way as laymen and laywomen, there is no precedent for their mastering the way. At the time of mastering the way, people invariably leave the household. How can those who cannot bear to leave the household succeed in the rank of buddhas?

Nevertheless, many of those who call themselves Zen monks in Great Song China have said for a couple of hundred years that the study of the way by the laity and the study of the way by home leavers are the same. Those who say such things are dogs who take in the urine and excrement [property] of laypeople.

At times they say to kings and ministers that there is no difference between the minds of rulers and the minds of buddha ancestors. The kings and ministers, without knowing authentic speech and true dharma, rejoice greatly and grant them the titles of masters, and so on.

Monks who make such statements are Devadattas. In order to eat the saliva and mucus of kings and ministers, they utter such childish, crazy words. How deplorable! They are not family members of the Seven Original Buddhas, but are beasts and demons. They are like this because they don't know the body-mind study of the way, don't study, and don't have the body-mind of leaving the household. They are like this because they are ignorant about kings and ministers governing with dharma, and they do not even dream of the great way of buddha ancestors.

Layman Vimalakirti, although he personally encountered the Buddha, had much he did not express and study. Layman Pangyun studied with some ancestors, but was not allowed to enter Yaoshan's chamber and was not as good as Mazu of Jiangxi. He stole the credit for studying but did not possess the fruit of it.

Other laity, including Li Fuma and Yang Wengong, regarded themselves as having filled up with study, but they hadn't even eaten a milk rice cake. How could they have eaten the painting of a rice cake? Even further, how could they have eaten buddha ancestors' gruel? They did not have eating bowls yet. What a pity that the skin bags of their lifetime were wasted!

Let me advise everyone—heavenly beings, human beings, dragon beings, and all other beings—to long for the Tathagata's dharma, quickly leave the household, practice the way, and succeed in the ranks of buddha and ancestor.

Do not listen to the words of unaccomplished Zen masters and others. They speak like this because they do not know the body and they do not know the mind. Or they say so because they do not have compassion for sentient beings. These human-faced dogs, human-skinned dogs who have turned into unwholesome dogs, have no intention of guarding buddha dharma; they just want to consume the urine and excrement of laypeople.

Do not sit with, speak with, or rely on such home leavers. They have already fallen into the animal realm while having human bodies. If these home leavers possess abundant urine and excrement, they may regard it as outstanding. They think so because they are not as good as beasts.

There is no mention in more than five thousand scrolls [of the entire Buddhist canon] and there is no trace of the statement for over two thousand years that the mind of the laity and the mind of home leavers are the same. There are no such words by fifty buddha ancestors of over forty generations.

Even a monk who breaks the precepts or keeps no precepts, with no dharma and no wisdom, excels a layperson who has wisdom and maintains the precepts. This is so because a monk's action is wisdom, enlightenment, and dharma.

A layperson may have a fair share of merit for having a wholesome root but may ignore acquiring the merit of having the wholesome root of body-mind. This being so, during the lifetime of the Buddha, no one attained the way as a layperson. The reason is that there are so many obstacles that home is not a practice place for studying the buddha way. When we investigate the bodies and minds of those who say that the minds of rulers and the minds of buddha ancestors are the same, we see that their bodies and minds are not the body-mind of buddha dharma. They do not transmit the skin, flesh, bones, and marrow of buddha ancestors. How pitiful it is that although they have encountered the true buddha dharma, they have become beasts!

This being so, Huineng, who would later be Old Buddha of Caoxi, all of a sudden bade farewell to his mother and started looking for a teacher. This was right action. Before arousing the aspiration for enlightenment upon hearing a passage of the *Diamond Sutra*, he was a householder and woodcutter. When he was permeated by the power of buddha dharma upon hearing this passage, he let go of his heavy obligation and left home.

Know that when you have buddha dharma in your body–mind, you cannot help leaving home. This has been so with all buddha ancestors.

The crimes of those who tell others not to leave their households are heavier than capital offenses, worse than Devadatta's. Do not speak with such people, keeping in mind that they are more guilty than the groups of the six monks, the six nuns, and the eighteen monks [of ancient times]. Our life span is too short to waste a moment speaking with such demons and beasts.

Furthermore, we have received our human body and mind due to the seed of seeing and hearing the buddha dharma in our past life. Our body and mind are like equipment in the common area [of the monastery]. We should not become a member of the demon clan. We should not associate with the demon clan. Without forgetting the benefaction of buddha ancestors, protect the nurturing of dharma milk and pay no attention to the howling of unwholesome dogs. Do not sit and eat with them.

When Bodhidharma, High Ancestor, Old Buddha of Mount Song, left the Buddha's country of India and traveled all the way to the remote nation of China, he personally brought the authentic dharma of buddha ancestors. Without his leaving the household and attaining the way, this would not have happened. Before Bodhidharma came from India, beings in the human and deva realms in the eastern land of China had never seen or heard the true dharma. In this way, know that the authentic transmission of the true dharma eye is just the benefaction of leaving the household.

Great Teacher Shakyamuni Buddha graciously left the palace and did not succeed in the position of his father king. It is not because the throne was not precious, but because he intended to succeed in the most precious buddha rank.

The buddha rank is the monk's rank. It is the position that all heavenly beings and human beings in the three realms revere. This position is not shared by Brahma or Indra. Even further, the buddha rank cannot be shared by human kings, or dragon kings in the lower realms.

It is a rank of unsurpassable, complete enlightenment. This rank expounds dharma, awakens beings, radiates light, and manifests miracles. Actions of this home leaver rank are right actions, embracing actions of all buddhas, including the Seven Original Buddhas.

These actions cannot be thoroughly experienced by those who are not "only buddha and buddha." Those who haven't left the household should serve, bow, and make offerings by dedicating their body and life to those who have left the household.

————————

Shakyamuni Buddha said, "Leaving the household and receiving the precepts is the seed of being a buddha. This is one who has received ordination."

Thus, know that ordination is to leave the household. Not to leave the household is to sink [in worldly defilement], which should be lamented.

In discourses during his lifetime, Shakyamuni Buddha extolled the virtue of home leaving countless times. The Buddha expounded it and all buddhas testified to it.

Even home leavers who break precepts and don't practice attain the way. There has not been a single layperson who has attained the way.

When the emperor bows to a monk or nun, the monk or nun does not bow back. When devas bow to monks and nuns, the monks and nuns do not bow back. This is because the merit of being a home leaver is excellent. If devas are bowed to by home-leaver monks or nuns, the devas' palaces, radiant light, and the wholesome results of their actions immediately crash and fall apart.

Since buddha dharma spread eastward to China, home leavers who have attained the way are as many as rice straws, flax, bamboo, and reeds. But there has not been a single layperson who attained the way. This is why when buddha dharma touches the eyes and ears, people rush to take on home leaving. Thus, we know that the household is not the abode of buddha dharma.

Therefore, those who say that the minds and bodies of rulers are no other than the minds and bodies of buddha ancestors have not seen or heard of buddha dharma. They are inmates in darkest hell, fools who haven't even heard their own statements; they are criminals of the nation. Because buddha dharma is excellent, rulers are pleased with the phrase that the minds and bodies of all people are no other than the minds and bodies of buddha ancestors.

Even if the minds of rulers became the same as the minds of buddha ancestors, these rulers' minds would not be the same as the minds of buddha ancestors becoming one with the minds of rulers. Those Zen masters who say that the minds of rulers are the same as the minds of buddha ancestors do not know how the mind of dharma moves and manifests. How can they even dream of the minds of buddha ancestors?

All kings, including Brahma, Indra, human kings, dragon kings, and demon kings, should not be attached to the karmic results of the three realms. They should immediately leave the household, receive the precepts, and learn the way of all buddhas and all ancestors. This will cause them to become a buddha in vast eons.

Don't you see? If Old Man Vimalakirti were to leave the household, we should see Monk Vimalakirti as more excellent than Layman Vimalakirti.

Today we see Subhuti, Shariputra, Manjushri, and Maitreya [in the *Vimalakirti Sutra*], but we don't see even half of Vimalakirti. Then, how can we see three, four, or five Vimalakirtis? If we don't see and know three, four, or five Vimalakirtis, we don't yet see, know, and acknowledge even one Vimalakirti. If we don't see, know, and acknowledge even one Vimalakirti, we don't see Vimalakirti Buddha.

If we don't see Vimalakirti Buddha, there is no Vimalakirti Manjushri, no Vimalakirti Maitreya, no Vimalakirti Subhuti, and no Vimalakirti Shariputra. Then, how can there be Vimalakirti mountains, rivers, and earth? How can there be Vimalakirti grass, trees, tiles, and pebbles; wind, rain, water, and fire; or past, present, future?

The reason why Vimalakirti has not seen the power of radiant light is that he has not yet left the household. If he had been a home leaver, he would have experienced such virtue.

Zen masters of the Tang and Song dynasties, however, without understanding this principle, mistakenly think that Vimalakirti got the point and say that Vimalakirti expressed the point. What a pity! These fellows who did not know the teachings by words were ignorant of buddha dharma.

There are also a number of those who think and say that the words by Vimalakirti and Shakyamuni Buddha are equal. They do not yet know and cannot access buddha dharma, the ancestral way, and even Vimalakirti.

Such people say that Vimalakirti remained silent and showed no words to all bodhisattvas and that this is equal to the Tathagata's words, "I teach people with no words."

I say that such people are quite ignorant of buddha dharma and lack the capacity to study the way. The Tathagata's words are different from those of others. His *no words* cannot be the same as the no words of other beings. Thus, the single silence of the Tathagata and the single silence of Vimalakirti cannot be compared.

If we investigate the capacity of those who imagined that even if speeches are different silence is the same, they cannot be regarded as those who are close to buddhas. How sad! They have not even seen and heard form and sound. How can they have the radiant light of leaping away from form and sound?

Furthermore, they don't know about studying the silence of silence and are not aware of such a thing. All beings have different ways of moving and being still. How can we discuss whether Shakyamuni Buddha and all beings are or are not the same? Those who have not studied inside the chamber of buddha ancestors speak in this way.

A number of mistaken people think and say that speeches and movements are temporary phenomena while silence and stillness are real. To speak in this way is not buddha dharma. This is a conjecture by those who have heard the scriptures of Brahma and Indra. How should buddha dharma be determined by movement or stillness? Investigate thoroughly whether buddha dharma does or does not have movement or stillness, whether buddha dharma touches movement or stillness, or is touched by movement or stillness. Latecomers to study nowadays should not be lax in this investigation.

When I see today's Great Song China, it appears that those who have studied the great way of buddha ancestors are extinct. It is not that there are even two or three such people. All people think that Vimalakirti is genuine by having a single silence, and that not having a single silence falls short of Vimalakirti. This is no vital path of buddha dharma.

There are also those who think that the single silence of Vimalakirti is no other than the single silence of Shakyamuni Buddha. This is not the radiant light of discernment. I should say that those who speak in this way have never seen and heard buddha dharma. Do not regard this as buddha dharma although it happens in Great Song China.

This principle is easy to clarify. Right actions are monks' actions. This is not known by teachers of treatises and scriptures.

Monks' actions are endeavor in the cloud hall [monks' hall], bowing in the buddha hall, and cleansing in the wash house. Further, putting palms together, greeting, burning incense, and boiling water are all right actions. It is not replacing the tail with the head, but replacing the head with the head, replacing the mind with the mind, replacing the buddha with the buddha, and replacing the way with the way. This is the right action path limb.

If you go astray and try to fathom buddha dharma other than this, your eyebrows and beard will fall out and your face will break up.

The right livelihood path limb is having the morning meal in early morning and the midday meal at midday, playing with the spirit in the monastery, and pointing directly from the teaching chair. Old Man Zhaozhou's assembly with fewer than twenty monks was right livelihood actualized. Yaoshan's assembly with fewer than ten monks was a life vein of right livelihood. Fenyang's assembly with seven or eight monks lived right livelihood. This is because they were free from a variety of crooked livelihood.

Shakyamuni Buddha said, "Shravakas have not attained right livelihood."

In this way, shravakas' teaching, practice, and realization are not yet right livelihood. But nowadays people in mediocre schools say that shravakas and bodhisattvas should not be distinguished, and that the guidelines and precepts of both schools should be used. They judge the bodhisattva guidelines in comparison with the guidelines for shravakas in the Lesser Vehicles.

Shakyamuni Buddha said, "A shravaka's keeping the precepts is a bodhisattva's breaking the precepts."

In this way, what shravakas regard as keeping the precepts is breaking the precepts in light of the bodhisattva precepts. The rest of the three learnings—samadhi and wisdom—are also like this.

Although the aspects of not killing and so on appear to be common between shravakas and bodhisattvas, they are certainly different, more apart from each other than heaven from earth. Even further, how is it possible that the teaching authentically transmitted by buddhas and ancestors could be the same as the teaching of shravakas?

There is not only right livelihood but also pure livelihood. Studying with buddha ancestors alone is right livelihood. Do not adopt the views of teachers of treatises.

Because they *have not attained right livelihood*, theirs is not genuine livelihood.

Right effort path limb is the activity of plucking out the entire body. It is plucking out the entire body and hitting a human face with it. It is to ride the buddha hall upside down and move in a circle. Because you ride two, three, four, and five times, it is nine times nine equals eighty-one circles. It is one thousand and ten thousand greetings. It is changing the heads freely, changing the faces freely. It is entering the abbot's room, ascending the teaching seat. It is meeting at the Land View Pavilion, meeting at Crow Stone Peak. It is an encounter in front of the monks' hall, an encounter inside the buddha hall. It is two mirrors facing each other creating three reflections.

The right mindfulness path limb is to be fooled by oneself and achieve eight or nine out of ten. To think that from mindfulness comes the aspiration for wisdom is to abandon your own father and escape [to a foreign land]. To think that within mindfulness there is the aspiration for wisdom is an extreme trap. To say that having no mindfulness is the right mindfulness is to be a person outside the way.

Also, do not regard spirits of earth, water, fire, and air as mindfulness. Do not call confusion of consciousness mindfulness. Indeed, "You have attained my skin, flesh, bones, and marrow" is itself the right mindfulness path limb.

The right samadhi path limb is dropping away buddha ancestors, dropping away right samadhi. It is letting someone else take it up. It is drilling the head top and making nostrils. It is holding up an udumbara blossom within the treasury of the true dharma eye. It is hundreds and thousands of Mahakashyapas smiling inside an udumbara blossom. It is using this activity for a long time and breaking a wooden dipper. Thus, weeds keep dropping for six years and blossoms open overnight. Tremendous fires blaze and a billion worlds crumble and disappear all of a sudden.

———————

These thirty-seven wings of enlightenment are the eyeball, nostrils, skin, flesh, bones, marrow, hands, feet, and face of buddha ancestors. The onefold buddha ancestor is being studied as the thirty-seven wings of enlightenment. Thus, this is one thousand three hundred sixty-nine [thirty-seven times thirty-seven] fundamental points, wings of enlightenment, actualized. Cut through them by sitting. Drop them away.

Presented to the assembly of the Yoshimine Temple, Echizen Province, on the twenty-fourth day, the second month, the second year of the Kangen Era [1244].

74

TURNING THE DHARMA WHEEL

RUJING, MY LATE master, Old Buddha Tiantong, ascended the teaching seat and declared:

The World-Honored One said, "When one person opens up reality and returns to the source, all the space in the ten directions disappears."

My teacher [Xuedou Zhijian] said, "Since this is a statement by the World-Honored One, it cannot help being an extraordinary formulation." I, Rujing, would say it otherwise: when one person opens up reality and returns to the source, a mendicant smashes his rice bowl.

Wuzu Fayan said, "When one person opens up reality and returns to the source, pounding and crackling resounds throughout the space in the ten directions."

Fuxing Fatai said, "When one person opens up reality and returns to the source, the space in the ten directions is just the space in the ten directions."

Keqin, Zen Master Yuanwu of Mount Jia, said, "When one person opens up reality and returns to the source, in the space throughout the ten directions flowers are added on brocade."

I, Daibutsu, say, "When one person opens up reality and returns to the source, the space throughout the ten directions opens up reality and returns to the source."

The words *When one person opens up reality and returns to the source, all the space in the ten directions disappears* come from the *Shurangama Sutra*. This saying has been commented on by these several buddha ancestors. It is indeed the bones, marrow, and eyeballs of buddha ancestors.

There is a debate whether the *Shurangama Sutra*, which is composed of ten scrolls, is apocryphal or not. The argument has lasted until now. Among the existing translations, the newest one from the Xinlong Era [705–707] is particularly suspect.

However, Fayan, Fatai, and Rujing have all commented on this saying. Thus, these words have already been turned by the dharma wheel of buddha ancestors. The buddha ancestors are turning this dharma wheel. In this way, these words turn the buddha ancestors, and these words have already expounded the buddha ancestors. Because these words have been turned by buddha ancestors and have turned buddha ancestors, even if this sutra is spurious, it has become a genuine buddha sutra and ancestor sutra, an intimate and familiar dharma wheel. Even a tile or a pebble, a fallen leaf, an udumbara blossom, or even a brocade robe, when taken up and turned by buddha ancestors, is the buddha dharma wheel and the buddha treasury of the true dharma eye.

Know that when sentient beings leap beyond and attain true awakening, they are buddha ancestors, disciples and teachers of buddha ancestors, and the skin, flesh, bones, and marrow of buddha ancestors. They are no longer the siblings of any ordinary sentient beings, but the siblings of buddha ancestors.

Likewise, even if the words in the ten-scroll *Shurangama Sutra* are inauthentic, the saying discussed above is an extraordinary buddha saying and ancestor saying that cannot be compared with usual words. However, even if these words go beyond, do not regard the entire text of the sutra as buddha words and ancestor words; do not regard the entire text as the eyeball of study.

There are many reasons that this saying should not be compared with usual words. I will present some of the reasons. What is called turning the dharma wheel is the activity of buddha ancestors. There have been no buddha ancestors who do not turn the dharma wheel. How the dharma wheel is turned is by taking up sound and form and smashing sound and form, by leaping out of sound and form and turning the dharma wheel, by plucking out the eyeball and turning the dharma wheel, or by raising a fist and turning the dharma wheel. The dharma wheel also turns by itself when the nostrils are grabbed and empty space is grasped. Taking up the saying discussed above at this immediate moment is taking up the morning star, nostrils, peach blossoms, or empty space. This is no other than taking up buddha ancestors and taking up the dharma wheel. This is the essence of clearly turning the dharma wheel.

Turning the dharma wheel is to practice without separating from the monastery for a whole lifetime, to ask for instructions, and to whole-heartedly engage the way on the sitting platform.

Presented to the assembly of the Yoshimine Temple, Echizen Province, on the twenty-seventh day, the second month, the second year of the Kangen Era [1244].

75

SELF-REALIZATION SAMADHI

WHAT HAS BEEN authentically transmitted by all buddhas, including the Seven Original Buddhas, is self-realization samadhi. It calls for following a teacher and following a sutra. This is the eyeball of buddha ancestors.

———

One time, Huineng, Old Buddha Caoxi, asked a monk, "Do you depend upon practice and enlightenment?"

The monk replied, "It's not that there is no practice and no enlightenment. It's just that it's not possible to divide them."

This being so, know that the undividedness of practice and enlightenment is itself the buddha ancestors. It is the thunderstorm of the buddha ancestors' samadhi.

———

At the very moment of following a teacher, you encounter with half a face or half a body. Or, you encounter with the entire face or the entire body. At times you encounter half a self and half another. You realize a spirit's hairy head and practice a demon's horned face. At times you follow others while traveling in the midst of different beings. At other times you travel differently while being born with those who have the same kind of birth.

In this way, you let go of yourself for the sake of dharma without knowing how many thousands of times you do so. You seek dharma for the sake of yourself without knowing in how many billions of eons you do so. This is the vital activity of following a teacher. This is the activity of practicing yourself and following yourself. In this way, at the time of blinking [by the Buddha], there is smiling [by Mahakashyapa]; at the occasion of bowing to receive the marrow [as Huike did], there is cutting off an arm.

From the time before and after the Seven Original Buddhas to the time of Huineng, the Sixth Chinese Ancestor, teachers who saw through the self were not limited to one or two, and teachers who have seen through others are not limited to then or now.

When you follow a sutra, you thoroughly experience your skin, flesh, bones, and marrow. When you drop away your skin, flesh, bones, and marrow, all of a sudden the emergence of the eye of [seeing] peach blossoms is encountered; the roaring sound of bamboo is heard in your ear consciousness.

When you follow and study a sutra, it emerges. A sutra means the entire world of the ten directions—mountains, rivers, the earth, grass, trees, self, and others. It is having a meal, putting on a robe, and engaging in activities. When you study the way, following a sutra, thousands and myriads of sutras that have never existed emerge and become present.

There are phrases that clearly affirm. There are verses that completely deny. By encountering these phrases and studying them with the entire body and mind, however long the eons you exhaust, and however long the eons you take up, there is always a place where you arrive with full mastery. By studying the letting go of body and mind, even if you pluck out the beginningless eon and fly beyond the beginningless eon, you will always achieve the experience of receiving and maintaining the sutra.

At the present time there are less than half a myriad of scrolls of scriptures translated from Sanskrit into Chinese. There are the Three Vehicles, the Five Vehicles, the Nine Divisions, and the Twelve Divisions among these scriptures. These are sutras to follow and study. Even if you try to avoid and not follow them, it will not be possible. This being so, they become the eye, and "my marrow." Their heads are right. Their tails are right.

When you receive a sutra from someone and give it to someone else, it becomes the vital emergence of the eye, dropping away self and other. It is just the entrusting of "my marrow," penetrating self and other. Because the eye, or "my marrow," is not self and not other, buddha ancestors have authentically transmitted it since olden times and have entrusted it from right now to right now.

———————

There is a sutra of a walking stick, expounding vertically and horizontally, crushing emptiness and crushing existence. There is a sutra of a whisk, rinsing snow and rinsing frost. There is a sutra of zazen, in one assembly and two assemblies. There is a sutra of the kashaya in one scroll and ten wrappings. These have been protected and maintained by buddha ancestors. Following sutras in this way, you practice, realize, and attain the way. With a deva face, a human face, a sun face, or a moon face, you actualize the practice of following sutras.

Thus, both following a teacher and following a sutra are following yourself. A sutra is no other than a sutra as yourself. A teacher is invariably a teacher as yourself. This being so, to visit teachers everywhere is to visit yourself everywhere. To take up one hundred grasses is to take up yourself. To take up myriad trees is to take up yourself. Study yourself that always endeavors thus. In this study, drop away, merge with, and realize yourself.

———————

Thus, in the great way of buddha ancestors, there are the essentials of self-realization and self-enlightenment. These cannot be authentically transmitted unless one is a direct successor of a buddha ancestor. The essentials transmitted from heir to heir cannot be authentically transmitted unless one is the bones and marrow of buddha ancestors. Because you study in this way, when this is transmitted to another, there is the entrusting of "You have attained my marrow," "I have the treasury of the true dharma eye. I entrust it to Mahakashyapa."

To speak to another [in this way] does not necessarily divide self and other. Speaking to another is self speaking to self. It is self and self, hearing and speaking together. One ear speaks and one ear hears. One tongue speaks and one tongue hears. Eyes, ears, nose, tongue, body, mind, root, consciousness, and objects are all like this. Furthermore, one body and one mind realize and practice. This is the ear itself hearing and speaking, the tongue itself hearing and speaking.

Even if you spoke of the dharma of impermanence to others yesterday, you speak of the dharma of permanence to yourself today. Such a sun face [one aspect] continues, such a moon face [another aspect] continues. To speak of dharma and practice for others is to hear dharma, to clarify dharma, and to realize dharma, birth after birth. If you have a sincere heart in speaking of dharma to others in this birth, your attaining dharma is easy. Or, if you assist and support others hearing dharma, your study of dharma receives a wholesome effect. You receive the effect in your body and in your mind. On the other hand, if you obstruct others from hearing dharma, your hearing of dharma is obstructed.

To speak dharma and to hear dharma birth after birth means to hear dharma lifetime after lifetime. Further, it is to hear in this world the dharma you have authentically received from the past. Because you are born in dharma and die in dharma, if you authentically receive dharma in the entire world of the ten directions, you hear it birth after birth and practice it body after body. Because you actualize dharma birth after birth, and make body after body into dharma, you bring forth a single particle, as well as the entire world of phenomena, and help them to realize dharma.

This being so, if you hear a phrase from someone in a far-eastern region, speak it for another in a far-western region. Endeavor in hearing and speaking equally with a single self. Practice and realize an east self and a west self.

Rejoice, hope for, and have the aspiration for bringing buddha ancestors' dharma, the ancestral way, closer to your body and mind. Extend this practice from one hour to one day, then to one year and to one lifetime. Make buddha ancestors' dharma the essential spirit and play with it. This is to live your life meaningfully.

So, do not think that you should not speak of dharma to others until you master it. If you wait until you master it, it will not be possible for countless eons. Even if you have mastered human buddhas, you need to master celestial buddhas. Even if you have mastered the heart of mountains, you need to master the heart of waters. Even if you have mastered the dharma of birth with causation, you need to master the dharma of birth beyond causation. Even if you have mastered the realm of buddha ancestors, you need to master going beyond buddha ancestors. Trying to speak to others after mastering all of these in one lifetime is not an endeavor of a person, and it is not the study.

Studying the way of buddha ancestors is to raise the aspiration as high as heaven for speaking to others from the moment of studying one dharma and one procedure. Thus, you drop away [become free from] self and others. Further, studying yourself thoroughly is studying others thoroughly. Studying others thoroughly is studying yourself thoroughly.

This practice of buddhas cannot be experienced with the body without receiving it from a teacher, even if you have knowledge by birth. Knowledge by birth does not know knowledge beyond birth, and beyond knowledge beyond birth. Even those who have knowledge by birth would not know the great way of buddha ancestors unless they study it.

To experience yourself with the body and to experience others with the body is the great road of buddha ancestors. Just turn the study of your beginner's mind and study simultaneously with others' beginners' minds. When self and others study together with the beginner's mind, you arrive together at the ultimate realm. In this way, your own endeavor encourages the endeavor of others.

However, hearing the words "self-realization" and "self-enlightenment," foolish people think that this is receiving transmission without a teacher and that one only needs to study by oneself. This is a great mistake. Those who make a crooked interpretation of self-realization without receiving instructions from a teacher are the same as those outside the way in India who believed in spontaneous enlightenment. How can those who do not understand this be considered practitioners of the buddha way?

Furthermore, those who hear the word "self-realization" and assume that this is the accumulation of the five skandhas are simply abiding in the practice of "self-control" in the Lesser Vehicles. There are many of those who do not understand the Great and Lesser Vehicles who call themselves descendants of buddha ancestors. Who with clear eyes would be fooled by them?

In the Shaoxing Era [1131–1162] of Great Song China, there was someone called Zonggao, Zen Master Dahui, of Mount Jing. He was originally a student of scriptures and treatises. While wandering [in search of a master], he studied Yunmen's commentaries on ancient words, and Xuedou's commentaries and verses on ancient words, under Shaoli, a Zen master of Xuan Province. This was the beginning of his practice and study. He could not understand Yunmen's style, and went to study with Dongshan Daowei, who did not allow him into his inner chamber. Daowei, a dharma child of Furong Daokai, cannot be viewed shoulder to shoulder with ordinary people who sit in lower positions. Although Zonggao studied with Daowei for a fair amount of time, he could not touch upon Daowei's skin, flesh, bones, and marrow. Furthermore, he was not aware that there is an eye in the midst of the objects of the senses.

One day, Zonggao heard about the practice of burning incense on one's elbow [to show determination] upon receiving a document of heritage. He kept asking Daowei to transmit a document of heritage to him. But Daowei would not do so. He said, "If you want to receive transmission of dharma, you should endeavor wholeheartedly and not be hasty. Buddha ancestors have not received and transmitted dharma groundlessly. It is not that I spare transmission, but that you do not yet have the eye."

Zonggao said, "The true eye one originally has is self-realization, self-enlightenment. How is it possible to transmit dharma groundlessly?"

Daowei just smiled and was silent.

Later, Zonggao studied with Zhantang Wenzhun [of Mount Baofeng]. One day Zhantang asked him, "How come one of your nostrils is missing today?"

Zonggao said, "It is studying at Mount Baofeng."

Zhantang said, "A coarse Zen student."

Later, when Zonggao was reading a sutra, Zhantang asked, "What sutra are you reading?"

Zonggao said, "The *Diamond Sutra*."

Zhantang said, "Dharma is equal with nothing high and nothing low. How come Mount Yunju is high and Mount Baofeng is low?"

Zonggao said, "Dharma is equal with nothing high and nothing low."

Zhantang said, "You have become a lecturer."

Another day, seeing the images of the Ten Kings [of Hell] being decorated, Zhantang asked senior monk Zonggao, "What is the family name of these officials?"

Zonggao said, "Liang."

Zhantang rubbed his head and said, "My family name is also Liang. How come I am not wearing a headdress?"

Zonggao said, "You are not wearing a headdress, but your nostrils look like theirs."

Zhantang said, "A coarse Zen student."

Another day, Zhantang said to Zonggao, "Senior Monk Gao, you have understood Zen in my place all at once. When I ask you to speak, you speak. When I ask you to practice, you practice. When I ask you to make a commentary, make a verse commentary, give an unscheduled talk, give a talk to the assembly, or ask questions, you can do any of those things. But there is one thing missing. Do you know what it is?"

Zonggao asked, "What is missing?"

Zhantang said, "You don't understand this one point. Indeed, this is the point you don't understand: When I am at the abbot's quarters and speak to you, there is Zen. But as soon as you step out of the abbot's quarters, it disappears. When you are clearly thinking, there is Zen. But when you are asleep, it disappears. If so, how can you grab hold of birth and death?"

Zonggao said, "That is exactly what I am questioning."

Some years later, Zhantang showed a sign of illness.

Zonggao said, "After your death, whose help should I get to complete my clarifying the great matter?"

Zhantang said, "There is someone called Qinbazi [Keqin of Ba Region]. I haven't met him. But if you meet him, you will certainly complete your study. After meeting him, do not wander around anymore. You will certainly bring out the fruition of your study."

When we examine these stories, we see that Zhantang did not yet approve Zonggao. Although Zonggao often tried to open up for one phrase of enlightenment, he was lacking a single experience. He could not take hold of or drop away from this single experience. Earlier, Daowei did not give Zonggao a document of heritage and encouraged him to try harder. Daowei's observation of his student was clear and trustworthy.

Indeed, Zonggao did not thoroughly study, drop away, and crush the point of doubt. He did not have a great doubt. He was not immersed in doubt. His request for transmitting a document of heritage groundlessly was a coarse action—an extreme example of having no aspiration for the way, not following the authentic procedure. It was a lack of deep consideration. He was not a vessel of the way and was completely ignorant of the study. He tried to invade the inner chamber of buddha ancestors with the intention of grabbing fame and loving benefit. How pitiful that he did not understand the phrases of buddha ancestors!

Because Zonggao did not understand that learning from the ancients is self-realization, and he did not hear and study that to examine myriad generations is self-enlightenment, he made such a mistake and had such self-delusion. Thus, among students of Zonggao, there is not one or even half a person who is truly worth grabbing by the nose. Many of them are expedient teachers. They do not understand buddha ancestors' dharma and do not go beyond understanding buddha ancestors' dharma in this way. Monks nowadays should study this in detail without neglect.

After Zhantang passed away, Zonggao followed his recommendation and went to study with Keqin, Zen Master Yuanwu of the Tianning Monastery in Dongjing. One day, Yuanwu ascended the teaching seat. Zonggao said he had a divine enlightenment and presented it to Yuanwu.

Yuanwu said, "Not yet. You understand in this way, but you haven't clarified the great matter."

Another day, Yuanwu ascended the teaching seat and explained Wuzu Fayan's words "having a phrase" and "having no phrase." Hearing this, Zonggao immediately said that he had attained the dharma of great ease and bliss, and presented his understanding.

Yuanwu said, "I do not want to fool you."

These are stories of Zonggao studying with Yuanwu. He served as secretary in Yuanwu's community. But from beginning to end, he did not seem to have a unique point of understanding. He did not show any point of understanding in his own lectures or talks. Know that the recorder of his words mentioned that he had had divine enlightenment or dharma of great ease and bliss, but did not admit that he had actually had realization. Do not take him seriously. He was merely a student.

Yuanwu was an old buddha, most revered in the ten directions. After Huangbo there had not been a venerable teacher like Yuanwu. He was an old buddha, rare in any world. But few humans and devas in this Saha Land know this. It is pitiable.

If we take up Yuanwu's words and examine senior monk Zonggao, we see that he did not have wisdom close to that of his teacher and he did not have wisdom equal to his teacher. Furthermore, it seems that he had never dreamed of wisdom beyond his teacher. Thus, know that Zonggao had less than half the capacity of his teacher. He only memorized lines from the *Avatamsaka Sutra* and the *Shurangama Sutra* and spoke about them. He was not yet the bones and marrow of buddha ancestors.

Zonggao regarded the views expressed by various hermits who follow the spirits abiding in grass and trees as buddha ancestors' dharma. Because he thought in this way, we know that he had not thoroughly studied the great road of buddha ancestors. After studying with Yuanwu, Zonggao did not wander around and visit teachers. Groundlessly, he became the abbot of a large monastery and led monks. The words he left cannot come close to great dharma.

However, ignorant people think that Zonggao was not less than earlier masters. But those who see and know agree that he did not have clear understanding. Without clarifying the great dharma, he merely chattered groundlessly. We know that Daowei did not make the mistake of acknowledging him and thus became an example for later generations. Students of Zonggao still resent Daowei. But Daowei just did not accept his understanding. Even further, Zhantang did not accept his understanding. Whenever Zhantang saw Zonggao, he scolded him. How shameful it is that those in the past and present have resented Zhantang for that!

There are a number of people in Great Song China who call themselves descendants of buddha ancestors. But there are few who study the truth, and there are few who teach the truth. This can be understood through these stories. It was like this in the Shaoxing Era. It is worse nowadays. These times cannot be compared. Today, those who do not know the great way of buddha ancestors have become leaders of monks.

Know that the Qingyuan Line has the authentic transmission of a document of heritage through buddhas and ancestors in both India and China. From the Qingyuan Line, the Dongshan Line started. The rest of the world has not seen it. All those who have this realization are descendants of Dongshan, and are highly regarded among monks.

Zonggao did not understand the words "self-realization," and "self-enlightenment" when he was alive. Then, how could he have examined other cases thoroughly? Even more so, how can descendants of old Zonggao understand the word "self-enlightenment"?

Thus, in the words of buddha ancestors, for themselves and for others, there is always the body-mind of buddha ancestors, and the eye of buddha ancestors. Because these words ["self-realization" and "self-enlightenment"] are the bones and marrow of buddha ancestors, their skin cannot be grasped by mediocre people.

Presented to the assembly while residing at the Yoshimine Temple on the twenty-ninth day, the second month, the second year of the Kangen Era [1244].

76

GREAT PRACTICE

BAIZHANG, ZEN MASTER Dazhi of Mount Baizhang, Hao Region, was the dharma heir of Mazu. His priest name is Huaihai. When Baizhang gave teachings to the assembly, an old man would often appear and listen to his dharma talks. The old man usually left after the talks, but one day he remained behind.

Baizhang asked, "Who are you?"

The old man said, "I am not actually a human being. In ancient times, at the time of Kashyapa Buddha, I lived and taught on this mountain. One day a student asked, 'Does a person who has cultivated great practice still fall into cause and effect?' I said to him, 'No, such a person does not fall into cause and effect.' Because of this I was reborn as a wild fox for five hundred lifetimes. Venerable Master, please say a turning word and free me from this body of a wild fox." Then he asked Baizhang, "Does a person who has cultivated great practice still fall into cause and effect?"

Baizhang said, "Do not ignore cause and effect."

Immediately the old man had great realization. Bowing, he said to Baizhang, "I am now liberated from the body of a wild fox. Master, will you perform for me a funeral service for a deceased monk? You will find the body of a dead fox in the mountain behind the monastery."

Baizhang asked the practice coordinator to hit the han and inform the assembly that funeral services for a monk would be held after the midday meal. The monks asked one another, "What's going on? Everyone is well; there is no one sick in the Nirvana Hall [infirmary]." After their meal, Baizhang led the assembly to a large rock behind the monastery and pointed out with his staff the body of a dead fox. Then, following the customary procedure, they cremated the body. That evening during his lecture in the dharma hall Baizhang talked about what had happened during the day.

Huangbo asked him, "A teacher of old gave a mistaken answer and was reborn as a wild fox for five hundred lifetimes. What if he hadn't given a mistaken answer?"

Baizhang said, "Come closer and I will tell you."

Huangbo approached and slapped Baizhang's face.

Laughing, Baizhang clapped his hands and said, "I thought only barbarians had red [extraordinary] beards, but you too are a red-bearded barbarian."

The fundamental point actualized now is great practice. According to the old man, there was already a Mount Baizhang of Hao region in the distant past at the time of Kashyapa Buddha, and during the present era of Shakyamuni Buddha there is also a Mount Baizhang of Hao region. This is a turning word actualized.

Now, Mount Baizhang in the distant past of Kashyapa Buddha and Mount Baizhang in the present era of Shakyamuni Buddha are not one and not two; neither three three before nor three three after [not many in the past or future]. It is not that Mount Baizhang in the past has become Mount Baizhang of the present; nor is it that Mount Baizhang right now was the Mount Baizhang at the time of Kashyapa Buddha. Yet there is the fundamental point of *I lived and taught on this mountain.*

My response to you would be exactly like what the present Baizhang said. What you should ask should be exactly like what the old man asked. If you take up one, you cannot take up another. If you neglect one, you fall into the secondary.

One day on Mount Baizhang a student asked, *"Does a person who has cultivated great practice still fall into cause and effect?"* Indeed, this question is not easily understood. For the first time since the buddha dharma was introduced to China during the Yongping Era [58–67] of the later Han Dynasty and since Bodhidharma transmitted the teaching from India in the Pudong Era [520–527] of the Liang Dynasty, this former student's question had been heard through the words of this old fox. It had never been heard before. Thus, this is rare indeed.

Investigating great practice is nothing but cause and effect itself. Because cause and effect are invariably comprehensive and completely full, they are beyond a discussion of falling or not falling, or considerations of ignoring or not ignoring. If not falling into cause and effect is a mistake, not ignoring cause and effect may also be a mistake. Whenever mistakes surpass mistakes, there is falling into a wild fox body and there is liberation from a wild fox body. It is possible that not falling into cause and effect was a mistake during the time of Kashyapa Buddha but not a mistake during the time of Shakyamuni Buddha. It is also possible that even though there is liberation from a wild fox's body during the present time of Shakyamuni Buddha, during the time of Kashyapa Buddha a different principle was actualized.

Regarding the old man's words *I was reborn as a wild fox for five hundred lifetimes*, what does it mean to be reborn as a wild fox? It is not that there was originally a wild fox and it lured the earlier Baizhang to fall into cause and effect, nor is it possible that the earlier Baizhang was originally a wild fox. To say that the earlier Baizhang's spirit went out and became a wild fox's skin bag is a statement of someone outside the way. It is not that a wild fox came and suddenly swallowed the earlier Baizhang. If you say the earlier Baizhang fell into the body of a wild fox, then there must be the liberation of the earlier Baizhang's body for the fox to fall into. And yet, Baizhang may fall into the body of a wild fox again, later. It is not that Baizhang was transposed into a wild fox's body.

How could it be that cause and effect are like this? Cause and effect are not original existence, and do not begin just now. It is not that cause and effect that are inactive wait for someone. Even if the answer *does not fall into cause and effect* is a mistaken response, it is not that the one who says so always falls into a wild fox's body. If such a response to a student's question necessarily causes a teacher to fall into the body of a wild fox, then recent teachers like Linji, Deshan, and their descendents would have become thousands of foxes. Careless elders of the last two or three hundred years would have become wild foxes. However, we have never heard that they have become wild foxes. If there were many such cases, we certainly would have heard about them. Although there are few who give such answers, there are many whose answers are far more confused than *does not fall into cause and effect*. There are quite a few who should not even be allowed within the neighborhood of buddha dharma. Those who have the eye of practice can discern this point. Those without it do not understand.

Thus, we know. We do not say that one becomes a wild fox because of a mistaken answer, and one does not become a wild fox because of a correct answer. In this story there is no mention of what happens after becoming free of the body of a wild fox, but presumably there is a pearl wrapped within the [wild fox's] skin bag.

Regarding this, those who have not seen or heard the buddha dharma say, "Becoming free of the wild fox body, he returns to the essential ocean of original enlightenment. As a result of delusion he became a fox for a while, but after his great enlightenment the wild fox body returned to the original essence."

This view of returning to the original self is not buddha dharma, but from outside the way. This is not buddha dharma. To say that a wild fox is not original nature and does not have original enlightenment is not buddha dharma. To say that after great enlightenment the wild fox body is discarded is not the wild fox's great enlightenment. This merely belittles the wild fox. Do not speak in such a way.

The story states that because of the turning word of the current Baizhang, the former Baizhang—an old fox for five hundred lifetimes— immediately became liberated from the body of a fox. Understand the meaning of this story. If you assert that a turning word by an outsider can liberate a wild fox, then there must be innumerable turning words by mountains, rivers, and the great earth from the incalculable past. However, to say that there had never been the liberation from a wild fox body in the past, but the current Baizhang's turning words alone liberated the wild fox, is to deny the way of the ancestors. To say that mountains, rivers, and the great earth have never uttered a single turning word is to say that there is no place for the current Baizhang to even open his mouth.

It has also been asserted by many teachers, one after another, that not falling into cause and effect is not different from ignoring cause and effect. But they have never realized the bodily experience of falling into or not ignoring cause and effect within the stream of those very words. They consequently neither experience the skin, flesh, bones, and marrow of falling into the body of a wild fox, nor experience the skin, flesh, bones, and marrow of being liberated from the body of a wild fox. When the beginning is not right, the end is never right.

In the old man's words, *Since then I have fallen into the body of a wild fox for five hundred lifetimes*, who has fallen and into what has he fallen? In the very moment of falling into the body of a wild fox, what form and color does the world continuing from the past have at present? Why five hundred repetitious births? Where did the dead body of the wild fox come from?

To say *Such a person does not fall into cause and effect* is to fall into the body of a wild fox. To hear *Do not ignore cause and effect* is to be liberated from the body of a wild fox. These instances of falling into and being liberated are just the cause and effect of the wild fox.

Nevertheless, since ancient times people have said, "Because *such a person does not fall into cause and effect* is an expression which seems to refute cause and effect, the speaker falls down." This assertion is without reason, spoken by those who are ignorant. Even if the former Baizhang said, *Such a person does not fall into cause and effect*, his great practice would not delude others and he would not refute cause and effect.

It has also been said, "The meaning of *Do not ignore cause and effect* is that because great practice transcends cause and effect, it liberates the body of a wild fox." Truly, this is realization eight or nine out of ten of the eye of practice.

Thus, in the time of Kashyapa Buddha the old man lived on this mountain. In the time of Shakyamuni Buddha he is living on this mountain. Former body and present body—sun face and moon face [in either case]—he covered the spirit of a wild fox, and manifested the spirit of a wild fox.

How could the wild fox know its life for five hundred lifetimes? If you say that it knows five hundred lifetimes with the intelligence of a wild fox, the wild fox's intelligence does not even know the matter of a single lifetime, much less a life rammed into a wild fox's skin bag. That a wild fox knows its falling down in five hundred lives is the fundamental point actualized. While it does not completely know the whole of one life, there are things that a wild fox knows and things it does not know. Even if the body and intelligence were permanent, the fox could not count five hundred lifetimes. As there is no way of counting so many rebirths, the words *five hundred lifetimes* may be a fiction.

If someone says that a wild fox knows by using the intelligence other than a wild fox's intelligence, then it is not the wild fox's knowing. What person can know these five hundred lives on behalf of the wild fox? Without having a clear path of realization through knowing and not knowing, you cannot speak of *falling into the body of a wild fox*. If there is no falling into the body of a wild fox, it is impossible to become liberated from the body of a wild fox. If there is no falling into and becoming liberated from a wild fox body, there can be no former Baizhang. If there is no former Baizhang, there can be no current Baizhang—this cannot be conceded at random. Investigate this matter in great detail with a discerning eye and crush the incomplete theories so prevalent throughout the Liang, Chen, Sui, Tang, and Song dynasties.

The old nonhuman said to the current Baizhang, *Will you perform for me a funeral service for a deceased monk?* This is not an appropriate thing to ask. Ever since the time of Baizhang there have been numerous teachers who have not been surprised at this statement and who have never doubted it. The fact of the matter is: how can a dead fox be regarded as a deceased monk without having received the precepts, without having participated in summer practice periods, without having awesome presence, and without the status of a monk? If one were to groundlessly perform a funeral service in the manner of one for a deceased monk for such a being, all those who have never left the household—lay men and women—should also be accorded the rites of a deceased monk. If we look for such precedents, there has never been anything like it. It is unheard of and such a case has not been authentically transmitted in the buddha way. Even if one wanted to perform such a ceremony, it would not be possible to do so.

It is said that Baizhang cremated the body of the wild fox following the customary procedure. This is not clear; perhaps there is a mistake. Know that funeral services for a deceased monk, from the moment of entering the Nirvana Hall to the practice of arriving at the Bodhi Garden [place of death], all have set procedures and cannot be changed at random. Even if the wild fox lying at the foot of a cliff claims it is the former Baizhang, how could this be the practice of a great monk, the bones and marrow of buddha ancestors? Who could clearly testify that this was the former Baizhang? Do not groundlessly regard the transmogrification of a wild fox spirit as authentic, and do not make light of the dharma standards of buddha ancestors.

As descendents of buddha ancestors, value the excellence of their dharma standards. Do not go along with such an inappropriate request as it appears Baizhang did. A single matter, a single dharma, is rare to encounter. Do not be affected by worldly customs and human sentiments. In this country of Japan, the form and manner of the buddhas and ancestors are hard to encounter and difficult to hear. As you now have the rare opportunity of hearing and seeing them, treasure them more than a pearl in the topknot. Those without such great fortune do not have the opportunity to honor them. This is sad indeed. Without realization of the lightness and gravity of matters, they lack the wisdom of five hundred years, the wisdom of a thousand years.

Thus, it is necessary to encourage yourself and others. Receiving the authentically transmitted tradition from the buddha ancestors—even one prostration or a single upright sitting—is rare indeed; greatly rejoice and celebrate this great fortune. Those who lack this heart will not possess a single virtue or acquire any benefit even if they were to encounter the emanation of a thousand buddhas. There are people outside the way who have mistakenly been entrusted with the buddha dharma. Though they may sound like they are learned in the buddha dharma, the buddha dharma they expound lacks the fruits of realization.

This being so, if kings and ministers, or even Brahma or Indra, who are not monks, come to you and ask for a funeral service of a deceased monk, do not permit it. Tell them that they should leave the household, receive the precepts, cultivate the life of a monk, and then return. If those who are attached to karmic results in the three realms, and do not aspire to actualize the life within the three treasures, bring forth ten thousand dead skin bags and try to disregard the funeral precedent for a deceased monk, do not permit it. That would not be conducive of any merit. If they wish to establish a favorable connection with the merit of buddha dharma, they should immediately leave the household, receive the precepts according to buddha dharma, and undertake to cultivate the life of a monk.

That evening the current Baizhang ascended the teaching seat and talked about what had happened during the day. The point of his talk is highly unclear. What did he talk about? It seems he said that the old man, having already completed five hundred lifetimes as a fox, became liberated from the body of the past. Are the five hundred lifetimes spoken of here counted in terms of the human world or in the manner of a wild fox? Or are they counted in the manner of the buddha way? Furthermore, how could the eyes of the old wild fox catch a glimpse of Baizhang? What is seen through the eyes of a wild fox must be the spirit of a wild fox. What is seen through the eyes of Baizhang are buddha ancestors.

In this regard, Facheng [Jingyin] Kumu, commented on the story in verse:

> Baizhang personally met the wild fox;
> questioned by it, his heart was greatly perturbed.
> Now, I ask you, practitioners of the way,
> have you completely spat out the wild fox's saliva, or not?

In this way, the wild fox is the eye of Baizhang's intimate experience. Even half the wild fox's saliva spat out is the wide, long tongue sticking out, uttering a turning word of transformation. This very moment is liberation from the wild fox body, liberation from Baizhang's body, liberation from the old nonhuman body, liberation from the entire world body.

Huangbo asked Baizhang, *A teacher of old gave a mistaken answer and was reborn as a wild fox for five hundred lifetimes. What if he hadn't given a mistaken answer?*

This question is a buddha ancestor's words actualized. Among the venerable teachers in the lineage of Nanyue there was no one like Huangbo, either before or after him. Nevertheless, the old man did not say he had given a mistaken answer to the student. Nor did Baizhang say that the old man had given a mistaken answer. Why did Huangbo dare to say, *A teacher of old gave a mistaken answer?* If Huangbo meant that this mistaken answer became the cause of falling into a wild fox's body, Huangbo had not yet grasped the great intention of Baizhang. It is as though Huangbo had not thoroughly investigated the mistaken answers and the answers beyond mistake spoken by buddhas and ancestors. Understand that in this story the former Baizhang did not mention a mistaken answer, nor did the current Baizhang.

Even so, using five hundred skins of a wild fox three inches thick, the former Baizhang lived and taught on the mountain for the benefit of practitioners, and expressed his understanding to a student. Because the pointed strands of hair on the wild fox skin dropped off, the current Baizhang is one stinky skin bag. I presume that this is dropping off half a wild fox's skin. This is freedom from falling, which at every moment is beyond mistakes. This is cause and effect, which at every moment speaks for another. This is bright and clear, great practice with great intention.

If Huangbo were to appear right now and ask, *What if he hadn't given a mistaken answer?* say, "He would still fall into the body of a wild fox." If Huangbo should ask, "How is this so?" say, "You spirit of a wild fox!"

Nevertheless, this is neither a mistake nor not a mistake. Do not concede that Huangbo's question was well asked. Again, if Huangbo were to ask, "What would he have become?" say, "Have you grasped the skin of your own face, or not?" Further say, "Have you become free of the wild fox's body?" Also say, "Can you answer students saying, *does not fall into cause and effect?*"

When Baizhang said, *Come closer and I will tell you,* he already answered the question, *What if he hadn't given a mistaken answer?* Huangbo went closer, having forgotten about the past and being oblivious of the future, and slapped Baizhang. This slap is Huangbo being possessed by countless transmogrifications of wild foxes.

Laughing, Baizhang clapped his hands and said, *I thought only barbarians had red beards, but you too are a red-bearded barbarian.* This expression lacks the vitality of being ten out of ten; it is only eight or nine out of ten complete realization. Even if we were to admit that it is eight or nine out of ten, this is still not eight or nine out of ten. Even admitting that it is ten out of ten, there is not more than eight or nine out of ten complete realization.

So, say, "Baizhang's words pervade the ten directions, though he is not yet out of the wild fox's cave. Huangbo's heels touch the ground, though he is still stuck on the [narrow] path of a praying mantis. Slapping and clapping hands are one, not two. The red-bearded barbarian is a barbarian with a red beard."

Presented to the assembly of the Yoshimine Temple, Echizen Province, on the ninth day, the third month, the second year of the Kangen Era [1244].

DAIBUTSU
MONASTERY PERIOD

———

1245–1246

77

SPACE

PROVOKED BY THE question "What is right here?" the way actualizes and buddha ancestors emerge. The actualization of the buddha ancestors' way has been handed down heir by heir. Thus, the whole
body of skin, flesh, bones, and marrow hangs in empty space.

Space is not classified within the twenty types of emptiness. Indeed,
emptiness is not limited merely to the twenty types of emptiness. There
are eighty-four thousand types of emptiness and more.

———————

Shigong, who would later become Zen Master Huizang of Fu
Region, asked his younger dharma brother Xitang, who would later
become Zen Master Zhizang, "Do you know how to grasp space?"

Xitang said, "Yes, I do."

Shigong said, "How do you grasp it?"

Xitang stroked the air with his hand.

Shigong said, "You don't know how to grasp space."

Xitang responded, "How do you grasp it, elder brother?"

Shigong poked his finger in Xitang's nostril and yanked his nose.

Xitang grunted in pain and said, "You're killing me! You tried to pull
off my nose."

Shigong said, "You can grasp it now."

Shigong said, *Do you know how to grasp space?* He was asking whether the entire body is hands and eyes.

Xitang said, *Yes, I do.* Space is one piece but is divided with a touch. As soon as it is divided, space has fallen to the ground.

Shigong said, *How do you grasp it?* Even if you call it thusness, it changes quickly. Although it changes, it slips away as thusness.

Xitang stroked the air with his hand. He knew how to ride on a tiger's head, but didn't know how to grab its tail.

Shigong said, *You don't know how to grasp space.* Not only did Xitang not know how to grasp it, but he had never dreamed of space. The gap between them was profound, yet Shigong did not want to speak for the other.

Xitang responded, *How do you grasp it, elder brother?* Thus, Xitang wanted Shigong to speak, not depending on him to say it all.

Shigong poked his finger in Xitang's nostril and yanked his nose. Know that Shigong hid his body in Xitang's nostril. This is the same as Shigong poking his own nostril. Thus, space is one ball which bounces here and there.

Xitang grunted in pain and said, *You're killing me! You tried to pull off my nose.* He thought he had met another person, but right there he actually met himself. At this moment, isolating himself was not possible. This is how you should study yourself.

Shigong said, *You can grasp it now.* This is certainly a way to grasp space. It is not that Shigong and another Shigong reached out together with one hand; it is not that one space and another space reached out together with one hand. No effort was needed [for grasping space].

There is no gap in the entire world to let space in, but this story has been a peal of thunder in space. From the time of Shigong and Xitang there have been many practitioners regarded as masters of the Five Schools, but few of them have seen, heard, and understood space. Some of those before and after Shigong and Xitang tried to play with space, but there are few who have reached it. Shigong took up space but Xitang did not see it.

Let me respond to Shigong. You grabbed Xitang's nose. If this was to grasp space, you should have grasped your own nose. You should have grasped your own finger with a finger. You have some understanding of grasping space. Even if you have a good finger to grasp space, you should penetrate the inside and outside of space. You should kill space and give life to space. You should know the weight of space. You should trust that the buddha ancestors' endeavor of the way in aspiration, practice, and enlightenment through challenging dialogues is no other than grasping space.

———

Rujing, my late master, Old Buddha Tiantong, said, "The entire body [of a wind bell] is a mouth hanging in emptiness."

Thus, we know that the entire body of space is hanging in emptiness.

———

Once, Lecturer Liang of Mount Xi, Hong Region, studied with Mazu, who said, "Which sutra do you teach?"

Liang said, "The *Heart Sutra.*"

Mazu said, "How do you teach it?"

Liang said, "I teach it with the heart."

Mazu said, "The heart is like a main actor. The will is like a supporting actor. The six types of consciousness are like their company. How do they understand your teaching of the sutra?"

Liang said, "If the heart doesn't understand it, does emptiness understand it?"

Mazu said, "Yes, it does."

Liang flipped his sleeves and started to walk away.

Mazu called, "Lecturer."

Liang turned his head around.

Mazu said, "Just this, from birth till death."

At this moment Liang had realization. He hid himself at Mount Xi, and no one heard about him any longer.

In this way buddha ancestors all expound sutras. What expounds sutras is empty space [boundlessness]. Without being empty space, no one can expound even one single sutra. Expounding the *Heart Sutra* and expounding the body sutra are both done with empty space. With empty space, thinking is actualized and beyond thinking is actualized. Empty space is wisdom with a teacher, wisdom without a teacher, knowing by birth, knowing by learning. Becoming a buddha, becoming an ancestor is also empty space.

Vasubandhu, the Twenty-first Ancestor, said:

> Mind is like the world of space
> equally bringing forth things of emptiness.
> When you realize space,
> there is nothing good or bad.

Now, the person who faces the wall meets the wall that faces the person. Here is the mind of a wall, the mind of a decayed tree. This is *the world of space*. Awakening others with this body, manifesting this body to speak dharma, is *equally bringing forth things of emptiness*. Being used by the twelve hours of the day and using the twelve hours of the day is, *When you realize space*. If the rock's head is large, its base is large. If the rock's head is small, its base is small. This is, *There is nothing good or bad*.

Investigate the fact right now that empty space is the treasury of the true dharma eye, the wondrous heart of nirvana.

This was presented to the assembly of the Daibutsu Monastery, Echizen Province, on the sixth day, the third month, the third year of the Kangen Era [1245].

78

EATING BOWL

THE AUTHENTIC TRANSMISSION has been conveyed from beyond the Seven Original Buddhas to the Seven Original Buddhas, from within the Seven Original Buddhas to the Seven Original Buddhas, from the total Seven Original Buddhas to the total Seven Original Buddhas, from the Seven Original Buddhas to the twenty-eight Indian ancestors. Bodhidharma, the Twenty-eighth Ancestor, went to China and gave authentic transmission to Huike, the Second Chinese Ancestor, Great Master Zhengzong Pujiao. This was handed down through six generations and reached Huineng.

Thus, in India and China, the teachers of all fifty-one generations transmitted the treasury of the true dharma eye, the wondrous heart of nirvana—the robes and the eating bowls. Earlier buddhas maintained the authentic transmission of the earlier masters. Thus, authentic transmission has been conducted from buddha to buddha, from ancestor to ancestor.

Accordingly, those who study with buddha ancestors with skin, flesh, bones, and marrow, with fist and eyeball, have their own expressions. Some understand that the eating bowls are the body and mind of buddha ancestors. Some understand that the eating bowls are the rice eating bowls of buddha ancestors. Some understand that the eating bowls are the eyeball of buddha ancestors. Some understand that the eating bowls are the radiant light of buddha ancestors. Some understand that the eating bowls are the true body of buddha ancestors. Some understand that the eating bowls are the treasury of the true dharma eye, the wondrous heart of buddha ancestors. Some understand that the eating bowls are the place of turning the body of buddha ancestors. Some understand that the eating bowls are the mouth and bottom of the eating bowls of buddha ancestors. The essential understanding of those who study in this way is expressed differently, but there can be further understanding.

Upon assuming the abbacy of the Tiantong Monastery in the first year of the Baoxin Era [1225], Rujing, my late master, Old Buddha Tiantong, ascended the teaching seat and said:

> I remember that Bhaizhang was asked by a monk, "What is extraordinary?"
>
> Bhaizhang said, "To sit alone on Daoxiong Peak. You cannot move this person. Let the person sit through for the moment."
>
> Now, someone may come up and ask me, "What is extraordinary?"
>
> I would reply, "The eating bowls of Jingci [where I was abbot] have moved to Tiantong and eat meals."

Know that *what is extraordinary* happens to an extraordinary person; an extraordinary utensil is used for an extraordinary thing. This is an extraordinary moment. Thus, where what is extraordinary is actualized, there are extraordinary eating bowls.

Thus, the Four Deva Kings protect the eating bowls and all dragon kings guard them. This is a profound procedure of the buddha way. This being so, we dedicate eating bowls to buddha ancestors and are entrusted with eating bowls by buddha ancestors.

Those who have not studied inside the chamber of buddha ancestors say that the buddha kashaya is made of silk, cotton, or celestial thread. They also say that the buddha eating bowls are made of stone, slate, or iron. They say this because they have not yet obtained the eye of study.

The buddha kashaya is the buddha kashaya; it should not be viewed as silk or cotton. To view it as silk or cotton is to fall into a conventional view. The buddha eating bowls are the buddha eating bowls. Do not call them stone, slate, iron, or wood.

The buddha eating bowls are not made. They neither arise nor perish, neither come nor go, neither gain nor lose. They are not limited to new or old, ancient or present.

Although the eating bowls of buddha ancestors are actualized by the assembling of clouds and water [monks], they are not limited to clouds and water. Although they are actualized by the assembling of grass and trees, they are not limited to grass and trees.

Water is water as a compound of all things. Clouds are clouds as a compound of all things. Clouds are assembled as clouds and water is assembled as water. The eating bowls are eating bowls as a compound of all things. The eating bowls are assembled as all things. The total mind is assembled as the eating bowls. The empty space is assembled as the eating bowls. The eating bowls are assembled as the eating bowls. The eating bowls are immersed in the eating bowls, and divided by the eating bowls.

The eating bowls transmitted to monks now were dedicated to the Buddha by the Four Deva Kings. The bowls wouldn't exist had they not been dedicated by the Four Deva Kings. The eating bowls, authentically transmitted by buddha ancestors of all directions who have transmitted the treasury of the true dharma eye, are eating bowls that leap beyond ancient and present.

Thus, these eating bowls penetrate the old views of an iron person, and are not bound by the analysis of a wooden stalk [stagnant thinker]. They go beyond the sound and form of tiles and pebbles. They are not hindered by the experience of stone or jade. Do not call them stone or tile. Do not call them wooden stalks.

Thus it has been understood.

Presented to the assembly of the Daibutsu Monastery, Echizen Province, on the twelfth day, the third month, the third year of the Kangen Era [1245].

79

PRACTICE PERIOD

IN AN INFORMAL talk to open the summer practice period, Rujing, my late master, Old Buddha Tiantong, presented this poem:

> Piling up bones in an open field,
> gouging out a cave in empty sky,
> break through the barrier of dualism
> and splash in a bucket of pitch-black lacquer.

To grab hold of this spirit, to train constantly for thirty years, eating meals, sleeping, and stretching your legs—this requires unstinting support. The structure of the ninety-day summer practice period provides such support. It is the head and face of buddhas and ancestors. It has been intimately transmitted as their skin, flesh, bones, and marrow. You turn the buddha ancestors' eyes and heads into the days and months of the ninety-day summer practice period. Regard the whole of each practice period as the whole of the buddhas and ancestors.

From top to bottom, the summer practice period is buddha ancestors. It covers everything without an inch of land or a speck of earth left out. The summer practice period is an anchoring peg that is neither new nor old, that has never arrived and will never leave. It's the size of your fist and takes the form of grabbing you by the nose. When the practice period is opened, the empty sky cracks apart and all of space is dissolved. When the practice period is closed, the earth explodes, leaving no place undisturbed.

When the koan of opening the summer practice period is taken up, it looks as if something has arrived. When the fishing nets and birds' nests of the summer practice period are all thrown away, it looks as if something has left. However, those who participated intimately in the practice period have been covered with opening and closing all along. An inch of grass has not appeared for ten thousand miles, so you might say, "Give me back the meal money for these ninety days."

Priest Sixin of Mount Huanglong said, "My pilgrimage of more than thirty years amounts to one ninety-day summer practice period, not a day more, not a day less."

Thus, after a pilgrimage of more than thirty years you develop an eye that sees summer itself as a ninety-day practice period. Even if you try to stretch it or contract it, the ninety days will always bounce back and be just ninety days. You yourself cannot leap over the boundary of ninety days, but if you use the ninety days as your hands and feet, you can make the leap. Although the ninety-day summer practice period serves as a support for us, the buddha ancestors did not create it on our behalf. They only handed it down to us from the past, heir to heir, authentically.

This being so, to experience a summer practice period is to experience all buddhas and all ancestors. To experience a summer practice period is to see buddhas and ancestors directly. Buddhas and ancestors have been produced by the summer practice period for a long, long time. Although the ninety-day summer practice period is only as long as your forehead, it is beyond time. One kalpa, ten kalpas, one hundred, one thousand, or innumerable kalpas cannot contain it. Although ordinary events can be contained within one thousand or innumerable kalpas, the ninety days contain one hundred, one thousand, or innumerable kalpas. Even if the innumerable kalpas experience the ninety days and see the buddhas, the ninety days are still free of innumerable kalpas.

Thus, investigate that the ninety-day summer practice period is as long as an eyeball. The body and mind of the practice period is just like that.

To become fully immersed in the liveliness of the summer practice period is to be free of the liveliness of the summer practice period. Although it has origination and cause, it has not come from another place or another time, nor has it arisen here and now. When you grasp for the origination of the ninety-day period, it immediately appears. When you search for the cause of the ninety-day period, it's immediately right here. Although ordinary people and sages use the ninety-day period as their abode and sustenance, it is beyond the boundary of ordinary and sacred. It is also beyond the reach of discernment and nondiscernment, and even beyond beyond the reach of discernment and nondiscernment.

———————

During a dharma talk that the World-Honored One gave in the country of Magadha, he announced his intention to go into a summer retreat. He said to Ananda, "My advanced disciples, the four types of human and celestial practitioners, are not truly paying attention to my dharma talk, so I have decided to enter Indra's cave and spend the ninety days of summer in sitting practice. If people should come to ask about the dharma, please give them your explanation on my behalf. All things are beyond birth, beyond death."

Then he closed the entrance to his meditation chamber and sat. It has been two thousand one hundred ninety-four years since then. Today is in the third year of the Kangen Era [1245].

Those who haven't entered the inner chamber regard the World-Honored One's retreat in the country of Magadha as proof of expounding the dharma without words. These confused people think, "The Buddha's closing off his chamber and spending the summer in solitary sitting shows that words and speech are merely skillful means and cannot indicate the truth. Cutting off words and eliminating mental activity is therefore the ultimate truth. Wordlessness and mindlessness is real; words and thoughts are unreal. The Buddha sat in the closed chamber for ninety days in order to cut off all human traces."

Those who say such things are greatly mistaken about the World-Honored One's true intention.

If you really understand the meaning of cutting off words, speech, and mental activity, you will see that all social and economic endeavors are essentially already beyond words, speech, and mental activity. Going beyond words and speech is itself all words and speech, and going beyond mental activity is nothing but all mental activity. So it is a misunderstanding of this story to see it as advocating the overthrow of words, speech, and mental activity. Reality is to go into the mud, enter the weeds, and expound dharma for the benefit of others; turning the dharma and helping all beings is not something optional. If people who call themselves descendants of the Buddha [leaders in the monastery] say that the Buddha's ninety days of solitary summer sitting means that words and speech are cut off, you should demand a refund for those ninety days of summer sitting.

Also, do not misunderstand the Buddha's further words to Ananda, *Please give them your explanation on my behalf. All things are beyond birth, beyond death.* Since the Buddha's closing the room and sitting through the summer is not merely an activity without words and speech, ask the World-Honored One, in Ananda's place, "What is the meaning of *all things are beyond birth, beyond death* and how do we practice it?" In light of your question, examine the World-Honored One's teaching.

This story about the Buddha contains the primary truth and the primary beyond-truth of his expounding and turning the dharma. It is a mistake to use it as proof that the Buddha taught abandonment of words and speech. If you see it that way, it is like taking a three-foot dragon-fountain sword and hanging it up on the wall of a potter's shop [to be used as a shaping knife].

Thus, sitting for ninety days of summer is an ancient method used by authentic buddha ancestors for turning the dharma wheel. The important part of this story is just the Buddha announcing his intention to go into a summer retreat. This makes it quite clear that sitting the ninety-day summer practice period is something to be done without fail. Not to practice in this way is to be outside the way.

When the World-Honored One was alive he held the summer practice period in Tushita Heaven, or he held it with five hundred monks in a hall on Vulture Peak. It didn't matter to him which of the five parts of India he was in; he always held a summer practice period when the time came. Buddha ancestors for generations up to the present have been practicing it as the essential matter; it is the unsurpassable way of practice and enlightenment. In the *Indra's Net Sutra* the winter practice period is mentioned, but that tradition has not been passed on; only the ninety-day summer practice period has come down to us, authentically transmitted for fifty-one generations up to the present.

The *Guidelines for Zen Monasteries* says: "When a seeker comes to a monastery wanting to join in a practice period, the person should arrive half a month in advance so that the welcoming tea and other entering rituals can be performed without haste."

Half a month in advance means the last part of the third month. Thus, seekers should arrive sometime in the third month. The season for traveling to enroll in a monastery ends before the first day of the fourth month. After that, the guest office and the visitors' room close. By then, according to tradition, all monks wishing to reside in a monastery should have their traveling bags hanging either in the monks' quarters, or in the nearby quarters for laypeople. This is the style of the buddha ancestors, and it should be respected and practiced. By then the fists and nostrils [teachers and elders] should also have their bags in place.

Nevertheless, a group of demons say that what is essential is the development of the Mahayana view, and that the summer practice period is a Hinayana training and should not be followed. Those who say such things have never seen or heard the buddha dharma. A ninety-day summer practice period of sitting is itself unsurpassable, complete enlightenment. Both Mahayana and Hinayana have fine teachings and practices; these are all branches, leaves, flowers, and fruits of the ninety-day practice period.

After the morning meal on the third day of the fourth month, the official preparation begins. Preceding this, from the first day of the fourth month, the practice coordinator prepares a preliminary list of the names of the participants according to their dharma ordination seniority.

On the third day of the fourth month, after the morning meal, the preliminary list is posted on the lattice window to the right of the entrance
to the study hall. The list is posted every day after the morning meal
and taken down after the bell that signals the end of the practice for the
day. It is displayed this way from the third day until the fifth day of the
fourth month.

Care must be taken with the order in which the names are arranged
on the preliminary list. They are not listed according to the monastic
offices held, but according to seniority in ordination date. However, the
titles of those who have served as officers in other monasteries should
be written on the list, especially if they have served as head monk or
administrator. If they have served in several positions, the title pertain-
ing to the highest position they reached should appear on the list. Those
who have been abbots should have the title "former abbot" added to
their names. Sometimes people who have served as abbots in small temples unknown to most monks prefer out of modesty not to be acknowledged as former abbots.

Also, there are monks who have served as senior teachers in monks'
halls, and as such have sat in the "former abbot" seat in the hall, without
actually having served as abbots. The listing of such monks should not
include the title "former abbot." In such cases the term "senior monk"
can be used. If such senior monks volunteer to serve as humble caretak-
ers of the abbot's robes and bowls, or as the abbot's incense attendants,
as they often do, this can be an excellent example. The senior monks
can be appointed to other positions by the teacher. Some monks who
have previously trained in small monasteries, including those who have
been abbots of small temples, might be invited to serve as the head monk,
secretary, treasurer, or administrator in large monasteries. Since it is not
unusual for people to make fun of positions in minor monasteries or temples, such monks may prefer their past positions not to be acknowledged.

The following is an example of such a list of participants:

In such-and-such monastery on such-and-such mountain in such-and-
such province of such-and-such country, the names in the ocean assembly forming the summer practice period are [for example] as follows:

Venerable Ajnatakaundinya [the first disciple of the Buddha], Chief Monk, Priest _____, Abbot

    Ordained in the first year of the Kempo Era
        _____, Senior monk
        _____, Librarian
        _____, Senior monk
        _____, Senior monk
    Ordained in the second year of the Kempo Era
        _____, Former abbot
        _____, Ino
        _____, Head monk
        _____, Senior monk
        _____, Bathhouse keeper
    Ordained in the first year of the Kenreki Era
        _____, Work leader
        _____, Attendant monk
        _____, Head monk
        _____, Head monk
        _____, Guest coordinator
        _____, Lay contact monk
        _____, Senior monk
        _____, Tenzo
        _____, Infirmary manager
    Ordained in the third year of the Kenreki Era
        _____, Secretary
        _____, Senior monk
        _____, Former abbot
        _____, Head monk
        _____, Senior monk
        _____, Senior monk

I respectfully present this preliminary list. Please notify me if there is a mistake.

                Sincerely yours, monk [so-and-so], Ino
                The third day, the fourth
                month, the year _____.

This is calligraphed in formal script on a white sheet of paper. Cursive or decorative script is not used. This list is fastened to a paperboard with a flax string, about the thickness of two grains of rice, and hangs like a screen. It is removed at the end of the break from zazen on the fifth day of the fourth month.

————————

On the eighth day of the fourth month, the Buddha's Birthday is celebrated.

On the thirteenth day, after the midday meal, the study hall monks are served tea and treats and do melodic sutra chanting in the study hall. The study hall director is in charge of this event, boiling the water and offering the incense. The study hall director sits at the end of the hall, in the middle [the place of highest honor], while the study hall head monk is positioned to the left of the enshrined image. It is the study hall director who rises to offer incense. The head monk and officers of the monastery do not join in this sutra chanting. Only the study hall monks participate in this ceremony.

The practice coordinator hangs the revised list of participants on the east wall in front of the monks' hall after the morning meal on the fifteenth. It hangs above the front platform on the south side near the center [where the monastery officers sit]. The *Guidelines for Zen Monasteries* says, "The practice coordinator prepares the list of participants beforehand and offers incense and flowers, and hangs the list in front of the monks' hall."

On the fourteenth day of the fourth month after the midday meal, a sign announcing the chanting ceremony is hung in front of the monks' hall as well as other halls. By the evening, officers have set up incense and flowers in front of the sign outside the shrine of the local earth deity, and the monks assemble.

This is the procedure for the ceremony: After the monks assemble, the abbot offers incense, then the officers and the heads of departments offer incense in a way similar to the style of offering made during the ceremony of bathing the Buddha. Then the practice coordinator comes forward, makes a standing bow to the abbot, faces north, bows to the local earth deities, and chants as follows:

> As we reflect quietly, fragrant winds waft over the fields, and the god of summer holds dominion in all directions. At this time, the Dharma King ordains that the monks remain secluded in the monastery, and on this day the children of Shakyamuni invoke the life-protecting deities. We assembled here respectfully worship the shrine of spirits, and chant the great names of myriad virtues, dedicating offerings to the deities enshrined here. We pray for protection and for the complete accomplishment of the practice period.
>
> Now we invoke the venerable ones (after each of the following names a small bell is struck): Pure Dharmakaya Vairochana Buddha, Complete Sambhogakaya Vairochana Buddha, Uncountable Nirmanakaya Shakyamuni Buddhas, Future Maitreya Buddha, All Buddhas throughout space and time, Great Sacred Manjushri Bodhisattva, Great Sacred Samantabhadra Bodhisattva, Great Compassion Avalokiteshvara Bodhisattva, All Venerable Bodhisattva Mahasattvas, Maha Prajna Paramita.
>
> We dedicate the merit of our chanting and offerings to the dragon deities of the earth who protect the true dharma. May the wondrous light illuminate and activate this merit so that pure enjoyment and selfless happiness will arise. We again invoke All Buddhas throughout space and time, All Venerable Bodhisattva Mahasattvas, and Maha Prajna Paramita.

The drum is hit and the monks go for ceremonial tea in the monks' hall. Serving the tea is the responsibility of the monastery administrator. The monks enter the hall with a formal circumambulation and sit in their positions facing the center of the hall; the officer in charge opens the ceremony with an incense offering. The *Guidelines for Zen Monasteries* says, "This ceremony is usually conducted by the monastery administrator but the practice coordinator may substitute."

Prior to the chanting ceremony the officer in charge writes an announcement of invitation to the tea ceremony and presents it to the head monk in the following manner: The officer, wearing the kashaya and carrying the folded bowing cloth, faces the head monk, spreads the bowing cloth twice [on the floor, spreading it in two folds, standing up, folding it up, and spreading it again] and makes three formal bows, then presents the announcement to the head monk. The head monk responds by bowing in the same way. The invitation is placed on a fine silk cloth spread over [the lid of] a box. This box is carried ceremonially by an assistant. The officer bringing the invitation is escorted into, and later, out of the hall, by the head monk. The invitation reads:

> This evening I will serve tea in the monks' hall for the head monk and everyone in the assembly to initiate the practice period. Please kindly attend.
>
> Respectfully yours,
> Monk so-and-so,
> Monastery Administrator
> The fourteenth day of the fourth month,
> the third year of the Kangen Era

This is signed with the first ideograph of the administrator's name. After presenting the invitation to the head monk, the administrator has his assistant post it in front of the monks' hall. There is a varnished bulletin board to the south of the front entrance, to which envelopes for announcements are fastened with bamboo pegs. The envelope for tea invitations is posted next to them. There is a traditional format for writing such an invitation. The size of ideographs should not exceed five *bu* [approximately half an inch]. On the front of the envelope, write: "Attention: Head Monk and Assembly. From Monastery Administrator." This announcement is removed after tea is served.

———

Before the morning meal of the fifteenth day of the fourth month, the monastery officers, heads of work crews, junior monks, and dharma associates assemble at the abbot's quarters to greet the abbot. However, the abbot may exempt the monks from this procedure by placing, on the previous day, a poetic statement of dharma words on the eastern side of the entrance to his room, the abbots quarters, or in front of the monks' hall.

After the dharma talk is delivered from the high seat in the dharma hall, the abbot descends the steps, stands on the northern end of the bowing mat placed in the center, and faces south. The monastery officers approach the abbot and make a ceremonial greeting by spreading their bowing cloths twice [on the floor] and making three bows in the following manner: First they spread their bowing cloths on the floor and say, "In this practice period of seclusion we have the opportunity to serve you intimately. With the beneficence of your dharma guidance we are confident that no disturbance will occur." Then they [fold up their bowing cloths, stand up, and] spread the bowing cloths again, offer a seasonal greeting, and make three semiformal bows [with their heads touching their cross-folded bowing cloths placed on the floor].

Offering this seasonal greeting is done in the following manner: They spread their bowing cloths and make three formal bows. They then fold up their bowing cloths, place them on their arms under their sleeves, and approach closer to the abbot, where they say, "Now it is the beginning of the summer, and the days are gradually getting warmer. This is the time of year when the Dharma King first established a practice period. We are all grateful that you now enjoy good health in motion and stillness. This is very auspicious." Then they make three semiformal bows and remain silent. The abbot returns the bows each time.

The abbot replies, "We are extremely fortunate to be able to have this practice period together. I hope that Head Monk so-and-so, Monastery Administrator so-and-so, and other leaders will support one another so as to prevent any disturbance from arising."

The head monk and the assembly of monks then come forward and repeat the same process of greeting with the abbot. At this time the head monk, officers, and other monks all face north and bow. The abbot alone faces south and stands in front of the dharma seat steps. The abbot's bowing cloth is spread on the main bowing mat.

Then the head monk and the entire assembly spread their bowing cloths twice, making three formal bows to the abbot. As they do this, those who are not fully participating in the practice period, including the junior monks, the attendant monks, the senior dharma associates, as well as the novices, stand to the side along the east wall of the dharma hall. However, if there are strips of paper with donors' names on the east wall, they should stand near the big drum [in the northeast corner] or along the west wall.

After these bows, the officers go to the kitchen and stand in the ceremonial location. The head monk leads the assembly there and greets the officers with three semiformal bows. During this time the junior monks, the attendant monks, and the senior dharma family members all pay their respects to the abbot in the dharma hall in the following manner: Senior dharma family members spread their bowing cloths twice and make three formal bows. The abbot returns their bows. The junior monks and attendant monks make nine formal bows. The abbot does not return their bows. Novices may make nine or twelve bows. The abbot responds to these bows by merely putting his palms together.

After the ceremony in the kitchen, the head monk and the assembly proceed to the monks' hall. The head monk stands outside on the north side near the entrance, facing south toward the monks who are gathered outside. The monks make three semiformal bows to the head monk.

Then the head monk enters the monks' hall followed by the assembly in the order of ordination seniority, and they circumambulate the hall. After this, the monks stand in their respective positions. The officers enter the hall, spread their bowing cloths fully open on the floor [without folding them], and make three most formal bows to the enshrined image. They get up and make three semiformal bows in front of the head monk [to the assembly]. The assembly returns their bows. The officers circumambulate the hall once, go to their positions, and stand with their hands folded.

The abbot then enters the hall, offers incense to the enshrined image, fully spreads the bowing cloth, makes three most formal bows, and stands. During this time, the junior monks [who have entered the hall after the assembly] are standing behind the enshrined image, while the senior dharma family members are standing behind the assembly. The abbot goes to the head monk and makes three semiformal bows, then goes to the abbot's seat, stands facing west, and makes three semiformal bows. These bows are returned by the head monk and the assembly.

The abbot circumambulates the hall and then exits. The head monk stands at the south side of the doorway of the hall in order to bow to the abbot as he leaves. Then the head monk and the assembly face each other, make three bows, and say, "We now have the good fortune to participate in this practice period. May unwholesome karma of body, speech, and thought not arise, and may we practice with compassion for one another." These bows are done after spreading the bowing cloths.

The head monk, secretary, head of the storehouse, and other officers go back to their offices. The monks who live in the monks' residence hall make three semiformal bows to the hall director and the head monk of the hall, and make the same statement that was made in the monks' hall.

———

The abbot then makes the rounds of the monastery buildings starting with the kitchen and ending with the abbot's quarters. This procedure is conducted as follows: First the abbot greets the officers in the kitchen and leaves the kitchen in procession followed by the officers. Following them are those who have been standing along the eastern hallway. The abbot goes down the eastern hallway past the main monastery gate without entering the infirmary. When he passes the gate, those stationed in the buildings near the gate now join the procession. The abbot goes up the western hallway toward the north, visiting the monks' living quarters along the way. Here the elderly practitioners, retired officers, officers on leave, aged teachers, other monks living in private quarters, and cleaning monks join the procession. The practice coordinator and head monk also join here, followed by the monks in the study hall. Thus, various monks join the procession in turn each at the place associated with their duties. This is called "the procession of amassing the assembly."

The abbot then proceeds to his quarters, ascends the stairs to the west, and stands in front of the main building, facing south in formal shashu posture. The assembly and the officers all face north, toward the abbot, and make a standing bow to him. This standing bow should be particularly formal and deep. The abbot returns their bow, and the assembly retires. Rujing, my late master, did not bring the assembly to the abbot's quarters; instead he brought the assembly into the dharma hall and stood in shashu in front of the steps of the dharma seat, facing south. The assembly made a standing bow to him and then retired. This is also an authentic tradition.

Then, the monks greet one another in various ways, according to their relationships. "Greet" here means that they bow to one another.

For example, groups from the same home region greet one another with a feeling of celebration, appreciating the opportunity to share the same practice period together. Tens of monks make these greetings in the Hall of Light [study hall]; others greet one another along the hallways. The monks may use the greeting phrases used in the monks' hall ceremony, or they may say something spontaneous. When disciples meet their root teachers, they greet them with nine formal bows. The dharma family members of the abbot greet him by spreading their bowing cloths twice and making three formal bows, or by spreading their bowing cloths fully and making three most formal bows. Monks accompanying the dharma family members make their greeting in the same way. Among others who should be greeted formally are dharma uncles, those who sit nearby on the meditation platform, and those who have practiced together in the past. Those monks who live in the private quarters, the head monk, the secretary, the librarian, the guest coordinator, and the bath master as well as the treasurer, monastery administrator, practice coordinator, tenzo, work leader, former abbots of other monasteries, senior nuns, and Daoist practitioners should visit one another's quarters and offer greeting bows.

If the entrances to the common quarters become crowded with monks so that it is difficult to enter, a note is left attached to the doorway. The note, on a small piece of white paper about one *sun* [about 1 inch] wide and two *suns* tall, should read, "Monk so-and-so of such and such quarters offers greetings," or the note may be from several monks: "Monks Soun, Esho (and others if there are any), offer greetings." Other options for the note are "Salutations from Monk so-and-so," "Respectful greetings from Monk so-and-so," "With greetings from Monk so-and-so," or "With bows from Monk so-and-so." These are several examples, but there are many other ways this card can be written. It is not unusual for there to be many cards attached to the doorways, always on the right-hand side, never on the left [considered the higher side], to be respectful. The director of each of the quarters removes the cards after the midday meal. On this day all the living quarters, large and small, have their entrance screens rolled up.

Traditionally, at this point the abbot, monastery administrator, and the head monk in turn serve tea; however, in remote monasteries, on distant islands, or in the deep mountains, this custom may be omitted.

Retired elders and those who have been head monks serve tea for officers and heads of crews in their own quarters.

After opening the practice period with this thorough ceremony, monks now make endeavors in the way. Those who have not participated in a summer practice period, regardless of other ways they may have practiced, are not descendents of buddha ancestors, nor can they themselves be buddha ancestors. The practice of the Jeta Grove and Vulture Peak are all actualized by the way of practice period. Practice period is the field of enlightenment, the mind seal of buddha ancestors, where buddha ancestors dwell.

The summer practice period draws to a close with the following events.

On the thirteenth day of the seventh month, sutras are chanted in the study hall, followed by formal serving of tea and refreshments. The monk who is serving as head of the study hall for that month officiates at these ceremonies.

On the fourteenth day of the seventh month there is a chanting ceremony in the evening.

On the fifteenth day of that month the abbot ascends the dharma seat to give a formal talk. The procedure of individual greetings, formal visits to the living quarters, and tea ceremony are similar to those at the opening of practice period. However, the words for the announcement of the tea ceremony should be written as follows:

> The administrator will serve refreshments in the monks' hall this evening to honor the head monk and the assembly in celebration of our completion of the practice period. The attendance of all is requested.
>
> Yours respectfully,
> Monk so-and-so, Administrator

Also, the chant at the shrine for the earth-guarding deities is presented as follows:

The golden wind blows over the fields and the god of autumn begins to govern the four quarters. Now it is time to release the practice period of the King of Enlightenment; on this day the dharma year is complete. The ninety days have passed without obstruction and the assembly is at ease. We chant the high names of all buddhas and make offerings to the enshrined spirits. The assembly of monks chants these words with deep respect.

The invocation of buddhas' names that follows is the same as at the beginning of practice period.

After the abbot's talk is over, the officers say in gratitude, "We respectfully rejoice that the dharma year has been completed without obstruction. This is due to the guidance of the master. We are extremely grateful."

The abbot responds by saying, "Now the dharma year is complete. I would like to express my gratitude to Head Monk so-and-so, to Monastery Administrator so-and-so, and to all others whose dharma efforts mutually supported the practice period. I am extremely grateful."

The head monk and the assembly of the monks' hall, the head of the dormitory, and others all say in gratitude: "During the ninety-day summer period our unwholesome acts of body, speech, and thought may have disturbed the assembly. If so, we beg forgiveness and ask for your compassion."

The officers and heads of crews say, "Fellow practitioners in the assembly, if any of you are going traveling, please do so at your convenience after the concluding tea." Some may leave earlier if necessary.

Since the time of the King of the Empty Eon there has been no practice higher than this practice. Buddha ancestors have valued it exclusively, and it is the only thing that has remained free of the confusion caused by demons and deluded people outside the way. In India, China, and Japan all descendents of buddha ancestors have participated in the practice period, but deluded people outside the way have never engaged in it. Because it is the original heart of the single great matter of buddha ancestors, this teaching of practice period is the content of what is expounded from the morning of the Buddha's attaining the way until the evening of pari-nirvana. There are Five Schools of home leavers in India, but they equally maintain a ninety-day summer practice period and without fail practice it and realize the way; and in China none of the monks in the Nine Schools have ever ignored the summer practice period. Those who have never participated in the summer practice period in their lifetimes cannot be called buddha disciples or monks. Practice period is not only a causal factor; it is itself practice-realization, it is itself the fruit of practice. The World-Honored One, the Great Enlightened One, practiced and realized without missing one summer practice period in his whole lifetime. Know that summer practice period is buddha realization within the fruit of enlightenment.

This being so, those who call themselves descendents of buddha ancestors without engaging in the practice realization of a ninety-day summer practice period should be ridiculed. In fact, ridicule would be more than they deserve! Simply pay no attention whatsoever to them: do not speak with them, do not sit with them, and do not walk in the same paths with them. In buddha dharma the ancient way to cure those with such mistaken views is simply to shut them out with silence.

Understand and maintain a ninety-day summer practice as the buddha ancestors themselves. The authentic transmission of the practice period tradition was handed down from the Seven Original Buddhas to Mahakashyapa, and through him it was authentically transmitted heir to heir to Bodhidharma, the Twenty-eighth Indian Ancestor. He in turn went to China and authentically transmitted it to Huike, the Second Ancestor, Great Master Zhengzong Pujiao, who authentically transmitted it heir to heir down to the present day. Thus, the tradition of practice period entered China and has been authentically transmitted in the assemblies of buddha ancestors, and accordingly it has been authentically transmitted to Japan.

By sitting zazen in the ninety-day summer practice period within this assembly of authentic transmission, you authentically receive the dharma of summer. Living with a true teacher and fully participating in the practice period makes the practice period a true practice period. Because the tradition of practice period has been transmitted face to face, heir to heir, directly from the practice periods practiced during the

Buddha's own lifetime, it is the authentic and personal transmission of buddha face, ancestor face, the complete merging with the realization of buddha ancestors' body and mind intimately and immediately.

Therefore, to see a practice period is to see buddha; to realize a practice period is to realize buddha; to practice a practice period is to practice buddha; to hear a practice period is to hear buddha; and to study a practice period is to study buddha. Now, a ninety-day practice period is the inviolable dharma of all buddha ancestors. This being so, even kings of the human world, the Indra world, or the Brahma world should make an effort to participate in a practice period as monks even for one summer; to do so is to actually see buddha. Humans, devas, or dragons should participate in a ninety-day practice period as monks or nuns even if it is only once in a lifetime: to practice this practice period is to actually see buddha, and all those who have joined the assembly of buddha ancestors to practice a ninety-day practice period have seen buddhas.

If we are fortunate enough to practice a summer practice period before our dewlike life drops down, whether in the realm of humans or devas, we will surely replace our skin, flesh, bones, and marrow with the skin, flesh, bones, and marrow of buddha ancestors. During every practice period it is the buddha ancestors who come to practice with everyone, and everyone who participates in the practice period practices as a buddha ancestor. Because of this, those who engage in a practice period are called "one thousand buddhas and ten thousand ancestors." The reason for this is that a practice period is the skin, flesh, bones, and marrow as well as the mind, consciousness, and body of buddha ancestors. Practice period is the top of the head, the eye, the fist, the nostrils, and the buddha-nature circle drawn in the air, as well as the whisk, the wooden staff, the bamboo stick, and the sitting mat of buddha ancestors. Practice period is neither creating something new nor reusing something old.

The World-Honored One said to Complete Enlightenment Bodhisattva and all those in the assembly, as well as to all beings:

Those who participate in the three-month summer practice period should abide as pure bodhisattvas, their minds free from the world's chattering, uninvolved with the world's opinions. On the opening day of the practice period, make a statement like this in front of the buddha image: I—Monk, Nun, Layman, or Laywoman so-and-so—now mount the bodhisattva vehicle in order to activate the practice of tranquillity and together with all beings enter the true mark of purity and abide in it so that we can all make complete enlightenment our temple. The wisdom of equanimity and the freedom of nirvana are without boundary; I pay homage to them. Without being influenced by the opinions of the world, I will engage in the three-month practice period with all the tathagatas and great bodhisattvas of the ten directions. Because I am now embarking on the practice of the great cause of the unsurpassable, wondrous enlightenment of all bodhisattvas, I am free of the bondage of the world. Good people, this is a practice period that manifests bodhisattvas.

Thus, when monks, nuns, laymen, or laywomen participate in a three-month practice period, they invariably practice the great cause of unsurpassable, wondrous enlightenment together with tathagatas and great bodhisattvas in the ten directions. Note that it is not only monks and nuns who participate in the practice period; laymen and laywomen also participate.

The place of this practice period is great, complete enlightenment. This being so, Vulture Peak and Jeta Grove are equally tathagatas' temples of great, complete enlightenment. Hear and understand the World-Honored One's teaching that tathagatas and great bodhisattvas of the ten directions practice together with you in the three-month practice period.

The World-Honored One held a ninety-day practice period in a monastery. On the last day, when all the monks are to confess their faults and ask for forgiveness, Manjushri suddenly appeared in the assembly.

Mahakashyapa asked Manjushri, "Where have you spent the summer practice period?"

Manjushri replied, "In three places" [a demon's palace, a wealthy man's house, and a house of prostitution].

Mahakashyapa immediately assembled the monks to announce that Manjushri would be expelled; he lifted the mallet and was about to strike the sounding block of wood when suddenly he saw countless monasteries appear and in each of them there were a Manjushri and a Mahakashyapa. Just at the moment Mahakashyapa raised the mallet and was about to strike the sounding block signaling the expulsions of the multiple Manjushris that were in the multiple monasteries, the World-Honored One said to Mahakashyapa, "Which of these Manjushris are you going to expel?" Mahakashyapa was dumbfounded.

Keqin, Zen Master Yuanwu, commented on this: "An unstruck bell won't ring; an unbeaten drum won't sound. Mahakashyapa made it to the ferry station; Manjushri's sitting rides the waves through unlimited space. This is an excellent enactment of the buddha scene, but unfortunately Mahakashyapa missed one move. He should have responded to Old Man Shakyamuni's question by striking the sounding block; then he would have seen how the old one destroys the whole world at once."

Keqin added a capping verse to this:

> A great elephant doesn't play in a rabbit hutch.
> Swallows and sparrows don't have the heart of an eagle.
> Careful precision, yet flowing with the wind,
> hitting the mark and biting off the arrowhead.
> The entire world is Manjushri.
> The entire world is Mahakashyapa.
> Solemnly they face each other—
> who can be punished by Mahakashyapa?
> One good swing—the Golden Ascetic [Mahakashyapa]
>   dropped it.

Thus, although the World-Honored One practiced a practice period in one place while Manjushri practiced in three places, Manjushri was not a nonparticipant in the practice period. Those who are nonparticipants in the practice period are nonbuddhas and nonbodhisattvas. There are no descendents of buddha ancestors who are nonparticipants in practice period. Know that all practice period participants are always descendents of buddha ancestors.

Participation in the practice period is the body and mind, eye, and life energy of buddha ancestors. Those who do not abide peacefully in practice period are neither buddha ancestors nor descendents of buddha ancestors. Buddhas and bodhisattvas made of mud, wood, metal, or the seven precious substances all sit the three-month summer practice period together. Practice period is the buddha's instruction, an authentic custom that maintains the buddha-dharma-sangha treasure. Those within the house of buddha ancestors should therefore wholeheartedly sit the three-month summer practice period.

Presented to the assembly of the Daibutsu Monastery, Echizen Province, on the thirteenth day, the sixth month, during the summer practice period, in the third year of the Kangen Era [1245].

80

SEEING OTHERS' MINDS

Huizhong, National Teacher Dazheng of the Guangzhai Monastery in Xijing, was from Zhuji, Yue Province. His family name was Ran. After receiving the mind seal, he resided in Dangzi Valley, Mount Boya of Nanyang, for over forty years without going out of the monastery gate.

His practice was known in the imperial capital [of Chang'an]. In the second year of the Shangyuan Era [761] of the Tang Dynasty, Emperor Su dispatched Sun Zhongjin as his messenger, invited Huizhong to the palace, and asked him to be his teacher. The emperor appointed Huizhong abbot of the Xichan Temple of the Qianfu Monastery.

Later, Emperor Dai visited Huizhong and asked him to be abbot of the Guangzhai Monastery, where Huizhong resided for sixteen years, expounding dharma on occasion.

There was a man called Tripitaka Master Daer from India. He claimed that he had mastered the power of seeing others' minds. Emperor Dai asked Huizhong to test him.

Daer saw Huizhong, bowed to him, and stood on the right side of him.

Huizhong said, "Have you mastered the art of seeing others' minds?"
Daer said, "Not really."

Huizhong said, "Tell me where this old monk is."

Daer said, "You are the teacher of the nation, reverend. Why are you in the West River enjoying the racing boats?"

Huizhong paused for a while and said, "Tell me where this old monk is now."

Daer said, "You are the teacher of the nation, reverend. Why are you on the Tianjin Bridge watching monkeys play?"

Huizhong again said, "Tell me where this old monk is at this very moment."

Daer tried to see for some time but could not see where Huizhong was.

Huizhong yelled: "You are possessed by the spirit of a wild fox. You don't have the power of seeing others' minds."

Daer remained silent.

A monk asked Zhaozhou, "Why didn't Daer see where Huizhong was the third time?"

Zhaozhou said, "Huizhong was on top of Daer's nostrils, so he could not see Huizhong."

A monk asked Xuansha, "Why did Daer not see Huizhong, who was on top of his nostrils?"

Xuansha said, "Because he was too close."

A monk asked Yangshan, "Why could Daer not answer the third time?"

Yangshan said, "The first two times Daer was dealing with an object of mind. But later, Huizhong entered receptive samadhi. That's why Daer could not see him."

Haihui Shouduan said, "If Huizhong was on top of Daer's nostrils, why was it difficult to see? Because Daer did not know that Huizhong was inside his eyeball."

Also, Xuansha criticized Daer by saying, "Say! Did you actually see Huizhong the first two times?"

Xuedou [Zhongxian], Zen Master Mingjue, said, "You lost. You lost."

––––––––––

A number of stinky fists [determined practitioners], particularly these five masters, have spoken of this story of Huizhong testing Tripitaka Master Daer.

These five masters strike the point but still miss Huizhong's practice. It's like saying Daer did not get it the third time but did the first two times. This is how they miss it. Those who study later should be aware of it.

I have two doubts about these five masters. One: they did not know why Huizhong had tested Daer. Two: they did not know the body and mind of Huizhong.

Now, the reason I say that they did not know why Huizhong had tested Daer is this: First of all, Huizhong said, *Tell me where this old monk is.* This is how he asked Daer if he had the eye to see and hear buddha dharma. He is asking Daer if he had mastered seeing others' minds in buddha dharma.

If Daer had understood buddha dharma, he would have had a way to go beyond discriminatory thoughts or would have had a means to directly experience thusness when Huizhong asked this question.

Huizhong's question, *Tell me where this old monk is,* was like saying, "Who am I?" Asking, *Tell me where this old monk is,* was asking, "What is the time right now?" *Tell me where* is no other than asking, "Where is this?" It is just like inquiring, "What do you call this old monk?" Huizhong is not necessarily the old monk. The old monk is a fist [an accomplished practitioner].

Although Daer was from India, he did not see through Huizhong's mind because he had not understood buddha dharma. He had only studied views of ordinary people or of the Two Lesser Vehicles.

Huizhong said again, *Tell me where this old monk is now.* For this Daer presented another fruitless statement.

Huizhong finally asked, *Tell me where this old monk is at this very moment.* Daer thought about it for some time but did not say anything. He was dumbfounded. Then Huizhong scolded him and said, *You are possessed by the spirit of a wild fox. You don't have the power of seeing others' minds.* But Daer could not say anything. He had no way to penetrate the way.

Regarding this case, all of the five masters thought that Huizhong's criticism indicated that Daer knew where he was the first two times but he did not the third time.

It is not so. Huizhong scolded Daer that he had not even dreamed of buddha dharma. It is not that Daer knew where he was the first two times but he did not the third time. Huizhong scolded Daer for being unable to see through others' minds though he claimed to be able to do so.

Huizhong's first point was to test Daer by asking if there was the power of seeing others' minds in buddha dharma. Daer said *Not really,* but, in fact, he meant there was.

Then Huizhong thought that Daer would be right if he said there was the power of seeing others' minds in buddha dharma and let the power be manifested in buddha dharma. But if he could not prove what he said, this would not be buddha dharma.

Even if Daer had a right answer the third time, what he said the first two times was not right expression; he should be scolded altogether. The reason why Huizhong asked him three times was to see if Daer had understood the true meaning of the question.

Secondly, I say that these five masters did not understand Huizhong's mind. The reason is this: The body and mind of Huizhong were not easily known and understood by Daer. They cannot be reached by bodhisattvas of the ten stages or three classes, or known by bodhisattvas whose enlightenment is equal to buddhas', being close to becoming buddhas. How could an ordinary person like Daer know the entire body of Huizhong? Clearly understand this.

Be sure of this. To say that the body and mind of Huizhong can be known by a scholar of the Tripitaka is to slander buddha dharma. To think that Huizhong is only equal to a master of sutras and treatises is extreme confusion. Do not assume that those who have the power of seeing others' minds can tell Huizhong's whereabouts.

The art of seeing others' minds is a folk practice of India, and there were some who had mastered it. But it is not based on the aspiration for enlightenment, nor on the right Mahayana view. There have been no known examples of such practitioners who realized buddha dharma with the art of seeing others' minds.

It is possible to enter realization of buddha dharma for those who have mastered the art of seeing others' minds, if they arouse the aspiration for enlightenment and practice like ordinary people. If the art of seeing others' minds had the power to help understand the buddha way, all ancient sages would have first acquired the art of seeing others' minds and understood the fruit of buddhahood with its power. However, this has never been the case for the emergence of one thousand or ten thousand buddhas. What would they do without knowing the way of buddha ancestors? I must say that such an art would be of no use in the buddha way. There is no difference in maintaining buddha nature between those who have mastered the art of seeing others' minds and those who have not.

You who study buddha dharma should not think that the five or six miraculous powers of those outside the way or those in the Two Lesser Vehicles surpass ordinary people. It is just that those who have way-seeking mind and want to study buddha dharma surpass those who have mastered the five or six miraculous powers. It is like the singing voice of a karavinka chick inside an egg already surpassing the voices of all other birds.

Furthermore, what is called the art of seeing others' minds in India should be seen as the art of seeing others' thoughts. Although practitioners of the art can relate to thoughts that have arisen, they have no idea about thoughts that have not yet arisen. It is ridiculous.

Even further, mind is not necessarily thought; thought is not necessarily mind. When mind is thought, however, one who has mastered the art of seeing others' minds does not know it. When thought is mind, one who has mastered the art of seeing others' minds does not know it.

Thus, those who have mastered five or six miraculous powers in India do not come up to those who cut weeds and work on rice fields in this country. Such miraculous powers are useless. Because they are not essential, the earlier teachers in China and eastward never favored or practiced such powers.

A foot-wide jade may be more useful than such powers. And yet, a foot-wide jade is not a treasure. A moment of time is most essential.

Who, among those who value each moment, has time to practice such powers? Thus, remind yourself that the power of seeing others' minds does not come close to the realm of buddha wisdom.

Nevertheless, the five masters all thought that Daer had known where Huizhong was the first two times. It is a great mistake. Huizhong was a buddha ancestor. Daer was an ordinary person. How could they understand each other?

Huizhong first said, *Tell me where this old monk is.* There is nothing hidden in this question. It was not Daer's fault that he did not understand its true meaning. But it was a mistake that the five masters could not hear and see it.

Huizhong's question was *Tell me where this old monk is.* He did not say, "Tell me where my mind is," or "Tell me where my thought is." This is the point that one needs to notice and examine. But the five masters did not notice and examine this point. Because of that, they did not understand Huizhong's body and mind. The one who has the point of this teaching is Huizhong, and the one who does not is not Huizhong.

The five masters could not know Huizhong, as his body and mind were neither large nor small, neither self nor other. It seems that they forgot that Huizhong had a head top and nostrils. Although he practiced continuously, how could he have intended to become a buddha? Thus, one should not take up a buddha and give dualistic interpretations.

Huizhong did have the body and mind of buddha dharma. Do not try to understand him with the practice of miraculous powers. Do not discuss him by emptying thought and forgetting relationships. He was not where discernment and beyond discernment could hit the point.

Huizhong neither had buddha nature nor did not have buddha nature. He was not the body of void. The body and mind of Huizhong were ungraspable. In the assembly of Huineng at Caoxi, beside Qingyuan and Nanyue, only Huizhong, National Teacher Dazheng, was a buddha ancestor.

The five masters' views should be altogether seen through:

Zhaozhou said, *Huizhong was on top of Daer's nostrils, so he could not see Huizhong.* This statement did not hit the point. How could Huizhong be on top of Daer's nostrils? Daer didn't have nostrils. Had he had nostrils, Huizhong would have had a true encounter with him. Had Huizhong had a true encounter with him, it would have been nostrils seeing nostrils. Daer, however, did not have a true encounter with Huizhong.

Xuansha said, *Because he was too close.* Daer was not even close. He was not in Huizhong's neighborhood. How could Xuansha say *too close*? He did not know what was too close, and he did not practice what was too close. Although he knew that what is too close is not true encountering, he did not know that true encountering is too close. I should say that Xuansha was far, far away in buddha dharma. If he meant that Daer was too close only at the third time, the first two times would be much too close.

Let me ask Xuansha now: What do you regard as too close? A fist? An eyeball? From now on, do not say what is too close is not worth examining.

Yangshan said, *The first two times Daer was dealing with an object of mind. But later, Huizhong entered receptive samadhi. That's why Daer could not see him.* Although his fame as Small Shakyamuni prevailed in India, his statement is completely wrong. It is not that merging with the object of mind and receptive samadhi are different. So he should not have said that Daer had not seen Huizhong because merging with the object of mind and receptive samadhi are different. Thus, although Yangshan presented a reason why Daer had not seen Huizhong the third time, his statement was not yet a [correct] statement.

If one did not see another in receptive samadhi, receptive samadhi would not manifest and actualize receptive samadhi. If Yangshan assumed that Daer had known Huizhong's whereabouts the first two times, he could be someone who understood buddha dharma.

Daer did not know or see Huizhong's whereabouts the third time, or the first two times. As Yangshan made such a statement, neither Daer nor Yangshan knew Huizhong's whereabouts.

Let me ask Yangshan: where is Huizhong now? When Yangshan is about to speak, I will give him a shout.

Xuansha criticized Daer by saying, *Did you actually see Huizhong the first two times?* This statement appears to express what needs to be expressed. But Xuansha ought to examine his own statement. This is a good statement. But it is like seeing without seeing. Thus, it is not right.

Xuedou, Zen Master Mingjiao, said upon hearing Xuansha, *You lost. You lost.* Xuedou should have said so if he had approved Xuansha. He should not have said so if he did not.

Haihui Shouduan said, *If Huizhong was on top of Daer's nostrils, why was it difficult to see? Because Daer did not know that Huizhong was inside his eyeball.* He only discussed the third time. He should have denied Daer's seeing of Huizhong the first two times, but he didn't. How could he know that Huizhong was on top of Daer's nose or inside his eyeball?

As Haihui said this, we should say that he did not hear Huizhong. Daer did not have nostrils or an eyeball. Even if he had his eyeball and nostrils, if Huizhong had entered Daer's eyeball and nostrils, they would have exploded. If they had exploded, they would not have been Huizhong's cave or basket [abode].

None of these five masters was clear about Huizhong's teaching. Huizhong is a buddha who excelled in his time, a tathagata of the world. He had clarified and authentically received transmission of the Buddha's treasury of the true dharma eye. Certainly maintaining the soapberry-pit [complete] eye, he transmitted dharma to himself, who was buddha, and to others who were buddhas.

Although Huizhong practiced simultaneously with Shakyamuni Buddha, he also practiced simultaneously with the Seven Original Buddhas. He attained the way before the King of the Empty Eon, after the King of the Empty Eon, and at the very time of the King of the Empty Eon.

Naturally, Huizhong abides in the Saha World, but his Saha World is not necessarily in the world of phenomena, or in the entire world of the ten directions. Shakyamuni Buddha, who presides over the Saha World, will not take away or hinder Huizhong's land. It is just like buddha ancestors from the past and future who will not rob or hinder each other. This is so, because attaining the way of buddha ancestors from the past and future is totally immersed in attaining the way.

Clearly understand that Daer's not knowing Huizhong can be a proof that shravakas and pratyeka-buddhas in the Lesser Vehicles cannot even come close to buddha ancestors. Study the meaning of Huizhong's criticism of Daer.

If Huizhong's whereabouts had been guessed the first two times and he had criticized Daer the third time, it would not have been a point of teaching. Guessing two out of three would be no different from guessing all three times. This would not be a criticism. If Huizhong had criticized in this way, Daer would not have been criticized for complete ignorance. What Daer guessed would have been Huizhong's shame. If so, who would have trusted Huizhong? People would have criticized him for what Daer had guessed.

Huizhong's intention was to criticize Daer for never knowing his whereabouts, his thoughts, his body and mind, these three times. He criticized Daer for not having seen, heard, or studied buddha dharma. Because of this intention, Huizhong asked the same question three times.

First Daer said, *You are the teacher of the nation, reverend. Why are you in the West River enjoying the racing boats?* But Huizhong did not utter words. He did not admit that Daer knew his whereabouts. He just kept asking the same question. Without knowing the true meaning of his intention, for hundreds of years after Huizhong, masters of various places have mistakenly expressed their opinions.

None of these five masters' statements express Huizhong's intention, nor do they fit the meaning of buddha dharma. What a pity that the old gimlets before and after are all mistaken!

———————

If you say that there is the art of seeing others' minds in buddha dharma, there should be the art of seeing others' bodies, the art of seeing others' fists, and the art of seeing others' eyeballs. If so, there should be the art of seeing through the mind of the self and the art of seeing through the body of the self. And if so, the self taking up the mind of the self is the art of seeing through the mind of the self. To manifest such a statement is the art of seeing others' minds, by the self and by the mind.

Now ask: "Is it all right to take up the art of seeing others' minds?"

Or, "Is it all right to take up the art of seeing through the mind of the self?" Answer quickly. Answer quickly.

Setting these questions aside, "You have attained my marrow" is no other than the art of seeing others' minds.

Presented to the assembly of the Daibutsu Monastery, Echizen Province, on the fourth day, the seventh month, the third year of the Kangen Era [1245].

81

KING WANTS THE SAINDHAVA

EXPRESSING WITH WORDS and without words is like a wisteria vine entwined around a tree, herding a donkey and a horse, or penetrating water and cloud.

Thus, the World-Honored One said in the *Great Maha Pari-nirvana Sutra*:

> It is like a great king telling his courtiers to bring the saindhava. The word *saindhava* indicates any of four things: water, salt, cup, or horse. These four things are called by the same name.
>
> A wise courtier understood this word well. When the king was about to wash his hands and wanted the saindhava, the courtier would bring water. When the king was about to have a meal and wanted the saindhava, the courtier would bring some salt. When the king finished eating and asked for the saindhava so he could have a drink, the courtier would bring the cup. When the king desired to go out and requested the saindhava, the courtier would bring the horse.
>
> This wise courtier thoroughly understood the great king's subtle use of this word.

This story of the king wanting the saindhava and the courtier bringing it has been handed down for a long time. It has been transmitted just like a dharma robe.

As the World-Honored One did not fail to bring it up, his descendants often quoted him. I suspect that those who practice together with the World-Honored One journey with the saindhava. Those who do not practice together with the World-Honored One should buy sandals and take one step of the journey to understand it.

The saindhava subtly permeates the house of buddha ancestors, just as it did in the house of the great king.

Hongzhi, Old Buddha of Mount Tiantong, Qingyuan Prefecture of Great Song, ascended the teaching seat and spoke to the assembly:

> A monk asked Zhaozhou, 'What about the moment the king wants the saindhava?'
> Zhaozhou bent his body forward and held his hands together.
> Xuedou later commented: "When the king wanted salt, the courtier brought the horse."
> Xuedou established a house one hundred years ago. Zhaozhou was an old buddha who lived for one hundred twenty years. If Zhaozhou was right, Xuedou was not right. If Xuedou was right, Zhaozhou was not right.
> Say it now. Ultimately, what is this?
> I cannot help adding comments. If there is a hairbreadth of discrepancy, I would miss it by ten thousand *li*.
> Even if you understand it, it is like scaring a snake by hitting the grass. Even if you don't understand it, it is like burning paper coins to attract the spirit of the dead. If you don't plow an unattended field, it will be like Old Monk Juzhi [who would always hold up one finger]. I just let my hand take it up.

When Rujing, my late master, ascended the teaching seat, he would often mention Old Buddha Xuedou. The only one who encountered Xuedou was Rujing, my late master, Old Buddha. At the time of Xuedou, there was someone called Zonggao, Zen Master Dahui of Mount Jing, a remote descendant of Nanyue. People all over Song China think he equaled or even excelled Xuedou. This mistake was made because monks and laypeople in Song China are shallow in their studies and their eyes are not clear; they do not discern true persons, nor do they have the power to discern themselves.

Hongzhi's words expressed the true heart. Thus, study the meaning of *Zhaozhou bent forward and held his hands together.* At this very moment, is it the king wanting the saindhava, or is it the courtier bringing the saindhava?

Study Xuedou's words, *When the king wanted salt, the courtier brought the horse.* Wanting salt and bringing the horse are also the king wanting the saindhava and the courtier wanting the saindhava.

The World-Honored One wanted the saindhava and Mahakashyapa smiled. Bodhidharma wanted the saindhava and his four disciples brought the horse, the salt, the water, and the cup. Study the key point that when the horse, the salt, the water, and the cup want the saindhava, the horse is brought and the water is brought.

———————

One day Nanquan saw Deng Yinfeng coming. He pointed to a water jar and said, "That jar is an object. There is water in it. Bring me the water without moving the object."

Deng Yinfeng brought the jar and poured out the water in front of Nanquan.

Nanquan shut up.

When Nanquan wanted water, the ocean dried out to the bottom. When Deng Yinfeng brought the jar, he tilted it and poured out the water. Thus, investigate water in an object and an object in water. Water has not moved, the object has not moved.

———————

Xiangyan, Great Master Xideng, was asked by a monk, "What is the meaning of the king wanting the saindhava?"

Xiangyan said, "Get over here."

The monk got closer.

Xiangyan said, "Human stupidity is deadly."

Now, let me ask you: do the words by Xiangyan, *Get over here,* indicate wanting the saindhava or bringing the saindhava? Tell me. I ask you.

Responding to Xiangyan's words, the monk got closer. Was it what Xiangyan wanted? Was it what Xiangyan brought forth? Had it been just as expected by Xiangyan? If it had not been expected, Xiangyan would not have said, *Human stupidity is deadly.*

Even if these words were Xiangyan's utmost statement, he could not have avoided the lack of vitality. It sounds like the commander of a lost battle boasting about the fight.

Expounding yellow and speaking in detail of black [expressing this way and that], through head top and eye, is the wanting and the bringing of the saindhava. Who doesn't know about taking up a staff and taking up a whisk? And yet, this cannot be done by those who try to keep a stringed instrument in tune by gluing down its movable bridges [causing a lack of flexibility]. As they do not understand the effect of gluing down the bridges, they do not have the capacity to keep the koto in tune.

———

One day the World-Honored One ascended the teaching seat.

Manjushri struck a bell with a mallet and said to the assembly, "Contemplate the Dharma King's teaching. The Dharma King's teaching is just like this."

The World-Honored One descended the seat.

Xuedou Zhongxian, Zen Master Mingjiao, commented on this story: "In the assembly of sages, only masters know that the dharma of the Dharma King is not like that. If there had been a person of the saindhava in the assembly, how would Manjushri have struck the bell with his mallet?"

Thus, Xuedou suggested in this statement that if this single mallet is entirely without fault, both striking and not striking are dropped away without fault. If it is so, a single striking of the mallet is the saindhava.

If you are a person of thusness, you are a person of the saindhava in the assembly [of the Buddha]. This being so, the dharma of the Dharma King is thus. Activating the twelve hours of the day is to want the sain-

dhava. Being activated by the twelve hours of the day is to want the saindhava. Want a fist and bring a fist. Want a whisk and bring a whisk.

Those who are called elders in monasteries in China, however, have
never dreamed of the saindhava. How painful! How terrible that the
ancestral way is declining! Don't be negligent in your endeavor of the
way. Receive and maintain the buddha ancestors' life vein.

For example, ask, "What is buddha?" Or say, "Mind is itself buddha."
What does it mean? Is it not the saindhava?

Thoroughly investigate who is "Mind is itself buddha." Who knows
the poundings and cracklings of the saindhava?

*Presented to the assembly of the Daibutsu Monastery on the twenty-second day,
the tenth month, the third year of the Kangen Era [1245].*

EIHEI MONASTERY PERIOD

1246–1253

82

INSTRUCTIONS ON KITCHEN WORK

Presented to the assembly on the sixth day, the eighth month, the fourth year of the Kangen Era [1246].

Regarding the method of serving meals to the community of monks, it is said [in the *Guidelines for Zen Monasteries*], "Make respect the essence of this pure practice."

The method that has been authentically transmitted from faraway India to neighboring China, after the pari-nirvana of the Tathagata, is to serve the offerings from the devas to the Buddha and monks, and to dedicate the kingly meals to the Buddha and monks. In addition, there are meals offered from the households of wealthy families and lay practitioners, and also from the households of those in the merchant and untouchable classes.

Such offerings should be equally respected and handled with utmost care. The deepest bows and the most venerated words among humans and devas should be employed for serving the food. Even on a deep and remote mountain the authentic manner and speech found in the monastery kitchen should be maintained. This is how humans and devas learn the buddha dharma.

Call the morning meal *onkayu* [the honorific form of *kayu*], and do not bluntly call it *kayu*. Call the midday meal *ontoki* [the honorific form of *toki*], and do not call it *toki*. Call the midday meal time *saiji* [in a formal way].

Say "Yone mairaseyo" or "Shirome maira seyo" ["Please serve the rice" in a formal way], and don't say "Yone tsuke yo" ["Put the rice on" in a disrespectful way]. Say "Jomai shi maira seyo" ["Please clean the rice" in a formal way], and do not say "Yone kase" ["Wash the rice" in a disrespectful way].

Say "Osai wo eri maira seyo" ["Please select vegetables (in the honorific form) for cooking"], and don't say "Sai ere" ["Pick vegetables"]. Say "Oshiru no mono, shi mairase yo" ["Please cook the soup" in a respectful way], but don't say "Shiru niyo." Say "On atsunomono shi mairase yo," ["Make hot vegetables," in the honorific form] and don't say "Atsumono seyo."

Say "Ontoki [or] onkayu wa mumase sase tamai taru" ("The midday meal or the morning meal is fully cooked" in an honorific form). All the materials being prepared for the midday or morning meals should be referred to with respect in this way. Being disrespectful to materials causes disaster and brings forth no merit.

When you prepare the midday or morning meal, don't blow onto the rice, vegetables, or any other food. Do not let the sleeves of your work clothes touch any food, even food that is dry.

Do not touch the utensils or food for the midday or morning meal with the hand you have used to touch your head or face; first wash your hands. From the time you select good rice grains until the time you cook the rice and vegetables, always wash your hands if you happen to scratch yourself.

When you cook, chant lines from a sutra or words of a buddha ancestor. Do not make worldly or unnecessary conversation.

Use honorific forms of verbs for describing how to handle rice, vegetables, salt, and soy sauce; do not use plain language for this.

When passing by food prepared for the morning or midday meal, monks and workers should make a standing bow toward the food with hands joined together. Dropped grains of rice or pieces of vegetables should be used later. Do not disrupt the meal serving [by picking them up and trying to use them right away].

Carefully protect the tools for cooking meals, and do not use them for anything else. Do not let those from lay households touch the tools before they have washed their hands. Purify unwashed vegetables and fruit from lay households with water, incense, and fire before you offer them to the three treasures and the assembly of monks.

Nowadays, in monasteries on various mountains of Great Song China, when bean cakes, milk cakes, or steamed cakes are brought from lay households, they are steamed again and then offered to the assembly of monks. This is to purify the food; without this procedure the food is not offered to the monks.

These are some of the many guidelines. Grasp the essential meaning of them and practice them in the kitchen. Do not be negligent.

These guidelines are the life vein of buddha ancestors, the eyeball of monks. Those who are outside the way do not know them. Heavenly demons do not bear them. Only children of the Buddha receive transmission of them. The officer in charge of the kitchen should understand these guidelines clearly and not ignore them.

Instructed by Dogen, Founding Monk.

POSTSCRIPT

To the officers of the Eihei Monastery: From now on, if you happen to receive meal offerings from donors to the monastery, hold them until the following day. However, noodles, cakes, and various kinds of gruel should be distributed in the evening. These are medicinal snacks [supper] in the assemblies of buddha ancestors. There are excellent precedents for such practice in Great Song China. Just as the Tathagata permitted the wearing of double clothes in the Snow Mountains [Himalayas], medicinal snacks during the time of snow are permitted in this monastery.

Founding monk of the Eihei Monastery, Kigen [Dogen].

83

LEAVING THE HOUSEHOLD

THE *GUIDELINES FOR Zen Monasteries* says:

It is taught that all buddhas in the past, present, and future leave the
household and attain the way. The twenty-eight ancestors in India and
the six early ancestors in China who transmitted the Buddha's mind seal
were all monks. They are distinguished in the three realms by strictly
observing the precepts. Thus, precepts are primary for practicing Zen
in pursuit of the way. How can one become a buddha ancestor without
becoming free from faults and preventing wrongdoing?

In preparation for receiving the precepts you should have three
types of robes, eating bowls and utensils, and new and purified clothes.
If new clothes are not available, use freshly washed clothes. Do not borrow clothes or eating bowls for stepping onto the platform to receive
the precepts. Concentrate your mind and do not be concerned with
other matters. To take a form of the Buddha, to embody the precepts of
the Buddha, and to acquire what the Buddha received are not a trifle.
You should not be casual about it. If you borrow someone's robes and
bowls, you do not actually receive the precepts, even if you step onto
the platform and receive them. Without actually receiving the precepts,
you will be one without precepts, mistakenly associated with the gate of
emptiness [buddha dharma] and falsely accepting faithful donations.

Beginning practitioners may not be familiar with the guidelines. Without a teacher's advice, they may make such mistakes. So, here is some advice. Keep it in mind.

If you have already received the bhikshu precepts, receive the bodhisattva precepts. This is the beginning of entering the dharma.

Clearly know that the attainment of the way by all buddhas and ancestors is only accomplished by leaving the household and receiving the precepts. The life vein of all buddhas and ancestors is no other than leaving the household and receiving the precepts. None of those who have not left the household are buddha ancestors. To meet a buddha and to meet an ancestor is to leave the household and receive the precepts.

Mahakashyapa followed the World-Honored One, aspired to leave the household, and expressed hope to awaken all beings.

The World-Honored One said, "Come, monk."

Then, Mahakashyapa's hair dropped all by itself and a kashaya wrapped around his body.

This is an excellent example of leaving the household and receiving the precepts when one studied with the Buddha and hoped to liberate all beings.

The *Maha Prajna Paramita Sutra* quotes the Buddha, the World-Honored One, in its third fascicle:

Some bodhisattvas, great beings, may think in this way:

"Someday I will abandon my country and my position, and leave my household. On that day I will attain unsurpassable, complete enlightenment and turn the dharma wheel. I will help innumerable sentient beings to become free from dust and defilement and give rise to a pure dharma eye. I will also help innumerable sentient beings to keep transforming delusion and attain unsurpassable, complete enlightenment without remitting."

If such bodhisattvas, great beings, want to fulfill such a vow, they should study the manifestation of prajna.

In this way, unsurpassable enlightenment is fulfilled at the moment you leave the household and receive the precepts. It is not fulfilled other than on this day.

Thus, you take up the day of leaving the household and actualize the day of attaining unsurpassable enlightenment. Taking up the day of attaining unsurpassable enlightenment is the day of leaving the household.

To turn cartwheels on the day of leaving the household is to turn the wondrous dharma wheel. This leaving the household makes innumerable sentient beings unremitting in unsurpassable enlightenment.

Know that to fulfill benefiting the self and benefiting the other and to be unremitting in unsurpassable enlightenment are leaving the household and receiving the precepts. Attaining unsurpassable enlightenment in turn actualizes the day of leaving the household.

Know that the day of leaving the household goes beyond one or many. On the day of leaving the household, you practice and realize countless eons. On the day of leaving the household, you cross over the boundless ocean of eons and turn the wondrous dharma wheel.

The day of leaving the household is not the length of a mealtime. It is not sixty small eons. It goes beyond the past, present, and future. It drops away from the top of the head. The day of leaving the household goes beyond the day of leaving the household. This being so, by crushing baskets and traps, the day of leaving the household becomes the day of leaving the household. The day of attaining the way becomes the day of attaining the way.

The *Treatise on Realization of Great Wisdom* says in its thirteenth fascicle:

When the Buddha was at Jeta Grove, there was a drunken Brahman. He went to see the Buddha and asked him to make him a monk. The Buddha told his monks to shave the Brahman's head and let him wear a buddha robe. When the man became sober, he was shocked to see himself turned into a monk, so he ran away.

The monks asked the Buddha, "Why did you allow that drunken Brahman to become a monk? When he saw what you had done, he ran away."

The Buddha said, "That Brahman would never intend to leave the household even for innumerable eons. But, because he aroused a faint aspiration when he was drunk, due to such causes and conditions he will leave the household and attain the way in the future.

"In this way, there are a variety of causes and conditions for leaving the household. Breaking the precepts as a home leaver is better than keeping them as a layperson. You cannot experience emancipation by keeping the precepts as a layperson."

Thus, the essence of the Buddha's teaching is clear. His teaching makes home leaving primary. Those who have not left the household are not in buddha dharma. When the Tathagata was living in the world, a number of those outside the way wanted to give up their wrong paths and take refuge in him, so first they asked his permission to leave the household.

The Tathagata would accept them by saying, "Come, monk." And when he asked his monks to shave their heads and faces, helping them to leave the household and receive the precepts, the procedure of leaving the household and receiving the precepts was immediately complete.

Know that when Mahakashyapa accepted the Buddha's teaching in his body and mind, his hair dropped spontaneously from his head and his body was wrapped by a kashaya. Without the permission of buddhas, his hair and beard would not have been shaved off, his body would not have been wrapped by the kashaya, and he would not have received the precepts. Thus, leaving the household and receiving the precepts are no other than being personally given the prediction of enlightenment by buddha tathagatas.

———————

Shakyamuni Buddha said:

Good people, the Tathagata, seeing that sentient beings pursue minor matters, being thin in their virtue and heavy in their defilement, tells them, "I left the household when I was young and attained unsurpassable, complete enlightenment. Truly, I have been a buddha for a long time. I teach sentient beings with skillful means and speak in this way for the sake of letting them enter the buddha way."

Thus, *I have been a buddha for a long time* is because *I left the household when I was young. Unsurpassable, complete enlightenment* is *I left the household when I was young.* When the Buddha says *I left the household when I was young,* sentient beings who *pursue minor matters, being thin in their virtue and heavy in their defilement,* follow the Buddha and leave the household when they are young.

When sentient beings see, hear, and study the Buddha's words *I left the household when I was young,* they encounter the Buddha's *unsurpassable, complete enlightenment.* When the Buddha awakens sentient beings *thin in their virtue and heavy in their defilement,* he tells them, *I left the household when I was young* and *I attained unsurpassable, complete enlightenment.*

Even though this is so, ask, "How much is the merit of leaving the household?"

If someone asks in this way, say, "To the top of the head."

Presented to the assembly of the Eihei Monastery, Echizen Province, on the fifteenth day, the ninth month, the fourth year of the Kangen Era [1246].

84

EIGHT AWAKENINGS
OF GREAT BEINGS

ALL BUDDHAS ARE great beings. What great beings practice is called the eight awakenings. Practicing these awakenings is the basis for nirvana. This is the last teaching of our original teacher Shakyamuni Buddha, which he gave on the night he entered pari-nirvana.

———————

[The *Buddha's Pari-nirvana Admonition Outline Sutra* (*Buddha's Willed Teaching Sutra*) says:]

The first awakening is to have few desires. To refrain from widely coveting the objects of the five-sense desires is called "few desires."

The Buddha said, "Monks, know that people who have many desires intensely seek fame and gain; therefore they suffer a great deal. Those who have few desires do not seek fame and gain and are free from them, so they are without such troubles. Having few desires is itself worthwhile. It is even more so because it creates various merits: Those who have few desires need not flatter to gain others' favor. Those who have few desires are not compelled by their sense organs; they have a serene mind and do not worry because they are satisfied with what they have and do not have a sense of lack. Those who have few desires experience nirvana. This is called 'few desires.'"

The second awakening is to know how much is enough. Even if you already have something, you set a limit for yourself for using it, so you should know how much is enough.

The Buddha said, "Monks, if you want to be free from suffering, you should contemplate knowing how much is enough. By knowing it, you are in the place of enjoyment and peacefulness. If you know how much is enough, you are content even when you sleep on the ground. If you don't know it, you are discontent even when you are in heaven. You can feel rich even if you are poor. You can feel poor even if you have much wealth. You may be constantly compelled by the five-sense desires and pitied by those who know how much is enough. This is called 'to know how much is enough.'"

The third awakening is to enjoy serenity. This is to be away from noise and confusion, and stay alone in a quiet place. Thus, it is called "to enjoy serenity in seclusion."

The Buddha said, "Monks, if you want to have the joy of serene nondoing, you should be away from the crowds and stay alone in a quiet place. A still place is what Indra and other devas revere. By leaving behind your relations as well as others', and by living in a quiet place, you may contemplate the conditions of suffering. If you are attached to the crowds, you will receive suffering, just like a tree that attracts a great many birds and gets killed by them. If you are bound by worldly matters, you will drown in troubles, just like an old elephant who is stuck in a swamp and cannot get out. This is called 'to enjoy serenity in seclusion.'"

The fourth awakening is diligent effort. It is to engage ceaselessly in wholesome practices. That is why it is called "diligent effort." It is refinement without mixing in other activities. You keep going forward without turning back.

The Buddha said, "Monks, if you make diligent effort, nothing is too difficult. That is why you should do so. It is like a thread of water piercing through a rock by constantly dripping. If your mind continues to slacken, it is like taking a break from hitting stones before they spark; you can't get fire that way. What I am speaking of is 'diligent effort.'"

The fifth awakening is not neglecting mindfulness. It is also called maintaining right mindfulness. This helps you to guard the dharma so you won't lose it. It is called "to maintain right mindfulness" or "not to neglect mindfulness."

The Buddha said, "Monks, for seeking a good teacher and good protection, there is nothing like not neglecting mindfulness. If you practice this, robbers of desire cannot enter you. Therefore, you should always maintain mindfulness in yourself. If you lose it, you will lose all merits. When your mindfulness is solid, you will not be harmed even if you go into the midst of the robbers of the five-sense desires. It is like wearing armor and going into a battlefield, so there is nothing to be afraid of. It is called "not to neglect mindfulness."

The sixth awakening is to practice meditation. To abide in dharma without being confused is called "stability in meditation."

The Buddha said, "Monks, if you gather your mind, it will abide in stability. Then, you will understand the birth and death of all things in the world. You will continue to endeavor in practicing various aspects of meditation. When you have stability, your mind will not be scattered. It is like a house where water is used sparsely, or an embankment that holds water. You practitioners are like this. Because you have the water of wisdom, you practice stability and the water of wisdom is not wasted. This is called 'stability in meditation.'"

The seventh awakening is "to cultivate wisdom." It is to listen, contemplate, practice, and have realization.

The Buddha said, "Monks, if you have wisdom, you are free from greed. You will always reflect on yourself and avoid mistakes. Thus, you will attain liberation in the dharma I am speaking of. If you don't have wisdom, you will be neither a follower of the way nor a lay supporter of it, and there will be no name to describe you. Indeed, wisdom is a reliable vessel to bring you across the ocean of old age, sickness, and death. It is a bright lamp that illuminates in the darkness of ignorance. It is an excellent medicine for all who are sick. It is a sharp ax to cut down the tree of delusion. Thus, you can deepen awakening through the wisdom of listening, contemplation, and practice. If you are illuminated with wisdom, even if you use your physical eyes, you will have clear insight. This is called 'to cultivate wisdom.'"

The eighth awakening is not to be engaged in hollow discussions. It is to experience realization and be free from discriminatory thinking, with the thorough understanding of the reality of all things. It is called "not to be engaged in hollow discussions."

The Buddha said, "Monks, if you get into hollow discussions, your mind will be scattered. Then, you will be unable to attain liberation even if you have left the household. So, you should immediately leave behind a scattered mind and hollow discussions. If you wish to attain the joy of serenity, you need to cure the sickness of hollow discussions. This is called 'not to be engaged in hollow discussions.'"

These are the eight awakenings. Each awakening contains all eight, thus there are sixty-four awakenings. When awakenings are practiced thoroughly, their number is countless. When they are practiced in summary, there are sixty-four.

These are the last words of the Great Teacher Shakyamuni Buddha, the ultimate admonition of the Mahayana teaching. He said at midnight of the fifteenth day of the second month, "Monks, always endeavor wholeheartedly to search for the way of liberation. All things in the world, whether they are in motion or not, are insecure and bound to decay. Now, all of you be still and do not speak. Time is passing and I am going to cross over. This is my last admonition to you." Without expounding dharma any further, the Buddha entered pari-nirvana.

All disciples of the Buddha should study this teaching. Those who don't learn or know about it are not his disciples. Indeed, this is the Tathagata's treasury of the true dharma eye, the wondrous heart of nirvana. However, there are many who do not know about this teaching, as there are few who have studied it. Many may have been confused by demons, and those who have few wholesome conditions from the past do not have the opportunity to see or hear this teaching.

In the Ages of True Dharma and Imitation Dharma, all disciples of the Buddha knew about this teaching and practiced it. But nowadays, less than one or two out of a thousand monks seem to know about it. How regrettable! The world has declined since those times. While the true dharma prevails in the billion worlds and the Buddha's pure teaching is still intact, you should immediately practice it without negligence.

It is rare to encounter the buddha dharma even in the span of countless eons. A human body is difficult to attain. A human body in the Three Continents of the world is preferable. A human body in the Southern

Continent, Jambudvipa, is particularly so, as it can have the chance to see the Buddha, hear the dharma, leave the household, and attain the way. But those who entered nirvana and died before the pari-nirvana of the Tathagata could not learn and practice these eight awakenings of great beings.

Now you can see, hear, and practice these awakenings because of the merit of your wholesome conditions from the past. By practicing and nurturing these awakenings birth after birth, you can certainly arrive at unsurpassable enlightenment and expound these eight awakenings to all beings, just as Shakyamuni Buddha did.

Written at the Eihei Monastery on the sixth day, the first month, the fifth year of the Kencho Era [1253].

FASCICLES NOT DATED BY DOGEN

85

KARMA IN THE THREE PERIODS

VENERABLE KUMARALABDHA, THE Nineteenth Ancestor, journeyed to Central India, where he met a seeker called Jayata, who asked him, "My parents follow the path of the three treasures, but they have been sick and nothing they do goes well. Our next-door neighbors have been engaged in the low practice of slaughtering animals, yet they are healthy and content. How come they are happy while we are so unfortunate?"

Kumaralabdha said, "Why should you doubt? The results from our wholesome and unwholesome actions take effect in the three periods. But people only see that the peaceful die young and the violent live long, or that the unrighteous prosper and the righteous decline. They deny the law of cause and effect and say that our sins and good deeds are without consequences. They do not know that the shadows and echoes follow our actions without a hairbreadth gap. The results of our actions don't get worn away even in one hundred, one thousand, or ten thousand eons."

Hearing these words, Jayata was freed from his doubt.

Kumaralabdha is the nineteenth-generation ancestor who was entrusted with the dharma. His name was predicted by the Tathagata. He not ony clarified and authentically transmitted Shakyamuni Buddha's dharma, but also illuminated the dharma of all buddhas of the past, present, and future.

After posing this question, Jayata studied the Tathagata's true dharma with Kumaralabdha and became the Twentieth Ancestor. It was also foretold that he would be the Twentieth Ancestor by the World-Honored One.

———

This is how the investigation of buddha dharma should be conducted. Do not join those with crooked views who do not know the law of cause and effect, who do not clarify the results of their actions, who ignore the relationship between the past, present, and future, and who do not make a distinction between wholesome and unwholesome deeds.

What Kumaralabdha meant by *the results from our wholesome and unwholesome actions take effect in the three periods* is:

One: the result received in this lifetime.
Two: the result received in the next lifetime.
Three: the result received in a lifetime after the next.

These are called the three periods. From the beginning of learning the way of buddha ancestors, we study and clarify the principle of the effects of karma in the three periods. If we don't, many of us will make a mistake and fall into crooked views. Not only do we fall into crooked views, we get into unwholesome realms and experience suffering for a long time. When we do not maintain wholesome roots, we lose a great deal of merit and are obstructed for a long time from the path of enlightenment. Would this not be regrettable?

———

The karmic effects in the three periods apply to both wholesome and unwholesome karma. First are the results in this lifetime:

It is taught that if one's karma is created and continued, and one receives various effects of this karma in this lifetime, they are called the results in this lifetime. In this case one receives the effects of wholesome or unwholesome action in this lifetime.

Here is an example of taking an unwholesome action and receiving unwholesome results in this lifetime:

Long ago there was a woodcutter who got lost after sunset in the snow on a mountain. He was close to freezing to death. He kept walking and saw a bear in the woods. It had a blue body and flaming eyes. The woodcutter was scared and almost fainted. He did not know it was a bodhisattva taking the form of a bear.

Seeing that the woodcutter was scared, the bear said, "Don't be afraid. Even if parents and their children have different minds, I will never harbor bad intentions."

Then the bear carried the woodcutter into a cave, warmed up his body, and revived him. She brought fruit and roots to feed him. Fearing that the coldness was not going away, she lay with him in her arms. She took care of him in this way for six days.

On the seventh day the weather cleared up and the road became visible. The woodcutter came back to himself. Noticing it, the bear brought some sweet fruit and gave it to him as a farewell gift. She took him out of the forest and tenderly said good-bye to him.

The woodcutter knelt down and said in gratitude, "What can I do to return your kindness?"

The bear said, "I don't want anything in particular from you. But you could protect me just as I have protected you."

The woodcutter promised to do so and climbed down the mountain carrying wood.

Then he met two hunters who asked, "Have you seen any birds or animals?"

The woodcutter said, "I didn't see any birds or animals except a bear."

The hunters asked him to show them where the bear was.

The woodcutter said, "I will show you if you give me two-thirds of what you get."

The hunters agreed. The three men went together, killed the bear, and divided the meat three ways.

When the woodcutter was going to pick up his share of meat, his unwholesome action caused both of his arms to drop off like a broken necklace or cut-off lotus roots. The hunters were shocked and asked him what made this happen. Fully ashamed, the woodcutter explained.

The hunters scolded him and said, "How could you dare to do such an evil thing to the bear who had been so kind to you? It is amazing that your body has not completely rotted."

The three men together donated the meat to a Buddhist temple. A senior monk there with his wondrous wisdom entered samadhi and observed the meat. Then he understood that it was the meat of a great bodhisattva who brings forth benefit to all beings. The monk came out of samadhi and told people about it. They were awed, gathered together fragrant firewood, and burnt the meat. They built a stupa to enshrine the remaining bones, and held ceremonies of dedication.

One receives the results of such an unwholesome action either immediately or soon after the action.

This is called "receiving the results of an unwholesome action in this lifetime."

If you receive kindness, aspire to return the kindness. If you give kindness, do not expect the kindness to be returned. It is also true nowadays that if you harm someone who has been kind to you, you will certainly receive the results of the unwholesome action.

Sentient beings should never have an intention like this woodcutter. Outside the forest he bade farewell in gratitude to the bear and asked, *What can I do to return your kindness?* But upon meeting the hunters at the foot of the mountain, he wanted two-thirds of the bear's meat. Pulled by his greed, the woodcutter harmed that great kind being.

Both laity and home leavers should never exercise such forgetfulness. The power of an unwholesome action cuts the arms faster than a sword.

Here is an example of making a wholesome action and receiving the results in this lifetime:

Long ago there was a eunuch who was managing the court affairs for King Kanishka of the country of Gandhara. When he went outside the city, he saw as many as five hundred oxen entering the city. He asked the man who was driving the herd, "What are you going to do with these oxen?"

The man said, "I am going to have them neutered."

The eunuch said to himself, "Because of my past unwholesome

karma, I have received an emasculated body. Now I want to use my resources to save these oxen from their misfortune."

So the eunuch paid the man and freed all the oxen. This wholesome deed transformed the eunuch into having a male body. He was delighted and went back to the city. He stood at the palace gate, sent a messenger to the king, and asked for his audience. The king called him in and asked what had happened. The former eunuch reported the incident to the king. The king was amazed, awarded him with treasures, gave him a high position, and had him manage external affairs.

One receives the results of such a wholesome action either immediately or soon after the action.

From this story we clearly know that those who help the well-being of oxen, usually not regarded as valuable, receive immediate wholesome effects. How much more so for those who honor the fields of kindness [parents] and the fields of virtue [buddha ancestors] and practice various wholesome actions! This is called "receiving wholesome results in this lifetime."

Examples of receiving wholesome and unwholesome results are countless, and it is impossible to speak about them.

———————

The second type of karmic effect is that the effect of one's action in this lifetime grows and one receives the result in the next lifetime. It is called the result received in the next lifetime.

Those who commit one of the five types of avichi crimes are certain to fall into Avichi Hell in the next lifetime. "Next lifetime" means the life after this lifetime, which is also called the second lifetime.

Some of those who commit other types of crimes also fall into hell in the next lifetime. Some others fall into hell in the life after the next one if they are bound to do so. But those who commit one of the five types of avichi crimes will certainly fall into Avichi Hell in the next lifetime. The five types of avichi crimes are: killing one's father, killing one's mother, killing an arhat, causing a buddha body to bleed, and harming the community of practitioners of the dharma wheel.

Those who commit any of these crimes inevitably fall into Avichi Hell in the next lifetime. Some of them commit all five crimes, like Monk Padmottara at the time of Kashyapa Buddha. Some commit one crime, like King Ajatashatru, who killed his father at the time of Shakyamuni Buddha. Some others commit three crimes, like Ajata, who killed his father, his mother, and an arhat when he was a layman. Later he was allowed to leave the household.

Devadatta, also known as Dipadaduo or Dipadadou [in Chinese], meaning "Heavenly Heat," committed three types of avichi crimes: harming the community of practitioners of the dharma wheel, causing a buddha body to bleed, and killing an arhat.

Devadatta talked five hundred ignorant novices into climbing to the top of Mount Gaya to conduct a new type of ceremony. This is the crime of harming the practicing community. Shariputra detested this crime and made him sleep deeply. Maudgalyayana led the group of novices and they climbed down the mountain. When Devadatta woke up, he swore to take revenge. He picked up a rock thirty *hasta* long and fifteen *hasta* wide, and threw it at the World-Honored One, trying to kill him. The rock was blocked by a mountain spirit and crushed. A small broken piece flew and struck a toe of the Tathagata, which caused the toe to bleed. According to this story, Devadatta's crime of harming the community preceded causing the Buddha to bleed. There are other versions, and it is unclear which crime he committed first.

He also struck Nun Utpalavarna, who was a great arhat, with his fist and killed her. This was the crime of killing an arhat. Thus, it is said that Devadatta committed three avichi crimes.

There are two types of crime that harm the practicing community: breaking the rituals and breaking the dharma wheel. Breaking the rituals of the practicing community can take place in the Three Continents but not in the Northern Continent [where buddha dharma is not practiced]. This has happened from the time when the Tathagata lived in this world until today. Breaking the dharma wheel of the practicing community took place only when the Tathagata lived in this world. In other times it has happened only in the Southern Continent, and not in the other Three Continents. This is the more serious crime.

Because Devadatta committed these three grave crimes, he fell into Avichi Hell in the next lifetime. There are people who commit all five grave crimes. Others commit one. Devadatta committed three. All these people fall into Avichi Hell. One grave crime should result in being in Avichi Hell for one eon. Those who commit the five avichi crimes should fully receive the result of the five types of punishment in one eon, in addition to before and after.

An earlier teacher said, "Both in the *Agama Sutra* and in the *Parinirvana Sutra,* there is equally one eon. But the fires [of punishment] vary." The teacher also said, "There is just increasing suffering."

As Devadatta committed three grave crimes, he was bound to receive suffering three times as much as those who committed one grave crime. But at the end of his life, he became slightly free from his unwholesome heart by saying, "I take refuge." It is regrettable that he did not fully say, "I take refuge in the Buddha." In Avichi Hell, however, he did say, "I take refuge in the Buddha." His wholesome effect is not far in the future.

Further, there were [four] Devadattas at the time of the four Buddhas. Monk Gokal was among the one thousand members of the Shakya Clan who left the household [at the time of Shakyamuni Buddha]. When he and Devadatta left the city, the horses they were riding suddenly fell down, so they were thrown off and their hats went flying. People who saw this predicted that these men would not be benefited by buddha dharma. Later, Kokalika falsely accused Shariputra and Maudgalyayana of grave crimes. The World-Honored One gently advised him to take it back, but he would not. The heavenly king Brahma also advised him, but he would not stop. For this false accusation, Kokalika fell into hell in the next lifetime. He has not yet encountered a condition to have a wholesome root.

Also, the Monk of the Fourth-Stage Meditation slandered the Buddha at the end of his life. Because of this, the intermediary realm for the fourth stage of meditation disappeared; instead, a vision of Avichi Hell emerged. He fell into Avichi Hell after his life ended.

Such cases are called "receiving the effect in the next lifetime."

The five effects of avichi [ceaseless] crimes are as follows:

Taking the effect is without cease, therefore it is called "ceaseless." As the effect is received in the next lifetime after the present body is given up, it is called "ceaseless."

Receiving the effect is without cease, therefore it is called "ceaseless." As the five grave crimes cause birth in Avichi Hell, with continuous suffering for one eon without having pleasure, it is called "ceaseless."

The amount of time is without cease, therefore it is called "ceaseless." As life in Avichi Hell is never cut off during the eon, it is called "ceaseless."

The life span is without cease, therefore it is called "ceaseless." As the life span of one who has committed grave crimes and is born in Avichi Hell is never cut off, it is called "ceaseless."

The body shape is without limit, therefore it is called "ceaseless." One who committed grave crimes is born in Avichi Hell. It is eighty-four thousand *yojana* wide and long. When even one person enters, the hell is full. When all people enter, it is full and they do not hinder one another. Thus, it is called "ceaseless."

————

Receiving the results after the next lifetime means that the effect of one's action in this lifetime grows into the third or fourth lifetime. Or, passing these lifetimes, one receives various results even after a hundred or a thousand eons.

Thus, one who creates an action, either wholesome or unwholesome, experiences the effects of the action in the third or fourth lifetime, or even after a hundred or thousand eons. This is receiving the results after the next lifetime.

The merit of bodhisattvas' practices throughout innumerable eons often brings forth results after the next lifetime. Practitioners who don't know this principle frequently have doubts, just like Jayata when he was a layperson. His doubt would not have been resolved had he not met Venerable Kumaralabdha. If the practitioners' thoughts are wholesome, their unwholesomeness disappears. If their thoughts are unwholesome, their wholesomeness immediately disappears.

There were two people in the city of Shravasti. One of them always practiced wholesomeness, and the other unwholesomeness.

The one who practiced wholesomeness always created wholesome deeds and never created unwholesome deeds. On the other hand, the one who practiced unwholesomeness always created unwholesome deeds and never created wholesome deeds.

On his deathbed, the one who practiced wholesomeness faced the realm intermediate to hell because of some unwholesome results [instead of the wholesome results] he was going to receive in the lifetime after his next life.

Then, he said to himself, "I have been practicing wholesomeness and have never created unwholesome deeds. I ought to be reborn in the deva realm. Why am I facing the realm intermediate to hell?"

But he thought, "It must be that I carry effects to receive in the lifetime after next, which I need to receive now. That is why I am facing the realm intermediate to hell."

So he meditated on the wholesome deed he had created and aroused deep joy. As the thoughts of excellent wholesomeness became present, the realm intermediate to hell disappeared, and, in its place, the realm intermediate to the deva realm appeared. Thus, when his life ended, he was reborn in the deva realm.

This person realized that he was carrying unwholesome karma and had to receive the results. But, he further thought of the results of his wholesome action. That is why he aroused deep joy. As his concentrated thought was sincere, the realm intermediate to hell disappeared and the realm intermediate to the deva realm appeared so that he could attain birth in the deva realm.

If he had been an unwholesome person and had to face the realm intermediate to hell on his deathbed, he would have thought: "The wholesome actions I have practiced have no effect. Otherwise, why am I facing the realm intermediate to hell?" Then he would deny causation, and slander the three treasures. In that way he would have fallen into hell. Because this man was not like that, he was reborn in the deva realm. Clarify this principle.

The one who practiced unwholesomeness faced the realm intermediate to the deva realm on his deathbed because of the wholesome results he was going to receive in the lifetime after his next life.

Then, he said to himself, "I have been practicing unwholesomeness and have never created wholesome deeds. I ought to be reborn in hell. Why am I facing the realm intermediate to the deva realm?"

He then aroused crooked views and denied various fruits of wholesome and unwholesome actions. Because of his crooked views, the realm intermediate to the deva realm disappeared and the realm intermediate to hell appeared. His life ended, and he was reborn in hell.

This person not only kept on taking unwholesome actions without taking a single wholesome action in his lifetime, but also failed to recognize on his deathbed the results he was going to receive in a lifetime after the next. So, he said to himself: "Although I have been taking unwholesome actions throughout my life, I am going to be reborn in the deva realm. From this I assume that there is no difference between wholesome and unwholesome actions."

Because of his wrong views that denied the difference between wholesome and unwholesome actions, the realm intermediate to the deva realm disappeared and the realm intermediate to hell appeared. So, he fell into hell after his life ended.

Thus, you practitioners should not hold crooked views. Study in detail until you clarify the difference between wrong views and right views.

To deny cause and effect, to slander buddha, dharma, and sangha, to deny the past, present, and future, and to deny emancipation are all crooked views. Know that you do not have two or three selves in this lifetime. Isn't it regrettable if you fall into wrong views and unfortunately receive unwholesome results by doing so? You receive unwholesome results by creating unwholesomeness and denying it, although you may hope that there will be no unwholesome results.

———————

Imperial Attendant Haoyue asked Priest Changsha Jingcen, "An ancient teacher said, 'If you have completed practice of the way, the hindrance of karma is essentially empty. If you haven't, you need to repay your past debt.' How can Venerable Simhabhikshu and Huike [who were both killed] repay their debts?"

Changsha said, "Reverend, you don't understand essential emptiness."

Haoyue asked, "What is essential emptiness?"

Changsha said, "The hindrance of karma."

Haoyue asked again, "What is the hindrance of karma?"

Changsha said, "Essential emptiness."

Haoyue remained silent.

Then Changsha instructed him with a verse:

> A temporal being is not being.
> A temporal death is not nonbeing.
> Nirvana and paying debt—
> one nature with no significant difference.

Changsha Jingcen, a senior student of Nanquan Puyuan, was known for his longtime practice. He often expressed himself with right understanding, but in this story he showed no understanding at all. He did not understand the recent words of Yongjia, nor did he clarify Kumaralabdha's admonition. It seems that he had never dreamed of the World-Honored One's talks on karma. If he had not understood these buddha ancestors, who would revere him?

The hindrance of karma is one of the three hindrances: the hindrance of karma, the hindrance of effect, and the hindrance of desire. The hindrance of karma is also called the five types of karma of Avichi Hell.

Haoyue's question follows his predecessor's words. It is based on the point that karma does not disappear, and so he asks about its effect in the future birth.

Changsha's mistake was that when he was asked what essential emptiness is, he said, "The hindrance of karma." This is grossly wrong. How can the hindrance of karma be originally empty? If karma is not created, there is no hindrance of karma. If karma is created, it is not originally empty. What has been created [unwholesome karma] should not have been created. Not removing the carrier of the hindrance of karma, and calling it emptiness, is a view of those outside the way.

Sentient beings who believe in the original emptiness of the hindrance of karma and create karma in self-indulgence would have no moment of emancipation. If there were no time for emancipation, there would be no emergence of buddhas. If there were no emergence of buddhas, Bodhidharma would not have come from India. If Bodhidharma had not come from India, there would be no Nanquan. If there were no Nanquan, who would replace your eye of study?

Responding to the question *What is the hindrance of karma?* by saying *It is essential emptiness* appears to be a traditional tautology. However, it seems to me that Changsha answered Haoyue with a lack of capacity; without completing the study, he uttered such an outrageous statement.

Then Changsha said in a verse, *Nirvana and paying debt—one nature with no significant difference.*

What is *one nature*? How does it fit with the three natures [the wholesome action nature, the unwholesome action nature, and the neutral nature]? I suspect Changsha did not know *one nature*.

What are *Nirvana and paying debt*? What kind of nirvana is it—that of shravakas, pratyeka-buddhas, or buddhas? Whichever it might be, nirvana is not the same as *paying debt*. What Changsha says is not the buddha ancestors' expression. He should buy straw sandals and travel in search of the way.

Venerable Simha [the Twenty-fourth Indian Ancestor, Simhabhikshu] and Huike [the Second Chinese Ancestor] were killed by rascals. But this should not be the cause of doubt [on the effect of karma]. What they had was not final lives or life existing in nothing. How would they not receive effects in their future birth? As the effects they are bound to receive later are already maturing, have no doubt about their future lives. Thus, it is clear that Changsha had not clarified karma in the three periods.

Those who study buddha dharma should clarify the karma of the three periods just as Kumaralabdha did. This is the essential teaching of karma in the ancestral school. Do not neglect it.

Besides the karma of the three periods, there are eight types of karma of indefinite time. Study this extensively.

Without knowing this, the true dharma of buddha ancestors will not spread. Those who have not clarified karma of the three periods should not groundlessly be regarded as teachers of humans and devas.

The World-Honored One said, "Effects of an action will never perish, even after one hundred and one thousand eons. One receives the results when the causes and conditions meet. Know that dark actions bring forth dark results, bright actions bring forth bright results, and mixed actions bring forth varied results. So, refrain from taking dark and mixed actions, and endeavor to take bright actions."

The assembly of those who heard the Buddha's discourse accepted it with joy and trust.

As the World-Honored One says, once wholesome or unwholesome actions are created, they will not perish even after one hundred, one thousand, or ten thousand eons. One receives the results when the causes and conditions meet. However, unwholesome actions disappear or turn to lighter results by repentance. Wholesome actions increase by rejoicing. This is called *never perish*. It is not that they do not have effects.

This was copied at the head monk's office at the Eihei Monastery on the ninth day, the third month, the fifth year of the Kencho Era [1253]. Ejo.

86

FOUR HORSES

ONE DAY SOMEONE outside the way asked the World-Honored One, "I am not asking you for a teaching with words, or a teaching without words."

Then the World-Honored One sat silently for some time.

The person outside the way bowed and admired him: "How splendid is the World-Honored One! With great compassion you have cleared out the cloud of delusion and helped me to enter realization." Then he bowed and left.

After the person outside the way was out of sight, Ananda asked the Buddha, "What caused that man to say that he had entered realization and praise you before he left?"

The World-Honored One said, "He is like a good horse that runs upon seeing a shadow of the whip."

From the time Bodhidharma came from India to China, many teachers have taken up this story and explained it to those who study the way. After studying this story for days, months, or years, some students clarify the meaning and enter the buddha dharma. This is called "a story of someone outside the way asking the World-Honored One a question."

Know that the World-Honored One has two methods of guiding—noble silence and noble speech. All those who enter the way with either of these methods are *like a good horse that runs upon seeing a shadow of the whip.* Those who enter the way without these methods are also like this.

———

Ancestor Nagarjuna said, "When a phrase of guidance is spoken, an excellent horse sees a shadow of the whip and gets to the right path."

To encounter various situations and hear the dharma of birth and beyond birth, and the teaching on the Three Vehicles and the One Vehicle, is to see a shadow of the whip and get to the right path, instead of the common tendency to follow the wrong path.

When you follow a master and encounter a true person, there is no place a guiding phrase is not presented; there is no moment when you don't see a shadow of the whip. Whether you see a shadow of the whip right away, or after immeasurable eons, you are able to enter the right path.

———

According to the *Samyuta Agama Sutra,* the Buddha said to the monks:

There are four types of horses. The first type of horse becomes startled upon seeing a shadow of the whip and follows the rider's intention. The second type of horse is startled by being whipped on its mane and follows the rider's intention. The third type of horse is startled upon being whipped on its flesh. The last type of horse becomes startled when it is whipped to its bones.

The first horse is like someone who hears about the impermanence of a village and arouses the thought of leaving home. The second horse is like someone who hears about the impermanence of one's own village and arouses the thought of leaving home. The third horse is like someone who hears about the impermanence of one's parents and arouses the thought of leaving home. The last horse is like someone who experiences suffering of one's own disease and arouses the thought of leaving home.

This teaching is called "the *Agama's* four types of horses," which is often studied when studying the buddha dharma. Those who emerge as true teachers among humans and devas, as well as ancestors and messengers of the Buddha, unfailingly study this teaching and transmit it to their students. Those who don't know it are not teachers of humans and devas. If students have nurtured wholesome roots and are close to the buddha way, they do not fail to hear this teaching. Those who are far from the buddha way do not hear it. This being so, teachers should consider teaching this right away. Students should hope to hear it right away.

In regard to *arousing the thought of leaving home*, it is taught: "When the Buddha expounds the dharma with a single voice, sentient beings understand it in accordance with their capacity. Some are frightened, some rejoice, some arouse the thought of leaving home, and others doubt."

According to the *Maha Pari-nirvana Sutra*, the Buddha said:

Good person, there are four ways to command a horse: touching the hair, touching the skin, touching the flesh, and touching the bones. The horse always follows the rider's command according to where it is touched.

The Tathagata likewise subdues sentient beings in four ways. First, the Buddha speaks of birth for sentient beings, who accept his words just as the horse follows the rider's command by being touched on the hair. Second, the Buddha speaks of birth and old age for sentient beings, who accept his words just as the horse follows the rider's command by being touched on the hair and the skin. Third, the Buddha speaks of birth, old age, and sickness for sentient beings, who accept his words just as the horse follows the rider's command by being touched on the hair, skin, and flesh. Finally, the Buddha speaks of birth, old age, sickness, and death for sentient beings, who accept his words just as the horse follows the rider's command by being touched on the hair, skin, flesh, and bones.

Good person, there is no fixed way for a rider to command the horse. The way the Tathagata, the World-Honored One, guides sentient beings is never in vain. Thus, the Buddha is called the Excellent Tamer.

This is called "the *Nirvana Sutra's* four types of horses." There are no students who do not study this teaching. There are no buddhas who do not speak of it.

You follow the Buddha and hear about this teaching. You see the Buddha, make offerings to the Buddha, and hear about it. For eons, every time you transmit buddha dharma to sentient beings, you explain this teaching without negligence. Even after arriving at the buddha fruit, just at the time of arousing the beginner's mind, you speak of this teaching to the assemblies of bodhisattvas, shravakas, humans, and devas. In this way, the seeds of the buddha-dharma-sangha treasure are not destroyed.

Thus, these teachings of the Buddha [in the early scriptures] are rather different from that of Bodhisattva Nagarjuna [in the Mahayana scriptures].

Know that there are four ways for a rider to command the horse—to touch the hair, the skin, the flesh, or the bones. It appears not clear what touches the hair, but teachers who transmit dharma interpret it as a whip.

However, sometimes a whip is used and sometimes a whip is not used for commanding a horse. Commanding is not limited to using a whip.

What is called Dragon Horse is said to be eight feet high. There are few humans who can ride it. What is called One-Thousand-Li Horse can travel one thousand *li* in a day. It sweats blood while going the first five hundred *li*, then it begins to be fresh and runs fast. There are also few humans who can ride and command it. There is no such horse in China, but it exists in a foreign land. It does not appear that frequent whipping is needed for such horses.

On the other hand, an ancient teacher said, "Commanding a horse is always done with a whip. Without a whip, commanding a horse is not possible." This is normally how to command a horse. It is done by touching the hair, the skin, the flesh, and the bones.

You cannot touch the skin without touching the hair. You cannot touch the flesh and bones without touching the hair and skin. Thus, we know that a whip should be used.

The description of commanding a horse is not sufficient without mentioning a whip. There are a number of insufficient descriptions in sutras.

The Tathagata, the World-Honored One, the Excellent Tamer, also guides sentient beings with four types of dharma, never in vain. There are those who accept the Buddha's words when he explains birth. There are those who accept the Buddha's words when he explains birth and old age. There are those who accept the Buddha's words when he explains birth, old age, and sickness. And there are those who accept the Buddha's words when he explains birth, old age, sickness, and death.

Those who hear the last three teachings do not skip the first. It is just like there is no touching the skin, flesh, and bones without touching the hair.

To explain birth, old age, sickness, and death is to explain birth, old age, sickness, and death as taught by the Tathagata, the World-Honored One.

This teaching is not to keep sentient beings away from birth, old age, sickness, and death. It is not to explain and let sentient beings understand that birth, old age, sickness, and death are the way. This teaching is to explain birth, old age, sickness, and death in order to help sentient beings attain unsurpassable, complete enlightenment.

This being so: *The way the Tathagata, the World-Honored One, guides sentient beings is never in vain. Thus, the Buddha is called the Excellent Tamer.*

On a summer practice day of the seventh year of the Kencho Era [1255], I have copied my late master's draft. Ejo.

87

VIRTUE OF HOME LEAVING

ACCORDING TO NAGARJUNA Bodhisattva [in the *Treatise on Real-ization of Great Wisdom*]:

Question: It is taught that those who receive lay precepts will be born in the deva world, attain the bodhisattva way, and experience nirvana. What, then, is the use of receiving the precepts for home leavers?

Answer: Those who receive both types of precepts become awakened. But one type is difficult and the other is easy. Laypeople engage in various works. If they wish to concentrate on the dharma of the way, their business declines. If they are focused on their business, their activity of the way declines. Without choosing one and abandoning the other, laypeople need to practice dharma. This is difficult. Those who have left the household can be free from worldly affairs, distant from confusion, and practice the way wholeheartedly. So, this is easy.

Further, laypeople are noisy and confused while being occupied in many things. The roots of their driving forces are the center of all unwholesome actions. That is why lay practice is difficult. Leaving the household is similar to going out into an empty field where there are no people. They can keep their minds unified and free from thinking. As their thoughts inside retreat, their affairs outside also disappear. It is said in a verse:

Sitting leisurely among trees,
quietly letting go of all unwholesome actions,
and attaining a single mind free from desire—
this is pleasure beyond a deva's bliss.
People seek wealth, profit, fame,
and desire comfortable clothes and furniture.
Such pleasure is not true comfort,
wanting profit brings no satisfaction.
While begging food in a patched robe,
in motion or stillness the mind is always unified.
The eye of wisdom observes the reality of all things.
Within various dharma gates, all equally enter this insight.
The wisdom of understanding is serene,
incomparable in the three realms.

In this way we know that maintaining the home leaver's precepts is very easy.

Also, if you leave the household and maintain the precepts, you attain immeasurable wholesome merit, which is fulfilled. For this reason, laypeople should leave the household and receive all of the [home leaver's] precepts.

On the other hand, leaving the household is difficult from the beginning.

Once Brahmans of the Jambudvipa World asked Shariputra, "What is most difficult in the buddha dharma?"

Shariputra said, "Leaving the household is most difficult."

They asked, "What is difficult about being a home leaver?"

Shariputra said, "Enjoying the life of a home leaver is difficult."

They asked, "What is difficult in enjoying the life of a home leaver?"

Shariputra said, "Practicing all types of wholesome deeds is difficult. That is why it is good to leave the household."

Now, when someone leaves the household, the Demon King says in lamentation, "This person wants to reduce the urge of desire, will certainly attain nirvana, and will join a group of the sangha treasure."

Again, even if those who have left the household in the buddha dharma break the precepts and commit a crime, they can be liberated after the crime is over. It is like a story told in the *Sutra on the Former Birth of Nun Utpalavarna:*

[Nagarjuna continues:] At the time when the Buddha was in this world, Nun Utpalavarna attained six miraculous powers and became an arhat. She visited noble householders and talked about the life of home leavers. She encouraged noble women to become nuns.

They said, "We are young and beautiful. It would be hard to keep the precepts."

Utpalavarna said, "It's all right to break the precepts. Leave the household first."

The women said, "If we break the precepts, we will fall into hell. How can we do that?"

Utpalavarna said, "Then go ahead and fall into hell."

They laughed and said, "We would be punished in hell. How can we allow ourselves to fall into hell?"

Utpalavarna said, "Reflecting on my former life, I was an entertainer, putting on various costumes and speaking memorized lines. Once I put on a nun's clothes for a joke. As a result of this action, I was reborn as a nun at the time of Kashyapa Buddha. Because of my high status and proper conduct, I grew arrogant and broke a precept. I fell into hell and experienced various punishments. In my next birth I met Shakyamuni Buddha, left the household, attained six miraculous powers, and became an arhat. From this I know that if you leave the household and receive precepts, even if you break a precept, you can become an arhat because of the merit of the precepts you received. But you cannot attain the way if you only create unwholesome deeds without receiving the precepts. I was once a criminal falling in and out of hell. If a mere criminal dies and enters hell, no merit has been attained. So, you should know that even if you break a precept, you can receive the fruit of the way."

Also, when the Buddha was at Jeta Grove, a drunken Brahman went up to him and requested that he be made a monk. The Buddha asked Ananda to shave the Brahman's head and let him put on a dharma robe. When the Brahman became sober, he was so shocked he had become a monk that he ran away.

The disciples asked the Buddha, "Why did you make that Brahman a monk?"

The Buddha said, "He would otherwise never have the aspiration for leaving the household, even for immeasurable eons. He aroused a faint aspiration because he was drunk. Due to such causes and conditions, he will leave the household and attain the way in the future. The merit of these causes and conditions and leaving the household is immeasurable."

Thus, holding the five precepts as a layperson does not equal leaving the household. [Thus said Nagarjuna.]

The World-Honored One allowed a drunk Brahman to leave the household and receive the precepts. He regarded this as planting the first seed for attaining the way. From this we clearly know that since olden times sentient beings without the merit of leaving the household have not been able to attain enlightenment—the buddha fruit—for a long time. Because this Brahman was drunk, he aroused a faint aspiration, had his head shaved, received the precepts, and became a monk. Although he became sober soon after that, he could preserve his merit and nurture the wholesome root of attaining the way. This is the golden admonition that expresses the World-Honored One's profound intention, the original meaning of the emergence of the Tathagata into this world.

All sentient beings should clearly receive this teaching with trust and practice it in the past, present, and future. Indeed, arousing the aspiration and attaining the way always take place in one moment. This Brahman's merit of momentarily leaving the household is like this. How much more so is the limited and unlimited merit for a human being who leaves the household and receives the precepts! How can the merit be less than that of this drunken Brahman?

One of the wheel-turning kings emerged when he was over eighty thousand years old and, decorated with seven treasures, presided over the Four Continents. These continents were like a Pure Land. The kings' pleasure cannot be described in words. It is said that one of the kings presided over a billion worlds. There are wheels made of gold, silver, copper, and iron for presiding over one, two, three, or four continents. The bodies of those who turn these wheels are not defiled by the ten unwholesome actions.

A wheel-turning king is filled with such privileges. When he finds a strand of white hair on his head, he gives the throne to his crown prince and immediately leaves the household. He puts on a kashaya, practices in a mountain or forest, and when his life ends, is invariably reborn in the world of the Brahma King. The white strand of his hair is put into a silver box treasured at his palace. This is transmitted to the next wheel-turning king. When the next wheel-turning king becomes old, he does the same as the previous king.

The life span of a wheel-turning king after leaving the household is so long that it cannot be compared to that of humans in our time. It is said that the life span of a wheel-turning king is over eighty thousand years and his body is equipped with the thirty-two marks, to which people today cannot come close. However, seeing white hair and knowing the impermanence of life, a wheel-turning king leaves the household without fail and practices the way in order to engage in pure conduct and accomplish merit.

Kings nowadays are not like the wheel-turning kings. If they waste the passage of time in greed without leaving the household, they may regret it in the next lifetime. Furthermore, this is a small country in a remote land, where there is a king who lacks the virtue of a king. People are greedy without end. If they leave the household and practice the way, all devas will protect them with delight. The dragon god will revere and guard them. The buddha eye of all buddhas will clearly confirm them with joy.

Without having faith, the courtesan put on a nun's robe for a joke. She was perhaps at minor fault for this action, but with the power of wearing this robe she encountered the buddha dharma in her next lifetime. A nun's robe means a kashaya. As a result of wearing a kashaya for a joke, she left the household, received the precepts, and became a nun called Utpalavarna at the time of Kashyapa Buddha. Although she broke precepts and fell into hell for punishment, her merit did not perish, and finally she encountered Shakyamuni Buddha. She saw the Buddha, listened to the dharma, aroused the aspiration for enlightenment, and practiced. Thus, she became free from the three realms and became a great arhat. She had mastered the six miraculous powers, including the three extraordinary types of knowledge. She was certainly unsurpassable in the way.

If so, the growing merit of those who have trust from the beginning and receive a kashaya with the pure heart of faith for the sole sake of unsurpassable enlightenment should be more immediate than the merit of this courtesan. Even further, the merit of those who arouse the aspiration for enlightenment, leave the household, and receive the precepts for the sake of unsurpassable enlightenment should be immeasurable. Without having a human body, it is rare to achieve this merit.

Although there are a great number of bodhisattvas and ancestors, whether they are householders or home leavers in India and China, none of them come close to Ancestor Nagarjuna. He particularly took up the stories of the drunken Brahman and the courtesan to encourage sentient beings to leave the household and receive the precepts. Ancestor Nagarjuna's enlightenment was predicted by the golden mouth of the World-Honored One.

The World-Honored One said, "There are four most excellent occurrences in the Southern Continent. They are: seeing the Buddha, hearing the dharma, leaving the household, and attaining the way."

Know clearly that these four most excellent occurrences surpass the activities in the Northern Continent and in all deva worlds. Now, led by the root power of wholesome actions in past lives, you have received the most excellent body [human body]. Rejoice, leave the household, and receive the precepts. Do not waste your most excellent body and leave the dewdroplike life to the wind of impermanence. If, birth after birth, you live as a home leaver, your merit and virtue will accumulate.

The World-Honored One said:

In buddha dharma, the effect of leaving the household is wondrous. The merit of building a stupa of seven treasures, as high as the Heaven of Thirty-three Devas, is not as large as the merit of leaving the household. The reason is that an evil, stupid person can destroy a stupa of seven treasures but cannot destroy the merit of leaving the household. This being so, if you teach men and women, let go of servants, pardon criminals, and let yourself leave the household—entering the way—the merit is immeasurable.

Thus, the World-Honored One let the amounts of merit be known and compared them. Shrivaddhi heard this, and, although he was one hundred twenty years old and frail, he determined to leave the household and receive the precepts. He sat on a seat lower than youths, practiced, and became a great arhat.

Know that, through causes and conditions, a human body in this lifetime is a temporary assemblage of the four great elements and the five skandhas. It always contains eight sufferings. Further, it is born and perishes moment by moment without ceasing. It is born and perishes at each of the sixty-five moments contained within one finger snap, but because of ignorance we don't notice it. There are six billion, four hundred million, ninety-nine thousand, nine hundred eighty moments in a day and night, and the five skandhas are born and perish at each moment, but we don't notice it. What a pity that although we are born and perish at each moment, we don't notice it! The amount of births and deaths at each moment is known only by the Buddha—the World-Honored One—and Shariputra. There are many other sages, but none of them know it. With this law of birth and death in each moment, sentient beings create wholesome and unwholesome actions. Also, with this law of birth and death in each moment, sentient beings arouse the aspiration for enlightenment and attain the way.

What is born and perishes in this way is the human body. Even if you cling to it, it will not stay where it is. Since olden times there has not been a single person who clung to the body and made it stay. Thus, the human body does not belong to the self. Yet, if you turn around, leave the household, and receive the precepts, you realize unsurpassable, complete enlightenment, realized by buddhas of the past, present, and future, which is the indestructible diamond buddha fruit. Who among the wise would not joyously seek this?

This being so, all the eight children of the Chandra Surya Pradipa Buddha in the past gave up their monarchy of ruling the world of the four directions and left the household.

All sixteen children of Maha Abhijna Jnana Abhibhu Buddha also left the household. When this buddha was in samadhi, he expounded the *Lotus Sutra* for all beings, and now he is a tathagata of the ten directions. All the eight trillion beings led by the wheel-turning king, the father of this buddha, saw the king's sixteen children leave the household and asked the king for permission to leave the household. The king gave all of them permission to do so.

Also, King Shubhavyuha's two children, as well as his father and queen, all left the household.

Know that when great sages emerge it is an authentic custom for them to leave the household. No one can say that they do so out of ignorance. If you learn that they leave the household out of their wisdom, you should wish to do the same.

In this present time span of Shakyamuni Buddha, Rahula, Ananda, and others all left the household. One thousand, or it is also said twenty thousand, members of the Shakya Clan also left the household. Their actions are indeed excellent precedents. From the Five Monks to Subhadra [the Buddha's first disciples to the last], those who took refuge in the Buddha all left the household. Know that the virtue is immeasurable.

This being so, if people care about their children and their grandchildren, let them leave the household as soon as possible. If they care about their parents, encourage them to leave the household.

Thus, it is said in a verse:

> If there had been no past world,
> there would have been no past buddhas.
> If there had been no past buddhas,
> there would have been no home leaving
>   and precept receiving.

This is a verse of all buddha tathagatas. It denies the negation of the past world spoken of by those outside the way. So, know that home leaving and precept receiving are the dharma of all buddhas in the past. As we have the fortune of encountering the time of home leaving and precept receiving, which are the wondrous dharma of all buddhas, how could we wastefully miss the opportunity to leave home and receive precepts? It would be difficult to understand the hindrance to doing so. Attaining the highest merit with the lowliest body is the highest achievement in the Jambudvipa World or in the three realms. Do not fail to leave the household and receive the precepts before the Jambudvipa's human body perishes.

Ancient sages said [in the *Abhidharma Mahashastra Treatise*]:

> Even if they break the precepts, those who have left the household excel householders who maintain the precepts. For this reason, the kindness of those who expound a sutra and encourage others to leave the household is difficult to repay. Those who encourage others to leave the household help them practice venerable actions. The reward they receive excels that of King Yama, the Wheel-Turning King, and Indra. For this reason, the kindness of those who expound a sutra and encourage others to leave the household is difficult to repay. Encouraging others to receive the precepts of supporting the dharma [lay practice] is not as valuable. To stay in laity is not recommended in sutras.

In this way, know that even if they break the precepts, those who have left the household excel householders who maintain the precepts. Taking refuge in the Buddha, leaving the household, and receiving the precepts are always excellent. The reward for encouraging others to leave the household excels that of King Yama, the Wheel-Turning King, and Indra. Even common people or untouchables who have left the household excel the nobles. They even excel King Yama, the Wheel-Turning King, and Indra. Receiving lay precepts is not like this. Therefore, leave the household.

Know that the immeasurable teachings of the World-Honored One were extensively collected by the World-Honored One and the five hundred great arhats [in the *Abhidharma Mahashastra Treatise*]. From this we know, indeed, that principles are clear in the buddha dharma. Ordinary teachers of recent times cannot fathom one arhat's wisdom, three types of extraordinary knowledge, or six miraculous powers. Then, how can they understand the wisdom of the five hundred arhats? Although these arhats knew what ordinary teachers of recent times didn't know, saw what they didn't see, and mastered what they didn't master, it is not that the arhats didn't know what ordinary teachers of recent times know. Therefore, do not compare the ignorant and foolish theory of these ordinary teachers with the words of arhats and three types of outstanding knowledge.

The *Abhidharma Mahashastra Treatise* says in chapter 120, "Even those who have aroused the aspiration for enlightenment and left the household are called sages. How much more so is it true of those who have attained the dharma of patience?"

Know in this way that those who have aroused the aspiration for enlightenment and left the household are called sages.

Among the five hundred great vows of Shakyamuni Buddha, his one hundred thirty-seventh vow says, "May I attain a true awakening in the future and may people who want to leave the household in my dharma have no hindrance—such as being lazy, forgetful, crazy, arrogant, lacking reverence and wisdom, being driven by many desires, or having scattered minds. Until this is achieved, I will not be fully awakened."

His one hundred thirty-eighth vow says, "May I attain a true awakening in the future, and may women who want to leave the household in my dharma, study the way, and receive the great precepts accomplish their wishes. Until this is achieved, I will not be fully awakened."

His three hundred fourteenth vow says, "May I attain a true awakening in the future, and if there are sentient beings who have little wholesome roots but arouse enjoyment in these wholesome roots, may I let them leave the household and study the way in the buddha dharma in their future lifetime, and let them abide at ease in the ten pure precepts. Until this is achieved, I will not be fully awakened."

Know that all the good men and good women who have left the household now have been helped by the power of the World-Honored One's great vows in the past, have left the household, and received the precepts without hindrance. The Tathagata made these vows and caused them to leave the household. They clearly know that this is a great merit, most venerable and unsurpassable.

The Buddha said, "If you make offerings to those who follow my teaching, shave off their hair, and wear a patch of kashaya, but have not received the precepts, you will enter the castle of no fear. Because of that, I speak in this way."

From this we know that if you make offerings to people who have shaved off their hair and wear a kashaya, but have not received the precepts, you may enter the castle of no fear.

He also said, "Even if they haven't received the precepts, if you harm those who have left the household with me, shaved off their hair, and wear a piece of kashaya, you will harm the dharma body and the reward body of all buddhas in the past, present, and future, and so you will fill the three unwholesome paths."

———

The Buddha also said:

> If sentient beings leave the household for me, shave off their hair, and wear a kashaya, even if they have not received the precepts, they will all be marked with a sign of nirvana. If you harm those who have left the household for me but haven't received the precepts; if you annoy, insult, or denounce them; if you beat, bind, cut them with a hand, a sword, or a stick, or take away their robes and bowls; or if you take away their tools for livelihood, you will harm the true reward bodies of all buddhas in the past, present, and future, and challenge the eyes of all humans and devas. Thus, you will conceal the seeds of authentic dharma among the three treasures, make all devas fall into hell, depriving them of receiving benefaction, and expand and fill the three unwholesome paths.

From this, know that those who shave their heads and wear ink-dyed robes, even if they have not received the precepts, are marked with a sign of unsurpassable, great nirvana. If you confuse them, you would harm the reward bodies of all buddhas of the past, present, and future. Your offense would be the same as murdering your parents. Thus, we know that the merit of leaving the household is being intimate with all buddhas of the past, present, and future.

———

The Buddha said, "You, home leavers, should not arouse an unwholesome mind. If you do, you are not home leavers. You, home leavers, your action and speech should be in accord with each other. If they aren't, you are not home leavers. I abandoned my parents, siblings, family members, relatives, and teachers to leave the household and practice the way. Indeed, this is the time to assemble wholesome awakening. It is not the time to assemble unwholesome awakening. Wholesome awakening is to have a tender heart toward all sentient beings as if they were babies. Unwholesome awakening is not like this."

Thus, the self nature of a home leaver is having a tender heart toward all sentient beings as if they were babies. This is *not arouse an unwholesome mind*. This is *your action and speech should be in accord with each other*. When you take the form of a home leaver, you have such virtue as this.

———————

The Buddha said:

Now, Shariputra, if bodhisattvas, great beings, wish to attain unsurpassable, complete enlightenment on the day they leave the household, turn the dharma wheel on the same day, and have sentient beings of uncountable eons become free from dust and attain pure dharma eyes, have sentient beings of uncountable eons become free from attachment and attain liberation from desires, and have sentient beings of uncountable eons practice unremittingly in unsurpassable, complete enlightenment, the bodhisattvas, great beings, should study realizing wisdom beyond wisdom.

The study of *realizing wisdom beyond wisdom* spoken of here is transmitted from one ancestor to another. Unsurpassable, complete enlightenment matures on the very day of leaving the household. However, in practicing and realizing for uncountable eons and for innumerable eons, it is not bound by having limitations or beyond having limitations. Those who study should know this.

———————

The Buddha said:

> If, on the day they leave the household, bodhisattvas, great beings, arouse the thought of declining their royal heritage and wish to attain unsurpassable, complete enlightenment, they will immediately turn the dharma wheel. They will free uncountable sentient beings from dust and help them to attain pure dharma eyes. They will free uncountable sentient beings from attachment and with wisdom mind liberate them from desires. They will help uncountable sentient beings to attain unsurpassable, complete enlightenment and unremitting practice. If these bodhisattvas, great beings, arouse this thought, they should study realizing wisdom beyond wisdom.

This merit [of leaving the household] is expounded in this way by Shakyamuni Buddha, who was born in the palace as the bodhisattva of the final body, declined his royal heritage, attained enlightenment, turned the dharma wheel, and awakened sentient beings.

———————

[The *Sutra on the Buddha's Deeds in His Former Lives* says:]

> Prince Siddhartha went to his chariot driver, Chanda, and took up a sword with its handle decorated with wish-granting jewels and seven treasures. He pulled the sharp blade from the sheath with his right hand and grabbed his snail-shaped blue lotus-colored hair with his left hand. He cut the hair off and threw it up in the air. Indra saw him do so, greatly rejoiced in Siddhartha's rare aspiration, and caught the bundle of the prince's hair with his heavenly robe, keeping it from dropping on the ground. Then, all the devas presented their supreme heavenly offerings.

This was when Shakyamuni Buddha was a crown prince. He climbed over a wall of the palace at midnight, went into the mountains the next day, and cut off his own hair. Then the Deva of Suddha Avasa Heaven came down, shaved his head, and made an offering of a kashaya to him. This is an auspicious event of the emergence of the Tathagata in this world. Such an occasion is normal for all buddhas, world-honored ones.

Not even one of the buddhas of the past, present, and future in the ten directions became a buddha as a householder. Because there were buddhas in the past, there is leaving the household and receiving the precepts. The attainment of the way by sentient beings invariably depends on their leaving the household and receiving the precepts. Because leaving the household and receiving the precepts is the definitive way of all buddhas, the merit is immeasurable.

Although, in the scriptures, there is a teaching about a layperson becoming a buddha, it is not an authentic transmission. Although there is a teaching of a woman becoming a buddha [by turning into a man], it is not an authentic transmission. What is authentically transmitted by buddha ancestors is leaving the household and becoming a buddha.

———

[The *Jingde Record of Transmission of the Lamp* says:]

Dhitika, the son of a wealthy man, went to see Venerable Upagupta, the Fourth Ancestor, and expressed his wish to leave the household.

Upagupta said, "Do you want to leave the household for the benefit of your body or mind?"

Dhitika said, "I want to leave the household, but not for my body or mind."

Upagupta said, "Who leaves the household if not for the benefit of body or mind?"

Dhitika said, "A home leaver does not have a self or self-possession. Because of having no self or self-possession, the mind is not born and does not perish. Not to have the mind that is born or perishes: this is an unchanging dharma. All buddhas practice this way. Neither their minds nor their bodies have marks."

Upagupta said, "You are greatly enlightened and your mind has been illuminated. You should take refuge in the buddha, dharma, sangha and nurture the sacred seed [of buddhahood]."

Thus, Upagupta allowed Dhitika to leave the household and receive the precepts.

Now, to encounter the dharma of all buddhas and leave the household is the supreme result. The dharma is not for the self or self-possession. It is not for body or mind. It is not that you leave the household for the benefit of body or mind. This is the meaning of *leaving the household is not for body or mind*. Because it is not for the self or self-possession, it is the dharma of all buddhas. This is the way of all buddhas. Because this is the way of all buddhas, it is not for the self or self-possession, and not for the body or mind.

There is nothing equal to this in the three realms. Thus, leaving the household is the supreme dharma. It is not sudden, not gradual, not permanent, not impermanent. It is not coming, not going, not abiding, not making. It is not wide, not narrow, not large, not small. It is not becoming, and not not-becoming. There are no ancestors transmitting buddha dharma person to person that have not left the household or have not received the precepts.

This is how Dhitika first met Venerable Upagupta and asked about leaving the household. In this way, Dhitika left the household, received the precepts, practiced with Upagupta, and finally became the Fifth Ancestor.

[The *Jingde Record of Transmission of the Lamp* says:]

Sanghanandi, the Seventeenth Ancestor, was a prince of King Ratnavyuha of Shrasvasti. He could speak soon after his birth and kept praising the Buddha's teaching. At age seven he detested worldly pleasure and presented this verse to his parents:

> Bow to my compassionate father.
> Veneration to my blood mother.
> I now wish to leave the household,
> begging you to kindly accept my plea.

But his parents insistently discouraged him. So, the prince refused to eat. Finally, his parents allowed him to leave the household while staying in the palace. They named him Sanghanandi and asked monk Dhyanartha to be his teacher. For nineteen years Sanghanandi didn't tire of his practice. He said to himself daily, "While living at home, how can I be a home leaver?"

One night he saw a heavenly light descending all of a sudden and illuminating a straight road. Without noticing, he walked slowly on the road for ten *li*. When he came to a grotto in front of a huge rock, he went inside and sat quietly. Knowing that his son had left, the King expelled Dhyanartha and searched all over the country, looking for the prince. But he could not find him. Ten years later, Sanghanandi attained dharma, had his enlightenment confirmed, became a wandering teacher, and got to the country of Madhya.

This is the first time that becoming a home leaver while being at home has been heard of. However, with the help of his wholesome action in the past, he found a straight way in the heavenly light. Then, he left his palace and got to the grotto. Indeed, it is an excellent precedent. One who detests worldly pleasure and is cautious about common dust is a sage. One who loves the five desires and does not reject them is an ordinary fool.

————————

Emperors Dai and Su practiced intimately with monks but they still clung to their thrones and did not abandon them.

Layman Lu [Huineng] left his parents and became an ancestor. It is the merit of leaving the household. On the other hand, Layman Pang abandoned treasure but did not throw away the dust of the world. It should be regarded as extreme foolishness. You cannot compare Lu's power of the way with Pang's study of the ancient way. Those who are clear leave the household. Those who are ignorant stay in the household, which becomes the causes and conditions of dark [unwholesome] actions.

————————

One day, Nanyue Huairang, said with admiration, "Home leaving is done to practice the way to become free from birth. There is nothing that excels this in the deva and human worlds."

The way to become free from birth is the true dharma of the Tathagata. Thus, it is excellent *in the deva and human worlds*. In the deva worlds, there are six deva worlds in the desire realm, eighteen deva worlds in the form realm, and four types of worlds in the no-form realm. None of them excel the path of home leavers.

————————

Panshan, Zen Master Baoji, said, "Virtuous practitioners of Zen, studying the way in our school is like the earth holding mountains without knowing how steep they are, or a stone containing a jewel without knowing how flawless it is. One who practices like this is called a home leaver."

The true dharma of buddha ancestors is not necessarily concerned with knowing or not knowing. As leaving the household is the true dharma of buddha ancestors, its merit is clear.

Linji Yixuan of Zhen Region, said, "Home leavers should discern what is right in everyday views, buddha from demon, and what is genuine, false, ordinary, or sacred. Those who discern in this way are called true home leavers. Those who cannot distinguish a buddha from a demon are like those who leave one home only to enter another home. They are called sentient beings who create karma, and cannot be called true home leavers."

What is right in everyday views spoken of here means identifying with cause and effect, and identifying with the three treasures. *Discern buddha* means to clearly reflect on the merit of the causes and effects of being a buddha. It is to clearly understand what is genuine and what is false, what is ordinary and what is sacred. If you don't clarify the distinction between a demon and a buddha, you will relapse and destroy the study of the way. If you are aware of a demon's affairs and do not follow them, your endeavor of the way is unremitting. This is called the dharma of true home leavers. There are many who groundlessly regard demons' affairs as buddha dharma. This is a mistake of recent times. You students should quickly know demons' affairs and clarify, practice, and realize buddhahood.

[The *Maha Pari-nirvana Sutra* says:]

When the Tathagata was entering pari-nirvana, Kashyapa Bodhisattva said to him, "World-Honored One, the Tathagata, you understand all the roots [potentials] of human beings. You must have known that Sunakshatra was going to cut off his wholesome roots. Then, why did you allow him to leave the household?"

The Buddha said:

Good disciple, in the past, after I left the household, my brother Nanda, my cousins Ananda and Devadatta, and my son Rahula all followed me, left the household, and practiced the way. If I had not allowed Sunakshatra to leave the household, he would have succeeded to his father's throne. Using his authority, he would have destroyed buddha dharma. For this reason, I permitted him to leave the household and practice the way.

Good disciple, if Sunakshatra had not left the household, he would have lost his wholesome roots and would have received no benefit in the uncountable lifetimes. As he has left the household, even if he has lost his wholesome roots now, if he maintains the precepts, venerates and makes offerings to old, senior, and virtuous ones, and practices the first to fourth stages of meditation, these will be wholesome causes. Wholesome causes give rise to wholesome dharma. If wholesome dharma rises, the way is practiced. If the way is practiced, unsurpassable, complete enlightenment is attained. That is why I allowed Sunakshatra to leave the household.

Good disciple, if I hadn't allowed Sunakshatra to leave the household and receive the precepts, people would not be able to call me the Tathagata who embodies the ten powers.

Good disciple, the Buddha observes the wholesome and unwholesome potential sentient beings carry with them. Although they have these two types of potential, some of them quickly cut off all wholesome roots and maintain unwholesome roots. Why so? Because such people do not associate with wholesome friends, do not listen to the true dharma, do not think of wholesome things, and do not act according to dharma. For this reason, they lose wholesome roots and maintain unwholesome roots.

From this, know that although the Tathagata, the World-Honored One, clearly knows that some sentient beings are going to lose their wholesome roots, he allows them to leave the household for the sake of giving them wholesome causes. This is great compassion. Losing wholesome roots is caused by not associating with wholesome friends, not listening to the true dharma, not thinking of wholesome things, and not acting according to dharma. Students nowadays should always associate with wholesome friends. Wholesome friends say that there are buddhas and teach that there are crimes and beneficial activities. Those who do not deny cause and effect are wholesome friends and wholesome teachers. What is explained by these people is the true dharma. To think of this principle is wholesome thinking. To act in this way is wholesome action.

This being so, encourage sentient beings to leave the household and receive the precepts whether you are close to them or not. Do not reflect on their future relapsing or not. Do not worry about their practicing or not. This is indeed the true dharma of Shakyamuni Buddha.

―――――――

The Buddha said to the monks, "Know that King Yama [King of Hell] said, 'When can I be liberated from this suffering, attain a human body, leave the household, shave off my hair, wear the three dharma robes, and practice the way as a home leaver?' Even King Yama makes his wish in this way. Then, why shouldn't you? You already have attained human bodies and have become monks. This being so, monks, be mindful of the practice of the body, speech, and thought, and do not be negligent. Put an end to the five delusions and work on the five sense organs. Such monks can keep practicing the way."

Hearing these words of the Buddha, all monks rejoiced and followed his teaching.

From this, we clearly know that even King Yama looks for birth in the human world. Those who are already born as humans should quickly shave off their hair, put on three dharma robes, and practice the buddha way. This is a merit of being in the human world more excellent than that in other paths. Therefore, although being born as a human, it is utmost foolishness to greedily pursue the path of worldly, official realms, passing the whole of life in a dream as a servant of kings and ministers, while going toward darkness in the future and having no place to rely upon.

You have not only received a human body, which is rare to achieve, but you also have encountered buddha dharma, which is rarer to encounter.

Quickly abandon all relations, leave the household, and practice the way. You can always encounter kings, ministers, and family members. On the other hand, buddha dharma is as difficult to encounter as an udumbara blossom.

When impermanence arrives with no time, none of the kings, ministers, intimate friends, servants, family members, or rare treasures can help you. You go to the Yellow Spring [the underworld of the dead] by yourself. The only things that accompany you are wholesome and unwholesome karmas. Also, when you are about to lose your human body, you will probably have a deep desire to maintain your human body. If so, while you have your human body, leave the household as soon as possible. This is indeed the true dharma of all buddhas in the past, present, and future.

There are four types of practice for home leavers, called the four dependences. They are: sitting under trees for a lifetime, wearing a robe of excrement-cleaning cloths for a lifetime, begging food for a lifetime, and taking medicine made of urine and excrement in case of sickness for a lifetime. If you conduct these practices, you are regarded as a monk. If you don't, you are not regarded as a monk. Thus, these are the practices of home leavers.

What has been authentically transmitted until now by buddha ancestors from India and China are these practices of home leavers. If you do not leave the monastery for a lifetime, these four dependences are practiced. Know that contradicting this and creating five dependences [as Devadatta did] is a wrong practice. Who would receive them with trust? Who would have patience to listen to such teaching? What has been authentically transmitted by buddha ancestors [as the four dependences] is the true dharma. Humans who leave the household according to these four dependences are the most auspicious, unsurpassable, and the most venerable.

Thus, in India, Nanda, Ananda, Devadatta, Aniruddha, Mahanaman, and Bhadrika are all grandchildren of King Simhahanu, noblest of all nobles. They left the household in early times. They are excellent examples for later generations. Now, those who are not nobles should not spare their positions. What positions are spared by those who are not princes? Turning what is most venerable in the Jambudvipa World into what is most venerable in the entire three realms is home leaving. Kings of other small nations and citizens of the nations groundlessly spare what should not be spared, are proud of what they should not be proud of, and remain in what should not be remained in, and so they do not leave the household. Who should not regard them as worthless? Who should not regard them as foolish?

Venerable Rahula was the son of the Bodhisattva [who became Shakyamuni Buddha] and a grandson of King Shuddhodana. The king wanted to pass on the throne to Rahula. But the World-Honored One encouraged him to leave the household. Thus, know that home leaving is the most venerable dharma. As the World-Honored One's primary disciple with thorough practice and as the field of benefaction for sentient beings, Rahula still abides in this world, not having entered nirvana.

Among the ancestors who transmitted the treasury of the true dharma eye in India, there are a number of princes who left the household. Bodhidharma, the First Ancestor of China, was the third prince of the king of the Xiangxi Kingdom. Not regarding kingship as weighty, Bodhidharma transmitted authentic dharma to China.

Know clearly that home leaving is most precious. While you need to leave the household quickly, how can you wait for tomorrow, leading a life that is not close to the lives of these princes? Your exhalation will not wait for your inhalation. It is wise to leave the household as soon as possible. Also know that the benefaction of your teacher at the time of your home leaving and receiving the precepts equals that of your father and mother.

The *Guidelines for Zen Monasteries* says in its first chapter:

It is taught that all buddhas in the past, present, and future have left the household and attained the way. The twenty-eight ancestors in India and the six early ancestors in China transmitted the buddha mind seal. They all were monks. They strictly observed the pure precepts and were models over the three realms. This being so, those who practice Zen and inquire about the way make the precepts a priority. How can you attain buddhahood and become an ancestor if you do not stay away from fault and prevent wrongdoing?

Even a monastery of the declining age is a fragrant forest of gardenia bushes that cannot be compared with ordinary trees or grass. Its community is like milk mixed with water. When you use milk, use milk that is mixed with water. Do not use anything else.

In this way, the authentic transmission of *it is taught that all buddhas in the past, present, and future have left the household and attained the way* is most precious. There are no buddhas in the past, present, and future who have not left the household. This is the unsurpassable enlightenment of the treasury of the true dharma eye, the wondrous heart of nirvana, authentically transmitted by buddhas and ancestors.

A day during the summer practice period, the seventh year of the Kencho Era [1255]. [Copied by Ejo.]

88

MAKING OFFERINGS TO BUDDHAS

T HE BUDDHA SAID, "Without the past worlds, there would be no
past buddhas. Without past buddhas, there would be no leaving
home and receiving the precepts."

Clearly know that there are always buddhas in the past, present, and
future. Do not say that past buddhas had a beginning or did not have
a beginning. To fall into such theoretical discussion is not the study of
buddha dharma. Instead, to make offerings to past buddhas, leave the
household, and follow them is a crucial way to become buddhas.

You become buddhas by the merit of making offerings to buddhas.
How can a sentient being who has not made offerings to even one buddha become a buddha? There is no becoming a buddha without cause.

According to the *Sutra of the Buddha's Original Practice*, the Buddha
said to Maudgalyayana:

In a vision I had of a past life, I was with innumerable, boundless world-
honored ones, planting various wholesome roots, and seeking unsurpassable, complete enlightenment. Maudgalyayana, in my vision, I became a

wheel-turning king and encountered three billion buddhas. They all had the same name and were called Shakyamuni. I made four types of sufficient offerings to tathagatas and shravakas, and served and venerated them. The four types of sufficient offerings are clothes, food, bedding, and medicine. But at that time those buddhas did not predict: "You will attain unsurpassable, complete enlightenment and become the Knower of the World, the Teacher of Devas, and the Buddha, the World-Honored One."

Maudgalyayana, in my vision of a past life, I became a wheel-turning king and encountered eight hundred million buddhas. They all had the same name and were called Dipankara. I made four types of offerings to tathagatas and shravakas, and served and venerated them. The four types of offerings included clothes, food, bedding, medicine, banners, canopies, flowers, and incense. But at that time those Buddhas did not predict: "You will attain unsurpassable, complete enlightenment and become the Knower of the World, the Teacher of Devas, and the Buddha, the World-Honored One."

Maudgalyayana, in my vision of a past life, I became a wheel-turning king and encountered three hundred million buddhas. They all had the same name and were called Pusya. I made four types of sufficient offerings to tathagatas and shravakas, and served and venerated them. But at that time those buddhas did not predict: "You will become a buddha."

Other than this, Shakyamuni Buddha in his former lives made offerings to a number of buddhas. A wheel-turning king presides over the Four Worlds. So, he must have had abundant things to offer. A great wheel-turning king must preside over a billion worlds. It is impossible nowadays for ordinary people to fathom the amount of his offerings. Even the Buddha himself would be unable to measure them completely.

———————

According to "Pure Seeing," the eighth chapter of the *Buddha's Treasury Sutra*, the Buddha said:

Shariputra, in a vision of a past life, I met three billion buddhas through my search for unsurpassable, complete enlightenment. They were all called Shakyamuni Buddha. I became a wheel-turning king and made sufficient offerings of clothes, food, bedding, and medicine to the buddhas and their disciples throughout my lifetime. I did this in search of unsurpassable, complete enlightenment. And yet, those buddhas did not predict: "You will become a buddha in the next lifetime." Why not? Because I had done so with a grasping mind.

Shariputra, in a past life, I met eight thousand buddhas. They were all called Dipankara. I became a wheel-turning king and made sufficient offerings of clothes, food, bedding, and medicine to the buddhas and their disciples throughout my lifetime. I did this in search of unsurpassable, complete enlightenment. And yet, those buddhas did not predict: "You will become a buddha in the next lifetime." Why not? Because I had done so with a grasping mind.

Shariputra, in my vision of a past life, I met sixty thousand buddhas. They were all called Prabha. I became a wheel-turning king and made sufficient offerings of clothes, food, bedding, and medicine to the buddhas and their disciples throughout my lifetime. I did this in search of unsurpassable, complete enlightenment. And yet, those buddhas did not predict: "You will become a buddha in the next lifetime." Why not? Because I had done so with a grasping mind.

Shariputra, in my vision of a past life, I met three hundred million buddhas. They were all called Pusya. I became a wheel-turning king and made sufficient offerings to the buddhas and their disciples throughout my lifetime. And yet, those buddhas did not predict: "You will become a buddha in the next lifetime." Why? Because I did my practice with a grasping mind.

Shariputra, in my vision of a past life, I met eighteen thousand buddhas. They were all called Parvataraja. The eon was called High Eight. At the place of the eighteen thousand buddhas I shaved my head and practiced for unsurpassable, complete enlightenment. And yet, those buddhas did not predict: "You will become a buddha in the next lifetime." Why? Because I was doing my practice with a grasping mind.

Shariputra, in my vision of a past life, I met five hundred buddhas. They were all called Padmottara. I became a wheel-turning king and offered everything to the buddhas and their disciples throughout my lifetime. I did this in search of unsurpassable, complete enlightenment. And yet, no buddhas predicted that I would be enlightened, because I did my practice with a grasping mind.

Shariputra, in my vision of a past life, I met five hundred buddhas. They were all called Prabhava. I offered everything to them. And yet, none of them gave me a prediction of enlightenment, because I did my practice with a grasping mind.

Shariputra, in one vision of a past life, I met two thousand buddhas. They were all called Kaundinya. I became a wheel-turning king and offered everything to these buddhas. And yet, none of them predicted that I would be enlightened, because I did my practice with a grasping mind.

Shariputra, in my vision of a past life, I met nine thousand buddhas. They were all called Kashyapa. I made four types of offerings to these buddhas and their disciples. And yet, none of them predicted that I would be enlightened, because I did my practice with a grasping mind.

Shariputra, in a vision I had of a past life, there were no buddhas for myriad eons. Then, for the next five hundred eons there were ninety thousand pratyeka-buddhas. I offered clothes, food, bedding, and medicine to all of them, and venerated and praised them. In the next five hundred eons I made four types of offerings to eighty trillion pratyeka-buddhas, and venerated and praised them.

Shariputra, after these one thousand eons, there were no more pratyeka-buddhas. I died in the Jambudvipa World and was born in the Brahma Heaven and became King Brahma. For the next five hundred eons, I transmigrated in the Brahma Heaven and was always born as King Brahma, without being born in the Jambudvipa World. After that, I was born in the Jambudvipa World and presided over it. When my life ended, I was born in the Heaven of the Four Deva Kings. After that, I was born in Tushita Heaven and became Indra. I transmigrated in this way for five hundred eons. Then I was born in the Jambudvipa World. After another five hundred eons, I was born in the Brahma Heaven and became King Brahma.

Shariputra, for the next nine thousand eons, I was always born in deva worlds, except once in the Jambudvipa World. When the eon was exhausted and the world exploded, I was born in Abhasvara Heaven. After the next world was formed, I went back to the Brahma World. I was never born in the human realm in these nine thousand eons. Shariputra, during this time there were no buddhas and pratyeka-buddhas. A number of sentient beings fell into unwholesome paths.

Shariputra, after more than ten thousand eons, a buddha emerged who was called Universal Protection Tathagata, Worthy of Offering, True Encompassing Knower, Clear Walker, Well Gone, Knower of the World, Unsurpassable Warrior, Excellent Tamer, Teacher of Humans and Devas, and Buddha, the World-Honored One. I had just finished a life as the Brahma King and was born in the Jambudvipa World to be a wheel-turning king called Heaven Sharer. I was ninety thousand years old in human age. Throughout my time I made offerings of excellent things to the Buddha and nine billion monks. I was in search of unsurpassable, complete enlightenment. But Universal Protection Tathagata did not predict: "You will become a buddha in the next lifetime." Why not? Because at that time I was not able to understand the reality of all things but only had a mind greedy for attainment.

Shariputra, in these eons one hundred buddhas with different names emerged. Every time, I became a wheel-turning king and made offerings through my lifetime to the buddha and his disciples of that time, in pursuit of unsurpassable, complete enlightenment. But none of these buddhas predicted, "You will become a buddha in the next lifetime," because I had a mind greedy for attainment.

Shariputra, in a vision I had of a past life, I met one thousand Buddhas in the seven hundredth uncountable eon. They were all called Jambunada. I made four types of offerings to them, but none of them predicted that I would be enlightened, because I had a mind greedy for attainment.

Shariputra, in my vision of a past life, I met six million two hundred thousand Buddhas in the seven hundred uncountable eons. They were all called Sarvarthadarsha. I became a wheel-turning king and made all types of comfortable offerings to these Buddhas and their disciples throughout my lifetime, but none of them predicted that I would be enlightened because I had a mind greedy for attainment.

Shariputra, in one vision I had of a past life, I met eighty-four Buddhas in the seven hundred uncountable eons. They were all called Indra Ketu. I became a wheel-turning king and made all types of splendid offerings to these Buddhas and their disciples throughout my lifetime, but none of them predicted that I would be enlightened, because I had a mind greedy for attainment.

Shariputra, in my vision of a past life, I met fifteen Buddhas in the seven hundredth uncountable eon. They were all called Suryarashmi. I became a wheel-turning king and made all types of comfortable offerings to these Buddhas and their disciples throughout my lifetime, but none of them predicted that I would be enlightened, because I had a mind greedy for attainment.

Shariputra, in my vision of a past life, I met sixty-two Buddhas in the seven hundredth uncountable eon. They were all called Shanta. I became a wheel-turning king and made all types of splendid offerings to these, but none of them predicted that I would be enlightened, because I had a mind greedy for attainment.

In this way I transmigrated and saw Dipankara Buddha and attained patience beyond birth. Dipankara Buddha predicted, "In the next life after passing uncountable eons, you will become a buddha and be called Shakyamuni Tathagata, Worthy of Offering, True Encompassing Knower, Clear Walker, Well Gone, Knower of the World, Unsurpassable Warrior, Excellent Tamer, Teacher of Humans and Devas, and Buddha, the World-Honored One.

From the time of meeting three billion Shakyamuni Buddhas and making offerings to them until the time of meeting Dipankara Buddha, the bodhisattva [former life of Shakyamuni Buddha] always took the form of a wheel-turning king and made offerings to Buddhas. Many wheel-turning kings are said to live more than eighty thousand years. During the lifetimes of eighty or ninety thousand years, he made his splendid offerings. Dipankara Buddha is the same as Lamp-Burning Tathagata. The *Sutra of Buddha's Original Practice* and the *Buddha's Treasury Sutra* also talk about his meeting three billion Shakyamuni Buddhas.

———————

[The *Abhidharma Kosha Treatise* says:]

Bodhisattva Shakyamuni met and made offerings to seventy-five thousand Buddhas in the first set of uncountable eons, when his name was Shakyamuni at first and Ratnachuda at the end. He met and made offerings to seventy-six thousand Buddhas in the second set of uncountable eons, when his name was Ratnachuda at first and Dipankara at the end. He met and made offerings to seventy-seven thousand Buddhas in the third set of uncountable eons, when his name was Dipankara at first and Vipashyin at the end. While he was practicing actions that nurture different types of effects, he met and made offerings to six Buddhas in ninety-one eons. His name was Vipashyin at first and Kashyapa at the end.

In making offerings during these three sets of uncountable eons, Bodhisattva Shakyamuni did not spare his own body and life, nor did he spare his nation, palace, wife, children, seven treasures, men, and women [followers]. It is beyond ordinary thinking. He made offerings sometimes by filling a silver bowl with golden millet, and sometimes by filling a gold and silver bowl with the millet of seven treasures. He made offerings of red beans, sandalwood, aloeswood, and flowers from both water and land. He made offerings to Dipankara Buddha of five stalks of blue lotus flowers purchased for five hundred coins, and of deerskin robes.

Making offerings to buddhas does not mean providing buddhas with what they need. It is dedicating moments of your life to buddhas without wasting any moment. What use can buddhas make even if gold and silver are offered? What benefit can buddhas receive if incense and flowers are offered? However, buddhas receive the offerings with great compassion to help increase the merit of sentient beings.

According to chapter 22 of the *Maha Pari-nirvana Sutra*, the Buddha said:

Good people, in my vision of a past life, countless and boundless trillion eons ago, there was a world called Saha. There was a buddha called Shakyamuni Tathagata, Worthy of Offering, True Encompassing Knower, Clear Walker, Well Gone, Knower of the World, Unsurpassable Warrior, Excellent Tamer, Teacher of Humans and Devas, and Buddha, the World-Honored One. This Buddha expounded the *Maha Pari-nirvana Sutra* for various beings. At that time, while at a good friend's place, I heard that the Buddha was expounding this sutra. I rejoiced and wanted to make offerings.

Since I was poor and had nothing where I lived, I wanted to be hired, but unfortunately no one wanted to hire me. On my way home I met someone and said, "I want to offer myself. Will you please hire me?"

The man said, "No one can bear the work in my house. But if you are willing to do it, I will hire you."

I asked, "What kind of work is it?"

The man replied, "I have a very bad disease. My doctor says the cure is to eat three ounces of human flesh every day. If you agree to give me three ounces of your flesh every day, I will give you five coins."

Hearing this, I rejoiced and said to the man, "Please give me the money and let me have seven days. When I am done with what I need to do, I will get to work."

The man said, "Seven days are not possible. If you want to do this, I will let you have one day."

Good people, I got the money, went to the Buddha, bowed at his feet by putting my head to the ground, and offered him all of my possessions. After doing this I sincerely listened to the sutra. Although I heard the sutra, I was stupid and could only receive this verse:

The Tathagata realizes nirvana.
Forever he becomes free from birth and death.
If you listen with utmost sincerity,
you will attain immeasurable bliss.

After receiving this verse, I went to the sick man's house.

Good people, although I gave three ounces of my flesh to the sick man every day, my mind was concentrated on this verse and I did not feel pain. This continued every day until a month had passed.

Good people, because of this endeavor, the man was cured. I was healed and did not possess a single scar. Furthermore, I aroused the aspiration for unsurpassable, complete enlightenment.

The power of one verse is like this. How much more so if you completely receive the sutra and chant it? Seeing that this sutra has such power, I further aroused the aspiration for enlightenment, and vowed to attain the buddha way and be called Shakyamuni Buddha in the future.

Good people, because of the power of my connection to this verse, I am moved to expound this sutra in this assembly of devas and humans.

Good people, as you see in this story, the *Maha Pari-nirvana Sutra* is beyond thinking and brings forth immeasurable, boundless merit. This sutra is a storehouse of very profound secrets of all buddha tathagatas.

The bodhisattva who offered himself became Shakyamuni Buddha in the next life. According to other sutras, this was the beginning of the first set of uncountable eons when the bodhisattva made offerings to the ancient Shakyamuni Buddha. The bodhisattva was a slate roofer and his name was Mahaprabha. In venerating the ancient Shakyamuni Buddha and his disciples, he made three kinds of offerings: grass cushions, sugar water, and candles. He also made a vow: "May my land, title, long span of life, and disciples all be equal to the present Shakyamuni Buddha." This vow has been fulfilled to the present day.

Thus, when you make offerings to the Buddha, don't say you are poor, and don't say your family is poor. To offer oneself and make offerings is the true dharma of Great Master Shakyamuni. Who will not rejoice for him? For this practice, he met a master who took three ounces of flesh from him daily. This is something other people could not have endured, however advanced their practice might be. But with the help of the deep aspiration to make offerings, he was able to receive this merit.

Now we hear the Tathagata's true dharma. This is to receive a share of the bodhisattva's past practice of scarifying his flesh. This verse of four lines cannot be purchased with five coins. This is what those buddhas and this buddha have realized without regard to receiving or letting go of birth for countless, boundless eons. Indeed, this verse has unthinkable power. Disciples of the dharma left by the Buddha should deeply bow to, receive, and maintain it. The Tathagata explained the power of this verse in this way. This teaching is, indeed, vast and profound.

———————

The *Lotus Sutra* says:

> If you venerate and make offerings of flowers, incense, banners, and a canopy to a jeweled or painted image of the Buddha in a stupa; if you make offerings of all the exquisite sounds by having musicians hit the drums, blow the horns and flutes, and play the harp and double hand-bells; or if you praise virtues of the Buddha by singing with joy; even a small sound can lead any of you to attain the buddha way. If, even with a scattered mind, you make offerings of a flower to a painted image of the Buddha, you will immediately see countless buddhas. Or, if you make offerings of bowing, just joining your palms together, raising one hand, or lowering your head to a painted image of the Buddha, you will soon see countless buddhas, attain unsurpassable enlightenment, and widely awaken countless beings.

This is the skull and eyeball of buddhas in the past, present, and future. Seeing a wise person and wanting to be like that, you should exert your power and endeavor to make offerings. Do not waste moments in your life.

———————

Shitou, Great Master Wuji, said, "Do not vainly pass your time."

All those who practice this virtue become buddhas. This is the same for the past, present, and future. There are not two or three different ways for this. Attaining the effect of becoming a buddha through the cause of making offerings to buddhas is like this.

———

Ancestor Nagarjuna said, "If you want the effect of being a buddha, recite one verse of praise, chant one refuge, burn a pinch of incense, or offer one flower. Even with such a small practice, you will certainly become a buddha."

Even if this had been spoken only by Ancestor Nagarjuna Bodhisattva, you should venerate it. But, he authentically transmitted and expounded great master Shakyamuni Buddha's words. With great fortune we now climb on the treasure mountain of the buddha way, enter the treasure ocean of the buddha way, and acquire the treasure. Rejoice in this more than anything else. This is the effect of making offerings to buddhas for vast eons. Do not doubt that *you will certainly become a buddha*. It is determined. What Shakyamuni Buddha explained was also like this.

[Ancestor Nagarjuna also said,] "A small cause can bring forth a large effect. A small condition can bring forth a large result. If you seek the buddha way, recite one verse of praise, chant one refuge, and burn a pinch of incense, then you will certainly become a buddha. Furthermore, if you learn and understand that the reality of all things is not beyond birth, beyond death, beyond beyond birth, beyond beyond death, and practice the act of causation, you will never miss it."

This is a clear teaching of the World-Honored One, authentically transmitted by Ancestor Nagarjuna. This golden expression of truth has been authentically transmitted and received. As this was a statement by Nagarjuna, it could not be compared to the statements of other teachers. Thus, you have encountered an authentic transmission and spreading of the World-Honored One's teaching. Rejoice. Do not compare this sacred teaching to the false statements of mediocre teachers in China.

[According to the *Treatise on Realization of Great Wisdom:*]

Ancestor Nagarjuna said, "Because buddhas venerate the dharma, they make offerings to the dharma and regard it as the teacher. How is it so? Because, all buddhas in the past, present, and future regard the reality of all phenomena as the teacher."

He was asked, "How come buddhas don't make offerings to the dharma within themselves, but make offerings to the dharma outside themselves?"

Nagarjuna replied, "Because they follow the convention of the world. If monks want to make offerings to the dharma treasure, they do not make offerings to the dharma within themselves, but they make offerings to other people's maintaining, knowing, and understanding of dharma. Buddhas are also like this. Although there is dharma within them, they make offerings to dharma in other buddhas."

He was asked, "Since the Buddha doesn't want to receive benefaction, why do we make offerings to him?"

Nagarjuna replied, "For countless eons the Buddha has conducted various meritorious deeds and practiced wholesome actions without seeking reward. Because we venerate his merit, we make offerings."

When the Buddha was in this world, there was a blind monk. Without seeing, he used his hands to sew a robe. When a thread came off from the needle, he said to himself, "Who is going to benefit me by threading the needle?"

Then the Buddha went to him and said to the blind monk, "I love beneficial merit. So, let me thread the needle for you."

Noticing that the voice was the Buddha's, the blind monk quickly put on his robe, bowed at the Buddha's feet, and said, "The Buddha is complete with merit. How come you say you love beneficial merit?"

The Buddha said, "Although I am already complete with merit, I deeply understand the cause, effect, and power of merit. The reason why I excel most among all sentient beings is because of this merit. Therefore, I love beneficial merit."

After praising merit for the sake of this blind monk, the Buddha spontaneously expounded dharma. Then the monk attained the pure dharma eye and also became able to see with his eyes.

I was told this story in an evening talk by Rujing, my late master. Later, I compared it with the *Treatise on Realization of Great Wisdom*. The admonition by Rujing, the dharma transmitting ancestor, had been correct with nothing lacking. This passage is found in the tenth chapter of the *Treatise on Realization of Great Wisdom*. Thus, it is clear that all buddhas regard the reality of all phenomena as their great teacher. Shakyamuni Buddha also realized the permanent dharma of all buddhas.

To regard the reality of all phenomena as their great teacher means to venerate and make offerings to the three treasures—buddha, dharma, and sangha. Buddhas in countless eons accumulate a great deal of merit—the wholesome root—without seeking reward, and only venerate and make offerings. Even after the Buddha reached the rank of having enlightenment—the buddha fruit—still he loved minor merits, and so he threaded the needle of a blind monk. If you want to clarify the merit of the buddha fruit, this story clearly demonstrates it.

In this way, the merit of enlightenment—the buddha fruit—and the principle of the reality of all phenomena are not like what ordinary people nowadays think they are. They think that creating unwholesomeness is the reality of all phenomena and that only those who are greedy for attainment can reach the buddha fruit of enlightenment. Those who have such a crooked view may know about eighty thousand eons but will not be able to escape the view of original eons and declined eons. How can they understand the reality of all phenomena, which is thoroughly understood by "only a buddha and a buddha"? The reason is that what is thoroughly understood by "only a buddha and a buddha" is the reality of all phenomena.

There are ten types of offerings:

Offerings to the Buddha himself; offerings to a chaitya [place of veneration] for the Buddha; offerings to the Buddha himself and to a chaitya for the Buddha; offerings to the invisible Buddha and to a chaitya for the Buddha; offerings by yourself; offerings you have others make; offerings of materials; excellent offerings; unstained offerings; and offerings of the ultimate way.

The first type of offering is for the physical form of the Buddha.

———————

The second type of offering to the Buddha is for a chaitya [sacred site] of the Buddha. They are called chaitya offerings.

The *Great Sangha Precepts* says, "A place of veneration where the relics are enshrined is called a stupa. A place of veneration where relics are not enshrined is called a chaitya. Sometimes both of these are called a chaitya. These are also called thuba in Sanskrit.

In China, *chaitya* is translated as a "square tomb" or "sacred shrine." The *Agama Sutra* uses the term *chaitya*.

What are called a stupa and a chaitya appear to be the same thing. But Nanyue Huisi says in his *Method of the Lotus Samadhi Repentance*, "Wholeheartedly I venerate all the relics, sacred images, chaityas, wondrous stupas, Prabhutaratna Tathagata, whose entire body is a stupa treasure." From here it is possible to assume that chaityas and wondrous stupas are different, just as relics and sacred images are.

———————

It is said in chapter 33 of the *Great Sangha Precepts:*

In regard to the way of building a stupa, once the Buddha lived in the country of Kaushala and was traveling. A Brahman who was plowing saw the Buddha passing by, pushed his cane onto the soil, and bowed to the Buddha.

The World-Honored One smiled. Then the monks asked, "Please tell us why you smiled."

The Buddha replied, "This Brahman just bowed to two World-Honored Ones."

The monks said, "Why two buddhas?"

The Buddha replied, "When he bowed to me, there was a stupa of Kashyapa Buddha below his cane."

The monks said, "We would like to see the Kashyapa Buddha's stupa."

The Buddha said, "Follow this Brahman and look under the ground."

So, the monks dug up the ground and looked for the tower under the guidance of the Brahman. When they found it, the World-Honored

One allowed a seven-treasure stupa of Kashyapa Buddha to appear. It was one *yojana* high and half a *yojana* wide.

Seeing this, the Brahman said to the Buddha, "World-Honored One, my family name is Kashyapa. This is my Kashyapa stupa."

The World-Honored One went to the Brahman's house and started building a stupa of Kashyapa Buddha.

Then, monks said to the Buddha, "World-Honored One, may we bring some dirt?"

"Yes, you may." Then the Buddha spoke this verse:

> Transporting hundreds of cartfuls of genuine gold
> and making offerings do not equal
> bringing a lump of dirt with a venerating heart
> to build a stupa for the Buddha.

After this, the Buddha completed a stupa of Kashyapa Buddha. Its ground story was square with a railing around it. The two stories above it were round with the roof joints sticking out from the four sides. Banners and canopies stood above these stories, and the wheel of space [symbolizing one of the five great elements] was added on top.

The Buddha said, "This is how to build a stupa." Then, the Buddha bowed respectfully to Kashyapa Buddha of the past.

The monks said, "World-Honored One, may we also bow?"

"Yes." And the Buddha said this verse:

> Transporting hundreds of cartfuls of genuine gold
> and making offerings do not equal
> respectfully bowing to a buddha tower
> with a single wholesome heart.

Hearing that the World-Honored One had built a stupa, people in the world brought incense and flowers and gave them to him. The Buddha received them and respectfully offered them to the tower of Kashyapa Buddha of the past.

The monks said, "May we make offerings?"

"Yes." And the Buddha recited this verse:

> Transporting hundreds of cartfuls of genuine gold
> and making offerings do not equal

the offering of flowers and incense to a stupa
with a single wholesome heart.

A multitude of people assembled like clouds.

The Buddha said to Shariputra, "I will expound dharma for these people." Then he recited this verse:

Hundreds of Jambudvipa Worlds filled with
the offerings of genuine gold
do not equal the offering of one dharma
to be followed and practiced.

In this assembly there were those who had attained the way. The Buddha said in a verse:

Hundreds of Jambudvipa Worlds filled with
offerings of genuine gold
do not equal the offering of one dharma
followed by the realization of truth.

Then, the Brahman attained indestructible trust and made a meal offering to the Buddha and monks in front of the stupa.

Hearing that the World-Honored One had a stupa built for Kashyapa Buddha, King Prasenajit brought seven hundred cartfuls of slate to the Buddha, bowed to the Buddha's feet by putting his face to the ground, and said, "World-Honored One, I wish to make this stupa larger. May I do so?"

"Yes." Then the Buddha said to the king, "In the past, when Kashyapa Buddha entered pari-nirvana, there was a king called Gridra. He wanted to build a seven-treasure stupa. One of the courtiers said to the king, 'In the future there may be people who break laws and want to destroy the stupa. I suggest that we build the stupa with slate and cover it with gold and silver. Then, even if the gold and silver are taken away, the slate of the stupa will remain intact.'

"The king followed the courtier's advice and had the stupa built with slate covered with gold. It was one *yojana* high and half a *yojana* wide. The balcony railing was made of bronze. It took seven years, seven months, and seven days to complete it. Then he made offerings of incense and flowers to the Buddha and monks."

King Prasenajit said to the Buddha, "That king must have been very wealthy and had many rare treasures. What I am going to build may not be as good." Then he built the stupa in seven months and seven days. After its completion he made offerings of incense and flowers to the Buddha and monks.

The way to build a stupa is to have the ground story square with a railing around it. The two higher stories are round with the joints of the roof sticking out from the four sides. Banners and canopies stand above these stories. The wheel of space is added on top. If you say, "The World-Honored One spoke of himself as having become free from greed, hatred, and delusion, then why would he need such a stupa?" then this would break the precept [of not slandering the three treasures]. Such an offence is serious and prohibited according to the stupa principles.

The stupa principles require selecting a suitable site when constructing a temple building. A stupa should be in the east or north of the temple compound but not in the south or west. The monks' quarters should not be in the Buddha's quarters [stupa], and the Buddha's quarters should not be in the monks' quarters. If the site of the stupa is close to a place for leaving corpses, build a fence so dogs don't pollute the ground by scattering bones. The monks' quarters should be built in the west or south of the temple. Water from the monks' quarters should not flow to the Buddha's quarters, but may flow from the Buddha's quarters to the monks' quarters. Therefore, the stupa should be built on higher ground. [At the site of the stupa] Do not wash clothes, wear sandals, cover the head or shoulders, or spit on the ground. If you say, "The World-Honored One spoke of himself as having become free from greed, hatred, and delusion, then why would he need such a stupa?" this would break the precept. The result of this action [insulting the Buddha or a stupa for him] is serious and prohibited according to the stupa principles.

In regard to stupa altars, King Prasenajit went to see the Buddha, bowed to the Buddha's feet by putting his face to the ground, and said, "World-Honored One, I have built a stupa for Kashyapa Buddha. May I make altars?"

"Yes." The Buddha said, "In the past when Kashyapa Buddha entered pari-nirvana, King Gridra built a stupa for the Buddha. He built altars with balconies that had railings on all four sides, and images of lions and various paintings above them. In those balconies there were places for flowers. Inside the altars, banners and canopies were hung. If you say, 'The World-Honored One speaks of himself as having become free from greed, hatred, and delusion, but he gets himself decorated and receives bliss,' this would break the precept. The result of this action is serious. These are called stupa altar principles."

Thus, we clearly know that to build a stupa for an ancient buddha and make offerings in veneration of enlightenment, the buddha fruit, are customs for buddhas. There are many precedents like this, but I am only presenting this for the time being.

In buddha dharma the teaching of the Sarva Asti Vada School is outstanding. The *Maha Sangha Precepts* is the most basic teaching of the school. Monk Faxian went to India by clearing a way through wild lands. He climbed Vulture Peak and brought this teaching to China for the first time. The teaching transmitted from ancestor to ancestor corresponds to that of the Sarva Asti Vada School.

The third type of offering is to the Buddha himself or to a chaitya for the present Buddha.

The fourth type of offering is the making of extensive offerings to the invisible Buddha or to a chaitya for the Buddha. It is said: There are offerings to the Buddha himself or to a chaitya for the present Buddha, and there are offerings to the invisible Buddha or to a chaitya for the invisible Buddha. By making offerings to the Buddha himself or to a chaitya for the present Buddha, you attain great merit. By making offerings to what is invisible, you attain extremely great merit, because the field of offerings is very extensive. If you combine making offerings to the visible and invisible, you attain the greatest merit.

The fifth type of offering is an offering made by yourself to the Buddha or to a chaitya for the Buddha.

The sixth type of offering is an offering you have others make to the Buddha or to a chaitya for the Buddha. If others have materials, you have them make an offering without negligence. It is said, "Offerings made by the self and others are done together." If you make offerings by yourself, you attain great merit. If you have others make offerings, you attain extremely great merit. If you combine making offerings by yourself and others, you attain the greatest merit.

The seventh type of offering is making an offering of materials to the Buddha or to a chaitya for the Buddha. It is said, "There are three kinds of materials: things for livelihood such as clothes and food, things for veneration such as incense and flowers, and things for decoration, including all other things, to create a magnificent sacred space."

The eighth type of offering is excellent offerings. There are three kinds: general offerings; appropriate offerings in accordance with pure trust in the weightiness of the Buddha's virtue; and offerings of the dedicated heart—the merit of one's practice—in seeking the buddha heart.

The ninth type of offering is unstained offerings. There are two kinds: an unstained heart free from all faults, and unstained materials free from all faults.

The tenth type of offering is making an offering of the ultimate way. Here, the offering follows its effect. The effect of being a buddha is being at the ultimate place. The practice of making offerings brings you to this place. This being so, it is called making offerings of the ultimate way. It is also called making offerings of dharma or making offerings of practice. There are three kinds: offerings of materials regarded as offerings of the ultimate way; offerings of delight [at others' wholesome actions] regarded as offerings of the ultimate way; and offerings of practice regarded as offerings of the ultimate way.

These are the ten types of offerings to the Buddha. Offerings made to the dharma and to the sangha are similar. It is said, "Making offerings to the dharma is making them to the principle, teaching and practice expounded by the Buddha, as well as to the scriptures. Making offerings to the sangha is making them to all sacred members of the Three Vehicles, the chaitya, images, and shrines, as well as to ordinary monks."

There are six types of hearts that make offerings: an unsurpassable heart in the field of benefaction, which is the most excellent of those aroused in the field of benefaction; an unsurpassable heart of gratitude, where all wholesome enjoyment is aroused by the three treasures; a heart that arouses the most excellent heart of all sentient beings; a heart rare to encounter like an udumbara blossom; a heart rare in the billion worlds; and a heart that embodies the principles that are depended on in the world and beyond the world.

If you make even small offerings to the three treasures with these six types of heart, you attain immeasurable, boundless merit. How much more so if you make many offerings?

These offerings should always be made with a sincere heart. This is what buddhas have practiced. Since examples of this practice are widely shown in sutras and teachings on the precepts, this practice has been authentically transmitted by buddha ancestors.

The days and months of assisting your master and engaging in labor are the time of making offerings. Guidelines for enshrining buddha images and relics, venerating and bowing, as well as building stupas and chaityas, have been authentically transmitted in the house of buddha ancestors alone, and not by those who are not descendants of buddha ancestors.

If the guidelines are not authentically transmitted, there will be discrepancies. If there are discrepancies, offerings will not be genuine. If the offerings are not genuine, there is no merit. Make sure to authentically receive the correct way of making offerings.

Zen Master Lingdao spent years attending to the tomb of Huineng at Caoxi. Worker Lu [Huineng] pounded rice ceaselessly for the assembly of monks day and night. These were both appropriate ways of making offerings. These examples are a few out of many that are impossible to list.

[Edited by Ejo during] The summer practice period, the seventh year of the Kencho Era [1265].

89

TAKING REFUGE IN BUDDHA, DHARMA, AND SANGHA

THE FIRST OF one hundred twenty questions in the *Guidelines for Zen Monasteries* says, "Do you revere buddha, dharma, and sangha, or not?"

Thus, it is clear that what the buddhas and ancestors in India and China have authentically transmitted is reverence to buddha, dharma, and sangha. Without taking refuge, there is no reverence. Without reverence, there is no taking refuge.

The act of taking refuge in buddha, dharma, and sangha is achieved through mutual affinity and interaction. Whether you are in a deva realm, a human realm, hell, a demon realm, or an animal realm, when you have mutual affinity and interaction with buddha, dharma, and sangha, you invariably take refuge in them.

Taking refuge in the three treasures, you nurture yourself wherever you are, birth after birth, world after world. You accumulate merit, assemble virtue, and attain unsurpassable, complete enlightenment. Even if you are misled by unwholesome friends, obstructed by demons, cut off from your wholesome roots, and become an icchantika, in the end you will regain your wholesome roots and increase merit. The power of taking refuge in the three treasures will never decay.

————————

To take refuge in the three treasures, whether at the time of the Tathagata or after the Tathagata's pari-nirvana, fill yourself with pure trust, put your hands together, bow, and recite in this way:

> I, so-and-so, from this body through the
>   attainment of a buddha body, take refuge in
>   Buddha, take refuge in Dharma, and take
>   refuge in Sangha.
> I take refuge in Buddha, the most revered of those
>   with two feet.
> I take refuge in Dharma, the most revered way to
>   become free from delusion.
> I take refuge in Sangha, the most revered assembly.
> I have taken refuge in Buddha,
> I have taken refuge in Dharma,
> I have taken refuge in Sangha.

Initiate this vow aspiring for enlightenment, the fruit of buddhahood. Even though your body-mind is born and dies moment by moment, your dharma body surely grows and attains enlightenment.

————————

"Taking refuge in" means returning and relying upon. "Returning" is like children returning to their parents. "Relying upon" is like citizens relying on the king. This phrase implies that you are liberated by doing so.

You take refuge in buddha because he is a great master. You take refuge in dharma because it is good medicine. You take refuge in sangha because it is an excellent friend.

————————

[A Chinese commentary called the *Meaning of the Mahayana* says:]

"Why do you return exclusively to these three treasures?

"The reason why these three are the ultimate place of return is that they help sentient beings to become free from birth and death, and realize great enlightenment."

These three treasures have wondrous power.

Buddha is a word from India. It is translated as "awakened one" in China. It means one who has unsurpassable, complete enlightenment.

Dharma is a word [in Sanskrit] from India. It is also called *dhamma* [in Pali]. There are a variety of Indian sounds for it. In China it is translated as "law." Although everything that is wholesome, unwholesome, or neutral is also dharma, the dharma in which we take refuge is the dharma that is the law.

Sangha is also a word from India. It is translated as "harmonious assembly" in China.

These three treasures have been venerated in this way.

The three treasures that have been maintained are:

The buddha treasure, such as buddha images and stupas; the dharma treasure transmitted as scripture on red or yellow scrolls; and the sangha treasure of precepts, including shaving the head, wearing a dyed robe, and following the precepts and dharma procedures.

The three treasures that function as teaching are: the buddha treasure of Shakyamuni Buddha, the World-Honored One; the dharma treasure transmitted as the turning of the dharma wheel, the spreading of sacred teaching; and the sangha treasure of the Five Monks [who listened to the Buddha's first discourse], including Ajnatakaundinya.

The three treasures that are the essence of reality are: the buddha treasure of the five types of dharma body; the dharma treasure of nirvana that is beyond change; and the sangha treasure of the merit of learning what is beyond learning.

The three treasures as one treasure are: the buddha treasure of fully realizing reality; the dharma treasure of being pure and free of defilement;

and the sangha treasure of living in accord with reality, being harmonious, and being free from stagnation.

You take refuge in these three treasures. Those unfortunate ones who lack virtue do not even hear the name of the three treasures; how can they take refuge in them?

The *Lotus Sutra* says, "These beings, because of their unwholesome conditions, cannot hear the name of the three treasures, even for uncountable kalpas."

The *Lotus Sutra* describes the great causes and conditions of buddha tathagatas. The *Lotus Sutra* is the king, the great master of the sutras expounded by Shakyamuni Buddha. All other sutras and dharmas are its subjects and relations.

The words in the *Lotus Sutra* are genuine. Other sutras that include skillful means are not necessarily the essential teachings of the Buddha. To rely on the words in other sutras in order to criticize the *Lotus Sutra* is upside down. Without the influence of the *Lotus Sutra*, there can be no other sutras. Other sutras assemble to take refuge in the *Lotus Sutra*. This sutra speaks of those who cannot hear the name of the three treasures. Thus, know that the merit of the three treasures is unequalled.

The World-Honored One said:

Many of you are fearful of suffering and take refuge in mountains, in gardens, in forests, under trees, or in shrines. This refuge is neither excellent nor valuable. You cannot be liberated from suffering by taking refuge in them.

On the other hand, if you take refuge in buddha, and if you take refuge in dharma and sangha, you can always abide in the four noble truths. With this wisdom, you always observe and understand suffering and the arising of suffering, you know how to go beyond suffering forever. You know the eightfold path. This refuge is the most excellent and most valuable of all. You will certainly become free from all suffering by taking this refuge.

The World-Honored One clearly taught all sentient beings not to take refuge in mountain deities, demon spirits, and so on, or in shrines of those outside the way, with their fear of suffering. It is not possible to be liberated from various sufferings by taking refuge in those. People follow the crooked teachings of those outside the way, and follow the ways of cows, deer, demons, those who practice not speaking, those who practice not hearing, dogs, chickens, peacocks, or those who put ash on their bodies, grow long hair, sacrifice sheep on the seasonal rites after chanting mantras, worship the fire for four months, or bow to the wind for seven days. They dedicate numerous flowers to devas and pray for attaining what they desire. There is no reason why these practices would cause liberation. Thus, people suffer in vain without receiving wholesome results. This is not recommended by those who are wise.

Thus, make sure that you don't mistakenly fall into such crooked paths. Do not take refuge in any practices that are similar to these.

Human birth is difficult to acquire and buddha dharma is rarely encountered. Do not spend your life in the company of demons and waste many lifetimes among those who have crooked views. This would be deplorable. Instead, immediately take refuge in the three treasures of buddha, dharma, and sangha, and not only be liberated from all suffering but also attain enlightenment.

———————

The *Rarity Sutra* says, "Even if you guided the four worlds and the six deva realms of desire, and helped all beings there to attain the arhat fruit, the merit could not be compared with that of helping one person take refuge in the three treasures."

The four worlds means the Eastern, Western, Southern, and Northern Continents. The Northern Continent is where the teaching of the Three Vehicles cannot reach. To teach beings there and help them to become arhats would be an extraordinary thing. The merit, however, is not even close to the merit of teaching and helping one person to take refuge in the three treasures. Also, the six heavenly realms of devas are where there are few who attain the way. Even if you would help them to attain the four fruits, it cannot compare with the great and deep merit of helping one person take refuge in the three treasures.

The *Ekottarika* says:

The king of Tushita Heaven showed the five signs of decay and was about to be reborn as a boar. Indra heard his desperate voice, called to him, and said, "You should take refuge in the three treasures." The king followed his teaching and escaped being reborn as a boar.

Shakyamuni Buddha said in a verse:

> By taking refuge in the buddha,
> beings will not fall into the three unwholesome realms.
> Free from desire, abiding in human or deva realms,
> they will reach nirvana.

This king took refuge in the three treasures and was born in a wealthy man's family. He left his household and achieved the state beyond study. In this way, the merit of taking refuge in the three treasures is immeasurable and boundless.

[The *Great Collection of Sutras* says:]

When the World-Honored One was alive, two billion six hundred million hungry dragons went to see him, all shedding tears like rain, and said, "We beg you to rescue us, World-Honored One of great compassion. Upon reflection, we realize that although we left the household and entered buddha dharma in our past lives, because of various unwholesome deeds we have remained in the three unwholesome realms for immeasurable eons. Then, due to other causes, we were born in the dragon realm and have been suffering a great deal."

The Buddha said to the dragons, "You should immediately take refuge in all three treasures and practice wholesomeness single-heartedly. As a result, you will be able to meet the final buddha named Ruchi Buddha in this present kalpa. Your sins will disappear during this buddha's time."

Upon hearing these words, all the dragons received and maintained the three treasures with utmost sincerity until their lives ended.

Thus, when the Buddha rescued the dragons, he used no other methods or techniques than just presenting the three treasures. Although in their past lives these dragons had left the household and received the three treasures, because of their unwholesome karma they became hungry dragons and there was no other way for the Buddha than to offer them refuge in the three treasures.

Know that the merit of taking refuge in the three treasures is venerable, unsurpassable, inconceivable, and profound. The World-Honored One already proved this. Sentient beings should receive them with trust.

Without having the dragons chant the names of buddhas in the ten directions, the World-Honored One just encouraged them to take refuge in the three treasures. Who can fathom the depth of his intention? Thus, sentient beings nowadays should immediately take refuge in the three treasures instead of chanting various buddhas' names. Do not miss this great merit through stupidity and ignorance.

[The *Great Collection of Sutras* says:]

Among these dragons, there was a blind female dragon whose mouth looked like excrement, rotten and full of insects. Her body was eaten all over by mosquitoes and flies; it shed blood and pus from their bites. She smelled disgusting and it was impossible for others to be near her.

Seeing the dragon suffering so much, the World-Honored One asked with great compassion, "Sister, how come you have such an unwholesome body? What did you do in your past life?"

The dragon replied, "World-Honored One, I have all kinds of suffering which does not stop even for a moment. It's beyond description. When I reflect on the past three billion six hundred million years, for one hundred thousand years during that time I was among unwholesome dragons and received pain day and night without end. I remember that ninety-one kalpas ago I was a nun in the dharma of Vipashyin Buddha, but I thought of carnal affairs even more than a drunkard would. Although I was a home leaver, I could not follow the dharma. I would spread a mat in the temple and often engaged in impure conduct. In satisfaction of my desire, I had much carnal pleasure. Also, I was greedy for possessions and undeservedly received excessive donations from believers. Because of all this, I have been continuously in the three unwholesome realms and have received all kinds of burning tortures. Even after ninety-one kalpas I cannot receive a deva body."

The Buddha inquired further, "Then, after this kalpa is over, what are you going to be born into?"

Hearing these words, the dragon said, "As the result of this past karma, even if I were to be born into a better world, when that karma is exhausted, a wind of unwholesome karma will blow, and I will be born in this place once again." Then the dragon said, "Great compassionate World-Honored One, please, please save me."

The Buddha scooped up water with his hands and said, "I call this wish-granting water. I will speak the truth to you. In the past I gave up my life in order to save a dove. I had no doubt and did not hold on to myself with the mind of self-clinging. If what I say to you is true, all your unwholesome sickness will be healed."

Then, the World-Honored One put the water in his mouth and sprayed it over the blind dragon's body. Instantly, all her sickness was healed.

The dragon said to the Buddha, "I wish to take refuge in the three treasures from you."

Thus, the World-Honored One gave her refuge in the three treasures.

This dragon had been a nun in the dharma of Vipashyin Buddha. Although she had broken the precepts, she was familiar with buddha dharma. Seeing Shakyamuni Buddha in person, she asked for and took refuge in the three treasures. This is certainly nurturing the wholesome root.

The benefaction of seeing the Buddha undoubtedly depends on taking refuge in the three treasures. Even though you are not a blind dragon and do not have an animal body, if you have not encountered the Tathagata and taken refuge in the three treasures, you are far away from seeing the Buddha; you should be pitied.

The World-Honored One himself gives refuge in the three treasures. Know that the merit of taking refuge in the three treasures is both profound and immeasurable.

Indra bowed to a wild fox and took refuge in the three treasures. This is all due to the unequaled merit of taking refuge in the three treasures.

When the Buddha was at the Banyan Grove in Kapilavastu, Mahanaman of the Shakya Clan came to him and said, "What is a layperson?"

The Buddha said, "If a good man or a good woman whose senses are open takes refuge in the three treasures, the person is called a layperson."

Mahanaman said, "What is a partial layperson?"

The Buddha said, "Mahanaman, one who takes refuge in the three treasures and receives even one precept [receiving the five precepts in stages], that person is called a partial layperson."

Thus, in becoming a disciple of the Buddha, you take refuge in the three treasures. Whatever precept you receive, you take refuge in the three treasures and then receive other precepts. In this way, you receive the precepts as a result of taking refuge in the three treasures.

According to the *Dharmapada* [the Sanskrit version of the *Dhammapada*]:

> Long ago Indra knew that he was about to die and be reborn as a donkey. He was worried and thought the Buddha, World-Honored One, alone could save him from his trouble. So, he went to the Buddha, prostrated, and took refuge in him. His life ended before he stood up and he entered a donkey's womb. Then the donkey broke her bit, went into a potter's house, and destroyed many pots. Getting angry, the potter hit the donkey and harmed her womb. Indra thus regained his life.
>
> The Buddha said, "Your sins have ended as you took refuge in the three treasures at the end of your life."
>
> Hearing this, Indra attained the first fruit [becoming a sage, a stream enterer].

No one equals the Buddha, World-Honored One, for relieving the suffering in the world. This is why Indra rushed to see him. While he was prostrating, his life ended and he entered a donkey's womb. With the merit of taking refuge in the Buddha, the donkey's bit was broken and she destroyed pots in the potter's house. The owner of the pots hit her, injuring her body and breaking open her womb. Thus, Indra returned to his body. Hearing the Buddha's words, he received the first fruit. This is due to the merit of taking refuge in the three treasures.

In this way, to be free from the suffering of the world and realize unsurpassable enlightenment is undoubtedly due to the merit of taking refuge in the three treasures. With the power of taking refuge in the three treasures, Indra not only became free from the three unwholesome realms, but he also returned to his body. He not only received the reward of being in the deva realm, he also became a sage, a stream enterer. Indeed, the ocean of merit of the three treasures is immeasurable and boundless.

When the World-Honored One was alive, humans and devas had great fortune. What can humans and devas do during the last set of five hundred years after the Tathagata's pari-nirvana [the period of decline of the dharma]? However, the Tathagata's images, relics, and so on are still present in the world. By taking refuge in them, you can still receive merit.

———————

According to the *Unprecedented Causation Sutra:*

The Buddha said, "I recall that innumerable kalpas ago, on Mount Shita in the great country of Vimana, a wild fox was chased by a hungry lion. While running, the fox fell into a well and could not get out. After three days, when he was ready to die, he settled his mind and said in a verse:

> Due to misfortune, I suffer today
> and am about to die inside this well.
> All things are impermanent.
> It would have been better if I had been eaten by the lion.
> I take refuge in the buddhas of the ten directions.
> Please know that my mind is selfless and pure.

When Indra heard the fox calling out the buddhas' names, he was shocked, thought of ancient buddhas, and said to himself, "I am on my own without a teacher, immersed in the five desires and drowning in them."

He flew down to the well together with eighty thousand devas to talk with the fox. Seeing the fox unsuccessfully trying to climb out from the bottom of the well, Indra inquired, "Does a sage not have skillful means? I see a fox, but you must be a bodhisattva with something valuable to teach. Would you please expound essential dharma for us devas?"

The fox looked up and replied, "You are the king of devas but do not behave well. The dharma teacher is down here and you are up there. You are asking for essential dharma without expressing respect. The dharma water is pure and capable of saving beings. Why do you regard yourself as higher?"

Hearing this, Indra was greatly ashamed, while the accompanying devas were surprised and said in laughter, "The king of devas came down with no effect."

Indra said to them, "Don't be surprised. I have been stubborn and without virtue. I need to ask about essential dharma." Then, he hung down his celestial robe, picked up the fox, and got him out. The devas prepared the food of nectar for the fox, who took it and regained vitality. Unexpectedly meeting good fortune in the midst of calamity, the fox rejoiced immeasurably and expounded essential dharma for Indra and devas.

This is called the story of Indra taking an animal as a teacher. In this way we clearly learn that the names of buddha, dharma, and sangha are rarely heard. Thus, Indra took the fox as his teacher.

———————

With the help of our wholesome deeds in past lives, we have a chance day and night to encounter and hear the names of the three treasures and the dharma left by the Tathagata. Such an opportunity does not recede in the course of time. This is the essential dharma.

Even the demon Papiyas takes refuge in the three treasures and escapes disaster. How much more so will others who arouse effort and accumulate merit by taking refuge in the three treasures!

In the practice of the way by children of the Buddha, people always pay respect to and invoke the three treasures in the ten directions, burn incense, sprinkle flowers, and engage in various practices. This is an ancient path and the authentic practice of buddha ancestors. Know that any practice that does not depend upon taking refuge in the three treasures is the way of outsiders, or that of demons.

The dharma of buddhas and ancestors always begins with taking refuge in the three treasures.

Copying of this draft written by Dogen, my late master, was completed on a day of the summer practice period in the seventh year of the Kencho Era [1255]. Dogen could not make revised and final manuscripts. He would have made some additions and deletions in the process of editing. Since this is no longer possible, I have preserved his draft. Ejo.

90

IDENTIFYING WITH CAUSE
AND EFFECT

EVERY TIME BAIZHANG, Zen Master Dazhi, gave a dharma talk, an old man would come to listen. He usually left after the talk, but one day he remained behind. Baizhang asked, "Who is there?"

The man said, "I am not actually a human being. I lived and taught on this mountain at the time of Kashyapa Buddha. One day a student asked me, 'Does a person who practices completely still fall into cause and effect?' I said to him, 'No, such a person does not fall into cause and effect.' Because I said this, I was made to be reborn as a wild fox for five hundred lifetimes. Reverend master, please say a turning word for me and free me from this wild fox body." Then he asked Baizhang, "Does a person who practices completely still fall into cause and effect?"

Baizhang said, "Do not ignore cause and effect."

Immediately the man had great realization. Bowing, he said, "I am now liberated from the body of a wild fox. I will stay in the mountain behind the monastery. Master, could you perform the usual services for a deceased monk for me?"

Baizhang asked the practice coordinator to inform the assembly that a funeral service for a monk would be held after the midday meal. The monks asked each other, "What's going on? Everyone is well; there is no one sick in the Nirvana Hall."

After their meal, Baizhang led the assembly to a large rock behind the monastery and showed them a dead fox at the rock's base. Following the customary procedure, they cremated the body.

That evening during his lecture in the dharma hall, Baizhang talked about what had happened that day.

Huangbo asked him, "A teacher of old gave a wrong answer and became a wild fox for five hundred lifetimes. What if he hadn't given a wrong answer?"

Baizhang said, "Come closer and I will tell you."

Huangbo went closer and slapped Baizhang's face.

Laughing, Baizhang clapped his hands and said, "I thought it was only barbarians who had red beards. But you too have a red beard!"

This story is in the *Tiansheng Extensive Record of the Lamp*. Still, students do not understand the principle of causation and mistakenly deny cause and effect. What a pity! Things are deteriorating and the ancestral way has degenerated. Those who say *does not fall into cause and effect* deny causation, thereby falling into the lower realms. Those who say *Do not ignore cause and effect* clearly identify with cause and effect. When people hear about identifying with cause and effect, they are freed from the lower realms. Do not try to escape this. Do not doubt this. Many contemporaries who consider themselves students of Zen deny causation. How do we know? They confuse *not ignore* with *not fall into*. Thus, we know that they deny cause and effect.

———

Venerable Kumaralabdha, the Nineteenth Ancestor in India, said:

We see both wholesome and unwholesome results in the three periods. Ordinary folks deny cause and effect when they see kind, fair-minded people suffer and die young, while violent and unjust people prosper into old age. Such ordinary folks say that neither crimes nor beneficial acts bring consequences. They do not realize that the consequences of our actions follow us for one hundred, one thousand, or ten thousand eons.

We clearly know from this that Kumaralabdha does not deny cause and effect. But students today do not understand this. They do not revere or follow the ancient way. Calling themselves teachers of humans and devas, they are robbers of humans and devas—enemies of practitioners. Followers of the ancestral teaching should not instruct later generations to deny causation, because that is a crooked view, not the dharma of buddha ancestors. People fall into this crooked view because their studies are shallow.

———

Nowadays, monks in China say, "Those of us who have received human bodies and encountered buddha dharma don't remember even one or two past lives, but the wild fox on Mount Baizhang remembered as many as five hundred past lives. He did not become a fox because of past actions. Stopped at the entrance door by a golden chain [trapped by a limited view of enlightenment], he was transmigrating only in the animal realm." Many who are regarded as great teachers talk like this, but such a view is not acceptable among buddha ancestors.

In the realms of humans, foxes, and others, some may be born with the capacity to see past lives. Such a capacity may be the result of unwholesome action and not necessarily a seed of enlightenment. The World-Honored One has cautioned us in detail about such a point. Not to understand it reflects a lack of study. Regrettably, to know as many as one thousand or ten thousand lifetimes is not necessarily to understand buddha dharma. There are those outside the way who remember eighty thousand eons, but do not understand buddha dharma. Compared with such capacities, this fox who could recall five hundred lifetimes is not significant.

The most serious mistake made by those who study Zen in China is to believe that a person who practices completely does not fall into cause and effect. What a pity! There have been an increasing number of those who deny cause and effect, even though they witness the Tathagata's true dharma being transmitted from ancestor to ancestor. So, those who study the way should urgently clarify this teaching. The point of Baizhang's words *Do not ignore cause and effect* is that we should not be ignorant of causation.

Thus, the significance of practicing cause and realizing effect is clear. This is the way of buddhas and ancestors. Those who themselves have not yet clarified buddha dharma should not superficially explain it to humans and devas.

———————

Ancestor Nagarjuna said, "If you deny cause and effect in the worldly realm, as some people outside the way do, you negate this present life as well as future lives. If you deny cause and effect in the realm of practice, you reject the three treasures, the four noble truths, and the four fruits of shravakas."

Clearly know that those who deny cause and effect are outside the way, whether they are living a worldly or a renunciate life. They say that the present life is unreal and that their transient body is in this world, but that their true nature abides in enlightenment. They believe that their true nature is mind, and that mind and body are separate.

There are also those who say that people return to the ocean of true nature when they die. Without having studied buddha dharma, they say that transmigration through birth and death ends and there are no future births after they return to the ocean of enlightenment. Those who hold this view of annihilation are outside the way. They are not buddha's disciples even if they look like monks. They are indeed outside the buddha dharma. Because they deny cause and effect, they deny present and future lives. They deny causation because they have not studied with true teachers. Those who have studied deeply with true teachers should abandon mistaken views which deny causation. Have faith in and pay respect to the compassionate teaching of Ancestor Nagarjuna.

———————

Yongjia, Great Master Zhenjiao, Priest Xuanjiao, was a senior student of Huineng of Mount Caoxi, the Sixth Ancestor. He had initially been a student of the Lotus School on Mount Tiantai, and a dharma brother of Zuoxi Xianlang. While he was reading the *Maha Pari-nirvana Sutra,* a golden light filled the room and he awakened beyond birth and death. He went to Mount Caoxi to present his realization to Huineng, who gave him his seal of approval.

Yongjia later composed a verse called "The Song of Realizing the Way," in which he wrote: "Carefree views of emptiness ignore cause and effect, and invite endless calamity."

It is true that ignoring causation invites disaster. Past sages clarified cause and effect, but students have become confused in recent times. Those of you who have a pure aspiration for enlightenment and want to study buddha dharma for the sake of buddha dharma should clarify causation as past sages did. Those who reject this teaching are outside the way.

Hongzhi, Old Buddha, commented in a verse on the wild fox:

> A foot of water has expanded to a wave ten feet tall.
> Helplessly wandering through five hundred births,
> the fox who struggles with not falling or not ignoring
> remains entangled in twining vines.
> Ha! Ha! Do you get it?
> If you are not stuck,
> you will let me continue my "goo goo wa wa."
> Shrine songs and dance emerge spontaneously
> during clapping and cheering.

By the lines *The fox who struggles with not falling or not ignoring remains entangled in twining vines,* Hongzhi means that not falling is itself not ignoring.

This story of the fox is not complete. It says that the old man did become free from a wild fox's body, but it does not say whether he was then born in the world of humans, devas, or elsewhere. This makes people wonder. If the old man is reborn in a wholesome realm, free from a wild fox's body, it must be the realm of either devas or humans. Otherwise, he would be reborn in one of the four unwholesome realms. There is no shortage of locations for rebirth. But those outside the buddha way mistakenly believe that sentient beings return to the ocean of permanence or to the great self after death.

Keqin, Zen Master Yuanwu of Mount Jia, commented in verse on this ancient case:

> A fish swims, making the water murky.
> A bird flies, shedding its feathers.
> The ultimate mirror is difficult to escape.
> The great void is boundless.
> Once you go, you go endlessly.
> By virtue of causation, the one who practices completely
> lives five hundred lifetimes.
> Thunder cracks the mountains and storms shake the ocean.
> The color of purified gold does not change.

This poem still has a view of a permanent self and a sense of denying cause and effect.

Zonggao, Zen Master Dahui, of Mount Jing, Hang Region, commented:

> Not falling and not ignoring
> are like a pebble and a lump of clay.
> When they show up together on a footpath,
> the silver mountain opens up.
> Seeing it, the silly Priest Budai of Ming
> claps his hands and bursts out laughing.

People in China nowadays regard Zonggao as an established ancestor. However, his view does not equal even the expedient teachings in the buddha dharma. It resembles a view of spontaneous enlightenment by people outside the way.

More than thirty masters have written poems or commentaries on this story. Not one of them understands the saying *a person of complete practice does not fall into cause and effect* as a denial of causation. What a pity!

Such people waste their lives by not clarifying cause and effect. In studying buddha dharma you should first understand causation. By denying causation, you generate outrageously crooked views and cut off wholesome roots.

After all, causation is self-evident; there are no exceptions. Those who act in an unwholesome way decline, and those who act in a wholesome way thrive. There is not a hairbreadth of discrepancy. If cause and effect had been ignored or denied, buddhas would not have appeared and Bodhidharma would not have come from India; sentient beings would not have seen Buddha or heard the dharma. The principle of cause and effect is not clarified by Confucius or Laozi. Buddhas and ancestors alone have transmitted it. Students in these decadent times seldom meet a genuine teacher or hear the true dharma. That is why they do not clarify cause and effect.

If you deny causation, endless harm results. Even if you do nothing more than deny cause and effect, this is a disastrous, poisonous view. Immediately clarify all causes and all effects if you want to make the aspiration for enlightenment your priority, and so respond to the boundless gift of buddha ancestors.

During the summer practice period in the seventh year of the Kencho Era [1255], I copied Dogen's draft. There may be a second or final version edited by him, but I have used his draft for the time being. Ejo.

91

MONK OF THE FOURTH-STAGE
MEDITATION

NAGARJUNA, THE FOURTEENTH Ancestor, said [in the *Treatise on Realization of Great Wisdom*]:

There was a monk among the Buddha's disciples who experienced the fourth stage of meditation, grew arrogant, and said that he had attained the fourth fruit.

Prior to that, upon experiencing the first stage of meditation, he said he had attained the fruit of entering the stream. Upon experiencing the second stage, he said he had attained the fruit of returning once. Upon experiencing the third stage, he said he had attained the fruit of no return. And, upon experiencing the fourth stage, he said he had attained the fruit of being an arhat. Believing this, he became proud and stopped practicing further.

When his life was about to end, the monk saw an image of the realm intermediate to the next life, formed a mistaken view, and said, "There is no such thing as nirvana [with no more rebirth]. The Buddha has deceived me." Because of this mistaken view, the image of the intermediary realm disappeared and an image of the realm intermediate to Avichi Hell appeared. When he died, he was reborn in Avichi Hell.

His fellow monks asked the Buddha, "Where was that monk of solitary practice born after his life ended?"

The Buddha said, "He was born in Avichi Hell."

The monks were surprised: "How could this happen to someone who practiced meditation and kept the precepts?"

The Buddha answered, "This happened because he grew arrogant. Upon experiencing the fourth stage of meditation, he said he had attained the fourth fruit. At the end of his life, he saw an image of the intermediary realm, formed a mistaken view, and thought, 'There is no nirvana. I am an arhat, but I am about to move on to another life. The Buddha has given a false teaching.' Then, he saw an image of the realm intermediate to Avichi Hell, and he fell into Avichi Hell."

Then the Buddha spoke in verse:

Learning extensively, keeping the precepts,
and practicing meditation are not yet being free of delusion.
They all have merit,
but it is hard to have trust in them.
Falling into hell is due to slandering the Buddha
and has nothing to do with the fourth stage of meditation.

This monk is called the Monk of the Fourth-Stage Meditation or the Monk of No-Learning. One is cautioned not to confuse the experience of the fourth stage of meditation with attaining the fourth fruit, and not to slander the Buddha. All humans and devas in the great assembly know this. From the time when the Buddha was alive to this day, in western and eastern lands, one is cautioned not to be attached to what is not correct as correct. This is ridiculed as mistaking the fourth stage of meditation for the fourth fruit.

————————

Let me examine the case of this monk who made three mistakes:

First, because he was a person of no learning who could not distinguish the fourth stage of zazen from the fourth fruit, he left his teacher groundlessly and practiced all by himself. As he had the fortune of living at the time when the Tathagata was in the world, if he had visited the Buddha constantly, seen the Buddha, and listened to the dharma, he would not have made this mistake. However, as he lived in a solitary place, did not visit the Buddha's place, and did not hear and listen to the Buddha, he made such a mistake. Even if he had not visited the Buddha, he should have visited various great arhats and asked for instructions. To live in a solitary place groundlessly was a mistake caused by his arrogance.

Second, to regard the first stage of meditation as the first fruit, the second stage as the second fruit, the third stage as the third fruit, and the fourth stage as the fourth fruit is a mistake. The aspects of the first, second, third, and fourth stages of meditation and the aspects of the first, second, third, and fourth fruits do not resemble each other and cannot be compared. His mistake is based on his ignorance due to his having no learning and no teacher.

[Zhanran said:]

Among the disciples of Upagupta, there was a monk who had left the household with aspiration, experienced the fourth stage of meditation, and thought he had attained the fourth fruit. Using skillful means, Upagupta sent the monk to another land. On the monk's way, Upagupta magically made robbers and five hundred traders appear. The robbers attacked and slaughtered the traders. The monk was frightened by the scene and said to himself, "I am not an arhat. I have merely experienced the third fruit."

After the monk left the traders, he saw one of their daughters. She said to him, "Please, reverend, take me with you."

The monk said, "The Buddha wouldn't allow me to travel with a woman."

The woman said, "I will follow you and keep you in sight."

The monk pitied her and let her follow him. Upagupta then made a wide river appear. The woman said, "Reverend, would you please cross the river with me?"

So the monk went into the river downstream and the woman went in upstream. She fell into the water and cried, "Reverend, please help me."

The monk took her hand and pulled her out. As he thought of her delicate body, his carnal desire was aroused. As a result, he realized that he hadn't attained the third fruit of no return. He was extremely attracted to the woman, led her to a secluded place, and was about to make love to her when the monk realized that it was his own master [creating an illusion]. Fully ashamed, he stood up quickly and made many bows.

Upagupta said to him, "You thought you were an arhat. How come you are doing such an awful thing?"

Upagupta took the monk to the assembly, made him repent, expounded essential dharma, and caused him to be an arhat.

Although this monk had a self-generated mistaken view, he was frightened by the scene of slaughter and realized that he was not an arhat. But he thought he had experienced the third fruit. Later he thought of the delicate body of the woman, aroused carnal desire, and realized that he had not experienced the fruit of no return. He did not arouse the thought of slandering the Buddha, did not intend to slander the dharma, and did not have the thought of going against the sacred teaching. He was not the same as the Monk of the Fourth-Stage Meditation. Rather, because of the power of having studied the sacred teaching, he realized that he was not an arhat and had not experienced the fruit of no return.

Nowadays, because those of no learning do not know what arhats and buddhas are, they do not realize that they are not arhats or buddhas; they groundlessly think and say that they are buddhas. This is a great mistake. It is a deep offense. Those who study the way should first learn what buddhas are.

An ancient teacher [Zhanran] said, "Those of you who study the sacred teaching should know what comes next. Even if you try to skip stages, you would come to know the truth."

How true this ancient teacher's words are! Even if you have a mistaken view about the next birth, you will not deceive yourself or be deceived by others if you study buddha dharma even a little bit.

[Zhanran said:]

I have heard: Someone thought that he had become a buddha. He waited for dawn but it did not arrive. He thought this was due to a demon's obstruction. Finally, the day broke, but he was not asked by Brahma to expound dharma. As a result, he realized that he had not become a buddha, but he did think he was an arhat. Later, insulted by another, he became angry and realized that he was not an arhat. He thought he had merely attained the third fruit. But, when seeing a woman, he aroused his carnal desire and realized that he was not a sage. He realized all of this because he understood various aspects of the teaching.

Now, those who know buddha dharma realize their faults in this way and quickly cast off their mistakes. Those who don't know it remain ignorant for the rest of their lives. To receive rebirth after this birth is also like this.

This disciple of Upagupta experienced the fourth stage of meditation and thought it was the fourth fruit, but he had the wisdom to realize that he was not an arhat. If the Monk of the Fourth-Stage Meditation had seen an image of the intermediary realm when he was about to die and realized that he was not an arhat, he would not have slandered the Buddha. Further, since he had experienced the fourth stage of meditation for a long time, how did he not realize that it was not the fourth fruit? If he had realized that it was not the fourth fruit, how would he not have changed his view? Instead, he remained in his mistaken thought and was drowned in his crooked view.

The third mistake made by the Monk of the Fourth-Stage Meditation took place at the end of his life. Because his offense was so deep, he fell into Avichi Hell. Even if he had thought that the fourth stage of meditation was the fourth fruit, if he had seen an image of the intermediary realm of the fourth stage at the end of his life, he would have repented for his mistake and realized that it was not the fourth fruit. How could he have thought that the Buddha had deceived him and formed a notion that nirvana did not actually exist? This is the fault of not learning and the fault of slandering the Buddha. In effect, an image of the realm intermediate to Avichi Hell appeared, and he fell into Avichi Hell after his death.

How can even a sage of the fourth fruit be equal to the Tathagata? Shariputra was a sage of the fourth fruit for a long time. If you assemble all the wisdom that is found in the billion worlds, except for that of the

Tathagata, make it one portion, and compare it with one-sixteenth of Shariputra's wisdom, the former does not come close to the latter. However, when Shariputra heard the Tathagata expound the dharma that had never been spoken, he did not think that the Tathagata's teaching was different from past and future buddhas' teachings, and that the Tathagata was deceiving him. Even the demon king praised the Tathagata's teaching by saying that such a teaching did not exist in the demon world. The Tathagata awakened the old man Shrivaddhi, but Shariputra did not awaken Shrivaddhi.

The enormous difference between the fourth fruit and the buddha fruit is like this. Even if Shariputra and other disciples like him [shravakas who have attained the four fruits] were to fill the world of the ten directions, none of them could measure the Buddha's wisdom.

Confucius and Laozi did not have such wisdom. How should those who study buddha dharma measure the teachings of Confucius and Laozi? Those who study Confucius and Laozi have never been able to measure buddha dharma. Nowadays, those in Great Song China advocate the theory of the accord of Confucius and Laozi with buddha dharma. It is an outrageously wrong view. I will discuss this in a while.

The Monk of the Fourth-Stage Meditation had a mistaken belief and thought that the Tathagata had deceived him. Thus, he was against the buddha way for a long time. It is extreme stupidity, equal to that of the six teachers outside the way [around the Buddha's time].

An ancient teacher [Zhanran] said, "Even when the Great Teacher was alive, there were those who had self-generated mistaken views. Then, after his pari-nirvana, would it ever be possible to accomplish meditation without a teacher?"

The Great Teacher refers to the Buddha, the World-Honored One. Indeed, when he was alive, even those who had left the household and received the precepts but did not listen to his teachings could not escape having self-generated views. Then, in the last five hundred years of the three periods [of five hundred years each] after the pari-nirvana of the

Tathagata, in a remote and lowly land, aren't there mistakes? Those who have entered the fourth stage of meditation are like this. Even more so, those who sink vainly in their greed for name and love of benefit, and those who enjoy official positions and worldly paths without having entered the fourth stage of meditation, are not worth mentioning.

———————

Nowadays in Great Song China there are many such people who are foolish and have learned little. They insist that buddha dharma and the ways of Confucius and Laozi accord with one another and are not different paths.

During the Jiatai Era [1201–1205] of Great Song China, a monk called Zhengshou compiled the [Jiatai] Record of the Universal Lamp in thirty fascicles. He said [in the preface]:

> I, a subject of His Majesty, have learned Gushan Zhiyuan's words: "My path is like a tripod worship bowl. The Three Teachings are like three legs of the bowl. If one leg is missing, the bowl tips over." I came to admire his personality and follow his theory. What is essential in Confucius' teaching is sincerity. What is essential in Laozi's teaching is empty mind. What is essential in Shakyamuni Buddha's teaching is seeing through human nature. Sincerity, empty mind, and seeing through human nature have the same essence with different names. If you thoroughly experience their original source, there is nothing that does not fit the buddha way.

Many others beside Zhiyuan and Zhengshou have self-generated mistaken views. Their mistakes are deeper than those who experience the fourth stage of meditation and regard it as the fourth fruit. It is slandering the buddha, slandering the dharma, and slandering the sangha. It is denying emancipation, denying the past, present, and future, and denying cause and effect; there is no doubt that his theory brings forth huge calamity. Such people are equal to those who don't believe in the three treasures, the four noble truths, and the four fruits of shramanas.

What is essential in buddha dharma is not seeing through human nature. Who, among the Seven Original Buddhas and the twenty-eight Indian ancestors, regards buddha dharma merely as seeing through human nature? There are the words "seeing through human nature" in the *Sixth Ancestor's Platform Sutra*. It is an apocryphal text and not a text by someone who was entrusted with the dharma treasury. "Seeing through human nature" are not words by Huineng. This is not a text to be depended upon by descendants of buddha ancestors. Because Zhengshou and Zhiyuan did not know about even one part of buddha dharma, they believed in the wrong view of one bowl with three legs.

A teacher of old [Zhanran] said:

Laozi and Zhuangzi did not know what to advocate and what to deny in the Hinayana teaching. Even further, they did not know what to advocate and what to deny in the Mahayana teaching. Thus, their teachings are not the same as that of buddha dharma. Foolish worldly people are confused about names and forms. Those who have loose ideas about Zen are ignorant of the true principle. They think that the virtue of the way [taught by Laozi] and the wandering around [taught by Zhuangzi] are the same as the teaching of emancipation in buddha dharma. How would it be possible?

In this way, since ancient times those who are confused by names and forms, and those who are ignorant of the true principle, have equated buddha dharma with the teachings of Laozi and Zhuangzi. On the other hand, those practicing buddha dharma even a little have never valued Laozi and Zhuangzi.

The *Sutra of Pure Dharma Conduct* says, "Moonlight Bodhisattva is called Yanhui [a student of Confucius], Pure Light Bodhisattva is called Confucius, and Kashyapa Bodhisattva is called Laozi."

From ancient times, some people have quoted this sutra and said that because Confucius and Laozi are bodhisattvas, their teachings should be subtly equal to that of the Buddha. Others have said that because they are messengers of the Buddha, their words should, in fact, be those of the Buddha. Such statements are all wrong.

An ancient teacher [Zhanran] said, "According to various lists, all of the sutras say that this sutra [*Sutra of Pure Dharma Conduct*] is suspected as an apocryphal text."

If we follow this explanation, it is even clearer that buddha dharma is different from the teachings of Confucius and Laozi. [This apocryphal sutra says that] Confucius and Laozi are regarded as bodhisattvas. However, bodhisattvas' achievements are not the same as the buddha fruit.

The practice of softening the light [of wisdom, becoming close to sentient beings] and emerging as regional sages is only done by buddhas and bodhisattvas of the past, present, and future. This cannot be done by ordinary people in the dusty world. How can ordinary people who participate in worldly activities have the power to transform themselves into regional sages?

Confucius and Laozi did not talk about [buddhas and bodhisattvas] transforming into regional sages. Furthermore, they did not know about earlier causes [from past lives] and their effects in this lifetime. They merely made loyalty to the lord and governing the family essentials of their teachings. They never talk about the future life. They must be part of the group of people who believe in views of annihilation. The one [Zhanran] who excluded Zhuangzi and Laozi and said that they did not know the Hinayana, and even further the Mahayana, is a clear master of the ancient time.

Those who advocate the accord of the Three Teachings are Zhiyuan, Zhengshou, and ignorant ordinary people of the later times of decline. With what brilliance do they put down an earlier master of ancient times and groundlessly say that buddha dharma is equal to the teachings of Confucius and Laozi? Their view is short of covering the buddha dharma. They should wear a traveling basket on their shoulders and look for masters of clear understanding. Zhiyuan and Zhengshou knew neither Hinayana nor Mahayana teachings. It is more ignorant than experiencing the fourth stage of meditation and regarding it as the fourth fruit. How deplorable that there are so many little demons when the wind of decline blows!

An ancient teacher [Zhanran] said, "The words of Confucius and Lord Zhou, as well as the teachings of the Three Kings and the Five Emperors [of China], expound governing the family with filial piety, governing the nation with loyalty, and serving the country, benefiting the subjects. This is merely a matter of one lifetime and does not cover past and future lifetimes. It is not the same as buddha dharma, which benefits lifetimes of the past, present, and future. Do not be mistaken on this point."

Indeed, this statement by the ancient teacher touches upon the ultimate principle of buddha dharma and clarifies the principles of worldly teachings. The teachings by the Three Kings and the Five Emperors do not come close to that of a wheel-turning king, and should not be compared with words by Brahma and Indra. Their realms and the effects of their past actions are far inferior to those of Brahma and Indra. Therefore, wheel-turning kings, Brahma, and Indra do not come close to a monk who has left the household and received the precepts. How can they be equal to the Tathagata?

Books by Confucius and Lord Zhou cannot get close to the *Eighteen Large Brahmanist Texts* of India, and, in particular, cannot be compared with the Four Vedic Scriptures among them. However, Brahmanism in India is not the same as the Buddha's teaching; it does not even equal the Hinayana, which is the teaching for shravakas. What a pity that in the remote, small country of China there is a mistaken view called the accord of the Three Teachings!

———————

Bodhisattva Nagarjuna, the Fourteenth Ancestor, said, "Great arhats and pratyeka-buddhas understand eighty thousand great eons. Bodhisattvas and buddhas understand uncountable eons."

Confucius, Laozi, and others do not yet understand the past and future of even one generation. How do they have the power to understand past lives, not to speak of one eon, or even further, one hundred and one thousand eons? Then, how do they understand eighty thousand eons or uncountable eons? Those who compare buddhas and bodhisattvas, who are as familiar with such past lives as seeing their own palms, with Confucius, Laozi, and others are not even worth calling ignorant. Cover your ears and don't listen to the theory of the accord of the Three Teachings. It's the most crooked theory among all wrong views.

———————

Zhuangzi said, "Noble and lowly, pain and pleasure, right and wrong, gain and loss, are all natural."

This view is similar to that of spontaneous origin, held by those outside the way in India. Noble and lowly, pain and pleasure, right and wrong, gain and loss, are all effects of wholesome and unwholesome actions. People who believe in spontaneous origin do not understand individual karma and collective karma. As they do not clarify past and future lives, they are ignorant of the present life. How can their views be equal to buddha dharma?

Someone said:

Because buddha tathagatas broadly realize the world of phenomena, the realm of a minute particle is all that is realized by buddhas. Thus, both effects [of actions]—the subject and its environs—are what is realized by tathagatas. In this way, mountains, rivers, the great earth, the sun, the moon, and the stars, as well as the three poisons and four confusions are all that is realized by tathagatas. To see mountains and rivers is to see tathagatas. The three poisons and four confusions cannot escape being buddha dharma. Seeing a minute particle is the same as seeing the world of phenomena. Even a casual, temporary experience is unsurpassable, complete enlightenment. This is called great emancipation, directly pointing to the ancestral way transmitted from person to person.

There are numberless people, both officials and commoners, who speak in this way in Great Song China. However, it is not clear whose descendants they are. Altogether, they don't know the way of buddha ancestors. Even if mountains, rivers, and the great earth are what is realized by buddhas, it is not the view of mountains, rivers, and the great earth of ordinary people. Those who speak in this way have not studied and learned what is realized by buddhas.

They say that seeing a minute particle is the same as seeing the world of phenomena. It is like saying that the subjects of a king are equal to the king. Why, then, don't they say that seeing the world of phenomena is equal to seeing a minute particle? If you would regard the view of these people as the great way of buddha ancestors, buddhas and ancestors would not have emerged in this world, and sentient beings would not be able to attain the way. Even if they might have experienced birth as beyond birth, their view would not be correct.

Tripitaka Master Paramartha said, "There are two fortunate things for China: there are no demons and there are no people outside the way [Brahmanists]."

This is a statement by someone who came from India, a country filled with people outside the way. Although there are no people outside the way who can perform the arts of miracles in China, it's not that there are no people who hold the views of those outside the way. Demons are not seen there, but there are some schools of those outside the way. Because China is a small country in a remote land, some people study buddha dharma, but they are not realized. It is not like the central country of India.

An ancient teacher [Zhanran] said, "There are many who have returned to laity. Trying to avoid service to the Emperor, they join those outside the way. Stealing the principles of buddha dharma, with a little understanding of Confucius and Zhuangzi, they create a mixture of these teachings. They confuse beginning students who do not know the difference between right and wrong. Their Vedic views [outside of buddha dharma] are created in this way."

Know that those who confuse and mix up beginning students, by not knowing which is right and which is wrong between buddha dharma and the teachings of Zhuangzi and Laozi, are Zhiyuan and Zhengshou, the ones I have discussed. Not only are they extremely foolish, but they also have not studied ancient teachings. This is evident and clear.

Nowadays, among monks in the Song Dynasty, there are none who know that the teachings of Confucius and Laozi do not come close to buddha dharma. Although there are countless people who call themselves descendants of buddha ancestors filling the mountains and fields of the nine regions of China, not a single person or half a person clearly understands that buddha dharma is distinct from the teachings of Confucius and Laozi. Rujing, my late master Old Buddha Tiantong, alone clearly understood that buddha dharma and the teachings of Confucius and Laozi are not one. He explained this day and night.

Teachers of sutras and treatises are called lecturers, but none of them understand that buddha dharma far exceeds the realms of Confucius and Laozi. A number of lecturers in these one hundred years have studied Zen and tried to steal its essential teaching, but they are fundamentally mistaken.

The writings of Confucius speak of knowledge by birth, whereas teachings by the Buddha don't. In buddha dharma, there are statements about relics, whereas Confucius and Laozi didn't know whether relics existed or not. Even if you tried to mix up these teachings and speak extensively, regarding them as one, it would be impossible to fully explain it.

The *Treatises* by Confucius says, "To have knowledge by birth is supreme. To have knowledge by learning is next. To have knowledge by struggling follows that. People regard struggling without learning as the worst."

If there is knowledge by birth, this may be seen as having no cause. In buddha dharma, there is no statement about having no cause.

The Monk of the Fourth-Stage Meditation committed the crime of slandering the Buddha at the end of his life. To see buddha dharma as the same as the teachings of Confucius and Laozi is a heavier crime than slandering the Buddha throughout one's lifetime. You, students, should quickly throw away such a mistaken view. In the end, those who maintain this view without giving it up will fall into an unwholesome realm.

You, students, should clearly know that Confucius and Laozi did not know the teaching of the past, present, and future. They did not know the principle of cause and effect. They did not know about the peaceful establishment of One Continent. Then, how can they know about the peaceful establishment of the Four Continents? They did not know about the six heavens of the desire realm; then how could they know about the three realms and the nine grounds? They do not know about the thousand worlds; how can they see and know about the million worlds or the billion worlds?

A subject of a king cannot be compared with the Tathagata, who is the king of the billion worlds. The Tathagata is the one who is honored and served day and night by Brahma, Indra, wheel-turning kings, and others, and is requested by them to expound dharma. Confucius and Laozi did not have such virtue; they were ordinary people who floated around [in birth and death] and did not know the path of leaving the world and becoming emancipated. Then, how could they thoroughly experience the reality of all things? If they hadn't thoroughly experienced it, how could they be equal to the World-Honored One? As Confucius and Laozi lacked the inner virtue and outer facility, they did not come close to the World-Honored One. How could people express the wrong view of the accord of the Three Teachings?

Confucius and Laozi did not understand the world's boundary and beyond boundary. They did not know and see what is broad and what is vast, and did not see an extremely minute form and know the length of a split second. On the other hand, the World-Honored One clearly saw an extremely minute form and knew the length of a split second. Thus, how can we regard him as equal to Confucius and Laozi? Confucius, Laozi, Zhuangzi, and Huizi are mere ordinary people. They cannot even come close to stream enterers of the Lesser Vehicles. How, then, can they come close to those who have attained the second or the third fruit, or to arhats who have attained the fourth fruit?

Nevertheless, some students are ignorant enough to regard them as equal to buddhas. It is delusion on top of delusion. Not only do Confucius and Laozi not know the past, present, and future, as well as multiple eons, they also do not know a single thought and a single mind. They cannot be compared with the sun, the moon, or the sky. They cannot come close to the Four Great Deva Kings or all devas. To compare them with the World-Honored One is to confuse those in and beyond the worldly realm.

The *Biographies of Courtiers* says:

Xi, who became a courtier of Lord Zhou, was good at astronomy. Once, he saw an extraordinary sign in heaven. He went toward the east, looked, and found Laozi, whom he asked to write a book of over five thousand words. He himself also wrote a book of nine chapters and titled it *Barrier Station Officer*. It was written after the style of Laozi's *Teachings for Barbarians*.

Later, Laozi went west of the border and Xi wanted to accompany him. Laozi said, "If you really want to go with me, bring seven decapitated heads including those of your parents. Then you may go with me."

Without hesitation Xi followed his instruction. Later, the seven decapitated heads turned into the heads of boars.

Regarding this, an ancient teacher [Zhanran] said:

According to the custom of the common world, those who are dedicated to their parents honor even wooden statues of their parents. On the other hand, it is said that Laozi instructed a student and had him kill his parents. The basis of the Tathagata's teaching is compassion; how can it be related to an upside-down teaching like Laozi's?

In the past there were groups of crooked people who regarded Laozi as equal to the Tathagata. Nowadays, there are foolish people who regard both Confucius and Laozi as equal to the World-Honored One. What a pity! Confucius and Laozi cannot come close to even wheel-turning kings who teach the world with ten types of wholesome actions. How can the Three Emperors and the Five Kings, decorated with seven treasures and guarded by one thousand soldiers, come close to the king of gold, silver, copper, and iron wheels, who transforms the worlds of the four directions and the billion worlds? Confucius and Laozi cannot even come close to them. For buddhas and ancestors of the past, present, and future, the basis of their teaching is dedication to parents, dharma teachers, and the three treasures, and making offerings to those who are sick and so forth. They have never made the murder of their parents the basis of teaching.

In this way, the teaching of Laozi and buddha dharma are not one. It is inevitable for those who murder their parents to receive the effects of their actions and fall into hell in their next lifetime. Even if Laozi talked groundlessly about the void, those who harm their parents cannot help receiving these effects in their next lifetime.

––––––––––

According to the [*Jingde*] *Transmission of the Lamp,* Huike, the Second Ancestor, would often lament: "The teachings of Confucius and Laozi are limited to manners and guidelines. The texts of *Zhuangzi* and the *Ijing* have not yet thoroughly explained the wondrous principle. These days I hear that Great Master Bodhidharma is staying at the Shaolin Monastery. As this man of deep understanding lives nearby, I would like to experience his profound teaching."

You in the present day should clearly know that the authentic transmission of buddha dharma in China is solely due to the power of Huike's practice. Even if Bodhidharma came to China, buddha dharma would not have been transmitted without having Huike as the Second Ancestor. If Huike had not transmitted buddha dharma, there would have been no buddha dharma in China. Thus, Huike should not be regarded as similar to others.

––––––––––

The [*Jingde*] *Transmission of the Lamp* says, "Monk Shenguang [Huike] was a man of extensive study. He lived near the Yi and Luo rivers, read a great number of books, and discussed the profound principle."

The extensive reading of Huike in the past and the extensive study of people in later times are different by far. Even after attaining dharma and receiving the robe, Huike did not say that his earlier understanding, *the teachings of Confucius and Laozi are limited to manners and guidelines,* had been a mistake. Know that Huike thoroughly understood that the teachings of Confucius and Laozi are not the same as buddha dharma. How should his remote descendants nowadays contradict their dharma grandfather and insist on the accord among Confucius and Laozi's teachings with buddha dharma? Know that this is a wrong view. If you are a remote descendant of Huike, how can you accept theories by Zhengshou and others? As you are a descendant of Huike, do not speak of an accord of the Three Teachings.

———————

[According to Zhanran:]

When the Tathagata was alive in this world, there was a man outside the way called Debate Power [Vivadabala]. Since he thought of himself as having an unmatchable capacity in debate, he called himself Debate Power. Having received a donation from five hundred members of the Vaishali Clan, he selected five hundred difficult questions with which to challenge the World-Honored One. He went to see the World-Honored One and asked, "Is the unsurpassable way one or many?"

The World-Honored One said, "The unsurpassable way is one."

Debate Power said, "Each of our teachers speaks of the unsurpassable way. Those outside the way all regard their own teachings as correct and put down others'. In this manner they speak of right and wrong. Thus, there are many ways."

By that time the World-Honored One had taught Migasisa and helped him to realize the fruit of no more learning. Migasisa was standing near the Buddha. Buddha asked Debate Power, "Among the many ways, who is the most advanced?"

Debate Power said, "Migasisa is."

The Buddha said, "If Migasisa is the most advanced, how come he gave up his own way, became my disciple, and entered into my way?"

Debate Power understood, was fully ashamed, made bows, took refuge, and entered the way.

Then, the Buddha expounded the principle with a verse:

> All are attached to their own teachings,
> calling theirs unsurpassable,
> claiming they are right and others are wrong.
> But none of their teachings are unsurpassable.
> They go into debate
> trying to clarify the meaning of nirvana,
> speaking of right and wrong,
> while agonizing in competition.

The winners fall into the pit of pride
and the losers fall into the hell of agony.
So, wise ones are not stuck
to either side.
Debate Power, you should know
the teaching for my disciples
is neither false nor true;
which do you seek?
If you want to destroy my discourse
there is no way to do it,
and no wisdom can clarify it;
you will end up destroying yourself.

The golden words of the World-Honored One are like this. Ignorant sentient beings in China should not go against the Buddha's teaching and say that there are ways that are equal to buddha dharma. That would be slandering the Buddha and slandering the dharma. India's Migasisa, Vivadabala (Debate Power), or Brahman Dirghanakha, or Brahman Shrenika were people of extensive studies. There has not been anyone like that in China. Confucius and Laozi cannot be compared with them.

These Brahmans all gave up their own paths and took refuge in the buddha way. Even those who listen to the comparison between buddha dharma and common people like Confucius and Laozi will be at fault. Furthermore, even arhats and pratyeka-buddhas will be bodhisattvas in the end, and none of them will remain in the Lesser Vehicles. How can you regard Confucius and Laozi, who have not yet entered the buddha way, as equal to buddhas? This is a greatly crooked view.

The fact that the Tathagata, the World-Honored One, is far beyond all beings, has been known and honored by buddha tathagatas, great bodhisattvas, Brahma, and Indra. This has been known by the twenty-eight ancestors in India and the six early ancestors in China. All those who have the ability to study know this. Those who are born in this later time should not accept the insane theory of the accord of the Three Teachings advocated by ignorant people of the Song Dynasty, which is the result of a lack of study.

Copied from a draft [by Dogen] during the practice period of the seventh year of the Kencho Era [1255]. Ejo.

92

Only a Buddha and a Buddha

Buddha dharma cannot be known by a person. For this reason, since olden times no ordinary person has realized buddha dharma; no practitioner of the Lesser Vehicles has mastered buddha dharma. Because it is realized by buddhas alone, it is said [in the *Lotus Sutra*], "Only a buddha and a buddha can thoroughly master it."

When you realize buddha dharma, you do not think, "This is realization just as I expected." Even if you think so, realization inevitably differs from your expectation. Realization is not like your conception of it. Accordingly, realization cannot take place as previously conceived. When you realize buddha dharma, you do not consider how realization came about. Reflect on this: what you think one way or another before realization is not a help for realization.

Although realization is not like any of the thoughts preceding it, this is not because such thoughts were actually bad and could not be realization. Past thoughts in themselves were already realization. But since you were seeking elsewhere, you thought and said that thoughts cannot be realization.

However, it is worth noticing that what you think one way or another is not a help for realization. For this reason, you become cautious not to be small-minded. Indeed, if realization came forth by the power of your prior thoughts, it would not be trustworthy.

Realization does not depend on thoughts, but comes forth far beyond them; realization is helped only by the power of realization itself. Know that then there is no delusion, and there is no realization.

When you have unsurpassed wisdom, you are called a buddha. When a buddha has unsurpassed wisdom, it is called unsurpassed wisdom. Not to know what it is like on this path is foolish. What is it like being undivided? To be undivided does not mean that you try forcefully to exclude intention or discrimination, or that you establish a state beyond intention. Being undivided cannot be intended or discriminated at all.

Being undivided is like meeting a person and not considering what the person looks like. Also, it is like not wishing for more color or brightness when viewing flowers or the moon.

Spring has the feeling of spring, and autumn has the look of autumn; there is no escaping it. So when you want spring or autumn to be different from what it is, notice that it can only be as it is. Or, when you want to keep spring or autumn as it is, reflect that it has no unchanging nature.

That which is accumulated is without self, and no mental activity has self. The reason is that not one of the four great elements or the five skandhas can be understood as self or identified as self. Therefore, the form of the flowers or the moon in your mind should not be understood as being self, even though you may think it is self. Still, when you clarify that there is nothing to be disliked or longed for, then the original face is revealed by your practice of the way.

A teacher of old said:

Although the entire universe is nothing but the dharma body of the self, you should not be hindered by the dharma body. If you are hindered by the dharma body, you will not be able to turn freely, no matter how hard you may try. But there should be a way to be free from hindrance. What, then, is the way for all people to be free from hindrance? If you cannot say clearly how to free all people, you will soon lose even the life of the dharma body and sink in the ocean of suffering for a long time.

If you are asked in this way, how can you answer so as to keep the dharma body alive and avoid sinking in the ocean of suffering?

In this case, say, "The entire universe is the dharma body of the self." If you say that the entire universe is the dharma body of the self, still, words cannot express it. When words cannot express it, would you understand that there is nothing to be said? Without words, ancient buddhas said something.

There is birth in death, and there is death in birth. Death is entirely death, and birth is entirely birth. This is so not because you make it so, but because dharma is like this. This being so, when a buddha turns the dharma wheel, there is insight such as this and expression such as this. Know that it is also like this when a buddha manifests a [buddha] body and awakens sentient beings. This is called "awareness beyond birth."

"A buddha manifests a body and awakens sentient beings" means that awakening sentient beings is itself the manifestation of the buddha body. In the midst of awakening sentient beings, do not pursue manifestation. Seeing manifestation, do not doubt awakening.

Understand that in the midst of awakening sentient beings, the buddha dharma is totally experienced. Explain it and actualize it this way. Know that it is the same with manifestation and having the buddha body.

This is so because a buddha manifests a buddha body and awakens sentient beings. This principle is clarified from the morning of attaining the way until the evening of pari-nirvana; it is expounded freely, without words getting in the way.

An ancient buddha said:

> The entire earth is the true human body.
> The entire earth is the gate of liberation.
> The entire earth is the single eye of Vairochana.
> The entire earth is the dharma body of the self.

The true human body means your own true body. Know that the entire earth is your own true body, which is not a temporary body.

If someone asks you why we do not usually notice this, say, "Just reflect within yourself that the entire earth is the true human body." Or say, "The entire earth is the true human body—you already know this."

Also, *The entire earth is the gate of liberation* means that you are not at all entangled or captivated. What is called *the entire earth* is intimate—not divided from the moment, the ages, mind, and words. This limitless and boundless experience is the entire earth. Even if you seek to enter or go through this gate of liberation, it cannot be done. How is this so? Reflect on the question raised. If you intend to seek outside what it is, nothing will be attained.

The entire earth is the single eye of Vairochana means that buddhas have a single eye. Do not suppose that a buddha's eye is like those of human beings.

Human beings have two eyes, but when you say "the human eye," you don't say "two eyes" or "three eyes." Those who study the teaching should not understand that "the eye of a buddha," "the eye of dharma," or "the celestial eye" is like the two eyes of human beings. To believe that it is like human eyes is lamentable. Understand now that there is only a buddha's single eye, which is itself the entire earth.

A buddha may have one thousand eyes or myriad eyes. But at present it is said that the entire earth is the single eye. Thus, it is not mistaken to say that this eye is one of many eyes of a buddha, just as it is not mistaken to understand that a buddha has only one eye. A buddha, indeed, has many kinds of eyes—three eyes, one thousand eyes, or eighty-four thousand eyes. Do not be surprised to hear that there are eyes such as these.

Also, learn that the entire earth is itself the dharma body.

To seek to know the self is always the wish of living beings. However, those who see the true self are rare. Only buddhas know the true self. People outside the way regard what is not the self as the self. On the other hand, what buddhas call the self is the entire earth. Thus, there is never an entire earth that is not the self, with or without our knowing it. On this matter, refer to the words of the ancient buddhas.

———————

Long ago a monk asked a master, "When hundreds, thousands, or myriads of objects come all at once, what should be done?"

The master replied, "Don't try to control them."

What he means is that in whatever way objects come, do not try to change them. Whatever comes is the buddha dharma, not objects at all. Do not understand the master's reply as merely a brilliant admonition, but realize that it is the truth. Even if you try to control what comes, it cannot be controlled.

———————

An ancient buddha said, "Mountains, rivers, and earth are born at the same moment with each person. All buddhas of the past, present, and future are practicing together with each person."

If we look at mountains, rivers, and earth when a person is born, this person's birth does not seem to be bringing forth additional mountains, rivers, and earth on top of the existing ones. Yet, the ancient buddha's words should not be a mistake. How should we understand this? Even if you do not understand it, do not ignore it, but be determined to understand it. Since these words are already expounded, listen to them. Listen until you understand.

This is how to understand: Is there anyone who knows what a person's birth is like in its beginning or end? No one knows either birth's end or its beginning; nevertheless everyone is born. Similarly, no one knows the extremities of mountains, rivers, and earth, but all see this place and walk here. Do not think with regret that mountain, rivers, and earth are not born with you. Understand that the ancient buddha teaches that your birth is not separate from mountains, rivers, and earth.

Again, all buddhas of the past, present, and future have already practiced, attained the way, and completed realization. How should we understand that those buddhas are practicing together with us? First of all, examine a buddha's practice. A buddha's practice is to practice in the same manner as the entire earth and all beings. If it is not practice with all beings, it is not a buddha's practice. This being so, from the moment of arousing the aspiration for enlightenment to the moment of attaining enlightenment, all buddhas realize and practice the way together with the entire earth and all beings.

You may have doubts about this. But the ancient buddha's word was expounded in order to clarify your confused thinking. Do not think that buddhas are other than you. According to this teaching, when all buddhas of the past, present, and future arouse the aspiration for enlightenment and practice, they never exclude our body-and-mind. Understand this. To doubt this is to slander buddhas of the past, present, and future.

When we reflect quietly, it appears that our body-and-mind has practiced together with all buddhas of the past, present, and future, and has aroused the aspiration for enlightenment together with them. When we reflect on the past and future of our body-and-mind, we cannot find the boundary of self or others. With what delusion do we believe our body-and-mind is apart from all buddhas of the past, present, and future? Such delusion is groundless. How, then, can delusion hinder the arousing of the aspiration for enlightenment and practice of the way by all buddhas of the past, present, and future? Thus, understand that the way is not a matter of your knowing or not knowing.

A teacher of old said, "Chopping down is nothing other than chopping down; moving about is beyond discussion. Mountains, rivers, and earth are the entirely revealed body of the dharma king."

A person of the present should study this phrase of the teacher of old. There is a dharma king who understands that the body of the dharma king is not different from chopping down, just as mountains are on earth and the earth is holding up mountains.

When you understand this, a moment of beyond understanding does not come and hinder understanding, and understanding does not break beyond understanding. Instead, understanding and beyond understanding are just like spring and autumn.

However, when you do not understand, the pervasive voice of dharma does not reach your ears; in the midst of the voice your ears remain idle. But when you understand, the voice has already reached your ears; samadhi has emerged.

Do not think that understanding is small and that beyond understanding is large.

Know that beyond understanding cannot be discerned by a self; the dharma king's understanding is just like this.

In the dharma king's body the eye is just like the body, and the mind is the same as the body. There is not the slightest gap between mind and body; everything is fully revealed. Similarly, understand that in illumination and discourse the dharma king's body is revealed.

———————

There has been a saying since olden times: "No one except a fish knows a fish's heart; no one except a bird follows a bird's trace."

Yet those who really understand this point are rare. To think that no person knows a fish's heart or a bird's trace is mistaken. Know that fish always know one another's heart, unlike people who do not know one another's heart. When the fish try to go up through the Dragon Gate [a waterfall], they know one another's intention and have the same heart. Or they share the heart of breaking through the Nine Great Bends. Those who are not fish hardly know this.

Again, when a bird flies in the sky, beasts do not even dream of finding or following its trace. As they do not know that there is such a thing, they cannot even imagine this. However, a bird can see traces of hundreds and thousands of small birds having passed in flocks, or traces of so many lines of large birds having flown south or north. Those traces may be even more evident than the carriage tracks left on a road or the hoofprints of a horse seen in the grass. In this way, a bird sees birds' traces.

Buddhas are like this. You may wonder how many lifetimes buddhas have been practicing. Buddhas, large or small, although they are countless, all know their own traces. You never know a buddha's trace when you are not a buddha.

You may wonder why you do not know. The reason is that, while buddhas see these traces with the buddha's eye, those who are not buddhas do not have the buddha's eye: they merely notice buddhas' attributes.

All who do not know this should search out the trace of the buddhas' path. If you find footprints, you should investigate whether they are the buddhas'. Upon investigation, the buddhas' trace is known; and whether it is long or short, shallow or deep, is also known. To illuminate your trace is accomplished by studying the buddhas' trace. Accomplishing this is buddha dharma.

93

BIRTH AND DEATH

As a buddha is in birth and death, there is no birth and death."
It is also said, "As a buddha is not in birth and death, a buddha is not deluded by birth and death."

These statements are the essence of the words of the two Zen masters Keqin [Jiashan] and Dingshan. Never neglect them, as they are the words of those who attained the way.

Those who want to become free from birth and death should understand the meaning of these words. If you search for a buddha outside of birth and death, it will be like trying to go to the southern country of Yue with your spear heading toward the north, or like trying to see the Big Dipper while you are facing south; you will cause yourself to remain all the more in birth and death, and miss the way of emancipation.

Just understand that birth-and-death is itself nirvana. There is nothing such as birth and death to be avoided; there is nothing such as nirvana to be sought. Only when you realize this are you free from birth and death.

———

It is a mistake to suppose that birth turns into death. Birth is a phase that is an entire period in itself, with its own past and future. For this reason, in buddha dharma birth is understood as beyond birth. Death is a phase that is an entire period in itself, with its own past and future. For this reason, death is understood as beyond death.

In birth there is nothing but birth, and in death there is nothing but death. Accordingly, when birth comes, face and actualize birth, and when death comes, face and actualize death. Do not avoid them or desire them.

———————

This birth-and-death is the life of a buddha. If you try to exclude it, you will lose the life of a buddha. If you cling to it, trying to remain in it, you will also lose the life of a buddha, and what remains will be the mere form of a buddha. Only when you don't avoid birth-and-death or long for it do you enter a buddha's mind.

However, do not analyze or speak about it. Just set aside your body and mind, forget about them, and throw them into the house of the buddha; then all is done by the buddha. When you follow this, you are free from birth and death, and become a buddha without effort or scheme. Who, then, remains in the mind?

There is a simple way to become a buddha: When you refrain from unwholesome actions, are not attached to birth and death, and are compassionate toward all sentient beings, respectful to seniors and kind to juniors, not excluding or desiring anything, with no thoughts or worries, you will be called a buddha. Seek nothing else.

94

HEART OF THE WAY

IN SEEKING THE buddha way, make the heart of the way primary. Those who know how the heart of the way should be are rare. Inquire of those who clearly know it.

There are those in the world who have a heart of the way but in fact lack the true heart of the way. There are also those who have a true heart of the way but are not known by others. Thus, it is hard to know whether one does or does not have the heart of the way.

Above all, do not listen to and trust those who are unwholesome. Also, do not make your desire primary, but make the dharma expounded by the Buddha primary. Keep well in mind, day and night, how the heart of the way ought to be. Wish and pray by all means to realize genuine enlightenment in this world.

In this declining world, there is a general lack of those who have the true heart of the way. However, for the time being, keep your mind on impermanence; do not forget that this world is transient and that human life is precarious. But do not be preoccupied with reflecting on the impermanence of the world. Determine to regard the dharma as weighty, and your body and life as lightly weighted. For the sake of dharma, do not withhold any part of your body and life.

Then, deeply respect the three treasures—buddha, dharma, and sangha. Vow to respect and dedicate yourself to the three treasures even if your life or body changes. Asleep or awake, think of the merit of the three treasures. Asleep or awake, chant the three treasures.

When you leave this life, and before you enter the next life, there is a place called an intermediary realm. You stay there for seven days. You should resolve to keep chanting the names of the three treasures without ceasing while you are there. After seven days, you die into another intermediary realm and remain there for no more than seven days. At this time you can see and hear without hindrance, like someone with a celestial eye. Resolve to encourage yourself to keep chanting the names of the three treasures without ceasing: "I take refuge in the Buddha. I take refuge in the Dharma. I take refuge in the Sangha."

After passing through the intermediary realm, when you approach your parents to be conceived, resolve to maintain authentic wisdom. Keep chanting refuge in the three treasures in your mother's womb. Do not neglect chanting while you are being born. Resolve deeply to dedicate yourself to chant and take refuge in the three treasures through the six sense roots.

When your life ends, your eyesight will suddenly become dark. Know that this is the end of your life, and be determined to chant, "I take refuge in the Buddha." Then, all buddhas in the ten directions will show compassion to you. Even if, due to conditions, you are bound to an unwholesome realm, you will be able to be born in the deva realm or in the presence of the Buddha. Bow and listen to the Buddha.

After darkness arises in your eyes, continue to chant refuge in the three treasures until you enter the intermediary realm and further.

Thus, keep chanting, birth after birth, world after world, until you reach enlightenment, the buddha fruit. This is the way all buddhas and bodhisattvas have practiced. It is the way to deeply realize dharma. It is an embodiment of the buddha way. Resolve not to involve yourself with thoughts other than this.

Work to create a buddha image in your lifetime. Once it is created, dedicate three types of offerings: a mat, sugar water, and candles. Purify them and offer them to the image.

Also, create copies of the *Lotus Sutra* in your lifetime. Write it or make a print of it and maintain it. Place it on your head and then bow to it. Offer flowers, incense, candles, food, drink, and clothing. Be sure your head is clean before you place the sutra on it.

Do zazen regularly with your kashaya on. There is a precedent for attaining the way in the second next lifetime as the result of wearing a kashaya in this lifetime. It is the robe of all buddhas in the past, present, and future. Its merit is immeasurable. Zazen is not a method of the three realms. It is the method of buddha ancestors.

95

RECEIVING THE PRECEPTS

THE *GUIDELINES FOR Zen Monasteries* says:

It is said that all buddhas in the past, present, and future have left the household and accomplished the way. The twenty-eight ancestors of India and the six early ancestors of China who transmitted the seal of buddha mind were all monks. Their strict observance of the precepts made them excellent models in the three realms. Thus, in practicing Zen in pursuit of the way, observing the precepts is a prerequisite. If you do not refrain from making mistakes and avoid taking wrong actions, how can you become a buddha, become an ancestor?

To receive the precepts, you should first prepare bowls and clean, new robes. If you cannot get new robes, you should have freshly washed and purified robes. Do not borrow someone else's bowls for receiving the precepts at the platform [site of ceremony]. Be single-minded, unconcerned with other matters. Taking the form of the Buddha, embodying the precepts of the Buddha, and maintaining the receptive samadhi of the Buddha are no small matter. How can you take it lightly?

If you were to borrow someone else's robes and bowls, you would not actually receive the precepts you are given at the platform. Without receiving them, you would be a person of no precepts all your life who has mistakenly entered the gate of emptiness and falsely received gifts from faithful donors.

When you enter the way as a beginner, you may not fully remember the guidelines and precepts. If the teacher does not caution the student, the student may fall into a mistake. This is my advice. Please keep this in mind.

After receiving the bhikshu precepts, receive the bodhisattva precepts. This is the beginning of entering the way.

In the western and eastern lands where buddha ancestors have transmitted dharma, entering dharma is always receiving the precepts. Without receiving the precepts, one is not a disciple of buddhas, not a descendant of ancestors. "Refrain from unwholesome action" is no other than practicing Zen in pursuit of the way. The words *observing the precepts is a prerequisite* are indeed the treasury of the true dharma eye.

Because becoming a buddha and becoming an ancestor is no other than transmission of the treasury of the true dharma eye, ancestors who authentically transmit the treasury of the true dharma eye always receive and maintain the buddha precepts. There can be no buddha ancestors who do not. Whether they practice with the Tathagata or with his disciples, they receive and maintain the buddha precepts. This is receiving the life vein.

The buddha precepts authentically transmitted up to today from buddha to buddha, from ancestor to ancestor, were originally transmitted to China by Bodhidharma, the First Ancestor of Mount Song, and reached Huineng, the High Ancestor of Caodong, through five transmissions. The authentic transmission through Qingyuan and Nanyue is still being maintained, but there are some ignorant elders who are not aware of it. This should be most pitied.

Receive the bodhisattva precepts. This is the beginning of entering the way. Those who practice the way should know about this. The procedure of receiving the bodhisattva precepts is invariably transmitted to those who study in the inner chamber of buddha ancestors. This is not received by those who are coarse and negligent.

———————

The preliminary procedure for the ceremony is that the recipient burns and offers incense, makes formal bows to the ancestral teacher, and asks for permission to receive the bodhisattva precepts.

After permission is granted, the recipient cleanses the body, spreads flower petals, burns incense, bows respectfully to the new or freshly washed robes, and puts them on. Then the recipient bows to all sacred images, the three treasures, and the elders, and removes all hindrances, maintaining a pure body and mind. This procedure has long been authentically transmitted in the inner chamber of buddha ancestors.

At the practice place, the officiant or the instructor guides the recipient to make formal bows and then to say while kneeling:

(The recipient chants this three times, repeating the last line three times on the third chant.)

> I take refuge in the Buddha.
> I take refuge in the Dharma.
> I take refuge in the Sangha.

> I take refuge in the Buddha as the most venerable
>   one among two-legged beings.
> I take refuge in the Dharma as the most venerable
>   teaching that frees me from clinging.
> I take refuge in the Sangha as the most venerable of
>   all assemblies.

> I have taken refuge in the Buddha.
> I have taken refuge in the Dharma.
> I have taken refuge in the Sangha.

> The Tathagatha with true, unsurpassable
>   enlightenment is my great teacher. I have now
>   taken refuge in him. I will not take refuge in evil
>   spirits or those outside the way.

> May you be compassionate.
> May you be compassionate.

[The officiant says:]

Good person. You have given up incorrect views and taken refuge in the true teaching. The precepts surround you.

Now, take the three universal pure precepts.

(The officiant asks the recipient each of the following questions three times. The recipient affirms it each time.)

One: The precept of observing guidelines.
Will you maintain this precept from now until you attain a buddha body?

Yes, I will maintain it.

Two: The precept of taking wholesome actions.
Will you maintain this precept from now until you attain a buddha body?

Yes, I will maintain it.

Three: The precept of benefiting all beings.
Will you maintain this precept from now until you attain a buddha body?

Yes, I will maintain it.

None of these three universal pure precepts should be violated. Will you maintain them from now until you attain a buddha body?

Yes, I will maintain them.

Please maintain them.

(The recipient makes three formal bows and kneels.)
[The officiant says:]

Good person, you have received the three universal pure precepts. Now receive the ten [prohibitory] precepts. These are the great pure precepts of all buddhas and bodhisattvas.

(The officiant asks the recipient each of the following questions three times. The recipient affirms at each time.)

One: Not to kill.
Will you maintain this precept from now until you attain a buddha body?

Yes, I will maintain it.

Two: Not to steal.
Will you maintain this precept from now until you attain a buddha body?

Yes, I will maintain it.

Three: Not to misuse sex.
Will you maintain this precept from now until you attain a buddha body?

Yes, I will maintain it.

Four: Not to make false statements.
Will you maintain this precept from now until you attain a buddha body?

Yes, I will maintain it.

Five: Not to sell or buy alcohol.
Will you maintain this precept from now until you attain a buddha body?

Yes, I will maintain it.

Six: Not to discuss the faults of other home-leaver bodhisattvas.
Will you maintain this precept from now until you attain a buddha body?

Yes, I will maintain it.

Seven: Not to praise yourself and insult others.

Will you maintain this precept from now until you attain a buddha body?

Yes, I will maintain it.

Eight: Not to withhold dharma or treasure.
Will you maintain this precept from now until you attain a buddha body?

Yes, I will maintain it.

Nine: Not to be angry.
Will you maintain this precept from now until you attain a buddha body?

Yes, I will maintain it.

Ten: Not to slander the three treasures.
Will you maintain this precept from now until you attain a buddha body?

Yes, I will maintain it.

None of these ten precepts should be violated. Will you maintain them from now until you attain a buddha body?

Yes, I will maintain them.

Please maintain them.
(The recipient makes three formal bows.)
(The officiant makes three formal bows.)
[The officiant says:]

These three refuges, three universal pure precepts, and ten prohibitory precepts have been maintained by all buddhas. Will you or will you not maintain these sixteen precepts from now until you attain a buddha body?
Yes, I will maintain them.
Please maintain them.

(The recipient makes three formal bows.)

The recipient sings the Sanskrit song "Living in This World," then chants:

> I take refuge in the Buddha.
> I take refuge in the Dharma.
> I take refuge in the Sangha.

(Finally the recipient leaves the practice place.)

———————

This procedure for receiving the precepts has been authentically transmitted by buddhas and ancestors without fail. Danxia Tianran and novice Gao of Mount Yaoshan both received these precepts. There have been ancestors without receiving the bhikshu precepts, but there have been no ancestors who have not received these bodhisattva precepts authentically transmitted by buddha ancestors. All ancestors receive these precepts.

96

ONE HUNDRED EIGHT GATES
OF REALIZING DHARMA

[THE *Sutra of the Buddha's Practices in Former Lives* says:]

Bodhisattva Realization Protector [a former life of Shakyamuni Buddha] was in Tushita Heaven at a celestial palace called High Banner that spread in a square sixty *yojana* on each side. At various times, the bodhisattva expounded essential dharma there.

Once, he meditated on the place of his birth in his next life [in the human realm]. Then, sitting in the palace, he called to the devas of Tushita Heaven:

> I want all of you to assemble here because I am going to descend to the human realm soon. I would like to offer a teaching that is called "the gates of skillful means for entering all aspects of dharma." This will be the last time I offer you guidance. This is for you to memorize. Rejoice when you hear me and learn about these dharma gates.

Hearing his call, a great number of devas with all of their family members, including jeweled women of heaven, assembled together.

Before expounding this dharma, Bodhisattva Realization Protector made a new palace appear and placed it on top of the High Banner Palace. It was high and broad, decorated with jewels, and it covered the entire world. Its magnificence was incomparable. There was nothing like it among palaces in the desire realm. Devas in the form realm saw that this illusory palace was like a kingly tomb.

Bodhisattva Realization Protector had conducted valuable practices, planted wholesome roots, accomplished benevolence in the past, and possessed great merit. When he was seated on the high lion seat, innumerable treasures were spread around him in glory. Various celestial robes were laid out on his seat, and all types of wondrous scents permeated the air. Incense was burnt in countless incense bowls, and petals of fragrant flowers were sprinkled on the ground. Rare treasures surrounded the high seat, and hundreds, thousands, and millions of splendid rays illuminated the palace.

Jeweled nets were spread above and below the palace walls. Golden bells hanging from them rang with exquisite sound. This great jeweled palace radiated innumerable kinds of radiant light. Thousands of banners and canopies reflecting hues of wondrous colors covered the palace, which was adorned with all types of swinging tassels.

Each of the hundreds, thousands, and millions of celestial women held seven types of treasures, played tunes, and sang their admiration of the boundless merit of the bodhisattva's practice in the past. Hundreds, thousands, and millions of the four types of protectors of the world stood on the right and left sides, guarding the palace. Thousands of Indras bowed to the palace, and thousands of Brahmas paid homage. Countless bodhisattvas guarded the palace, and all buddhas in the ten directions protected it with mindfulness. Their practices, realizations, and beneficial results from hundreds, thousands, and countless eons in the past were actualized. The causes and effects were completed, and their benefit increased day and night. Immeasurable merit was adorned in this way, which is impossible to explain.

The bodhisattva sat on the high lion seat of great splendor and said to all the devas:

Now, Devas, those of you bodhisattva mahasattvas who abide in Tushita Heaven and are about to be born in the human realm should expound to other devas the one hundred eight gates of realizing dharma. You should leave this teaching for them, let them memorize it, and then make your descent.

Now, Devas, listen and accept the truth wholeheartedly. I am going to explain it:

What are the one hundred eight gates of realizing dharmas?

Right trust is a gate of realizing dharma; it keeps determined aspiration from breaking. Pure heart is a gate of realizing dharma; it is not defiled. Rejoicing is a gate of realizing dharma; it keeps the mind calm and at ease. Love of enjoyment is a gate of realizing dharma; it keeps the heart pure.

Right practice of the body is a gate of realizing dharma, for the three actions [of body, speech, and thought] are kept pure. Pure practice of speech is a gate of realizing dharma; it keeps us from the four types of unwholesomeness. Pure practice of mind is a gate of realizing dharma; it keeps the mind from the three types of poison.

Mindfulness of the Buddha is a gate of realizing dharma; it visualizes the buddha in purity. Mindfulness of dharma is a gate of realizing dharma; it visualizes dharma in purity. Mindfulness of sangha is a gate of realizing dharma; it makes attaining the way sustained.

Mindfulness of giving is a gate of realizing dharma; it makes you free from wanting a reward. Mindfulness of the precepts is a gate of realizing dharma; it fully contains all vows. Mindfulness of heaven is a gate of realizing dharma; it arouses vast aspiration.

Compassion is a gate of realizing dharma; it encompasses wholesome roots in all realms of birth. Grieving is a gate of realizing dharma; it keeps you from harming sentient beings. Joy is a gate of realizing dharma; it keeps you from all joyless matters. Letting go is a gate of realizing dharma; it frees you from the five types of desire.

Visualizing impermanence is a gate of realizing dharma; it illustrates the desires of the three realms. Visualizing suffering is a gate of realizing dharma; it frees you from all wishes. Visualizing no-self is a gate of realizing dharma; it frees you from the self. Visualizing serene samadhi is a gate of realizing dharma; it keeps your heart and mind from being stirred.

Repentance is a gate of realizing dharma; it keeps your inner mind in serene samadhi. Shame is a gate of realizing dharma; it destroys outer unwholesomeness. Realness is a gate of realizing dharma; it does not deceive devas and humans. Truthfulness is a gate of realizing dharma; it does not deceive you. Practice of dharma is a gate of realizing dharma; it engages the practice of dharma. Taking refuge in the three [treasures] is a gate of realizing dharma; it purifies the three unwholesome paths.

Knowing another person's kindness is a gate of realizing dharma; it keeps the wholesome roots from being abandoned. Repaying another person's kindness is a gate of realizing dharma; it does not ignore the debt. Not deceiving yourself is a gate of realizing dharma; it does not allow you to praise yourself.

Helping sentient beings is a gate of realizing dharma; it does not allow you to slander others. Helping dharma is a gate of realizing dharma; it lets you practice in accordance with dharma. Being aware of time is a gate of realizing dharma; it does not allow you to speak lightly. Being patient is a gate of realizing dharma; it fulfills wisdom. Not arousing unwholesome intention is a gate of realizing dharma; it protects the self and others. Not being hindered is a gate of realizing dharma; it keeps your mind free from doubt. Understanding with trust is a gate of realizing dharma; it clarifies the matter of primary significance.

Visualizing impurity is a gate of realizing dharma; it abandons the desire for defilement. Not fighting is a gate of realizing dharma; it keeps you from anger and argument. Not being ignorant is a gate of realizing dharma; it keeps you from killing.

Enjoying the meaning of dharma is a gate of realizing dharma; it seeks the meaning of dharma. Love of realizing dharma is a gate of realizing dharma; it leads to realizing dharma. Seeking extensive learning is a gate of realizing dharma; it leads to right awakening to aspects of dharma. Right skillful means is a gate of realizing dharma; it embodies right action. Knowing names and forms is a gate of realizing dharma; it removes various hindrances.

Removing the views of causes is a gate of realizing dharma; it leads to emancipation. The intention not to resent those close to you is a gate of realizing dharma; it creates the heart of oneness in the midst of resenting those who are close. Subtle skillful means is a gate of realizing dharma; it knows all forms of suffering. A great sense of equality is a gate of realizing dharma; it leads to freedom from all things that are composed. Entering is a gate of realizing dharma; it leads to the practice of the right path. Not having to arouse patience is a gate of realizing dharma; it realizes the truth of eliminating [causes of suffering].

The ground of mindfulness of the body is a gate of realizing dharma; it leads all things to serenity. The ground of mindfulness of perception is a gate of realizing dharma; it frees all perceptions. The ground of mindfulness of the mind is a gate of realizing dharma; it sees the mind as not different from a phantom. The ground of mindfulness of dharma is a gate of realizing dharma; it leads to wisdom with no obscuration.

The four types of right effort are a gate of realizing dharma; they prevent all unwholesome actions and lead to wholesome actions. The four types of fulfillment are a gate of realizing dharma; they lead to lightness of body and mind.

The root of trust is a gate of realizing dharma; it does not follow others' words. The root of effort is a gate of realizing dharma; it attains various types of wisdom. The root of mindfulness is a gate of realizing dharma; it leads to various wholesome actions. The root of samadhi is a gate of realizing dharma; it keeps the mind pure. The root of wisdom is a gate of realizing dharma; it sees all things as they are.

The ability to trust is a gate of realizing dharma; it excels all demonic power. The ability to make effort is a gate of realizing dharma; it is not remitting. The ability of mindfulness is a gate of realizing dharma; it does not blindly go along with others. The ability of samadhi is a gate of realizing dharma; it becomes free from all thoughts. The ability of wisdom is a gate of realizing dharma; it goes beyond dualism.

Branches of mindfulness are a gate of realizing dharma; they are like wisdom about all things. Branches of awakening with dharma are a gate of realizing dharma; they illuminate all things. Branches of making effort are a gate of realizing dharma; they perceive well. Branches of joy are a gate of realizing dharma; they lead to various types of samadhi. Branches of letting go are a gate of realizing dharma; they discern actions. Branches of samadhi are a gate of realizing dharma; they know the oneness of all things. Branches of letting go are a gate of realizing dharma; they become secluded from all living things.

Right view is a gate of realizing dharma; it leads to exhaustion of desire and attainment of the noble path. Right thinking is a gate of realizing dharma; it leads to freedom from thinking and beyond thinking. Right speech is a gate of realizing dharma; it knows that all names, sounds, and phrases are mere echoes. Right livelihood is a gate of realizing dharma; it prevents all unwholesome paths. Right action is a gate of realizing dharma; it leads you to the other shore. Right mindfulness is a gate of realizing dharma; it leads to freedom from thoughts on all things. Right samadhi is a gate of realizing dharma; it attains undivided concentration.

The aspiration for enlightenment is a gate of realizing dharma; it keeps the three treasures from being cut off. Dependence [on enlightenment] is a gate of realizing dharma; it keeps you from desiring the Lesser Vehicles. Right trust is a gate of realizing dharma; it leads to attaining the most excellent dharma. Improvement is a gate of realizing dharma; it leads to attaining all wholesome roots.

The realization of giving is a gate of realizing dharma; it leads to attaining a joyful appearance each moment, embellishing the buddha land, and freeing sentient beings from greed. The realization of precepts is a gate of realizing dharma; it keeps away the hindrance of unwholesome paths and guides sentient beings who have broken the precepts. The realization of patience is a gate of realizing dharma; it lets go of all anger, pride, flattery, and amusement, and guides sentient beings who are filled with such emotions. The realization of making effort is a gate of realizing dharma; it attains all wholesome things and guides lazy sentient beings. The realization of meditation is a gate of realizing dharma; it attains all types of meditation and miraculous actions, and guides sentient beings whose minds are scattered. The realization of wisdom is a gate of realizing dharma; it cuts off the darkness of ignorance and attachment to all views, and guides foolish sentient beings.

Skillful means is a gate of realizing dharma; it manifests guidance in accordance with the awesome presence viewed by sentient beings, and accomplishes the dharma of all buddhas. The four methods of guidance are a gate of realizing dharma; they include all sentient beings, help them to be enlightened, and offer them dharma. Teaching sentient beings is a gate of realizing dharma; it does not bring unwholesome pleasure and indulgence. Accepting true dharma is a gate of realizing dharma; it transforms the delusions of sentient beings. Assembling benefaction is a gate of realizing dharma; it benefits sentient beings.

Practice of meditation is a gate of realizing dharma; it fulfills the ten types of abilities. Serene samadhi is a gate of realizing dharma;

it accomplishes and maintains the samadhi of the Tathagata. Insight of wisdom is a gate of realizing dharma; it accomplishes and fulfills wisdom.

Entering unhindered understanding is a gate of realizing dharma; it acquires and completes the dharma eye. Entering all types of practice is a gate of realizing dharma; it acquires and completes the buddha eye.

Accomplishing dharani is a gate of realizing dharma; it hears and maintains the dharma of all buddhas. Attaining unhindered understanding is a gate of realizing dharma; it causes all sentient beings to rejoice.

Practicing patience is a gate of realizing dharma; it accords with the dharma of all buddhas. Attaining patience beyond birth is a gate of realizing dharma; it attains the prediction of enlightenment.

The ground of unremitting practice is a gate of realizing dharma; it embodies the dharma of all past buddhas. Following and reaching the ground of wisdom are a gate of realizing dharma; it sprinkles wisdom water on the head and achieves all wisdom. The ground of sprinkling wisdom water on the head is a gate of realizing dharma; it brings forth birth, leaving the household, and unsurpassable, complete enlightenment.

Thus, Bodhisattva Realization Protector finished expounding this dharma and said to all the devas, "Devas, these are the one hundred eight gates of realizing dharma, which I offer to you. Accept and maintain them. Always keep them in mind and do not forget them."

[Dogen says:]

These are the one hundred eight gates of realizing dharma. It is customary in the buddha world that when bodhisattvas who taught throughout their lives in Tushita Heaven are about to descend to the Jambudvipa Continent [where humans abide], they expound this teaching to devas.

Bodhisattva Realization Protector is the name of Shakyamuni Buddha when he was a bodhisattva teaching throughout his life in the Fourth Heaven. When Li Fuma compiled the *Tiansheng Extensive Record of the Lamp,* he added "One Hundred Eight Gates of Realizing Dharma" to the title of the book.

Not many of those who study know about this teaching. Those who are unaware of it are as many as straws, flax, bamboo, and reeds.

I am showing this teaching to beginners and latecomers. Those who may ascend to the lion seat and become teachers of humans and devas should study this thoroughly. Those who do not teach throughout their lives in Tushita Heaven [before descending to the human realm] are not buddhas. Practitioners, do not be proud of yourselves. The bodhisatt-vas who teach throughout their lives do not have intermediary realms [before rebirth into the human realm].

AFTERWORD

THE COMPLETION OF the translation of Dogen's great work, the *Treasury of the True Dharma Eye,* is a milestone in Zen's coming-of-age in the Western world. This work and Shasta Abbey's recently completed translation of the text mark the absorption of Dogen's lifework by Zen practitioners outside of Japan, and establishes the mind relic of Dogen's written teaching in the English-speaking world.

Shunryu Suzuki Roshi came to the United States in 1959. Kazuaki Tanahashi began his English translation of Dogen in 1964. It has taken this amount of time for Soto Zen to lay down its roots here in North America. While more than thirty teachers and practitioners from San Francisco Zen Center and beyond have collaborated on the translation, Kaz's contribution stands out—combining the roles of coach, teacher, cheerleader, and wordsmith—and his flexibility and integrity shine through. Knowing when to give time for a word or phrase to become ripe, a good translator demonstrates a remarkable patience and skill set.

The difficulty of translation cannot be underestimated. Kaz himself noticed that it wasn't until he started to translate Dogen into English that he was able to complete his translation of Dogen from medieval into modern Japanese. Suzuki Roshi was a respected teacher in Japan, but when he spoke in English his teaching was outstanding. His creative expression in a different social linguistic context demonstrated the depth of his understanding. My own experience with translation is that I may understand something a little bit, but to express it in another language takes a deeper intimacy with the material. For many of us cotranslators this project has been a stretching and testing of our dharma limits.

In closing, I would like to acknowledge the committed sangha whose sincere and daily practice of the buddha way has supplied the background and context of the teaching in this book. My hope is that its publication continues to inspire a new expression of the dharma for this age: *May the dharma floursh in the ten directions!*

DAIRYU MICHAEL WENGER
Beginner's Mind Temple,
San Francisco Zen Center
December 8, 2008

APPENDIX I
Recommending Zazen to All People
Dogen

———

THE REAL WAY CIRCULATES everywhere; how could it require practice or enlightenment? The essential teaching is fully available; how could effort be necessary? Furthermore, the entire mirror is free of dust; why take steps to polish it? Nothing is separate from this very place; why journey away?

And yet, if you miss the mark even by a strand of hair, you are as distant as heaven from earth. If the slightest discrimination occurs, you will be lost in confusion. You could be proud of your understanding and have abundant realization, or acquire outstanding wisdom and attain the way by clarifying the mind. Still, if you are wandering about in your head, you may miss the vital path of letting your body leap.

You should observe the example of Buddha Shakyamuni of the Jeta Grove, who practiced sitting up straight for six years even though he was gifted with intrinsic wisdom. Still celebrated is the Master Bodhidharma of Shaolin Temple who sat facing the wall for nine years, although he had already received the mind seal. Ancient sages were like this; who nowadays does not need to practice as they did?

Hence, you should stop searching for phrases and chasing after words. Take the backward step and turn the light inward. Your body-mind of itself will drop off and your original face will appear. If you want to attain just this, immediately practice just this.

For zazen, a quiet room is appropriate. Drink and eat in moderation. Let go of all involvements and let myriad things rest. Do not think good

or bad. Do not judge right or wrong. Stop conscious endeavor and ana-
lytic introspection. Do not try to become a buddha. How could being a
buddha be limited to sitting or not sitting?

In an appropriate place for sitting, set out a thick mat and put a
round cushion on top of it. Sit in either the full- or half-lotus posture.
For the full-lotus posture, first place the right foot on the left thigh, then
the left foot on the right thigh. For the half-lotus posture, place the left
foot on the right thigh. Loosen the robes and belts and arrange them
in an orderly way. Then place the right hand palm up on the left foot,
and the left hand on the right hand, with the tips of the thumbs lightly
touching each other.

Sit straight up without leaning to the right or left and without bending forward or backward. The ears should be in line with the shoulders
and the nose in line with the navel. Rest the tongue against the roof of
the mouth, with lips and teeth closed. Keep the eyes open and breathe
gently through the nose.

Having adjusted your body in this manner, take a breath and exhale
fully, then sway your body to left and right. Now sit steadfastly and think
not-thinking. How do you think not-thinking? Beyond thinking. This is
the essential art of zazen.

The zazen I speak of is not learning meditation. It is simply the
dharma gate of enjoyment and ease. It is the practice-realization of complete enlightenment. Realize the fundamental point free from the binding of nets and baskets. Once you experience it, you are like a dragon
swimming in the water or a tiger reposing in the mountains. Know
that the true dharma emerges of itself, clearing away hindrances and
distractions.

When you stand up from sitting, move your body slowly and rise
calmly, without haste. We understand from past precedents that going
beyond ordinary and sacred, where sitting and standing are effortless and
boundless, depends solely on the power of zazen.

Furthermore, bringing forth the turning point by using a finger, a
pole, a needle, or a mallet, or leading people to enlightenment with a
whisk, a fist, a stick, or a shout, cannot be understood by discriminatory
thinking. How can it be understood by the use of supernatural powers?
Zazen is an awesome presence outside form and color. How is it not the
path preceding concept?

Thus, do not be concerned with who is wise and who is stupid. Do not discriminate the sharp from the dull. To practice wholeheartedly is the true endeavor of the way. Practice-realization is not defiled with specialness; it is a matter for every day.

Now, in this world and in other worlds, in India and China, buddha ancestors equally carry the buddha seal and teach to sit immersed in steadfastness. Although circumstances may vary in a thousand ways, wholeheartedly practice Zen, giving yourself fully to the way. Why give up the sitting platform of your own house and wander uselessly in the dust of a remote land? Once a wrong step is taken, you depart from the way.

Having received a human life, do not waste the passing moments. Already upholding the buddha way, why would you indulge in the sparks from a flint? After all, form is like a dewdrop on the grass. Human life is like a flash of lightning, transient and illusory, gone in a moment.

Honored practitioners of Zen, please do not grope for the elephant or try to grasp the true dragon. Strive to hit the mark by directly pointing. Revere the mind that goes beyond study and surpasses all doings. Experience the enlightenment of the buddhas, correctly inheriting the samadhi of the ancestors. Practice thusness continuously, and you will be thus. The treasury will open of itself for you to use as you wish.

Written at the Kannondori Monastery on the fifteenth day, the midyear [seventh month], the first year of the Tempuku Era [1233].

APPENDIX 2
Dogen's Life and Teaching
Keizan Jokin

————————

PRIEST EIHEI DOGEN, THE fifty-first ancestor, practiced with priest Rujing of Tiantong. One day during the late evening zazen, Rujing said to the assembly, "Practicing Zen is dropping away body and mind."

Upon hearing this, Dogen suddenly had great realization. Immediately [after zazen], he went up to the abbot's quarters and offered incense to Rujing, who said, "Why are you offering incense to me?"

Dogen said, "I have dropped away body and mind."

Rujing said, "You have dropped away body and mind. Your body and mind have been dropped away."

Dogen said, "This is a temporary matter. Please don't approve me easily."

Rujing said, "I am not approving you easily."

Dogen said, "What is not approving easily?"

Rujing said, "Dropping away body and mind."

Dogen bowed deeply.

Rujing said, "Dropping away has dropped away."

At that moment the attendant monk Guanping from Fu Region said, "This person from a foreign country has achieved what-it-is. Indeed, this is not a minor thing."

Rujing said, "How many blows of the fist have you received with this understanding? Dropping away serene composure is thunder and lightning."

Dogen's family name was Minamoto. Dogen was the name he was given when he was ordained. Born in the second year of the Shoji Era [1200], he was a ninth-generation descendent of Emperor Murakami and an eighth-generation descendant of Prince Gochusho.

After his birth, an astronomer saw him and said, "The double rings around his pupils show that he is a sacred child who is destined to be a great vessel. However, according to an old book, after a sacred child is born, his mother's life is endangered. She will die when he is seven years old." Hearing these words, Dogen's mother was neither surprised nor frightened, but loved the child all the more. She died when Dogen was eight years old. People said, "Although there was one year's discrepancy, the astronomer's prediction was right."

Earlier than that, in the winter of his fourth year, Dogen read one hundred poems by Li Jiao while sitting on his grandmother's lap. In the autumn of his seventh year he copied out a poem from the Shu Dynasty and presented it to his grandfather. Those who were learned regarded the child as extraordinary and called him a genius.

Dogen was deeply saddened by the loss of his mother. Seeing the incense smoke during the funeral at the Takao Temple [in Kyoto], he realized the impermanence of birth and death, and aroused the aspiration for enlightenment.

In the spring of his ninth year, Dogen read Vasubandhu's *Abhidharma Kosha Treatise*. Mature practitioners said that Dogen was like Manjushri, a great vessel of Mahayana. At a young age he memorized ancient teachings and studied hard.

There was a man called Lord of the Pine Palace who served as Regent of the nation, and his retired name was Zenjo Kaku (Dhyana Hall). He was the most respected courtier in the country and an exemplary figure for kings and ministers. He adopted Dogen as a child and transmitted to him the essentials of both family affairs and governing. When Dogen was thirteen years old, the lord wanted to hold a ceremony for him to assume manhood, and put him on the path to becoming a key retainer of the imperial court.

However, Dogen quietly left the lord's residence on Mount Kobata and went to the foot of Mount Hiei. He visited a monk called Ryokan, a senior member of the [Tendai School] community and a teacher of Exoteric and Esoteric Buddhism, who was a secular uncle of Dogen's.

Dogen entered his chamber and asked him for ordination. Much surprised, Ryokan asked, "You are about to reach manhood. If you leave the household, your father and foster father will be upset. What do you think about that?"

Dogen said, "Before my mother died, she asked me to leave the household and study the way. This is also what I want to do instead of being mixed with secular dust. In order to repay the kindness of my mother, grandmother, and nursing mother, I want to become a monk."

Ryokan was moved to tears, agreed to give Dogen instructions, and allowed him to stay at the Senko Temple of the Shuryogon Monastery in Yokawa [at Mount Hiei]. On the ninth day, the fourth month, the first year of the Kempo Era [1213], Dogen bowed formally to Bishop Koen, the head monk of the Tendai School, and got his head shaved. On the following day, Dogen received the bodhisattva precepts at the Precept Platform Temple of Mount Hiei and became a monk. From that time on, he studied the shamatha [quieting the mind] and vipashyana [insight] practices of the school, as well as esoteric teachings from India. At age eighteen he began to read through the entire Buddhist canon.

Soon after that, Dogen asked Bishop Koin of the Mii Monastery, a famed dharma teacher and also a secular uncle of his, about an essential teaching of the Tendai School, the reason why Buddhas of the three times practice even though they are already enlightened.

Koin said, "What you are asking now is the most advanced question of our school. This theme has been passed on orally from generation to generation by great masters Dengyo [Saicho] and Jikaku [Ennin]. I cannot fully elucidate it, but I hear that Bodhidharma transmitted the buddha seal from India to China; his teaching prevails all over China now and it is called the Zen School. If you want to have a definite answer to your question, you should enter the chamber of Bishop Eisai of the Kennin Monastery [in Kyoto] and ask him. You should also go to China in search of the way."

Thus, at age eighteen, on the twenty-fifth day, the eighth month, the fifth year of the Kampo Era [1217], Dogen joined the assembly of Priest Myozen, Bishop Eisai's successor at the Kennin Monastery. Earlier, when Bishop Eisai had been teaching, he had allowed students to wear a priest's robe only after three years of study. However, when Dogen joined, Myozen allowed Dogen to wear a priest's robe in the ninth month, and then he allowed Dogen to wear a great robe in the eleventh month, regarding him a vessel of dharma.

Myozen was the only dharma heir of Eisai, receiving the transmission of the three teachings—Exoteric, Esoteric, and Buddha Heart (Zen) teachings. According to a record in the Kennin Monastery, Eisai said, "I entrust the treasury of dharma to Myozen alone. Those who want to inquire of my dharma should see Myozen."

Dogen entered Myozen's inner chamber and received the bodhisattva precepts again, as well as the robe and eating bowl. Earlier, Dogen had mastered the Esoteric rites for one hundred thirty-four deities and the transmission of the fire ceremonies [of the Tani Sect of Esoteric Buddhism]. He had also studied the precepts as well as shamatha and vipashyana. Now he heard the teaching of the Rinzai School for the first time and received an authentic transmission of Exoteric, Esoteric, and Buddha Mind teachings. Thus, Dogen became the sole successor of Myozen.

Seven years later, at age twenty-four, on the twenty-second day, the second month, the second year of the Teio Era [1223], Dogen bade farewell to Eisai's tomb at the Kennin Monastery. He went to China and hung his traveling stick at the Tiantong Monastery. It was the sixteenth year of the Jiading Era [1223] of the Song Dynasty.

In China, while visiting various monasteries, he met Priest Ruyan of Mount Jing, who said, "When did you arrive?"

Dogen said, "In the fourth month of last year."

Ruyan said, "Did you come with others?"

Dogen said, "No, I didn't come with others. How is it to come?"

Ruyan said, "You have already come with others."

Dogen said, "How is it to have come with others?"

Ruyan clapped his hands and said, "There is someone who talks a lot."

Dogen said, "If there is not someone who talks a lot, how is it?"

Ruyan said, "Sit down and have some tea."

Later, Dogen visited Xiaocuiyan in Tai Region, met Priest Sizhuo, and asked, "What are buddhas?"

Sizhuo said, "Those in the hall."

Dogen said, "If they are in the hall, how is it that they are everywhere in the countless worlds?"

Sizhuo said, "They are just in the countless worlds."

Dogen said, "Your words are accompanying them."

After having such conversations with various masters, Dogen became proud of himself, thinking that he was matchless in Japan and China. So, he planned to return to Japan, when a monk called Laojin said, "The only person in Great Song China who has a dharma eye is Old Man Rujing. You would certainly get something from him." However, more than a year passed before Dogen found the opportunity to study with Rujing.

Then, Wuji Liaopai left the abbacy of Tiantong, and Rujing moved in as abbot. Dogen thought this was an auspicious karmic turning point unfolding from the past. Therefore, he went to ask Rujing questions, and his spearhead was immediately broken. Thus, Dogen became a student of Rujing's. With the hope of studying more deeply, Dogen wrote to him:

> When I was young I aroused the aspiration for enlightenment and visited various monasteries in my country. I had some understanding of the principle of cause and effect; however I was not able to clarify the real source of buddha dharma. I was only seeing the outer forms, the marks and names. Later, I entered the chamber of Eisai, Zen Master Senko, and for the first time heard the teaching of the Linji School. Now I have accompanied Monk Myozen to Great Song and entered your dharma assembly. This is the fortunate result of my wholesome roots from the past.
>
> Great Compassionate Teacher, grant me permission to ask you about the way.

Rujing wrote back: "Dogen, you can come informally to ask questions anytime, day or night, from now on. Do not worry about formality; we can be like father and son."

After that, Dogen entered Rujing's inner chamber day and night and intimately received essential teachings.

At one point, Rujing asked Dogen to be his attendant monk. Dogen declined, saying, "I am from a foreign country. If I am given the honor of being your attendant at this great monastery in this great nation, people in the monastic community may become jealous. I only wish to study with you day and night."

Rujing said, "You are very modest and what you say has a point."

In this way, Dogen received instructions from Rujing by continuing to ask questions.

One day during the late evening zazen time, Rujing entered the hall and cautioned the assembly against dozing: "Practicing Zen is dropping away mind and body. It is not pivotal to offer incense, bow, chant buddhas' names, make repentance, or read sutras. Just wholeheartedly sit so you will attain what you are pursuing."

Hearing this, Dogen immediately had great realization. This is the occasion that I mentioned earlier.

After the first encounter with Rujing, Dogen endeavored to practice the way day and night ceaselessly, not veering off even for a moment and without lying down. Rujing often said to him, "Your practice is as pure as that of ancient buddhas. You will extensively spread the ancestral way. I have you with me just as Shakyamuni Buddha had Mahakashyapa."

Thus, in the first year of the Baoqing Era [1225], which corresponds to the first year of the Karoku Era, Rujing installed Dogen as the fifty-fifth ancestor.

Entrusting dharma to Dogen, Rujing said, "Return to your country as soon as possible and widely spread the ancestral way. Retreat and live in a deep mountain and keep nourishing the sacred womb."

In addition to practicing with Rujing in this way, Dogen had opportunities to see documents of heritage of the Five Houses:

First, when Dogen met Visiting Abbot Weiyi [at Mount Tiantong], a former abbot of the Guangfu Monastery, Weiyi said, "Ancient scrolls that are worth seeing are treasures of humankind. How many of them have you seen?"

Dogen said, "I have not seen any."

Then Weiyi said, "I have a scroll of old writing. I will show it to you." He brought it to Dogen. It was a document of heritage of the Fayan lineage that he had obtained from items left behind by an old master; so it was not what Weiyi himself had received. It was written in a certain format, but I won't explain this now.

At another time, Dogen was shown a document of heritage of the Yunmen lineage by elder Zongyue, who was filling the position of head monk at Mount Tiantong. Dogen asked Zongyue, "Reverend, there is some difference among the Five Schools in the arrangement of names on the documents of heritage. Why is that so? If it came directly from India, why is there such a difference?"

Zongyue said, "Even if there is a vast difference, just understand that buddhas of Mount Yunmen are like this. For what reason is the venerable Shakyamuni revered? He is revered for his way of awakening. For what reason is great master Yunmen revered? He is revered for his way of awakening."

Upon hearing these words, Dogen had some understanding.

Earlier, there had been a priest named Chuan, a descendant of Qingyuan, the Zen Master Fuyan of Longmen. This Chuan, a librarian, also had a document of heritage. At the beginning of the Jiading Era [1208–1224], when librarian Chuan was sick, senior monk Ryuzen, a Japanese man, took good care of him. Because Ryuzen worked hard, librarian Chuan, grateful for help during his illness, took out his document of heritage and let Ryuzen see it, saying, "This is a thing not commonly shown, but I will let you pay homage to it."

Some years after that, in the autumn of the sixteenth year of the Jiading Era [1223], when Dogen first came to Mount Tiantong, Ryuzen cordially requested that librarian Chuan show this document of heritage to Dogen. This was one transmitted in the Yangqi Line [of the Linji School]. Also, on the twenty-first day, the first month, the seventeenth year of the Jiading Era [1224], Dogen saw the document of heritage of priest Wuji Liaopai of the Tiantong Monastery. Wuji said, "Few people know about this, and now you do, elder. This is a fulfillment of your practice of the way." Dogen was very pleased.

Dogen visited Mount Tiantai and Mount Yadang later in the Baoqing Era [1225–1227] and got to the Wannian Monastery of Pingtian, on Mount Tiantai. The abbot there was priest Yuanzi of Fu Region. Upon first greeting him, Yuanzi talked about the teaching of the buddha ancestors. When he mentioned Yangshan's dharma succession from Great Guishan, he said, "You haven't seen the document of heritage here in my quarters, have you?"

Dogen replied, "No, unfortunately I haven't."

Abbot Yuanzi got up, took out the document of heritage, and, holding it up, said:

Following the dharma admonition of buddha ancestors, I have not shown this even to a close disciple or an old attendant monk. But when I went to the city to see the governor and stayed there as I occasionally do, I had a dream. In this dream a distinguished priest who seemed to be Zen Master Fachang of Mount Damei appeared, holding up a branch of plum blossoms. He said, "If a true person comes who has disembarked from a boat, do not withhold these flowers." And he gave me the plum blossoms. Still in the dream, I exclaimed, "Why shouldn't I give him thirty blows before he leaves the boat?" Then, before five days had passed, you came to meet me, elder. Of course you have disembarked from a boat, and this document of heritage is written on brocade that has a design of plum blossoms. Since you must be the one Damei was referring to, in accordance with the dream I have taken this document out. Do you wish to inherit dharma from me? I will not withhold it if you do.

Dogen could not help being moved. Although he could have requested to receive a document of heritage from him, Dogen only offered incense, bowed, and paid homage to him with deep respect. At that time there was present an incense attendant named Faning. He said that it was the first time he had ever seen the document of heritage.

Dogen said to himself, "This event indeed could not have happened without the invisible help of buddha ancestors. As a foolish man from a remote country, by what fortune have I been able to see a document of heritage once again?" Tears wet his sleeves.

Later, Dogen stayed at the entry hall of the Husheng Monastery, on Mount Damei. At that time he had an auspicious dream that the ancestor Damei came to him and gave him a branch of plum blossoms in full bloom.

Indeed, as Dogen opened his eye of the way as the ancient sages had done, he was able to view several ancient documents of heritage and was acknowledged by various masters.

Having received Rujing's seal of enlightenment, Dogen realized the great matter and received the teachings from generations of ancestors.

At age twenty-eight, in the third year of the Baoqing Era in China—the first year of the Antei Era in Japan [1227]—Dogen returned to Japan. He temporarily got settled at the Kennin Monastery of his late teacher [Myozen] and practiced for some time.

He visited near and far and examined thirteen properties his supporters offered as places for retreat, but none of them satisfied him. When he
was thirty-four years old, he moved to the side of the Gokuraku Temple in Fukakusa, Uji County, near Kyoto. His teaching style gradually
became known, and monks gathered and formed a community of over
fifty. After staying there for ten years, Dogen moved to Echizen Province.

He went deep into the mountains in the region of Shihi, where
he cleared away thorn bushes, built a thatched-roof hall, hauling dirt
and stones, and upheld the ancestral way. This is the present-day Eihei
Monastery.

Earlier, when Dogen resided at the Kosho Monastery, divine spirits received the precepts and joined every repentance ceremony. At the
Eihei Monastery, a dragon god came and asked to receive the eight pure
precepts and have them chanted in dedication to him daily. So, Dogen
wrote the eight pure precepts and chanted them to the dragon god every
day. This is still practiced at the Eihei Monastery without fail.

Now, Dogen raised true dharma for the first time in the seven hundred years since buddha dharma came to Japan. In the past, buddha
images were brought to Japan from the [Korean] kingdom of Shila in
the thirteenth year of Emperor Kimmei's reign [551], one thousand five
hundred years after the pari-nirvana of the Buddha. In the following
year, two scrolls of buddha images were enshrined. Then, the miraculous
power of buddha dharma began to reveal itself. Eleven years later, in the
third year of Emperor Yomei's reign, Prince Shotoku was born holding the Buddha's relics in his hand. After he lectured on the scriptures,
including the *Lotus Sutra* and *Shrimala Devi Sutra,* the teachings of names
and forms spread all over Japan.

At the request of former empress Tachibana, a successor of National
Teacher Qi'an came to Nara, but only a monument remains. As he has
no more dharma descendants, his teaching has not been transmitted in
Japan. Later, Kakua Katsudo became an authentic heir of Zen Master
Fuyan Qingyuan and brought his teaching from China to Japan, but his
teaching did not flourish. Also, Bishop Eisai succeeded Donglin Huai-
chang and intended to spread the teaching as the eighth-generation mas-
ter of the Huanglong lineage [of the Linji School]. He wrote a text called
"Raising Zen to Protect the Nation" and presented it to the emperor.
But he was opposed by Buddhists in Nara and Kyoto, and could not

keep his teaching purely Zen. Instead, he taught three types of ways: Exoteric, Esoteric, and Buddha Mind practices

Dogen mastered the Linji style of Zen as a direct dharma descendant of Eisai, and yet he also studied with Rujing, realized his life's quest, returned home, and widely spread the true dharma. This is indeed good fortune for the nation and brings happiness to the people. Just as Bodhidharma, the Twenty-eighth Indian Ancestor, entered China and became the First Chinese Ancestor, so Dogen became the Fifty-first Chinese Ancestor and the First Ancestor in Japan. Thus, Dogen is revered as the Founding Ancestor of our gate.

Although China was full of authentic teachers, if Dogen had not met a true master and penetrated his study, how could we have unfolded and clarified his treasury of the true dharma eye?

In this age of decline and in the last era of dharma, the buddha dharma has been degraded and true masters are rarely encountered in China. Although Wuji Liaopai and Ruyan Zheweng were the abbots of famed monasteries, there was something they had not reached. Dogen thought there was nobody who could teach him, and he wanted to return to Japan. Then, Rujing, who maintained the authentic vein of ancestors as the twelfth-generation heir of Dongshan, but had not revealed his mystery to others, intimately transmitted to Dogen the entire ancestral teaching, withholding nothing. This is unique and extraordinary.

Further, for me to be a [third-generation] dharma heir of Dogen is as fortunate as it was for Dogen to encounter the Third and Fourth Ancestors of China. The essential teaching has not fallen away. Although the teaching has journeyed through three countries, what has been transmitted has not changed at all. What you need to penetrate is no other than this: you need to clarify your mind.

Dogen first attained the way with Rujing's words of encouragement: "To practice Zen is to drop away body and mind." Thus, in practicing Zen, abandon your body and become free from your mind. Without being liberated from body and mind, what you practice is not the way.

You might think that the body is skin, flesh, bones, and marrow. If you examine closely, not even a particle of them belongs to you.

You see two types of mind. One is discriminatory mind. You might think this discernment is the mind. The other is serene and immovable consciousness, clear and vast. You might think this is the mind, without knowing that you are not free from the root of consciousness. Ancient teachers call it a clear, vast, and immovable place. However, you should not remain in this place or regard it as mind.

When you start to examine, you see three types of mind. Discriminating mind likes and dislikes. It judges right and wrong. Feeling knows hot and cold, pain and itch. Awareness does not divide right and wrong, nor does it feel pain or itch. It is like wood, stone, or a wall. This awareness experiences serenity, with no eyes and ears. When you speak with this awareness, you are like a wooden person or an iron person. Although you have eyes, you don't see. Although you have ears, you don't hear. In this awareness, speech and thought don't prevail. This awareness is deeper than feelings of hot and cold, pain and itching. Our discriminating mind [as opposed to awareness] operates right here. But do not regard this discriminating mind as the original mind.

Do not think that studying the way is limited to body and mind. To study the way is to drop away discrimination, feeling, and awareness. Beyond them there is something mysteriously radiant, timeless, and firm. Investigate thoroughly, and make sure to experience it. If you clarify this awareness, body and mind cannot take over and the selves of all things do not get hold of you. Thus, it is said that body and mind drop away.

If you look from this place, even if you look around with one thousand eyes, there is not a particle of skin, flesh, bones, and marrow, and there is nothing separated as discernment, feeling, or awareness. Then, how do you know hot and cold, or feel pain and itching? How do you judge right and wrong, or likes and dislikes? Thus, it is said that even if you look, there is not one thing.

When Dogen reached this precise point, he said, "I have dropped away body and mind." Rujing said in approval, "You have dropped away your body and mind. Your body and mind have been dropped away." Then he said, "Dropping away has dropped away."

Get to this field and be like a basket with no bottom or a bowl with a hole drilled in the center. What pours out does not cease, and what goes in does not fill. When you get there, you drop away the bottom of the barrel.

However, if you think that you are enlightened by even a hairbreadth or that you have attained something, it is not the way. It is merely the activity of a fooling spirit.

All of you, fully realize this point and practice thoroughly. Understand that you have a body that has no skin, flesh, bones, or marrow. Even if you try to become free from this body, it is not possible. Even if you try to throw away this body, it is not possible. Thus, this place is described as the place where all things are exhausted and there is emptiness that cannot be grasped.

If you fully clarify this, you will have no doubt about what is spoken by the old priest of the world as well as buddhas of the past, present, and future. How is this? Listen!

> Bright and clear, no inside and outside.
> Have you dropped away body and mind?

APPENDIX 3
Dogen's Editions of the Book

AFTER WRITING "LEAVING THE Household" in 1246 C.E., Dogen edited and restructured all available fascicles of the *Treasury of the True Dharma Eye*. With Ejo's help, he organized them into two groups—the older and newer versions, as Ejo's colophon to "Eight Awakenings of Great Beings" suggests. The former is the seventy-five-fascicle version and the latter the twelve-fascicle version. The "newer version," however, includes texts that were written in earlier times, such as "Power of the Robe." Dogen himself added the number of each fascicle to its beginning and ending titles, samples of which are seen in Dogen's extant handwritten manuscripts, such as the "Mountains and Waters Sutra" and "Document of Heritage." In the last seven years of his life, 1246–1253, Dogen seems to have spent much of his time in an effort to enhance the integrity of the writings contained in these two versions.

	SEVENTY-FIVE-FASCICLE VERSION		OUR VERSION
1	Genjō Kōan	Actualizing the Fundamental Point	3
2	Maka Hannya Haramitsu	Manifestation of Great Prajna	2
3	Busshō	Buddha Nature	23
4	Shinjin Gakudō	Body-and-Mind Study of the Way	38
5	Sokushin Zebutsu	The Mind Itself Is Buddha	6
6	Gyōbutsu Iigi	Awesome Presence of Active Buddhas	24
7	Ikka Myōju	One Bright Pearl	4
8	Shin Fukatoku	Ungraspable Mind	19

SEVENTY-FIVE-FASCICLE VERSION		OUR VERSION
9	Kobutsu Shin	Old Buddha Mind	45
10	Daigo	Great Enlightenment	27
11	Zazen Gi	Rules for Zazen	58
12	Zazen Shin	The Point of Zazen	28
13	Kai'in Zammai	Ocean Mudra Samadhi	32
14	Kūge	Flowers in the Sky	44
15	Kōmyō	Radiant Light	37
16	Gyōji, Jō	Continuous Practice, Part One	31a
16	Gyōji, Ge	Continuous Practice, Part Two	31b
17	Immo	Thusness	30
18	Kannon	Avalokiteshvara	34
19	Kokyō	Old Mirror	21
20	Uji	The Time Being	12
21	Juki	Confirmation	33
22	Zenki	Undivided Activity	42
23	Tsuki	The Moon	43
24	Gabyō	Painting of a Rice Cake	41
25	Keisei Sanshoku	Valley Sounds, Mountain Colors	10
26	Bukkōjō Ji	Going Beyond Buddha	29
27	Muchū Setsumu	Within a Dream Expressing the Dream	39
28	Raihai Tokuzui	Receiving the Marrow by Bowing	9
29	Sansuikyō	Mountains and Waters Sutra	15
30	Kankin	Reading a Sutra	22
31	Shoaku Makusa	Refrain from Unwholesome Action	11
32	Den'e	Transmitting the Robe	14
33	Dōtoku	Expressions	40
34	Bukkyō	The Buddhas' Teaching	25
35	Jinzū	Miracles	26
36	Arakan	Arhat	35
37	Shunjū	Spring and Autumn	66
38	Kattō	Twining Vines	47
39	Shisho	Document of Heritage	17
40	Hakujushi	Cypress Tree	36
41	Sangai Yuishin	Three Realms Are Inseparable from Mind	48
42	Sesshin Sesshō	Speaking of Mind, Speaking of Essence	49

	TWELVE-FASCICLE VERSION		OUR VERSION
1	Shukke Kudoku	Virtue of Home Leaving	87
2	Jukai	Receiving the Precepts	95
3	Kesa Kudoku	Power of the Robe	13
4	Hotsu Bodai Shin	Arousing the Aspiration for Enlightenment	70
5	Kuyō Shobutsu	Making Offerings to Buddhas	88
6	Kie Buppōsō	Taking Refuge in Buddha, Dharma, and Sangha	89
7	Shinjin Inga	Identifying with Cause and Effect	90
8	Sanji Gō	Karma in the Three Periods	85
9	Shime	Four Horses	86
10	Shizen Biku	Monk of the Fourth-Stage Meditation	91
11	Ippyakuhachi Hōmyō Mon	One Hundred Eight Gates of Realizing Dharma	96
12	Hachi Dainin Gaku	Eight Awakenings of Great Beings	84

APPENDIX 4
Lineage of Chinese Zen Ancestors

———

Bodhidharma ——┬—— Dazu Huike ——————— Jianzhi Sengcan ——— Dayi Daoxin ———
                   ├— Daoyu
                   ├— Daofu
                   └— Zongchi

The teacher–student relationship of Chinese Zen practitioners mentioned in the main text is shown here. For the Indian lineage, please see "Buddha Ancestors," p. 165.

< >	Repeated from the previous page
( )	Not mentioned in the main text
[ ]	Japanese
- - - -	Generations are skipped in this chart
....	Direct relationship is questionable
Bold	Founder/Cofounder

Generation

    I   2   3   4

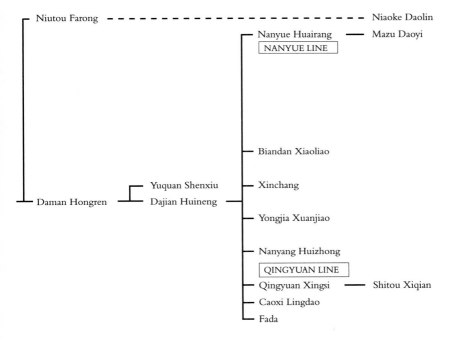

Niutou Farong - - - - - - - - - - - - - - - - - Niaoke Daolin

Nanyue Huairang — Mazu Daoyi
NANYUE LINE

Biandan Xiaoliao

Yuquan Shenxiu
Daman Hongren — Dajian Huineng — Xinchang

Yongjia Xuanjiao

Nanyang Huizhong

QINGYUAN LINE
Qingyuan Xingsi — Shitou Xiqian
Caoxi Lingdao
Fada

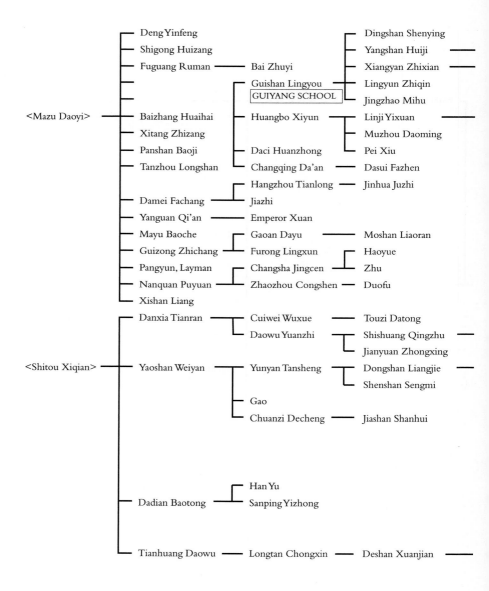

Deng Yinfeng		Dingshan Shenying
Shigong Huizang		Yangshan Huiji
Fuguang Ruman	Bai Zhuyi	Xiangyan Zhixian
	Guishan Lingyou	Lingyun Zhiqin
	GUIYANG SCHOOL	Jingzhao Mihu
Baizhang Huaihai	Huangbo Xiyun	Linji Yixuan
Xitang Zhizang		Muzhou Daoming
Panshan Baoji	Daci Huanzhong	Pei Xiu
Tanzhou Longshan	Changqing Da'an	Dasui Fazhen
	Hangzhou Tianlong	Jinhua Juzhi
Damei Fachang	Jiazhi	
Yanguan Qi'an	Emperor Xuan	
Mayu Baoche	Gaoan Dayu	Moshan Liaoran
Guizong Zhichang	Furong Lingxun	Haoyue
Pangyun, Layman	Changsha Jingcen	Zhu
Nanquan Puyuan	Zhaozhou Congshen	Duofu
Xishan Liang		

<Mazu Daoyi>

Danxia Tianran	Cuiwei Wuxue	Touzi Datong
	Daowu Yuanzhi	Shishuang Qingzhu
		Jianyuan Zhongxing
Yaoshan Weiyan	Yunyan Tansheng	Dongshan Liangjie
		Shenshan Sengmi
	Gao	
	Chuanzi Decheng	Jiashan Shanhui

<Shitou Xiqian>

Dadian Baotong	Han Yu
	Sanping Yizhong

Tianhuang Daowu	Longtan Chongxin	Deshan Xuanjian

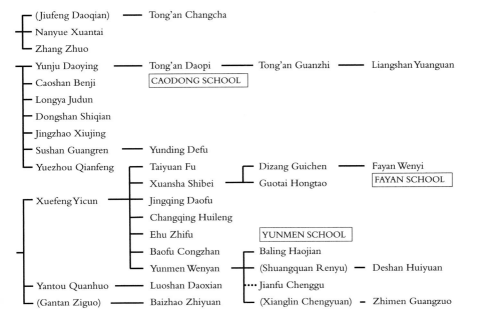

12   13   14   15

```
                                              ┌─ Langye Huijiao ──┬─ (Xingjiao Tan) ────
                                              │                   └─ Changshui Zixuan
<Shoushan Xingnian> ┬─ Fenyang Shanzhao ──────┼─ Ciming Chuyuan ──┬─ Huanglong Huinan ──
                    ├─ Shexian Guixing        │                   │  ┌─────────────────┐
                    │                          │                   │  │ HUANGLONG ORDER │
                    │                          │                   │  └─────────────────┘
                    ├─ (Guyin Yuncong) ── Li Fuma                  ├─ (Ciyan Kejing) ────
                    │                          │                   │
                    └─ (Yuanlian) ──────── Yang Wengong            └─ Yangqi Fanghui ────
                                                                      ┌──────────────┐
                                                                      │ YANGQI ORDER │
                                                                      └──────────────┘


<Liangshan Yuanguan> ┬─ Dayang Jingxuan ──── Touzi Yiqing ──── Furong Daokai ────
                     └─ Shimen Huiche


<Fayan Wenyi> ──── Baoen Xuanze


<Deshan Huiyuan> ──── (Kaixian Shanxian) ── Fuyin Liaoyuan
                                                               ┌─ (Fayun Faxiu) ────
<Zhimen Guangzuo> ── Xuedou Zhongxian ── (Tianyi Yihuai) ──────┤- - - - - - - - - -


         <15>              16                     17                    18
```

Ruizhu Shaoli

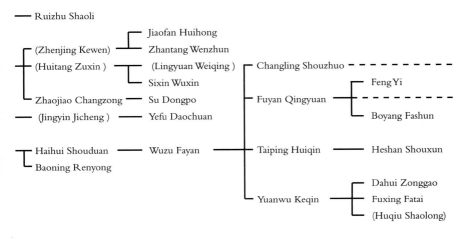

(Zhenjing Kewen)

(Huitang Zuxin)
    Jiaofan Huihong
    Zhantang Wenzhun
    (Lingyuan Weiqing) — Changling Shouzhuo - - - - - - - -
    Sixin Wuxin

Zhaojiao Changzong — Su Dongpo
    Fuyan Qingyuan
        Feng Yi - - - - - - - -
        Boyang Fashun

(Jingyin Jicheng) — Yefu Daochuan

Haihui Shouduan — Wuzu Fayan — Taiping Huiqin — Heshan Shouxun
Baoning Renyong

Yuanwu Keqin
    Dahui Zonggao
    Fuxing Fatai
    (Huqiu Shaolong)

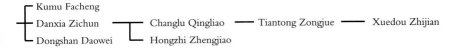

Kumu Facheng

Danxia Zichun — Changlu Qingliao — Tiantong Zongjue — Xuedou Zhijian

Dongshan Daowei — Hongzhi Zhengjiao

Fuguo Weibai
- - Leian Zhengshou

19   20   21   22

- - - - - - - - - [Myoan Eisai] ——— [Butsuju Myozen]

[RINZAI SCHOOL]

- - - - - - - - - Chuan

<Dahui Zonggao> ——— Zhuoan Deguang ——— Wuji Liaopai ——— Xuechuang Zongyue

<Huqiu Shaolong> ——— Ying'an Tanhua ——┬— (Wuzhun Shifan) ——— Huanxi Weiyi
                                        └— Dehui

<Xuedou Zhijian> ——— Tiantong Rujing ——— [Eihei Dogen]

[SOTO SCHOOL]

<22>   23   24   25

APPENDIX 5
Maps Related to the Text

KASHMĪRA

GANDHĀRA

PAÑJĀB

Himālaya

MATSYA

MATHURĀ

Kānyakubja

Gaṅgā

Shrāvastī   Kapilavastu
            Lumbinī
KAUSHALA

MALLA   Kushinagara

SHŪRASENA

Vaishālī

Vārāṇasī

KĀSHI   Gridhrakūṭa
        Rājagriha

Buddhagayā   ANGA
         Kukkutapada

MAGADHA

AVANTI

VANGA

Gayā

SUNĀPARANTA   ASHVAKA

KALINGA

ANDHRA

DRAVIDA

KERALAPUTRA

Bold   Kingdom
△   Mountain
◎   City
○   Town/Village

Ancient India

Chinese Zen Sites

Bold   Province
△   Mountain
◎   City
○   Region
■   Monastery

Jiang

Lu △

Yunju △   △ Fengqi

Letan ■   Jianfu △

△ Daxiong
(Baizhang)

△ Huanglong   △ Dong

Zhongling ○

Rui ○

△ Mo   Ehu △

△ Yangqi

Su △

Cao △

△ Yang   Shigong △

Qingyuan △

△ Mountain
◎ City
○ Region
■ Monastery

Jiangxi, China

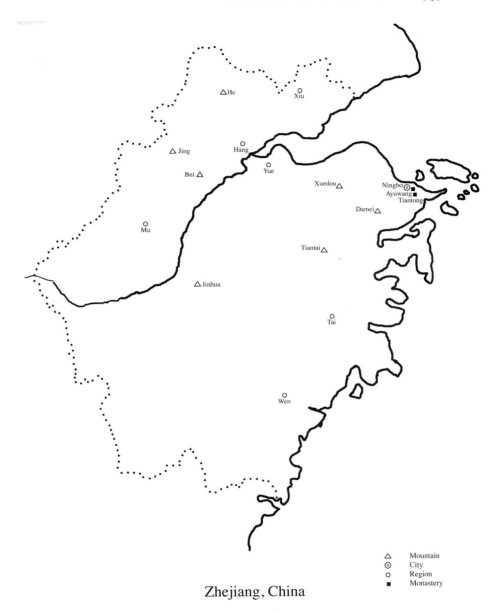

He
Xiu
Jing
Hang
Bei
Yue
Xuedou
Ningbo
Ayuwang
Tiantong
Damei
Mu
Tiantai
Jinhua
Tai
Wen

△   Mountain
◎   City
○   Region
■   Monastery

Zhejiang, China

HONSHŪ

■ Eihei

Kamakura ◉

Kyōtō ◉ △Hiei
■ Kōshō

Hakata ◉

SHIKOKU

KYŪSHŪ

△ Mountain
◉ City
■ Monastery

Japan, Sites Related to Dogen

APPENDIX 6
Eihei-ji Presumed Original Layout

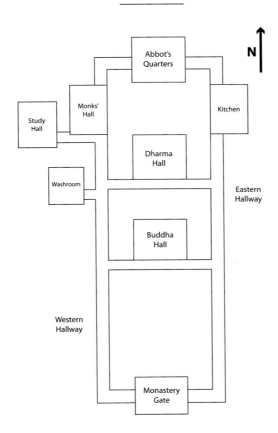

EIHEI-JI: PRESUMED ORIGINAL LAYOUT. *The ground plan of the Eihei Monastery at Dogen's time no longer exists. The original buildings were burned in 1473. The presumed layout presented here is based on the 1752 map of the reconstructed buildings. It has been modified in accordance with Dogen's accounts in "Practice Period," which imply the approximate location of other buildings: east side, south of the kitchen—infirmary; west side, south of the monks' hall (from north)—the offices of the ino and the head monk, monks' private quarters.*

APPENDIX 7
Monks' Hall

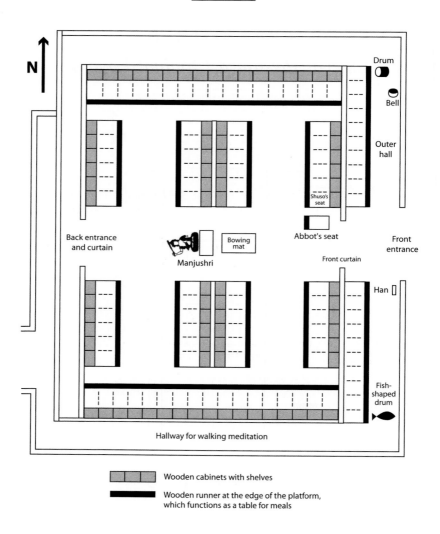

MONKS' HALL. *A presumed floor plan at the Daibutsu/Eihei Monastery during Dogen's time. Reconstructed from the current floor plan at the Eihei Monastery, drawn by Shohaku Okumura (Dogen's "Pure Standards for the Zen Community").*

APPENDIX 8
Time System

ACCORDING TO THE TRADITIONAL East Asian system, the daytime from sunrise to sunset is divided into six (five and two half) hours. The nighttime is similarly divided into six hours. Hence, the lengths of daytime hours and nighttime hours change daily, while the positions of noon and midnight do not change. These diagrams illustrate the cases of a day in the summer and a day in the winter.

There are five night periods, each of which is divided into five segments. According to Dogen's instructions for monastic practice, a night period is signaled by so many strikes of a drum, and a segment by so many strikes of a bell.

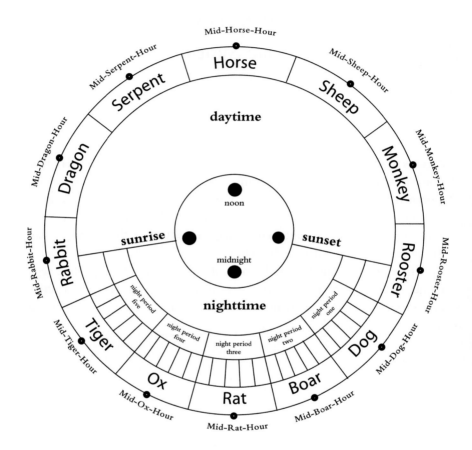

Summer

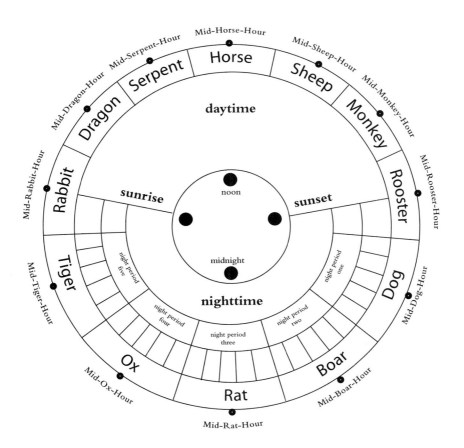

Winter

GLOSSARY

———

THIS GLOSSARY BRIEFLY explains terms, titles of writings, and mythological and historical names mentioned in the main text. Some entries only provide linguistic information. All entries are listed in alphabetical order. Readers should note the order of entries: a word followed by a comma appears prior to entries of the same word followed immediately by a phrase or another word without an interceding comma (i.e., *Buddha, Vipashyin* is followed by *buddha activity*).

We include traditional forms of ideographs. English and Chinese entry terms are followed by their Japanese equivalents in phonetic transliteration within brackets. Sanskrit spellings are a simplified form of transliteration with macrons indicating long vowels. Plurals of Sanskrit words are rendered by adding the English suffix -*s*. When the syllable –*su* is added to a Japanese noun, it turns that noun into a verb. Language abbreviations include J. (Japanese), C. (Chinese), and Skt. (Sanskrit). Years are from the common era (C.E.) unless specified otherwise.

Phrases are often reversed so they may be alphabetized by the more significant word. For example, *truths, four noble*. Titles, such as *Buddha, Emperor, King,* and *Minister,* precede names in order to facilitate searching and comparing. Personal names of laypersons are in alphabetical order by family name. Since Japanese names give the family name first, these names are not reversed for alphabetization. Dharma or Buddhist names are also not reversed.

An original term is often translated according to the context into a variety of English words in different parts of speech. For a typical English term, you will find the original term in the glossary, and in the same entry you will find other translations of the original term, which may appear to be unrelated to one another. This glossary thus reflects the richness of the meanings and ambiguity of the original terms. Also, some of the unusually stretched translations—such as "all are" being used as a compound noun, and "as"—are in the entries.

This glossary includes page references. While the page numbers of names are exhaustive, page numbers for terms are selective. Selective page entries are indicated by ellipses at the end of the last number.

abbot: 堂頭 [dōchō], literally, head of the hall. Also, 住持 [jūji] or 住持人 [jūjinin], literally, one who abides in and maintains. 席主 [sekishu], literally, head seat. 粥飯頭 [shukuhantō], literally, head of (one who takes) meals. The spiritual leader and administrative chief of a Zen monastery. (Later, in large Japanese monasteries, the latter function became independent from the abbotship.) 171, 173, 227, 729–39.

abbot, former: 西堂 [seidō], literally, west hall. Also, visiting abbot. 729, 737, 916.

abbot's quarters: 方丈 [hōjō], literally, ten feet square. Room or building in a Zen temple or monastery. Later it became a large structure in a Zen monastery. 223, 618, 733.

abbot's room, plaque signaling permission to enter the: 入室牌 [nisshitsu hai]. 528.

abbot's room, receive guidance in the: 入室 [nisshitsu]. Enter the inner chamber (of the master). 174.

Ābhāsvara Heaven: 光音天 [Kō'on Ten]. A heaven Shākyamuni Buddha was born into in one of his former lives. 822.

Abhidharma Mahāvibhāsha Shastra: 阿毘達磨大毘婆沙論 [Abidatsuma Daibibasha-ron]. An ancient Indian compilation of pre-Mahāyāna treatises. 658.

abide (in): 住持す [jūji-su]. 3, 289, 290, 539, 742.

abide in each moment: See *abide in one's condition.*

abide in one's condition: 住法位 [jū hōi], 住位 [jūi], literally, abiding in (dharma) position(s). Abide in each moment; at each moment. 269.

ability: 力量 [rikiryō]. Power; understanding. 449, 469, 605.

abode, ancestors': 祖域 [soiki]. 515.

abundance and lack: 豊儉 [hōken]. Affirmation and negation; dualism and monism. 29.

acacia powder: 皂莢 [sōkyō]. Used as soap. 68.

accept: 承當(す) [jōtō(-su)]. Realize; hit the mark; exact point. 8, 584, 599, 600.

accept what is as it is: 聽許 [chōko], literally, listen and allow. 458.

accept with trust: See *trust, accept with.* 424, 498.

accomplishment, gain: 得力 [tokuriki], literally, attain power. 173.

accord, imperceptibly: 冥す [meisu]. 7.

achieve, finally: 究竟の果上 [kukyō no kajō], literally, ultimate fruit. 102.

acquired enlightenment: See *enlightenment, acquired.*

action: 行取 [gyōshu], literally, action taken. 動容 [dōyō], literally, state of movement. 95, 288, 679, 702.

action(s), pure: 梵行 [bongyō]. 16.

action, beneficial: 利行 [rigyō]. One of a bodhisattva's four methods of guidance. 473, 475.

action, dark: 黒業 [kokugō]. Unwholesome action. 790.

action, deluded: 妄業 [mōgō]. 14.

action, do wholesome: 101, 102, 445. See also *Refrain from unwholesome actions.*

action, increasing power of: 業增上力 [gōzōjō riki]. 業增上 [gōzōjō]. Increasing effect of action. 235.

action, monk's: 僧業 [sōgō]. 682, 684.

action, past: 報地 [hōchi], literally, ground of reward (effect). 425.

action, refrain from unwholesome: 離過防非 [rika bōhi], literally, separating from mistakes and preventing violation (of the way). 96, 97, 101, 102, 445, 885. See also *Refrain from unwholesome actions.*

action, unwholesome: 惡業 [akugō]. 360, 779–82.

action, wholesome past: 宿善 [shukuzen]. 118, 134, 152, 362.

action(s) that nurture different types of effect(s): 相異熟業 [sōi juku gō]. For example, situation where a wholesome or unwholesome action creates a neutral effect. 824.

activities: 活計消息 [kakkei shōsoku], literally, activity, disappearing and resting. 155, 410, 666.

activities, daily: 茶飯 [sahan], literally, tea and rice. 26, 287, 343, 371.

activities, everyday: 去就 [kyoshū], literally, go away or get on. 204, 257, 262, 636.

activities, three: 三業 [sangō]. Body, speech, and thought.

activities of the (buddha) house: 家業 [kagō], literally, work of the house. 148.

activity: 云爲 [un'i]. Natural activities; literally, words and actions. 機關 [kikan], working; dynamic work; undivided activity. Also, 機 [ki]. Capacity; potential; person. 活計(す) [kakkei(-su)]. Everyday activity; vital activity; experience; activate; struggle; carry on; think superficially; theme. 消息 [shōsoku], fluctuation; fluctuating circumstances; how it is; personal correspondence, literally, disappearing and resting. 造次 [zōji], action; happening; making; work; behavior; thoughts; literally, making next. 運用 [un'yō], literally, carry and use. 56, 225, 589, 598, 696.

activity, celestial: 神境通 [shinkyōtsū], literally, mastering celestial state. 125.

activity, engage in: 造次動容 [zōji dōyō], literally, behavior and movement. 6.

activity, inessential: 雜用 [zōyō], literally, trivial function. 410.

activity, mental: 心行 [shingyō], literally, mind movement. 663, 726, 727, 877.

activity, mutual: 通消息 [tsū shōsoku], literally, to encompass disappearing and resting. 95.

activity, undivided: 全機 [zenki]. 全 [zen]: entire, whole, together. 機 [ki]: possibility, capacity, response, function, working, total experience. 404, 429, 450–52.

activity, unsurpassable: 上上の機 [jōjō no ki], literally, highest of high activity. 88.

actualization: 證驗 [shōken], literally, realization proof. 26.

actualization, complete: 舉力 [koriki], literally, total strength; complete effort. 盡力 [jinriki], literally, entire strength. 487.

actualization, utmost: 全舉 [zenko], literally, totally raise. 487.

actualize: 現成(す) [genjō(-su)], literally, appear and complete. Appear; let appear; realize; manifest; complete. 差排す [sahai-su], literally, exclude discrepancy. 證會す [shōe-su], literally, realize and understand. 6, 28, 100, 282, 500, 540.

actualize, fully: 圓成す [enjō-su]. 究竟す [kukyō-su], literally, actualize the ultimate realm. 107, 391.

actualize, immediately: 速證 [sokushō]. 97, 122, 132, 164, 454, 660.

actualize expression: 道現成 [dō genjō]. 276, 433, 560, 617.

actualize the fundamental point: 現成公案 [genjō kōan]. 100. See also *actualize; kōan.*

Actualizing the Fundamental Point: 現成公案 [Genjō Kōan]. Third fascicle of this book. xliv, xlv, xlvii, xlviii, liv, lv, lxv, lxxvi, xcii, xcvi, 29–33.

Adbhuta-dharma: 283, 285. See also *Divisions, Twelve.*

add a little to a lot: 多處添些子 [tasho ten shasu]. 299.

add eyelids on top of eyelids: 眼皮上更添一枚皮 [gampi jō kōten ichimai hi]. 228.

administrator: 377, 729, 732, 733, 737, 738. See also *officers, six.*

admonition: 制誡 [seikai]. 21, 774, 918.

admonition, golden: 誠諦ノ金言 [jōtai no kongon], literally, sincere and truthful golden words. 800.

adoration: 戀慕 [rembo]. 573.

advanced: 老大 [rōdai], literally, old and great. 251, 632.

affairs, secular: 世緣 [se'en], literally, world connection. 40.

affirm: 肯然 [kōnen]. 145, 440, 696.

afflictions, all: 諸漏 [shoro], literally, various leakings (desires). 404.

Āgama: Pali, Skt. 阿含 [Agon], 阿笈摩 [Agyūma]. Early Buddhist teaching, literally, that which comes (from the source). 133, 140, 143, 152, 241, 794.

Āgama Midiaka Sūtra: 中阿含經 [Chū Agon Kyō]. The Sanskrit version of one of the early sutras, Āgama. 133.

Āgama School(s): 阿笈摩教 [Agyūma Kyō]. Early Buddhist school(s), later called Hīnayāna by Mahāyāna practitioners. 179, 238.

Āgama Sūtra(s): 阿含經 [Agon Kyō]. Early Buddhist sūtra(s). Many of the Sanskrit versions were translated into Chinese. 134, 143, 152, 241, 785, 793, 831.

age of declining dharma: xxxiv. See also *three periods.*

Ajata: 阿逸多 [Aitta]. Official for King of Kaushala, ancient India. Later he was allowed to leave the household by the Buddha. 784.

Ājñātakaundinya: Skt. 阿若憍陳如 [Anyakyōjinnyo], 陳如尊者 [Jinnyo Sonja]. Kaundinya, 憍陳如 [Kyōjinnyo]. One who was enlightened first among the five earliest disciples of Shākyamuni Buddha. 566, 730, 841.

Akshobhya: 479. See also *Buddhas, Five.*

aligned: 52, 382, 383. See also *arise sequentially.*

alike, all worlds are: 界等 [kai tō]. 427.

all are: 234–36, 252, 644, 665. See also *buddha nature.*

all-inclusive: 等 [tō], literally, equal. 96, 98, 100.

all-inclusive study: 遍参 [henzan]. 1. Visiting and studying with masters in various places. 2. In Dōgen's usage, realizing the entire teaching of the buddha by penetrating a single dharma. 609, 614 . . .

All-Inclusive Study: 遍参 [Henzan]. Sixty-second fascicle of this book. lxxxi, 609–14.

all over China: 九州 [kushū], literally, nine lands (of China). 50, 533, 669, 913.

all things: 3, 28, 518–23, 598. See also *dharma.*

aloeswood: 沈香 [jinkō], literally, sinking incense. Fine incense made of hardwood that sinks in water. Related to daphne shrub. 54, 55, 61, 121, 231, 564, 825.

Alone above and below the heavens, I am the honored one: 天上天下唯我獨尊 [tenjō tenge yui ga dokuson]. Birth verse of Shākyamuni Buddha. According to legend, when he was born he took seven steps in each of the four directions, raised his right hand, and spoke these words. 584.

altar, stūpa: 塔龕 [tōgan]. 834, 835.

Amitābha. Buddha of Infinite Light. See *Buddhas, Five.*

Amitāyus. Buddha of Infinite Life, another name for Amitābha. See also *Buddhas, Five.*

Amoghasiddhi. See *Buddhas, Five.*

Āmrapāli Grove: Skt. 菴羅衞林 [Anrae Rin]. Grove of myrobalan (also translated as mango) fruit in the city of Vaishālī, central India. Known as a place where Shākyamuni Buddha often gave discourses. 573.

amulet of protection: 護身符子 [goshin fusu]. 514.

analyze: 度量 [takuryō], literally, measure degree. 183, 262, 266, 331, 632, 885.

Ānanda: 阿難陀 [Ananda], 阿難 [Anan]. A cousin of Shākyamuni Buddha. Became his disciple and attendant. Known as the foremost learner of the Buddha's teaching, who remembered and narrated the sūtras after the Buddha's death. Dharma heir of Mahākāshyapa, and regarded as the Second Ancestor in the Zen tradition. 19, 166; and Mahākāshyapa, 172, 509, 521; and Nanda, 482, 814, 816; and Rāhula, 570, 804; and Shākyamuni Buddha, 170, 593, 726, 727, 792, 799.

Anavatapta Lake: 阿耨達池 [Anokudatsu Chi], 阿那婆達池 [Anabadatsu Chi]. A lake at the center of the world in Buddhist cosmology.

Described in sūtras as always cool and refreshing without scorching heat. 61, 119, 607.

Anavatapta Lake, Dragon King of: 阿那婆達多龍王 [Anabadatsuta Ryū Ō]. 138, 606.

Anavatapta Lakes, four: 四阿耨達池 [shi Anokudatsu Chi]. Mystic lakes in the Northern Continent of Uttarakuru. 423.

ancestor: 祖 [so]. 祖師 [soshi], literally, ancestor [so] teacher. An earlier teacher of the dharma lineage, who inherits and transmits dharma. Also called buddha ancestor. Sometimes translated as "patriarch." 4, 112, 479, 889.

Ancestor: 祖師 [Soshi]. Sometimes indicates Bodhidharma. 478–80, 538, 586.

ancestor, go beyond: See *go beyond ancestor.*

ancestor sickness: 祖病 [sobyō]. Hindrance of attachment to becoming a buddha and ancestor. 464.

ancestors, five early Chinese: 東地五代 [tōchi go dai]. 586.

ancestors, surpassing the: 越祖 [osso]. 447. See also *go beyond ancestor.*

ancient teaching: 古教 [kokyō]. 228, 229, 328, 869, 912.

Aniruddha: 阿那律 [Anaritsu]. One of the ten major disciples of Shākyamuni Buddha. A grandson of King Simhahanu, he left the household life with other members of Shākya Clan. Scolded by the Buddha for dozing while listening to discourse, he made a vow not to sleep and lost his eyesight, but attained celestial eyes. 816.

annihilation: 斷滅 [dametsu], literally, cut off and destroy. Freedom from desire. 496, 854, 866.

antagonist nods and smiles, even an: 怨家笑點頭 [onke shō tentō]. 432.

apparent: 32, 86, 314, 333, 434. See also *Ranks, Five.*

appear spontaneously: 新成 [shinjō], literally, newly formed. 488.

appears like a spirit and disappears like a demon: 神出鬼没 [shinshutsu kibotsu], literally, spirits emerge and demons vanish. 406.

approve: 許可 [kyoka]. 343, 527, 576, 702, 911.

area, back: 後架 [goka]. Added area behind the monks' hall; sink behind the hall. Later meaning, toilet, 62.

arhat: Also arhant. Skt., literally, worthy or venerable one. 阿羅漢 [arakan], 羅漢 [rakan]. A follower of the Buddha's path who has attained nirvāna. Among the four fruits (achievements) of the way, arhatship was the ultimate goal in early (pre-Mahāyāna Buddhism). 26, 404–8, 799.

Arhat: 阿羅漢 [Arakan]. Thirty-fifth fascicle of this book. lxx, 404–8.

arhat fruit: 阿羅漢果 [arakan ka]. See *arhat.*

arise and fall, things that: 造次顛沛 [zōji tempai], literally, creating next and stumbling. Casual, temporary experience. 20.

arise at this moment: 今有 [kon'u], literally, currently existing. 488.

arise sequentially: 相待す [sōtai(-su)], literally, wait for each other. Aligned; to be separate; face one another. 380.

arm is cut off: 断臂 [dampi]. 427. See also *Dazu Huike.*

armband: 臂鞲 [hikō]. 578.

arms are long but the sleeves are short: 臂長衫袖短 [hi chō sanshū tan]. 410.

arms, extend one's: 垂手 [suishu]. Reach out to guide (others). 634.

Arousing the Aspiration for Enlightenment: 發菩提心 [Hotsu Bodai Shin]. Seventieth fascicle of this book. xlvi, lxxxiv, 655–63.

Arousing the Aspiration for the Unsurpassable: 發無上心 [Hotsu Mujō Shin]. Sixty-ninth fascicle of this book. lxxxiv, 646–54.

arrive: 到 [tō]. To have complete experience. 110.

arrive, not: 不到 [futō]. 未到 [mitō], literally, have not yet arrived. 1. To be not yet realized or experienced. 2. In Dōgen's usage, not seen as different from arriving or having already arrived. To be free from arriving. 258, 362, 423, 861.

arrowhead and the shaft crush each other: 箭鋒相拄 [sempō sōshu]. A situation of being completely blocked. 274.

art, excellent: 妙術 [myōjutsu]. Splendid method. 5, 7, 19.

as: 時節 [jisetsu], literally, when . . . For example, "*As* all things are buddha dharma, there are delusion, realization, practice, birth and death, buddhas and sentient beings" ("Actualizing the Fundamental Point"). The first word in other translations is usually *when.* But for Dōgen, "when . . ." can mean "all the time." 29.

as it is: 聻 [nii]. Just as it is without changing anything; just as they are. 如是 [nyoze]. Thusness. 190, 270, 651.

ascetic practices, twelve: 十二頭陀 [jūni zuda]. Skt., dhūta. Types of asceticism. See also fascicle 31a, "Continuous Practice, Part One." 334, 335.

ash, cold: 635. See also *ash, dead.*

ash, dead: 死灰 [shikai]. Meditation in complete stillness. 冷灰 [reikai], literally, cold ash. 357, 413, 428, 502, 541, 627.

Ashoka, (Great) King: 阿育王 [Aiku Ō], 阿育大王 [Aiku Daiō]. Third king of Maurya Empire in India, reigning ca. 270–230 B.C.E. After waging a brutal conquest, he realized the misery of war and stopped violent aggression. Ruled as a great supporter of Buddhism and sent missionaries to foreign lands. Shākyamuni Buddha's year of birth and parinirvāna are counted back from Ashoka's coronation dates according to the Pāli chronicles. Known through legendary biography of him, *King Ashoka Sūtra,* in premodern times. 474, 606, 607.

Ashvaghosha: 馬鳴 [Memyō]. Twelfth Ancestor of the Zen tradition in India. Born into a wealthy home in Vārānasī but became a monk. *The Awakening of Faith in the Mahāyāna,* a very important text in East Asian Buddhism, though apocryphal, is mythically attributed to him. 166, 238.

ask for a turning word: See *turning word, ask for a.*

aspiration: 志気 [shiiki], literally, spirit of determination. 73, 332, 372, 698.

aspiration for enlightenment: See *enlightenment, aspiration for.*

aspiration, initial: 初一念 [shoichinen]. 321.

aspiration, joyful: 欣求 [gonku]. 91.

asura: Skt. 阿修羅 [ashura]. Fierce and wrathful deity or fighting spirit. Three heads and eight arms, 三頭八臂 [sanzu happi]. See also *paths, six; guardians, eight types of.*

Assaji: 阿濕卑 [Ashippi]. 566. See also *monks, five.*

assembly: 會 [e]. Community of dharma practitioners. 衆 [shu], 一衆 [isshu]. Literally, gathering. 4, 18, 28, 733 . . .

assembly, harmonious: 和合衆 [wagōju], literally, harmonious and united gathering. 39, 209, 244, 528, 729.

assembly, good: 諸賢 [shoken], literally, wise ones. 121, 123.

ātman: See *soul.*

attached to, something to be: 愛處 [aisho], literally, place to love. 156.

attachment: 愛惜 [aijaku]. 29, 130, 382, 433, 808, 809, 901.

attain, directly: 即得(す) [sokutoku(-su)]. 598, 599.

attain buddhahood: 121, 122, 241, 392, 669. See also *buddha, become a.*

attain liberation: 度脱す [dodatsu-su]. 124, 301, 773, 774, 808.

attain the way: See *way, attain the.*

attendant, incense: 燒香侍者 [shōkō jisha]. Assists the officiant in ceremonial offering of incense. 177, 729, 918.

attendant monk: 侍者 [jisha]. A monk high in seniority who works for the abbot as a secretary and sometimes as an assistant teacher. 176, 355, 442, 599, 734.

authenticated: 正決を得 [shōketsu wo u]. 279.

authenticity: 嫡意 [tekii], literally, mind of (authentic) heir. 11, 70.

authenticity, determine the: 決擇す [ketsujaku-su]. 279.

autumn, god of: See *god of autumn.*

Avadāna: 283, 285. See also *Divisions, Twelve.*

Avalokiteshvara: Skt. 觀音 [Kannon], literally, observer of voices; 觀世音菩薩 [Kanzeon Bosatsu], bodhisattva who is observer of voices (cries of suffering) in the world; 觀自在菩薩, [Kanjizai Bosatsu], bodhisattva who sees freely; 大悲菩薩 [Daihi Bosatsu], bodhisattva of great compassion. Sometimes described as having one thousand hands and eyes. lxix, 37, 382, 435, 681, 732, 924; monastery name after, liii, lvi. Also, title of the Thirty-fourth fascicle of this book. lxix, 397–403.

Avatamsaka School: Skt. 華嚴宗 [Kegon Shū]. (Chinese) Huayan School. Established by Fazang, it flourished during the Tang Dynasty along with the Tiantai School before the Zen School became dominant in China. Provided a theoretical background for much of Zen thought. The teaching is based on the principle in the *Avatamsaka Sūtra* of all things interacting with one another without obstruction. As the Kegon School in Japan, it became one of the six schools of Buddhism in the Nara Period (710–794). 9.

Avatamsaka Sūtra: 華嚴經 [Kegon Kyō]. A major Mahāyāna sūtra, known for its magnificent cosmic view of all things interreflecting, centering on Vairochana Buddha. xxxiii, lxxvi, 49, 54, 63, 68, 487, 653, 703.

avatar: Skt. avatāra. 權者 [gonsha]. Manifestation of a Buddhist deity as a god in local religion. 81.

aversion: 棄嫌 [kiken]. Hatred or avoidance. Opposite of attachment. 29.

avīchi crimes, five types of: 五無間業 [go mugengō]. Killing one's father, killing one's mother, killing an arhat, causing a buddha body to bleed, and harming the community of dharma. Those who commit any of these crimes will fall into Avīchi Hell in the next lifetime. 783.

Avīchi Hell: Skt. Transliteration: 阿鼻 [Abi]. Translation: 無間 [Mugen], literally, no interval. The hell of unceasing suffering, the worst of all hells. 161, 783–86, 858.

avoid, no place to: 無迴避處 [muehisho]. 405.

awaken others: 覺他 [kakuta]. 107, 347, 657, 659.

awaken sentient beings, expound dharma to: 度生説法 [doshō seppō]. 337, 401.

awakening: 覺 [kaku], enlightenment. 度 [do], bringing (sentient beings) across the ocean of birth and death to the shore of enlightenment; saving (sentient beings). 44, 260, 448, 878.

awakening, have thorough: 豁然として大悟す [katsunen to shi te daigo-su]. 87.

awakening is seen within: 證中見證 [shōchū kenshō], literally, in realization seeing realization. 431.

awakening of the way: 悟道 [godō]. 5, 172.

awakening, ocean of: 佛海 [bukkai], literally, buddha sea. 85.

awesome manifestation: 威儀 [iigi]: Awesome presence; dignified form; noble conduct. Expression of buddha dharma through a home leaver's posture and behavior. 555.

Awesome Presence of Active Buddhas: 行佛威儀 [Gyōbutsu Iigi]. Twenty-fourth fascicle of this book. xlv, lxv, 260–75.

awesome virtue: 威徳 [itoku]. 668.

bad: 14, 356, 428, 506, 781, 825, 876 . . . See also *unwholesome.*

Baiyun Shouduan: See *Haihui Shouduan.*

Baizhang Huai Hai: 百丈懷海 [Hyakujō Ekai]. 749–814, China. Dharma heir of Mazu Daoyi, Nanyue Line. Many of Huaihai's students from all over built a monastery on Mount Daxiong in Hao Region (Jiangxi). Even when he was older he always participated in communal labor and is known for his words "A day of no work is a day of no eating." As compiler of the first known Zen monastic guidelines, he contributed greatly to the establishment of monastic practice suited to Chinese seekers. He produced outstanding students including Guishan Lingyou and Huangbo Xiyun. His posthumous name is Zen Master Dazhi, 大智禪師 [Daichi Zenji]. P. 930, Generation 9. 403, 543, 622; and wild fox, 705–14, 851–53; students of, 287, 322, 369, 370, 510; teacher of, 338; words of, 136, 252, 253, 295, 329, 408, 427, 575–58.

Bai Zhuyi: 白居易 [Haku Kyoi]. 772–846, China. Bo Letian (Bai Jui). One of the most reknowned poets of the Tang Dynasty. He lived in the suburb of the capital city Luoyang (Henan) accompanied by poetry, wine, and lute. He worked as a government official and called himself

Layman Xiangshan. Studied with Niaoke Daolin of the Niutou School. P. 930, Generation 10. 101.

Baizhao Zhiyuan: 白兆志圓 [Hakuchō Shien]. Ca. ninth–tenth century, China. Also called Qinfeng. Dharma heir of Gantan Ziguo, Qingyuan Line. Taught at Zhugan Monastery, Mount Bozhan, An Province (Hubei). Qingfeng was the first teacher of Baoen Xuanze. When Xuanze asked him, "What is the self of a Zen student?" Qingfeng replied, "The fire spirits are here to look for fire." Later, when he studied with Fayan, Xuanze understood Qingfeng's meaning. His posthumous name is Great Master Xianjiao 顯教大師 [Kenkyō Daishi]. P. 931. Generation 13. 18, 930.

balanced equilibrium: 平 [hei]. 435.

balancing scale: 秤子 [hyōsu]. 435.

Baling Haojian: 巴陵顥鑑 [Haryō Kōkan]. Ca. ninth–tenth century, China. Dharma heir of Yunmen Wenyan, Yunmen School. Taught at Xinkai Monastery, Baling, Yue Region (Hunan). Called Multiple Mouth Hao for his eloquence. P. 931, Generation 14. 930.

ball, red flesh: 赤肉團 [shaku nikudan]. Bare human body. 678.

ball (you are holding a): 一團子 [ichi dansu]. 218.

bamboo, tall: 脩竹 [shūchiku]. 447, 448.

bamboo node: 破節 [hasetsu]. Become free from dualistic thinking. 75, 380.

bamboo pipes, breaking: 竹筒 [chikutō]. 318.

bamboo pole, top of a one-hundred-foot: See *pole, top of a one-hundred-foot bamboo.*

bandits: 種賊 [shuzoku]. 613.

banner: 幖幟 [hyōshiki]. Identifying symbol raised in a temple or monastery. 19, 76, 118, 129, 131, 328.

banner, wind and the: 76. See also *wind and the banner.*

banner pole: 刹竿 [sekkan]. 19.

Banyan Grove: Skt., Nyagrodha Vana. 尼拘陀林 [Nikuda Rin]. Located in Kapilavastu. This is where the Buddha stayed when he visited his hometown. 847.

Baoche: See *Mayu Baoche.*

Baoen Xuanze: 報恩玄則 [Hō'on Gensoku]. Ca. ninth–tenth century, China. First studied with Qingfeng and then with Fayan Wenyi, Fayan School. He was enlightened as a student of Fayan Wenyi and became his dharma heir. Taught at Baoen Monastery, Jinling (Jiangsu). P. 932, Generation 16. 931.

Baofu Congzhan: 保福從展 [Hofuku Jūten]. d. 928. Dharma heir of Xuefeng Yicun, Qingyuan Line. He became a student of Xuefeng at fifteen and was ordained at eighteen. Founded Baofu Monastery, Zhang Region (Fujian), where he always had more than seven hundred students. When he became ill at the end of his life, he refused medicine, told his monks his time had come, crossed his legs, and passed away. P. 929, Generation 13. 930.

Baoji: See *Panshan Baoji.*

Baojing: See *Xiangshan Baojing.*

Baoning Renyong: 保寧仁勇 [Honei Nin'yū]. Ca. eleventh century, China. Dharma heir of Yanqi Fanghui, Linji School. As a young man he was dignified and intelligent. He traveled on pilgrimage for more than twenty years and studied with many Zen teachers. Eventually he settled and taught at Baoning Monastery, Jinling (Jiangsu). P. 933, Generation 19. 607.

Baotong: See *Dadian Baotong.*

barbarian, when a: 胡來胡現 [korai kogen]. 205, 209, 210, 212, 213.

barbarian, red-bearded: 赤鬚胡 [shakushu ko]. 273, 706, 714.

barbarians' invasion: 胡亂 [uron]. 676.

barbarians with red beards: 胡鬚赤 [koshu shaku]. 273.

barrel with no bottom: 脱底桶 [dattei tō]. 541.

Barrier Station Officer: 關令子 [Kanreishi]. Book by Xi, Lord Zhou, a follower of Laozi. 872.

barrier, arrive at a: 始到牢關 [shi tō rōkan], literally, begin to arrive at a prison gate. 408.

barrier, pass through the: See *pass through the barrier.*

barrier, penetrate the: 透關 [tōkan]. Become free from dualistic thinking. 108.

base, true: 正本 [shōhon]. 149.

basket, great: 大藏 [daizō]. Buddhist canon. 643.

beads: 珠數 [juzu], literally, jewels for counting. Most commonly, rosaries of 108 beads are used for subduing that many kinds of delusions. Used in some schools of Buddhism for counting mantras or prostrations. 41, 318.

become a buddha: See *buddha, become a.*

bee inside the sleeves, holding a stinging: そてのなかに蜂あり [sode no naka ni hachi ari]. To have sharp understanding within. 194.

before and after, born together: 前後生 [zengo shō]. 207.

before and after, independent of: 前後際断 [zengo sai dan], literally, past (zensai) and future (gosai) are cut off (from the present). Dōgen's view of time is not that it is a simplistic sequence of past, present, and future. He explains that every moment of the present is inclusive of the entire period of time. Thus, there is no past or future separate from the present moment. 30.

before form arose: 朕兆已前 [chinchō izen], 朕兆未萌 [chinchō mibō], 朕兆不打 [chinchō fuda], 未萌以前 [mibō izen]. Timeless beginning. 154, 155.

begging: 乞食 [kotsujiki], literally, begging food. Walking and asking for donation, an important practice of home leavers. 334, 798, 811, 816.

beginner: 初心 [shoshin], beginner(s), literally, beginner's mind. 初心始學 [shoshin shigaku], literally, beginner's mind; one who starts to study. 93, 101, 321, 890.

beginning, middle, and end: 初中後 [sho chū go]. 98, 102, 297, 383, 462, 522, 523 ...

beginning, middle, and end, independent from one another: 初中後際断 [sho chū go sai dan]. 523. See also *before and after, independent of.*

being: 有 [u]. 98, 104–111, 458, 591.

being, a temporal: 假有 [keu]. 789.

being, embryonic: 始有 [shiu]. 235.

being, great: 大人 [dainin]. Buddha, bodhisattva, or mature practitioner of dharma. 771, 775.

being, imaginary: 妄有 [mōu]. 235.

being, inconceivable: 妙有 [myōu]. 235.

being, insentient: 非情 [hijō], 無情 [mujō]. A being that does not have feelings, for example, a plant, stone, or cloud. 297, 531, 549–57.

beings, all: 群類 [gunrui], literally, various groups. 5, 6.

beings, many: 群品 [gumbon], literally, group of things. 364.

beings, myriad: 百頭 [hyakutō], literally, one hundred heads. 7.

beings, sentient: 衆生 [shujō], literally, assembly of (those with) life. Also, ordinary unenlightened beings, as opposed to buddhas. 有情 [ujō], those who have feelings. 生 [shō], living beings. 26, 29, 164, 234, 767.

beings, various: 群生 [gunjō], literally, group of (those with) life. 234.

beings with spirits: 含靈 [ganrei], literally, holding spirit. Living beings. 463, 464.

Beita Guangzuo: See *Zhimen Guangzuo.*

bend forward in a formal manner: 曲躬如法 [kyokukyū nyohō], literally, arching in accordance with dharma. 564.

bend self and push others without ceasing: 屈己推人也未休 [kutsuko suinin ya mikyū]. 628.

Bends, Nine Great: 九浙 [kyūsetsu]. The Huang River, which in its entirety, is said to have nine great curves. 882.

beneficence: うるほひ [uruoi], literally, moisturizing (by rain). 8, 361, 362, 734.

beneficence: 恩 [on]. Kindness (by someone senior or in a higher position); worldly obligation to return kindness. 8, 361, 362, 734.

beneficial action: See *action, beneficial.*

Benji: See *Caoshan Benji.*

beyond: 無 [mu], 不 [fu], 非 [hi], literally, no, not, non-. Also represents transcendental negation; such as "not one, not many." 237, 303, 574.

beyond, inquire: 向上の問著 [kōjō no monjaku], literally, question in going beyond. 326.

beyond buddha, go: See *go beyond buddha.*

beyond birth: 不生 [fushō], literally, no birth. 30, 462, 464, 885.

beyond consciousness, realm: 非想 [hisō]. 430.

beyond death: 不滅 [fumetsu], literally, no destruction. 30, 463, 885.

beyond deluded, person who is: 不迷者 [fumei sha], literally, one who is not deluded. 497.

beyond enlightenment: 6, 217, 296, 326, 346, 566, 616. See also *enlightenment.*

beyond grasping: 不得 [futoku]. 677.

beyond knowing: 不識 [fushiki], literally, not knowing. 189, 190, 235.

beyond knowledge: 不知 [fuchi]. 190, 226, 699.

beyond perception: 不覺 [fukaku]. 189, 190.

beyond purpose, merit: 無爲の功德 [mui no kudoku], literally, virtue of not doing. 648.

beyond thinking: See *thinking, beyond.*

beyond this buddha: 不是佛 [fuzebutsu]. 412.

beyond this mind: 不是心 [fuzeshin]. 412.

beyond this object: 不是物 [fuzemotsu]. 412.

beyond unconsciousness, realm: 非非想 [hi hisō]. 430.

beyond understanding: 不會 [fue]. 105, 157, 881, 882 . . .

beyond words and speech: 言語道斷 [gongo dōdan], literally, words that cut through expression. 727.

beyond-express a beyond-expression: 不道得を不道 [fudōtoku wo fudō]. 440.

beyondness: 一如 [ichinyo], literally, one thusness. A state beyond dualism. Going beyond.

Bhadrapāla: 跋陀婆羅 [Batsudabara]. Bodhisattva, regarded as a dharma descendant of Prajñātāra, Bodhidharma's teacher. 113.

Bhadrika: 拔提 [Batsudai], 婆提 [Badai]. One of the five monks who practiced with the Buddha after he left the palace. The second one (after Ājñātakaundinya) who was enlightened upon hearing the Buddha's first discourse. A grandson of King Simhahanu. 566, 816.

Bhaishajyarāja Bodhisattva: 藥王菩薩 [Yaku Ō Bosatsu], literally, Medicine King Bodhisattva. 393, 394, 598, 664.

Biandan Xiaoliao: 匾擔曉了 [Hentan Gyōryō]. Ca. seventh–eighth century, China. Student of Sixth Ancestor Huineng. Taught at Mount Biandan (Zizhiou). It is said he picked acorns for his meals. P. 929, Generation 7. 371, 928, 938.

billion worlds: 大千界 [daisen kai]. Billion worlds of phenomena, literally, great thousand realms. 大千法界 [daisen hokkai], literally, great thousand dharma worlds. Also called 三千世界 [sanzen sekai], literally, three thousand (but meaning, one thousand cubed) worlds. Sahā Worlds. 39, 113, 666, 862.

binding the self with no rope: 無繩自縛 [mujō jibaku]. Although there is in reality nothing to bind the mind with, one is bound up with one's own delusions. 424.

bird: Often represents freedom. 31, 311, 856, 882.

bird's path: 鳥道 [chōdō]. 351, 340.

birth, beyond: 不生 [fushō], 無生 [mushō], literally, unborn. 30, 395, 584, 699, 854.

birth, egg: 20, 264. See also *birth, four forms of.*

birth, four forms of: 四生 [shishō]. Ways in which living beings are born: womb birth, 胎生 [taishō]; egg birth, 卵生 [ranshō]; moisture birth, 濕生 [shisshō]; and transformation (magical) birth, 化生 [keshō]. Devas born as a result of karma are classified in the last category. 90.

birth, moisture: 20, 264. See also *birth, four forms of.*

birth, previous: 夙生 [shukushō]. 21.

birth, those who already have understanding at: 生知 [shōchi]. 296, 297.

birth, transformation: 20, 264. See also *birth, four forms of.*

birth, womb: 20, 264. See also *birth, four forms of.*

birth after birth: 生生 [shōshō]. 139, 251, 698, 775, 802.

birth and death: 生死 [shōji]. Life and death. Life is seen as a number of births and deaths at each moment of a person. That is why "life" is often called "birth" in Buddhism. 1. The ongoing cycle of birth, death, and rebirth, which in Buddhism is viewed as suffering. 2. Life viewed as a continuous occurrence of birth and death moment by moment. 3. Birth as a complete, independent experience in the present moment without reference to other moments; death in the same manner. xxiii, xlvi, lv, xcv, 13, 40, 264, 653, 659, 884.

birth-and-death: Birth and death seen as not separable. xxiii, xlvi, 425, 429, 464, 884.

Birth and Death: 生死 [Shōji]. Ninety-third fascicle of this book. xlvi, xcv, 884–85.

birth and death, coming and going of: 生死去来 [shōji korai]. 35, 426, 446, 520.

birth-and-death, detachment from: 出生死 [shutsu shōji]. Literally, leaving birth-and-death. 450.

birth-and-death, let go of: 捨生死 [sha shōji]. 450, 827.

birth and death, pass through: 流轉生死 [ruten shōji]. 659.

birth-and-death, penetration of: 入生死 [nisshōji]. Literally, entering birth-and-death. 450.

birth and death, sea of: A cycle of transmigration seen as continuous suffering. A way toward the shore of enlightenment. 380.

birth-and-death, vitalize: 度生死 [do shōji], literally, bringing birth-and-death (to the other shore of enlightenment.) 450.

birth and death at each moment: 剎那生滅 [setsuna shōmetsu]. 659.

bits and pieces: 片片 [hempen]. 片片條條 [hempen jōjō], literally, pieces and strips. Sometimes means moment-by-moment actualizing practice. 36, 107, 184, 481, 483 . . .

bitter gourd has a bitter root: 苦瓠連根苦 [kuka renkon ku]. 609.

black stone tortoise: See *tortoise, black stone.*

blind one leads a blind one: 一盲引一盲 [ichimō in ichimō]. Blind leads the blind: 一盲引衆盲 [ichimō in shumō]. 386.

blink: 44, 109, 111, 459, 493, 584. See also *treasury of the true dharma eye.*

bliss, dharma: See *dharma bliss.*

blood vein: 血脈 [kechimyaku]. Continuation of the dharma and precept lineage. 552, 628, 629.

blossom: 華 [hana]. 170, 503, 569, 837 . . .

blossom, spring: 春華 [shunka]. 643.

blossom, wondrous: 妙華 [myōke]. 158.

blows, thirty: 三十棒 [sanjūbō]. Hitting with a stick thirty times, as a means to awaken a student. 176, 295, 350, 433, 594 . . .

blue-eyed: 碧眼 [hekigan]. Bodhidharma. 611.

board rolls on a pearl: 盤走珠 [ban sō ju]. 521, 634.

boar hat, wild: 猪皮冠 [chohi kan]. 636.

boat, treasure: 寶乘 [hōjō]. 432.

bodhi: 436, 539, 655, 669. See also *enlightenment; way, attain the.*

bodhi tree: The tree under which the Buddha attained enlightenment. 436, 669.

bodhi tree, glorious one under the: 覺樹王 [kakuju'ō], literally, bodhi tree king. 6.

Bodhidharma: Skt. 菩提達磨 [Bodaidaruma]. Ca. fifth–sixth century, India and China. Reportedly a prince of 香至 Xiangxi Kingdom, of which the Sanskrit name is unknown. Regarded as the Twenty-eighth Indian Ancestor and the First Chinese Ancestor in the Zen tradition. Dharma heir of Prajñātāra, India. According to legend, he had a dialogue with Emperor Wu of the southern kingdom of Liang, but Wu did not understand him. Then he went to the northern kingdom of Wei and sat at Shaolin Temple, Shaoshi Peak, Mount Song (Henan). He taught Huike, Daoyu, Daofu, and the nun Zongchi. The dharma lineage of Huike, the Second Chinese Ancestor, has flourished. P. 928, Generation 1. lxxxi, 484, 494, 502, 505, 609–11, 707, 873; and Emperor Wu, 216, 355, and dharma descendants, 11, 12, 360; and Huike, 363–65, 416, 504, 565, 569, 578, 598, 721, 873; and students, lxii, 479, 480, 482, 483, 752; and Zen school, 505; at Mount Song, 92; dharma transmission of, 171, 177, 416, 478, 480, 483, 669, 721, 740, 890, 913; facing the wall, 4, 5, 11, 357, 372, 502, 669, 907; lineage of, xxviii, 4, 166, 478, 503, 537, 544, 569, 574, 585, 586, 740, 920; meaning of coming from India, xxx, xxxi, 109, 280, 411, 412, 442, 638, 641, 644; robe of, 113, 117, 126, 144, 574.

Bodhidharma School: 達磨宗 [Daruma Shū]. A Japanese Zen school founded by Dainichi Nōnin in the late twelfth century. 505.

Bodhiruchi: 菩提流支 [Bodairushi]. Ca. fifth–sixth century, China. An Indian monk who arrived in Luoyang (Henan) in 508 and engaged in translation of sūtras into Chinese. Purportedly one of the monks who accused and attempted to oppress Bodhidharma. 92, 356.

bodhisattva: Skt. Transliteration: 菩提薩埵 [bodaisatta]. Abbreviated as 菩薩 [bosatsu]. 1. In early Buddhism, a former life of the Buddha who endeavors to become a buddha in a future birth. 2. Later in Mahāyāna Buddhism, a seeker of enlightenment (bodhi) who dedicates his or her life to awakening others and practicing the pāramitās (realizations), and who is destined to become a buddha. The bodhisattva in this sense is regarded as an ideal practitioner of dharma. 130, 522, 656, 809.

Bodhisattva, Moonlight: 月光菩薩 [Gakkō Bosatsu]. Skt., Chandraprabha. Commonly known as attendant of Medicine Buddha. 865.

Bodhisattva, Prajñā Kūta: 智積菩薩 [Chishaku Bosatsu]. A speaker in the *Lotus Sūtra* who had dialogue with Mañjushrī. 666.

Bodhisattva, Pure Light: 光淨菩薩 [Kōjō Bosatsu]. Skt., Prabhāsvara. Identified as Confucius in the *Sūtra of Pure Dharma Conduct.* 865.

Bodhisattva, Vajragarbha: 金剛藏菩薩 [Kongōzō Bosatsu]. A deity who conveys Vairochana's universal enlightenment to sentient beings who raise the thought of enlightenment. Regarded as dharma heir of Vairochana, and as Second Ancestor of Esoteric Buddhism. 455.

bodhisattva mahāsattva: Skt. 菩薩摩訶薩 [botatsu makasatsu]. Bodhisattva who is a great being. 897.

bodhisattva of great compassion: 397–99. See also *Avalokiteshvara.*

bodhisattva precepts: 菩薩戒 [bosatsu kai]. Mahāyāna precepts. 129, 690, 767, 890, 891, 895, 913, 914.

Bodhisattva Realization Protector: 護明菩薩 [Gomyō Bosatsu]. A former life of the Buddha. 896, 897, 902.

Bodhisattva Vehicle: 282. See also *Vehicles, Three.*

bodhisattva who is a candidate to be a buddha: 補處(の)菩薩 [fusho (no) bosatsu], literally, bodhisattva at the place (status) of replacement. 補處等覺 [fusho tōgaku], literally, one whose enlightenment is equal (to buddha's) at the place of standing by. 一生補處(の)菩薩 [isshō fusho (no) bosatsu], literally, bodhisattva standing by only one lifetime (to be a buddha next lifetime). 199, 200, 661.

Bodhisattva's Four Methods of Guidance: 菩提薩埵四攝法 [Bodaisatta Shi Shōhō]. Forty-sixth fascicle of this book. lxxv, 473–77.

bodhisattvas, countless: 那由他衆 [nayuta shu], literally, niyuta people. Skt. niyuta: ten to the eleventh power. 897.

bodhisattvas of the last ten stages approaching buddha's enlightenment: 十地等覺 [jitchi tōgaku], literally, ten grounds and equal enlightenment. See also *bodhisattvas of the ten stages and three classes.* 310.

bodhisattvas of the ten stages and three classes: 十聖三賢 [jisshō sangen], literally, ten stages and three wise ones. According to Tiantai and Huayan doctrines, bodhisattvas are classified into the forty-two stages based on their maturity. The beginning thirty degrees are called three classes (ten stages of abiding, ten stages of practice, ten stages of dedication). The more advanced ten degrees are called the ten stages or the ten grounds. That makes forty stages. There are yet two more stages before becoming a buddha: stages of enlightenment equal to the Buddha's and of inconceivable enlightenment. 145, 178, 266, 289, 418.

bodies crushed and shattered: 粉碎其身 [funsai goshin]. 317.

bodies of all buddhas: 諸佛體 [sho buttai]. 245, 246, 247, 490, 807.

bodily presences, four: 四儀 [shigi]. The noble forms in everyday practice: walking, standing, sitting, and lying down. 11, 12.

body: 身 [shin]. 1. The material structure and substance of a human being. 2. Buddha body. 3. Truth itself. 422, 667, 887.

body, all over the: 遍身 [henshin]. 401, 402.

body, cast off the: 脱體 [dattai]. Drop away the body; become free from the body. 110.

body, drop: 身沒 [shimbotsu], literally, disappear body. 553.

body, drop away the: 棄身す [kishin-su]. To become free of attachment and preconceived ideas. 586.

body, entire: 渾身 [konshin]. 25, 481, 718, 719.

body, final: 最後身 [saigoshin]. The state of being free from rebirth. Body of an arhat; or in Mahāyāna, of a bodhisattva whose enlightenment is equal to Buddha's. 59, 406, 426, 809.

body, form of the: 身相 [shinsō]. 159.

body, forthright: 直身 [jiki shin]. 669.

body, hiding the: 蔵身 [zōshin]. Dropping away body and mind; complete identity of teacher and student. 269, 644, 682.

body, mind, and environs: 依正 [eshō]. 依報 [ehō], literally, dependence reward; plus 正報 [shōhō], literally, right reward. The "dependence reward" is something the body and mind depend upon; land and the world. The "right reward" means body and mind. 58, 120, 162, 235, 419, 451, 455.

body, place of turning the: 轉身處 [tenshin sho]. 722.

body, practice with the: 體究(す) [taikyū(-su)]. Embody or thoroughly take hold of what is essential. 297.

body, see through with the: 體達(す) [taitatsu(-su)]. Realize through bodily experience.

body, short dharma: 短法身 [tan hosshin]. Dharma body is truth itself, which is manifested in the unique characteristics (such as shortness or tallness) of each person. 243, 628, 674.

body, tall dharma: 長法身 [chō hosshin]. Dharma body is truth itself, which is manifested in the unique characteristics (such as shortness or tallness) of each person. 243, 628, 674.

body, three parts of female: Anus, vagina, and mouth. Organs used for sexual activities according to the *Precept Scripture.* 79.

body, true: 實體 [jittai]. True form. 眞實體 [shinjitsu tai]. 37, 481, 520, 879 . . .

body, true dharma: 眞法身 [shin hosshin]. 99, 453.

body, true human: 眞實人體 [shinjitsu nintai]. 103, 465, 488, 521. See also *buddha body.*

body, turn: 轉身 [tenshin]. Become free of stagnation; have a breakthrough. 585.

body, twirl one's: 翻身 [honshin]. 640.

body, two parts of a male: Anus and penis. Organs used for sexual activities according to the *Precept Scripture.* 79.

body, unconditioned: 清淨身 [shōjō shin], literally, pure body. 86–88.

body and capacity, same: 同身同機 [dōshin dōki]. 652.

body and flap the brain, freely turn the: See *turn the body and flap the brain, freely.*

body and mind: 正報 [shōhō], literally, right reward. Pursued and fortunate effect from past action, meaning body and mind. 40, 42, 48, 58 . . .

body and mind, drop away: 身心脱落す [shinjin datsuraku-su]. To become fully liberated. 5, 6, 376, 540, 920.

body and mind, fully engage: 身心を擧ぐ [shinjin wo agu]. Literally, upholding body and mind. 30.

body and mind are not separate: 身心一如 [shinjin ichinyo], literally, body and mind one thusness. 15.

Body-and-Mind Study of the Way: 身心學道 [Shinjin Gakudō]. Thirty-eighth fascicle of this book. lxxi, lxxvi, 422–30.

body born from the mother: 孃生 [jōshō], literally, young woman birth. 673.

body dimension: 身量 [shinryō]. 642.

body first and mind last: 身先心後 [shinsen shingo]. 553.

body is straight: 身直 [shinjiki]. 669.

body-mind: 身心 [shinjin]. Body and mind experienced as inseparable. 49–51, 379, 584 . . .

body reaches, wherever the: 通身 [tsūshin]. 277, 402, 465.

bones and marrow: 骨髓 [kotsuzui]. 158, 347, 697.

born together: 同生 [dōshō]. 205–7, 414.

bound: 拘牽(せらる) [kōken(-se raru)]. 202, 222, 723.

boundary: 邊表 [hempyō], literally, superficial (views). 邊量 [henryō], literally, limited amount. 邊際 [henzai], environ. 際限 [saigen], literally, limited bound. 6, 32, 296, 554.

boundlessness: 空 [kū], literally, sky, emptiness. 25, 217, 719.

bow: 禮拜 [raihai]. Prostrating oneself. 137, 230, 564–68.

bow, hitting: 頓首拜 [tonshu hai]. 565.

bow, spread the bowing cloth and: 展坐具禮拜す [ten zagu raihai-su]. 565, 732, 734–37.

bow, standing: 問訊 [monjin], literally, inquiring or greeting. Bowing with hands together in front of the chest while standing. 曲躬す [kyokkyū-su]. literally, bend the body. 230, 231, 732, 736, 764.

bowed to, one who is: 所禮 [shorei]. 61.

bowing, utmost: 最上禮 [saijōrei]. Bowing by hitting the floor with one's head. 565.

bowing cloth: 坐具 [zagu]. A rectangular patched cloth spread fully or half folded on the floor or bowing mat by an ordained person for full bowings (prostrations). It is folded into a strap and carried over the left forearm under the robe when not spread during a ceremony. 528, 564, 565, 732, 734, 735–37.

bowing cloth, fully spread the: 大展 [daiten], literally, great spread. The most formal way to make prostrations.

bowing cloth twice and make three formal bows, spread the: See *spread the bowing cloth twice and make three bows.*

bowing down with the head touching the floor: 稽首拜 [keishu hai]. 565.

bowing mat: 拜席 [haishiki/hasshiki]. A straw mat placed on the floor in front of the altar, on which the officiant of a ceremony or service makes full bows to the enshrined image. 733, 734.

bowl, monk's: 鉢盂 [hou/hatsuu]. 623.

bowl, same: 一盂 [ichi u], literally, one bowl. 334.

bowls and utensils, eating: 鉢具 [hogu]. Used for meals and begging practice. 766.

bows, indefinite: 不住拜 [fujū hai]. 565.

bows, make three formal: 三禮 [sanrai]. 565, 734, 735.

bows, nine formal: 九拜 [kyūhai]. Most formal bow on the floor over the spread bowing cloth. 735, 737.

bows, one who: 能禮 [nōrei]. 61.

bows, semiformal: 觸禮 [sokurei]. Placing the bowing cloth cross-folded on the floor and making a bow by touching the mat with forehead. 565, 734, 735, 736.

bows, spread the bowing cloth twice and make three: See *spread the bowing cloth twice and make three bows.*

Boxiang: See *Wang Boxiang.*

Brahmā Heaven: 梵天 [Bon Ten]. 梵世 [Bonse], literally, Brahmā World. Heaven where Brahmā resides. Heaven of purity. 822.

Brahmā, King: See *King Brahmā.* 131, 822.

Brahmā World: 822. See also *Brahmā Heaven.*

Brāhman: Skt. Transliteration: 婆羅門 [baramon]. A priest of the priest caste in Brāhmanism or Hinduism. 梵志 [bonshi], literally, seeker of Brahman, the Absolute. 11, 356, 802, 831.

Brāhman, a drunk: 醉婆羅門 [sui baramon]. 800.

Brāhman, Dīrghanakha: 長爪梵志 [Chōso Bonshi], literally, Long Nail Brāhman. Uncle of Shāriputra. As a Brāhman he made a vow not to cut his nails until he attained the way. He became one of the ten great disciples of the Buddha. Named Kushinagara, he was known as the best debater. 875.

Brāhmanism: 婆羅門教 [Baramon Kyō]. Religious practice related to Vedas, prevalent in ancient India. 867.

Brāhmanist Texts, Eighteen Large: 十八大經 [jūhachi daikyō]. Four Vedic scriptures, six supplementary scriptures, and eight commentaries. 867.

brain, freely turn the body and flap the: See *turn the body and flap the brain, freely.*

branches and vines: 蔓枝 [manshi]. 596.

breaking an eggshell by pecking from the inside and outside at once: 啐啄の迅機 [sottaku no jinki], literally, swift timing of spitting and pecking. 571.

break away: 出離 [shutsuri]. 89.

break open: 329, 642. See also *illuminate and break open.*

breathing in: 入息 [nissoku]. 190, 289.

breathing out: 出息 [shussoku]. 190, 290.

breezes, freely circulates like the flowing: 轉風流 [ten fūryū]. 432.

brick, polishing a: 磨塼 [masen]. Just as polishing a brick does not make it into a mirror, sitting zazen with a desire to become a buddha will not make a person a buddha. Based on a story about Nanyue Huairang and Mazu Daoyi. 428.

brightness comes meet it with brightness, when: 明頭來明頭打 [meitō rai meitō da]. Puhua's words. Brightness represents duality. 208.

brilliance and obscure traces, hide: 韜光晦跡 [tōkō kaiseki]. 40.

bring: 將來す [shōrai-su], literally, pull and come. 244, 299, 681, 832.

bring across: 662. See also *awakening.*

bring forth: 拈來 [nenrai]. Take up; touch; quote. 97, 631, 698.

bring here, take away: 擔來擔去 [tanrai tanko].

brings forth: 推出す [suishutsu-su], literally, push out. 391, 399.

brush, take up the: 援筆 [empitsu]. 173.

Budai: Gan Budai 慤布袋 [Kan Hotei], literally, Heavy Cloth Bag. d. 916, China. A fat-bellied person from Ming Region (Zhejiang). Wandering about and begging with all his possessions in a cloth bag, he later became a symbol of freedom and was regarded as an incarnation of Maitreya Bodhisattva. 856.

buddha: Skt., literally, awakened one. 佛 [butsu; hotoke]. One who has attained unsurpassable, complete enlightenment and teaches others. One of the three treasures. 4, 43–47, 537–47, 884, 885.

Buddha: 1. See *Buddha, Shākyamuni.* 2. An enlightened being described in scriptures. 3. Mythological or deified personification of enlightenment, i.e., Vairochana Buddha. 8, 26, 596–608, 801–7.

Buddha, accept: 佛信受 [butsu shinju], literally, trust and accept Buddha. 169.

buddhas, active: 行佛 [gyōbutsu]. 260–64, 266–71, 275, 470, 574. See also *Awesome Presence of Active Buddha.*

buddha, become a: 成佛 [jōbutsu]. 作佛 [sabutsu], literally, create a buddha. Attain buddhahood. 241, 304–6, 387, 652.

Buddha, bondage to: 佛縛 [butsubaku]. 261.

Buddha, Dīpankara: 定光佛 [Jōkō Butsu], literally, Solid Light Buddha. 然燈如來 [Nentō Nyorai], literally, Lamp-Burning Tathāgata. A mystic Buddha said to be the first one to give a prediction of enlightenment to a bodhisattva, one of the former lives of Shākyamuni Buddha. 824, 825.

buddha, earlier: 前佛 [zembutsu]. 92, 93, 95, 143, 549.

Buddha, eighty appearances of the: 八十種好 [hachijisshu kō]. 293.

buddha, enter the realm of: 佛に入る [butsu ni iru]. 304.

buddha, everyone's mind becomes: 是心作佛 [zeshin sabutsu]. 9.

buddha, go beyond: See *go beyond buddha.*

Buddha, Kanakamuni: 拘那含牟尼佛 [Kunagon'muni Butsu]. 金色仙 [Konjiki Sen], literally, Golden Sage. Fifth of the six mythological Buddhas among the Seven Original Buddhas. 178.

Buddha, Kāshyapa: 迦葉佛 [Kashō Butsu], 迦葉波佛 [Kashōha Butsu]. 飲光 [Inkō], literally, Drinking Light. Sixth and last of the mythological Buddhas among the Seven Original Buddhas. Regarded as the dharma teacher of Shākyamuni, the seventh Original Buddha. 115, 128, 165–67, 170, 171, 178, 242, 266, 705–7, 784, 799, 801, 831, 832–34, 851.

buddha, kill: 殺佛 [satsubutsu]. Go beyond buddha. 308.

Buddha, Krakucchanda: 拘留孫佛 [Kuruson Butsu]. 金仙人 [Kin Sennin], literally, Golden Wizard. Fourth of the six mythological Buddhas among the Seven Original Buddhas. 178. 128, 242; Lineage of, 170, 171, 178, 179, 266; Buddha(s) named, 831, 832; time of, 115, 705–7, 709, 784, 799, 801, 851; tower for, 833, 834.

Buddha, Mahā Abhijñā Jñānā Abhibhū: 大通智勝佛 [Daitsū Chishō Butsu]. Buddha described in the *Lotus Sūtra.* 803.

Buddha, Moon-Face: 月面佛 [Gachimen Butsu]. 455, 596. See also *Buddha, Sun-Face.*

buddha, not-: 非佛 [hibutsu]. Beyond buddha. 308, 317, 318, 592.

buddha, old: 古佛 [kobutsu]. Ancient buddha. 37, 74 . . .

Buddha, Ratnakosha: 寶藏佛 [Hōzō Butsu]. One of the Buddhas to whom Shākyamuni Buddha made offerings in his former lifetime. 121–23.

buddha, realized: 證佛 [shōbutsu]. 12, 94, 749, 876.

buddha, reward-body: See *buddha body.*

Buddha, Ruchi: 樓至佛 [Rōshi Butsu]. Last Buddha of the present eon. 844.

Buddha, Shākyamuni: Ca. 566–ca. 486 B.C.E., according to Western and Indian scholarship. Many contemporary Japanese scholars support the dates ca. 448–ca. 368 B.C.E., based on the northern textual tradition. Dōgen's understanding of the Buddha's dates is 908–828 B.C.E. (Fascicle 23, "Buddha Nature," gives a clue to the year of the Buddha's attaining the way, which is calculated to be 878 B.C.E. Fascicle 31a, "Continuous Practice, Part One," says the Buddha was thirty years old then and entered pari-nirvāna fifty years later.)

The founding teacher of Buddhism who taught in the plain along the Ganges, central to eastern part of northern India. Dōgen refers to him in a number of ways: Skt. Shākyamuni, 釋迦牟尼 [Shakamuni], literally, practitioner of silence from Shākya Clan. Family name, Gautama, 瞿曇 [Kudon]. Royal title, Prince Siddhārtha, 悉達太子 [Shidda Taishi]. Also in Buddhism, Shākyamuni Tathāgata, 釋迦牟尼如來 [Shakamuni Nyorai]; Venerable Shākya, 釋尊 [Shakuson]. Particularly in Zen, Great Master Shākya, 釋迦大師 [Shaka Daishi]; Old Man Shākya, 釋迦老子 [Shaka Rōshi]; 釋迦老漢 [Shaka Rōkan]; Old Gautama, 老瞿曇 [Rō Kudon]. His honorary titles include: the Buddha, Tathāgata, and the World-Honored One.

Born in Kapilavastu (present-day central southern Nepal) as son of King Shuddhodana and Queen Māyā. Married Princess Yashodharā and had a son named Rāhula. Left the palace to seek the way, visited Brāhman teachers, sat alone and attained the way in Buddhagaya (currently called Bodhgaya), in the western part of the kingdom of Magadha. As the Buddha, he gave his first teaching (turning of the dharma wheel) at Deer Park in Vārānasī, the central city of Brāhmanism, located in the northwest of Buddhagaya. For almost five decades he taught monks and nuns as well as laypeople of all kinds. His summer retreats took place at Jeta Grove, Shrāvastī, in the kingdom of Kaushala. Vulture Peak in Magadha is often described in scriptures as the place where he gave dharma discourses. He entered pari-nirvāna in Kushinagara in the northwest of Magadha at age eighty.

After the Buddha's death, his teachings were recalled and collected by his disciples and dharma descendants; centuries later these were recorded as scriptures. Buddhist scriptures developed in response to the needs of practitioners in each era. However, until modern scholarship started to develop in the nineteenth century, it was common for Buddhists, including Dōgen, to believe that all Buddhist sūtras were direct discourses of the Buddha himself.

In the Mahāyāna Buddhist tradition, the Buddha's becoming enlightened simultaneously with the awakening of all sentient beings is emphasized. His enlightenment is seen as the result of his search in former lifetimes as a variety of beings called bodhisattvas. It is also seen as an inheritance of the universal enlightenment transmitted by his earlier buddhas; Shākyamuni is regarded as the last of the Seven Original Buddhas, six of whom are mythological. Inspired by his teaching, different types of deified Buddhas and their iconographic images, along with other deities, evolved in the Buddhist pantheon. According to the Zen tradition, he transmitted dharma to Mahākāshyapa, the First Ancestor. xxvi, 89, 188, 515, 536, 743, 830; and Avalokiteshvara, 402; and bodhisattvas, 80, 181, 896, 902; and buddhas, 142, 180, 181, 186, 188, 287, 437, 532, 820, 824–26; and Kāshyapa Buddha, 128, 171, 178, 179, 242, 266, 501; and Mahākāshyapa, lxxxiii, 4, 11, 12, 115, 171, 277, 279, 334, 335, 389, 478, 503, 504, 536, 569–71, 574, 642, 656, 696, 743, 769, 916; and sutras, lxxxv, 842; attaining the way, xxiv, 19, 81, 170; bowing to, 571, 572; children of, 732; confirmation by, 390, 391; descendants of, 112, 136, 172, 304, 324, 356, 359, 409, 416, 469, 560, 612, 752, 779, 828, 864; discourses of, 28, 73, 234, 393, 405, 406, 435, 453, 455, 461, 487, 488, 490, 518, 522, 549, 591, 599–601, 603, 604, 646, 651, 665, 668, 674, 677, 678, 682, 686, 690, 769, 771, 809, 844; dharma of, 123, 125, 190, 200, 815, 827; dharma, transmitting, 4, 7,

545, 574, 577; dharma blossoms of, lxiii; enlightenment of, 650, 917; Gautama, 527, 585, 593, 643; image of, 232; lineage of, xcvii, 165, 501, 570; offering to, 568; on Vulture Peak, 8, 598, 602, 664; one with, 47, 775; pagodas of, 573; practice of, 163, 334, 373, 528, 666, 669, 685, 907; rains retreats, liv; robe of, 114, 115, 121, 123, 135, 139, 141–43, 153, 567; seeing, lxxxi, 120, 292, 605–7, 799, 801, 846; Siddhārtha, 809; silence of, 689; Small, 203, 751; spread of buddha-dharma, 57; students of, 12, 26, 124, 489, 588, 817, 916; three treasures of, 841; time of, xxxiv, 17, 20, 69, 138, 468, 706, 707, 709, 784, 785, 804; treasury of the true dharma eye of, 115, 140, 279, 389, 478, 503, 504, 569, 574, 639, 642; vow of, 806; words of, xcii, 8, 18, 180, 251, 274, 293, 394, 436, 507, 520, 523, 561, 592, 688, 774.

Buddha, Sun-Face: 日面佛 [Nichimen Butsu]. According to the *Buddhas' Names Sūtra,* Sun-Face Buddha lives for 1,800 years, while Moon-Face Buddha lives for one day and night. These Buddhas represent immeasurable time and short moments. 455, 596.

buddha, true: 眞佛 [shimbutsu]. 17, 96, 294, 362, 684.

Buddha, Universal Protection: 普守如來 [Fushu Nyorai]. One of the Buddhas to whom Shākyamuni Buddha made offerings in his former lifetime.

Buddha, Vairochana: Skt. 毘盧遮那佛 [Birushana Butsu], 毘盧 [Biru]. Vairochana Tathāgata, 毘盧遮那如來 [Birushana Nyorai]. 盧舍那佛 [Rushana Butsu]. The dharma body buddha, manifestation of reality of the universe; literally, illumination buddha. Called Mahā Vairochana Buddha in Esoteric Buddhism. See also *Buddhas, Five; dharma body.* 186, 433, 732.

buddha, vicinity of: 佛邊 [buppen]. Realm of buddhas. 261.

Buddha, Vipashyin: Transliteration: 毘婆尸佛 [Bibashi Butsu]. Translations: 勝觀 [Shōkan], literally, Excellent Observation; 広説 [Kōsetsu], literally, Boundless Discourse. First of the six mythological Buddhas among the Seven Original Buddhas. (Shākyamuni is the seventh Buddha.) 503.

buddha activity/activities: 佛事 [butsuji]. 6, 122, 600.

buddha ancestor: An earlier awakened teacher of the dharma lineage. 7, 27, 113, 169, 724, 890.

buddha ancestor, forthright: 直佛祖 [jiki busso]. 669.

buddha ancestor, grasp the: 拈得佛祖 [nentoku busso]. 611.

buddha ancestor, mature: 參飽の佛祖 [sambō no busso]. 298.

Buddha Ancestors: 佛祖 [Busso]. Sixteenth fascicle of this book. lxi, 165–67.

buddha ancestors, activity of: 佛祖儀 [busso gi]. 296, 304, 383, 433, 598, 626, 693.

buddha ancestors, powers as: 佛祖力 [busso riki]. 622.

buddha ancestors, realm of: 有佛祖處 [ubusso sho]. 431, 534, 699.

buddha ancestors, realm of going beyond: 無佛祖處 [mubusso sho]. literally, place of no buddha ancestors. 534.

buddha ancestors, turning of: [ten busso] 轉佛祖. 598.

buddha ancestors' perception: 佛量祖量 [butsuryō soryō], literally buddha thinking, ancestor thinking. 247.

buddha and a buddha, only between a: 唯佛與佛 [yuibutsu yobutsu]. A buddha together with a buddha. 491.

buddha body: Skt., buddha kāya. 佛身 [busshin]. Three bodies or aspects of buddha: (1) Dharma kāya, 法身 [hosshin]—dharma body, which is the absolute aspect of truth, equal to the whole universe of phenomena. (2) Sambhoga kāya, 報身 [hōjin]—reward, enjoyment, bliss, or purified body, associated with the fruit of practice. (3) Nirmāna kāya, 応身 [ōjin]—manifestation body that appears in the world and acts for the benefit of beings. The buddha body that has these three aspects is also known as the true human body. 6, 118, 546, 892–94.

buddha cause: 佛因 [butsuin]. 102.

buddha dharma: Skt. 佛法 [buppō]. Truth taught by a buddha; reality experienced by an awakened one. 4, 29, 199, 501, 707.

buddha dharma, authentic: 眞實の佛法 [shinjitsu no buppō]. 5, 525.

buddha dharma, essential: 天眞の佛法 [tenshin no buppō], literally, natural and true buddha dharma. 6.

buddha dharma, matter of: 佛法邊事 [buppō henji].

buddha dharma, pure, single: 純一の佛法 [jun'itsu no buppō]. 5.

buddha dimension: 佛量 [butsuryō]. 642.

buddha effect: 102. See also *buddha fruit.*

Buddha entrusting the dharma: 佛勅 [butchoku]. 21.

buddha eyes: 441, 462. See also *eyes, five.*

buddha fruit: 佛果 [bukka]. Also, buddha effect. 49, 522, 657, 795.

buddha ground: 佛地 [butchi]. 406.

buddha hall. 佛殿 [butsuden]. Building in a monastery where the main buddha image is enshrined and services take place. 232, 270, 644, 689.

buddha hall upside down and move in a circle, ride the: 690. See also *ride the buddha hall upside down and move in a circle.*

buddha heir: 佛子 [busshi], literally, buddha child. 169, 181, 454, 547.

buddha heritage: 佛嗣 [busshi]. 169, 179.

buddha house: 佛家 [bukke]. 1. Practicing community of buddha dharma. 2. Practitioner of buddha dharma. 4, 33, 103, 295, 538.

buddha kāshāya: 佛袈裟 [butsu kesa]. 113, 115, 121, 129, 140, 147, 722.

buddha knowledge: 佛之知見 [butsu no chiken]. 181, 182, 186, 505.

buddha land: 佛國 [bukkoku], 佛國土 [bukkokudo]. A land where a Buddha has appeared. 21, 55, 160, 515, 588.

buddha land, southern: 南方佛國土 [nampō bukkokudo]. Southern Continent, Jambudvipa. 188. See also *Continents, Four.*

buddha light: 佛光 [bukkō]. 佛光明 [butsu kōmyō], literally, buddha illumination. 67, 150, 309, 416, 417, 418, 420.

buddha mind: 佛心 [busshin]. Mind that is inseparable from the great activity of the universe. 91, 118, 197, 574.

Buddha Mind School: 佛心宗 [Busshin Shū]. A name for the Zen school. xli, 505, 514.

buddha name, chanting: 念佛 [nembutsu]. 5.

buddha nature: 佛性 [busshō]. 1. The capacity for becoming a buddha, which is inherent in all sentient beings according to Mahāyāna Buddhist teaching. 2. Dōgen interprets *Mahā Pari-nirvāna Sūtra's* statement "All sentient beings have buddha nature," 一切衆生悉有佛性 [Issai shujō shitsu u busshō], as "Living beings all are buddha nature." (He reads "all have" 悉有 [shitsu u] as "all are.") 45, 234–47, 412, 648.

Buddha Nature: 佛性 [Busshō]. Twenty-third fascicle of this book. xlvii, lxiv, lxv, 234–59.

buddha-nature circle: 圓相佛性 [ensō busshō]. 741.

buddha nature, does a dog have: 狗子還有佛性也無 [kushi kan'u busshō ya mukushi ni mata busshō ari ya nashi ya]. Famous kōan of Zhaozhou Congshen. 255, 256.

buddha nature, ocean of: 佛性海 [busshō kai]. 238, 239, 385.

buddha nose: 佛尖 [bussen], literally, buddha pointed. 574.

buddha oldness: 佛古 [bukko]. 470.

buddha precept: 佛戒 [bukkai]. 86, 151, 890.

buddha procedure: 佛儀 [butsugi]. Buddha practice; buddha guidelines. Also, stories about the Buddha. 56, 57.

buddha radiance: 佛光明 [bukkōmyō]. 91.

buddha rank: 佛位 [butsui]. 685, 686.

buddha robe: 佛衣 [butsue]. 112–15, 137.

buddha seal: 佛印 [butchin]. Unchanging reality experienced by a buddha. Also, recognition of the buddha mind and entrustment of the teaching. 佛心印 [busshin 'in], literally, buddha mind seal. 5, 9, 16, 909, 913.

buddha seed: 佛種 [busshu]. 98, 125.

buddha sickness: 佛病 [butsubyō]. Driven by the desire to become a buddha. 464.

Buddha Sūtras: 佛經 [Bukkyō]. Fifty-third fascicle of this book. lxxviii, 537–47.

buddha tathāgata: 5. See also *tathāgata.*

buddha thought: 佛量 [butsuryō]. 304, 331.

buddha tongue: 佛舌 [butsuzetsu]. 235, 574.

Buddha Vehicle: 181, 184. See also *Vehicle, One.*

buddha virtue: 佛德 [buttoku]. 6.

buddha way: 佛道 [butsudō]. Also called the great way of all buddhas, 諸佛の大道 [shobutsu no daidō]. The path of awakened ones, which is actualized through each person's practice. This term is often used in contrast to scriptural studies. 4, 29, 502, 544, 886.

buddha way, contemplate the: 思惟佛道 [shiyui butsudō]. 653.

Buddha Way, The: 佛道 [Butsudō]. Fiftieth fascicle of this book. lxxvii, xcvi, 501–17.

buddha wind: 佛風 [buppū]. Buddha's style of teaching. 102, 181.

buddha wisdom: 佛知 [butchi], 佛智慧 [butchie]. 7, 15, 186, 750.

buddha words: 佛語 [butsugo]. 148, 235, 693.

buddha work: 佛業 [butsugō]. 57, 543.

Buddha's abdomen: 佛腹 [buppuku].

Buddha's birthday: Shākyamuni Buddha's birthday is traditionally celebrated on the eighth day of the fourth month in East Asia. 731.

buddha's enlightenment, equal to: 等覺 [tōgaku], literally, equal enlightenment. See also *bodhisattva who is a candidate to be a buddha.*

buddha's form: 佛相 [bussō]. 308.

buddha's heir buddha: 佛嗣佛 [butsushi butsu]. 170.

buddha's instruction: 佛訓 [bukkun]. Admonitions of the Buddha. 744.

Buddha's life: 一代 [ichidai], literally, one lifetime. 80, 187, 334, 487, 502, 570, 624.

Buddha's life span: 佛壽量 [butsu juryō]. 187.

buddha's mudrā: 佛印 [butsuin/butchin]. 1. A hand gesture of a buddha. 2. The mind of a buddha, that is unchangeable. See also *mudrā.*

Buddha's Pari-nirvāna *Admonition Outline Sūtra:* 佛垂般涅槃略説教誡經 [Busshi Hatsu Nehan Ryakusetsu Kyōkai Kyō]. Also called *Buddha's Willed Teaching Sūtra,* 佛遺教經 [Butsu Yuikyō Gyō]. 771.

Buddha's teaching was transmitted eastward: 佛法東漸 [buppō tōzen]. 21.

buddha's transformation: 佛化 [bukke]. Buddha's teaching. 6, 7.

Buddha's womb: 佛胎 [buttai]. 666.

buddha-as-self: 自佛 [jbutsu]. 596.

buddhas: 諸佛 [shobutsu]. 3, 29, 43, 771, 889.

buddhas, enter: 入佛 [nyūbutsu]. 140, 186.

Buddhas, Five: 五佛 [Gobutsu]. Mahā Vairochana, Akshobhya, Prabhūta-ratna, Amitāyus (Amitābha), and Amoghasiddhi. The manifestations of the fourfold wisdom of Mahā Vairochana in Vajrayāna (Esoteric) Buddhism is represented by the four other Buddhas. 9.

Buddhas, Four: 四佛 [Shibutsu]. Shākyamuni Buddha, plus three preceding Buddhas: Krakucchanda, Kanakamuni, and Kāshyapa. 785.

buddhas, incarnated: 化佛 [kebutsu]. Incarnate-body buddhas. Buddhas taking forms of others to guide beings. 602, 603.

buddhas, miracle: 神通佛 [jinzū butsu]. 289, 290.

buddhas, presence of all: 諸佛の佛儀 [shobutsu no butsugi]. 170.

buddhas, self-manifested: 自性身佛 [jishō shin butsu]. 260.

Buddhas, Seven Original: 七佛 [Shichi Butsu]. Succession of six mythological buddhas before Shākyamuni Buddha, plus Shākyamuni Buddha. 9, 57, 169, 569, 864. See fascicle 16, "Buddha Ancestors."

Buddhas' Teaching, The: 佛教 [Bukkyō]. Twenty-fifth fascicle of this book. xlviii, lxv, lxvi, lxxii, 276–86.

buddhas, throughout: 互佛 [gōbutsu].

buddhas and ancestors: 佛佛祖祖 [butsubutsu soso]. 43, 115, 309, 854, 895.

buddhas and ancestors, form and manner of the: 佛儀祖儀 [butsugi sogi]. 711.

buddhas as many as the sands of the Ganges: 恒沙佛 [gōsha butsu]. 598, 599.

buddhas before Shākyamuni Buddha: 過去の諸佛 [kako no shobutsu], literally, past buddhas. 287.

buddhas manifested from others: 他性身佛 [tashōshin butsu]. 260.

Buddhist practitioners: 佛衆 [busshu], literally, buddha assembly. 548.

Butsuju Myōzen: 佛樹明全. 全公 [Zen Kō], literally, honorable Myōzen. 1184–1225, Japan. Dharma heir of Myōan Eisai. As abbot of the Kennin Monastery, Kyōto, he taught Rinzai Zen to Dōgen. He took Dōgen to China but died at the Tiantong Monastery during his study. P. 934, Generation 24. xxxvi, xxxvii, xxxix, xl, 914.

cage and snare: 籠籮 [rōra]. Traps of words and concepts. 304, 433.

cage or a fishing net, bird: 籠羅 [rōra]. Being confined by delusion. 202.

calf: 牛兒 [gyūji]. 228, 527.

call and actualize: 喚作 [kansa]. 671.

calmness, place of: 平穩地 [heion chi]. 304.

candle, blew at a: 吹滅紙燭 [suimetsu shishoku]. 194.

canon, rotate the: 轉大藏經 [ten daizō kyō]. Ceremoniously and symbolically chant the entire body of sūtras. 226–28.

Caodong School: 曹洞宗 [Sōtō Shū]. One of the Five "Houses" of Zen in China. The dharma lineage derived from Dongshan Liangjie. Sometimes his successor Caoshan Benji is regarded as cofounder. There is also a theory that the name of this school is a combination of *Caoxi*, where the Sixth Ancestor Huineng lived, and *Dongshan Liangjie*. Dōgen brought this teaching to Japan and is regarded as founder of its Japanese form, the Sōto School. 5, xxxviii, xli, lxvii, lvii, 514.

Caoshan Benji: 曹山本寂 [Sōzan Honjaku]. 840–901, China. Dharma heir of Dongshan Liangjie. Sometimes regarded as cofounder of Caodong School along with his teacher, Dongshan. Studied Confucianism as a youth and entered Lingshi Monastery in Fuzhou at nineteen. After becoming Dongshan's dharma heir, he started a monastery at Mount Cao, Fu Region (Jiangxi). He used Dongshan's "Five Ranks" as a method of instruction, thereby widening its use. He was known for his commentary on the verses of the poet Hanshan. His posthumous name is Great Master Yuanzheng 元證大師 [Genshō Daishi]. P. 931, Generation 12. 319, 930.

Caoxi: See *Dajian Huineng.*

Caoxi Lingdao: 曹渓令韜 [Sōkei Reitō]. 666–760, China. Dharma heir of Sixth Ancestor Huineng. Tended to the stūpa that enshrined Huineng's robe after his death, declining imperial invitations. His posthumous name is Zen Master Daxiao, 大曉禪師 [Daigyō Zenji]. P. 929, Generation 7. 838.

capacity, excellent: 上根 [jōkon], literally, high root. 183.

capacity, great: 大機 [daiki], literally, large function. 8, 137, 251, 443.

capacity, human: 人根 [ninkon], literally, person's root. 271, 296.

capacity, in accordance with the listener's: 隨機 [zui ki]. 赴機 [fuki]. 794.

capacity, minor: 小量の機根 [shōryō no kikon]. 544.

capacity, sharp: 利根 [rikon]. 282, 369.

capacity, true: 實力 [jitsuriki]. True power. 520.

capping verses: 頌古 [juko]. Commentary verses on a kōan. 636.

careless: 杜撰 [zusan]. 12, 157, 243, 304, 323, 483, 504, 516.

cart, white-ox: 白牛車 [byaku gossha]. 182, 183, 185.

carts, three types of: 三車 [sansha]. Carts pulled by a sheep, a deer, and an ox, representing the Three Vehicles. The One Vehicle is symbolized by a great white-ox cart. This analogy is told in the *Lotus Sūtra.* 183.

cases, master: 極則 [gokusoku]. To master kōans. 644.

cast away: 抛却 [hōkyaku]. Hurl away. *Kyaku* is a suffix indicating emphasis. 239, 546.

cast off: 放下(す) [hōge(-su)]. 371, 862. See also *body, cast off the.*

causal beings: 緣有 [en'u]. 235.

causal conditions: 緣起 [engi]. 269, 333.

causal relations, power of the: 因緣力 [innen riki]. 473.

causal relationship, excellent: 結良緣 [ketsu ryōen], literally, forming good conditions. 583.

causation, imaginary: 妄緣起 [mōengi]. 235.

causation, produced by: 因緣生 [innen shō]. Arise through causes and conditions. 488.

causation, this very moment of: いまの時節因緣 [ima no jisetsu innen]. 470.

causation, twelvefold: 十二輪転 [jūni rinden], 十二因緣 [jūni innen]. The chain of the "dependent origination" [innen] of pain and despair in the cycle of birth, death, and rebirth: ignorance; karma-formations; consciousness; name-and-form (corporeality); six sense fields (the spheres of sense activities); contact; feeling (sensation); craving (thirst); grasping (clinging); becoming (action); birth (rebirth); and decay (old age, sickness) and death. The logical formula is as follows: "Ignorance is the cause of karma-formations. Karma-formations are the cause of consciousness," and so on to "decay and death." 10, 281.

cause and effect: 因果 [inga]. 37, 98, 705, 851.

cause and effect over time: 時節因縁 [jisetsu innen]. Also for Dōgen, this moment of enlightenment. 237, 238.

cause and effect, deny: 撥無因果 [hatsumu inga]. 662, 788, 815, 852–54, 857.

cause and effect, not fall into: 不落因果 [furaku inga]. 705, 707–9, 713, 851–53, 856.

cause and effect, not ignore: 不昧因果 [fumai inga], literally, not obscure cause and effect. 705, 709, 851, 852, 853.

cause, true: 實因 [jitsuin]. 184, 520.

causes and conditions: 因縁 [innen]. Also, an explanation of causes; story for studying; materials to study. 7, 98, 100, 677, 769–91 . . .

causes and conditions, cease through: 因縁滅 [innen metsu]. 98

causes, practice: 修因 [shuin]. 458.

cave and basket: 窟籠 [kutsurō]. Limited dualistic views. 191, 255, 752.

celestial activity: 125. See also *activity, celestial.*

celibate: 孤獨潔白 [kodoku keppaku], literally, solitary and pure. 77.

ceremony, chanting: 念誦 [nenju]. 731, 732, 738.

chair, bent-wood teaching: 曲木の床 [kyokumoku no shō]. Cross-legged chair, 交椅 [kōi]. Foldable chair with a bent piece of wood for the back and arm rest. 559.

chaitya: Skt. Transliteration: 支提 [shidai], 制多 [seita]. Shrine, tower. Sometimes indicates stūpa. 830, 831, 835–37.

Chanda: 車匿 [Shanoku]. Chariot driver of King Shuddhodana in Kapilavastu. He escorted Prince Siddhārtha out with a horse, brought back his clothing and possessions, and reported the prince's leaving the household to the king. 809.

Chandra Sūrya Pradīpa Buddha: 日月燈明佛 [Nichigatsu Tōmyō Butsu], literally, Sun and Moon Lamp Buddha. Described in the *Lotus Sūtra* as one who expounded the sūtra incalculable eons ago. 521, 803.

Changcha: See *Tong'an Changcha.*

change, not subject to: 無有變易 [mu'u hen'yaku]. 234.

changes, one thousand: 千變 [sempen]. 216.

Changling Shouzhuo: 長靈守卓 [Chōrei Shutaku]. 1065–1123, China. Dharma heir of Lingyuan Weiqing, Linji School. Taught at Tianning Wanshou Monastery, Dongjing (Henan). P. 933, Generation 21. 635.

Changlu Qingliao: 長蘆清了 [Chōro Seiryō]. 1089–1151, China. Also called Zhenxie Qingliao. Dharma heir of Danxia Zichun, Caodong School. Changlu became a monk at eleven. After passing his exam on the *Lotus Sūtra* at eighteen, he visited famous teachers and sacred mountains. He taught at a number of monasteries, including Changlu Monastery, Jiangning (Jiangsu), until the downfall of the Northern Song Dynasty and the ensuing social unrest caused him to become itinerant again. His posthumous name is Zen Master Wukong, 悟空禪師 [Gokū Zenji]. P. 933, Generation 20. 932, 938.

Changqing Da'an: 長慶大安 [Chōkei Daian]. 793–883, China. Dharma heir of Baizhang Huaihai, Nanyue Line. Called the Second Guishan. Also called Lazy An. As a young man he traveled in search of truth until he met Master Baizhang and ended his search. Da'an's dharma brother was Guishan Lingyou, who established a temple at Mount Gui, Tan Region (Hunan). After Guishan Lingyou's death, Da'an was invited to become abbot there. He taught the importance of staying still and training the mind. Later taught at the Changqing Monastery, Fu Region (Fujian). His posthumous name is Zen Master Yuanzhi, 圓智禪師 [Enchi Zenji]. P. 930, Generation 10. 338.

Changqing Huileng: 長慶慧稜 [Chōkei Eryō]. 854–932, China. Dharma heir of Xuefeng Yicun, Qingyuan Line. Taught at Chanqing Monastery, Quan Province (Fujan). His posthumous name is Great Master Chaojiao, 超覺大師 [Chōkaku Daishi]. P. 931, Generation 13. 930.

Changsha Jingcen: 長沙景岑 [Chōsha Keishin]. Ca. eighth–ninth century, China. Dharma heir of Nanquan Puyuan, Qingyuan Line. Taught at Luyuan Monastery, Changsha (Hunan). Once, he saw Yangshan Huiji and kicked him right away. Since Yangshan remarked Jingcen was as rough as a tiger, he was called Tiger Cen 岑大蟲 [Shin Daichū]. Jingcen encouraged students to take one step from the top of a hundred-foot pole. His posthumous name is Great Master Zhaoxian 招賢大師 [Shōken Daishi]. P. 930, Generation 10. 257, 788, 789.

Changshui Zixuan: 長水子璿 [Chōsui Shisen]. d. 1038, China. Dharma heir of Langye Huijiao, Linji School. Taught in Changshui, Shen Region

(Zhejiang). Wrote a commentary on *Shūraṅgama Sūtra.* P. 932, Generation 18. 931.

Changzong: 86. See also *Zhaojiao Changzong.*

chant quietly: 默誦 [mokuju]. 134, 152.

Chaozhou Dadian: See *Dadian Baotong.*

chase the self: 36. See also *self and make it into things, chase the.*

check (a person) out: 勘過す [kanka-su]. 442, 443.

Chen, Venerable: 349, 542. See also *Muzou Daoming.*

Chenggu: See *Jianfu Chenggu.*

Chenggui: 成桂 [Jōkei]. Ca. thirteenth century, China. Guest coordinator of Ayuwang Mountain Guanli Monastery (Zhejang), when Dōgen visited. 249.

China: 神丹國/震旦國 [Shintan Koku], literally, country of China. 東地 [tōchi], literally, eastern land. 4, 43, 74, 502, 863, 889.

Chinese person comes a Chinese person appears, when a: 漢來漢現 [kanrai kangen]. 205, 209, 210, 213.

Chinese person learns a Chinese way of walking: 唐人赤脚學唐步 [tōnin shakkyaku gaku tōho], literally, Chinese person learns barefooted Chinese walking. 681.

chitta: Skt. 心 [shin]. Seat of mental and emotional activities. 655, 658.

Chongjing: See *Liu Chongjing.*

Chongxin: See *Longtan Chongxin.*

chop down: 撲落 [bokuraku]. Same as, drop away. 881.

Chuan: 傳 [Den]. Ca. thirteenth century, China. Librarian at Tiantong Jingde Monastery when Dōgen visited. A descendant of priest Qingyuan, Zen Master Fuyan of Longmen. P. 934, Generation 23. 173, 174, 917, 933.

Chuanzi Decheng: 船子德誠 [Sensu Tokujō]. Ca. eighth–ninth century, China. Studied with Yaoshan Weiyan, Qingyuan Line, for thirty years and became one of his heirs. Under the persecution of Buddhism by Emperor Wu of the Tang Dynasty, he disguised himself as a boatman on Wu River, in Huating (Jiangsu), and taught. After transmitting dharma to Jiashan Shanhui, he turned over the boat and disappeared into the water. P. 930, Generation 10. 929.

Chuyuan: See *Ciming Chuyuan.*

Ciming Chuyuan: 慈明楚圓 [Jimyō Soen]. 987–1040, China. Dharma heir of Fenyang Shanzhao, Linji School. Also called Shishuang Chuyuan.

Ciming trained assiduously, jabbing himself in the leg with an awl if he ever felt sleepy during evening meditation. Taught at Mount Shishuang, Tan Region (Hunan). Teacher of Huanglong Huinan and Yangqi Fanghui, regarded as founders of the two major orders of the Linji School. P. 932, Generation 17. 86, 175, 931.

circle: 圓相 [ensō], literally, circle form. Represents enlightenment. 團圞 [danran], literally, circle round. Represents intimacy. 174, 227, 248, 249, 295, 592, 690, 741.

circle of the way: 道環 [dōkan], literally, way ring. For Dōgen, each person's practice of the way at each moment encompasses aspiration (for enlightenment), practice, enlightenment, and nirvāna. Also, each person's practice is actualized by the practice of all buddhas throughout time, and at the same time actualizes the great way of all buddhas. Thus, the circle of the way has its micro aspect (the former) and macro aspect (the latter). xxiv, 268, 332 . . .

circle, creating a: 打一圓相 [da ichi ensō]. 227.

circle, draw a: 作一圓相 [sa ichi ensō]. 592.

circle, rotating a: 回環 [kaikan]. 418.

circulate: 周旋す [shūsen-su]. 101, 538.

circumambulation: 巡堂 [jundō]. Greeting circuit in the monks' hall. 41, 230, 231, 732.

circumstances: 時處 [jisho], literally, time and place. 156, 231, 269, 289, 407, 476, 909.

circumstances, turn: 轉境 [tenkyō]. 156.

clarifying dharma, gate of: 法明門 [hōmyō mon]. 661.

class, warrior: 刹利種 [setsuri shu]. 356.

cleaning monk: 淨頭 [jinjū]. 736.

Cleansing: 洗淨 [Senjō]. Seventh fascicle of this book. xlviii, lvii, 48–57.

clear: 玲瓏 [reirō], literally, crystal clear. 205, 303, 591, 854.

cloud: 雲 [un/kumo]. Represents freedom of moving about, not having a fixed abode. Often indicates a monk's life. Also represents the realm of nonduality. 62, 755.

cloud and water: 雲箇水箇 [unko suiko]. 箇 [ko] is a suffix with no additional meaning. 507, 723, 755.

cloud hall: 62, 69, 616, 618, 689. See also *monks' hall.*

cloud or a waterweed, wander about like a: See *wander about like a cloud or a waterweed.*

cloud robes and mist sleeves: 雲衲霞袂 [unnō kabei]. Monk who wears Buddhist robes. 77, 193, 343, 445.

Clouds and moon are one, valleys and mountains are separate: 雲月是同渓山各別 [ungetsu zedō, keizan kakubetsu]. The Buddha's original teaching is one but it is expressed and experienced in myriad ways. 586.

clouds arising below one's feet: 足下雲生 [sokka unshō]. 109.

coin: 寶貝 [hōbai], literally, treasure shell. 249.

cold/heat. 寒暑 [kansho]. Represents birth/death. 631–37 . . .

come forward, not: 不進 [fushin]. 291.

coming and going: 去来 [kyorai]. 1. Conventional way of viewing birth and death, past and future, as coming from somewhere and going somewhere else. 2. In Dōgen's usage, total experience of the continually arising moment of now. 46, 103, 418, 446, 489.

comment: 拈古 [nenko], literally, take up ancient (words). Commentary. 頌古 [juko], literally, poem on ancient (words); commentary in verse. 132, 270, 274, 411, 693, 712, 743 . . .

commentaries and verses: 頌古拈古 [juko nenko]. 700.

commentary: 典釋 [tenshaku], literally, interpreting text. 疏釋 [soshaku], literally, clarification and interpretation. 章疏 [shōso], literally, clarification. 191, 196, 349, 701, 840, 951.

common people and sages: 凡聖 [bonshō]. 6.

community: 會下 [eka], literally, under the assembly. 18, 172, 481, 652.

compassion: 慈悲 [jihi]. Identification with those who are suffering (Skt., karunā) and sharing wisdom and joy with them (maitrī). 16, 356, 736.

compassionate admonition: 慈誨 [jikai]. 223, 227.

Compiled Precepts in Ten Sections for Chanting: 十誦律 [Jūju Ritsu]. Collection of precepts of Sarvāstivādin School, one of the twenty early Buddhist schools of India. 56.

Complete Enlightenment Bodhisattva: 圓覺菩薩 [Engaku Bosatsu]. One who receives the Buddha's teaching in the *Sūtra of Complete Enlightenment*. 741.

completion: 全圓 [zen'en], literally, entire circle. 18, 738, 834, 905.

composure: 雍容 [yōyō]. 269, 366, 378, 627, 911.

composure, magnificent: 巍巍堂堂 [gigi dōdō]. 298.

comprehension: 了知 [ryōchi]. 120, 270, 312, 571.

conceal: 藏 [zō]. Also, treasure; treasury. 86, 531–33, 535, 536, 807.

concentration, learn to do: 習禪 [shūzen]. A process of gradual attainment through increasingly advanced stages employing various methods of meditation.

condition: 緣 [en]. Circumstance. 依 [e], literally, dependence: 法位 [hōi]. State of each thing, literally, dharma position. 30, 308, 518, 785.

condition, abide in one's: See *abide in one's condition.*

condition, true: 實緣 [jitsuen]. 520.

condition complete this moment: ひとときのくらゐ/一時の位 [hitotoki no kurai], literally, position of one time. Dharma position or state of being itself, 法位 [hōi], at each moment which carries all time. An entire period of itself. The unique, nonrepeatable stage of a thing's existence at any given moment. 31.

conditioned by karma: 業報 [goppō], literally, reward of karma; unwholesome karma. 266.

conditions: 衆緣 [shuen]. 224, 269, 538.

conditions that increase: 増上緣 [zōjō en]. 658.

conditions, gate of abiding in: 住位門 [jūi mon]. 538.

conditions, one who enters with ripened: 從緣入者 [jūen nissha]. 88.

conditions, pressing: 現前の衆緣 [genzen no shuen], literally, conditions that are present. 253.

conditions, worldly: 世緣. 464.

confirm: 證明 [shōmyō]. Confirmation. Also, clarification. 392–94, 801.

Confirmation: 授記 [Juki]. Thirty-third fascicle of this book. lxix, 387–96.

confirmed, those who have not yet: 未證據者 [mishōko sha]. 107.

Confucius: 孔子 [Kōshi]. Kongzi. Ca. sixth–fifth century B.C.E., China. Social thinker, writer, and educator. Author of *Analects.* 544, 545, 604, 857, 863–73, 875.

confused: 動著 [dōjaku]. Move, sway. 疑著 [gijaku], literally, doubt. 動執 [dōshū], literally, move and be attached. 156, 272, 294, 595, 602.

confusions, four: 四倒 [shitō], literally, four fallings. To be attached to permanence, bliss, self, and purity. 61, 868.

Congshen: See *Zhaozhou Congshen.*

Congzhan: See *Baofu Congzhan.*

consonants and vowels: 字母 [jimo], literally, mother letters (vowels). 567.

contemplate the buddha way: See *buddha way, contemplate the.*

contemplation, straw sandal: 草鞋思惟 [sōai shiyui]. 677.

Continents, Four: 四洲 [shishū]. According to sūtras, the world consists of Eight Seas among Nine Mountains that lie around Mount Sumeru. Four Continents lie in the Eight Seas. Among them, the Great Northern Continent, Uttarakuru, is where inhabitants live for one thousand years and don't know suffering. Therefore, they indulge in the pleasure of the present moment. The Southern Continent, Jambudvīpa, is our world on earth, where we humans live with suffering, but where there is the potential for awakening. 264, 473, 800, 870.

Continuous Practice: 行持 [Gyōji]. Thirty-first fascicle of this volume (Parts One and Two). xlv, xlvi, xlviii, lviii, lxviii, 332–53, 354–79.

continuous practice, solid: 行持堅固 [gyōji kengo]. 366.

Continuous Transmission of the Lamp: See *Jianzhong Jingguo Continuous Transmission of the Lamp.*

control: 管す [kan-su]. 66, 699, 880.

cooking monk: 行粥飯僧 [gyō shukuhan sō / an shukuhan sō], literally, monk who works on breakfast and midday meal. 87.

cotton, fine: Skt., kārpāsaka 屈眴 [kutsujun]. Cloth of core cotton threads. 149.

Cotton Robe Tai: See *Nanyue Xuantai.*

country: 刹土 [setsudo]. Transliteration of Skt. kshetra [setsu], "field," plus ideograph for "land" [do]. 4, 5, 17, 19, 20, 21 . . .

craving: 愛 [ai], literally; love, attachment. See also *causation, twelvefold.*

cream: 酥酪 [soraku]. 醍醐 [daigo]. 33, 334.

create or measure, attempt to: 有作有量 [usa uryō]. 186.

creating, not-: 無作 [musa]. Beyond doing. 282.

crime, grave: Skt., pārājayika. Transliteration: 波羅夷 [harai]. Offenses to the practicing community. Cause for being expelled from the sangha. 79, 83, 784–86.

crimes, one who commits serious: 逆人 [gyakunin], literally, upside down person. 17, 648.

criticize: 勘破 [kampa], literally, discern and crush. 203, 204, 753, 842. See also *respond and discern; turn around.*

cross over, help: 得度 [tokudo], literally, attain and help arrive (at the shore of enlightenment). わたす [watasu]. 656.

Crow Stone Peak: 烏石嶺 [Useki Rei]. Located in Mount Xuefeng, Fu Region (Fujian), China. Known for its excellent view. 421. See also *Land View Pavilion.*

crown: 頂上 [chōjō], literally, headtop. 115, 341, 433, 800, 809.

crush (one's) bones: 粉骨 [funkotsu], literally, pound (one's own) bones to powder. 85.

crush: 打破 [daha], literally, beat and break. 31, 68, 270, 274, 506, 702, 710.

crush underfoot: 踏著 [tōjaku]. 635.

crushing, vital: 活碎 [kassai]. 617.

crystal: 頗瓈樹 [hari ju]. 459, 591, 679 . . .

crystal, eight facets of clear: 八面玲瓏 [hachimen reirō]. Eight facets, 八面 [hachimen]. Crystal clarity like an eight-faceted jewel. 431.

cuckoo: 杜宇 [tou]. 527.

Cuiwei Wuxue: 翠微無學 [Suibi Mugaku]. Ca. eighth–ninth century, China. Dharma heir of Danxia Tianran, Qingyuan Line. Taught at Cuiwei Monastery, Mount Zhongnan (Shanxi). Given the title of Great Master Guangzhao, 廣照大師 [Kōshō Daishi] by the Emperor. P. 930, Generation 10. 557, 929.

cult: 黨類 [tōrui]. 261.

Cunjiang: See *Xinghua Cunjiang.*

cushion: 坐蒲 [zafu]. A round padded seat placed under the buttocks for sitting zazen.

custom, authentic: 古儀 [kogi], literally, old form. 故實 [kojitsu], literally, old truth. 78, 81, 744, 804.

customary in the dharma: 如法 [nyohō], literally, as it is in dharma. 常法 [jōhō], literally, permanent method. 60.

cut off arm: 斷臂 [dampi]. 72, 364, 372.

cut through: 截斷 [saidan], literally, chop off. 得斷 [tokudan], literally, achieve cutting. 直截 [jikisetsu], literally, cut straight. 6, 93, 98, 532, 545.

cut to the original source: 根源を截斷す [kongen wo saidan-su]. 328.

Cypress Tree: 柏樹子 [Hakujushi]. Thirty-sixth fascicle of this book. 子 [shi] is a suffix with no special meaning. lxx, 409–14.

Da'an: See *Changqing Da'an.*

Daci Huanzhong: 大慈寰中 [Daiji Kanchū]. 780–862, China. Dharma heir of Baizhang Huaihai, Nanyue Line. Returned to laity during the persecution of Buddhism by Emperor Wu, but later became a monk and taught at Mount Daci, Hang Region (Zhejiang). *Huanzhong* means

"Boundless World." His posthumous name is Great Master Xingkong, 性空大師 [Shōkū Daishi]. P. 930, Generation 10. 345.

Dadian Baotong: 大顛寶通 [Daiten Hōtsū]. 732–824, China. Also called Chaozhou Dadian, 潮州大顛 [Chōshū Daiten]. Dharma heir of Shitou Xiqian, Qingyuan Line. Taught at Mount Ling, Chao Region (Guangdong). P. 930, Generation 9. 337, 929.

Daer, Tripitaka Master: 大耳三藏 [Daini Sanzō]. Ca. eighth century. Known for his debate with Huizhong after arriving in China from a western country. Named *Dae* (Large) *Er* (Ears) for his large ears. 197, 198, 204, 745–48, 750–53.

Daguang: 大光 [Daikō]. Ca. twelfth–thirteenth century, China. Abbot of Ayuwang Monastery (Zhejiang), when Dōgen visited. Biography unknown. 249.

Dahui Zonggao: 大慧宗杲 [Daie Sōkō]. 1089–1163, China. Dharma heir of Yuanwu Keqin. Attacked Caodong Zen as "silent-illumination Zen" and advocated a formal kōan Zen practice, especially for laypeople. Revived the teaching at Mount Jing, Hang Region (Zhejiang), and was regarded as the restorer of the Linji School. Author of *Treasury of the True Dharma Eye,* not to be confused with Dōgen's book of the same title. In some writings Dōgen strongly criticized him. His posthumous name is Zen Master Dahui, 大慧禪師 [Daie Zenji]. P. 933, Generation 22. xxxvii, 756; missing the point, 495, 497, 704; lineage of, 175; life of, 700–703; words of, 494, 856.

Daibutsu: 大佛. Dōgen referred to himself by this name when he resided in the Daibutsu Monastery. 692.

Daibutsu Monastery: 大佛寺 [Daibutsu-ji]. "Great Buddha" Monastery. After moving to Echizen Province, Japan, in 1243, Dōgen founded this monastery in the following year. Renamed Eihei Monastery in 1246. 720, 723, 744, 754, 759.

daily activities: see *activities, daily.*

Dajian Huineng: 大鑑慧能 [Daikan Enō]. 638–713, China. Also called Laborer Huineng, 慧能行者 [Enō Anja]; Worker Lu, 盧行者 [Ro Anja]; Sixth Ancestor, 六祖 [Rokuso]; Caoxi, 曹渓 [Sōkei]; Old Buddha Caoxi, 曹谿古佛 [Sōkei Kobutsu]. Born into a poor family of Xin Region (Guangdong). Sold firewood for a living. At age twenty-four he joined Fifth Ancestor Hongren's community. After cleaning rice for

eight months, he secretly received dharma transmission from Hongren and escaped angry senior monks by fleeing to the south. Hid in
a hunter's house for four years and then became a monk. Taught at
Baolin Monastery, Caoxi, Shao Region (Guangdong). While Hongren's senior student, Shenxiu, emphasized gradual enlightenment
in northern China, Huineng emphasized immediate enlightenment.
As a teacher, he produced a group of excellent students who transmitted his teaching, called the Southern School of Zen. Some of
his stories and dharma discourses are included in the *Sixth Ancestor's Platform Sūtra*, although this text is considered spurious, both by
Dōgen and modern scholars, especially the story about the poetry
contest Huineng supposedly won to gain dharma transmission. His
posthumous name is Zen Master Dajian 大鑑禪師 [Daikan Zenji].
P. 929, Generation 6. 189, 568; descendants of, 321, 469, 510, 574; lineage of, 5, 166, 177, 178, 181, 468, 501, 523, 569, 586, 721, 890; poems
of, 208, 223; practice of, 12, 290, 838; robe of, 112, 119, 120, 129, 136,
141, 144, 148, 149, 374, 539; story of, 76, 241, 242, 328, 330, 337, 547,
684, 812; students of, 45, 182–84, 348, 349, 390, 470, 505, 513, 526, 750,
854; time of, 696; words of, 48, 169, 224, 243, 262, 331, 382, 598, 610,
673, 695, 865.

Daman Hongren: 大滿弘忍 [Daiman Kōnin]. 688–761, China. Also called
Huangmei. Dharma heir of Fourth Ancestor Dayi Daoxin. As Fifth
Chinese Ancestor of the Zen School, taught at Mount Huang-
mei, later called Mount Wuzu (Mount Fifth Ancestor), Qi Region
(Hubei). He had two outstanding students, Shenxiu and Huineng.
Hongren is regarded as the one who established the Dongshan (East
Mountain) School [Tozan Shū] (not to be confused with Dong-
shan Liangjie's Caodong School), in contrast to the contemporary
Niutou School. His posthumous name is Zen Master Daman 大滿
禪師 [Daiman Zenji]. P. 929, Generation 5. 166; practice of, 579, 652;
robe of, 112, 538; story of, 239, 374; students of, 136, 148, 208, 242, 330,
337, 539, 547; words of, 240, 241.

Damei Fachang: 大梅法常 [Daibai Hōjō]. 752–839, China. Grew up in
Xiangyang (Hubei). Enlightened in the community of Mazu Daoyi,
Nanyue Line, and became one of his dharma heirs. Secluded in Mount
Damei (Great Plum Mountain), Ningbo (Zhejiang), for forty years,
and praised Mazu's "This very mind is buddha." At Mount Damei he

founded Husheng Monastery, where more than six hundred monks practiced. P. 930, Generation 9. 628.

Danxia Tianran: 丹霞天然 [Tanka Tennen]. 739–824, China. Dharma heir of Shitou Xiquan. Tianran spent his youth as a scholar and hoped to work as a civil servant, but on his way to take the exam he met a Zen monk in an inn and decided to study Buddhism instead. He practiced with both Mazu and Shitou. His iconoclastic way included outrageous behavior such as climbing onto a sacred statue in one temple, and burning a wooden Buddha to warm himself in another. He taught at Mount Tianran, Nanyang (Henan). His posthumous name is Zen Master Zhitong 智通禪師 [Chitsū Zenji]. P. 930, Generation 9. 895.

Danxia Zichun: 丹霞子淳 [Tanka Shijun]. 1064–1117, China. Dharma heir of Furong Daokai, Caodong School. Taught at Mount Danxia, Nanyang (Henan). Teacher of Hongzhi Zengjiao. P. 933, Generation 19. 166.

Daochuan: See *Yefu Daochuan.*

Daofu: See *Jingqing Daofu.*

Daofu: 道副 [Dōfuku]. Ca. sixth century, China. A disciple of Bodhidharma. Biography unknown. P. 928, Generation 2. 479, 480, 673, 930.

Daoying: See *Yunju Daoying.*

Daoism: 道教 [Dō Kyō]. Also, Taoism. 524, 544.

Daoist: 道士 [dōshi], literally, Daoist practitioner. 道家流 [dōkaryū], literally, follower of the Daoist House. 137, 344, 345, 378, 544, 737.

Daokai: See *Furong Daokai.*

Daolin: See *Niaoke Daolin.*

Daoming: See *Muzhou Daoming.*

Daopi: See *Tong'an Daopi.*

Daosheng: 道昇 [Dōshō]. Ca. thirteenth century, China. A Daoist studying Zen with Rujing at Tiantong Monastery when Dōgen stayed there. Biography unknown. 378.

Daowei: See *Dongshan Daowei.*

Daowu: 320. See also *Tianhuang Daowu.*

Daowu Yuanzhi: 道吾圓智 [Dōgo Enchi]. 769–835, China. Dharma heir of Yaoshan Weiyan, Qingyuan Line. Also called Daowu Zongzhi. He studied with Baizhang Niepan and received ordination from him before practicing with Yaoshan. Traveled for many years to various Zen monasteries, then resided and taught at Mount Daowu, Tan Region (Hunan). Biological and dharma brother of Yunyan Tansheng. A number of dialogues between them remain, and were commented on by Dōgen. Posthumous name, Great Master Xiuyi 修一大師 [Shūichi Daishi]. P. 930, Generation 10. xxxvii, xxxviii, 320, 321, 337, 397–402, 614.

Daowu Zongzhi: See *Daowu Yuanzhi.*

Daoxian: See *Luoshan Daoxian.*

Daoxin: See *Dayi Daoxin.*

Daoxuan, Precept Master: 道宣律師 [Dōsen Risshi]. 596–667, China. Regarded as founder of the Precept School in China. Taught at Mount Zhongnan, also called Mount Nan. 368.

Daoyi: 368. See also *Mazu Daoyi.*

Daoyu: 道育 [Dōiku]. Ca. sixth century, China. A disciple of Bodhidharma. Biography unknown. P. 928, Generation 2. 479, 480.

dark action: See *action, dark.*

darkness: 暗頭 [antō]. Also, night, which often represents the realm of nonduality. 312, 375, 385.

darkness arises meet it with darkness, when: 暗頭來暗頭打 [antō rai antō da]. Puhua's words. Darkness represents nonduality. 311, 384.

Dasui Fazhen: 大隋法眞 [Daizui Hōshin]. 834–919, China. Dharma heir of Changqing Da'an, Nanyue Line. He experienced great enlightenment while quite young. Traveled extensively and studied with various teachers (in addition to his dharma father, Guishan,) including Dongshan Liangjie. Taught at Mount Dasui (Sichuan), where he lived for more than ten years in a large hollow tree. His posthumous name is Great Master Shenzhao 神照大師 [Shinshō Daishi]. P. 930, Generation 11. 929.

Datong: See *Touzi Datong.*

Daxiong Peak: 大雄峯 [Daiyū Hō], literally, Great Hero Peak. Another name for Mount Baizhang. Located in Nanchang (Jianxi), China. ("Great Hero" is a name of the Buddha.) Cf.: A monk asked Baizang, "What is extraordinary?" Baizang said, "Sitting alone on Daxiong Peak." 622, 623.

Daxiu: See *Tiantong Zongjue.*

day of no work is a day of no eating, a: 一日不作一日不食 [ichinichi fusa ichinichi fujiki]. A saying of Baizhang Huaihai. 338.

Dayang: See *Furong Daokai.*

Dayang Jingxuan: 大陽警玄 [Taiyō Kyōgen]. 942–1027, China. Dharma heir of Liangshan Yuanguan, Caodong School. Taught for thirty years at Mount Dayang, Ying Region (Hubei). His posthumous name is Great Master Ming'an, 明安大師 [Myōan Daishi]. His lineage was passed posthumously to Touzi Yiqing by Dayang's friend, the Linji School teacher Fushan Fayuan. P. 932, Generation 16. 621, 931, 938.

Dayi Daoxin: 大醫道信 [Daii Dōshin]. 580–651, China. The Fourth Ancestor, 四祖 [Shiso], of the Zen School. Also called Shuangfeng, 双峰 [Sōhō]. Dharma heir of the Third Ancestor, Jianzhi Sengcan. Taught for thirty years at Mount Shuangfeng (Twin Peaks Mountain), also called West Mountain or Broken Top Mountain, Huangmei, Qi Region (Hubei). Had five hundred students, the first large assembly in Zen Buddhism. His posthumous name is Zen Master Dayi 大醫禪師 [Daii Zenji]. P. 928, Generation 4. 166; practice of, 614; story of, 366, 367; students of, 113, 239, 322; words of, 240, 241.

Dayu: 75. See also *Gaoan Dayu.*

Dazu Huike: 大祖慧可 [Taiso Eka]. 487–593. Monk name: Shenguang, 神光 [Jinkō]. Dharma heir of Bodhidharma. The Second Ancestor of Chinese Zen. According to legend, when he visited Bodhidharma at Shaolin Monastery and asked for instruction, Bodhidharma would not reply. Finally, while standing in the snow, Huike cut off his arm and gave it to Bodhidharma as a sign of his sincerity. Thus, he received instruction. Later, taught in the northern capital of Ye (Hebei). His posthumous names are Great Master Zhengzong Pujiao 正宗普覺大師 [Shōshū Fukaku Daishi], and Zen Master Dazu. P. 928, Generation 2. 166, 416, 435, 504, 565, 568; attaining the marrow, 89, 365, 440, 479, 480, 481, 574, 696; cutting off his arm, 72, 85, 364, 372, 539; descendants of, 874; harmonizing blood, 177; lineage of, 4, 478, 569, 721, 740; not go to India, 35, 609, 610, 611; practice of, 598, 614; story of, 363, 364, 495, 496, 788, 790; words of, 463, 873.

dead or alive: 殺活の因縁 [shakkatsu no innen], literally, cause and condition of being dead or alive. 159.

death, demons of: 死魔 [shima]. 662, 663.

death, temporal: 假滅 [kemetsu]. 789.

death find life, in: 死中得活 [shichū toku katsu], literally, in death attain vitality. 493, 500.

Debate Power: See *Vivādabala.*

debt, pay: 償債 [shōsai].

decadent, groups of those who are: 破落黨 [haraku tō]. 50.

decay, five signs of: 五衰 [gosui]. Signs that appear before a deva dies. 844.

decayed teaching: 173. See also *three periods.*

decayed tree: 枯木 [koboku]. A tree that has been chopped down with just the trunk remaining—sitting upright like someone doing zazen, never lying down. Sitting zazen with no seeking mind. 428, 635.

deception: 瞞 [man]. 208, 209, 624.

Decheng: See *Chuanzi Decheng.*

decline of the dharma: See *three periods.*

decline, last age of: 末代惡世 [matsudai akuse], literally, last era, unwholesome world. 17.

deepest and most intimate teaching: 極之極 [goku shi goku], literally, extreme of extremes. 667.

deeply impressed with this: 深然之 [jinnen shi]. 609.

defilement: 染汚 [zenna]. Also, divided. 49, 418, 686.

Defu: See *Yunding Defu.*

Deguang: See *Zhuoan Deguang.*

Dehui: 德徽 [Tokki]. Ca. twelfth century, China. A monk trained at the monastery of Ying'an Tanhua, Linji School. P. 932, Generation 24. 526.

deluded action: See *action, deluded.*

deluded thought, recognizing the shadow of: 迷頭認影 [meitō nin'yō]. 268.

delusion: Not enlightened. Viewing enlightenment as separate from practice. 迷 [mei], まとひ [madoi], literally, being lost. 煩惱 [bonnō], translation of Skt. klesha, consisting of greed, hatred, and ignorance. 惑執 [wakushū], literally, worrying and attachment. 漏 [ro], literally, leaking. 29, 130, 150, 299, 773.

delusion and enlightenment: 迷悟 [meigo]. 10, 224, 393, 656.

delusion, become free from: 斷惑 [dan'waku]. Literally, cutting of delusion. 82, 840.

delusions, demons of: 煩惱魔 [bonnō ma]. 662.

delusions, five: 五結 [goketsu]. Greed, anger, pride, jealousy, and stinginess. 815.

demon: 魔 [ma]. Abbrevriated transliteration of Skt. māra, literally, killer. 羅刹 [rasetsu], transliteration of Skt. rākshasa, eater of humans. 92, 362, 660, 662.

demon, heavenly: 天魔 [temma]. 404, 524, 541. See also *Pāpīyas*.

demon, outsider: 魔外 [mage]. 244.

demon, statement of: 魔説 [masetsu]. 662.

Demon School: 魔黨 [Matō]. 503.

demon's cave on the black mountain: 黑山鬼窟裏 [kokuzan kikutsu ri]. 35, 37, 38.

demons, celestial king of: 天子魔 [tenshima]. 662, 663.

demons, enter the realm of: 入魔 [nyūma]. 304.

demons, place of heavenly: 天魔界 [temma kai]. 82.

demons of delusions: See *delusions, demons of.*

demons of the five skandhas: 五衆魔 [goshuma]. 662, 663.

Deng Yinfeng: 鄧隱峯 [Tō Impō]. Ca. eighth–ninth century, China. Dharma heir of Mazu Daoyi, Nanyue Line. Deng is his family name. He was eccentric, known for dying while standing on his head. Yinfeng is a peak at Mount Wutai (Shanxi). P. 930, Generation 9. 757.

Denguang: See *Zhuoan Deguang.*

deny the way of the ancestors: 疑殺古先 [gisetsu kosen], literally, doubt and kill the ancient. 708.

depend upon letters and interpret their meaning: 依文解義 [emon gegi]. 509.

dependences, five: 五依 [goe]. Devadatta tried to establish these practices in an attempt to alter home leavers' four dependences taught by the Buddha. 816.

dependences, four: 四依 [shie]. Types of practices for home leavers: (1) Sitting under trees for a lifetime. (2) Wearing a robe of excrement-cleaning cloths for a lifetime. (3) Begging food for a lifetime. (4) Taking medicine made of urine and excrement in case of sickness for a lifetime. 816.

descendant: 兒孫 [jison], literally, child and grandchild. 51, 172, 287, 874.

descendant, dharma: 法孫 [hōson], literally, dharma grandchild. Dharma heir of a dharma heir of a master, or further down. Dharma offspring. 110, 115, 634.

describe roughly or in detail: 説細説麁 [sessai sesso]. 59.

Deshan Xuanjian: 德山宣鑒 [Tokusan Senkan]. 780–865, China. He was a well-known commentator on the *Diamond Sūtra* and was called周金剛王 Diamond King Chou after his family name. Unable to answer a rice-cake seller's simple question, he became a Zen student. Later he became a dharma heir of Longtan Chongxin, Qingyuan Line. Taught at Mount De, Ding Region (Hunan). Known for teaching by shouting and striking his students. His posthumous name is Great Master Jianxing 見性大師 [Kenshō Daishi]. P. 930, Generation 11. 317, 350, 483, 507, 536; and a rice cake seller, 84, 191–94, 196, 197; descendants of, 557, 707; student of, 216.

desire: 有漏 [uro], literally, have leaking. 353, 355.

desire, freedom from: See *miraculous powers, six.*

desire, wisdom of: 有漏智 [uro chi]. 237.

desire realm: 128, 151, 663, 812, 871, 897. See also *realms, three.*

desires, remove: 漏盡 [rojin], literally, exhaust leaking. 125.

desires in the three realms, free of: 三界欲を斷す [sangai yoku wo danzu], literally, cut off desires of the three realms. 336.

destiny of the nation, turn the: 迴天 [kaiten], literally, turn heaven (or change the mind of Emperor). 475.

determination: 意樂 [igyō], literally, will and wish. 656. See also *mind art.*

determination, towering: 衝天す [shōten-su], literally, thrust heaven. 553.

deva: Skt. 天 [ten]. Celestial being, in the highest of the six paths of transmigration. Dharma teaching is often given to humans and devas. 119, 393, 839. See also *paths, six.*

deva kings: 天王 [tennō]. 393, 660.

Deva Kings, Four: 四天王 [Shi Tennō]. Lords of the Heaven of Four Kings on Mount Sumeru, serving Indra. Guardians of the four directions in Buddhism. Dhritarāshtra (east), Virūdhaka (south), Virūpāksha (west), and Vaishravana (north). 722, 723, 822.

Deva Kings, Six: 六天 [Roku Ten]. Lords of Six Heavens in the desire worlds. 151.

Deva Vehicle: The teaching for celestial beings. See also *Vehicles, Five.*

deva worlds, eighteen: 十八天 [jūhachi ten]. Heavens in the form realm: three heavens in each of the first to third stages, plus nine heavens in the fourth stage of meditation. 812.

deva worlds, six: 六天 [reku ten]. Six heavens of the desire realm. 812.

Devadatta: 提婆達多 [Daibadatta], 達多 [Datta], 調達多 [Chōdatta]. A grandson of King Simhahanu, Shākya Clan. Elder brother of Ānanda, he was a cousin of Shākyamuni Buddha. Became a student of the Buddha along with other members of the clan and practiced hard for twelve years but could not become enlightened. Jealous of the Buddha's reputation, he tried to split the community but failed. He then attempted to kill the Buddha but could only slightly injure him. Because of these grave crimes, it is said that he fell into unceasing hell. 92, 189, 676, 784, 785, 814, 816.

devas who pull the cart: 堅行天子 [Kengyō Tenshi], literally, solid going deva(s). 660.

dewdrop: 彌露 [miro], literally, abundant dew. 31, 353, 366, 432, 909, 951.

dhamma: 曇無 [damma]. Pāli equivalent of Skt. *dharma*. 841.

dhāranī: Skt. Transliteration: 陀羅尼 [darani]. Translation: 総持 [sōji], literally, maintaining all. 1. Magical verses chanted in Esoteric Buddhism. 2. In Dōgen's usage, bowing and offering respect to the teacher, which is no other than bowing to the Buddha. 149, 327, 443, 563–68, 648, 902.

Dhāranī: 陀羅尼 [Darani]. Fifty-sixth fascicle of this book. lxxix, 563–68.

dhāranī, teachers of: 呪術師 [jujutsu shi]. 171.

dhāranī nurtured in the past: 宿殖陀羅尼 [shukujiki darani]. 58, 567.

dharma: Skt. 法 [hō]. 1. Ultimate law, reality, or truth. 2. Teaching of truth. One of the three treasures. 3. A thing, all things or phenomena. 4. Procedure. 5. Custom. 3, 35, 95, 113, 458, 839.

dharma, against: 非法 [hihō]. 50, 51.

dharma, awakening with: 法度 [hatto]. 331, 900.

dharma, buddha: See *buddha dharma.*

dharma, enter: 入法 [nippō]. 767.

dharma, essential: 法要 [hōyō]. 65, 849, 861, 896.

dharma, hue of: 風彩 [fūsai]. 366.

dharma, inconceivable: 妙法 [myōhō]. Wondrous dharma. 3, 218, 393.

dharma, indiscernible: 無分別法 [mufumbetsu hō]. 549.

dharma, inherit: 嗣法 [shihō]. 170, 171, 177, 178, 242, 577, 918.

dharma, inquire about: 問法 [mombō]. 73, 237, 339.

dharma gates, eighty thousand: 八萬法門 [hachiman hōmon]. 198.

dharma gates, eighty-four thousand: 八萬四千門 [hachiman shisen mon]. 八萬四千部 [hachiman shisen bu], literally, eighty-four thousand sections (books). Entire Buddhist scriptures. 82.

dharma hall: 法堂 [hattō]. One of the main buildings of a Zen monastery, where formal dharma talks are given. 350, 528, 733–36.

dharma heir: 法嗣 [hassu]. Immediate and certified dharma successor. 86, 246, 327, 577.

dharma instruction: 法益 [hōyaku], literally, dharma benefit. 565.

Dharma King: 法王 [hō'ō]. Shākyamuni Buddha. 732, 734, 758.

dharma king's body: 法王身 [hō'ō shin]. 132, 882.

Dharma King's teaching: 法王法令 [hō'ō hōrei], literally, Dharma King's law. 758.

dharma nature: 法性 [hosshō]. The reality of all phenomena. 159, 261, 265, 269, 558–62, 648.

Dharma Nature: 法性 [Hosshō]. Fifty-fifth fascicle of this book. xlvii, lxxix, 558–62.

dharma of impermanence: 不定法 [fujōhō], literally, dharma of things not fixed or stable. 698.

dharma of the manifested buddha body: 現身説法 [genshin seppō]. 86.

dharma procedure: 法儀 [hōgi]. 57, 522, 841.

dharma standard: 法謨 [hōmo]. 557, 711.

dharma talk: 道話 [dōwa], literally, talk of the way. 普説 [fusetsu], literally, extended talk. An informal talk presented by a dharma teacher. 223, 227, 244, 298, 376, 377, 401, 527–29.

dharma teacher: 法師 [hosshi]. 173, 192, 416, 598.

dharma teaching, receive: 法益をかうふる [hōyaku wo kōburu], literally, be allowed to receive dharma benefit. 565.

dharma thought: 法量 [hōryō]. 304.

dharma transmission: 傳法 [dempō]. Acknowledgment of mastery and entrustment of buddha dharma from teacher to disciple; also, the inheritance of the dharma. Dōgen emphasizes that this transmission remains unique and unchanged throughout all generations of buddha ancestors. 4, 76, 339, 532, 576.

dharma treasure: 法財 [hōzai]. Precious dharma. 90, 148, 334, 829, 841.

dharma treasury, entrusted with the: 付法藏 [fuhōzō]. 865.

dharma uncle: 師伯 [shihaku]. Dharma brother of the teacher. 493, 499, 737.

dharma vessel: 法器 [hōki]. Holder of dharma or one who has potential for dharma. 239, 364.

dharma way: 法道 [hōdō]. 95.

dharma wheel: 法輪 [hōrin]. The full, continuous, and dynamic teaching of the Buddha. The wheel is a symbol of a monarch in ancient India, representing justice and the crushing of hindrances. 6, 9, 57, 103, 234, 242, 270, 271, 272, 273, 276, 279, 280, 428, 431, 432, 433, 436, 437, 454, 534, 567, 573, 582, 583, 592, 617, 693, 694, 727, 767, 783, 784, 808, 809, 841, 878.

dharma wheel, break the: 破法輪僧 [ha hōrin sō]. Destroy the teaching and practice of a sangha. 280, 784.

dharma words: 法語 [hōgo]. 38, 172, 173, 373, 374, 583, 733.

Dharmapada: Skt. 法句經 [Hokku Kyō]. An early Buddhist scripture. Its Pāli counterpart is *Dhammapada.* 847.

Dharmaratna: 竺法蘭 [Jiku Hōran]. Ca. first century, c.e. A monk from central India who introduced Buddhism to China together with Kāshyapamātanga in 67 c.e., during the reign of Emperor Xiaming of the Later Han Dynasty. Also pioneered translation of Sanskrit scriptures into Chinese. Dharmaratna's Chinese name is Zhu Falan. (*Zhu* in this case means "of India.") 415.

Dhītika: 提多迦 [Daitaka]. Monk from the kingdom of Mathurā, central northern India. Taught in central India as the Fifth Ancestor of the Zen tradition. 810, 811.

dhyāna: 禪那 [zenna]. 10, 11. See also *Zen; pāramitās, six.*

dhyāna, realization of: See *pāramitās, six.*

Dhyānārtha: 禪利多 [Zenrita]. Monk who taught the young Sanghānandi in the palace of his father the king. 811, 812.

diamond samādhi: See *samādhi, diamond.*

diamond seat: See *seat, diamond.*

difficult situations, eight: 八難處 [hachi nanjo], literally, eight difficult places. Places or situations where attaining enlightenment is hindered: hell, realm of hungry ghosts, realm of animals, devas of very long life, those in remote places, those with sense defects, those who are attached to wrong views, and time before and after the time of buddhas. 656.

Dingshan Shenying: 定山神英 [Jōzan Shin'ei]. Ca. eighth–ninth century, China. Guiyang School. Dharma heir of Guishan Lingyou. Taught at Mount Ding, Chu Region (Anhui). P. 930, Generation 11. 884, 929.

Dīpankara Buddha: See *Buddha, Dīpankara.*

dipper with a missing handle, broken: 沒柄破木杓 [moppei ha mokushaku]. 1. A useless thing. 2. In Dōgen's usage, body and mind dropped away. 404.

dipper, wooden: 木杓 [mokushaku]. 278, 318, 442, 538, 541, 691.

direct: 端的 [tanteki]. 1. Direct expression; direct understanding beyond words or thoughts. 2. Essential meaning. 3. Straightforward teaching. 305, 478, 646.

direct way: 直道 [jikidō]. 242.

directions are all-inclusive: 方等 [hōtō]. 427.

directly point: 直指 [jikishi]. Experience without words and concepts. 195, 277, 350, 868.

directly point to the human mind: 直指人心 [jikishi ninshin]. 277, 330.

director: 40, 731, 736, 737. See also *officers, six.*

director of the guesthouse: 廨院主 [kai'in ju]. 75.

director of the monks' hall: 229. See also *officers, six.*

Dīrghanakha: See *Brāhman Dīrghanakha.*

disappear, both: 俱隱 [kuin]. 213, 454.

discernment: 分別 [fumbetsu]. 思量分別 [shiryō fumbetsu], literally, discrimination and discernment. 識 [shiki], literally, knowable, consciousness. 59, 245, 281, 312. See also *skandhas, five.*

discourses: 廣語 [kōgo], literally, broad words. 11, 222, 323, 514, 515, 686.

discrimination: 取舍 [shusha], literally, take and throw away. 308, 311, 312, 877.

discussion, philosophical: 論議 [rongi]. 283.

distinction: 同別 [dōbetsu], literally, same or different. 149, 279, 780, 813.

divided: 同隔 [dōkaku], literally, same or separate. 261, 271.

divided, not: 無差別 [mushabetsu], literally, not discriminated. 18, 333, 382, 383, 487, 529, 879.

divine heads: 神頭 [jinzu]. 445, 594.

Divisions, Nine: 九部 [kubu]. Classification of scriptures: 1. Sūtra. 2. Gāthā. 3. Itivrittaka. 4. Jātaka. 5. Adbhuta-dharma. 6. Nidāna. 7. Avadāna. 8. Geya. 9. Upadesha. 284, 285, 696. See also *The Buddha's Teaching; Divisions, Twelve.*

Divisions, Twelve: 十二分教 [jūni bunkyō], 十二部 [jūni bu]. Classifications of the Buddhist scriptures: (1) Sūtra—a scripture in prose. (2) Geya—a teaching to be sung. (3) Vyākarana—a prediction of enlightenment. (4) Gāthā—a verse. (5) Udāna—a teaching expounded not in response to a question. (6) Nidāna—an explanation of causes [of unwholesome things]. (7) Avadāna—a parable. (8) Itivrittaka—a past life [of a disciple of the Buddha]. (9) Jātaka—a past life [of the Buddha]. (10) Vaipulya—a broad teaching. (11) Adbhuta-dharma—an unprecedented [magical] story. (12) Upadesha—a philosophical discussion. 109, 277, 278, 280–84, 643, 696.

Dizang Guichen: 地藏桂琛 [Jizō Keichin]. 867–928, China. Also called Luohan Guichen 羅漢桂琛 [Rakan Keichin]. Dharma heir of Xuansha Shibei, Qingyuan Line. From early childhood, he spoke very well and chose not to eat meat. At first he followed the teachings of the precepts with Wuxiang, but then he declared that adhering to the precepts was not enough. He studied with Xuefeng Yicun and then with Xuefeng's disciple, Xuansha, who brought him to full awakening. He taught at Dizang Monastery and later at Luohan Monastery, in Zhang Region (Fujian). His teaching style was down-to-earth, unmasking those who used fancy words. Teacher of Fayan Wenyi, founder of the Fayan School of Zen. His posthumous name is Great Master Zheying 眞應大師 [Shin'ō Daishi]. P. 931, Generation 14. 930.

dō: See *way, expression.*

Document of Heritage: 嗣書 [Shisho]. Seventeenth fascicle of this book. lxi, 168–79.

dog: 狗子 [kushi]. A person who does not practice the way. 255, 256, 257, 634, 674.

dog have buddha nature?, does a: See *buddha nature?, does a dog have.*

Dōgen: See *Eihei Dōgen.*

doing, purposeful: 有爲 [ui]. 648.

donation, give a: 施淨財 [se jōzai], literally, give pure material. 226.

Dongpo: See *Su Dongpo.*

Dongshan Daowei: 洞山道微 [Tōzan Dōbi]. Ca. eleventh–twelfth century. Dharma heir of Furong Daokai, Caodong School. Taught at Mount Dong, Rui Region (Jiangxi). P. 933, Generation 19. 700.

Dongshan Liangjie: 洞山良价 [Tōzan Ryōkai]. 807–869, China. Became a monk in childhood, studied extensively with teachers including Nanquan and Guishan. Later became dharma heir of Yunyan Tansheng, Qingyuan Line. Taught at Mount Dong, Rui Region (Jiangxi). Author of "Song of Precious Mirror Samādhi," *Baojing Sanmeike* [Hōkyō Zammaika], the text that established the Five Ranks of the teaching, the philosophical underpinning of Caodong practice. Regarded as a founder of the Caodong School, one of the Five Schools of Chinese Zen. His posthumous name is Great Master Wuben, 悟本大師 [Gohon Daishi]. P. 930, Generation 11. 291, 929.

Dongshan School: 洞山宗 [Tōzan Shū]. 324, 514.

donkey, blind: 瞎驢 [katsuro]. 76, 511, 512.

donkey and horse, herd: 餧驢餧馬 [iro iba]. 755.

donkey comes before and horse comes after: 驢前馬後漢 [rezen bago (no) kan], literally, one who is in front of a donkey and behind a horse. One who is not oneself. 257.

donkey has not left, yet the horse has arrived: 驢事未去馬事到來 [roji miko baji tōrai]. Also reads: 驢事いまだおはらされとも馬事到來す [roji imada owara zare domo baji tōrai su]. While delusion has not left, enlightenment has arrived. Doing two things at once. Being inclusive and not divided. 101.

donkey, fins of a: 驢腮 [rosai]. That which is invisible or impossible. 238.

donkey, hoof of a: 驢馬の脚蹄 [roba no kyakutei]. Freedom from intellect and hierarchy. 423.

donkey womb, enter into a: 生身入驢胎 [shōshin nyū rotai]; 入驢胎 [nyū rotai], literally, be reborn with a body in the womb of a donkey. 676, 679, 847.

donor: 施主 [seshu]. 150, 227, 229–32.

dormitory, head of the: 寮主 [ryōshu]. 739.

doubt: 自魔 [jima], literally; self demon, self-killer. 584, 589.

doubt, ground of no: 不疑之地 [fugi no chi].

doubt, have a great: 大疑す [daigi-su]. 702.

doubtful: 不信 [fushin]. Lacking in trust. 7, 93.

dragon: 龍 [ryū]. Often represents an enlightened person. Same as *true dragon.* 114, 117, 139, 627–29, 668.

dragon, blind female: 盲龍女 [mōryūnyo]. 845.

dragon, true: 眞龍 [shinryū]. True practitioner of dharma. 89, 90, 164, 305, 599, 909.

Dragon Gate: 龍門 [Ryūmon]. Rapids midway up the Huang River, where fish who pass are said to turn into dragons. 882.

dragon head, snake tail: 龍頭蛇尾 [ryūtō dabi]. Usually meaning the beginning is not matched by what follows. For Dōgen a snake tail can be as powerful as a dragon head. 215.

dragon king: 龍王 [ryūō]. 117, 393, 686, 687, 722.

dragon replaces, bones a: 龍の換るか骨 [ryū no kauru ga hone]. 45.

dragon song: Fresh, joyous, and vast awareness. 629.

Dragon Song: 龍吟 [Ryūgin]. Sixty-fifth fascicle of this book. lxxxii, 627–30.

dragons, hungry: 餓龍 [garyū]. 844, 845.

dragons and elephants: 龍象 [ryūzō]. Excellent practitioners of dharma. 85, 340, 369, 410, 547.

dream: 1. Illusory vision. 2. In Dōgen's usage, direct and nondual experience of reality. 45, 288, 431–38.

dream, actualize the: 證夢 [shōmu]. 436.

dream, phantom, and empty flower: [mugen kūge] 夢幻空華. 20.

dreams, direct: 夢直 [muchoku]. 432.

drift: 流浪 [rurō]. 429.

drink tea and eat rice: 茶飯 [sahan], literally, tea and rice. 621.

drop away: 脱落(す) [datsuraku(-su)]. Let go; be released. To experience complete freedom beyond delusion and enlightenment, with nonattachment to body and mind. 落處 [rakusho], literally, place of dropping. 1. To be stagnant, to be stuck with narrow views. 2. To be in a state of complete freedom. 30, 440, 579, 596–99, 696.

drop off facility: 落便宜 [raku bengi]. Drop away initial understanding.

drops off completely, skin: 皮膚脱落盡 [hifu datsuraku jin]. Experiencing freedom from body.

drum, big: 法鼓 [hōku]. literally, dharma drum. 734.

dualism, barrier of: 兩重關 [ryōjūkan], literally, heavy barrier of two. 724.

duck: 鴛鴦 [en'ō]. 279.

dullness: 昏昧 [kommai]. 353.

dumbfounded: 茫然 [bōzen]. Astonished; gone blank. 192, 543, 638, 743, 747.

Duofu: 多福 [Tafuku]. Ca. ninth century, China. Dharma heir of Zhaozhou Congshen, Nanyue Line. Taught in Hang Region (Zhejiang). P. 930, Generation 11. 385, 929.

dushkrita: Skt. Transliteration: 突吉羅 [tokira]. Light wrongdoing, for which repentance may be made to oneself or another sangha member. 55.

dust, extra speck of: 客塵 [kakujin]. Delusion that comes from outside. 235.

dust, red: 紅塵 [kōjin]. Worldly matter. 237.

dusts, six: 六塵 [rokujin]. Objects of the six senses: form, sound, smell, taste, touch, and mind. 60.

dynamic work: 488. See also *activity.*

ear, celestial: 125, 535. See also *miraculous powers, six.*

early morning zazen: 朝參 [chōsan]. 41.

earth deity, shrine of the local: 土地堂 [tochi dō]. 731.

earth, emerge from the: See *emerge from the earth.*

earthworm: 蚯蚓 [kyūin]. 257, 258, 619.

east mountains travel on water: See *water, east mountains travel on.*

Eating Bowl: 鉢盂 [Hou]. Seventy-eighth fascicle of this book. lxxxviii, 721–23.

effect(s): See *action(s) that nurture different types of effect(s).*

effect, realize: 感果 [kanka]. Experience the effect.

effect, true: 實果 [jikka]. 520.

effective: 得益あり [tokuyaku ari], literally, having benefit. 553.

effort: ちから [chikara], literally, strength, power. 功夫 [kufū]. Practice. 精進 [shōjin]. Vigor. 8, 40, 90, 504, 505, 666, 718.

effort, accumulate: 積功 [shakku]. 665.

effort, complete: 108. See also *actualization, complete.*

efforts, four right: 四正勤 [shishōgon]. Not arousing an unwholesome action that has not arisen, stopping an unwholesome action that has arisen, arousing a wholesome action that has not arisen, and allowing a wholesome action that has arisen to increase. 675.

Ehu Zhifu: 鵞湖智孚 [Gako Chifu]. Ca. ninth–tenth century, China. Student of Xuefeng Yicun, Qingyuan Line. Biography unknown. P. 931, Generation 13. 420, 421.

Eight Awakenings of Great Beings: 八大人覺 [Hachi Dainin Gaku]. Eighty-fourth fascicle of this book. xcii, xcvi, 771–75.

eight or nine out of ten are accomplished before questioning: 機先の八九成あり [kisen no hakkujō ari]. 97.

eight- or sixteen-foot body: 丈六八尺 [jōroku hasshaku]. Shākyamuni Buddha is characterized as being sixteen feet tall when standing and eight feet tall when sitting. 104–6.

eight precepts: See *precepts, eight.*

Eight Seas: See *Seas, Eight.*

eight types of karma: 八種の業 [hasshu no gō]. Each of the following four types of karma is divided into two categories: matured result is definite and indefinite. (1) Effect received in this lifetime. (2) Effect received in the next lifetime. (3) Effect received in the lifetime(s) after next. (4) Effect received in an indefinite lifetime. 790.

eighteen items: See *items, eighteen.*

Eighteen Large Brāhmanist Texts: See *Brāhmanist Texts, Eighteen Large.*

eightfold noble path: See *path, eightfold noble.*

eighty-four thousand: 八万四千 [hachiman shisen]. A commonly used number in Buddhism to indicate a great many. 79, 398, 428, 879.

Eihei: 永平. Dōgen referred to himself as Eihei after the Daibutsu Monastery was renamed Eihei (Eternal Peace) Monastery in 1246. 66, 911.

Eihei Dōgen: 永平道元. See also Editor's Introduction and "Texts in Relation to Dogen's Life" for Dōgen's biography and main writings: *Treasury of the True Dharma Eye*: 正法眼藏 [Shōbō Genzō]. (See also *Treasury of the True Dharma Eye.*) Other major writings of Dōgen's are: 1. "Recommending Zazen to All People," 普勧坐禪儀 [Fukan Zazen Gi] (see appendix 1). 2. *Extensive Record of Priest Eihei Dōgen,* 永平道元和尚広録 (Eihei Dōgen Oshō Kōroku), also called *Eihei Kōroku.* A collection of Dōgen's monastic guidelines, lectures, words, and poems compiled soon after his death by his students Sen'e, Ejō, and Gien. Published in 1672. 3. *Monastic Guidelines of Eihei,* 永平清規 (Eihei Shingi), formally called *Monastic Guidelines of Dōgen Zenji, First Ancestor of the Sōto School, Japan.* A collection of six texts of monastic rules, published in 1667. 4. *Journal of My Study in China.* Commonly known as *Record of the Baoqing Era,* 宝慶記 [Hōkyō Ki], a draft record of Dōgen's study with his teacher, Rujing. Discovered and edited by Ejō after Dōgen's death. 5. *Treasury of the True Dharma Eye, Record of Things Heard:* 正法眼藏随聞記 [Shōbō Genzō Zuimon-ki]. A collection of Dōgen's informal evening talks recorded by Ejō during Katei Era (1235–1238), probably edited later by one of Ejō's students. P. 934, Generation 24. 911.

Eihei Monastery: 永平寺 [Eihei-ji]. Named in 1246. Formerly called Daibutsu Monastery. Zen training center in Shibi County, Echizen Province (present Fukui Prefecture), Japan, founded by Dōgen. Eihei—literally, eternal peace; Japanese transliteration of *Yongping*, an era in the Later Han Dynasty, 58–75, when Buddhism was officially introduced to China. Its "mountain name" is 吉祥山 [Kichijō Zan], literally, Auspicious Mountain. 63, 71, 765, 770, 775, 791, 919.

Eisai: See *Myōan Eisai.*

Ekottarika Āgama Sūtra: 増一阿含經 [Zōichi Agon Kyō]. Sanskrit version of one of the *Āgama Sūtras*—early Buddhist scriptures. Translated into Chinese. *Ekota* means increasing by one. In this sūtra, ungrouped terms, as well as those classified in groups of two, three, and so on, up to eleven, are explained.

elder: 耆年老宿 [ginen rōshuku], literally, elderly person, old teacher. 62, 69.

elements or objects: 大塵 [daijin], literally, great dust. Four great elements, plus five skandhas. 427.

elements, five: 五行 [gogyō]. 五才 [gosai]. Ancient Chinese classification: wood, fire, soil, metal, and water. 210, 211.

elements, five great: 五大 [godai]. Ancient Indian classification: earth, water, fire, air, and space. 161, 832.

elements, four great: 四大 [shidai]. Ancient Indian classification: earth, water, fire, and air. 77, 161, 297, 479, 652.

elements, six great: 六大 [rokudai]. Ancient Indian classification: earth, water, fire, air, space, and consciousness. 161, 292.

elements, three: 三才 [sansai]. Ancient Chinese classification: heaven, earth, and humans. 628.

elucidate: 解説 [gesetsu]. 18, 182, 665, 913.

emancipated right where one is: 當處解脱 [tōjo gedatsu]. 218.

emancipation: 解脱 [gedatsu]. Liberation. Freedom from bondage, like a fish escaping the net. Liberation from delusion or suffering. 81, 102, 769, 884.

emancipation, eight types of: 八解脱 [hachi gedatsu]. Steps of meditation toward freedom from attachment: (1) See all things as impure and reduce desire. (2) Reduce attachment to external phenomena. (3) Avoid giving rise to illusion. (4) Contemplate boundless space transcending all form. (5) Contemplate boundless consciousness. (6) Contemplate nonsubstantiality. (7) Contemplate the state beyond thought. (8) Attain a state where all mental activity ceases. 336.

emancipation, gate of: 解脱門 [gedatsu mon]. Also translated as gate of liberation. 5.

emancipation, state of great: 大解脱地 [daigedatsu chi]. 5.

embody, originally: 本具す [hongu-su].

emerge from the earth: 地涌 [chiyū]. 187, 467.

emotion: 汗栗多心 [karida shin]. Transliteration of Skt. hridaya, heart. 422.

emotions arise wisdom is pushed aside, while: 情生智隔 [jōshō chikyaku]. 36.

Emperor Dai: 代宗 [Daisō]. Eighth emperor of the Tang Dynasty, China. Reigned 762–779. 112, 137, 745.

Emperor Gao: 高宗 [Kōsō]. Third Emperor of Tang Dynasty, China. Reigned 649–683. 367.

Emperor Guangwu: 光武皇帝 [Kōbu Kōtei]. First Emperor of the Later Han Dynasty, China. Reigned 25–57.

Emperor Jing: 敬宗 [Keisō]. Thirteenth emperor of Tang Dynasty, China. Reigned 824–826. 415.

Emperor Kimmei: 欽明天皇 [Kimmei Tennō]. 509–571, Japan. Reigned 539–571. Buddhism was officially introduced shortly before or during his reign. 21, 919.

Emperor Mu: 穆宗 [Bokusō]. Twelfth emperor of Tang Dynasty, China. Reigned 820–824. 350, 912.

Emperor Ning: 寧宗 [Neisō]. 1168–1224, China. 嘉定聖主 [Katei Shōshu] /嘉定の皇帝 [Katei no Kōtei], meaning Emperor in the Jiading Era. Fourth emperor of the Southern Song Dynasty, China. Reigned 1194–1224. Ning is his posthumous name; named after the era of his reign, as customary in East Asia. 374, 377.

Emperor of Wei: 魏主 [Gi Shu]. The ruler of Wei when Bodhidharma arrived in the northern country of Wei was Emperor Xiaoming (reigned 516–528). 92.

Emperor Ren: 仁宗皇帝 [Jinsō Kōtei]. Fourth emperor of Northern Song Dynasty, China. Reigned 1022–1063. 575.

Emperor Shōmu: 聖武天皇 [Shōmu Tennō], 聖武皇帝 [Shōmu Kōtei]. 701–756, Japan. Reigned 724–749. A great supporter of Buddhism. Sponsored the construction of Tōdai Monastery with the gigantic image of Vairochana Buddha in Nara. 129.

Emperor Shun: 舜 [Shun]. A legendary virtuous ruler of ancient China. Regarded as the successor of Emperor Yao. 16, 344, 621, 622.

Emperor Shun: 順宗 [Junsō]. Tenth emperor of the Tang Dynasty China. Reigned in 805. 16, 344, 621, 622.

Emperor Su: 肅宗 [Shukusō]. Seventh emperor of the Tang Dynasty, China. Reigned 756–762. 198, 745.

Emperor Tai: 太宗 [Taisō]. 598–649, China. Second emperor of the Tang Dynasty. Reigned 626–649. Supported the translation project of the Buddhist canon from Sanskrit to Chinese, headed by Xuanzong, who had traveled to India and brought back a number of scriptures. 211, 366, 367, 474.

Emperor Tai: 太祖 [Taiso]. 155–220, China. Called Caocao while alive. Founder of the northern kingdom of Wei. His successor, Emperor Wen, the first monarch of Wei, gave him this posthumous title. Also called Emperor Wu. 211, 366, 367, 474.

Emperor Wen: 文宗 [Bunsō]. Fourteenth emperor of Tang Dynasty, China. Reigned 826–840. 351, 417, 508, 516.

Emperor Wu: 武宗 [Busō]. Fifteenth emperor of Tang Dynasty. Reigned 840–846. Oppressed Buddhism during his reign. 129, 216, 355, 357, 416.

Emperor Wu of Liang: 梁武帝 [Ryō Butei]. Founder of the southern kingdom of Liang. Reigned 502–549. Regarded as one who had a dialogue with Bodhidharma upon his arrival in China. 357.

Emperor Xian: 憲宗 [Kensō]. Eleventh emperor of Tang Dynasty, China. Reigned 805–820. 37, 350, 415, 417, 418.

Emperor Xiaoming: 孝明皇帝 [Kōmei Kōtei]. Second emperor of Later Han Dynasty. Reigned 57–75. He sent a messenger to India to invite monks, which resulted in the first official introduction of Buddhism to China in 67. 115, 140, 355, 415.

Emperor Xuan: 宣宗 [Sensō]. Sixteenth emperor of Tang Dynasty. Reigned 846–859. Treated brutally by his brother Emperor Wu, he left the palace and became a wanderer. As Monk Dazong, he studied with Xiangyan Zhixian, Guiyang School. After ascension, he abolished Wu's persecution of Buddhism. P. 928, Generation 10. 350, 351, 352, 417, 700.

Emperor Yang of the Sui Dynasty: 隋の煬帝 [Zui no Yōdai]. Second emperor of the Sui Dynasty, China. Reigned 604–618. 129.

Emperor Yao: 堯 [Gyō]. Legendary virtuous ruler of ancient China. 344.

Emperor Yōmei: 用明天皇 [Yōmei Tennō]. d. 587, Japan. Reigned 585–587. There was a major conflict among his retainers whether to support Buddhism or stay with the indigenous belief, Shintoism. 21, 919.

Emperor Zong: 中宗 [Chūsō]. Fourth and seventh emperor of Tang Dynasty, China. Reigned 683–684 and 705–710. 112, 136.

Emperor, Yellow: 黃帝 [Kōtei]. Legendary ruler of ancient China. Regarded as creator of the calendar, music, literature, and medicine. 163, 210, 344.

Emperors, Five: 五帝 [gotei]. Heavenly rulers of four directions, plus Yellow Emperor in the center. The four rulers are: Green Emperor (east, in charge of spring), Red or Flame (south, summer), White (west, autumn), and Black (north, winter). There are other lists, too. 867.

emptiness: 空 [kū], literally, sky. Skt., shūnyatā, literally, zeroness. Formless, boundless, and nonseparate nature of all things. Space, void. Also, illusory. liv, 7, 98, 279, 643, 717.

emptiness, a piece of rock hanging in: See *rock hanging in emptiness, a piece of.*

emptiness, flower of: 空華 [kūge]. Also, flower in the sky. 10, 21, 44, 79.

emptiness, gate of: 空門 [kūmon]. 766, 890.

emptiness, twenty types of: 二十空 [nijukkū]. Aspects of emptiness (shūnyatā): (1) Internal emptiness. (2) External emptiness. (3) Internal and external emptiness. (4) Emptiness of emptiness. (5) Great emptiness (that of the four noble truths and twelvefold causation). (6) Lesser emptiness (that of four fruits). (7) Emptiness of truth. (8) Emptiness of conditional form. (9) Emptiness of unconditional elements. (10) Absolute emptiness. (11) Unoriginated emptiness. (12) Caused form emptiness. (13) Unchangeable form emptiness. (14) Original nature emptiness. (15) Self-form emptiness. (16) Common form emptiness. (17) All existences emptiness. (18) Unobtainable emptiness. (19) Non-nature emptiness. (20) Self-nature emptiness. 717.

empty, originally: 性空寂 [shō kūjaku], literally, (self) nature is empty and serene. 61, 479, 789.

empty and serene: 空寂 [kūjaku]. 355.

Empty Eon, King of the: 威音王 [Ion Ō], 威音王佛 [Ion Ō Butsu]. The four stages in a world cycle are: becoming, abiding, decaying, and empty. The buddha who appears in the Empty Eon is called the King of the Empty Eon or King of Emptiness, 空王 [Kū Ō], king of beginningless kalpa 空劫 [kūgō]. Regarded as symbol of the original face. after, 155, 739; before, 408, 540, 548, 606, 752; before and/or after, 564, 586, 676; realm of, 647.

encompass: 覆藏す [fukuzō-su], literally, cover and store. 蓋 [gai], literally, cover. 囊括 [nōkatsu], literally, bag and bind. 132, 247, 257, 267, 289, 290, 554, 604.

encompass, fully: 正當覆藏 [shōtō fukuzō], literally, exactly covering and treasuring. 257.

encounter: 相見(す) [shōken(-su)], literally, seeing each other. 相逢 [sōhō], literally, meeting each other. 1. Dualistic opposition. 2. Meeting between teacher and disciple. 3. Understanding. 72, 299, 544, 695, 751.

encountering Buddha: 值佛 [chi butsu]. 418.

encourage: 誨勵 [kairei]. 376.

end of the break from zazen: 放參罷 [hōsan ha]. 731.

end of the practice for the day: 放參 [hōsan]. Also, a day of rest from scheduled monastic activities. 729.

endeavor of the way, concentrated: See *way, concentrated endeavor of the.*

endeavor, conscious: 心意識 [shin'ishiki]. 579, 908.

enemy: 讐家 [shūke]. 182, 223, 348, 475.

enjoyment and ease: 大安樂 [dai anraku], literally, great ease and bliss. 12, 908.

enjoyment, four practices of: 四安樂行 [shi anraku gyō]. Taught in *Lotus Sūtra.* (1) Wholesome action by the body. (2) Wholesome action by speech. (3) Wholesome action by mind. (4) Vow to awaken sentient beings. 58.

enlighten: 證(す) [shō(su)]. 107.

enlightened, naturally: 性覺 [shōkaku]. 260.

enlightenment: Skt. bodhi. Awakening. Transliteration: 菩提 [bodai]. Translation: 覺 [kaku] (awakening); 悟/さとり [go/satori] (enlightenment, realization); 證 [shō] (enlightenment, realization); 道 [dō] (way, enlightenment). 1. Shākyamuni Buddha's great realization under the bodhi tree. 2. Original manifestation of buddha nature, inseparable from practice. 3. Fundamental awareness of reality beyond dualism. 4. Sudden and direct experience of reality, which is often sought as a goal separate from practice. Dōgen emphasizes that one must go beyond enlightenment in this sense. xxiv, 5, 30, 261, 287, 655.

enlightenment, acquired: 始覺 [shikaku]. Enlightenment attained by becoming free of delusion; initial enlightenment. 267, 269.

enlightenment, arousing the aspiration for: 發菩提心 [hotsu bodai shin]. Having the thought of enlightenment. See also *enlightenment, aspiration for; enlightenment, thought of.*

enlightenment, aspects of: 菩提相 [bodai sō]. 395.

enlightenment, aspiration for: 菩提心 [bodai shin]. Skt. bodhi chitta. The wish and quest for enlightenment that establishes one's determination to practice. 73, 646–52, 655–63.

enlightenment, attain: 取證 [shushō]. 8, 94, 107, 656, 800, 843.

enlightenment, attain authentic: 成正覺 [jō shōgaku]. 497, 539.

enlightenment, complete: Transliteration: 三菩提 [sambodai]. Skt., sambodhi. Translation: 圓覺 [engaku]. 335, 445, 567, 648, 657, 868. See also *enlightenment, unsurpassable, complete.*

enlightenment, depend upon: 假悟 [kego]. 301.

enlightenment, equal to buddha's: See *bodhisattva who is a candidate to be a buddha; bodhisattvas of the ten stages and three classes.*

enlightenment, filled with great: 參飽大悟 [sambō daigo]. 297.

enlightenment, go beyond: See *go beyond enlightenment.*

enlightenment, gradual: 漸悟 [zengo]. A method of practice or cultivation that leads step by step to enlightenment.

enlightenment, great: 大悟 [daigo], 大覺 [daigaku], 大菩提 [daibodai]. 157, 268, 296–302, 616.

enlightenment, great, complete: 大圓覺 [dai engaku]. 673, 742.

enlightenment, immediate realization of: 直證菩提 [jikishō bodai]. 9.

enlightenment, inconceivable: [myōkaku]. The highest stage of bodhisattvas. 674. See also *bodhisattvas of the ten stages and three classes.*

enlightenment, letting-go limb of: 捨覺支 [sha kakushi]. 680, 681.

enlightenment, mistaken views of spontaneous or natural: 自然天然の邪見 [jinen tennen no jaken]. 428.

enlightenment, original: 本覺 [hongaku]. Enlightenment that is intrinsic to each person, that is actualized by practice. 237, 267, 269, 381, 461, 708.

enlightenment, painting of: 證畫 [shōga]. 449.

enlightenment, play with: 弄悟 [rōgo].

enlightenment, prediction of: 授記 [juki]. Confirmation of present or future enlightenment. 142, 676.

enlightenment, retreat limb of: 除覺支 [jo kakushi]. 680, 681.

enlightenment, seven limbs of: 七等覺支 [shichi tō kakushi]. 680.

enlightenment, spontaneous: 天然 [tennen]. "Claimed enlightenment" without practice or verification from an authentic teacher. 自然 [jinen], 自然見 [jinen ken], literally, (view of) natural enlightenment. 158, 170, 178, 237, 427, 699, 856.

enlightenment, sudden. 頓悟 [tongo]. Immediate realization of buddha nature without going through a series of stages.

enlightenment, take up: 拈悟 [nengo]. 297.

enlightenment, thirty-seven wings of: 三十七品菩提分法 [sanjūshichi hon bodai bumpō]. 三十七部 [sanjūshichi bu], 三十七品 [sanjūshichi hon]. Thirty-seven *bodhipākshikas,* or conditions favorable to enlightenment: four applications of mindfulness, four right efforts, four elements of supernormal power, fivefold controlling power, fivefold moral power, seven limbs of enlightenment, and eightfold noble path. 82, 573, 651, 671, 682, 691.

enlightenment, those without: 422. See also *icchantika.*

enlightenment, thought of: 道念 [dōnen]. The aspiration for enlightenment.

enlightenment, trace of: 悟迹 [goshaku]. 30.

enlightenment, unfold: 開悟 [kaigo]. 665.

enlightenment, unsurpassable, complete: Skt., anuttara samyak sambodhi. Transliteration: 阿耨多羅三藐三菩提 [anokutara sammyaku sambodai]. 阿耨菩提 [anoku bodai]. 無上菩提 [mujō bodai], literally, bodhi (that has) nothing higher. 3, 28, 393–95 …

enlightenment, without: 無覺 [mukaku]. 260.

enlightenment, wondrous: 妙覺 [myōgaku]. 81, 82, 461, 522, 545, 674, 742.

enlightenment thought: 悟量 [goryō]. 304.

entangle: 纏 [ten]. Entangled, 結纏 [ketten], literally, tied and entangled. 479.

entangled vines, slash: 葛藤斷句 [kattō dan ku], literally cut off phrases that are like twining vines. 157.

enter homeless life: 出家 [shukke]. Become a monk or nun. 424, 426.

enter so deep inside that no one can guide the person: 深入裏許無人接渠 [jinnyūri kyo munin sekkyo]. 599.

enter the chamber: 堂奥 [dōō], literally, deep inside the hall. To receive personal instruction in the abbot's room. 583, 913. See also *abbot's room, receive guidance in the.*

entire body: 渾身 [konshin]. 25, 404, 616, 643.

entire body upholds the entire body: 渾身是已掛渾身 [konshin ze i ka konshin]. 643.

entire sky collapses: 蓋地撲落 [gaichi bokuraku]. 46.

entire world of the ten directions: 盡十方世界 [jinjuppō sekai]. 35, 208, 592–94, 696.

entrust: 附授 [fuju]. 10, 170, 389, 517, 642, 697, 914 . . .

entrust, intimately: 親附 [shimpu]. 570, 678.

entrusted of the dharma treasury: See *dharma treasury, entrusted of the.*

entrustment, intimate: 密付 [mippu]. 263, 570.

entry hall: See *hall, entry.*

environs: See *body, mind, and environs.*

eon, last: 過去莊嚴劫 [kako shōgen gō]. 169.

eon, present: 現在賢劫 [genzai kengō]. This present kalpa: 賢劫 [kengō]. 169, 178.

eons, countless: Skt. tri kalpa asankhyeya. 三阿僧祇劫 [san'asōgi kō], literally, three [san] plus, (Skt.) kalpa [kō] asankhyeya [asōgi]. Also, 三阿僧祇 [san'asōgi]. Three stages of countless kalpas for bodhisattvas to become buddhas. 阿僧企耶 [asōgiya] means, incalculable. Also, 三祇百劫 [sangi hyakkō], literally, three countless, one hundred kalpas. 568, 656, 829.

eons, dormant for boundless: 曠劫未明 [kōgō mimyō]. 85.

eons, great: 大劫 [daikō]. 317, 428, 587, 656, 669, 867.

eons, many: 多劫 [tagō]. 9, 532, 656.

eons, one hundred million: Skt. niyuta kalpa. Transliteration: 那由他劫 [nayuta kō]. *Niyuta* is ten to the eleventh power.

ephemeral: はかなし [hakanashi]. 15.

equal: 平等 [byōdō]. 一等 [ittō], literally, one and the same. Inseparable. 14, 462, 526, 701.

Equal Wisdoms, Ten: 十同眞智 [jū dōshinchi]. Ten types of wisdom for a Zen teacher for guiding a student, taught by Fenyang Shanzhao. (1) Oneness between teacher and student. (2) Equal great matter. (3) Total study with all phenomena. (4) Equal genuine wisdom. (5) Equal universal understanding. (6) Equal embodiment (of buddha nature). (7) Common gain and loss (in practice). (8) Shared life and death. (9) Shared voice. (10) Nondual entering. 507.

Esoteric Buddhism: 密教 [mikkyō]. The ultimate development in Mahāyāna Buddhism, which views the universe as a manifestation of Mahā Vairochana Buddha. The practice is based on rituals involving mudrās, mantras, and visualizations of various deities. 912, 914. See also *Mantra School; Tendai School.*

essence: 的旨 [tekishi], literally, target meaning. 自性 [jishō], literally, self nature. 9, 29, 655.

essence and form: 性相 [shōsō]. Also, essential. 142, 212, 652.

essence, marks, substance, and activity: 性相體力 [shōsō tairiki]. 102.

essential, most: 要樞 [yōsū], literally, central pivot. 531, 749.

essential, not: 不用得 [yō futoku], literally, not usable. 263, 280, 281, 284, 540, 547, 749.

Essentials, Three: 三要 [san'yō]. Classification of words by Linji: (1) Unintended words. (2) Words that lead one thousand students into profundity. (3) Words that are beyond words. 507.

Etatsu: 慧達. Ca. thirteenth century, Japan. Practitioner of chanting the *Lotus Sutra.* Then a student of Dōgen at Kōshō Hōrin Monastery. Further biography unknown. 190.

evenly and broadly: 平展 [heiten]. 296.

everyday activity: 家常 [kajō], literally, normal thing in the (buddha) house. 56, 296, 621, 626.

Everyday Activity: 家常 [Kajō]. Sixty-fourth fascicle of this book. xlviii, lxxxii, 621–26.

everyday speech: 家常語 [kajō go]. 415.

evil: 132, 782, 802, 891. See also *unwholesome.*

exact point: 94. See also *accept.*

exactly: 是 [ze], literally; be correct. 106, 217, 254, 554.

examine: 辨肯 [benkō], literally, clarify and affirm. 參究 [sankyū], study all the way, investigate thoroughly. 30, 108, 597, 727.

example, excellent: 勝躅 [shōchoku]. 75, 343, 568, 767.

excellence, a person of: 祖席の英雄 [soseki no eiyū], literally, hero on the ancestral seat. 21, 505.

Excellent Tamer: 調御丈夫 [Chōgyo Jōbu]. One of the ten principal titles of the Buddha. 794, 796, 822, 824, 825.

existence, future: 當本有 [tō hon'u], literally, future original existence. 659.

existence, original: 本有 [hon'u]. Originally present; original possession. 707.

existences, twenty-five: 二十五有 [nijūgo u]. Types of beings in the three worlds: fourteen in the desire world, seven in the form world, and four in the formless world. 10. See also *realms, three.*

expectation, without: 無圖 [muto]. 171, 314, 443.

experience, thorough ancestral: 祖究盡 [so gūjin]. 169.

experience, thoroughly: 究盡(す) [gūjin(-su)]. Fully investigate; thoroughly practice; fully understand; penetrate the essential matter. 82, 186, 612, 864.

expound: 演説 [enzetsu], literally, present and explain. 開演 [kaien], literally, open and present. 説著 [setsujaku], literally, explain. 説盡 [setsujin], literally, expound fully. 6, 25, 99, 270, 727.

express thoroughly: 道得盡 [dōtoku jin]. 139, 398, 400.

expressed beyond: 向上に道取 [kōjō ni dōshu], literally, expression in going beyond. 73.

expression: 道 [dō]. The Chinese *dao* (on which the Japanese term is based), usually means "way." But in this case it means "word," "speak," or "express." 道得 [dōtoku] literally, expression competed. Complete expression; true expression. Coming up with one phrase. Presenting a case. Thorough expression of realization. Statement. 道取 [dōshu], literally, expression taken. 衔道 [kandō], literally, holding words in mouth. 語話 [gowa], words; statement. 96, 154, 276, 439–43, 682.

expression, complete: 道著 [dōjaku]. Saying a word. Statement. 254, 607, 624.

expression, ultimate: 究竟説 [kukyō setsu]. 207.

Expressions: 道得 [Dōtoku]. Fortieth fascicle of this book. lxxii, 439–43.

expressions in the past: 曽道取 [sō dōshu], literally, having spoken before. 483.

expressions of dharma, amassing of: 説法蘊 [seppō'on], literally, assemblage of speaking dharma.

Extensive Record of the Lamp: See *Tiansheng Extensive Record of the Lamp.*

extra: 剩法 [jōhō], literally, leftover thing. 46, 107, 235, 371, 390, 406, 434, 517.

extraordinary: 特地 [tokuchi]. 地 [chi] is a suffix meaning "that which is." 393.

extremely fine: 極微 [gokumi]. 424.

extremely large is small: 極大同小 [gokudai dō shō]. 264.

extremely small is large: 極小同大 [gokushō dō dai]. 264.

eye: 眼 [gen]. True seeing, understanding, or experience. Often represents awakening. 207, 398, 415, 569, 593.

eye, a single: 一隻眼 [ichi sekigen]. 228, 255, 592, 879.

eye, authentic: 正眼 [shōgen]. 286.

eye, blossoms in an: 眼中華 [gan chū ke]. 617.

eye, celestial: 125, 344, 535, 879, 887. See also *miraculous powers, six.*

eye, covered: 眼礙 [genge]. 263.

eye, half an: 半隻眼 [han sekigen]. 228.

eye, hear with the: 眼處聞聲 [gensho monshō]. 93.

eye, open: 活眼 [katsugen], literally, vital eye. 97, 406, 423.

eye, shramana's single: 沙門(の)一隻眼 [shamon (no) isseki gen]. 488.

eye, tip of the: 眼頭尖 [gantō sen], literally, the head of the eye is pointed. 616.

eye, true dharma: See *true dharma eye.*

eye becomes lofty through the entire world: 眼高一世 [gankō isse]. 270.

eye of practice: 31, 515, 708, 709. See also *eye of study.*

eye of seeing the Buddha: 見佛眼 [kembutsu gen]. 604, 607.

eye of study: 參學眼 [sangaku gen]. 參學眼力 [sangaku ganriki], literally, eye power of study. Also, eye of practice. (For Dōgen, "study" often means practice.) 50, 323, 563.

eyeball: 眼睛 [ganzei]. That which represents true seeing or understanding; hence, buddha ancestor. Also, essence. 223, 615–20, 827.

Eyeball: 眼睛 [Ganzei]. Sixty-third fascicle of this book. lxxxi, 615–20.

eyeball, crush the: 打失眼睛 [dashitsu ganzei]. 228, 617.

eyeball, diamond: 金剛眼睛 [kongō ganzei]. 619.

eyeball, fool with an: 弄眼睛 [rōganzei]. Seeing through. 406.

eyeball, pluck the: 抉出眼睛 [kesshutsu ganzei]. Annihilate and transcend views or understanding. 406.

eyeball, vital: 活眼睛 [katsu ganzei]. 222, 617, 632, 652.

eyeball has been switched to a black bead by someone else: 眼睛被別人換却木槵子 [ganzei hi betsunin kankyaku mokkansu]. Represents being blinded, going beyond discrimination. 594.

eyebrows, raise one's: 揚眉 [yōbi]. 44, 109, 111, 605.

eyes, blind: 瞎眼 [katsugen]. 462.

eyes, five: 五眼 [gogen]. Fleshly eyes, heavenly eyes, wisdom eyes, dharma eyes, and buddha eyes. Heavenly or celestial eyes are those of devas. Wisdom eyes are those of shrāvakas and pratyeka-buddhas. Dharma eyes are those of bodhisattvas. 584.

eyes, obscured: 翳眼 [eigen]. 460–62.

eyes, one thousand: 千眼 [sengen]. Avalokiteshvara, the great bodhisattva of compassion who hears the cries of the world, is sometimes described or portrayed as having one thousand arms, with an eye on each hand. 402, 465, 556, 584, 879, 921.

eyes, wisdom: See *eyes, five.*

face: 面目 [memmoku], literally, face and eye. Original face, or buddha nature, which is inherent in every sentient being. 37, 569–95, 631, 724.

face, demon: 鬼面 [kimen]. 216, 445, 594.

face, demon's horned: 鬼面の戴角 [kimen no taikaku]. 695.

face, deva: 天面 [temmen]. 697.

face, exchange: 換面 [kammen]. To turn the ordinary face into the original face. 36.

face, human: 人面 [ninmen]. 92, 211, 362, 690, 697.

face, luminous: 面光 [menkō]. 572.

face, original: 本面目 [hommemmoku], literally, original face and eyes. 本來面目 [honrai (no) memmoku], literally, face and eyes originally come. Same as original self. Buddha nature, or compete and nondual reality, inherent to each person. 5, 98, 588, 877.

face, serene: 面目雍容 [memmoku yōyō]. 298.

face, skin, flesh, bones, and marrow, to exchange: 換面目皮肉骨髄 [kan memmoku hiniku kotsuzui]. To turn the ordinary self into the original self.

face after one's parents were born, one's: 父母所生の面目 [bumo shoshō no memmoku]. Represents timelessness of the present moment. 445.

face before one's parents were born, one's: 父母未生の面目 [bumo mishō no memmoku]. 445. See also *face*.

face skin is ten feet thin: 面皮薄一丈 [mempi haku ichi jō]. 572.

face skin is three inches thick: 面皮厚三寸 [mempi kō san zun]. 572.

face-to-face transmission: See *transmission, face-to-face.*

Face-to-Face Transmission: 面授 [Menju]. Fifty-seventh fascicle of this book. xlvii, xlix, lxxx, 569–78.

Fachang: See *Damei Fachang; Kumu Facheng.*

facility, achieve: 得便宜 [toku bengi]. 94.

Fada: 法達 [Hōtatsu]. Ca. seventh–eighth century, China. Originally a practitioner of chanting *Lotus Sūtra*. Dharma heir of Sixth Ancestor Huineng. Taught at Nanhua Monastery, Shao Region (Guangdong). P. 929, Generation 7. 182–84, 223, 224.

fall off the straight line: 曠然繩墨外 [kōzen jōboku gai], literally, far out of the line (drawn) with an inked string. 251.

fame and gain: 名利 [myōri]. 4, 39, 375, 379.

family member: 眷屬 [kenzoku]. 207, 683, 735, 737, 808, 816.

fan: 扇 [ōgi]. 32, 33.

Fang Xuanling: See *Minister Fang.*

Fanghui: See *Yangqi Fanghui.*

farewell: 珍重 [chinchō], literally, treasure (yourself). 291, 354.

Farong: See *Niutou Farong.*

Fatai: See *Fuxing Fatai.*

fathom: 卜度 [bokutaku], literally, guess and measure. 258.

fault: 非 [hi]. 19, 41, 801.

Faxian: 法顯 [Hōken]. 340–420?, China. After becoming a monk, realized the incomplete knowledge of precepts in China. Left for India in 399 and journeyed for ten years. Brought and translated into Chinese *Mahā Sangha Precepts* and *Mahā Pari-Nirvāna Sūtra.* 835.

Fayan: See *Wuzu Fayan.*

Fayan School: 法眼宗 [Hōgen Shū]. The lineage of Fayan Wenyi. One of the Five Schools of Chinese Zen Buddhism. 5, 506, 512.

Fayan Wenyi: 法眼文益 [Hōgen Mon'eki/Bun'eki]. 885–958, China. Dharma heir of Dizang Guichen, Qingyuan Line. Abbot of Baoen Monastery, Jinling (Jiangsu). Author of many poems and commentaries, including the *Ten Admonitions for the Zen School.* His posthumous name is Zen Master Great Fayan, 大法眼禪師 [Daihōgen Zenji].

Regarded as founder of the Fayan School. P. 931, Generation 15. descendant of, 197; discourse of, 597; lineage of, 171, 175, 366, 513, 916; story of, 512; student of, 18, 19; words of, 317, 598.

Fazhen: See *Dasui Fazhen.*

feature: 相 [sō]. Also form, essence. 31.

feeling: 25, 225, 559, 663. See also *skandhas, five.*

fellow, bald-headed: 禿頭漢 [tokutō kan]. 157, 612.

Fengxue Yanzhao: 風穴延昭 [Fūketsu Enshō]. 896–973, China. Dharma heir of Nanyuan Huiyong, Linji School. Taught at Mount Fengxue, Ru Region (Henan). Later taught for twenty years at Guanghui Monastery, Ying Region (Hubei), where he had over one thousand students. The subsequent Linji lineage descended from him. P. 931, Generation 14. 175.

Fenyang Shanzhao: 汾陽善昭 [Fun'yō Zenshō]. 947–1024, China. Dharma heir of Shoushan Xingnian, Linji School. Fenyang traveled widely and studied with many teachers before receiving the mind seal of Shoushan. He refused invitations to assume the abbacy of eight well-known monasteries, but when his teacher Shoushan died, he was persuaded to become abbot of Mount Fenyang, Fen Region (Shanxi), where he taught for thirty years. Fenyang is known for his use of Zen stories in his teaching and for developing the first kōan collections, which were included in the *Recorded Sayings of Zen Master Fenyang Wude.* Although he was of the Linji School, he had also studied in the Caodong lineage, and he introduced the Five Ranks into the Linji teaching. Stories from all the Zen schools were included in his texts, along with verses. Later on, commentaries were added, and the kōan collections we know today, like the *Blue Cliff Record,* came into being. His posthumous name is Zen Master Wude, 無德禪師 [Mutoku Zenji]. P. 932, Generation 16. 175.

field, reach the: 到田地 [tō denchi], literally, arrive at a rice field. 499.

field of benefaction: 福田 [fukuden], literally, rice field of good fortune. 118, 130, 131, 134, 146, 151, 817, 837.

fighting spirits: 293, 294, 425, 538. See also *paths, six.*

file a file: 43. See also *mistake after mistake.*

fill: 参飽(す) [sambō(-su)]. Also, filled, satisfied. 31.

final body: See *body, final.*

fine: 罰油 [batsu'yu], literally, oil for punishment. Monks are asked to pay for a small portion of oil for the lamps, when they make careless mistakes. 41.

finger, raise one: 竪一指 [ju isshi]. Tianlong and his successor Juzhi raised one finger whenever asked a question. 204.

fingers, snap: 彈指 [danshi]. Gesture for warning, awakening, approval, or cleansing. 53.

fire on one's head, brush off the: 頭燃をはらふ [zunen wo harau]. 72.

fire, blink of: 星火 [seika], literally, star fire. 459.

fire, raging: 猛火 [mōka]. 159.

firewood, carry: 搬柴 [hansai]. 290, 291, 392, 547, 781.

fist: 拳頭 [kentō]. 頭 [tō] is a suffix. 223, 286, 725, 747.

fist, a single: 拳頭一隻 [kentō isseki]. 591.

fist, blow of a: 喫拳 [kikken], literally, receiving a fist. 317.

fist, enter a: 入拳頭裏 [nyū kentō ri]. 405.

fist, held-up: 拈拳頭 [nenkentō]. 236.

fist, raise a: 拳頭を擧起す [kentō wo koki-su]. Expresses direct understanding. 542.

fist, vital: 活拳頭 [katsuketō]. 222.

fists, stinky: 臭拳頭 [shūkentō]. 747.

fists and nostrils: 拳頭鼻孔 [kentō bikū]. Teachers and elders. 728.

fit exactly: 的當 [tekitō], literally, hit the mark.

Five Buddhas: See *Buddhas, Five.*

Five Gates: 5. See also *Schools, Five.*

Five Houses: 19, 515, 916. See also *Schools, Five.*

Five Houses, different flavors of the: 五家門風 [goke mompū]. 509.

five monks: See *monks, five.*

Five Ranks. See *Ranks, Five.*

Five Schools: See *Schools, Five.*

five skandhas: See *skandhas, five.*

Five Vehicles: See *Vehicles, Five.*

fivefold power: 五力 [goriki]. The power of: trust, effort, mindfulness, samādhi, and wisdom. Included in the thirty-seven wings of enlightenment. 679.

five sense organs: See *organs, five sense.*

flame: 火焰 [kaen]. 271, 286, 490.

flavors, hundred: 百味珍饈 [hyaku mi chinshū], literally, one hundred tastes and rare delicacies. 372.

flaws, free of: 無漏 [mro]. 436.

flesh, lump of red: 赤肉團 [shakuniku dan]. Body. 426.

flow: 經歷(す) [kyōraku(-su)], literally, passing through or continuous passage. For Dōgen, experience of all time—past, present, and future—as the present moment. 108, 561.

flower canopy: 華蓋 [kegai]. 206.

flower in the sky: 虚空華 [kokūge]. Illusory flowers; illusory vision. See also *emptiness, flower of.*

flower, heavenly: 天華 [tenge]. 418, 664.

Flowers in the Sky: 空華 [Kūge]. Forty-fourth fascicle of this book. lxxiv, 458–67.

flowery words: 言華 [gonka]. 413.

fluctuation: 437, 448. See also *activity.*

fly beyond: 趯飛 [chōhi]. 696.

flying, activity of: 飛空 [hikō]. 313.

follow all the way through: 隨他去 [zui ta ko]. 301.

force: 強爲 [gōi]. Forcefully assert, wield authority. 156, 241, 312.

force, vital: 命 [myō]. 614.

foretell: 記す [ki-su]. Predict one's enlightenment.

form: 色 [shiki]. Translation of Skt. rūpa: color, form, or phenomena. 象 [shō], literally, shape. 37, 154, 268, 279, 573.

form, color, and measurements: 體色量 [tai shiki ryō]. 129.

form, conceal the body and reveal the: 藏身彌露 [zōshin yō miro].

form, essence, body, and power: 相性體力 [sōshō tairiki]. 627.

form, fixed: 定相 [jōsō]. 97, 308.

form, genuine: 本色 [honjiki], literally, original color. 正儀 [shōgi], authentic procedure. 373, 407, 437.

form, no: 無相 [musō]. 232, 246, 293, 294, 526, 598.

form, original: 本樣 [hon'yō]. 144.

form, perception, feeling, inclination, and discernment: 色受想行識 [shiki ju sō gyō shiki]. Five skandhas. 225, 559.

form, venerable: 尊儀 [songi]. 583.

form is emptiness: 色即是空 [shiki soku ze kū]. 25, 188, 241.

form is revealed: 露影 [roei], literally, image is revealed. 319.

form realm: 128, 195, 812, 897. See also *realms, three.*

formless realm: See *realms, three.*

forms, beyond: 非相 [hisō], literally, not form. 596–98.

forms, myriad: 萬象 [manzō]. 25, 393, 446, 453, 454.

forthright practice-realization: 直修證 [jiki shushō]. 669.

foundation, master the: 達本 [tappon]. 498.

four bodily presences: See *bodily presences, four.*

Four Continents: See *Continents, Four.*

four dependences: See *dependences, four.*

Four Deva Kings: See *Deva Kings, Four.*

four fruits: See *fruits, four.*

four groups of practitioners: See *practitioners, four groups of.*

Four Horses: 四馬 [Shime]. Eighty-sixth fascicle of this book. xciii, 792–96.

four noble truths: See *truths, four noble.*

four right efforts: See *efforts, four right.*

four stages of meditation: See *meditation, four stages of.*

four types of practice: 行法に四種 [gyōhō ni shishu]. 816. See also *dependences, four.*

Four Understandings: See *Understandings, Four.*

four worlds: See *worlds, four.*

Fourth Heaven: 第四天 [daishi ten]. Fourth of the six heavens in the desire realm. Tushita Heaven. 902.

fourth stage of meditation: See *meditation, four stages of; Monk of the Fourth Stage of Meditation.*

fox, spirit of a wild: 野狐精 [yako zei]. 198, 709, 746.

fox, wild: 野干 [yakan]. 72, 705–714, 846, 851.

free, float: 遊戯(す) [yuke(-su)]. Free oneself. 435.

free, not yet: 未脱 [midatsu], literally, not yet off. 495, 534.

freedom: 自在 [jizai], literally, being oneself. 404.

freedom from attachment: 執爲斷 [shui dan], literally, cut off attachment. 382.

friend and enemy: 怨親 [onshin] 475.

from beginning to end: 頭正尾正 [zushin bishin], literally, head correct and tail correct. 38 . . .

from head to toe: 把尾收頭 [habi shūtō], literally, grabbing tail and taking head. 670.

from root to twig: 搆本宗末 [kōhon shūmatsu]. 408.

front of oneself, in: 當面 [tōmen], literally, hitting face. 53, 306, 423, 564, 633.

fruit, first: See *fruits, four.*

fruit, realize the: 證果 [shōka]. Fruits of realization. 97, 574, 874. See also *fruits, four.*

fruit of no returning: 阿那含果 [anagon ka]. Skt., anāgāmin, literally, one who does not return. Transliteration: 阿那含 [anagon]. Third of the four fruits of shramanas, wandering monks. See also *fruits, four.*

fruits, four: 四果 [shika]. The four stages of shramanas (wandering monks) in the progression of becoming an arhat. Achievements of a practitioner as: a stream enterer who has become free from delusions; once-returner and never-returner who have become free from desires; and one who has no more need to study. The last stage is called the fruit of an arhat. 20, 294, 408, 863.

Fu: See *Taiyuan Fu.*

Fuguang Ruman: 佛光如滿 [Bukkō Nyoman]. Ca. eighth–ninth century. Dharma heir of Mazu Daoyi, Nanyue Line. Abbot of Fuguang Monastery, Luoyang (Henan), the capital city of dynasties including Tang. Renowned poet Bai Jui was a lay student of his. P. 930, Generation 9. 101.

Fuguo Weibai: 佛國惟白 [Bukkoku Ihaku]. Eleventh–twelfth century. Dharma heir of Fayun Faxiu, Yunmen School. Compiled *Jianzhong Jingguo Continuous Transmission of the Lamp* (Continuous Transmission of the Lamp). P. 933, Generation 19. 577.

full moon, shape of a: 滿月輪 [mangetsu rin]. 244–47, 249.

full-lotus position: 結跏趺坐 [kekka fuza]. Sitting with both legs crossed over each other. 579.

fully manifest: 獨露 [dokuro]. 381, 451, 584.

Fuma: See *Li Fuma.*

function: 功德 [kudoku], literally, effort and virtue. Ability, possibility, active power, activity, aspect, characteristics, merit, effect, value, virtue. 功 [kō]. 106, 184, 502, 841.

function, great: 大用 [daiyū]. 36, 311.

function, transformative: 化機 [keki]. 260, 274.

fundamental point: 32, 46, 531, 593, 631, 671. See also *kōan.*

furnace: 火爐 [karo]. 217, 218, 639.

furnace and bellows: 爐鞴 [rohai]. 1. The practice place where the master trains the students, like tempering a furnace. 2. Entire daily activity. 623.

furnishing: 家具 [kagu]. Furniture. 調度 [chōdo]. Accoutrement, equipment, instrument, utensil. Things needed for the daily activities of the buddha house. 220.

Furong Daokai: 芙蓉道楷 [Fuyō Dōkai]. 1043–1118, China. Dharma heir of Touzi Yiqing, Caodong School. Also called Dayang, 大陽 [Taiyō]. Before he studied Zen, he engaged in Daoist sorcery. He taught at Mount Dayang, Ying Region (Hubei), and later at Lake Furong, (Shandong). His reputation as a teacher led Emperor Hui to offer Furong favors and demand that he teach near the palace, but Furong refused on both counts, incurring the Emperor's wrath. Later, the Emperor forgave him and built him a temple at Furong, where he moved and taught many students for the rest of his life, revitalizing the monastic standards of the Caodong School. P. 932, Generation 18. 167; discourse of , 154, 371–73; practice of, 370; robe of, 174; story of, 621; student of, 700.

Furong Lingxun: 芙蓉靈訓 [Fuyō Reikun]. Ca. ninth century, China. Dharma heir of Guizong Zhichang, Nanyue Line. Taught at Mount Furong, Fu Region (Fujian). His posthumous name is Great Master Hongzhao, 弘照大師 [Kōshō Daishi]. P. 930, Generation 10. 368, 465.

future: 末上 [matsujō], literally, upward-pointing twigs. 301, 326.

Fuxing Fatai: 佛性法泰 [Busshō Hōtai]. Ca. eleventh–twelfth century, China. Dharma heir of Yuanwu Keqin, Linji School. Abbot of Mount Gui (Dagui), Tan Region (Hunan). His posthumous name is Zen Master Fuxing, 佛照禪師 [Busshō Zenji]. P. 933, Generation 22. 635, 692, 693.

Fuyan Qingyuan: 佛眼清遠 [Butsugen Seion]. 1067–1120, China. Dharma heir of Wuzu Fayan, Linji School. Taught at Longmen Monastery, near Luoyang (Henan). Given the title of Zen Master Fuyan, 佛眼禪師 [Butsugen Zenji], by the Emperor. P. 933, Generation 21. 173, 917, 919.

Fuyin Liaoyuan: 佛印了元 [Butchin Ryōgen]. 1032–1098, China. Dharma heir of Kaixian Shanxian, Yunmen School. Taught at many monasteries, including Mount Yunju, Hong Region (Jiangxi). His posthumous name is Zen Master Fuyin, 佛印禪師 [Butchin Zenji]. Known for his association with Su Dongpo. P. 932, Generation 17. 86.

Fuzhao: See *Zhuoan Deguang.*

Gandhara: 健馱羅國 [Kendara Koku]. An ancient kingdom northwest of India, in present-day Pakistan and Afghanistan. 782.

gandharva: 122, 123, 393. See also *guardians, eight types of.*

Ganges: Skt., Gangā. 恒河 [gōga]. A river in northern India, flowing from the Himālaya Mountains generally eastward through a vast plain. Buddhism rose and developed along this river. Sacred to Brāhmanism in ancient times and Hinduism in later times up to the present day. 184, 286, 464, 599.

Ganges, sands of the: 恒河沙 [gōga sha], 恒沙 [gōsha]. 恒河沙數 [gōga shasū], literally the number of the sands of the Ganges. An innumerable amount. 7, 114, 139, 362.

Gao, novice: 高沙彌 [Kō Shami]. Ca. eighth–ninth century. A student of Yaoshan Weiyan, Qingyuan Line. After leaving Mount Yaoshan, he lived in a hut and taught passersby. P. 930, Generation 10. 233, 895.

Gaoan Dayu: 高安大愚 [Kōan Daigu]. Ca. ninth century, China. Dharma heir of Guizong Zhichang, Nanyue Line. He taught in Gaoan, Rui Region (Jiangxi), where his teaching was instrumental in the enlightenment of Linji Yixuan, founder of the Linji School. He was also the teacher of Moshan Liaoran, the most prominent female teacher in the early Zen School. P. 930, Generation 10. 75, 349, 469, 511, 542.

gardenia bush: 薝蔔の林 [sempuku no rin]. 818.

garuda: 122, 132, 393. See also *guardians, eight types of.*

gasshō: J., 合掌. Gesture of placing palms together in front of the chest, expressing respect. Often accompanied with bowing, it is used for greeting, chanting, and offering or receiving something. 230, 231.

gate, ancestral: 祖門 [somon]. 144–46.

gate, front: 正門 [shōmon]. Front entrance, 前門 [zemmon]. 7.

gate, hammer open the: 擊關 [kyakukan]. Pound open a barrier. 75.

gate, universal: 普門 [fumon]. 403.

Gates, Five: 5. See also *Schools, Five.*

gāthā: Skt. 伽陀 [kada]. Verse for chanting. One of the Twelve Divisions of the teaching. See also *Divisions, Twelve.* 231, 283.

Gautama: See *Shākyamuni Buddha.*

Gayā, Mount: 伽耶山 [Gaya San]. Located near Vulture Peak in the country of Magadha, ancient India. This is where Devadatta tried to cause a split in the Buddha's practicing community. 784.

Gayashata: 伽耶舍多 [Kayashata]. Monk from Madhya, northern India. Family name, Uddaka-Rāmaputta. Dharma heir of Sanghānandi. Eighteenth Ancestor of the Zen tradition in India. 166, 205, 206, 327.

generosity: 布施 [fuse]. 25. See also *giving.*

genius: 軼才 [issai]. 85, 607, 912.

gentle curving: 圓陀陀地 [en dadachi]. 地[chi] is a suffix.

genuineness: 眞僞 [shingi], literally, true or false. 9.

get all the way through: 打得徹 [datoku tetsu]. 打 [da] is a prefix for emphasis. 610.

get into: 撞入 [tōnyū], literally, push in. 256, 257, 463, 774, 780.

geya: Skt. 祇夜 [giya]. Teaching reiterated in verse. One of the Twelve Divisions of the teaching. 282, 285.

giant radish: 大蘿蔔頭 [dairafu tō]. 頭 [tō] is a suffix with no special meaning. 607.

gift, great: 大恩 [dai'on]. 361, 365, 366.

gimlet, old: 老古錐 [rō kosui]. Sharp, penetrating Zen master. 骨律錐 [kotsu rissui], literally, bone discipline awl. Strong, determined practitioner. 376, 407, 586, 641, 753.

give and take: 與奪 [yodatsu]. Also, give or take. 412.

giving: 布施 [fuse]. One of the six pāramitās. Also, one of the bodhisattva's four methods of guidance. 365, 473.

giving, act of: 布施の檀度 [fuse no dando], literally, pāramitā (度 [do]) of giving (布施 [fuse], 檀 [dan]). 布施の功業 [fuse no kugō], literally, meritorious action of giving. 474.

giving, pāramitā of: 檀波羅蜜 [dan haramitsu]. 282.

go and study all over: 35. See also *all-inclusive study.*

go back and forth: 進步退步 [shimpo taiho]. 611.

go beyond: 出身 [shusshin], literally, bringing out one's body. Emerge, leap beyond, leave bondage behind. 超越(す) [chō'otsusu(-su)], transcend. 149, 269, 297, 559, 723.

go beyond ancestor: 越祖 [osso], literally, surpass ancestor. 315, 379, 521.

go beyond buddha: 佛向上 [bukkōjō], literally, buddha going up. Also translated as buddha going beyond; ongoing buddhahood. Acting freely and concretely within practice-and-enlightenment without attachment to it. Cf. "*Going beyond buddha* means that you reach buddha, and going further, you continue to see buddha" ("Going Beyond Buddha"). 超佛 [chōbutsu], literally, transcending buddha. 6, 260, 315–18, 431.

go beyond enlightenment: 悟出 [goshutsu], literally, exit enlightenment. 6.

go beyond the dharma body: See *dharma body, go beyond the.*

go downward: 向下 [kōge]. 161.

go game: 著碁 [chaku ki]. The second ideograph is often pronounced *go* in Japanese. 633.

go through: 徹 [tetsu]. 329, 879.

go toward: 趣向(す) [shukō(-su)]. Intention, trying to. 49, 464, 609.

goal, true: 本期 [hongo], literally, original expectation. 301.

goat, mountain: 羚羊 [reiyō]. 634.

god of autumn: 白帝 [Hakutei], literally, White Emperor. Deity of the western direction. 739. See also *Emperors, Five.*

god of spring: 東君 [Tōkun]. Deity of the eastern direction, in charge of spring. 329. See also *Emperors, Five.*

god of summer: 炎帝 [Entei], literally, flame emperor. One of the five heavenly rulers. Resides in the southern heaven. 732. See also *Emperors, Five.*

god's head and a demon face: 神頭鬼面 [jinzu kimen]. 216.

Going Beyond Buddha: 佛向上事 [Bukkōjō Ji], literally, matter of buddha going up. Twenty-ninth fascicle of this book. lvii, 315–23.

golden body, sixteen-foot: 丈六(の)金身 [jōroku (no) konjin]. 46, 107, 195, 651.

gong, shang, jue, zhi, yu: C. 宮商角徵羽 [kyū shō kaku chi u]. Notes of a musical scale. 628.

goo goo wa wa: 哆哆和和 [tatawawa]. Baby talk. 855.

good: See *wholesome.*

good, not thinking of: 善也不思量 [zen ya fu shiryō]. 579.

gourd: 葫蘆 [koro]. Twining vine; succession of the dharma lineage. 479, 556, 609, 630.

gourd, bitter: See *bitter gourd has a bitter root.*

grasp: 取 [shu], literally, take. 搆 [kō], literally, trap. 把定 [hajō], 把定了 [jōha ryō], literally, grab solidly. 策把す[sakuha-su], 把捉 [hasoku], literally, catch. 269, 611, 717, 726.

grasp, easy to: 肯易參 [kōisan]. 390.

grasp, reach over to: 體取 [taishu], literally, take with the body. 263.

grasp, vitally: 得活 [tokukatsu]. 596.

grasp cases through words: 向言中取則 [kō gonchū shusoku]. 312.

grasp clearly: 明得 [myōtoku]. 466.

grass, drop: 落草 [rakusō]. Become free of delusions; to be emancipated. 480.

grass, hold up: 拈草 [nensō]. 480.

grass, one blade of: 一莖草 [ikkyōsō]. 一草 [issō]. 164, 195, 462, 647.

grasses, one hundred: 百草 [hyakusō]. Infinite phenomena, all things. 25, 45, 489, 538.

grass, trees, and forests: 草木叢林 [sōmoku sōrin]. 244, 550.

grass, trees, land, and earth: 草木國土 [sōmoku kokudo]. 250.

grass for ten thousand miles, not an inch of: 萬里無寸草 [banri mu sunsō]. 725.

grasses are bright and clear, one hundred: 明明百草 [meimei hyakusō]. 390.

Great Collection of Sūtras: 大集経 [Daishū Kyō]. Korean collection of Mahā-yāna sūtras, rendered in Chinese by different translators. 844, 845.

great death: 大死 [daishi]. A death met with complete readiness for death, thereby being free from death. Termination of ignorance or delusion, leading to liberation. 448.

great elements, five: 五大 [godai]. Four great elements (earth, water, fire, and air), plus space. 161, 832.

great enlightenment: Enlightenment without leaving a trace of it. 109, 296, 574, 616.

Great Enlightenment: 大悟 [Daigo]. Twenty-seventh fascicle of this book. lxvi, lxxiv, 296–302.

great enlightenment is black: 大悟頭黒 [daigo tō koku]. 頭 [tō] is a suffix with no special meaning. 302.

great enlightenment is white: 大悟頭白 [daigo tō haku]. 頭 [tō] is a suffix with no special meaning. 302.

great house: 大家 [taike/taika], literally, big house. Assembly, audience of the master's lecture. 589, 594, 613, 634.

great matter: 4, 173, 411, 542. See also *matter, single essential*.

great matter, break open the: 大事打開 [daiji dakai]. 173.

great matter of the way, settle the: See *settle the great matter of the way*.

Great Practice: 大修行 [Dai Shugyō]. Seventy-sixth fascicle of this book. lxxxvi, xcv, 705–14.

Great Sangha Precepts [Scripture]: 摩訶僧祇律 [Maka Sōgi Ritsu]. Collection of precepts from the Mahāsamghika School, one of the eighteen early Buddhist schools of India. This school became an early source of Mahāyāna Buddhism. 57, 63, 831.

Great Vehicle: See *Vehicles, Three.*

great way of all buddhas: 450. See also *buddha way.*

Great Wisdom, Treatise on Realization of: See *Treatise on Realization of Great Wisdom.*

greed: 貪 [ton]. 408, 773, 801, 834.

green mountains are always walking: 青山常運歩 [seizan jō umpo]. 154.

greeting circuit: 巡堂 [jundō]. The abbot or practice leader goes around inside the monks' hall to greet all practitioners. Circumambulation. 230–32.

greeting, formal: 人事 [ninji], literally, human matter. 1. Greetings in monastery. 2. Gift. 3. *Ninji* also means worldly affairs. 564, 567.

grip: 把定 [hajō]. Hold, take hold. 440.

grope for: 摸索 [mosaku]. Look for. 262, 909.

grotto hut: 窟宅 [kuttaku]. Cave, abode. 594.

ground: 露地 [roji], literally, bare earth. 185, 343, 621.

grounds, nine: 九地 [kuchi/ kyūchi]. Also, nine types of existences. One ground in the desire realm, and four grounds each in the form and no-form realms. 871.

gruel, satisfied with: 粥足 [shuku soku]. 407.

Guangcheng: 廣成 [Kōsei]. Legendary sorcerer of ancient China who taught the Yellow Emperor. 163, 210, 344.

Guangren: See *Sushan Guangren.*

Guangtong Huiguang: 光統慧光 [Kōzu Ekō]. 468–537, China. Precept Master who advocated precepts that are classified in four divisions. Purportedly one of the monks who accused and attempted to oppress Bodhidharma. 92.

Guangzuo: See *Zhimen Guangzuo.*

Guanxi Zhixian: 灌溪志閑 [Kankei Shikan]. d. 895, China. Dharma heir of Linji Yixuan, Linji School. Taught at Guanxi, Changsha (Hunan). P. 931, Generation 12. 74, 75.

Guanzhi: See *Tong'an Guanzhi.*

Guanzi: 管子 [Kanshi]. A book by Guanzhong (d. 645 B.C.E.), prime minister of Qi Kingdom. 476.

guard: 護持 [goji]. 21, 62, 309, 722.

guardian spirit of the monastery buildings: 護伽藍神 [gogaran jin]. 345.

guardians, eight types of: A deva, dragon, yaksha (flying demon), gandharva (heavenly musician), asura (fighting spirit), garuda (bird god), kinnara (heavenly singer), and mahoraga (land dragon). Often revered as protectors of dharma. 82.

guest and host: 賓主 [hinju]. Student and teacher. 41.

guest office: 接待 [settai]. 728.

Guichen: See *Dizang Guichen.*

guidance: 化導 [kedō], literally, transform and guide. 13, 242, 275, 404.

guide other: 爲他 [ita], literally, make other. 50.

guide the person: 接渠 [sekkyo], literally, touch the person. 213, 599.

guideline, pure: 清規 [shingi], literally, pure regulation. 42.

Guidelines for Zen Monasteries: C. Chanyuan Qinggui, 禪苑清規 [Zennen Shingi], literally, pure rules for Zen gardens. Compiled by Changlu Zongze of Yunmen School, eleventh–twelfth century, China. Published in 1103. The oldest extant collection of monastic guidelines, as most of the earlier guidelines, attributed to Baizhang, had been lost. Basis for later monastic guidelines. 12, 53, 55, 66, 660, 728, 731, 732, 763, 766, 817, 839, 889.

guidelines, what are the: いかなる規矩かある [ikanaru kiku ka aru]. 280.

guidepost: 榜樣 [bōyō]. Example. 標傍 [hyōbō]. Standard. 389, 431.

guiding a person: 爲人接人 [inn setsunin], literally, making and touching a person. 480.

Guishan Lingyou: 潙山靈祐 [Isan Reiyū]. 771–853, China. Dharma heir of Baizhang Huaihai, Nanyue Line. Along with his co-student Huangbo Xiyun, Guishan was a renowned Zen teacher of Tang Dynasty China. Taught at Mount Gui, Tan Region (Hunan). He had forty-one room-entering (senior) students, one of whom was Yangshan Huiji. Guishan and Yangshan are regarded as cofounders of the Guiyang School, the first of the Five Schools of Chinese Zen to come into existence. His posthumous name is Zen Master Dayuan 大圓禪師 [Daien Zenji]. P. 930, Generation 10. 483, 510; and Yangshan, 46, 176, 255, 288, 289, 511, 563, 917; discourse of, 251, 338, 339, 625; lineage of, 287; practice of, 369, 370; Second, 338; students of, 87, 88, 349, 638; words of, 252, 289.

Guixing: See *Shexian Guixing.*

Guiyang School: 潙仰宗 [Igyō Shū]. One of the Five Schools of Chinese Zen Buddhism. Regards Guishan Lingyou and Yangshan Huiji as its founders. 5, 510–12.

Guizong Zhichang: 歸宗智常 [Kisu Chijō]. Ca. eighth century, China. Dharma heir of Mazu Daoyi, Nanyue Line. Taught at Guizong Monastery, Mount Lu (Jiangxi). His teaching was well known, and he was frequently visited by the famous Tang Dynasty poet and statesman Bai Zhuyi. At the end of his life he was known as Red-Eyed Guizong because the medicine he used for cataracts turned his eyes red. His posthumous name is Zen Master Zhizhen 至眞禪師 [Shishin Zenji]. P. 930, Generation 9. 465.

Guotai Hongtao: 國泰弘瑫 [Kokutai Kōtō]. Ca. ninth–tenth century, China. Dharma heir of Xuefeng Yicun, Qingyuan Line. Taught at Anguo Monastery, Fu Region (Fujian). His posthumous name is Great Master Mingzhen, 明眞大師 [Myōshin Daishi]. P. 931, Generation 14. 219.

Gushan Zhiyuan: 孤山智圓 [Kozan Chien]. Dates unknown, China. His theory of the Three Teachings as one is quoted in the preface of the *Record of the Universal Lamp.* 18, 864–66, 869.

Ha!: 咦 [nii]. 613, 620, 855.

Haihui Shouduan: 海會守端 [Kaie Shutan]. 1025–1072, China. Also, Baiyun Shouduan. Dharma heir of Yangqi Fanghui, Linji School. Taught at Haihui Monastery on Mount Baiyun, Shu Region (Anhui). P. 933, Generation 19. 175, 200, 203, 746, 752.

hair breathing in the vast ocean, tuft of: 毛吞巨海 [mō don kokai]. 289, 290, 292.

hairbreadth: 毫釐 [gōri]. 189, 680, 756, 857.

half-lotus position: 半跏趺坐 [hanka fuza]. Sitting with one leg crossed over the other. 579, 580.

hall, auxiliary cloud: 重雲堂 [jū'undō]. A hall for zazen, eating, and sleeping, attached to the main monks' hall. 39.

hall, entry: 旦過寮 [tangaryō], literally, passing the dawn dormitory. Special building or quarters for those seeking entry to the monastery or staying overnight. Visitors' room. 177, 918.

hall, meditation: 坐禪堂 [zazendō]. 12.

hall, monks': 僧堂 [sōdō]. 雲堂 [undō], literally, cloud hall, because a monk who wanders about in search of the way is called 雲水 [unsui], meaning cloud and water. This hall is where monks engage in zazen, have morning and midday meals, and sleep. 41, 229, 376, 419, 644.

hall, relic: 舍利殿 [shari den]. 249.

hall, study: 衆寮 [shuryō], literally, dormitory of assembly. 照堂 [shōdō], literally, illumination hall, hall of light. 本寮 [honryō], literally, main dormitory. A building in the Zen monastery where monks read, drink tea, and have evening meals. 62, 729, 731, 736–38.

hall for sleeping: 寝堂 [shindō]. 616.

han: J. 版 / 板. A hanging wooden board struck by a wooden mallet as a signal in a monastery. 170, 572, 645, 706.

Han Dynasty: 漢 [Kan]. Former Han, 202–28 B.C.E. Later Han, 25–220 C.E. 5, 115, 140, 415, 707.

Han Yu: 韓愈 [Kan'yu]. 768–828, China. Government official and outstanding writer, exiled and pardoned twice. Studied with Dadian Baotong, Qingyuan Line. His posthumous name is Lord Wen. P. 930, Generation 10. 417, 418.

hands and eyes, countless: Referring to one thousand arms and one thousand eyes of Bodhisattva Avalokiteshvara. 382, 403.

hang on emptiness: 空にかかる [kū ni kakaru]. 435.

hang up traveling staff: 掛錫 [kashaku]. Stay at a monastery. 352, 416.

Hangzhou Tianlong: 杭州天龍 [Kōshū Tenryū]. Ca. eighth–ninth century, China. Dharma heir of Damei Fachang, Nanyue Line. His teaching was always raising one finger, known as Tianlong's One Finger Zen, which was famously taken up by his student Juzhi. P. 930, Generation 10. 342, 611.

Haojian: See *Baling Haojian.*

Haoyue, Imperial Attendant: 皓月供奉 [Kōgetsu Gubu]. Ca. eighth–ninth century, China. Student of Changsha Jingcen, Qinguan Line. Biography unknown. P. 930, Generation 11. 788–90.

hasta: Skt. 肘 [chū]. Measuring unit. The length from elbow to middle fingertip. 126, 127, 784.

hat, wild boar: See *boar hat, wild.*

have some tea: 喫茶去 [kissa ko], literally, go and drink tea. 625, 914.

head, shave the: 剃頭 [teitō]. To become a monk or nun. 190.

head, turn one's: See *turning one's head.*

head as it is: 頭顳 [zu nii]. 433.

head but no tail, one who has: 有頭無尾漢 [utō mubi kan]. 592.

head monk: 首座 [shuso], literally, head seat. One who assists the abbot in teaching during one practice period as part of the training. 230, 729–39.

head monks, those who have been: 立僧の首座 [rissō no shuso]. 738.

head of the garden: 園頭 [enjū]. 75.

head on top of another, placing one: 頭上安頭 [zujō anzu]. Head above head-top. 384.

head to tail, from: 頭正尾正 [zushin bishin], literally, the head is correct and the tail is correct. 102, 492, 603, 678.

heads, divine: 神頭 [jinzu]. 445, 594.

heads are right, their: 頭角正 [zukaku shin], literally, head horn is correct. 697.

heads of work crew: 頭首 [chōshu]. 733.

hear sounds with entire eye: 滿眼聞聲 [mangen monshō]. 269.

Heart of the Way: 道心 [Dōshin]. Ninety-fourth fascicle of this book. xcvi, 886–88.

heaven: 天堂 [tendō], literally, heavenly halls. Heavenly world. 264, 583, 772.

Heaven of No Thought: 無想天 [musōten]. Skt., Āsamjñika. The realm of meditation where all mental activity is stopped. 161.

heaven of purity: 130. See also *Brahmā Heaven.*

Heaven of Shining Banner: 光明旛世界 [Kōmyō Ban Sekai]. 128.

Heaven of Thirty-three Devas: 三十三天 [Sanjūsan Ten]. One of the six heavens of the desire world above Mount Sumeru. Indra is surrounded by thirty-two other devas—eight in each of the four directions. Also called Tushita Heaven. 802.

Heaven Share: 共天 [Kuten]. King, one of the former lives of Shākyamuni Buddha. 823.

Heaven, Tushita: See *Tushita Heaven.*

heavenly beings: 天衆 [tenshu]. Devas. 16, 108, 555.

heavenly eyes: See *eyes, five.*

heels have not yet touched the ground: 脚跟未點地在 [kyakkon mitten chi zai]. 217–19.

heir, direct: 親嫡嗣 [shin tekishi], literally, intimate heir. 315, 501, 531.

heir, new: 新嗣 [shishi]. 172, 174.

heir to heir: 嫡嫡 [tekiteki]. 76, 356, 725.

heir-buddha: 嗣佛 [shibutsu]. Same as buddha's heir [busshi]. Holder of an authentic dharma heritage. 170, 181.

hell: Skt., niraya. Transliteration: 泥犁 [nairi]. Translation: 地獄 [jigoku], literally, underground prison. 124, 783, 799, 839.

help invisibly: 冥資 [myōshi], 冥助 [myōjo]. 6, 172.

helper, young: 童行 [zunnan]. Young worker or youth who is not yet ordained. 230.

herbs, three types of: 三草 [sansō]. Classification in the *Lotus Sūtra*. Excellent herbs: Bodhisattva Vehicle. Medium herbs: Shrāvaka and Pratyeka-buddha Vehicles. Lesser herbs: Human and Deva Vehicle. 188.

here, it is right: 只在者裏 [shi zai shari]. 313.

here, right: 當處 [tōjo]. 448, 726.

here, what is right: 這裏是什麼處在 [shari ze jūmosho zai]. 352, 717.

heretic thinkers, six types of: 六群禿子 [rokugun tokushi]. See *monks, group of the six.*

heritage, document of: 嗣書 [shisho]. A genealogical record given by a teacher to a disciple as a proof of dharma transmission. The names of the buddha ancestors and the new heir are written by the heir, and the teacher adds words of approval with a signature and seals. xxxix, 170–77, 700.

heritage, mutual: 相嗣 [sōshi]. Realization outside of time; beyond, before, and after. In the merged realization of teacher and disciple, disciple inherits dharma from the teacher, and the teacher inherits dharma from the disciple. (Document of Heritage: "Shākyamuni Buddha inherited dharma from Kāshyapa Buddha. . . . Kāshyapa Buddha inherited dharma from Shākyamuni Buddha.") 169.

heritage, our: 宗門 [shūmon], literally, spiritual gate. 5.

hero: 英雄 [eiyū]. 419.

Heshan Shouxun: 何山守珣 [Kazan Shujun]. Ca. eleventh–twelfth century, China. Dharma heir of Taiping Huiqin, Linji School. Taught at Mount He (Zhejiang). His posthumous name is Zen Master Fudeng 佛燈禪師 [Buttō Zenji]. P. 933, Generation 22. 636.

hidden in the entire world, nothing is: See *world, nothing is hidden in the entire.*

hidden, apparent, existent, or not existent: 隱顯存沒 [onken zommotsu]. 333.

high ancestor: 高祖 [kōso]. For Dōgen, *high ancestor* refers to an outstanding ancestor, such as Yunyan or Dangshan. 12, 141, 197, 291, 346, 513.

High Banner Palace: 高幢本天宮 [Kōtō Hon Tengū]. 897.

High Eight: 上八 [Jōhatsu]. 821.

Himālāyas: Described in sūtras as the place where Shākyamuni Buddha practiced in his former life. 287, 300, 646, 765. See also *Snow Mountains.*

Hīnayāna: 82, 116, 117, 202, 278, 406, 728, 865–67. See also *Vehicles, Three.*

hindrance: 罣礙(す) [keige(-su)], 礙 [ge]. 1. Hinder, obstructing, being sheltered, contradicted, covered. Separation from reality. 2. For Dōgen, being completely covered, immersed, undivided. Being one with reality. 37, 93, 248, 464, 617.

hindrance in the study of the way: 障道 [shōdō]. 93.

hindrances of unwholesome actions: 罪障 [zaishō]. 573.

Hinokuma Shrine: 日前杜 [Hinokuma Sha]. Shinto shrine in Akitzuki, Kii Province (present Wakayama Prefecture), Japan. Enshrines Great Deity of Hinokuma [Hinokuma Ōkami]. 211.

hiro: J. 尋. Measuring unit. Sixty *sun.* 177.

hit the mark: 一當 [ittō], literally, one strike. 496.

Hōjō, Tokiyori: 1227–1263. Became the head of the Kamakura government as Regent of Japan in 1246. His monk name is Dōsū Saimyōji. He invited Dōgen to give dharma discorses in Kamakura. xc, xci.

hold on fully: 但惜 [tan shaku], literally, only be attached. xc, xci, 262.

hold up a flower and blink: 拈華瞬目 [nenge shummoku]. 533. See also *treasury of the true dharma eye.*

hold up grass: 粘草 [nensō]. Have realization. 480.

hollow discussion: 戲論 [keron]. Theoretical discussion, groundless theory. 773, 774.

homage to: 稽首 [keishu], literally, lower the head (to the ground). 208.

home leaver: 出家 [shukke]. Monk or nun. 出家人 [shukkenin], person who has left his or her household to join the sangha. 16, 410, 769, 797–99.

home leaving and entry into the practice of the way: 出家修道 [shukke shudō]. 190.

home leavers, Five Schools of: 五部の僧衆 [gobu no sōshu]. 740.

Hongren: See *Daman Hongren.*

Hongtao: See *Guotai Hongtao.*

Hongzhi Zhenjiao: 宏智正覺 [Wanshi Shōgaku]. 1091–1157, China. Dharma heir of Danxia Zichun, Caodong School. When he was abbot at

Mount Tiantong, his monastery flourished with as many as twelve hundred monks in residence. In a period when Zen practice was in decline, he revived the Caodong tradition. Regarded as leader of "silent-illumination Zen," he was a prolific writer who poetically articulated Caodong meditation practice. Author of *Hongzhi's Capping Verses,* which became the basis of the *Book of Serenity.* His posthumous name is Zen Master Hongzhi, 宏智禪師 [Wanshi Zenji]. P. 933, Generation 20. and the guardian spirit, 345; discourse of, 756; Old Buddha, 313, 469; story of, 345; verse of, lxvii, 310–13, 855; words of, 263, 633, 757, 764.

honorarium: 俵錢 [hyōsen], literally, straw bag full of coins. 231, 232.

Honored One: 大和尚 [dai oshō], literally, great priest. 165–67.

horizontally and vertically, maneuver: 橫擔竪擔 [ōtan jutan]. 446.

horn on the head, break a: 頭角觸折 [zukaku shokusetsu].

horn on the head, grow a: 頭角生 [zukaku shō]. Arouse desire. 629.

horn, painted: 畫角 [gakaku]. 590.

horns, hide the body but expose the: 藏身露角 [zōshin rokaku]. 269.

horse, beak of: 馬觜 [bashi]. Something that does not exist. 238.

horse, command a: 調馬 [chōba]. 794, 795.

horse's womb, enter the: 入馬胎 [nyū batai]. 679.

host: 主人 [shujin], literally, main person. 39, 41, 77, 99, 230–32, 591.

hours of a day, utilizes the twelve: 使得十二時 [shitoku jūniji]. 191.

hours of Horse and Sheep: Horse is the seventh hour of the day. Sheep is the eighth hour of the day. 107.

hours of the day, twelve: 十二時 [jūni ji]. In East Asia a day was divided into twelve hours. See also Time System (appendix 8) 98, 210, 381, 526 . . .

house where water is used sparsely: 惜水之家 [sekisui no ie]. 773.

house, burning: 火宅 [kataku]. 184, 185, 224.

house, in one's own: 自家屋裏 [jike okuri]. 251, 909.

house, in the: 屋裏 [oku ri]. Domain, teaching of the buddha house. 211, 216, 219, 233, 469, 517, 837 . . .

household, merit of leaving the: 出家功德 [shukke kudoku]. 770, 800, 802, 807, 812.

Houses, Five: See *Schools, Five.*

how: 爲體 / ていたらく [teitaraku]. 1. How it is, how it works. 2. Meaning (of a word or phrase). 43, 168, 223, 560.

How does this expression of thusness emerge?: See *thusness emerge?, How does this expression of.*

how to maintain them, how not to violate them, how to be open to them, and how to control oneself: 持犯開遮 [jibon kaisha]. Ways to work on precepts. 66.

Huaihai: See *Baizhang Huaihai.*

Huairang: See *Nanyue Huairang.*

Huangbo Xiyun: 黃檗希運 [Ōbaku Kiun]. d. 850, China. Dharma heir of Baizhang Huaihai, Nanyue Line. Born in Fu Region (Fujian) and ordained on Mount Huangbo of the region. After attaining deep insight with Baizhang and teaching for some time, he moved to a mountain at Zhongling (Jiangxi) at invitation of Minister Pei Xiu and called it Huangbo after his place of ordination; his teaching flourished there. Known for striking with a staff as a teaching device. Linji Yixuan was one of his successors. Pei Xiu compiled Huangbo's words, *Transmission of Heart, Essential Dharma.* His posthumous name is Zen Master Duanji, 斷際禪師 [Dansai Zenji]. P. 930, Generation 10. 107, 543; and Baizhang, 575, 706, 852; and Linji, 75, 350, 511, 542; and Nanquan, 253; and Xuan, 351, 352; descendants of, 512, 703; discourse of, 322; student of, 349; view of, 576; words of, 254, 255, 323, 577, 712–14.

Huangbo's striking with a staff: 黃檗の行棒 [Ōbaku no gyōbō], literally, Huangbo's practice stick. 157, 538.

Huanglong Huinan: 黃龍慧南 [Ōryū Enan]. 1002–1069, China. Dharma heir of Shishuang Chuyuan, Linji School. His teaching with the use of kōans flourished at Mount Huanglong (Jiangxi). Regarded as founder of the Huanglong Order of Linji School. His posthumous name is Zen Master Pujiao, 普覺禪師 [Fugaku Zenji]. P. 932, Generation 18. 86, 514, 725.

Huangmei: Hongren of, 538, 547; Mount, 112, 119, 136, 148, 149, 208, 239–41, 330, 337, 374, 570, 579. See also *Daman Hongren.*

Huanxi Weiyi: 環溪惟一 [Kankei Iichi]. 1202–1281, China. Dharma heir of Wuzhun Shifan, Linji School. Abbot of several renowned training centers, including Ruiyuan Monastery and Tiantong Jingde Monastery, both in Ming Region (Zhejiang). A visiting abbot of Jingde Monastery when Dōgen visited. P. 934, Generation 25.

Huanzhong: See *Daci Huanzhong.*

Huayan School: Also called Avatamsaka School. In China, it developed profound dialectic of Mahāyāna philosophy that was the basis for much Zen thought.

hub: 要 [yō]. Center of a folding fan. 310, 311, 314.

Huiche: See *Shimen Huiche.*

Huiguang: See *Guangtong Huiguang.*

Huiji: See *Yangshan Huiji.*

Huijiao: See *Langye Huijiao.*

Huike: See *Dazu Huike.*

Huileng: See *Changqing Huileng:*

Huinan: See *Huanglong Huinan.*

Huineng: See *Dajian Huineng.*

Huiqin: See *Taiping Huiqin.*

Huiran: See *Sansheng Huiran.*

Huisi: See *Nanyue Huisi.*

Huitang Zuxin: 晦堂祖心 [Kaidō Soshin]. 1025–1100, China. Dharma heir of Huanglong Huinan, Linji School. He traveled back and forth for seven years between Yunfeng Wenyue and Huanglong before attaining clarity with Huanglong. He taught at Mount Huanglong (Jiangxi), emphasizing clear seeing and self-understanding. His posthumous name is Zen Master Baojiao 寶覺禪師 [Hōgaku Zenji]. P. 933, Generation 19.

Huiyan Zhizhao: See *Zhicong.*

Huiyong: See *Nanyuan Huiyong.*

Huizang: See *Shigong Huizang.*

Huizhong: See *Nanyang Huizhong.*

Human and Deva Vehicles: 人天乘 [ninden jō]. 304. See also *Vehicles, Five.*

human stupidity is deadly: 鈍置殺人 [donchi satsunin]. 757, 758.

humans and devas: 人天 [ninden]. 5, 524, 651, 853. See also *deva.*

humans, things, body, and mind: 人物身心 [nimmotsu shinjin]. 244.

hunger: 飢 [ki]. 1. Hunger as opposed to satisfaction. 2. In Dōgen's usage, emptiness or ultimate truth. 444–46, 449, 623.

hungry ghost: 餓鬼 [gaki]. 122, 425. See also *paths, six.*

hunting dog: 獵狗 [ryōku]. 634.

hurl insightful flashes: See *unroll the matter and hurl insightful flashes.*

hut: 菴 [an]. 444–46, 449, 623.

hut, grass-roof: 草菴 [sōan]. 201.

hut, pounding: 碓房 [taibō]. 330.

Hutou Zhao: 虎頭昭 [Kotō Shō]. Ca. ninth–tenth century. A student of Xiangyan Zhixian. Biography unknown. P. 931, Generation 12. 638.

huts, residential: 菴内 [annai]. 62.

I am always intimate with this: 吾常於此切 [go jō o shi setsu]. 295, 445, 609.

I am originally in this land: 吾本來此土 [go honrai shi do]. 458, 585.

icchantika: Skt. Abbreviated transliteration: 闡提 [sendai] 1. Someone who is unable or does not wish to become a buddha. 2. In Dōgen's usage, a buddha who goes beyond buddha. 318, 839.

identify with and actualize: 信受奉行 [shinju bugyō], literally, accept dharma with trust and practice.

Identifying with Cause and Effect: 深信因果 [Shinjin Inga]. Ninetieth fascicle of this book. lxxxvii, xcv, 851–57.

identity action: 同事 [dōji], literally, same thing. One of the bodhisattva's four methods of guidance. See also fascicle 46, "Bodhisattva's Four Methods of Guidance." 473, 476, 477.

if the top of a stone is large, the bottom is large: 石頭大底大 [seki tō dai tei dai]. 611.

if the top of the stone is small, the bottom is small: 石頭小底小 [seki tō shō tei shō]. 611.

ignorance: Skt., avidyā, 無明 [mumyō]. 261, 281, 773. See also *causation, twelvefold.*

ijing/Ijing: C. 易經 [eki kyō/ Eki Kyō]. Also, *i-ching.* Ancient Chinese philosophy on change and human actions, including methods of making predictions. Originally, *Book of Changes.* 357, 502, 873.

illuminate: 開明す [kaimei-su], literally, open and clarify. 17.

illuminate, auspiciously: 放光現瑞 [hōkō genzui].

illuminate all the ten directions, broadly: 遍照於十方 [henshō o jippō]. 82.

illuminate and break open: 照破 [shōha]. 329.

illumination: [kōmyō] 光明. 36, 104, 311, 882. See also *Radiant Light.*

illumination, splendid: 莊嚴光明 [shōgon kōmyō]. 469.

Illumination and Function, Four Positions of: 四照用 [shishōyū]. Linji's teaching on Serenity—寂照 [jakushō] (essence) and its function: (1) Serenity first. (2) Function first. (3) Serenity and function are not simultaneous. (4) Serenity and function are simultaneous. 507.

illusion: 妄法 [mōhō], literally, illusory dharma (thing). 257, 258, 314, 461, 861.

illusion, no: 莫妄想 [maku mōzō]. 258, 314.

images, sacred: 形像 [gyōzō]. 831, 891.

imagine: 想憶 [sō'oku]. 10, 30, 108, 199, 261, 364, 882.

immature: 未練 [miren], literally, not yet kneaded. 155, 157, 192, 358, 497, 515.

immature person, foolish: 小獃子 [shōgaisu], literally, small, stupid person. 157.

immediate: 直下 [jikige]. Directly beneath one's feet. 6, 235, 314.

immediately: 忽爾 [kotsuji]. 驀地 [makuchi]. 地 [chi/ji] is a suffix with no special meaning. 97, 267, 438.

immersed: 礙 [ge]. See *hindrance.*

immersed, totally: 埋没す [maibotsu-su], literally, buried. 412, 413, 752.

immovability: 不動著 [fudōjaku]. 著 [chaku/jaku] is a suffix with no special meaning. 627.

imperial advisor: 供奉 [gubu].

impermanence of all things: 諸行無常 [shogyō mujō], literally, everything that is created (shogyō; Skt., sanskāra) is impermanent. 181, 663, 676.

impermanent: 無常 [mujō]. 40, 45, 811, 848.

impulse: 40. See also *skandhas, five.*

incarnate body: 化身 [keshin]. A buddha body attained by miraculous power. 119, 147, 260.

incense burner, portable: 手爐 [shuro]. 230, 231.

incense offering: 燒香 [shōkō], literally, burn incense. 5, 667, 732.

incense sticks: 棧香 [senkō]. 231.

incense, distribute to the monks: 行香 [ankō]. Making a gift to monks during a meal offering. 606.

inclination: 25, 225, 281, 282, 559, 663. See also *skandhas, five.*

inclination skandha: 行衆 [gyōshu], literally, inclination assembly. 663. See also *skandhas, five.*

inclusion: 全收 [zenshū], literally, totally including. 599.

inconceivable: 不可思議 [fukashigi]. 密有 [mitsu'u], literally, intimate being. 3, 32, 287, 845.

inconceivable cause, inconceivable effect: 妙因妙果 [myōin myōka]. 102.

incorrect views: 不是處 [fuzesho], literally, point that is not right. 398, 892.

indefinite: 不必 [fuhitsu], literally, not necessarily. 458, 565, 790.

independent of before and after: See *before and after, independent of.*

indestructible: 堅牢 [kenrō], literally, solid and firm. 59, 185, 253, 385, 448, 803, 833.

indestructible body: 不壊身 [fueshin]. 59, 253.

India: 天竺 [Tenjiku]. 竺乾 [Jikuken]. 西天 [Saiten], literally, Western Heaven. 5, 78, 660, 727, 867.

India and China: 乾唐 [Ken Tō]. 5, 140, 149, 181, 839, 909 . . .

Indian sounds: 梵音 [bon'on]. 841.

Indra: Skt., Shakra Devānām Indra, literally, Shakra (mighty one), who is the lord of devas. Transliteration: 釋迦提桓因陀羅 [Shaka Daikan Indara]. (Dōgen refers to this deity in the following ways.) Abbreviated: 釋提桓因 [Shaku Daikan In]. Also, Deva Lord Shakra, 天帝釋 [Ten Taishaku]; Lord Shakra, 帝釋 [Taishaku]; Deva Lord, 天帝 [Ten Tei]; Shakra Deva, 釋天 [Shaku Ten]; Shakra King, 釋王 [Shaku Ō]. Originally a Vedic deity, regarded in Buddhism as a main guardian deity of dharma. Resides in the Heaven of Thirty-three Devas (Tushita Heaven) above Mount Sumeru. 83, 199, 564, 686, 711, 867; and three treasures, 844, 846–48; asking questions, 26, 27, 73, 74, 204, 849; becoming, 822; Buddhas called, 823, 875; catching Siddhārtha's hair, 809; cave of, 726; defeating a fighting spirit, 294; king of deva worlds, 138, 151, 687, 772, 805, 871; palace of, 470; testing practitioners, 92; world, 741.

Indra Ketu: 帝相 [Taisō], literally, King Form. Shākyamuni Buddha made offerings in his former lifetime to many Buddhas with this name. 823.

Indra's Cave: 因沙臼室 [Inshakyū Shitsu]. The cave on Mount Veda in the ancient Indian kingdom of Magadha. Known as the first place the Buddha had a summer retreat. 726.

Indra's Net Sūtra: 梵網經 [Bommō Kyō]. *Indra's Net Bodhisattva Precepts Sūtra,* 梵網菩薩戒經 [Bommō Bosatsu Kai Kyō]. Mahāyāna sūtra, revered for its elucidation of the bodhisattva precepts. 728.

inessential activity: See *activity, inessential.*

infirmary: 延壽院 [enju in], literally, hall for prolonging longevity. 706, 736.

inherit, individually: 單傳す [tanden-su]. Also, transmit person to person. 12.

initial enlightenment: 381. See also *enlightenment, acquired.*

inner chamber: 屋裏 [okuri], literally, inside the house. 堂奥 [dō'ō], literally, deep inside the hall. 閫奥 [kon'ō], literally, deep inside the threshold. Domain. Teacher, or inner meaning of the teaching. 162, 364, 503, 726.

inner chamber, enter the: 353, 575. See also *abbot's room, receive guidance in the.*

innumerable eons: 五百塵點 [gohyaku jinten], literally, five hundred particle (eons). 189, 559, 576, 808 . . .

inquire: 咨問す [shimon-su]. 10, 132, 339.

insentient beings: See *being, insentient.*

Insentient Beings Speak Dharma: 無情説法 [Mujō Seppō]. Fifty-fourth fascicle of this book. xlviii, lxxix, 548–57.

inseparable, close and: 親密 [shimmitsu], literally, parent intimate. 535.

insight into others' minds: 125. See also *miraculous powers, six.*

insightful flashes: See *unroll the matter and hurl insightful flashes.*

insightful flashes at each other, hurl: 互換投機 [gokan tōki]. Tossing back and forth of deep understanding. 270, 274.

insightful response, launch the: 投機 [tōki]. 270.

instruction: 啓發 [keihatsu], literally, guide and express. 12, 343, 530, 872.

instruction for zazen practice: 修行の用心 [shugyō no yōjin], literally, use of mind for practice. 12.

instruction, compassionate: 慈悲指示 [jihi shiji]. 330.

instruction, give: 爲示(す) [iji(-su)]. 12.

Instructions on Kitchen Work: 示庫院文 [Ji Kuin Mon]. Eighty-second fascicle of this book. lxxxix, 763–65.

instructor: Skt. āchārya. Transliteration: 阿闍梨 [ajari], 闍梨 [jari]. Reverend, teacher. 891.

intellect: Skt. (possibly), vriddha, literally, expanded (traditionally interpreted as, accumulated mind). Transliteration: 矣栗多 [iriddha]. Translation: 心識 [shinshiki], literally, mind and knowing. 慮知 [ryochi], literally, thinking and knowing. 有智 [uchi], literally, having wisdom. 8, 32, 226, 422, 494.

intellect and awareness: 慮知念覺 [ryochi nengaku]. 494.

intellectual: 擬議量 [gigiryō], literally, discuss measurement. 20, 101, 204, 294, 295, 380.

intention, considerate: 老思 [rōshi], literally, old person's thought. 269.

intention, true: 正意 [shōi]. 545, 726.

intentionally: 知而 [chini], literally, knowing and then. 256, 257, 503.

interact with, not: 不礙 [fuge]. 468.

interchangeable and not interchangeable: 回互不回互 [ego fu ego]. Interpenetrating and beyond interpenetrating one another. 312.

interfere, not: 不干 [fukan]. 635.

intermediary realm: 中有 [chū'u]. In-between realm, intermediary existence. A realm between this life and the next life. 中陰相 [chū'insō], literally, in-between invisible form. 785, 858, 859, 862, 887, 903.

interpretation: 釋 [shaku]. 76, 248, 327, 632, 699, 750 . . .

intimate: 親切 [shinsetsu], 親 [shin], literally, parent. 切 [shin], literally, close, deep. 密 [mitsu], literally, tight, secret. 親曽 [shinzō], literally, parent ever. Immediate experience. Close and inseparable. 237, 299, 393, 507, 693.

intimate, fully: 全靠密 [zenkōmitsu], literally, totally close and secret. 535.

intimate attention, with: 綿密 [memmitsu], literally, (woven) cotton tight secret. 296.

Intimate Language: 密語 [Mitsugo]. Fifty-second fascicle of this book. xlviii, lxxviii, 531–36.

intimate with or remote from: 親疎 [shinso]. *Shin* means intimate, and *so* means distant. 307.

intimately observe: 當觀(す) [tōkan(-su)], literally, see right in front. 237, 238.

introspection: 念想觀 [nensōkan], literally, memory, recollection [nen]; thought, ideas [sō], and observation or insight [kan]. Dōgen indicates that zazen is not visualization, insight, or analytical observation. 16, 579, 908.

investigate: 商量(す) [shōryō(-su)], literally, discuss and measure. 局量 [kyokuryō], literally, border measure. Analyze. 檢點 [kenten], literally, examine. 73, 264, 399, 726.

investigate, thoroughly: 功夫參究 [kufū sankyū], literally, endeavor and study all the way. 95, 489, 492.

involvements, various: 諸緣 [shoen], literally, various relationships. Outside conditions. 16.

iron, a single rail of: 一條鐵 [ichijō tetsu]. Solid rail of iron, one straight rod of iron. 236.

iron, one rod of: See *one rod of iron, ten thousand miles long.*

iron person: 鐵漢 [tekkan]. Person of determination, or someone who has attained the way. 255, 429, 447, 623, 723, 921.

iron tree blossoms: 鐵樹華開 [tetsuju kekai]. 274.

Ise Shrine: 伊勢神宮 [Ise Jingū]. Primary Shinto shrine of Japan, located in Ise Province (present-day Mie Prefecture). Consists of Kōtai Jingū (Inner Shrine) and Toyouke Jingū (Outer Shrine). The former enshrines Sun Goddess [Amaterasu Ōkami] and the latter, Harvest God [Toyouke Ōkami]. 211.

items, eighteen: 十八種物 [jūhachi shu motsu]. What a home leaver carries for engaging in ascetic practice or traveling: a willow twig, washing powder, three robes, a jar, bowls, a sitting mat, a walking stick, an incense bowl, a water bag, a towel, a knife, a flint stone, tweezers, a straw mat, sūtras, a precept book, a Buddha image, and a bodhisattva image. 66.

Itivrittaka: 283. See also *Divisions, Twelve.*

Jambudvīpa: Skt. 50, 180, 264, 661, 775, 822. See *Continents, Four.*

Jambunada: 閻浮檀 [Embudan], literally, Jambu Wood Platform. Shākyamuni Buddha made offerings in his former lifetime to many buddhas with this name. 823.

Jaradhara Garjita Ghosha Susvara Nakshatra Rāja Sankusumitābhijña Buddha: 雲雷音宿王華智佛 [Unrai On Shuku Ō Kechi Butsu], literally, Cloud Thunder Constellation King Flower Wisdom Buddha. Described in *Lotus Sūtra* as the buddha who, an incalculable time ago, expounded the sūtra to King Subhavyūha. 603.

Jātaka: 283, 285. See also *Divisions, Twelve.*

Jayata: 闍夜多 [Shayata]. Monk from northern India. Twentieth Ancestor of the Zen tradition in India. 166, 779, 780, 786.

Jeta Grove: 祇園／祇桓 [Gion], literally, Je Garden. [Kodoku On], Garden of Solitude. In the south of the city of Shrāvastī, Kaushala Kingdom, central northern India. According to sūtras, this is where Shākyamuni Buddha's community practiced together in the monastery during the rainy season. Donated by Prince Jeta, a son of King Prasenajit of Kaushala. 373, 514, 738, 742, 768, 799, 907.

Jeta, Prince: Son of King Prasenajit of Kaushala Kingdom, India. He donated the Jeta Grove to Shākyamuni as a site for a monastery.

jewel: 瓔珞 [yōraku]. Jeweled ornament. 31.

jewel in the banded hair, bright: 髻中の明珠 [keichū no meiju]. According to the *Lotus Sūtra,* a precious jewel that a wheel-turning king wore in his tied-up hair and gave to a retainer for his meritorious service. 347.

jewel, Bian's giant: 卞璧 [Ben peki]. Bianhe (Bian), 卞和 [Benka] of the country of Chu in Zhou Dynasty, found a large jade stone and dedicated it to two successive kings. Each time he was punished for making a false statement, but finally the third king had it polished and a most precious jewel emerged. 137.

jewel, to attract a: See *tile to attract a jewel, hurl a.*

jewel, wish-granting: 摩尼珠 [mani ju]. 159, 809.

jewels, four: 四寶 [shihō]. Also called 四蔵 [shizō], literally, four treasuries. Sūtras, precepts, treatises, and dhāraṇīs. 446.

Jiaofan Huihong: 覺範慧浩 [Kakuhan Ekō]. 1071–1128, China. Also called Shimen (Rock Gate). Dharma heir of Zhenjing Kewen, Linji School. Taught at Qingliang Monastery, Rui Region (Jianxi) but was falsely accused by other monks and imprisoned four times. After being pardoned, he lived in Xiangxi (Hunan) and concentrated on writing. Author of books including *Record within the Forests.* P. 933, Generation 20.

Jianfu Chenggu: 薦福承古 [Sempuku Shōko]. d. 1045, China. Studied with Nanyue Liangya, Yunmen School. Had realization when he heard about Yunmen's words. Claimed to have received dharma transmission from Yunmen without actually meeting him. Taught at Jianfu Monastery, Mount Jianfu, Rao Region (Jiangxi). P. 929, Generation 14. 575–77.

Jianyuan Zhongxing: 漸源仲興 [Zengen Chūkō]. Ca. eighth–ninth century, China. Dharma heir of Daowu Yuanzhi, Qingyuan Line. Taught at Mount Jianyuan, Tan Region (Hunan). His posthumous name is Zen Master Zhongxing, 仲興大師 [Chūkō Daishi]. P. 930, Generation 11. 471.

Jianzhi Sengcan: 鑑智僧璨 [Kanchi Sōsan]. d. 606, China. Third Chinese Ancestor of Zen School. Dharma heir of Second Ancestor Dazu Huike. Due to harsh government persecution of Buddhism, Sengcan lived in hiding as a homeless wanderer for much of his teaching life, and was a leper who was eventually cured. Nevertheless, Sengcan was found by Dayi Daoxin, who came to him as a fourteen-year-old novice, attained enlightennment, served as Sengcan's attendant for many years, and became his successor, the Fourth Ancestor. Later, Sengcan taught at Mount Sikong, Shu Region (Anhui). Regarded as the author of a poem titled "Engraving of Trust Mind" [Shinjin-mei]. Sengcan died standing up. His posthumous name is Zen Master Jianzhi, 鑑智禪師 [Kanchi Zenji]. P. 928, Generation 3. 166, 207, 366, 614.

Jianzhong Jingguo Continuous Transmission of the Lamp: Jianzhong Jingguo Xudeng-lu 建中靖国續燈録 [Kinchū Seikoku Zokutōroku]. Compiled by Foguo Weibai of Yunmen School and dedicated to the Emperor in the first year of Jianzhong Jingguo Era (1101). Organized historical Zen masters according to their dharma lineages.

Jiashan Shanhui: 夾山善會 [Kassan Zenne]. 805–881, China. First taught at Zhulin Monastery, Jingkou, Run Region (Jiangsu). Then he became a dharma heir of "the boatman" Chuanzi Decheng, Qingyue Line, before the latter disappeared in the river. After that, Jiashan dwelt deep in the mountains for thirty years before teaching at Mount Jia, Feng Region (Hunan). His posthumous name is Great Master Chuanming, 傳明大師 [Demmyō Daishi]. P. 930, Generation 11. 163, 407, 884.

Jiatai Record of the Universal Lamp: Jiatai Pudeng-lu, 嘉泰普燈録 [Katai Futōroku]. Compiled by Leian Zhengshou. Dedicated in the fourth year of Jiatai Era (1204) to the Emperor, who allowed it into the Buddhist canon. Unlike earlier collections of historical Zen materials, it includes stories of nuns, kings, officials, and commoners. 310.

Jiazhi: 迦智 [Kachi]. Ca. eighth–ninth century, Korea. Dharma heir of Damei Fachang. Taught in Korea. P. 930, Generation 10. 342.

jin: C. 斤 [kin]. Measuring unit. 596.82 grams (1.31 pounds) in Tang and Song dynasties. Sometimes we translate it as "pound." 406, 591.

Jingcen: See *Changsha Jingcen.*

Jingde Record of Transmission of the Lamp: Jingde Chuandeng-lu, 景德傳燈録 [Keitoku Dentōroku]. Compiled in the first year of Jingde Era (1004), probably by Yong'an Daoyuan of Fayan School. A primary collection of words and deeds of 1,701 masters. A common Zen expression, "1,700 kōans," derives from this number. 144, 310, 810, 811.

Jingqing Daofu: 鏡清道怤 [Kyōshō Dōfu]. 864–937, China. Dharma heir of Xuefeng Yicun, Qingyuan Line. Taught at Jingqing Monastery, Yue

Region (Zhejiang). Honorary title: Great Master Shunde 順德大師 [Juntoku Daishi]. P. 931, Generation 13. 338, 479, 480, 673.

Jingxuan: See *Dayang Jingxuan.*

Jingyin Facheng: See *Kumu Facheng.*

Jingzhao Mihu: 京兆米胡 [Kyōchō Beiko]. Ca. eighth–ninth century, China. Guiyang School. Dharma heir of Guishan Lingyou. *Mihu* means "foreigner." Jingzhao taught in the ancient Chinese capital city of Jingzhao. He said, "If there's a Buddha to be seen, it's not other than all beings." He was known for his wonderful beard. P. 930, Generation 11. 301.

Jingzhao Xiujing: 京兆休靜 [Keichō Kyūjō]. Ca. ninth century, China. Dharma heir of Dongshan Liangjie, cofounder of the Caodong School. Taught at Jingzhao Huayan Monastery, Mount Zhongnan, south of the city of Chang'an (Shanxi). Also called Huayan Xiujing. His posthumous name is Great Master Baozhi 寶智大師 [Hōchi Daishi]. P. 931, Generation 12. 298.

Jinhua Juzhi: 金華俱胝 [Kinka Kutei/Gutei]. Ca. ninth century, China. Dharma heir of Hangzhou Tianlong, Nanyue Line. Juzhi always responded to dharma questions by simply raising his finger. Old Monk Juzhi, 老俱胝 [Rō Kutei]. P. 930, Generation 11. 219, 342, 756.

join palms together: 388, 827. See also *gasshō.*

journey among other types of beings: 異類中行 [irui chū gyō]. Walk in the midst of various beings. 617.

joy, boundless: 福德無量 [fukutoku murō], literally, immeasurable bliss and virtue. 668.

Judun: See *Longya Judun.*

Jui: See *Bai Jui.*

Juñānaprabha: 智光 [Chikō]. Monk student of Shākyamuni Buddha. Formerly a wealthy man in a small country far away in the northeast of Rājagriha. 130, 131.

just as they are: 法爾 [hūni], literally, dharma thus. 290, 530.

just now: 而今 [nikon]. 8, 36, 245, 297, 302, 456, 560, 707.

just sit: 打坐 [taza]. *Ta* is a prefix for emphasis. *Za* means "sit" or "sitting." 只管打坐/祇管打坐 [shikan taza], literally, single-minded sitting: practice of zazen with no attempt to solve questions or expectation of attainment or enlightenment, and without either repressing or holding on to thoughts and feelings. Sometimes contrasted to meditation with kōan studies. xxiii, xxxiii, xxxviii, xlvi, 8, 220, 248, 376, 540, 644, 678.

just this: 57, 401, 585, 719.

Juzhi: See *Jinhua Juzhi.*

kalpa: Skt. Transliteration: 劫波 [kōha], 劫 [kō]. Eon; an incalculable span of time. 歴劫 [ryakukō], literally, passing many kalpas. 47, 183, 725, 842.

kalpa, this present: Skt., bhadra kalpa, literally, good kalpa. Translation: 賢劫 [gengō / kengō], literally, kalpa of sages. 844.

kalpas, limitless: 長劫 [chōgō], literally, long kalpas. Timeless eon. 117.

Kānadeva: 迦那提婆 [Kanadaiba], literally, One-Eyed Deva. Originally a Brāhman from southern India. Fifteenth Ancestor of Zen tradition as successor of Nāgārjuna. Resented and killed by those outside the way. 166, 244–48.

Kanakamuni Buddha: See *Buddha, Kanakamuni.*

Kannondōri-in: See *Kōshō Hōrin Monastery.*

Kānyakubja: 曲女城 [Kyokunyo Jō]. A city on the upper part of the Ganges in central northern India (Uttar Pradesh). Sometimes regarded as the place where Shākyamuni Buddha descended from the Heaven of Thirty-three Devas (Tushita Heaven) above Mount Sumeru. 573.

Kapilavastu: 迦毘羅衞 [Kabirae], literally, town of Kapila, center of Shākya Clan's region (present-day central southern Nepal, bordering India). Siddhārtha's father, King Shuddodana, ruled this region. Lumbinī Garden, where Siddhārtha was born, is in the western side of the town. 847.

Kapimala: 迦毘摩羅 [Kabimara/Kabimora]. Monk from Magadha. As Thirteenth Ancestor of the Zen tradition, he taught in southern and western India. Regarded as Nāgārjuna's teacher. 166, 238.

karavinka: Skt. Also, kalavinka. 迦陵頻伽 [karyōbinga], 頻伽 [binga]. Mythical bird who sings with celestial voice. 749.

karma: Skt. 業 [gō]. Action; visible or invisible effect of action. xliii, lxxx-vii, xciii, 659, 780, 783, 813.

karma, collective: 引業 [ingō]. Karma that brings forth a common form, such as a human being. 868.

karma, driven by: 業にひかる [gō ni hikaru], literally, pulled by karma.

karma, hindrance of: 業障 [gosshō]. 788–90.

karma, individual: 滿業 [mangō]. Karma that brings forth individual differences. 868.

karma, practice, body-mind, and environs: 業道依正 [gōdō eshō]. 業道 [gōdō], literally, karma way. 250. See also *body, mind, and environs.*

karma consciousness: 業識 [gosshiki]. Action consciousness; consciousness resulting from past deluded action; total ignorance. 677.

karma consciousness, vast: 業識茫茫 [gosshiki bōbō]. 677.

Karma in the Three Periods: 三時業 [Sanji Gō]. Eighty-fifth fascicle of this book. xciii, 779–91.

karma-formations: See *causation, twelvefold.*

karmic results: 果報 [kahō], literally, effect reward. 業報 [gōhō], literally, karma reward. 687, 711.

kāshāya: Skt. Transliteration: 袈裟 [kesa]. お袈裟 [okesa], an honorific Japanese spoken expression. 衲衣 [nōe], literally, patched robe. A patched robe worn over one shoulder by a Buddhist monk or nun. Shoulder robe. Also represents a monk or nun. 51, 113–18, 120, 128–35, 800.

kāshāya, three types of: 三衣 [sanne]. 三法衣 [sanhō'e], three dharma robes. (1) Great robe, most formal robe; Skt., sanghātī, 僧伽梨衣 [sōgyari'e]. 大袈裟 [daikesa]. Consists of nine to twenty-five panels. (2) Formal robe; Skt., uttarāsangha: 嗢呾羅僧伽衣 [uttarasōgya'e]. Consists of seven panels. (3) Indoor robe, informal robe, minor robe; Skt. antarvāsa, 安陀衣 [anda'e]. Consists of five panels. 中著衣 [chūjaku'e]. See also fascicle 13, "Power of the Robe." 115, 126.

kāshāya, wear the: 搭袈裟 [takkesa]. To put on the Buddhist shoulder robe. 116, 131, 139, 143, 564, 579.

Kāshyapa Bodhisattva: 迦葉菩薩 [Kashō Bosatsu]. Mahākāshyapa. 656, 865.

Kāshyapa Buddha: See *Buddha, Kāshyapa.*

Kaundinya: 憍陳如 [Kyōjinnyo]. 1. Ājñātakaundinya, one of the first disciples of the Buddha. 2. Shākyamuni Buddha made offerings in his former lifetime to many Buddhas with this name. 822.

Kaushala: Skt. 拘薩羅國 [Kōsara Koku / Kyōsatsura Koku], literally, country of Kaushala or Kosala. A large ancient kingdom on the Ganges, in central northern India near Nepal (Uttar Pradesh). West of the kingdom of Maghada; northwest of the kingdom of Kāshi; southwest of the region of the Shākya Clan. Shrāvastī was its capital, where King Prasenajit ruled during Shākyamuni Buddha's time. Jeta Grove, where the Buddha's community retreated in summer, is in the south of Shrāvastī.

Kausika: 憍尸迦 [Kyōshika]. Another name for Indra. 26, 27.

keep it in mind: 心術とす [jinjutsu to su], literally, make it mind art. 411, 767.

keep precept: 持戒 [jikai]. One of the six pāramitās. 124, 690, 700, 799, 859.

Kefu: See *Zhiyi Kefu.*

Keqin: See *Yuanwu Keqin.*

Kewen: See *Zhenjing Kewen.*

key to this barrier: 關棙(子) [kanrei(su)]. Key point, essential matter, mechanism of time. 318, 322, 323.

kind speech: 愛語 [aigo]. One of the bodhisattva's four methods of guidance. See also fascicle 46, "Bodhisattva's Four Methods of Guidance." 473, 475.

kindness, fields of: 恩田 [onden]. 783.

King Ajātashatru: 阿闍世王 [Ajase Ō]. Son of King Bimbisāra of Maghada, one of the sixteen kingdoms of India during the time of Shākyamuni Buddha. Ajātashatru became king by poisoning his father, who later died in prison. He agonized over his crime but reached peace of mind by taking refuge in the Buddha's teaching. He supported the first assembling of the sūtras soon after the Buddha's pari-nirvāna. 784.

King Brahmā: 梵王 [Bonnō]. Brahmā Deva 梵天 [Bon Ten]. Great Brahmā King, 大梵王 [Dai Bonnō]. Highest god of Brāhmanism. Regarded as one of the former lives of the Buddha, an initial listener of the Buddha's discourse, and a guardian deity who protects Buddhist teachings. 131, 822.

King Gridra: 吉利王 [Kitsuri Ō]. Mythological king at the time of Kāshyapa Buddha. 833, 834.

King Kanishka: 迦膩色迦王 [Kanishika Ō]. Ca. second century, India. King of Gandhāra. A great supporter of buddha dharma. Studied with Pārshva and Ashvaghosha, ancestors of Zen. 782.

King of Samādhis: 三昧王三昧 [Sammai Ō Zammai]. Literally, samādhi that is king of samādhis. Seventy-second fascicle of this book. lxxxv, 667–70.

King Prasenajit: 波斯匿王 [Hashinoku Ō]. Monarch of Kaushala, a large nation in central northern India near Nepal, who lived in the city of Shrāvastī. About the same age as the Buddha, he was a devoted follower and great supporter of Shākyamuni Buddha and his community. But he was ousted by his son Prince Virūdhaka and died in misery while the Buddha was alive. 64, 65, 587, 588, 604, 605, 833, 834.

King Ratnabyūha: 寶莊嚴王 [Hōshōgon Ō]. King in Shrāvastī of the ancient Indian kingdom of Kaushala. Father of Sanghānandi, the Seventeenth Ancestor. 811.

King Shuddhodana: 淨飯王 [Jōbonnō]. Monarch of the Shākya Clan, based in Kapilavastu (present-day central southern Nepal, bordering India). The first son of King Simhahanu. Father of Siddhārtha by Queen Māyā. He is also the father of Nanda by Queen Mahāprajāpatī, whom he married after the death of Māyā. 817.

King Simhahanu: 師子頰王 [Shishikyō Ō]. Monarch of Shākya Clan, based in Kapilavastu, ancient India. Father of King Shuddhodana. Grandfather of Siddhārtha. 816.

King Subhavyūha: 妙莊嚴王 [Myōshōgon Ō], literally, Wondrously Adorned King. One who was told about his former life story in the *Lotus Sūtra* by Jaradhara Garjita Ghosha Susvara Nakshatra Rāja Sankusumitābhijña Buddha. 603.

King Wants the Saindhava: 王索仙陀婆 [Ō Saku Sendaba]. Eighty-first fascicle of this book. lxxxix, 755–59.

King Wen: 文王 [Bunnō]. Ca. eleventh century B.C.E., China. Xibai Chang, 西伯昌 [Seihaku Shō]. Xibai is his title as head of lords in western China. After his death, his son King Wu defeated Empire of Yan and founded Zhou Dynasty. His posthumous name is King Wen of Zhou. 508, 516.

king, wheel-turning/King, Wheel-Turning: 轉輪王 [tenrinnō]. 輪王 [rinnō]. See *dharma wheel.* 轉輪聖王 [tenrin jō-ō], literally, wheel-turning sacred king. 83, 820–24, 867, 871, 872 . . .

kingfisher: 翡翠 [hisui]. 632.

Kings, Three: 三皇 [sankō]. Mythological rulers of China—emperors of heaven, earth, and humans. 867.

kinnara: Skt. 122, 393. See also *guardians, eight types of.*

kitchen: 庫院 [kuin], literally, storehouse. 香積局 [kōjaku kyoku], literally, place of accumulating fragrance. 230, 734, 764.

kitchen assistant: 陪饌役送 [baisen ekisō], literally, assisting to cook and serve up. 87.

kneeling: 長跪 [chōki], literally, kneeling tall. 891.

knot and wood grain: 節目 [setsumoku]. Also, nodes in bamboo or knots in wood. Concepts and theories. 311, 543.

know, intuitively: 靈知す [reichi-su], literally, know with spirit. 44.

know and trust: 決定信解す [ketsujō shinge-su], literally, determine and resolve with faith. 649.

Knower of the World: 世間解 [Seken Ge]. One of the ten primary names of the Buddha. 820, 822, 824, 825.

knowing, beyond: 未識 [mishiki], literally, not yet know. 185, 189, 190, 235, 270, 435, 534.

knowing, correct pervasive: 正遍知 [shōhin chi]. 45.

knowing, seeing, understanding, and merging: 知見解會 [chiken ge'e].

knowledge: 知見 [chiken], literally, knowing and seeing. 32, 181–84, 381.

knowledge, excellent: 善知識 [zenchishiki]. Also, teacher. 72.

knowledge, three types of: 124, 125, 336. See also *miraculous powers, six.*

kōan: J. 公案. 1. Fundamental point, first principle, truth that is experienced directly. 2. An exemplary story pointing to this realization. 3. Story used to lead students to experience this realization. Dōgen uses this word mainly in the first sense. *Kōan* is a Japanese transliteration of the Chinese *gongan*, which referred to official records or cases. The ideogram *gong* represents "official" or "public," and *an* represents "a case at law" or "legal records." Often Dōgen's commentators interpret the first syllable as "universal" and the second as "particular." xxxvi, 312, 412, 725.

kōan, a: 一則公案 [issoku kōan]. A kōan case. 312.

Kōen: 公圓. Ca. twelfth–thirteenth century, Japan. Seventieth Head Priest (Zasu) of Tendai School, based on Mount Hiei, in 1213. Around this time, Dōgen studied both Esoteric and Exoteric Buddhism with him. xxxv, 913.

Kōin: 公胤. d. 1216, Japan. Bishop and Head Priest of Onjō Monastery, Tendai School, Ōmi Province, east of Kyōto. In his young age, Dōgen received instruction from him. xxxvi, 913.

Kokālika: 倶伽離 [Gukari/Kukari]. An associate of Devadatta. He became a follower of the Buddha along with Devadatta and other members of Shākya Clan. Later he tried to split the practicing community and fell into unceasing hell. xxxvi, 785.

Kosala: Pāli. See *Kaushala.*

Kōshō Hōrin Monastery: 興聖寶林寺 [Kōshō Hōrin-ji]. Originally a temple called Kannondōri-in 觀音導利院, existed on the remains of An'yō-in 安養院, a part of Gokuraku Monastery 極楽寺 [Gokuraku-ji], located in Fukakusa, just south of Kyōto. Dōgen moved into this temple in 1233, added some buildings, and renamed it Kōshō Hōrin-ji in 1236. He retained the original name as its mountain name, or first name, so its full name became Kannondōri Kōshō Hōrin-ji 觀音導利興聖寶林寺. (He also used 護國 [Gokoku], meaning "Protecting Nation," as one of the monastery titles.) Dōgen lived there for eleven years until his community moved to Echizen. Since 1649, the site of this temple has been in Uji, further south of Fukakusa. 103, 111, 204, 233, 259, 302, 314, 323, 443, 467; Kannondori Kosho Horin Monastery, 38, 47, 57, 70, 78, 94, 135, 153, 164, 167, 179, 190, 194, 221, 295, 331, 379, 386, 396, 408, 421, 438, 449, 457, 484; Kannondori Monastery, 28, 414, 909.

Koun Ejō: 1198–1280, Japan. 孤雲懷弉 After studying Zen with Kakuan of the Japan Daruma School, he became Dōgen's student in 1234 and, later, the first head monk. As the most advanced student, he assisted Dōgen, edited many of his writings, and became his dharma heir. He was appointed second abbot of the Eihei Monastery by Dōgen in 1253. xxix, xl, lv, lxii, lxxvii, xc, xcii, xciv, xcv, xcvii, 791, 796, 818, 838, 850, 857, 875.

Krakucchanda Buddha: See *Buddha, Krakucchanda.*

Kuangren: See *Sushan Guangren.*

Kumāralabdha: 鳩摩羅多 [Kumorata]. Originally a Brāhman, he became a monk and Nineteenth Ancestor of the Zen tradition in India. 779, 780, 786, 790, 852, 853.

kumbhānda: Skt. 狗辨荼 [kuhanda]. Demon who flies like wind and consumes human spirits. 122.

Kumu Facheng: 枯木法成 [Koboku Hōjō]. 1071–1128, China. Also called Jingyin Facheng. Became dharma heir of Furong Daokai, Caodong School, on Mount Dahong, Sui Region (Hubei). Accompanied Daokai when he moved to Jingyin Monastery, Dongjing (Henan). Later became its abbot. He was called Kumu, meaning "tree stump," because of his devotion to sitting in silent meditation day and night, as he had learned to do from his teacher, Shishuang Qingzhu. Kumu was one of the teachers of Hongzhi Zhengjiao and inspired his emphasis on "silent illumination Zen," which later became the defining practice of the Caodong School. His posthumous name is Great Master Puzheng, 普證大師 [Fushō Daishi]. P. 933, Generation 19. 318, 632, 712.

Laborer Huineng: 374. See also *Dajian Huineng.*

lacquer, bucket of pitch-black: 黑漆桶 [koku shittsū]. Complete darkness, ignorance. 724.

lake without heat: 無熱池 [munetsu chi]. 無熱惱池 [munetsunō chi], literally, lake of no suffering from heat. 423.

lamp: 燈 [tō]. Represents dharma that is transmitted. 55, 194, 350, 436, 571, 773.

land of eternal serene light: 常寂光土 [jōjakkō do]. 186.

land on earth, not an inch of: 大地無寸土 [daichi mu sundo]. 46, 219, 610.

Land View Pavilion: 望州亭 [Bōshū Tei]. Located in Mount Xuefeng, Fu Region (Fujian). Known for its excellent view. 690. See also *Crow Stone Peak.*

language, intimate: 密語 [mitsugo], literally, secret words. 263, 531–36.

Langye Huijiao: 瑯瑘慧覺 [Rōya Ekaku]. Ca. tenth–eleventh century, China. Dharma heir of Fenyang Shanzhao, Linji School. Taught at Mount Langye, Chu Region (Anhui). Langye decided to become a monk after visiting an ancient monastery at the top of Mount Yao and feeling as though he already knew the place. His teachings and those of Master Xuedou Chongxian were known as "the two gates of sweet dew." Given the title Zen Master Guangzhao 廣照禪師 [Kōshō Zenji]. P. 932, Generation 17. 89.

lantern: 燈籠 [tōrō]. Originally a bamboo container for a lamp with paper at the sides. Often represents insentient being. 73, 98, 425, 630.

Laozi: 老子 [Rōshi]. Ca. sixth–fifth century, China. Sage regarded as founder of Daoism. Attributed author of the Daoist classic *Daode Jing* (*Tao-te Ching*), "The Way and Its Power." descendants of, 524; not clarified by, 857, 863, 865–68; regarded as bodhisattva, 866; student of, 872; teachings compared with buddha dharma, 544, 864, 869, 870, 873, 875; teachings of, 545, 604, 864.

lapels, pull open the: 開襟 [kaikin]. 554.

lapis lazuli: 瑠璃 [ruri]. 205, 601, 602, 634.

last eon: 莊嚴劫 [shōgen kō], literally, kalpa of magnificence. 169.

latecomer: 晚學 [bangagu], 後學 [kōgaku], literally, one who studies later. One who recently started. 晚進 [banshin], literally, one who advances afterward. 晚流 [banru], literally, later stream. 101, 419, 527, 542.

Later Han Dynasty: 後漢 [Gokan]. 5, 115, 140, 415. See also *Han Dynasty.*

laughing kills people: 笑也笑殺人 [shō ya shōsetsu nin]. 248.

lay men and women: 在俗の男女 [zaizoku no nannyo]. 16, 129, 151, 173, 710.

layperson: 俗人 [zokunin]. 白衣 [byakue], literally, white robe, as opposed to black robe representing a monk or nun. 128, 800.

Lazy An: See *Changqing Da'an.*

leap, make the: 跳脱す [chōdatsu-su], literally, jump and drop away. 725.

leap beyond: 一超す [itchō-su], literally, take one leap. 6, 224, 296, 469, 674, 693, 723. See also *go beyond.*

leap beyond ancient and present: 透脱古今底 [chōdatsu kokon tei]. 底[tei] is a suffix meaning "that which is." 723.

leap into: 跳入 [chōnyū]. 617.

leap out: 跳出 [chōshutsu]. Leap clear. Become free. 679.

leap over: 参跳 [sanchō], literally, study and jump. 跳翻 [chōhon], literally, jump and flap. 59, 622, 667, 725.

learn from the ancients: 稽古 [keiko]. Revere and follow the ancient way, study the past. Also, ancient custom.

learn to do concentration: 習禪 [shūzen]. Step-by-step practice of learning meditation.

learning, extensive: 多聞 [tamon], literally, much hearing. 381, 899.

learnings, three: 三學 [sangaku]. Practice of precepts, samādhi, and prajñā. 10, 11, 690.

Leave bondage behind: See *go beyond.*

leave no trace: 不留朕跡 [furyū chinshaku], literally, not leaving a sign of traces. 295, 401.

Leaving the Household: 出家 [Shukke]. Eighty-third fascicle of this book. xc, xciv, xcvi, 766–70.

lecture: 講誦 [kōju]. 377, 400, 706, 852.

lecture, informal: 陞座 [shinzo], literally, ascend the (teaching) seat. 174.

lecture on scripture: 講經 [kōkyō]. 116.

lecturer: 講者 [kōsha]. 講師 [kōshi], literally, lecturing teacher. 座主 [zasu], literally, head of seats. One who teaches Buddhist scriptures. 89, 192, 196, 330, 590, 701.

leg, invisible: 失脚來 [shikkyaku rai], literally, lost leg comes. 572.

legs, crossed: 累足 [ruisoku]. 579.

Leian Zhengshou: 雷庵正受 [Raian Shōju]. Ca. twelfth–thirteenth century, China. Compiler of *Jiatai Record of the Universal Lamp.* Advocated the accord of the Three Teachings (Buddhism, Confucianism, and Daoism). P. 933, Generation 19. 864–66, 869, 874.

leisurely person: 閑道人 [kandōnin], literally, leisurely way person. 526.

Lesser Vehicles: 45, 81, 200–3, 525, 875 . . . See also *Vehicles, Three.*

Letan Zhantang: See *Zhantang Wenzhun.*

let flow, freely: 通暢す [tsūchō-su]. 413.

let go: 放 [hō]. 捨 [sha], literally, throw away. 失 [shitsu], literally, lose. 放行 [hō gyō], literally, practice letting go. 拈放 [nempō], literally, take up and let go. 雙放す [sōhō-su], literally, let go both. 243–46, 521.

level, ultimate: 究竟位 [kukyōi]. 321.

level balance: 平平 [heihei], literally, even and even. 435, 436.

li: C. 里 [ri]. Measuring unit. One *li* was approximately 559.8 meters (0.348 miles) in Tang Dynasty and 553 meters (0.343 miles) in Song Dynasty. 66, 497, 606, 795, 812.

Li Fuma: 李駙馬 [Ri Fuba]. d. 1038, China. Government official. Studied with Guyin Yuncong, Linji School, and received seal of approval. Developed friendship with a number of Zen masters. Compiled *Tiansheng Extensive Record of the Lamp* during Tiansheng Era (1023–1032). P. 932, Generation 17. 683, 902.

Li, Minister: See *Minister Li.*

liang: C. 兩 [ryō]. Measuring unit. One *liang* was approximately 37.3 grams (1.31 ounces) in Tang and Song dynasties. Sometimes we translate it as "ounce." 591.

Liang: See *Xishan Liang.*

Liang: 梁 [Ryō]. Southern kingdom of China, 502–557. 357, 416, 494, 502; Epmeror Wu of, 92, 129, 355, 357; time of, 116, 359, 707, 710.

Liang, Lecturer: 亮座主 [Ryō Zasu]. Ca. eighth century, China. A student of Mazu Daoyi, Nanyue Line. After realization, he secluded himself on Mount Xi, Hong Region (Jiangxi). 719.

Liangjie: See *Dongshan Liangjie.*

Liangshan Yuanguan: 梁山緣觀 [Ryōzan Enkan]. Ca. tenth century, China. Dharma heir of Tong'an Guanzhi, Caodong School. Taught at Mount Liang, Ding Region (Hunan). P. 931, Generation 15. 167, 467.

Liaoran: See *Moshan Liaoran.*

Liaoyuan: See *Fuyin Liaoyuan.*

liberation, gate of: 解脱門 [gedatsu mon]. 878, 879. See also *emancipation, gate of.*

liberation, pure: 清淨解脱 [shōjō gedatsu]. 159.

librarian: 藏主 [zōsu]. 173, 174, 737, 917.

life, before and after: 身先身後 [shinsen shingo]. Also, before and after this lifetime. 495.

life, limited: 命者 [myōsha]. Those who live a transient life. 32.

life, renounce worldly: 捨命 [shamyō]. 427.

life, vitalize: 活命 [katsumyō]. 640.

life root: 命根 [myōkon]. 643, 678.

life span: 壽命 [jumyō]. 99, 127, 261, 663, 665, 786, 801.

life span, timeless: 壽量 [juryō]. Timeless activity. 181, 187, 660.

life stream, forthright: 直命脈 [jiki myōmyaku]. 669.

life vein: 命脈 [myōmyaku]. Life stream. Continuous transmission of dharma through buddha ancestors. 75, 373, 521, 584, 890.

life vein, tip of the: 命脈一尖 [myōmyaku issen]. 611.

lifetime, details of a: 一化の始終 [ikke no shijū], literally, from beginning to end of one transformation (guidance). 592.

life's study of the great matter: See *great matter.*

lifetimes, many: 累生 [ruishō]. 94, 379, 545, 843, 882.

light to shine within, turn the: See *turn the light to shine within.*

light, radiate: 放光 [hōkō]. 401.

light, soften the: 和光 [wakō]. Reduce the radiance of enlightenment and mingle with the ordinary. 866.

Lingdao: See *Caoxi Lingdao.*

lingering trace: 255. See also *wind and stream.*

Lingnan: 嶺南 [Reinan]. South of the Nanling Mountains, which divide China into north and south. Worker Lu (later, Sixth Ancestor Huineng) came from Xin Region (Guangdong) in this area. 241.

linguistics: 依主隣近 [eshu ringon], literally, modifier, the modified, the neighbor, and the close. A way of classifying a compound noun and an alternative expression. 327.

Lingxun: See *Furong Lingxun.*

Lingyou: See *Guishan Lingyou.*

Lingyun Zhiqin: 靈雲志勤 [Reiun Shigon]. Ca. ninth century, China. Studied with Guishan Lingyou, Guiyang School. After practicing for thirty years, had realization upon seeing peach blossoms. Taught at Mount Lingyun, Fu Region (Fujian). P. 930, Generation 11. 88, 645.

Linji School: 臨濟宗 [Rinzai Shū]. One of the Five Schools of Chinese Zen Buddhism. Regards Linji Yixuan as founder. In the eleventh century. Chiming Chuyuan's heirs, Huanglong Huinan and Yangqi Fanghui, became founders of the two sects of this school, Huanglong Order and Yangqi Order. The former spread first. but the latter became dominant in China in the twelfth century. A Japanese form of Linji School is the Rinzai School. xxxvi, xxxvii, 5, 175, 338, 511, 512, 915, 917, 919.

Linji Yixuan: 臨濟義玄 [Rinzai Gigen]. d. 867, China. Dharma heir of Huangbo Xiyun, Nanyue Line. Taught at Linji Monastery, Zhen Region (Hebei). Known for his shouting and dynamic teaching. Regarded as founder of Linji School, one of the Five Schools of Chinese Zen. His posthumous name is Great Master Huizhao 慧照 大師 [Eshō Daishi]. P. 930, Generation 11. xxviii, xxxvi, xxxvii, lxxvii, 317, 350, 483, 507, 536, 557, 613, 707. descendants of, 172, 304, 604; discourse of, 110, 293, 297, 813; lineage of, 174, 175, 177, 337; practice of, 349, 350, 511, 652; students of, 74, 75, 216, 511, teachings of, 506, 542, 920; understanding of, 403, 543; words of, 298, 458, 499, 512.

Linji's shout: 臨濟の擧喝 [Rinzai no kokatsu]. 157.

lion, combatting: 師子奮迅 [shishi funjin]. 577.

lion roar: 師子吼 [shishi ku]. 103, 234, 627, 628, 681.

lips, smack: 鼓兩片皮をこととす [kuryōhempi wo koto-to-su], literally, busy moving two skins of the drum (lips).

list of the names of the participants according to their dharma ordination seniority: 戒臘牌 [kairō hai], literally, dharma age plaque. 728.

Liu Chongjing: 劉崇景 [Ryū Sōkei]. Ca. eighth century, China. Nation's Chief General under Emperor Dai of Tang Dynasty. 112, 137.

Liu, Old Man: 劉氏翁 [Ryū Shi Ō]. Ca. ninth–tenth century, China. Planted pine trees at the monastery of Dongshan Shiqian, Mount Dong, Rui Region (Jiangxi). 652.

livelihood, pure: 淨命 [jōmyō]. 134, 690.

livelihood, right: 正命 [shōmyō]. True life. 304, 681, 689, 690. See also *path, eightfold noble.*

Living beings all are buddha nature: 234, 242, 251, 252. See also *buddha nature.*

logic, beyond: 理會およひかたし [rie oyobi gatashi], literally, logical understanding cannot reach. 157.

logical thought, phrases of: 念慮の語句 [nenryo no goku]. 158.

long for the ancient way: 慕古(す) [bōko(-su)]. Long for the authentic teaching. 56, 91, 411.

Long Nail Brāhman: See *Brāhman, Dīrghanakha.*

long river: 長河 [chōga]. 33.

Longshan: See *Tanzhou Longshan.*

Longtan Chongxin: 龍潭崇信 [Ryūtan Sōshin]. Ca. eighth–ninth century, China. Dharma heir of Tanhuang Daowu, Qingyuan Line. Lived in a hut in Longtan, Feng Region (Hunan). Deshan Xuanjian's teacher. P. 930, Generation 10. 192, 194, 196, 197.

Longya Judun: 龍牙居遁 [Ryūge Kodon]. 835–923, China. Dharma heir of Dongshan Liangjie, Caodong School. After studying with Cuiwei and Deshan, joined Dongshan's community and received dharma transmission. Taught at Miaoji Monastery, Mount Longya, Tan Region (Hunan). His posthumous name is Great Master Zengkong 證空大師 [Shōkū Daishi]. P. 931, Generation 12. 21, 94.

look into deeply: 看看 [kankan], literally, see and see.

look into this: 試擧看 [shi kokan], literally, try to bring up seeing. 28, 252, 267.

look through a bamboo pipe at a corner of the sky: 一隅ノ管見 [ichigū no kanken].

Lord Wen: See *Han Yu.*

lose one's life: 喪身失命 [sōshin shitsumyō]. To become free from one's limited self.

lotus blossom: 蓮華 [renge]. 189, 264, 459, 582.

Lotus Samādhi Repentance, Method of the: 法華懺法 [Hokke Sembō]. Treatise written by Nanyue Huisi on lotus samādhi, a method to experience reality by contemplating the teaching of the *Lotus Sūtra.*

Lotus School: 法華宗 [Hokke Shū]. Tiantai School, 天台宗 [Tendai Shū]. Established by Zhiyi at Mount Tiantai, Tai Region (Zhejiang), China, in the sixth century. Based on Zhiyi's classification of the entire canon. Central to this school are the *Lotus Sūtra* and the meditation practices of shamatha (Skt., ceasing of wavering mind) and vipashyanā (insight). 9, 854.

Lotus Sūtra: Skt., *Saddharma Pundarīka,* "Sūtra of Wondrous Dharma Blossoms," 妙法蓮華經 [Myō Hōrenge Kyō], 妙法華經 [Myō Hokke Kyō]. *Dharma Blossom Sūtra,* 法華經 [Hokke Kyō]. (The Sanskrit title does not include "Sūtra.") Full of parables and poetic imagery, this scripture is one of the most revered in the Mahāyāna canon. Other sūtras are considered provisional teachings, as opposed to the "complete" or supreme teaching of the *Lotus.* Unique to this sūtra are the teachings of One Vehicle, and of Buddha's enlightenment from the beginningless past. xxxiii, xxxiv, lxii, lxiii, xcv, xcvi, 919; as king of sūtras, 842; assemblies described in, 403, 437, 440, 611; chanting, 182, 184, 223, 224, 231, 232; copying, 888; bodhisattva's words in, 666; Buddha's verses in, 436, 439; Buddha's words in, 261, 274, 383, 384, 405, 406, 518, 520–22, 644, 657; dharma blossoms in, 180; expounding, 129, 803; parables in, 37, 188; receiving, 600; teaching of cleansing in, 58; teaching of making offering in, 827; transmission of, 189; words in, 185, 329, 404, 405, 416, 650, 680, 876.

Lotus Sūtra, assembly described by the: 法華會 [Hokke'e].

lower one leg: 垂一足 [sui issoku].

luminous: 昭昭靈靈 [shōshō ryōryō], literally, bright bright mysterious mysterious. 44, 312, 328, 572.

Luohan Guichen: See *Dizang Guichen.*

lute, song, and wine: 琴詩酒 [kin shi shu]. 476.

Madhya: 摩提國 [Madai Koku]. An ancient kingdom of India. Details unknown. 205, 812.

Magadha: 摩竭陀國 [Makada], literally, country of Magadha; 摩竭 [Makatsu]. An ancient kingdom of northeastern India, currently southern Bihār, bordering Nepal. Buddhagayā (present-day Bodhgaya), where Shākyamuni Buddha was enlightened, is located in this region, and much of his dharma discourses, later recorded in scriptures, took place on Vulture Peak near its capital city, Rājagriha. The Buddha's pari-nirvāna took place in Kushinagara in this country. 726.

Mahā Abhijñā Jñanā Abhibhū Buddha: 大通智勝佛 [Daitsū Chishō Butsu]. King whose sixteen children left the household. He expounded the teaching of the *Lotus Sūtra* upon entering nirvāna. 803.

Mahā Pari-nirvāna Sūtra: Skt. 大般涅槃經 [Dai Hatsu Nehan Gyō], 涅槃經 [Nehan Gyō]. 大經 [Dai Kyō], literally, great sūtra. A Mahāyāna scripture, regarded as describing the last discourse of the Buddha, a major source of teachings about buddha nature. Most of the Sanskrit version is lost. xlvii, 755, 794, 813, 825, 826, 854.

Mahā Prajñā Pāramitā Heart Sūtra: Skt. 摩訶般若波羅蜜多心經 [Maka Hannya Haramitta Shin Gyō]. Brief Mahāyāna sūtra. Excerpt of *Mahā Prajñā Pāramitā Sūtra.* Seventh-century Chinese translation by Xuanzang is most common in East Asia. A longer version is recited in Tibet and Mongolia. 25.

Mahā Prajñā Pāramitā Sūtra: Skt. 大般若波羅蜜經 [Dai Hannya Haramitsu Kyō]. Comprehensive collection of Prajñā Pāramitā scriptures, some of which are among the earliest Mahāyāna texts, formed around first century B.C.E. A seventh-century Chinese translation by Xuanzang contains 600 fascicles—largest of all Buddhist scriptures. 767.

Mahā Sangha Precepts: See *Great Sangha Precepts.*

Mahākarunā Bodhisattva: Skt. 大悲菩薩 [Daihi Bosatsu], literally, Great Compassion Bodhisattva. One of the former lives of Shākyamuni Buddha. 121, 123.

Mahākāshyapa: Skt. Transliteration: 摩訶迦葉 [Makakashō], 迦葉 [Kashō]; 迦葉波 [Kashōha]. 迦葉大士 [Kashō Daishi], literally, great person Kāshyapa. 迦葉尊者 [Kashō Sonja], literally, venerable person Kāshyapa. A senior disciple of Shākyamuni Buddha who engaged in rigorous ascetic practice. Regarded as the First Ancestor of the Zen School. lxxxiii, 509, 531, 534, 536, 916; and Ānanda, 482, 521, 532; and Mañjushrī, 742, 743; becoming a monk, 767, 769, Buddha entrusting dharma to, 246, 277, 389, 478, 504, 570, 574, 585, 587, 697; descendants of, 390, 503, 533, 535, 740; lineage of, 4, 11, 166, 171, 172, 208, 225, 279, 504, 572; meeting the Buddha, 501; practice of, 12, 21, 80, 334, 335, 571; robe of, 115, 503; smile of, 195, 365, 503, 534, 577, 642, 644, 691, 696; verse of, 656.

Mahānāman: Skt. 摩訶摩南 [Makamanan], 摩訶男 [Makanan], 摩男 [Manan]. One of the five monks who practiced with the Buddha after he left the palace. Elder brother of Aniruddha. A grandson of King Simha-hanu. Later, he returned to be a lay practitioner and became King of Kapilavastu while the Buddha was alive. 566, 816.

Mahāprabhā: Skt. 大光明 [Daikōmyō]. A slate roofer who was one of the former lives of Shākyamuni Buddha. 826.

mahāsattva: Skt. Transliteration: 摩訶薩 [makasatsu]. Translation: 大士 [dai-shi], literally, great person. Honorary way of referring to a bodhisattva. Often used as "bodhisattva mahāsattvas." 393, 732, 897.

Mahāyāna: 9, 81, 728, 866. See also *Vehicles, Three.*

Mahāyāna, Meaning of the: 大乘義章 [Dajō Gisho]. An extensive, eluci-dating text of the Mahāyāna teaching by Huiyuan of Sui Dynasty [581–617]. 840.

mahoraga: 122, 393. See also *guardians, eight types of.*

maintain: 保任(す) [honin(-su)], literally, keep and undertake. Fully pres-ent, enact, confirm. 奉覲(す) [bugon(-su)], literally, respectfully see. See in veneration. 奉覲承事 [bugon shōji], literally, respectfully see and uphold. 護念 [gonen], literally, protect with mindfulness. 49, 138, 668, 780.

Maitreya: 彌勒 [Miroku]. Maitreya Bodhisattva. Maitreya Tathāgata, 彌勒如來 [Miroku Nyorai]. Venerable Buddha Maitreya, 彌勒尊佛 [Miroku Sombutsu]. The future Buddha. Predicted to come down from Tushita Heaven to the Continent of Jambudvīpa 5,670,000,000 years in the future as the next Buddha and awaken those who missed the teaching of Shākyamuni Buddha. 37, 101, 128, 181, 395, 396, 687, 732.

make: 施爲 [sei], literally, conduct a deed, activities. 造作 [zōsa]. By inten-tion, create. 45, 92, 392, 780.

Making Offerings to Buddhas: 供養諸佛 [Kuyō Shobutsu]. Eighty-eighth fascicle of this book. xciv, 819–38.

Malaya, Mount: 摩黎山 [Mari Sen], also 摩羅耶山 [Maraya Sen]. Known as a place in the ancient kingdom of Dravida in southern India where incense from white chandana trees was produced. 61.

māndāra blossoms: Skt., māndāra, 曼陀羅華 [mandara ge]. Also, great māndāra blossoms, 摩訶曼陀羅華 [maka mandara ge]. Flowers of the heavenly world with colors and fragrance that make people joyous. The plant has many leaves, giving people shade and comfort. 584.

manifest: 示現 [shigen], literally, show and appear. 5, 184, 554, 753.

Manifestation of Great Prajñā: 摩訶般若波羅蜜 [Maka Hannya Haramitsu]. Second fascicle of this book. liii, lxv, liv, 25–28.

mañjūshaka blossoms: Skt. 曼殊沙華 [manjusha ge]. Also, great mañjūshaka blossoms: 摩訶曼殊沙華 [maka manjusha ge]. Soft white blossoms, which are rained down by heavenly beings and free the viewers from wrong actions. 584.

Mañjushrī: 文殊 [Monju]. Mañjushrī Bodhisattva, 文殊師利菩薩 [Monjushiri Bosatsu]. Mañjushrī Buddha, 文殊師利佛 [Monjushiri Butsu]. Bodhisattva of wisdom, whose figure is often enshrined as the Sacred Monk in the center of the monks' hall in a Zen monastery. 101, 687, 912; and Mahākāshyapa, 742, 743; praying to, 732; words of, 180, 181, 758.

mantra: Skt. 眞言 [shingon], literally, true word. 呪 [ju], magical spell. Indicates a dhāranī, especially a short one. Regarded as having a specific psycho-spiritual effect. A mantra is Sanskrit-based, but its sound is often unlike any known word. 16, 68, 843.

Mantra School: 眞言宗 [Shingon Shū]. Esoteric Buddhist teaching which was widely practiced but not organized as a school in China. It was brought to Japan in 806 by Kūkai, who soon established the Shingon School. *Mantra* (J. *shingon,* "true word") indicates the expression of dharma in mystical syllables. The Shingon School, along with the Tendai School, was influential before and during Dōgen's time. 9.

mark on top of missing the mark, miss the: 錯錯 [shaku shaku]. 412.

mark, hit the: 的當 [tekitō]. 103, 349, 371, 401, 435, 743 · · ·

mark, not hit the: 即不中 [soku fuchū], literally, just not hitting. 93, 233, 263, 284, 562.

mark, off the: 蹉跎 [sada], literally, stumble. 157, 248.

mark, right on the: 正的 [shōteki]. 384.

marketplace, confiscate goods from the: 攙奪行市 [zandatsu kōshi]. 400.

marks, missing of one hundred: 百不當 [hyaku futō], literally, not hit one hundred. 496.

marks, thirty-two: 三十二(相) [sanjūni (sō)]. Extraordinary physical characteristics of the Tathāgata as described in sūtras. They include a golden body, full cheeks like a lion's, a hair tuft on the forehead, and a raised area on top of the head. 293, 446, 605, 801.

marrow, attain the: 得髓 [tokuzui]. 72, 482. See also *skin, flesh, bones, and marrow.*

marrow, you have attained my: Bodhidharma's words to his students. Skin, flesh, bones, marrow—each represents the essence of teaching. 382.

master: 宗匠 [sō-shō], literally, craft person of the essential teaching. 通徹す [tsūtetsu-su], literally, be thoroughly familiar. 了達す [ryōtatsu-su], literally, complete arriving. 4, 32, 72, 270, 322, 469.

master, ancient: 古先 [kosen], literally, ancient and early one. 古徳 [kotoku], literally, old virtuous one. 18, 46, 129, 157, 236, 459.

master, guiding: 導師 [dōshi]. 5, 67, 129, 514, 524 . . .

master, thoroughly: 通達(す) [tsūdatsu(-su)]. Fully explore, fully experience. 262, 427, 429, 589, 876.

master, true: 眞善知識 [shin zenchishiki], literally, true good knower. 91, 157, 174, 511, 533, 920.

master and disciple: 師資 [shishi]. 274, 319, 511.

masteries, eight: 八達 [hattatsu]. Experiencing feely. 212, 240, 392.

mat: 草座 [sōza], literally, grass seat. 888.

mat, thick: 坐蓐 [zaniku]. 579, 908.

Mātanga: 摩騰迦 [Matōgya], Kāshyapamātanga, 迦葉摩騰迦 [Kashōmatōgya]. Monk from central India. Arrived in Luoyang, the capital of Han Dynasty, in the tenth year of the Yongping Era (67 C.E.) with Dharmaratna. Translated the *Forty-two-Chapter Sūtra.* This marked the official introduction of buddha dharma into China. 415.

match: 相委 [sōi], literally, mutually entrust. 144, 267, 402, 480, 492.

material: 物 [motsu]. Thing, an object. 473.

material, pure: 淨財 [jōzai]. 133, 134, 147, 150.

materials to study: 565.

matter, great: 大事 [daiji]. Most essential issue in understanding dharma. 11, 21, 36, 40, 702, 740, 918 . . .

matter, heart of the: 理 [ri]. 308.

matter, life's quest of the great: 一生參學の大事 [isshō sangaku no daiji]. 4.

matter, single essential: 一大事 [ichidaiji], literally, single great matter. 唯一大事 [yiitsu daiji], literally, only one great matter. 一大事因縁 [ichi daiji innen], literally, a great matter of causes and conditions. Essential matter; matter of grave importance. According to Buddhist teaching, all events are results of prior causes and conditions, and they themselves serve as causes and conditions for future events. 182.

matters, three: 三法 [sambō]. What is essential to sustain one's body and mind: consciousness, warmth, and life. 663.

mature: 熟脱 [jukudatsu], literally, ripen and get off. 92, 379, 634.

mature, not yet: 未便 [miben], literally, not yet favorable. 94, 251.

matures of itself: 自然成 [jinen jō], literally, naturally become. 585, 643.

maturing, heterogeneous: 異熟 [ijuku], literally, ripen differently. Wholesome and unwholesome cause brings forth a neutral effect. 102.

Maudgalyayana: 目犍連 [Mokkenren]. 目連 [Mokuren]. One of the ten major disciples of the Buddha. Born to a Brāhman family near Rājagraha. Together with his close friend Shāriputra, he became a student of the Buddha. Known for his mastery of miraculous powers. 128, 288, 784, 785, 819, 820.

may I ask how you are: 不審 [fushin], literally, (I do) not know details (about you). 475.

Mayu Baoche: 麻谷寶徹 [Mayoku Hōtetsu]. Ca. eighth–ninth century, China. Dharma heir of Mazu Daoyi, Nanyue Line. Taught at Mount Mayu, Pu Region (Shanxi). P. 930, Generation 9. 32, 403.

Mazu Daoyi: 馬祖道一 [Baso Dōitsu]. 709–788, China. Dharma heir of Nanyue Huairang, Nanyue Line. Taught at Kaiyuan Monastery, Zhongling (Jiangxi). Along with Shitou Xiqian, considered one of the two great jewels of Zen in his time. Had 139 enlightened disciples and made the Nanyue Line of the Southern School flourish. Initiated the Zen tradition of "recorded sayings," collections of informal dialogues and lectures. Also called Jiangxi, 江西 [Kōsei]. His posthumous name is Zen Master Daji, 大寂禪師 [Daijaku Zenji]. P. 929, Generation 7. 107, 468, 543, 683; and Nanyue, 220, 305–7, 309, 373, 377; descendants of, 101, 322; practice of, 219, 337, 526; students of, 109, 251, 290, 338, 575–77, 705, 719; words of, 250, 340, 342, 559–62, 676.

meal offering: 齋 [sai]. A midday meal hosted by a donor to home leavers. 227, 606, 765, 833.

meal time, morning: 粥時 [shuku ji], literally, gruel time. 229.

meal, satisfied with each: 粥足飯足 [shuku soku han soku], literally, satisfied with gruel (morning meal) and satisfied with cooked rice (midday meal). 647.

meals: 齋粥 [saishuku], literally, gruel and cooked rice. Morning and midday meals. Traditionally, only two meals were served in a Zen monastery, in the morning and at noon. 763–65.

meaning: こころ [kokoro], literally, mind. 宗趣 [shūshu], literally, source reason. 形段 [gyōdan], literally, shape and steps. 8, 106, 168, 708, 884.

meaning behind: 句裏 [kuri], literally, deep inside the phrase. 242.

Meaning of Bodhidharma's Coming from India, The: 祖師西來意 [Soshi Sairai I]. Sixty-seventh fascicle of this book. lxxxiii, 638–41.

meaning, essential: 大意 [taii], literally, large intention. Fundamental meaning. 13, 101, 349.

means, skillful: 善巧 [zengyō], literally, good and skillful. 善巧方便 [zengyō hōben], literally, good and skillful method. 348, 475, 726.

measure: 測度 [shikitaku], literally, measure degrees. 105, 313, 444, 863.

measure, beyond: 過量 [karyō], literally, pass the measure. 67, 218, 448, 474, 593 · · ·

meditation, first stage of: 初禪 [shozen]. 858, 860. See also *meditation, four stages of.*

meditation, four stages of: 四禪定 [shi zenjō], 四靜慮 [shijōryo]. (1) Having joy and ease by becoming free from desire. (2) Having joy and ease through samādhi. (3) Having ease of body by abandoning joy. (4) Free from joy and suffering. 28.

meditation, learning: 356, 357, 502, 908. See also *learn to do concentration.*

meditation, pāramitā of: 282. See also *six pāramitās.*

meditation, walking: See *walking meditation.*

meditation, Zen: 禪定 [zenjō], literally, Zen samādhi. 502, 503, 505, 506.

meditation posture: 跏趺 [kafu], literally, crossed legs. 606, 647, 667–70.

meet even one person, not: 不逢一人 [fuhō ichinin].

melodic sūtra chanting, do: 諷經す [fugin-su]. 731.

mendicant: 乞兒 [koji], literally, begging child. 130, 131, 692.

mental activity: See *activity, mental.*

merge in realization: 證入 [shōnyū], literally, enter realization. 6.

merge with realization: 契心證會 [kaishin shōe], literally, merge minds and realize understanding. 494, 496, 497.

merging, beyond: 不回互 [fuego]. Going beyond merging in complete merging of realization.

merit: 功德 [kudoku], literally, function and virtue. 功 [kō], literally, function. Ability to awaken self and/or others. 7, 113, 388, 775, 798–802.

merit beyond making: 無作の功德 [musa no kudoku], literally, function and virtue of not doing. 648.

merit, great: 大功 [daikō]. 140, 146, 431, 806, 835 ...

merit, have: 有功 [ukō]. 138, 859.

merit, visible: 有爲の功 [ui no kō], literally, effect of having (intentional) creation. 20.

merits, ten excellent: 十勝利 [jisshōri]. See fascicle 13, "Power of the Robe." 130–32.

method: 作法 [sahō], literally, dharma of making (conduct). 49.

Miaoxin: 妙信 [Myōshin]. Ca. ninth century, China. Nun who was a student of Yangshan Huiji, Guiyang School. Served as director of the guesthouse in Yangshan's monastery. P. 931, Generation 12. 75, 76.

midpoints, four: 四維 [shiyui]. Southeast, northeast, southwest, and northwest. 427.

Migasīsa: 鹿頭 [Rokutō]. Originally a Brāhman in the kingdom of Kaushala, known as an outstanding scholar. Became a student of the Buddha and attained arhathood. 874, 875.

Mihu: See *Jingzhao Mihu.*

mind art: 心術 [shinjutsu]. Also, determination. 74.

mind, all things are inseparable from: 萬法唯心 [mambō yuishin], literally, myriad dharmas are mind only. 269.

Mind Itself Is Buddha, The: 即心是佛 [Sokushin Zebutsu]. Sixth fascicle of this book. xlviii, lvii, 43–47.

mind, make up: 決定(す) [ketsujō(-su)], literally, determine and settle. Be clear about, resolve, understand. 597.

mind, through countless springs there is no change of: 幾度逢春不變心 [kido hōshun fu henshin]. 341, 385.

mind, way-seeking: Skt., bodhi chitta. 道心 [dōshin]. literally, heart of the way, or mind of the way. Aspiration for enlightenment. 39, 131, 369, 749.

mindfulness is present: 繫念 [kenen], literally, fasten mindfulness. 669.

mindfulness, four abodes of: 四念住 [shinenjū]. Four objects of contemplation: (1) Impurity of the body. (2) The perception of suffering. (3) Impermanence of the mind. (4) Things have no independent and permanent self. Also called four places of mindfulness, 四念處 [shinenjo]. 671, 674.

Minister Fang: 1. 防相國 [Bō Shōkoku]. Probably refers to Pei Xiu. See *Minister Pei.* 2. 房相國 [Bō Shōkoku]. Fang Xuanling, 房玄齡 [Bō Genrei]. 578–648, China. Prime Minister for fifteen years serving Emperor

Tai, second emperor of Tang Dynasty. Also a historian, participated in compilation of the *History of Jin*. 16.

Minister Feng: 馮相公 [Hyō Shōkō]. d. 1153, China. Feng Yi. 馮揖 [Hyō Shū]. A lay student of Fuyan Qingyuan, Linji School. Governor of Qiong Region (Sichuan). P. 933, Generation 22. 17.

Minister Li: 李相國 [Ri Shōkoku]. Ca. ninth century, China. Studied Zen with Yaoshan Weiyan, Qingyuan Line. 16.

Minister Pei: 裴相國 [Hai Shōkoku]. Pei Xiu, 裴休 [Hai Kyū]. 797–870, China. A lay student of Huangbo Xiyun, Nanyue Line, Pei also studied with other masters, including Guishan. Compiler of Huangbo's *Transmission of Heart, Essential Dharma*. P. 930, Generation 11. 350.

Minister Tai: 太公 [Taikō]. Named Wang, 望 [Bō]. Ca. eleventh–century, B.C.E. Assisted King Wen, then his son King Wu, and defeated Empire of Yan. Later founded Kingdom Qi in Zhou Dynasty. Author of the military manual *Liutao*. 508, 516.

miracle: 神通 [jinzū], literally, divine reaching. Also, a supernormal event. 287, 289–91, 294, 673.

miracle, minor: 小神通 [shōjinzū]. For Dōgen, a magical event. 289, 291.

Miracles: 神通 [Jinzū]. Twenty-sixth fascicle of this book. lxvi, 287–95.

miracles, great: 大神通 [dai jinzū]. For Dōgen, the everyday activity of an awakened person. 289, 291, 292.

miracles going beyond buddha: 佛向上神通 [bukkōjō jinzū]. 289.

miracles of buddha: 佛神通 [butsu jinzū]. 289, 563.

miraculous power: See *power, miraculous.*

miraculous powers, five or six: 五通六通 [gotsū rokutsū]. 289, 749.

miraculous powers, practice: 神通修證 [jinzū shushō], literally, practice and realization of miracles. 202.

miraculous powers, six: 六神通 [roku jinzū], 六通 [rokutsū]. The celestial feet, the celestial eye, the celestial ear, seeing others' minds, knowing the past, and the power to be free from desire. The last three are called three types of knowledge, 三明 [sammyō], three miraculous powers. 124, 292, 336, 749.

miraculous powers, three: 三明 [sammyō]. Three types of knowledge; three of the six miraculous powers: knowing the past, celestial eye, power to be free from desire. 447, 558.

mirror: 鏡 [kyō/kagami]. A round bronze mirror represents unmarred awakening. 30, 205–21, 306, 620.

miss: 蹉過(す) [shaka(-su)], literally, stumble and pass. Ignore, be ignorant. 10, 197, 214, 747. 錯 [shaku], literally, mistake. 轉疎轉遠 [tenso ten'on], literally, turn remote and turn far.

miss one hundred marks: See *marks, miss one hundred.*

missing the mark: See *mark on top of missing the mark, miss the.*

mistake after mistake: 將錯就錯 [shōshaku jushaku], literally, take a file (rasp) and work on the file. File a file about something. Take up a mistake and settle in with the mistake. Mistakes surpass mistakes. 錯錯 [shakushaku]. 204.

mistaken: 不是 [fuze], literally, not correct. 202, 297, 490, 858.

model: 慣節 [kansetsu], literally, precedented form. 龜鑑 [kikan], literally, tortoise (timeless) mirror. 75, 149, 216, 338.

moment: 一念 [ichinen], literally, a flash of thought. Skt., kshana. Transliteration: 刹那 [setsuna]. Skt., muhūrta, 須臾 [shuyu]. 刹那須臾 [setsuna shuyu]. An instant. 寸陰 [sun'in], literally, an inch of (the movement of) a shadow. 39, 44, 72, 75, 117, 747.

moment, at each: 107, 658, 659, 803. See also *abide in one's condition.*

moment, at this very: 正當恁麼時 [shōtō immo ji], literally, just this time. 37, 234, 495, 757.

moment, condition complete this: See *condition complete this moment.*

moment, great: 大節 [dai setsu], literally, large division. 346.

moment, myriad years in one: 一念萬年 [ichinen mannen], literally, moment of a thought (that is) ten thousand years. 205.

moment, myriad years of this: 直須萬年 [jikishu mannen]. Directly (experiencing) this moment (as) ten thousand years. 455.

moment, one hairbreadth: 一毛許 [ichimōko], literally, one hair amount. 189.

moment of a thought: 一念頃 [ichinen kyō]. 587.

moments as uncountable as the sands of the Ganges: 恒刹那 [gōsetsuna]. 658.

monasteries, high-ranking: 甲刹 [kassetsu]. 309.

monastery: 叢林 [sōrin], literally, grove and forest. 叢席 [sōseki], literally, grove seats. 院門 [immon], literally, temple gate. 精藍 [shōran]. Abbreviation of 精伽藍 [shōja garan]. 精舍 [shōja], literally, hall of effort. 伽藍 [garan], abbreviated transliteration of Skt. sangha ārāma, quiet place for home leavers' assembly. 19, 57, 176, 727.

monastery, join the: 掛搭 [kata], literally, hang a (travel) bag. 583.

monastery, Zen: 禪林 [zenrin], literally, Zen forest. 378.

monastery officer: 231, 411, 731, 733. See also *officers, six.*

monk: Skt., bhikshu. Transliteration: 比丘 [biku], 苾芻 [bissū]. 僧家 [sōke], literally, sangha house (person). 18, 26, 526, 858.

monk, blind: 盲比丘 [mō biku]. 829, 830.

monk, junior: 小師 [shōshi], literally, minor teacher. 733–35.

monk, old: 老僧 [rōsō]. 198, 747.

monk, patch-robed: 衲僧 [nōsō]. 407, 581, 582, 615.

Monk, Sacred: 聖僧 [shōsō]. Statue, usually of Mañjushrī, enshrined in the center of the monks' hall. 230, 231.

monk, senior: 上座 [jōza], literally, high seat. 335, 729, 782.

monk, sūtra chanting: 念經僧 [nenkin sō]. 224.

monk of solitary practice: See *solitary practice, monk of.*

Monk of the Fourth Stage Meditation: 四禪比丘 [Shizen Biku]. Ninety-first fascicle of this book. xcv, 858–75.

monkey: 獼猴 [mikō]. 46, 270, 274.

monk's action: See *action, monk's.*

monks, five: 五比丘 [gobiku]. Ājñātakaundinya, Assaji, Mahānāman, Bhadrika, and Vappa, who heard the first expounding of dharma by the Buddha after he attained the way. Also called Five Sangha Treasures, 五人僧寶 [gonin sōhō]. 566.

monks, group of the eighteen: 十八群比丘 [jūhachi gun biku]. Group of dharma practitioners who break the precepts. 685.

monks, group of the six: 六群比丘 [rokugun biku]. Monks during Shākyamuni Buddha's time who engaged in wrongdoing and caused the need for precepts. 685.

monks, ocean of: 海衆 [kaishu], literally, ocean of assembly. 618.

monks' hall: See *hall, monks'.*

monks' quarters: 菴裏 [anri], literally, inside the huts. 728, 834.

monograms: 華字 [kaji], literally, flowery character. Used for signature. 174.

moon: 月 [getsu/tsuki]. Usually represents enlightenment. 9, 31, 244–50, 521.

Moon, The: 都機 [Tsuki], meaning "moon" by pronunciation while the ideographs mean "entire" (*tsu*) and "function" (*ki*). Forty-third fascicle of this book. lxxiii, 453–57.

moon face: 月面 [gachimen]. 37, 211, 698, 709 . . . See also *Buddha, Sun-Face.*

Moon-Face Buddha: 455, 596. See also *Buddha, Sun-Face.*

Moonlight Bodhisattva: See *Bodhisattva, Moonlight.*

moon thusness: 月如 [getsunyo]. 453.

morning star: 明星 [myōjō]. Represents Shākyamuni Buddha's enlightenment, based on a legend that he attained the way when he saw the morning star while sitting under the bodhi tree. 19, 618, 672, 694.

mortar, stone: 石碓 [sekitai]. 643.

Moshan Liaoran: 末山了然 [Massan Ryōnen]. Ca. ninth century, China. Nun. Dharma heir of Gaoan Dayu, Nanyue Line. Taught at Mount Mo, Yun Region (Jiangxi). She was a prominent female teacher in the early, male-dominated Zen School. One of her students, Guanxi Xian, said of her, "I received half a ladle at Father Linji's place and half a ladle at Mother Moshan's. Since I took that drink, I've never been thirsty." P. 930, Generation 11. 75, 175.

mosquito biting an iron bull: 蚊子の鐵牛にのほる [bunsu no tetsugyū ni noboru]. Phrase indicating that something is incomprehensible by intellectual thinking.

Most Excellent King Sūtra: 最勝王經 [Saishō Ō Kyō]. One of the translations of *Suvarna Prabhāsottama King Sūtra.* 232.

mountain: 山 [san/yama] 1. Mountain in the usual sense. 2. Nature. 3. One's state of meditation. 99, 155, 423, 880.

mountains and waters, bear hardships traveling through: 山水に辛苦す [sansui ni shinku-su]. 360.

Mountains and Waters Sūtra: 山水經 [Sansui Kyō]. Fifteenth fascicle of this book. xlviii, lxi, lxxvii, 154–64.

Mountains are mountains, waters are waters: 山是山 水是水 [san ze san, suii ze sui]. Qingyuan Weixin's words. 164.

Mountains, Nine: 157, 291, 470. See also *Sumeru.*

mountains, rivers, and earth: 山河大地 [senga daichi]. 46, 97, 403, 615.

move, a single: 一著 [ichijaku]. As in the *go* game. 269.

move delusions in samādhi and pull them out with wisdom: See *samādhi and pull them out with wisdom, move delusions in.*

move forward: 進歩 [shimpo]. Walk forward, go beyond. 106, 426.

moved by the words: 語脈ノ翻身 [gomyaku no honshin], literally, turn the body by the word vein. 611.

movement, before a: 機先 [kisen]. 537.

movement, within a: 機中 [kichū]. 537.

mu: J. 無. C., wu. No, nothing, or nothingness. A monk asked Zhaozhou, "Does a dog have buddha nature or not?" Zhaozhou said, "No [mu]." This "no" is regarded as an understanding beyond "yes" or "no." 349–51, 417.

mud, go into the: 泥水す [deisui-su]. Stained by muddy water; to be in the ordinary world to awaken beings. 727.

mud, lump of: 泥團 [deidan], 泥彈子 [deidan su]. Mud ball. 221, 610.

mud, stone, sand, and pebbles: 土石砂礫 [deseki sharyaku]. 278.

mud and water, enter into: 入泥入水 [nyūdei nissui]. 574.

mud ball, twiddling with a: 弄泥團 [rō deidan]. 296.

mudrā: Skt. 印 [in]. Seal, proof, shape, or form. What is definite. The symbol of a buddha's or bodhisattva's original vow. Also, a physical gesture or posture in meditation. 5, 380, 381, 383, 384, 386, 521.

mustard seed storing Mount Sumeru: 芥納須彌 [ke nō Shumi]. 289.

mutual activity: See *activity, mutual.*

mutual affinity and interaction: 感應道交(す) [kannō dōkō(-su)], literally, responding feeling and the ways cross. A buddha responds to the feeling of a sentient being, and vice versa. 839.

Muzhou Daoming: 睦州道明 [Bokushū Dōmyō]. 780–877, China. Also called Venerable Chen, 陳尊宿 [Chin Sonshuku], by his family name. Dharma heir of Huangbo Xiyun, Nanyue Line. Taught more than one hundred students at Longxing Monastery, Mu Region (Zhejiang). Then left his students and made straw sandals to support his mother. P. 930, Generation 11. 483.

Myōan Eisai: 明庵榮西 [also, Myōan Yōsai]. 1141–1225, Japan. 西和尚 [Sai Oshō], literally, Priest Eisai. Went to China in 1168 and brought back Tiantai texts. Made a second visit to China between 1185 and 1191 to study Zen. Dharma heir of Xuan Huaichang, Linji School. Author of *On Raising Zen and Protecting the Nation* [*Kōzen Gokoku-ron*]. Founded Shōfuku Monastery in Hakata, Jufuku Monastery in Kamakura, and Kennin Monastery in Kyōto. Regarded as founder of Rinzai School, the Japanese form of Linji School. P. 934, Generation 23. xxxvi, xxxvii, 4, 68, 913–15, 919, 920.

Myōzen: See *Butsuju Myōzen.*

myriad things: 萬事 [banji], literally, ten thousand things. 萬法 [mambō], literally, ten thousand dharmas. 9, 102, 278, 590, 611 . . .

myrobalan fruit: 菴羅果 [anra ka]. Skt. āmura. Sometimes translated as "mango." 474, 661.

mystery of mysteries: 玄之玄 [gen no gen]. 433.

Nāgārjuna: Skt. Transliteraton: 那伽閼剌樹那 [Nagaarujuna]. Translation: Dragon Tree, 龍樹 [Ryūju]; Dragon Excellence, 龍勝 [Ryūshō]; Dragon Ferocity, 龍猛 [Ryūmyō]. Also, Ancestor Nāgārjuna, 龍樹祖師 [Ryūju Soshi]; Nāgārjuna Bodhisattva, 龍樹菩薩 [Ryūju Bosatsu]. Ca. second–third century, India. Pioneered a philosophical investigation on the Mahāyāna doctrines, centering on the concept of shūnyatā or emptiness. Known as the founder of the Mādhyamika School based on the *Mahā Prajñā Pāramitā* scriptures and his own writings. Author of treatises as well as "Verses on the Foundation of the Middle Way." Regarded as the Fourteenth Indian Ancestor in the Zen tradition. 802; descendants of, 247; lineage of, 166; manifesting a full moon, 245, 246, 248, 249; story of, 244; verse of, 245; words of, 124, 244, 662, 663, 793, 795, 797, 799, 800, 828, 829, 854, 867.

name and concept: 名相 [myōsō], 名色 [myō shiki], literally, names and forms. 359.

name, hide one's: 韜名 [tōmyō]. 407.

name, what is your: 汝何姓 [nyo ka shō]. Asking the family name. 239, 319.

nameless: 無名 [mumyō]. 214–16.

Nanda: 難陀 [Nanda]. A half brother of Siddhārtha, a son of King Shuddodana and Queen Mahāprajāpatī. After the Buddha's enlightenment, Nanda was about to be installed as king of the Shākya Clan in Kapilavastu, but the Buddha used his skillful means and made him leave the household. He served the Buddha's monastery as an officer and became an arhat. 814, 816.

Nanquan Puyuan: 南泉普願 [Nansen Fugan]. 748–834, China. After studying Buddhist philosophy, became a Zen student. Dharma heir of Mazu Daoyi, Nanyue Line. Lived at Mount Nanquan, Chiyang (Anhui), for thirty years cutting wood, raising cattle, and plowing. Taught many students including Changsha Jingcen and Zhaozhou Congshen. He called himself Old Master Wang. P. 930, Generation 9. xxxi; and Huangbo, 253, 254; and Zhaozhou, 339, 409, 410, 607; practice of, 614; students of, 757, 789; words of, 254, 345.

Nanquan's story of a sickle: 南泉の鎌子話 [Nansen no kensu wa]. Nanquan was once on the mountain working. A monk came by and asked him, "What is the way that leads to Nanquan?" The master raised his sickle and said, "I bought this sickle for thirty cents." The monk said, "I am not asking about the sickle you bought for thirty cents. What is the way that leads to Nanquan?" The master said, "It feels good when I use it." 157.

Nanyang Huizhong: 南陽慧忠 [Nan'yō Echū]. d. 775, China. Dharma heir of Sixth Ancestor Huineng. Taught at Nanyang (Henan) for forty years and taught Zen while emphasizing scriptural studies. Emperor Su asked Nanyang to be his teacher. Regarded as a master of the Northern Chinese Zen. His posthumous name is National Teacher Dazheng 大證國師 [Daishō Kokushi]. P. 929, Generation 7. defeating Daer, 198–204, 746–53; memorial site of, 87, 349; on view of soul/permanent nature, 14, 44, 45; story of, 470, 745; words of, 549–53, 647.

Nanyuan Huiyong: 南院慧顒 [Nan'in Egyō]. 860–930?, China. Dharma heir of Xinghua Cunjiang, Linji School. Nanyuan was considered the most important teacher of the third generation from Linji. He taught at Nanyuan Temple of Baoying Monastery, Ru Region (Henan), and was known for the strictness of his teaching. P. 931, Generation 13. 175.

Nanyue Huairang: 南嶽懷讓 [Nangaku Ejō]. 677–744, China. Studied fifteen years with Sixth Ancestor Huineng and became his heir along with Qingyuan Xingsi. Taught at Bore Monastery, Nan Peak (Mount Heng), Heng Region (Hunan). The teaching lineages derived from Nanyue and Qingyuan became the main streams of the Chinese Zen tradition. Regarded as founder of the Nanyue Line; he was teacher of Mazu. His posthumous name is Zen Master Dahui 大慧禪師 [Daie Zenji]. P. 929, Generation 7. 5, 48, 348, 513, 812.

Nanyue Huisi: 南嶽慧思 [Nangaku Eshi]. 515–577, China. Studied lotus samādhi with Huiwen of the Kingdom of Qi and reached enlightenment through contemplating the *Lotus Sūtra*. Practiced Zen for eight years at Nanyue (Mount Heng), Heng Region (Hunan), during the last part of his life. Teacher of Zhiyi, he established the Tiantai School and authored *Mahe Fuchuan* 摩訶止観 [Maka Shikan] (Great Shamatha and Vipashyanā). 831.

Nanyue Xuantai: 南嶽玄泰 [Nangaku Gentai]. Ca. ninth century, China. Dharma heir of Shishuang Qingzhu, Qingyuan Line. Known as a poet and called Cotton Robe Tai. Lived on Nanyue (Mount Heng), Heng Region (Hunan). P. 931, Generation 12. 371.

nature: 性 [shō]. Fundamental characteristics. 13, 33, 234–47, 493–95.

nature, ocean of: 性海 [shōkai]. 14.

nature, original: 本性 [honshō]. Basic characteristics. 44, 269, 277, 518–22, 708.

nature, other: 他性 [tashō]. Fundamental characteristics of other, as opposed to self. 656.

nature, self: 自性 [jishō]. Fundamental characteristics of self. 460, 656, 808.

nature, true: 實性 [jisshō]. 理性 [rishō], literally, reason nature. 44, 277, 520, 854.

natures, three: 三性 [sanshō]. The wholesome action nature, the unwholesome action nature, and the neutral nature. 96, 99, 790.

necessarily, not: 不必 [fuhitsu]. 何必 [kahitsu], literally, how is it always? Beyond one's knowledge. 29, 390, 412, 463.

negations, one hundred: 百非 [hyappi]. Negations upon negations. 592.

nest, old: 舊巢 [kyūsō]. Stagnating. Staying in comfortable, conventional views or understanding. 144, 437, 488.

net of pearls: 眞珠網 [shinju mō]. 204.

neutral: 無記 [muki]. Neither wholesome nor unwholesome. 35, 96, 277, 425, 592, 790, 841.

new, something: 新條 [shinjō], literally, new twig. Fresh and extraordinary. 549, 599, 741.

Niaoke Daolin: 鳥窠道林 [Chōka Dōrin]. 741–828, China. Dharma heir of Jiashan Faqin, Niutou School. As he lived on a limb of a long pine tree, he was called Zen Master Bird Nest (Niaoke). P. 929, Generation 8. 101–3.

Nidāna: 283, 285. See also *Divisions, Twelve.*

night: 夜 [ya/yoru]. Darkness, which sometimes represents the realm of nonduality. 154, 183, 453, 454, 771.

night period: 更 [kō]. One fifth of the time from sunset to sunrise. 61, 421.

nihilistic view: 斷見 [danken], literally, cutting off seeing. View of annihilation. The belief that nothing exists. 293, 675.

nine realms of sentient beings: See *realms of sentient beings, nine.*

Nine Schools: See *Schools, Nine.*

Nine Ties of Teaching: See *Ties of Teaching, Nine.*

nirvāna: Skt. Transliteration: 涅槃 [nehan], 泥洹 [naion]. Translation: 寂滅 [jakumetsu], literally, serene extinction. The state of enlightenment attained by Shākyamuni Buddha, or by any other buddha. Literally, extinction of fire, meaning extinction of desires, or liberation from the cycle of birth, death, and rebirth. In Mahayana Buddhism, nirvāna is viewed as not separate from birth and death, as opposed to extinction of birth and death. In Dōgen's usage, nondualistic experience. One of the four elements of the "circle of the way." 15, 131, 332, 771. See also *way, circle of the.*

nirvāna, great: 大涅槃 [dai nehan]. 646, 807.

nirvāna, path of: 涅槃の道法 [nehan no dōhō], literally, way dharma of nirvāna. 663.

nirvāna, wondrous heart of: 涅槃妙心 [nehan myōshin]. 322, 405, 502, 569, 774. See also *treasury of the true dharma eye.*

nirvāna by skillful means, manifesting: 方便現涅槃 [hōben gen nehan]. 185.

Nirvāna Hall: 涅槃堂 [nehan dō]. Building in a monastery for residents who are very ill. 706, 710, 852.

Niutou Farong: 牛頭法融 [Gozu Hōyū]. 594–657, China. Said to be a dharma heir of Fourth Ancestor Daoxin. His lineage is called Niutou School or Ox-Head School, in contrast to Fifth Ancestor Hongren's East Mountain School. His teaching emphasized thoroughness and logic. His posthumous name is Great Master Farong, 法融大師 [Hōyū Daishi]. P. 929, Generation 5. 113, 322, 323.

no more studying and no more doing: 絶學無爲 [zetsugaku mui]. 526.

no small matter: 不同小小 [fu dō shōshō], literally, not the same as small small. 288, 289, 291, 889.

noble conduct: See *awesome manifestation.*

noble path, eightfold: See *path, eightfold noble.*

noble truths, four: See *truths, four noble.*

no-expression: 不道 [fudō]. Beyond expression. 441.

no-form: 無相 [musō]. 232, 246, 293, 294, 526, 710.

noise and confusion: 憒閙 [kainyō]. 772.

nondifference: 不違 [fui]. 476.

nongreed: 不貪 [futon]. 473.

nonhuman: 非人 [hinin]. 123, 710, 712.

Northern Continent, Great: 北俱盧洲 [hoku kuroshū]. 423. See also *Continents, Four.*

nose appears, sharpened: 尖鼻來 [senbi rai]. 572.

nose, grab hold of the: 巴鼻 [ha bi]. 469.

nose, truly worth grabbing by the: 眞巴鼻 [shin habi]. 702.

no-self. 無我 [muga]. The understanding that there is no truly existing, separate self—the interdependence and impermanence of sentient beings and all things as seen through the eye of nonduality. 391, 898.

nostril: 鼻孔 [bikū]. That which is essential. Same as original face, eyeball, bones, and marrow. 225, 301, 405, 420, 603, 717.

nostrils, lose one's: 失却鼻孔 [shikkyaku bikū]. 611.

nostrils, vitalize the: 活鼻孔 [katsubikū]. 595. See also beyond.

not buddha: 非佛 [hibutsu]. Buddha who is free from being a buddha. 66, 459, 506, 882.

not hearing: 不聞 [fumon]. Direct experience of realization through the body.

not knowing. 不知 [fuchi], 不識 [fushiki]. Direct realization, or knowing outside of words. 328, 358, 753.

not necessarily: See *necessarily, not.*

notice: 覺知 [kakuchi]. 29, 155, 333, 803.

not-thinking: 303, 304, 423, 638 . . . See also *thinking, beyond.*

novice: Skt., shrāmanera. Transliteration: 沙彌 [shami]. 56, 233, 409, 410, 895 . . .

now and then: 亙古亙今 [gōko gōkon]. 102.

now, begin just: 始起 [shiki]. 707.

now, eternal: 長今 [chōkon], literally, long now. 506.

now, just this right: 即今の遮裏 [sokkon no shari], literally, within this right now. 560.

nuns, group of the six: 六群尼 [rokugun ni]. Nuns whose wrongdoings caused the precepts to be expanded. 685.

object: 境 [kyō]. Objective. 79, 81, 411, 757.

objects of the senses: 塵中 [jinchū], literally, in the dust. Dust [jin] represents the six-sense objects. 700. See also *dusts, six.*

obligation and love: 恩愛 [on'ai], literally, benefit by a person of higher position, such as a parent, and love. Worldly obligations. 329.

obscure: くらし [kurashi], literally, dark. 407, 434, 516, 534.

obscure traces: See *brilliance and obscure traces, hide.*

obstruct: 乖向 [kekō], literally, go against. 犯 [hon], literally, commit (wrong-doing). 155, 468, 698.

obstruction, beyond: 無礙 [muge], literally, no hindrance. 267.

occasion, on: 隨機 [zuiki], literally, according to circumstances. 745.

occupied, not being: 不區區 [fukuku]. 366, 678.

occur equally: 同條 [dōjō], literally, same twig. 287.

occurrences, four most excellent: 四種最勝 [shishu saishō]. Benefits of living in Southern Continent, Jambudvīpa: seeing the Buddha, hearing the dharma, leaving the household, and attaining the way. 802.

ocean dries up and yet does not reveal the bottom: 海枯不到露底 [kaiko futō rotei]. 209, 653.

ocean mouth: 海口 [kaikō]. 593.

Ocean Mudrā Samādhi: 海印三昧 [Kai'in Zammai]. Thirty-second fascicle of this book. xliv, lxviii, lxix, 380–86.

ocean, inexhaustible: 無盡法界海 [mujin hokkai kai]. 290.

offer sand: See *sand, offer.*

offering: 供養 [kuyō]. 恩給 [onkyū], literally, beneficial giving. 120, 582, 809, 822.

offering, faithful: 信施 [shinse]. 651, 652.

offerings, four types of: 四事 [shi ji]. Offering of things necessary for dharma practitioners, including food, clothes, bedding, and medicine. Sometimes, banners, canopies, flowers, and incense are included. 372, 820, 822, 823.

offerings, revere and make: 恭敬供養 [kugyō kuyō]. 114.

offerings, six types of hearts that make: 供養心有六種 [kuyōshin u rokushu]. A heart (1) in the field of benefaction, (2) of gratitude, (3) that arouses the most excellent heart of all sentient beings, (4) rare to encounter, (5) rare in the billion worlds, (6) that embodies the principles that are depended on in the world and beyond the world. 837.

offerings, ten types of: 供養に十種 [kuyō ni jusshu]. Offerings (1) to the Buddha himself; (2) to a place of veneration for the Buddha; (3) to the Buddha himself and to a place of veneration for the Buddha; (4) to the invisible Buddha as well as to a place of veneration for the Buddha; (5) by oneself; (6) that one has others make; (7) of materials; (8) that is excellent; (9) that is unstained; (10) of the ultimate way. 830, 837.

offerings, three types of: 三種の供養 [sanshu no kuyō]. Offering to a Buddha image: a mat, sugar water, and candles. 888.

officer, retired: 前資 [zenshi]. 736.

office: 寮 [ryō]. Also, living quarters. 211, 728, 791.

officers, six: 六知事 [roku chiji]. Six main officers in a Zen monastery. 知事 [chiji], literally, those who understand the matter: (1) 都寺 [tsūsu], director or chief administrator (also called 庫司 [kusu]) (2) 監寺 [kansu], assistant director (also called 監院 [kan'in], 院主 [inju]); (3) 副寺 [fūsu], treasurer; (4) 維那 [ino], practice coordinator in charge of activities in the monks' hall and ceremonies (also called 堂司 [dōsu], director of the monks' hall); (5) 典座 [tenzo], head cook; (6) 直歳 [shissui], work leader.

officiant: 和尚 [oshō]. 891–94. Also, *honorable.*

Old Buddha Caoxi: See *Dajian Huineng.*

Old Buddha Mind: 古佛心 [Kobutsu Shin]. Forty-fifth fascicle of this book. lxxiv, 468–72.

Old Buddha Tiantong: See *Tiantong Rujing.*

Old Mirror: 古鏡 [Kokyō]. Twenty-first fascicle of this book. xlv, lxiv, 205–21.

old shrine: 古祠 [koshi]. 412.

OM MANI SHRĪ SŪRYA: Skt. 唵摩尼悉哩蘇嚧 [om mani shiri soro]. Mantra that means "Homage to the jewel that shines like the sun." 607.

On the Endeavor of the Way: 辦道話 [Bendōwa], literally, talk on the endeavor of the way. First fascicle of this book. xliv, xlvii, xlviii, lii, liii, lxxvii, 3–22.

once-returner: 28. See also *fruits, four.*

one: 一 [ichi]. 1. One as opposed to two or many. 2. 一如 [ichinyo]. The inseparableness of two, such as practice and enlightenment. 261, 451, 474, 519, 797.

One Bright Pearl: 一顆明珠 [Ikka Myōju]. Fourth fascicle of this book. lvi, 34–38.

One Hundred Eight Gates of Realizing Dharma: 一百八法明門 [Ippyaku Hachi Hōmyō Mon]. Ninety-sixth fascicle of this book. xcvi, 896–903.

One Hundred One Practices of the Sarvāstivādin School. 根本説有部百一羯磨 [Kompon Setsuubu Hyaku-ichi Komma]. Guidelines of one of the pre-Mahāyāna schools in India. xcvi.

one or many ways: 一條兩條 [ichi jō ryōjō], literally, one or two strips. 399.

one or two stalks are bent and three or four stalks are leaning: 一莖兩莖曲なり、三莖四莖斜なり [ikkyō ryōkyō kyoku nari, sankyō shikyō sha nari]. 385.

one piece: 同條 [dōjō]. Also, single avenue. 271.

one rod of iron, ten thousand miles long: 萬里一條鐵 [ban ri ichijō tetsu]. 261, 391.

one thing: 一法 [ippō], literally, one dharma. Also, oneness, single matter. 32, 263, 650, 661.

One Vehicle: See *Vehicle, One.*

One Vehicle, dharma of the: 一乘法 [ichijō hō]. 591.

one who buys gold sells gold: 賣金須是買金人 [maikin shuze maikinnin]. 433.

one, clouds and moon are: 雲月是同 [ungetsu ze dō]. 586.

oneness or difference: 一異 [ichi i]. 444.

Only a Buddha and a Buddha: 唯佛與佛 [Yuibutsu Yobutsu]. Ninety-second fascicle of this book. xcv, xcvi, 876–83.

open the summer: 結夏 [ketsuge], literally, form a summer (practice period). 724.

open up: 開發す [kaihatsu-su]. 536, 610, 702.

openings and blockages: 通塞 [tsūsoku]. 494, 497.

opportunity: 便宜 [bengi]. Also, facility. 474, 734.

opportunity, time of surging: 激揚のとき [gekiyō no toki]. 4.

opposite: 相對 [sōtai], literally, face each other. Separate; arise in alignment; sequential. 231, 429.

ordinary humans, cannot be grasped by: 匪從人得 [hijū nintoku]. 532.

ordinary person, constantly being an: 常凡 [jōbon]. 243.

ordination: 得度 [tokudo], literally, attain crossing over (to the shore of enlightenment). 355, 686, 728, 729, 735, 913.

organs and six sub-organs, five: 五臟六腑 [gozō roppu]. Ancient Chinese classification: heart, kidney, lung, liver, and spleen; colon, small intestine, stomach, gallbladder, bladder, and three jiaos (burners), 三焦 [samsō] (an area that includes lower heart and upper stomach). 60.

organs and their objects, six sense: 六入 [rokunyū], literally, six enterings. 663.

organs, five sense: 五根 [gokon] literally, five roots. Eyes, ears, nose, tongue, and body. 815.

organs, sense: 諸根 [shokon]. 318, 771. See also *organs, six sense.*

25

organs, six sense: 六根 [rokkon], literally, six roots. 六情 [rokujō], literally, six feelers. Eyes, ears, nose, tongue, body, and mind. 294, 295, 318, 559, 560, 663.

original enlightenment: See *enlightenment, original.*

originally in this land, the ancestor was: 祖師本來茲土 [soshi honrai shi do]. 582.

other-power: 他力 [tariki]. Guidance of a Buddha or bodhisattva to lead one to enlightenment. 312.

ounce: See *liang.*

outlook: 形興 [gyōkō], literally, form rising. 217.

outside the way, six teachers: 六師 [rokushi], literally, six teachers. Six liberal thinkers who lived around the time of Shākyamuni Buddha. 65, 863.

outside the way, those: 外道 [gedō], literally, outside the way. Often implies those who follow Brāhmanism. 12, 43, 157, 853, 891.

outside the way who believe in spontaneous enlightenment, people: 天然外道 [tennen gedō], literally, natural (enlightenment) outside the way. 170, 178, 237.

outside-inside, intimate: 表裏團圞 [hyōri danran]. 584.

outstanding disciple: 神足 [jinsoku], literally, divine feet. 5, 216.

outstanding seeing: 見徹獨拔 [kentetsu dokubatsu], literally, seeing through alone and distinguished. 93.

Overnight Jiao: See *Yongja Xuenjiao.*

ox, white: 白牛 [byakugyū]. 270, 625.

Padmottara: 華上比丘 [Kejō Biku], literally, Flower Top Monk. Monk who committed the five avīchi crimes at the time of Kāshyapa Buddha. 784, 821.

Pagodas, Eight: 八塔 [hattō]. Stūpas built in the eight places related to Shākyamuni Buddha's life. 573, 574.

painting: 畫 [ga/e]. 1. Expression intended to represent reality. 2. Experience of nonduality. 3. In Dōgen's usage, a painting or picture represents the expression of enlightenment. 87, 248, 444–49, 588.

Painting of a Rice Cake: 畫餅 [Gabyō]. Literally, painted rice cake. Forty-first fascicle of this book. xlviii, lxxii, lxxiv, 444–49.

painting of a rice cake does not satisfy hunger: 畫にかけるもちひは、うゑをふさくにたらす [e ni kake ru mochii wa ue wo fusagu ni tara zu]. 87, 192, 197, 444, 445, 446.

painting spring: 春を畫く [haru wo egaku]. To experience truth directly, free from forms or concepts. 588.

panels: 條 [jō]. Strips of cloth used to create a kashāya. 116, 126, 127, 141, 142, 151.

Pangyun, Layman: 龐蘊居士 [Hō'on (Hō'un) Koji], 龐居士蘊公 [Hō Koji On Kō]. 740–808, China. Also known as Layman Pang. A lay student of Mazu Daoyi, Nanyue Line, who also studied with Shitou. Lived in Xiang Region (Hubei) and made his living by making baskets and having his daughter Lingzhao sell them in town. His teachings are found in *Recorded Sayings of Layman Pang.* P. 930, Generation 9. 290, 683.

Panshan Baoji: 盤山寶積 [Banzan Hōshaku]. 720–814, China. Dharma heir of Mazu Daoyi, Nanyue Line. Taught at Mount Pan, You Region (Hebei). Panshan was awakened when he heard a customer in the market ask a butcher for meat of the best quality, and the butcher replied "Where is there any that is not the best quality?" P. 930, Generation 9. 320, 454, 813.

paper, strips of: 垂箔 [suihaku]. 734.

Pāpīyas: Skt. 波旬 [Hajun]. 魔波旬 [Ma Hajun], literally Māra (Demon) Pāpīyas. 天魔波旬 [Tenma Hajun], literally, Celestial Māra Pāpīyas. A demon who tried to tempt and obstruct the practice of Shākyamuni Buddha and his disciples. 92, 503, 662, 849.

parable: 譬喩 [hiyu]. Also, analogy. 182, 283.

Paramārtha: 眞諦 [Shintai], literally, Genuine Truth. 527–596. An Indian monk who held the title of Tripitaka Master. Invited by Emperor Wu of the kingdom of Liang and arrived in China in 546. Translated sixty-four Buddhist texts, including *Golden Beam (Most Excellent) King Sūtra.* 869.

pāramitā: Skt. Transliteration: 波羅蜜 [haramitsu]. Translation: 度 [do], literally, ferrying or crossing over. Arriving at the other shore (of enlightenment through the ocean of delusions). Manifestation; realization. Sometimes translated as perfection. 282. See also *prajñā pāramitā; pāramitās, six.*

pāramitās, six: 六波羅蜜 [roku haramitsu]. 六度 [rokudo], literally, six crossings over (to the shore of enlightenment). Six types of realization. The basis for a bodhisattva's practice leading to the shore of nirvāna: giving, 檀 (那)[dan(na)]; keeping precepts, 尸羅 [shira]; patience, 屬提

[sendai]; vigor, 毘梨耶 [biriya]; meditation, 禪那 [zenna]; and prajñā (beyond wisdom), 般若 [hannya]. 282, 474.

parent: 父 [chichi], literally, father. 187.

parent and child: 父子 [fushi], literally, father and child. 214, 489.

parents were born: 87, 311, 445, 540, 553.

pari-nirvāna: Skt. Transliteration: 般涅槃 [hatsu nehan], 般泥洹 [hatsu naion], literally, perfect nirvāna. The Buddha's death. 276, 771, 833.

pari-nirvāna, great: 大般涅槃 [dai hatsu nehan]. Great death of the Buddha. 244, 661.

pari-nirvāna, manifestation of: 滅度現 [metsudo gen], literally, realization of dying and crossing (people) over (to the shore of enlightenment). 266.

pari-nirvāna, unsurpassable great: 無上大般涅槃 [mujō dai hatsu nehan]. 661.

Pari-nirvāna Sūtra, Mahā: See *Mahā Pari-nirvāna Sūtra.*

Pārshva: 波栗湿縛 [Barishiba]. Legendary monk regarded as the Tenth Ancestor of the Zen tradition in India. As he engaged in the practice of not lying down, he was called Venerable Undefiled Sides, 脇尊者 [Kyō Sonja]. 166, 335, 336.

part of: 少許 [shōko], literally, a small portion. 392, 523.

part, one: 一隅 [ichigū], literally, one corner. 264, 389, 428, 649, 865.

particle, most minute: 一極微 [ichi gokumi]. 47.

particle, one: 一塵 [ichijin]. One speck of dust. 389, 428, 649.

particle of dust: 微塵 [mijin], literally, minute dust. 9, 389, 428, 430, 474, 651.

particles, crack open: 微塵を破す [mijin wo ha-su]. 540.

Parvatarāja: 山王 [San'ō], literally, Mountain King. Shākyamuni Buddha made offerings in his former lifetime to many Buddhas with this name. 821.

pass on person to person: 嫡嫡相承 [tekiteki sōjō]. 309.

pass on the original nourishment: 還他本分草料 [gen ta hombun sōryō], literally, returning to another the original grass to feed the person. 594.

pass through the barrier: 超關 [chōkan]. Go beyond the barrier of dualism. 3.

passage, this: 一句の道著 [ikku no dōjaku], literally, expression of one phrase. 487, 685, 830.

passed on, be: 受業す [jugō-su], literally, receiving the work (accomplishment). 144, 247, 309, 448, 728, 913.

past: 向來 [kōrai], literally, come toward (now). 前頭來 [zentō rai], literally, former (life) coming (toward now). 頭 [tō] is a suffix. 宿命 [shukumyō], 宿生 [shukushō], literally, past life. 105, 114, 309, 325, 359, 641.

past, future, (or) present: 三際 [sansai], literally, three boundaries. 7, 14, 160, 396, 522.

past, illuminate the: 照古 [shōko].

past, knowing: 125. See also *miraculous powers, six.*

past, planted in the: 宿殖 [shukujiki]. 142, 145, 146.

past, present, and future: 過現當 [ka gen tō], 過現當來 [ka gen tōrai]. 59, 99, 392, 488, 864. See also *worlds, three.*

past, reflect on the: 照後 [shōgo], literally, illuminate back. 508, 516, 845, 881.

past and future: 前程後程 [zentei kōtei]. 382, 386.

past life [of a disciple of the Buddha]: 本事 [honji]. 283.

past life, knowledge of a: 宿住智 [shukujū chi]. 宿命通 [shukumyōtsū]. 宿通 [shukutsū]. 558.

path, authentic: 正道 [shōdō]. 473.

path, complete: 全道 [zendō]. 11.

path, eightfold noble: 八正道 [hasshōdō]. Fourth of the four noble truths: right understanding, right thoughts, right speech, right action, right livelihood, right effort, right mindfulness, and right concentration. 681. See also *enlightenment, thirty-seven wings of.*

path, invisible: 通霄 [tsūshō], literally, penetrating the clouds. Vast sky. Celestial path, 通霄路 [tsūshō ro]. 441.

path, single: 隻條道 [sekijō dō]. 73, 229, 268, 320, 598.

path, vital: 活路 [katsuro]. 33, 158, 267, 671.

path of letting go: 出路 [shutsuro], literally, road for going out. 3.

paths, five: 五道 [godō]. 418, 471. See also *paths, six.*

paths, six: 六道 [rokudō], 六趣 [rokushu]. The "roads" or "destinations" in the cycle of birth, death, and rebirth: realms of devas (gods or celestial beings), human beings, fighting spirits (asuras), animals, hungry ghosts, and hell beings. The first three are considered wholesome. The last three are called unwholesome realms, 惡趣 [akushu]; three lower paths, 三途 [sanzu]; or three unwholesome paths 三惡道 [san'akudō]. Sometimes called five realms, when hungry ghosts and hell beings are classified together. 5, 38, 44, 309, 418, 460.

paths, three lower: 5. See also *paths, six.*

patience: 安忍 [annin]. 25. See also *pāramitās, six.*

patience, pāramitā of: 282. See also *pāramitās, six.*

pavilion, wind-and-string: 管絃樓 [kan gen rō]. 613.

pay respect: 禮敬 [raigyō]. 28, 73, 122, 123, 849, 854.

peaceful establishment: 安立 [anryū]. 870.

pearl, a: 一顆珠 [ikka ju]. 37, 209.

pearl, dragon's bright: 驪珠 [ri ju]. Pearl said to be hidden under a dragon jar. Symbol of enlightenment. 347.

pearl, one bright: Complete and nondual reality. 35–38, 217, 269, 329, 594. See also *One Bright Pearl.*

pearl from the gill: 頷珠 [ganju]. 194.

pearl hidden in the hair: 髻珠 [keiju]. Pearl in the topknot. 188.

pearl rolls on the board: 珠の盤をはしる [tama no ban wo hashiru]. 521, 634.

pearl sewn inside the robe: See *robe, pearl sewn inside the.*

pebble from Mount Yan: 燕石 [En seki]. A rock that looks like a jewel but is actually worthless. Mount Yan is in present-day Hebei, China.

peg, anchoring: 一橛 [ikkitsu], literally, one peg. 724.

Pei Xiu: See *Minister Pei.*

penetrate: 透脱 [tōdatsu]. Break through, jump beyond, see through, free from, free and transparent, emancipation. 參徹 [santetsu], literally, practice through. 究辨 [kyūben], literally, inquire thoroughly, ultimate study. 說透 [settō], literally, speak through. 透擔來 [tōtanrai], literally, carry through. 透體 [tōtai], literally, go through the body. 透過す [tōka-su], literally, pass through. 36, 154, 251, 320, 624, 723.

penetration: 通 [tsū]. Direct experience; thorough understanding beyond discriminatory thinking. 102, 450, 574.

penetrations, seven: 七通 [shichitsū]. Knowing freely. 212, 240, 392.

people, good: 善男子 [zen nanshi], literally, good men. 742, 769, 825, 826.

people, mediocre: 庸流 [yōru], literally, ordinary stream. Also, mediocre lineage. 160, 494, 499, 545, 704.

people of excellence: 哲匠 [tesshō], literally, wise artisan. 21.

people outside: 傍觀 [bōkan], literally, (those who) see at a side. 155, 481, 711.

perception: 662. See also *skandhas, five.*

perception skandha: 受衆 [jushu], literally, perception assembly. 662. See also *skandhas, five.*

period of decline: 848. See also *three periods.*

permanence, dharma of: 定法 [jōhō]. 698.

permanent: 常住 [jōjū], literally, continuously abiding. Unchanged. 13, 30, 44.

permanent self, view of a: See *self, view of a permanent.*

Persian person looks for ivory: 南海波斯求象牙 [nankai hashi gu zōge]. 681.

person, idle: 閑人 [kanjin]. 144.

person, iron: 鐵漢 [tekkan]. 255, 429, 447, 623, 723, 921.

person, know the very: 當知是人 [tōchi zenin]. 600.

person, make a true: 爲人 [inin], literally, make a person. Teach someone. 220.

person, original: 本來人 [honrainin]. 235, 259.

person, true: 人 [nin], literally, person. 148, 515, 793.

person, Zen: 禪人 [Zennin]. 190, 636.

person as the very person, very: 如是當人 [nyo ze tōnin]. 600.

person beyond: 無人 [munin], literally, no person. 434, 498, 499.

person beyond measure, great: 沒量大人 [motsuryō taijin]. 593.

person in the ultimate realm: See *realm, person in the ultimate.*

person to person, pass on: See *pass on person to person.*

person who is beyond enlightened: 不悟者 [fugosha], literally, one who is not enlightened. 497.

perspective, lofty: 高著眼 [kōchakugan]. 389.

perturbed: 太心麁 [tai shinso], literally, very coarse mind. 712.

petals, five: 五葉 [goyō]. 458, 460, 582, 585, 586, 643.

phenomena, all: 萬象森羅 [manshō shinra], literally, myriad forms, many arraying. 萬回 [bankai], literally, myriad rotations. 268, 459, 559.

phenomena, inexhaustible worlds of: 無盡法界 [mujin hokkai]. 94.

phenomena, temporary: 假法 [kehō]. 688.

phenomena, world of: 法界 [hokkai]. 161, 186–89, 310, 868.

phrase, dead: 死句 [shiku]. 499.

phrase, single: 一句子 [ikkusu]. 子 [su] is a suffix with no special meaning. 一道 [ichi dō], literally, one expression. 37, 49, 274, 434.

Phrases, Three: 三句 [sanku]. Three lines that outline the essence of Zen. Separately taught by Linji Yixuan, Yantou Quanhuo, Fenyang Shanzhao, Yunmen Wenyan, and Taiping Huiqin. 507, 542.

pick it up or let it go: 一拈一放 [ichinen ippō], literally, taking up one, letting go one. 97.

picture, enter into and see the: 入畫看 [nyū ga kan]. 610.

pieces, one hundred broken: 百雜碎 [hyakuzassui]. 209, 214.

pilgrimage: 巡禮 [junrei]. 41, 725.

pillar, bare: 露柱 [rochū]. An unpainted column in the lecture hall or buddha hall. Represents insentient existence. Synonym for walls or bricks and pebbles. 425, 591, 594.

pillar walks in the sky: 露柱步空行 [rochū ho kū gyō]. 681.

pillow, someone asleep at night searching for the: 如人夜間背手摸枕子 [nyo nin yakan haishu mo chinsu]. 399, 542.

Pindola: 賓頭盧 [Binzuru]. Formerly a retainer of a king. Left the household and attained supernormal powers. At the Buddha's request, he taught in southwestern India, not entering nirvāna. Foremost of the sixteen arhats—the Buddha's disciples. 587, 588, 604–7.

pishācha: Skt. 毘舍遮 [bisasha]. Flesh-eater. A type of demon. 122.

pit: 窠窟 [kakutsu]. 窟坑 [kukkō]. Old pit: 舊窠 [kyūka]. Conventional views. Old pit of demons: 舊窠の鬼窟 [kyūka no kikutsu]. Pit of confusion. 179, 261, 549, 555, 559, 752, 875.

pivotal, not: 不要 [fuyō]. Not essential. 667, 916.

place that contains one's body: 容身の地 [yōshin no chi]. 579.

place, communal: 公界 [kugai]. Common area in a monastery where things for common use are kept. 298, 377.

place, this: 遮頭 [shatō]. Just this. 頭 [tō] is a suffix. 520.

place, this very: 這裏 [shari], literally, this within. 279, 297, 907.

plantain: 芭蕉 [bashō]. 447, 448.

plaque announcing a sūtra recitation: 看經牌 [kankin hai]. 229.

platform, front: 前架 [zenka]. A raised, long seating area on the south side of the monks' hall, near the center (where the monastery officers sit). 731.

platform, long sitting: 長連床 [chōrenjō]. A raised seat in the monks' hall on which five to ten monks do zazen side by side. Each assigned unit is called a tan. A cabinet is attached to the back of each tan for storing bedding and personal items. 134, 152, 173, 232.

platform, meditation: 禪床 [zenshō]. A long platform on which practitioners sit side by side. 55, 226, 227, 351, 672, 737.

platforms, sitting: 連床 [renjō]. 339, 343, 411, 694, 909.

play with: 弄(す) [rō(-su)]. Fool with. 698, 718.

pluck out: 抉出 [kesshutsu]. 617, 618, 696.

Plum Blossoms: 梅華 [Baika]. Fifty-ninth fascicle of this book. xliv, lxxx, lxxxi, 581–90.

point: 一究 [ikkyū], literally, one thorough investigation. 指示 [shiji], literally, point to and show. 道處 [dōsho], literally, place of expression. Make a statement. 道理 [dōri]. Expression of understanding; reality; truth; teaching. 32, 191, 263, 607, 747.

point, deepest: 徹地の堂奥 [tetchi no dō'ō], literally, inside the hall of penetration. 93.

point, fundamental: 32, 46, 631, 671, 706. See also *kōan.*

point, get the: 作得是 [satoku ze], literally, attain just this. 687.

point, grasp the: 取則 [shusoku], literally, get the case (kōan). 269.

point, have a: 一隅の搆得 [ichigū no kōtoku], literally, a corner (bit) of having arrived. 242, 560.

point, miss this: 猶滯 [yūtai], literally, further stagnant. 374.

point, pivotal: 要機 [yōki]. Essential point; essential method. 307, 309.

point, this very: 正當 [shōtō], literally, correct hit. 432.

point, turning: See *turning point.*

point, understanding this one: 這一解 [sha ichige]. 701.

Point of Zazen, The: 坐禪箴 [Zazen Shin]. Literally, bamboo needle on zazen. *Shin* also means admonition. Twenty-eighth fascicle of this book. xlviii, lxvi, lxxii, lxxx, 303–14.

poisons, three: 三毒 [sandoku]. Greed, hatred, and delusion. 61, 91, 868.

pole, top of a one-hundred-foot bamboo: 百尺竿頭 [hyaku shaku kantō]. 677.

polishing a brick: See *brick, polishing a.*

poppy seed: 芥子 [keshi]. 346, 666.

portrait: 頂相 [chinsō], literally, form of head top. 172.

pound: 240, 330, 423, 547, 692. See also *jin.*

pounding and crackling: 築著磕著 [chikujaku katsujaku]. Hit a stone and sound the stone. Bounce here and there. 692.

power: 功力 [kuriki], literally, effort and strength. 547, 553. See also *ability.*

Power of the Robe: 袈裟功德 [Kesa Kudoku]. Thirteenth fascicle of this book. xlviii, lx, lxi, 112–35.

power, miraculous: 神力 [jinriki]. Extraordinary power. 124, 416, 602.

powers, ten: 十力 [jūriki]. Extraordinary wisdom of the Buddha. Power to: discern what is reasonable and not; know each cause and effect; know various type of samādhis; distinguish abilities of sentient beings; know wishes of sentient beings; understand the nature of all beings; know the realms to which sentient beings are destined to go; recall the past lives of the self and others; know the death and rebirth of sentient beings; know the way to be free from desire. 814.

Prabhā: 光明 [Kōmyō], literally, Radiant Light. Shākyamuni Buddha made offerings in his former lifetime to many Buddhas with this name. 821.

Prabhāva: 威德 [Itoku], literally, Awesome Virtue. Shākyamuni Buddha made offerings in his former lifetime to many Buddhas with this name. 821.

Prabhūtaratna Tathāgata: See *Tathāgata, Prabhūtaratna.*

practice: 修行 [shugyō], 修 [shu], 行 [gyō]. Continuous daily activity centered on zazen. A moment-by-moment process of actualizing enlightenment, according to Dōgen. 修練 [shuren], literally, practice and train. 行李/行履 [anri], literally, traveling case / traveling sandal. Activity; daily activity; vital process; workings; 行業 [gyōgō], literally, taking action. 辦道 [bendō], literally, endeavor of the way. 3, 32, 58, 405, 646–54.

practice, bodhisattva's original: 本行菩薩道 [hongyō bosatsudō]. 189.

practice, complete: 行足 [gyōsoku], literally, sufficient practice. 450, 614, 856.

practice, difficult and rigorous: 難行苦行 [nangyō kugyō]. 368, 496, 666.

practice, engage in early morning: 朝上朝參 [chōjō chōsan]. 618.

practice, intimate: 密行 [mitsu gyō]. Also, thorough practice. 263, 535, 599.

practice, original: 本行 [hongyō]. Fundamental practice; practice in past life. 本修行 [honshugyō]. Practice that in essence is realization. 7, 49, 180, 184, 186, 282, 388.

practice, person of leisurely: 閑功夫漢 [kan kufū kan]. 600.

practice, pure: 操行 [sōgō]. 129, 411, 763, 898.

practice, temper: 練磨 [remma], literally, temper and polish. 215, 370.

practice, thorough: 107, 186, 309, 450, 817. See also *practice, full.*

practice, thoroughly: 參學 [sangaku]. Also, student. 參究(す) [sankyū(-su)], investigate thoroughly. 行盡 [gyōjin], literally, exhaust practice. 155, 268, 450.

practice, true: 正修行 [shō shugyō]. 94, 740.

practice, unchanging: 宛然なり [ennen nari], literally, as it is. 573.

practice, wholeness of: 同修 [dōshu], literally, same practice. Practice that includes enlightenment. 7.

practice, wondrous: 妙修 [myōshu]. Also, inconceivable practice that is not outside of realization. 12.

practice and enlightenment, undividedness of: 不染汚の修證 [fuzenna no shushō]. Oneness or wholeness of practice and enlightenment. 695.

practice and realization: 修證 [shushō]. Also, practice and enlightenment. 6, 59, 222, 573, 650.

practice and realization, depend on: 假修證 [ka shushō]. 610.

practice and understanding, merge the: 行解相應 [gyōge sō'ō]. 668.

practice continuously: 展轉廣作す [tenden kōsa-su], literally, unfolding and turning broadly. 6, 365, 373.

practice coordinator: 410, 706, 728, 851. See also *officers, six.*

practice-enlightenment: xxiv, xxv, lxxi, 32, 107, 321, 535. See also practice within realization.

practice for sudden or gradual realization: 頓漸修行 [tonzen shugyō]. 8.

practice instruction, evening: 暮請 [boshō]. Literally, evening request. Personal instruction in the abbot's room. 41.

practice mutually: 同參究 [dō sankū]. 481, 482.

practice period: 安居 [ango], literally, "peaceful dwelling." A three-month period of intensive practice. In Dōgen's time the summer practice period ran from the fifteenth day of the fourth month to the fifteenth day of the seventh month of the lunar calendar. It actually consisted of eighty-five days, but the number is rounded off, as is customary in East Asia, so that it is called a ninety-day practice period. (The winter practice period, which ran from the fifteenth day of the tenth month to the fifteenth day of the first month, was also known. But Dōgen says, "The tradition of winter practice period has not been passed on.") 65, 528, 724–29.

Practice Period: 安居 [Ango]. Seventy-ninth fascicle of this book. xlviii, 724–44.

practice period, completion of the: 解制 [kaisei], literally, undue restriction. 738.

practice period, summer: 夏臘 [gerō]. 710. See also *practice period.*

practice period draws to a close: 解夏 [kaige], literally, undue summer. 738.

practice place: 道場 [dōjō], literally, place, way, or field of enlightenment. 選佛道場 [sembutsu dōjō], literally, place of practice for selecting buddhas. 6, 55, 614, 684, 891.

practice-realization: 修證 [shushō], originally, practice and realization/enlightenment. xxiv, 47, 157–59, 673. See also *practice within realization.*

practice within realization: 證上の修 [shōjō no shū], literally, realization on top of practice. Practice that is inseparable from enlightenment or realization of buddha nature. A central teaching of Dōgen. 12.

practices completely, person who: 大修行底人 [dai shugyō tei nin]. 底 [tei] is a suffix meaning "one who." 851, 853.

practices, seven-type: 七種の行處 [shichishu no gyōsho]. Taught in *Lotus Sūtra.* Receive, chant, memorize, study, and copy *Lotus Sūtra,* plus see Shākyamuni Buddha and become Shākyamuni Buddha. 600.

practicing: 依行 [egyō], literally, depend on practice. 47, 59, 86, 88, 94.

practitioner: 仁者 [jinsha], literally, virtuous person. 作家 [sakke], literally, house (person) who makes or becomes (a buddha). 117, 594. *practitioners, four groups of:* 四衆 [shishu]. The Buddha's four types of disciples: monks, nuns, laymen, and laywomen. 436.

prajñā: Skt. Transliteration: 般若 [hannya]. Translation: 智慧 [chie]. Wisdom to see directly beyond dualistic views; wisdom beyond wisdom. 4, 25–28, 282.

prajñā pāramitā: Skt. Transliteration: 般若波羅蜜多 [hannya haramitta], 般若波羅蜜 [hannya haramitsu]. Arriving at prajñā; manifestation of prajñā; realization of wisdom beyond wisdom. 25, 732, 767. See also *pāramitās, six.*

prajñā, base of: 般若臺 [hannya dai]. 204.

prajñā, eighteenfold: 十八枚の般若 [jūhachi mai no hannya]. Prajñā of eyes, ears, nose, tongue, body, and mind; the prajñā of sight, sound, smell, taste, touch, and objects of mind; also the prajñā of the corresponding consciousness of eyes, ears, nose, tongue, body, and mind. 25.

prajñā, right seed of: 般若の正種 [hannya no shōshu]. 20.

prajñā, twelvefold: 般若波羅蜜十二枚 [hannya haramitsu jūni mai]. Prajñā that understands the twelvefold causation. 25.

Prajñā Kūta Bodhisattva: See *Bodhisattva, Prajñā Kūta.*

Prajñātara: 般若多羅 [Hannyatara]. Ca. fifth–sixth century, India. Bodhidharma's teacher. Originally a Brāhman in eastern India; taught in southern India. Regarded as the Twenty-seventh Ancestor in the Indian Zen tradition. 113, 166, 224, 225, 354, 478, 540.

pratyeka-buddha: Skt. Transliteration: 辟支迦佛 [byakushika butsu]. Abbreviated as 辟支佛 [byakushi butsu], 支佛 [shi butsu]. Translation: 緣覺 [engaku], literally, one who realizes causation. 獨覺 [dokkaku], literally, (one who was) awakened alone. Solitary awakened person who did not study with an authentic teacher. Mahāyāna word for a sage of earlier-style Buddhism. 28, 77, 125, 466.

Pratyeka-buddha Vehicle: 281. See also *Vehicles, Three.*

praying mantis: 蟷螂 [tōrō]. 714.

precedent, ancient: 先蹤 [senshō]. Example. 568, 599.

precept: Skt., vinaya. Transliteration: 毘尼 [bini]. Translation: 戒律 [kairitsu], literally, precepts. 律學 [ritsugaku], literally, study (practice) of the precepts. 15, 120, 797, 801, 804, 889–95.

precept, break the: 越毘尼罪 [otsu bini zai], literally, crime of transgressing vinaya. 124, 798, 799, 805, 834, 835.

precept, buddha: See *buddha precept.*

precept, general: 通戒 [tsūkai]. 95.

Precept School: 律宗 [Risshū]. One of the Nine Schools of Buddhism in China, based on the Mahāyāna system of precepts. Daoxuan (596–667) is regarded as founder. 117, 146, 148, 509.

precepts: See *precepts, ten; unwholesome actions, ten; precepts, come and receive the.*

precepts, eight: 八戒 [hakkai]. Precepts observed by laypeople on six particular days of purification in a month: (1) not to kill; (2) not to steal; (3) not to misuse sex; (4) not to make false statements; (5) not to sell or buy alcohol; (6) not to decorate one's hair and not to see or listen to music performance; (7) not to sleep on a high, wide bed; (8) not to eat outside the mealtime. 426.

precepts, forty-eight minor: 四十八輕 [shijūhachi kyō]. 66.

precepts, hold to the: 持戒 [jikai]. 16.

precepts, pāramitā of: 282. See also *pāramitās, six.*

precepts, receive the: 受具 [jugu]. 800–805.

precepts, ten: 十戒 [jikkai]. Ten pure precepts, 梵淨十戒 [bonjō jikkai]. 十重 [jū jū], literally, ten grave precepts. Guiding admonitions observed by Buddhists. The ten Mahāyāna precepts quoted by Dōgen's "Receiving the Precepts" literally read: (1) not to kill; (2) not to steal; (3) not to misuse sex; (4) not to make false statements; (5) not to sell or buy alcohol; (6) not to discuss the faults of other home-leaver bodhisattvas; (7) not to praise yourself and insult others; (8) not to withhold dharma or treasure [the Buddha's teaching or materials]; (9) not to be angry; (10) not to slander the three treasures. These precepts correspond to those in the *Indra's Net Sūtra.* 894.

prediction: 記莂 [kibetsu]. Of enlightenment. 122.

prepare: 料理す [ryōri-su]. 551.

present in the three realms: 今此三界 [konshi sangai]. 488.

Priest Rock Head: See *Shitou Xiqian.*

primary beyond-truth: 第一無諦 [daiichi mutai], literally, primary no-truth. 727.

primary truth: 第一義諦 [daiichi gitai]. 727.

Prince Shōtoku: 聖徳太子 [Shōtoku Taishi]. 574–622, Japan. Second son of Emperor Yōmei. As Regent of Emperor Suiko, he established a constitution and sent an envoy to China. A practitioner and pioneering supporter of Buddhism in Japan. xxxiii, 129, 919.

principle, clarify the: 究理 [kyūri]. Realize the great matter. 411, 780.

*principle, profound:*玄理 [genri]. 玄旨 [genshi]. 法則 [hōsoku], literally, law. 4, 873.

procedure: 儀則 [gisoku]. Also, rules of practice; occasions. 134, 152.

procedure, essential: 本儀 [hongi]. 566.

procedure, not following the authentic: 無稽古 [mukeiko], literally, not respecting the ancient. 702.

procession of amassing the assembly: 大衆相送 [daishu sōsō]. 736.

profundity: 奥玄 [ōgen], literally, inner subtlety. 181, 494, 495.

prose: 長行 [jōgō], literally, long line. 132, 282.

protect: 守護す [shugo-su]. 27, 113, 137–39, 567, 661.

provisional name: 虚名 [komyō], literally, hollow name. 293.

Puhua: 普化 [Fuke]. Ca. ninth century, China. Dharma heir of Panshan Baoji, Nanyue Line. Lived in Zhen Region (Hebei). A friend of Linji, he was known for eccentric conduct such as making a cartwheel and overturning tables at feasts provided by donors. Known as "one who has a head but no tail." The Japanese Fuke School of Zen, which incorporates playing shakuhachi flute music with meditation practice, is named after Puhua. 385.

pure action(s): See *action(s), pure.*

Pure Land: 淨土 [jōdo]. 1. A pristine world, free from delusion, where buddhas and bodhisattvas abide. 2. Paradise in the western direction where Amitābha Buddha presides. 185, 268, 800.

purification, dharma of: 淨法 [jōhō]. 58.

pushing others: 628, 680.

Pusya: 弗沙 [Fusha/Hossha]. Shākyamuni Buddha made offerings in his former lifetime to many Buddhas with this name. 820, 821.

Puyuan: See *Nanquan Puyuan.*

Qi'an: See *Yanguan Qi'an.*

Qianfeng: See *Yuezhou Qianfeng.*

Qici: See *Budai.*

Qinfeng: See *Baizhao Zhiyuan.*

Qingliao: See *Changlu Qingliao.*

Qinglin Shiqian: See *Dongshan Shiqian.*

Qingyuan: See *Fuyan Qingyuan.*

Qingyuan Xingsi: 青原行思 [Seigen Gyōshi]. d. 740, China. Dharma heir of Sixth Ancestor Huineng. Abbot of Jingju Monastery, Mount Qingyuan, Ji Region (Jiangxi). Students included Shitou Xiqian. Regarded as founder of the Qingyuan Line, from which the Caodong, Yunmen, and Fayan schools derived. His posthumous name is Great Master Hongji, 弘濟禪師 [Kōsai Zenji]. P. 929, Generation 7. 107; and Nanyue, 5, 115, 181, 216, 366, 468, 504, 890; and Shitou, 284, 366, 390, 505; descendants of, 135, 513, 530, 531, 917; document of heritate of, 177, 178, 704; words of, 282.

Qingzhu: See *Shishuang Qingzhu.*

Quanhuo: See *Yantou Quanhuo.*

quarters, individual: 單寮 [tanryō]. Private quarters in a monastery. 62.

quarters, other: 諸寮 [shoryō]. 229.

question: 問處 [monsho], literally, point of inquiry. Question: 問著 [mon-jaku], 問頭 [montō]. 著 [chaku/jaku] and 頭 [tō] are both suffixes. 擬議 す [gigi-su], literally, discuss. 159, 192, 470, 622.

quiescent, heart is: 得胸襟無事了 [toku kyōkin buji ryō], literally, getting the chest and lapels not eventful. 304.

quietude: 悄然の機 [shōzen no ki], literally, opportunity of being quiet. 88.

Radiant Light: 光明 [Kōmyō]. Thirty-seventh fascicle of this book. lxx, 415–21.

radiate light, cause the land to: 國土放光 [kokudo hōkō]. 401.

Rāhula: 羅睺羅 [Ragora]. Son of Siddhārtha before he became Shākya-muni Buddha. His mother was Princess Yashodharā. When the Bud-dha visited the Shākya Clan, Rāhula became a novice. Later he became one of the ten great disciples. Known for strict observance of the precepts. 56, 57, 570, 804, 814, 817.

raise it overhead: 戴著 [taijaku]. 著 [chaku/jaku] is a suffix. 635.

raise one's eyebrows: 揚眉 [yōbi]. 111.

Rājagriha: 王舍城 [Ōsha Jō], literally, king's city of residence. Capital city of the ancient Indian kingdom Magadha. Much of Shākyamuni Bud-dha's teaching activity took place around this city. 64.

rank, monk's: 出家位 [shukke'i]. 685.

rank, true person of no: 無位眞人 [mui shinnin]. 458.

Ranks, Five: 五位 [goi]. Dongshan Liangjie's theory of understanding reality, which consists of two elements: C. zheng 正 [shō] and pian, 偏 [hen]. *Zheng,* literally, correct or upright, can be translated here as oneness, real, general, complete, universal, noumenal, or absolute. *Pian,* literally, eccentric or one-sided, can be interpreted as differ-entiation, apparent, special, partial, particular, phenomenal, or rela-tive. Dongshan's original theory consists of: (1) pian within zheng, (2) zheng within pian, (3) zheng alone, (4) pian alone, (5) zheng and pian together. There are also later versions of the Five Ranks. 507, 542, 543, 633, 635.

rarity of meeting, extreme: 難値難遇 [nanchi nangū]. 573.

Ratnachūda: 寶髻 [Hōkei], literally, Crest (hair). One of the Buddhas to whom Shākyamuni Buddha made offerings in his former life. 824.

reach one thing: 一法通 [ippō tsū]. 444.

read, silently: 念 [nen]. 229.

Reading a Sūtra: 看經 [Kankin]. Twenty-second fascicle of this book. lxiv, 222–33.

readiness of those who hear it, in response to the: 機縁に逗す [kien ni zu-su]. 273.

reading, single path of silently: 一條の念底 [ichijō no nentei]. 229.

real: 正 [shō], literally, true; right. 實 [jitsu], literally, genuine. 眞實 [shin-jitsu], literally, genuine and true. 10, 218, 432, 526, 688.

reality: 實相 [jissō], literally, true form; genuine forms. 眞實相 [shinjitsu sō], literally, true and genuine form. 96, 518–25, 773.

reality, enter: 入理門 [nyūri mon]. 403.

reality, mudrā of: 實相印 [jissōin]. 521.

reality, open up: 發眞 [hosshin]. 692, 693.

reality, scale of: 實相量 [jissōryō]. 664.

reality, three treasures that are the essence of: See *treasures that are the essence of reality, three.*

reality as it is: 如是實相 [nyoze jissō]. 651.

reality of all things: 諸法實相 [shohō jissō]. Things as they are, which are not outside of ultimate truth. Cf. *Lotus Sūtra,* "Skillful Means": Only a buddha and a buddha can finally master the reality of all things. 181, 518–23, 871.

Reality of All Things, The: 諸相實相 [Shohō Jissō]. Fifty-first fascicle of this book. lxxvii, lxxviii, 518–30.

realization: 證 [shō]. Body and mind experience of reality; enlightenment. 證著 [shōjaku], literally, realization completed. 悟/さとり [go/satori], enlightenment. 覺 [kaku], 覺智 [kakuchi], awakening, understanding. 現成 [genjō], actualization, actualizing the fundamental point. 機 [ki], insightful flashes. 現前 [genzen], manifesting right in front. 3, 29, 108, 340, 450, 511. See also *pāramitā.*

realization, before or after: 機先機後 [kisen kigo]. Beyond the moment of having insight flashes. See also *realization.*

realization, enter: 入證 [nisshō], 得入 [tokunyū]. 16, 381, 749, 792.

realization, fruit of: 證實 [shōjitsu]. 657.

realization, immediate: 直證 [jikishō]. 6, 9.

realization, in: 證上 [shōjō], literally, on top of realization. 3, 6, 12, 478, 479, 495.

realization, intimate: 密證 [misshō]. 263, 534.

realization, mark of: 證相 [shōsō]. 7.

realization, merge with: 證契(す). [shōkai(-su)]. 407, 494, 496, 497.

realization, original: 本證 [honshō]. 6, 12.

realization, receive: 證嗣 [shōshi], literally, inherit realization. 168.

realization, receive through: 證傳 [shōden]. Inherit dharma upon being enlightened. 478.

realization, seal of: 印證 [inshō]. Seal of enlightenment; certification of realization. 168, 169, 178.

realization, wholeness of: 同證 [dōshō]. One realization, literally, same realization. 7.

realization itself: 證則 [shōsoku], literally, realizing a case (of kōan). 6, 7, 877.

realization thought: 會量 [eryō]. 304.

realization without a teacher: 無師獨悟 [mushi dokugo]. Usually means self-proclaimed enlightenment, which is cautioned against in the Zen School. In Dōgen's usage, a teacher's selfless realization and a student's selfless realization completely merge. 168, 558.

realization without self: 無自獨悟 [muji dokugo]. 168. See also *realization without a teacher.*

realize: 5, 379, 469, 887. See also *accept.*

realize and manifest: 修證現成 [shushō genjō], literally, actualize practice and realization. 642.

realm: 田地 [denchi], literally, rice field land. 85, 389, 527, 551.

realm, human: 人道 [nindō]. 137, 839, 896, 897, 903 . . .

realm, person in the ultimate: 究竟人 [kukyōnin]. 389.

realm beyond: 430.

realm of beyond merging: 不回互 [fuego], literally, not turn each other. 314.

realms of sentient beings, nine: 九道 [kudō]. Favorable realms where sentient beings abide: human realm, four realms in the form realm, and four in the no-form realm. 135.

realms, all: 彌界 [mikai]. 265, 282, 555, 898.

realms, three: 三界 [sangai], roughly meaning the entire world of phenomena and beyond. (1) Desire realm, 欲界 [yokukai], including the six paths. (2) Form realm, 色界 [shikikai], of those who are free from desire. (3) Formless realm, 無色界 [mushikikai], of those who have attained the highest worldly mental states through meditative exercises. 78, 278, 487, 651, 889.

realms, visible and invisible: 冥陽 [meiyō]. 10, 108.

reborn as a wild fox: 墮野狐身 [da yakoshin], literally, fall into a wild fox body. 705, 706, 707, 851.

receive: 稟受(す) [bonju(-su)]. Respectfully receive. 137, 170, 334, 889–92.

receive, intimately: 密受 [mitsuju]. 309, 337, 915.

receive instructions: 請參す [shinsan-su], literally, ask for study (with the teacher). 353.

receive the entire earth: 大地全收 [daichi zenshū]. 270.

Receiving the Marrow by Bowing: 禮拜得髓 [Raihai Tokuzui]. Ninth fascicle of this book. lviii, 72–84.

Receiving the Precepts: 受戒 [Jukai]. Ninety-fifth fascicle of this book. xcvi, 889–95.

recent member of the community: 後生 [goshō], literally, born later. 18.

receptive samādhi: See *samādhi, receptive.*

recitation hall: 看經堂 [kankindō]. 232, 233.

recitation of a gāthā: 梵音 [bonnon], literally, Indian sound. 231.

recognize, fully: 錯認 [shakunin], literally, recognize mistakenly. See also *mistake after mistake.*

recognize it even though you are facing it, not: 對面不相識 [taimen fu sōshiki], literally, to face but not know each other. 589.

recognize the thief as one's own child: 認賊爲子 [ninzoku ishi]. 299.

Record within the Forests: Linjian-lu, 林間録 [Rinkan-roku]. Collection of Zen Buddhist stories edited by Jiaofan Huihong, also called Shimen, of the Linji School, China. Published in 1107. "Forests" represent monasteries. 356, 502.

red, brilliant: 赤赤 [shakushaku], literally, red and red. 677.

reflect: 回光す [ekō-su], literally, turn around the light. Reflect: 照顧 [shōko], literally, illuminate back. 嘗觀す [shōkan-su], literally, taste and observe. 15, 242, 550.

Refrain from Unwholesome Action: 諸惡莫作 [Shoaku Makusa]. Eleventh fascicle of this book. xlvi, xlvii, xlviii, 95–103.

Refrain from unwholesome actions. Do wholesome actions: 諸惡莫作 衆善奉行 [shoaku makusa, shuzen bugyō]. The Seven Original Buddhas' precepts take this imperative form. According to Dōgen's interpretation, in practice within realization it is not possible to be engaged in unwholesome actions, and wholesome actions are invariably carried out. xlvi, 95–99, 101, 102, 445, 885, 890. See also *wholesome; unwholesome*.

refresh oneself: 點心 [tenjin], literally, lighten the mind. Also, snack. 192.

refuge, take: 敬禮 [kyōrai], literally, respect and bow. 26, 118, 839–46.

Regulations for the Auxiliary Cloud Hall at the Kannondōri Kōshō Gokoku Monastery: 觀音導利興聖護國寺重雲堂式 [Kannondōri Kōshō Gokoku-ji Jū'undō Shiki]. Fifth fascicle of this book. xlviii, lvi, 39–42.

rejoicing, extraordinary oneness of: 特地一條の歡喜 [tokuchi ichijō no kangi]. 393.

rejoicing, fully: 遍歡喜 [hen kangi]. 393.

relationships, all: 萬緣 [ban'en], literally, ten thousand conditions. 40.

relevant, not: 不用得 [fuyōtoku], literally, not able to use. 256.

relics: 舍利 [shari]. 138, 417, 664–66, 831, 837 . . .

remain free of administrative duties: 薙草の繁務なし [chisō no hammu nashi], literally, no busy duty of cutting weed. 366.

Renyong: See *Baoning Renyong*.

repent: 發露 [hotsuro], literally, begin to reveal. 93, 94, 118, 143, 148, 861.

repentance: 修懺 [shusan], literally, practice repentance. 5, 376, 540, 667.

repentance, formal: 禮拜懺悔 [raihai zange], literally, bow and repent. 41.

replace the tail with the head: 以頭換尾 [itō kambi]. 689.

replete with: 受用(す) [juyō-(su)], literally, receive and utilize. Be fulfilled, be enriched. Experience receptive samādhi. 10.

resource: 智略 [chiryaku], literally, wisdom and plan. 508, 783.

respond: 感應 [kannō]. 77.

respond, invisibly: 冥感 [myōkan]. 172.

respond, not: 無對を拈す [mutai wo nen-zu], literally, take up no answer. 420, 633, 640, 641.

response, mistaken: 錯對 [shakutai]. 707.

result: 報業 [hōgō], literally, reward of action. 所感 [shokan], literally, what is experienced. 賞 [shō], literally, award. 780, 853.

result received in a lifetime after the next: 順後次受 [jungoji ju]. 780.

result received in the next lifetime: 順次生受 [junjishō ju]. 780, 783.

result received in this lifetime: 順現法受 [jungenhō ju]. 780.

retired officers: 勤舊 [gonkyū]. 736.

retreat: 掩室 [enshitsu], literally, close the room. 726, 727.

return to be a sentient being: 還作衆生 [gen sa shujō]. 300.

return to the source and manifest a buddha body: 從本垂迹 [jūhon suijaku]. 300.

return to the source and origin: 還源返本 [gengen hempon]. 83, 292, 310.

returning once, fruit of: 斯陀含果 [shiidagon ka]. 斯陀含 [shiidagon] is a transliteration of Skt. sakrid āgamin, once coming. 果 [ka] means fruit. One who is reborn once to be enlightened. Second of the four stages of becoming an arhat. 858.

reveal: 露 [ro]. 206, 615.

reveal each other: 相顯 [sōken]. 316.

revered, deeply: 大尊貴生 [taison kisei]. Having great value, magnificent. The last ideograph, *sei*, is a suffix with no special meaning. 585.

reward, meritorious: 福報 [fukuhō]. 389, 391.

reward, true: 實報 [jippō]. 520, 807.

reward body: See *buddha body*.

rice cake: 餅 [mochii]. 81, 192–94, 444–47.

rice cake, painted: 畫餅 [gabyō]. 1. Xiangyan said, "A painting of a rice cake does not satisfy hunger." This is usually interpreted as "studying words and letters does not help one to realize ultimate truth." 2. Dōgen's interpretation is that words and letters as an expression of enlightenment cannot be separated from the ultimate truth. Thus, "painted rice cake" means an expression of enlightenment. 192, 194, 197, 248, 249, 445–47, 449. See also fascicle 41, "Painting of a Rice Cake."

rice plants, flax, bamboo, or reed, widely spread: 稻麻竹葦 [tōma chikui]. A great number of things. 73.

rice water: 漿 [konzu]. 647.

rice, husking: 米白 [bei haku]. 643.

rice, satisfied with cooked: 飯足 [han soku]. 407.

ride the buddha hall upside down and move in a circle: 倒騎佛殿打一匝 [tōki butsuden ta issō]. 690.

ride the robber's horse to chase the robber: 騎賊馬逐賊 [ki zokuba chiku zoku]. 36.

right now: 而今 [nikon]. This particular moment, here and now. 106, 154, 299, 706.

right now, all-inclusively: 蓋時節 [gai jisetsu], literally, cover the time period. 36.

right path limb, eightfold: 八正道支 [hasshōdō shi]. See fascicle 73, "Thirty-seven Wings of Enlightenment."

right shoulder uncovered: 偏袒右肩 [hendan uken] 116, 143.

right to the point: 是 [ze], literally, this, correct, right. 492.

Rinzai School: 臨濟宗 [Rinzai Shū]. Japanese form of Linji School. One of the two major schools of Japanese Zen Buddhism. Myōan Eisai is regarded as founder. In the eighteenth century this school was revitalized by Hakuin, a dharma descendent of Xutang Zhiyu. 4, 914.

ritual: Skt., karman. Transliteration: 羯摩 [komma]. Manners. Precept transmission ceremony. 59, 231.

Rivers, Four: 四瀆 [shitoku]. Great rivers of China: the Yangzi, the Yellow, the Zhun, and the Ji. 211.

rivers, four great: 四大河 [sh daiga]. Mythological rivers in general. 423.

road, inconceivable: 玄路 [genro], literally, subtle path. 317.

robe: 衣衫 [esan]. *E* is kashāya, and *san* is upper robe. Represents an entire garment. 52, 112–16, 136–41.

robe, antarvāsa: Skt. 安呾婆娑衣 [andabasha]. Inner robe. 127.

robe, brocade: 金襴衣 [kinran'e]. The robe that is said to have been handed from Shākyamuni Buddha to Mahākāshyapa and from Mahākāshyapa to Ānanda. 170, 174, 391, 423, 693.

robe, combined: 直裰 [jikitotsu], 裰子 [tossu]. One-piece robe. Upper robe (jacket) and lower robe (skirt) combined. 375.

robe, dharma: 法衣 [hōe]. 51, 65, 127, 815.

robe, double: 重複衣 [jūfuku e]. 127. See also *robe, sanghātī.*

robe, great: 大衣 [dai e]. 115, 116, 122, 126, 127, 143, 914. See also *robe, sanghātī.*

robe, informal: 小衣 [shōe], literally, small robe. 127.

robe, inner: 内衣 [nai e]. See *robe, antarvāsa.*

robe, lay: 俗服 [zokufuku]. 129.

robe, less formal: 中衣 [chū e], literally, middle robe. 127.

robe, outer: 上衣 [jōe], literally, high robe. Uttarasangha robe. 51, 52, 54, 127, 142, 143.

robe, patched: 21, 798. See also *kashāya.*

robe, pearl sewn inside the: A story in the *Lotus Sūtra.* A man went to see a dear friend, got drunk, and fell asleep. As a gift, a friend sewed a priceless jewel inside the man's robe while he was asleep. When the man awoke, he did not notice the pearl, so he never knew he had received this gift. 149.

robe, pure: 淨衣 [jō e]. New or fresh robe. 130, 334.

robe, sanghātī. 僧迦梨衣 [sōngari e], 僧迦胝衣 [sōngaji e] Also called great robe and double robe. A formal robe for visiting and teaching. 115, 127.

robe, shoulder: See *kashāya*.

robe, single stitch: 單縫 [tanhō]. 129.

robe, supreme: 一頂衣 [itchō e], literally, single peak robe. 138.

robe, teaching of the: 衣法 [ehō]. 112, 114, 136.

robe, two-piece: 裙褊衫 [kun henzan]. *Kun* (skirt) and *henzan* (upper robe) in separate pieces. 61.

robe, under: 下衣 [ge 'e]. Another name for the inner robe. 127.

robe, uphold the: 頂戴 [chōdai]. Putting the folded *kashāya* on one's head before wearing it. Gesture of handling a sacred object.

robe, upper: 褊衫 [hensan], 衫 [san]. Jacket, day robe, upper robe. 52.

robe, uttarāsangha: Skt. 嗢呾羅僧伽衣 [uttarasōgya'e]. See *robe, outer*.

robe, work: 作務衣 [samu e]. 127.

robe beyond form: 無相衣 [musō e], literally, a robe of no-form. 118, 130, 134, 146, 151.

robe of a field of benefaction: 福田衣 [fukuden 'e]. 118.

robe of compassion: 慈悲衣 [jihi e]. 146.

robe of discarded cloth: 糞掃衣 [funzō e], literally, robe of excrement-cleaning cloth. 119.

robe of emancipation: 解脱服 [gedappuku]. Robe of liberation. 139, 146.

robe of patience: 忍辱衣 [ninniku e]. 118, 146.

robe of the Tathāgata: 如來衣 [Nyorai e]. 146.

robes, black and white: 緇白 [shihaku]. Black robes worn by home leavers and white robes worn by lay practitioners. 137.

rock, dissolve a: 消石 [shōseki]. 256.

rock hanging in emptiness, a piece of: 空裏一片石 [kū ri ippen seki]. 241.

rolling the pearl and turning the jewel: 玉轉珠迴 [gyokuten shukai]. 264.

Rooster-Foot, Mount: Skt., Kukkutapada. 雞足山 [Keisoku San]. Located in southeast of Gayā (Brahmā Gayā), in the country of Magadha, ancient India. Known as the place where Mahākāshyapa engaged in ascetic practice and also passed away. 21.

root: 根源 [kongen], literally, root and source. 5, 327, 478.

root, branch, and beyond: 本末究竟 [hommatsu kukyō], literally, root, branch, and the ultimate realm. 518–20.

root, capacity, awakening, and the noble path: 根力覺道 [kon riki kaku dō]. The [fivefold] root, the [fivefold] power, the limbs of enlightenment, and the noble path. 447.

root, unwholesome: 罪根 [zaikon], literally, root of crime. 267, 814.

root, wholesome: 善根 [zenkon]. 149, 474, 800, 839.

root or branch: 本末 [hommatsu]. 262.

roots, six sense: See *organs, six sense.*

rough, pretty: 大麁生 [taisosei]. 生 [sei] is a suffix with no special meaning. 352.

round cushion: 蒲團 [futon]. Also 坐蒲 [zafu]. A cushion for sitting zazen. Nowadays in Zen, *futon* indicates a rectangular sitting mat. 579, 908.

Ruchi Buddha: See *Buddha, Ruchi.*

Ruizhu Shaoli: 瑞竹紹理 [Zuichiku Shōri]. Ca. eleventh–twelfth century, China. Dharma heir of Xingjiao Dan, Linji School. A teacher of Dahui Zonggao. P. 933, Generation 19. 700.

Rujing: See *Tiantong Rujing.*

Rules for Zazen: 坐禪儀 [Zazen Gi]. Fifty-eighth fascicle of this book. lxxx, 579–80.

Ruman: See *Fuguang Ruman.*

run barefoot: 赤脚走 [shakkyaku sō]. 425.

ryō: J. 417. See *liang.*

Ryōkan: 良觀. Ca. twelfth–thirteenth century, Japan. Also known as, 良顯 [Ryōken] according to an early biography. Dōgen's uncle. A monk of the Tendai School who practiced in a hermitage on Mount Hihei. xxxv.

Ryūzen: 隆禪. Ca. twelfth–thirteenth century, Japan. Originally a student of Myōan Eisai. Monk who was practicing at Tiantong Monastery before and during the time Dōgen practiced there. Further biography unknown. 173, 174, 917.

Sacred Monk: See *Monk, Sacred.*

sage: 聖人 [seijin], literally, sacred person. 81, 162, 502, 847.

sage, ancient: 先聖 [senshō]. 先哲 [sentetsu], literally, early wise one. 先德 [sentoku], literally, early virtuous one. 4, 81, 344, 371, 372, 632, 749.

sage, constantly being a: 常聖 [jōshō]. 243.

sage, emerge as regional: 應迹 [ōjaku], literally, appear in response (to the need of people in the region). 866.

sage, enlightened: 證果の賢聖 [shōka no kenshō], literally, wise one and sage with fruit of realization. 474.

sage, great: 大聖 [daishō]. 91, 162, 448, 804.

sages, seven or ten: 七聖十聖 [shichishō jisshō]. Those who are in one of the seven stages of practice in early Buddhism; also called 七賢 [shichiken]. Or, those in one of the ten stages [jisshō]. 442. See also *bodhisattvas of the ten stages and three classes.*

Sahā World: Skt. 娑婆世界 [shaba sekai], 娑婆國土 [shaba kokudo]. The cosmos within the reach of Shākyamuni Buddha's teaching, literally, world of endurance, referring to the hardship of inhabitants, which requires the development of patience. Sūtras say that there are a billion such worlds, each consisting of Mount Sumeru and the Four Continents that surround it. 34, 56, 206, 437, 591, 601, 602, 752.

saindhava: Skt. 仙陀婆 [sendaba]. Meaning variously, salt, vessel, water, and horse. According to the *Mahā Pari-nirvāna Sūtra,* when a king asked his retainers to bring saindhava, a wise retainer understood which saindhava the king referred to without receiving further explanation. Thus, *saindhava* indicates direct communication. 318, 319, 593, 755–59.

salt and vinegar, not short of: 不曾闕鹽醋 [fuzō ketsu enso]. 676.

samādhi: Skt. Transliteration: 三昧 [sammai]. Translation: 定 [jō], literally, stability. Concentration; serene, settled, and collected state of body and mind in meditation. xxi, 3, 668, 679–91, 882 . . .

samādhi, dharma-nature: 法性三昧 [hosshō zammai]. 558–61.

samādhi, diamond: 金剛定 [kongō jō]. 672.

samādhi, practice of: 定學 [jōgaku], literally, study of samādhi. One of the three learnings: precepts, samādhi, and prajñā. 10.

samādhi, receptive: 自受用三昧 [jijuyū zammai], literally, self receiving and utilizing samādhi. The buddha's realizing and utilizing the joy of samādhi. Contrasted with *tajuyū zammai*—extending samādhi for helping other beings. 5, 200, 746.

samādhi, serene subtle: 安詳三昧 [anshō zammai]. 180.

samādhi, shūrangama: 首楞嚴定 [shuryōgon jō]. Taught in *Shūrangama Sūtra.* A method of meditation for swiftly removing defilement and attaining enlightenment. 672.

samādhi, sit in: 坐定 [zajō]. 5, 580.

samādhi and pull them out with wisdom, move delusions in: 定動智拔 [jōdō chibatsu.] 257.

samādhis in formlessness, four: 四無色定 [shimushiki jō]. 28.

Samantabhadra: 普賢 [Fugen]. Bodhisattva of awakened practice. An image of this bodhisattva, along with that of Mañjushrī, often accompanies that of Shākamuni Buddha. 180, 181, 600, 732.

Samyuta Āgama Sūtras: 雜阿含經 [Zō Agon Kyō]. Collection of miscellaneous and short sūtras in early Buddhist tradition. 793.

sand, count grains of: 算沙 [sansha]. Fully depend on scriptures. 267.

sand, offer: According to the *King Ashoka Sūtra,* Buddha and Ānanda were on the road begging one day when they came upon two young boys playing with sand. One of the boys was deeply taken with Buddha's deportment. Urged by a strong wish to offer something, he placed a handful of sand—the only thing he had—into the Buddha's begging bowl. The Buddha made the prediction that the boy would be born in his next life as King Ashoka and be a great supporter of buddha dharma. 474.

sandals, change: 換鞋 [kan'ai]. 53.

sandals, straw: 草鞋 [sōai]. Represents nonintellectual understanding. 76, 253, 578, 790.

sandals and socks: 鞋襪 [aibetsu]. 564.

sands of the Ganges: See *Ganges, sands of the.*

sangha: Skt. 僧迦 [sōgya]. A practitioners' community. Universal community of dharma practitioners. 839–43. See also *treasures, three.*

sangha āsanika: Skt. 僧迦僧泥 [sanka sunnai]. Skt. *Āsanika* is a meal. The single meal taken once a day by the sangha, or practitioners' community. One of the ascetic practices engaged in by Mahākāshyapa. 334.

sangha naishadika: Skt. 僧泥沙者偈 [sunnai sashaku]. Not to lie down day or night, but to practice walking meditation and sleep sitting up. One of the twelve ascetic practices engaged in by Mahākāshyapa. 334.

Sanghānandi: 僧伽難提 [Sōgyanandai]. A prince of King Ratnavyuha in the city of Shrāvastī, Kingdom of Kaushala. He could speak soon after his birth and kept praising the Buddha's teaching. In his youth, he was allowed to leave the household and study with monk Dhyanartha while staying in the palace. But he left the palace at night and became a wandering monk. He became the Seventeenth Ancestor in the Zen tradition. 166, 206, 207, 327, 811, 812.

Sanping Yizhong: 三平義忠 [Sampei Gichū]. 781–872, China. Dharma heir of Dadian Baotong, Nanyue Line. Taught at Mount Sanping, Zhang Region (Fujian). P. 930, Generation 10. 338.

Sansheng Huiran: 三聖慧然 [Sanshō Enen]. Ca. ninth–tenth century. Linji School. After becoming a dharma heir of Linji Yixuan, visited and studied with Yangshan, Deshan, and Xuefeng. Taught at Sansheng Monastery, Zhen Region (Hebei). Traditionally regarded as the compiler of the *Record of Linji.* On his deathbed, Linji is said to have claimed that his teaching would perish with this "blind donkey" (Sansheng). P. 931, Generation 12. 214–16, 511, 512.

Sanskrit: 梵 [Bon]. 115, 696, 831, 841, 847, 895.

Sarvārthadarsha: 見一切儀 [Ken'issaigi]. A number of Buddhas of this name to whom Shākyamuni Buddha made offerings in one of his former lives.

Sarvastivāda School: 有部 [ubu]. Abbreviation of 説一切有部 [Setsu Issai Ubu], literally, group of those who insist that all things exist. The most influential school in early Buddhism. 126, 256.

save sentient beings: 救生 [gushō]. 356.

say quickly: 速道 [sokudō]. 255, 540, 629.

say something (about oneself): 一句を道取す [ikku wo dōshusu], literally, express one phrase. 87, 313, 316, 319, 326, 737.

scale: 量 [ryō]. Measurement. See also *balancing scale.*

scholars with extensive knowledge: 恒沙の遍學 [gōsha no hengaku], literally, study as extensive as the innumerable sands of the Ganges. 381.

Schools, Five: 五宗 [Goshū]. 五家 [goke], literally, five houses. 五門 [gomon], literally, five gates. The major schools of Zen Buddhism after the late Tang Dynasty China: Fayan, Guiyang, Caodong, Yunmen, and Linji schools. Dōgen denies that these schools offer separate teachings. 4, 507, 718.

Schools, Nine: 九宗 [kushū]. A classification of Buddhist schools: (1) Kosha [Kusha] School, based on *Abhidharma-kosha Treatise* by Vasubandhu; (2) Satyasiddhi [Jōjitsu] School, based on *Satyasiddhi Treatise* by

Harivarman; (3) Precept [Ritsu] School; (4) Three Treatises [Sanron] School, based on Nāgārjuna's *Mādhyamika Treatise* and *Twelve Gate Treatise*, as well as Āryadeva's *One Hundred Treatises;* (5) Tiantai [Tendai] School; (6) Avatamsaka [Kegon] School; (7) Dharma-lakshana [Hossō] School; (8) Mantra [Shingon] School, and (9) Zen School. 740.

scriptural school: 教家 [kyōke]. Zen Buddhist way of naming other schools of Buddhism whose teaching is based on specific sūtras or treatises. Zen Buddhists explain that Zen teaching is based directly on Shākyamuni Buddha's enlightenment without depending upon any particular sūtras. This theory is described as "transmission outside of scriptures." 18, 256.

scriptural school, view of: 聽教の解 [chōkyō no ge]. 178.

scripture-burning platform: 焚經臺 [hunkyō dai]. 415.

scriptures, net of: 教網 [kyōmō]. 171.

scriptures, teachings of Buddhist: 教籍 [kyōjaku], literally, teaching text. 5.

scriptures, transmission outside of: See *transmission outside of scriptures.*

scroll, yellow: 黄卷 [ōkan]. 669, 841.

seal of approval: 印可 [inka]. 83, 577, 854.

seal of realization: See *realization, seal of.*

seal, buddha: See *buddha seal.*

seal, intimate: 密印 [mitsuin]. Person-to-person confirmation of enlightenment. 337.

seal, mind: 心印 [shin'in]. Confirmation of the merging of the minds of teacher and disciple. 195, 305, 337, 669.

seamless tower: A standing-egg-shaped one-piece tombstone for home leavers. 389, 391, 639.

Seas, Eight: 八海 [hakkai]. 291, 385, 470. See also *Continents, Four.*

Seas, Four: 四海 [shikai]. Seas in all quarters, representing the world. 211, 343, 376, 611.

seasonal greetings: 寒暄 [kanken], literally, cold or warm. 565.

seat, ancestral: 祖席 [soseki]. 290, 350, 419, 632.

seat, diamond: 金剛座 [kongōza]. The name for the seat beneath the bodhi tree where Shākyamuni Buddha was sitting when he attained enlightenment. 377, 579.

seat, teaching: 師子座 [shishi za], literally, lion seat. 505, 533.

secluded area: 結界 [kekkai], literally, bound realm. 81–84.

Second Guishan: See *Changqing Da'an.*

second next lifetime: 第三生 [daisan shō], literally, the third birth. 888.

second person: 第二人 [daini nin]. 235.

secondary: 第二 [daini]. 301, 302, 467.

secondary, fall into the: 落第二頭 [raku daini tō]. 301, 706.

secretary of the monastery: 書記 [shoki]. 351.

see: 見る [miru]. Direct experience without separation between subject and object. 137, 193, 596–606.

see beyond seeing: 覷不見 [cho fuken], literally, see not see. 85.

see buddha: 見佛 [kembutsu]. Realize buddha beyond the dualism of seeing and seen, subject and object. 93, 596, 657, 725.

see colors with entire ear: 滿耳見色 [manni kenshiki]. 269.

see spring in a branch of plum blossoms: 見梅梢春 [ken bai shō shun]. 606.

see through: 見得 [kentoku]. 98, 321, 647, 747, 748 . . .

see through immediately: 急著眼 [kyū chakugan]. 228.

seed, bloom, and fall: 種熟脱 [shu juku datsu].

seed, wholesome: 善種 [zenshu]. 142, 474.

Seeing Others' Minds: 他心通 [Tashin Tsū]. Eightieth fascicle of this book. lxxxviii, 745–54. See also *miraculous powers, six.*

Seeing the Buddha: 見佛 [Kembutsu]. Sixty-first fascicle of this book. xlviii, lxxxi, 596–608.

seeing, way of: 見處 [genjo], literally, point of seeing. 148, 255.

seek eloquence beyond words: 言外求巧 [gonge gukō]. 269.

seek, nothing to: 無處覓 [mushomyaku], literally, no place to seek. 618.

self: [jiko] 自己. 1. Ego as an independent and permanent entity. 我 [ga]. Buddhism denies the existence of self in this sense. See also *skandhas, five.* 2. A person. 自家 [jike], literally, one's house. 3. A person who has realized selflessness that is not separate from the universe. True self. 7, 29, 89, 154, 673–76, 695–700. See also *self, original.*

self, chase things and make them into the: 逐物爲己 [chikumotsu iko]. 36.

self, heavenly: 自己天 [jikoten], literally, self heaven. Highest self. 294.

self, original: 本分人 [hombun nin], literally, person of original share. 1. Same as original face. 2. 本我 [honga], a non-Buddhist idea of permanent, universal self. 20, 30, 507, 583, 708.

self, radiant light of the: 自己光明 [jiko kōmyō]. 415, 416, 418, 525, 593, 594.

self, scheming: 計我 [keiga]. 59.

self, view of a permanent: 常見 [jōken]. 856.

self, without a permanent and independent: 無我 [muga]. 671, 674.

self, without an abiding: われにあらさる [ware ni ara zaru]. 29.

self and make it into things, chase the: 逐己爲物 [chikuko imotsu]. 36.

self and other: 自他 [jita]. 18, 44, 297, 522, 697.

self-awakening: 自覺 [jikaku]. Also, self awareness. 7.

self-control: 自調 [jichō]. 699.

self-deception: 自熱瞞 [jinetsuman]. 624.

self-direction: 自方 [jihō]. All ten directions experienced within the self, at this moment. 591.

self existence: 我有 [gau]. Existence of a permanent "self" according to a non-Buddhist view. 235.

self-interest: 己利 [kori]. 404.

Self-Realization Samādhi: 自證三昧 [Jishō Zammai]. Seventy-fifth fascicle of this book. lxxxvi, lxxxviii, 695–704.

Sengcan: See *Jianzhi Sengcan.*

Sengmi: See *Shenshan Sengmi.*

senior disciple: 上足 [jōsoku], literally, high feet. 4, 45.

senior monk: 具壽 [guju], literally, equipped with long life. 84, 173, 335, 547, 638 . . .

senior nun: 尼師 [nishi], literally, nun teacher. 737.

senior student: 勤舊前資 [gonkyū zenshi]. One who has served as a monastery officer; retired officer. 75, 789, 854.

seniority in ordination date: 戒臘 [kai rō]. 729.

sense organs: 諸根 [shokon], literally, various roots. See also *organs, six sense.*

senses, six: 六情 [rokujō]. 25.

sentient: 情 [jō]. 142, 297, 550–53.

sentient beings: See *beings, sentient.*

sentient beings that are numberless, vow to save: 衆生無邊誓願度 [shujō muuhen seigan do]. 80.

separate, not: 無對 [mtai], literally, not facing. 444, 446.

serene: 寂靜 [jakujō]. 327, 771, 898.

serenely composed: 安穩 [annon]. 42.

serve: 勤恪(す) [gonkaku(-su)], literally, work respectfully. Also, endeavor. 358, 563 . . .

set aside: 放捨す [hōsha-su], literally, let go and throw away. 9, 254, 579, 668, 885.

set up: 施設(す) [sesetsu(-su)]. Structure; present; guide; explain. 51, 232, 278, 564, 731.

settle the great matter of the way: 大道を決擇す [daidō wo ketsujaku-su], literally, make a selection and decision on the great way. 338.

settling point: 治象 [chishō], literally, sign of (peaceful) governing. 557.

Seven Original Buddhas: See *Buddhas, Seven Original.*

seven paths vertical and eight paths horizontal: 七縦八横 [shichijū hachiō]. Free in countless ways. 158.

shaku: J. 尺. Measuring unit. Ten *sun.* 55, 61, 67, 176, 177.

Shākya Clan: 釋 [Shaku]. Based in the ancient kingdom of Kapilavastu. Shākyamuni Buddha, who came from this clan, encouraged many of its members to practice dharma. 804, 847.

Shākya Clan, one thousand members of the: 千釋 [sen Shaku]. 785.

Shākya Clan, twenty thousand members of the: 二萬釋 [niman Shaku]. 804.

Shākyamuni Buddha: See *Buddha, Shākyamuni.*

shamatha and vipashyanā: Skt. 止觀 [shikan]. Literally, stopping (*shi*) and observing (*kan*). The technique of sitting meditation, consisting of calming the mind (shamatha) and analytical introspection or insight (vipashyanā). Not to be confused with *shikan taza* (see *just sit*). 914.

Shānavāsin: 商那和修 [Shōnawashu]. Monk from Mathurā, central northern India. Received dharma from Ānanda. Third Indian Ancestor of the Zen tradition. 120, 149, 166, 570, 673.

Shanhui: See *Jiashan Shanhui.*

Shānta: 善寂 [Zenjaku], literally, Wholesome Serenity. Shākyamuni Buddha made offerings in his former lifetime to sixty-two Buddhas with this name. 823.

Shanzhao: See *Fenyang Shanzhao.*

Shaoli: See *Ruizhu Shaoli.*

Shaolin Temple: Situated on Mount Song (Henan), China, where Bodhidharma sat facing the wall for nine years. 11, 355, 357, 363, 416, 584, 669, 907.

Shāriputra: Skt., literally, heron child, child of Shāri (his mother's name); sometimes interpreted as relic child. Transliteration: 舍利弗 [Sharihotsu]. Translation: 鶖子 [Shūji], literally, heron child; 身子 [Shinshi],

literally, body (relic) child. Combination of transliteration and translation: 舍利子 [Sharishi]. Regarded as the best listener among disciples
of the Buddha. Many sūtras take the form of the Buddha delivering
discourses to him. 288, 687, 785, 862; and Devadatta, 784; addressed
by Buddha, 28, 808, 820–23, 833; practice of, 51; wisdom of, 370, 803,
863; words of, 798.

shashu: J. 叉手. A mindful way of holding hands on the chest. One hand
covers the other, inner hand closed in a fist. In traditional Chinese
way, the left hand covers the right fist. The current Sōtō way is the
right hand over the left. This hand position is used in walking or
standing when one's hands are not in gasshō. 52, 230, 565, 736.

Shenguang: 873. See also *Dazu Huike.*

Shenshan Sengmi: 神山僧密 [Shinzan Sōmitsu]. Ca. eighth–ninth century,
China. Dharma heir of Yunyan Tansheng, Qingyuan Line. Traveled
for twenty years with his dharma junior brother Dongshan Liangjie.
A number of their dialogues have beeen recorded. Dongshan's stu-
dents respectfully called him Dharma Uncle Mi (Mi Shibo). P. 930,
Generation 11. 493, 498–500.

Shenxiu: See *Yuquan Shenxiu.*

Shenying: See *Dingshan Shenying.*

Shexian Guixing: 葉縣歸省 [Sekken Kisei]. Ca. tenth century, China.
Dharma heir of Shoushan Xingnian, Linji School. Taught at Guangjiao
Monastery, She Prefecture, Ru Region (Henan). He traveled widely.
His teaching style was confrontational, and some of the kōans men-
tion his throwing or breaking things. P. 932, Generation 16. 110.

Shibei: See *Xuansha Shibei.*

shielded. 遮 [sha]. Entirely covered. 塞却 [sokukyaku], literally, blocked. 却
[kyaku] is a suffix indicating the completion of action. 316.

Shigong Huizang: 石鞏慧藏 [Shakkyō Ezō]. Ca. eighth century, China.
Dharma heir of Mazu Daoyi, Nanyue Line. Previously a hunter, he
arrived at Mazu's while chasing a deer. Taught at Mount Shigong, Fu
Region (Jiangxi). P. 930, Generation 9. 717, 718.

shikan taza: See *just sit.*

Shimen Huiche: 石門慧徹 [Sekimon Etetsu]. Ca. tenth–eleventh century,
China. Dharma heir of Liangshan Yuanguan, Caodong School. P. 932,
Generation 16. 467.

Shingon School: See *Mantra School.*

Shiqian: See *Dongshan Shiqian.*

Shishuang Qingzhu: 石霜慶諸 [Sekisō Keisho]. 807–888, China. Dharma heir of Daowu Yuanzhi, Qingyuan Line. Taught at Mount Shishuang, Tan Region (Hunan), for twenty years. He and his students sat like decayed trees without lying down. As a result, they were called the "Dead Stump Assembly." His posthumous name is Great Master Puhui, 普會大師 [Fue Daishi]. 371, 463, 628.

Shitā, Mount: 徒陀山 [Shida San]. Mountain in the mythological country of Vimana. 848.

Shitou Xiqian: 石頭希遷 [Sekitō Kisen]. 700–790, China. Ordained by Sixth Ancestor Huineng, after whose death he studied with Qingyuan Xingsi and became his dharma heir. As he did zazen continually in a hut built on a rock at Nan Monastery (also called Nanyue), Mount Heng (Hunan), he was called Priest Rock Head (Shitou). Author of poems "Merging of One and Many" and "Song of the Grass Hut." His posthumous name is Great Master Wuji 無濟大師 [Musai Daishi]. P. 929, Generation 8. and Mazu, 107, 290, 465, 468, 506; and Qingyuan, 284, 390; and Yaoshan, 109, 330, 331, 513; practice of, 366; verse of, 622; words of, 320, 321, 505, 828.

Shiva: Skt. 自在天 [Jizai Ten], literally, Deva of Freedom—a Buddhist epithet of Shiva of Brāhmanism: Īshvara, the Lord of the Universe. 101.

Shizi: 尸子. A book written by Shijiao of the Warring Period [503–222 B.C.E.], China. It has survived in fragments. 344.

shō: J. 升. Measuring unit. Approximately 1.8 liters. 622.

shore, arrive at the other: 彼岸到 [higan tō]. See *pāramitā.*

Shouchu: See *Dongshan Shouchu.*

Shouduan: See *Haihui Shouduan.*

shoulder to shoulder, put: 齊肩す [seiken-su]. 236.

shoulders, cover both: 通兩肩搭 [tsū ryōken ta]. A way to wear a kashāya. 116, 143.

Shoushan Xingnian: 首山省念 [Shuzan Shōnen]. 926–993, China. Dharma heir of Fengxue Yanzhao, Linji School. Founded a monastery at Mount Shou, Ru Region (Henan). P. 931, Generation 15. 110, 175.

Shouxun: See *Heshan Shouxun.*

Shouzhuo: See *Changling Shouzhuo.*

shramana: Skt. 沙門 [shamon]. A wanderer or a monk. 100, 131, 153, 183, 415, 488, 864.

shramanas, four fruits of: 864. See also *fruits, four.*

shrāvaka: Skt. 聲聞 [shōmon], literally, a listener; a disciple of the Buddha's whose goal is arhatship. Mahāyāna word for a sage of "Hīnayāna" Buddhism. 80, 656, 682, 795.

Shrāvaka Vehicle: 281. See also *Vehicles, Three.*

Shrāvastī: 786. See also *Kaushala.*

Shrenika: 先尼 [Senni]. A Brāhman scholar described in the *Mahā Parinirvāna Sūtra* who asserted permanency of soul but was argued down by Shākyamuni Buddha. 14, 43, 45, 235, 875.

Shrīmālā Devī Sūtra: Skt. 勝鬘經 [Shōman Gyō]. Mahāyāna sūtra describing the dedication of Queen Shrīmālā. Expounds the teaching of One Vehicle and is also an early source for teaching about tathāgata garbha [literally, buddha womb, matrix, seed or essence], related to teaching of buddha nature. 129, 919.

shrine: 70, 133, 412, 731, 831, 842. See also *chaitya.*

Shrīvaddhi: 福增 [Fukuzō], literally, Happiness Increase. Wealthy man who lived in the city of Rājagriha, Magadha. Ordained at age one hundred twenty by Maudgalyayana with permission of the Buddha, who was at Kalandaka Bamboo Grove, north of Rājagriha. After ordination, he extensively studied dharma. 802, 863.

Shuangfeng: See *Dayi Daoxin.*

Shuklāyāh: 鮮白 [Senbyaku], literally, Pure White. Woman from Kapilavastu who wanted to be ordained by the Buddha. When the Buddha said, "Come, Nun," her mundane clothes turned into a kashāya. 120.

Shūrangama Sūtra: 首楞嚴經 [Shuryōgon Kyō], 楞嚴經 [Ryōgon Kyō]. Mahāyāna scripture explaining the meaning of *shūrangama samādhi*, a valiant state of meditation. 403, 693, 703.

shut one out with silence: 梵壇の法 [bondan no hō]. Skt. brāhman danda. Transliteration: 梵壇 [bondan]. Refers to the practice in which members of the sangha do not speak to a fellow member who has committed wrongdoing. This practice—法 [hō]—of punishment is defined by a precept. 740.

Siddhārtha: 809. See also *Buddha, Shākyamuni.*

silence, noble: 聖默 [shōmoku]. 793.

silent, be: 休す [kyū-su]. Literally, come to rest. 53.

silk cloth, fine: 複袱子 [fufukusa su]. 733.

Simhabhikshu: 師子 [Shishi], literally, Lion Monk. Twenty-fourth Ancester of the Zen tradition in India. Taught in Kashmīra, northwestern kingdom of India, but was killed by a king who persecuted buddha dharma. 166, 788, 790.

simultaneously attain the way: See *way, attain the.*

single great matter: See *matter, single essential.*

sit at ease: 燕坐す [enza-su], literally, sit like a swallow. 357, 367.

sit facing the wall: 壁面打坐 [hekimen taza]. 面壁 [mempeki], literally, facing the wall. A common way to sit in zazen, individually or in community. 406.

sit in samādhi: See *samādhi, sit in.*

sit, just: See *just sit.*

sit solidly: 兀兀 [gotsugotsu]. Solid; steadfast. 兀坐 [gotsuza], sitting like a rock. 248, 580.

sit through: 坐斷(す) [zadan(-su)]. Cut through by sitting. 坐殺 [zasatsu], literally, sit and kill. 312, 722.

sit through the skin you were born with: 坐破嬢生皮 [zaha jōshō hi]. 312.

sit upright: 端坐 [tanza]. 5, 6, 21, 580.

sitting, endeavor in: 打坐功夫 [taza kufū]. 618.

sitting, steadfast: 303, 304, 313, 441. See also *sit solidly.*

sitting form: 坐相 [zasō]. 308.

sitting platform, long: See *platform, long sitting.*

situation: 機縁 [kien], literally, capacity and conditions. 119, 260, 340, 392, 443.

Six Excellent Places: 六殊勝地 [Roku Shushōchi]. A garden at the Guangli Monastery, Mount Ayuwan (Zhejiang). 249.

six pāramitās: See *pāramitās, six.*

six paths: See *paths, six.*

six sense organs: See *organs, six sense.*

six sense roots: See *organs, six sense.*

six senses: See *organs, six sense.*

Sixin Wuxin: 死心悟新 [Shishin Goshin]. 1043–1114, China. Dharma heir of Haihui Shouduan, Linji School. Taught at Mount Huanglong (Jiangxi). Legend says he was born with purple skin on his shoulders and right side, as if he was wearing a monk's robe. Awakened upon hearing a thunderclap while on pilgrimage. He once shouted at a monk who was talking a lot, "Stop! Stop! Can you feed people by talking about food?" P. 933, Generation 20. 725.

Sixth Ancestor: See *Dajian Huineng.*

Sixth Ancestor's Platform Sūtra: 六祖壇經 [Rokuso Dankyō]. Collection of Chinese Six Ancestor Huineng's words. Some parts were added by later writers. Dōgen regards the entire text as apocryphal. 865.

skandha, discernment: 識衆 [shiki shu], literally, discernment assembly. 663. See also *skandhas, five.*

skandha, feeling: 想衆 [sōshu], literally, feeling assembly. 663. See also *skandhas, five.*

skandha, form: 色衆 [shiki shu], literally, form or matter assembly. 662. See also *skandhas, five.*

skandhas, eighty thousand: 八萬蘊 [hachiman on]. 八萬法蘊 [hachiman hō'on]. A number of dharma teachings. 539, 647.

skandhas, five: Skt. 五蘊/ 五陰 [go'on]. 五衆 [goshu], literally, five types of aggregate or assembly. Five streams of body and mind: (1) form (matter), 色 [shiki]. (2) feeling, 受 [ju], literally, receiving. (3) perception, 想 [sō], literally, visioning. (4) inclination or impulse, 行 [gyō], literally, go or act. Voluntary and involuntary mental facility that forms action. Sometimes translated as mental formation. (5) discernment, 識 [shiki], literally, consciousness. Facility to discriminate. With the understanding of five skandhas, what is commonly seen as a self is explained as a continuous interaction of these elements, not a fixed and independent entity. 25, 247, 479, 658.

skandhas, realm of: 蘊界 [onkai]. 225, 246.

skillful means: Skt., upāya. 方便 [hōben]. Expedient method to remove deluded people's doubts and lead them to realize true dharma. Expedient phrase. 185, 769, 842, 860.

skillful means, gate of: 方便門 [hōben mon]. 522–24, 538.

skin bag: 皮袋 [hitai]. 皮袋子 [hitaisu]; 袋皮 [taihi]. Human being described as a collection of bones enclosed in a bag of skin. Human or animal. 89, 275, 707–9.

skin bag, stinky: 臭皮袋 [shūhitai]. 313, 360, 416, 541, 713.

skin, flesh, bones, and marrow: 皮肉骨髓 [hiniku kotsuzui]. Each represents the essence of teaching. Originally, Bodhidharma's words of confirming his four disciples. 123, 297, 303, 724.

skin, flesh, bones, and marrow, you have attained my: 汝得吾皮肉骨髓 [nyo toku go hi ni kotsu zui]. Bodhidharma's words to each of his four students are combined in this way. 235.

skull: 髑髏 [dokuro]. Sitting in stillness. 318, 627–29, 827 . . .

skull covers the entire field: 髑髏遍野 [dokuro hen'ya]. 628.

sky, boundless: 漫天 [manten]. 426, 677.

sky, entire: 彌天 [miten]. 5, 31, 46, 275, 332, 451, 623.

slightest hint: 毫忽之兆 [gōkotsu no chō]. 311, 312.

Small Vehicles: See *Vehicles, Three.*

smash: 打失(す) [tashitsu(-su)]. 218.

smash sound and form: 聲色を打失す [shōshiki wo tashitsu-su].

smile: 195, 319, 372, 503, 534, 584, 639. See also *treasury of the true dharma eye.*

smile, breaking into a: 破顔微笑 [hagan mishō]. 248, 389, 394, 482, 534, 539, 587. See also *treasury of the true dharma eye.*

snap the sleeves and walk away: 拂袖便行 [hosshū benkō]. A gesture usually made before an emphatic departure. In Dōgen's usage, activity that is free and leaves no traces. 457.

snow blossom: 雪華 [sekka]. 643.

Snow Mountains: 雪山 [Sessen]. Himālaya Mountains, where Shākyamuni Buddha practiced in a former life according to *Mahā Prajñā Pāramitā Sūtra.* 584, 646, 765.

Snow Palace: 雪宮 [Setsu Gū]. 584. Same as *Snow Mountains.*

soapberry pit: 木槵子 [mokukan su]. 752.

softening the light and emerging as regional sages: 和光同塵 [wakō dōjin]. Refers to a Buddha not fully manifesting the light of wisdom, becoming close to sentient beings, and appearing as a local deity. 866.

solitary practice: Skt., aranya. Transliteration: 阿蘭若 [arannya], literally, wilderness. 859.

somersaults, turning: 翻巾斗 [honkinto]. Also, turn cartwheels. 425.

Song: 宋 [Sō]. Song Dynasty, 960–1279. Great Song China, 大宋國 [Dai Sōkoku]. Also means China. 4, 301, 338, 569.

sorcerer: 仙人 [sennin]. 神仙 [shinsen], literally, divine sorcerer. 292, 293.

Sōtō School: 曹洞宗 [Sōtō Shū]. Japanese form of Chinese Caodong School. One of the two major schools of Zen Buddhism in Japan. Dōgen is regarded as its founder. xli, lii, liii, xcvii *soul:* Skt., ātman 霊知 [reichi]. Everlasting identity or consciousness throughout a series of transmigrations. Dōgen denies existence of such a permanent self. 14, 43, 44.

sounding block: 犍槌 [kentsui]. 743.

sounds, different: 異音 [ion]. 414.

source beyond words, directly clarify the: 直須旨外明宗 [jikishu shige myōshū]. 312.

source, original: 本地 [honji]. 5, 328, 864.

source, return to the: 歸源 [kigen]. 實歸 [jikki], literally, true return. 83, 292, 310.

south of Xiang, north of Tan: 湘之南潭之北 [shō no nan tan no hoku]. Xiang Region is in the south of Tan Region near Changsha (Hunan). This phrase means everywhere. 37.

Southern Continent: 50, 264, 656, 784, 802. See also *Continents, Four.*

space: 虚空 [kokū]. Open sky; boundless realm. 26, 717–20, 725.

Space: 虚空 [Kokū]. Seventy-seventh fascicle of this book. lxxxvii, lxxxviii, 717–20.

space, play with: 弄虚空 [rō kokū]. 718.

space is one piece but is divided with a touch: 虚空一塊觸而染污 [kokū ikkai soku ni zenna]. 718.

space throughout the ten directions: 十方虚空 [jippō kokū]. 692, 693.

sparks of a gimlet: 鑽火 [sanka]. 459.

sparrow, sick: 病雀 [byōjaku]. 361, 475.

speaking about it won't hit the mark: 説似一物即不中 [setsuji ichimotsu soku fuchū]. 349, 539, 610.

Speaking of Mind, Speaking of Essence: 説心説性 [Sesshin Sesshō]. Forty-ninth fascicle of this book. xlvii, lxxxvi, 493–500.

specks of gold in human eyes: 金屑 [kinsetsu]. 248.

speech: 語端 [gotan], literally, edge of words. 593.

speech, noble: 聖説 [shōsetsu]. 793.

speechless: 啞漢 [akan], literally, one who is unable to speak. 340, 441, 442.

spirit: 精魂 [zeikon]. 神 [jin]. 72, 227, 239, 388, 698, 707.

spirit, corpse with no: 無魂屍子 [mukon shisu]. 194.

spirit, full activity of playing with the: 弄精魂の活計 [rō zeikon no kakkei]. 317.

spirit, playing with the: 弄精魂 [rō zeikon]. Twiddling with spirit. 317, 644, 689.

spirit being: 神道 [shindō]. 神物 [jimmotsu]. 神 [jin]. Deva, fighting spirit, or demons. 10, 142, 476.

spirit's hairy head: 神頭の被毛 [jinzu no himō]. 695.

spirits, fighting: 293, 294, 425, 538. See also *paths, six.*

splattered by mud and soaked in water: 入泥入水 [nyūdei nyūsui]. Identification with sentient beings in guiding them. 267.

splendor: 莊嚴 [shōgon]. Adornment. 9, 59, 156, 284, 897.

spoken, what cannot be: 說不得底 [setsu fu toku tei]. 底 [tei] is a suffix meaning "that which is." 346.

spread the bowing cloth twice and make three bows: 兩展三拜 [ryōten sampai]. The way a monastic trainee expresses respect to the abbot: spreads the bowing cloth fully on the floor and makes three full bows, stands up and folds the bowing cloth, spreads it threefold on the floor and makes three full bows, stands up and folds it, then makes three semiformal bows. Customarily, at the beginning, the abbot gestures to simplify the procedure so that the trainee skips the first two sets of three full bows, but still spreads the bowing cloth twice.

spread the teaching: 弘法 [guhō]. 266, 513, 919.

spread widely: 弘通(す) [guzū(-su)]. Prevail everywhere. 17, 129, 256.

spring: 春 [haru]. Often meaning total experience of the world. 31, 108, 462, 521, 877.

Spring and Autumn: 春秋 [Shunjū]. Sixty-sixth fascicle of this book. xlviii, lxxxii, lxxxiii, 631–37.

spring, god of: 東君 [Tōkun], literally, lord of east. 329.

sprout: 才生す [saishō-su]. 131.

squeeze out: 敲出す [kōshutsu-su]. 591.

staff: 拄杖 [shujō]. A long walking stick carried by a traveling monk, or used by a Zen master when lecturing or encouraging students. Thus, it represents a person who practices or teaches. 286, 446, 595, 741.

staff, arched bamboo: 竹箆 [shippei]. A ceremonial staff used by a Zen teacher. 170.

staff, iron: 鐵拄杖 [tetsu shujō]. 446.

stage, ultimate: 果位 [kai], literally, stage of fruit. 413.

stages, ten: 十地 [jutchi]. 168, 310, 660. See also *bodhisattvas of the ten stages and three classes.*

stained: 染 [sen]. Separated by dualistic conception. 46, 133, 316, 591.

stake: 木橛 [mokketsu], literally, wooden stick. 627, 639.

stake, withered: 枯椿 [koshō]. 628.

stand alone: 獨步 [dokuho], literally, walk alone. 607.

stand like a wall: 壁堅す [hikiryū-su]. 472.

stand on one's toes: 翹足 [gyōsoku]. 72.

standard: 規矩 [kiku], literally, rule, custom. 量局 [ryōkyoku], literally, measure and boundary. 風規 [fūki], literally, style and rule. 45, 63, 126, 163, 172, 240, 241, 327, 411, 547, 557 …

standing bow: See *bow, standing.*

statement: 話頭 [watō]. Outstanding statement; words. 頭 [tō] is a suffix meaning "that which is (spoken)." 215, 419, 629.

statement, confused: 胡説亂道 [usetsu rondō], literally, barbarians' speech and confused words. 218, 500.

statement, false: 虛設 [kosetsu]. Fiction. 306, 828, 893.

statement is just right: 道是 [dō ze]. 275.

statement that kills doubt: 疑殺話頭 [gisatsu watō]. 420.

status: 地位 [chi'i]. 413.

steadfast sitting: 303, 304, 313, 441. See also *sit solidly.*

steadfastness: 兀爾 [gotsuji]. 268, 909.

stick: 179, 251, See also *staff.*

stick and shout: 棒喝 [bō katsu]. 615.

stick swallowing both people, a single: 一條拄杖吞兩人 [ichijō shujō don ryōnin]. 251.

still and serene: 澄湛 [chōtan]. 494, 498.

still, remain: 恬靜 [tenjō], literally, peaceful and quiet. 498.

stone or tile: 礫甎 [rokusen]. 723.

stone woman gives birth to a child at night: 石女夜生兒 [sekinyo ya shōji]. 154, 156.

stoppings, four right: 四正斷 [shishōdan]. Not arousing an unwholesome action that has not arisen, stopping an unwholesome action that has arisen, arousing a wholesome action that has not arisen, and allowing a wholesome action that has arisen to increase. Part of the thirty-seven wings of enlightenment. 675.

storm, vairambhaka: 毘嵐風 [birampū]. 毘嵐 [biran] is transliteration of Skt. vairambhaka. Horrendous storm that blows at the beginning and the end of an eon. 99.

story for studying: See *causes and conditions.*

story, illogical: 無理會話 [murie wa]. 157.

straight ahead: 驀直 [makujiki]. 594, 677.

straight ahead, go: 劈面來 [hekimen rai]. 594.

straight on: 直趣 [jikishu]. 240.

straightforward: 正直 [shōjiki]. Direct. 5, 423, 425, 511, 593 …

straightforward by nature: 質直 [jitsujiki]. 20.

straightforward expression: 赤心片片 [sekishin hempen], literally, bits and pieces of red heart. 189.

stream, authentic: 正脈 [shōmyaku], literally, authentic vein. 297.

stream, enter the: Skt., srota āpanna. Transliteration: 須陀洹 [shudaon]. Translation: 預流 [yoru], literally, entering the stream (of buddha dharma). First of the four stages for becoming an arhat. 578. See also *fruits, four.*

stream, homogenous: 等流 [tōru]. Cause and effect are similar. 102.

stream enterer. 28, 847, 848, 871. See also *fruits, four.*

strict observance: 嚴淨 [gonjō], literally, solemnly pure. 889.

strike a person: 打人 [tanin]. 617, 618.

stringed instrument in tune, keep a: 調絃 [chōgen]. 758.

strings attached, soar with no: 足下無絲去 [sokka mushi ko]. 609.

strive whole-heartedly: 行業純一 [gyōgō jun'itsu], literally, practice single and pure. 350.

stroke the air: 以手撮虛空 [i shu satsu kokū]. 717, 718.

student, a coarse Zen: 杜撰禪和 [zusan zenna]. 700, 701.

student, thorough: 資強 [shikyō], literally, disciple is strong. 309.

student, true: 眞流 [shinru], literally, true stream. 4, 22.

student, Zen: 禪和子 [zenna su]. 19, 502.

students, good: 諸禪德 [shozentoku]. Addressing Zen students. 318.

study, begin to: 咨參 [sisan], literally, question and study. For Dōgen, *study* often means practice. 427.

study, deep: 玄學 [gengaku]. 327.

study, definitive: さたまれる參究 [sadama reru sankyū], literally, defined thorough study. 304.

study, further: 趣向の參學 [shukō no sangaku], literally, study going toward. 298, 524, 607.

study, going beyond: 絕學 [zetsugaku], literally, cut off study. 349.

study all the way: See *examine.*

study and investigate thoroughly: 究徹 [kyūtetsu]. 156, 413, 434.

study shoulder to shoulder: 同參齊肩 [dōsan seiken]. 398.

study simultaneously and all-inclusively: 同参遍参 [dōsan henzan]. 611, 612, 699.

study together: 同参(す) [dōsan(-su)], literally, same going. One practice; those who study together; investigate together; practice mutually; go together; arise simultaneously. 699.

stūpa: Skt. Transliteration: 偸婆 [tōba]. 塔婆 [tōba]. thūpa (in Pāli). Shrine or tower for relics. 647, 650–54, 831–35.

stūpa principle: 塔事 [tō ji]. 834.

stūpa shrine: 塔廟 [tō byō]. 651.

Stūpas, Eight: See *Face-to-Face Transmission.*

styles, one thousand: 千品 [sembon], literally, one thousand things. 266.

Su Dongpo: 蘇東坡 [So Tōba]. 1036–1101, China. Shi 軾 of the Su 蘇 family. Initiatory name: Zidan 子瞻 [Shisen]. Renowned poet of Song Dynasty, also a high government offical. Lay student of Zhaojiao Changzong. Later studied with Foyin Liaoyuan. P. 933, Generation 20. 85–87.

Subhadra: 須跋陀羅 [Shubatsudara]. The last student of the Buddha. As a one-hundred-twenty-year-old Brāhman, he went to meet the Buddha, heard his last dharma talk, and attained arhathood. 804.

Subhūti: Skt. Transliteration: 須菩提 [Shubodai]. Translation: 具壽善現 [Guju Zengen], literally, Holding Long Life (elder), Actualizing Wholesomeness. Born in Shrāvastī in the kingdom of Kaushala. Heard the Buddha's discourse and became a monk when Jeta Grove opened. Regarded as the one who best understood emptiness among the Buddha's disciples. 26, 27, 687.

subtle: 微 [bi], literally, minute. 6, 26, 312, 555, 755 . . .

subtle and pivotal: 祕要 [hiyō]. 555.

successive: 相繼 [shōkei]. 392.

suchness, form as: 是相 [zesō]. 180.

suchness, one: 如一 [nyoichi]. 437.

suddenly: 忽然 [kotsunen]. 34, 427, 582, 660, 785 . . .

suffering: 苦 [ku], literally, bitterness. 661, 671, 772, 842.

suffering, truth of: 苦諦 [kutai]. The first of the four noble truths. 281.

suffering, truth of the causes of: 集諦 [shūtai]. The second of the four noble truths. 281.

suffering, truth of the cessation of: 滅諦 [metsutai]. The third of the four noble truths. 281.

sufferings, eight: 八苦 [hakku]. Four sufferings (birth, old age, sickness, and death) plus: parting with loved ones, encountering resented and hated ones, not getting what is wanted, and caused by the five skandhas. 803.

Sui: 隋 [Zui]. Chinese dynasty, 581–619. 116, 129, 360, 416, 710.

Sumeru: Skt. Transliterations: 須彌 [Shumi], 迷盧 [Meiro]. According to Indian mythology there are nine mountains and eight oceans in the world around Four Continents, with Mount Sumeru at the center. 157, 289, 290, 291, 346, 374, 388, 423, 431, 448, 464.

Sumeru, Great: 大須彌 [dai Shumi]. See *Sumeru.*

Sumeru, Small: 小須彌 [shō Shumi]. See *Sumeru.*

summer practice period, ninety-day: 九夏 [kyūge], literally, nine (ninety-day) summer. 724–29, 740–42.

summer retreat: 白夏 [byakuge], literally, summer with announcement. Summer practice period is called in this way as daily cautions to participants are given. 726, 727.

sun: J. 寸. Measuring unit. Approximately 3 cm (1.18 inches). Corresponds to Chinese *cun*, which was 3.11 cm in Tang Dynasty and 3.072 cm in Song Dynasty. 50, 64, 142, 176.

sun face: 日面 [nichimen]. 37, 211, 698, 709 . . .

sun face and moon face: 日面月面 [nichimen gachimen]. See *Buddha, Sun-Face.*

Sun Zhongjin: 孫朝進 [Son Chōshin]. Ca. eighth century, China. A courtier for Emperor Su of Tang Dynasty. Sent to invite Huizhong to be the emperor's teacher. 745.

sun, moon, and stars: 日月星辰 [nichigetsu seishin]. 250.

Sunakshatra: 善星 [Zenshō]. Prince of Shākya Clan. Although he became a monk under Shākyamuni Buddha, he was not obedient and always had wrong schemes. He returned to laity and spoke ill of the Buddha. 814.

Sun-Face Buddha: See *Buddha, Sun-Face.*

supernormal powers, practitioners of: 神通變化のやから [jinzū henge no yakara], literally, those of miracles, transforming (things magically). 442.

supporter: 檀那 [danna]. Lay supporter of a practicing community. Cf., Skt. dāna, literally, giving. 773.

surging opportunity, time of: See *opportunity, time of surging.*

surpass ancestor: See *go beyond ancestor.*

surrender and reject: 任違 [nin'i]. 269.

surrender, totally: 任任 [ninnin]. 一任 [ichinin]. 268.

Sūryarashmi: 日明 [Nichimyō], literally, Sun Bright. Fifteen Buddhas of this name to whom Shākyamuni Buddha made offerings in his former life. 823.

Sushan Guangren: 疎山光仁 [Sozan Kōnin]. Also, Sushan Kuangren, 疎山匡 仁 [Sozan Kyōnin]. Ca. ninth–tenth century, China. Dharma heir of Dongshan Liangjie, Caodong School. Taught at Mount Su, Linchuan (Jiangxi). P. 931, Generation 12. 469, 627.

Sushan Kuangren: See *Sushan Guangren.*

sūtra: Skt. 經 [kyō], literally, warp as in weaving, later meaning principle of the teaching. Now refers to Indian Buddhist scriptures which take the form of discourses by Buddha as heard and verified by one of his disciples. Chinese transliteration: sudanlan, 素呾纜 [sotanran]. 縑緗 [kenshō], literally, thin silk for mounting books. 182, 222–33, 282, 496, 538, 539. See also *Divisions, Twelve; Buddha Sūtras.* ("Sūtras," created outside of India are regarded as apocryphal.)

sūtra, chant a: 誦經 [zukyō]. 227, 647.

sūtra chanting, do melodic: See *melodic sūtra chanting, do.*

sūtra, copying a: 書經 [shokyō]. 665.

Sūtra, Lotus: See *Lotus Sūtra.*

sūtra, maintain a: 持經 [jikyō]. 222.

sūtra, read a: 看經 [kankin]. Reading or chanting a scripture, literally, looking at a sūtra. 228, 229, 231, 233.

sūtra, receive a: 受經 [jukyō]. 697.

sūtra, shrāvaka: 聲聞經 [shōmon kyō]. Scriptures of Shrāvaka Vehicle. Early Buddhist sūtras. 406.

sūtra, study a: 經書をひらく [kyōsho wo hiraku], literally, open a sūtra. 222, 558, 696.

sūtra, turn the: 轉經す [tenkyō-su]. Ceremonially chant a sūtra. 540.

Sūtra of the Three Thousand Guidelines for Pure Conduct: 三千威儀經 [Sanzen Iigi Kyō]. A Mahāyāna sūtra on daily activities for home leavers. The two hundred fifty precepts are called for in each of the four bodily presences in three times—past, present, and future. 48, 55.

sūtra recitation, plaque announcing a: See *plaque announcing a sūtra recitation.*

sūtras, entire treasury of the: 一大藏教 [ichi daizō kyō]. Buddhist canon. 269.

Suvarna Prabhāsottama King Sūtra: Skt. 金光明經 [Kon Kōmyō Kyō]. *Golden Beam King Sūtra.* In East Asia this Mahāyāna scripture was often recited and enshrined for the protection of the nation. It explains that the four guardian deities protect the king in ruling the nation. 231.

swallow: 燕子 [ensu]. Bird. 子 [su] is a suffix. 106, 292, 454, 455, 633.

swallowing up everything in one gulp: 一口吞盡 [iku donjin]. 268.

sway, fall, prosper, and decline: 搖落盛衰 [yōraku seisui]. 405.

sweet dew, gate of: 甘露門 [kanro mon]. 364.

sweet melon: 甜熟瓜 [tenjuku ka]. 609, 673.

sweet melon has a sweet stem: 甜瓜徹蒂甜 [tenka tettai ten]. 609.

swordmaster: 劍客 [kenkaku]. 88.

table: 臺盤 [daiban]. 53, 475, 528, 641.

table, small: 棹子 [takusu]. 232.

Taibai Peak: 大白峯 [Taihaku Hō]. 大白名山 [Taihaku Meizan], literally, renowned Taibai Mountain. Also called Mount Tiantong, 天童山 [Tendō Zan]. Tiantong Jingde Monastery, where Dōgen studied, is located on this mountain. 4.

tails are right: 尾條正 [bijō shin]. 697.

Taiping Huiqin: 太平慧懃 [Taihei Egon]. 1059–1117, China. Dharma heir of Wuzu Fayan, Linji School. Taught at Xingguo Monastery, Mount Taiping (Anhui), where he was abbot. An official of the imperial court presented Taiping with the ceremonial purple robe and gave him the name Fujian, or "Buddha Mirror"—Zen Master Fujian 佛鑑 禪師 [Bukkan Zenji]. P. 933, Generation 21. 636.

Taiyuan Fu: 太原孚 [Taigen Fu]. Ca. ninth–tenth century, China. Student of Xuefeng Yicun, Qingyuan Line. Served as head of the bathhouse. Remained as a senior Zen student. P. 931, Generation 13. 590.

take care: 別處安排 [bessho ambai], literally, bring (the person) and get settled. 373, 410, 576.

take in: 雙收す [sōshū-su], literally, receive both. 36, 270, 683.

take out a little from a little: 少處減些子 [shōsho gen shasu]. 299.

take refuge: 歸依(す) [kie(-su)]. Pay homage. 26, 91, 422, 839–48.

take up: 拈 [nen]. 把拈す [hanen-su], literally, grab and take up. 拈得 [nen-toku], literally, manage to take up. 拈擧 [nenko], literally, take up and raise. Investigate. 161, 207, 633, 639, 646.

take up images and cast the mirror: 拈像鑄鏡 [nenzō shukyō]. 209.

take up one view: 拈一 [nen'ichi], take up another view. 162.

Taking Refuge in Buddha, Dharma, and Sangha: 歸依佛法僧 [Kie Buppōsō]. Eighty-ninth fascicle of this book. xciv, 839–50.

talk: 言談祗對 [gondan shitai], literally, speak and respond. 84, 214, 300, 315–17, 507, 701.

talk, formal: 上堂 [jōdō], 陞堂 [shindō], literally, ascending (in) the hall. Ascending the (teaching) seat. Giving a discourse in the dharma hall. 50, 232, 375, 415, 738.

talk, informal: 小參 [shōsan], literally, small study. 50, 724.

talks on profundity and wonder: 談玄談妙 [dangen dammyō], literally, talk on profundity and talk on excellence. 494, 495.

tallow beads: 木槵子 [mokukansu]. 318.

Tang Dynasty: 唐朝 [Tōchō]. 唐 [Tō]. Tang China. 618–907. Golden age of Zen in China. 74, 101, 112, 136, 137, 198, 211, 350, 367, 417, 474, 500, 745.

Tanhua: See *Ying'an Tanhua.*

Tansheng: See *Yunyan Tansheng.*

Tanzhou Longshan: 潭州龍山 [Tanshū Ryūzan]. Ca. ninth century, China. Dharma heir of Mazu Daoyi, Nanyue Line. Secluded on a mountain till the end of his life. Also called Yinshan. P. 930, Generation 9. 371.

tathāgata: Skt., literally, one who has thus gone; one who has thus come; or one who has come from thusness. Honorific name for Shākyamuni Buddha, also indicating buddhas in general. 如來 [nyorai]. Buddha tathāgatas, 諸佛如來 [shobutsu nyorai]. 9, 456, 665, 769, 859.

Tathāgata, Prabhūtaratna: 多寶如來 [Tahō Nyorai], literally, Many Jewels Tathāgata. 寶勝如來 [Hōshō Nyorai], literally, Excellent Treasure Tathāgata. Ancient Buddha who emerged from underground to demonstrate the true meaning of *Lotus Sūtra*. Whenever this sūtra is being expounded, Prabhūtaratna appears in his stūpa or reliquary floating in mid-air. He opened his stūpa to allow Shākyamuni Buddha to sit side-by-side with him, a primary motif of the *Lotus Sūtra*. 831.

Tathāgata, reclining: 臥如來 [ga nyorai]. Image of the pari-nirvāna of the Buddha. 409.

Tathāgata's Entire Body: 如來全身 [Nyorai Zenshin]. Seventy-first fascicle of this book. lxxxv, 664–66.

tea and rice, daily: 家常(の)茶飯 [kajō (no) sahan], literally, usual house tea and rice. Everyday matter. 240.

tea and treats, serve: 煎點 [sen ten]. 731.

tea room: 茶堂 [sadō], literally, tea hall. 253, 372.

teach: 設化 [sekke], literally, set up for transformation. 266.

teach the assembly: 示衆 [jishu], literally, show the assembly. Give a discourse. Present a talk. 50, 318, 506, 612, 622–24 …

teach, ask to: 請問 [shōmon], literally, request for questioning. 76.

teacher: 知識 [chishiki], literally, one who knows. 8, 96, 235, 558, 695.

teacher, authentic: 正師 [shōshi]. 9, 13, 192, 197, 327, 662, 920 …

teacher, earlier: 先達 [sendatsu], literally, earlier mastering. Pioneering teacher. 241, 749, 785.

teacher, enlightened: 有道の宗師 [udō no shūshi], literally, teacher of the (Zen) school who holds the way. 290.

teacher, great: 大善知識 [dai zenchishiki]. 45, 140, 234, 830, 853, 891 …

teacher, incapable: 邪師 [jashi], literally, crooked teacher. 4.

teacher, ordinary: 凡師 [bonshi]. 115, 805.

teacher, revered: 尊宿 [sonshuku], literally, honored abode. Master. 74, 368.

teacher, root: 本師 [honshi]. One who ordains or gives dharma transmission to the student. 564, 566, 568, 737.

teacher giving the document: つきかみの師 [tugikami no shi], literally, teacher giving joined sheets of paper. 172.

teacher is excellent: 師勝 [shishō]. 262.

Teacher of Humans and Devas: 天人師 [Tennin Shi]. One of the honorary names of the Buddha. 822, 824, 825.

teacher(s), aged: 頤堂 [idō]. 736.

teaching: 家風 [kafū], literally, wind (style) of the house. 4, 30, 334, 503–7.

teaching, ancestral: 祖宗 [soshū]. Ancestral school; ancestral source. 468, 498, 513, 557, 853.

teaching, broad: 方廣 [hōkō], literally, directions vast. 283.

teaching, essential: 宗旨 [shūshi]. Essence, essential meaning, teaching, heart of the teaching, various doctrines. 21, 45, 309, 389, 565.

teaching, expedient: 假立の法 [keryū no hō], literally, dharma that is temporarily established. 445, 856.

teaching, practice, and enlightenment: 教行證 [kyō gyō shō], Also, teaching, practice, and realization. 95, 97, 289.

teaching, practice, practitioner, and essence: 教行人理 [kyō gyō nin ri], literally, teaching, practice, person, and principle. 117.

teaching, profound: 玄旨 [genshi]. 玄訓 [genkun], literally, deep admonition. 玄境 [genkyō], literally, deep state. 120, 338, 343, 360, 507, 873.

teaching, Shākyamuni Buddha's: 釋教 [Shakukyō]. Buddhism. 14, 544, 864.

teaching, true: 眞訣 [shinketsu], literally, true formula. True understanding, essence, essence of the teaching. 11, 114, 245, 356, 360, 509, 892.

teaching expounded not in response to a question: 無問自説 [mumon jisetsu]. 283.

teaching word: 下語 [agyo], literally, words (that are brought) down.

Teachings, Three: 三教 [sankyō]. Buddhism, Daoism, and Confucianism. 524, 545, 864, 871, 874, 875.

Teachings are in accord, Three: 三教は一致なり [sankyō wa itchi nari]. 607.

temple: 梵刹 [bonsetsu]. 梵 [bon] means, pure. 刹 [setsu] is transliteration of Skt. kshetra, literally, land. 345, 547.

temple building: Skt., sangha ārāma. Transliteration: 僧伽藍摩 [sōgyaramma], 僧伽藍 [sōgyaran]. 369, 834.

ten directions: 十方 [jippō]. North, south, east, west, their midpoints, plus up and down. 5, 56, 425, 591–95, 742, 845.

Ten Directions: 十方 [Jippō]. Sixtieth fascicle of this book. lxxx, 591–95.

ten directions, penetrates the: 十方通 [jippō tsū]. 270, 428.

Ten Kings: 十王 [Jū Ō]. Lords of hell, including King Yama. The concept of this group of kings derived from China. 701.

ten names: 十號 [jū gō]. Ten principle titles of, or ten honorific ways of referring to Shākyamuni Buddha: Worthy of Offering, True Encompassing Knower, Clear Walker, Well Gone, Knower of the World, Unsurpassable Warrior, Excellent Tamer, Teacher of Humans and Devas, Buddha, the World-Honored One. 447.

ten stages: 168, 310, 660. See also *bodhisattvas of the ten stages and three classes.*

ten unwholesome actions: See *unwholesome actions, ten.*

Tendai School: 天台宗 [Tendai-shū]. Japanese form of the Tiantai School. Founded by Saichō in the ninth century. Mount Hiei, northeast of

Kyōto, is its center. A distinguishing element of this school is the addition of Esoteric Buddhist practices to the Chinese Tiantai way. Dōgen first studied Buddhism and became a monk at Mount Hiei. xxxiii, xxxv, 912, 913.

tenzo: xxxvii, 421, 737. See also *officers, six.*

thing beyond suchness: 不恁麼事 [fuimmo ji]. Literally, thing that is not suchness. 434.

thing, extra: 剩法 [jōhō]. 406.

thing, one: 一境 [ikkyō], literally, one object. 159.

things as they are: 法爾 [hōni]. 235, 400. See also *thusness.*

things, all: 諸法 [shohō]. 26, 29, 195, 518–23, 649. See also *dharma.*

things, flower of all: 諸法華相 [shohō kesō], literally, flower form of all dharmas. 465.

things, reality of all: See *reality of all things.*

things, turn: 轉物 [tenmotsu]. 449.

things, turned by: 物轉 [motten]. 449.

think beyond thinking: 無念念 [munen nen]. 182, 223.

think deeply: 遠慮 [enryo]. Also, deep understanding. 463, 574.

think one hundred times: 百思 [hyakushi]. 38.

thinking: 思量 [shiryō]. 20, 59, 534, 555, 720, 908, 915 . . .

thinking, beyond: 非思量 [hi shiryō], literally, nonthinking; not thinking. In contrast to thinking, 思量 [shiryō]; and not-thinking, 不思量 [fu shiryō]; beyond thinking or nonthinking describes the unrestricted mind in zazen where one tries neither to develop nor to suppress thoughts which are continually arising. These terms come from the following dialogue: When Yaoshan was sitting, a monk asked him, "In steadfast sitting, what do you think?" Yaoshan said, "Think not-thinking." "How do you think not-thinking?" Yaoshan replied, "Beyond thinking." 59, 224, 289, 682, 720, 826 . . .

thinking, deluded: 情量 [jōryō]. 266.

thinking, discriminatory: 測量 [shikiryō], literally, measuring. 思量分別 [shiryō fumbutsu], literally, thinking, measuring, and discriminating. 292, 773, 908.

thinking, give rest to: 息慮 [sokuryo]. 648.

thinking, human: 人處 [ninsho], literally, human place. 85.

thinking, ordinary: 凡慮 [bonryo]. 凡情 [bonjō], literally, ordinary feeling. 10, 148, 456, 550, 825.

thinking, thinking about: 有念念 [unen nen]. 182, 223.

thinking and be still, cease: 息慮凝寂 [sokuryo gyōjaku]. 310.

thinking of bad, not: 惡也不思量 [aku ya fu shiryō]. 579.

thinking of good, not: 善也不思量 [zen ya fu shiryō]. 579.

third child of Zhang and fourth child of Li: 張三李四 [Chō san Ri shi]. Zhang and Li are common names in China, so this expression refers to ordinary people. 388.

thirty blows: 三十棒 [sanjū bō]. Master striking a student with a stick. 176, 295, 350, 594, 621 . . .

thirty blows, I grant you: 放儞三十棒 [hō ni sanjū bō]. 433.

thirty-seven wings of enlightenment: See *enlightenment, thirty-seven wings of.*

Thirty-seven Wings of Enlightenment: 三十七品菩提分法 [Sanjūshichi Hon Bodai Bumpō]. Seventy-third fascicle of this book. lxxxv, lxxxvi, 671–91.

thirty-two marks: See *marks, thirty-two.*

this, be one with just: 即此 [sokushi], literally, be this. 110, 111.

this, free from just: 離此 [rishi], literally, apart from this. 111.

this, just: 即是 [soku ze]. 如今 [nyokon], literally, now as it is. 57, 88, 432, 501.

this, what is: 作麼生 [somo san]. 生 [san] is a suffix. 249, 315, 414, 454, 470, 653, 756.

thorn branches: 荊棘 [keikyoku]. 582, 585.

thorough going: 遍學 [hengaku], literally, study all over.

thought: 念慮 [nenryo]. 157, 201.

thought, crooked: 邪念 [janen]. 245.

threads as incarnated bodies of the tree god: 化絲 [keshi]. 119.

three classes: See *bodhisattvas of the ten stages and three classes.*

Three Continents: 三洲 [sanshū]. The Four Continents minus the Northern Continent. 774, 784.

three heads and eight arms: 104, 105, 107. See also *asura.*

three lower realms. Worlds of animals, hungry ghosts, and hell beings. See also *paths, six.*

three periods: 三時 [sanji]. 1. The three stages (five hundred years each) of Buddhist teaching after Shākyamuni Buddha passed away: the period of the true dharma, 正法 [shōbō], when teaching, practice, and enlightenment exist; the period of the imitative dharma, 像法 [zōhō], when teaching and practice remain; the period of the decline of the dharma, 末法 [mappō], when there remains only teaching. This concept was not found in sūtras but was believed by a number of Chinese and Japanese Buddhists, and was very influential in Japanese Buddhism, though not believed by Dōgen. In Japan there was a theory that 1051 C.E. was the first year of the period of the dharma's decay. 2. This lifetime, next lifetime, and lifetime(s) after the next. See also fascicle 85, "Karma in the Three Periods." 69, 779, 780, 790, 852, 863.

Three Phrases: See *Phrases, Three.*

three realms: See *realms, three.*

Three Realms Are Inseparable from Mind: 三界唯心 [Sangai Yuishin]. Forty-eighth fascicle of this book. lxxvi, lxxvii, 487–92.

three realms, leave the: 出離三界 [shutsuri sangai]. 488.

three teaching: See *teachings, three.*

three three after: See *three three before, three three after.*

three three before, three three after: 前三三後三三 [zen sansan go sansan]. Many beings in front and back; first and last nine days of a month. 238, 453, 455, 459, 706.

three treasures: See *treasures, three.*

Three Vehicles: See *Vehicles, Three.*

three virtues: See *virtues, three.*

threshold: 道閫 [dōkon]. 633.

thunder: 霹靂 [byakuryaku]. 132, 316, 624, 718.

thunderstorm: 霹靂風雷 [byakuryaku fūrai]. 695.

thūpa: See *stūpa.*

thusness: 恁麼 [immo], pronounced *renmo* in Chinese. Originally a Chinese colloquial expression, meaning this, that, such, in this way, or how. In Zen usage, reality itself, which is limitless. Suchness. As it is; things as they are. 72, 186, 324, 331, 518 . . .

Thusness: 恁麼 [Immo]. Thirtieth fascicle of this book. xlviii, lvii, lviii, 324–31.

thusness, aspects of: 如是相 [nyozo sō]. 561.

thusness, buddha nature of: 眞如佛性 [shinnyo busshō], literally, true thusness of buddha nature. 561, 651.

thusness, knowledge of: 如實知見 [nyojitsu chiken]. 181.

thusness, ocean of: 性海 [shōū kai], literally, ocean of (original) nature. 291.

thusness, timeless: 有如無始 [unyo mushi], literally, having thusness without beginning. 37.

thusness, true: 眞如 [shinnyo]. 164, 464, 593, 648, 649.

thusness emerge?, how does this expression of: 爲甚麼恁麼道 [i jimmo immo dō] 328.

thusness within: 如中 [nyochū]. 453.

Tianhuang Daowu: 天皇道悟 [Tennō Dōgo]. 748–807, China. Dharma heir of Shitou Xiqian, Qingyuan Line. Abbot of Tianhuang Monastery, Jing Region (Hubei). Previously studied with Mazu. He was said to have a noble appearance and was known for the diligence of his practice. His reputation as a teacher was widely known, and many practitioners came to study with him. He treated his visitors equally, whether they were humble or influential. P. 930, Generation 9. 320, 321, 337, 397–402, 614.

Tianlong: See *Hangzhou Tianlong.*

Tianning. 635, 702. See also *Changling Shouzhuo.*

Tianran: See *Danxia Tianran.*

Tiansheng Extensive Record of the Lamp: Tiansheng Guangdeng-lu, 天聖廣燈録 [Tenshō Kōtōroku]. Compiled by Layman Li Zunxu. Dedicated to the Emperor on the seventh year of the Tiansheng Era (1029). Includes biographies and sayings of over three hundred seventy masters in the Zen lineage, starting with Shākyamuni Buddha. 852, 902.

Tiantong Rujing: 天童如淨 [Tendō Nyojō]. Old Buddha Tiantong, 天童古佛 [Tendō Kobutsu]. Dōgen calls him "My late master," 先師 [Senji]. 1163–1228, China. Dharma heir of Xuedou Zhijian, Caodong School. Between 1210 and 1225 he was successively abbot of Qingliang Monastery, Jiankang (Jiangsu); Ruiyan Monastery, Tai Region (Zhejiang); and Jingci Monastery, Hang Region (Zhejiang). In 1225 he became abbot of Jingde Monastery, Mount Tiantong (Mount Taibai), Ming Region (Zhejiang), where he transmitted dharma to Dōgen. His teaching is included in the *Recorded Sayings of Priest Rujing.* P. 934, Generation 23. 167, 668; and Dōgen, xxxviii, xxxix, xlvii, lxxxvii, 167, 507, 529, 569, 575, 911, 915, 916, 918, 920, 921; as abbot, 61, 736; death of, lii; descendants of, 50, 174, 178, 376, 509, 514, 525, 528, 540, 542, 613, 630, 667, 722; lineage of, xli, lxi, 234, 569; monastery of, lviii; practice of, 174, 374, 375, 377, 378; teachings of, lxviii, lxxi, lxxviii, lxxxii, 227, 506, 507, 524, 546, 583, 589, 756, 830, 870; transmission from, xxvi; verses of, xxviii, xliv, lxxx, 27, 527, 582, 586–89, 605, 615, 618–20, 623, 624, 626, 645; words of, xxvi, xlv, lxii, 90, 171,

228, 313, 447, 469, 479, 556, 568, 594, 604, 617, 618, 692, 693, 719, 724.

Tiantong Zongjue: 天童宗珏 [Tendō Sōkaku]. 1091–1162, China. Dharma heir of Changlu Qingliao and a link in the Caodong lineage. He was abbot of Yuelin Monastery, Ningbo (Zhejiang), for twenty-three years, before he went on to teach at Mount Xuedou and Mount Tiantong, both in Ming Region (Zhejiang). Called himself Daxiu, so he was called Zen Master Daxiu, 大休禪師 [Daikyū Zenji]. P. 933, Generation 21.

Ties of Teaching, Nine: 九帶 [kyūtai]. Taught by Fushan Fayuan, dharma heir of Shexuan Guixing of Linji School: (1) Treasury of the true dharma tie. (2) Treasury of buddha dharma tie. (3) Penetrating the reality tie. (4) Phenomena tie. (5) Phenomena and reality interaction tie. (6) Bending and hanging tie. (7) Wondrous inclusive tie. (8) Gold needle and double chain tie. (9) Everyday ordinary tie. 507.

tiger, trap a: 陷虎 [kanko]. 255.

Tiger Cen: See *Changsha Jingcen.*

tile: 塼 [sen]. 219, 305–7.

tile to attract a jewel, hurl a: 抛塼引玉 [hōsen ingyoku]. 307, 680.

tiles and pebbles: 瓦礫 [garyaku]. Represents insentient beings. 723.

time, arrival of: 時節到來 [jisetsu tōrai]. 381.

time, at the same: 俱時 [kuji]. 306, 382, 456, 489, 572, 612, 643.

time, from beginningless: 無始劫來 [mushi kō rai]. 259, 371.

time, passage of: 光陰 [kōin], literally, shadow of (sun) light. 41, 358, 376, 801.

time, passage of: 步暦 [horeki], literally, walk of calendar. 353, 367, 431, 448, 529 . . .

time, throughout: 互時 [gōji]. 39, 260, 313, 411, 573, 642.

Time Being, The: 有時 [Uji]. Twelfth fascicle of this book. xliv, xlv, xlix, lx, lxi, 104–11.

time being, for the: 有時 [uji]. Once in a while. 4, 104, 107, 109, 110, 198, 324, 422, 462, 544, 835, 857, 886.

time span, a vast: 年代深遠 [nendai jinnen], literally, generation deep and far. 229.

timeless life, those who live: 壽者 [jusha]. Unlimited life. 602.

timelessly passing away: 久滅度 [ku metsudo], literally, long pari-nirvāna. 189.

timelessness, tides of: 時節劫波 [jisetsu kōha]. 554.

times, all: 彌時 [miji]. 55, 97, 260, 555.

ting-ting, ting-ting, ting-ting: 滴丁東了滴丁東 [tekitei tōryō tekitei]. 27.

titles as Zen masters: 師號 [shigō]. 174.

to: J. 斗. Measuring unit. Ten shō. Approximately 18 liters (4.75 gallons). 166.

tomb: 塔頭 [tatchū], literally, tower. 頭 [tō/chū] is a suffix. 360, 361, 838, 897, 914.

tomb, square: 方墳 [hōfun]. 831.

Tong'an Changcha: 同安常察 [Dōan Jōsatsu]. Ca. ninth–tenth century, China. Dharma heir of Jiufeng Daoqing, Qingyuan Line. Taught at Tong'an Monastery, Mount Fengqi, Hao Region (Jiangxi). P. 931, Generation 13. 459.

Tong'an Daopi: 同安道丕 [Dōan Dōhi]. Ca. ninth–tenth century, China. Dharma heir of Yunju Daoying and a link in the Caodong lineage. Taught at Tong'an Monastery, Mount Fengqi, Hao Region (Jiangxi), and passed the dharma seal on to Tong'an Guanzhi. When a monk asked about how to practice the way, Daopi said, "Eat gruel. Eat rice." P. 931, Generation 13. 167.

Tong'an Guanzhi: 同安観志 [Dōan Kanshi]. Ca. tenth century, China. Dharma heir of Tong'an Daopi, and a link in the continuing Caodong lineage. Taught at Tong'an Monastery, Jianchang (Jiangxi). P. 931, Generation 14. 167.

tongue: 舌端 [zettan], literally, tip of the tongue. 214.

tongue, click one's: 咄之 [tosshi]. 616.

tongue, long broad: 廣長舌 [kōchōzetsu]. The Buddha's tongue. 86, 87.

topple: 倒 [tō]. 261.

tortoise climb up a tree backward, black: 烏龜倒上樹 [uki tōjōju]. 577.

tortoise, a captured: 窮龜 [kyūki]. 361.

tortoise, black stone: 石烏龜 [seki uki]. Represents beyond conceptual thinking. 446.

total: 都盧 [toro], literally, entire bucket. 256, 261, 340, 455, 489, 499, 563, 596, 597, 599, 721, 723.

totality: 總章 [sōshō], literally, entire structure. 557.

Touzi Datong: 投子大同 [Tōsu Daidō]. 819–914, China. Dharma heir of Cuiwei Wuxue, Qingyuan Line. Datong lived and taught in obscurity at Mount Touzi, Shu Region (Anhui), for more than thirty years, but many practitioners found him there and came to study with him. He told the monks: "There is no mystery that can be compared with you yourself." During a period of civil unrest, a knife-wielding bandit entered the temple, and after hearing Touzi's calm dharma discourse, he took off his clothes and left them as an offering. Touzi's posthumous name is Great Master Ciji, 慈濟大師 [Jisai Daishi]. P. 930, Generation 11. 353, 371, 455, 557, 627, 628.

Touzi Yiqing: 投子 義青 [Tosu Gisei]. 1032–1083, China. Dharma heir of Dayang Jingxuan, Caodong School. Taught at Mount Touzi, Shu Region (Anhui). Restored the Caodong School. Touzi left home to become a monk at the age of seven, and over his lifetime he studied various traditions (such as Huayan) with many teachers, including Fushan Fayuan, who transmitted the Caodong lineage to Touzi for Dayang Jingxuan. Touzi's reputation as a teacher was widespread. P. 932, Generation 17. 167, 621.

trace, no: 無迹 [mushaku]. 30, 211.

track, single: 一條 [ichijō]. 346, 440.

train for a long time: 久修練行 [kushu rengyō]. Longtime practitioner. 81.

transform: 化す [ke-su]. Give guidance. 接す [ses-su], literally, encounter. 開托 [kaitaku], literally, open and entrust. 267, 271, 407, 521, 866.

transform devas: 化天 [keten]. 267.

transform humans: 化人 [kenin]. 267, 407.

transformation, miraculous: 神變 [shimpen]. 神變神怪 [shimpen shinge], literally, miraculous transformation, miraculous wonder. 567.

transformations, ten thousand: 萬化 [banka]. 149, 216.

transformative function: 化儀 [kegi]. 260, 274.

transforming guidance of the spreading sky: 亙天の化導 [gōten no kedō]. 275.

transmigration: 輪迴 [rinne], 輪轉 [rinden], literally, wheel turning. 81, 90, 268, 309, 854.

transmission, authentic: 正傳 [shōden]. authentic, 10, 33, 114, 573, 890. See also *dharma transmission.*

transmission, direct: 單傳 [tanden], literally, single conveying. Person-to-person, single-lined transmission of dharma. 5, 9, 129, 478.

transmission, face-to-face: 面授 [menju]. 面授相承 [menju sōjō], literally, face-to-face giving and mutually holding. 115, 569–75, 588.

Transmission of the Lamp: See also *Jingde Record of Transmission of the Lamp.*

transmission outside of scriptures: 教外別傳 [kyōge betsuden], literally, separate transmission outside the teaching. 277.

transmit: 相承 [sōjō], literally, mutually holding. 114, 239, 265, 289, 517.

transmit, intimately: 密受(せしむ) [mitsju (se shimu)], literally, allow to receive intimately. 5, 115, 141, 219, 571, 724, 920.

transmit dharma: 239, 354, 359, 458, 585, 700, 795. See also *dharma transmission.*

transmit mind with mind: 以心傳心 [ishin denshin]. 479, 552.

Transmitting the Robe: 傳衣 [Den'e]. Fourteenth fascicle of this book. xlviii, lx, lxi, 136–53.

traps and snares: 筌罘 [sentei]. 10.

travel, way-seeking: See *way-seeking travel.*

treasures, ocean of the three: 三寶の海 [sambō no umi]. 652.

treasures, seven: 七寶 [shippō]. Gold, silver, lazuli, moonstone, agate, coral, and amber. (The list varies according to the sūtra.) 156, 446, 800, 872.

treasures, three: 三寶 [sambō]. Buddha, dharma, sangha. Buddhists are those who take refuge in the three treasures. 118, 647–49, 839–50, 901. See also fascicle 89, "Taking Refuge in Buddha, Dharma, and Sangha."

treasures as one treasure, three: 一體三寶 [ittai sambō]. 841.

treasures that are the essence of reality, three: 理體三寶 [ritai sambō]. 841.

treasures that function as teaching, three: 化儀三寶 [kegi sambō]. 841.

treasures that have been maintained, three: 住持三寶 [jūji sambō]. 841.

treasury, small: 小藏 [shōzō]. Canon of early Buddhist scriptures. 278.

treasury of the true dharma eye: 正法眼藏 [shōbō genzō]. According to Zen legend: Once, at an assembly on Vulture Peak, Shākyamuni Buddha took up an udumbara flower and blinked. Mahākāshyapa smiled. Then, Shākyamuni Buddha said, "I have the treasury of the true dharma eye, the wondrous heart of nirvāna. This I entrust to Mahākāshyapa." Although not found in Indian scriptures, this story is traditionally used as a proof of authenticity of the Zen tradition. 11, 115, 534, 569, 642.

Treasury of the True Dharma Eye: 正法眼藏 [Shōbō Genzō; Shōbōgenzō]. 1. Three hundred cases of kōans collected by Dōgen at Kōshō Hōrin Monastery. Dated 1235. Written in Chinese, probably to serve as notes for his main text of the same title (number 2 below). Also called *Shinji Shōbō Genzō,* or the *Chinese-Language Treasury of the*

True Dharma Eye. 2. The lifework of Dōgen, written in Japanese and divided into numerous parts or "fascicles." (See "Preface and Acknowledgments" and "Editor's Introduction" for more detailed information.) There are several versions of this text: (a) 75-fascicle edition, Dōgen's primary version; (b) 12-fascicle version, a later version by Dōgen; (c) 60-fascicle version, edited by Giun (1252–1333), fifth abbot of Eihei-ji; (d) 28-fascicle version, called the "Secret Shōbō Genzō," a collection of fascicles not included in the 60-fascicle version. A 95-fascicle version edited in chronological order around 1690 by Kōzen, thirty-fifth abbot of Eihei-ji, and published in 1815. In addition to these three main forms of the text, there are also 83- and 84-fascicle versions. Our book is based on the 95-fascicle version, plus "One Hundred Eight Gates of Realizing Dharma" from the 60-fascicle version. 905.

Treatise on Realization of Great Wisdom: 大智度論 [Daichido Ron]. 大論 [Dai Ron]. An extensive commentary in Sanskrit on the *Mahā Prajñā Pāramitā Sūtra* by Nāgārjuna. Kumālajīva made an abridged translation of this work in Chinese entitled *Dazhidu Lun.* 662, 678, 768, 797, 829, 830, 858.

treatises, master of: 論師 [ronji]. Commentator. 115, 140, 148, 168, 748.

tree, cypress: 柏樹 [hakuju]. 411–14, 429.

tree, decayed: 枯木 [koboku]. 341, 357, 428, 502, 541, 635, 678, 720.

tree, rootless: 無根樹 [mukon ju]. 647.

tree, withered: 枯木 [kosboku]. Sitting in stillness. 413, 627, 628, 629.

treeness: 樹功 [jukō], literally, tree function. 413, 582.

trees and rocks: 若樹若石 [nyaku ju nyaku seki], literally, whether (they are) trees or whether (they are) rocks. 73, 135, 152, 162, 223.

trees, two types of: 二木 [ni boku]. Classification in the *Lotus Sūtra.* (1) Separate teaching for bodhisattvas. (2) Common teaching for shrāvakas, pratyeka-buddhas, and bodhisattvas. 188.

tripitaka: Skt. 三藏 [sanzō]. "Three baskets" of Buddhist teaching: sūtras, precepts, and commentaries. Entire canon. Also, a master of the canon. 244, 295, 336, 356, 745.

tripod of a worshipping vessel: 鼎の三脚 [kanae no sankyaku]. The three legs of a ceremonial bronze pot of ancient China are compared to the Three Teachings. 524, 544. See also *Teachings, Three.*

troublemaker: 禍胎 [katai]. 613.

true dharma eye: 正法眼 [shōbō gen]. Understanding and experience of authentic dharma. 37, 563.

true human body: 103, 465, 488, 521 . . . See also *buddha body.*

true person: See *person, make a true.*

true person, become a: 人に相逢す [nin ni sō'ō-su], literally, encounter a person. 449, 667.

true person inside: 箇中人 [kochū nin], literally, person inside this. 667.

trunk and branches: 本枝 [honshi]. 571.

trust: 淨信 [jōshin], literally, pure faith. 93, 137, 840.

trust, accept with: 信受(す) [shinju(-su)]. 424, 498.

trust, complete: 全靠 [zenkō], literally, total dependence. 507.

trust, genuine: 正信 [shōshin]. True faith. 8, 20, 21.

trust, practice: 信行 [shingyō]. 100.

trust, realize: 證信す [shōshin-su]. 597.

trust, true body of: 正信身 [shō shinjin]. 94.

trust, true heart of: 正信心 [shō shinjin]. 94.

truth: 諦實 [taijitsu], literally, truth and reality. 如實 [nyojitsu], literally, reality as it is. 156, 880.

truth, foremost sacred: 聖諦第一義諦 [shōtai daiichigi tai]. 355.

truth, realizing the: 證理 [shōri]. 80.

truth, sacred: 聖諦 [shōtai]. 321, 357.

truth doesn't do anything, sacred: 聖諦亦不爲 [shōtai yaku fui]. 609.

truth of the path: 道諦 [dōtai]. The fourth of the four noble truths. 281.

truths, four noble: 四諦 [shitai]. One of the earliest teachings of the Buddha. The truth of suffering; the truth of the causes of suffering; the truth of the cessation of suffering; and the truth of the (eightfold) path. 281, 842, 854, 864.

tuft on forehead, white: 白毫 [byakugō]. 181.

tumble over: 壁落 [hekiraku], literally, wall falling down. 425.

tune, same: 同調 [dōchō]. 414.

turn: 轉 [ten]. 180, 693.

turn heads and exchange faces: 回頭換面 [katō kammen]. See *face, exchange.*

turn the body and flap the brain, freely: 翻身回腦 [honshin kainō]. 429.

turn the dharma wheel: 轉法輪 [tenbōrin]. The Buddha expounding dharma. 273, 534, 567, 808. See also *dharma wheel.*

turn the light to shine within: 迴光返照／回光返照 [ekō henshō]. Turn the light inward and illuminate oneself. 268.

turning one's head: 回頭 [kaitō]. Turning around. 307, 436.

turning point: 轉処 [tensho]. 轉機 [tenki], literally, turning event. A place where delusion is transformed into enlightenment. 246, 321, 908, 915.

turning the body in the word vein: 語脈に轉身す [gomaku ni tenshin-su]. Being free from intellectual, verbal thinking. 629.

Turning the Dharma Wheel: 轉法輪 [Tembōrin]. Seventy-fourth fascicle of this book. lxxxvi, 692–94.

turning the head and pivoting the brain: 回頭轉腦 [kaitō tennō]. 436.

turning word(s): See *word(s), turning.*

turning word, ask for a: 請一轉語 [shō ittengo]. 214.

Tushita Heaven: Skt. Transliteration: 兜率陀 [Tosotsuda]. Also, transliteration plus "heaven" [Ten]: 忉利天 [Tōri Ten], 覩史多天 [Toshita Ten], 兜率天 [Tosotsu Ten]. A heaven in the desire realm presided over by Indra. Believed to be an abiding place for bodhisattvas who are bound to go down to the human realm and become buddhas. Also called Heaven of Thirty-three Devas. 266–68, 661, 727, 896.

Twelve Divisions: See *Divisions, Twelve.*

twelvefold causation of rebirth: See *causation, twelvefold.*

twining vines: 葛藤 [kattō], literally, a plant called kuzu or kudzu, and wisteria. 1. Words and concepts that are a hindrance to understanding. 2. Entanglement. 3. In Dōgen's usage, transmission and heritage of dharma through dynamic interaction and oneness of teacher and disciple. 4. Condition of being immersed. 5, 255, 478, 488.

Twining Vines: 葛藤 [Kattō]. Forty-seventh fascicle of this book. xlviii, lxxv, 478–84.

two kinds (of birth and death): 二種(生死) [nishu (shōji)]: (1) Individual birth and death: ordinary beings transmigrate with bodies of particularities. (2) Changeable birth and death: those whose vow is believed to have the ability to alter their direction of birth and death. 159, 836.

Two Lesser Vehicles. 45, 200, 271, 288, 747 . . . See also *Vehicles, Three.*

Udāna: 283. See also *Divisions, Twelve.*

udumbara blossom: Skt. 優曇華 [udon ge], 優曇 [udon], 曇華 [don ge]. A mythological flower that blooms once in three thousand years when the Tathāgata appears. 170, 503, 642, 644 . . . See also *treasury of the true dharma eye.*

Udumbara Blossom: 優曇華 [Udon Ge]. Sixty-eighth fascicle of this book. lxxxiv, 642–45.

ultimate: 究竟 [kukyō]. Utmost teaching, understanding, or realm. 6, 116, 651, 867 . . .

umpan: J. 雲板, literally, "cloud board." Metal board in the shape of a rising cloud, hung in the kitchen or the study hall for sounding signals. 231.

unconditioned: 無爲 [mui]. Skt. *asamskrita.* Same as unconstructed, 無造作 [muzōsa]. Completely at rest, beyond causes and conditions. Nonthinking, nonintending, nonattaining. Free of expectations. Place of no effort. 3, 6, 16, 86, 87, 88.

unconditioned, originally: 清淨本然 [shōjō honnen], literally, originally pure. 89.

unconstructed, realm of the: 無爲の地 [mui no chi]. 12.

unconstructedness: 無造作 [muzōsa], literally, not constructing. 6.

undefiled: 不染汚 [fuzenna]. Also, undivided. Not colored with dualistic separation, especially between practice and realization. 48, 49, 130, 295, 335. See also *What has thus come?*

understand: 會 [e], literally, merge. 會宗 [eshū], literally, realize the essential meaning. 覺了す [kakuryō-su], literally, awakening completed. 領覽 [ryōran], literally, realize and see. 諦觀す [taikan-su], literally, see the truth. 解路 [gero], literally, unfold the path.

understand through study: 學而知 [gaku ni chi]. 297.

understand without teachers, those who: 無師知者 [mushi chi sha]. 297. See also *realization without a teacher.*

understanding: 4, 35, 398–401, 532, 902. See also *ability.*

understanding, fundamental: 得本 [tokuhon]. 154.

understanding, half-: 一知半解 [itchi hange], literally, know one and understand half.

understanding, human: 人慮の測度 [ninryo no shikitaku], literally, measurement by human thinking. 163.

Understandings, Four: 四料簡 [shiryōken]. Four positions of subject and object taught by Linji: denying subject and not denying object; denying object and not denying subject; denying both subject and object; not denying either subject or object. 542, 543.

understood with trust: 信解す [shinge-su]. 601.

undivided: 不染汚 [fuzenna], literally, nondefilement, unstained. 不曾染汚 [fuzō zenna], literally, not ever defiled. 580, 877.

undivided activity: See *activity, undivided.*

Undivided Activity: 全機 [Zenki]. Forty-second fascicle of this book. xlvi, lxxii, lxxiii, xcvi, 450–52.

unfolding the stillness: 開静 [kaijō]. Leaving the seat after the end of a zazen period.

ungraspable: 悟不得 [go futoku], literally, cannot attain realization. 會不得 [e futoku], literally, cannot attain understanding. 191–93, 195–98, 331.

Ungraspable Mind: 心不可得 [Shin Fukatoku]. Nineteenth fascicle of this book. lxiii, lxxxviii, 191–94.

Ungraspable Mind, Later Version: 後心不可得 [Go Shin Fukatoku]. Twentieth fascicle of this book. 195–204.

Unicorn Sūtra: 佛麟經 [Butsurin Kyō]. Not an actual scripture, "Unicorn Sūtra" is Dōgen's poetic expression for the buddhas' unique teaching. 637.

Universal Lamp: See *Jiatai Record of the Universal Lamp.*

universe: 乾坤 [kenkon]. 36, 329, 545, 620.

Unprecedented Causation Sūtra: 未曾有經 [Mizōu Kyō]. One of the Twelve Divisions of sūtras. 848.

unroll the matter: 展事 [tenji]. Opening a question. 269, 270, 423, 446.

unroll the matter and hurl insightful flashes: 展事投機 [tenji tōki]. Teacher and student open an essential question and harmonize their understanding. 269, 270, 423, 446.

unsurpassable activity: See *activity, unsurpassable.*

unsurpassably: 無等等の [mutōdō no], literally, not equaled at all. 6.

unwholesome: 惡 [aku]. Commonly translated as bad, wicked, or evil. 95–99, 779–83, 885.

unwholesome action, refrain from: See *Refrain from Unwholesome Action.*

unwholesome actions, ten: 十惡 [jūaku]. Actions prohibited by precepts: (1) to kill; (2) to steal; (3) to misuse sex; (4) to make false statements; (5) to buy or sell alcohol; (6) to discuss the faults of other home-leaver bodhisattvas; (7) to praise yourself and insult others; (8) to withhold dharma or treasure; (9) to be angry; (10) to slander the three treasures. 83, 426, 800.

unwholesome realms: 780, 844, 846, 848, 855. See also *paths, six.*

unwholesome time: 惡時世 [akujisei]. 118, 146.

up, down, or the cardinal directions: 上下四維 [jōge shiyui]. 161.

Upadesha: 283, 285. See also *Divisions, Twelve.*

Upagupta: 優婆毱多 [Ubakikuta]. Son of a merchant in the kingdom of Mathulā, central northern India. Taught in his youth by Shānavāsin. Achieved arhathood as soon as he was ordained. Fourth Ancestor of Zen tradition. 166, 810, 811, 860–62.

Upāli: 鄔波離 [Ubari]. After being a barber, he became a student of the Buddha and became an advanced student. Known for understanding and maintaining the precepts. He recited precepts at the first assembling of the Buddha's teachings soon after the latter's pari-nirvāna. 126, 127.

uphold: 禀持 (す) [bonji(-su)], literally, receive and hold. 5, 9, 28, 90, 114, 165, 644.

uphold in veneration: 舉拈 [konen]. 165.

uplift, vigorously: 激揚す [gekiyō-su]. 6.

urgency: 死急 [shikyū], literally, death fast. 72, 215, 216.

utilize: 使用す [shiyō-su], literally, make use. 使得(す) [shitoku(-su)], literally, attain usage. Activate, engage in. 253, 280, 312, 596.

utmost actualization: See *actualization, utmost.*

utpala blossom: Skt. 優鉢羅華 [upara ge]. Blue lotus blossom. 459.

Utpalavarnā: Skt. Utpala Blossom, 優鉢羅華 [Upara Ge], literally, Lotus Blossom Color. Translation: 蓮華色 [Renge Shiki]. Nun originally from Rājagriha. The foremost female disciple of Shākyamuni Buddha. Known for attaining the six miraculous powers and becoming an arhat. 124, 125, 784, 798, 799, 801.

Utpalavarnā, Sūtra on the Former Birth of Nun: 優鉢羅華比丘尼本生經 [Upara Ge Bikuni Honshō Kyō]. 123, 798.

utterance, complete: 道得是 [dōtoku ze]. Expressing the point. 272.

utterance, make one brief: 道得一句 [dōtoku ikku], literally, say one phrase. 434.

Vaipulya: 282. See also *Divisions, Twelve.*

vairambhaka: See *storm, vairambhaka.*

Vairochana Buddha: See *Buddha, Vairochana.*

Vairochana, stepping over the head of: 毘盧頂上行 [Biru chōjō kō]. 614.

Vairochana's ocean storehouse: 毘盧藏海 [Biru zōkai]. 385.

Vaishālī Clan: 梨昌 [Rishō]. Based in the ancient Indian kingdom of Vaishālī (Braj in modern India), located in the north of Magadha. 874.

Valley Sounds, Mountain Colors: 谿聲山色 [Keisei Sanshoku]. Tenth fascicle of this book. xliv, lix, 85–94.

valley where no shouts echo: 喚不響谷 [kan fukyō koku]. 433.

valleys and mountains are separate: 谿山各別 [keizan kakubetsu]. 586.

values, worldly: 事相の善 [jisōno zen], literally, goodness of the practical aspects of matters. 20.

vanish: 打失 [dashitsu], literally, be lost. 打 [da/ta] is an emphatic prefix. 270, 274.

Vappa: 婆敷 [Bafu]. 566. See also *five monks.*

Vārānasī: 波羅奈 [Harana]. City on the Ganges in central northern India. The Buddha gave his first dharma discourse in Deer Park there. Capital city of the ancient kingdom of Kāshī. Most sacred center of ancient Brāhmanism and the later Hinduism. 682.

vast spirit has no contradiction: 豁達靈根無向背 [kattatsu reikon mu kōhai]. 412.

vast, empty, and clear: 廓然虚明 [kakunen komei]. 244, 247.

Vasubandhu: 婆修盤頭 [Bashubanzu]. Twenty-first Ancestor of the Zen tradition in India. A legendary figure, possibly named after the famous Mahāyāna commentator in fifth-century India. 166, 720.

Vedic Scriptures, Four: 四韋陀 [shiida]. Veda, Sāma Veda, Atharva Veda, and Yajur Veda. 867.

veer off, not: 不退 [futai]. 83, 291, 916.

Vehicle, Bodhisattva: 282. See also *Vehicles, Three.*

Vehicle, Buddha: 181, 184. See also *Vehicle, One.*

Vehicle, Great: 8, 119, 189, 273, 286, 495, 682 . . . See also *Vehicles, Three.*

Vehicle, One: 一乘 [ichijō]. Buddha Vehicle, 佛乘 [butsujō]. The teaching that carries sentient beings over the ocean of birth and death to the shore of nirvāna. According to the *Lotus Sūtra*, the Three Vehicles are expedient means to arrive at the One Vehicle. 181–85, 330, 445, 591, 793.

Vehicle, Pratyeka-buddha: 281. See also *Vehicles, Three.*

Vehicle, Shrāvaka: 281. See also *Vehicles, Three.*

Vehicle, Small: See *Vehicles, Three.*

Vehicle, Supreme: 上乗 [Jōjō]. One Vehicle. 252, 253, 277, 278.

Vehicles, Five: 五乗 [gojō]. Three Vehicles plus Human Vehicle and Deva Vehicle. 10, 250, 696.

Vehicles, Lesser: 119, 699, 871, 901. See also *Vehicles, Three.*

Vehicles, Three: 三乗 [sanjō]. According to the traditional Mahāyāna Buddhist view, the Buddha's teaching is classified into three ways: the Shrāvaka (listener) Vehicle, 聲聞乗 [shōmon jō]; the Pratyeka-buddha (solitary awakened one) Vehicle, 緣覺乗 [engaku jō]; and the Mahāyāna or Great Vehicle, 大乗 [daijō]. The first two are called in a derogatory way the Hīnayāna or Lesser (Small) Vehicle(s), 小乗 [shōjō]. They are also called Two Vehicles, 二乗 [nijō]. The Great Vehicle, which emphasizes bringing all sentient beings to enlightenment, is also called the Bodhisattva Vehicle, 菩薩乗 [bosatsu jō]. 109, 183, 250, 330, 843 . . .

vein: See *blood vein.*

venerable: 尊者 [sonja]. 4, 114, 498, 816.

Venerable Chen: See *Muzhou Daoming.*

verse: 頌 [ju]. 偈 [ge], 偈頌 [geju]. 86, 117, 278, 855.

verse, capping: 頌古 [juko]. 636, 743.

verse, four-line: 四句偈 [shiku ge]. 138, 207, 294, 408.

verse, teaching reiterated in: 重頌 [jūju]. 282.

verses, eighty-four thousand: 八萬四千偈 [hachiman shisen ge]. 86, 93, 94.

very person as the very person: See *person as the very person, very.*

vessel of the way: 道機 [dōki]. 171, 702.

vessel, tripod of a worshipping: See *tripod of a worshipping vessel.*

view, carefree: 豁達 [kattatsu]. 855.

view, distorted: 邪見 [jaken]. 邪計 [jakei], literally, crooked thinking. 158.

view, mistaken: 僻見 [hekiken], literally, one-sided view. 495, 502, 858.

view, narrow: 小見 [shōken], literally, small view. 小量の見 [shōryō no ken], literally, small-scale view. 367, 374, 453, 456.

view, self-generated: 生見 [shōken], literally, view on living (being). To think there is something solid as sentient beings. 863.

views, confused: 胡亂の説 [uron no setsu], literally, talk of revolting barbarians. 416.

views, five wrong: 五見 [goken], literally, five views. (1) Attachment to the self and possession. (2) Extreme views. (3) Denial of cause and effect. (4) Regarding one's own view as the highest. (5) Trust in outsiders' practice. 131.

views, four: 四句 [shiku], four basic modes of discernment: affirmation; negation; partial affirmation and partial negation; negation or doubt of both affirmation and negation. 480, 592.

views, outrageously crooked: 猛利の邪見 [mōri no jaken]. 58, 857.

vigorousness: See *pāramitās, six.*

village, mystic: 帝郷 [teikyō], literally, hometown of the emperor. 624.

Vimalakīrti: Skt. Transliteration: 維摩詰 [Yuimakitsu]. Layman Vimalakīrti, 維摩居士 [Yuima Koji]. Translation: 淨名 [Jōmyō], literally, Pure Name. An enlightened layman who is the main figure of the Mahāyāna text *Vimalakīrti Sūtra.* 275; as a layman, 683, 687, 688; Hall, 177; silence of, 270, 689; words of, 45, 395, 396.

Vimalakīrti Sūtra: 維摩經 [Yuima Gyō]. Mahāyāna sūtra presenting stories of Vimalakīrti, an enlightened lay disciple of the Buddha. 229, 687.

Vimana, the great country of: 毘摩大國 [Bima Taikoku]. A mythological country. 848.

vines: See *twining vines.*

Vipashyin Buddha: See *Buddha, Vipashyin.*

virtue: 福德 [fukutoku], literally, beneficial virtue. 668, 828.

virtue, develop: 累德 [ruitoku], literally, accumulate virtue. 496.

virtue, field of: 德田 [tokuden]. 783.

virtue, guiding: 導利 [dōri], literally, guiding benefit. 72.

Virtue of Home Leaving: 出家功德 [Shukke Kudoku]. Eighty-seventh fascicle of this book. xciv, 797–818.

virtues, five: 五常 [gojō]. Love, righteousness, formality, wisdom, and trust. Taught in Confucianism. 211.

virtues, three: 三德 [santoku]. Excellent qualities of cooked food: mildness, cleanliness, and formality.

Virtuous King Sūtra: 仁王經 [Ninnō Kyō]. Mahāyāna sūtra expounding the essentials of protecting the nation. Revered by rulers in East Asia. 232.

visage, motion and stillness of one's: 容止動靜 [yōshi dōyō]. 263.

visiting abbot: See *abbot, former.*

visitors' room: 728. See also *hall, entry.*

visualization: 觀練薫修 [kanren kunju], literally, refine seeing and practice fragrance. 310, 674.

vital: 活鱍 [kappatsu]. 活鱍鱍 [kappatsupatsu], literally, very vital. 活鱍鱍地 [kappatsupatsu chi]. 地 [chi] is a suffix meaning "that which is." Lively, active, vigorous. 活鱍鱍ならしむ [kappatsupatsunara shimu], literally, cause to be vital. Enliven. 599.

Vivādabala: 論力 [Ronriki], literally, Debate Power. A Brāhman who regarded himself as a great debater and who challenged the Buddha. He learned that Migasīsa, who was known as the best scholar, had already become the Buddha's student. Ashamed, he himself became a follower of the Buddha. 874, 875.

voice that stops all sound: 揚聲止響 [yōshō shikyō]. 427.

voice, a single: 一音 [itton]. One sound. 794.

voice, in one: 一口同音 [ikku dō'on], literally; one mouth, same sound. 419.

void: 83, 405, 873. See also *emptiness.*

voidness and send back an echo, receive: 承虚接響 [shōko sekkyō].

vow: 行願 [gyōgan], literally, vow of practice. Vow for enlightenment. 87, 477, 649.

vow, chant a: 呪願す [jugan-su]. 63.

vow, great: 大期 [daigo], literally, great expectation. 538, 806.

Vulture Peak: Skt., Gridhrakūta. Transliteration: 耆闍崛 [Gishakkutsu]. Translation: 靈鷲山 [Ryōju Sen], literally, spiritual vulture mountain; 鷲峯山 [Jubu Sen], literally, vulture peak mountain; 靈山 [Ryō Zen], literally, spiritual mountain. A mountain in the northeast of Rājagriha City, the capital of Magadha, India. Sūtras mention this mountain as a place where Shākyamuni Buddha gave discourses. 514, 570, 602, 727, 738, 742, 835; as lotus flowers, 181; assemblies on, 4, 8, 11, 181, 188, 533, 574, 602; confirmation on, 389, 390, 503; dharma transmission on, 246, 478, 512, 569, 602; in the tower, 188, 189; equinimity of, 185; kings and ministers on, 21; teachings at, 598, 601, 664.

Vyākarana: 283. See also *Divisions, Twelve.*

walk backward: 退步 [taiho]. Move backward. 155, 388.

walking: 步 [ho]. 1. One of the four postures. 2. In Dōgen's usage, continuous practice. 672.

walking meditation: 經行す [kinhin-su], literally, pass and go. 60, 334, 343.

walking, abiding, sitting, and lying down: 行住坐臥 [gyōjū zaga]. 98.

wall: 牆壁 [shōheki]. A stone or brick wall, symbol of insentient beings. 11, 159, 472, 566.

walls, tiles, and pebbles: 牆壁瓦礫 [shōheki garyaku]. 46, 404, 424, 674.

wander about like a cloud or a waterweed: 雲遊萍寄 [un'yū hyōki]. 4.

wander around: 跉跰 [reihei]. 81, 339, 359, 701, 703, 865.

wander at ease: 逍遥す [shōyō-su]. 10.

Wang Boxiang: 王伯庠 [Ō Hakushō]. 1106–1173, China. Writer and government official. Author of *Biography of Zen Master Hongzhi*. 345.

warn: 烱誡(す) [keikai(-su)]. Admonish. 346.

wash house: 厠 [shi]. 51, 53, 55, 56, 57, 689.

washing powder: 澡豆 [sōzu], literally, bath beans. 65.

Washing the Face: 洗面 [Semmen]. Eighth fascicle of this book. lvii, lxxix, xci, 58–71.

water: 1. Water in the usual sense. 2. River, ocean. 3. Thusness. 4. One's state of meditation. 158–64, 311–14, 453–55, 521.

water, east mountains travel on: 東山水上行 [tōzan suijō kō]. 155–58.

water, fetch: 運水 [unsui]. 290, 291, 442.

water, sugar: 石蜜漿 [shakumitsu shō]. 826, 888.

water buffalo: 水牯牛 [suikogyū]. Sometimes refers to a person who realizes original face through practice. 254, 339, 625, 681.

water buffalo comes out and bellows: 一頭水牯牛出來道吽吽 [ittō suikogyū shutsurai dō un'un]. 254.

water by four types of beings, views of: 四見 [shiken], literally, four views: Devas see water as a jewel palace; humans see it as water; hungry ghosts see it as pus and blood; fish see it as a place of abode. 336.

water chestnut: 菱 [hishi]. 425.

water draws water: 水引水 [sui in sui]. 617.

water of eight virtues: 八功德水 [hakkudoku sui]. Water in paradise or around Mount Sumeru has qualities such as: sweet, chilly, soft, light, pure, free of smell, not hurting the throat, and not hurting the stomach. 61.

water thusness: 水如 [suinyo]. 453.

waves: 波 [ha/nami]. Often represent vital life or activity. 46, 354, 383, 604, 618, 743.

waves, follow waves to chase: 隨波逐浪 [zuiha chikurō]. 604.

way: 道 [dō]. Path of spiritual pursuit for and actualization of enlightenment. Buddha way. Enlightenment. Eightfold noble path. Expression.
To express, to speak. 3, 475–81, 500–513.

way, ability of the: 道力 [dōriki]. 659.

way, ancestor: 祖道 [sodō]. 169, 174, 480, 500.

way, attain the: 成道 [jōdō], 得道 [tokudō]. Completion of practice, including Shākyamuni Buddha's enlightenment under the bodhi tree. In
this case "way" is the translation of Skt. *bodhi* (enlightenment). Cf.
Shākyamuni Buddha's words: "I, simultaneously with all sentient
beings and the great earth, attained the way." 大地有情同時成道 [daichi
ujō dōji jōdō]. Arousing the unsurpassable mind. 7, 89, 647, 775, 799.

way, awakening of the: 覺道 [kakudō]. 5, 172.

way, bones of the: 道骨 [dōkotsu]. 478, 513.

way, circle of the: See *circle of the way.*

way, concentrated endeavor of the: 功夫辦道 [kufū bendō]. 3, 349.

way, cultivate the: 耕道 [kōdō]. 353.

way, decisive: 至道 [shidō]. 296.

way, flavor of the: 道味 [dōmi]. 366, 543.

way, follower of the: 道流 [dōru], literally, way stream. 773.

way, fruit of the: 道果 [dōka]. 124, 573, 799.

way, go against the: 非道 [hidō]. 511.

way, in every possible: 千端萬端 [sentan mantan], literally, one thousand
edges, ten thousand edges. 667.

way, intellectual: 有心の趣向 [ushin no shukō], literally, going forward with
mind (thought). 101.

way, long for the ancient: See *long for the ancient way.*

way, maintain the: 有道 [udō], literally, have the way. 50, 353.

way, opening of the: 運啓 [unkei], literally, opening of the fortune. 163.

way, penetrate the: 通路 [tsūro], literally, way for passing. 748.

way, practice of the: 行道 [gyōdō]. Also, chanting while circumambulating.
41, 83, 130, 788, 849 . . . See also *way, study the.*

way, practitioner of the: 道人 [dōnin], literally, way person. 9, 337.

way, settle the great matter of the: See *settle the great matter of the way*

way, single: 一道 [ichidō]. 555.

way, students of the: 參學閑道の人 [sangaku kandō no hito], literally, person
of study, leisure in the way. 4.

way, study the: 學道 [gakudō]. Also, practice the way. 17, 423, 469, 861.

way, this and that: 七通八達 [shichitsū hattatsu], literally, seven penetrations and eight masteries. 94, 219, 758.

way, those outside the: See *outside the way, those.*

way, vessel of the: 道器 [dōki]. 171, 702.

way, voice of the: 道聲 [dōshō]. 103, 340.

way-seeking eyes: 道眼 [dōgen], literally, eyes of the way. 462.

way-seeking mind: See *mind, way-seeking*

way-seeking travel: 行脚 [angya]. 254.

ways, a number of: 衆品 [shubon], literally, various things. 462.

ways, various: 許多般の法 [kyotahan no hō], literally, many things. 96, 143, 496, 566, 736.

wear: 搭著 [tatsujaku]. 564, 567.

weeds: 草 [sō/kusa]. Delusions or the world of delusions. 22, 29, 38, 407, 635, 691, 749.

weeds, enter the: 入草す [nissō-su]. 727.

weeds, gather and bind: 草料をむすふ [sōrō wo musubu]. 38.

Weibai: See *Fuguo Weibai.*

Wei Dynasty: 魏 [Gi]. Northern dynasty in China, 385–556.

Weiqing: See *Lingyuan Weiqing.*

Weiyan: See *Yaoshan Weiyan.*

Weiyi: See *Huanxi Weiyi.*

Well Gone: 善逝 [Zenzei]. One of the ten principal titles of the Buddha. 822, 824, 825.

Wengong: See *Yang Wengong.*

Wenyan: See *Yunmen Wenyan.*

Wenyi: See *Fayan Wenyi.*

Wenzhun: See *Zhantang Wenzhun.*

What degrees can there be?: 何階級之有 [ga kaikyū shi yū]. 609.

What has thus come?: 什麼物恁麼來 [jūmo motsu immo rai]; also read as nani mono ka immon ni kitaru, literally, what thing thus comes? Originally, Huineng's question to Nanyue, roughly meaning "Who is here?" One of the essential Zen questions. 218, 234, 235, 539, 562.

What is it here?: 這裏是什麼所在 [shari ze jūmo sho zai]. 59.

What is the meaning of Bodhidharma's coming from India?: 如何是祖師西來意 [ika naru ka kore soshi sairai i]. This can also be read: いかにあらんかこれ祖師西來意 [ika ni ara n ka kore soshi sairai i], literally, what is the meaning of the ancestor coming from the west? 280, 411, 412, 442.

what it is, understanding of: 什麼心行 [jūmo shingyō], literally, what (it is) of mind movement. 386.

what's there: 那邊事 [nahen ji]. 263.

wheel, dharma: See *dharma wheel.*

wheel, wondrous dharma: 妙法輪 [myō hōrin]. 26, 433, 493, 768.

wheel of dharma, turning the: 轉法輪 [ten bōrin]. 234.

wheel-turning king: See *king, wheel-turning.*

whisk: 拂子 [hossu]. A ceremonial implement used by and thus representing a Zen master. 98, 170, 605, 741.

whisk, raise the: 舉拂 [kohotsu]. 390.

white-ox cart: See *cart, white-ox.*

wholeheartedly: 一向に [ikkōni], literally, in a single direction. 5, 76, 797.

wholeness: 一如 [ichinyo], literally, one thusness. 一等 [ittō], literally, one and equal. Inseparableness. Not one, not two. Also translated as "oneness." 7, 446, 487, 506.

wholesome: 善 [zen]. Commonly translated as good. 98–102, 425, 546, 779.

wholesome action, do: 95, 99, 101, 102, 445. See also *Refrain from Unwholesome Action.*

wholesome actions, ten: [jūzen] 十善. Refraining from engaging in the ten unwholesome actions. 130.

wholesome at the beginning, middle, and end: 初中後善 [sho chū go zen]. 181.

wicked time: 惡時 [akuji]. 173.

willing: 願樂 [gangyō], literally, wish and enjoy. 367, 474, 475, 825.

willow: 楊柳 [yōryū]. 63–68, 70, 410, 462, 465, 587.

willow twig: 楊枝 [yōji]. 63–68, 70, 410.

willows, plums, peaches, or apricots: 楊梅桃李 [yō bai tō ri]. 588.

wind: 風 [fū/kaze]. Often represents style of teaching. 4, 32, 372, 843.

wind, nature of: 風性 [fūshō]. 32, 33.

wind, unobstructed: 無礙風 [mugefū]. 252, 253.

wind and stream: 風流 [fūryū]. Activity of all things, or pure practice. Also, lingering trace. 163, 457.

wind-and-string pavilion: See *pavilion, wind-and-string.*

wind and the banner: 風幡 [fūban]. 76.

window, bright: 明窓 [myōsō]. 40, 348, 512.

window, lattice: 棧子 [renji]. 729.

winter solstice: 一陽 [ichi yō], literally, one sun. 564, 619.

wisdom, all-: 薩婆若 [sabanya]. Skt., sarva jña, literally, all-wisdom; all-knower. 291, 902.

wisdom, cultivation of: 熏修 [kunju]. 253, 446.

wisdom, realization of: 知見波羅蜜 [chiken haramitsu], literally, pāramitā of knowing and seeing. 186, 901.

wisdom and practice, complete: 明行足 [myō gyōsoku]. 262.

wisdom beings, seven: 七賢 [shichiken]. Stages of early Buddhist practice. 442.

wisdom beings, three: 三賢 [sangen]. Stages of early Buddhist practice. Also, three classes; see *bodhisattvas of the ten stages and three classes.*

wisdom beyond desire: 無漏智 [muro chi], literally, no-desire wisdom. 237.

wisdom equaling the master: 智等于師 [chitō ushi]. 274.

wisdom eyes: 623. See also *eyes, five.*

wisdom is pushed aside, while emotions arise: See *emotions arise wisdom is pushed aside, while.*

wisdom surpassing the master: 智勝于師 [chishō ushi]. 274.

Wise and Fools Sūtra: 賢愚經 [Gengu Kyō]. Collection of sixty-nine stories. Titled thus in China. 64, 65.

wise people: 賢人 [kenjin]. 92, 162, 163, 320, 508.

wishes, four aspects of the fulfillment of: 四如意足 [shinyoisoku]. Four bases of practice for enlightenment: (1) Wish for excellent meditation. (2) Effort for excellent meditation. (3) Controlling of mind. (4) Contemplation and observation with wisdom. 677.

wisteria, entwined around a tree like: 如藤倚樹 [nyotō iju]. 316.

wisteria vines entangled with each other, like: 如藤倚藤 [nyotō itō]. 316, 427.

withered stake: See *stake, withered.*

withered tree: See *tree, withered.*

Within a Dream Expressing the Dream: 夢中説夢 [Muchū Setsumu]. Thirty-ninth fascicle of this book. xlvi, lxxi, lxxii, lxxiv, 431–38.

within, turn the light to shine: See *turn the light to shine within.*

woman, old: 老婆子 [rōbasu]. 子 [su] is a suffix with no special meaning. 81, 192, 196, 226, 542, 681.

woman becoming a buddha, a: 女身成佛 [nyoshin jōbutsu]. There was an ancient belief that a woman could not become a buddha. An early Mahāyāna response was that a woman can turn her body into a male body in this lifetime and gain enlightenment. Dōgen denies this theory and asserts that everyone can be enlightened. (In his later life, he emphasizes that one can become a buddha only by leaving the household.) 810.

womb: 胎裏 [tairi], literally, inside the womb. 206, 674 . . .

womb, sacred: 聖胎 [shōtai]. Body that contains the potential of a buddha. 674, 916.

womb birth, egg birth, moisture birth, transformation birth: 胎卵濕化 [tai ran shitsu ke]. 490.

women, heavenly: 天女 [tennyo]. 82.

wonder of wonders: 妙之妙 [myō no myō]. 433.

wondrous: 妙 [myō]. 逞風流 [tei fūryū], literally, express wind and stream. 96, 138, 311, 401.

wondrous, most: 極妙 [gokumyō]. 77, 294, 524.

Wondrous Plateau: 妙高臺 [Myōkō Dai]. The abbot's quarters at the Tiantong Monastery. 528.

wooden dipper, broken: 破木杓 [ha mokushaku]. Useless. Fully immersed in sitting. 278, 318, 541.

wooden stalk: 木橛 [bokuketsu]. 723.

word vein: 語脈 [gomyaku]. Continuous expression. Ceaseless murmuring. 629.

word(s), turning: 轉語 [tengo]. Statement that crushes delusion and leads to liberation. 593, 598, 705, 851.

words: 言端 [gontan], literally, edge of speech. 道底 [dōtei], literally, expression. 底 [tei] is a suffix meaning "that which is." 言語 [gongo]. 言句 [gonku], literally, word and phrase. 句 [ku], literally, phrase. 1. Limited dualistic expressions, which are a hindrance to realization. 2. In Dōgen's usage, the entire expression of enlightenment, including silence. 9, 34, 487, 532, 592, 890.

words, after the: 句後 [kugo], literally, after the phrase. 537.

words, conversational: 通語 [tsūgo], literally, ordinary talk. 607.

words, golden: 金言 [kingen]. 91, 665, 875.

words, profound: 玄談 [gendan]. 390.

words, truthful: 誠言 [jōgon]. 465, 601.

words, with: 有句 [uku]. 8, 10, 540, 640, 755, 792, 867.

words and phrases, confined to: 滯言滯句 [taigon taiku]. 156.

words are all-inclusive: 語等 [gotō], literally, words that are equal. 426.

work: 功業 [kugō], literally, effect of the work. Accomplishment. 41, 277, 488, 888.

work leader: 737. See also *officers, six.*

work of the way: 道業 [dōgō]. Activity of the way, understanding. 41, 144, 543.

work on: 修理す [shuri-su], literally, practice the principle. 撈摝(す) [rōroku(-su)], literally, scoop up and roll. 243, 551, 749, 815.

worker: 行者 [anja]. Assistant. 76, 230, 231, 547.

Worker Lu: 547, 838. See also *Dajian Huineng.*

working: 247, 306, 338, 376, 399, 403, 661. See also *activity.*

working, part of the: 一造次 [ichi zōji], literally, one creating. 247.

world, all-embracing: 遍界 [hengai], literally, all over the world. 遍法界 [hen-hokkai], literally, all over the dharma world. Whole world of phenomena. 432.

world, dusty: 塵界 [jinkai]. Ordinary world. 塵勞 [jinrō], literally, dusty labor. 31, 67, 407, 470, 866 . . .

world, entire: 盡界 [jinkai], 渾界 [konkai]. 59, 105–8, 276, 582.

world, floating: 浮世 [ukiyo]. 34, 348.

world, heavenly: 上界 [jōkai], literally, upper world. 11, 582.

world, leave the dusty: 出塵 [shutsujin]. 34.

world, material: 器世間 [kiseken]. Realm of insentient beings. 459, 461.

world, nothing is hidden in the entire: 遍界不曾藏 [hengai fu sōzō]. 235, 263.

world beyond conditions: 格外 [kakugai], literally, outside frameworks. Beyond worldly scales or ordinary thinking. 31.

World-Honored One: Skt., bhagavān. Transliteration: 薄伽梵 [Bagyabon]. Translation: 世尊 [Seson], literally, world-revered. One of the ten primary titles of the Buddha. 佛世尊 [Butsu Seson]; Buddha, the World-Honored One. Shākyamuni Buddha. 49, 118, 595, 841.

world of blossoming flowers arises: 華開世界起 [kekai sekai ki]. A line in the transmission poem from Prajñātāra to Bodhidharma. 582, 609, 643.

world of phenomena, most honored in the: 法界中尊 [hokkai chū son]. 584.

worldly life, renounce: See *life, renounce worldly.*

worlds, billion: See *billion worlds.*

worlds, four: 四天下 [shitenge]. Four mythological continents around Mount Sumeru. 843.

worlds, three: 三世 [sanze]. Past, present, and future. 102, 103, 549.

Wuji Liaopai: 無際了派 [Musai Ryōha]. 1149–1224, China. Dharma heir of Zhuoan Deguang, Linji School. Abbot of Mount Tiantong when Dōgen first visited the monastery. P. 934, Generation 24. 175, 915, 917, 920.

Wuxin: See *Sixin Wuxin.*

Wuxue: See *Cuiwei Wuxue.*

Wuzu Fayan: 五祖法演 [Goso Hōen]. d. 1104, China. Dharma heir of Haihui Shouduan, Linji School. Taught at Mount Wuzu, Qi Region (Hubei), and spread teachings of the Yangqi Order. His successors included Fuyan Qingyuan, Taiping Huiqin, and Yuanwu Keqin. P. 933, Generation 20. 342, 590, 633, 636, 692, 702 . . .

Xiangshan Baojing: 香山寶静 [Kōzan Hōjō]. Ca. sixth century. Taught at Mount Xiang, Luoyang (Henan). Sent Dazu Huike to study with Bodhidharma. 363.

Xiangyan Zhixian: 香嚴智閑 [Kyōgen Chikan]. d. 898. Guiyang School. Ordained by Baizhang Huaihai and studied with Guishan Lingyou. Left Guishan and was enlightened by the sound of a pebble striking bamboo while he was sweeping at the graveyard of Nanyang Huizhong on Mount Wudang, Jun Region (Hubei). Became dharma heir of Guishan and taught at Xiangyan Monastery, Deng Region (Henan). His posthumous name is Great Master Xideng, 襲燈大師 [Shūtō Daishi]. P. 930, Generation 11. and Guishan, 87, 288; and Xuan, 351; awakening of, 87, 88; practice of, 349; verse of, 360; words of, 218, 444, 628, 629, 638–41, 757, 758.

Xianlang: See *Zuoxi Xian lang.*

Xiantong Era: 咸通年中 [Kantsū nenchū]. 860–873, Tang Dynasty, China. This is when Xuansha Shibei aspired to leave the household at age thirty. Signifies a particular time, also, anytime. 34, 367, 424.

Xiaoang: 蕭昂 [Shōgō]. Ca. sixth century, China. Known as the Governor of Guang Province, Liang Kingdom, who greeted Bodhidharma when he arrived from India. 355.

Xiaoliao: See *Biandan Xiaoliao.*

Xinchang: 行昌 [Gyōshō]. Ca. seventh–eighth century, China. A student of Sixth Ancestor Huineng. Biography unknown. P. 929, Generation 7. 243.

Xinghua Cunjiang: 興化存獎 [Kōke Sonshō]. 830–888, China. Dharma heir of Linji Yixuan, Linji School. Taught at Xinghua Monastery, Weifu (Hebei). Supervised the compilation of *Linji Record*. His posthumous name is Great Master Guanji, 廣濟大師 [Kōsai Daishi]. P. 931, Generation 12. 175.

Xingnian: See *Shoushan Xingnian.*

Xingsi: See *Qingyuan Xingsi.*

Xinlong: 青龍 [Sheiryū]. A temple in Chang'an where monk Daoyin wrote a commentary on the *Diamond Sūtra.* 693.

Xiqian: See *Shitou Xiqian.*

Xishan Liang: 西山亮 [Seizan Ryō]. Ca. eighth–ninth century, China. Dharma heir of Mazu Daoyi, Nanyue Line. Retreated to Mount Xi, also called Mount Shuangfeng, Huangmei, Qi Region (Hubei). Biography unknown. P. 930, Generation 9. 719.

Xitang Zhizang: 西堂智藏 [Seidō Chizō]. 735–814, China. Dharma heir of Mazu Daoyi, Nanyue Line. Zhizang, Huahai, and Nanquan Puyuan were the three most outstanding students of Mazu, who praised the former two by saying, "Zang's head is white, Hai's head is black." His posthumous name is Zen Master Dajiao, 大覺禪師. P. 930, Generation 9. 717, 718.

Xiujing: See *Jingzhao Xiujing.*

Xiyun: See *Huangbo Xiyun.*

Xuanjian: See *Deshan Xuanjian.*

Xianjiao: See *Yongjia Xianjiao.*

Xuansha Shibei: 玄沙師備 [Gensha Shibi]. 835–908, China. Third son of Xie Family, 謝三郎 [Sha Sanrō]. Engaged in fishing in childhood. Studied with Xuefeng Yicun and was called Ascetic Bei, 備頭陀 [Bi Zuda], for his severe observance of precepts. Celebrated by Dōgen for his statement "The entire world of the ten directions is one bright pearl." Abbot of Xuansha Monastery, Fu Region (Fujian). Given title Great Master Zongyi, 宗一大師 [Sōichi Daishi] by the emperor. P. 931, Generation 13. and Xuefeng, lvi, lxxxi, 34, 35, 209, 217, 389, 609, 610; descendant of, 512; story of, lvi, 34, 367, 368; words of, 36–38, 200, 202, 203, 210, 212, 213, 217–19, 270–75, 280, 281, 284, 391, 470, 491, 492, 529, 530, 556, 594, 611–13, 746, 751, 752.

Xuantai: See *Nanyue Xuantai.*

Xuanze: See *Baoen Xuanze.*

Xuechuang Zongyue: 雪窓宗月 [Sessō Sōgetsu]. Ca. thirteenth century, China. Head monk at Tiantong Jingde Monastery when Dōgen was practicing there. P. 934, Generation 25. 172, 916, 917.

Xuedou Zhijian: 雪竇智鑑 [Setchō Chikan]. 1105–1192, China. Dharma heir of Tiantong Zongjiao, Caodong School. Taught at Mount Xuedou, Ming Region (Zhejiang), where many students came to hear his dharma, including his famous dharma heir, Tiantong Rujing. As a boy, he saw the marks of the Buddha on his hands. As an adult, he became enlightened late one night despite seeing a hundred ghosts. P. 933, Generation 22. 167, 692.

Xuedou Zhongxian: 雪竇重顯 [Setchō Jūken]. 980–1052, China. Dharma heir of Zhimen Guangzuo, Yunmen School. Taught at Mount Xuedou, Ming Region (Zhejiang). As he was a noted poet, his selection of kōans became the basis of the *Blue Cliff Record.* His posthumous name was Zen Master Mingjiao, 明覺禪師 [Myōkaku Zenji]. P. 932, Generation 16. 200, 557, 634, 641, 747, 758.

Xuefeng Yicun: 雪峯義存 [Seppō Gison]. 822–908, China. Dharma heir of Deshan Xuanjian, Qingyuan Line. Taught at Mount Xuefeng, Fu Region (Fujian), where his congregation of monks rose to fifteen hundred. He emphasized direct, wordless experience in his teaching. It was Xuefeng who famously tipped over the rice pot when his teacher Dongshan asked him whether he would strain the rice from the sand or the sand from the rice. His posthumous name is Great Master Zhenjiao, 眞覺大師 [Shinkaku Daishi]. P. 931, Generation 12. 317, 347, 412, 512; and Xuansha, 34, 35, 209, 210, 368, 389, 391, 609, 610; and Yunmen, 419, 543; practice of, 352, 353; shaving a hermit, 442; words of, 212–75, 420, 443, 469, 483, 523.

yaksha: 393. See also *guardians, eight types of.*

Yama, King: Skt. 琰魔王 [Emma Ō]. 閻羅王 [Enra Ō]. Lord of hell. 805, 815.

Yang Wengong: 楊文公 [Yō Bunkō]. 楊億 [Yō Oku]. 974?–1020?, China. Poet and government official. Lay student of Shoushan Xingnian, Linji School. Supervised *Jingde Record of Transmission of the Lamp.* P. 932, Generation 17. 683.

Yangqi Fanghui: 楊岐方會 [Yōgi Hōe]. 993–1046, China. Dharma heir of Ciming Chuyuan, Linji School. Taught at Mount Yangqi, Yuan Region (Jiangxi). Regarded as founder of the Yangqi Order of the Linji School. He became a monk after he got into trouble as a tax administrator and was forced to flee the city. He taught that enlightenment is to be found in everyday events. P. 932, Generation 18. 175, 343, 917.

Yangshan Huiji: 仰山慧寂 [Gyōzan/Kyōzan Ejaku]. 803–887, China. Opposed by his parents, he cut off two fingers to show his determination to become a monk. When young, studied with Baizhang Huaihai. He was like Shāriputra, who gave one hundred answers to ten questions, and he was called Small Shākyamuni. Attending Guishan Lingyou, he spent three years watching over a buffalo. Became dharma heir of Guishan. Taught at Mount Yang, Yuan Region (Jiangxi). Sometimes said to have had prophetic talents, he also used symbolic circular diagrams in his teaching. Guiyang School was partly named after him. P. 930, Generation 11. 510, 511; and Guishan, 46, 176, 255, 288, 289, 370, 917; and Mihu, 301; practice of, 563; student of, 75, 76; words of, 200, 203, 302, 746, 751.

Yanguan Qi'an: 鹽官齊安 [Engan Sai'an]. 750–842, China. Dharma heir of Mazu Daoyi, Nanyue Line. He had an unusual appearance, and Mazu recognized him as a "great vessel." Taught at Haichang Monastery, Yanguan, Hang Region (Zhejiang). Known as an accomplished teacher of the precepts. The famous kōan of the rhinoceros fan—"If the fan is broken, then bring me the rhinoceros"—is his teaching. His posthumous name is National Teacher Qi'an, 齊安國師 [Seian Kokushi]. P. 930, Generation 9. 250, 251, 341, 351, 919.

Yanhui: 顏回 [Gankai]. Top student of Confucius. Lived in poverty, enjoyed the Heaven's decree, and engaged in virtuous conduct. 865.

Yantou Quanhuo: 巖頭全奯 [Gantō Zenkatsu]. 828–887, China. Dharma heir of Deshan Xuanjian. Traveled widely with his friend Xuefeng Yicun. Taught at Yantou near Lake Dongting (Hunan), where many monks came to study with him. He was attacked and killed by bandits while sitting in meditation. Without losing his composure he made a great shout that could be heard ten miles away. P. 931, Generation 12. 317.

Yanzhao: See *Fengxue Yanzhao.*

Yaoshan Weiyan: 藥山惟儼 [Yakusan Igen]. 745–828, China. He was an earnest student of the precepts, but when he grew weary of the repetitive observances, he went to study with Shitou Xiqian, Qingyuan Line, and became his dharma heir. Taught at Mount Yao, Feng Region (Hunan). Noted by Dōgen for replying to a monk that during meditation he thought of not-thinking, which is beyond thinking. Once, when the monks entered the hall to hear his lecture, he descended the dharma seat without saying a word. His posthumous name is Great Master Hongdao, 弘道大師 [Kōdō Daishi]. P. 930, Generation 9. xxix, xlv, 683; and Mazu, 109; and Shitou, 330, 331; and Yanyan, 513; assembly of, 309, 398, 689; dharma brother of, 321; lineage of, 304; students of, 337, 895; teachings of, 223, 228; verse of, xxix, xlv, 104; words of, 233, 303, 682.

Yefu Daochuan: 治父道川 [Yafu Dōsen]. Ca. eleventh–twelfth century, China. Dharma heir of Jingin Jicheng, Linji School. P. 933, Generation 20. 228.

Yicun: See *Xuefeng Yicun.*

yin and yang: C. 陰陽 [in'yō]. 二柄 [nihei], literally, two stems, two powers. Passive and active forces. 210, 212, 357, 358, 448, 502.

Yinfeng: See *Deng Yinfeng.*

Ying'an Tanhua: 應菴曇華 [Ōan Donge]. 1103–1163, China. Dharma heir of Huqiu Shaolong, Linji School. Taught at Mount Tiantong (Zhejiang). Regarded as one of the Two Nectar Gates of Linji School, along with Dahui Zonggao. P. 934, Generation 23. 526, 527.

Yiqing: See *Touzi Yiqing.*

Yixuan: See *Linji Yixuan.*

Yizhong: See *Sanping Yizhong.*

Yō Kōshū: 楊光秀. Ca. thirteenth century, Japan. An early lay student of Dōgen's. Resided in Kyūshū Island. Further biography unknown. liv, lv, 33.

yojana: Skt. 由旬 [yujun]. Measuring unit. Seven to nine miles. Distance for an ancient king to travel per day. 188, 391, 832, 833, 896.

Yongjia Xuanjiao: 永嘉玄覺 [Yōka Genkaku]. d. 713. Came from Yongjia Prefecture, Wen Region (Zhejiang). After studying the Tiantai meditation of the Lotus School, he studied Zen. Upon meeting and exchanging a few words with Sixth Ancestor Huineng, he received dharma transmission and stayed overnight at his community, so he was called Overnight Jiao (Awakening). He went back to Wen Region and taught. Wrote a poem, "Song of the Realization of the Way." His posthumous name is Great Master Zhenjiao, 眞覺大師 [Shinkaku Dai-shi]. P. 929, Generation 7. 295, 402, 673, 789, 854, 855.

Yongping Era: 永平年中 [Eihei nenchū]. In the tenth year of the Yongping Era [67 C.E.] , during the reign of Emperor Xiaoming of the Later Han Dynasty, Buddhism was formally introduced to China from India. 295, 402, 673, 789, 854, 855.

Yoshimine Temple: 吉峰寺 /吉嶺寺 [Yoshimine-dera, also Kippō-ji]. Located in Echizen Province, Japan. Dōgen's community resided in the thatched-roof building of this abandoned temple while the nearby Daibutsu Monastery was under construction, 1243–1244. 70, 302, 314, 500, 517, 530, 536, 547, 557, 562, 568, 575, 580, 589, 595, 645, 654, 663, 666, 670, 691, 694, 704, 714.

you and I are just this: 儞我渠 [niga ko]. 72.

you have attained my marrow: See *marrow, you have attained my.*

Yuanguan: See *Liangshan Yuanguan.*

Yuanwu Keqin: 圜悟克勤 [Engo Kokugon]. 1063–1135, China. Also called Jiashan. Dharma heir of Wuzu Faya n, Linji School. Taught at Jiashan Monastery (Hunan). Had over one thousand students. Compiled the *Blue Cliff Record* by adding comments and verses to Xuedou's one hundred cases. His posthumous name is Zen Master Zhenjiao, 眞覺禪師 [Shinkaku Zenji]. P. 933, Generation 21. and Zonggao, 701, 702; student of, 175; verses of, 429, 633, 634, 743, 856; words of, 208, 270, 271, 274, 275, 407, 451, 469, 692, 743, 884.

Yuanzhi: See *Daowu Yuanzhi.*

Yuezhou Qianfeng: 越州乾峯 [Esshū Kempō]. Ca. ninth century, China. Caodong School. Dharma heir of Dongshan Liangjie. Taught in Yue Region (Zhejiang). When asked by a monk about all buddhas' road to nirvāna, he responded by drawing a line on the ground with his walking stick. P. 931, Generation 12. 595.

Yun'an Kewen: See *Zhenjing Kewen.*

Yunding Defu: 雲頂德敷 [Unchō Tokufu]. Ca. ninth–tenth century, China. Dharma heir of Sushan Guangren, Caodong School. Biography unknown. P. 931, Generation 13.

Yunju Daoying: 雲居道膺 [Ungo Dōyō]. d. 902, China. Caodong School. Dharma heir of Dongshan Liangjie. He founded Jenru (True

Thusness) Monastery on Mount Yunju, Hong Region (Jiangxi), and taught many monks there for more than thirty years. His posthumous name is Great Master Hongjiao, 弘覺大師 [Kōkaku Zenji]. P. 931, Generation 12. 514; and Dongshan, 319, 338, 384; teaching of, 229, 257, 324, 347, 531–33.

Yunmen School: 雲門宗 [Ummon Shū]. A lineage from Yunmen Wenyan. One of the Five Schools of Zen in China. 5, 512.

Yunmen Wenyan: 雲門文偃 [Ummon Bun'en]. 864–949, China. After becoming dharma heir of Xuefeng Yicun, he traveled widely and established a monastery at Mount Yunmen, Shao Region (Guangdong). His community grew to include one thousand monks. His teaching flourished, and he is considered founder of the Yunmen School. Known for expressing buddha dharma in pithy single phrases. Given the title Great Master Daciyun Kuangzhen, 大慈雲匡眞大師 [Daijiun Kyōshin Daishi] by the Emperor. P. 931, Generation 13. 483, 506, 512, 917; and Xuefeng, 543; descendant of, 634; lineage of, 172, 197, 366, 513, 575–78, 916; commentaries of, 700; teaching of, 542; words of, 157, 317, 403, 419–21, 447, 604.

Yunyan Tansheng: 雲巖曇晟 [Ungan Donjō]. 782–841, China. Studied with Baizhang Huaihai for twenty years. Then he became a disciple of Yaoshan Weiyan, Qingyuan Line, and became his dharma heir. Taught at Yunyan, Tan Region (Hunan). Many dialogues are recorded between Yunyan and his dharma and biological brother, Daowu Yuanzhi. Dongshan Liangjie, who studied with several famous teachers, regarded the lesser-known Yunyan as his dharma teacher because Yunyan never explained anything directly. His posthumous name is Great Master Wuzhu, 無住大師 [Mujū Daishi]. P. 930, Generation 10. and Daowu, 397; and Dongshan, 291, 315, 319, 551, 552, 616; lineage of, 337, 513; practice of, 614; words of, 398, 400–402, 553–56, 617.

Yuquan Shenxiu: 玉泉神秀 [Gyokusen Jinshū]. d. 706, China. Dharma heir of Fifth Ancestor Daman Hongren, he was the most senior student among over seven hundred peers. Taught at Mount Dangyang, Jing Region (Hubei). Regarded as founder of Northern School of Zen, while his dharma brother Huineng is regarded as founder of Southern School of Zen. P. 929, Generation 6. 149, 374, 547.

zazen: J. 坐禅. A Chinese compound of *zuo* [za], sitting, and *chan* [zen], meditation. Total concentration of body and mind in upright seated meditation posture, which is the basis of Zen Buddhist practice. xxi, 6, 303–10, 579 · · ·

Zazen School: 坐禅宗 [Zazen Shū]. 11.

Zazen, The Point of: See *Point of Zazen, The.*

Zen: J. 禅. Originally, Skt. dhyāna. Its Chinese transliteration is *channa,* 禅那 [zenna]. Abbreviated as *chan* [zen]. Translated as 静慮 [jōryo], literally, quiet thinking. 1. Meditation; contemplation. 2. Zen Buddhist practice. 3. Zen School of Buddhism. 4. In Dōgen's usage, the buddha way. 304, 338, 503–6, 865,

Zen, practice: 参禅 [sanzen], literally, visiting (and studying) Zen (with a teacher). 17, 250, 376, 817, 909, 920.

Zen master: 禅師 [zenji]. 1. Accomplished meditation teacher. 2. Title given by the Emperor. 416, 597, 684, 884.

Zen monastery: 禅院 [zen'in]. 378.

Zen School: 禅宗 [Zen Shū]. Zen Gate, 禅門 [Zemmon]. xli, 11, 356, 502–6, 511, 512, 913 · · ·

Zen student: 学人 [gakunin], literally, studying person. 19, 502, 700, 701.

Zen text: 禅册 [zensatsu], literally, Zen bundle (of books). 40, 310.

Zhang Zhuo: 張拙 [Chō Setsu]. Ca. ninth century, China. Scholar. Had realization after exchanging a few words with Shishuang Qingzhu. P. 931, Generation 12. 104, 252, 388, 394, 463.

Zhanran: 湛然 [Tannen]. 711–782, Tiantai School sixth ancestor and scholar who articulated the teaching potential of grasses and trees and more generally the buddha nature of nonsentient beings. These were important philosophical background materials for Dōgen's teachings about worldview and buddha nature. Author of *Zhiguan Fu Xingchuan Hongjue,* 止観輔行伝弘決 (Biological Study of the Buddha's Practice That Supported Shamatha and Vipashyanā)—a large commentary on *Mahe Fuchuan* 摩訶止観 [Maka Shikan] (Great Shamatha and Vipashyanā) by Zhiyi, founder of the Tiantai School. Dōgen quotes this book of Zhanran, while referring to him as an ancient teacher. 860, 861, 863, 865–67, 869, 872, 874.

Zhantang Wenzhun: 湛堂文準 [Tandō Monjun]. 1061–1115, China. Studied with Zhenjing Kewen, Linji School, and became his dharma heir.

Abbot of Letan Monastery, Nanchang (Jiangxi). P. 933, Generation 20. 635, 700–3.

Zhao: see *Hutou Zhao.*

Zhao, Superintendent: 趙提舉 [Chō Teiko]. Ca. thirteenth century, China. Government officer, grandson of Emperor Ning of the Song Dynasty. A lay student of Tiantong Rujing. 377.

Zhaojiao Changzong: 照覺常總 [Shōkaku Jōsō]. 1025–1091, China. Dharma heir of Huanglong Huinan, Linji School. Taught at Donglin Monastery, Jiang Region (Jiangxi). Teacher of Su Dongpo. His posthumous name is Zen Master Zhaojiao, 照覺禪師 [Shōkaku Zenji]. P. 933, Generation 19. 86.

Zhaozhou Congshen: 趙州從諗 [Jōshū Jūshin]. 778–897, China. Dharma heir of Nanquan Puyuan, Qingyuan Line. Aroused aspiration for enlightenment at age sixty-one. Taught for forty years at Guanyin Monastery, Zhao Region [Zhaozhou] (Hebei). His teachings are collected in *Recorded Sayings of Zen Master Zhenji of Zhaozhou.* A great many of his sayings, and anecdotes about him, are used as kōans, including the kōan *mu*, about a dog's buddha nature. His posthumous name is Great Master Zhenji, 眞際大師 [Shinzai Daishi]. P. 930, Generation 10. 469, 470; and Nanquan, 409, 410; on a cypress tree; xxxi, lxx, 411–14; on a dog's buddha nature, 255, 256; practice of, 371, 689; teaching of, 226, 756, 757; story of, 74, 339; words of, xxxi, 340, 411, 441, 482, 483, 491, 607, 625, 626, 746, 750.

Zhengjiao: See *Hongzhi Zhengjiao.*

Zhengshou: See *Leian Zhengshou.*

Zhenxie Qingliao: See *Changlu Qingliao.*

Zhichang: See *Guizong Zhichang.*

Zhicong: 智聰 [Chisō]. Ca. twelfth century, China. Also named Huiyan Zhizhao. Dharma heir of Zhuoweng Ruyan, Linji School. Visited monasteries for twenty years and compiled *Human and Deva Eyes.* 515.

Zhifu: See *Ehu Zhifu.*

Zhijian: See *Xuedou Zhijian.*

Zhimen Guangzuo: 智門光祚 [Chimon Kōso]. Ca. tenth century, China. Dharma heir of Xianglin Chengyuan, Yunmen School. He first taught at Shuangchuan in Suizhou and later became Abbot of Zhimen Monastery, Sui Region (Hubei), from which he derived his name. Also known as Beita Guangzuo. P. 931, Generation 15. 320, 634.

Zhiqin: See *Lingyun Zhiqin.*

Zhixian: See *Guanxi Zhixian; Xiangyan Zhixian.*

Zhiyi Kefu: 紙衣克符 [Shie Kokufu]. Ca. ninth century, China. Linji School. Student of Linji Yixuan. Called Ascetic Paper Robe (Zhiyi) because of his clothes. Also called Zhuozhou Kefu. P. 931, Generation 12. 371.

Zhiyuan: See *Gushan Zhiyuan.*

Zhizang: See *Xitang Zhizang.*

Zhongjian: 宗鑑 [Sōkan]. Ca. twelfth–thirteenth century, China. Abbot of Wannian Monastery on Mount Tiantai (Zhejiang) before Dōgen visited. Biography unknown. 176.

Zhongjin: See *Sun Zhongjin.*

Zhongxian: See *Xuedou Zhongxian.*

Zhongxing: See *Jianyuan Zhongxing.*

Zhou, Lord: 周大夫 [Shū Taifu]. Ca. twelfth century B.C.E. Named Ji Dan. Son of King Wen and brother of King Wu. Established legal system of the Zhou Dynasty. Regarded as an ideal ruler by Confucius. 867, 872.

Zhu, Government Secretary: 竺尚書 [Chiku Shōsho]. Ca. ninth century, China. Studied with Changsha Jingcen, Qingyuan Line. Biography unknown. P. 930, Generation 11. 257.

Zhu Falan: See *Dharmaratna.*

Zhuangzi: 莊子 [Sōji (Sōshi)]. Also, Chuang-tzu. Ca. fourth century B.C.E., China. Zhuangzhou, author of *Zhuangzi,* one of the main texts of ancient Daoism. Known for his wit, colorful parables, and deep insight. 524, 865, 866, 868, 869, 871, 873.

Zhuo: See *Zhang Zhuo.*

Zhuoan Deguang: 拙菴德光 [Setsuan Tokkō]. 1121–1203. Dharma heir of Dahui Zonggao, Linji School. The Emperor gave him the honorary title Zen Master Fuzhao, 佛照禪師 [Bussō Zenji]. Abbot of Ayuwang Monastery, Ming Region (Zhejiang), when Dōgen's teacher Rujing visited. Later taught at Lingying Monastery and Mount Jia, both in Hang Region (Zhejiang). His posthumous name is Great Zen Master Puhui Zongjiao, 普慧宗覺大禪師 [Fue Shūkaku Daizanji]. P. 934, Generation 23. 175, 376.

Zhuozhou Kefu: See *Zhiyi Kefu.*

Zhiyuan: See *Bozhao Zhiyuan.*

Zichun: See *Danxia Zichun.*

Zidan: 85. See also *Su Dongpo.*

Zixuan: See *Changshui Zixuan.*

Zongchi, Nun: 尼總持 [Ni Sōji]. Ca. sixth century, China. A disciple of Bodhidharma. Biography unknown. Described in apocryphal legends as the daughter of Emperor Wu, whom Bodhidharma first encountered upon arrival in China. P. 928, Generation 2. 479, 480.

Zonggao: See *Dahui Zonggao.*

Zongjiao: See *Tiantong Zongjiao.*

Zongyue: See *Xuechuang Zongyue.*

Zunxu: See Li Zunxu.

Zuoxi Xianlang: 左谿玄朗 [Sakei Genrō]. Ca. seventh–eighth century, China. Dharma brother of Yongjia Xuanjiao when he was practicing in the Lotus School. 854.

Zuxin: See *Huitang Zuxin.*

SELECTED BIBLIOGRAPHY

FOR FURTHER DETAILS ABOUT Dogen's major writings, please see the entry *Eihei Dōgen* in the glossary.

ENGLISH

Books about or by Dogen

Abe, Masao. *A Study of Dogen: His Philosophy and Religion.* Albany: State University of New York Press, 1992.

Bielefeldt, Carl. *Dogen's Manuals of Zen Meditation.* Berkeley: University of California Press, 1988.

Bielefeldt, Carl, and Griffith Foulk, eds. *Soto Zen Text Project.* Translations of Soto texts including Dogen. An initiative of the Sotoshu Shumucho International Division. http://hcbss.stanford.edu/research/projects/sztp/index.html.

Cleary, Thomas, trans. *Rational Zen: The Mind of Dogen Zenji.* Boston: Shambhala Publications, 1993.

————, trans. *Record of Things Heard: The Shobogenzo Zuimonki, Talks of Zen Master Dogen as Recorded by Zen Master Ejo.* Boulder, Colo.: Prajna Press, 1980.

————, trans. *Shobogenzo: Zen Essays by Dogen.* Honolulu: University of Hawaii Press, 1986.

Cook, Francis. *How to Raise an Ox: Zen Practice as Taught in Zen Master Dogen's Shobogenzo.* Los Angeles: Center Publications, 1978.

————. *Sounds of Valley Streams: Enlightenment in Dogen's Zen.* Albany: State University of New York Press, 1989.

Eto Sokuo. *Zen Master Dogen as Founding Patriarch.* Trans. Shohei Ichimura. Woodville, Wash.: North American Institute of Zen and Buddhist Studies, 2001.

European Committee for the Organization of the 750th Commemoration of Dogen Zenji's Entering Nirvana, eds. *Dogen Zenji's Mind Here and Now.* Tokyo: Shotoshu Shumucho, 2001.

Heine, Steven. *A Blade of Grass: Japanese Poetry and Aesthetics in Dogen Zen.* New York: Peter Lang, 1989.

_____. *Did Dogen Go to China?: What He Wrote and When He Wrote It.* New York: Oxford University Press, 2006.

_____. *Dogen and the Koan Tradition: A Tale of Two Shobogenzo Texts.* Albany: State University of New York Press, 1994.

_____. *Existential and Ontological Dimensions of Time in Heidegger and Dogen.* Albany: State University of New York Press, 1985.

_____. *The Zen Poetry of Dogen: Verses from the Mountain of Eternal Peace.* Boston: Tuttle Publishing, 1997.

Ichimura, Shohei, trans. and ed. *Zen Master Eihei Dogen's Monastic Regulations.* Woodville, Wash.: North American Institute of Zen and Buddhist Studies, 1993.

Jaffe, Paul, trans. *Flowers of Emptiness: Dogen's Genjokoan with Commentary by Yasutani Roshi.* Boston: Shambhala Publications, 1997.

Kim, Hee Jin. *Dogen on Meditation and Thinking: A Reflection on His View of Zen.* Albany: State University of New York Press, 2007.

_____. *Eihei Dogen: Mystical Realist.* Boston: Wisdom Publications, 2004.

Kim, Hee Jin, trans. *Flowers of Emptiness: Selections from Dogen's Shobogenzo.* Lewiston, N.Y.: Edwin Mellen Press, 1985.

Kodera, Takashi James. *Dogen's Formative Years in China: An Historical Study and Annotated Translation of the Hokyo-ki.* Boulder, Colo.: Prajna Press, 1980.

Kopf, Gereon. *Beyond Personal Identity: Dogen, Nishida, and a Phenomenology of No-Self.* Richmond, Surrey: Curzon Press, 2001.

LaFleur, William R., ed. *Dogen Studies.* Honolulu: Kuroda Institute, University of Hawaii Press, 1985.

Leighton, Taigen Dan. *Songs for the True Dharma Eye: Verse Comments on Dogen's Shobogenzo.* San Francisco: Browser Books, 2007.

_____. *Visions of Awakening Space and Time: Dogen and the Lotus Sutra.* New York: Oxford University Press, 2007.

Leighton, Taigen Dan, and Okumura Shohaku, trans. with introductions. *Dogen's Extensive Record: A Translation of the* Eihei Koroku. Boston: Wisdom Publications, 2004.

_____, trans. *Dogen's Pure Standards for the Zen Community: A Translation of* Eihei Shingi. Albany: State University of New York Press, 1996.

Masunaga, Reiho. *A Primer of Soto Zen: A Translation of Dogen's* Shobogenzo Zuimonki. Honolulu: University of Hawai'i Press, 1978.

Merzel, Dennis Genpo. *Beyond Sanity and Madness: The Way of Zen Master Dogen.* Boston: Charles E. Tuttle, 1994.

Myers, Bob. *First Dogen Book.* Scott Valley, Calif.: CreateSpace, 2008.

Nearman, Hubert, trans. *The Shobogenzo: A Trainee's Translation of Great Master Dogen's Spiritual Masterpiece.* www.urbandharma.org/udharma12/shobo.html.

Nishijima, Gudo Wafu, and Chodo Cross, trans. *Master Dogen's Shobogenzo.* 4 vols. Woods Hole, Mass.: Windbell Publications, 1994–1998.

Nishijima, Gudo. *Master Dogen's Shinji Shobogenzo.* Woods Hole, Mass.: Windbell Publications, 2003.

Nishiyama, Kosen, and John Stevens. *Dogen Zenji's Shobogenzo (The Eye and Treasury of the True Law).* 4 vols. Sendai, Japan: Daihokkaikaku, 1975–1983.

Okumura, Shohaku, trans. and ed. *Dogen Zen.* Kyoto: Kyoto Soto Zen Center, 1988.

_____, trans. *Shobogenzo Zuimonki: Sayings of Eihei Dogen Zenji, Recorded by Koun Ejo.* Kyoto: Kyoto Soto Zen Center, 1987.

_____, ed. *Dogen Zen and Its Relevance for Our Time: An International Symposium Held in Celebration of the 800th Anniversary of the Birth of Dogen Zenji.* San Francisco: Soto Zen Buddhism International Center, 2003.

Okumura, Shohaku, and Taigen Dan Leighton, trans. *The Wholehearted Way: A Translation of Eihei Dogen's* Bendowa *with Commentary by Kosho Uchiyama Roshi.* Boston: Charles Tuttle and Co., 1997.

Rajneesh, Osho. *Dogen the Zen Master: A Search and a Fulfillment.* Cologne, West Germany, Rebel Publishing House, 1988.

Shasta Abbey Buddhist Monastery. *Shobogenzo.* www.shastaabbey.org/shobogenzo1.htm.

Shimano, Eido, and Charles Vacher, trans. *Shobogenzo Bussho: The Buddha Nature / La nature donc bouddha.* La Versanne, France: Encre Marine, 2002.

_____, trans. *Shobogenzo Uji: Être-temps (Being time).* La Versanne, France: Encre Marine, 1997.

_____, trans. *Shobogenzo yui butsu yo butsu, shôji / Seul bouddha connaît bouddha, vie-mort.* La Versanne, France: Encre Marine, 1999.

Stambaugh, Joan. *Impermanence Is Buddha-Nature: Dogen's Understanding of Temporality.* Honolulu: University of Hawai'i Press, 1990.

Tanahashi, Kazuaki, ed. and trans. *Beyond Thinking: A Guide to Zen Meditation by Zen Master Dogen.* Boston: Shambhala Publications, 2004.

————, ed. *Enlightenment Unfolds: The Essential Teachings of Zen Master Dogen.* Boston: Shambhala Publications, 1999.

————, ed. *Moon in a Dewdrop: Writings of Zen Master Dogen.* New York: North Point Press, 1985.

Tanahashi, Kazuaki, and John Daido Loori, trans., with commentary and verse by John Daido Loori. *The True Dharma Eye: Zen Master Dogen's Three Hundred Koans.* Boston: Shambhala Publications, 2005.

Waddell, Norman, and Abe Masao, trans. *The Heart of Dogen's Shobogenzo.* Albany: State University of New York Press, 2002.

Warner, Brad. *Sit Down and Shut Up: Punk Rock Commentaries on Buddha, God, Truth, Sex, Death, and Dogen's Treasury of the Right Dharma Eye.* Novato, Calif.: New World Library, 2007.

Warner, Jisho, Okumura Shohaku, John McRae, and Taigen Dan Leighton, eds. *Nothing Is Hidden: Essays on Zen Master Dogen's* Instructions for the Cook. New York: Weatherhill, 2001.

Wright, Thomas, trans. *Refining Your Life: From the Zen Kitchen to Enlightenment* by Zen Master Dogen and Kosho Uchiyama. New York: Weatherhill, 1983.

Yokoi, Yuho, trans. *The Shobogenzo.* Tokyo: Sankibo Buddhist Bookstore, 1986.

Yokoi, Yuho, with Daizen Victoria. *Zen Master Dogen: An Introduction with Selected Writings.* New York: Weatherhill, 1976.

Books with Material Concerning Dogen

Anderson, Reb. *Being Upright: Zen Meditation and the Bodhisattva Precepts.* Berkeley: Rodmell Press, 2001.

————. *Warm Smiles from Cold Mountains: Dharma Talks on Zen Meditation.* Berkeley: Rodmell Press, 1999.

Barnhart, Bruno, and Joseph Wong, eds. *Purity of Heart and Contemplation: A Monastic Dialogue between Christian and Asian Traditions.* New York: Continuum, 2001.

Bodiford, William M. *Soto Zen in Medieval Japan.* Honolulu: Kuroda Institute, University of Hawai'i Press, 1993.

Cleary, Thomas, trans. and ed. *Minding Mind: A Course in Basic Meditation.* Boston: Shambhala Publications, 1995.

————, ed. and trans. *Timeless Spring: A Soto Zen Anthology.* Tokyo: Weatherhill, 1980.

Faure, Bernard. *Visions of Power: Imagining Medieval Japanese Buddhism.* Princeton: Princeton University Press, 1996.

Heine, Steven. *Shifting Shape, Shaping Text: Philosophy and Folklore in the Fox Koan.* Honolulu: University of Hawai'i Press, 1999.

_____. *Zen Skin, Zen Marrow: Will the Real Zen Buddhism Please Stand Up?* New York: Oxford University Press, 2008.

Heine, Steven, and Dale Wright, eds. *Zen Ritual: Studies of Zen Buddhist Theory in Practice.* New York: Oxford University Press, 2008.

Kasulis, T. P. *Zen Action / Zen Person.* Honolulu: University of Hawai'i Press, 1981.

Katagiri, Dainin. *Each Moment Is the Universe: Zen and the Way of Being Time.* Boston: Shambhala Publications, 2007.

_____. *Returning to Silence, Zen Practice in Daily Life.* Boston: Shambhala Publications, 1988.

Leighton, Taigen Dan. *Faces of Compassion: Classic Bodhisattva Archetypes and Their Modern Expressions.* Boston: Wisdom Publications, 2003.

Leighton, Taigen Dan, and Yi Wu, trans. *Cultivating the Empty Field: The Silent Illumination of Zen Master Hongzhi.* Boston: Tuttle Publishing, 2000.

Loori, John Daido, ed. *The Art of Just Sitting: Essential Writings on the Zen Practice of Shikantaza.* Boston: Wisdom Publications, 2002.

Nearman, Hubert, trans. *The Denkoroku: The Record of the Transmission of the Light, by Zen Master Keizan Jokin.* Mount Shasta, Calif.: Shasta Abbey Press, 1993.

Okumura, Shohaku, trans. and ed. *Shikantaza: An Introduction to Zazen.* Kyoto: Kyoto Soto Zen Center, 1985.

Okumura, Shohaku, ed. *Soto Zen: An Introduction to Zazen.* Tokyo: Soto Shu Shumucho, 2002.

Okumura, Shohaku, and Thomas Wright, trans. *Opening the Hand of Thought.* New York: Arkana; Viking Penguin, 1994.

Payne, Richard, and Taigen Dan Leighton, eds. *Discourse and Ideology in Medieval Japanese Buddhism.* London: Routledge, 2006.

Snyder, Gary. *Mountains and Rivers without End.* Washington, D.C.: Counterpoint, 1996.

_____. *The Practice of the Wild.* New York: North Point Press, 1990.

Suzuki, Shunryu. *Not Always So: Practicing the True Spirit of Zen.* New York: HarperCollins, 2002.

_____. *Zen Mind, Beginner's Mind.* New York: Weatherhill, 1970.

Tanahashi, Kazuaki, and Tensho David Schneider, eds. *Essential Zen.* San Francisco: Harper, 1994.

Williams, Duncan Ryuken. *The Other Side of Zen: A Social History of Soto Zen Buddhism in Tokugawa Japan.* Princeton: Princeton University Press, 2005.

JAPANESE

Books about Dogen

Ito Shuken. *Dogen Zen Kenkyu* (Study of Dogen Zen). Tokyo: Daizo Shuppan, 1998.

Kagamishima Genryu. *Dogen In'yo Goroku no Kenkyu* (Study of Quoted Materials by Dogen). Tokyo: Soto Shugaku Kenkyujo, 1995.

_____. *Dogen Zenji to Sono Shufu.* Tokyo: Shunjusha, 1994.

_____, trans. *Genbun-taisho Gendaigo-yaku Dogen Zenji* Zenshu (modern Japanese translation: Collected Works of Zen Master Dogen). Vols. 10–13. Tokyo: Shunjusha, 1999.

Kato Shuko, ed. *Shobo Genzo Yogo Sakuin* (*Shobo Genzo* Concordance). 2 vols. Tokyo: Rishosha, 1963.

Kawamura Kodo, ed. *Eihei Kaisan Dogen Zenji Gyojo Kenzei-ke, Shohon Taiko* (Kenzei's Biography of the Founder Dogen of Eihei, compared versions). Tokyo: Daishukan Shoten, 1975.

_____, ed. *Shohon Taiko: Eihei Kaisan Dogen Zenji Gyojo Kenzei Ki* (compared versions: Kenzei's Biography of Zen Master Dogen, Founder of Eihei). Tokyo: Daishukan Shoten, 1975.

Kosaka Kiyu and Suzuki Kakuzen, eds. *Dogen Zenji Zenshu* (Collected Works of Zen Master Dogen). 7 vols. Tokyo: Shunjusha, 1989.

Masutani Fumio, trans. *Gendaigo-yaku Shobo Genzo* (Modern Japanese translation: Treasury of the True Dharma Eye). 8 vols. Tokyo: Kadokawa Shoten, 1973–1975.

Mizuno Yaoko, ed. *Shobo Genzo.* 4 vols. Tokyo: Iwanami Shoten, 1993.

Nakamura Soichi; Nakamura Sojun; and Tanahashi Kazuaki, trans. *Zen'yaku Shobo Genzo* (complete modern Japanese translation: Treasury of the True Dharma Eye). 4 vols. Tokyo: Seishin Shobo, 1971–1972.

Nakaseko Shodo. *Shin Dogen Zenji Den Kenkyu* (New Study of Zen Master Dogen's Biography). Tokyo: Kokusho Kankokai, 2002.

Nishijima Kazuo, trans. *Gendaigo-yaku Shobo Genzo* (modern Japanese translation: Treasury of the True Dharma Eye). 4 vols. Tokyo: Bukkyosha, 1975.

Okubo Doshu, ed. *Dogen Zenji Zenshu* (Entire Work of Zen Master Dogen). 2 vols. Tokyo: Chikuma Shobo, 1970.

Sakai Tokugen, Kagamishima Genryu, Sakurai Hideo, supervisors; Suzuki Gakuzen, Kawamura Kodo, Kosaka Kiyu, eds. *Dogen Zenji Zenshu* (Entire Work of Zen Master Dogen). 7 vols. Tokyo: Shunjusha, 1988–1993.

Sawaki Kodo. *Dogen Zen Sanky* (Thorough Study of Dogen Zen). Tokyo: Chikuma Shobo, 1976.

Sekiryu Mokudo, trans. *Gendaigo-yaku Kenzei-ki Zue* (Modern Japanese translation: Illustrated Biography of Dogen by Kenzei). Tokyo: Kokusho Kanko-kai, 2000.

Suganuma Akira. *Dogen Jiten* (Dogen Dictionary). Tokyo: Tokyodo Shuppan, 1999.

Takahashi Kenchin, trans. *Zenkan Gendai-yaku Shobo Genzo* (all-fascicles modern Japanese translation: Treasury of the True Dharma Eye). 2 vols. Tokyo: Risosha, 1961–1962.

Takeuchi Michio. *Dogen*. Tokyo: Yoshikawa Kobunkan, 1962, rev. 1992.

Tamaki, Koshiro, trans. *Gendaigo-yaku Shobo Genzo* (modern Japanese translation: Treasury of the True Dharma Eye). 6 vols. Tokyo: Okura Shuppan, 1994.

References

Hirakawa Akira, ed. *Bukkyo Kanbon Daijiten* (Buddhist Chinese-Sanskrit Dictionary). Tokyo: Reiyukai, 1997.

Koga Hidehiko, ed. *Zengo Jiten* (Dictionary of Zen Terms). Kyoto: Shibunkaku, 1991.

Komazawa Daigaku Shiten Hensanjo, ed. *Zengaku Daijiten* (Extensive Dictionary of Zen Studies). 3 vols. Tokyo: Daishukan Shoten, 1978.

Nakamura Hajime, ed. *Bukkyogo Daijiten* (Dictionary of Buddhist Terms). Tokyo: Tokyo Shoseki Shuppan, 1981.

CREDITS

Material from *Moon in a Dewdrop: Writings of Zen Master Dogen,* edited by Kazuaki Tanahashi, ©1985 by San Francisco Zen Center, is here revised and reprinted by permission of North Point Press, a division of Farrar, Straus and Giroux: "Rules for Zazen," "Bodhisattva's Four Methods of Guidance," "Regulations for the Auxiliary Cloud Hall," "Actualizing the Fundamental Point," "Birth and Death," "The Time-Being," "Undivided Activity," "Body-and-Mind Study of the Way," "Mountains and Waters Sutra," "Spring and Autumn," "Plum Blossoms," "Everyday Activity," "The Moon," "Painting of a Rice-cake," "On the Endeavor of the Way," "Only Buddha and Buddha," "Twining Vines," "Face-to-Face Transmission," "Buddha Ancestors," "Document of Heritage," "All-Inclusive Study," "Going beyond Buddha."

Part of the text from the following two books published by Shambhala Publications has been revised and reprinted: *Enlightenment Unfolds: The Essential Teachings of Zen Master Dogen,* edited by Kazuaki Tanahashi, ©1999 by San Francisco Zen Center. *Beyond Thinking: A Guide to Zen Meditation,* edited by Kazuaki Tanahashi, ©2004 by San Francisco Zen Center.

The enso design on the book cover is by Shunryu Suzuki and is reproduced by permission of San Francisco Zen Center.